UNIVERSITY DEGREE COURSE OFFERS

Choosing Your University And Degree Course...And Completing Your UCAS Application

Why not contact HEAPS (*Higher Education Advice and Planning Service***) for a telephone consultation for advice on such issues as:**

- **Choosing A-level subjects (which are the best and required subjects and for which degree courses)**
- **Degrees and Diploma courses (making the right choice from a list of thousands!)**
- **Completing your UCAS application (will the admissions tutor remember your personal statement?)**
- **Choosing the right university or college (the best ones for you and your courses)**

For details of services and consultation fees contact:

**The Higher Education Advice and Planning Service
Email heapservice@gmail.com**

MPW

Mander Portman Woodward

UNIVERSITY DEGREE COURSE OFFERS

The essential guide to winning
your place at university

Brian Heap

49th edition

HEAP 2019: UNIVERSITY DEGREE COURSE OFFERS

In order to ensure that *Heap 2019: University Degree Course Offers* retains its reputation as the definitive guide for students wishing to study at UK universities and other higher education institutions, hundreds of questionnaires are distributed, months of research and analysis are undertaken, and painstaking data checking and proofing are carried out.

Every effort has been made to maintain absolute accuracy in providing course information and to ensure that the entire book is as up to date as possible. However, changes are constantly taking place in higher education so it is important for readers to check carefully with prospectuses and websites before submitting their applications. The author, compilers and publishers cannot be held responsible for any inaccuracies in information supplied to them by third parties or contained in resources and websites listed in the book.

We hope you find this 49th edition useful, and would welcome your feedback as to how we can ensure the 50th edition is even better.

Author Brian Heap
Advertising Sales Crimson Publishing Services
Contact Simon Connor on 020 8445 4464 or email simonc@crimsonpublishingservices.co.uk

This 49th edition published in 2018 by Trotman Education an imprint of Crimson Publishing Ltd, 21d Charles Street, Bath BA1 1HX
www.trotman.co.uk

© Brian Heap 2018

A CIP record for this book is available from the British Library

ISBN 978 1 911067 88 7

Typeset by IDSUK (DataConnection) Ltd
Printed by Gambia Centro Gráfico, Spain

QUOTES

'An excellent, inclusive and thorough guide which ALL careers libraries should include, not just schools with sixth forms and colleges. If I were forced to narrow down my choices of higher education materials to one resource, it would be this one.'
Ray Le Tarouilly, Careers Adviser, The Midlands Academies Trust, 2018

'HEAP helps you make informed choices about university course offers.'
Angie Stone, Librarian, Pate's Grammar School, 2018

'Invaluable – HEAP is my 'go to' resource.'
Wendy Kerley, Freelance Careers Adviser, 2018

'If I only had the budget to buy one careers book, it would be HEAP. Doing my job would be much harder without it!'
Celia Golding, Careers Guidance Manager, Langley Grammar School, 2017

'Up-to-date information, easy to use and accurate.'
Kenneth Nolan, Careers Adviser, Xaverian College, 2017

'A very useful starting point for exploration of degree courses. Supplements our UCAS programme and careers advice very effectively.'
Paul Meadway, Head of Careers, Hymers College, 2017

'Our first stop for students sourcing university information and the courses they are interested in.'
Lorraine Durrands, Careers Co-ordinator, Kesteven & Grantham Girls' School, 2016

'The students find it an invaluable resource.'
Rebecca Mockridge, Sixth Form Administrator, Queen's College Taunton, 2016

'It's a really quick way of getting an overview of the standard offer for a particular course or course type ... and is helpful in terms of advising both on offer conditions, but also when choosing A-level subjects for particular interests.'
Etta Searle, Careers Co-ordinator, Wyke 6th Form College, 2016

'The definitive guide to university degree course offers ... clearly laid out and remarkably easy to navigate ... should be stocked in every sixth form library.'
Teach Secondary, October 2015

'Degree Course Offers is probably the UK's longest running and best known reference work on the subject.'
Education Advisers Limited, 2015

'HEAP University Degree Course Offers is simply "The Bible" for careers advisors and students alike.'
Stephen King, MA (Lib), School Librarian and Careers Coordinator, The Duke of York's Royal Military School, 2015

'We buy this book every year and use it all the time, it offers essential careers and higher education advice.'
Dr Beth Linklater, Director of Student Support, Queen Mary's College, 2015

'A fantastic and invaluable resource for UCAS advisers, university applicants and their parents.'
Mark Collins, Head of Economics/Business & Careers, St Teresa's School, 2015

'An invaluable guide to UK degree entry requirements. My "go to" handbook when kick-starting the UCAS process.'
Susan Gower, Head of Year 9 and Careers, Croydon High School, 2015

'I've been a UCAS adviser for most of the past 25 years and I've come to rely on HEAP for clear guidance and up to date info.'
Gabe Crisp, Aspire Co-ordinator, Worthing College, 2015

'An excellent one-stop shop for finding out information on different universities and courses.'
Oswestry School, 2013

'Degree Course Offers is my bible and I couldn't be without it … it gives students focus and saves them time.'
South Thames College, 2013

'Degree Course Offers remains an essential component of our careers library, providing a quick reference to entry requirements and course specific tips for university applications.'
Mid Kent College, 2013

'Degree Course Offers … will keep aspirations realistic.'
www.tes.com/new-teachers, 2011

'An extremely useful guide ….'
Woodhouse Grove School, 2010

'Look out for Brian Heap's excellent books on choosing higher education courses.'
Carre's Grammar School, 2010

'Degree Course Offers by Brian Heap – not to be missed. Invaluable.'
Maidstone Grammar School, 2010

'Degree Course Offers … a really good resource.'
www.sueatkinsparentingcoach.com, 2009

'The guru of university choice.'
The Times, 2007

'For those of you going through Clearing, an absolute must is the Degree Course Offers book. This guide operates subject by subject and gives you each university's requirements, standard offers and, most importantly, "course features".'
The Independent, August 2007

'Brian Heap, the guru of university admissions.'
The Independent, September 2007

'I would like to take this opportunity to congratulate you in maintaining the quality and currency of the information in your guide. We are aware of its wide range and its reputation for impartiality.'
University Senior Assistant Registrar, 2007

'This guide contains useful, practical information for all university applicants and those advising them. I heartily recommend it.'
Dr John Dunford, General Secretary, Association of School and College Leaders, 2005

'An invaluable guide to helping students and their advisers find their way through the maze of degree courses currently on offer.'
Kath Wright, President, Association for Careers Education and Guidance, 2005

'No one is better informed or more experienced than Brian Heap in mediating this range of information to university and college applicants.'
Careers Education and Guidance, October 2005

'The course-listings bible.'
The Guardian, June 2005

CONTENTS

AUTHOR'S ACKNOWLEDGEMENTS

This book and the website www.heaponline.co.uk are a team effort, in which I, my editor Della Oliver, with Emma Davies and Courtney Lawrence and a supporting team at Trotman Publishing, make every effort each year to check the contents for accuracy, including all offers from official sources, up to the publication deadline in March. My team's effort throughout the months of preparation therefore deserves my gratitude and praise. In respect of the offers however, the reader should recognise that offers are constantly changing depending on the range and abilities of candidates and therefore are shown as 'typical' or target offers.

In the ever-changing world of higher education, research must be on-going and each year many individuals are involved in providing additional up-to-date information. These include Caroline Russell at UCAS, Sarah Hannaford at the Cambridge Admissions Office, Helen Charlesworth at the University of Oxford Public Relations Office and also my daughter Jane Heap for her valuable guidance and assistance. In addition, my appreciation goes to HEIST for information on graduate destinations, the many universities and colleges which annually update information, and individual admissions staff who return our requests for information, along with the many teachers and students who furnish me with information on their experiences. To all, I add my grateful thanks.

Brian Heap BA, DA (Manc), ATD
May 2018

Choosing Your University And Degree Course...And Completing Your UCAS Application

Why not contact HEAPS (*Higher Education Advice and Planning Service***) for a telephone consultation for advice on such issues as:**

- **Choosing A-level subjects (which are the best and required subjects and for which degree courses)**
- **Degrees and Diploma courses (making the right choice from a list of thousands!)**
- **Completing your UCAS application (will the admissions tutor remember your personal statement?)**
- **Choosing the right university or college (the best ones for you and your courses)**

For details of services and consultation fees contact:

**The Higher Education Advice and Planning Service
Email heapservice@gmail.com**

ABOUT THIS BOOK

Heap 2019: University Degree Course Offers for 49 years has been a first-stop reference for university and college applicants choosing their courses in higher education by providing information from official sources about how to choose courses and how admissions tutors select students. **Brand new content for this year's edition includes new degree apprenticeship course listings in Chapter 7.**

For 2019/20 higher education applicants, this edition of *Heap 2019: University Degree Course Offers* again aims to provide the latest possible information from universities to help equip them to obtain a degree course place in a fiercely competitive applications process. This level of competition will make it essential for every applicant to research carefully courses and institutions.

Schools, colleges and students quite rightly focus on getting through examinations, particularly when employers and, more so, universities, require specific exam grades in a variety of subjects. But once out of the exam room, where to next? There are many students who restrict their applications to a small number of well-known universities. They must realise that in doing so they are very likely to receive rejections from all of them. Applicants must spread their choices across a wide range of institutions. There are also many students who limit their choice to their best subject, but in doing so miss out on some good alternatives.

How do applicants decide on a strategy to find a place on a degree course? There are more than 1200 separate degree subjects and over 50,000 Joint and Combined Honours courses so how can applicants choose a course that is right for their futures? What can applicants do to find a course place and a university or college that is right for them, when there are over 150 of them? For the past 48 years, for hundreds of students, the answers have been in the next 600 pages of this book.

Heap 2019: University Degree Course Offers is intended to help applicants find their way through these problems by providing the latest possible information about university course offers from official sources, and by giving guidance and information about:

- **Degree courses** – what Honours level courses involve, the range and differences between them, and what applicants need to consider when choosing and deciding on subjects and courses
- **Degree apprenticeships** – what courses are available in different subject areas
- **Universities and higher education colleges** – the range and differences between universities and colleges, and the questions applicants might ask when deciding where to study
- **Admissions information** for every university (listed in **Chapter 3**)
- **Target A-level grades/UCAS points offers** (listed in points order in the subject tables in **Chapter 7**) for 2019 entry to Honours degree courses in universities and colleges, with additional Appendix data for applicants with Scottish Highers/Advanced Highers, the Advanced Welsh Baccalaureate – Skills Challenge Certificate, the International Baccalaureate Diploma, BTEC Level 3 National Extended Diploma, the Extended Project, Music examinations and Art and Design Foundation Studies qualifications
- **The UCAS applications process** – what to do, when to do it and how to prepare the personal statement in the UCAS application
- **Your course** – how to choose by school subjects or career interests
- **Universities' and colleges' admissions policies** – how admissions tutors select students
- **Which universities, colleges and courses use admissions tests for entry**

- Finance, fees and sources of help
- Graduate destinations data for each subject area
- **Action after results day** – and what to do if your grades don't match your offer
- Entry to UK universities and higher education colleges for international students

Heap 2019: University Degree Course Offers provides essential information for all students preparing to go into higher education in 2019, covering all stages of researching, planning, deciding and applying to courses and universities. To provide the latest possible information the book is compiled each year between October and March for publication in May and includes important data from the many universities and colleges responding to questionnaires each year.

Every effort is made to ensure the book is as up to date as possible. Nevertheless, the increased demand for places is expected to lead to offers changes during 2019/20, and after prospectuses have been published. Some institutions may also discontinue courses as a result of government cuts and the changes in tuition fees. It will be essential for applicants to check institutions' websites **frequently** to find out any changes in offers, course availability and requirements. If you have any queries, contact admissions staff without delay to find out the latest information as institutions, for many courses, will be looking for a very close, if not precise, match between their requirements and what you offer in your application, qualifications and grades.

Heap 2019: University Degree Course Offers is your starting point for moving on into higher education and planning ahead. Used in conjunction with *Choosing Your Degree Course & University* (see **Appendix 4**) it will take you through all the stages in choosing the course and place of study that is right for you. Now go for it!

Brian Heap
May 2018

Every effort has been made to maintain absolute accuracy in providing course information and to ensure that the entire book is as up to date as possible. However, changes are constantly taking place in higher education so it is important for readers to check carefully with prospectuses and websites before submitting their applications.

The problem You and 600,000 students (including 100,000 from the EU and overseas) are applying for university places in the UK this year. You have a choice of about 1200 degree subjects and many of these are joint or combined courses from over 150 universities and colleges.

The Choice It depends what you want. There are three types of degrees. 1. Academic courses, eg History, Anthropology, Geography and Philosophy. Don't worry about graduate employment yet; many occupations are open to you when you graduate and commence specialist training, eg law, accountancy, business. 2. Vocational courses, eg medical careers, engineering and hospitality management. Some courses have opportunities to spend part of your degree course in full time employment with pay as part of the course. 3. Practical courses, eg Art and Design, Drama, Music and Sports Studies.

There are two possible options for choosing your degree course:

Many students want to follow a degree course by way of their favourite and best subject. **See Section A**. School subjects are listed along with other degree courses which have some similarities.

Section B lists careers which may appeal to you and the degree courses which are linked to them.

SECTION A
Choosing your course by school subjects
Accounting Accountancy, Accounting, Actuarial Mathematics, Banking and Finance, Business Studies (Finance), Economics, Finance Investment and Risk, Financial Mathematics, Financial Software Engineering, Management Sciences, Mathematics. See also **Section B**.

Ancient history Archaeology, Biblical Studies, Classical Greek, Classics and Classical Civilisation, Latin, Middle and Near Eastern Studies.

Arabic Arabic. See also **Languages** below.

Art and design Art, Fine Art, Furniture Design, Graphic Design, Photography, Textile Design, Theatre Design, Three-Dimensional Design, Typography and Graphic Communication. See also **Section B**.

Bengali Bengali. See also **Languages** below.

Biblical Hebrew Hebrew, Religious Studies, Theology.

Biology Agricultural Sciences, Animal Behaviour, Audiology, Bioinformatics, Biological Sciences, Biology, Biomedical Sciences, Biotechnology, Dental Hygiene, Ecology and Conservation, Environmental Sciences, Genetics, Human Embryology, Infection and Immunity, Life Sciences, Medicine, Microbiology, Molecular Sciences, Natural Sciences, Physiology, Plant Biology, Plant Science, Veterinary Science, Zoology. See also **Section B**.

Business Accounting, Banking, Business Management, Business Statistics, Computing, Economics, Entrepreneurship, Finance, Hospitality Management, Human Resource Management, Information Systems, Logistics, Management Sciences, Marketing, Mathematics, Publishing, Retail Management, Transport Management, Web Design and Development. See also **Section B**.

Chemistry Biochemistry, Cancer Biology, Chemical Engineering, Chemical Physics, Chemistry, Dentistry, Environmental Sciences, Fire Engineering, Forensic Sciences, Medicinal Chemistry, Medicine, Microbiology, Natural Sciences, Nutritional Biochemistry, Pharmacology, Pharmacy, Veterinary Science, Virology and Immunology. See also **Section B**.

Chinese Chinese. See also **Languages** below.

Classics and classical civilisation Ancient History, Archaeology, Classical Studies, Classics, Greek (Classical), Latin.

Computer science Artificial Intelligence, Business Information Systems, Computer Engineering, Computer Science, Computing, Cybernetics, E-Commerce, Electronic Engineering, Games Technology, Intelligent Product Design, Multimedia Systems Engineering, Network Management and Security, Robotics, Software Engineering. See also **Section B**.

Dance Arts Management, Ballet Education, Choreography, Dance, Drama, Education, Music, Musical Theatre, Performance Management, Performing Arts, Sport and Exercise, Street Arts, Theatre and Performance, Theatre Arts, Writing Directing and Performance. See also **Section B**.

Design technology Food Technology, Manufacturing Engineering, Product Design, Sport Equipment Design, Systems and Control. See also **Section B**.

Drama and theatre studies Acting, Community Drama, Costume Production, Creative Writing, Dance, Drama, Education Studies, English Comedy: Writing and Performance, International Theatre, Music, Performing Arts, Scenic Arts, Scriptwriting, Set Design, Stage Management, Theatre Arts, Theatre Practice. See also **Section B**.

Economics Accountancy, Banking, Business Administration, Business Economics, Business Studies, Development Studies, Economics, Estate Management, Finance, Management Science, Mathematics, Political Economy, Politics, Quantity Surveying, Sociology, Statistics.

Electronics Computing, Electronics, Engineering (Aeronautical, Aerospace, Communication, Computer, Software, Systems), Mechatronics, Medical Electronics, Multimedia Technology, Technology. See also **Section B**.

English language and literature Communication Studies, Comparative Literature, Creative Writing, Drama, Education, English Language, English Literature, Information and Library Studies/Management, Journalism, Linguistics, Media Writing, Philosophy, Publishing, Scottish Literature, Scriptwriting, Theatre Studies.

Environmental sciences Biological Sciences, Biology, Earth Sciences, Ecology, Environment and Planning, Environmental Management, Environmental Sciences, Forestry, Geography, Geology, Land Management, Marine Biology, Meteorology, Oceanography, Outdoor Education, Plant Sciences, Sustainable Development, Wastes Management, Water Science, Wildlife Biology, Wildlife Conservation, Zoology.

French French, International Business Studies, International Hospitality Management, Law with French Law. See also **Languages** below.

Geography Development Studies, Earth Sciences, Environmental Policy, Environmental Sciences, Estate Management, Forestry, Geographical Information Science, Geography, Geology, Land Economy, Meteorology, Oceanography, Surveying, Town and Country Planning, Urban Studies, Water Science.

Geology Earth Sciences, Geography, Geology, Geophysical Sciences, Geosciences, Meteorology, Mining Engineering, Natural Sciences, Oceanography, Palaeontology and Evolution, Planetary Sciences, Water and Environmental Management. See also **Section B**.

German German, International Business Studies, International Hospitality Management, Law with German Law. See also **Languages** below.

Government/Politics Development Studies, Economics, Global Politics, Government, History, Human Rights, Industrial Relations, International Politics, Law, Peace Studies, Politics, Public Administration, Social and Political Science, Social Policy, Sociology, Strategic Studies, War Studies.

Gujarati Gujarati. See also **Languages** below.

History African Studies, American Studies, Ancient History, Archaeology, Art History, Classical Civilisations, Classical Studies, Education, Egyptology, Fashion and Dress History, History, International Relations, Law, Literature, Medieval Studies, Museum and Heritage Studies, Philosophy, Politics, Russian Studies,

Scandinavian Studies, Scottish History, Social and Economic History, Theology and Religious Studies, Victorian Studies.

Italian Italian. See also **Languages** below.

Japanese Japanese. See also **Languages** below.

Languages Languages, Modern Languages, Translating and Interpreting. **NB** Apart from French and German – and Spanish for some universities – it is not usually necessary to have completed an A-level language course before studying the many languages (over 60) offered at degree level. Many universities provide opportunities to study a language in a wide range of degree courses. See also **The Erasmus+ Programme** details in **Chapter 4**.

Law Criminal Justice, Criminology, European Business Law, Human Rights, International Business, International Relations, Law, Legal Studies, Police Sciences, Social Sciences, Sociology, Youth Justice. See also **Section B**.

Mathematics Accountancy, Actuarial Mathematics, Aeronautical Engineering, Astrophysics, Business Management, Chemical Engineering, Civil Engineering, Computational Science, Computer Systems Engineering, Control Systems Engineering, Cybernetics, Economics, Engineering Science, Ergonomics, Financial Mathematics, Further and Additional Mathematics, Geophysics, Management Science, Materials Science and Technology, Mechanical Engineering, Meteorology, Naval Architecture, Physics, Quantity Surveying, Statistics, Systems Analysis, Telecommunications.

Media studies Advertising, Animation, Broadcasting, Communication Studies, Creative Writing, English, Film and Television Studies, Journalism, Mass Communication, Media courses, Media Culture and Society, Media Production, Media Technology, Multimedia, Photography, Publishing, Radio Production and Communication, Society Culture and Media, Translation Media and French/Spanish, Web and Broadcasting. See also **Section B**.

Modern Greek Greek. See also **Languages** above.

Modern Hebrew Hebrew. See also **Languages** above.

Music Audio and Music Production, Creative Music Technology, Education, Music, Music Broadcasting, Music Informatics, Music Management, Music Systems Engineering, Musical Theatre, Musician, Performance Arts, Popular and World Musics, Sonic Arts. See also **Section B**.

Persian Persian. See also **Languages** above.

Philosophy Classical Studies, Cultural Studies, Divinity, Educational Studies, Ethics, History of Ideas, History of Science, Law, Mathematics, Natural Sciences, Philosophy, Politics Philosophy and Economics, Psychology, Religious Studies, Social Sciences, Theology.

Physics Aeronautical Engineering, Architecture, Astronomy, Astrophysics, Automotive Engineering, Biomedical Engineering, Biophysics, Chemical Physics, Civil Engineering, Communications Engineering, Computer Science, Cybernetics, Education, Electrical/Electronic Engineering, Engineering Science, Ergonomics, Geophysics, Materials Science and Technology, Mechanical Engineering, Medical Physics, Meteorology, Nanotechnology, Naval Architecture, Oceanography, Optometry, Photonics, Planetary Science, Quantum Informatics, Radiography, Renewable Energy, Telecommunications Engineering.

Polish Polish. See also **Languages** above.

Portuguese Portuguese. See also **Languages** above.

Psychology Advertising, Animal Behaviour, Anthropology, Artificial Intelligence, Behavioural Science, Childhood Strudies, Cognitive Science, Counselling Studies, Criminology, Education, Human Resource Management, Marketing, Neuroscience, Nursing, Politics, Psychology, Social Sciences, Sociology, Speech and Language Therapy. See also **Section B**.

Punjabi Punjabi. See also **Languages** above.

Religious studies Abrahamic Religions (Christianity, Islam and Judaism), Anthropology, Archaeology, Biblical Studies, Christian Youth Work, Comparative Religion, Divinity, Education, Ethics, History of Art, International Relations, Islamic Studies, Jewish Studies, Philosophy, Psychology, Religious Studies, Social Policy, Theology.

Russian Russian. See also **Languages** above.

Sport and physical education Chiropractic, Coaching Science, Community Sport Development, Dance Studies, Exercise and Health, Exercise Science, Fitness Science, Football Studies, Golf Studies, Osteopathy, Outdoor Pursuits, Physical Education, Physiotherapy, Sport and Exercise Science, Sport and Health, Sport Coaching, Sport Equipment Design, Sport Management, Sport Marketing, Teaching (Primary) (Secondary).

Statistics Actuarial Studies, Business Analysis, Business Studies, Informatics, Management Sciences, Statistics. See also **Mathematics** above and **Section B** Mathematics-related careers.

Turkish Turkish. See also **Languages** above.

Urdu Urdu. See also **Languages** above.

SECTION B
Choosing your course by career interests

Accountancy Accountancy, Accounting, Actuarial Science, Banking, Business Studies, Economics, Finance and Business, Finance and Investment, Financial Services, Management Science, Real Estate Management, Risk Management.

Actuarial work Actuarial Mathematics, Actuarial Science, Actuarial Studies, Financial Mathematics, Risk Analysis and Insurance.

Agricultural careers Agri-Business, Agricultural Engineering, Agriculture, Animal Sciences, Aquaculture and Fishery Sciences, Conservation and Habitat Management, Countryside Management, Crop Science, Ecology, Environmental Science, Estate Management, Forestry, Horticulture, Landscape Management, Plant Sciences, Rural Resource Management, Soil Science, Wildlife Management.

Animal careers Agricultural Sciences, Animal Behaviour and Welfare, Biological Sciences, Bioveterinary Science, Equine Management/Science/Studies, Veterinary Nursing, Veterinary Practice Management, Veterinary Science, Zoology.

Archaeology Ancient History, Anthropology, Archaeology, Bioarchaeology, Classical Civilisation and Classics, Egyptology, Geography, History, History of Art and Architecture, Viking Studies.

Architecture Architectural Design, Architectural Technology, Architecture, Building, Building Conservation, City and Regional Planning, Civil Engineering, Conservation and Restoration, Construction Engineering and Management, Interior Architecture, Stained Glass Restoration and Conservation, Structural Engineering.

Art and Design careers Advertising, Animation, Architecture, Art, Design, Digital Media Design, Education (Art), Fashion and Textiles, Fine Art, Games Art and Design, Glassware, Graphic Design, Illustration, Industrial Design, Jewellery, Landscape Architecture, Photography, Stained Glass, Three-Dimensional Design.

Astronomy Astronomy, Astrophysics, Mathematics, Natural Sciences, Planetary Geology, Physics, Quantum and Cosmological Physics, Space Science, Space Technology and Planetary Exploration.

Audiology Audiology, Education of the Deaf, Human Communication, Nursing, Speech and Language Therapy.

Banking/Insurance Accountancy, Actuarial Sciences, Banking, Business Studies, Economics, Financial Services, Insurance, Real Estate Management, Risk Management.

Biology-related careers Agricultural Sciences, Animal Sciences, Biochemistry, Biological Sciences, Biology, Biomedical Sciences, Biotechnology, Cell Biology, Ecology, Education, Environmental Biology, Environmental Sciences, Freshwater Science, Genetics, Immunology, Life Sciences, Marine Biology,

Medical Biochemistry, Medicine, Microbiology, Molecular Biology, Natural Sciences, Oceanography, Pharmacy, Plant Science, Physiology, Wildlife Conservation, Zoology.

Book Publishing Advertising, Business Studies, Communications, Creative Writing, Illustration, Journalism, Media Communication, Photography, Printing, Publishing, Science Communication, Web and Multimedia.

Brewing and Distilling Biochemistry, Brewing and Distilling, Chemistry, Food Science and Technology, Viticulture and Oenology.

Broadcasting Audio Video and Digital Broadcast Engineering, Broadcast Documentary, Broadcast Media, Broadcast Technology and Production, Digital Media, Electronic Engineering (Broadcast Systems), Film and TV Broadcasting, Media and Communications Studies, Media Production, Multimedia, Music Broadcasting, Outside Broadcast Technology, Radio Journalism, Television Studio Production, TV Production, Video and Broadcasting.

Building Architecture, Building Conservation, Building Services Engineering, Building Studies, Building Surveying, Civil Engineering, Estate Management, General Practice Surveying, Land Surveying, Quantity Surveying.

Business Accountancy Advertising, Banking, Business Administration, Business Analysis, Business Studies, Business Systems, E-Commerce, Economics, Estate Management, European Business, Hospitality Management, Housing Management, Human Resource Management, Industrial Relations, Insurance, Logistics, Management Sciences, Marketing, Property Development, Public Relations, Publishing, Supply Chain Management, Transport Management, Tourism.

Cartography Geographic Information Systems, Geographical Information Science, Geography, Land Surveying.

Catering Consumer Studies, Culinary Arts Management, Dietetics, Food Science, Hospitality Management, International and Hospitality Business Management, Nutrition.

Chemistry-related careers Agricultural Science, Biochemistry, Botany, Ceramics, Chemical Engineering, Chemistry, Colour Chemistry, Education, Environmental Sciences, Geochemistry, Materials Science and Technology, Medical Chemistry, Nanotechnology, Natural Sciences, Pharmacology, Pharmacy, Physiology, Technologies (for example Food, Plastics).

Computing Artificial Intelligence, Bioinformatics, Business Computing, Business Studies, Computer Engineering, Computer Games Development, Computer Science, Computers, Electronics and Communications, Digital Forensics and System Security, Electronic Engineering, Games Design, Information and Communication Technology, Internet Computing, Mathematics, Multimedia Computing, Physics, Software Systems, Telecommunications, Virtual Reality Design.

Construction Architectural Technology, Architecture, Building, Building Services Engineering, Civil Engineering, Construction Management, Fire Risk Engineering, Landscape Architecture, Quantity Surveying, Surveying, Town and Country Planning.

Dance Ballet Education, Choreography, Dance, Drama, Movement Studies, Performance/Performing Arts, Physical Education, Theatre Studies.

Dentistry Biochemistry, Dental Materials, Dental Technician, Dentistry, Equine Dentistry, Medicine, Nursing, Oral Health Sciences, Pharmacy.

Drama Dance, Drama, Education, Movement Studies, Musical Theatre, Scenic Arts, Teaching, Theatre Management.

Education Ballet Education, British Sign Language, Childhood Studies, Coach Education, Deaf Studies, Early Years Education, Education Studies, Education with QTS, Education without QTS, Music Education, Physical Education, Primary Education, Psychology, Secondary Education, Social Work, Special Educational Needs, Speech and Language Therapy, Sport and Exercise, Teaching, Technology for Teaching and Learning, Youth Studies.

Electronics Automotive Electronics, Avionics, Computer Systems, Computer Technology, Computing, Digital Electronics, Digital Media Technology, Electronic Design, Electronic Engineering, Electronics,

Information Systems, Internet Engineering, Mechatronics, Medical Electronics, Motorsport Electronic Systems, Multimedia Computing, Software Development, Sound Engineering.

Engineering Engineering (including Aeronautical, Aerospace, Chemical, Civil, Computing, Control, Electrical, Electronic, Energy, Environmental, Food Process, Manufacturing, Mechanical, Motorsport, Nuclear, Product Design, Software, Telecommunications), Geology and Geotechnics, Horology, Mathematics, Physics.

Estate Management Architecture, Building, Civil Engineering, Economics, Estate Management, Forestry, Housing Studies, Landscape Architecture, Property Development, Real Estate Management, Town and Country Planning.

Food Science and Technology Biochemistry, Brewing and Distilling, Chemistry, Culinary Arts, Dietetics, Food and Consumer Studies, Food Safety Management, Food Science and Technology, Food Supply Chain Management, Fresh Produce Management, Hospitality and Food Management, Nutrition, Public Health Nutrition, Viticulture and Oenology.

Forestry Arboriculture, Biological Sciences, Countryside Management, Ecology, Environmental Science, Forestry, Horticulture, Plant Sciences, Rural Resource Management, Tropical Forestry, Urban Forestry.

Furniture Design Furniture Design, Furniture Production, History of Art and Design, Three-Dimensional Design, Timber Technology.

Geology-related careers Chemistry, Earth Sciences, Engineering (Civil, Minerals), Environmental Sciences, Geochemistry, Geography, Geology, Land Surveying, Oceanography, Soil Science.

Graphic Design Advertising, Graphic Design, Photography, Printing, Web Design.

Health and Safety careers Biomedical Informatics, Biomedical Sciences, Community and Health Studies, Environmental Health, Exercise and Health Science, Fire Science Engineering, Health and Social Care, Health Management, Health Promotion, Health Psychology, Health Sciences, Holistic Therapy, Nursing, Occupational Safety and Health, Paramedic Science, Public Health, Public Services Management. (See also **Medical careers**.)

Horticulture Agriculture, Crop Science, Horticulture, Landscape Architecture, Plant Science, Soil Science.

Hospitality Management Business and Management, Culinary Arts Management, Events and Facilities Management, Food Science, Food Technology, Heritage Management, Hospitality Management, Human Resource Management, International Hospitality Management, Leisure Services Management, Licensed Retail Management, Spa Management, Travel and Tourism Management.

Housing Architecture, Estate Management, General Practice Surveying, Housing, Social Administration, Town and Country Planning.

Law Business Law, Commercial Law, Consumer Law, Criminal Justice, Criminology, European Law, Government and Politics, International History, Land Management, Law, Legal Studies, Politics, Sociology.

Leisure and Recreation Adventure Tourism, Airline and Airport Management, Business Travel and Tourism, Community Arts, Countryside Management, Dance, Drama, Event Management, Fitness Science, Hospitality Management, International Tourism Management, Leisure Management, Movement Studies, Music, Physical Education, Sport and Leisure Management, Sport Development, Sports Management, Theatre Studies, Travel and Tourism.

Library and Information Management Administration, Business Information Systems, Digital Media, Education Studies, Information and Communication Studies, Information and Library Studies, Information Management, Information Sciences and Technology, Management and Marketing, Media and Cultural Studies, Media Communications, Museum and Galleries Studies, Publishing.

Marketing Advertising, Business Studies, Consumer Science, E-Marketing, Health Promotion, International Business, Marketing, Psychology, Public Relations, Retail Management, Sports Development, Travel and Tourism.

Materials Science/Metallurgy Automotive Materials, Chemistry, Engineering, Glass Science and Technology, Materials Science and Technology, Mineral Surveying, Physics, Polymer Science, Sports Materials, Textile Science.

Mathematics-related careers Accountancy, Actuarial Science, Astronomy, Banking, Business Decision Mathematics, Business Studies, Computer Studies, Economics, Education, Engineering, Financial Mathematics, Mathematical Physics, Mathematics, Physics, Quantity Surveying, Statistics.

Media careers Advertising, Broadcasting, Communications, Computer Graphics, Creative Writing, Film/Video Production, Journalism, Media, Multimedia, Photography, Public Relations, Psychology, Visual Communication.

Medical careers Anatomy, Biochemistry, Biological Sciences, Biomedical Sciences, Chiropractic, Dentistry, Genetics, Human Physiology, Immunology, Medical Engineering, Medical Sciences/Medicine, Nursing, Occupational Therapy, Orthoptics, Osteopathy, Pathology and Microbiology, Pharmacology, Pharmacy, Physiotherapy, Psychology, Radiography, Speech and Language Therapy, Sports Biomedicine, Virology.

Music Commercial Music, Creative Music Technology, Digital Music, Drama, Folk and Traditional Music, Music, Music Composition, Music Education, Music Industry Management, Music Performance, Music Production, Music Studies, Musical Theatre, Performance/Performing Arts, Popular Music, Sonic Arts, Sound and Multimedia Technology, Theatre Studies.

Nautical careers Marine Engineering, Marine Studies, Nautical Studies, Naval Architecture, Oceanography, Offshore Engineering, Ship Science.

Naval Architecture Boat Design, Marine Engineering, Marine Studies, Naval Architecture, Offshore Engineering, Ship Science, Yacht and Powercraft Design, Yacht Production.

Nursing Anatomy, Applied Biology, Biochemistry, Biological Sciences, Biology, Dentistry, Education, Environmental Health and Community Studies, Health Studies, Human Biology, Medicine, Midwifery, Nursing, Occupational Therapy, Orthoptics, Physiotherapy, Podiatry, Psychology, Radiography, Social Administration, Speech and Language Therapy, Veterinary Nursing. (See also **Medical careers**.)

Nutrition Dietetics, Food Science and Technology, Health Promotion, Human Nutrition, Nursing, Nutrition, Sport and Fitness.

Occupational Therapy Art, General and Mental Nursing, Occupational Therapy, Orthoptics, Physiotherapy, Psychology, Social Sciences, Speech and Language Therapy.

Optometry Applied Physics, Optometry, Orthoptics, Physics.

Photography/Film/TV Animation, Communication Studies (some courses), Digital Video Design, Documentary Communications, Film and Media, Graphic Art, Media Studies, Moving Image, Multimedia, Photography.

Physics-related careers Applied Physics, Astronomy, Astrophysics, Avionics and Space Systems, Education, Electronics, Engineering (Civil, Electrical, Mechanical), Laser Physics, Mathematical Physics, Medical Instrumentation, Molecular Physics, Nanotechnology, Natural Sciences, Optometry, Physics, Planetary and Space Physics, Quantum and Cosmological Physics, Theoretical Physics.

Physiotherapy Chiropractic, Exercise Science, Nursing, Orthoptics, Osteopathy, Physical Education, Physiotherapy, Sport and Exercise, Sports Rehabilitation.

Production Technology Engineering (Manufacturing, Mechanical), Materials Science.

Property and Valuation Management Architecture, Building Surveying, Estate Agency, Property Investment and Finance, Property Management and Valuation, Quantity Surveying, Real Estate Management, Residential Property, Urban Land Economics.

Psychology Advertising, Animal Sciences, Anthropology, Applied Social Studies, Behavioural Science, Business, Cognitive Science, Criminology, Early Childhood Studies, Education, Human Resource Management, Human Sciences, Linguistics, Marketing, Neuroscience, Occupational Therapy, Psychology

(Clinical, Developmental, Educational, Experimental, Forensic, Health, Occupational, Social, Sports), Psychosocial Sciences, Public Relations, Social Sciences, Sociology.

Public Administration Applied Social Studies, Business Studies, Public Administration, Public Policy Investment and Management, Public Services, Social Administration, Social Policy, Youth Studies.

Quantity Surveying Architecture, Building, Civil Engineering, Construction and Commercial Management, Environmental Construction Surveying, Surveying (Building, Land and Valuation), Surveying Technology.

Radiography Anatomy, Audiology, Biological Sciences, Clinical Photography, Diagnostic Imaging, Diagnostic Radiography, Digital Imaging, Imaging Science and Technology, Medical Imaging, Moving Image, Nursing, Orthoptics, Photography, Physics, Physiology, Physiotherapy, Radiography, Radiotherapy, Therapeutic Radiography.

Silversmithing/Jewellery Design Silversmithing and Jewellery, Silversmithing Goldsmithing and Jewellery, Silversmithing Metalwork and Jewellery, Three-Dimensional Design.

Social Work Abuse Studies, Applied Social Science, Community Work, Counselling Studies, Early Childhood Studies, Education, Health and Social Care, Human Rights, Journalism, Law, Nursing, Playwork, Politics and Government, Psychology, Public Administration, Religious Studies, Social Administration, Social Policy, Social Work, Sociology, Town and Country Planning, Youth Studies.

Speech and Language Therapy Audiology, Education (Special Education), Linguistics, Nursing, Occupational Therapy, Psychology, Radiography, Speech and Language Therapy.

Sport and Physical Education Coaching Sciences, Exercise Sciences, Fitness Science, Health and Fitness Management, Leisure and Recreation Management, Physical Education, Sport and Recreational Studies, Sport Journalism, Sports Psychology, Sports Science, Sports Studies.

Statistics Business Studies, Economics, Informatics, Mathematics, Operational Research, Population Sciences, Statistics.

Surveying Building Surveying, General Practice Surveying, Property Development, Quantity Surveying, Real Estate Management.

Technology Audio Technology, Dental Technology, Design Technology, Food Science and Technology, Football Technology, Logistics Technology, Medical Technology, Music Studio Technology, Paper Science, Polymer Science, Product Design Technology, Sports Technology, Technology for Teaching and Learning, Timber Technology.

Textile Design Applied Art and Design, Art, Clothing Studies, Fashion Design, Interior Design, Textile Design (Embroidery, Constructive Textiles, Printed Textiles), Textile Management.

Theatre Design Drama, Interior Design, Leisure and Recreational Studies, Theatre Design, Theatre Management, Theatre Studies.

Three-Dimensional Design Architecture, Industrial Design, Interior Design, Theatre Design, Three-Dimensional Design.

Town and Regional Planning Architecture, Architecture and Planning, City and Regional Planning, Environmental Planning, Estate Management, Geography, Housing, Land Economy, Planning and Development, Population Sciences, Property Planning and Development, Spatial Planning, Statistics, Sustainable Development, Town and Regional Planning, Transport Management, Urban and Regional Planning.

Transport Air Transport Engineering, Air Transport Operations, Air Transport with Pilot Training, Business Studies, Civil and Transportation Engineering, Cruise Operations Management, Industrial Design (Transport), Logistics, Planning with Transport, Supply Chain Management, Sustainable Transport Design, Town and Regional Planning, Urban Planning Design and Management.

Typography and Graphic Communication Design (Graphic and Typographic Design), Digital Graphics, Fine Art (Print and Digital Media), Graphic Communication and Typography, Graphic Design, Illustration, Illustration and Print, Printmaking, Publication Design, Publishing, Visual Communication.

Veterinary careers Agricultural Sciences, Agriculture, Anatomical Science, Animal Behaviour and Welfare, Animal Sciences, Bioveterinary Sciences, Equine Dentistry, Equine Science, Medicine, Pharmacology, Pharmacy, Veterinary Medicine, Veterinary Nursing, Veterinary Practice Management, Zoology.

COURSE TYPES AND DIFFERENCES
The options
You will then need to decide on the type of course you want to follow. The way in which Honours degree courses are arranged differs between institutions. For example, a subject might be offered as a single subject course (a Single Honours degree), or as a two-subject course (a Joint Honours degree), or as one of two, three or four subjects (a Combined Honours degree) or a Major/Minor degree (75% and 25% of each subject respectively).

Entry requirements
Courses in the same subject at different universities and colleges can have different subject requirements so it is important to check the acceptability of your GCE A-levels and GCSE subjects (or equivalent) for all your preferred courses. Specific GCE A-levels, and in some cases, GCSE subjects, may be stipulated. (See also **Chapter 6** and **Appendix 1** for information on Scottish Highers/Advanced Highers, the Advanced Welsh Baccalaureate – Skills Challenge Certificate, the International Baccalaureate Diploma, BTEC Level 3 National Extended Diploma, the Extended Project, Music examinations and Art and Design Foundation Studies, and **Appendix 2** for international qualifications.)

SANDWICH COURSES AND PROFESSIONAL PLACEMENTS
The benefits
Media coverage on student debt and tuition fees highlights the importance of sandwich courses. Many vocational courses offer sandwich periods and placements of 6 or 12 months in which students spend time away from their university or college in industry, commerce or in the public sector as part of a four-year degree course. The advantages of these courses can be quite considerable. Not only may students receive an income from the company, but contacts made can lead to permanent employment on graduation.

Work-based learning (WBL) programmes
Some colleges also offer work-based learning programmes in which placements last a few weeks when students can gain experience of different careers.

Students report ...
'I was able to earn £15,000 during my year out and £4000 during my three-month vacation with the same firm.' (**Bath** Engineering)

'There's really no other better way to find out what you want to do for your future career than having tried it for a year.' (**Aston** Human Resources Management)

'It was a welcome break in formal university education: I met some great people including students from other universities.' (**Kingston** Biochemistry)

'Having experienced a year in a working environment, I am more confident and more employable than students without this experience.' (**Aston** Business Studies)

'At Sanofi in Toulouse, I learned to think on my feet – no two days were the same.' (**Aston** European Studies)

'I have seen how an organisation works at first-hand, learned how academic skills may be applied in a working environment, become proficient in the use of various software, acquired new skills in interpersonal relationships and communications and used my period away to realign my career perspectives.' (**Aston** European Studies)

'I was working alongside graduate employees and the firm offered me a job when I graduated.' (**Bath** Mathematics)

Employers, too, gain from having students ...
'We meet a lot of enthusiastic potential recruits who bring new ideas into the firm, and we can offer them commercially sponsored help for their final year project.'

'The quality of this student has remained high throughout the year. He will do well for his next employer, whoever that may be. However, I sincerely hope that it will be with us.'

University staff advise ...
'We refer to sandwich courses as professional placements, not "work experience" which is a phrase we reserve for short non-professional experiences, for example summer or pre-university jobs. The opportunity is available to all students but their success in gaining a good placement depends on academic ability.' (**Bath**)

'Where a placement year is optional, those who opt for it are more likely to be awarded a First or an Upper Second compared to those who don't, not because they are given more marks for doing it, but because they always seem to have added context and motivation for their final year.' (**Aston**)

When choosing your sandwich course, check with the university (a) that the institution will guarantee a list of employers, (b) whether placement experience counts towards the final degree result, (c) that placements are paid and (d) that placements are validated by professional bodies. Finally, once you start on the course, remember that your first-year academic performance will be taken into account by potential employers. Now read on!

What do employers require when considering students?
Aston (Biol) Successful second year undergraduates; (Bus) Number of UCAS points, degree programme, any prior experience; (Eng) UCAS points scores and expected degree classification; (Mech Eng) Students interviewed and selected by the company according to student ability, what they are studying and specific needs of the job. **Bath** (Chem) 'Good students': Upper Second or above and non-international students (those without work visas). Students with strong vivisection views rejected; (Mech Elec Eng) Subject-based, eg electronics, aerospace, computing and electrical engineering; (Mech Eng) Good communication, IT and social skills; (Maths) Interest in positions of responsibility, teamwork, integrity, self-motivation, analytical ability, communication, recent work experience, knowledge of the company, desire to work for the company, predicted 2.1; (Phys) Many organisations have cut-offs regarding students' first-year performance (eg must be heading for a 2.1 although some require better than this), some need students to be particularly good in some areas (eg lab work, computer programming), many require UK nationality with minimum residency condition. **Brunel** Requirements not usually specified except for IT jobs since they need technical skills. **Cardiff Met** (Clsrm Asst) Disclosure and Barring Service (DBS) checks. **Kingston** (Bus Law) Theoretical knowledge and a stated interest in certain areas (eg finance, human resources, marketing, sales, IT), excellent communication skills, teamwork, ability to prioritise, time management and a professional attitude; (Sci) Grades are rarely mentioned: it's usually a specific module or course requirement undertaken by the students that they are looking for, as well as a good attitude, motivation, initiative: a good all-rounder. **Loughborough** (Civ Eng) Target specific courses.

What are the advantages of placements to the students?
Aston (Biol) Many take jobs with their placement employers (eg NHS), gaining valuable research and clinical experience; (Bus) Graduate job offers, sponsorship through the final year of the course, gym membership, staff discounts; (Eng) Some students are fast-tracked into full-time employment and, in some cases, have been given higher starting salaries as a result of the placement with the company; (Mech Eng) Offers of full-time employment on graduation, bursaries for their final year of study, final year projects following placements, better class of degree. **Bath** (Chem) Sponsorships for final year project work, offers of full-time employment, PhD offers and work-to-study courses, industrial references, establishment of prizes; (Maths) Sponsorship in the second year, graduate employment, bonuses during placement, travel abroad during placement, sponsorship during final year; (Phys) Job offers on graduation, sponsored final year, improved study skills for final year, job market awareness, career decisions. **Brunel** Higher percentage of students get Firsts, many students get a job offer from the placement provider, higher salaries often paid to sandwich course students, some students get exemptions from

professional exams, eg ACCA, ACA and IMechE. **Cardiff Met** (Clsrm Asst) Good experience in team work, classroom experience, coaching, mentoring: decisions made whether or not to follow a teaching career. **Kingston** (Bus Law) Sponsorships fewer these days but students return with more confidence and maturity and better able to complete their final year; 70% receive job offers on completion of a successful placement; (Sci) Full-time employment on graduation and occasionally part-time work in the final year; many students are encouraged to write their final year dissertation whilst on placement and benefit from the company's support, subject matter and validation. **Loughborough** (Civ Eng) Most students are sponsored by their firms and perform better in their final examinations; (Prod Des) Final year bursary for some students, offer of employment by the sponsor and a final year design project for the sponsor.

DEGREE APPRENTICESHIP COURSES

Degree apprenticeship courses combine a full degree with practical work. They are designed in partnership with employers – apprentices will be employed throughout and earning a wage, with part-time study taking place at a university. They can be completed to bachelor's or master's degree level and take between three and six years to complete, depending on the level of the course. Currently, the scheme operates across England and Wales only, although applications may be made from all parts of the UK. Since degree apprenticeships are new, there are only a limited number of vacancies available at present. It is anticipated that the number of vacancies will grow over the coming years. See www.ucas.com/degree-apprenticeships for further details.

MATURE APPLICANTS

There are a great many mature students following first degree courses in UK universities and colleges. The following is a list of key points a group of mature students found useful in exploring and deciding on a university course.

- Check with your nearest university or college to find out about the courses they can offer, for example degrees, diplomas, full-time, part-time.
- Some institutions will require examination passes in some subjects, others may not.
- An age limit may apply for some vocational courses, for example Medicine, Dentistry and Teaching.
- If entry requirements are an obstacle, prospective students should approach their local colleges for information on Access or distance-learning courses such as those offered by the National Extension College. These courses are fast-growing in number and popularity, offering adults an alternative route into higher education other than A-levels. They are usually developed jointly by colleges of further education and the local higher education institution.
- Demands of the course – how much time will be required for study? What are the assignments and the deadlines to be met? How is your work assessed – unseen examinations, continuous assessment, practicals?
- The demands on finance – cost of the course – loan needed – loss of earnings – drop in income if changing to another career – travel requirements – accommodation – need to work part-time for income?
- The availability and suitability of the course – geographical location – competition for places – where it will lead – student support services, for example childcare, library.
- What benefits will you derive? Fulfilment, transferable skills, social contacts, sense of achievement, enjoyment, self-esteem, career enhancement?
- Why would employers want to recruit you? Ability to adapt to the work scene, realistic and balanced approach, mature attitude to work?
- Why would employers not want to recruit you? Salary expectations, inability to fit in with younger colleagues, limited mobility? However, some employers particularly welcome older graduates: civil service, local authorities, health service, religious, charitable and voluntary organisations, teaching, social/probation work, careers work, housing.

MODULAR COURSES AND CREDIT ACCUMULATION AND TRANSFER SCHEMES (CATS)

Courses can also differ considerably not only in their content but in how they are organised. Many universities and colleges of higher education have modularised their courses which means you can choose modules of different subjects, and 'build' your course within specified 'pathways' with the help and approval of your course tutor. It also means that you are likely to be assessed after completing each module, rather than in your last year for all your previous years' learning. In almost every course the options and modules offered include some which reflect the research interests of individual members of staff. In some courses subsidiary subjects are available as minor courses alongside a Single Honours course. In an increasing number of courses these additional subjects include a foreign language, and the importance of this cannot be over-emphasised, as language skills are increasingly in demand by employers, and studying a language may also open up opportunities for further study abroad. A popular option is the Erasmus+ programme (see **Chapter 4**) which enables university students to apply for courses in Europe for periods of up to a year, with some of the courses being taught in English. Please note that following the UK's vote to leave the EU in the June 2016 referendum, the UK's future access to the Erasmus+ scheme, once it exits the EU, has yet to be determined. At present, the UK will continue to access the scheme until the end of 2020. The terms of the UK's continued participation in the Erasmus+ scheme are to be negotiated as part of wider discussions with the other EU Member States. Many institutions have introduced Credit Accumulation and Transfer Schemes (CATS). These allow students to be awarded credits for modules or units of study they have successfully completed which are accumulated towards a certificate, diploma or degree. They can also put their completed modules towards higher education study in other universities or colleges. Students wanting to transfer their credits should talk to the admissions office of the university they want to enter as there may be additional special subjects or module requirements for the degree they want to study.

FOUNDATION DEGREES AND FOUNDATION COURSES

Foundation courses, not be confused with Foundation degrees, normally require two years' full-time study, or longer for part-time study. They are also often taught in local colleges and may be taken part-time to allow students to continue to work. In comparison a Foundation degree can lead into the second or final year of related Honours degree courses when offered by the university validating the Foundation degree. Two-year Higher National Diplomas will also qualify for entry into the second or final year of degree courses. These, too, are often offered at universities as well as colleges of further education and partnership colleges linked to universities.

Part-time degrees and lifelong learning or distance learning courses are also often available and details of these can be found on university websites and in prospectuses. Some universities publish separate prospectuses for part-time courses.

NEXT STEPS

When choosing your course remember that one course is not better than another – it is just different. The best course for you is the one which best suits you. To give some indication of the differences between courses, see **Chapter 3** and also *Choosing Your Degree Course & University*, the companion book to *Heap 2019: University Degree Course Offers* (see **Appendix 4**). After provisionally choosing your courses, read the prospectuses again carefully to be sure that you understand what is included in the three, four or more years of study. Each institution differs in its course content even though the course titles may be the same and courses differ in other ways, for example:

- methods of assessment (eg unseen examinations, continuous assessment, project work, dissertations)
- contact time with tutors
- how they are taught (for example, frequency and size of lectures, seminars)
- practicals; field work requirements
- library, computing, laboratory and studio facilities
- amount of free study time available.

These are useful points of comparison between courses in different institutions when you are on an Open Day visit or making final course choices. Other important factors to consider when comparing courses include the availability of opportunities for studying and working abroad during your course, professional body accreditation of courses leading to certain professional careers (see **Appendix 3**), and the career destinations of previous graduates.

Once you have chosen your course subject(s) and the type of course you want to follow, the next step is to find out about the universities and colleges offering courses in your subject area, how much a higher education course will cost you and what financial help is available. The next chapter, **University Choice and Finance** provides information to help you do this.

TAKING A GAP YEAR

Choosing your course is the first decision you need to make, the second is choosing your university and then, for an increasing number, the third is deciding whether or not to take a Gap Year. But there lies the problem. Because of the very large number of things to do and places to go, you'll find that you almost need a Gap Year to choose the right one (although a read through *Your Gap Year* by Susan Griffith (see **Appendix 4**) is a good place to start)!

Planning ahead is important but, in the end, bear in mind that you might be overtaken by events, not least in failing to get the grades you need for a place on the course or at the university you were counting on. This could mean repeating A-levels and re-applying, which in turn could mean waiting for interviews and offers and deferring the start of your 'gap'.

Once you have decided to go, however, it's a question of whether you will go under your own steam or through a Gap Year agency. Unless you are streetwise, or preferably 'world wise', then an agency offers several advantages. Some agencies may cover a broad field of opportunities whilst others will focus on a specific region and activity, such as the African Conservation Experience, offering animal and plant conservation work in game and nature reserves in southern Africa.

When making the choice, some students will always prefer a 'do-it-yourself' arrangement. However, there are many advantages to going through specialist agencies. Not only can they offer a choice of destinations and opportunities but also they can provide a lot of essential and helpful advice before your departure on issues such as health precautions and insurance. Support is also available in the case of accidents or illnesses when a link can be established between the agency and parents.

Finally, in order to enhance your next university or college application, applying for a job for the year could be an even better option than spending a year travelling. Not only will it provide you with some financial security but it will also introduce you to the world of work, which could be more challenging than the Inca Trail!

CHOOSING YOUR UNIVERSITY OR COLLEGE

The choice

You choose a holiday because of its location (noisy or quiet), the accommodation and the facilities. It's the same with universities or colleges, some are in or near a city; others are in quiet rural locations. Some have good accommodation for students. Some not. Some are easy to reach others are at a distance. You already know where some of the very popular universities are located, others you have no idea! Don't let that put you off. Find out where they are.

So once you have chosen your degree find out as much as you can about the universities or colleges offering it and go and pay a visit and **talk to the students, particularly those taking your choice of degree** – they will tell you the good and not so good points about the university and the course. Institutions always arrange open days, although you can walk on to the campuses at any time without prior arrangement.

ACTION POINTS

Before deciding on your preferred universities and courses, check out the following points.

Teaching staff

How do the students react to their tutors? Do staff have a flair and enthusiasm for their subject? Are they approachable? Do they mark your work regularly and is the feedback helpful, or are you left to get on with your own work with very little direction? What are the research interests of the staff?

Teaching styles

How will you be taught, for example, lectures, seminars, tutorials? Are lectures popular? If not, why not? How much online learning will you have? How much time will you be expected to work on your own? If there are field courses, how often are they arranged and are they compulsory? How much will they cost?

Facilities

Are the facilities of a high standard and easily available? Is the laboratory equipment 'state of the art' or just adequate? Are the libraries well-stocked with software packages, books and journals? What are the computing facilities? Is there plenty of space to study or do rooms and workspaces become overcrowded? Do students have to pay for any materials?

New students

Are there induction courses for new students? What student services and facilities are available? Is it possible to buy second-hand copies of set books?

Work placements

Are work placements an optional or compulsory part of the course? Who arranges them? Are the placements popular? Do they count towards your degree? Are work placements paid? How long are they?

Transferable skills

Transferable skills are now regarded as important by all future employers. Does the department provide training in communication skills, teamwork, time-management and information technology as part of the degree course?

Accommodation
How easy is it to find accommodation? Where are the halls of residence? Are they conveniently located for libraries and lecture theatres? Are they self-catering? Alternatively, what is the cost of meals in the university refectory? Which types of student accommodation are the most popular? What is the annual cost of accommodation? If there is more than one campus, is a shuttle-bus service provided?

Costs
Find out the costs of materials, accommodation and travel in addition to tuition fees (see below) and your own personal needs. What are the opportunities for earning money, on or off campus? Does the department or faculty have any rules about part-time employment?

FINANCE: WHAT WILL IT COST AND WHAT HELP IS THERE?
Tuition fees and other costs
Tuition fees are charged for degree courses in England, Wales and Northern Ireland. Precise details of the level of the tuition fee to be charged will appear on each university and college website since levels may vary. The maximum fee currently set for English institutions is £9,250 per year, in Wales it is £9,000, and in Northern Ireland £3,925 for their home students only, but the full fee for students from the rest of the UK. Eligible students in Scotland pay £1,820 which is covered by the Student Award Agency for Scotland (SAAS); other UK students pay the full fee in Scottish universities. Tuition fee loans are available and are repaid once the student has graduated and is earning above a certain threshold; for students in England and Wales this is when they are earning more than £25,000.

Students also face additional charges covering university accommodation (usually, the highest single cost in a typically weekly budget and may vary between universities), on top of which there are personal living costs, and possibly travel expenses. Certain courses will also require students to pay for special equipment, particularly for courses of a practical nature such as Art, Architecture, and Music.

Maintenance loans are available for students to help with living costs, which are means-tested. Details are available from local authorities and university websites. Disabled Students' Allowances (DSAs) (non-repayable) are also available to those who live in England, to cover some of the extra costs because of mental health problems, physical disabilities, long-term illness or learning difficulties, for example dyslexia or dyspraxia. These allowances come on top of any other student finance and do not depend on household income. (See www.gov.uk/disabled-students–allowances-dsas and www.thestudentroom.co.uk/student-finance.)

University scholarships These are usually merit-based and are often competitive although some universities offer valuable scholarships to any new entrant who has achieved top grades at A-level. Scholarships vary considerably and are often subject-specific, offered through faculties or departments, so check the availability of any awards with the subject departmental head. Additionally, there are often music, choral and organ awards, and scholarships and bursaries for sporting achievement. Entry scholarships are offered by several universities which normally stipulate that the applicant must place the university as their first choice and achieve the specified high grades. Changes in bursaries and scholarships take place every year so it is important to check university and college websites.

University bursaries These are usually paid in cases of financial need: all universities charging course fees are obliged to offer some bursaries to students from lower-income families. The term 'bursary' is usually used to denote an award to students requiring financial assistance or who are disadvantaged in various ways. Universities are committed to fair access to all students from lower income backgrounds and individual universities and colleges have bursaries, trust funds and sponsorships for those students, although reports suggest that many such students fail to claim the money due to them. These non-repayable awards are linked to the student's family income and vary between universities.

Useful websites   Students from England www.gov.uk/student-finance
Students from Scotland www.saas.gov.uk
Students from Wales www.studentfinancewales.co.uk
Students from Northern Ireland www.studentfinanceni.co.uk

For comprehensive finance information see the useful websites above and other sources listed in **Appendix 4**.

INFORMATION SOURCES

Prospectuses, websites and Open Days are key sources of the information you need to decide where to study and at the back of this book a directory of institutions is provided, with full contact details, for you to use in your research. Other sources of information include the books and websites listed in **Appendix 4**, the professional associations listed in **Appendix 3**, and the websites given in the subject tables in **Chapter 7**. It is important to take time to find out as much as you can about your preferred universities, colleges and courses, and to explore their similarities and differences. The following chapter **University and College Course and Admissions Profiles** gives you information about the types of courses offered by each university and how they are organised. This is important information that you need to know when choosing your university or college because those factors affect, for example, the amount of choice you have in what you study, and the opportunities you have for sandwich placements (see **Chapter 1**). You therefore need to read **Chapter 3** to give you an insight into universities so that you can find the one that is right for you.

UNIVERSITY AND COLLEGE COURSE AND ADMISSIONS PROFILES

UNIVERSITIES, COLLEGES AND THEIR COURSES

Choosing a degree subject is one step of the way to higher education (see **Chapter 1**), choosing a university or college is the next stage (see **Chapters 2** and **9**). However, in addition to such features as location, entry requirements, accommodation, students' facilities and the subjects offered, many universities differ in the way they organise and teach their courses. The course profiles which follow aim to identify the main course features of each of the institutions and to provide some brief notes about the types of courses they offer and how they differ.

Although universities and colleges have their own distinct identities and course characteristics, they have many similarities. Apart from full-time and sandwich courses, one-year Foundation courses are also offered in many subjects which can help the student to either convert or build on existing qualifications to enable them to start an Honours degree programme. All universities and colleges also offer one-year international Foundation courses for overseas students to provide a preliminary introduction to courses and often to provide English language tuition.

ADMISSIONS POLICIES

Although the UCAS application process is standard for all undergraduate Honours degree courses (see **Chapter 4**) the admissions policies adopted by individual departments in universities and colleges often differ, and will depend on the popularity of the course and the quality of applicants.

Mature students (defined as those aged over 21 on entry) are often interviewed. Normal published offers may not apply to mature students. In all institutions certain courses require Disclosure and Barring Service (DBS) checks or medical examinations; students should check these requirements before applying for courses.

The acceptance of deferred entry varies, depending on the chosen course, and many admissions tutors ask that the intention to take a Gap Year be included on the application if firm arrangements have been made.

Several universities and colleges advise that if a student fails to achieve the grades required for an offer, they may still be awarded a place; however, they may receive a changed offer for an alternative course. Applicants are strongly advised to be wary of such offers, unless the course is similar to the original course choice.

Applicants for places at popular universities or for popular courses cannot assume that they will receive an offer even if their predicted grades are the same or higher than a stated standard offer. Even though the government has now removed the cap on the number of places that universities in England are able to offer, meaning that they can admit an unlimited number of home and EU undergraduates for most courses, not every institution has adopted these reforms.

All institutions have a number of schemes in place to enable admissions tutors to identify and make offers to applicants who, for example, may have had their education affected by circumstances outside their control. A major initiative is Widening Participation in which various schemes can assist school and college students in getting into university. These programmes focus on specific groups of students and communities including:

- students from low participation areas
- low-performing schools and colleges or those without a strong history of progression to higher education
- students with disabilities

- people living in deprived geographical areas, including deprived rural areas
- students from black or ethnic minority backgrounds
- students from the lower socio-economic groups 4–8 including mature learners
- students requiring financial assistance or who are disadvantaged in various ways
- families with little or no experience of higher education
- students from homes with low household incomes
- students returning to study after a period of time spent away.

Applicants are strongly advised to check prospectuses and websites for up-to-date information on admissions and, in particular, on alternative qualifications to A-levels as well as any entrance test to be taken (see also **Chapter 5**). Applicants whose first language is not English should refer to **Chapter 8** for details of the English Language entry requirements.

The following information provides a selection of relevant aspects of admissions policies and practice for the institutions listed.

COURSE AND ADMISSIONS PROFILES

Aberdeen One of the oldest universities in the UK, based on two campuses. Students applying for the MA degree in Arts and Social Sciences are admitted to a degree rather than a subject, selecting from a range of courses in the first year, leading up to the final choice of subject and Honours course in the fourth year. The BSc degree is also flexible but within the Science framework. Engineering students follow a common core course in Years 1 and 2, specialising in Year 3. There is less flexibility, however, in some vocational courses such as Accountancy, Law, Medicine and Dentistry. For some degree programmes, highly qualified applicants may be admitted to the second year of the course. Courses include Divinity and Theology, Education, Music, Life Sciences, Medical Sciences and Business.

In personal statements and the referees' reports, selectors look for evidence of subject knowledge and understanding, commitment, motivation and responsibility, and the ability to cope with a university education.

Abertay A city centre university in Dundee. Courses have a strong vocational bias and are offered in the Schools of Science, Engineering and Technology, Business, Social and Health Sciences, Arts, Media, and Computer Games which is a centre of excellence.

Only applicants for the Mental Health Nursing degree are interviewed. Applicants for the Computer Arts degree are required to provide a portfolio of artworks. Make sure to check the website for the most up-to-date information before applying.

Aberystwyth The University offers Single, Joint and Major/Minor Honours courses on a modular basis. In Year 1 core topics related to the chosen subject are studied alongside optional subjects. This arrangement allows some flexibility for change when choosing final degree subjects in Years 2 and 3 provided appropriate pathways and module prerequisites are followed. Some students take a year in industry or commerce between Years 2 and 3.

All offers are made on the basis of academic criteria, and personal statements and references are important. Offers will be made predominantly on the basis of the application form but interviews are required for some subjects. Candidates will not normally be interviewed unless there are special reasons for doing so, eg the candidate has been away from study for a long time. Decisions are normally made within four weeks of receiving the application and all those receiving an offer will be invited to visit the University and their chosen academic department.

AECC (UC) AECC University College specialises in chiropractic and other healthcare disciplines.

For information on admissions procedures see their website: www.aecc.ac.uk.

Anglia Ruskin The University has campuses in Cambridge, Chelmsford, London and Peterborough. Courses are modular which enables students to choose from a range of topics in addition to the compulsory subject core modules. Courses are delivered by five faculties: the Lord Ashcroft International Business School, Faculty of Arts, Law & Social Sciences, Faculty of Science & Technology, Faculty of Health,

Social Care & Education and Faculty of Medical Science. Many programmes have a strong vocational focus, with a focus on employability, and opportunities for placements and/or study abroad. Anglia Ruskin is now recruiting medical students for its new School of Medicine based at its Chelmsford campus, with 100 student places available from September 2018.

The University interviews all shortlisted applicants for Art and Design, Paramedic Science, Nursing, Social Work, Midwifery, English, Media, Law, Humanities and Social Sciences courses. Maths and English testing is also used for Nursing, Midwifery, Paramedic Science and Social Work courses. For details of entry to the School of Medicine, see the university website.

Arden This private university offers career-focused online distance learning courses worldwide, as well as blended learning study at their following UK study centres: Ealing, Tower Hill, Holborn, Birmingham and Manchester.

The admissions team will make sure you don't enrol on a course that is the wrong level for you. See the website for details of how to apply.

Arts London University of the Arts London (UAL) is Europe's largest specialist art and design university, comprising six colleges: Camberwell College of Arts, Central Saint Martins, Chelsea College of Arts, London College of Communication, London College of Fashion and Wimbledon College of Arts. Together, the colleges offer a wealth of courses at pre-degree, undergraduate and postgraduate level in Art, Design, Fashion, Media, Communication and Performing Arts.

In addition to formally qualified applicants, UAL welcomes applications from candidates who can demonstrate equivalent skills and knowledge gained from work or life experience. The application process varies depending on the chosen course and whether the applicant is from the UK, EU or from a country outside the EU. Many courses require candidates to submit a portfolio of work and attend an interview as part of the selection process.

Aston A campus university in Birmingham city centre. The University offers modular courses in Single Honours degrees and Joint Honours (usually in related areas). Most degrees allow students to spend the third year on a one-year sandwich placement. Courses are taught in the Schools of Engineering and Applied Science, Languages and Social Sciences, Life and Health Sciences, Aston Medical School and in the Aston Business School.

Offers are not normally made simply on the basis of UCAS points. Interviews are only used in special cases, for example, mature students, or those with non-standard entry qualifications. BTEC awards are acceptable and a mix of BTEC and A-levels welcomed. High-achieving Level 3 Diploma students in relevant subjects will be considered. Key Skills will be taken into account but will not be included in offers; Access programmes are accepted.

Bangor Bangor University is situated in North Wales between the mountains and the sea. There is a wide range of subjects to choose from including Ocean Sciences, Psychology, Medical Sciences, Linguistics, Chemistry, Engineering and Law. Students can study a Single Honours course or choose to combine the study of two subjects from a range of Joint Honours courses. Some courses offer a four-year undergraduate degree eg MEnvSci, MSci, MArts, MEng, MChem.

The University considers each application on its merit – assessing your potential to succeed on and benefit from the course. It uses the UCAS Tariff when making offers in addition to programme-specific requirements. For a degree course, the points total should include at least two GCE A-levels or equivalent Level 3 qualifications (eg BTECs, Access, Irish Highers, International Baccalaureate, Welsh Baccalaureate, Scottish Advanced Highers and others). The University also welcomes applications from mature applicants, individuals with European qualifications and international applicants (subject to minimum English language requirements).

Bath The University is situated on a large campus outside the city centre. The academic year is divided into two semesters with Single and Combined Honours degrees composed of core units and optional units, allowing students some flexibility in shaping their courses with 10–12 units taken each year. A central feature of all programmes is the opportunity to take a professional placement as part of the degree: this is usually taken as either one 12-month placement or two periods of six months.

Some departments interview promising applicants; those not receiving an offer can obtain feedback on the reasons for their rejection. Students are encouraged to take the Extended Project and to provide details on their personal statement.

Bath Spa Bath Spa offers a full complement of creative, cultural and humanities-based courses, alongside social sciences and sciences. Most courses – Single Honours awards, specialised awards and Combined Honours awards – are part of a flexible modular scheme with students taking up to six modules per year.

All eligible candidates for Art & Design and Music & Performing Arts courses are invited to attend an interview or audition. Applicants with offers for subjects which do not require an audition or interview, and are not taught at a partner college, will be invited to an Applicant Visit Day. Gap years are acceptable for most courses.

Bedfordshire The campuses of Bedfordshire University are situated in Luton, Bedford, Milton Keynes, Aylesbury and Putteridge Bury. Its courses place a strong focus on entrepreneurship, not just employability. Many courses receive professional accreditation. A current Student Internship Scheme (SIS) operates, providing students with the opportunity to gain paid-for work experience, with flexible hours to fit around their studies. A Go Global programme gives students the opportunity to participate in two-week language and cultural programmes with one of Bedfordshire's partner universities. There is also a Get Into Sport programme offering students free membership throughout the year.

The University offers advice and guidance to enquirers and applicants throughout the admissions process via its website, www.beds.ac.uk/howtoapply/admissions or via its live chat function. The University considers applicants with a wide range of Level 3 qualifications and will hold interviews and auditions for a number of courses.

Birmingham The University is situated on a large campus on the edge of the city centre. Single subject and Joint Honours courses are offered. In Joint Honours courses the two chosen subjects may have common ground or can be disparate, for example Mathematics and a modern language. Some Major/Minor combinations are also possible. The modular system provides opportunities for students to study a subject outside their main degree. An International Foundation Year (Birmingham Foundation Academy) is available for overseas students from 12-year secondary education systems.

An Unconditional Offers Scheme applies (see website). Courses are academic and 75% of the personal statement should relate to why the applicant wants to study the subject for which they have applied. The Extended Project Qualification (EPQ) is accepted in addition to three A-levels with applicants being made an alternative offer of one grade lower plus the EPQ in addition to the standard offer. The University now has a standard overall IB points requirement for every course and makes offers relating to the higher level subject scores. Gap years are acceptable and should be mentioned on the UCAS application or as soon as arrangements have been made.

Birmingham (UC) The University College offers degrees within the hospitality and tourism sectors, which are awarded by the University of Birmingham. It is Europe's leading specialist in management courses for the culinary arts, hospitality and tourism management, and is also situated in the heart of Birmingham. Teaching benefits from its central location too: it's based in the conference and hotel quarter, which means opportunities for practical experience are on its doorstep. Its vocational degree courses, experienced tutors and strong links with business give students the skills they need to tackle a career in a range of rapidly expanding industries. There are international study-exchange opportunities including industrial placement opportunities throughout Europe, the USA and the UK.

Applications must be made through UCAS. Students can apply online at www.ucas.com. Students wishing to apply for part-time courses should apply direct to the University College. Please contact the Admissions Office for further information.

Birmingham City Courses are offered on three main campuses and additional sites throughout the city. Many courses have a vocational focus and include sandwich placements. Music and Acting is offered through the Birmingham Conservatoire. There is also an extensive International Exchange Programme, with many courses abroad being taught in English.

Admissions are administered centrally through the Admissions Unit in the Academic Registry. Some applicants will be called to interview and others invited to the department before an offer is made. If the required grades of an offer are not achieved it may still be possible to be accepted on to a course. Deferred entry is acceptable.

Bishop Grosseteste A single-site university campus close to Lincoln city centre. It has a strong reputation in Primary Education courses but also offers a varied selection of subjects at Foundation and Single Honours degree as well as a very large number of joint degrees in subject areas such as psychology, sport and the creative arts. Employability is central to all courses with most incorporating work placements and live projects.

Candidates are advised to attend an Open Day prior to applying. Applicant days are held for students who have applied for a non-teaching course or a course that does not require an interview.

Bolton A small, tight-knit university family in Bolton, with an excellent reputation for student support. A range of courses are offered, designed with the workplace in mind, with many offering vocational or professional content and work experience elements.

Academic offers are based on UCAS points from at least two A-levels (or equivalent) for most courses. The University is committed to giving equal consideration to factors other than formal academic qualifications such as work experience and vocational qualifications – any relevant information should be listed in the application.

Bournemouth The University has a strong focus on employability and offers a range of undergraduate degrees leading to BA, BSc and LLB. Courses are designed with direct input from employers, there's a work placement opportunity for every student (including opportunities to work and study abroad), and courses are accredited by the biggest names in industry. The University offers subjects in all aspects of Management, Media & Communication, Science & Technology and Health & Social Sciences.

Academic qualifications are an important part of the application, but this is not the only factor the University takes into account when assessing applications. It looks at each application on an individual basis and offer places based on a student's potential to succeed on the course they're applying for. Their offer making will typically be based on A-level equivalent qualifications, including any required subjects. Additional study may be valuable for breadth of study, and the university will look at a range of qualifications and subjects, including the AS and Extended Project Qualification.

Bournemouth Arts The University specialises in arts, performance, design and media courses.

The University interviews the majority of applicants who meet or potentially will meet entry requirements or invites them to a post-offer Applicant Day. There is a selection process which is based on each applicant's UCAS application, qualifications and an electronic portfolio.

BPP A private university with study centres throughout England. Courses focus on business and the professions covering Business, Law, Accountancy, Psychology and Health subjects.

A range of qualifications will be considered.

Bradford A city centre university. Honours degree courses are offered, many of which are vocational, leading to professional accreditation, and include sandwich placements in industry and commerce. Subjects are taught in the Faculty of Engineering and Informatics, the Faculty of Health Studies, the Faculty of Life Sciences, the Faculty of Management and Law and the Faculty of Social Sciences.

Offers will be based on UCAS points. Many courses require specific subjects to A-level standard or the equivalent, with particular grades. The University's typical offers are a guide; other factors other than academic achievement will be taken into account, such as evidence of relevant experience, skills or ability. GCSE English at grade 4 or C and above – or the equivalent – is a standard requirement for all courses and GCSE Mathematics at grade 4 or C is required for many more. Some courses require an interview as part of the selection criteria. Full details are online at: www.bradford.ac.uk/undergraduate. All students whose first language is not English need to demonstrate a minimum standard in English language such as IELTS 6.0 or the equivalent, with no subtest less than 5.5.

Brighton BA, BSc and BEng courses are offered, many with industrial placements including some in Europe, the USA and Canada. Over 500 courses are on offer at this popular university on the south coast.

The University welcomes applications from students with qualifications and experience other than traditional A-levels. Access courses and BTEC are acceptable alternative qualifications. Courses usually requiring interview include Art and Design, Nursing, Medicine, Pharmacy, Paramedic Practice, Physiotherapy, Product Design, Social Work and Teaching.

Brighton and Sussex (MS) Students have the opportunity to use facilities on the University of Brighton and the University of Sussex campuses, and in Year 1 can choose on which campus they would like to live. However, as the BSMS term dates currently fall outside of the term dates advertised by the University of Sussex and the University of Brighton, applicants have the choice of living at Lewes Court Halls of Residence at Sussex or Paddock Fields Halls of Residence at University of Brighton. All Year 1 Medical School students are guaranteed accommodation as long as they apply by the deadline (some students who live in the immediate local area may not be able to apply for accommodation due to more applicants requiring housing than rooms available). Students spend their first two years on the Falmer campus and then move on to associated teaching hospitals and community settings. Teaching is 'systems integrated' so students are exposed to the clinical environment from Year 1. Cadaver dissection is also part of the course from Year 1, so students get a real understanding of human anatomy, enhancing their learning experience. As the Medical School is small, so are class sizes, meaning that students have a strong relationship with academic and support staff.

Standard offers usually include three A grades at A-level with a minimum of an A grade in biology and chemistry. All applicants, to include graduates and Access applicants, are required to have a grade B or above or grade 6 or above in GCSE Mathematics and English Language or English Literature.

Bristol A leading research university offering Single or Joint Honours degrees. A number of courses include a year of industrial experience or the opportunity to study or work abroad. Most courses take three or four years to complete and are modular in structure. Dentistry, Medicine and Veterinary Science are longer in duration and take five or six years to complete. Most Science and Engineering courses offer a choice of four-year integrated master's (MEng, MSci) as well as the three-year bachelor's (BEng, BSc) courses.

Bristol is a popular university with a high level of competition for places on all courses. A* grades may be included in the offers for some applicants depending on the application and the course applied for; where it may be included, this is shown in the typical offers published in the online course finder. Students choosing to take the Extended Project may receive two offers, one of which includes the Extended Project, for example, AAA or AAB plus the Extended Project. The University does not generally use unit grade information when making a decision, but it may be used if applicants do not meet the terms of their offer. Most subjects will consider an application to defer entry, but you should indicate your intention to defer in your personal statement, giving information about your plans. In fairness to applicants applying in the next admissions cycle, the number of deferred places may be limited. Applicants for Law will be required to sit the LNAT (see Chapter 5). The acceptability of resitting qualifications varies depending on the course, and is outlined in each course's admissions statement. The following courses always hold interviews before making an offer: Dentistry, Medicine, Veterinary Nursing and Bioveterinary Science and Veterinary Science. Further information is available on the applicants' web pages: http://bristol.ac.uk/applicants. Information on how to apply can be found in the online course finder: www.bristol.ac.uk/study/undergraduate/apply.

Brunel A campus-based university in West London (Uxbridge). All courses are made up of self-contained modules enabling students, within their scheme of studies, to choose a broad range of topics or greater specialisation as they prefer. Some modern language modules may be taken, depending on the timetable of the chosen subjects. Almost all degree courses are available in a three-year full-time mode or in four-year thick or thin sandwich courses which combine academic work with industrial experience organised through a very successful on-campus placement centre. Some exchange schemes also operate in Europe, USA and other worldwide locations. Degree programmes are offered across three Colleges: College of Engineering, Design and Physical Science (including Computing and Maths), College of Business, Arts and Social Sciences (including Theatre, Education, Journalism, English and Law) and the College of Health and Life Science (including Biomedical Science, Psychology, Physiotherapy, Occupational

Therapy and Sport Science). Many courses are accredited by professional institutions recognised by employers. Please follow this link to view available courses: www.brunel.ac.uk/courses/course-finder.

All applicants are interviewed for Design, Electrical Engineering, Physiotherapy, Occupational Therapy, Journalism, Theatre and Education courses. The required grades for your course must normally come from at least three full A-level passes, although candidates offering a combination of AS and A-levels or BTEC and A-level courses may be considered. All applicants would usually need to have a minimum of five GCSEs at grade C or grade 4 or above, including English and Maths. Some courses may require a higher grade at GCSE in English and/or Maths, and some courses specify other additional subjects – all GCSE requirements are listed on the relevant course pages.

Buckingham The private University of Buckingham has around 2,000 students and all facilities are within 10 minutes' walking distance. It specialises in subjects where employment prospects are good. Its Law school puts a heavy emphasis on international and commercial subjects, while its Business school has developed a strong service management specialism, and is the first to establish an undergraduate Venture Creation Programme (Business Enterprise). The University's Computing courses offer career development opportunities with flexible modes of study. It is the first university to launch an independent medical school. The University offers a range of undergraduate programmes, with entry points in January, July and September and students can complete a traditional three year Honours degree in just two years.

Candidates apply through UCAS in the normal way or directly online via the University's website. Following the recent reforms of A-levels and GCSEs, and the changes to the UCAS Tariff, the University now makes only grade offers based on the best three A-levels taken.

Bucks New Students choose from a wide range of subjects in two faculties – Design, Media and Management (Art, Design, Music, Policing, Media, Business, Travel & Tourism, Computing, Law and Sport) and Society and Health (Nursing, Social Work, Operating Department Practitioner, Health and Social Care, Psychology, Social Sciences). The Uxbridge campus is just a short walk from a London Underground tube station and the High Wycombe campus is 40 minutes to Central London.

The University is happy to consider applicants on a case by case basis and mature students (aged 21+) with relevant experience/interest are encouraged to apply. It accepts a range of equivalent qualifications at Level 3 and requires Level 2 maths and English for the majority of its courses. Admissions tests will be used for entry to Nursing and Social Work courses. The university offers an unconditional offer scheme for certain courses.

Cambridge The University has 29 undergraduate colleges located throughout the city: Christ's, Churchill, Clare, Corpus Christi, Downing, Emmanuel, Fitzwilliam, Girton, Gonville and Caius, Homerton, Hughes Hall (mature students only), Jesus, King's, Lucy Cavendish (mature, female students only), Magdalene, Murray Edwards (female students only), Newnham (female students only), Pembroke, Peterhouse, Queens', Robinson, St Catharine's, St Edmund's (mature students only), St John's, Selwyn, Sidney Sussex, Trinity, Trinity Hall, and Wolfson (mature students only). Undergraduate courses are offered in Arts and Sciences. Three-year degree courses (Triposes) provide a broad introduction to the subject followed by options at a later stage, and are divided into Part 1 (one or two years) and Part 2. In some Science and Engineering courses there is a fourth year (Part 3). Students studying courses in Modern and Medieval Languages and Asian and Middle Eastern Studies participate in a year abroad. In college-based teaching sessions (supervisions), essays are set for discussion to support university lectures, seminars and practicals.

The typical A-level offer for arts subjects (excluding Economics) and for Psychological and Behavioural Sciences is A*AA. For science subjects (excluding Psychological and Behavioural Sciences) and Economics it is A*A*A. Colleges modify offers to take account of individual circumstances. Self-discipline, motivation and commitment are required together with the ability to think critically and independently, plus passion or, at the very least, real enthusiasm for the chosen course. If examination predictions are good then the chance of admission may be better than one in five. Applicants are encouraged to take the Extended Project although it will not be a requirement of any offer. Critical thinking is not considered acceptable as a third A-level subject for any course at Cambridge. The colleges at the University of Cambridge use common-format written assessments, to be taken by applicants for all subjects except Mathematics and

Music. Applicants will take the written assessments either pre-interview or at interview, depending on the course for which they apply. Please see www.undergraduate.study.cam.ac.uk/applying/admission-assessments and www.admissionstesting.org for further information on these assessments, and Chapter 5 for information you need to know before completing and submitting your application. Natural Sciences receives the most applications, Classics (four years) receives the fewest. Cambridge is strongly in favour of and will continue to use UMS scores at the end of Year 12 as long as they are available. Students are strongly encouraged to take at least three and possibly four subjects, reformed or not, at the end of Year 12. Information should appear in the UCAS reference in cases where school policy limits the student's opportunity to take AS subjects. See www.undergraduate.study.cam.ac.uk. The University of Cambridge does not accept applications through Clearing.

Canterbury Christ Church The University offers a wide range of BA, BSc, LLB and BMus programmes as well as an extensive Combined Honours scheme. The University has a main campus at Canterbury as well as a campus at Medway where a number of Health and Education programmes are taught. The University offers undergraduate initial teacher training (primary and secondary), a wide range of degrees that lead to professions within the National Health Service as well as subjects in Arts and Humanities, Social and Applied Sciences, Childhood and Education Sciences, and Health Studies. Canterbury Christ Church University and the University of Kent have been awarded funding to establish a new medical school, with places due to become available for 2020 entry.

Applications are considered individually and the University takes into account academic qualifications in addition to paying great attention to the personal statement and the reference(s) provided. All offers are tailored to individual applications. Currently the University asks for between 88–120 UCAS points for entry onto Year 1 of an undergraduate degree. Some courses require you to achieve specific grades and for some you need to have studied a particular subject. The University offers a range of extended degrees where students can study a foundation year (Year 0) and then progress onto Year 1 (Level 4) of the degree programme. For details about the new forthcoming medical school, see the website.

Cardiff A city centre university. All students taking the very flexible BA degree study three subjects in the first year and then follow a Single or Joint Honours course in their chosen subject(s). Similarly, BSc Economics courses offer the option to transfer to an alternative degree course at the end of Year 1, depending on the subjects originally chosen. Many degree schemes have a vocational and professional content with a period of attachment in industry, and there are well-established links with universities abroad.

Applicants are required to take only three A-levels for degree courses. Deferred entry is acceptable. The 14–19 Diploma is an acceptable qualification for entry. Key Skills should be mentioned in an application but will not form part of an offer.

Cardiff Met Campuses are located at Llandaff, Cyncoed and in the city centre Howard Gardens. Cardiff Metropolitan University specialises in courses that are career-orientated and have been designed in conjunction with business and industry. All of the courses are created with the working world in mind and include work placements, visiting lecturers, and options for sandwich courses.

Students from Foundation degree courses or with HNC/HND qualifications should contact the course director before applying.

Central Lancashire The University is based on a single site campus in Preston city centre, with a smaller campus at Burnley and another campus in Cyprus. It has 20 academic schools covering a wide range of subjects. Many subjects offer optional modules which gives extra choice within programmes. Foundation entry route is available for most Honours degree programmes. A number of integrated master's courses are offered, in addition to sandwich courses.

For entry onto Honours degree programmes, the University looks for a minimum of 104–120 points at A-level or equivalent, or 72 points at A-level or equivalent for Foundation entry. Some courses also require an interview, audition or portfolio.

Chester The University of Chester offers an extensive range of Single and Combined Honours courses across its six sites: from Arts and Media, Science and Engineering, Social Sciences, Humanities, Business and Management, and specialist vocational pathways to nursing and education. Over at its Warrington

Campus it runs well-established courses in Media, Business, Public Services, and Sport. The University also accredits innovative and entrepreneurial degree courses at the University Centre Shrewsbury. Further to this, our new Faculty of Agriculture and Veterinary Science is located at University Centre Reaseheath in Nantwich, one of the leading land-based colleges in the UK.

For entry requirements and to see what qualifications the University accepts, refer to the specific course page on the University of Chester's website (www1.chester.ac.uk/study/undergraduate). Interviews, workshops and portfolios are required for some courses to support applications. Any questions should be directed to the admissions team using the details above.

Chichester Degree courses are offered in a range of subjects covering Acting, Dance, English & Creative Writing, Fine Art, History, Music, Musical Theatre, PE, Philosophy, Politics, Psychology, Sport & Exercise Sciences and Theology at Chichester, and Business & Management, Creative & Digital Technologies, Education, Engineering & Design and Maths at the Bognor Regis campus.

Applicants will be interviewed for professional programmes (eg Early Childhood; Teacher Training). Applicants for programmes in the creative arts (eg Dance) will be auditioned. Most other decisions are made on the basis of the application form. The University of Chichester does not make unconditional offers to applicants still awaiting their exam results.

City The University offers a wide range of three-year and four-year programmes leading to degrees in Business, Management, Finance and Accounting, Computing, Engineering and Mathematical Sciences, English, Health Sciences including Nursing Radiography and Speech Therapy, History, Law, Music and Social Sciences. Some schools and departments provide a common first year, allowing students to make a final decision on their degree course at the end of the first year. Students in some subject areas may apply to study abroad.

Most typical offers are made on the basis of three A-levels or alternative equivalent qualifications. There will also be flexible offers whereby an applicant's offer may be reduced in return for putting City as the firm choice through UCAS. In some instances an applicant may be made an unconditional offer in return for putting City as the firm choice. This only occurs after a strict triage of the application and including a review of all past achievements and the personal statement.

Coventry Coventry University courses are designed with employability in mind. Most courses offer the chance to spend a year working in industry or working or studying abroad. Most courses also include a mandatory Add+vantage module that allows students to study their choice of a wide range of career-related subjects as part of their degree. Individual programmes of study are usually made up of compulsory modules, core options from a prescribed list and free choice modules.

The University is committed to excellence in admissions and aims to provide a professional, fair, equal and transparent service to all applicants. The University operates a centralised admissions service for full-time undergraduate applications. Applications from UK students are managed by the Recruitment and Admissions Office. Applications from the EU and overseas are managed by the International Office. The University also welcomes applications from those who have significant work or life experience and who may not necessarily meet the published academic requirements for their chosen course. Coventry University makes offers for full degree courses based on three A-levels (or equivalent). AS are not usually included in these offers, and there are no plans at present to make any changes to this approach. Those applicants whose school or college chooses to purely offer the new linear A-levels will therefore not be disadvantaged in any way if applying without additional qualifications.

Creative Arts Foundation and Honours degree courses are offered covering Art and Design, Architecture, Media and Communications at this specialist university with campuses at Canterbury, Epsom, Farnham and Rochester.

Interviews and portfolios are not required for all courses. There is no minimum age requirement for entry to undergraduate courses.

Cumbria The University of Cumbria offers a wide range of courses, both taught and research-based, spanning arts, business, education, health, humanities, law, policing, social science, sport, STEM and the outdoors. The University has an extensive portfolio at both undergraduate level and postgraduate level and many courses have the option to undertake placements which gives students the much needed practical experience.

The University accepts a wide range of qualifications for course entry. Required Tariff points vary across all disciplines and some courses have specific GCSE requirements. All entry requirements and course codes can be found on its website, in its prospectus or on the UCAS website. Its institutional code is C99. The University also offers undergraduate courses with Foundation entry. A new addition to the wide range of opportunities it already offers, Foundation entry is an alternative route to accessing higher education and all the experiences you'd expect as a full-time student.

De Montfort De Montfort University Leicester (DMU) offers a wide range of undergraduate and postgraduate courses, both full-time and part-time, tailored to meet the needs of today's employers.

DMU welcomes applications from UK, European and international students with a wide range of qualifications and experience. Current entry and admissions requirements are published on its website. These may differ from criteria in the printed undergraduate prospectus or course brochures – the online information is always the most up-to-date.

Derby Courses at the Derby campus are offered across three subject areas: Arts, Design and Technology, Business and Education, and Health and Sciences, whilst at the Buxton campus Foundation degrees are offered as well as some BA and BSc degrees. There is also a comprehensive Joint Honours programme offering two subjects and Combined Honours courses with a choice of up to three subjects. Major/Minor courses are also available. Courses are offered at three campuses, Derby, Buxton and Chesterfield. Check website.

The Level 2 Diploma is regarded as equivalent to GCSEs and the Level 3 Diploma to A-levels. Students without formal qualifications can take an Access course or the Modular Foundation course to gain entry to degree programmes.

Dundee The University of Dundee offers a wide range of undergraduate degrees. Many of its courses are vocational and offer professional accreditation. Its academic schools cover Art and Design; Science and Engineering; Education and Social Work; Humanities; Social Sciences; Life Sciences; Dentistry; Nursing and Health Sciences; and Medicine.

All applicants will be invited to visit the University after receiving an offer. Some courses interview as part of the admissions process. Advanced entry is available for most courses. For most subjects the entry requirements are shown as 'minimum' and 'typical'. Please note that the University offers a wide range of degree programmes and some have a higher level of competition for places than others. For programmes with a higher level of demand, it will make offers around the 'typical' rather than the 'minimum' level. Offers to applicants who are repeating their examinations will remain the same as any previous offer.

Durham A competitive collegiate university consisting of 16 colleges. Degree options include Single and Joint Honours courses to which subsidiary subjects can be added. There are named routes in Natural Sciences and courses in Liberal Arts and Combined Honours in Social Sciences in which students may design their own degree course by choosing two to three subjects from a wide range.

The Durham admissions policy (www.dur.ac.uk/study/ug/apply/policy) states that the following factors are considered when an application is reviewed: A-level or equivalent grades; GCSE performance; the personal statement; the school/college reference; motivation for the chosen degree programme; independence of thought and working; skills derived from non-academic activities, eg sport, the arts, and voluntary and community work; and contextual evidence of merit and potential. Students applying for more than one type of course or institution may submit a substitute personal statement: please see www.dur.ac.uk/study/ug/apply/ucas/personalstatement/substitute for further details. Admission decisions are made by admissions selectors. Successful applicants will be informed of the decision on their application before a college is allocated. Durham does not use interviews as a means of selection except in specific circumstances. These include applications to courses where external bodies determine that interviewing is compulsory (for example, applicants to Primary Education), applications to the Foundation Centre, applications where the candidate is without recent and/or relevant qualifications and applications where applicants have had a break in their study prior to application. The need for an interview will be determined by academic departments on an individual basis having considered all the information provided in the application.

Dyson Dyson offers a unique four-year Bachelor of Engineering degree alongside real-world job experience and mentorship within their Global Engineering team.

There are four stages of assessment on application. See the website for more details: www.dysoninstitute. com/apply/.

East Anglia A campus university on the outskirts of Norwich that has four faculties (Arts and Humanities, Medicine and Health Sciences, Science and Social Sciences). The University maintains an extensive network of international exchanges in which students studying certain degree programmes are able to spend up to a year. During these placements, our students are fully integrated into the culture of the host university.

Offers are normally made in terms of three A-levels. Critical Thinking and General Studies A-levels are not accepted for most courses. Interviews are necessary for some courses. Deferred entry is acceptable.

East London The University, based on the Stratford, Docklands and University Square Stratford campuses in East London, offers Single Honours and Combined Honours programmes. Courses provide a flexibility of choice and are based on a modular structure with compulsory and optional course units. A very large number of extended degrees are also available for applicants who do not have the normal university entrance requirements.

Candidates are advised to apply as soon as possible and results are normally announced within seven days. Some students may be called for interview and in some cases an essay or a portfolio may be required. The interviewers will be looking for evidence of a real interest in the chosen subject. Rejected applicants may receive an offer of a place on an extended degree or on another course.

Edge Hill The University in Ormskirk, Lancashire has three-year programmes including Business, English, Film, Geographical Sciences, History, Law, Media, Midwifery, Nursing, Performance Studies, Social and Psychological Sciences, Sport and Teacher Training. The university will offer a new access to medicine course from 2019, and train doctors from 2020.

With the exception of courses in Journalism, Animation, Media (Film and TV), TV Production, Performing Arts, Teacher Training, Nursing and Midwifery, most decisions are made without an interview. Those applicants who receive offers are invited to visit the University. For details of entry to the new medicine course, see the university website.

Edinburgh Scottish degree programmes are designed to include four years of study giving a broad and flexible education. Most programmes in the arts, humanities, engineering, sciences or social sciences allow students to study a range of subjects in Years 1 and 2, before specialising in the next two. There is a considerable choice of subjects although there may be restrictions in the case of high-demand subjects such as English, Economics and Psychology. General or Ordinary degrees take three years and Honours degrees take four years. Joint Honours degrees are also offered.

Admission decisions are made by the admissions offices of the University's three colleges: the College of Arts, Humanities and Social Science, the College of Science and Engineering and the College of Medicine and Veterinary Medicine. Decisions on the majority of applications will be made after the UCAS deadline, once all applications have been received. All offers will be expressed in grades, not Tariff points. Make sure to check the website for the latest up-to-date information before applying.

Edinburgh Napier Students choose between Single and Joint Honours degrees from a wide range of subjects.

Entry requirements for all courses can be found at www.napier.ac.uk/courses. Applications are screened and decisions are made centrally by the Admissions Team, using entry criteria which have been agreed by the academic department. Where the admissions selection process involves an interview, audition or portfolio review, the application will be sent to the academic department for consideration. This applies to the following programmes: Nursing, Vet Nursing, Journalism, Design programmes, Music, Acting, Film, Photography and Television.

Essex The main University campus is located near Colchester. Undergraduate departments are grouped in schools of study covering Humanities, Social Sciences, Law and Sciences, Health and Engineering. Degree schemes in Health and Business are also offered at the Southend campus and degree schemes in Performing Arts are offered at both Southend and Loughton campuses.

The wide range of qualifications the University considers include the following: A-levels, BTEC qualifications, International Baccalaureate Diploma and Diploma Programmes, QAA Approved Access to HE Diplomas, Open University courses and practising professional qualifications. The typical offer for most courses requires applicants to achieve specific grades in three A-levels (or equivalent), although the University considers additional qualifications.

Exeter The University has six Academic Colleges: the Business School; the College of Engineering, Maths and Physical Sciences; the College of Humanities; the College of Life and Environmental Sciences; the College of Social Sciences and International Studies; and the University of Exeter Medical School. Most courses include an optional study abroad opportunity. Courses are taught across three main campuses, two in Exeter and one in Cornwall at Penryn near Falmouth. Subjects taught in Cornwall include Biosciences, English, History, Geology and Mining Engineering.

The University welcomes applications from students from all backgrounds. Key indicators include predicted and achieved academic performance in Level 2 and 3 qualifications; candidates would normally be expected to take three A-levels (or the equivalent). Deferred applications are welcome. The subjects interviewing all candidates are Applied Psychology (Clinical), Drama, Medical Imaging, Medicine and Physics programmes.

Falmouth A south coast university. The courses focus on Art and Design, Music and Theatre Arts, Film and TV, Photography and Journalism.

For most courses, samples of work and/or interviews will be required.

Glasgow Applicants choose a degree from the Colleges of Arts; Medical, Veterinary & Life Sciences; Science & Engineering; Social Sciences. The flexible degree structure in Arts, Sciences and Social Sciences allows students to build their own degree programme from the courses on offer. Honours degrees normally take four years, with the decision for Honours taken at the end of Year 2. Primary Education, Health & Social Policy, and Environmental Science & Sustainability can be studied at the Dumfries Campus.

The University does not accept applications after the 15 January deadline. Offers are made until late March. The University does not interview applicants except for entry to Dentistry, Education, Medicine, Music and Veterinary Medicine. Deferred entry is not guaranteed for all subjects so check with the University. See the University website for up-to-date information.

Glasgow Caledonian The University offers a wide range of career-focussed programmes offered by its Academic Schools: Glasgow School for Business and Society, School of Engineering and Built Environment, and School of Health and Life Sciences.

The University accepts a wide range of qualifications for entry, depending upon the chosen programme. Please check the website for programme-specific entry requirements.

Gloucestershire The University is located in Cheltenham and Gloucester with courses made up of individual study units (modules). Some are compulsory for the chosen course but other modules can be chosen from other subjects. All courses have strong employability focus with many opportunities to undertake placements and internships.

Students failing to meet the UCAS Tariff requirements may be eligible for entry based on life or work experience following an interview. Entry with BTEC, NVQ Level 3, International Baccalaureate Diplomas and Access to Higher Education qualifications is acceptable.

Glyndŵr Glyndŵr University is based in Wrexham, North East Wales. The University offers a wide range of courses covering areas such as Art and Design, Business, Computing, Creative Media Technology,

Education, Engineering, Health, Social Science and Sport. It also has a dedicated rural campus in nearby Northop for Animal and Environment based courses. The University places a big emphasis on developing employability and linking courses with industry requirements. As well as traditional degree pathways, it has a range of four-year degree options that allow students to incorporate either a Foundation year or integrated master's year into their degree.

Offers for all courses are made through the Admissions and Enquiries team, and are usually based on UCAS Tariff point requirements. General entry requirements for three-year bachelor's degrees are 112 UCAS Tariff points, with 120 Tariff points for four-year integrated master's courses and 48 Tariff points for courses including a Foundation year. UCAS points may be counted from a wide variety of qualifications but offers are usually made based on points from GCE A-levels or equivalent. An interview is always required for Occupational Therapy and Social Work, and usually required for all Art and Design courses, Theatre, Television and Performance, Complementary Therapies, Health and Social Care, and Youth and Community. Other subject areas do not interview as standard, but may decide to interview applicants if deemed appropriate. Deferred applications for Occupational Therapy and Social Work are not accepted. Applications are welcomed from candidates who do not possess the standard qualifications but who can demonstrate their capacity to pursue the course successfully. Entrance can be based on past experience, skills, organisational capabilities and the potential to succeed, particularly for entry onto a programme including a Foundation year.

Greenwich Many courses are on offer and there is also a flexible and comprehensive Combined Honours degree programme offering two Joint subjects of equal weight or, alternatively, Major/Minor combinations.

For information on admissions procedures see the University website: www.gre.ac.uk/study/apply.

Harper Adams Based in Newport, Shropshire, the University focuses on agricultural, food chain and rural subjects.

Applicants for Agriculture, Engineering, Veterinary Nursing, Veterinary Physiotherapy and the Extended Foundation Degree Programme will be required to attend an interview.

Heriot-Watt This campus university near Edinburgh has five schools offering courses in Energy, Geoscience, Infrastructure and Society, Engineering and Physical Sciences, Social Sciences, Mathematical and Computer Sciences, and Textiles and Design which is based at our second campus in Galashiels.

Admissions decisions are made through the Faculty 'Hubs'. The personal statement is regarded as highly important and students are advised to include all relevant interests and work experience. The University welcomes a wide range of entry qualifications.

Hertfordshire Full-time and sandwich courses are offered as well as Joint courses. All Hertfordshire students have a work exposure strand in their degrees and the close links with employers contribute to a consistently good work placement and graduate employment record. All students have the opportunity to develop self-employment skills through tailor-made packages in addition to their subject expertise and proficiency.

Applicants wanting to take a gap year should finalise their arrangements before asking for deferment and accepting a place. Once a place has been accepted for the following year it will not be possible to change their application for entry to the current year. They would need to withdraw their application and apply again through Clearing. Offers to applicants who are repeating examinations are the same.

Huddersfield The modular approach to study provides a flexible structure to all courses, which are offered as full-time or sandwich options. All students also have the opportunity to study a modern language either as a minor option or by studying part-time through the Modern Languages Centre. Most courses are vocational.

For information on admissions procedures see the University website: www.hud.ac.uk.

Hull All full-time courses are made up of core and optional modules and are taught on the Hull campus. The opportunity to learn a language is available for all students irrespective of their degree course subject.

All criteria for selection are set by the academic faculty. A mandatory interview process operates for shortlisted applicants for Nursing, Operating Department Practice, Midwifery, Teaching (QTS), Legislative Studies and Social Work. A wide range of qualifications are accepted for entry to degree courses. Applications are also welcomed from those who can demonstrate Level 3 work-based learning such as Advanced Apprenticeships and NVQ 3. Bridging study may be recommended by way of a Foundation year. Most courses welcome applications for deferred entry although this should be stated on the application.

Hull York (MS) The Medical School is a partnership between the Universities of Hull and York with teaching and learning facilities on both campuses.

See Medicine in Chapter 7.

Imperial London The central site is in South Kensington. Medicine is mainly based at St Mary's Hospital, Royal Brompton Hospital, Chelsea and Westminster Hospital, Charing Cross Hospital and Hammersmith Hospital. The College offers world-class programmes in Science, Medicine, Engineering and Management. Joint Honours courses and degree courses with a year abroad are also available. Science courses are offered primarily in one principal subject, but flexibility is provided by the possibility to transfer at the end of the first year and by the choice of optional subjects in the later years of the course. A Humanities programme is also open to all students with a wide range of options, whilst the Imperial College Business School offers Management courses which form an integral part of undergraduate degrees. Work experience and placements are a feature of all courses.

Applicants are normally required to have three A-levels, but applicants with other qualifications of equivalent standard and students with other competencies are also welcome. The College considers candidates with the Advanced Engineering Diploma if they also have A-levels in specified subjects which meet the College's entry requirements. Applicants for entry to Year 2 of some courses can also be considered if they have completed the first year of a comparable degree at another institution with a high level of achievement, but they need to contact the relevant department before applying. A College Admissions and Appeals and Complaints procedure is available to applicants dissatisfied with the way their application has been considered. Applicants should note the College's policy on dress, health and safety published on its website. An offer for an alternative course may be made to rejected applicants.

Keele Keele University's campus in Staffordshire, in the heart of the UK, is near to cities north and south, accessible to Manchester, Birmingham and London. Flexibility is provided through either interdisciplinary Single Honours degrees, bringing together a number of topics in an integrated form, or Dual Honours degrees in which two principal subjects are studied to degree level to the same depth as a Single Honours course.

Keele's conditional offers to candidates are usually made in terms of specified grades from the qualifications they are studying. Some of its degree courses require a specific subject background and for applicants applying for a Dual Honours or Major/Minor degree, the subject-specific requirements should be met for both subjects. It welcomes applications from candidates with non-traditional qualifications and will take into consideration prior learning and experience and alternative qualifications. Applicants are normally required to have completed a period of study in the last three years. Keele has taken into consideration the changes that were made to A-level and GCSE qualifications in the recent reforms and reviewed its entry requirements to ensure the new post-16 curriculum does not disadvantage students in their higher education journey. Further information about its approach and entry requirements for September 2019 can be found on the following web page: www.keele.ac.uk/studyatkeele/undergraduatestudy/howtoapply/admissionsfaqs.

Kent The University's main campuses are in Canterbury and Medway in the South East of England, with specialist centres in Europe where study and research are underpinned by the exceptional facilities and resources of locations in Brussels, Paris, Athens and Rome. Many courses have a year in industry, giving valuable practical experience ahead of your final year of study. The majority of programmes offer the opportunity to study or work abroad. Single Honours courses can include the option of taking up to 25% of the degree in another subject, or to change the focus of a degree at the end of the first year. Many social sciences and humanities subjects are available as Joint Honours programmes on a 50/50 basis or as Major/Minor Honours degrees. The University of Kent and Canterbury Christ Church University have been awarded funding to establish a new medical school, with places due to become available for 2020 entry.

The University accepts a wide range of qualifications. Applicants returning to study after a long break are advised to contact the admissions staff before making a UCAS application. The University offers integrated Foundation year study in a number of degree subjects and an international Foundation year programme is available to non-UK students. Deferred entry is acceptable but should be mentioned on the UCAS application. The University regards the personal statement as important and recommends that applicants research their chosen courses thoroughly, and show an understanding of the curriculum. The University does not use the UCAS Tariff when making offers. For details about the new forthcoming medical school, see the website.

Kingston Kingston University is based in Kingston upon Thames, a busy riverside town in Surrey which is only 25 minutes away from central London. It has five campuses, each with its own character, but all of which combine state-of-the-art facilities with a friendly study environment. Its courses have a modular structure, and several of them are available to study as Joint Honours which allows students to combine two different subjects. The two subjects can be studied equally (half-field), or one subject can be focused on more than the other (major minor fields). All students have the opportunity to study abroad during their degree and can choose from 36 countries spanning five continents. They can also learn one of 10 languages through the Kingston Language Scheme for free during their time at the University.

Once the University has received an application from UCAS, it looks carefully at each applicant's academic record, references and personal statement. Some courses at Kingston University have an interview as part of the selection process where one or two people will interview you to find out if you have the intellectual capability, knowledge and passion to benefit from your chosen course. If you don't have an interview, you'll be invited to an applicant day instead where you will get to experience taster sessions of the course you have applied for.

Lancaster The University is situated on a large campus some distance from the city and consists of several colleges. Each college has its own social activities and events. The degree programme is split into Part 1 (Year 1) and Part 2 (Years 2 and 3). Students study up to three subjects in Year 1 and then choose to major in one or a combination of subjects in Years 2 and 3. Single and Joint courses are offered in a wide range of subjects. There are study opportunities abroad in the USA and Canada, the Far East and Australasia.

The University accepts a wide range of qualifications and offers are based on the best three A-level (or equivalent) results. Some departments interview applicants prior to making an offer. All applicants are invited to an informal post-offer Applicant Visit Day which encourages discussions with admissions tutors and current students.

Leeds One of the largest city-based single-site campuses in the UK and a member of the Russell Group, the University of Leeds offers excellence in learning and teaching in a wide range of courses in most subject areas, including an extensive offering of Joint Honours degrees. The size and breadth of the University allows Leeds to offer a complete student experience; studying abroad and/or industrial placements are offered as part of most courses. The research-based curriculum, combined with an unparalleled range of opportunities to complement their degree, allows students to develop skills needed for the future.

The University welcomes students with a variety of qualifications. Some courses do not accept A-levels in General Studies or Critical Thinking. Check the University's course finder for details of accepted qualifications: https://courses.leeds.ac.uk.

Leeds Arts BA courses in Art and Design, Fashion and Textiles, Fine Art and Graphics and Photography.

The University accepts a wide range of qualifications and experience.

Leeds Beckett Many of the degrees are vocational with links to industry and commerce. Courses are modular with core studies and optional modules. Degree programmes are offered in 13 different schools including the School of Clinical and Applied Sciences, Carnegie School of Education and the Leeds Business School.

Most offers are made in UCAS Tariff points, and interviews are held before an offer is made for some courses. Deferred entry is acceptable although applicants should be aware that some courses may change slightly each year.

Leeds Trinity An employer-focused, campus university located a few miles from Leeds city centre. The University offers Foundation and undergraduate degrees in a wide range of subject areas, including Business, Management and Marketing; Childhood and Education; Criminology; English; History; Journalism; Media, Film and Culture; Psychology; Secondary Education; Sociology; Sport, Health and Nutrition; and Theology and Religious Studies. Professional work placements are embedded into every undergraduate degree, and most courses include the opportunity to study abroad. Leeds Trinity is one of three UK universities with a Catholic foundation but is committed to providing maximum support to all students irrespective of their faith.

All applicants receiving an offer for non-interviewing courses will be invited to an Applicant Day. This gives them (and their families and friends) the opportunity to visit the campus, get a taste of student life and receive specific details about their chosen course. Some courses do require an interview – these courses are specified in the UCAS entry requirements. The University makes Tariff-based offers for most courses, with only a few offers based on grades. All entry requirements, whether Tariff or grade-based, are listed in the course-specific entry requirements on the University's website and through UCAS. Personal statements and references are always taken into account, alongside students' academic profiles. All information is correct at the time of going to print, but please check the University website for the most up-to-date information.

Leicester Single Honours courses are offered in all the main disciplines and are taken by 75% of students. The main subject of study may be supported by one or two optional modules. Joint Honours courses, which are split equally between the subjects, and Major/Minor courses are also offered. For Major/Minor courses, a core area is studied in depth (75%) while an additional area (25%) is also explored. Apart from Medicine, all programmes have a common modular structure with compulsory modules and a wide choice of optional modules.

Most courses do not interview applicants although invitations to visit the University will follow any offers made. Most typical offers are made on the basis of three A-levels. For some courses the University will give an offer if an EPQ is being taken with three A-levels. Other qualifications are considered, including the Access to HE Diploma, BTEC Nationals. Applications from suitably qualified students are also considered for second year entry. Contact the subject department for further information.

LIBF A private university college. Courses focus on financial services and related professions.

Applications are submitted through UCAS. All applications made before the closing date will be considered equally against the stated selection criteria and in the context of the number of available places. The Institute will consider late applications only for courses where places are still available.

Lincoln A city centre university made up of the College of Arts, College of Science, College of Social Science and the Lincoln International Business School. Single and Joint subject degrees are offered on a modular basis, with some subjects offering the chance to study abroad. A collaboration with the University of Nottingham sees a new medical school opening, with an initial 80 places available from September 2019. The degree at the new University of Nottingham Lincoln Medical School will be delivered by the University of Nottingham, with placements based in Lincoln.

On some courses, notably Art and Design and Architecture, an interview with a portfolio is sometimes required before an offer can be made. The University accepts a wide range of qualifications but students without the standard entry requirements may still be offered a place on the basis of prior experience and qualifications. For details of entry to the Medical School, see the university website.

Liverpool The University offers degrees in the Faculties of Humanities and Social Sciences, Science and Engineering and Health and Life Sciences. Apart from courses with a clinical component, programmes are modular. In some cases they include placements in industry or in another country and there is the opportunity for students studying many subjects to spend a year of their degree in China. The Faculty of Humanities and Social Sciences offers the 'Honours Select' programme allowing students to combine subjects from across the Faculty as Joint (50:50) or Major/Minor (75:25) degrees.

Decisions on offers for most schools/departments are made centrally. The exceptions are in the Schools of Medicine, Dentistry, Health Sciences and Veterinary Science. Most departments will invite applicants to visit the University before or after an offer is made. Some departments require interviews. Offers are normally based on three A-levels or equivalent (a wide range of qualifications are accepted). Entry requirements are reviewed annually.

Liverpool Hope Liverpool Hope offers a wide range of Single and Combined Honours undergraduate degrees. The University offers small group teaching, which means students are taught by research-active lecturers and benefit from insights into their research.

Each application is assessed on its own merits. The policy is to select those candidates who demonstrate they have an academic ability and personal motivation to succeed in their chosen programme of study. The admissions decision will rest primarily on the qualifications and also on the aspirations of the applicant in relation to their chosen programme of study. Selectors will take into account the evidence provided on the application form against the criteria for that particular course.

Liverpool John Moores Courses are offered in the Faculties of Arts, Professional & Social Studies, Business, Education, Health and Community, Science and Engineering & Technology. The majority of courses provide the opportunity for work-based learning or for a year-long industrial placement. The majority of programmes in the Faculty of Science and Faculty of Engineering & Technology also offer a Foundation pathway.

Admissions decisions are made through the Faculty 'Hubs' (Science; Education, Health and Community; Engineering and Technology; Arts, Professional and Social Studies). The personal statement is regarded as highly important and students are advised to include all relevant interests and work experience. The University welcomes a wide range of entry qualifications. If an applicant fails to receive an offer for their chosen course then an offer for an alternative course may be made. All candidates are interviewed for Dance, Primary Education, Pharmacy (including an admissions test), Nursing, Midwifery and Paramedic Practice courses and also the following specific courses: Drama, Drama and Creative Writing, Drama and English, Fashion, Film Studies, Fine Art, Graphic Design and Illustration, Journalism and Media Production.

London (Birk) Part-time and full-time evening courses are offered for mature students wishing to read for first and higher degrees. Courses are offered in the schools of Arts; Business, Economics and Informatics; Law; Science; and Social Sciences, History and Philosophy.

All applications are made online. Part-time undergraduate, all certificate and short course and all postgraduate applications are made directly through its website. Full-time undergraduate applications are made through UCAS.

London (Court) The Courtauld offers one undergraduate degree programme, the BA (Hons) History of Art. This seeks to attract students of the highest calibre, who are driven by an insatiable curiosity to learn about the visual arts and their histories.

The University welcomes applicants who have a serious interest in, and enthusiasm for, the study of art history. Entry is competitive; however, The Courtauld is committed to admitting students with the best ability and potential regardless of their educational background or financial resources. You will not be required to have studied history of art previously, however, advanced study in the humanities is recommended.

London (Gold) Goldsmiths is situated in New Cross, south-east London. The University takes an innovative and interdisciplinary approach to its degree courses, which include Art, Design, Drama, Computing, Media, the Arts, Education and Social Sciences. An undergraduate degree is made up of 360 credits from core and optional modules – 120 at each level. A standard module is worth 60 credits, although some degrees also contain 15-credit modules or can be made up of higher-value parts, such as a dissertation or a Major Project.

It welcomes applications from students with A-levels or equivalent qualifications. While entry requirements are stipulated, candidates are assessed individually and may receive an offer that differs from the published grades. Some applicants are interviewed, in particular those for Art and Design degrees for which examples of current art and design work are required before interview. Applicants requiring deferred entry (which may or may not be acceptable depending on the course) should contact the admissions tutor before applying.

London (Inst Paris) The Institute was established as part of London University in 1969 and offers three year courses in French Studies leading to a London University BA. Courses are taught in French.

For information on admissions procedures see Institute website: https://ulip.london.ac.uk.

London (King's) The College on the Strand offers more than 200 degree programmes in the Faculty of Arts and Humanities, Faculty of Life Sciences and Medicine, The Dickson Poon School of Law, Florence Nightingale Faculty of Nursing and Midwifery, Faculty of Natural and Mathematical Sciences, Insitute of Psychiatry, Psychology and Neuroscience and the Faculty of Social Science and Public Policy and King's Business School at the Guy's, Strand, Waterloo, Denmark Hill and St Thomas's campuses. The degree course structure varies with the subject chosen and consists of Single Honours, Joint Honours, Combined Honours (a choice of over 60 programmes) and Major/Minor courses.

The majority of courses require three A-levels. Applicants to the Department of Mathematics are required to take Further Mathematics to at least AS. Currently, Medicine and Dentistry require students to present either an additional AS subject at grade B, or the EPQ. Where students are unable to take an AS, King's College will waive the requirement, but a statement about their school or college's AS policy must be included in the first few lines of the UCAS reference. A-level General Studies and Critical Thinking are not included in offers, though their contribution to a student's overall development is valued. Deferred entry is acceptable.

London (QM) Queen Mary University of London (QMUL), based in the heart of east London, is a member of the Russell Group of leading UK universities and in the top 200 universities in the world. Its flexible approach enables students to choose from a wide range of compulsory and optional modules to develop a degree programme to suit their interests. In addition, many of its degrees are accredited by professional bodies, which can give graduates a head-start in their chosen career. Many of its students also take advantage of study abroad and industrial experience opportunities, ranging from internships to a year in industry.

For all full-time programmes, students should apply online at ucas.com. The institution code for QMUL is Q50. It may be possible for students to join undergraduate degree programmes at the beginning of the second and sometimes the third year. Those wishing to transfer their degree studies from another UK higher education institution may be considered but should contact the subject department before applying.

London (RH) The University is situated in Egham, Surrey. It offers Single, Joint and Major/Minor undergraduate Honours degrees in a wide range of subjects across three faculties: Arts and Social Sciences, Management, Economics and Law, and Science. Many courses offer a year in industry and/or the opportunity to study abroad.

Royal Holloway is committed to operating a fair, transparent and professional admissions process. Applicants likely to meet the entry requirements will either be made an offer or contacted for further information.

London (RVC) Campuses in London and in Hertfordshire. Courses are offered in Veterinary Medicine, Biological Sciences and Bioveterinary Sciences (the latter two do not qualify graduates to practise as veterinary surgeons). There is also a Veterinary Gateway course and Veterinary Nursing programme.

Applications for deferred entry are considered but the offer conditions must be met in the same academic year as the application. Applicants holding offers from RVC who fall slightly below the grades required are always reconsidered and may be offered entry if places are available.

London (St George's) Courses are offered in Biomedical Science, Medicine, Occupational Therapy, Paramedic Science, Healthcare Science, Physiotherapy and Diagnostic and Therapeutic Radiography.

Interviews are required for most courses and admissions tests are required for some courses. Candidates will be interviewed for all courses in Medicine, Physiotherapy, Occupational Therapy, Paramedic Science,

Healthcare Science and Therapeutic and Diagnostic Radiography. Once admitted students are not allowed to change courses.

London (SOAS) Single-subject degrees focusing on Asia, Africa and the Near East include compulsory and optional units, with two-thirds of the total units studied in the chosen subject and the remaining units or 'floaters' from a complementary course offered at SOAS or another college of the University of London. In addition, two-subject degrees give great flexibility in the choice of units, enabling students to personalise their degrees to match their interests.

Particular attention is paid to past and predicted academic performance and offers may be made without an interview. SOAS is happy to consider deferred entry, which should be stated on the UCAS application.

London (UCL) Subjects are organised in Faculties: Arts and Humanities, Brain Sciences, Built Environment (the Bartlett), Engineering Sciences, Laws, Life Sciences, Mathematical and Physical Sciences, Medical Sciences (including the UCL Medical School), Population Health Sciences, Social and Historical Sciences. In addition, there is the School of Slavonic and East European Studies and the UCL Institute of Education. UCL also offers a cross-disciplinary degree in Arts and Sciences, based on the US Liberal Arts model.

UCL welcomes applications from students proposing to spend a pre-university year engaged in constructive activity in the UK or abroad. About 9% of UCL's undergraduates take a gap year. Those wanting to enter the second year of a degree programme should make early contact with the relevant subject department to obtain approval. Applications are assessed on the basis of the personal statement, reference and the predicted academic performance, as well as additional assessment methods such as essays, questionnaires, aptitude tests and interviews. Decisions on admission are final and there is normally no right of appeal.

London LSE The School offers 38 degrees across a wide range of social science subjects, taught in 19 departments. Degrees are three years long, except Philosophy, Politics and Economics (PPE), which is a four-year programme. All undergraduates study a compulsory course called 'LSE 100: Understanding the causes of things' which actively challenges them to analyse questions of current public concern and develops their critical skills.

A wide range of international qualifications are accepted for direct entry to the School. The standard entry requirements for the majority of the School's undergraduate programmes are based on three A-levels (or equivalent). LSE also values the breadth of study gained by students taking AS examinations or the EPQ. The School continues to use AS grades in its admissions assessments and recommends that students, wherever possible, sit AS exams at the end of year 12. Students will not be disadvantaged if they have not been able to take AS examinations at their school or college, but the School asks that referees advise on such circumstances. In these circumstances, the School will use the information presented on the application form to make its decision (possibly in conjunction with some form of additional assessment). Applicants normally offer A-levels in LSE's preferred subjects, which do not include AS/A-level Accounting, Art and Design, Business Studies, Citizenship Studies, Communication and Culture, Creative Writing, Design and Technology, Drama and Theatre Studies, Film Studies, Health and Social Care, Home Economics, ICT, Law, Leisure Studies, Media Studies, Music Technology, Sports Studies, Travel and Tourism. Standard offers range from AAB to A*AA – applicants should check individual degree requirements. Intense competition for places means that high predicted grades on the application will not guarantee an offer. Great weight is placed on the personal statement and advice on writing this can be found on the School's website. Applications are considered on a rolling basis, but they are often held in a 'gathered field' and decisions made only when all on-time applications have been received. It is unlikely there will be any vacancies when A-level results are published.

London Met Single and Joint Honours courses are made up of compulsory and optional modules allowing students some flexibility to follow their particular interests.

Applicants may be required to sit a test or to submit a portfolio of work.

London Regent's Regent's private university offers undergraduate and postgraduate programmes delivered in an international learning environment. Programmes range from US-style Liberal Studies degrees to industry-led UK degree programmes in Business, Psychology, Acting, Film, Media and Fashion.

Please visit the University website for specific admissions criteria.

London South Bank All courses have flexible modes of study and many vocational courses offer sandwich placements.

Applicants not achieving the grades required for their chosen course should contact the University, which may still be able to make an offer of a place. All applicants are interviewed for Midwifery, Nursing, Allied Health Professions and Architecture courses.

Loughborough Loughborough is a single-site campus university that offers a range of courses, across 19 different academic schools and departments. Degrees are structured using a combination of compulsory and optional modules so that study can be tailored to individual interest. All undergraduates have the option to incorporate a year of paid industry experience into study, where students can practise skills learned in a professional environment. As a result, Loughborough students have high graduate employment prospects and are often sought after by top national and international recruiters.

The University's admissions policy and supporting information for applicants can be found at www.lboro. ac.uk/study/apply/supporting.

Manchester A large popular university offering Single and Joint Honours courses which are divided into course units, some of which are compulsory, some optional, and some are taken from a choice of subjects offered by other schools and faculties. A comprehensive Combined Studies degree enables students to choose course units from Arts, Humanities, Social Sciences and Sciences, and this provides the flexibility for students to alter the emphasis of their studies from year to year.

Strong examination results are the main factor in the admission of students to courses and the University accepts a wide range of qualifications. All decisions are made by the academic departments according to their individual requirements. For example, some programmes may require the applicant to have GCSE Mathematics at grade C or 4 or above for entry, others may require a compulsory subject at A-level. Other factors that are considered are prior and predicted grades, evidence of knowledge and commitment in the personal statement, and teacher references. Some courses may also take into account performance at interview, aptitude tests and portfolios. Where places are limited, they are offered to those eligible applicants who best meet the selection criteria and who, according to the admissions team, are most likely to benefit from their chosen course and contribute to both their academic school and the wider university.

Manchester Met A large number of courses involve industrial and commercial placements. It is also possible to take Combined Honours degrees selecting a combination of two or three subjects. Many programmes have a modular structure with compulsory and optional core modules.

Admissions staff look for personal statements showing evidence of the applicants' motivation and commitment to their chosen courses, work or voluntary experience relevant to any chosen career, and extra-curricular activities, achievements and interests which are relevant to the chosen courses.

Medway Sch Pharm The School is part of a collaboration between the Universities of Greenwich and Kent. Offers undergraduate and Master's degrees in pharmaceutical courses, accredited by The General Pharmaceutical Council.

See Medicine in Chapter 7.

Middlesex Single and Joint Honours courses are offered on a modular basis, most programmes having an optional work placement.

Some courses start in January (see www.mdx.ac.uk/courses/help-with-your-application/january-start).

NCH London The New College of the Humanities is located in Bloomsbury and is a private university-level college. It offers liberal arts-inspired undergraduate programmes featuring Majors and Minors in subjects including Economics, English, History, Philosophy, and Politics & International Relations, and a Single Honours Law LLB. In addition to studying towards their degree, all students study eight core courses in subjects including Applied Ethics, Critical Reasoning, Science Literacy, and a unique professional development programme. To reflect this further study, students are awarded the NCH Diploma. Students typically experience lectures of fewer than 50 students, small group seminars and weekly one-to-one tutorials from eminent academics. Scholarships and bursaries are offered.

Students may apply direct to the College at any time or through UCAS. The application form is similar to the traditional UCAS form. NCH will consider applications individually and on their merits. Decisions are quick – usually within four to six weeks. As well as personal details and academic records, applicants are required to supply a reference and a piece of written work. An application to NCH can be made in addition to any application made to other universities through UCAS. All shortlisted students are interviewed. NCH accepts deferred entries for those wishing to take a Gap Year.

Newcastle Single, Joint and Combined Honours programmes are offered. Some programmes provide students with the opportunity to defer their choice of final degree to the end of the first or second year.

The University accepts a wide range of qualifications and combinations of qualifications for entry to its degree programmes. All qualifications that are of suitable academic level will be considered. Offers are made in terms of grades to be achieved (UCAS Tariff points are not used). Four per cent of applicants entering through Clearing drop out in Year 1.

Newman A full range of full-time and part-time degree courses can be chosen with a focus on Initial Teacher Training qualifications.

Applicants are advised to submit an accurate and well-presented application. Personal statements are applicants' chance to shine, show their qualities and convince admission tutors why they should offer them a place.

Northampton The University of Northampton offers Single Honours, Joint Honours, Foundation degrees, HNDs and top-up courses. The University also offers a Year 0 in some courses for those who do not meet its entry requirements. There are also placement opportunities in the third year for certain courses, particularly within the business school. A range of courses and learning options are available including full- and part-time, distance learning and two-year fast track degrees.

Entry requirements usually range from BCC to ABB for BA/BSc degrees depending on the course.

Northumbria The University is located in Newcastle and offers a wide range of courses with an emphasis on vocational studies. Single and Joint Honours courses are offered, and a Combined Honours course allows a choice of up to three subjects.

Interviews are compulsory for most courses in Art and Design and courses in Health and Teaching. There are no admissions tests.

Norwich Arts Courses focus on Art, Design and Media Studies.

For information on admissions procedures see the University website: www.nua.ac.uk.

Nottingham Single and Joint Honours courses are available, with some industrial placements. Programmes are modular with compulsory and optional modules, the latter giving some flexibility in the selection of topics from outside the chosen subject field. Degree programmes are offered in the Faculties of Arts, Engineering, Medicine and Health Sciences, Science and Social Sciences. In addition, study-abroad opportunities are currently offered at over 320 institutions worldwide, through schemes such as Universitas 21 and Erasmus+; almost all students can apply to spend a period of time abroad. Please check the university's website for further details about this. The University of Nottingham is delivering a new medicine degree in collaboration with the University of Lincoln. The new University of Nottingham Lincoln Medical School will offer an initial 80 places from September 2019, and a further 80 places planned for future years.

Although grade predictions may match the offers published for the course there is no guarantee that an offer can be made. For details of entry to the Medical School, see the university website.

Nottingham Trent Degree programmes are offered in a range of subjects. Many courses are vocational with industrial and commercial placements and some students are also able to spend periods of time studying at a partner university around the world.

The UCAS personal statement is seen as a key part of the application process; the University website provides a guide on its possible content and preparation.

Open University Distance learning and part-time higher education courses. Degree and diploma courses are offered in the following subject areas: Arts and Humanities, Business and Management, Childhood and Youth, Computing and ICT, Education, Engineering and Technology, Environmental Development and International Studies, Health and Social Care, Languages, Law, Mathematics and Statistics, Psychology, Science and Social Sciences. Students study at home and are sent learning materials by the OU, maintaining contact with their tutors by email, post and telephone.

There are no formal entry qualifications for admission to courses.

Oxford The University has 30 colleges and five private halls admitting undergraduates. Colleges: Balliol, Brasenose, Christ Church, Corpus Christi, Exeter, Harris Manchester (mature students only), Hertford, Jesus, Keble, Lady Margaret Hall, Lincoln, Magdalen, Mansfield, Merton, New, Oriel, Pembroke, St Anne's, St Catherine's, St Edmund Hall, St Hilda's, St Hugh's, St John's, St Peter's, Somerville, Queen's, Trinity, University, Wadham, Worcester. Permanent Private Halls: Blackfriars, Regent's Park College, St Benet's Hall, St Stephen's House, Wycliffe. Candidates apply to a college and for a Single or Joint Honours programme. Courses are offered with a core element plus a variety of options. Weekly contact with a college tutor assists students to tailor their courses to suit personal interests. Arts students are examined twice, once in the first year (Preliminary or Honour Moderations examinations) and at the end of the course (Final Honours School). Science students are similarly examined although in some subjects examinations also take place in the second year.

Entrance requirements range from A*A*A to AAA depending on the course. There are specific subject requirements for some courses, particularly in the sciences. Once any subject requirements are met, any other subjects at A-level are acceptable for admission purposes with the exception of general studies (and both general studies and critical thinking for Medicine). It is generally recommended that students take those subjects which they enjoy the most and those in which they are most likely to achieve top grades. However, as the selection criteria for the University of Oxford are entirely academic, it is also a good idea for students to consider how best they can demonstrate their academic abilities in their choice of subjects. Admissions tests and written work are often part of the application process. Other equivalent qualifications such as Scottish Advanced Highers, American APs/SAT/ACT and the International Baccalaureate are also very welcome. Oxford does not participate in UCAS Clearing, Extra or Adjustment. Please see www.ox.ac.uk/enreqs for further details. There are full details on admissions tests at www.ox.ac.uk/tests.

Oxford Brookes Single Honours courses are offered with modules chosen from a field of study or, alternatively, Combined Honours courses in which two subjects are chosen. These subjects may be in related or unrelated subjects.

Conditional offers are now expressed in terms of UCAS Tariff points rather than in grades. Applicants will benefit from greater flexibility (i.e. for the majority, there will be no uncertainty over the security of their place regardless of whether they achieve BBC, A*CD, or any other combination as long as the total number of points required is achieved); they also find a growing number of applicants offering a mixture of qualifications (eg 1 A-level plus BTEC National Diploma, or 2 A-levels plus 1 Cambridge Pre-U Certificate) and these applicants will also find simpler, more consistent offers.

Plymouth A broad portfolio of degree courses is available. Single Honours courses are offered, with many vocational programmes offering work placements.

The University looks for evidence in the UCAS personal statement of your understanding of the course, good numeracy and literacy skills, motivation and commitment, work experience or placement or voluntary work, especially if it is relevant to your course, any sponsorships or placements you have applied for, and your possible plans for a gap year.

Portsmouth Around half of the students at Portsmouth are on courses that lead to professional accreditation, and many more study on courses that offer real-life learning. Simulated learning environments include a mock courtroom, a newsroom, a health simulation suite, a £1m model pharmacy and a forensic house, where criminologists work on staged crime scenes. Placement opportunities are available in many subjects and there is also the opportunity for all students to learn a foreign language.

Applications are considered using a variety of methods and a range of the following are taken into account depending on the course applied for: actual and predicted grades, references, personal statements, interviews and tests. Different courses use different criteria and selection methods to reflect the nature and demands of the course. For all courses, academic achievement through prior learning or experience is important, as is the potential to succeed, as demonstrated through commitment to the subject.

Queen Margaret QMU offers a wide range of professionally relevant courses in the areas of Healthcare; Social Sciences; Performing Arts; Film, Media and PR; and Business, Tourism and Hospitality Management.

For information on admissions procedures see QMU's website: www.qmu.ac.uk/about-the-university/quality/committees-regulations-policies-and-procedures/regulations-policies-and-procedures.

Queen's Belfast The academic year is divided into two semesters of 15 weeks each (12 teaching weeks and three examination weeks), with degree courses (pathways) normally taken over three years of full-time study. Six modules are taken each year (three in each semester) and, in theory, a degree can involve any combination of six Level 1 modules. Single, Joint and Combined Honours courses are offered and, in addition, Major/Minor combinations; some courses include sandwich placements.

Applications for admission to full-time undergraduate courses are made through UCAS. Interviews are essential for Medicine and Dentistry.

Reading The University of Reading offers more than 220 undergraduate courses in arts, humanities, business, social science and science. The modular structure of its courses means you can specialise in the areas that interest you most, while still developing core subject knowledge. If you are interested in studying two related subjects, it also has a wide range of combined degrees to choose from. Because it recognises that it is training students for 21st-century career paths which are constantly evolving, all its courses are designed to equip you with the thinking, problem-solving and creative skills to allow you to thrive in any sector. You can gain professional experience that counts towards your degree by carrying out a work placement or an internship, or by spending a year working in your chosen industry. Its wide range of study abroad opportunities also offer an exciting way to enhance your future career options.

Approximately 80% of decisions on applications to undergraduate study are made by the central Admissions Office and 20% of decisions are recommended to the Admissions Office by academic departments/schools. This is agreed on an annual basis according to the requirements of the school or department. In all cases, the criteria on which successful applicants are admitted are agreed with the University's admissions steering group and the academic admissions tutor of the relevant school or department, who also maintains oversight of decisions during the year and will be involved in decisions on specific cases. Candidates are interviewed for Accounting and Business, Archaeology, Architecture, Art, Chemistry, Film and Theatre, Food and Nutritional Sciences, Graphic Communication, Meteorology, Pharmacy, Primary Education, Psychology (MSci course) and Speech and Language Therapy. Typical offers are presented in terms of A-level grades (with the exception of Single Honours Art degrees which use UCAS Tariff points), but applications are welcomed from those presenting a wide range of qualifications. For some courses, selection criteria will include interview, portfolio submission or attendance at a selection centre.

Richmond (Am Int Univ) The priavte University runs British and American courses. American courses are accredited by the Middle States Commission on Higher Education, an agency recognised by the US Department of Education. Courses are also approved by the Open University and can lead to Open University Validated Awards.

Candidates can apply through UCAS, directly to the institution, or through the Common Application. Students are encouraged to visit before applying.

Robert Gordon The University offers a wide range of vocational courses. Many courses offer work placements and there are some opportunities to study abroad in Europe, Canada and the USA.

Interviews are held for some courses, for example Nursing and Midwifery, Health Sciences, Art and Social Work.

Roehampton Roehampton has a 54-acre parkland campus in south-west London with historic buildings alongside modern, cutting edge facilities. The campus provides a close-knit community feel for students and is made up of four historic colleges and 10 academic departments. There are over 50 programmes offered at undergraduate level and Roehampton is also one of the largest providers of initial teacher training in the UK.

Tariffs for entry to undergraduate programmes vary depending on the programme; please check the website for full details. There may be additional requirements so please check before applying.

Rose Bruford (Coll) Situated in Sidcup, Kent, Rose Bruford College of Theatre and Performance offers a comprehensive list of degree courses focusing on Acting and Theatre Arts.

Courses usually require interview and/or audition. Check the website for more details.

Royal Agricultural Univ The University is based in Cirencester, Gloucestershire. It offers undergraduate degree courses in subjects as varied as Real Estate, Rural Land Management, International Business Management, British Wildlife Conservation, Bloodstock and Performance Horse Management, and of course Agriculture, amongst others. The RAU is ranked third in the UK for graduate employability.

For information on admissions procedures see the University website: www.rau.ac.uk/study/undergraduate.

St Andrews A very wide range of subjects is offered across the Faculties of Arts, Divinity, Medicine and Science. A flexible programme is offered in the first two years when students take several subjects. The decision of Honours degree subject is made at the end of second year when students choose between Single or Joint Honours degrees for the next two years. A broadly based General degree programme is also offered lasting three years. After two years of a General degree programme students may transfer onto a named Honours degree programme if they meet the requirements of the department(s).

The University highlights the importance of the personal statement and the quality of this is likely to decide which applicants receive offers. Admissions tutors prefer candidates to achieve their grades at the first sitting. Apart from Medicine, Gateway to Physics and Gateway to Computer Science, no candidates are interviewed.

St Mark and St John The University is based in Plymouth on the edge of the city and runs 100-plus programmes which place a high emphasis on being relevant to the labour market. Students will be provided with the relevant transferable skills in demand from employers and businesses – key skills that can help put students a step ahead of the competition. The University specialises in sport, education, languages and linguistics, journalism and creative arts.

The University welcomes applications from students with disabilities, who are well catered for on campus.

St Mary's Flexible, modular degree options allow a great deal of choice to both Joint and Single Honours students. Practical and theoretical studies are followed in the Acting course.

Offers are made through UCAS. Students for over-subscribed courses or programmes of a practical or professional nature may be called for interview and may be required to take tests.

Salford The University offers BA, BSc and BEng degrees with teaching methods depending on the degree. The University is equally likely to accept students with BTECs and Access qualifications as well as those with A-levels. There is a wide range of professionally accredited programmes, many involving work placements. All undergraduates may study a foreign language.

The University is committed to widening participation but it does not make lower offers on the basis of educational or social disadvantage.

Sheffield The teaching year consists of two semesters (two periods of 15 weeks). Courses are fully modular, with the exceptions of Dentistry and Medicine. Students register for a named degree course which has a number of core modules, some optional modules chosen from a prescribed range of topics, and some unrestricted modules chosen from across the University.

The University considers qualifications already achieved (including GCSEs), predicted grades and personal statements as the most important parts of an application. Interviews are not a prerequisite of admission, however some departments do interview to further assess the motivation and personal qualities of applicants. Departments that interview include Medicine, Dentistry, Orthoptics and Human Communication Science (for Speech Science). The Applicant Information Desk can help with any questions applicants have about the process of applying to Sheffield and the current status of their application.

Sheffield Hallam A large number of vocational courses are offered in addition to those in Arts, Humanities and Social Sciences. The University is the largest provider of sandwich courses in the UK with most courses offering work placements, usually between the second and third years. Most students are able to study an additional language from French, German, Italian, Spanish and Japanese.

For information on admissions procedures see the University website: www.shu.ac.uk.

South Wales The University has five campuses in Cardiff, Glyntaff, Treforest, Caerleon and in Newport City. Many of the courses are vocational and can be studied as Single or Joint Honours courses or Major/ Minor degrees.

Applicants for courses in Art and Design, Teacher Training and Social Work are interviewed.

Southampton A wide range of courses is offered in the Faculties of Business, Law and Art, Engineering and the Environment, Health Sciences, Humanities, Medicine, Natural and Environmental Sciences, Physical Sciences and Engineering and Social, Human and Mathematical Sciences. Programmes are generally for three years. All students have the chance to study a language as part of their degree and there are many opportunities for students to study abroad or on an Erasmus+ exchange programme whether or not they are studying modern languages.

The University looks for a well-considered personal statement, focusing on your reasons for choosing a particular course, the skills you would bring to it, information about any relevant work experience, your career ideas, your personal interests related to the course, and your thoughts about 'what makes you stand out in a crowd'.

Southampton Solent Courses are offered in many vocational subjects. There are opportunities for students to gain work experience in the form of industrial placements alongside academic study.

Admissions staff look for applicants' reasons for their course choice, and for evidence of their abilities and ambitions. UK and EU applicants who have demonstrated outstanding academic ability are able to apply for the Undergraduate Academic Merit Scholarship. Students who are eligible for this scholarship may also qualify for the unconditional offer scheme. An International Academic Merit Scheme is also in place. More information can be located on the University's website.

Staffordshire The main campus at Stoke-on-Trent offers a diverse range of courses in Art and Design, Business, Computing, Engineering, Film, Sound & Vision, Humanities, Law, Psychology, Social Sciences, Science and Sports Science. The Centres of Excellence in Stafford and Shrewsbury offer courses in Health Professions including Nursing, Midwifery, Paramedic Science and Operating Department Practice. Courses can be taught full-time or part-time, whilst a selection of courses can be taught on a 'Fast Track' two-year basis.

The University provides various ways to support prospective students with their applications and personal statements. This includes advice over the phone, workshops on campus or at schools and colleges, online information and tailored advice at Open Days.

Stirling A flexible system operates in which students can delay their final degree choice until midway through the course. The University year is divided into two 15-week semesters, from September to December and January to May with a reading/study block and exams at the end of each semester. Innovative January entry is possible to some degree programmes. There are 200 degree combinations with the opportunity to study a range of disciplines in the first two years. In addition to Single and Combined Honours degrees, there is a General degree which allows for greater breadth of choice. Subjects range across the Arts, Social Sciences and Sciences.

Admissions are administered through a central office. It is essential to include in the personal statement your reasons for choosing your specified course. The University also looks for evidence of your transferable skills, for example communication skills and teamwork, and how you acquired these, for example through work experience, voluntary work, academic studies, hobbies and general life experience.

Stranmillis (UC) This is a college of Queen's University, Belfast focusing on teacher training courses with European and international exchanges as part of the degrees.

Candidates for teacher training courses will be called for interview.

Strathclyde A credit-based modular system operates with a good degree of flexibility in course choices. The University offers many vocational courses in the Faculties of Engineering, Humanities and Social Sciences, Science and in the Strathclyde Business School. There are also degree programmes in arts subjects, Education and Law.

Formal interviews are required for some vocational courses; informal interviews are held by some science and engineering courses.

Suffolk The University of Suffolk is situated in central Ipswich and is based on the waterfront. It caters mainly for local and mature students. Several degree courses are offered, as listed in Chapter 7.

For information on course admissions see: www.uos.ac.uk/content/applications.

Sunderland The University of Sunderland provides a range of courses across four faculties: Arts, Design and Media, Business and Law, Education and Society and Applied Science. All courses are geared towards employability, with work placements and visiting lecturers from some of the biggest companies in the UK. Several courses can include an option to study abroad in various locations including Australia, USA, Germany, France and more. The University of Sunderland is opening a new School of Medicine, with a first intake of 50 students in 2019, and 100 in 2020.

The University holds informal interviews for certain courses, when applicants will be asked to present their portfolio, to give an audition, or to talk about themselves and why they want to study for that particular course. For details of entry to the School of Medicine, see the university website. The University's admissions team are able to guide applicants through the process, via telephone 0191 515 3154, or email: admissions@sunderland.ac.uk.

Surrey Based in Guildford, just 34 minutes from central London, the University of Surrey offers a wide variety of undergraduate degree programmes designed to reflect students' needs, and those of society and industry, whilst retaining academic rigour. The University works with over 2,300 partner organisations in the UK and overseas as it feels very strongly that professional training is an integral part of university life. A professional training year allows students to put their skills into practice and to experience a real professional environment.

The University is willing to consider deferring an application for one year, providing it considers that this will benefit the applicant's studies. Contact the admissions staff if you are considering deferred entry. Surrey will make some unconditional offers from 2018.

Sussex Teaching is structured around 12 schools of study and the Brighton and Sussex Medical School. Courses cover a wide range of subjects in Humanities, Life Sciences, Science and Technology, Social Sciences and Cultural Studies. Students are registered in a school depending on the degree taken. The flexible structure allows students to interrupt their degree programme to take a year out. In addition, students can customise their degree through a range of pathways, placements and study abroad programmes.

If you are applying to do an undergraduate course in Social Work, Pharmacy, Primary and Early Years Education (with Qualified Teacher Status) BA or Medicine, you will need to attend an interview. If you do not have formal academic qualifications, you may have to attend an interview. There are workshops within the admissions process for Drama Studies and portfolio reviews for Product Design. A Skype interview is also required for our BA in Journalism. If you are asked to come for an interview or workshop, this forms part of the selection process for deciding if the University can offer you a place. Interviews and workshops normally take place between January and April and the University tries to give you at least two weeks' notice. It aims to keep interviewing to a minimum but depending on your chosen subject, it may need to interview you to reach a decision on your application. However, it aims to make the interview or workshop part of a structured visit to the University. You should remember that it is a two-way process – allowing you to ask questions and helping it to reach a decision about your application.

Swansea Courses are offered in Arts and Social Sciences, Business, Economics and Law, Engineering, Languages, Medicine and Health Sciences and Science. Degree courses are modular with the opportunity to take some subjects outside the chosen degree course. Part-time degrees are available and study abroad arrangements are possible in several subject areas.

All applicants applying for undergraduate degrees (with the exception of 'professional' programmes where an interview is an integral part of the selection process) who apply offering the requisite subjects (and grades at GCSE) can expect to receive a conditional offer of a place.

Teesside The Middlesbrough campus offers courses at undergraduate and postgraduate level, emphasising professionalism through work placements, volunteering, live projects, accredited courses and graduate internships. Areas of study include Animation, Games, Petroleum Technology, Chemical Engineering, Network Systems, Applied Science, Business, Computing, Design, Media, Engineering, Forensic and Crime Scene Investigation, History, Law and Criminal Justice, Psychology, Sociology and Sport.

Interviews are held for a wide range of courses, and successful applicants are given an individualised offer. Conditional offers are made in UCAS Tariff points. For some courses you may need to include points from certain subjects in your Tariff points score.

Trinity Saint David The University's main campuses are situated in various locations in and around Swansea's city centre as well as in the rural towns of Lampeter and Carmarthen in South West Wales. Study at the Lampeter campus comprises Single and Joint Honours degrees in a wide range of Humanities and Carmarthen has a strong Art and Design focus.

The University guarantees to give equal consideration to all applicants irrespective of when their applications are received. Applicants who successfully complete the residential Wales Summer School at Lampeter, Aberystwyth or Carmarthen are offered a place on an appropriate course of study on completion of their current school or college course. All other candidates will be invited to an interview to discuss their course choice. Entry is based on individual merit.

UCO This is the largest and oldest osteopathic school in the UK, offering undergraduate and postgraduate qualifications.

Shortlisted applicants will be invited to attend an interview and evaluation day at the UCO.

UHI The University of the Highlands and Islands offers a range of courses at centres throughout Scotland including Argyll, Inverness, Perth, Orkney and Shetland.

Contact the institution regarding its requirements and procedures.

Ulster The Faculties of Computing, Engineering and the Built Environment, Life and Health Sciences, Arts, Humanities and Social Sciences and Ulster University Business School offer a wide range of courses. There are various styles of learning supported by formal lectures and many courses include periods of work placement.

Information is available via www.ulster.ac.uk/apply.

Univ Law The private University of Law offers undergraduate Law degrees with a variety of full-time, part-time and online study options, all based on a traditional three-year full-time Qualifying Law Degree. There is a choice of where to study across the country, with centres in Birmingham, Bristol, Chester, Guildford, Leeds, London and Manchester. The courses combine academic rigour and practical skills, taught by qualified lawyers, often in small group workshops, with a strong emphasis on individual tutor contact and feedback. Employability is built into the course, through learning materials and teaching. If you're looking for a career in law, it is also possible to continue postgraduate study with their Legal Practice Course (LPC) to practise as a solicitor or their Bar Professional Training Course (BPTC) to prepare you for life as a barrister. The University of Law: Business School offers undergraduate business degrees with a focus on providing the training employers are looking for so that you're ready to do business from day one. If you're interested in a particular business specialism, the school offers pathways in finance, marketing and human resource management. The flexible course structure also allows you to switch to an alternative route should your aspirations change. You can choose to study on campus at the London Bloomsbury centre in the heart of London's West End or entirely online for those seeking greater flexibility.

Apply through UCAS for full-time courses, and for part-time courses apply direct to the University of Law.

UWE Bristol The University consists of several campuses in Bristol including Frenchay (the largest), Bower Ashton (Creative Industries), Glenside (Health and Applied Sciences) and Gloucester (Nursing). The University offers Single and Combined Honours courses organised on a modular basis which gives much flexibility in the choice of options. Many courses include optional sandwich placements and, in addition, students on many programmes have the opportunity to undertake a period of study in another EU country.

Offers may vary between applicants since selection is based on individual merit. Students applying for courses 'subject to approval' or 'subject to validation' will be kept informed of the latest developments. Most offers will be made in terms of UCAS Tariff points with specific subjects required for some programmes.

Warwick Courses are offered by departments in the Faculties of Arts, Science and Social Studies and the Warwick Medical School, which only accepts graduate applications. The University's undergraduate students can either choose single-subject degrees or combine two or more subjects in a Joint Honours degree. Options offered in each course provide some flexibility for you to tailor your course to your own areas of academic interest. Whatever course you choose, you can apply to study abroad, and many of its courses have inbuilt overseas experiences. Some of its degrees offer work placements and/or professional accreditation.

Before you decide to apply, you should check the entry requirements for your course. You will find the typical offer levels at www.warwick.ac.uk/ugoffers. Advice on the completion of your application is available at www.warwick.ac.uk/go/study. Feedback can be provided if requested for candidates whose application has been unsuccessful. The University welcomes applications for deferred entry.

West London UWL provides a high quality experience connected to the world of work. Subjects offered cover Business and Accounting, Law and Criminology, Tourism, Aviation, Hospitality and Leisure, Computing and Engineering, Music and Performing Arts, Film, Media and Design, Nursing, Midwifery and Healthcare, Education, Forensic Science and Psychology. Credit-rated Honours courses are offered, many with year-long work placements between Years 2 and 3. There are some study-abroad arrangements in Europe and there is a large mature student intake.

The University accepts a wide range of qualifications for entry to all of its undergraduate courses. Average entry requirements range between 112 UCAS Tariff points (A-level BBC, BTEC DMM) and 128 UCAS points (A-level ABB, BTEC DDM). It is also possible to transfer credits achieved at another university to a course at this university.

West Scotland UWS has campuses in Ayr, Dumfries, Lanarkshire, London and Paisley and provides a range of vocationally related courses, with a combination of links with employers, practical opportunities and professional recognition.

Applications are considered by the Admissions Office against previously agreed academic entry qualifications provided by the following Schools: Business and Enterprise; Engineering and Computing; Media, Culture and Society; Health, Nursing and Midwifery; Education; and Science and Sport. Within the Schools of Education; Media, Culture and Society; Health, Nursing and Midwifery; Engineering and Computing; and Science and Sport, applicants may be invited to attend an audition or interview prior to an offer being made.

Westminster Based in the heart of London with over a million businesses within a 20-mile radius, the University of Westminster offers a wide range of practice-based and career-focused courses that help students gain the skills and experience required to succeed in professional life. The University has one of the country's largest university scholarship schemes available, awarding over £2.9 million per year in scholarships.

Interviews are usually required for Media, Art and Design courses and Complementary Therapy courses. Applicants for creative courses should bring a portfolio of practical work to interviews. The University accepts transfers into Years 1, 2 and 3 of a full-time degree programme if students have studied similar units to the chosen Westminster course, and have passed Year 1 and Year 2, each with 120 credits, excluding all Westminster Business School degrees, Fashion Design and Film.

Winchester The University offers undergraduate and postgraduate study on a range of subjects within the arts, humanities, social sciences, business, law, sport, education, and health and social care. Single Honours courses generally encompass core modules, complemented by a range of optional modules which enable students to tailor their degree towards their own interests.

Interviews are required for a number of courses, including Choreography & Dance, Comedy (Performance and Production), Social Work and Theology, Religion & Ethics. Please make sure to check the website for the most up-to-date information before applying.

Wolverhampton A large number of specialist and Joint Honours degrees are offered and many have work placements at home or abroad. Except for courses linked to specific professional requirements, programmes are modular providing flexibility of choice.

Admissions staff make decisions on the basis of the application, and may invite applicants for interview or audition. If an applicant cannot meet the entry requirements for the chosen course, the University may offer an alternative course, or give the applicant feedback about why it was unable to offer a place.

Worcester A wide range of undergraduate courses in Education, Health, Sport, Arts, Humanities, Sciences and Business are on offer with Single and Joint Honours degrees available. The University is close to Worcester city centre, and most of its halls of residence, many of which are en-suite, are right on campus.

The University accepts a wide range of qualifications including Access to HE Diplomas. The majority of offers are based on UCAS Tariff points but some courses have specific subject or GCSE requirements. Many courses require interviews before an offer is made, including Primary Education and Nursing courses. The personal statement is highly important and applicants are advised to reflect on interests, work experience, voluntary experience, extra-curricular activities and achievements relevant to their chosen course. If the applicant fails to receive an offer for their chosen course then an offer for an alternative course may be made.

Writtle (UC) The College is situated in Chelmsford, Essex and is one of the largest land-based colleges in the UK. Higher and further education courses include Agriculture, Animal Sciences, Bioveterinary Science, Equine Studies, Landscape and Garden Design and Veterinary Physiotherapy.

Application details for the full range of courses offered are available on the College's website.

York Thirty departments and centres cover a range of subjects in the arts and humanities, sciences, social sciences and medicine. The 'Languages for All' programme enables any student to take a course in any one of a number of languages, in addition to which there are several opportunities to build a period abroad into a degree course.

Decisions on offers are made in the following ways. Centralised decision making: Archaeology, Economics, Education, History, History of Art, Language and Linguistic Science, Management, PEP, Philosophy, Politics, Psychology, Social Policy, Social and Political Sciences, Sociology. Semi-centralised decision making: Law, Mathematics, Physics. Devolved decision making in academic departments: Biology, Biochemistry, Biomedical Science, Chemistry, Computer Science, Electronics, English, Environment, Hull York Medical School, Music, Nursing and Midwifery, Natural Sciences, Social Work, Theatre Film and Television. All candidates are interviewed for Biology, Chemistry, Health Sciences, Law, Medicine, Music, Natural Sciences, Physics, Social Work and Theatre Film and Television. There are optional interviews for Maths.

York St John A city centre university with nine schools: Art and Design, Education, Health Sciences, Humanities, Religion and Philosophy, Languages and Linguistics, Performance and Media Production, Psychological and Social Sciences, Sport, and York Business School. These offer a range of specialist degrees with Joint Honours courses offered in Business, Counselling, Education, Health Studies, Information Technology, Languages and Linguistics, Management, Psychology and Sport.

Interviews are compulsory for Physiotherapy and Primary Education courses.

ENTRY REQUIREMENTS

Before applying to universities and colleges, be sure that you have the required subjects and qualifications for entry to your chosen course. Details of entry requirements are available direct from the universities and colleges. You will need to check:

 (i) the general entry requirements for courses
 (ii) any specific subject requirements to enter a particular course, for example, study of specified GCE A-levels and (where required) AS, Scottish Highers/Advanced Highers, GCSEs, Scottish Nationals, or BTEC qualifications (for example, Diploma, Certificate). The course requirements are set out in prospectuses and on websites
(iii) any age, health, Disclosure and Barring Service (DBS; formerly CRB) clearance or other requirements for entry to particular courses and universities and colleges. For entry to some specific courses such as Medicine and Nursing, offers are made subject to health screening for hepatitis B, for example, and immunisation requirements. Owing to government regulations, some universities will insist on a minimum age at entry of 18 years. Check university and college websites and prospectuses for these particular course requirements
(iv) admissions tests required by a number of universities for a range of subjects, including Dentistry, Law, Medicine and Veterinary Science/Medicine. Offers of places made by these universities are dependent on an applicant's performance in the relevant test. It is important to find out full details about universities' course requirements for possible admissions tests well before submitting the UCAS application and to make all the necessary arrangements for registering and taking any required admissions tests. See **Chapter 5** and check university/college and admissions tests websites for the latest information.

Potential applicants should ask the advice of teachers, careers advisers and university and college advisers before submitting their application.

APPLICATIONS FOR UNIVERSITY AND COLLEGE COURSES THROUGH UCAS

UCAS, the organisation responsible for managing applications to higher education courses in the UK, deals with applications for admission to full-time and sandwich first degrees, Foundation degrees, Diploma of Higher Education and Higher National Diploma courses and some full-time Higher National Certificate courses in nearly all universities (but not the Open University), university colleges, colleges and institutes of higher education, specialist colleges and some further education colleges. The UCAS Undergraduate scheme also is applicable for those applying for teacher training courses in Scotland.

The UCAS application process

Full details of application procedures and all course information can be found on the UCAS website (www.ucas.com).

Applications are made online at www.ucas.com using **Apply**. This is a secure web-based application system, which has been designed for all applicants whether they are applying through a UCAS-registered centre, such as a school or college, or applying independently from anywhere in the world.

Applications for 2019 entry can be sent to UCAS from 5 September 2018. The first deadline is 15 October by 18.00 (UK time) for applications to the universities of Oxford or Cambridge and applications for most courses in Medicine, Dentistry and Veterinary Science/Medicine. The deadline for UK and EU applicants to apply for all other courses is 15 January by 18.00 (UK time), except for some Art and Design courses that have a 24 March by 18.00 (UK time) deadline. You can still apply after these deadlines up to 30 June, but institutions may not be able to consider you.

On the UCAS application, you have up to five course choices unless you are applying for Dentistry, Medicine or Veterinary Science/Medicine. For these courses only four choices are permitted; however, you can make another subject your fifth choice.

Each university or college makes any offer through the UCAS system. UCAS does not make offers, or recruit on behalf of universities and colleges. It does not advise applicants on their choice of subject although it does publish material which applicants may find useful.

Applicants may receive an 'unconditional' offer in the case of those who already hold the required qualifications, or, for those awaiting examination results, a 'conditional' offer or a rejection. When all decisions have been received from universities or colleges, applicants may finally hold up to two offers: a firm choice (first) offer and an insurance offer. Applicants who have made five choices and have no offers or have declined any offers received can use **Extra**. Applicants are told if they become eligible for **Extra** and can apply online for one further course at a time using **Track** at www.ucas.com. **Extra** runs from 25 February until 4 July. Courses available in **Extra** can be found in the search tool at www.ucas.com. Applicants not placed through this system will be eligible to contact institutions with vacancies in **Clearing** from 5 July.

If you already have your qualifications and are not waiting for any exam results, your place can be confirmed at any time after you send in your application. However, for thousands of applicants confirmation starts on the day when the A-level examination results are released. Clearing vacancies are listed in the search tool from early July to late-September. Applicants meeting the conditions of their offers for their firm choice will receive confirmation from their university or college and may still be accepted even if their results are slightly lower than those stipulated in the original offer. If rejected by their firm choice university/college, applicants will have their places confirmed by their insurance choice institution providing they have obtained the right grades. Applicants who are unsuccessful with both their institutions will be eligible to go into **Clearing** in which they can select an appropriate course in the same or a different institution where places are available. In 2017, a record high of 66,865 applicants obtained places through **Clearing**, and 6,370 applicants found a place though **Extra**.

Each year some applicants pass their exams with better results than expected. This may mean that some will not only have met the conditions of their firm choice, but will have exceeded them. UCAS introduced **Adjustment** for these applicants – it provides an opportunity to reconsider where and what to study whilst holding a confirmed place. The **Adjustment** process is available from A-level results day (15 August 2019) until 31 August.

UCAS timetable

5 September 2018	UCAS begins accepting applications.
15 October	Deadline for UCAS to receive applications to Oxford University or the University of Cambridge, and applications to most courses in Medicine, Dentistry or Veterinary Medicine/Science.
15 January 2019	Deadline for UCAS to receive applications from UK and EU applicants for all other courses, except for some Art and Design courses that have a 24 March deadline. Use the search tool at www.ucas.com to find out whether Art and Design courses have a 15 January or 24 March deadline.
16 January–30 June	Applications received by UCAS are forwarded to the institutions for consideration at their discretion. Applications received after 30 June are processed through **Clearing**.
25 February–4 July	Applicants who have made five choices and have no offers or who have declined any offers received can use **Extra** to apply for one further course at a time on **Track** at www.ucas.com. Institutions will show which courses have vacancies in **Extra** on the UCAS website. Details of the **Extra** service can be found at www.ucas.com/extra.
24 March	Deadline for UCAS to receive applications for some Art and Design courses. Use the search tool at www.ucas.com to find out whether Art and Design courses have a 15 January or 24 March deadline.
1 May	Applicants who have received all their decisions from universities and colleges by the end of March are asked to reply to their offers by this date.

6 June	Applicants receiving decisions from all their choices by 2 May must reply to their offers by this date.
30 June	Last date for receiving applications. Applications received after this date are entered directly into **Clearing**. On 5 July **Clearing** starts.
TBC	Scottish SQA results published.
15 August	GCE A-level and AS results published. (See **What To Do on Results Day ... and After** below.)

PLEASE NOTE

- You are not required to reply to any university/college offers until you have received your last decision.
- Do not send a firm acceptance to more than one offer.
- Do not try to alter a firm acceptance.
- If you decide not to go to university or college this year you can go to **Track** to completely cancel your application. But don't forget, you will not be able to reapply until next year.
- Remember to tell the institutions and UCAS if you change your address, or change your examination board, subjects or arrangements.

Information on the special arrangements for applications for Law, Medicine and Dentistry can be found under separate headings in Chapter 5.

APPLICATIONS FOR ART AND DESIGN COURSES

All art and design courses use one of two application deadlines: 15 January or 24 March. The later closing date is to allow students taking a Diploma in Foundation Studies (Art and Design) time to identify their specialisation and put together a portfolio of work which they will need to present at interview. The deadline for each course is given in the UCAS search tool.

APPLICATIONS FOR MUSIC COURSES AT CONSERVATOIRES

UCAS Conservatoires handles applications for practice-based music, dance, drama and musical theatre courses. Applications can be made simultaneously to a maximum of six of the conservatoires listed below and simultaneous applications can also be made through both UCAS Undergraduate and UCAS Conservatoires systems. Full details of UCAS Conservatoires are given on www.ucas.com/conservatoires. The conservatoires taking part in this online admissions system are:

- Bristol Old Vic Theatre School www.oldvic.ac.uk
- Leeds College of Music www.lcm.ac.uk
- Royal Academy of Music www.ram.ac.uk
- Royal Birmingham Conservatoire www.bcu.ac.uk/conservatoire
- Royal College of Music www.rcm.ac.uk
- Royal Conservatoire of Scotland www.rcs.ac.uk
- Royal Northern College of Music www.rncm.ac.uk
- Royal Welsh College of Music & Drama www.rwcmd.ac.uk
- Trinity Laban Conservatoire of Music & Dance www.trinitylaban.ac.uk

The Guildhall School of Music & Drama is not part of the UCAS Conservatoires scheme, so students wishing to apply will have to make their applications directly to the school. There is an application fee, which varies depending on the course for which you apply; the fee includes the audition fee, which is charged by all conservatoires. For more details, see the Guildhall website. Similarly, applications for the Conservatoire for Dance and Drama (a group of eight specialist colleges) and the Royal Central School of Speech and Drama should be made directly to the schools as they are not part of the UCAS Conservatoires scheme either.

APPLICATIONS FOR TEACHER TRAINING COURSES

Applicants intending to start a course of initial teacher training in England, Northern Ireland and Wales leading to Qualified Teacher Status can find information on the Get Into Teaching website https://getintoteaching.education.gov.uk. See also www.ucas.com/teaching-in-the-uk for full details of applying for undergraduate (and postgraduate) training courses. Scottish students should apply through UCAS Undergraduate for teacher training courses.

APPLICATIONS FOR DEGREE APPRENTICESHIP COURSES

Applications for degree apprenticeship courses in England are handled by GOV.UK (www.gov.uk/apply-apprenticeship). It is likely that the employer and university will jointly recruit for their vacancies, to ensure that both are satisfied that the applicant can meet their respective requirements. You can use UCAS' career finder tool to see details of a number of new degree apprenticeship vacancies. Deadlines for vacancies vary so you'll need to keep an eye on these. Please also see page 11.

THE UCAS APPLICATION

In the choices section of **Apply**, all your university/college choices (a maximum of five) are to be listed, but remember that you should not mix your subjects. For example, in popular subject areas such as English, History or Physiotherapy, it is safer to show total commitment by applying for all courses in the same subject and not to include second and/or third subject alternatives on the form. (See advice in separate tables in **Chapter 7** for **Medicine**, **Dentistry** and **Veterinary Science/Medicine**.)

A brief glance at the subject tables in **Chapter 7** will give you some idea of the popularity of various courses. In principle, institutions want the best applicants available so if there are large numbers of applicants the offers made will be higher. For Medicine and a number of other courses, offers in terms of A-level grades are now reaching AAA or A* grades, and sometimes with additional grades at AS, where school policy does not limit your opportunity to take AS subjects (in which case alternative A-level offers may be given). Conversely, for the less popular subjects, the offers can be much lower – down to CCC.

Similarly, some institutions are more popular (not necessarily better) than others. Again, this popularity can be judged easily in the tables in **Chapter 7**: the higher the offer, the more popular the institution. Popular universities often are located in attractive towns or cities such as Bristol, Exeter, Warwick, Bath or York. Because of the intense competition for places at the popular universities, applications to five of them could result in rejections from all of them! (If you are not good enough for one of them you won't be good enough for the other four!) Spread your choice of institutions.

When you have chosen your courses and your institutions, look again at the offers made and compare these with the grades projected by your teachers. It is most important to maximise your chances of a place by choosing institutions which might make you a range of offers. When all universities have considered your application you can hold only two offers (one firm and one insurance offer) and naturally it is preferable for one to be lower than the other in case you do not achieve the offer grades or equivalent points for your first choice of university or college.

The other section of the UCAS application that deserves careful thought is the personal statement. This seems simple enough but it is the only part of the application where you can put in a personal bid for a place! In short, you are asked to give relevant background information about yourself, your interests and your choice of course and career. Give yourself plenty of time to prepare your personal statement as this part of your application could make all the difference to getting an offer or not.

The personal statement

The statement is your only opportunity to make a personal bid for your chosen courses. The University of Surrey advises applicants to include the following information:

- Why you want to study the course you have chosen. Show why you are passionate about the field.
- How your current studies have helped you to prepare for university. Be reflective – explain why you have made certain choices and what you have learnt, but do not go into lots of detail.
- How you have gone above and beyond the curriculum to demonstrate your interest in the subject (for example, books you have read, taster sessions you have attended).

- Your skills and experiences (including work and placements) and how you feel they will help you to succeed on your chosen course.
- The achievements that you are particularly proud of. Be honest – you may be asked about them at interview!
- What you hope to gain from university, and your career aspirations.
- Your interests and hobbies. It is recommended that 75% of your statement be academic/course related, while the other 25% can focus on extra-curricular activities.

Motivation to undertake your chosen course is very important. You can show this by giving details of any work experience and work shadowing you have done (and for History courses, for example, details of visits to places of historical interest). It is a good idea to begin your statement with such evidence and explain how your interest in your chosen subject has developed. In the subject tables in **Chapter 7** under **Advice to applicants and planning the UCAS personal statement**, advice is given on what you might include in your personal statement. You should also include various activities in which you have been involved in the last three or four years. Get your parents and other members of the family to refresh your memory – it is easy to forget something quite important. You might consider planning out this section in a series of sub-sections – and if you have a lot to say, be brief. The sub-sections can include the following.

- **School activities** Are you a prefect, chairperson or treasurer of a society? Are you involved in supervisory duties of any kind? Are you in a school team? Which team? For how long? (Remember, team means any team: sports, chess, debating, even business.)
- **Intellectual activities** Have you attended any field or lecture courses in your main subjects? Where? When? Have you taken part in any school visits? Do you play in the school orchestra or have you taken part in a school drama production – on or off stage? Do you go to the theatre, art galleries or concerts?
- **Out-of-school activities** This category might cover many of the topics above, but it could also include any community or voluntary work you do, or Duke of Edinburgh Awards, the Combined Cadet Force (CCF), sport, music and drama activities etc. The countries you have visited might also be mentioned, for example, any exchange visits with friends living abroad.
- **Work experience** Details of part-time, holiday or Saturday jobs could be included here, particularly if they have some connection with your chosen course. Some applicants plan ahead and arrange to visit firms and discuss career interests with various people who already work in their chosen field. For some courses such as Veterinary Science, work experience is essential, and it certainly helps for others, for example Medicine and Business courses.
- **Functional/Essential Skills** These cover maths, English and information technology (the basics) and also advanced skills involving teamwork, communication, problem solving and improving your own learning. If you are not offering the qualifications then evidence of your strengths in these areas may be mentioned in the school or college reference or you may include examples in your personal statement relating to your out-of-school activities.

Finally, plan your personal statement carefully. Although you are not required to write in continuous prose, it is advisable to do so as this is likely to make a better impression on admissions tutors. Your statement should be written in good, clear English, and it is essential that your spelling and grammar be accurate throughout. Keep a copy of your complete application for reference if you are called for interview. Almost certainly you will be questioned on what you have written.

Admissions tutors always stress the importance of the confidential reference from your head teacher or form tutors. Most schools and colleges will make some effort to find out why you want to apply for a particular course, but if they do not ask, do not take it for granted that they will know! Consequently, although you have the opportunity to write about your interests on the form, it is still a good idea to tell your teachers about them. Also, if you have to work at home under difficult conditions or if you have any medical problems, your teachers must be told since these points should be mentioned on the reference.

Deferred entry
Although application is usually made in the autumn of the year preceding the proposed year of entry, admissions tutors may be prepared to consider an application made two years before entry, so that the applicant can, perhaps, gain work experience or spend a period abroad. Policies on deferred entry may differ from department to department, so you should check with admissions tutors before applying. Simply

remember that there is no guarantee that you will get the grades you need or a place at the university of your first choice at the first attempt! If not, you may need to repeat A-levels and try again. It may be better not to apply for deferred entry until you are certain in August of your grades and your place.

APPLICATIONS TO THE UNIVERSITY OF CAMBRIDGE

The universities of Oxford and Cambridge offer a wealth of resources and opportunities to students, including highly personalised teaching in tutorials (at Oxford) or supervisions (at Cambridge), where groups of two or three students meet to discuss their work with a tutor (Oxford) or supervisor (Cambridge). The college system is also a key advantage of an Oxbridge education, as students gain all the benefits of studying at a large and internationally acclaimed university, as well as the benefits of life in the smaller college community.

If you are a UK or EU applicant applying to Cambridge, you need only complete the UCAS application. You will then receive an email from the University, confirming the arrival of your application and giving you the website address of their online Supplementary Application Questionnaire (SAQ) which you will then need to complete and return by the specified date. International students and prospective organ scholars also need to submit a Cambridge Online Preliminary Application (COPA) by the required deadline; further details are available on the Cambridge website. Check with the Admissions Office or on www.study.cam.ac.uk/undergraduate/apply for the latest information.

Your UCAS application listing Cambridge as one of your university choices must be sent to UCAS by 15 October, 18.00 (UK time). If you are applying for Medicine or Veterinary Medicine you must include your BMAT registration with your application. You can indicate your choice of college or make an Open application if you have no preference. Open applicants are allocated by a computer program to colleges that have had fewer applicants per place for your chosen subject.

The Extenuating Circumstances Form (ECF) has been designed to ensure that the Cambridge colleges have the information they require in order to accurately assess any applicant who has experienced particular personal or educational disadvantage through health, personal problems, disability or difficulties with schooling. The ECF should normally be submitted by the applicant's school/college by 15 October. Further details can be obtained at www.study.cam.ac.uk/undergraduate/apply/ecf.html.

Interviews take place in Cambridge in the first three weeks of December, although some may be earlier. The colleges at the University of Cambridge use common-format written assessments to be taken by all applicants for all subjects, except Mathematics and Music. Applicants will take the written assessments either pre-interview or at interview, depending on the course for which they apply. Pre-interview assessments will take place on 2 November, on the same day as those set by the University of Oxford, whilst at-interview assessments will form part of the December interview period. Please see www.undergraduate.study.cam.ac.uk/applying/admissions-assessments for further information on these assessments and **Chapter 5** for information you need to know before completing and submitting your application.

In January applicants receive either an offer conditional upon certain grades in examinations to be taken the following summer, or a rejection. Alternatively, you may be placed in a pool for further consideration. Decisions are made on the basis of academic record, reference, personal statement, submitted work/test results and interviews. The conditions set are grades to be obtained in examinations such as A-levels, Scottish Highers/Advanced Highers or the International Baccalaureate. Offers made will include Sixth Term Examination Papers (STEP) in mathematics (see **Chapter 5** under *Mathematics*). The STEPs are taken in June and copies of past papers and full details are available from www.admissionstesting.org.

College policies

All colleges that admit undergraduates use the selection procedures described in **Chapter 5**. However, there will be some minor variations between the various colleges, within each college and also between subjects. Further information about the policies of any particular college can be found in the Cambridge Undergraduate Prospectus and may also be obtained from the admissions tutor of the college concerned. No college operates a quota system for any subject except Medicine and Veterinary Medicine, for which there are strict quotas for the University from which places are allocated to each college.

Full details of the admissions procedures are contained in the current Cambridge Undergraduate

Prospectus. Copies of the prospectus are available from Cambridge Admissions Office, Fitzwilliam House, 32 Trumpington Street, Cambridge CB2 1QY, or via the website www.undergraduate.study.cam.ac.uk.

APPLICATIONS TO THE UNIVERSITY OF OXFORD

Applications for undergraduate courses at Oxford are made through UCAS in the same way as applications to other UK universities but candidates must submit their application by 15 October, 18.00 (UK time) for entry in the following year.

You can only apply to one undergraduate course at Oxford. You can also express a preference for a particular college if you wish, or you can make an Open application. This is just like saying that you don't mind which college you go to and your application will then be allocated to a college which has relatively fewer applications for your subject in that year. The colleges have far more in common than they have differences, and all offer the same high standard of academic teaching and support, so please do not worry too much about college choice.

Applicants for most courses are required to sit a written test as part of their application, or to submit examples of their written work. See **Chapter 5** for more information and www.ox.ac.uk/apply for full details. Separate registration is required for any tests, so it's really important to check the details for your subject in good time.

When considering your application, tutors will take into account all the information that has been provided, in order to assess your suitability and potential for your chosen course. This includes your academic record, personal statement, academic reference and predicted grades, along with any written tests or written work required. If you haven't done particularly well in one area, you may still be successful if you have performed strongly in other aspects of your application. Each application is considered carefully on its individual merits, including contextual information about candidates' educational background.

A shortlist of the very best candidates will be invited to Oxford for interview, which is an important part of the selection procedure. Candidates will usually be interviewed at their college of preference and also may be interviewed by other colleges. Those from outside Europe who are not able to travel may be interviewed by telephone or Skype or some other remote means, although if you are applying for Medicine and are shortlisted, you will need to travel to Oxford for the interview. The University works hard to ensure that the best candidates are successful, whichever college you have applied to. Any college may make you an offer of a place.

Successful candidates who have not completed their school-leaving examinations will be made conditional offers based on final grades. This will be probably be between A*A*A and AAA at A-level, 38–40 points in the International Baccalaureate, including core points, or other equivalent qualifications. Decisions are notified to candidates via UCAS by the end of January.

To find out more
The University holds three Open Days a year: two in late June or early July, and one in mid-September. These are highly recommended as a great way to visit the city and the University, meet tutors and current students and find out more. Visit the website at www.ox.ac.uk/study for further information, and details of other events around the UK and beyond.

APPLICATIONS TO THE RUSSELL GROUP

The Russell Group universities are:
University of Birmingham; University of Bristol; University of Cambridge; Cardiff University; Durham University; University of Edinburgh; University of Exeter; University of Glasgow; Imperial College London; King's College London; University of Leeds; University of Liverpool; London School of Economics and Political Science; University of Manchester; Newcastle University; University of Nottingham; University of Oxford; Queen Mary University of London; Queen's University Belfast; University of Sheffield; University of Southampton; University College London; University of Warwick; University of York. (See also under London (LSE) in **Chapter 3**.)

The Russell Group has published information on what it terms 'facilitating subjects', ie subjects they would prefer to be studied by A-level students. The subjects they view as 'facilitating subjects' are maths and further maths, physics, biology, chemistry, history, geography, modern and classical languages, and English literature.

APPLICATIONS TO IRISH UNIVERSITIES

All applications to universities, colleges of education and institutes of technology in the Republic of Ireland are made through the Central Application Office, Tower House, Eglinton Street, Galway, Ireland; see www.cao.ie or telephone 091 509 800. In addition, applications to some specialist colleges are made through the Central Application Office (CAO). The CAO website gives full details of all 44 institutions and details of the application procedure. Applications are made by 1 February. Individual institutions publish details of their entry requirements for courses, but unlike applications through UCAS in the UK, no conditional offers are made. Applicants are judged purely on their academic ability. The results are published in August when institutions make their offers and when successful students are required to accept or decline the offer.

APPLICATIONS TO COMMONWEALTH UNIVERSITIES

Details of universities in 40 commonwealth countries (all charge fees) are published on www.acu.ac.uk or for those in Australia, on www.idp.com/australia, and for those In Canada, www.studyincanada.com.

APPLICATIONS TO AMERICAN UNIVERSITIES

There is a very large number of universities and colleges offering degree course programmes in the USA; some institutions are independent and others state-controlled. Students applying to study in the USA can apply to over 600 colleges through the Common Application, the central admissions system. However, unlike the UK, where UCAS controls nearly all university and college applications, it is still necessary to apply to certain American institutions directly; a full list of participating Common Application colleges can be downloaded from the website at www.commonapp.org. Most American universities will expect applicants to have A-levels or IB qualifications and in addition, usually require students to complete either the SAT or ACT admissions tests. The SAT Reasoning Test covers mathematical and evidence-based reasoning abilities. In some cases applicants may be required to complete a writing task as part of the reasoning test, as well as taking SAT II tests which are based on specific subjects. The ACT tests English, maths, comprehension and scientific reasoning. Some universities require applicants to take the ACT with writing, which includes an additional writing task. Both the SAT and the ACT can be taken at centres in the UK: see www.collegeboard.org and www.act.org respectively for details.

Unlike the usual specialised subject degrees at UK universities, 'Liberal Arts' programmes in the USA have considerable breadth and flexibility, although subjects requiring greater specialised knowledge such as Medicine and Law require further study at Medical or Law School.

Because of the complexities of an application to American universities, such as financial implications, visas etc, students should initially refer to www.fulbright.co.uk. It is also important to be able to identify the differences between and the quality of institutions and valuable guides can be sourced through www.petersons.com.

THE ERASMUS+ PROGRAMME

Many universities in the UK have formal agreements with partner institutions in Europe through the Erasmus+ programme which enables UK university students to apply for courses in Europe for periods up to one year. Some of these courses are taught in English and students can receive help with accommodation and other expenses through the Erasmus+ Student Grant scheme.

The Erasmus+ programme is for undergraduates in all subject areas who would like to study or do a work placement for three to twelve months as part of their degree course in one of 32 other European countries. Most universities offer it although it is not available with every course so students are advised to check with their chosen universities before making an application. Students do not pay any fees to the European university they visit and those who go for the full academic year (24 weeks) have their UK tuition fees reduced. Following the 23 June 2016 European Union referendum, in which the UK voted to leave the EU, the UK's future participation in the Erasmus+ programme is to be determined as part of formal discussions with the EU. While the UK remains a member of the EU, and until it has finalised the terms of its withdrawal with the other Member States, students will continue to have access to the Erasmus+ scheme under the current terms of the programme, until the end of 2020.

AND FINALLY ... BEFORE YOU SEND IN YOUR APPLICATION

CHECK that you have passes at grade C or 4 or higher in the GCSE (or equivalent) subjects required for the course at the institutions to which you are applying. FAILURE TO HAVE THE RIGHT GCSE SUBJECTS OR THE RIGHT NUMBER OF GRADE C OR 4 PASSES OR HIGHER IN GCSE WILL RESULT IN A REJECTION.

CHECK that you are taking (or have taken) the GCE A-level and, if required, AS (or equivalent) subjects required for the course at the institution to which you are applying. FAILURE TO BE TAKING OR HAVE TAKEN THE RIGHT A-LEVELS WILL ALSO RESULT IN A REJECTION.

CHECK that the GCE A-levels and other qualifications you are taking will be accepted for the course for which you are applying. Some subjects and institutions do not stipulate any specific A-levels, only that you are required to offer two or three subjects at GCE A-level. In the view of some admissions tutors NOT ALL GCE A-LEVELS CARRY THE SAME WEIGHT (see **Chapter 1**).

CHECK that you can meet the requirements for all relevant admissions/interview tests.

CHECK that you have made all the necessary arrangements for sitting any required admissions tests.

CHECK that you can meet any age, health and DBS requirements for entry to your listed courses.

WHAT TO DO ON RESULTS DAY ... AND AFTER

BE AT HOME! Do not arrange to be away when your results are published. If you do not achieve the grades you require, you will need to follow an alternative course of action and make decisions that could affect your life during the next few years. Do not expect others to make these decisions for you. If you achieve the grades or points which have been offered you will receive confirmation of a place, but this may take a few days to reach you. Once your place is confirmed contact the accommodation office at the university or college and inform them that you will need a place in a hall of residence or other accommodation.

If you achieve grades or points higher than your conditional firm (CF) choice you can reconsider where and what to study by registering with UCAS to use the **Adjustment** process in **Track**. This is available from A-level results day until 31 August and you have five days to register and secure an alternative course. You must check very carefully all the **Adjustment** information on the UCAS website (www.ucas.com/adjustment) to make sure that you are eligible and that a vacancy is available. There is no guarantee of a vacancy on a course you are aiming for, and it is very unlikely that competitive courses will have places. If you decide definitely to change courses advise the university or college immediately, but check with www.ucas.com and your school/college adviser for the latest information.

If your grades or points are higher than you expected and you are not holding any offers you can telephone or email the admissions tutor at the universities and colleges which rejected you and request that they might reconsider you.

If you just miss your offers then telephone or email the universities and colleges to see if they can still offer you a place. ALWAYS HAVE YOUR UCAS PERSONAL ID AVAILABLE WHEN YOU CALL. Their decisions may take a few days. You should check the universities and colleges in your order of preference. Your first choice must reject you before you contact your second choice.

If you have not applied to any university or college earlier in the year then you can apply through the **Clearing** scheme which runs from early July. Check the tables in **Chapter 7** to identify which institutions normally make offers matching your results, check **Clearing** vacancy listings, and then telephone or email the institution before completing your application.

If you learn finally that you do not have a place because you have missed the grades in your offer you'll know you're in **Clearing** if your **Track** status says 'You are in **Clearing**' or '**Clearing** has started', and your **Clearing** number will be displayed.

If an institution has vacancies they will ask you for your grades. Get informal offers over the phone – maybe from a variety of universities and colleges – then decide which one you want to accept. If you're given an offer you want to accept, and you have permission from the university or college, you can add a **Clearing** choice in **Track**. You can only add one choice at a time, but if the university or college doesn't confirm your place, you'll be able to add another.

If you have to re-apply for a place, check the vacancies on the UCAS website (www.ucas.com), in the national press and through your local careers office. If there are vacancies in your subject, check with the university or college that these vacancies have not been taken.

REMEMBER – There are many thousands of students just like you. Admissions tutors have a mammoth task checking how many students will be taking up their places since not all students whose grades match their offers finally decide to do so!

IF YOU HAVE AN OFFER AND THE RIGHT GRADES BUT ARE NOT ACCEPTING THAT OR AN ALTERNATIVE PLACE – TELL THE UNIVERSITY OR COLLEGE. Someone else is waiting for your place! If you are applying for a place through **Clearing** it may even be late September before you know you have a place so BE PATIENT AND STAY CALM!

Good luck!

5 | ADMISSIONS TESTS, SELECTION OF APPLICANTS AND INTERVIEWS

The selection of applicants by universities and colleges takes many forms. However, with rising numbers of applicants for places (especially in the popular subjects) and increasing numbers of students with high grades, greater importance is now attached not only to applicants' predicted A-level grades and GCSE attainments, but also to other aspects of their applications, especially the school reference and the personal statement and, for some courses and some institutions, performance at interview, and performance in admissions tests.

ADMISSIONS TESTS

Admissions tests are now increasingly used for undergraduate entry to specific courses and specific institutions. These include national subject-based tests such as LNAT, BMAT and UKCAT (see below) which are used for selecting applicants for entry to specified courses at particular institutions in subjects such as Law, Medicine, Dentistry and Veterinary Sciences. Admissions tests are also set by individual universities and colleges (or commercial organisations on their behalf) for entry, again, to particular courses in the individual institutions. Examples of these include the Thinking Skills Assessment (TSA) used by, for example, the University of Oxford, and the Health Professions Aptitude Test (HPAT) used by Ulster University for entry to some health-related courses. Other examples include the subject-based admissions tests used by many universities and colleges for entry to particular courses in subjects such as Art, Dance, Construction, Design, Drama and other Performance-based courses, Education and Teacher Training, Economics, Engineering, Journalism, Languages, Music, Nursing and Social Work.

Admissions tests are usually taken before or at interview and, except for courses requiring auditions or portfolio inspections, they are generally timed, unseen, written, or online tests. They can be used on their own, or alongside other selection methods used by university and college admissions staff, including:

- questionnaires or tests to be completed by applicants prior to interview and/or offer
- examples of school work to be submitted prior to interview and/or offer
- written tests at interview
- mathematical tests at interview
- practical tests at interview
- a response to a passage at interview
- performance-based tests (for example, for Music, Dance, Drama).

With regard to tests, applicants should check prospectuses and subject websites as soon as possible since, in some cases, early registration is required. This is especially important for applicants to Oxford and Cambridge and for those applying for Law, Medicine, Dentistry and Veterinary Science who may be required to take the LNAT, UKCAT or BMAT.

Here is a list of commonly used admissions tests, and this is followed by degree subject lists showing subject-based and individual institutions' admissions tests.

English
English Literature Admissions Test (ELAT)
The ELAT is a pre-interview admissions test for applicants to English courses at the Universities of Oxford and Cambridge (see the ELAT pages on the Admissions Testing Service website www.admissionstesting.org).

Health Professions
Health Professions Admissions Test (HPAT)-Ulster
The HPAT-Ulster is used by Ulster University for entry to courses including Dietetics, Occupational Therapy, Physiotherapy, Podiatry, Radiography, Radiotherapy and Oncology, and Speech and Language Therapies.

History
History Aptitude Test (HAT)
The HAT is a two-hour test sat by all candidates applying for History courses and joint schools at Oxford University (see *History* below). See www.history.ox.ac.uk.

Law
Cambridge Law Test (CLT)
This is a one-hour, two-part question test designed and used by the University of Cambridge with Law applicants who are called for interview. No prior knowledge of law is required for the test. See http://ba.law.cam.ac.uk/applying/cambridge_law_test for full details.

Law National Aptitude Test (LNAT)
The LNAT is an on-screen test for applicants to specified undergraduate Law programmes at Bristol, Durham, Glasgow, London (King's), London (UCL), Nottingham, Oxford and SOAS universities. (See *Law* below, and **Law** in the subject tables in **Chapter 7**.) Applicants need to check universities' websites and the LNAT website (www.lnat.ac.uk) for the UCAS codes for courses requiring applicants to sit the LNAT. (**NB** Cambridge does not require Law applicants to take the LNAT but see above and the Cambridge entry under *Law* below.) Details of LNAT (which includes multiple-choice and essay questions), practice papers, registration dates, test dates, test centres and fees are all available on the LNAT website.

Mathematics
Sixth Term Examination Paper (STEP)
Applicants with offers for Mathematics courses at Cambridge and Warwick universities are usually required to take STEP. Bath, Bristol and Oxford Universities, and Imperial London also encourage applicants for their Mathematics courses to take STEP. For details, see the STEP pages on the Admissions Testing Service website (www.admissionstesting.org).

Mathematics Admissions Test (MAT)
The MAT is required by the University of Oxford for Mathematics, Computer Science courses and joint schools, and by Imperial London for its Mathematics course. Details of the test can be found on the MAT pages on the Admissions Testing Service website (www.admissionstesting.org).

Medicine, Dentistry, Veterinary Science/Medicine, and related subjects
Most medical schools require applicants to sit the UK Clinical Aptitude Test (UKCAT) or the BioMedical Admissions Test (BMAT) or, for graduate entry, the Graduate Australian Medical Schools Admissions Test (GAMSAT) for specified Medicine courses. Applicants are advised to check the websites of all universities and medical schools offering Medicine for their latest admissions requirements, including admissions and aptitude tests, to check the UKCAT website www.ukcat.ac.uk or the BMAT pages on www.admissionstesting.org (and for graduate entry www.gamsat.co.uk) for the latest information.

The BioMedical Admissions Test (BMAT)
This is a pen-and-paper admissions test taken by undergraduate applicants to Medicine and Veterinary Medicine at Cambridge, Medicine and Biomedical Sciences at Oxford, Medicine and Dentistry at Leeds, and Medicine courses at Imperial London, London (UCL), Brighton and Sussex (MS), Lancaster and Keele (international applicants only). Applicants for Graduate Medicine at Imperial are also required to take the BMAT. A list of the courses requiring BMAT is available on the BMAT pages of the Admissions Testing Service website (www.admissionstesting.org) and also on university websites and in their prospectuses. It is important to note BMAT's early closing date for entries and also the test dates. The two-hour test consists of three sections:

- aptitude and skills
- scientific knowledge and applications
- writing task.

Applicants sit the test only once and pay one entry fee no matter how many courses they apply for. However, if they re-apply to universities the following year they will need to re-take the BMAT and pay another fee. Past question papers are available (see website) and an official study guide *Preparing for the BMAT* is also available at www.pearsonschoolsandfecolleges.co.uk. Results of the BMAT are first sent to the universities, and then to the BMAT test centres. Candidates need to contact their test centres direct for their results. See **Dentistry**, **Medicine** and **Veterinary Science/Medicine** below and relevant subject tables in **Chapter 7**.

The UK Clinical Aptitude Test (UKCAT)
The UKCAT is a clinical aptitude test used by the majority of medical and dental schools in the selection of applicants for Medicine and Dentistry, alongside their existing selection processes, for undergraduate entry. The tests are not curriculum-based and do not have a science component. No revision is necessary; there is no textbook and no course of instruction. In the first instance, the UKCAT is a test of cognitive skills involving problem-solving and critical reasoning. With over 150 test centres, it is an on-screen test (not paper-based), and is marked electronically. Some bursaries are available to help towards the cost of the test. Applicants who require extra time due to a disability or medical condition should register for the UKCATSEN. Further details (including the most recent list of universities requiring applicants to sit the UKCAT) are found on the website www.ukcat.ac.uk. See also the **Dentistry** and **Medicine** subject tables in **Chapter 7**, the entries for **Dentistry** and **Medicine** below, and **Chapter 4** for application details. See www.ukcat.ac.uk.

Modern and Medieval Languages
The Modern and Medieval Languages Admissions Assessment (MMLAA)
This written test is used by the University of Cambridge for selecting applicants for entry to courses involving modern and medieval languages. See www.mml.cam.ac.uk/applying/involve.

General Admissions Tests
Thinking Skills Assessment (TSA)
The TSA is a pen-and-paper test that tests applicants' critical thinking and problem-solving skills. The test is used by the University of Cambridge for applicants to Land Economy, by University College London for European, Social and Political Studies, and by the University of Oxford for entry to several courses (see below and the TSA web pages on www.admissionstesting.org). Both the TSA Cambridge and TSA UCL tests consist of 50 multiple-choice questions, which applicants have 90 minutes to complete. However, the TSA Oxford has an additional section, the Writing Task, where candidates are given 30 minutes to answer one essay question out of a possible four questions.

LSE UG Admissions Assessment (UGAA)
The LSE UGAA is used for some applicants with non-traditional educational backgrounds. The test is not subject or course specific and consists of English comprehension exercises, essay questions and mathematical problems.

DEGREE SUBJECT EXAMPLES OF UNIVERSITIES AND COLLEGES USING TESTS AND ASSESSMENTS
Many universities and colleges set their own tests for specific subjects so it is important to check the websites for your preferred institutions and courses for the latest information about their applications and selection processes. The following list provides a guide to the subjects and some of the institutions requiring admissions tests and other forms of assessment. Due to the constant changes in admissions policies, this is not a complete list. However, applicants for these subjects should be guided as to the requirements of those universities requiring tests.

Adult Nursing
Bolton Numeracy and literacy test.

Anglo Saxon, Norse and Celtic
Cambridge ASNCAA pre-interview. Check college websites for submitted work requirements.

Animal Management
Kirklees (Coll) Mature applicants screening test.

Anthropology
Oxford See Archaeology.

Archaeology
Cambridge Shortlisted applicants take the ARCHAA at interview. Check college websites for submitted work requirements.

Oxford (Arch Anth) Two recent marked essays are required, preferably in different subjects, plus a statement of no more than 500 words in response to a set question – required before interview. No written test at interview. (Class Arch Anc Hist) Written work required. No written test at interview. Check www.ox.ac.uk/tests.

Architecture
Cambridge ARCHITAA taken at interview. Check college websites for details.

Cardiff (Archit, Archit Eng) Samples of work to be sent before interview.

Dundee Samples of work required before interview.

Huddersfield Portfolio of work required.

Liverpool Portfolio and selection workshop.

London Met Portfolio of work required.

London South Bank Samples of work to be sent before interview.

Manchester Met Portfolio of work required.

Nottingham Portfolio of work required.

Nottingham Trent Examples of work are required.

Plymouth Digital portfolio of work required.

Portsmouth Interview required.

Sheffield Portfolio required.

Art and Design
Arts London Portfolio required.

Bolton (Fash) You may be required to attend for interview and provide a portfolio of appropriate work.

Bournemouth (Comp Animat Art) Maths, logic and life-drawing tests at interview, and portfolio of work required.

Brunel (Des Eng) All applicants are required to attend an interview including a portfolio review as part of the selection process.

Chester (Fash des) Applicants may be required to attend a portfolio interview.

Hertfordshire (Fash Des) Portfolio interview required.

Oxford (Fn Art) No written work required. Portfolio to be submitted in November. Practical examination. Two pieces in different media from a number of possible subjects. Check www.ox.ac.uk/tests.

Ravensbourne Verbal examination. (Animat) Written test.

Sussex (Prod Des) Interview and portfolio review required.

Asian and Middle Eastern Studies
Cambridge AMESAA pre-interview. Check www.cam.ac.uk/assessment.

Biomedical Sciences
Oxford BMAT is required. Check www.ox.ac.uk/tests.

Portsmouth Test of motivation and knowledge of the subject, the degree and careers to which it leads.

Business Courses
Arts London (CFash) School work to be submitted before interview. Degree subject-based test and numeracy test at interview.

Buckingham (Bus Man) Informal interview required.

Newcastle Some shortlisted applicants will be given a variety of assessment tests at interview.
Plymouth (Cruise Mgt) Informal interview required.

Chemistry
Oxford No written work required. All candidates must take the TSA Chemistry (section 1 of the TSA Oxford). Check www.ox.ac.uk/tests.
Reading During the interview, applicants will be asked a series of chemistry-related questions from a select list. Applicants are required to discuss these in detail and may be asked to draw molecular formulas.

Classics (see also Archaeology)
Cambridge Shortlisted applicants take the CAA at interview, with separate tests for the three- and four-year courses. Check college websites for submitted work requirements.
Oxford For all Classics courses, two essays or commentaries required, normally in areas related to Classics, and submitted in November. CAT also required. Check www.ox.ac.uk/tests.

Classics and English
Oxford Two pieces of written work required, one relevant to Classics and one to English. CAT and ELAT also required. Check www.ox.ac.uk/tests.

Classics and Modern Languages
Oxford Two Classics essays and two modern language essays required, one in the chosen language and one in English. CAT and MLAT also required. Check www.ox.ac.uk/tests.

Classics and Oriental Studies
Oxford CAT; two pieces written work also required, at least one should be on a classical topic if already studying a classical subject. Check www.ox.ac.uk/tests.

Community Learning and Development
Dundee Written question response form.

Computer Science
Cambridge Shortlisted applicants take the CSAT. Check www.cam.ac.uk/assessment.
Oxford No written work required. MAT required. See also **Mathematics**. Check www.ox.ac.uk/tests.
Winchester (Comp Aid Des) Interview required.

Dance
Chichester (Perf Arts) Group practical test.

Dental Nursing
Bolton (Dntl Tech) A manual dexterity test is taken at interview.
Portsmouth (Dntl Hyg Dntl Thera) Interview.

Dentistry
Glasgow UKCAT.
Leeds BMAT
London (King's) UKCAT.
Manchester UKCAT and interview.

Dietetics
Hertfordshire Literacy and numeracy tests are used at interview.
London Met (Diet Nutr) Interview required.
Ulster HPAT: see https://hpat-ulster.acer.org and www.ulster.ac.uk before completing the UCAS application.

Drama
Liverpool (LIPA) (Actg) Applicants will be expected to perform one devised piece, one Shakespearean piece and a song and give a short review of a performance they have seen recently.
London (Royal Central Sch SpDr) Written papers and/or tests.
Reading (Thea) Applicants undertake a practical assessment and an interview.

Economics
Cambridge ECAA pre-interview. Check college websites for submitted work requirements.
Oxford (Econ Mgt) No written work required. Oxford TSA required. Check www.ox.ac.uk/tests.

Education Studies (see also Teacher Training)
Cambridge Shortlisted applicants take the EAA at inteview. Check www.cam.ac.uk/assessment and college websites for written work requirements.
Cumbria Literacy and numeracy Professional Skills tests.
Newman (P Educ) Basic numeracy and literacy tests.

Engineering
Cambridge ENGAA pre-interview. Check www.cam.ac.uk/assessment.
Oxford No written work required. All candidates take the PAT. Check ox.ac.uk/tests.
Southampton Mathematics test may be required for Foundation course applicants.

English
Bristol Samples of work may be required.
Cambridge ELAT pre-interview. Check college websites for submitted work requirements.
London (UCL) After interview, applicants are asked to write a critical commentary on an unseen passage of prose or verse.
Oxford (Engl Lang Lit) ELAT and one recent marked essay. (Engl Modn Langs) ELAT and MLAT. One English essay and two modern language essays required, one in the chosen language and one in English. Check www.ox.ac.uk/tests.
Portsmouth (Crea Writ) All applicants will be required to submit a short piece of creative writing to the admissions office.

European and Middle Eastern Languages (see also Modern and Medieval Languages)
Oxford Two pieces of written work, one in the chosen language and one in English. MLAT and OLAT required. Check www.ox.ac.uk/tests.

Film Studies
Bournemouth Arts (Film Prod) Portfolio including a five minute showreel of the applicant's work.
Creative Arts (Film Prod) Portfolio at interview.
Reading There are three stages to the interview process: a practical, a film seminar and an interview.
South Wales Piece of written work required at interview.

Film, TV and Radio
Portsmouth (Film Prod) Applicants without relevant qualifications may be asked to submit a digital portfolio.
Staffordshire Interview with portfolio required.

Geography
Cambridge GAA pre-interview. Check college websites for submitted work requirements.
Cardiff Test for some Joint Honours courses.
Oxford No written work required. All candidates must take the Oxford TSA. Check www.ox.ac.uk/tests.
Worcester Interview required.

Healthcare Science
Hertfordshire Literacy and numeracy tests are used at interview.

History
Cambridge HAA pre-interview. Check college websites for submitted work requirements.
Liverpool John Moores Mature students not in education must submit an essay.
London (Gold) Samples of written work from non-standard applicants and from those without academic qualifications.
Oxford An essay on a historical topic is required as well as the HAT. (Hist Modn Langs) Written work; HAT and MLAT required. Check www.ox.ac.uk/tests.

History of Art
Cambridge Shortlisted applicants take the HAAA at interview. Check college websites for submitted work requirements.
Oxford Two pieces of work required: (a) a marked essay from an A-level or equivalent course and (b) no more than 750 words responding to an item of art, architecture or design to which the applicant has had first-hand access with a photograph or photocopy of the item provided if possible. No written test at interview. Check www.ox.ac.uk/tests.

Human Sciences
Oxford No written work required. All candidates must take the Oxford TSA. Check www.ox.ac.uk/tests.

Human, Social and Political Sciences
Cambridge HSPSAA pre-interview. Check college websites for submitted work requirements.

Journalism (see also Media Studies)
Brighton (Spo Jrnl) Test for those called to interview: contact admissions tutor.
City Written test.
Edinburgh Napier (Jrnl) Samples of work before interview.
Kent English language and academic tests for all candidates, relating to requirements of the accrediting professional bodies.
Portsmouth Journalism and Broadcast Journalism candidates are subject to an interview and an admissions test.
South Wales Test and interview.

Land Economy
Cambridge Shortlisted applicants take the TSA Cambridge at interview. Check college websites for individual requirements.

Law
Bradford (Coll) Academic tests at interview may be required for mature students.
Bristol LNAT.
Cambridge Shortlisted applicants take the CLT at interview. Check college websites for submitted work requirements.
Durham LNAT.
Glasgow LNAT.
London (King's) LNAT.
London (UCL) LNAT.
Manchester Met LNAT.
Nottingham LNAT.
Oxford No written work required. All applicants take the LNAT. (Law; Law St Euro) LNAT plus, at interview, a possible oral test in the modern language for students taking a joint language, except for those taking Dutch Law options. Check www.ox.ac.uk/tests.

Linguistics
Cambridge Shortlisted applicants take the LAA. Check college websites for submitted work requirements.

Materials Science
Oxford No written work required. All candidates must take the PAT. Check www.ox.ac.uk/tests.

Mathematics
Cambridge STEP. Check www.cam.ac.uk/assessment.
Imperial London MAT. The paper takes two and a half hours and sample tests are available online. Students unable to sit the MAT must complete the STEP.
Oxford No written work required. MAT required. Check www.ox.ac.uk/tests.

Media Studies
Coventry Interview and portfolio.
Hull (Coll) Essay required before interview.

Liverpool John Moores Questionnaire to be completed before interview. Degree subject-based test at interview.

Medicine
Aston (UKCAT) 5-year course.
Birmingham UKCAT.
Brighton and Sussex (MS) BMAT.
Cambridge BMAT test required. Check www.cam.ac.uk/assessment.
Exeter UKCAT or GAMSAT required.
Glasgow UKCAT.
Imperial London BMAT.
Lancaster BMAT.
Leeds BMAT
London (King's) UKCAT.
London (St George's) GAMSAT is required for the four-year Graduate Stream course. UKCAT is required for the five-year course.
London (UCL) (Six-year course) BMAT.
Manchester UKCAT and interview.
Nottingham UKCAT.
Oxford No written work required. BMAT test required. Check www.ox.ac.uk/tests.

Medicine/Dentistry
Liverpool Entrants require UKCAT. Graduate entrants to Medicine must complete GAMSAT.

Meteorology
Reading (Meteor Clim (MMet)) All applicants will be asked to attend an interview prior to an offer being made.

Midwifery
Anglia Ruskin Literacy and numeracy tests.
Canterbury Christ Church Literacy test at interview.
Hertfordshire Literacy and numeracy tests are used at interview.
Liverpool John Moores Literacy and numeracy tests.

Modern and Medieval Languages (see also Asian and Middle Eastern Studies, Oriental Studies and separate languages)
Cambridge Shortlisted applicants take the MMLAA. Check college websites for submitted work requirements.
Oxford (Modn Langs; Modn Lang Ling) MLAT. Two marked essays, one in chosen language and one in English. (Euro Mid E Langs) MLAT and OLAT required. One essay required in English an for the European language but none for the Middle Eastern language. Check www.ox.ac.uk/tests.

Music
Bath Spa (Commer Mus) Interview requirements include performance of an original piece of work.
Birmingham City Portfolio required for some courses.
Cambridge Check college websites for assessment details and submitted work requirements.
Cardiff Interview requirements include performance or extracts for analysis.
Chichester Interview requirements include performance.
City Interview requirements include performance.
Colchester (Inst) Interview requirements include performance, aural, keyboard skills and essay.
Coventry Audition held alongside an interview.
Derby Interview requirements include performance.
Edinburgh Interview requirements include performance, harmony and counterpoint (written), essay and sight-singing.
Edinburgh Napier Audition and theory test.
Glasgow Interview requirements include performance and sight-singing.
Guildhall (Sch Mus Dr) Interviews mostly held at the School but also at Newcastle and in the USA.
Huddersfield Audition.

Liverpool Hope Interview requirements include performance, keyboard tests and harmony and counterpoint (written).

London (Gold) Interview requirements include performance.

London (King's) Only borderline applicants or candidates with non-standard qualifications are interviewed.

London (RAcMus) (Mus) Interview requirements include performance, keyboard skills, harmony and counterpoint (written), and extracts for analysis.

Oxford Interview requirements include the performance of a piece/s on the candidate's principal instrument or voice. Candidates without keyboard skills to grade 5 may be asked to take a keyboard sight-reading test. Two pieces of marked work (with at least one on music), plus one or two examples of marked harmony and counterpoint required, plus examples of composition (optional). Check www.ox.ac.uk/tests.

RCMus Interview requirements include performance and sight-singing.

RConsvS Interview requirements include performance, sight-singing and aural.

Royal Welsh (CMusDr) Interview requirements include performance and essay.

West London Students required to produce a portfolio of work and attend an audition: see www.uwl.ac.uk.

Wolverhampton Interview requirements include performance and a musical theory test.

York Interview requirements include performance.

Natural Sciences
Cambridge NSAA pre-interview. Check www.cam.ac.uk/assessment.

Nursing
Anglia Ruskin Literacy and numeracy tests.

Birmingham City Literacy and numeracy tests prior to interview.

Bucks New Tests for BSc Nursing.

Canterbury Christ Church Literacy and numeracy tests at interview.

City Written test.

Coventry Literacy and numeracy tests.

Cumbria (Nurs; Midwif) Numeracy test.

Derby Literacy and numeracy tests at interview.

East Anglia Tests.

Essex Numeracy and literacy test alongside an interview.

Hertfordshire Literacy and numeracy tests are used at interview.

London South Bank (Nurs A/C/MH) On-campus literacy and numeracy tests before interview.

Suffolk Interview and tests.

UWE Bristol Selection event involving numeracy and literacy test, group activity and individual interview.

West London Numeracy and literacy tests.

Wolverhampton Tests.

Nursing and Midwifery
Cardiff Multiple Mini Interview (MMI).

Occupational Therapy
Essex Numeracy and literacy test alongside an interview.

Ulster HPAT: see https://hpat-ulster.acer.org and www.ulster.ac.uk before completing the UCAS application.

UWE Bristol Interview.

Optometry
Hertfordshire Literacy and numeracy tests are used at interview.

Oriental Studies
Oxford Two essays required. OLAT required for certain course combinations. Check www.ox.ac.uk/tests.

Paramedic Science
Anglia Ruskin Literacy and numeracy tests.

Hertfordshire Literacy and numeracy tests are used at interview.

Pharmacology/Pharmaceutical Sciences
Portsmouth Test of motivation, knowledge of the subject, degree course and the careers to which it leads.

Pharmacy
Hertfordshire Literacy and numeracy tests are used at interview.
Liverpool John Moores Aptitude test.
Portsmouth (A-level students) Test of motivation and knowledge of pharmacy as a profession. (Other applicants) Test of chemistry and biology, plus literacy and numeracy tests.

Philosophy
Cambridge Shortlisted applicants take the PAA at interview. Check college websites for submitted work requirements.
Oxford (Phil Modn Langs) MLAT. Two pieces of written work required; one in English and one in the chosen language. (Phil Theol) Philosophy Test and one piece of written work. (Phil Pol Econ (PPE)) Oxford TSA; no written work required. Check www.ox.ac.uk/tests.

Physical Education
Chichester Physical test.

Physics
Oxford PAT; no written work required. Check www.ox.ac.uk/tests.

Physiotherapy
Cardiff Multiple Mini Interview (MMI).
East Anglia Tests.
Essex Numeracy and literacy test alongside an interview.
Hertfordshire Literacy and numeracy tests are used at interview.
Robert Gordon Practical testing varies from year to year.
Ulster HPAT: see https://hpat-ulster.acer.org and www.ulster.ac.uk before completing the UCAS application.

Podiatry
Ulster HPAT: see https://hpat-ulster.acer.org and www.ulster.ac.uk before completing the UCAS application.

Politics
Oxford See (Phil Pol Econ (PPE)) under Philosophy.

Popular Music
South Wales Audition.

Product Design
Dundee Portfolio and interview will determine the appropriate entry point for candidate (Level 1 or 2).

Psychological and Behavioural Sciences
Cambridge PBSAA pre-interview. Check college websites for submitted work requirements.

Psychology
London (UCL) Questionnaire may be required.
Oxford (Expmtl Psy) Oxford TSA; no written work required. Check www.ox.ac.uk/tests.

Radiography
Hertfordshire Literacy and numeracy tests are used at interview.
Ulster HPAT: see https://hpat-ulster.acer.org and www.ulster.ac.uk before completing the UCAS application.

Social Work
Anglia Ruskin Literacy and numeracy tests.
Birmingham Shortlisted applicants may be required to complete a written test.
Birmingham City Written test at interview.
Bucks New Tests.

Cardiff Met Group task, individual interview and written test.
Derby Literacy and numeracy tests at interview.
Dundee Written question response form.
Durham New (Coll) Written test at interview.
East Anglia Test.
Essex Literacy test alongside an interview.
Hertfordshire Literacy and numeracy tests are used at interview.
Kent Written test followed by an interview and observed group discussions.
London (Gold) Questions on social work practice and the applicant's experience of working in the social work/social care field.
London Met Pre-interview literacy test and, if successful, an interview.
Manchester Met (Yth Commun Wk) Tests.
Newman (Yth Commun Wk) Written exercise for candidates with no qualifications but considerable experience.
Portsmouth Test.
Stirling Assessments.
Suffolk Interview and test.
UWE Bristol Written test and interview.
Wolverhampton Tests.

Speech Pathology/Sciences/Therapy
Ulster HPAT: see https://hpat-ulster.acer.org and www.ulster.ac.uk before completing the UCAS application.

Teacher Training
Bishop Grosseteste Literacy and numeracy tests are part of the selection criteria at interview.
Brighton Written test at interview.
Canterbury Christ Church All candidates are interviewed in groups of 8–10 and assessments are made based on the results of a written English test and performance in the group interview.
Cardiff Met Literacy and numeracy tests.
Chester Literacy and numeracy tests.
Chichester Written test at interview.
Dundee Literacy and numeracy tests.
Durham Literacy and numeracy tests.
Hertfordshire Admissions test.
Liverpool John Moores (P Educ) Literacy and numeracy tests.
Plymouth Mathematical test at interview. Written test at interview.
Reading Applicants are required to take part in both a group activity and an individual interview as well as completing a short essay-based written test.
Roehampton Written test at interview.
St Mary's National Skills Test in English and mathematics.
Sheffield Hallam Interview with numeracy and literacy tests.
UWE Bristol Literacy test at interview.
Winchester Literacy test at interview.

Theatre and Performance
Glyndŵr An audition is required for Theatre and Performance.

Theology and Religious Studies
Cambridge TAA pre-interview. Check college websites for submitted work requirements.
Oxford (Theol Relgn) No test; one piece of marked written work required or response to a marked unseen exam question. (Theol Orntl St) OLAT for certain strands; two pieces of written work required, one on religious studies and one on any subject. Check www.ox.ac.uk/tests.

Veterinary Science/Medicine
Cambridge BMAT test required. Check www.cam.ac.uk/assessment.
Glasgow (Vet Med) Computer-based ethical reasoning test for candidates attending interviews.
Myerscough (Coll) (Vet Nurs) Subject-based test at interview.

SELECTION OF APPLICANTS

University and college departmental admissions tutors are responsible for selecting candidates, basing their decisions on the policies of acceptable qualifications established by each institution and, where required, applicants' performance in admissions tests. There is little doubt that academic achievement, aptitude and promise are the most important factors although other subsidiary factors may be taken into consideration. The outline which follows provides information on the way in which candidates are selected for degree and diploma courses.

- Grades obtained by the applicant in GCE A-level and equivalent examinations and the range of subjects studied may be considered. Some universities require an additional AS grade for certain courses, such as Medicine. Where school policy limits a student's opportunity to take AS subjects, alternative A-level offers may be given (check websites).
- Applicant's performance in aptitude and admissions tests, as required by universities and colleges.
- Academic record of the applicant throughout his or her school career, especially up to A-level, Highers, Advanced Highers or other qualifications and the choice of subjects. If you are taking general studies at A-level confirm with the admissions tutor that this is acceptable.
- Time taken by the applicant to obtain good grades at GCSE/Scottish Nationals and A-level/Scottish Highers/Advanced Highers.
- Forecast or the examination results of the applicant at A-level (or equivalent) and head teacher's report.
- The applicant's intellectual development; evidence of ability and motivation to follow the chosen course.
- The applicant's range of interests, both in and out of school; aspects of character and personality.
- The vocational interests, knowledge and experience of the applicant particularly if they are choosing vocational courses.

INTERVIEWS

Fewer applicants are now interviewed than in the past but even if you are not called you should make an effort to visit your chosen universities and/or colleges before you accept any offer. Interviews may be arranged simply to give you a chance to see the institution and the department and to meet the staff and students. Alternatively, interviews may be an important part of the selection procedure for specific courses such as Law, Medicine and Teaching. If they are, you need to prepare yourself well. Most interviews last approximately 20–30 minutes and you may be interviewed by more than one person. For practical subjects such as Music and Drama almost certainly you will be asked to perform, and for artistic subjects, to take examples of your work. For some courses you may also have a written or other test at interview (see above).

How best can you prepare yourself?

Firstly, as one applicant advised, 'Go to the interview – at least you'll see the place.'

Secondly, on the question of dress, try to turn up looking smart (it may not matter, but it can't be wrong).

Two previous applicants were more specific: 'Dress smartly but sensibly so you are comfortable for travelling and walking round the campus.'

More general advice is also important

- 'Prepare well – interviewers are never impressed by applicants who only sit there with no willingness to take part.'
- 'Read up the prospectus and course details. Know how their course differs from any others you have applied for and be able to say why you prefer theirs.'
- 'They always ask if you have any questions to ask them: prepare some!' For example, How many students are admitted to the course each year? What are the job prospects for graduates? How easy is it to change from your chosen course to a related course?

Questions which you could ask might focus on the ways in which work is assessed, the content of the course, field work, work experience, teaching methods, accommodation and, especially for vocational courses, contacts with industry, commerce or the professions. However, don't ask questions which are already answered in the prospectus!

These are only a few suggestions and other questions may come to mind during the interview which, above all, should be a two-way flow of information. It is also important to keep a copy of your UCAS application (especially your personal statement) for reference since your interview will probably start with a question about something you have written.

Usually interviewers will want to know why you have chosen the subject and why you have chosen their particular institution. They will want to see how motivated you are, how much care you have taken in choosing your subject, how much you know about your subject, what books you have read. If you have chosen a vocational course they will want to find out how much you know about the career it leads to, and whether you have visited any places of work or had any work experience. If your chosen subject is also an A-level subject you will be asked about your course and the aspects of the course you like the most.

Try to relax. For some people interviews can be an ordeal; most interviewers know this and will make allowances. The following extract from the University of Manchester's website will give you some idea of what admissions tutors look for.

- 'You should remember that receiving an interview invite means that the admissions tutors are impressed with your application so far and you are in the running for an offer of a place at that university. It is an opportunity for you to discuss a subject that you and the interviewer share an interest in.'
- 'Interviewers will be looking for you to demonstrate how you met the criteria advertised in the prospectus and UCAS entry profiles, but will not always ask you about them directly. Some examples of criteria used by admissions tutors include: interest, motivation and commitment to the subject; the ability to study independently; the ability to work with others; the ability to manage time effectively; an interest in the university.'

In the tables in **Chapter 7** (**Selection interviews**, **Interview advice and questions** and **Reasons for rejection**) you will also find examples of questions which have been asked in recent years for which you might prepare, and non-academic reasons why applicants have been rejected! **Chapter 4**, **Applications**, provides a guide through the process of applying to your chosen universities and courses and highlights key points for your action.

The subject tables in the next chapter represent the core of the book, listing degree courses offered by all UK universities and colleges. These tables are designed to provide you with the information you need so that you can match your abilities and interests with your chosen degree subject, prepare your application and find out how applicants are selected for courses.

At the top of each table there is a brief overview of the subject area, together with a selection of websites for organisations that can provide relevant careers or course information. This is then followed by the subject tables themselves in which information is provided in sequence under the following headings.

Course offers information
- Subject requirements/preferences (GCSE/ A-level/other requirements)
- NB Offers statement
- Your target offers and examples of degree courses
- Alternative offers

Examples of colleges offering courses in this subject field

Choosing your course
- Universities and colleges teaching quality
- Top universities and colleges (research)
- Examples of sandwich degree courses

Admissions information
- Number of applicants per place
- Advice to applicants and planning the UCAS personal statement
- Misconceptions about this course
- Selection interviews
- Interview advice and questions
- Reasons for rejection (non-academic)

After-results advice
- Offers to applicants repeating A-levels

Graduate destinations and employment (Higher Education Statistics Agency (HESA))
- HESA data on graduate destinations
- Career note

Other degree subjects for consideration

When selecting a degree course it is important to try to judge the points score or grades that you are likely to achieve and compare them with the offers listed under **Your target offers and examples of degree courses**. However, even though you might be capable of achieving the indicated grades or UCAS Tariff points, it is important to note that these are likely to be the minimum grades or points required and that there is no guarantee that you will receive an offer: other factors in your application, such as the personal statement, references, and admissions test performance will be taken into consideration (see also **Chapters 3** and **5**).

University departments frequently adjust their offers, depending on the numbers of candidates applying, so you must not assume that the offers and policies published now will necessarily apply to courses starting in 2019 or thereafter. Even though offers may change during the 2018/19 application cycle, you can assume that the offers published in this book represent the typical academic levels at which you should aim.

Below are explanations of the information given under the headings in the subject tables. It is important that you read these carefully so that you understand how they can help you to choose and apply for courses that are right for you.

COURSE OFFERS INFORMATION
Subject requirements/preferences
Brief information is given on the GCSE and A-level requirements. Specific A-level subject requirements for individual institutions are listed separately. Other requirements are sometimes specified, where these are relevant to the course subject area, for example, medical requirements for health-related courses and Disclosure and Barring Service (DBS) clearance. Check prospectuses and websites of universities and colleges for course requirements.

GCSE reforms Reformed GCSEs in English language, English literature and maths have been taught in schools in England, with the first results issued in August 2017. Further subjects will see new GCSEs introduced over the following two years. Under the reformed GCSEs, the grading system has changed from letter to numerical grading, with students no longer receiving their results graded as A*–G but as 9–1. We have included the numerically adjusted GCSEs alongside the letter grading for reference, but please check university websites for their exact requirements. For further details about the reforms, see the government website.

Your target offers and examples of degree courses
Universities and colleges offering degree courses in the subject area are listed in descending order according to the number of UCAS Tariff points and/or A-level grades they are likely to require applicants to achieve. The UCAS Tariff points total is listed down the left-hand side of the page, and to the right appear all the institutions (in alphabetical order) likely to make offers in this Tariff point range. (Information on the UCAS Tariff is given in **Appendix 1** and guidance on how to calculate your offers is provided on every other page of the subject tables in this book. Please also read the information in the **Important Note** box on page 76.)

The courses included on the offers line are examples of the courses available in the subject field at that university or college. You will need to check prospectuses and websites for a complete list of the institution's Single, Joint, Combined or Major/Minor Honours degree courses available in the subject. For each institution listed, the following information may be given.

Name of institution
Note that the name of an institution's university college or campus may be given in brackets after the institution title, for example London (King's) or Kent (Medway Sch Pharm). Where the institution is not a university, further information about its status may also be given to indicate the type of college – for example (UC) to mean University College or (CAg) to mean College of Agriculture. This is to help readers to differentiate between the types of colleges and to help them identify any specialisation a college may have, for example art or agriculture. A full list of abbreviations used is given under the heading **INSTITUTION ABBREVIATIONS** later in this chapter.

Grades/points offer
After the institution's name, a line of offers information is given, showing a typical offer made by the institution for the courses indicated in brackets. **Offers, however, may vary between applicants and the published grades and/or points offers should be regarded as targets to aim for and not necessarily the actual grades or points required**. Offers may be reduced after the publication of A-level results, particularly if a university or college is left with spare places. However, individual course offers listed in the tables in **Chapter 7** are abridged and should be used as a first source of reference and comparison only. It is not possible to publish all the variables relevant to each offer: applicants must check prospectuses and websites for full details of all offers and courses.

Depending on the details given by institutions, the offers may provide information as follows.

- **Grades** The specific grades, or average grades, required at GCE A-level or at A-level plus AS in some cases, where available, or, if specified, EPQ for the listed courses. (**NB** Graded offers may require specific grades for specific subjects.) A-level grades are always presented in capital letters; AS and EPQ grades are shown in lower case. The offer BBBc would indicate three grade Bs at A-level, plus an additional AS at grade c. The offer AAB+aEPQ would indicate two grade As and one grade B at A-level, plus an additional EPQ at grade a. Where necessary, the abbreviation 'AL' is used to indicate

A-level, 'AS' to indicate AS and EPQ to indicate that an Extended Project Qualification is part of the offer. Offers are usually shown in terms of three A-level grades although some institutions accept two grades with the same points total or, alternatively, two A-level grades accompanied by AS grades.

NB Unit grade and module information, now introduced into the admissions system, is most likely to be required by universities where a course is competitive, or where taking a specific unit is necessary or desirable for entry. Check with institutions' websites for their latest information.

- **The UCAS Tariff points system** A-levels, AS, International Baccalaureate (IB), Scottish Highers, the Progression Diploma and a range of other qualifications have a unit value in the UCAS Tariff system (see **UCAS 2019 Entry Tariff Points Tables** in **Appendix 1**). Where a range of Tariff points is shown, for example 112–120 points, offers are usually made within this points range for these specified courses. Note that, in some cases, an institution may require a points score which is higher than the specified grade offer given. This can be for a number of reasons – for example, you may not be offering the standard subjects that would have been stipulated in a grades offer. In such cases additional points may be added by way of AS grades, Functional/Essential Skills, the Extended Project Qualification, etc.

Unit value of A-level grades in the UCAS Tariff points system:

A* = 56 pts; A = 48 pts; B = 40 pts; C = 32 pts; D = 24 pts; E = 16 pts

Some universities make offers for entry to each course by way of A-level grades, others make Tariff points offers while others will make offers in both A-level grades and in Tariff points. Applicants should be sure that the A-level subjects they are taking are acceptable for their chosen course and for A-level grades and points offers.

A Tariff points offer will not usually discriminate between the final year exam subjects being taken by the applicant unless otherwise stated, although certain GCSE subjects may be stipulated eg English or mathematics.

Admission tutors have the unenviable task of trying to assess the number of applicants who will apply for their courses against the number of places available and so judging the offers to be made. However, since the government removed the cap on the number of places that universities in England are able to offer, English universities can admit an unlimited number of home and EU undergraduates, though not every institution has adopted these reforms. Nevertheless, it is still important when reading the offers tables to be aware that variations occur each year. Lower offers or equivalents may be made to disadvantaged students, mature and international applicants.

The offers published in this edition therefore are based on expected admission policies operating from September to January 2018/19. They are targets to be achieved and in the case of popular courses at popular universities they should be regarded as minimum entry qualifications.

See **Chapter 3** for information from universities about their admissions policies including, for example, information about their expected use of A*, unit grades, the Progression Diploma, the Extended Project Qualification and the Cambridge Pre-U in their offers for applicants. See **Appendix 1** for **UCAS 2019 Entry Tariff Points** tables.

- **Admissions tests for Law, Medicine and Veterinary Science/Medicine** Where admissions tests form part of a university's offer for any of these subjects, this is indicated on the offers line in the subject tables for the relevant university. This is shown by '+LNAT' (for Law), '+BMAT' or '+UKCAT' (for Medicine), and '+BMAT' (for Veterinary Science/Medicine). For example, the offers lines could read as follows:

Cardiff – AAA incl chem+biol+interview+UKCAT (Med 5 yrs) (IB 36 pts HL 666 incl chem/biol+sci/maths)
Durham – A*AA +LNAT (Law) (IB 38 pts)
London (RVC) – AAA–AAB incl chem+biol +BMAT (Vet Med)

Entry and admissions tests will be required for 2019 by a number of institutions for a wide range of subjects: see **Chapter 5** and the subject tables in **Chapter 7** for more information and check university websites and prospectuses.

Course title(s)

After the offer, an abbreviated form of the course title(s) to which the offers information refers is provided in brackets. The abbreviations used (see **COURSE ABBREVIATIONS** at the end of this chapter) closely relate to the course titles shown in the institutions' prospectuses. When the course gives the opportunity to study abroad this can be indicated on the offers line by including 'St Abrd' after the abbreviated course title. For example:

Lancaster – AAB incl maths (Econ (St Abrd)) (IB 35 pts HL 6 maths)

When experience in industry is provided as part of the course (not necessarily a sandwich course) this can be indicated on the offers line by including 'Yr Ind' after the abbreviated course title. For example:

Liverpool – ABB (Bus Mgt (Yr Ind)) (IB 33 pts)

Sometimes the information in the offers line relates to more than one course (see **Worcester** below). In such cases, each course title is separated with a semicolon.

Worcester – 112 pts (PE Spo St; PE Dance)

When a number of joint courses exist in combination with a Major subject, they may be presented using a list separated by slashes – for example '(Int Bus Fr/Ger/Span)' indicates International Business with French or German or Spanish. Some titles may be followed by the word 'courses' – for example, (Hist courses):

Bishop Grosseteste – 96–112 pts (Hist courses; Arch Hist)

This means that the information on the offers line refers not only to the Single Honours course in Archaeology History, but also to the range of History courses. For some institutions with extensive Combined or Joint Honours programmes, the information given on the offers line may specify (Comb Hons) or (Comb courses).

For Engineering courses, BSc is included as an abbreviation in the subject line if the course is also offered at the same institution as a BEng degree with different entry requirements. For example:

Anglia Ruskin – 96 pts (Civ Eng (BSc)) (IB 24 pts)

Sometimes, where relevant, the offers line shows integrated master's degree courses (four year courses which combine three years of undergraduate study with a fourth year of postgraduate level study). In such cases, an abbreviation showing the type of degree course appears at the end of the course offer. For example:

Bristol – AAA–ABB incl maths (Elec Electron Eng (MEng)) (IB 36–32 pts HL 6 maths)

Courses awaiting validation are usually publicised in prospectuses and on websites. However, these are not included in the tables in **Chapter 7** since there is no guarantee that they will run. You should check with the university that a non-validated course will be available.

To help you understand the information provided under the **Your target offers and examples of degree courses** heading, the box below provides a few examples with their meaning explained underneath.

OFFERS LINES EXPLAINED

136 pts [University/University College name] – AAB (Acc Fin)
For the Accounting Finance course the University requires grades of AAB (136 pts) at A-level.

152 pts [University/University College name] – A*AA incl chem+biol +BMAT (Med 6 yrs)
For the 6 year Medicine course the University requires one A and two A grades at A-level, with two of these subjects in Chemistry and Biology, plus the BMAT.*

104 pts [University/University College name] – 104–120 pts (Geog)
For Geography, the University usually requires 104 UCAS Tariff points, but offers may range up to 120 UCAS Tariff points.

Alternative offers
In each of the subject tables, offers are shown in A-level grades or equivalent UCAS Tariff points, and in some cases as points offers of the International Baccalaureate Diploma (see below). However, applicants taking Scottish Highers/Advanced Highers, the Advanced Welsh Baccalaureate – Skills Challenge Certificate, the International Baccalaureate Diploma, BTEC, the Extended Project, Music examinations and Art and Design Foundation Studies should refer to **Appendix 1 – UCAS 2019 Entry Tariff Points**. For more information, see www.ucas.com/how-it-all-works/explore-your-options/entry-requirements/tariff-tables or contact the institution direct.

IB offers
A selection of IB points offers appears at the end of some university/subject entries, along with any requirements for points gained from specific Higher Level (HL) subjects. Where no specific subjects are named for HL, the HL points can be taken from any subject. For comparison of entry requirements, applicants with IB qualifications should check the A-level offers required for their course and then refer to **Appendix 1** which gives the revised IB UCAS Tariff points for 2019 entry. The figures under this subheading indicate the number or range of International Baccalaureate (IB) Diploma points likely to be requested in an offer. A range of points indicates variations between Single and Joint Honours courses. Applicants offering the IB should check with prospectuses and websites and, if in doubt, contact admissions tutors for the latest information on IB offers.

Scottish offers
Scottish Honours degrees normally take four years. However, students with very good qualifications may be admitted into the second year of courses (Advanced entry). In some cases it may even be possible to enter the third year.

This year we have included some offers details for Advanced entry. Any student with sufficient A-levels or Advanced Highers considering this option should check with the university to which they are applying. The policies at some Scottish universities are listed below:

Aberdeen Advanced entry possible for many courses, but not for Education, Law or Medicine.
Abertay Possibility of advanced entry largely dependent on content of current course.
Dundee Advanced entry possible for many courses, but not Education or Medicine.
Edinburgh Advanced entry possible for Science, Engineering, and Art and Design courses.
Edinburgh Napier Advanced entry to Stages 2, 3 or 4 of a programme, particularly for those with an HNC/HND or those with (or expecting to obtain) good grades in Advanced Highers or A-levels.
Glasgow Advanced entry possible in a range of subjects, including Neuroscience, Sociology and Civil Engineering.
Glasgow Caledonian Advanced entry available in a wide range of courses, including Business, Journalism and Biological Sciences.
Queen Margaret Advanced entry for some courses.
St Andrews Advanced entry for some courses.
Stirling Advanced entry for some courses.
Strathclyde Advanced entry for some courses.
West Scotland Advanced entry for some courses.

For others not on this list, please check individual university and college websites.

EXAMPLES OF DEGREE APPRENTICESHIPS IN THIS SUBJECT FIELD
Examples of degree apprenticeships offered by some universities, designed in partnerships with employers. To check degree apprenticeship vacancies and details, refer to GOV.UK (www.findapprenticeship.service.gov.uk/apprenticeshipsearch).

EXAMPLES OF COLLEGES OFFERING COURSES IN THIS SUBJECT FIELD
Examples of courses offered by some local colleges – but also check your local college. To check details of courses, refer to college websites and **Chapter 9** Sections 2 and 3.

IMPORTANT NOTE ON THE COURSE OFFERS INFORMATION

The information provided in **Chapter 7** is presented as a first reference source as to the target levels required. Institutions may alter their standard offers in the light of the qualifications offered by applicants.

The offers they publish do not constitute a contract and are not binding on prospective students: changes may occur between the time of publication and the time of application in line with market and student demand.

The points levels shown on the left-hand side of the offers listings are for ease of reference for the reader: not all universities will be making offers using the UCAS Tariff points system and it cannot be assumed that they will accept a points equivalent to the grades they have stipulated. Check university and college prospectuses, and also their websites, for their latest information before submitting your application.

CHOOSING YOUR COURSE

The information under this heading (to be read in conjunction with **Chapter 1**) covers factors that are important to consider in order to make an informed decision on which courses to apply for. The information is organised under the following subheadings.

Universities and colleges teaching quality

The Unistats website (https://unistats.ac.uk) provides official information where available for different subjects and universities and colleges in the UK to help prospective students and their advisers make comparisons between them and so make informed choices about what and where to study. Information is updated annually and is available for each subject taught at each university and college (and for some further education colleges). The Quality Assurance Agency (www.qaa.ac.uk) reviews the quality and standards of all universities and colleges and official reports of their reviews are available on their website but it is important to note their dates of publication.

Top research universities and colleges (REF 2014)

In December 2014 the latest Research Excellence Framework was undertaken covering certain subject areas. The leading universities in the relevant subject areas are listed in the order of achievement. It should be noted that not all subjects were assessed. The next REF is due in 2021.

Examples of sandwich degree courses

This section lists examples of institutions that offer sandwich placements for some of their courses in the subject field shown. The institutions listed offer placements of one-year duration and do not include language courses or work experience or other short-term placements. Check with the institutions too, since new courses may be introduced and others withdrawn depending on industrial or commercial arrangements. Further information on sandwich courses with specific information on the placements of students appears in **Chapter 1**.

NB During a period of economic uncertainty, universities and colleges may have problems placing students on sandwich courses. Applicants applying for courses are therefore advised to check with admissions tutors that these courses will run, and that placements will be available.

ADMISSIONS INFORMATION

Under this heading, information gathered from the institutions has been provided. This will be useful when planning your application.

Number of applicants per place (approx)

These figures show the approximate number of applicants initially applying for each place before any offers are made. It should be noted that any given number of applicants represents candidates who have also applied for up to four other university and college courses.

Advice to applicants and planning the UCAS personal statement
This section offers guidelines on information that could be included in the personal statement section of your UCAS application. In most cases, applicants will be required to indicate why they wish to follow a particular course and, if possible, to provide positive evidence of their interest. See also **Chapters 4** and **5**.

Misconceptions about this course
Admissions tutors are given the opportunity in the research for this book to set the record straight by clarifying aspects of their course they feel are often misunderstood by students, and in some cases, advisers!

Selection interviews
A sample of institutions that normally use the interview as part of their selection procedure is listed here. Those institutions adopting the interview procedure will usually interview only a small proportion of applicants. It is important to use this section in conjunction with **Chapters 3** and **5**.

Interview advice and questions
This section includes information from institutions on what candidates might expect in an interview to cover, and examples of the types of interview questions posed in recent years. Also refer to **Chapters 3** and **5**: these chapters provide information on tests and assessments which are used in selecting students.

Reasons for rejection (non-academic)
Academic ability and potential to suceed on the course are the major factors in the selection (or rejection) of applicants. Under this subheading, admissions tutors give other reasons for rejecting applicants.

AFTER-RESULTS ADVICE
Under this heading, information for helping you decide what to do after the examination results are published is provided (see also the section on **What to do on Results Day ... and After** in **Chapter 4**). Details refer to the main subject area unless otherwise stated in brackets.

Offers to applicants repeating A-levels
This section gives details of whether second-time offers made to applicants repeating their exams may be 'higher', 'possibly higher' or the 'same' as those made to first-time applicants. The information refers to Single Honours courses. It should be noted that circumstances may differ between candidates – some will be repeating the same subjects taken in the previous year, while others may be taking different subjects. Offers will also be dictated by the grades you achieved on your first sitting of the examinations. Remember, if you were rejected by all your universities and have achieved good grades, contact them by telephone on results day – they may be prepared to revise their decision. This applies particularly to medical schools.

GRADUATE DESTINATIONS AND EMPLOYMENT (2015/16 HESA)
The information under this heading has been provided by the Higher Education Statistics Agency (HESA) and is taken from their most recent report *Destinations of Leavers from Higher Education 2015/16*, released in July 2017. The report can be obtained from www.hesa.ac.uk.

Details are given of the total number of graduates surveyed whose destinations have been recorded – not the total number who graduated in that subject. Employment figures relate to those in full-time permanent paid employment after six months in a variety of occupations not necessarily related to their degree subject (part-time employment figures are not included). Figures are also given for those in voluntary, unpaid work. 'Further study' includes research into a subject-related field, higher degrees, private study or, alternatively, career training involving work and further study. The 'Assumed unemployed' category refers to those students who were believed to be unemployed for various reasons (eg travelling, personal reasons) or those students still seeking permanent employment six months after graduating. The figures given do not equal the total number of graduates surveyed as we have chosen only to include the most relevant or interesting areas.

Career note
Short descriptions of the career destinations of graduates in the subject area are provided.

OTHER DEGREE SUBJECTS FOR CONSIDERATION
This heading includes some suggested alternative courses that have similarities to the courses listed in the subject table.

ABBREVIATIONS USED IN THE SUBJECT TABLES IN CHAPTER 7

INSTITUTION ABBREVIATIONS

The following abbreviations are used to indicate specific institutions or types of institution:

Ac	Academy
AI	Arts Institute
ALRA	Academy of Live and Recorded Arts
AMD	Academy of Music and Drama
Birk	Birkbeck (London University)
BITE	British Institute of Technology, England
CA	College of Art(s)
CAD	College of Art and Design
CAFRE	College of Agriculture, Food and Rural Enterprise
CAg	College of Agriculture
CAgH	College of Agriculture and Horticulture
CAT	College of Advanced Technology or Arts and Technology
CComm	College of Communication
CDC	College of Design and Communication
CECOS	London College of IT and Management
CFash	College of Fashion
CHort	College of Horticulture
CmC	Community College
CMus	College of Music
CMusDr	College of Music and Drama
Coll	College/Collegiate
Consv	Conservatoire
Court	Courtauld Institute (London University)
CT	College of Technology
CTA	College of Technology and Arts
Educ	Education
Gold	Goldsmiths (London University)
GSA	Guildford School of Acting
HOW	Heart of Worcestershire College
IA	Institute of Art(s)
IFHE	Institute of Further and Higher Education
Inst	Institute
King's	King's College (London University)
LeSoCo	Lewisham Southwark College
LIBF	London Institute of Banking and Finance
LIPA	Liverpool Institute of Performing Arts
LSE	London School of Economics and Political Science
LSST	London School of Science and Technology
Met	Metropolitan
MS	Medical School
NCC	New City College
NCH	New College of the Humanities
QM	Queen Mary (London University)
RAc Dance	Royal Academy of Dance
RAcMus	Royal Academy of Music
RConsvS	Royal Conservatoire of Scotland
RCMus	Royal College of Music
Reg Coll	Regional College

Reg Fed	Regional Federation (Staffordshire)
RH	Royal Holloway (London University)
RNCM	Royal Northern College of Music
RVC	Royal Veterinary College (London University)
SA	School of Art
SAD	School of Art and Design
Sch	School
Sch SpDr	School of Speech and Drama
SMO	Sabhal Mòr Ostaig
SOAS	School of Oriental and African Studies (London University)
SRUC	Scotland's Rural College
UC	University College
UCEM	University College of Estate Management
UCFB	University College of Football Business
UCL	University College (London University)
UCO	University College of Osteopathy
UHI	University of the Highlands and Islands
Univ	University

COURSE ABBREVIATIONS

The following abbreviations are used to indicate course titles and admissions tests:

Ab	Abrahamic
Abrd	Abroad
Acc	Accountancy/Accounting
Accs	Accessories
Acoust	Acoustics/Acoustical
Acq	Acquisition
Act	Actuarial
Actg	Acting
Actn	Action
Actr	Actor
Actv	Active
Actvt(s)	Activity/Activities
Acu	Acupuncture
Add	Additional
Adlscn	Adolescence
Adlt	Adult
Admin	Administration/Administrative
Adt	Audit
Adv	Advertising
Advc	Advice
Advnc	Advanced
Advntr	Adventure
Aero	Aeronautical/Aeronautics
Aerodyn	Aerodynamics
Aero-Mech	Aero-mechanical
Aerosp	Aerospace
Aeroth	Aerothermal
Af	Africa(n)
Affrs	Affairs
Age	Ageing
Agncy	Agency
Agribus	Agribusiness
Agric	Agriculture/Agricultural
Agrofor	Agroforestry
Agron	Agronomy
Aid	Aided
Aircft	Aircraft
Airln	Airline
Airpt	Airport
Airvhcl	Airvehicle
Akkdn	Akkadian
ALN	Additional Learning Needs
Am	America(n)
Amen	Amenity
AMESAA	Asian and Middle Eastern Studies Admissions Assessment
Analys	Analysis
Analyt	Analytical/Analytics
Anat	Anatomy/Anatomical
Anc	Ancient
Anim	Animal
Animat	Animation
Animatron	Animatronics
Anth	Anthropology
Antq	Antique(s)
App(s)	Applied/Applicable/Applications
Appar	Apparel
Appr	Appropriate
Apprsl	Appraisal
Aqua	Aquaculture/Aquatic
Ar	Area(s)
Arbc	Arabic
Arbor	Arboriculture
Arch	Archaeology/Archaeological
ARCHAA	Archaeology Admissions Assessment

Archit	Architecture/Architectural	**Bioelectron**	Bioelectronics
ARCHITAA	Architecture Admissions Assessment	**Bioeng**	Bioengineering
		Biogeog	Biogeography
Archvl	Archival	**Biogeosci**	Biogeoscience
Aroma	Aromatherapy	**Bioinform**	Bioinformatics
Arst	Artist	**Biokin**	Biokinetics
Artfcts	Artefacts	**Biol**	Biological/Biology
Artif	Artificial	**Biom**	Biometry
As	Asia(n)	**Biomat**	Biomaterials
ASNCAA	Anglo-Saxon, Norse and Celtic Admissions Assessment	**Biomed**	Biomedical/Biomedicine
		Biomol	Biomolecular
Ass	Assessment	**Biophys**	Biophysics
Assoc	Associated	**Bioproc**	Bioprocess
Asst	Assistant	**Biorg**	Bio-organic
Assyr	Assyriology	**Biosci**	Bioscience(s)
Ast	Asset	**Biotech**	Biotechnology
Astnaut	Astronautics/Astronautical	**Biovet**	Bioveterinary
Astro	Astrophysics	**Bkbnd**	Bookbinding
Astron	Astronomy	**Bld**	Build(ing)
A-Sxn	Anglo-Saxon	**Bldstck**	Bloodstock
Ated	Accelerated	**Blksmthg**	Blacksmithing
Atel	Atelier	**Blt**	Built
Atlan	Atlantic	**Bngli**	Bengali
Atmos	Atmospheric/Atmosphere	**Braz**	Brazilian
Attrctns	Attractions	**Brew**	Brewing
Auc	Auctioneering	**Brit**	British
Aud	Audio	**Brnd**	Brand(ing)
Audiol	Audiology	**Broad**	Broadcast(ing)
Audtech	Audiotechnology	**Bspk**	Bespoke
Aus	Australia(n)	**Bty**	Beauty
Austr	Australasia	**Bulg**	Bulgarian
Auth	Author/Authoring/Authorship	**Burm**	Burmese
Auto	Automotive	**Bus**	Business
Autom	Automated/Automation	**Buy**	Buying
Automat	Automatic	**Byz**	Byzantine
Autombl	Automobile		
Autsm	Autism	**CAA**	Classics Admissions Assessment
AV	Audio Video	**CAD**	Computer Aided Design
Avion	Avionic(s)	**Callig**	Calligraphy
Avn	Aviation	**Can**	Canada/Canadian
Ay St	Ayurvedic Studies	**Canc**	Cancer
		Cap	Capital
Bank	Banking	**Cardio**	Cardiology
Bch	Beach	**Cardiov**	Cardiovascular
Bd	Based	**Carib**	Caribbean
Bdwk	Bodywork	**Cart**	Cartography
Bev	Beverage	**Cat**	Catering
BHS	British Horse Society	**CAT**	Classics Admissions Test
Bhv	Behaviour(al)	**CATS**	Credit Accumulation and Transfer Scheme
Bib	Biblical		
Bio Ins	Bio Instrumentation	**Cell**	Cellular
Bioarch	Bioarchaeology	**Celt**	Celtic
Bioch	Biochemistry/Biochemical	**Cent**	Century
Biocomp	Biocomputing	**Ceram**	Ceramics
Biodiv	Biodiversity	**Cert**	Certificate

Ch Mgt	Chain Management	**Commun**	Community
Chart	Chartered	**Comp**	Computation/Computer(s)/ Computerised/Computing
Chc	Choice		
Chch	Church	**Compar**	Comparative
Chem	Chemistry	**Complem**	Complementary
Cheml	Chemical	**Comput**	Computation(al)
Chin	Chinese	**Con**	Context
Chiro	Chiropractic	**Conc**	Concept
Chld	Child/Children/Childhood	**Concur**	Concurrent
Chn	Chain	**Cond**	Conductive
Chng	Change	**Condit**	Conditioning
Choreo	Choreography	**Cons**	Conservation
Chr	Christian(ity)	**Conslt**	Consultant
Chrctr	Character	**Constr**	Construction
Chtls	Chattels	**Consum**	Consumer
Cits	Cities	**Cont**	Contour
Civ	Civil(isation)	**Contemp**	Contemporary
Class	Classical/Classics	**Contnl**	Continental
Clim	Climate/Climatic	**Contr**	Control
Clin	Clinical	**Conv**	Conveyancing
Cllct	Collect(ing)	**Cord**	Cordwainers
Clnl	Colonial	**Corn**	Cornish
Cloth	Clothing	**Corp**	Corporate/Corporation
Clsrm	Classroom	**Cos**	Cosmetic
CLT	Cambridge Law Test	**Cosmo**	Cosmology
Cmbt	Combat	**Cr**	Care
Cmc	Comic	**Crcs**	Circus
Cmdy	Comedy	**Crdc**	Cardiac
Cmn	Common	**Crea**	Creative/Creation
Cmnd	Command	**Crft(s)**	Craft(s)/Craftsmanship
Cmplrs	Compilers	**Crim**	Criminal
Cmpn	Companion	**Crimin**	Criminological/Criminology
Cmpsn	Composition	**Crit**	Criticism/Critical
Cmpste(s)	Composite(s)	**Crm**	Crime
Cmwlth	Commonwealth	**Cro**	Croatian
Cncr	Cancer	**Crr**	Career
Cnflct	Conflict	**Crsn**	Corrosion
Cnma	Cinema/Cinematics/ Cinematography	**Crtn**	Cartoon
		Cru	Cruise
Cnslg	Counselling	**Crypt**	Cryptography
Cnsltncy	Consultancy	**CSAT**	Computer Science Admissions Test
Cnt	Central		
Cntnt	Content	**Cstl**	Coastal
Cntrms	Countermeasures	**Cstm**	Costume
Cntry	Country(side)	**Cstmd**	Customised
Cntxt	Context	**Ctln**	Catalan
Cnty	Century	**Ctlys**	Catalysis
Coach	Coaching	**Ctzn**	Citizenship
Cog	Cognitive	**Culn**	Culinary
Col	Colour	**Cult**	Culture(s)/Cultural
Coll	Collaborative	**Cur**	Curation
Comb	Combined	**Cy**	Cyber
Combus	Combustion	**Cyber**	Cybernetics/Cyberspace
Comm(s)	Communication(s)	**Cybercrim**	Cybercrime
Commer	Commerce/Commercial	**Cyberscrty**	Cybersecurity

Cybertron	Cybertronics	**E**	East(ern)
Cym	Cymraeg	**EAA**	Education Admissions
Cz	Czech		Assessment
		ECAA	Economics Admissions
Dan	Danish		Assessment
Decn	Decision	**Ecol**	Ecology/Ecological
Decr	Decoration/Decorative	**Ecomet**	Econometrics
Def	Defence	**e-Commer**	E-Commerce
Defer	Deferred Choice	**Econ**	Economic(s)
Deg	Degree	**Econy**	Economy/Economies
Demcr	Democratic	**Ecosys**	Ecosystem(s)
Dept	Department	**Ecotech**	Ecotechnology
Des	Design(er)	**Ecotour**	Ecotourism
Desr	Desirable	**Ecotox**	Ecotoxicology
Dest	Destination(s)	**Edit**	Editorial/Editing
Dev	Development(al)	**Educ**	Education
Devsg	Devising	**Educr**	Educare
Df	Deaf	**Efcts**	Effects
Diag	Diagnostic	**EFL**	English as a Foreign
Diet	Diet/Dietetics/Dietitian		Language
Dif	Difficulties	**Egypt**	Egyptian/Egyptology
Dig	Digital	**ELAT**	English Literature Admissions
Dip	Diploma		Test
Dip Ing	Diplom Ingeneur	**Elec**	Electrical
Dipl	Diplomacy	**Elecacoust**	Electroacoustics
Dir	Direct/Direction/Director/	**Electromech**	Electromechanical
	Directing	**Electron**	Electronic(s)
Dis	Disease(s)	**ELT**	English Language Teaching
Disab	Disability	**Ely**	Early
Disas	Disaster	**Emb**	Embryo(logy)
Discip	Disciplinary	**Embd**	Embedded
Diso	Disorders	**Embr**	Embroidery
Disp	Dispensing	**Emer**	Emergency
Dist	Distributed/Distribution	**Emp**	Employment
Distil	Distillation/Distilling	**Ener**	Energy
Div	Divinity	**Eng**	Engineer(ing)
d/l	distance learning	**ENGAA**	Engineering Admissions
Dlvry	Delivery		Assessment
Dnstry	Dentistry	**Engl**	English
Dntl	Dental	**Engmnt**	Engagement
Doc	Document(ary)	**Engn**	Engine
Dom	Domestic(ated)	**Ent**	Enterprise
Dr	Drama	**Enter**	Entertainment
Drg	Drawing	**Entomol**	Entomology
Drs	Dress	**Entre**	Entrepreneur(ship)
Dscrt	Discrete	**Env**	Environment(s)/Environmental
Dscvry	Discovery	**EPQ**	Extended Project
Dsply	Display		Qualification
Dtbs	Databases	**Eql**	Equal
Dth	Death	**Eqn**	Equine/Equestrian
Dvc	Device	**Equip**	Equipment
Dvnc	Deviance	**Equit**	Equitation
Dvsd	Devised	**Ergon**	Ergonomics
Dynmcs	Dynamics	**Est**	Estate
		Eth	Ethics

Ethl	Ethical	Frchd	Franchised
Eth-Leg	Ethico-Legal	Frcst	Forecasting
Ethn	Ethnic	Frm	Farm
Ethnol	Ethnology	Frmwk	Framework
Ethnomus	Ethnomusicology	Frshwtr	Freshwater
EU	European Union	Frst	Forest
Euro	Europe/European	Frsty	Forestry
Eval	Evaluation	Frtlty	Fertility
Evnglstc	Evangelistic	Fst Trk	Fast Track
Evnt(s)	Event(s)	Fstvl	Festival(s)
Evol	Evolution(ary)	Ftbl	Football
Ex	Executing	Ftre	Feature(s)
Excl	Excellence	Ftwr	Footwear
Exer	Exercise	Furn	Furniture
Exhib	Exhibition	Fut	Futures
Exmp	Exempt(ing)		
Exp	Export	GAA	Geography Admissions
Explor	Exploration		Assessment
Explsn	Explosion	Gael	Gaelic
Expltn	Exploitation	Gam	Gambling
Expmtl	Experimental	GAMSAT	Graduate Australian Medical
Expnc	Experience		School Admission Test
Expr	Expressive	Gdn	Garden
Ext	Extended	Gdnc	Guidance
Extr	Exterior	Gem	Gemmology
Extrm	Extreme	Gen	General
		Genet	Genetics
Fabs	Fabric(s)	Geochem	Geochemistry
Fac	Faculty	Geog	Geography
Fact	Factor(s)	Geoinform	Geoinformatics
Facil	Facilities	Geol	Geology/Geological
Fash	Fashion	Geophys	Geophysics
Fbr	Fibre	Geophysl	Geophysical
Fctn	Fiction	Geopol	Geopolitics
Fd	Food	Geosci	Geoscience
Fdn	Foundation	Geosptl	Geospatial
Fd Sc	Foundation degree in Science	Geotech	Geotechnics
Filmm	Filmmaking	Ger	German(y)
Fin	Finance/Financial	Gerc	Germanic
Finn	Finnish	GIS	Geographical Information
Fish	Fishery/Fisheries		Systems
Fit	Fitness	Gk	Greek
Fl	Fluid	Glf	Golf
Fld	Field	Gllry	Gallery/Galleries
Flex	Flexible	Glob	Global(isation)
Flm	Film	Gls	Glass
Flor	Floristry	Gm(s)	Game(s)
Fmaths	Further Mathematics	Gmg	Gaming
Fmly	Family	Gmnt	Garment
Fn	Fine	Gmtc	Geomatic
Foot	Footwear	Gndr	Gender
For	Foreign	Gnm	Genome/Genomics
Foren	Forensic	Gold	Goldsmithing
Foss	Fossil(s)	Gov	Government
Fr	French	Govn	Governance

Gr	Grade	Id	Idea(s)
Graph	Graphic(s)	Idnty	Identity
Grgn	Georgian	Illus	Illustration
Grn	Green	Imag	Image/Imaging/Imaginative
Guji	Gujerati	Immun	Immunology/Immunity
		Impair	Impairment
HAA	History Admissions Assessment	Incl	Including
HAAA	History of Art Admissions	Incln	Inclusion
	Assessment	Inclsv	Inclusive
Hab	Habitat	Ind	Industrial/Industry/Industries
Hack	Hacking	Indep St	Independent Study
Hard	Hardware	Indiv	Individual(s)
HAT	History Aptitude Test	Indsn	Indonesian
Haz	Hazard(s)	Inf	Information
Heal	Healing	Infec	Infectious/Infection
Heb	Hebrew	Infml	Informal
Herb	Herbal	Inform	Informatics
Herit	Heritage	Infra	Infrastructure
Hi	High	Inftq	Informatique
Hisp	Hispanic	Injry	Injury
Hist	History/Historical	Innov	Innovation
HL	IB Higher level	Ins	Insurance
Hlcst	Holocaust	Inst	Institute/Institution(al)
Hlnds	Highlands	Instln	Installation
Hlth	Health	Instr	Instrument(ation)
Hlthcr	Healthcare	Int	International
Hm	Home	Integ	Integrated/Integration
Hnd	Hindi	Intel	Intelligent/Intelligence
Hol	Holistic	Inter	Interior(s)
Hom	Homeopathic	Interact	Interaction/Interactive
Homin	Hominid	Intercult	Intercultural
Horol	Horology	Interd	Interdisciplinary
Hort	Horticulture	Intermed	Intermedia
Hosp	Hospital	Interp	Interpretation/Interpreting
Hous	Housing	Intlctl	Intellectual
HPAT	Health Professions Admissions	Intnet	Internet
	Test	Intr	Interest(s)
HR	Human Resource(s)	Intrmdl	Intermodal
Hrdrs	Hairdressing	Inv	Investment
Hrs	Horse	Invstg	Investigating/Investigation(s)/
Hse	House		Investigative
HSPSAA	Human, Social and Political	IPML	Integrated Professional Master
	Sciences Admissions Assessment		in Language
Hspty	Hospitality	Ir	Irish
Htl	Hotel	Is	Issues
Hum	Human(ities)	Isl	Islands
Hung	Hungarian	Islam	Islamic
Hydrog	Hydrography	Isrl	Israel/Israeli
Hydrol	Hydrology	IT	Information Technology
Hyg	Hygiene	Ital	Italian
		ITE	Initial Teacher Education
Iber	Iberian	ITT	Initial Teacher Training
Ice	Icelandic		
ICT	Information and	Jap	Japanese
	Communications Technology	Jew	Jewish

Jewel	Jewellery
Jrnl	Journalism
Jud	Judaism
Juris	Jurisprudence
Just	Justice
Knit	Knit(ted)
Kntwr	Knitwear
Knwl	Knowledge
Kor	Korean
KS	Key Stage
LAA	Linguistics Admissions Assessment
Lab	Laboratory
Lang(s)	Language(s)
Las	Laser
Lat	Latin
Lcl	Local
LD	Learning Disabilities
Ldrshp	Leadership
Lea	Leather
Leg	Legal
Legis	Legislative
Leis	Leisure
Lf	Life
Lfstl	Lifestyle
Lgc	Logic
Lib	Library
Librl	Liberal
Libshp	Librarianship
Lic	Licensed
Lic de Geog	Licence de Geographie
Lic de Let	Licence de Lettres
Ling	Linguistics
Lit	Literature/Literary/Literate
Litcy	Literacy
Lnd	Land(scape)
Lndbd	Land-based
Lns	Lens
Log	Logistics
Lrn	Learn
Lrng	Learning
Ls	Loss
Lsr	Laser
Ltg	Lighting
Ltr	Later
Lv	Live
Lvstk	Livestock
Mach	Machine(ry)
Mag	Magazine
Mait	Maitrise Internationale
Mak	Making/Maker
Mand	Mandarin

Manuf	Manufacture/Manufacturing
Map	Map(ping)
Mar	Marine
Marit	Maritime
Mark	Market(ing)
Masch	Maschinenbau
Mat	Material(s)
MAT	Mathematics Admissions Test
Mathem	Mathematical
Maths	Mathematics
Mbl	Mobile
Measur	Measurement
Mech	Mechanical
Mecha	Mechatronic(s)
Mechn	Mechanisation
Mechnsms	Mechanisms
Med	Medicine/Medical
Medcnl	Medicinal
Mediev	Medieval
Medit	Mediterranean
Ment	Mentoring
Metal	Metallurgy/Metallurgical
Meteor	Meteorology/Meteorological
Meth	Method(s)
Mgr	Manager
Mgrl	Managerial
Mgt	Management
Microbiol	Microbiology/Microbiological
Microbl	Microbial
Microcomp	Microcomputer/ Microcomputing
Microelec	Microelectronics
Mid E	Middle Eastern
Midwif	Midwifery
Min	Mining
Miner	Minerals
Mix	Mixed
Mkup	Make-up
MLAT	Modern Languages Admissions Test
Mling	Multilingual
Mltry	Military
MMath	Master of Mathematics
MMLAA	Medieval and Modern Languages Admissions Assessment
Mnd	Mind
Mndrn	Mandarin
Mnrts	Minorities
Mnstry	Ministry
Mnswr	Menswear
Mntl Hlth	Mental Health
Mntn	Mountain
Mntnce	Maintenance
Mny	Money

Mod	Modular
Modl	Modelling/Modelmaking
Modn	Modern
Modnty	Modernity
Mol	Molecular
Monit	Monitoring
MORSE	Mathematics, Operational Research, Statistics and Economics
MOst	Master's in Osteopathy
Mov	Movement/Moving
Mrchnds	Merchandise/Merchandising
Mrchnt	Merchant
Mrl	Moral
Msg	Massage
Mslm	Muslim
Mtl	Metal(s)
Mtlsmth	Metalsmithing
Mtlwk	Metalwork(ing)
Mtn	Motion
Mtr	Motor
Mtrcycl	Motorcycle
Mtrg	Motoring
Mtrspo	Motorsport(s)
Multid	Multi-disciplinary
Multim	Multimedia
Mus	Music(ian)
Muscskel	Musculoskeletal
Musl	Musical
Musm	Museum(s)
Mushp	Musicianship
Myan	Myanmar
N	New
N Am	North America
Nanoelectron	Nanoelectronics
Nanosci	Nanoscience
Nanotech	Nanotechnology
Nat	Nature/Natural
Natpth	Naturopathy
Navig	Navigation
Nbrhd	Neighbourhood
Nds	Needs
Neg	Negotiated
Net	Networks/Networking
Neuro	Neuroscience
Neuropsy	Neuropsychology
News	Newspaper
NGO	Non-Governmental Organisation(s)
NI	Northern Ireland/Northern Irish
Nnl	National
Norw	Norwegian
Npli	Nepali

Nrs	Norse
NSAA	Natural Sciences Admissions Assessment
Ntv	Native
Nucl	Nuclear
Num	Numerate
Nurs	Nursing
Nursy	Nursery
Nutr	Nutrition(al)
Nvl	Naval
NZ	New Zealand
Obj(s)	Object(s)
Obs	Observational
Occ	Occupational
Ocean	Oceanography
Ocn	Ocean
Ocnc	Oceanic
Oeno	Oenology
Ofce	Office
Off	Offshore
Offrd	Off-road
Okl	Oklahoma
OLAT	Oriental Languages Aptitude Test
Onc	Oncology
Onln	Online
Op(s)	Operation(s)
Oph	Ophthalmic
Oprtg	Operating
Opt	Optical
Optim	Optimisation
Optn/s	Optional/Options
Optoel	Optoelectronics
Optom	Optometry
OR	Operational Research
Ord	Ordinary
Org	Organisation(s)/Organisational
Orgnc	Organic
Orgnsms	Organisms
Orn	Ornithology
Orntl	Oriental
Orth	Orthoptics
Orthot	Orthotics
Oseas	Overseas
Ost	Osteopathy
Out	Outdoor
Out Act	Outdoor Activity
Outsd	Outside
Ovrs	Overseas
P	Primary
PAA	Philosophy Admissions Assessment
P Cr	Primary Care

Pacif	Pacific	Plntsmn	Plantsmanship
Pack	Packaging	Plt	Pilot
PActv	Physical Activity	Pltry	Poultry
Pal	Palaeobiology	PMaths	Pure Mathematics
Palae	Palaeoecology/Palaeontology	Pntg	Painting
Palaeoenv	Palaeoenvironments	Pod	Podiatry/Podiatric
Paramed	Paramedic(al)	Pol	Politics/Political
Parasit	Parasitology	Polh	Polish
Parl	Parliamentary	Pollut	Pollution
Part	Participation	Poly	Polymer(ic)
Pat	Patent	Pop	Popular
PAT	Physics Aptitude Test	Popn	Population
Path	Pathology	Port	Portuguese
Pathobiol	Pathobiological	Postcol	Postcolonial
Pathogen	Pathogenesis	PPE	Philosophy, Politics and
Patt	Pattern		Economics or Politics,
Pblc	Public		Philosophy and Economics
PBSAA	Psychological and Behavioural	PPI	Private Pilot Instruction
	Sciences Admissions	Ppl	People
	Assessment	Ppr	Paper
Pce	Peace	Pptry	Puppetry
PE	Physical Education	PR	Public Relations
Ped	Pedagogy	Prac	Practice(s)/Practical
Per	Person(al)	Practnr	Practitioner
Perf	Performance/Performed	Prchsng	Purchasing
Perfum	Perfumery	Prcrmt	Procurement
Pers	Personnel	Prdcl	Periodical
Persn	Persian	Precsn	Precision
Petrol	Petroleum	Pref	Preferable/Preferred
PGCE	Postgraduate Certificate in	Prehist	Prehistory
	Education	Prem	Premises
Pharm	Pharmacy	Proc	Process(ing)
Pharmacol	Pharmacology	Prod	Product(s)/Production/Produce
Pharml	Pharmaceutical	Prodg	Producing
Phil	Philosophy/Philosophies/	Prof	Professional/Proffesiynol/
	Philosophical		Professions
Philgy	Philology	Prog	Programme/Programming
Phn	Phone	Proj	Project
Phon	Phonetics	Prom	Promotion
Photo	Photography/Photographic	Prop	Property/ies
Photojrnl	Photojournalism	Pros	Prosthetics
Photon	Photonic(s)	Prot	Protection/Protected
Phys	Physics	Proto	Prototyping
Physio	Physiotherapy	Prplsn	Propulsion
Physiol	Physiology/Physiological	Prsts	Pursuits
Physl	Physical	Prt	Print
Pks	Parks	Prtcl	Particle
Plan	Planning	Prtd	Printed
Planet	Planetary	Prtg	Printing/Printmaking
Plas	Plastics	Prtshp	Partnership
Play	Playwork	Prvntn	Prevention
Plcg	Police/Policing	Pst	Post
Plcy	Policy	Pstrl	Pastoral
Plmt	Placement	Psy	Psychology
Plnt	Plant	Psychobiol	Psychobiology

Psyling	Psycholinguistics	**Rlwy**	Railway
Psysoc	Psychosocial	**Rmnc**	Romance
Psytrpy	Psychotherapy	**RN**	Registered Nurse
Pt	Port	**Rnwl**	Renewal
p/t	part-time	**Robot**	Robotic(s)
Ptcl	Particle	**Rom**	Roman
Pub	Publishing/Publication	**Romn**	Romanian
Pvt	Private	**Rsch**	Research
Pwr	Power	**Rspnsb**	Responsibility
Pwrcft	Powercraft	**Rsrt**	Resort
		Rstrnt	Restaurant
Qntm	Quantum	**Rtl**	Retail(ing)
Qry	Quarry	**Rts**	Rights
Qtrnry	Quaternary	**Rur**	Rural
QTS	Qualified Teacher Status	**Russ**	Russian
Qual	Quality	**Rvr**	River
Qualif	Qualification		
Quant	Quantity/Quantitative	**S**	Secondary
		S As	South Asian
Rad	Radio	**Sansk**	Sanskrit
Radiog	Radiography	**Sat**	Satellite
Radiothera	Radiotherapy	**Sbstnce**	Substance
Rbr	Rubber	**Scand**	Scandinavian
Rce	Race	**Sch**	School
Rcycl	Recycling	**Schlstc**	Scholastic
Rdtn	Radiation	**Schm**	Scheme
Realsn	Realisation	**Sci**	Science(s)/Scientific
Rec	Recording(s)	**Scn**	Scene
Reclam	Reclamation	**Scnc**	Scenic
Recr	Recreation	**Scngrph**	Scenographic/Scenography
Reg	Regional	**Scot**	Scottish
Regn	Regeneration	**Scr**	Secure
Rehab	Rehabilitation	**Script**	Scriptwriting
Rel	Relations	**Scrn**	Screen
Relgn	Religion(s)	**Scrnwrit**	Sreenwriting
Relig	Religious	**Scrts**	Securities
Reltd	Related	**Scrty**	Security
Rem Sens	Remote Sensing	**Sctr**	Sector
Ren	Renaissance	**Sculp**	Sculpture/Sculpting
Renew	Renewable(s)	**Sdlry**	Saddlery
Rep	Representation	**SE**	South East
Repro	Reproductive	**Sec**	Secretarial
Reqd	Required	**Semicond**	Semiconductor
Res	Resource(s)	**SEN**	Special Educational
Resid	Residential		Needs
Resoln	Resolution	**Serb Cro**	Serbo-Croat
Resp	Response	**Serv**	Services
Respir	Respiratory	**Set**	Settings
Restor	Restoration	**Sex**	Sexual
Rev	Revenue	**Sfty**	Safety
Rflxgy	Reflexology	**Sgnl**	Signal
Rgby	Rugby	**Ship**	Shipping
Rgstrn	Registration	**Silver**	Silversmithing
Rl	Real	**Simul**	Simulation
Rlblty	Reliability	**Sit Lrng**	Situated Learning

Sk	Skills	**Strf**	Stratified
Slav	Slavonic	**Strg**	Strength
Slf	Self	**Strt**	Street
Sln	Salon	**Struct**	Structural/Structures
Slovak	Slovakian	**Stry**	Story
Slp	Sleep	**Stt**	State
Sls	Sales	**Stwdshp**	Stewardship
Sml	Small	**Styl**	Styling
Smt	Smart	**Sub**	Subject
Smtc	Semitic	**Surf**	Surface
Snc	Sonic	**Surv**	Surveying
Snd	Sound	**Sust**	Sustainability/Sustainable
Sndtrk	Soundtrack	**Swed**	Swedish
Sndwch	Sandwich	**Swli**	Swahili
Sng	Song	**Sxlty**	Sexuality
Soc	Social	**Sys**	System(s)
Sociol	Sociology	**Systmtc**	Systematic
SocioLeg	Socio-Legal		
Socling	Sociolinguistics	**TAA**	Theology Admissions Assessment
Soft	Software		
Sol	Solution(s)	**Tam**	Tamil
Solic	Solicitors	**Tap**	Tapestry
Soty	Society	**Tax**	Taxation
Sov	Soviet	**Tax Rev**	Taxation and Revenue
Sp	Speech	**Tbtn**	Tibetan
Span	Spanish	**Tcnqs**	Techniques
Spat	Spatial	**Teach**	Teaching
Spc	Space	**Tech**	Technology/Technologies/ Technician/Technical
Spcrft	Spacecraft		
Spec	Special/Specialism(s)/ Specialist	**Technol**	Technological
		TEFL	Teaching English as a Foreign Language
Spec Efcts	Special Effects		
Sply	Supply	**Telecomm**	Telecommunication(s)
Spn	Spain	**Ter**	Terrestrial
Spo	Sport(s)	**TESOL**	Teaching English to Speakers of Other Languages
Spotrf	Sportsturf		
Spowr	Sportswear	**Testmt**	Testament
Sppt(d)	Support(ed)	**Tex**	Textile(s)
Sprtng	Supporting	**Thbred**	Thoroughbred
Sqnt	Sequential	**Thea**	Theatre
Srf	Surf(ing)	**Theol**	Theology
Srgy	Surgery	**Theor**	Theory/Theoretical
SS	Solid-state	**Ther**	Therapeutic
St	Studies/Study	**Thera**	Therapy
St Reg	State Registration	**Tht**	Thought
Stats	Statistics/Statistical	**Tiss**	Tissue
Std	Studio	**Tlrg**	Tailoring
STEM	Science, Technology, Engineering and Mathematics	**Tm**	Time
		Tmbr	Timber
Stg	Stage	**Tnnl**	Tunnel(ling)
Stgs	Settings	**Tns**	Tennis
Stnds	Standards	**Topog**	Topographical
STQ	Scottish Teaching Qualification	**Tour**	Tourism
Str	Stringed	**Tox**	Toxicology
Strat	Strategic/Strategy	**TQ**	Teaching Qualification

Tr	Trade	**Vit**	Viticulture
Tr Stands	Trading Standards	**Vkg**	Viking
Trad	Traditional	**Vntr**	Venture
Trans	Transport(ation)	**Vnu**	Venue
Transat	Transatlantic	**Voc**	Vocational
Transl	Translation	**Vol**	Voluntary
Transnl Med Sci	Translational Medical Science	**Vrtl Rlty**	Virtual Reality
Trav	Travel	**Vsn**	Vision
Trfgrs	Turfgrass	**Vstr**	Visitor
Trg	Training		
Trnrs	Trainers	**Wdlnd**	Woodland
Trpcl	Tropical	**Welf**	Welfare
Trpl	Triple	**Wk**	Work
Trstrl	Terrestrial	**Wkg**	Working
Tstmnt	Testament	**Wkplc**	Workplace
Ttl	Total	**Wlbng**	Well-being
Turk	Turkish	**Wldlf**	Wildlife
TV	Television	**Wls**	Wales
Twn	Town	**Wmnswr**	Womenswear
Typo	Typographical/Typography	**Wn**	Wine
		Wrbl	Wearable
Ukr	Ukrainian	**Writ**	Writing/Writer
Un	Union	**Wrld**	World
Undwtr	Underwater	**Wrlss**	Wireless
Unif	Unified	**Wst**	Waste(s)
Up	Upland	**Wstn**	Western
Urb	Urban	**Wtr**	Water
USA	United States of America	**Wtrspo**	Watersports
Util	Utilities/Utilisation	**Wvn**	Woven
		www	World Wide Web
Val	Valuation		
Vcl	Vocal	**Ycht**	Yacht
Veh	Vehicle	**Ychtg**	Yachting
Vert	Vertebrate	**Yng**	Young
Vet	Veterinary	**Yrs**	Years
Vib	Vibration	**Yth**	Youth
Vict	Victorian		
Vid	Video	**Zool**	Zoology
Viet	Vietnamese		
Virol	Virology	**3D**	Three-dimensional
Vis	Visual(isation)		

ACCOUNTANCY/ACCOUNTING

(see also **Finance**)

Accountancy and Accounting degree courses include accounting, finance, economics, law, management, qualitative methods and information technology. Depending on your chosen course, other topics will include business law, business computing, a study of financial institutions and markets, management accountancy, statistics, taxation and auditing, whilst at some institutions an optional language might be offered. Many, but not all, Accountancy and Accounting degrees give exemptions from the examinations of some or all of the accountancy professional bodies. Single Honours courses are more likely to give full exemptions, while Joint Honours courses are more likely to lead to partial exemptions. Students should check with universities and colleges about which professional bodies offer exemptions for their courses before applying. Most courses are strongly vocational and many offer sandwich placements or opportunities to study Accountancy/Accounting with a second subject.

Useful websites www.accaglobal.com/uk; www.cimaglobal.com; www.cipfa.org; www.tax.org.uk; www.icaew.com; www.ifa.org.uk

NB The points totals shown to the left of the institutions are for ease of reference only. It must not be assumed that Tariff points are always used by institutions or that they can be substituted for an offer in grades. The level of an offer is not necessarily indicative of the quality of a course.

COURSE OFFERS INFORMATION

Subject requirements/preferences GCSE English and mathematics required: popular universities may require A or A* (7 or 8/9). **AL** Mathematics (A or B) or accounting (A or B) required or preferred for some courses.

Your target offers and examples of degree courses
144 pts **Bath** – AAA–AAB+bEPQ incl maths (Acc Fin) (IB 36 pts HL 666)
   Bristol – AAA–ABB incl maths (Acc Fin; Acc Fin (St Abrd)) (IB 36–32 pts HL 6 maths); AAA–A*AB incl maths (Acc Mgt) (IB 36–32 pts HL 6 maths)
   City – AAA (Acc Fin) (IB 36 pts)
   Exeter – AAA–AAB (Bus Acc; Acc Fin (Euro St); Acc Fin (Yr Ind)) (IB 36–34 pts)
   Glasgow – AAA/A*AB incl maths (Acc Fin; Acc Maths) (IB 38 pts HL 666 incl maths)
   Leeds – AAA (Acc Fin) (IB 35 pts HL 17 pts incl 5 maths)
   London (QM) – AAA (Acc Mgt) (IB 36 pts HL 666)
   London LSE – AAA (Acc Fin) (IB 38 pts HL 666)
   Manchester – AAA (Acc) (IB 37 pts HL 666)
   Reading – AAA–AAB (Acc Mgt) (IB 35 pts); (Acc Fin) (IB 35–34 pts)
   Strathclyde – AAA–ABB incl maths (Acc Mark) (IB 36 pts HL 6 maths); (Acc Hspty Tour Mgt) (IB 38 pts HL 6 maths); AAA incl maths (Acc) (IB 36 pts HL 6 maths)
   Warwick – AAA incl maths/fmaths (Acc Fin) (IB 38 pts HL 5 maths)
136 pts **Aston** – AAB–ABB (Acc Mgt) (IB 32 pts HL 665–655)
   Birmingham – AAB (Acc Fin) (IB 32 pts HL 665)
   Cardiff – AAB incl Fr/Ger/Span (Acc Euro Lang (Fr/Ger/Span)) (IB 35 pts); AAB (Acc (Yr Ind); Acc) (IB 33–35 pts)
   Durham – AAB (Acc Fin; Acc Mgt) (IB 36 pts)
   Edinburgh – AAB (Acc Fin; Bus Acc) (IB 43 pts HL 776)

Lancaster – AAB (Acc Fin; Acc Mgt St) (IB 35 pts HL 16 pts)
Liverpool – AAB (Acc Fin) (IB 35 pts)
Loughborough – AAB (Acc Fin Mgt) (IB 35 pts HL 665)
Nottingham – AAB (Fin Acc Mgt; Acc) (IB 34 pts HL 18 pts)
Queen's Belfast – AAB (Acc Fr/Span; Acc)
Reading – AAB (Acc Bus) (IB 35–34 pts)
Southampton – AAB/ABB+aEPQ (Acc Fin; Acc Fin (Yr Ind)) (IB 34 pts HL 17 pts)
Surrey – AAB (Acc Fin) (IB 34 pts)
Sussex – AAB–ABB (Acc Fin (Yr Ind); Acc Fin) (IB 32 pts)
York – AAB (Acc Bus Fin Mgt) (IB 35 pts)

128 pts   **Abertay** – ABB (3 yr course) CCC (4 yr course) (Acc Fin) (IB 28 pts)
BPP – ABB (2 yr course) BBB (3 yr course) 128–120 pts (Acc Fin)
Bradford – ABB 128 pts (Acc Fin)
Coventry – ABB–BBB (Acc Fin) (IB 31–30 pts)
East Anglia – ABB (Acc Fin) (IB 32 pts)
Heriot-Watt – ABB (3 yr course) BBB (4 yr course) (Acc Fin; Acc Bus Law) (IB 34 pts
   (3 yr course) 29 pts (4 yr course))
Kent – ABB (Acc Fin; Acc Fin (Yr Ind)) (IB 34 pts HL 4 maths)
Leicester – ABB–BBB+bEPQ (Acc Fin) (IB 30 pts)
LIBF – ABB–BBC (Bank Fin) (IB 32–28 pts)
London (RH) – ABB (Acc Fin) (IB 32 pts HL 655 incl maths)
Northumbria – 128–136 pts (Acc) (HL 444)
Roehampton – 128 pts (Acc)
Sheffield – ABB (Acc Fin Mgt) (IB 33 pts)
Stirling – ABB incl acc+econ (3 yr course) BBB (4 yr course) (Acc) (IB 35 pts (3 yr course)
   32 pts (4 yr course))
Swansea – ABB–BBB (Acc; Acc Fin (Yr Ind)) (IB 33–32 pts)
Ulster – ABB–BBB incl maths (Acc Law; Acc) (IB 27 pts HL 13 pts)

120 pts   **Aberdeen** – BBB (Acc Leg St; Acc Bus Mgt) (IB 32 pts HL 555)
Aberystwyth – BBB (Acc Fin) (IB 28 pts)
Bangor – 120 pts (Acc Fin)
Bournemouth – 120–112 pts (Acc Tax) (IB 31–30 pts HL 555)
Brunel – BBB (Bus Mgt (Acc)) (IB 30 pts)
Buckingham – BBB–BCC +interview (Acc Fin) (IB 32–30 pts)
Coventry – BBB (Int Fin Acc) (IB 29 pts)
De Montfort – 120 pts (Acc Fin) (IB 30 pts)
Dundee – BBB (Acc Bus Fin; Acc) (IB 30 pts HL 555)
Edge Hill – BBB 120 pts (Acc)
Essex – BBB (Acc courses; Acc Fin) (IB 30 pts)
Greenwich – 120 pts (Acc Fin)
Huddersfield – BBB 120 pts (Acc Fin; Acc)
Kingston – 120 pts (Acc Fin) (IB 27 pts HL 664 incl 4 Engl lang)
Liverpool Hope – BBB–BBC 120–112 pts (Acc Fin)
London South Bank – BBB 120 pts (Acc Fin)
Middlesex – 120 pts (Acc Fin)
Nottingham Trent – BBB 120 pts (Acc Fin)
Oxford Brookes – BBB 120 pts (Acc Fin) (IB 31 pts)
Plymouth – 120 pts (Acc Fin) (IB 28 pts HL 4)
Sheffield Hallam – 120 pts (Acc Fin); 120–104 pts (Foren Acc)
Staffordshire – BBB 120 pts (Acc Fin)
UWE Bristol – 120 pts (Acc Fin)
Westminster – BBB (Acc) (IB 28 pts)

112 pts   **Birmingham City** – BBC 112 pts (Bus Acc) (IB 28 pts HL 14 pts)
Bournemouth – 112–120 pts (Acc Fin; Acc Law; Acc Bus) (IB 30–31 pts HL 55)
Brighton – BBC–CCC 112–96 pts (Acc Fin) (IB 28 pts HL 16 pts)

UCAS points Tariff: A* = 56 pts; A = 48 pts; B = 40 pts; C = 32 pts; D = 24 pts; E = 16 pts

Canterbury Christ Church – 112–88 pts (Acc Mgt; Acc)
Cardiff Met – 112 pts (Acc)
Central Lancashire – 112 pts (Acc Fin Mgt)
Chichester – BBC–CCC (Acc Fin) (IB 28 pts)
East London – 112 pts (Acc Fin) (IB 26 pts HL 15 pts)
Gloucestershire – BBC 112 pts (Acc Fin Mgt St)
Glyndŵr – 112 pts (Acc Fin)
Hull – 112 pts (Acc) (IB 30 pts)
Keele – BBC (Acc Comb Hons) (IB 30 pts)
Leeds Beckett – 112 pts (Acc Fin) (IB 25 pts)
Lincoln – BBC (Acc Fin) (IB 29 pts)
Liverpool John Moores – BBC 112 pts (Acc Fin) (IB 28 pts)
London (Birk) – 112 pts (Acc)
Oxford Brookes – BBC 112 pts (Acc Econ) (IB 30 pts)
Portsmouth – 112 pts (Acc Fin) (IB 30 pts HL 17 pts)
Robert Gordon – BBC (Acc Fin) (IB 29 pts)
Suffolk – BBC (Acc Fin Mgt)
Univ Law – BBC (Acc Fin)
West London – 112–120 pts (Acc Fin) (IB 26 pts)
Winchester – 112–120 pts (Acc Fin) (IB 26 pts)
Wolverhampton – BBC–CCC (Acc Fin; Acc Law)
Worcester – 112 pts (Bus Acc)

104 pts **Bangor** – 104–96 pts (Acc Ital)
Bath Spa – BCC–CCC (Bus Mgt (Acc))
Bolton – 104 pts (Acc)
Chester – BCC–BBC (Acc Fin) (IB 26 pts)
Derby – 104 pts (Acc Fin)
Edinburgh Napier – BCC (Acc Law; Acc) (IB 27 pts HL 654)
Glasgow Caledonian – BCC (Acc) (IB 26 pts)
Manchester Met – BCC–BBC 104–112 pts (Bank Fin; Acc Fin) (IB 26 pts)
Northampton – BCC (Acc Comb Hons)
Salford – BCC–BBC (Acc Fin) (IB 30–31 pts)

96 pts **Anglia Ruskin** – 96–112 pts (Acc Fin) (IB 24 pts)
Hertfordshire – 96–112 pts (Acc)
London Met – CCC 96 pts (Acc Fin)
Middlesex – 96 pts (Bus Acc)
Newman – 96 pts (Acc Fin)
York St John – 96–112 pts (Acc Bus Mgt; Acc Fin)

88 pts **Derby** – 88–120 pts (Acc Comb Hons)
Trinity Saint David – 88 pts +interview (Acc)

80 pts **Bedfordshire** – 80 pts (Acc)
Bucks New – 80–96 pts (Acc Fin)
South Wales – BCC–CDD 104–80 pts (Acc Fin) (HL 655–445)
Teesside – 80–96 pts (Acc Fin)

24 pts **UHI** – (Acc Fin)

Alternative offers
See **Chapter 6** and **Appendix 1** for grades/UCAS Tariff points information for other examinations.

EXAMPLES OF COLLEGES OFFERING COURSES IN THIS SUBJECT FIELD

Accrington and Rossendale (Coll); Barking and Dagenham (Coll); Bath (Coll); Blackburn (Coll); Blackpool and Fylde (Coll); Bournemouth and Poole (Coll); Bradford (Coll); Bridgwater and Taunton (Coll); Bury (Coll); Chesterfield (Coll); Cornwall (Coll); Craven (Coll); Derby (Coll); East Riding (Coll); Exeter (Coll); Farnborough (CT); Grimsby (Inst Group); Hartlepool (CFE); HOW (Coll); Leeds City (Coll); LeSoCo; London City (Coll); London South East (Coll); Macclesfield (Coll); Manchester (Coll); Mont Rose

(Coll); NCC Redbridge; Neath Port Talbot (Coll); Nescot; North Notts (Coll); North West London (Coll); Norwich City (Coll); Nottingham (Coll); Oldham (Univ Campus); Pearson (Coll); Peterborough (Coll); Plymouth City (Coll); Redcar and Cleveland (Coll); Richmond-upon-Thames (Coll); St Helens (Coll); South City Birmingham (Coll); South Gloucestershire and Stroud (Coll); Sussex Coast Hastings (Coll); Tameside (Coll); Telford New (Coll); Westminster Kingsway (Coll); Weymouth (Coll); Yeovil (Coll).

CHOOSING YOUR COURSE (SEE ALSO CH.1)

Universities and colleges teaching quality See www.qaa.ac.uk; https://unistats.ac.uk.

Examples of sandwich degree courses Aston; Bath; Bedfordshire; Birmingham City; Bournemouth; Bradford; Brighton; Brunel; Canterbury Christ Church; Cardiff Met; Central Lancashire; Chester; Chichester; Coventry; De Montfort; Derby; Durham; Gloucestershire; Greenwich; Hertfordshire; Huddersfield; Hull; Kent; Lancaster; Leeds Beckett; Liverpool John Moores; Loughborough; Manchester Met; Middlesex; Northumbria; Nottingham Trent; Oxford Brookes; Portsmouth; Reading; Salford; Sheffield Hallam; South Wales; Surrey; Sussex; Teesside; Ulster; UWE Bristol; West London; Westminster; Wolverhampton; Worcester; York.

ADMISSIONS INFORMATION

Number of applicants per place (approx) Bath 15; Birmingham 8; Bristol 10; Dundee 5; Durham 5; East Anglia 6; Essex 7; Exeter 18; Glasgow 10; Heriot-Watt 6; Hull 5; Lancaster 5; Leeds 25; London LSE 14; Manchester 11; Oxford Brookes 8; Salford 8; Sheffield 6; Staffordshire 3; Stirling 7; Strathclyde 10; Ulster 10; Warwick 14.

Advice to applicants and planning the UCAS personal statement Universities look for good numerical and communication skills, interest in the business and financial world, teamwork, problem-solving and computing experience. On the UCAS application you should be able to demonstrate your interest in and understanding of accountancy and to give details of any work experience or work shadowing undertaken. Try to arrange meetings with accountants, work shadowing or work experience in accountants' offices, commercial or industrial firms, town halls, banks or insurance companies and describe the work you have done. Obtain information from the main accountancy professional bodies (see **Appendix 3**). Refer to current affairs which have stimulated your interest from articles in the *Financial Times*, *The Economist* or the business and financial sections of the weekend press. **Bath** Gap year welcomed. Extracurricular activities are important and should be described on the personal statement. There should be no gaps in your chronological history. **Bristol** Deferred entry accepted.

Misconceptions about this course Many students believe incorrectly that you need to be a brilliant mathematician. However, you do have to be numerate and enjoy numbers (see **Subject requirements/preferences**). Many underestimate the need for a high level of attention to detail. **Buckingham** Some students think it's a maths course. **Salford** Some applicants believe the course is limited to financial knowledge when it also provides an all-round training in management skills.

Selection interviews Yes Newcastle, Reading; **Some** Cardiff Met, Liverpool John Moores, Warwick, Wolverhampton; **No** Birmingham, Bristol, Cardiff, East Anglia, Essex, London LSE, Staffordshire, Surrey.

Interview advice and questions Be prepared to answer questions about why you have chosen the course, the qualities needed to be an accountant, and why you think you have these qualities! You should also be able to discuss any work experience you have had and to describe the differences in the work of chartered, certified, public finance and management accountants. See also **Chapter 5**. **Buckingham** Students from a non-English-speaking background are asked to write an essay. If their maths results are weak they may be asked to do a simple arithmetic test. Mature students with no formal qualifications are usually interviewed and questioned about their work experience.

Reasons for rejection (non-academic) Poor English. Lack of interest in the subject because they realise they have chosen the wrong course! No clear motivation. Course details not researched. **London South Bank** Punctuality, neatness, enthusiasm and desire to come to London South Bank not evident.

UCAS points Tariff: A* = 56 pts; A = 48 pts; B = 40 pts; C = 32 pts; D = 24 pts; E = 16 pts

AFTER-RESULTS ADVICE

Offers to applicants repeating A-levels Higher Manchester Met; **Possibly higher** Brighton, Central Lancashire, Leeds, Sheffield Hallam; **Same** Abertay, Aberystwyth, Anglia Ruskin, Bangor, Birmingham City, Bolton, Bradford, Brunel, Buckingham, Cardiff, Cardiff Met, Chichester, De Montfort, Derby, Dundee, Durham, East Anglia, East London, Edinburgh Napier, Heriot-Watt, Huddersfield, Hull, Liverpool John Moores, Loughborough, Northumbria, Oxford Brookes, Salford, Staffordshire, Stirling, Trinity Saint David, West London, Wolverhampton; **No** Glasgow.

GRADUATE DESTINATIONS AND EMPLOYMENT (2015/16 HESA)

Graduates surveyed 4,335 **Employed** 2,530 **In voluntary employment** 85 **In further study** 930 **Assumed unemployed** 270

Career note Most Accountancy/Accounting graduates enter careers in finance.

OTHER DEGREE SUBJECTS FOR CONSIDERATION

Actuarial Studies; Banking; Business Studies; Economics; Financial Services; Insurance; International Securities and Investment Banking; Mathematics; Quantity Surveying; Statistics.

ACTUARIAL SCIENCE/STUDIES

Actuaries deal with the evaluation and management of financial risks, particularly those associated with insurance companies and pension funds. Studies focus on business economics, financial mathematics, probability and statistics, computer mathematics, statistics for insurance, and mathematics in finance and investment. Most courses include compulsory and optional subjects. Although Actuarial Science/Studies degrees are vocational and give full or partial exemptions from some of the examinations of the Institute and Faculty of Actuaries, students are not necessarily committed to a career as an actuary on graduation. However, many graduates go on to be actuary trainees, leading to one of the highest-paid careers.

Useful websites www.actuaries.org.uk; www.soa.org; www.beanactuary.org

NB The points totals shown to the left of the institutions are for ease of reference only. It must not be assumed that Tariff points are always used by institutions or that they can be substituted for an offer in grades. The level of an offer is not necessarily indicative of the quality of a course.

COURSE OFFERS INFORMATION

Subject requirements/preferences GCSE Most institutions require grades A or B (7 or 5/6) in English and mathematics. **AL** Mathematics at a specified grade required.

Your target offers and examples of degree courses

152 pts **City** – A*AA incl maths (Act Sci) (IB 36 pts HL 6 maths)
Manchester – A*AA–AAA incl maths (Act Sci Maths) (IB 34 pts HL 6 maths)
Queen's Belfast – A*AA–AAA incl maths (Act Sci Risk Mgt)

144 pts **Heriot-Watt** – AAA incl maths (3 yr course) AAB incl maths (4 yr course) (Act Sci Dip Ind Trg; Act Sci) (IB 30 pts (3 yr course) 28 pts (4 yr course) HL 7 maths (3 yr course) 6 maths (4 yr course))
Kent – AAA incl maths (Act Sci; Act Sci (Yr Ind)) (IB 34 pts HL 6 maths)
Leeds – AAA–A*AB incl maths/AAB–A*BB incl maths+fmaths (Act Maths) (IB 35 pts HL 17 pts incl 6 maths)
London LSE – AAA incl maths (Act Sci) (IB 38 pts HL 766 incl 7 maths)
Southampton – AAA/AAB+aEPQ incl maths (Maths Act Sci) (IB 36 pts HL 6 maths)

136 pts **East Anglia** – AAB incl maths (Act Sci) (IB 33 pts HL 66 incl maths); AAB incl A maths (Act Sci (Yr Ind)) (IB 33 pts HL 66 incl maths)
Leicester – AAB/ABB+bEPQ incl maths (Maths Act Sci) (IB 32 pts HL 6 maths)
Liverpool – AAB incl maths (Act Maths) (IB 35 pts HL 6 maths)

120 pts **Essex** – BBB incl maths/fmaths (Act Sci; Act Sci (Yr Ind)) (IB 30 pts HL 6 maths)
Kingston – 120 pts inc maths (Act Sci)

Alternative offers
See **Chapter 6** and **Appendix 1** for grades/UCAS Tariff points information for other examinations.

CHOOSING YOUR COURSE (SEE ALSO CH.1)

Universities and colleges teaching quality See www.qaa.ac.uk; https://unistats.ac.uk.

Top research universities and colleges (REF 2014) See **Mathematics**.

Examples of sandwich degree courses East Anglia; Essex; Heriot-Watt; Kent; Kingston; Queen's Belfast.

ADMISSIONS INFORMATION

Number of applicants per place (approx) City 3; Heriot-Watt 4; London LSE 8; Southampton (Maths Act Sci) 9.

Advice to applicants and planning the UCAS personal statement Demonstrate your knowledge of this career and its training, and mention any contacts you have made with an actuary. (See **Appendix 3** for contact details of professional associations for further information.) Any work experience or shadowing in insurance companies should be mentioned, together with what you have learned about the problems facing actuaries. It is important to show motivation and sheer determination for training as an actuary as it is long and tough (up to three or four years after graduation). Mathematical flair, an ability to communicate and an interest in business are paramount.

Misconceptions about this course There is a general lack of understanding of actuaries' career training and of the career itself.

Selection interviews No East Anglia, Southampton.

Interview advice and questions In view of the demanding nature of the training, it is important to have spent some time discussing this career with an actuary in practice. Questions, therefore, may focus on the roles of the actuary and the qualities you need to succeed. You should also be ready to field questions about your AL mathematics course and the aspects of it you most enjoy. See also **Chapter 5**.

Reasons for rejection (non-academic) Kent Poor language skills.

AFTER-RESULTS ADVICE

Offers to applicants repeating A-levels Higher City; **Same** Heriot-Watt, Southampton.

GRADUATE DESTINATIONS AND EMPLOYMENT (2015/16 HESA)

See **Finance**.

Career note Graduates commonly enter careers in finance, many taking further examinations to qualify as actuaries.

OTHER DEGREE SUBJECTS FOR CONSIDERATION

Accountancy; Banking; Business Studies; Economics; Financial Risk Management; Financial Services; Insurance; Mathematics; Money, Banking and Finance; Statistics.

AFRICAN STUDIES

(see also **Languages**)

African Studies courses tend to be multi-disciplinary and cover several subject areas. These can include anthropology, history, geography, sociology, social psychology and languages. Most courses focus on Africa and African languages (Amharic (Ethiopia), Hausa (Nigeria), Somali (Horn of Africa), Swahili (Somalia and Mozambique), Yoruba (Nigeria, Sierra Leone, Ghana and Senegal), and Zulu (South Africa)). Courses will also include a wide range of optional topics covering African art, music, and literature, and the religions of Africa.

Useful websites www.britishmuseum.org; https://africanstudies.org; www.blackhistorymonth.org.uk; www.sasaonline.org.za

NB The points totals shown to the left of the institutions are for ease of reference only. It must not be assumed that Tariff points are always used by institutions or that they can be substituted for an offer in grades. The level of an offer is not necessarily indicative of the quality of a course.

COURSE OFFERS INFORMATION

Subject requirements/preferences GCSE Grade A–C (7–4) in mathematics and English may be required. **AL** For language courses a language subject or demonstrated proficiency in a language is required.

Your target offers and examples of degree courses
136 pts **London (SOAS)** – AAB–ABB (Swli Comb Hons; Af Lang Cult; Af St) (IB 35 pts HL 665)
  London (UCL) – AAB incl Fr (Fr As Af Lang) (IB 36 pts HL 6 Fr)
120 pts **Birmingham** – BBB (Af St; Af St Anth; Af St Dev) (IB 32 pts HL 555)

Alternative offers
See **Chapter 6** and **Appendix 1** for grades/UCAS Tariff points information for other examinations.

CHOOSING YOUR COURSE (SEE ALSO CH.1)

Universities and colleges teaching quality See www.qaa.ac.uk, https://unistats.ac.uk.

ADMISSIONS INFORMATION

Number of applicants per place (approx) Birmingham 5.

Advice to applicants and planning the UCAS personal statement Describe any visits you have made to African countries and why you wish to study this subject. Embassies in London may be able to provide information about the history, geography, politics, economics and the culture of the countries in which you are interested. Keep up-to-date with political developments in African countries. Discuss any aspects which interest you.

Selection interviews No Birmingham.

Interview advice and questions Questions are likely to be on your choice of country or geographical region, your knowledge of it and your awareness of some of the political, economic and social problems that exist. See also **Chapter 5**.

GRADUATE DESTINATIONS AND EMPLOYMENT (2015/16 HESA)

Graduates surveyed 10 **Employed** 0 **In voluntary employment** 0 **In further study** 0 **Assumed unemployed** 0

Career note The language skills and knowledge acquired in African Studies courses, particularly when combined with periods of study in Africa, are relevant to a wide range of careers.

OTHER DEGREE SUBJECTS FOR CONSIDERATION

Anthropology; Geography; History; Languages; Sociology.

AGRICULTURAL SCIENCES/AGRICULTURE

(including **Forestry**; see also **Animal Sciences, Food Science/Studies and Technology, Horticulture, Landscape Architecture, Surveying and Real Estate Management, Zoology**)

Courses in Agriculture recognise that modern farming practice requires sound technical and scientific knowledge, together with appropriate management skills, and most courses focus to a greater or lesser extent on all these requirements. Your choice of course depends on your particular interest and aims: some courses will give greater priority than others to practical application. Most graduates enter the agriculture industry whilst others move into manufacturing, wholesale and retail work. Agricultural courses specialise in crop and animal production and will also include agri-business and environmental issues. Forestry courses cover all aspects of the importance of forests from the biological, ecological, environmental, economic and sociological aspects with practical involvement in the establishment of forests and their control, growth, health and quality. Rural Estate and Land Management courses relate to the purchase and sale of country property, residential agency in towns, the management of commercial property, portfolios, investment funds and the provision of valuation and technical services. Countryside management courses cover the uses of the countryside including tourism, land use, and ecosystems and environmental aspects.

Useful websites www.gov.uk/government/organisations/department-for-environment-food-rural-affairs; www.gov.uk/government/organisations/natural-england; www.lantra.co.uk; www.forestry.gov.uk; www.nfuonline.com; www.nfyfc.org.uk; http://iagre.org; www.bbsrc.ac.uk; www.wwoof.org.uk

NB The points totals shown to the left of the institutions are for ease of reference only. It must not be assumed that Tariff points are always used by institutions or that they can be substituted for an offer in grades. The level of an offer is not necessarily indicative of the quality of a course.

COURSE OFFERS INFORMATION

Subject requirements/preferences GCSE English and mathematics usually required; chemistry sometimes required. Practical experience may be required. **AL** One or two maths/biological science subjects may be required or preferred. Geography may be accepted as a science subject. Similar requirements apply for Agricultural Business Management courses. (Crop Sci) Two science subjects may be required. (Cntry Mgt) Geography or biology may be preferred.

Your target offers and examples of degree courses

128 pts Newcastle – ABB–BBB (Agric; Agric Agron) (IB 32–30 pts)
  Nottingham – ABB–BBB incl sci (Agric Lvstk Sci; Agric Crop Sci; Agric) (IB 32–30 pts)
  Queen's Belfast – ABB–BBB (Agric Tech)
  Reading – ABB–BBB incl sci (Agric) (IB 32–30 pts); ABB–BBB (Agric Bus Mgt) (IB 32–30 pts)
120 pts CAFRE – BBB (Agric Tech)
  Edinburgh – BBB incl biol/chem (Agric Sci (Glob Agric Food Sec); Agric Sci (Anim Sci)) (IB 30 pts HL 6 biol/chem)
104 pts Aberystwyth – BCC incl sci (Cntry Mgt; Cntry Cons; Agric; Agric Anim Sci) (IB 28 pts HL 5 sci)
  Bangor – 104 pts incl sci (Frsty; Cons Frsty)
  Harper Adams – 104–120 pts (Agric courses)
  Myerscough (Coll) – 104 pts (Arbor Urb Frsty) (IB 24 pts)
  Royal Agricultural Univ – BCC (Agric; Rur Lnd Mgt) (IB 26 pts)
 96 pts Cumbria – 96–112 pts (Frst Mgt; Wdlnd Ecol Cons)
  Harper Adams – CCC–BBB 96–120 pts +interview (Agric Mechn)
  Hertfordshire – 96 pts (Env Mgt Agric) (HL 44)
  Royal Agricultural Univ – CCC (Bldstck Perf Hrs Mgt) (IB 26 pts)
  Writtle (UC) – 96 pts (Agric)

Alternative offers
See **Chapter 6** and **Appendix 1** for grades/UCAS Tariff points information for other examinations.

UCAS points Tariff: A* = 56 pts; A = 48 pts; B = 40 pts; C = 32 pts; D = 24 pts; E = 16 pts

EXAMPLES OF COLLEGES OFFERING COURSES IN THIS SUBJECT FIELD

Askham Bryan (Coll); Bicton (Coll); Bishop Burton (Coll); Bridgend (Coll); Bridgwater and Taunton (Coll); Craven (Coll); Duchy (Coll); Easton Otley (Coll); Hadlow (Coll); Hartpury (Coll); Moulton (Coll); Myerscough (Coll); Northumberland (Coll); Plumpton (Coll); Reaseheath (Coll); Sir Gâr (Coll); Sparsholt (Coll).

CHOOSING YOUR COURSE (SEE ALSO CH.1)

Universities and colleges teaching quality See www.qaa.ac.uk; https://unistats.ac.uk.

Top research universities and colleges (REF 2014) (Agriculture, Veterinary and Food Science) Warwick; Aberdeen; Glasgow; East Anglia; Bristol; Stirling; Queen's Belfast; Liverpool; Reading; Cambridge; Nottingham.

Examples of sandwich degree courses Aberystwyth; Bangor; CAFRE; Cumbria; Harper Adams; Newcastle; Nottingham; Queen's Belfast; Reading.

ADMISSIONS INFORMATION

Number of applicants per place (approx) Bangor (Frstry) 6; Newcastle 3; Nottingham 6; Royal Agricultural Univ (Agric) 2.

Advice to applicants and planning the UCAS personal statement First-hand farming experience is essential for most courses and obviously important for all. Check prospectuses and websites. Describe the work done. Details of experience of work with agricultural or food farms (production and laboratory work), garden centres, even with landscape architects, could be appropriate. Keep up-to-date with European agricultural and fishing policies and mention any interests you have in these areas. Read farming magazines and discuss any articles which have interested you. You may even have had first-hand experience of the serious problems facing farmers. Discuss your interest or experience in practical conservation work. Ability to work both independently or as a member of a team is important. (See also **Appendix 3**.)

Forestry Contact the Forestry Commission and the Woodland Trust and try to arrange visits to forestry centres, local community woodlands and forests and to the Woodland Trust's sites. Discuss the work with forest officers and learn about future plans for specific forest areas and describe any visits made. Mention any experience of forestry or wood processing industries (for example, visits to forests and mills, work experience in relevant organisations). (See also **Appendix 3**.) **Harper Adams** Applicants should be aware that our courses are academic and not necessarily totally vocational.

Misconceptions about this course Bangor Forestry That the course provides practical training in forestry (for example, in the use of chainsaws and pesticides) or wood processing. It does not: it is intended to educate future managers, for example. It is not intended to train forestry or mill workers.

Selection interviews Yes Bishop Burton (Coll), Harper Adams; **No** Reading, Royal Agricultural Univ.

Interview advice and questions You should be up-to-date with political and scientific issues concerning the farming community in general and how these problems might be resolved. You are likely to be questioned on your own farming background (if relevant) and your farming experience. Questions asked in the past have included: What special agricultural interests do you have? What types of farms have you worked on? What farming publications do you read and which agricultural shows have you visited? What is meant by the term 'sustainable development'? Are farmers custodians of the countryside? What are the potential sources of non-fossil-fuel electricity generation? See also **Chapter 5**.

Forestry Work experience or field courses attended are likely to be discussed and questions asked such as: What is arboriculture? On a desert island how would you get food from wood? How do you see forestry developing in the next hundred years? What aspects of forestry are the most important? See also **Chapter 5**.

Reasons for rejection (non-academic) Insufficient motivation. Too immature. Unlikely to integrate well. Lack of practical experience with crops or animals.

AFTER-RESULTS ADVICE

Offers to applicants repeating A-levels Possibly higher Harper Adams, Newcastle; **Same** Bangor (Forestry), Nottingham, Royal Agricultural Univ.

GRADUATE DESTINATIONS AND EMPLOYMENT (2015/16 HESA)

Agriculture graduates surveyed 1,250 **Employed** 615 **In voluntary employment** 25 **In further study** 310 **Assumed unemployed** 55

Forestry graduates surveyed 70 **Employed** 25 **In voluntary employment** 0 **In further study** 20 **Assumed unemployed** 5

Career note The majority of graduates entered the agricultural industry whilst others moved into manufacturing, the wholesale and retail trades and property development.

For Forestry, opportunities exist with the Forestry Commission as supervisors, managers and in some cases, scientists. Other employers include private landowners (especially in Scotland), co-operative forest societies, local authorities and commercial firms.

OTHER DEGREE SUBJECTS FOR CONSIDERATION

Agroforestry; Animal Sciences; Biochemistry; Biological Sciences; Biology; Biotechnology; Chemistry; Conservation Management; Ecology (Biological Sciences); Environmental Sciences; Estate Management (Surveying); Food Science and Technology; Forestry; Horticulture; Land Surveying; Landscape Architecture; Plant Sciences; Veterinary Science; Zoology.

AMERICAN STUDIES

(see also **Latin American Studies**)

Courses normally cover American history, politics and literature, although there are opportunities to study specialist fields such as drama, film studies, history of art, linguistics, politics or sociology. In some universities, a year, term or semester spent in the USA (or Canada) is compulsory or optional whilst at other institutions the course lasts three years without a placement abroad.

Useful websites www.historynet.com; www.americansc.org.uk; www.theasa.net

NB The points totals shown to the left of the institutions are for ease of reference only. It must not be assumed that Tariff points are always used by institutions or that they can be substituted for an offer in grades. The level of an offer is not necessarily indicative of the quality of a course.

COURSE OFFERS INFORMATION

Subject requirements/preferences GCSE Specific grades in some subjects may be specified by some popular universities. **AL** English, a modern language, humanities or social science subjects preferred.

Your target offers and examples of degree courses

136 pts Birmingham – AAB (Am Can St) (IB 32 pts HL 665–655)
East Anglia – AAB (Am Lit Crea Writ) (IB 33 pts)
Sussex – AAB–ABB (Am St courses) (IB 34 pts)
Swansea – AAB–BBB (Law Am St)

128 pts Kent – ABB (Am St) (IB 34 pts)
Manchester – ABB incl Engl lit/hist (Am St) (IB 32 pts HL 665)
Nottingham – ABB incl Engl (Am St Engl) (IB 32 pts HL 5 Engl); ABB incl hist (Am St Hist) (IB 32 pts HL 5 hist); ABB (Film TV St Am St; Am Can Lit Hist Cult) (IB 32 pts)

120 pts Essex – BBB (Am (US) St Film; Crimin Am St) (IB 30 pts)
Hull – 120 pts (Am St; Am St Modn Lang)
Keele – BBB/ABC (Am St) (IB 32 pts)
Leicester – BBB–BBC+bEPQ (Am St) (IB 30–28 pts)

       Northumbria – 120–128 pts (Am St) (HL 444)
       Swansea – BBB 120 pts (Am St) (IB 32 pts)
112 pts **Hertfordshire** – 112 pts (Am St Comb Hons) (HL 44)
       Richmond (Am Int Univ) – BBC (Am St) (IB 28 pts)
104 pts **Winchester** – 104–120 pts (Am St) (IB 26 pts)
 96 pts **Portsmouth** – 96–120 pts (Am St) (IB 26 pts)
       York St John – 96–112 pts (Am St courses)
 88 pts **Canterbury Christ Church** – 88–112 pts (Am St courses)
       Derby – 88–120 pts (Am St Comb Hons)

Alternative offers
See **Chapter 6** and **Appendix 1** for grades/UCAS Tariff points information for other examinations.

CHOOSING YOUR COURSE (SEE ALSO CH.1)
Universities and colleges teaching quality See www.qaa.ac.uk; https://unistats.ac.uk.

ADMISSIONS INFORMATION
Number of applicants per place (approx) Birmingham 6; East Anglia 5; Essex 6; Hull 5; Keele 7; Leicester 7; Manchester 6; Nottingham 4; Swansea 2.

Advice to applicants and planning the UCAS personal statement Visits to America should be described, and any knowledge or interests you have of the history, politics, economics and the culture of the USA should be included on the UCAS application. The US Embassy in London may be a useful source of information. American magazines and newspapers are good reference sources and also give a good insight to life in the USA. Applicants should demonstrate an intelligent interest in both North American literature and history in their personal statement. State why you are interested in the subject and dedicate at least half of your personal statement to how and why your interest has developed – for example through extra-curricular reading, projects, films and academic study. **Manchester** Due to the detailed nature of entry requirements for American Studies courses, the prospectus is unable to include full details. For complete and up-to-date information on entry requirements for these courses, please visit the website at www.manchester.ac.uk/study/undergraduate/courses.

Misconceptions about this course Swansea Some candidates feel that American Studies is a soft option. While we study many topics which students find interesting, we are very much a humanities based degree course incorporating more traditional subjects such as history, literature and English. Our graduates also find that they are as employable in the same jobs as those students taking other degrees.

Selection interviews No Birmingham, Derby, East Anglia, Essex, Hull, Kent, Winchester.

Interview advice and questions Courses often focus on history and literature so expect some questions on any American literature you have read and also on aspects of American history, arts and culture. You may also be questioned on visits you have made to America (or Canada) and your impressions. Current political issues might also be raised, so keep up-to-date with the political scene. See also **Chapter 5**.

Reasons for rejection (non-academic) If personal reasons prevent year of study in America. **Birmingham** Lack of commitment to the course. **Swansea** Lack of knowledge covering literature, history and politics.

AFTER-RESULTS ADVICE
Offers to applicants repeating A-levels Same Birmingham, Derby, East Anglia, Essex, Hull, Nottingham, Swansea, Winchester.

GRADUATE DESTINATIONS AND EMPLOYMENT (2015/16 HESA)
Graduates surveyed 410 **Employed** 190 **In voluntary employment** 10 **In further study** 105 **Assumed unemployed** 20

Career note All non-scientific careers are open to graduates. Start your career planning during your degree course and obtain work experience.

OTHER DEGREE SUBJECTS FOR CONSIDERATION

Business Studies; Cultural Studies; English Literature; Film Studies; Government; History; International History; International Relations; Latin-American Literature/Studies; Politics.

ANIMAL SCIENCES

(including **Equine Science**; see also **Agricultural Sciences/Agriculture, Biological Sciences, Biology, Physiology, Psychology, Veterinary Science/Medicine, Zoology**)

Animal Science is a broad-based subject including the study of farm and companion animals and wildlife conservation and management. The more specialised courses include a range of specialisms including animal biology, nutrition and health, behavioural studies and welfare. Equine Science involves specialised studies in areas such as breeding, equine business, horsemanship, performance, stud management, event management, veterinary techniques and injuries. Some scholarships are available.

Useful websites www.rspca.org.uk; www.bhs.org.uk; www.wwf.org.uk; www.bsas.org.uk

NB The points totals shown to the left of the institutions are for ease of reference only. It must not be assumed that Tariff points are always used by institutions or that they can be substituted for an offer in grades. The level of an offer is not necessarily indicative of the quality of a course.

COURSE OFFERS INFORMATION

Subject requirements/preferences GCSE Mathematics/science subjects required. Also check any weight limits on equitation modules. **AL** One or two science subjects usually required for scientific courses; biology and chemistry preferred.

Your target offers and examples of degree courses

144 pts **Manchester** – AAA–ABB (Zool Modn Lang) (IB 37–32 pts HL 5 sci)

136 pts **Exeter** – AAB–ABB incl sci/maths (Anim Bhv (Cornwall)) (IB 34–32 pts HL 5 sci/maths)
Sussex – AAB–ABB (Zool) (IB 32 pts HL 5 sci)

128 pts **Kent** – ABB incl nat sci (Wldlf Cons; Wldlf Cons (Yr Prof Prac)) (IB 34 pts HL 5 nat sci)
Newcastle – ABB–BBB incl biol+sci (Anim Sci) (IB 35–32 pts HL 6 biol)
Nottingham – ABB–BBB incl sci/maths (Anim Sci) (IB 32–30 pts)
Reading – ABB–BBB incl biol+sci (Anim Sci) (IB 32–30 pts incl biol+sci)
Stirling – ABB incl sci/maths (3 yr course) BBB incl biol+sci (4 yr course) (Anim Biol) (IB 35 pts (3 yr course) 32 pts (4 yr course))

120 pts **Aberdeen** – BBB incl maths/sci (Anim Bhv) (IB 32 pts HL 5 maths/sci)
Gloucestershire – BBB 120 pts (Anim Biol)
Lincoln – BBB incl biol (Anim Bhv Welf) (IB 30 pts HL 5 biol)
Plymouth – 120–128 pts incl B biol+C sci (Anim Bhv Welf) (IB 30 pts HL 5 biol+sci)

112 pts **Aberystwyth** – BBC–BBB incl biol (Anim Bhv; Anim Sci) (IB 30 pts HL 5 biol)
Anglia Ruskin – 112 pts incl biol/psy (Anim Bhv) (IB 24 pts HL biol/psy)
Bangor – 112–136 pts incl biol+sci (Zool Anim Bhv)
Glyndŵr – 112 pts (Eqn Sci Welf Mgt)
Liverpool John Moores – BBC incl biol/geog/sci 112 pts (Wldlf Cons) (IB 26 pts); BBC incl biol 112 pts (Anim Bhv) (IB 26 pts)
Nottingham Trent – BBC incl sci 112 pts (Wldlf Cons); BBC incl biol 112 pts incl biol (Anim Biol)
Oxford Brookes – BBC 112 pts (Anim Biol Cons; Eqn Sci; Eqn Sci Thbred Mgt) (IB 30 pts)

UCAS points Tariff: A* = 56 pts; A = 48 pts; B = 40 pts; C = 32 pts; D = 24 pts; E = 16 pts

104 pts **Aberystwyth** – BCC–BBC incl biol (Eqn Sci) (IB 30 pts HL 5 biol/chem)
Bournemouth – 104–120 pts (Ecol Wldlf Cons) (IB 28–31 pts HL 555)
Chester – BCC–BBC incl biol/chem (Anim Bhv Welf) (IB 26 pts HL 5 biol); BCC–BBC incl biol/chem/psy (Anim Bhv) (IB 26 pts HL 5 biol); BCC–BBC incl biol/chem/sci (Wldlf Cons Ecol) (IB 26 pts HL 5 biol/chem)
Edinburgh Napier – BCC (Anim Cons Biol)
Harper Adams – 104–120 pts incl biol +interview (Anim Prod Sci (MSci))
Manchester Met – BCC–BBC incl biol 104–112 pts (Anim Bhv (St Abrd)) (IB 26 pts HL 5 biol)
Northampton – 104–120 pts (Wldlf Cons)
Nottingham Trent – BCC incl sci 104 pts (Eqn Spo Sci)
South Wales – BCC–CDD incl biol+sci 104–80 pts (Int Wldlf Biol) (HL 655–445 incl biol); BCC–CDD incl sci 104–80 pts (Nat Hist) (HL 5 geog/maths)
SRUC – BCC incl biol+chem (App Anim Sci)
96 pts **CAFRE** – 96 pts incl sci (Eqn Mgt)
Cumbria – 96–112 pts (Anim Cons Sci); 96–112 pts +interview +portfolio (Wldlf Media)
Royal Agricultural Univ – CCC (Bldstck Perf Hrs Mgt) (IB 26 pts); CCC 96 pts (App Eqn Sci Bus) (IB 26 pts HL sci/tech)
Worcester – 96–104 pts incl biol+sci/maths/stats (Anim Biol)
Writtle (UC) – 96 pts (Eqn courses) (IB 24 pts)
88 pts **Canterbury Christ Church** – 88–112 pts incl sci (Anim Sci)
Harper Adams – 88–104 pts incl biol +interview (Anim Bhv Welf (Clin); Anim Bhv Welf (Non Clin); Anim Hlth Welf)
80 pts **Wolverhampton** – BB/CDD incl sci (Anim Bhv Wldlf Cons)
48 pts **Glyndŵr** – 48 pts (Anim St)

Alternative offers
See **Chapter 6** and **Appendix 1** for grades/UCAS Tariff points information for other examinations.

EXAMPLES OF COLLEGES OFFERING COURSES IN THIS SUBJECT FIELD
Barnsley (Coll); Bedford (Coll); Bicton (Coll); Bishop Burton (Coll); Brooksby Melton (Coll); Bury (Coll); Calderdale (Coll); Canterbury (Coll); Central Bedfordshire (Coll); Cornwall (Coll); Craven (Coll); Derby (Coll); Duchy (Coll); Easton Otley (Coll); Grimsby (Inst Group); Guildford (Coll); Hadlow (Coll); Hartpury (Coll); Kingston Maurward (Coll); Kirklees (Coll); Lancaster and Morecambe (Coll); Moulton (Coll); Myerscough (Coll); Northumberland (Coll); Pembrokeshire (Coll); Petroc; Plumpton (Coll); Reaseheath (Coll); Sir Gâr (Coll); South Devon (Coll); South Gloucestershire and Stroud (Coll); South Staffordshire (Coll); Sparsholt (Coll); Stamford New (Coll); Warwickshire (Coll); West Anglia (Coll); Weston (Coll); Wiltshire (Coll); Wirral Met (Coll).

CHOOSING YOUR COURSE (SEE ALSO CH.1)
Universities and colleges teaching quality See www.qaa.ac.uk; https://unistats.ac.uk.

Top research universities and colleges (REF 2014) See **Agricultural Sciences/Agriculture** and **Biological Sciences**.

Examples of sandwich degree courses Aberystwyth; Anglia Ruskin; Cumbria; Harper Adams; Liverpool John Moores; Manchester Met; Nottingham Trent; Royal Agricultural Univ.

ADMISSIONS INFORMATION
Number of applicants per place (approx) Harper Adams 4; Newcastle 3; Nottingham 6; Nottingham Trent (Eqn Spo Sci) 4; Reading 10; Royal Agricultural Univ 4.

Advice to applicants and planning the UCAS personal statement Describe any work you have done with animals which generated your interest in this subject. Work experience in veterinary practices, on farms or with agricultural firms would be useful. Read agricultural/scientific journals for updates on animal nutrition or breeding. For equine courses, details of practical experience with horses (eg BHS examinations, Pony Club tests) should be included.

Check **Chapter 3** for new university admission details and **Chapter 6** on how to read the subject tables.

Misconceptions about this course Students are not always aware that equine studies courses cover science, business management, nutrition, health and breeding. **Bishop Burton (Coll)** (Eqn Sci) Some students wrongly believe that riding skills and a science background are not required for this course which, in fact, is heavily focused on the scientific principles and practice of horse management.

Selection interviews Yes Bishop Burton (Coll), SRUC; **Some** Cumbria; **No** Anglia Ruskin, Harper Adams, Newcastle, Nottingham, Plymouth, Royal Agricultural Univ, Stirling, Writtle (UC).

Interview advice and questions Questions are likely about your experience with animals and your reasons for wishing to follow this science-based subject. Other questions asked in recent years have included: What do your parents think about your choice of course? What are your views on battery hens and the rearing of veal calves? The causes of blue-tongue disease, foot and mouth disease and BSE may also feature. (Eqn courses) Students should check the level of riding ability expected (eg BHS Level 2 or PC B-test level). Check the amount of riding, jumping and competition work on the course. (See also **Chapter 5**.)

Reasons for rejection (non-academic) Uncertainty as to why applicants chose the course. Too immature. Unlikely to integrate well.

AFTER-RESULTS ADVICE
Offers to applicants repeating A-levels Same Anglia Ruskin, Bishop Burton (Coll), Chester, Harper Adams, Liverpool John Moores, Nottingham, Royal Agricultural Univ, Stirling.

GRADUATE DESTINATIONS AND EMPLOYMENT (2015/16 HESA)
Graduates surveyed 1,170 **Employed** 520 **In voluntary employment** 35 **In further study** 395 **Assumed unemployed** 40

Career note The majority of graduates obtained work with animals whilst others moved towards business and administration careers. This is a specialised subject area and undergraduates should start early to make contacts with organisations and gain work experience.

OTHER DEGREE SUBJECTS FOR CONSIDERATION
Agriculture; Biological Sciences; Biology; Food Science; Natural Sciences; Veterinary Science; Zoology.

ANTHROPOLOGY

(including **Social Anthropology**; see also **Archaeology, Sociology**)

Anthropology is the study of people's behaviour, beliefs and institutions and the diverse societies in which they live, and is concerned with the biological evolution of human beings. It also involves our relationships with other primates, the structure of communities and the effects of diet and disease on human groups. Alternatively, social or cultural anthropology covers aspects of social behaviour regarding family, kinship, marriage, gender, religion, political structures, law, psychology and language. Anthropology is also offered in combination with several other subjects such as Archaeology (London (UCL) and Southampton) and the study of forensics (Dundee and Bradford).

Useful websites www.britishmuseum.org; www.therai.org.uk; www.theasa.org

NB The points totals shown to the left of the institutions are for ease of reference only. It must not be assumed that Tariff points are always used by institutions or that they can be substituted for an offer in grades. The level of an offer is not necessarily indicative of the quality of a course.

COURSE OFFERS INFORMATION
Subject requirements/preferences GCSE English and mathematics usually required. A foreign language may be required. **AL** Biology and geography preferred for some biological anthropological courses. (Soc Anth) No specific subjects required.

UCAS points Tariff: A* = 56 pts; **A** = 48 pts; **B** = 40 pts; **C** = 32 pts; **D** = 24 pts; **E** = 16 pts

Your target offers and examples of degree courses

152 pts **Cambridge** – A*AA +interview +HSPSAA (Hum Soc Pol Sci (Soc Anth)) (IB 40–41 pts HL 776); (Hum Soc Pol Sci (Assyr Egypt); Hum Soc Pol Sci; Hum Soc Pol Sci (Biol Anth)) (IB 40–42 pts HL 776)

144 pts **Oxford** – AAA +interview (Arch Anth) (IB 38 pts)

136 pts **Durham** – AAB (Anth Sociol; Anth Arch; Anth) (IB 36 pts)
Exeter – AAB–ABB (Anth; Sociol Anth; Arch Anth) (IB 34–32 pts)
London (SOAS) – AAB–ABB (Soc Anth) (IB 35 pts HL 665)
London (UCL) – AAB (Arch Anth) (IB 36 pts HL 17 pts)
London LSE – AAB (Soc Anth; Anth Law) (IB 37 pts HL 666)
St Andrews – AAB (Soc Anth courses) (IB 35 pts)

128 pts **Birmingham** – ABB–BBB (Anth courses) (IB 32 pts HL 655–555)
Bristol – ABB–BBC (Anth) (IB 32–29 pts HL 15–14 pts)
East Anglia – ABB (Arch Anth Art Hist) (IB 32 pts)
Edinburgh – ABB–AAA (Soc Anth courses) (IB 39 pts HL 655); ABB (Arch Soc Anth) (IB 34 pts HL 655)
Kent – ABB incl sci/maths (Biol Anth) (IB 34 pts); ABB (Anth; Soc Anth) (IB 34 pts)
Liverpool – ABB (Evol Anth) (IB 33 pts)
Manchester – ABB (Soc Anth Crimin; Relgn Anth) (IB 33 pts HL 655)
Southampton – ABB/BBB+aEPQ (Sociol Anth) (IB 32 pts HL 16 pts); ABB–BBB+aEPQ (Arch Anth) (IB 32–30 pts HL 16–15 pts)
Sussex – ABB–AAB (Anth courses) (IB 32 pts)

120 pts **Aberdeen** – BBB (Anth; Anth Fr/Ger) (IB 32 pts HL 555)
Brunel – BBB (Anth Sociol; Anth) (IB 30 pts)
Dundee – BBB incl biol (Foren Anth) (IB 30 pts HL 555)
Essex – BBB (Sociol Soc Anth) (IB 30 pts)
London (Gold) – BBB (Anth courses) (IB 33 pts)
Queen's Belfast – BBB (Soc Anth courses)

112 pts **Bradford** – BBC 112 pts (Foren Arch Anth)
Liverpool John Moores – BBC incl sci/soc sci 112 pts (Foren Anth)
Oxford Brookes – BBC 112 pts (Biol Anth; Soc Anth); BBC (Anth) (IB 30 pts)
Roehampton – 112 pts (Anth)

104 pts **Bournemouth** – 104–120 pts (Anth; Arch Anth; Sociol Anth) (IB 28–30 pts HL 555)
Central Lancashire – 104 pts (Arch Anth) (IB 26 pts)
Portsmouth – 104–120 pts incl biol (Palae) (IB 27 pts)
Winchester – 104–120 pts (Anth) (IB 26 pts)

96 pts **Trinity Saint David** – 96 pts (Anth)

Alternative offers
See **Chapter 6** and **Appendix 1** for grades/UCAS Tariff points information for other examinations.

CHOOSING YOUR COURSE (SEE ALSO CH.1)

Universities and colleges teaching quality See www.qaa.ac.uk; https://unistats.ac.uk.

Top research universities and colleges (REF 2014) (Anthropology and Development Studies) London LSE (Int Dev); Manchester (Anth); Oxford (Int Dev); Manchester (Dev St); London (Gold); Durham; East Anglia; Cambridge; Edinburgh.

Examples of sandwich degree courses Bournemouth; Bradford; Brunel; Liverpool John Moores.

ADMISSIONS INFORMATION

Number of applicants per place (approx) Bristol 9; Cambridge 2; Durham 3; Hull 5; Liverpool John Moores 4; London (Gold) 7; London (SOAS) 10; London (UCL) 5; London LSE 7; Manchester 5; Oxford Brookes 7; Queen's Belfast 10; Southampton 6; Sussex 10.

Advice to applicants and planning the UCAS personal statement Visits to museums should be discussed; for example, museums of anthropology (London, Oxford, Cambridge). Describe any aspect of the subject which interests you (including books you have read) and how you have pursued this interest. Give details of any overseas travel. Give reasons for choosing course: since this is not a school subject, you will need to convince the selectors of your knowledge and interest. **Bristol** Deferred entry acceptable. **Oxford** See **Archaeology**.

Selection interviews Yes Cambridge, Oxford (Arch Anth) 28%; **Some** Bristol; **No** Dundee, East Anglia, Hull, London (Gold), London (UCL), London LSE, Oxford Brookes, Roehampton.

Interview advice and questions This is a broad subject and questions will tend to emerge as a result of your interests in aspects of anthropology or social anthropology and your comments on your personal statement. Past questions have included: What stresses are there among the nomads of the North African desert? What is a society? What is speech? If you dug up a stone axe, what could you learn from it? What are the values created by a capitalist society? Discuss the role of women since the beginning of this century. **Cambridge** See **Chapter 5** and **Archaeology**. **Oxford** See **Chapter 5** and **Archaeology**.

Reasons for rejection (non-academic) Lack of commitment. Inability to deal with a more philosophical (less positivist) approach to knowledge.

AFTER-RESULTS ADVICE
Offers to applicants repeating A-levels Same Cambridge, Durham, East Anglia, Liverpool John Moores, London (UCL), Oxford Brookes, Roehampton.

GRADUATE DESTINATIONS AND EMPLOYMENT (2015/16 HESA)
Graduates surveyed 1395 **Employed** 635 **In voluntary employment** 55 **In further study** 335 **Assumed unemployed** 85

Career note All non-scientific careers are open to graduates. However, career planning should start early and efforts made to contact employers and gain work experience.

OTHER DEGREE SUBJECTS FOR CONSIDERATION
Archaeology; Egyptology; Heritage Studies; History; Human Sciences; Political Science; Psychology; Religious Studies; Social Science; Sociology.

ARABIC and ANCIENT NEAR and MIDDLE EASTERN STUDIES

(see also **History (Ancient)**, **Religious Studies**)

Arabic is one of the world's most widely used languages, spoken by more than 300 million people in over 20 countries in the Middle East and countries right across North Africa. Study of the language also includes Islamic and modern Middle Eastern history, whilst a course in Middle Eastern Studies will include an optional language such as Arabic, Persian or Turkish (Edinburgh, Exeter). Links between Britain and Arabic-speaking countries have increased considerably in recent years and most of the larger UK organisations with offices in the Middle East have only a relatively small pool of Arabic-speaking graduates from which to recruit future employees each year.

Useful websites www.ciol.org.uk; www.bbc.co.uk/languages; www.languageadvantage.com; www.languagematters.co.uk; www.upi.com; www.merip.org; www.memri.org; www.mei.edu

NB The points totals shown to the left of the institutions are for ease of reference only. It must not be assumed that Tariff points are always used by institutions or that they can be substituted for an offer in grades. The level of an offer is not necessarily indicative of the quality of a course.

COURSE OFFERS INFORMATION

Subject requirements/preferences GCSE English, mathematics and a foreign language usually required. A high grade in Arabic may be required. **AL** A modern language is usually required or preferred.

Your target offers and examples of degree courses

152 pts **Cambridge** – A*AA +interview +AMESAA (As Mid E St) (IB 40–42 pts HL 776)

Durham – A*AA (Comb Hons Soc Sci) (IB 38 pts)

St Andrews – A*AA incl maths (Arbc Maths) (IB 36 pts HL 6 maths)

144 pts **Exeter** – AAA–ABB incl lang (Arbc Islam St Comb Hons) (IB 34–32 pts HL 5 lang)

Oxford – AAA +interview +OLAT (Orntl St) (IB 39 pts HL 666); AAA +interview +CAT (Class Orntl St) (IB 39 pts HL 666)

St Andrews – AAA (Art Hist Mid E St) (IB 36 pts HL 6 hist); (Arbc Mid E St) (IB 36 pts HL 6 hist); (Arbc Econ) (IB 38 pts)

136 pts **Edinburgh** – AAB (Mid E St; Arbc courses; Persn Pol; Persn Soc Anth; Islam St; Persn St) (IB 37 pts HL 666)

Exeter – AAB–BBB (Mid E St) (IB 34–30 pts)

London (SOAS) – AAB–ABB (Arbc Comb Hons; Anc Near E St; Persn Comb Hons; Mid E St; Arbc Islam St; Heb Comb Hons; Heb Isrl St) (IB 35 pts HL 655)

128 pts **Leeds** – ABB (Mid E St; Arbc Islam St; Arbc Mid E St) (IB 34 pts HL 16 pts)

Manchester – ABB (Arbc St; Mid E St) (IB 32 pts HL 655)

Warwick – ABB incl Fr/Ger (Fr/Ger St Arbc) (IB 34 pts HL 5 Fr/Ger)

112 pts **Central Lancashire** – 112 pts (Mod Lang Int Bus); 112–128 pts (Modn Langs Arbc) (IB 28 pts)

104 pts **Westminster** – BCC (Arbc Ling) (IB 28 pts)

96 pts **Islamic (Coll)** – CCC (Islam St; Hawza St)

Alternative offers

See **Chapter 6** and **Appendix 1** for grades/UCAS Tariff points information for other examinations.

CHOOSING YOUR COURSE (SEE ALSO CH.1)

Universities and colleges teaching quality See www.qaa.ac.uk; https://unistats.ac.uk.

ADMISSIONS INFORMATION

Number of applicants per place (approx) Cambridge 2; Durham 5; Leeds 6; London (SOAS) 5.

Advice to applicants and planning the UCAS personal statement Describe any visits to, or your experience of living in, Arabic-speaking countries. Develop a knowledge of Middle Eastern cultures, history and politics and mention these topics on the UCAS application. Provide evidence of language-learning skills and experience.

Selection interviews Yes Cambridge, Oxford (Orntl St) 24%; **No** Leeds.

Interview advice and questions You will need to be able to justify your reasons for wanting to study Arabic or other languages and to discuss your interest in, and awareness of, cultural, social and political aspects of the Middle East. **Cambridge** See **Chapter 5** under **Modern and Medieval Languages**. **Oxford** See **Chapter 5** under **Modern and Medieval Languages**.

AFTER-RESULTS ADVICE

Offers to applicants repeating A-levels Higher Leeds, St Andrews; **Same** Exeter.

GRADUATE DESTINATIONS AND EMPLOYMENT (2015/16 HESA)

Graduates surveyed 130 **Employed** 40 **In voluntary employment** 10 **In further study** 45 **Assumed unemployed** 10

Career note Most graduates enter business and administrative work, in some cases closely linked to their language studies.

Check **Chapter 3** for new university admission details and **Chapter 6** on how to read the subject tables.

OTHER DEGREE SUBJECTS FOR CONSIDERATION
Anthropology; Archaeology; Classical Studies; Hebrew; History; Persian; Politics; Turkish.

ARCHAEOLOGY

(see also **Anthropology, Classical Studies/Classical Civilisation, History (Ancient)**)

Courses in Archaeology differ between institutions but the majority focus on the archaeology of Europe, the Mediterranean and Middle Eastern countries and on the close examination of discoveries of prehistoric communities and ancient, medieval and post-medieval societies. Hands-on experience is involved in all courses as well as a close study of the history of the artefacts themselves. All courses will involve excavations in the UK or abroad. A number of universities combine Archaeology with History and Anthropology whilst Bournemouth combines it with Forensic Sciences. Southampton also has a Centre for Maritime Archaeology.

Useful websites http://new.archaeologyuk.org; www.english-heritage.org.uk; www.britishmuseum. org; www.archaeologists.net

NB The points totals shown to the left of the institutions are for ease of reference only. It must not be assumed that Tariff points are always used by institutions or that they can be substituted for an offer in grades. The level of an offer is not necessarily indicative of the quality of a course.

COURSE OFFERS INFORMATION

Subject requirements/preferences GCSE English and mathematics or science usually required for BSc courses. **AL** History, Geography, English or a science subject may be preferred for some courses and two science subjects for Archaeological Science courses.

Your target offers and examples of degree courses

152 pts **Cambridge** – A*AA +interview +HSPSAA (Hum Soc Pol Sci (Arch); Hum Soc Pol Sci (Assyr Egypt); Hum Soc Pol Sci) (IB 40–42 pts HL 776); A*AA +interview +ARCHAA (Arch) (IB 40–42 pts HL 776)

144 pts **Durham** – AAA (Anc Hist Arch) (IB 37 pts)
Oxford – AAA +interview (Class Arch Anc Hist) (IB 39 pts HL 666); (Arch Anth) (IB 38 pts)
St Andrews – AAA (Mediev Hist Arch) (IB 36 pts HL 6 hist)

136 pts **Durham** – AAB (Arch; Anth Arch) (IB 36 pts)
East Anglia – AAB (Arch Anth Art Hist (St Abrd)) (IB 33 pts)
Edinburgh – AAB (Anc Hist Class Arch; Class Arch Gk; Archit Hist Arch) (IB 36 pts HL 665)
Exeter – AAB–ABB (Arch courses) (IB 34–30 pts); (Arch Anth) (IB 34–32 pts); AAB–BBB (Arch) (IB 34–30 pts)
Glasgow – AAB incl sci (Arch) (IB 36 pts HL 665 incl sci)
London (King's) – AAB (Class Arch) (IB 35 pts HL 665)
London (UCL) – AAB–ABB (Arch; Class Arch Class Civ; Egypt Arch) (IB 36–34 pts HL 17–16 pts); AAB (Arch Anth) (IB 36 pts HL 17 pts)
Southampton – AAB–ABB incl hist +interview (Arch Hist) (IB 34–32 pts HL 6 hist)

128 pts **Birmingham** – ABB (Arch courses) (IB 32 pts HL 655)
Bristol – ABB–BBC (Arch Anth) (IB 39–32 pts HL 16–14 pts)
Cardiff – ABB–BBC (Cons Objs Musm Arch) (IB 34–31 pts); (Arch courses) (IB 35–27 pts)
Edinburgh – ABB (Arch; Celt Arch; Arch Soc Anth) (IB 34 pts HL 655)
Leicester – ABB–BBB+bEPQ (Anc Hist Arch) (IB 30 pts)
Liverpool – ABB/BBB+aEPQ (Egypt) (IB 33 pts); ABB (Arch; Arch Anc Civ) (IB 33 pts)
London (SOAS) – ABB–BBB (Hist Art Arch courses) (IB 33 pts HL 555)
Manchester – ABB (Arch; Arch Anth) (IB 33 pts HL 655)
Newcastle – ABB–BBB (Arch) (IB 32 pts HL 555)

Nottingham – ABB (Anc Hist Arch; Arch Class Civ) (IB 32 pts); ABB incl hist (Arch Hist) (IB 32 pts); ABB–BBB incl sci (Arch) (IB 32–30 pts); ABB–BBB incl geog (Arch Geog) (IB 32–30 pts HL 5 geog)

Reading – ABB–BBB incl sci (Arch courses) (IB 30 pts HL 5 sci)

Southampton – ABB–BBB incl geog (Arch Geog) (IB 32–30 pts HL 6 geog); ABB–ABB incl sci +interview (Arch) (IB 34–32 pts IIL 17–16 pts)

Warwick – ABB (Anc Hist Class Arch) (IB 34 pts)

York – ABB–BBB (Arch; Bioarch; Hist Arch) (IB 34–31 pts)

120 pts **Aberdeen** – BBB incl maths/sci (Arch) (IB 32 pts HL 5 pts incl maths/sci)

Hull – 120 pts (Hist Arch) (IB 28 pts)

Queen's Belfast – BBB (Arch Palae; Arch)

Sheffield – BBB/BBC+bEPQ incl lang (Arch Langs (Yr Abrd)) (IB 32 pts HL 6 lang); BBB/BBC+bEPQ (Arch; Arch Comb Hons; Class Hist Arch) (IB 32 pts)

Swansea – BBB (Egypt Anc Hist) (IB 32 pts)

112 pts **Bangor** – 112–120 pts (Herit Arch Hist; Welsh Hist Arch)

Bradford – BBC 112 pts (Arch courses)

Brighton – BBC–CCC 112–96 pts (Arch Geog) (IB 28 pts)

104 pts **Bournemouth** – 104–120 pts (Arch Anth) (IB 28–30 pts HL 555); (Arch) (IB 28–31 pts HL 555); 104–120 pts incl maths/sci (Arch Foren Sci) (IB 28–31 pts IIL 555)

Central Lancashire – 104 pts (Arch) (IB 26 pts)

Chester – BCC–BBC (Arch courses) (IB 26 pts)

London (Birk) – 104 pts (Arch)

Portsmouth – 104–120 pts incl biol (Palae) (IB 27 pts)

Winchester – 104–120 pts (Arch) (IB 26 pts)

96 pts **Bishop Grosseteste** – 96–112 pts (Arch Hist)

Trinity Saint David – 96–104 pts +interview (Arch; Arch Prof Prac)

Winchester – 96–112 pts (Arch Prac) (IB 25 pts)

Worcester – 96–112 pts (Arch Herit St courses)

88 pts **Canterbury Christ Church** – 88–112 pts (Arch courses)

72 pts **UHI** – BC (Arch; Scot Hist Arch)

64 pts **UHI** – CC (Arch Env St)

Alternative offers

See **Chapter 6** and **Appendix 1** for grades/UCAS Tariff points information for other examinations.

EXAMPLES OF COLLEGES OFFERING COURSES IN THIS SUBJECT FIELD

Truro and Penwith (Coll).

CHOOSING YOUR COURSE (SEE ALSO CH.1)

Universities and colleges teaching quality See www.qaa.ac.uk; https://unistats.ac.uk.

Top research universities and colleges (REF 2014) (Geography, Environmental Studies and Archaeology) Glasgow (Geog); London (RH); London LSE; Bristol (Geog); Cambridge (Geog); Oxford (Geog Env St); London (QM); St Andrews; Newcastle (Geog); Southampton (Geog); London (UCL) (Geog); Reading (Arch); Sheffield (Geog); Oxford (Arch).

Examples of sandwich degree courses Bradford.

ADMISSIONS INFORMATION

Number of applicants per place (approx) Bangor 4; Birmingham 7; Bradford 4; Bristol 7; Cambridge 8; Cardiff 6; Durham 3; Leicester 5; Liverpool 6; London (UCL) 3; Manchester (Arch) 4; Newcastle 3; Nottingham 4; Sheffield 7; Southampton 6; Trinity Saint David 2; York 4.

Advice to applicants and planning the UCAS personal statement First-hand experience of digs and other fieldwork should be described. The Council for British Archaeology (see **Appendix 3**) can provide information on where digs are taking place. Describe any interests in fossils and any museum visits as well as details of visits to current archaeological sites. Your local university archaeological department or central library can also provide information on contacts in your local area (each county council employs an archaeological officer). Since this is not a school subject, the selectors will be looking for good reasons for your choice of subject. Gain practical field experience and discuss this in the personal statement. Show your serious commitment to archaeology through your out-of-school activities (eg fieldwork, museum experience) (see **Chapter 5**). (See also **Anthropology**.) **Bristol** Deferred entry accepted. **Cambridge** Many colleges require a school/college essay.

Misconceptions about this course Bristol We are not an elitist course: 75% of applicants and students come from state schools and non-traditional backgrounds. **Liverpool** (Egypt) Some students would have been better advised looking at courses in Archaeology or Ancient History and Archaeology which offer major pathways in the study of Ancient Egypt.

Selection interviews Yes Cambridge, Oxford (Arch Anth) 28%, (Class Arch Anc Hist) 25%, Southampton, Trinity Saint David, Winchester; **Some** Bristol; **No** Bangor, Birmingham, Bournemouth, Bradford, Cardiff, East Anglia, Leicester, London (UCL), Newcastle, Nottingham, Reading.

Interview advice and questions Questions will be asked about any experience you have had in visiting archaeological sites or taking part in digs. Past questions have included: How would you interpret archaeological evidence, for example a pile of flints, coins? What is stratification? How would you date archaeological remains? What recent archaeological discoveries have been made? How did you become interested in archaeology? With which archaeological sites in the UK are you familiar? See also **Chapter 5**. **Cambridge** See **Chapter 5**. **Oxford** Interviews involve artefacts, maps and other material to be interpreted. Successful entrants average 28% (see **Chapter 5**).

Reasons for rejection (non-academic) (Mature students) Inability to cope with essay-writing and exams. **Liverpool** (Egypt) Applicant misguided on choice of course – Egyptology used to fill a gap on the UCAS application.

AFTER-RESULTS ADVICE
Offers to applicants repeating A-levels Same Birmingham, Bradford, Cambridge, Chester, Durham, East Anglia, Leicester, Liverpool, London (UCL), Sheffield, Trinity Saint David, Winchester.

GRADUATE DESTINATIONS AND EMPLOYMENT (2015/16 HESA)
Graduates surveyed 575 **Employed** 210 **In voluntary employment** 25 **In further study** 185 **Assumed unemployed** 55

Career note Vocational opportunities closely linked to this subject are limited. However, some graduates aim for positions in local authorities, libraries and museums. A number of organisations covering water boards, forestry, civil engineering and surveying also employ field archaeologists.

OTHER DEGREE SUBJECTS FOR CONSIDERATION
Ancient History; Anthropology; Classical Studies; Classics; Geology; Heritage Studies; History; History of Art and Architecture; Land Economy; Medieval History.

ARCHITECTURE

(including **Architectural Engineering** and **Architectural Technology**; see also **Art and Design (Interior, Product and Industrial Design)**, **Building and Construction**, **Landscape Architecture**)

Courses in Architecture provide a broad education consisting of technological subjects covering structures, construction, materials and environmental studies. Project-based design work is an integral part of all courses and in addition, history and social studies will also be incorporated into degree programmes. After completing the first three years leading to a BA (Hons), students aiming for full professional status take a further two-year course leading to, for example, a BArch, MArch or Diploma, and after a year in an architect's practice, the final professional examinations are taken. There is also a close link between architecture and civil engineering in the construction of large projects eg The Shard, Sydney Opera House and the construction of bridges and other major projects. Several architectural engineering courses are offered, for example Bath, Loughborough and Glasgow offer courses which, whilst focussing on civil engineering, also introduce creative design elements working on inventive and imaginative design solutions.

Useful websites www.ciat.org.uk; www.architecture.com; www.rias.org.uk; www.ciob.org.uk; www. citb.co.uk

NB The points totals shown to the left of the institutions are for ease of reference only. It must not be assumed that Tariff points are always used by institutions or that they can be substituted for an offer in grades. The level of an offer is not necessarily indicative of the quality of a course.

COURSE OFFERS INFORMATION

Subject requirements/preferences GCSE English and mathematics, in some cases at certain grades, are required in all cases. A science subject may also be required. **AL** Mathematics and/or physics required or preferred for some courses. Art and design may be preferable to design and technology. Art is sometimes a requirement and many schools of architecture prefer it; a portfolio of art work is often requested and, in some cases, a drawing test will be set. MEng courses not listed below unless otherwise stated.

Your target offers and examples of degree courses

152 pts **Bath** – A*AA (Archit) (IB 36 pts HL 6 maths/phys); A*AA/AAA+aEPQ incl maths (Civ Archit Eng (MEng)) (IB 36 pts HL 766)

Cambridge – A*AA +interview +ARCHITAA (Archit) (IB 40–42 pts HL 776)

Southampton – A*AA/A*AB+aEPQ incl maths+sci/geog (Civ Eng Archit (MEng)) (IB 36 pts HL 6 maths+sci)

144 pts **Cardiff** – AAA (Archit) (IB 36 pts); AAA–ABB incl maths (Archit Eng) (IB 36–32 pts HL 5 maths+sci)

Edinburgh – AAA–ABB (Archit) (IB 40–34 pts); AAA incl maths+phys/eng/des tech (Struct Eng Archit) (IB 37 pts HL 555)

Leeds – AAA incl maths (Archit Eng) (IB 35 pts HL 5 maths)

Liverpool – AAA (Archit) (IB 36 pts)

Manchester – AAA (Archit) (IB 32 pts HL 666)

Manchester Met – AAA 144 pts +portfolio (Archit) (IB 32 pts HL 666)

Newcastle – AAA +portfolio (Archit) (IB 36 pts)

Nottingham – AAA incl maths/phys (Archit Env Des (MEng)) (IB 36 pts); AAA (Archit) (IB 36 pts)

Sheffield – AAA (Archit) (IB 36 pts); AAA–AAB+aEPQ incl maths (Archit Eng (MEng); Struct Eng Archit (MEng)) (IB 36 pts HL 6 maths)

UWE Bristol – 144 pts (Archit)

136 pts **Arts London** – AAB 136 pts +portfolio (Archit)

Birmingham City – AAB 136 pts (Archit) (IB 30 pts)

De Montfort – 136 pts +portfolio +interview (Archit) (IB 32 pts)

Edinburgh – AAB (Archit Hist Arch; Archit Hist Herit) (IB 36 pts HL 665)

Glasgow – AAB–BBB incl maths+phys (Civ Eng Archit) (IB 36–34 pts HL 665)

Huddersfield – AAB 136 pts (Archit (Int); Archit) (IB 32)

Kent – AAB (Archit) (IB 34 pts)

Liverpool – AAB incl maths (Archit Eng (MEng)) (IB 35 pts HL 5 maths)

London (UCL) – AAB +portfolio (Archit Interd St; Archit) (IB 36 pts)

Northumbria – 136–144 pts (Archit) (IB 33 pts)

Nottingham – AAB–ABB (Archit Env Eng) (IB 34–32 pts)

Oxford Brookes – AAB (Archit) (IB 34–32 pts)

Queen's Belfast – AAB incl maths+sci/tech/geog (Struct Eng Archit (MEng)); AAB (Archit)

UWE Bristol – 136 pts (Archit Plan)

Westminster – AAB (Archit) (IB 35 pts)

128 pts **Bournemouth Arts** – ABB (Archit) (IB 32 pts)
 Creative Arts – 128 pts (Archit)
 Glasgow (SA) – ABB (Archit)
 Greenwich – 128 pts (Archit)
 Kingston – 128 pts (Archit)
 Leeds Beckett – 128 pts +interview +portfolio (Archit) (IB 27 pts)
 Liverpool – ABB incl maths (Archit Eng) (IB 33 pts HL 5 maths)
 Liverpool John Moores – 128 pts (Archit) (IB 27 pts)
 Newcastle – ABB (Archit Urb Plan) (IB 32 pts)
 Plymouth – 128 pts +portfolio (Archit) (IB 32 pts)
 Reading – ABB–BBB (Archit) (IB 32–30 pts)
 Strathclyde – ABB 128 pts (Archit St) (IB 34 pts)
 UWE Bristol – 128 pts incl maths (Archit Env Eng) (HL 5 maths)
 Wolverhampton – ABB/AAC +interview +portfolio (Archit)
120 pts **Brighton** – BBB–AAB (Archit) (IB 34 pts)
 Cardiff Met – 120 pts (Archit Des Tech)
 Central Lancashire – 120 pts (Archit) (IB 30 pts)
 Coventry – BBB–BCC (Archit) (IB 30 pts); BBB (Archit Tech) (IB 30 pts)
 Dundee – BBB–BCC incl maths/phys (Archit) (IB 30 pts)
 East London – 120 pts incl art des (Archit) (IB 28 pts HL 15 pts)
 Heriot-Watt – ABC–BBB incl maths (Archit Eng) (IB 31 pts HL 5 maths)
 Leeds Beckett – 120 pts (Archit Tech) (IB 26 pts)
 London Met – 120 pts +portfolio (Archit)
 Loughborough – ABC–BBB incl sci (Archit Eng Des Mgt) (IB 32 pts)
 Northumbria – 120–128 pts incl maths+sci (Mech Archit Eng) (HL 444)
 Norwich Arts – BBB incl art/des (Archit) (IB 32 pts)
 Nottingham Trent – BBB 120 pts +portfolio (Archit)
 Portsmouth – 120–136 pts (Archit) (IB 26 pts)
 Ulster – BBB (Archit) (IB 26 pts)
112 pts **Anglia Ruskin** – 112 pts +portfolio (Archit) (IB 26 pts)
 Birmingham City – BBC 112 pts (Archit Tech) (HL 14 pts)
 Central Lancashire – 112 pts (Archit Tech) (IB 28 pts)
 East London – 112 pts (Archit Des Tech) (IB 26 pts HL 15 pts)
 Glyndŵr – 112 pts (Archit Des Tech)
 Lincoln – 112 pts (Archit)
 London South Bank – BBC (Archit)
 Northampton – 112 pts (Archit Tech)
 Plymouth – 112 pts (Archit Tech Env) (IB 28 pts)
 Portsmouth – 112–120 pts (Inter Archit Des) (IB 26 pts)
 Robert Gordon – BBC incl maths/sci (Archit MArch) (IB 29 pts)
 Salford – 112 pts (Archit) (IB 31 pts)
 Sheffield Hallam – 112 pts (Archit Tech)
 Southampton Solent – 112 pts (Archit Tech)
 UWE Bristol – 112 pts (Archit Tech Des)
 West London – 112 pts (Archit Des Tech)
 Westminster – BBC (Archit Tech) (IB 28 pts)
104 pts **Anglia Ruskin** – 104 pts (Archit Tech)
 Falmouth – 104–120 pts (Archit)
 Liverpool John Moores – 104 pts (Archit Tech)
 Northumbria – BCC (Archit Tech) (IB 30 pts)
 Nottingham Trent – 104 pts (Archit Tech)
 UHI – BCC incl maths/phys/tech (Archit Tech)
 Ulster – BCC incl sci/maths/tech (Archit Tech Mgt) (IB 24 pts)
96 pts **Derby** – 96–112 pts (Archit Tech Prac); 96–128 pts (Archit Des Comb Hons)
 Edinburgh Napier – CCC (Archit Tech) (IB 28 pts HL 555)

UCAS points Tariff: A* = 56 pts; A = 48 pts; B = 40 pts; C = 32 pts; D = 24 pts; E = 16 pts

London South Bank – CCC (Archit Tech)
Robert Gordon – CCC (Archit Tech) (IB 26 pts)
Trinity Saint David – 96 pts (Archit Tech)
80 pts **Wolverhampton** – BB/CCE (Archit Des Tech)
64 pts **Archit Assoc Sch London** – CC +portfolio (Archit)
Ravensbourne – CC (Archit) (IB 28 pts)

Alternative offers
See **Chapter 6** and **Appendix 1** for grades/UCAS Tariff points information for other examinations.

EXAMPLES OF COLLEGES OFFERING COURSES IN THIS SUBJECT FIELD
Bournemouth and Poole (Coll); Hull (Coll); London South East (Coll); Weymouth (Coll).

CHOOSING YOUR COURSE (SEE ALSO CH.1)
Universities and colleges teaching quality See www.qaa.ac.uk; https://unistats.ac.uk.

Top research universities and colleges (REF 2014) (Architecture, Built Environment and Planning) Bath; Glasgow; Cambridge; Loughborough; Aberdeen; Newcastle; Sheffield; Cardiff (Plan Geog); Liverpool; Reading; London (UCL); Sheffield Hallam.

Examples of sandwich degree courses Coventry; Derby; Glasgow (SA); Leeds Beckett; London South Bank; Loughborough; Northumbria; Nottingham Trent; Sheffield Hallam; Ulster; UWE Bristol; Wolverhampton.

ADMISSIONS INFORMATION
Number of applicants per place (approx) Archit Assoc Sch London 2; Bath 8; Bournemouth Arts 4; Cambridge 7; Cardiff 12; Cardiff Met 2; Creative Arts 4; Dundee 8; Edinburgh 10; Glasgow 16; London (UCL) 14; London Met 13; Manchester 7; Manchester Met 25; Newcastle 5; Nottingham 7; Oxford Brookes 6; Queen's Belfast 9; Robert Gordon 8; Sheffield 9; Southampton 10; Strathclyde 10.

Admissions tutors' advice The following universities require a portfolio and evidence of art/design ability – East London, Greenwich, Huddersfield, Liverpool, London South Bank, Nottingham, Nottingham Trent, Strathclyde. Check with other universities.

Bath Preference for applicants with high proportion of **GCSE**s at A* (8/9). A-level mathematics, physics and art or design technology highly desirable.

Cambridge Art provides a better preparation than design technology.

Liverpool A lower grade offer if portfolio impressive.

Manchester Two art and/or design A-levels not advised.

UWE Bristol Architecture and Environmental Engineering degree gives RIBA status.

Advice to applicants and planning the UCAS personal statement You should describe any visits to historical or modern architectural sites and give your opinions. Contact architects in your area and try to obtain work shadowing or work experience in their practices. Describe any such work you have done. Develop a portfolio of drawings and sketches of buildings and parts of buildings (you will probably need this for your interview). Show evidence of your reading on the history of architecture in Britain and modern architecture throughout the world. Discuss your preferences among the work of leading 20th and 21st century world architects (see **Chapter 4** and also **Appendix 3**). **Cambridge** Check College requirements for preparatory work.

Misconceptions about this course Some applicants believe that Architectural Technology is the same as Architecture. Some students confuse Architecture with Architectural Engineering.

Selection interviews The majority of universities and colleges interview or inspect portfolios for Architecture. **Yes** Archit Assoc Sch London, Cambridge, De Montfort, Dundee, East London, Glasgow (SA), Huddersfield, Kingston, London (UCL), London Met, London South Bank; **Some** Bath, Cardiff Met, Coventry, Leeds Beckett, Queen's Belfast; **No** Anglia Ruskin, Birmingham City, Cardiff, Derby,

Edinburgh, Falmouth, Kent, Liverpool, Manchester Met, Newcastle, Northumbria, Nottingham, Oxford Brookes, Portsmouth, Sheffield, Ulster, West London.

Interview advice and questions Most Architecture departments will expect to see evidence of your ability to draw; portfolios are often requested at interview and, in some cases, drawing tests are set prior to the interview. You should have a real awareness of architecture with some knowledge of historical styles as well as examples of modern architecture. If you have gained some work experience then you will be asked to describe the work done in the architect's office and any site visits you have made. Questions in the past have included the following: What is the role of the architect in society? Is the London Eye an eyesore? Discuss one historic and one 21st century building you admire. Who is your favourite architect? What sort of buildings do you want to design? How would you make a place peaceful? How would you reduce crime through architecture? Do you like the University buildings? Do you read any architectural journals? Which? What is the role of an architectural technologist? See also **Chapter 5**. **Archit Assoc Sch London** The interview assesses the student's potential and ability to benefit from the course. Every portfolio we see at interview will be different; sketches, models, photographs and paintings all help to build up a picture of the student's interests. Detailed portfolio guidelines are available on the website. **Cambridge** All candidates should bring with them their portfolio of work. We are interested to see any graphic work in any medium that you would like to show us – please do not feel you should restrict your samples to only those with architectural reference. All evidence of sketching ability is helpful to us. (NB All colleges at Cambridge and other university departments of architecture will seek similar evidence.) **Sheffield** Some Architecture and Landscape courses have portfolio requirements.

Reasons for rejection (non-academic) Weak evidence of creative skills. Portfolio of artwork does not give sufficient evidence of design creativity. Insufficient evidence of interest in architecture. Unwillingness to try freehand sketching. **Archit Assoc Sch London** Poor standard of work in the portfolio.

AFTER-RESULTS ADVICE
Offers to applicants repeating A-levels Higher Huddersfield; **Possibly higher** Brighton, De Montfort, Newcastle; **Same** Archit Assoc Sch London, Bath, Birmingham City, Cambridge, Cardiff, Cardiff Met, Creative Arts, Derby, Dundee, Greenwich, Kingston, Liverpool John Moores, London Met, London South Bank, Manchester Met, Nottingham, Nottingham Trent, Oxford Brookes, Queen's Belfast, Robert Gordon, Sheffield; **No** Glasgow.

GRADUATE DESTINATIONS AND EMPLOYMENT (2015/16 HESA)
Graduates surveyed 2,490 **Employed** 1,590 **In voluntary employment** 145 **In further study** 380 **Assumed unemployed** 160

Career note Further study is needed to enter architecture as a profession. Opportunities exist in local government or private practice – areas include planning, housing, environmental and conservation fields. Architectural technicians support the work of architects and may be involved in project management, design presentations and submissions to planning authorities.

OTHER DEGREE SUBJECTS FOR CONSIDERATION
Building; Building Surveying; Civil Engineering; Construction; Heritage Management; History of Art and Architecture; Housing; Interior Architecture; Interior Design; Landscape Architecture; Property Development; Quantity Surveying; Surveying; Town and Country Planning; Urban Studies.

ART and DESIGN (3D DESIGN)

(including **Ceramics, Design Crafts, Glass and Ceramics, Jewellery and Metalwork, Modelmaking** and **Silversmithing and Jewellery**; see also **Art and Design (General), Art and Design (Interior, Product and Industrial Design)**)

This field covers a range of specialisations which are involved in the manufacture of products in metal, ceramics, glass and wood and also digital design. Some courses approach the study in a broad, comprehensive manner whilst other universities offer specialised courses in subjects such as Silversmithing and Jewellery (Glasgow School of Art and Sheffield Hallam), or Contemporary Jewellery and Fashion Accessories (Staffordshire University). The Birmingham City University course in Horology is the only course in the UK offering the study of time measurement and watches and clocks, both mechanical and electronic.

Useful websites www.ergonomics.org.uk; www.creativefuture.org.uk; www.glassassociation.org.uk; www.naj.co.uk; www.cpaceramics.com; http://ccskills.org.uk; www.dandad.org; www.designcouncil.org.uk

NB The points totals shown to the left of the institutions are for ease of reference only. It must not be assumed that Tariff points are always used by institutions or that they can be substituted for an offer in grades. The level of an offer is not necessarily indicative of the quality of a course.

COURSE OFFERS INFORMATION

Subject requirements/preferences See **Art and Design (General)**.

Your target offers and examples of degree courses
128 pts **Dundee** – ABB incl art des +portfolio (Jewel Metal Des) (IB 34 pts HL 665)
      Edinburgh – ABB (Sculp) (IB 34 pts HL 655)
      Glasgow (SA) – ABB (Silver Jewel) (IB 30 pts HL 555)
120 pts **Cardiff Met** – 120 pts (Ceram)
      Hertfordshire – 120 pts incl art des +interview +portfolio (3D Comp Animat Modl)
        (HL 44 incl vis art)
      Northumbria – 120–128 pts (3D Des) (HL 444)
      Plymouth – 120 pts +interview +portfolio (3D Des courses) (IB 28 pts)
112 pts **Birmingham City** BBC 112 pts (Horol) (HL 14 pts)
      Bournemouth Arts – BBC–BBB 112–120 pts (Modl) (IB 30–32 pts)
      Creative Arts – 112 pts (Contemp Jewel; Silver Gold Jewel)
      De Montfort – 112 pts incl art des (Des Crfts) (IB 26 pts)
      Glyndŵr – 112 pts (App Arts)
      Manchester Met – 112 pts +interview +portfolio (3D Des) (IB 26 pts)
      Nottingham Trent – BBC 112 pts +portfolio (Decr Arts)
      Sheffield Hallam – 112–96 pts (Jewel Mtlwk)
      Staffordshire – 112 pts (3D Des (Contemp Jewel Fash Accs)); BBC (3D Des Mak)
      Sunderland – 112 pts (Gls Ceram)
      Wolverhampton – BBC (App Arts)
104 pts **Liverpool Hope** – BBC–ABB 104–136 pts +interview +portfolio (Des)
96 pts **Plymouth (CA)** – 96 pts (Ceram Gls; Jewel)
80 pts **Hereford (CA)** – 80 pts (Arst Blksmthg); 80 pts +interview +portfolio (Jewel Des)
72 pts **Robert Gordon** – BC incl art/des (3D Des) (IB 24 pts)
64 pts **Colchester (Inst)** – 64 pts (3D Des Crft)
48 pts **Birmingham City** – DD 48 pts (Jewel Silver) (IB 24 pts)
40 pts and below or other selection criteria (Foundation course, interview and portfolio inspection) Arts London; Arts London (Camberwell CA); Bath Spa; Hertfordshire; Northbrook Met (Coll); Staffordshire Reg Fed (SURF).

Alternative offers
See **Chapter 6** and **Appendix 1** for grades/UCAS Tariff points information for other examinations.

Check **Chapter 3** for new university admission details and **Chapter 6** on how to read the subject tables.

EXAMPLES OF COLLEGES OFFERING COURSES IN THIS SUBJECT FIELD
Barking and Dagenham (Coll); Bedford (Coll); Bury (Coll); Gloucestershire (Coll); Havering (Coll); HOW (Coll); London UCK (Coll); Oldham (Coll); Sir Gâr (Coll); York (Coll).

CHOOSING YOUR COURSE (SEE ALSO CH.1)
Universities and colleges teaching quality See www.qaa.ac.uk; https://unistats.ac.uk.

Top research universities and colleges (REF 2014) See **Art and Design (General)**.

ADMISSIONS INFORMATION
Number of applicants per place (approx) Bath Spa 3; Birmingham City 4 (Jewel) 5; Creative Arts 4; De Montfort 3; Dundee 6; Manchester Met 5.

Advice to applicants and planning the UCAS personal statement Describe your art studies and your experience of different types of materials used. Discuss your special interest in your chosen field. Compare your work with that of professional artists and designers and describe your visits to museums, art galleries, exhibitions etc. Portfolios of recent work should demonstrate drawing skills, visual awareness, creativity and innovation, showing examples of three-dimensional work in photographic or model form. See also **Art and Design (Graphic Design)**.

Selection interviews Most institutions will interview and require a portfolio of work. **Yes** Anglia Ruskin.

Interview advice and questions Questions focus on the artwork presented in the student's portfolio. See also **Art and Design (General)** and **Chapter 5**.

Reasons for rejection (non-academic) Lack of pride in their work. No ideas. See also **Art and Design (General)**.

AFTER-RESULTS ADVICE
Offers to applicants repeating A-levels Same Brighton, Creative Arts, Dundee, Manchester Met.

GRADUATE DESTINATIONS AND EMPLOYMENT (2015/16 HESA)
See **Art and Design (General)**.

Career note See **Art and Design (General)**.

OTHER DEGREE SUBJECTS FOR CONSIDERATION
Design Technology; see other **Art and Design** tables.

ART and DESIGN (FASHION and TEXTILES)

(including Printed Textiles and Surface Pattern Design)

Fashion Design courses involve drawing and design, research, pattern cutting and garment construction for clothing for menswear and womenswear, with specialisation often offered later in the course. First year Textiles courses will involve the study of constructed textile technology techniques such as knitting and stitching, leading to specialisation later. Within digital textiles, the focus is on fashion for interiors and students will experiment with techniques such as laser knitting and digital fabric printing. Courses may also cover design for textiles, commercial production and marketing. Some institutions have particularly good contacts with industry and are able to arrange sponsorships for students.

Useful websites www.fashion.net; www.londonfashionweek.co.uk; www.texi.org; www.creativefuture. org.uk; www.britishfashioncouncil.co.uk; www.designcouncil.org.uk

NB The points totals shown to the left of the institutions are for ease of reference only. It must not be assumed that Tariff points are always used by institutions or that they can be substituted for an offer in grades. The level of an offer is not necessarily indicative of the quality of a course.

UCAS points Tariff: A* = 56 pts; A = 48 pts; B = 40 pts; C = 32 pts; D = 24 pts; E = 16 pts

COURSE OFFERS INFORMATION

Subject requirements/preferences AL A textile-related subject may be required.

Your target offers and examples of degree courses

144 pts **Manchester** – AAA incl maths/phys/chem +interview (Tex Sci Tech) (IB 37 pts HL 666)

128 pts **Edinburgh** – ABB +portfolio (Fash; Jewel Silver; Tex; Perf Cstm) (IB 34 pts HL 655)

Glasgow (SA) – ABB +interview +portfolio (Fash Des)

Kingston – 128 pts +interview +portfolio (Fash)

Leeds – ABB incl art/des (Fash Des; Tex Des) (IB 34 pts HL 16 pts incl 5/6 art/vis/des)

Loughborough – ABB +interview +portfolio (Tex (Innov Des))

Northumbria – 128–136 pts +interview +portfolio (Fash Des Mark) (HL 444); 128 pts +interview +portfolio (Fash) (IB 31 pts)

120 pts **Bournemouth Arts** – BBB 120 pts (Fash Brnd Comm) (IB 30 pts)

Brighton – BBB–CCC 120–96 pts +interview +portfolio (Fash Bus St) (IB 30 pts)

Cardiff Met – 120 pts +interview +portfolio (Tex)

Heriot-Watt – BBB (Fash Tech) (IB 29 pts); BBB +portfolio (Fash Comm; Fash) (IB 29 pts)

Huddersfield – BBB 120 pts (Int Fash Buy Mgt); BBB 120 pts +interview +portfolio (Fash Des Tex; Fash Des Mark Prod; Fash Brnd Mark)

Norwich Arts – BBB incl art/des/media +interview +portfolio (Tex Des; Fash) (IB 32 pts)

Nottingham Trent – BBB 120 pts (Fash Comm Prom; Fash Mark Brnd)

Southampton (Winchester SA) – BBB (Fash Mark) (IB 30 pts HL 16 pts); BBB incl art/des +interview +portfolio (Fash Tex Des) (IB 30 pts HL 16 pts)

Trinity Saint David – 120 pts +interview +portfolio (Surf Patt Des (Fash Obj); Surf Patt Des (Tex Fash); Surf Patt Des (Tex Inter)) (IB 32 pts)

112 pts **Anglia Ruskin** – 112 pts incl art/des/media +interview +portfolio (Fash Des) (IB 24 pts)

Arts London (CFash) – 112 pts (Fash Mgt) (IB 25 pts); 112 pts +interview +portfolio (Fash Jrnl)

Birmingham City – BBC 112 pts +portfolio (Fash Bus Prom; Fash Des courses) (HL 14 pts)

Bournemouth Arts – BBC–BBB 112–120 pts +portfolio +interview (Mkup Media Perf) (IB 30–32 pts); BBC–BBB 112–120 pts +interview +portfolio (Fash; Cstm Perf Des; Tex) (IB 30–32 pts)

Central Lancashire – 112 pts +interview +portfolio (Fash Prom)

Coventry – BBC incl art/des (Fash) (IB 29 pts)

Creative Arts – 112 pts +portfolio (Fash Atel; Fash Jrnl; Tex Fash Inter; Fash Prom Imag); 112 pts +interview +portfolio (Hand Embr Fash Inter Tex Art)

De Montfort – 112 pts incl art des +interview +portfolio (Cont Fash; Fash Des; Tex Des; Fash Tex Accs) (IB 26 pts incl art des); 112 pts (Fash Buy courses) (IB 26 pts)

Derby – 112 pts +interview +portfolio (Tex Des; Fash)

East London – 112 pts +interview +portfolio (Fash Des) (IB 25 pts HL 15 pts)

Leeds Arts – BBC incl art des 112 pts +interview +portfolio (Prtd Tex Surf Patt Des; Fash (Comm); Fash (Des))

Liverpool John Moores – BBC 112 pts +interview +portfolio (Fash) (IB 28 pts)

London (Royal Central Sch SpDr) – BBC +interview +portfolio (Thea Prac (Cstm Constr))

Manchester Met – 112 pts +interview +portfolio (Fash; Tex Prac) (IB 26 pts)

Middlesex – 112 pts +interview +portfolio (Fash Tex; Fash Des)

Nottingham Trent – BBC 112 pts +portfolio (Cstm Des Mak; Fash Accs Des; Fash Des; Fash Kntwr Des Knit Tex; Tex Des)

Robert Gordon – BBC (Fash Mgt) (IB 29 pts)

Sheffield Hallam – 112–96 pts +interview +portfolio (Fash Des)

Southampton Solent – 112 pts +portfolio (Fash Styl)

Staffordshire – 112 pts +interview +portfolio (Tex Surf)

Sunderland – 112–120 pts (Fash Jrnl); 112 pts +portfolio (Fash Prod Prom)

UWE Bristol – 112 pts +portfolio (Fash Comm)

West London – 112 pts incl art des (Fash Tex); BBC 112 pts (Fash Brnd Mark; Fash Prom Imag)

Check **Chapter 3** for new university admission details and **Chapter 6** on how to read the subject tables.

Westminster – BBC +interview (Fash Mrchnds Mgt) (IB 29 pts)

Wolverhampton – BBC 112 pts +portfolio (Fash)

104 pts **Bath Spa** – BCC incl art des +interview +portfolio (Tex Des Fash Inter) (IB 27 pts HL 6 art); BCC +interview +portfolio (Fash Des) (IB 27 pts HL 6 art)

Bolton – 104 pts (Spec Efcts Cost Film TV)

Brighton – BCC–CCC +interview (Fash Drs Hist) (IB 27 pts)

Falmouth – 104–120 pts +interview +portfolio (Fash Des; Fash Photo; Perf Spowr Des; Tex Des)

Lincoln – BCC incl art/des/media st +interview +portfolio (Fash) (IB 28 pts)

Manchester Met – BCC–BBC 104–112 pts +portfolio (Fash Des Tech) (IB 26 pts); BCC–BBC 104–112 pts (Fash Buy Mrchnds; Int Fash Prom) (IB 26 pts)

Northampton – BCC (Fash Mark); BCC incl art/tex +interview +portfolio (Fash; Ftwr Accs; Fash (Tex Fash))

Portsmouth – 104–112 pts +interview +portfolio (Fash Tex Des) (IB 26 pts)

South Wales – BCC incl art des +interview +portfolio (Fash Des) (HL 655–445); BCC–CCD (Fash Mark Rtl Des) (HL 655–445); BCC–CCD incl art des +interview +portfolio (Fash Prom) (HL 655–445)

Ulster – BCC–BBB +portfolio (Tex Art Des Fash) (IB 24 pts HL 12 pts)

96 pts **Arts London (CFash)** – CCC 96 pts +interview +portfolio (Hair Mkup Pros Perf); 96 pts +interview +portfolio (Cstm Perf; Fash PR Comm)

Bolton – 96 pts incl art +interview +portfolio (Tex Surf Des)

Brighton – CCC–BBB +interview +portfolio (Tex Bus St) (IB 32 pts)

Cleveland (CAD) – 96 pts (Tex Surf Des; Body Cont Fash)

Hertfordshire – 96 pts incl art +interview +portfolio (Fash Des; Fash Fash Bus) (HL 44)

London Met – CCC/BC 96 pts (Fash Mark Bus Mgt)

Plymouth (CA) – 96–120 pts +interview +portfolio (Fash; Prtd Tex Des Surf Patt)

Salford – 96–112 pts incl art des +interview +portfolio (Fash Des) (IB 26 pts)

Southampton Solent – 96 pts (Fash courses; Fash Mgt Mark); 96 pts +interview +portfolio (Fash Graph)

80 pts **Bedfordshire** – 80 pts +portfolio (Fash Des)

Bradford (Coll) – 80 pts +interview +portfolio (Tex Surf Des; Fash)

Bucks New – 80–96 pts +interview +portfolio (Fash Des)

Hereford (CA) – 80 pts +interview +portfolio (Tex Des; Jewel Des)

72 pts **Robert Gordon** – BC incl art/des +portfolio (Fash Tex Des) (IB 24 pts)

64 pts **Arts London (CFash)** – CC 64 pts +interview +portfolio (Bspk Tlrg; Cord Fash Bags Accs (Prod Des Innov); Crea Dir Fash; Fash Cont; Fash Des Dev; Fash Des Tech (Mnswr); Fash Des Tech (Wmnswr); Fash Illus; Fash Jewel; Fash Photo; Fash Spowr; Fash Tex courses); CC +interview +portfolio (Cord Ftwr (Prod Des Innov))

Colchester (Inst) – 64 pts +interview +portfolio (Fash Tex)

Ravensbourne – CC +interview +portfolio (Fash; Fash Accs Des ; Fash Prom) (IB 28 pts)

UHI – CC incl Engl +portfolio (Contemp Tex); CC +interview +portfolio (Fn Art Tex)

40 pts and below or other selection criteria (Foundation course, interview and portfolio inspection) Arts London; Arts London (CFash); Arts London (Chelsea CA); Arts London (Wimb CA); Bath Spa; Bolton; Cardiff Met; East London; Hertfordshire; Kent; Kingston; Lincoln; Liverpool John Moores; London Met; Loughborough; Middlesex; Robert Gordon; Southampton (Winchester SA); South Wales; Staffordshire Reg Fed (SURF); Suffolk; UWE Bristol.

Alternative offers

See **Chapter 6** and **Appendix 1** for grades/UCAS Tariff points information for other examinations.

EXAMPLES OF COLLEGES OFFERING COURSES IN THIS SUBJECT FIELD

Check all art colleges. Barnet and Southgate (Coll); Barnfield (Coll); Basingstoke (CT); Bath (Coll); Blackburn (Coll); Blackpool and Fylde (Coll); Bournemouth and Poole (Coll); Bradford (Coll); Bury (Coll); Central Bedfordshire (Coll); Central Campus, Sandwell (Coll); Chelmsford (Coll); City and

Islington (Coll); Doncaster (Coll); Dudley (Coll); East Coast (Coll); Gloucestershire (Coll); Harrogate (Coll); Havering (Coll); HOW (Coll); Hull (Coll); Leicester (Coll); LeSoCo; Liverpool City (Coll); NCC Hackney; Newcastle (Coll); North Warwickshire and Hinckley (Coll); Northbrook Met (Coll); Rotherham (CAT); Sir Gâr (Coll); South City Birmingham (Coll); South Devon (Coll); South Essex (Coll); South Gloucestershire and Stroud (Coll); South Thames (Coll); Tresham (CFHE); Walsall (Coll); West Herts (Coll); West Kent (Coll); Wigan and Leigh (Coll); York (Coll).

CHOOSING YOUR COURSE (SEE ALSO CH.1)
Universities and colleges teaching quality See www.qaa.ac.uk; https://unistats.ac.uk.

Top research universities and colleges (REF 2014) See **Art and Design (General)**.

Examples of sandwich degree courses Arts London; Birmingham City; Brighton; Central Lancashire; Coventry; De Montfort; East London; Hertfordshire; Huddersfield; Manchester Met; Northumbria; Nottingham Trent; Portsmouth; South Wales; Ulster; Westminster; Wolverhampton.

ADMISSIONS INFORMATION
Number of applicants per place (approx) Arts London 5; Arts London (CFash) (Fash Mgt) 20; Bournemouth Arts 4; Central Lancashire 4; Creative Arts 8; De Montfort 5; Derby 4; Heriot-Watt 6; Huddersfield 4; Kingston 5; Leeds Arts 4; Liverpool John Moores 6; Manchester Met 3; Middlesex 5; Northampton 4; Nottingham Trent 8, (Tex Des) 3; Southampton (Winchester SA) 6; Staffordshire 3; Wolverhampton 2.

Advice to applicants and planning the UCAS personal statement A well-written statement is sought, clearly stating an interest in fashion and how prior education and work experience relate to your application. You should describe any visits to exhibitions and, importantly, your views and opinions. Describe any work you have done ('making' and 'doing' skills, if any, for example, pattern cutting, sewing) or work observation in textile firms, fashion houses, even visits to costume departments in theatres can be useful. These contacts and visits should be described in detail, showing your knowledge of the types of fabrics and production processes. Give opinions on trends in haute couture, and show awareness of the work of others. Provide evidence of materials handling (see also **Appendix 3**). Show good knowledge of the contemporary fashion scene. See also **Art and Design (Graphic Design)**.

Misconceptions about this course Some students expect the Fashion degree to include textiles. (Tex) Some applicants feel that it's necessary to have experience in textiles – this is not the case. The qualities sought in the portfolio are analytical drawing, good colour sense and a sensitivity to materials.

Selection interviews Most institutions interview and require a portfolio of work. You should be familiar with current fashion trends and the work of leading designers. **Yes** Bolton, Huddersfield, Leeds Beckett, Liverpool John Moores, Manchester, Northumbria, Salford; **Some** Chester, Westminster; **No** Falmouth, UWE Bristol, West London.

Interview advice and questions Questions mostly originate from student's portfolio. See also **Art and Design (General)** and **Chapter 5**. **Birmingham City** (Tex Des) What do you expect to achieve from a degree in Fashion? **Creative Arts** Describe in detail a specific item in your portfolio and why it was selected.

Reasons for rejection (non-academic) Portfolio work not up to standard. Not enough research. Not articulate at interview. Lack of sense of humour, and inflexibility. Narrow perspective. Lack of resourcefulness, self-motivation and organisation. Complacency, lack of verbal, written and self-presentation skills. Not enough experience in designing or making clothes. See also **Art and Design (General)**.

AFTER-RESULTS ADVICE
Offers to applicants repeating A-levels Same Birmingham City, Bournemouth Arts, Creative Arts, Huddersfield, Manchester Met, Nottingham Trent, South Essex (Coll), Staffordshire.

Check **Chapter 3** for new university admission details and **Chapter 6** on how to read the subject tables.

GRADUATE DESTINATIONS AND EMPLOYMENT (2015/16 HESA)
See **Art and Design (General)**.

Career note See **Art and Design (General)**.

OTHER DEGREE SUBJECTS FOR CONSIDERATION
History of Art; Retail Management; Theatre Design.

ART and DESIGN (FINE ART)

(including **Painting and Printmaking** and **Sculpture and Environmental Art**; see also **Art and Design (Graphic Design), Photography**)

Fine Art courses are essentially practice-based courses encouraging students to find their own direction through additional intellectual and theoretical studies. The work will involve a range of activities which cover painting, illustration and sculpture. Additional studies can also involve electronic media, film, video, photography and print, although course options will vary between institutions. A more specialised study in the field of Sculpture and Environmental Art is offered at Glasgow School of Art, taking sculpture outside art galleries and museums and into the public domain where students focus on drawing, wood and metal fabrication, photography, video, computers and sound. As in the case of most Art degrees, admission to courses usually requires a one-year Foundation Art course before applying.

Useful websites www.artcyclopedia.com; www.nationalgallery.org.uk; www.britisharts.co.uk; www.tate.org.uk; www.creativefuture.org.uk; www.a-n.co.uk/news; www.artscouncil.org.uk

NB The points totals shown to the left of the institutions are for ease of reference only. It must not be assumed that Tariff points are always used by institutions or that they can be substituted for an offer in grades. The level of an offer is not necessarily indicative of the quality of a course.

COURSE OFFERS INFORMATION
Subject requirements/preferences See **Art and Design (General)**.

Your target offers and examples of degree courses
144 pts Oxford – AAA +interview +portfolio (Fn Art) (IB 38 pts HL 666)
136 pts Lancaster – AAB–ABB +portfolio (Fn Art) (IB 35–32 pts HL 16 pts)
    Leeds – AAB +interview +portfolio (Fn Art) (IB 35–34 pts)
    Newcastle – AAB–BBB +interview +portfolio (Fn Art) (IB 35–32 pts HL 555)
128 pts Dundee – ABB incl art des +portfolio (Fn Art) (IB 34 pts HL 665)
    Edinburgh – ABB +portfolio (Fn Art; Illus) (IB 34 pts HL 655)
    Glasgow (SA) – ABB +interview +portfolio (Sculp Env Art; Pntg Prtg; Fn Art Photo)
    London (UCL) – ABB +interview +portfolio (Fn Art) (IB 34 pts HL 16 pts)
    London (UCL/Slade SA) – ABB +interview +portfolio (Fn Art) (IB 34 pts HL 16 pts)
    Loughborough – ABB +interview +portfolio (Fn Art)
120 pts Anglia Ruskin – 120 pts +interview +portfolio (Fn Art) (IB 24 pts)
    Brighton – BBB–CCC 120–96 pts +interview +portfolio (Fn Art Pntg; Fn Art Sculp; Fn Art Crit Prac) (IB 30 pts)
    Cardiff Met – 120 pts +interview +portfolio (Fn Art)
    Huddersfield – BBB 120 pts +interview +portfolio (Contemp Art)
    Leeds Beckett – 120 pts +interview +portfolio (Fn Art) (IB 26 pts)
    Liverpool Hope – BBB–BBC 120–112 pts +interview +portfolio (Fn Art) (IB 26 pts)
    Northumbria – 120–128 pts incl art/photo +interview +portfolio (Fn Art)
    Norwich Arts – BBB incl art/des/media +interview +portfolio (Fn Art) (IB 32 pts)
    Southampton (Winchester SA) – BBB incl art/des +interview +portfolio (Fn Art) (IB 30 pts HL 16 pts)
    Trinity Saint David – 120 pts +interview +portfolio (Fn Art (Std Site Con)) (IB 32 pts)

112 pts **Aberystwyth** – BBC incl art +portfolio (Fn Art; Fn Art Art Hist) (IB 30 pts)
Birmingham City – BBC 112 pts +portfolio (Fn Art) (HL 14 pts)
Bournemouth Arts – BBC–BBB 112–120 pts +interview +portfolio (Fn Art) (IB 30–32 pts)
Central Lancashire – 112 pts +interview +portfolio (Fn Art) (IB 28 pts)
Chester – 112 pts incl art des+Fr +interview +portfolio (Fn Art Fr) (IB 26 pts HL 5 vis arts+Fr)
Coventry – BBC incl art/des (Fn Art; Fn Art Illus) (IB 29 pts)
Creative Arts – 112 pts +portfolio (Fn Art courses)
Cumbria – 112 pts +interview (Fn Art)
De Montfort – 112 pts incl art des +interview +portfolio (Fn Art) (IB 26 pts)
Derby – 112 pts +interview +portfolio (Fn Art)
Gloucestershire – BBC 112 pts +interview +portfolio (Fn Art)
Glyndŵr – 112 pts +portfolio (Fn Art)
Kingston – 112 pts +interview +portfolio (Fn Art)
Leeds Arts – BBC 112 pts +interview +portfolio (Fn Art)
Liverpool John Moores – BBC incl art/des 112 pts +interview +portfolio (Fn Art) (IB 26 pts)
London Met – BBC 112 pts +interview +portfolio (Fn Art)
Manchester Met – 112 pts +interview +portfolio (Fn Art) (IB 26 pts)
Middlesex – 112 pts +interview +portfolio (Fn Art) (IB 28 pts)
Nottingham Trent – BBC 112 pts +portfolio (Fn Art)
Oxford Brookes – BBC incl art +interview +portfolio (Fn Art) (IB 30 pts)
Sheffield Hallam – 112–96 pts incl art des +interview +portfolio (Fn Art)
Southampton Solent – 112 pts +portfolio (Fn Art)
Staffordshire – 112 pts +interview +portfolio (Fn Art)
Sunderland – 112 pts +portfolio (Fn Art)
UWE Bristol – 112 pts +portfolio (Fn Art)
Wolverhampton – BBC 112 pts +portfolio (Fn Art)
104 pts **Bath Spa** – BCC +interview +portfolio (Fn Art) (IB 27 pts HL 6 art)
Chester – BCC–BBC incl art des/fn art +interview +portfolio (Fn Art) (IB 26 pts HL 5 vis arts)
Falmouth – 104–120 pts +interview +portfolio (Fn Art)
Lincoln – BCC incl art/des/media st +interview +portfolio (Fn Art) (IB 28 pts)
Northampton – BCC +interview +portfolio (Fn Art; Fn Art Pntg Drg)
Plymouth – 104 pts +interview +portfolio (Fn Art Art Hist; Fn Art) (IB 26 pts)
Ulster – BCC–BBB +portfolio (Fn Art) (IB 24 pts HL 12 pts)
Worcester – 104 pts +interview +portfolio (Fn Art)
York St John – 104–120 pts +interview +portfolio (Fn Art)
96 pts **Bolton** – 96 pts incl art +interview +portfolio (Fn Art)
Chichester – 96–120 pts incl art/photo/tex +interview +portfolio (Fn Art courses)
East London – 96 pts +interview +portfolio (Fn Art) (IB 24 pts HL 15 pts)
Hertfordshire – 96 pts incl art +interview +portfolio (Fn Art) (HL 44)
Plymouth (CA) – 96–120 pts +interview +portfolio (Fn Art)
Teesside – 96–112 pts +interview +portfolio (Fn Art)
Westminster – CCC/BB +interview +portfolio (Fn Art Mix Media) (IB 26 pts)
80 pts **Bedfordshire** – 80 pts +portfolio (Fn Art)
Hereford (CA) – 80 pts +interview +portfolio (Fn Art)
Reading – 80 pts +Art Fdn +interview +portfolio (Fn Art) (IB 24–35 pts)
64 pts **Colchester (Inst)** – 64 pts +interview +portfolio (Fn Art)
UHI – CC +interview +portfolio (Fn Art Tex; Fn Art)
40 pts **and below or other selection criteria (Foundation course, interview and portfolio inspection)** Arts London; Arts London (Camberwell CA); Arts London (Chelsea CA); Arts London (Wimb CA); Bath Spa; Bedfordshire; Cardiff Met; Central Lancashire; Creative Arts; De Montfort; Glyndŵr; Hertfordshire; Kent; Kingston; London (Gold); Middlesex; Staffordshire Reg Fed (SURF); Trinity Saint David; UWE Bristol.
32 pts **Reading** – 32–136 pts +interview +portfolio (Art courses) (IB 24–35 pts)

Check **Chapter 3** for new university admission details and **Chapter 6** on how to read the subject tables.

Alternative offers
See **Chapter 6** and **Appendix 1** for grades/UCAS Tariff points information for other examinations.

EXAMPLES OF COLLEGES OFFERING COURSES IN THIS SUBJECT FIELD
Most colleges. All are practical workshop courses. Bath (Coll); Blackpool and Fylde (Coll); Bradford (Coll); Bury (Coll); Central Bedfordshire (Coll); City and Islington (Coll); City of Oxford (Coll); Cornwall (Coll); Craven (Coll); Doncaster (Coll); Exeter (Coll); Grimsby (Inst Group); Grŵp Llandrillo Menai; Harrogate (Coll); Havering (Coll); Leicester (Coll); Liverpool City (Coll); Newcastle (Coll); Northbrook Met (Coll); St Helens (Coll); Sheffield (Coll); South Gloucestershire and Stroud (Coll); Stamford New (Coll); Sunderland (Coll); Tyne Coast (Coll); Weymouth (Coll).

CHOOSING YOUR COURSE (SEE ALSO CH.1)
Universities and colleges teaching quality See www.qaa.ac.uk; https://unistats.ac.uk.

Top research universities and colleges (REF 2014) See **Art and Design (General)**.

Examples of sandwich degree courses Coventry; Huddersfield; Ulster; Wolverhampton.

ADMISSIONS INFORMATION
Number of applicants per place (approx) Arts London (Chelsea CA) 5; Arts London (Wimb CA) (Sculp) 3; Bath Spa 8; Birmingham City 6; Bournemouth Arts 5; Cardiff Met 3; Central Lancashire 4; Creative Arts 2; Cumbria 4; De Montfort 5; Derby 4; Dundee 6; Gloucestershire 5; Kingston 9; Lincoln 4; Liverpool John Moores 3; London (Gold) 10; London (UCL) 23; London Met 11; Manchester Met 4; Middlesex 3; Newcastle 8; Northampton 3; Nottingham Trent 5; Sheffield Hallam 4; Solihull (Coll) 4; Southampton (Winchester SA) 6; Staffordshire 3; Sunderland 3; UHI 2; Wirral Met (Coll) 3.

Advice to applicants and planning the UCAS personal statement Since this is a subject area that can be researched easily in art galleries, you should discuss not only your own style of work and your preferred subjects but also your opinions on various art forms, styles and periods. Keep up to date with public opinion on controversial issues. Give your reasons for wishing to pursue a course in Fine Art. Visits to galleries and related hobbies, for example reading, cinema, music, literature should be mentioned. Show the nature of your external involvement in art. (See also **Appendix 3**.) **Oxford** No deferred applications are accepted for this course; successful applicants average 10%.

Misconceptions about this course That Fine Art is simply art and design. Sixth-form applicants are often unaware of the importance of a Foundation Art course before starting a degree programme. **Bournemouth Arts** Applicants need to make the distinction between fine art and illustration.

Selection interviews Most institutions interview and require a portfolio of work. **Yes** Arts London (Chelsea CA), Bolton, Brighton, Cardiff Met, Chichester, Leeds Beckett, Liverpool John Moores, Newcastle, Northumbria, Oxford (10%), Plymouth; **Some** Chester, Cumbria; **No** Falmouth, Kent, York St John.

Interview advice and questions Questions asked on portfolio of work. Be prepared to answer questions on your stated opinions on your UCAS application and on current art trends and controversial topics reported in the press. Discussion covering the applicant's engagement with contemporary fine art practice. Visits to exhibitions, galleries etc. Ambitions for their own work. How do you perceive the world in a visual sense? Who is your favourite living artist and why? See also **Art and Design (General)** and **Chapter 5**.

Reasons for rejection (non-academic) Lack of a fine art specialist portfolio. No intellectual grasp of the subject – only interested in techniques.

AFTER-RESULTS ADVICE
Offers to applicants repeating A-levels Same Anglia Ruskin, Arts London, Birmingham City, Cumbria, Manchester Met, Nottingham Trent, Staffordshire, Sunderland, UHI; **No** Oxford.

GRADUATE DESTINATIONS AND EMPLOYMENT (2015/16 HESA)
Graduates surveyed 2,650 **Employed** 1,015 **In voluntary employment** 110 **In further study** 520
Assumed unemployed 175

Career note See **Art and Design (General)**.

OTHER DEGREE SUBJECTS FOR CONSIDERATION
Art Gallery Management; History of Art; see other **Art and Design** tables.

ART and DESIGN (GENERAL)

(including **Drawing** and **Painting**; see also **Art and Design (3D Design), Art and Design (Graphic Design), Combined and Liberal Arts Courses, Communication Studies/Communication, Drama, Media Studies, Photography**)

Art and Design and all specialisms remain one of the most popular subjects. Many of the courses listed here cover aspects of fine art, graphic or three-dimensional design, but to a less specialised extent than those listed in the other Art and Design tables. Travel and visits to art galleries and museums are strongly recommended by many universities and colleges. Note that for entry to many Art and Design courses it is often necessary to follow an Art and Design Foundation course first: check with your chosen institution.

Art and Design degree courses cover a wide range of subjects. These are grouped together in six tables:

Art and Design (3D Design),
Art and Design (Fashion and Textiles),
Art and Design (Fine Art),
Art and Design (General),
Art and Design (Graphic Design),
Art and Design (Interior, Product and Industrial Design).
(History of Art and Photography are listed in separate tables.)

Useful websites www.artscouncil.org.uk; www.designcouncil.org.uk; www.theatredesign.org.uk; www.arts.ac.uk; www.dandad.org; www.csd.org.uk; www.creativefuture.org.uk

The points total shown to the left of the institutions are for ease of reference only. It must not be assumed that Tariff points are always used by institutions or that they can be substituted for an offer in grades. The level of an offer is not necessarily indicative of the quality of a course.

COURSE OFFERS INFORMATION

Subject requirements/preferences Entry requirements for Art and Design courses vary between institutions and courses (check prospectuses and websites). Most courses require an Art and Design Foundation course and a portfolio of work demonstrating potential and visual awareness. **GCSE** Five subjects at grades A–C (7–4), or a recognised equivalent. **AL** Grades or points may be required. (Des Tech) Design Technology or a physical science may be required or preferred. (Crea Arts courses) Music/art/drama may be required.

Your target offers and examples of degree courses
128 pts Edinburgh – ABB +portfolio (Pntg) (IB 34 pts HL 555)
         Leeds – ABB incl art/des (Art Des) (IB 34 pts HL 16 pts incl 5/6 art/des)
         Ulster – ABB (Interact Multim Des) (IB 27 pts HL 13 pts)
120 pts De Montfort – 120 pts incl art des +interview +portfolio (Gm Art) (IB 30 pts HL 6 art des)
         Huddersfield – BBB 120 pts +interview +portfolio (Contemp Art)
112 pts Birmingham City – BBC 112 pts (Art Des) (HL 14 pts)
         Bournemouth Arts – BBC–BBB 112–120 pts +interview (Crea Evnts Mgt) (IB 30–32 pts)

Check **Chapter 3** for new university admission details and **Chapter 6** on how to read the subject tables.

Coventry – BBC incl art/des +portfolio (Gm Art) (IB 29 pts)
Lincoln – BBC incl art/des 112 pts +interview +portfolio (Des Exhib Musms) (IB 29 pts HL 5 art/des/media st)
Manchester Met – 112 pts +interview (Interact Arts) (IB 26 pts)
Nottingham Trent – BBC 112 pts +portfolio (Decr Arts)
Portsmouth – 112 pts (Comp Animat Vis Efcts) (IB 26 pts)
Staffordshire – BBC 112 pts (Gms Art)
UWE Bristol – 112 pts (Drg Prt) (+interview +portfolio)

104 pts **Bath Spa** – BCC incl art/des +interview +portfolio (Contemp Arts Prac) (IB 27 pts HL 6 art)
Falmouth – 104–120 pts +interview +portfolio (Drg)
South Wales – BCC–CDD +interview +portfolio (Crea Ther Arts) (HL 655–445)
Worcester – 104 pts +interview +portfolio +written work (Art Des)

96 pts **Bolton** – 96 pts +interview +portfolio (Art Des)
Cardiff Met – CCC–BBB 96–120 pts (Arst Des (Mak))
Glasgow Caledonian – CCC incl art des +portfolio (Comp Gms (Art Animat)) (IB 24 pts)
Hertfordshire – 96 pts incl art +interview +portfolio (Des Crfts courses) (HL 44)
Rose Bruford (Coll) – 96 pts (Scnc Arts (Constr Props Pntg))
Salford – 96–112 pts incl art des +interview +portfolio (Vis Arts) (IB 26 pts)
Writtle (UC) – 96 pts +interview +portfolio (Contemp Art Des)

80 pts **Hereford (CA)** – 80 pts +interview +portfolio (Contemp Des Crfts; Illus)
Westminster – BB/CCC +portfolio (Illus Vis Comm)

72 pts **Robert Gordon** – BC incl art/des +portfolio +interview (Pntg) (IB 24 pts); BC +interview/portfolio (Contemp Art Prac) (IB 24 pts)

32 pts **Reading** – 32–136 pts +interview +portfolio (Art courses) (IB 24–35 pts)

Alternative offers
See **Chapter 6** and **Appendix 1** for grades/UCAS Tariff points information for other examinations.

EXAMPLES OF COLLEGES OFFERING COURSES IN THIS SUBJECT FIELD
All art colleges. Banbury and Bicester (Coll); Barnet and Southgate (Coll); Barnsley (Coll); Blackburn (Coll); Blackpool and Fylde (Coll); Bradford (Coll); Brighton Met (Coll); Chelmsford (Coll); Chesterfield (Coll); Chichester (Coll); Cornwall (Coll); Doncaster (Coll); Ealing, Hammersmith and West London (Coll); East Berkshire (Coll); East Coast (Coll); East Surrey (Coll); Exeter (Coll); Furness (Coll); Grimsby (Inst Group); Grŵp Llandrillo Menai; Highbury Portsmouth (Coll); Hugh Baird (Coll); Hull (Coll); Kingston (Coll); London UCK (Coll); Loughborough (Coll); Manchester (Coll); NCC Redbridge; North Notts (Coll); North Warwickshire and Hinckley (Coll); Northumberland (Coll); Norwich City (Coll); Nottingham (Coll); Pembrokeshire (Coll); Peter Symonds (Coll); Portsmouth (Coll); Richmond-upon-Thames (Coll); South Devon (Coll); South Essex (Coll); Southampton City (Coll); Southport (Coll); Stockport (Coll); Sunderland (Coll); Sussex Coast Hastings (Coll); Totton (Coll); Truro and Penwith (Coll); Tyne Coast (Coll); Wakefield (Coll); West Cheshire (Coll); West Herts (Coll); West Kent (Coll); Westminster City (Coll); Wirral Met (Coll); Yeovil (Coll).

CHOOSING YOUR COURSE (SEE ALSO CH.1)
Top research universities and colleges (REF 2014) (Art and Design: History, Practice and Theory) London (Court); Reading (Typo/Graph Comm); St Andrews; Westminster; Essex; Open University; London (UCL) (Hist Art); Manchester; Arts London; Newcastle; York; Birmingham; Lancaster; Leeds (Art); London (SOAS); Sheffield Hallam.

ADMISSIONS INFORMATION
Number of applicants per place (approx) Dundee 6; Manchester Met 10.

Advice to applicants and planning the UCAS personal statement Admissions tutors look for a wide interest in aspects of art and design. Discuss the type of work and the range of media you have explored through your studies to date. Refer to visits to art galleries and museums and give your opinions of the styles of paintings and sculpture, both historical and present day. Mention art-related hobbies. Good drawing skills and sketchbook work, creative and analytical thinking will be needed.

Check **Chapter 3** for new university admission details and **Chapter 6** on how to read the subject tables.

Misconceptions about this course Lincoln (Des Musm Exhib) This is a design course, not a museum course.

Selection interviews Most institutions interview and require a portfolio of work. **Yes** Bath Spa, Bolton, Dundee, Hertfordshire, Huddersfield, Reading, Robert Gordon, South Wales; **Some** Westminster; **No** Lincoln, Staffordshire.

Interview advice and questions Admissions tutors will want to see both breadth and depth in the applicant's work and evidence of strong self-motivation. They will also be interested to see any sketchbooks or notebooks. However, they do not wish to see similar work over and over again! A logical, ordered presentation helps considerably. Large work, especially three-dimensional work, can be presented by way of photographs. Video or film work should be edited to a running time of no more than 15 minutes. Examples of written work may also be provided. Past questions have included: How often do you visit art galleries and exhibitions? Discuss the last exhibition you visited. What are the reactions of your parents to your choice of course and career? Do you think that modern art has anything to contribute to society compared with earlier art? Is a brick a work of art? Show signs of life – no apathy! Be eager and enthusiastic.

Reasons for rejection (non-academic) Lack of enthusiasm for design issues or to acquire design skills. Poorly presented practical work. Lack of interest or enthusiasm in contemporary visual arts. Lack of knowledge and experience of the art and design industry.

GRADUATE DESTINATIONS AND EMPLOYMENT (2015/16 HESA)
Graduates surveyed 27,840 **Employed** 13,295 **In voluntary employment** 1,230 **In further study** 4,510 **Assumed unemployed** 1,715

Career note Many Art and Design courses are linked to specific career paths which are achieved through freelance consultancy work or studio work. Some graduates enter teaching and many find other areas such as retail and management fields. Opportunities for fashion and graphic design specialists exceed those of other areas of art and design. Opportunities in industrial and product design and three-dimensional design are likely to be limited and dependent on the contacts that students establish during their degree courses. Only a very limited number of students committed to painting and sculpture can expect to succeed without seeking alternative employment.

OTHER DEGREE SUBJECTS FOR CONSIDERATION
Animation; Architecture; Art Gallery Management; Communication Studies; Computer Studies; Education; Film Studies; History of Art; Media Studies; Photography; see other **Art and Design** tables.

ART and DESIGN (GRAPHIC DESIGN)

(including **Advertising, Animation, Design, Graphic Communication, Illustration** and **Visual Communication**; see also **Art and Design (Fine Art), Art and Design (General), Film, Radio, Video and TV Studies**)

Graphic Design ranges from the design of websites, books, magazines and newspapers to packaging and advertisements. Visual communication uses symbols as teaching aids and also includes TV graphics. An Art Foundation course is usually taken before entry to degree courses. Graphic Design students are probably the most fortunate in terms of the range of career opportunities open to them on graduation. These include advertising, animation, book and magazine illustration, film, interactive media design, typography, packaging, photography and work in publishing and television. Courses cover the essential element of creative thinking alongside the normal industrial practices of scriptwriting, character design, storyboarding, animation, and sound design.

Useful websites www.lifewire.com/learn-how-graphic-design-4160665; www.graphic-design.com; www.creativefuture.org.uk; www.designcouncil.org.uk

UCAS points Tariff: A* = 56 pts; A = 48 pts; B = 40 pts; C = 32 pts; D = 24 pts; E = 16 pts

NB The points totals shown to the left of the institutions are for ease of reference only. It must not be assumed that Tariff points are always used by institutions or that they can be substituted for an offer in grades. The level of an offer is not necessarily indicative of the quality of a course.

COURSE OFFERS INFORMATION

Subject requirements/preferences See **Art and Design (General).**

Your target offers and examples of degree courses

144 pts Arden – (Graph Des)

136 pts Reading – AAB–ABB +portfolio (Graph Comms) (IB 35–32 pts)

128 pts Dundee – ABB incl art des +interview +portfolio (Animat) (IB 34 pts HL 665); ABB incl art des +portfolio (Graph Des) (IB 34 pts)

East Anglia – ABB (Comp Graph Imag Multim) (IB 32 pts)

Edinburgh – ABB +portfolio (Graph Des; Intermed Art) (IB 34 pts HL 655)

Kent – ABB (Dig Art) (IB 34 pts)

Leeds – ABB incl art/des (Graph Comm Des) (IB 34 pts HL 16 pts incl 5/6 art/vis art/des)

Loughborough – ABB +interview (Graph Comm Illus)

Northumbria – 128–136 pts +interview +portfolio (Graph Des) (HL 444); 128 pts (Comp Sci Animat Graph Vsn) (IB 31 pts)

120 pts Birmingham City – BBB 120 pts (Film Tech Vis Efcts) (IB 32 pts)

Bournemouth – 120–128 pts +interview +portfolio (Comp Animat Arts Des) (IB 31–32 pts HL 655)

Brighton – BBB–CCC +interview +portfolio (Graph Des) (IB 32 pts)

Cardiff Met – 120 pts +interview +portfolio (Graph Comm)

Edge Hill – BBB 120 pts +interview (Animat)

Greenwich – 120 pts +interview +portfolio (Graph Dig Des)

Hertfordshire – 120 pts incl art des +interview +portfolio (3D Comp Animat Modl; 2D Animat Chrctr Dig Media) (HL 44 incl vis art)

Huddersfield – BBB 120 pts +interview +portfolio (Contemp Art Illus; Illus; Graph Des; Animat)

Leeds Beckett – 120 pts +interview +portfolio (Graph Arts Des) (IB 26 pts)

Norwich Arts – BBB incl art/des/media +interview +portfolio (Animat; Graph Comm; Graph Des; Illus; Film Mov Imag Prod) (IB 32 pts)

Southampton (Winchester SA) – BBB incl art/des +interview +portfolio (Graph Arts) (IB 30 pts HL 16 pts)

Trinity Saint David – 120 pts +interview +portfolio (3D Comp Animat; Illus; Graph Des) (IB 32 pts)

112 pts Aberystwyth – BBC (Comp Graph Vsn Gms) (IB 28 pts)

Anglia Ruskin – 112 pts incl art/des/media +interview +portfolio (Illus; Illus Animat) (IB 24 pts); 112 pts incl art/des/media +interview +portfolio (Graph Des) (IB 24 pts)

Birmingham City – BBC 112 pts +portfolio (Vis Comm (Film Animat)) (HL 14 pts)

Bournemouth Arts – BBC–BBB 112–120 pts +interview +portfolio (Animat Prod; Graph Des; Illus; Vis Comm) (IB 30–32 pts)

Central Lancashire – 112 pts +interview +portfolio (Graph Des; Adv) (IB 28 pts)

Coventry – BBC incl art/des +portfolio (Graph Des; Illus Graph; Illus Animat) (IB 29 pts)

Creative Arts – 112 pts +portfolio (Graph Comm; Animat); 112 pts +interview +portfolio (Graph Des)

Cumbria – 112 pts +interview +portfolio (Graph Des; Illus)

East London – 112 pts +interview +portfolio (Animat Illus) (IB 24 pts HL 15 pts)

Edinburgh Napier – BCC incl art/des +interview +portfolio (Graph Des) (IB 28 pts HL 654)

Gloucestershire – BBC 112 pts (Adv); BBC 112 pts +interview (Graph Des)

Glyndŵr – 112 pts +interview +portfolio (Des (Animat Vis Efcts Gm Art); Des (Graph Des Multim))

Hull – 112 pts +interview +portfolio (Dig Des) (IB 28 pts)

Kingston – 112 pts +interview +portfolio (Graph Des)

Leeds Arts – BBC incl art/des 112 pts +interview +portfolio (Animat; Vis Comm; Graph Des)

Lincoln – BBC incl art/des/media st +interview +portfolio (Animat; Graph Des; Illus) (IB 29 pts)

Liverpool John Moores – BBC 112 pts +interview +portfolio (Graph Des Illus) (IB 26 pts)

London Met – BBC 112 pts +interview +portfolio (Graph Des)

Manchester Met – 112 pts +interview +portfolio (Graph Des; Illus Animat) (IB 26 pts)

Middlesex – 112 pts +interview +portfolio (Animat; Graph Des; Illus)

Nottingham Trent – BBC 112 pts +portfolio (Graph Des)

Plymouth – 112 pts +interview +portfolio (Dig Art Tech; Graph Comm Typo; Gm Arts Des) (IB 28 pts)

Portsmouth – 112 pts +interview +portfolio (Animat) (IB 26 pts)

Sheffield Hallam – 112–96 pts +portfolio (Graph Des)

Southampton Solent – 112 pts +portfolio (Animat; Graph Des)

Staffordshire – 112 pts +interview +portfolio (Crtn Cmc Arts; Illus; Graph Des)

Suffolk – BBC +interview +portfolio (Graph Des; Graph Des (Graph Illus)); BBC (Graph Comm Des)

Sunderland – 112 pts +portfolio (Illus Des; Adv Des; Animat Gms Art); 112 pts +interview +portfolio (Graph Des)

Teesside – 112 pts +portfolio (Graph Des)

UWE Bristol – 112 pts +portfolio (Graph Des; Animat)

West London – BBC 112 pts (Gms Des Animat)

Wolverhampton – BBC +portfolio (Vis Comm)

104 pts **Bath Spa** – BCC +interview +portfolio (Graph Comm) (IB 27 pts HL 6 art)

Central Lancashire – 104 pts +interview +portfolio (Animat) (IB 28 pts)

Chester – BCC–BBC +interview +portfolio (Graph Des) (IB 26 pts HL 5 vis arts)

Chichester – 104–120 pts (3D Anim Vis Efcts) (IB 28 pts)

De Montfort – 104 pts incl art des +portfolio (Graph Des; Graph Des Illus; Animat) (IB 24 pts HL 5 art des)

Falmouth – 104–120 pts +interview +portfolio (Animat Vis Efcts; Graph Des; Illus)

Northampton – BCC +interview +portfolio (Graph Comm; Illus)

Sheffield Hallam – 104–96 pts +portfolio (Animat)

South Wales – BCC–CDD incl art des +interview +portfolio (Graph Comm); (Adv Des) (HL 655–445)

Ulster – BCC–BBB +portfolio (Graph Des Illust) (IB 24 pts HL 12 pts); BCC–BBB +interview +portfolio (Animat) (IB 24 pts HL 12 pts)

Worcester – 104 pts +interview +portfolio (Graph Des Multim; Animat)

96 pts **Bolton** – 96 pts +interview +portfolio (Animat Illus)

Derby – 96–112 pts (Animat); 96–112 pts +interview +portfolio (Graph Des; Illus)

East London – 96 pts +interview +portfolio (Graph Des) (IB 24 pts HL 15 pts)

Glasgow Caledonian – CCC incl art des +portfolio (Comp Gms (Art Animat)) (IB 24 pts)

Hertfordshire – 96 pts incl art +interview +portfolio (Graph Des) (HL 44)

Leeds Beckett – 96 pts (Gms Des; Comp Animat Vis Efcts)

Plymouth (CA) – 96–120 pts +interview +portfolio (Gm Arts; Graph Des; Animat; Illus)

Portsmouth – 96–112 pts +interview +portfolio (Illus; Graph Des) (IB 26 pts)

Teesside – 96–112 pts +interview (Comp Gms Des); 96–112 pts +interview +portfolio (Comp Gms Animat; Comp Gms Art)

Westminster – CCC +interview +portfolio (Animat) (IB 26 pts)

West Scotland – CCC (Comp Animat)

York St John – 96–112 pts +interview +portfolio (Graph Des)

88 pts **Canterbury Christ Church** – 88–112 pts (Animat Prod); 88–112 pts +interview +portfolio (Graph Des)

West Scotland – CCD incl art (Comp Animat Arts)

80 pts **Bedfordshire** – 80 pts (Adv Brnd Des); 80 pts +portfolio (Animat; Graph Des)

Blackburn (Coll) – 80 pts +interview +portfolio (Illus Animat)

Bucks New – 80–96 pts +interview +portfolio (Animat Vis Efcts; Crea Adv; Graph Arts)

Hereford (CA) – 80 pts +interview +portfolio (Graph Media Des; Illus)

Westminster – BB/CCC +interview +portfolio (Graph Comm Des); BB/CCC +portfolio (Illus Vis Comm)

64 pts   Colchester (Inst) – 64 pts +interview +portfolio (Graph Des)

Ravensbourne – CC +portfolio (Animat; Dig Adv Des; Mtn Graph) (IB 28 pts); CC +interview +portfolio (Graph Des) (IB 28 pts)

40 pts and below or other selection criteria (Foundation course, interview and portfolio inspection) Arts London; Arts London (Camberwell CA); Arts London (Chelsea CA); Bucks New; Greenwich; Hertfordshire; Kingston; Liverpool John Moores; Loughborough; Oxford Brookes; Southampton (Winchester SA); UWE Bristol.

Alternative offers

See **Chapter 6** and **Appendix 1** for grades/UCAS Tariff points information for other examinations.

EXAMPLES OF COLLEGES OFFERING COURSES IN THIS SUBJECT FIELD

Most colleges. Banbury and Bicester (Coll); Barking and Dagenham (Coll); Barnet and Southgate (Coll); Birmingham Met (Coll); Blackburn (Coll); Bristol City (Coll); Bury (Coll); Canterbury (Coll); Cleveland (CAD); Cornwall (Coll); Craven (Coll); Doncaster (Coll); Durham New (Coll); Exeter (Coll); Farnborough (CT); Harlow (Coll); Havering (Coll); Hugh Baird (Coll); Kirklees (Coll); Leicester (Coll); London UCK (Coll); Milton Keynes (Coll); NCC Redbridge; Newcastle (Coll); Northbrook Met (Coll); Nottingham (Coll); Oldham (Coll); Rotherham (CAT); St Helens (Coll); Sheffield (Coll); South Cheshire (Coll); South Gloucestershire and Stroud (Coll); Southport (Coll); Staffordshire Reg Fed (SURF); Stamford New (Coll); Stockport (Coll); Truro and Penwith (Coll); Tyne Coast (Coll); West Kent (Coll); West Suffolk (Coll); Weston (Coll); Wigan and Leigh (Coll); York (Coll).

CHOOSING YOUR COURSE (SEE ALSO CH.1)

Universities and colleges teaching quality See www.qaa.ac.uk; https://unistats.ac.uk.

Top research universities and colleges (REF 2014) See **Art and Design (General)**.

Examples of sandwich degree courses Aberystwyth; Arts London; Central Lancashire; Coventry; Hertfordshire; Huddersfield; Loughborough; Northumbria; Portsmouth; South Wales; Ulster; Wolverhampton.

ADMISSIONS INFORMATION

Number of applicants per place (approx) Anglia Ruskin (Illus) 3; Arts London 4; Bath Spa 9; Bournemouth Arts 4; Cardiff Met 5; Central Lancashire 5; Colchester (Inst) 3; Creative Arts 5; Derby 4; Edinburgh Napier 10; Hertfordshire 6; Kingston 8; Lincoln 5; Liverpool John Moores 7; Manchester Met 8; Middlesex 3; Northampton 3; Nottingham Trent 6; Ravensbourne 9; Solihull (Coll) 3; Staffordshire 3; Teesside 5; Trinity Saint David 10; Wolverhampton 5.

Advice to applicants and planning the UCAS personal statement Discuss your special interest in this field and any commercial applications that have impressed you. Discuss the work you are enjoying at present and the range of media that you have explored. Show your interests in travel, architecture, the arts, literature, film, current affairs (see also **Appendix 3** for contact details of relevant professional associations). Have an awareness of the place of design in society.

Misconceptions about this course Bath Spa Some students think that illustration is simply 'doing small drawings' and that Graphic Design is a soft option with little academic work. **Bournemouth** You need to have a good mix of artistic and mathematical/technical ability. **Plymouth** These courses also involve typography.

Selection interviews Most institutions interview and require a portfolio of work. **Yes** Bolton, Brighton, Chester, Cumbria, Huddersfield, Leeds Beckett, Liverpool John Moores, Plymouth, Reading, Salford; **Some** Edge Hill, Northumbria; **No** Falmouth, UWE Bristol, West London, York St John.

Interview advice and questions Questions may be asked on recent trends in graphic design from the points of view of methods and designers and, particularly, art and the computer. Questions are usually asked on applicant's portfolio of work. See also **Art and Design (General)** and **Chapter 5**.

Reasons for rejection (non-academic) Not enough work in portfolio. Inability to think imaginatively. Lack of interest in the arts in general. Lack of drive. Tutor's statement indicating problems. Poorly constructed personal statement. Inability to talk about your work. Lack of knowledge about the chosen course. See also **Art and Design (General)**.

AFTER-RESULTS ADVICE
Offers to applicants repeating A-levels Same Bath Spa, Bournemouth Arts, Cardiff Met, Creative Arts, Lincoln, Manchester Met, Nottingham Trent, Staffordshire.

GRADUATE DESTINATIONS AND EMPLOYMENT (2015/16 HESA)
See **Art and Design (General)**.

Career note See **Art and Design (General)**.

OTHER DEGREE SUBJECTS FOR CONSIDERATION
Art Gallery Management; Film and Video Production; History of Art; Multimedia Design, Photography and Digital Imaging. See also other **Art and Design** tables.

ART and DESIGN (INTERIOR, PRODUCT and INDUSTRIAL DESIGN)

(including **Footwear Design, Furniture Design, Interior Design, Product Design, Product Design Technology, Theatre Design** and **Transport Design**; see also **Architecture, Art and Design (3D Design)**)

The field of industrial design is extensive and degree studies are usually preceded by an Art Foundation course. Product Design is one of the most common courses in which technological studies (involving materials and methods of production) are integrated with creative design in the production of a range of household and industrial products. Other courses on offer include Furniture Design, Interior, Theatre, Automotive and Transport Design. It should be noted that some Product Design courses have an engineering bias. Interior Design courses involve architectural considerations and courses will include aspects of building practices, materials, products and finishes. Historical studies of period designs and styles will also be included: see **Subject requirements/preferences** below. These are stimulating courses but graduate opportunities in this field are very limited. Good courses will have good industrial contacts for sandwich courses or shorter work placements – check with course leaders (or students) before applying.

Useful websites www.ergonomics.org.uk; www.creativefuture.org.uk; www.productdesignforums.com; www.carbodydesign.com; http://shoe-design.com; www.bild.org.uk; www.csd.org.uk; www.designcouncil.org.uk; www.theatredesign.org.uk

NB The points totals shown to the left of the institutions are for ease of reference only. It must not be assumed that Tariff points are always used by institutions or that they can be substituted for an offer in grades. The level of an offer is not necessarily indicative of the quality of a course.

COURSE OFFERS INFORMATION
Subject requirements/preferences Interior Architecture Design courses require an art portfolio. **AL** Check Product Design, Industrial Design and Engineering Design course requirements since these will often require mathematics and/or physics.

Your target offers and examples of degree courses
144 pts **Glasgow** – AAA incl maths+phys (Prod Des Eng (MEng)) (IB 38–36 pts HL 666 incl maths+phys)
      Leeds – AAA +interview +portfolio (Prod Des) (IB 35 pts HL 18 pts)

136 pts **Brighton** – AAB–BBC incl tech 136–112 pts +interview +portfolio (Prod Des Tech (Prof Expnc)) (IB 34 pts); AAB–BBC incl tech +interview +portfolio (Spo Prod Des (Prof Expnc); Prod Des (Yr Ind)) (IB 34 pts)

Edinburgh Napier – AAB (3 yr course) BCC (4 yr course) +interview +portfolio (Prod Des) (IB 27 pts HL 654)

Glasgow – AAB incl maths+phys (Prod Des Eng) (IB 38 pts HL 666 incl maths+phys)

Liverpool – AAB/ABB+aEPQ incl maths+sci/des tech (Ind Des (MEng)) (IB 35 pts HL 5 maths+phys)

Nottingham – AAB–ABB incl maths (Prod Des Manuf) (IB 34–32 pts HL 5 maths)

Queen's Belfast – AAB incl maths+sci/des tech (Prod Des Eng (MEng))

Strathclyde – AAB incl maths+phys (4 yr course) BBB (5 yr course) (Prod Des Eng (MEng)) (IB 26 pts HL 5 maths+phys); (Prod Eng Mgt (MEng)) (IB 36 pts HL 5 maths+phys)

128 pts **Aston** – ABB–BBB incl sci/tech (Trans Prod Des) (IB 32 pts)

Brunel – ABB incl art/des/tech+maths/phys +interview +portfolio (Prod Des; Ind Des Tech; Prod Des Eng) (IB 31 pts HL 5 art/des/tech+maths/phys)

Edinburgh – ABB +portfolio (Inter Des; Prod Des) (IB 34 pts HL 555)

Edinburgh Napier – ABB (3 yr course) BCC (4 yr course) +interview +portfolio (Inter Spat Des) (IB 27 pts HL 654)

Glasgow (SA) – ABB +interview +portfolio (Inter Des) (IB 30 pts HL 18 pts); ABB incl lang +portfolio (Prod Des) (IB 30 pts HL 18 pts)

Liverpool – ABB/BBB+aEPQ incl maths+sci/des tech (Ind Des) (IB 33 pts HL 5 maths+phys)

Loughborough – ABB incl des tech/art des +interview +portfolio (Ind Des Tech) (IB 34 pts HL 655 incl des tech/art des); ABB incl maths/phys+des tech/art des +interview +portfolio (Prod Des Tech) (IB 34 pts HL 655 incl maths/phys+des tech/art des)

Northumbria – 128–136 pts +interview +portfolio (Inter Archit) (HL 444)

Oxford Brookes – ABB +interview +portfolio (Inter Archit) (IB 34–32 pts)

Strathclyde – ABB (3 yr course) BBB (4 yr course) (Prod Des Innov) (IB 34 pts HL 5 maths/ phys); (Prod Eng Mgt) (IB 34 pts HL 5 maths+phys)

Sussex – ABB–BBB incl art/des (Prod Des) (IB 32 pts)

UWE Bristol – 128 pts (Inter Archit)

120 pts **Aston** – BBB–ABB incl sci/tech (Ind Prod Des) (IB 32 pts)

Cardiff Met – 120 pts +interview +portfolio (Prod Des)

Coventry – BBB incl art/des +portfolio (Inter Des) (IB 31 pts)

Dundee – BBB incl art/des/sci/tech +portfolio (Prod Des) (IB 30 pts HL 665)

Huddersfield – BBB 120 pts +portfolio (Prod Des); BBB 120 pts +interview +portfolio (Inter Des)

Leeds Beckett – 120 pts incl art/des +interview +portfolio (Inter Archit Des)

London South Bank – BBB +portfolio (Prod Des)

Nottingham Trent – BBB 120 pts +portfolio (Inter Archit Des)

Plymouth – 120 pts +interview +portfolio (3D Des courses) (IB 28 pts)

Queen's Belfast – BBB incl maths+sci/des tech (Prod Des Eng)

Trinity Saint David – 120 pts +interview +portfolio (Auto Des; Prod Des) (IB 32 pts)

Ulster – BBB +portfolio (Prod Furn Des) (IB 26 pts HL 13 pts)

Westminster – BBB +portfolio (Inter Archit) (IB 28 pts)

112 pts **Anglia Ruskin** – 112 pts incl art/des/media +interview +portfolio (Inter Des) (IB 24 pts)

Birmingham City – BBC 112 pts (Prod Furn Des) (HL 14 pts); (Inter Archit Des) (IB 28 pts)

Bournemouth Arts – BBC–BBB 112–120 pts +interview +portfolio (Inter Archit Des) (IB 30–32 pts)

Central Lancashire – 112 pts +interview +portfolio (Prod Des; Inter Des) (IB 28 pts)

Coventry – BBC incl art/des +portfolio (Prod Des) (IB 29 pts)

Creative Arts – 112 pts +portfolio (Prod Des)

De Montfort – 112 pts incl art des +interview +portfolio (Prod Furn Des; Prod Des; Ftwr Des; Furn Des; Inter Des) (IB 26 pts)

Kingston – 112 pts incl art des +portfolio (Prod Furn Des; Inter Des)

Lincoln – BBC incl art/des/media st +interview +portfolio (Inter Archit Des; Prod Des) (IB 29 pts)

London Met – BBC 112 pts +interview +portfolio (Inter Archit Des; Furn Prod Des)

Manchester Met – 112 pts +interview +portfolio (Inter Des) (IB 26 pts)

Middlesex – 112 pts +interview +portfolio (Inter Des)

Nottingham Trent – BBC 112 pts +portfolio (Thea Des); BBC 112 pts +interview +portfolio (Furn Prod Des; Prod Des)

Portsmouth – 112–120 pts (Inter Archit Des) (IB 26 pts)

Sheffield Hallam – 112 pts incl art des +interview +portfolio (Prod Des (Furn)); 112–96 pts +interview +portfolio (Inter Des; Prod Des)

Southampton Solent – 112 pts +interview +portfolio (Prod Des; Inter Des Decr)

Staffordshire – BBC 112 pts +interview +portfolio (Prod Des); 112 pts +interview +portfolio (Trans Des)

Suffolk – BBC +interview +portfolio (Inter Archit Des); BBC (App Inter Des)

Teesside – 112 pts +portfolio (Prod Des; Inter Des)

UWE Bristol – 112 pts +portfolio (Prod Des; Prod Des Tech; Inter Des)

Wolverhampton – BBC (Inter Des; Prod Des)

104 pts **Bournemouth** – 104–120 pts +interview (Prod Des; Ind Des) (IB 28–31 pts HL 55)

Falmouth – 104–120 pts +interview +portfolio (Inter Des)

Leeds Beckett – 104 pts +interview +portfolio (Des Prod)

Manchester Met – BCC–BBC incl maths/tech/sci 104–112 pts (Prod Des Tech) (IB 26 pts)

Northampton – BCC +interview +portfolio (Inter Des); BCC incl art/des +interview +portfolio (Prod Des)

South Wales – BCC–CDD incl art des +interview +portfolio (Inter Des) (HL 445–655)

96 pts **Chichester** – CCC (Prod Des) (IB 28 pts)

Derby – 96–112 pts incl art des/des tech +interview +portfolio (Prod Des)

Dundee – CCC–BCC incl art/des +portfolio (Inter Env Des) (IB 30 pts HL 555)

East London – 96 pts incl art des +interview +portfolio (Inter Des; Prod Des) (IB 25 pts HL 15 pts)

Hertfordshire – 96 pts incl art +interview +portfolio (Inter Archit Des) (HL 44); 96 pts incl art/des tech/eng +interview +portfolio (Prod Ind Des) (HL 44); (Prod Des) (IB 24 pts HL 44)

Portsmouth – 96–120 pts (Prod Des Innov) (IB 26 pts)

Rose Bruford (Coll) – 96 pts (Ltg Des)

Salford – 96–112 pts incl art des/tech +interview +portfolio (Inter Des) (IB 29 pts)

York St John – 96–112 pts +interview +portfolio (Prod Des; Inter Des)

80 pts **Bangor** – 80–96 pts (Prod Des)

Bedfordshire – 80 pts (Inter Des Rtl Brnd)

64 pts **Liverpool (LIPA)** – CC 64 pts +interview +portfolio (Thea Perf Des; Thea Perf Tech)

London (Royal Central Sch SpDr) – 64–120 pts +interview+portfolio (Thea Prac (Prod Ltg)); 64–120 pts +interview +portfolio (Thea Prac (Prop Mak); Thea Prac (Scnc Art); Thea Prac (Scnc Constr)); 64–120 pts (Thea Prac (Thea Ltg Des))

London Regent's – CC +interview +portfolio (Inter Des)

Ravensbourne – CC (Des Prod; Inter Des Env Archit) (IB 28 pts)

40 pts and below or other selection criteria (Foundation course, interview and portfolio inspection) Arts London; Arts London (Chelsea CA); Arts London (Wimb CA); Bath Spa; Bournemouth Arts; Brighton; Heriot-Watt; Kingston; Southampton Solent.

Alternative offers
See **Chapter 6** and **Appendix 1** for grades/UCAS Tariff points information for other examinations.

EXAMPLES OF COLLEGES OFFERING COURSES IN THIS SUBJECT FIELD
Accrington and Rossendale (Coll); Banbury and Bicester (Coll); Barking and Dagenham (Coll); Bradford (Coll); Bury (Coll); Calderdale (Coll); Chichester (Coll); Doncaster (Coll); East Riding (Coll); Gloucestershire (Coll); Grimsby (Inst Group); Harrogate (Coll); Hartlepool (CFE); Havering (Coll); Hull

(Coll); Manchester (Coll); Moulton (Coll); Newcastle (Coll); North Warwickshire and Hinckley (Coll); Sir Gâr (Coll); South Essex (Coll); Stockport (Coll); Truro and Penwith (Coll); West Suffolk (Coll).

CHOOSING YOUR COURSE (SEE ALSO CH.1)

Universities and colleges teaching quality See www.qaa.ac.uk; https://unistats.ac.uk.

Top research universities and colleges (REF 2014) See **Art and Design (General)**.

Examples of sandwich degree courses Aston; Bournemouth; Brighton; Brunel; Coventry; De Montfort; Huddersfield; Lincoln; London South Bank; Loughborough; Manchester Met; Middlesex; Nottingham Trent; Portsmouth; Queen's Belfast; Sheffield Hallam; Sussex; UWE Bristol; Wolverhampton.

ADMISSIONS INFORMATION

Number of applicants per place (approx) Arts London 2; Arts London (Chelsea CA) 2; Aston 6; Bath Spa 4; Birmingham City (Inter Des) 9; Cardiff Met 6; Central Lancashire 7; Creative Arts 4; De Montfort 5; Derby 4; Edinburgh Napier 5; Manchester Met 2; Northampton (Prod Des) 2; Nottingham Trent (Inter Archit Des) 7, (Prod Des) 5; Ravensbourne (Inter Des) 4; Salford 6; Staffordshire 3; Teesside 3; Trinity Saint David 3.

Advice to applicants and planning the UCAS personal statement Your knowledge of design in all fields should be described, including any special interests you may have, for example in domestic, rail and road aspects of design, and visits to exhibitions, motor shows. **School/college reference:** Tutors should make it clear that the applicant's knowledge, experience and attitude match the chosen course – not simply higher education in general. Admissions tutors look for knowledge of interior design and interior architecture, experience in three-dimensional design projects (which include problem-solving and sculptural demands), model-making experience in diverse materials, experience with two-dimensional illustration and colour work, and computer skills. Knowledge of computer-aided design (CAD) and photography is also helpful. See also **Art and Design (Graphic Design)**.

Misconceptions about this course Theatre Design is sometimes confused with Theatre Architecture or an academic course in Theatre Studies. **Birmingham City** (Inter Des) Some applicants believe that it is an interior decorating course (carpets and curtains).

Selection interviews Most institutions will interview and require a portfolio of work. **Yes** Bournemouth, Brunel, Cardiff Met, Chester, Dundee, Huddersfield, Northumbria, Salford, Staffordshire, Sussex; **Some** UWE Bristol; **No** Falmouth, York St John.

Interview advice and questions Applicants' portfolios of artwork form an important talking-point throughout the interview. Applicants should be able to discuss examples of current design and new developments in the field and answer questions on the aspects of industrial design which interest them. See also **Art and Design (General)** and **Chapter 5**. **Creative Arts** No tests. Discuss any visits to modern buildings and new developments, eg British Museum Great Court or the Louvre Pyramid.

Reasons for rejection (non-academic) Not hungry enough! Mature students without formal qualifications may not be able to demonstrate the necessary mathematical or engineering skills. Poor quality and organisation of portfolio. Lack of interest. Inappropriate dress. Lack of enthusiasm. Insufficient portfolio work (eg exercises instead of projects). Lack of historical knowledge of interior design. Weak oral communication. See also **Art and Design (General)**. **Creative Arts** Not enough three-dimensional model-making. Poor sketching and drawing.

AFTER-RESULTS ADVICE

Offers to applicants repeating A-levels Same Birmingham City, Creative Arts, Nottingham Trent, Salford, Staffordshire.

GRADUATE DESTINATIONS AND EMPLOYMENT (2015/16 HESA)

See **Art and Design (General)**.

Career note See **Art and Design (General)**.

OTHER DEGREE SUBJECTS FOR CONSIDERATION
Architectural Studies; Architecture; Art Gallery Management; Design (Manufacturing Systems); History of Art; Manufacturing Engineering; Multimedia and Communication Design and subjects in other **Art and Design** tables.

ASIA-PACIFIC STUDIES

(including **East Asian Studies** and **South Asian Studies**; see also **Chinese, Japanese, Languages**)

These courses focus on the study of the cultures, the politics, economic issues and the languages of this region of the world, such as Korean, Sanskrit, Thai and Vietnamese. Leeds offers 12 Asia-Pacific Studies Joint Honours combinations. Work experience during undergraduate years will help students to focus their interests. Many courses have a language bias or are taught jointly with other subjects.

Useful websites www.dur.ac.uk/oriental.museum; http://bacsuk.org.uk

NB The points totals shown to the left of the institutions are for ease of reference only. It must not be assumed that Tariff points are always used by institutions or that they can be substituted for an offer in grades. The level of an offer is not necessarily indicative of the quality of a course.

COURSE OFFERS INFORMATION
Subject requirements/preferences GCSE A language at grade A–C (7–4) may be required. **AL** A language may be required.

Your target offers and examples of degree courses
152 pts **Cambridge** – A*AA +interview +AMESAA (As Mid E St) (IB 40–42 pts HL 776)
144 pts **Oxford** – AAA +interview +OLAT (Orntl St) (IB 39 pts HL 666)
128 pts **Leeds** – ABB (As Pacif St (Int); As Pacif St; Int Rel Thai St) (IB 34 pts HL 16 pts)
　　　　　London (SOAS) – ABB (S As St; SE As St courses; Viet Comb Hons) (IB 35 pts HL 665)
　　　　　Sheffield – ABB–BBB+bEPQ (Kor St Jap; Jap St Comb Hons; E As St; Jap St; Kor St) (IB 33 pts)
112 pts **Central Lancashire** – 112–128 pts (As Pacif St) (IB 28 pts)

Alternative offers
See **Chapter 6** and **Appendix 1** for grades/UCAS Tariff points information for other examinations.

CHOOSING YOUR COURSE (SEE ALSO CH.1)
Universities and colleges teaching quality See www.qaa.ac.uk; https://unistats.ac.uk.

Top research universities and colleges (REF 2014) See **Languages**.

Examples of sandwich degree courses Central Lancashire.

ADMISSIONS INFORMATION
Number of applicants per place (approx) London (SOAS) 4.

Advice to applicants and planning the UCAS personal statement Connections with, and visits to, South and South East Asia should be mentioned. You should give some indication of what impressed you and your reasons for wishing to study these subjects. An awareness of the geography, culture and politics of the area should also be shown on the UCAS application. Show your skills in learning a foreign language (if choosing a language course), interest in current affairs of the region, experience of travel and self-discipline.

Selection interviews Yes Cambridge, Oxford (Orntl St) 24%.

Interview advice and questions General questions are usually asked that relate to applicants' reasons for choosing degree courses in this subject area and to their background knowledge of the various cultures. See also **Chapter 5**.

GRADUATE DESTINATIONS AND EMPLOYMENT (2015/16 HESA)

South Asian Studies graduates surveyed 5 **Employed** 0 **In voluntary employment** 0 **In further study** 0 **Assumed unemployed** 0

Other Asian Studies graduates surveyed 65 **Employed** 25 **In voluntary employment** 0 **In further study** 15 **Assumed unemployed** 10

Career note Graduates enter a wide range of careers covering business and administration, retail work, education, transport, finance, community and social services. Work experience during university often helps students make decisions about their future career plans. Graduates may have opportunities for using their language skills in a range of occupations.

OTHER DEGREE SUBJECTS FOR CONSIDERATION

Anthropology; Development Studies; Far Eastern Languages; Geography; History; International Relations; Politics; Social Studies.

ASTRONOMY and ASTROPHYSICS

(including **Planetary Science with Astronomy** and **Space Science and Robotics**; see also **Geology/ Geological Sciences, Physics**)

All Astronomy-related degrees are built on a core of mathematics and physics which, in the first two years, is augmented by an introduction to the theory and practice of astronomy or astrophysics. Astronomy emphasises observational aspects of the science and includes a study of the planetary system whilst Astrophysics tends to pursue the subject from a more theoretical standpoint. Some universities have onsite observatories (Central Lancashire and Lancaster). Courses often combine Mathematics or Physics with Astronomy.

Useful websites www.ras.org.uk; www.scicentral.com; www.iop.org; www.britastro.org

NB The points totals shown to the left of the institutions are for ease of reference only. It must not be assumed that Tariff points are always used by institutions or that they can be substituted for an offer in grades. The level of an offer is not necessarily indicative of the quality of a course.

COURSE OFFERS INFORMATION

Subject requirements/preferences GCSE English and a foreign language may be required by some universities; specified grades may be stipulated for some subjects. **AL** Mathematics and physics usually required.

Your target offers and examples of degree courses

160 pts **Cambridge** – A*A*A incl sci/maths +interview +NSAA (Nat Sci (Astro)) (IB 40–42 pts HL 776)

Durham – A*A*A incl maths+phys (Phys Astron (MPhys)) (IB 38 pts HL 776 incl maths+phys)

Manchester – A*A*A–A*AA incl maths+phys (Phys Astro) (IB 37 pts HL 776–766 incl maths+phys)

152 pts **Birmingham** – A*AA incl maths+phys (Phys Astro) (IB 32 pts HL 766 incl 7 maths/phys)

Bristol – A*AA–AAB incl maths+phys (Phys Astro) (IB 38–34 pts HL 6 maths+phys)

Exeter – A*AA–AAB incl maths+sci (Nat Sci) (IB 38–34 pts HL 5 maths+sci); A*AA–AAB incl maths+phys +interview (Phys Astro (MPhys)) (IB 38–34 pts HL 6 maths/phys)

Nottingham – A*AA–AAA incl maths+phys (Phys Theor Astro; Phys Astron) (IB 36 pts HL 666 incl maths+phys)

144 pts **Cardiff** – AAA–ABB incl maths+phys (Astro) (IB 34–32 pts HL 6 maths+phys); AAA–AAB incl maths+phys (Astro MPhys) (IB 34–32 pts HL 6 maths+phys); (Phys Astron (MPhys)) (IB 36–34 pts HL 6 maths+phys)

Edinburgh – AAA incl maths+phys (Astro) (IB 37 pts HL 666)

Lancaster – AAA incl maths+phys (Phys Astro Cosmo (MPhys)) (IB 36 pts HL 16 pts incl maths/phys); (Phys Ptcl Phys Cosmo (MPhys)) (IB 36 pts HL 16 pts incl maths+phys)
London (RH) – AAA–ABB incl maths+phys +interview (Astro) (IB 32 pts HL 6 maths+phys)
London (UCL) – AAA incl maths+phys (Astro) (IB 38 pts HL 6 maths+phys)
St Andrews – AAA incl maths+phys (Astro) (IB 38 pts HL 6 maths+phys)
Sussex – AAA incl maths+phys (Astro) (IB 35 pts HL 6 maths+phys)

136 pts **Cardiff** – AAB–ABB incl maths+phys (Phys Astron) (IB 34–30 pts HL 6 maths+phys)
Glasgow – AAB–BBB incl maths+phys (Astron; Phys Astro) (IB 36 pts HL 665 incl 6 maths+phys)
Lancaster – AAB incl maths+phys (Phys Astro Cosmo; Phys Ptcl Phys Cosmo) (IB 35 pts HL 16 pts)
Leeds – AAB incl maths+phys (Phys Astro) (IB 35 pts HL 16 pts incl 5 maths+phys)
Leicester – AAB incl maths+phys (Phys Spc Sci) (IB 32 pts HL 5 maths+phys); (Phys Astro) (IB 32 pts)
London (QM) – AAB incl maths+phys (Astro (MSci)) (IB 34 pts HL 6 maths+phys)
Sheffield – AAB incl maths+phys (Phys Astro) (IB 35 pts HL 6 maths+phys)
Sussex – AAB–ABB incl maths+phys (Phys Astro) (IB 32 pts HL 5 maths+phys)
Swansea – AAB–BBB incl maths+phys (Phys Ptcl Phys Cosmo) (IB 34–32 pts HL 6 maths 6/5 phys)
York – AAB incl maths+phys +interview (Phys Astro) (IB 36 pts HL 6 maths+phys)

128 pts **Hertfordshire** – 128 pts incl maths+phys (Astro) (HL 555 incl maths+phys)
Kingston – 128–152 pts incl maths+sci (Aerosp Eng Astnaut Spc Tech (MEng))
Liverpool – ABB incl maths+phys (Phys Astron) (IB 33 pts HL 6 maths+phys)
Liverpool John Moores – ABB incl maths+phys 128 pts (Phys Astron)
London (QM) – ABB incl maths+phys (Astro) (IB 32 pts HL 6/5 maths+phys 6/5 phys+maths)
Loughborough – ABB incl maths+phys (Phys Astro Cosmo) (IB 34 pts)
Manchester – ABB incl maths/phys (Geol Planet Sci) (IB 33 pts HL 5 maths/phys)
Surrey – ABB incl maths+phys (Phys Astron; Phys Nucl Astro) (IB 32 pts)

120 pts **Central Lancashire** – 120 pts incl maths+phys (Astro) (IB 30 pts)
Kent – BBB incl maths+phys (Phys Astro) (IB 34 pts HL 5 maths+phys); BBB incl maths+phys (Astron Spc Sci Astro) (IB 34 pts)
London (Birk) – 120 pts (Planet Sci Astron)
Queen's Belfast – BBB incl maths+phys (Phys Astro)

112 pts **Aberystwyth** – BBC incl math+phys/comp sci (Spc Sci Robot) (IB 28 pts HL 5 maths+5 phys/comp sci)
Hull – 112 pts incl maths+phys (Phys Astro) (IB 28 pts HL 5 maths+phys)
Keele – BBC incl maths+phys (Astro Comb Hons) (IB 30 pts HL 5 maths+5/4 phys)
Kingston – 112–144 pts incl maths+sci (Aerosp Eng Astnaut Spc Tech)
Nottingham Trent – 112 pts incl maths+phys (Phys Astro)

Alternative offers
See **Chapter 6** and **Appendix 1** for grades/UCAS Tariff points information for other examinations.

CHOOSING YOUR COURSE (SEE ALSO CH.1)

Universities and colleges teaching quality See www.qaa.ac.uk; https://unistats.ac.uk.

Top research universities and colleges (REF 2014) See **Physics**.

Examples of sandwich degree courses Cardiff; Hertfordshire; Surrey.

ADMISSIONS INFORMATION

Number of applicants per place (approx) Cardiff 6; Durham 5; Hertfordshire 5; London (QM) 6; London (RH) 5; London (UCL) 7; Southampton 6.

Advice to applicants and planning the UCAS personal statement Books and magazines you have read on astronomy and astrophysics are an obvious source of information. Describe your interests and why you have chosen this subject. Visits to observatories would also be important. (See also **Appendix 3**.)

Misconceptions about this course Career opportunities are not as limited as some students think. These courses involve an extensive study of maths and physics, opening many opportunities for graduates such as geodesy, rocket and satellite studies and engineering specialisms.

Selection interviews Yes Cambridge; **No** Cardiff, London (QM), London (UCL).

Interview advice and questions You will probably be questioned on your study of physics and the aspects of the subject you most enjoy. Questions in the past have included: Can you name a recent development in physics which will be important in the future? Describe a physics experiment, indicating any errors and exactly what it was intended to prove. Explain weightlessness. What is a black hole? What are the latest discoveries in space? See also **Chapter 5**.

AFTER-RESULTS ADVICE
Offers to applicants repeating A-levels Higher St Andrews; **Same** Cardiff, Durham, London (UCL); **No** Cambridge.

GRADUATE DESTINATIONS AND EMPLOYMENT (2015/16 HESA)
Graduates surveyed 320 **Employed** 110 **In voluntary employment** 0 **In further study** 105 **Assumed unemployed** 30

Career note The number of posts for professional astronomers is limited although some technological posts are occasionally offered in observatories. However, degree courses include extensive mathematics and physics so many graduates can look towards related fields including telecommunications and electronics.

OTHER DEGREE SUBJECTS FOR CONSIDERATION
Aeronautical/Aerospace Engineering; Computer Science; Earth Sciences; Geology; Geophysics; Mathematics; Meteorology; Mineral Sciences; Oceanography; Physics.

BIOCHEMISTRY
(see also Biological Sciences, Chemistry, Food Science/Studies and Technology, Pharmacy and Pharmaceutical Sciences)

Biochemistry is the study of life at molecular level – how genes and proteins regulate cells, tissues and ultimately whole organisms – you! It's a subject which provides the key to understanding how diseases arise and how they can be treated, it is the core of many areas of biology and it is responsible for a large number of breakthroughs in medicine and biotechnology. At Newcastle, Year 1 of the course consists of modules in cell biology, biochemistry, microbiology and immunology, genetics, pharmacology and physiology with transfers between degrees possible at the end of the year. This is a pattern reflected in many other university courses. Many courses also allow for a placement in industry in the UK or in Europe or North America.

Useful websites www.biochemistry.org; www.bioworld.com; www.annualreviews.org; www.ibms.org; www.acb.org.uk; see also **Biological Sciences** and **Biology**.

NB The points totals shown to the left of the institutions are for ease of reference only. It must not be assumed that Tariff points are always used by institutions or that they can be substituted for an offer in grades. The level of an offer is not necessarily indicative of the quality of a course.

COURSE OFFERS INFORMATION
Subject requirements/preferences GCSE English, mathematics and science usually required; leading universities often stipulate A–B grades (7–5/6). **AL** Chemistry required and biology usually preferred by most universities; one or two mathematics/science subjects usually required.

Check **Chapter 3** for new university admission details and **Chapter 6** on how to read the subject tables.

Your target offers and examples of degree courses

160 pts Cambridge – A*A*A incl sci/maths +interview +NSAA (Nat Sci (Bioch)) (IB 40–42 pts HL 776)
152 pts Oxford – A*AA incl maths/sci +interview (Bioch (Mol Cell)) (IB 39 pts HL 766 incl 7 chem)
York – A*AA–AAA incl chem+sci/maths +interview (Chem Biol Medcnl Chem) (IB 36–35 pts HL 6 chem+sci/maths)
144 pts Bath – AAA/A*AB incl chem+sci/maths (Bioch) (IB 36 pts HL 6 chem+biol)
Bristol – AAA–AAB incl chem+sci/maths (Bioch Med Bioch; Bioch) (IB 36–32 pts HL 6 chem+sci/maths); AAA–ABB incl chem+sci/maths (Bioch Mol Biol Biotech) (IB 36–32 pts HL 6 chem+sci/maths)
Edinburgh – AAA incl biol+chem (Bioch) (IB 37 pts HL 666)
Imperial London – AAA–A*AA incl chem+sci/maths (Bioch; Bioch (Yr Ind/Rsch)) (IB 39 pts HL 6 chem+biol/maths); (Bioch courses) (IB 39 pts HL 6 chem+sci/maths)
Leeds – AAA–AAB incl chem+sci (Bioch; Med Bioch) (IB 35–34 pts HL 18–16 pts incl 6 chem+sci)
London (UCL) – AAA incl chem+sci/maths (Bioch) (IB 38 pts HL 6 chem 5 sci/maths)
Manchester – AAA–ABB incl chem+sci/maths +interview (Bioch (Yr Ind); Bioch; Med Bioch) (IB 37–32 pts HL 5/6 chem+sci)
Newcastle – AAA–AAB incl biol/chem+maths/sci (Bioch) (IB 35–34 pts HL 5 biol/chem+sci)
Sheffield – AAA–AAB incl sci (Med Bioch) (IB 36–34 pts HL 6 chem); AAA–AAB incl chem+sci (Bioch; Bioch Comb Hons) (IB 36–34 pts HL 6 chem+sci)
York – AAA–AAB incl chem+sci/maths (Bioch) (IB 36–35 pts HL 6 chem+biol/phys)
136 pts Birmingham – AAB incl chem+sci (Bioch (Genet); Bioch; Med Bioch) (IB 32 pts HL 665)
Cardiff – AAB–ABB incl biol+sci (Bioch) (IB 34 pts HL 6 biol+chem)
Dundee – AAB incl biol+chem (Bioch) (IB 30 pts HL 555)
East Anglia – AAB incl chem+maths/sci (Bioch (Yr Ind)) (IB 33 pts HL 6 chem+sci/maths)
Exeter – AAB–ABB incl biol+chem (Bioch) (IB 34–32 pts HL 5 biol+chem)
Glasgow – AAB incl biol/chem (Bioch) (IB 36 pts)
Lancaster – AAB incl chem+sci (Bioch Genet) (IB 35 pts HL 16 pts incl 6 chem+sci); (Bioch) (IB 35 pts HL 6 chem+sci/maths)
Leicester – AAB–ABB/BBB+bEPQ incl sci/maths (Biol Sci (Bioch)) (IB 32–30 pts HL 66 sci); AAB–ABB/BBB+bEPQ incl chem+sci/maths (Med Bioch) (IB 32–30 pts HL 6 chem 6 sci/maths)
London (King's) – AAB incl chem+biol (Bioch) (IB 35 pts HL 665 incl chem+biol)
Loughborough – AAB incl chem (Bioch) (IB 35 pts HL 665)
Nottingham – AAB incl chem+sci (Bioch Mol Med; Bioch; Bioch Genet; Bioch Biol Chem) (IB 34 pts HL 5/6 chem+sci)
St Andrews – AAB incl biol+sci/maths (Bioch) (IB 35 pts)
Southampton – AAB incl chem+sci (Bioch) (IB 34 pts HL 6 chem+sci)
Sussex – AAB–ABB incl biol+chem (Bioch) (IB 32 pts HL 5 biol+chem)
Swansea – AAB–BBB incl biol+chem 136–120 pts (Bioch; Bioch Genet) (IB 33–32 pts)
128 pts Aston – ABB–BBB incl biol (Biol Sci (Cell Mol Biol)) (IB 32 pts HL 6 biol)
East Anglia – ABB incl chem+sci/maths (Bioch) (IB 32 pts HL 5 chem+maths/sci)
Heriot-Watt – ABB incl chem+maths (3 yr course) BBB incl chem (4 yr course) (Chem Bioch (MChem)) (IB 35 pts (3 yr course) 30 pts (4 yr course) HL 6 chem+maths (3 yr course) 5 chem (4 yr course))
Keele – ABB incl chem+sci (Bioch) (IB 34 pts HL 6 chem/sci)
Liverpool – ABB incl biol+chem (Bioch) (IB 33 pts HL 6/5 biol/chem)
London (QM) – ABB incl chem (Bioch) (IB 34 pts HL 6/5 chem)
London (RH) – ABB–BBB incl biol+chem (Bioch; Med Bioch) (IB 32 pts HL 555 incl biol+chem); (Mol Biol) (IB 32 pts HL 555)
Reading – ABB–BBB incl biol+chem (Bioch) (IB 32–30 pts HL 5 biol+chem)
Surrey – ABB incl biol+sci (Bioch) (IB 32 pts)
Warwick – ABB incl biol+chem (Bioch) (IB 34 pts HL 5 biol+chem)
120 pts Aberdeen – BBB incl maths/sci (Bioch courses) (IB 32 pts HL 5 maths/sci)
Brunel – BBB incl sci (Biomed Sci (Bioch)) (IB 30 pts HL 5 sci)

Keele – ABC/BBB incl chem+sci (Bioch Comb Hons) (IB 32 pts HL 6 sci/maths)
Kent – BBB incl chem+biol (Bioch) (IB 34 pts HL 5 chem+biol)
Lincoln – BBB incl biol/chem (Bioch) (IB 30 pts HL 5 biol/chem)
Nottingham Trent – BBB incl biol 120 pts (Bioch)
Queen's Belfast – BBB–ABB incl chem+sci/maths (Bioch)
Reading – BBB–CCC (Biochem Fdn)
Strathclyde – BBB incl biol+chem (Bioch courses) (IB 34 pts HL 55 sci)

112 pts **Aberystwyth** – BBC–BBB incl chem (Genet Bioch) (IB 30 pts HL 5 chem)
Chester – 112 pts incl chem (Biochem) (IB 26 pts HL 5 chem)
East London – 112 pts incl biol/chem (Biotech Bioch) (IB 25 pts HL 15 pts incl biol+chem)
Huddersfield – BBC incl chem+sci 112 pts (Bioch); BBC incl sci 112 pts (Med Bioch)
Portsmouth – 112 pts incl biol+chem (Bioch) (IB 30 pts HL 17 pts incl 6 biol+chem)
Westminster – BBC incl sci (Bioch) (IB 26 pts HL 4 sci)

104 pts **Aberystwyth** – BCC–BBC incl chem (Bioch) (IB 30 pts HL 5 chem)
Essex – BCC incl chem+sci/maths (Bioch) (IB 28 pts HL 5 chem+sci/maths)
Hertfordshire 104 pts incl chem+sci (Bioch; Bioch (St Abrd)) (HL 4 biol/chem)
Kingston – 104–112 pts incl chem/biol+sci (Bioch; Med Bioch)
Liverpool John Moores – BCC 104 pts incl chem/biol (Bioch) (IB 24 pts)
Salford – 104–120 pts incl biol+chem (Bioch) (IB 28 pts)

96 pts **London Met** – CCC 96 pts (Bioch)
Sheffield Hallam – 96 pts incl biol+chem (Bioch)
Worcester – 96–104 pts incl biol+chem (Bioch)

80 pts **Wolverhampton** – BB/CDD incl biol/chem (Bioch)

Alternative offers
See **Chapter 6** and **Appendix 1** for grades/UCAS Tariff points information for other examinations.

CHOOSING YOUR COURSE (SEE ALSO CH.1)

Universities and colleges teaching quality See www.qaa.ac.uk; https://unistats.ac.uk.

Top research universities and colleges (REF 2014) See **Biological Sciences**.

Examples of sandwich degree courses Aston; Bath; Bristol; Brunel; Cardiff; East London; Essex; Hertfordshire; Huddersfield; Imperial London; Kent; Kingston; Leeds; Lincoln; Liverpool John Moores; Manchester; Nottingham Trent; Queen's Belfast; Sheffield Hallam; Sussex; York.

ADMISSIONS INFORMATION

Number of applicants per place (approx) Bath 10; Birmingham 5; Bradford 7; Bristol 7; Cardiff 6; Dundee 8; East Anglia 5; East London 5; Edinburgh 8; Essex 5; Imperial London 6; Keele 7; Leeds 10; Leicester (Med Bioch) 5; London (RH) 5; London (UCL) 8; Nottingham 10; Salford 4; Southampton 8; Strathclyde 7; Warwick 6; York 6.

Advice to applicants and planning the UCAS personal statement It is important to show by reading scientific journals that you have interests in chemistry and biology beyond the exam syllabus. Focus on one or two aspects of biochemistry that interest you. Attend scientific lectures (often arranged by universities on Open Days), find some work experience if possible, and use these to show your understanding of what biochemistry is. Give evidence of your communication skills and time management. (See **Appendix 3**.) **Bristol** Deferred entry accepted. **Oxford** No written or work tests; successful entrants 19%. Further information may be obtained from the Royal Society of Biology and the Royal Society of Chemistry.

Misconceptions about this course York Students feel that being taught by two departments could be a problem but actually it increases their options.

Selection interviews Yes Cambridge, Kent, Manchester, Oxford (75% (success rate 19%)), Sheffield; **Some** Aberystwyth (mature students only), Bath, Warwick; **No** Birmingham, Cardiff, Dundee, East Anglia, East London, Essex, Keele, Kingston, Leeds, Liverpool John Moores, London (RH), London (UCL), Salford, Surrey, Wolverhampton.

Check **Chapter 3** for new university admission details and **Chapter 6** on how to read the subject tables.

Interview advice and questions Questions will be asked on your study of chemistry and biology and any special interests. They will also probe your understanding of what a course in Biochemistry involves and the special features offered by the university. In the past questions have been asked covering Mendel, genetics, RNA and DNA. See also **Chapter 5**.

Reasons for rejection (non-academic) Borderline grades plus poor motivation. Failure to turn up for interviews or answer correspondence. Inability to discuss subject. Not compatible with A-level predictions or references. **Birmingham** Lack of total commitment to Biochemistry, for example intention to transfer to Medicine without completing the course.

AFTER-RESULTS ADVICE

Offers to applicants repeating A-levels Higher Leeds, Leicester, St Andrews, Strathclyde, Warwick; **Possibly higher** Bath, Bristol, Keele, Lancaster; **Same** Aberystwyth, Birmingham, Brunel, Cardiff, Dundee, East Anglia, Heriot-Watt, Liverpool, Liverpool John Moores, London (RH), London (UCL), Nottingham, Salford, Sheffield, Wolverhampton, York; **No** Cambridge.

GRADUATE DESTINATIONS AND EMPLOYMENT (2015/16 HESA)

Biochemistry, Biophysics and Molecular Biology graduates surveyed 2,145 **Employed** 760 **In voluntary employment** 50 **In further study** 935 **Assumed unemployed** 130

Career note Biochemistry courses involve several specialities which offer a range of job opportunities. These include the application of biochemistry in industrial, medical and clinical areas with additional openings in pharmaceuticals and agricultural work, environmental science and in toxicology.

OTHER DEGREE SUBJECTS FOR CONSIDERATION

Agricultural Sciences; Agriculture; Biological Sciences; Biology; Biotechnology; Botany; Brewing; Chemistry; Food Science; Genetics; Medical Sciences; Medicine; Microbiology; Neuroscience; Nursing; Nutrition; Pharmaceutical Sciences; Pharmacology; Pharmacy; Plant Science.

BIOLOGICAL SCIENCES

(including **Biomedical Materials Science, Biomedical Science, Brewing and Distilling, Forensic Science, Immunology, Medical Science** and **Virology and Immunology;** see also **Animal Sciences, Biochemistry, Biology, Biotechnology, Environmental Sciences, Genetics, Medicine, Microbiology, Natural Sciences, Neuroscience, Nursing and Midwifery, Pharmacology, Plant Sciences, Psychology, Zoology**)

Biological Science (in some universities referred to as Biosciences) is a fast-moving, rapidly expanding and wide subject area, ranging from, for example, conservation biology to molecular genetics. Boundaries between separate subjects are blurring and this is reflected in the content and variety of the courses offered. Many universities offer a common first year allowing final decisions to be made later in the course. Since most subjects are research-based, students undertake their own projects in the final year. It should be noted that some Medical Science courses provide a foundation for graduate entry to medical schools. Check with universities.

Useful websites www.ibms.org; www.scicentral.com; www.bbsrc.ac.uk; www.csofs.org; www. immunology.org; see also **Biochemistry** and **Biology**.

NB The points totals shown to the left of the institutions are for ease of reference only. It must not be assumed that Tariff points are always used by institutions or that they can be substituted for an offer in grades. The level of an offer is not necessarily indicative of the quality of a course.

COURSE OFFERS INFORMATION

Subject requirements/preferences GCSE English, mathematics and science usually required. **AL** Chemistry usually required plus one or two other mathematics/science subjects, biology preferred.

UCAS points Tariff: A* = 56 pts; A = 48 pts; B = 40 pts; C = 32 pts; D = 24 pts; E = 16 pts

(Ecol) Biology and one other science subject may be required or preferred. (Neuro) Mathematics/science subjects with chemistry and/or biology required or preferred.

Your target offers and examples of degree courses

160 pts **Cambridge** – A*A*A incl sci/maths +interview +NSAA (Nat Sci (Biol Biomed Sci)) (IB 40–42 pts HL 776)

152 pts **Bath** – A*AA/AAA+aEPQ incl maths+sci (Nat Sci) (IB 36 pts HL 766 incl maths+sci)

London (UCL) – A*AA–AAA incl biol (Bioproc N Med (Sci Eng)) (IB 39–38 pts HL 5 biol); A*AA–AAA incl sci (Bioproc N Med (Bus Mgt)) (IB 39–38 pts HL 5 sci)

Nottingham – A*AA incl sci/maths (Nat Sci) (IB 38 pts HL 6/7 sci/maths)

Oxford – A*AA incl sci/maths +Interview (Biol Sci) (IB 39 pts HL 7 sci/maths); A*AA incl sci/maths +interview +BMAT (Biomed Sci) (IB 39 pts HL 766)

144 pts **Bath** – AAA/A*AB–AAB+aEPQ incl biol+chem (Biomed Sci) (IB 36 pts HL 6 chem+biol)

Durham – AAA incl biol/chem+sci (Biol Sci) (IB 37 pts)

Edinburgh – AAA incl biol+chem (Biol Sci; Biol Sci (Immun)) (IB 37 pts HL 666 incl biol+chem)

Imperial London – AAA incl biol+sci/maths (Biol Sci; Med Biosci) (IB 38 pts HL 6 biol+sci/maths)

Leeds – AAA–AAB incl biol+sci (Biol Sci) (IB 35–34 pts HL 18–16 pts incl 6 biol+sci); AAA–AAB incl biol/chem+sci (Med Sci) (IB 35–34 pts HL 18–16 pts incl 6 biol/chem+sci)

London (UCL) – AAA incl biol+sci/maths (Biol Sci) (IB 38 pts HL 6 biol 5 sci/maths); AAA incl biol+chem (Biomed Sci) (IB 38 pts HL 5 biol+chem); AAA–AAB incl biol+chem (App Med Sci) (IB 38–36 pts HL 5 biol+chem)

Manchester AAA ABB (Zool Modn Lang) (IB 37–32 pts HL 5 sci); AAA–ABB incl sci/maths +interview (Biomed Sci; Biomed Sci (Yr Ind)) (IB 37–32 pts HL 5/6 sci)

Newcastle – AAA–ABB incl biol (Psy Biol) (IB 35 pts HL 6 biol); AAA–AAB incl biol/chem+maths/sci (Med Sci (Defer); Biomed Genet; Biomed Sci) (IB 35–34 pts HL 5 biol/chem+maths/sci)

Reading – AAA–ABB incl biol+sci (Biol Sci (Yr Ind)) (IB 30–32 pts HL 5 biol)

Sheffield – AAA–AAB incl sci (Med Bioch) (IB 36–34 pts HL 6 chem)

York – AAA–AAB incl biol+sci/maths (Biomed Sci) (IB 36–35 pts HL 6 biol+chem)

136 pts **Birmingham** – AAB incl biol+sci (Biol Sci; Biol Sci (Genet)) (IB 32 pts HL 665); AAB/ABB+aEPQ incl biol/chem+sci (Biomed Mat Sci) (IB 32 pts HL 665 incl chem+biol)

Bristol – AAB–BBB incl chem+sci/maths (Cell Mol Med) (IB 34–31 pts HL 6–5 chem+sci/maths); AAB–BBB/ABB+aEPQ incl chem+sci/maths (Canc Biol Immun) (IB 34–31 pts HL 6/5 chem+sci/maths); AAB–BBB incl biol+sci (Palae Evol (MSci)) (IB 34–31 pts HL 17–15 pts); AAB–ABB/ABC incl chem+sci/maths (Virol Immun) (IB 34–31 pts HL 6/5 chem+sci/maths)

Cardiff – AAB incl biol+sci (Biomed Sci (Physiol)) (IB 34 pts HL 6 biol+chem); AAB–ABB incl biol+sci (Biomed Sci (Anat); Biomed Sci; Neuro) (IB 34 pts HL 6 biol+chem)

Dundee – AAB–BBB incl biol+chem (Biol Sci) (IB 30 pts HL 555)

East Anglia – AAB incl chem+sci (Foren Invstg Chem (MChem)) (IB 33 pts HL 6 chem+sci/maths); AAB incl biol+maths/sci (Biomed) (IB 33 pts HL 6 biol+sci/maths); AAB incl biol (Biol Sci (Yr Ind); Biol Sci (Yr Abrd)) (IB 33 pts HL 6 biol)

Edinburgh – AAB incl biol+chem (Infec Dis; Med Sci) (IB 36 pts HL 6 biol+chem)

Exeter – AAB–ABB incl biol (Biol Sci) (IB 34–32 pts HL 5 biol); AAB–ABB incl biol+sci (Hum Biosci) (IB 34–32 pts HL 5 biol+sci); (Med Sci) (IB 34–32 pts HL 6 biol/sci)

Glasgow – AAB incl biol/chem (Immun) (IB 36–34 pts)

Lancaster – AAB incl biol+sci/maths (Biomed Sci) (IB 35 pts HL 16 pts incl 6 sci); AAB incl sci (Biol Sci courses) (IB 35 pts HL 16 pts incl 6 sci)

Leicester – AAB–ABB/BBB+bEPQ incl sci/maths (Biol Sci; Biol Sci (Genet)) (IB 32–30 pts HL 6 sci)

London (King's) – AAB incl chem+biol (Biomed Sci) (IB 35 pts HL 665 incl chem+biol)

London (QM) – AAB incl biol+sci (Biomed Sci) (IB 35 pts HL 6 biol+sci)

Newcastle – AAB–ABB incl biol (App Plnt Sci) (IB 35–32 pts)

> "
> The course has so many good optional modules that you can tailor it to whatever interests you most. I would like to go into a career within Animal Behaviour and Welfare, with some potential for working abroad. The University has helped me with these goals as there have been many lectures with organisations coming in to talk about what they do, and the careers/events that they offer.
>
> **Alex Muffatt,**
> BSc Zoology
> "

UNIVERSITY OF LEEDS

Biology
AT THE UNIVERSITY OF LEEDS

We want to inspire you to be part of the next generation of highly skilled, critical thinkers – shaping the world around you in years to come. Work alongside experienced researchers and become part of a thriving research team and environment.

Our courses include topics at the cutting edge of biological discovery and reflect the complexity of the subject area, encompassing everything from molecules to populations of organisms.

Study with us
You can benefit from our extensive research expertise and study at the forefront of knowledge. All our undergraduate courses offer you the opportunity to study at postgraduate level in your fourth year with our Integrated Masters option.

- BSc/MBiol Biology
- BSc/MBiol Biology with Enterprise
- BSc/MBiol Ecology and Conservation Biology
- BSc/MBiol Genetics
- BSc/MBiol Zoology

Flexible degree choices
Our courses have a common first year, providing you with a broad foundation as a scientist, flexibility, and the opportunity to specialise and follow your own biological interests in Years 2, 3 and 4.

Accredited courses
Our MBiol courses give you the benefit of recognised excellence by being awarded Advanced Accreditation by the Royal Society of Biology.

Enhance your experience
Take the opportunity to study abroad or do an industrial placement year as part of any of our degree courses. You could also participate in or conduct your own research, or do our summer studentship scheme.

In and outside the lab
You'll learn from experts in world-class facilities, and you can apply your knowledge and skills outside the lab – we offer a variety of exciting field courses from North Yorkshire and Spain to South Africa and Kenya.

Find out more at an open day
www.leeds.ac.uk/opendays

TOP 10 IN THE UK - THE TIMES AND SUNDAY TIMES GOOD UNIVERSITY GUIDE 2018

TOP 100 IN THE WORLD FOR LIFE SCIENCES - TIMES HIGHER EDUCATION WORLD UNIVERSITY RANKINGS 2018

COME AND
F I N D
YOUR
PLACE

> **"**
>
> I really enjoy the course as I like being able to choose which modules I study to tailor it more towards my own interests.
>
> The city and campus are a really good aspect of the university. The support services such as the employability team and careers centre are also really useful to be able to see what opportunities there are available to you after graduation.
>
> Luke Boothman,
> BSc Medical Sciences **"**

UNIVERSITY OF LEEDS

Biomedical and Sport Science

AT THE UNIVERSITY OF LEEDS

We want to inspire you to be part of the next generation of highly skilled, critical thinkers – shaping the world around you in years to come. Work alongside experienced researchers and become part of a thriving research team and environment.

Biomedical and sport science are fast moving and exciting research areas with fantastic career options. We're 1st in the UK for 'world leading' research in Sport and Exercise Sciences (RFF, 2014).

Study with us
You can benefit from our extensive research expertise and study at the forefront of knowledge. All our undergraduate courses offer you the opportunity to study at postgraduate level in your fourth year with our Integrated Masters option.

- BSc/MBiol Human Physiology
- BSc/MBiol Medical Science
- BSc/MBiol Neuroscience
- BSc/MBiol Pharmacology
- BSc/MSci Sport and Exercise Science
- BSc/MSci Sports Science and Physiology

Accredited courses
Our MBiol courses give you the benefit of recognised excellence by being awarded Advanced Accreditation by the Royal Society of Biology.

Enhance your experience
Take the opportunity to study abroad or do an industrial placement year as part of any of our degree courses. There are other opportunities where you can participate or conduct your own research, or do our summer studentship scheme.

In the lab
With a high level of practical teaching each week you will benefit from industry-standard research facilities, specialist equipment and the latest technology.

Find out more at an open day
www.leeds.ac.uk/opendays

TOP 10 IN THE UK - THE TIMES
AND SUNDAY TIMES GOOD
UNIVERSITY GUIDE 2018

TOP 100 IN THE WORLD FOR
LIFE SCIENCES - TIMES HIGHER
EDUCATION WORLD UNIVERSITY
RANKINGS 2018

COME AND
F I N D
YOUR
PLACE

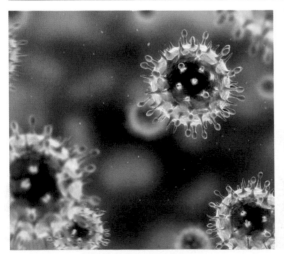

> **"**
>
> Biochemistry is such a fascinating subject, and has opened my eyes to the vast possibility of the scientific careers that Biochemistry can lead to.
>
> **Megan Bonsor,**
> MBiol Medical
> Biochemistry
>
> **"**

UNIVERSITY OF LEEDS

Molecular & Cellular Biology

AT THE UNIVERSITY OF LEEDS

We want to inspire you to be part of the next generation of highly skilled, critical thinkers – shaping the world around you in years to come. Work alongside experienced researchers and become part of a thriving research team and environment.

Understanding how cells and organisms function at the molecular level is fascinating. Our courses prepare you to work in a variety of settings, from cancer research and vaccine and drug development, to biotechnology and crop improvement.

Study with us

You can benefit from our extensive research expertise and study at the forefront of knowledge. All our undergraduate courses offer you the opportunity to study at postgraduate level in your fourth year with our Integrated Masters option.

- BSc/MBiol Biochemistry
- BSc/MBiol Biological Sciences (Biology with Enterprise)
- BSc/MBiol Medical Biochemistry
- BSc Medical Microbiology
- BSc/MBiol Microbiology

Accredited courses

Our MBiol courses give you the benefit of recognised excellence by being awarded Advanced Accreditation by the Royal Society of Biology.

Enhance your experience

Take the opportunity to study abroad or do an industrial placement year as part of any of our degree courses. There are other opportunities where you can participate or conduct your own research, or do our summer studentship scheme.

In the lab

With a high level of practical teaching each week you will benefit from industry-standard research facilities, specialist equipment and the latest technology.

Find out more at an open day
www.leeds.ac.uk/opendays

COME AND
FIND
YOUR
PLACE

EXPLORE THE BODY AT BANGOR

Why Medical Sciences at Bangor?

The degrees in Medical Sciences are grounded in modern medical practice and develop graduates with the skills to enter into a range of healthcare career pathways, including the potential for graduate entry into medicine and physician associate training.

Student satisfaction and student life

We offer our students an exceptional lifestyle, a few highlights of which are:

- Top 10 for 'Student Satisfaction' in the National Student Survey 2017.
- Unlike most universities, Bangor offers free membership of all clubs and societies.
- Bangor is a friendly, safe city whose nightlife is dominated by the influx of over 11,000 students. About 1 in 3 of the town's inhabitants are students!
- Best Clubs & Societies (WhatUni? 2017) & best Accommodation in the UK (WhatUni? 2016)
- Bangor is "one of the cheapest places in Britain" to be a student (*The Independent's A-Z of Universities*).

Bangor boosts your job prospects

To help you go further with your Bangor degree, you can develop additional skills, gain qualifications and complete work experience that's relevant both to your degree and to your future career.

- 12th in the UK for Graduate Prospects – Complete University Guide 2018

Undergraduate Degrees

- BSc Biomedical Sciences
- MBiol/BSc Medical Biology
- BMedSci Medical Sciences

Teaching excellence

We focus on caring for and supporting our students and have specialist International, Employability and Disability Tutors who can help you reach your maximum potential. Many staff also work for the local health board ensuring excellent exposure to practising clinicians.

"The highlight of my course is the opportunity to shadow doctors and clinicians at the local hospital. I have really enjoyed this valuable experience and it really helps seeing real life examples for use in my practical human anatomy module."

HARRI TATNELL
2nd Year Medical Sciences from Cardiff

Please feel free to contact us:
t. 01248 383244 **e.** medsciences@bangor.ac.uk
www.bangor.ac.uk/sms 🐦 @MedicalBangor

TEF Gold Teaching Excellence Framework

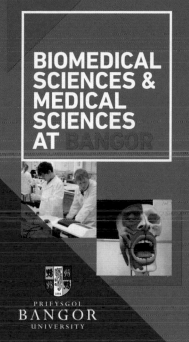

If you enjoy Biology and/or Chemistry have you considered a Medical Sciences related degree? Our courses are grounded in modern medical practice and provide an excellent gateway into health-related careers including the possibility of graduate entry to medicine.

Bangor's Medical Sciences School offers:
- BSc Biomedical Sciences, BMedSci Medical Sciences and BSc/MBiol Medical Biology
- Accreditation by the Institute of Biomedical Science
- 12th in the UK for Graduate Prospects – CUG 2018

Bangor University:
- Bangor is top 10 in the National Student Survey 2017
- WhatUni?: Best Clubs & Societies (2017) & Best Accommodation (2016)
- Affordable living costs in a beautiful, safe location with good transport links

More Information:
t. 01248 383244 **e.** medsciences@bangor.ac.uk
www.bangor.ac.uk/sms 🐦 @MedicalBangor

BIOMEDICAL SCIENCES & MEDICAL SCIENCES AT BANGOR

PRIFYSGOL
BANGOR
UNIVERSITY

 TEF Gold Teaching Excellence Framework IBMS

Reading – AAB–ABB incl biol+sci (Biomed Sci) (IB 34–32 pts HL 5 biol+sci)
Sheffield – AAB–ABB+bEPQ incl sci (Biomed Sci) (IB 34 pts); AAB/ABB+aEPQ incl biol+sci (Ecol Cons Biol) (IB 34 pts HL 6 biol+sci)
Southampton – AAB incl biol/chem+sci (Biomed Sci) (IB 34 pts HL 17 pts)
Surrey – AAB–ABB incl biol+chem/maths (Biomed Sci) (IB 34–32 pts HL 5 biol/chem)
Sussex – AAB–ABB incl biol+sci/maths (Biomed Sci) (IB 32 pts HL 5 biol+sci/maths)
Warwick – AAB–ABB incl biol (Biomed Sci; Biol Sci) (IB 36–34 pts HL 5 biol)

128 pts **Aberdeen** – ABB incl chem/biol+maths/sci (Biomed Sci) (IB 34 pts HL 6 chem/biol+maths/sci); ABB incl biol+chem (Biol Sci MSci) (IB 34 pts HL 6 biol+chem)
Aston – ABB–BBB incl biol (Microbiol Immun; Biol Sci; Biomed Sci) (IB 32 pts HL 6 biol)
Bangor – 128–112 pts incl biol+sci/maths (Med Sci); 128–112 pts incl biol (Biomed Sci)
East Anglia – ABB incl biol (Biol Sci) (IB 32 pts HL 5 biol); ABB (Biol Sci Educ) (IB 32 pts HL 5 biol)
Heriot-Watt – ABB (3 yr course) BBB (4 yr course) incl biol (Biol Sci; Brew Distil) (IB 32 pts (3 yr course) 27 pts (4 yr course) HL 6 biol (3 yr course) 5 biol (4 yr course))
Leicester – ABB–BBB incl chem (Chem Foren Sci) (IB 30 pts HL 5 chem)
Liverpool – ABB/BBB+aEPQ incl biol+sci (Biol Sci) (IB 33 pts HL 65 incl 6 biol); ABB/BBB+aEPQ incl biol+chem (Biol Med Sci) (IB 33 pts HL 6/5 biol/chem)
London (RH) – ABB–BBB incl biol+chem (Biomed Sci) (IB 32 pts HL 555 incl biol+chem); (Mol Biol) (IB 32 pts HL 555)
London (St George's) – ABB incl biol+chem (Biomed Sci) (IB 34 pts HL 16 pts incl 6/5 biol+chem)
Nottingham Trent – ABB incl biol+chem 128 pts (Foren Sci)
Plymouth – 128 pts incl biol+chem (Biomed Sci) (IB 30 pts HL 5 biol+chem)
Queen's Belfast – ABB–AAB incl biol/chem+sci (Biomed Sci)
Reading – ABB–BBB incl biol+sci (Biol Sci) (IB 30–32 pts HL 5 biol+sci)

Check **Chapter 3** for new university admission details and **Chapter 6** on how to read the subject tables.

Strathclyde – ABB incl chem+biol (3 yr course) BBB incl chem+biol (4 yr course) (Biomed Sci) (IB 32 pts HL 5 sci); (Immun (MSci)) (IB 34 pts HL 5 sci)

Swansea – ABB–BBB incl biol (Biol Sci Defer) (IB 33–32 pts HL 5 biol)

UWE Bristol – 128 pts incl biol/chem+sci (Biomed Sci) (HL 6 biol/chem 5 sci)

120 pts **Aberdeen** – BBB incl maths/sci (Immun) (IB 32 pts HL 5 maths/sci)

Bradford – BBB incl biol+chem 120 pts (Clin Sci; Biomed Sci)

Brunel – BBB incl sci (Biomed Sci (Genet); Biomed Sci) (IB 30 pts HL 5 sci); BBB (Lfe Sci) (IB 30 pts HL 5 sci)

Central Lancashire – BBB (Med Sci)

De Montfort – 120 pts incl biol/chem (Biomed Sci) (IB 30 pts HL 6 biol/chem); (Med Sci) (IB 28 pts HL 6 chem+sci)

Derby – 120–128 pts incl biol/chem (Foren Sci; Foren Sci Crimin)

Dundee – BBB incl biol (Foren Anth) (IB 30 pts HL 555)

Edinburgh Napier – BBB incl sci (Biol Sci) (IB 28 pts HL 5 sci)

Keele – ABC–BBB incl chem/biol (Foren Sci) (IB 32 pts HL 6 chem/biol)

Kent – BBB incl chem/biol (Foren Sci) (IB 34 pts HL 5 chem+biol); BBB incl biol (Biomed Sci) (IB 34 pts)

Leeds Beckett – 120 pts incl biol (Biomed Sci courses) (IB 26 pts HL 6 biol)

Lincoln – BBB incl biol/chem (Biomed Sci) (IB 30 pts HL 5 biol/chem)

London Met – 120 pts incl biol+chem (Biomed Sci)

Northumbria – 120–128 pts incl chem/biol/app sci (Foren Sci) (HL 444 incl chem/biol); 120–128 pts incl biol (Biomed Sci) (HL 444)

Nottingham Trent – BBB incl biol 120 pts (Biomed Sci)

Plymouth – 120 pts incl biol+maths/sci (Hum Biosci) (IB 28 pts HL 5 biol/chem); 120–128 pts incl biol+sci (Biol Sci) (IB 30 pts HL 5 biol+sci)

Portsmouth – BBB incl biol+sci/maths (Biomed Sci) (IB 31 pts HL 666 incl biol+chem/maths)

Queen's Belfast – BBB–ABB incl biol/app sci (Biol Sci)

Reading – BBB–CCC (Biol Sci Fdn; Biomed Sci Fdn)

Roehampton – 120 pts incl biol/chem (Biomed Sci)

Sheffield Hallam – 120–104 pts incl biol (Biomed Sci)

South Wales – BBB incl biol (Med Sci) (IB 32 pts HL 18 pts incl 6 biol+sci)

Ulster – BBB incl sci (Strf Med; Biomed Sci) (IB 26 pts HL 13 pts)

UWE Bristol – 120 pts incl biol/chem (Foren Sci) (HL 6 biol/chem)

112 pts **Anglia Ruskin** – 112 pts incl biol/chem (Foren Sci) (IB 26 pts)

Bedfordshire – 112 pts incl sci (Biomed Sci)

Bradford – BBC 112 pts (Foren Med Sci); BBC incl chem 112 pts (Foren Sci)

Brighton – BBC–CCC incl biol+chem 112–96 pts (Biomed Sci)

Cardiff Met – 112 pts incl biol+sci (Biomed Sci)

Central Lancashire – 112 pts incl biol/chem (Foren Sci) (IB 28 pts HL 5 biol/chem)

Coventry – BBC incl biol (Biomed Sci; Biol Foren Sci) (IB 30 pts HL 5 biol); (Med Pharmacol Sci) (IB 30 pts)

De Montfort – 112 pts incl sci (Foren Sci) (IB 26 pts)

East London – 112 pts incl biol/chem (Biomed Sci) (IB 25 pts HL 15 pts incl biol+chem)

Edinburgh Napier – BBC incl sci (Biomed Sci) (IB 28 pts HL 5 sci)

Glyndŵr – 112 pts incl sci (Foren Sci)

Greenwich – 112 pts incl biol+chem (App Biomed Sci; Biomed Sci); 112 pts incl maths/sci (Foren Sci; Foren Sci Crimin)

Huddersfield – BBC incl chem 112 pts (Foren Analyt Sci) (IB 30 pts HL 5 chem); BBC incl sci 112 pts (Med Bioch)

Hull – 112 pts incl biol/app sci (Biomed Sci) (IB 28 pts HL 5 biol); 112 pts incl chem/app sci (Chem (Foren Analyt Sci)) (IB 28 pts)

Kingston – 112–128 pts incl sci (Biomed Sci)

Liverpool John Moores – BBC incl sci/soc sci 112 pts (Foren Anth); BBC incl biol/chem 112 pts (Foren Sci) (IB 26 pts); BBC 112 pts incl sci (Biomed Sci) (IB 26 pts)

London (Birk) – 112 pts incl sci (Biomed)

Middlesex – 112 pts (Biomed Sci)

Oxford Brookes – BBC 112 pts (Biomed Sci; Biol Sci; Med Sci) (IB 30 pts)

Roehampton – 112 pts incl biol/chem (Biol Sci)

Staffordshire – 112 pts (Biomed Sci; Foren Biol); 112 pts incl biol/chem (Foren Sci)

Suffolk – BBC (Biosci)

Sunderland – 112 pts incl biol/chem (Biomed Sci)

Teesside – BBC incl biol/chem (Foren Sci); BBC incl biol (Foren Biol; Biol Sci)

UWE Bristol – 112 pts incl sci (Biol Sci) (HL 5 sci)

Westminster – BBC incl sci/maths (Biol Sci) (IB 26 pts HL 4 sci); BBC incl sci (Biomed Sci) (IB 26 pts HL 4 sci)

Wolverhampton – A*A*/BBC incl sci (Med Sci)

104 pts **Abertay** – BCC incl sci (Psy Foren Biol) (IB 29 pts)

Bournemouth – 104–120 pts incl maths/sci (Arch Foren Sci; Biol Sci; Foren Sci) (IB 28–31 pts HL 555)

Brighton – BCC–CCC incl biol 104–96 pts (Biol Sci) (IB 27 pts)

Chester – BCC–BBC incl biol/chem/app sci (Biomed Sci) (IB 26 pts HL 5 biol); BCC–BBC incl sci 104 pts (Immun) (IB 26 pts HL 5 biol/chem); BCC–BBC incl biol/chem/env sci/app sci (Foren Biol) (IB 26 pts HL 5 biol/chem)

Cumbria – 104–120 pts incl sci (Foren Invstg Sci)

De Montfort – 104 pts incl chem+sci (Pharml Cos Sci) (IB 24 pts HL 6 chem+sci)

Essex – BCC incl chem/biol+sci/maths (Biomed Sci) (IB 28 pts HL 5 chem/biol+sci/maths); BCC incl biol (Biol Sci) (IB 28 pts HL 5 biol)

Hertfordshire – 104 pts incl chem+sci/maths (Biol (St Abrd)); 104 pts incl biol/chem+sci (Biol Sci; Biomed Sci) (HL 44)

Kingston – 104–112 pts incl sci (Foren Sci; Biol Sci)

Lincoln – BCC incl biol/chem (Foren Sci)

Manchester Met – BCC–BBC incl biol 104–112 pts (Biomed Sci) (IB 26 pts HL 5 biol)

Northampton – BCC incl sci/psy/spo sci (Hum Biosci)

Nottingham Trent – BCC incl biol 104 pts (Biol Sci)

Robert Gordon – BCC incl chem+sci/maths (Foren Analyt Sci) (IB 28 pts HL 5 chem+sci/maths); BCC incl biol+sci (App Biomed Sci) (IB 28 pts HL 5 biol+sci)

South Wales – BCC–CDD incl chem+biol 104–80 pts (Foren Biol) (IB 29 pts HL 16 pts incl 5 chem+biol)

West London – 104–120 pts (Foren Sci)

96 pts **Abertay** – CCC incl chem+biol/phys (Foren Sci) (IB 28 pts); CCC incl biol (Biomed Sci) (IB 28 pts)

Glasgow Caledonian – CCC incl chem (Foren Invstg; Biomed Sci) (IB 24 pts)

London Met – CCC incl biol+chem 96 pts (Med Biosci); CCC 96 pts (Biol Sci)

Salford – 96–112 pts incl biol (Hum Biol Infec Dis) (IB 28 pts)

Wolverhampton – AA/CCC incl biol/chem +interview (Foren Sci); AA/CCC incl sci (Biomed Sci)

Worcester – 96–104 pts incl biol+sci/maths (Foren App Biol); 96–104 pts incl biol/chem (Biomed Sci)

88 pts **Canterbury Christ Church** – 88–112 pts (Biol; Foren Invstg)

London Met – CCD (Foren Sci)

London South Bank – CCD incl sci (Biosci); CCD incl sci 88 pts (Foren Sci)

West Scotland – CCD incl biol (App Biosci; App Biosci Zool) (IB 24 pts); CCD incl biol+sci (Biomed Sci) (IB 24 pts); CCD incl chem (Foren Sci) (IB 27 pts incl chem)

80 pts **Bedfordshire** – 80 pts (Foren Sci; Biol Sci)

Stirling – BB incl biol/chem (App Biol Sci) (IB 28 pts)

64 pts **Greenwich** – 64 pts (Biol Sci (Ext)) (IB 20 pts)

Alternative offers

See **Chapter 6** and **Appendix 1** for grades/UCAS Tariff points information for other examinations.

EXAMPLES OF COLLEGES OFFERING COURSES IN THIS SUBJECT FIELD

Birmingham Met (Coll); Brighton Met (Coll); Furness (Coll); Haringey, Enfield and North East London (Coll); Liverpool City (Coll); Nescot; Peterborough (Coll); Petroc; South Devon (Coll); Sunderland (Coll); Weymouth (Coll).

OTHER HIGHER EDUCATION COURSES IN THIS FIELD

Nottingham (Coll).

CHOOSING YOUR COURSE (SEE ALSO CH.1)

Universities and colleges teaching quality See www.qaa.ac.uk; https://unistats.ac.uk.

Top research universities and colleges (REF 2014) Oxford; Dundee; Newcastle; Sheffield; Birmingham; Imperial London; Edinburgh; York; Exeter; Kent; Leicester; Cambridge; East Anglia; Sussex.

Examples of sandwich degree courses See **Biology**. Reading; Stirling.

ADMISSIONS INFORMATION

Number of applicants per place (approx) Aston (Biomed Sci) 8; Bangor (Biol Sci) 4, (Med Sci) 5; Bath 7; Cardiff 5; Durham 8; East Anglia 5; Edinburgh 10; Essex 8; Lancaster (Biomed Sci) 5; Leeds (Med Sci) 25; Leicester 8; London (King's) 7; London (QM) 8; London (St George's) 15; London (UCL) 8; Newcastle 5; Nottingham 6; Southampton 8; York 9.

Advice to applicants and planning the UCAS personal statement Read scientific journals and try to extend your knowledge beyond the A-level syllabus. Discuss your special interests, for example, ecology, microbiology, genetics or zoology (read up thoroughly on your interests since questions could be asked at interview). Mention any voluntary attendance on courses, work experience, voluntary work, or holiday jobs. Demonstrate good oral and written communication skills and be competent at handling numerical data. Interest in the law for Forensic Science courses. See **Appendix 3**.

Misconceptions about this course Anglia Ruskin (Foren Sci) Some students are not aware that modules in management and quality assurance are taken as part of the course. **Birmingham** We offer a range of degree labels each with different UCAS codes, for example Biological Sciences Genetics, Biological Sciences Microbiology: all have the same first year and students can freely transfer between them. (Med Sci) Applicants often use this course as an insurance for a vocational course (usually Medicine). If they are unsuccessful for their first choice, they occasionally find it difficult to commit themselves to Medical Sciences and do not perform as well as their academic performance would predict. **Cardiff** Some students mistakenly believe that they can transfer to Medicine. **De Montfort** (Foren Sci) Students are often unaware of how much of the work is analytical biology and chemistry: they think they spend their time visiting crime scenes. **London (St George's)** It is not possible to transfer to Medicine after the first year of the Biomedical Science course. Students may be able to transfer to Year 3 of the Medical course on completion of the BSc degree. **Swansea** (Med Sci Hum) Some applicants think the course is a form of medical training – it isn't, but it is relevant to anyone planning graduate entry for courses in Medicine or paramedical careers. (Biol Sci Defer) Some applicants think that this is a degree in its own right. In fact, after the first year, students have to choose one of the other degrees offered by the School of Biological Sciences. This course allows students an extra year in which to consider their final specialisation.

Selection interviews Yes Manchester, Oxford (Bio Sci) 21%, (Biomed Sci) 12%, Sheffield, Stirling, Sunderland; **Some** Cardiff Met, East Anglia, Imperial London, Warwick; **No** Anglia Ruskin, Aston, Bangor, Birmingham, Cardiff, Derby, Dundee, Essex, Greenwich, Hull, Kent, Liverpool John Moores, London (RH), London (St George's), London (UCL), Newcastle, Nottingham, Nottingham Trent, Oxford Brookes, Reading, Roehampton, Salford, Sheffield Hallam, Staffordshire, Strathclyde, Surrey, Swansea, UWE Bristol, Wolverhampton.

Interview advice and questions You are likely to be asked about your main interests in biology and your choice of specialisation in the field of biological sciences or, for example, about the role of the botanist, specialist microbiologist in industry, your understanding of biotechnology or genetic engineering. Questions likely to be asked on any field courses attended. If you have a field course workbook, take it to interview. See also **Chapter 5**. **Oxford** No written or work tests. Interviews are rigorous but sympathetic; successful entrants average 21%. Applicants are expected to demonstrate their ability to understand whatever facts they have encountered and to discuss a particular aspect of biology in which they are interested. What problems does a fish face under water? Are humans still evolving?

Reasons for rejection (non-academic) Oxford Applicant appeared to have so much in his head that he tended to express his ideas in too much of a rush. He needs to slow down a bit and take more time to select points that are really pertinent to the questions. **Ulster** Reasons relating to health and/or police checks.

AFTER-RESULTS ADVICE
Offers to applicants repeating A-levels Higher London (St George's), Newcastle, Sheffield; **Possibly higher** Aston, Lancaster, Manchester Met; **Same** Abertay, Anglia Ruskin, Aston, Birmingham, Cardiff, Cardiff Met, De Montfort, Derby, Durham, East Anglia, East London, Edinburgh Napier, Essex, Exeter, Heriot-Watt, Huddersfield, Hull, Kingston, Leeds, Lincoln, Liverpool Hope, Liverpool John Moores, London (RH), Oxford Brookes, Plymouth, Robert Gordon, Roehampton, Salford, Sheffield Hallam, Stirling, West London, West Scotland, Wolverhampton, Worcester, York; **No** Cambridge, Glasgow.

GRADUATE DESTINATIONS AND EMPLOYMENT (2015/16 HESA)
See **Biology**.

Career note Degrees in biological science subjects often lead graduates into medical, pharmaceutical, veterinary, food and environmental work, research and education, in both the public and private sectors (see also **Biology**). Sandwich courses are offered at a number of institutions enabling students to gain paid experience in industry and commerce, often resulting in permanent employment on graduation. In recent years there has been a considerable increase in the number of Biomedical Science courses designed for students interested in taking a hands-on approach to studying the biology of disease. However, students should be warned that the ever-popular Forensic Science courses may not always pave the way to jobs in this highly specialised field.

OTHER DEGREE SUBJECTS FOR CONSIDERATION
Biochemistry; Biology; Biotechnology; Botany; Chemistry; Consumer Sciences; Ecology; Environmental Health; Environmental Science; Genetics; Genomics; Immunology; Microbiology; Pharmaceutical Sciences; Pharmacology; Pharmacy; Physiology; Plant Sciences; Psychology; Sport and Exercise Science; Toxicology; Virology; Zoology.

BIOLOGY

(including **Marine Biology**; see also **Animal Sciences, Biological Sciences, Biotechnology, Environmental Sciences, Microbiology, Plant Sciences, Zoology**)

The science of biology is a broad and rapidly developing subject that increasingly affects our lives. Biologists address the challenges faced by human populations such as disease, conservation and food production, and the continuing advances in such areas as genetics and molecular biology that have applications in medicine and agriculture. (See also under **Biological Sciences**.)

Useful websites www.rsb.org.uk; www.mba.ac.uk; www.bbsrc.ac.uk; see also **Biochemistry**.

NB The points totals shown to the left of the institutions are for ease of reference only. It must not be assumed that Tariff points are always used by institutions or that they can be substituted for an offer in grades. The level of an offer is not necessarily indicative of the quality of a course.

Check **Chapter 3** for new university admission details and **Chapter 6** on how to read the subject tables.

COURSE OFFERS INFORMATION

Subject requirements/preferences GCSE Mathematics and English stipulated in some cases. **AL** Biology and chemistry important, other science subjects may be accepted. Two and sometimes three mathematics/science subjects required including biology.

Your target offers and examples of degree courses

152 pts Durham – A*AA incl sci (Nat Sci) (IB 38 pts); A*AA incl sci/maths (Biol Comb Hons) (IB 38 pts)

144 pts Bath – AAA/A*AB incl biol+sci/maths (Biol) (IB 36 pts HL 6 biol+sci/maths)

Edinburgh – AAA incl biol+chem (Biol Sci (Evol Biol)) (IB 37 pts HL 555 incl biol+chem)

Imperial London – AAA incl biol+sci/maths (Ecol Env Biol; Biol Sci Ger Sci) (IB 38 pts HL 6 biol+sci/maths)

Lancaster – AAA incl sci (Biology (Yr Abrd)) (IB 36 pts)

Leeds – AAA–AAB incl biol (Biol Ent; Biol) (IB 35–34 pts HL 18–16 pts incl 6 biol+sci)

Manchester – AAA–ABB (Zool Modn Lang) (IB 37–32 pts HL 5 sci); AAA–ABB incl chem+sci/maths +interview (Mol Biol) (IB 37–32 pts HL 5/6 chem+sci); AAA–ABB incl sci/maths +interview (Cell Biol (Yr Ind)) (IB 37–32 pts HL 5/6 biol+chem); (Biol Modn Lang; Cell Biol Modn Lang) (IB 37–32 pts HL 5/6 sci+chem); (Biol; Cell Biol; Dev Biol; Biol Sci Soty; Biol (Yr Ind)) (IB 37–32 pts HL 5/6 sci)

Sheffield – AAA/AAB+aEPQ incl biol+sci (Biol (MBiolSci)) (IB 36 pts HL 6 biol+sci); AAA/AAB+aEPQ incl biol+sci +interview (Biol (Yr Abrd)) (IB 36 pts HL 6 biol+sci)

York – AAA–AAB incl biol+sci (Biol; Mol Cell Biol) (IB 36–35 pts HL 6 biol+chem/maths); AAA–AAB incl biol+chem/maths (Biol (Yr Abrd)) (IB 36–35 pts HL 6 biol+chem/maths)

136 pts Bangor – 136–112 pts incl biol (Biol; Mar Biol)

Birmingham – AAB incl biol+sci (Hum Biol) (IB 32 pts HL 665)

Bristol – AAB–BBB/ABB+aEPQ incl chem+sci/maths (Canc Biol Immun) (IB 34–31 pts HL 6/5 chem+sci/maths); AAB–BBB incl sci/maths (Biol) (IB 34–31 pts HL 6/5 sci/maths)

Edinburgh – AAB incl biol+chem (Repro Biol) (IB 36 pts HL 6 biol+chem)

Exeter – AAB–ABB incl sci/maths (Cons Biol Ecol; Evol Biol) (IB 34–32 pts HL 5 sci/maths)

Glasgow – AAB incl biol/chem (Mar Frshwtr Biol) (IB 36 pts)

Lancaster – AAB incl sci (Biol courses) (IB 35 pts HL 16 pts incl 6 sci)

London (King's) – AAB incl chem+biol (Anat Dev Hum Biol) (IB 35 pts HL 665 chem+biol)

Newcastle – AAB–ABB incl biol+sci/maths (Mar Biol Ocean) (IB 35–34 pts HL 6 biol); AAB–ABB incl biol+sci (Mar Biol) (IB 35–34 pts HL 6 biol); AAB–ABB incl biol (Biol) (IB 35 pts HL 6 biol)

Nottingham – AAB incl biol+sci/maths (Biol) (IB 34 pts HL 5/6 biol+sci)

St Andrews – AAB incl biol+sci/maths (Biol Arbc) (IB 36 pts HL 6 biol+sci); AAB incl sci/maths (Biol courses) (IB 36 pts HL 6 biol+sci)

Sheffield – AAA/ABB+bEPQ incl biol/sci (Biol) (IB 34 pts HL 6/5 biol+sci)

Southampton – AAB incl biol+sci (Biol) (IB 34 pts HL 6 biol+sci); AAB incl sci/maths/geog +interview (Mar Biol (MSci)) (IB 34 pts)

Sussex – AAB–ABB incl sci (Biol) (IB 32 pts HL 5 sci)

128 pts Aston – ABB–BBB incl biol (Biol Sci (Cell Mol Biol); Hum Biol) (IB 32 pts HL 6 biol)

Bangor – 128–112 pts incl biol (App Mar Biol)

Dundee – ABB incl biol+chem (Mol Biol) (IB 30 pts HL 555)

Heriot-Watt – ABB (3 yr course) BBB (4 yr course) (Mar Biol) (IB 32 pts (3 yr course) 27 pts (4 yr course) HL 6 biol (3 yr course) 5 biol (4 yr course))

Keele – ABB incl sci/geog/maths (Biol) (IB 34 pts HL 6 sci/maths)

Leeds – ABB incl biol (Biol Hist Phil Sci) (IB 34 pts HL 6 biol)

Liverpool – ABB/BBB+aEPQ incl biol+sci (Trpcl Dis Biol) (IB 33 pts HL 6 biol); ABB/BBB+aEPQ incl biol+sci/maths/geog (Mar Biol) (IB 33 pts HL 6 biol 5 sci)

London (QM) – ABB incl biol (Biol) (IB 34 pts HL 6/5 biol)

London (RH) – ABB–BBB incl biol (Biol) (IB 32 pts HL 555); ABB–BBB incl biol+chem (Mol Biol) (IB 32 pts HL 555)

Loughborough – ABB incl sci (Hum Biol) (IB 34 pts HL 655 incl 5 biol/sci)

UCAS points Tariff: A* = 56 pts; **A** = 48 pts; **B** = 40 pts; **C** = 32 pts; **D** = 24 pts; **E** = 16 pts

Nottingham – ABB–BBB incl sci/maths/geog (Env Biol) (IB 32–30 pts)

Southampton – ABB incl biol+sci/maths/geog +interview (Mar Biol Ocean) (IB 32 pts)

Stirling – ABB (3 yr course) BBB (4 yr course) incl sci/maths (Biol) (IB 35 pts (3 yr course) 32 pts (4 yr course))

Swansea – ABB–BBB incl biol (Biol) (IB 33–32 pts HL 5 biol)

120 pts   **Aberdeen** – BBB incl maths/sci (Mar Biol; Biol; Cons Biol) (IB 32 pts HL 5 maths/sci)

Bangor – 120 pts (App Trstl Mar Ecol); 120 pts incl biol (Physl Geog Ocean)

Dundee – BBB incl maths+sci (Mathem Biol) (IB 30 pts HL 555)

Edge Hill – BBB incl biol 120 pts (Biol)

Gloucestershire – BBB 120 pts (Biol; Anim Biol)

Keele – ABC–BBB incl sci (Biol Law) (IB 32 pts HL 6 sci/maths)

Kent – BBB incl biol (Biol courses) (IB 34 pts)

Lincoln – BBB incl biol/chem (Biol) (IB 30 pts HL 5 biol/chem)

Liverpool Hope – BBB–BBC incl sci 120–112 pts (Biol)

Plymouth – 120 pts incl biol+maths/sci (Hum Biosci) (IB 28 pts HL 5 biol/chem)

Queen's Belfast – BBB–ABB incl biol/app sci (Mar Biol)

Strathclyde – BBB incl chem+biol (Microbiol (MSci)) (IB 34 pts HL 5 sci)

112 pts   **Aberystwyth** – BBC–BBB incl biol (Plnt Biol; Biol; Mar Frshwtr Biol) (IB 30 pts HL 5 biol)

Anglia Ruskin – 112 pts incl biol (Mar Biol Biodiv Cons) (IB 24 pts)

Bangor – 112–136 pts incl biol (Mar Biol Zool)

Central Lancashire – 112 pts incl biol/chem/app sci (Foren Sci Mol Biol (MSci)) (IB 28 pts HL 5 biol/chem)

Chester – BBB–BBC (Cell Mol Biol)

Coventry – BBC incl biol (Hum Biosci) (IB 30 pts HL 5 biol)

Cumbria – 112 pts incl biol (Cons Biol)

Huddersfield – BBC incl sci 112 pts (Med Biol; Biol (Mol Cell))

Hull – 112 pts incl biol/app sci (Biol) (IB 28 pts HL 6 biol); 112 pts incl biol (Hum Biol) (28 pts HL 5 biol)

Liverpool John Moores – BBC incl sci (Biol) (IB 26 pts)

London (Birk) – 112 pts (Struct Mol Biol)

Middlesex – 112 pts (Biol)

Nottingham Trent – BBC incl biol 112 pts (Zoo Biol)

Oxford Brookes – BBC 112 pts (Biol) (IB 30 pts); BBC (Hum Biol) (IB 30 pts)

Portsmouth – 112 pts incl biol (Biol; Mar Biol) (IB 30 pts HL 17 pts incl 6 biol)

Sheffield Hallam – 112–96 pts incl biol (Hum Biol; Biol)

Staffordshire – 112 pts (Hum Biol)

Teesside – BBC incl biol (Foren Biol)

104 pts   **Bath Spa** – BCC–CCC incl biol/env sci (Biol) (IB 26 pts)

Chester – BCC–BBC incl biol/chem/env sci/app sci (Foren Biol) (IB 26 pts HL 5 biol/chem); BCC–BBC incl biol/chem/app sci (Biol courses) (IB 26 pts HL 5 biol)

Edinburgh Napier – BCC (Anim Cons Biol); BCC incl sci (Mar Frshwtr Biol) (IB 28 pts HL 5 sci)

Essex – BCC (Mar Biol) (IB 28 pts HL 5 biol)

Glasgow Caledonian – BCC incl chem (Cell Mol Biol) (IB 24 pts)

Manchester Met – BCC–BBC incl biol 104–112 pts (Biol (Yr Abrd/Yr Ind)) (IB 26 pts HL 5 biol)

Northampton – BCC (Biol)

South Wales – BCC–CDD incl chem+biol 104–80 pts (Foren Biol) (IB 29 pts HL 16 pts incl 5 chem+biol); BCC–CDD incl biol 104–80 pts (Biol) (HL 5 biol); BCC–CDD incl biol+sci 104–80 pts (Hum Biol) (HL 655–445); (Int Wldlf Biol) (HL 655–445 incl biol)

Ulster – BCC incl sci/maths (Biol)

96 pts   **Bolton** – 96 pts incl biol (Biol)

Derby – 96–112 pts incl biol (Biol)

Salford – 96–112 pts incl biol (Biol) (IB 28 pts)

Worcester – 96–104 pts incl biol (Biol)

Check **Chapter 3** for new university admission details and **Chapter 6** on how to read the subject tables.

88 pts   **Canterbury Christ Church** – 88–112 pts (Biol)
80 pts   **Queen Margaret** – BB incl chem/biol (Hum Biol) (IB 26 pts)
         Wolverhampton – BB/CDD incl sci (Genet Mol Biol; Microbiol; Hum Biol)

Alternative offers
See **Chapter 6** and **Appendix 1** for grades/UCAS Tariff points information for other examinations.

EXAMPLES OF COLLEGES OFFERING COURSES IN THIS SUBJECT FIELD
Bishop Burton (Coll); Blackpool and Fylde (Coll); Bournemouth and Poole (Coll); Brighton Met (Coll); HOW (Coll); Leeds City (Coll); Liverpool City (Coll); Manchester (Coll); North Hertfordshire (Coll); Solihull (Coll); South Devon (Coll); Sparsholt (Coll); SRUC; Sunderland (Coll); Truro and Penwith (Coll); Walsall (Coll); Warrington and Vale Royal (Coll).

CHOOSING YOUR COURSE (SEE ALSO CH.1)
Universities and colleges teaching quality See www.qaa.ac.uk; https://unistats.ac.uk.

Top research universities and colleges (REF 2014) See **Biological Sciences**.

Examples of sandwich degree courses Aston; Bath; Birmingham; Coventry; Dundee; Huddersfield; Kent; Leeds; Lincoln; Liverpool John Moores; Loughborough; Manchester; Manchester Met; Middlesex; Newcastle; Northumbria; Nottingham Trent; Queen's Belfast; Sheffield Hallam; Sussex; Teesside; Ulster; York.

ADMISSIONS INFORMATION
Number of applicants per place (approx) Aston 6; Bath 8; Bath Spa 8; Birmingham 9; Bristol 5; Dundee 6; Durham 8; Exeter 6; Heriot-Watt 4; Hull 5; Imperial London 4; Kent 8; Leeds 6; London (RH) 5; Newcastle (Mar Biol) 3; Nottingham 8; Oxford Brookes 7; Salford 3; Southampton 7; Stirling 8; Sussex 4; Swansea (Mar Biol) 8, (Biol) 4; York 8.

Advice to applicants and planning the UCAS personal statement See **Biochemistry**, **Biological Sciences** and **Appendix 3**.

Misconceptions about this course Sussex Many students think that a Biology degree limits you to being a professional scientist which is not the case. **York** Mature students often lack the confidence to consider the course.

Selection interviews Yes Manchester, SRUC; **Some** Bath, Southampton, York; **No** Anglia Ruskin, Aston, Bangor, Birmingham, Derby, Dundee, Essex, Kent, Liverpool John Moores, London (RH), Nottingham, Sheffield, Sheffield Hallam, Staffordshire, Stirling, Swansea, Wolverhampton.

Interview advice and questions Questions are likely to focus on your studies in biology, on any work experience or any special interests you may have in biology outside school. In the past, questions have included: Is the computer like a brain and, if so, could it ever be taught to think? What do you think the role of the environmental biologist will be in the next 40–50 years? Have you any strong views on vivisection? You have a micro-organism in the blood: you want to make a culture. What conditions should be borne in mind? What is a pacemaker? What problems will a giraffe experience? How does water enter a flowering plant? Compare an egg and a potato. Discuss a family tree of human genotypes. Discuss fish farming in Britain today. What problems do fish face underwater? See also **Chapter 5**. **York** Why Biology? How do you see your future?

Reasons for rejection (non-academic) Bath Spa Poor mathematical and scientific knowledge.

AFTER-RESULTS ADVICE
Offers to applicants repeating A-levels Higher East London, St Andrews, Strathclyde; **Possibly higher** Bath, Durham, Leeds, London (RH); **Same** Aberystwyth, Anglia Ruskin, Bangor, Chester, Derby, Dundee, Edinburgh Napier, Heriot-Watt, Hull, Liverpool John Moores, Loughborough, Manchester Met, Newcastle, Nottingham, Oxford Brookes, Plymouth, Sheffield, Southampton, Staffordshire, Stirling, Teesside, Wolverhampton, York.

GRADUATE DESTINATIONS AND EMPLOYMENT (2015/16 HESA)

Graduates surveyed 4,595 **Employed** 1,690 **In voluntary employment** 150 **In further study** 1,725 **Assumed unemployed** 290

Career note Some graduates go into research, but many will go into laboratory work in hospitals, food laboratories, agriculture, the environment and pharmaceuticals. Others go into teaching, management and other professional and technical areas.

OTHER DEGREE SUBJECTS FOR CONSIDERATION

Anatomy; Biochemistry; Biological Sciences; Biotechnology; Chemistry; Dentistry; Ecology; Environmental Health; Environmental Science/Studies; Food Science; Genomics; Health Studies; Medicine; Midwifery; Nursing; Nutrition; Optometry; Orthoptics; Pharmaceutical Sciences; Pharmacology; Pharmacy; Physiology; Physiotherapy; Plant Sciences; Radiography; Speech and Language Therapy; Zoology.

BIOTECHNOLOGY

(including **Prosthetics and Orthotics**; see also **Biological Sciences, Biology, Engineering (Medical), Microbiology**)

Biotechnology is basically the application of biology to improve the quality of life. It is a multi-disciplinary subject which can involve a range of scientific disciplines covering chemistry, the biological sciences, microbiology and genetics. At Bangor for example, the course involves medical and industrial applications, the environment, the food industry, and because of its very favourable coastal location it can add marine biotechnology and fisheries genetics to its programme. Medical engineering involves the design, installation, maintenance and provision of technical support for diagnostic, therapeutic and other clinical equipment used by doctors, nurses and other clinical healthcare workers.

Useful websites www.bbsrc.ac.uk; www.bioindustry.org; www.abcinformation.org

NB The points totals shown to the left of the institutions are for ease of reference only. It must not be assumed that Tariff points are always used by institutions or that they can be substituted for an offer in grades. The level of an offer is not necessarily indicative of the quality of a course.

COURSE OFFERS INFORMATION

Subject requirements/preferences GCSE Mathematics and science subjects required. **AL** Courses vary but one, two or three subjects from chemistry, biology, physics and mathematics may be required.

Your target offers and examples of degree courses

152 pts Imperial London – A*AA–A*A*A incl maths+phys+chem +interview (Biomat Tiss Eng (MEng)) (IB 38–40 pts HL 6 maths+phys+chem)

Leeds – A*AA incl maths+phys/sci +interview (Med Eng; Med Eng (MEng)) (IB 36 pts HL 18 pts incl 6 maths+phys)

144 pts Bristol – AAA–ABB incl chem+sci/maths (Bioch Mol Biol Biotech) (IB 36–32 pts HL 6 chem+sci/maths)

Edinburgh – AAA incl biol+chem (Biol Sci (Biotech)) (IB 37 pts HL 666)

Imperial London – AAA–A*AA incl chem+sci/maths (Biotech; Biotech (Yr Ind/Rsch)) (IB 39 pts HL 6 chem+biol/maths)

London (UCL) – AAA incl chem+sci/maths (Biotech) (IB 38 pts HL 6 chem 5 sci/maths)

Manchester – AAA–ABB incl sci/maths +interview (Biotech) (IB 37–32 pts HL 5/6 sci)

Sheffield – AAA–AAB incl maths+sci (Cheml Eng Biotech (MEng)) (IB 36 pts HL 6 maths+sci)

York – AAA–AAB incl biol+chem/maths (Biotech Microbiol) (IB 36–35 pts HL 6 biol+chem/maths)

136 pts Glasgow – AAB incl biol/chem (Mol Cell Biol (Biotech)) (IB 36–34 pts)

128 pts Nottingham – ABB–BBB incl biol+sci/maths (Biotech) (IB 32–30 pts)

Strathclyde – ABB–BBB incl maths+sci +interview (Pros Orthot) (IB 34 pts HL 6 maths)

Surrey – ABB incl biol+sci/maths (Biotech) (IB 32 pts)

Check **Chapter 3** for new university admission details and **Chapter 6** on how to read the subject tables.

120 pts **Aberdeen** – BBB incl maths/sci (Biotech (App Mol Biol)) (IB 32 pts HL 5 maths/sci)

112 pts **Bangor** – 112–136 pts incl biol (Biol Biotech)

Chester – 112 pts incl biol/chem/sci (Genet Evol) (IB 26 pts HL 5 biol/chem); 112 pts incl sci (Biotech) (IB 26 pts HL 5 biol/chem)

Middlesex – 112 pts (Biol (Biotech)) (IB 26 pts)

96 pts **London Met** – CCC incl biol+chem 96 pts (Biotech)

80 pts **Wolverhampton** – BB/CDD incl sci (Biotech)

Alternative offers
See **Chapter 6** and **Appendix 1** for grades/UCAS Tariff points information for other examinations.

CHOOSING YOUR COURSE (SEE ALSO CH.1)

Universities and colleges teaching quality See www.qaa.ac.uk; https://unistats.ac.uk.

Examples of sandwich degree courses Imperial London; Manchester; Surrey; York.

ADMISSIONS INFORMATION

Number of applicants per place (approx) Bristol 9; Imperial London 4; Leeds 7; London (UCL) 8; Strathclyde 4.

Advice to applicants and planning the UCAS personal statement See **Biological Sciences**, **Biochemistry** and **Appendix 3**.

Selection interviews Yes Manchester, Strathclyde; **No** Imperial London, Leeds, Surrey, Wolverhampton.

Interview advice and questions See **Biology**, **Biological Sciences** and **Chapter 5**.

AFTER-RESULTS ADVICE

Offers to applicants repeating A-levels Same Leeds, Nottingham, Wolverhampton.

GRADUATE DESTINATIONS AND EMPLOYMENT (2015/16 HESA)

Graduates surveyed 35 **Employed** 15 **In voluntary employment** 0 **In further study** 10 **Assumed unemployed** 0

Medical Technology graduates surveyed 1,320 **Employed** 1,140 **In voluntary employment** 0 **In further study** 65 **Assumed unemployed** 35

Career note Biotechnology, biomedical and biochemical engineering opportunities exist in medical, agricultural, food science and pharmaceutical laboratories. Some Bioengineering graduates apply for graduate medical courses and obtain both engineering and medical qualifications.

OTHER DEGREE SUBJECTS FOR CONSIDERATION

Agriculture; Biochemistry; Biological Sciences; Biomedicine; Chemistry; Food Technology; Genetics; Materials Science and Technology; Microbiology; Molecular Biology; Pharmacology.

BUILDING and CONSTRUCTION

(including **Building Services Engineering** and **Construction and Project Management**; see also **Architecture, Engineering (Civil), Housing, Surveying and Real Estate Management**)

The building and construction industry covers a wide range of specialisms and is closely allied to civil, municipal and structural engineering (see under **Engineering (Civil)**). The specialisms include Construction Management involving accountancy, economics, law and estimating in addition to main studies in building materials and methods, construction techniques, and health and safety. Then there is Building Surveying which not only involves modules on building technology but also the study of the history of building techniques and styles and enables the surveyor to diagnose and test all aspects of a building's performance and construction. Quantity Surveying is another specialism which relates to the financial planning of a building project covering costs (which can constantly change during the period of the project) as well as modifications which might be required to the original architect's plans. (See under **Surveying and Real Estate Management**.) Finally, there is Building Services Engineering, a career which involves specialised areas such as heating, lighting, acoustics, refrigeration and air conditioning. All university courses in these subjects will offer work placements.

Useful websites www.ciob.org.uk; www.cibse.org; www.citb.co.uk; www.rics.org; www.cstt.org.uk; www.cbuilde.com

NB The points totals shown to the left of the institutions are for ease of reference only. It must not be assumed that Tariff points are always used by institutions or that they can be substituted for an offer in grades. The level of an offer is not necessarily indicative of the quality of a course.

COURSE OFFERS INFORMATION
Subject requirements/preferences GCSE English, mathematics and science usually required. **AL** Physics, mathematics or a technical subject may be required for some courses.

Your target offers and examples of degree courses
136 pts **Edinburgh Napier** – AAB (Constr Proj Mgt)
128 pts **Heriot-Watt** – ABB (3 yr course) ABC/BBB (4 yr course) (Constr Proj Mgt) (IB 34 pts
(3 yr course) 29 pts (4 yr course))
London (UCL) – ABB (Proj Mgt Constr) (IB 34 pts HL 555)
Northumbria – 128–136 pts (Constr Proj Mgt)
Reading – ABB–BBB (Constr Mgt) (IB 32–30 pts)
120 pts **Coventry** – BBB–BBC (Bld Serv Eng) (IB 28 pts); (Constr Mgt) (IB 30 pts)
Huddersfield – BBB 120 pts (Surv (Bld Surv); Constr Proj Mgt)
London South Bank – BBB (Bld Surv)
Loughborough – BBB/ABC +interview (Constr Eng Mgt) (IB 32 pts HL 555)
Nottingham Trent – BBB 120 pts (Bld Surv)
Ulster – BBB incl maths/sci (Constr Eng Mgt) (IB 26 pts HL 13 pts)
112 pts **Aston** – BBC–BBB (Constr Proj Mgt) (IB 32 pts)
Birmingham City – BBC 112 pts +interview (Constr Mgt) (IB 30 pts)
Brighton – BBC–CCC 112–96 pts (Constr Mgt) (IB 28 pts)
Glasgow Caledonian – BBC (Bld Serv Eng)
Glyndŵr – 112 pts (Constr Mgt)
Leeds Beckett – 112 pts (Constr Mgt)
Liverpool John Moores – BBC incl maths/sci 112 pts (Bld Serv Eng) (IB 25 pts
HL 5 maths)
Nottingham Trent – BBC 112 pts (Quant Surv Constr Commer Mgt)
Oxford Brookes – BBC–BCC 112–104 pts +interview (Constr Proj Mgt) (IB 31–30 pts)
Plymouth – 112 pts +interview (Constr Mgt Env) (IB 28 pts)
Portsmouth – 112–120 pts (Constr Eng Mgt) (IB 26 pts)
Sheffield Hallam – 112–96 pts (Constr Proj Mgt)
Southampton Solent – 112 pts (Constr Mgt)
West London – 112–120 pts (Constr Proj Mgt)
Westminster – BBC (Constr Mgt) (IB 28 pts)
104 pts **Anglia Ruskin** – 104 pts (Constr Mgt) (IB 24 pts)
Central Lancashire – 104 pts incl maths (Bld Serv Sust Eng) (IB 28 pts HL
5 maths)
Greenwich – 104 pts (Des Constr Mgt; Quant Surv)
UWE Bristol – 104 pts (Constr Proj Mgt)
96 pts **Central Lancashire** – 96 pts (Constr Proj Mgt) (IB 26 pts)
Derby – 96–112 pts (Constr Mgt Prop Dev)

> **Glasgow Caledonian** – CCC (Constr Mgt) (IB 24 pts)
> **Kingston** – 96 pts (Constr Mgt) (IB 24 pts)
> **London South Bank** – CCC (Constr Mgt; Commer Mgt (Quant Surv))
> **Nottingham Trent** – CCC 96 pts (Constr Mgt)
> **Trinity Saint David** – 96 pts (Proj Constr Mgt)
> **UCEM** – 96 pts (Bld Serv)

80 pts **Colchester (Inst)** – 80 pts (Constr Mgt (Site Mgt); Constr Mgt (Commer Mgt))
> **Wolverhampton** – BB/CCE (Constr Mgt)

Alternative offers
See **Chapter 6** and **Appendix 1** for grades/UCAS Tariff points information for other examinations.

EXAMPLES OF DEGREE APPRENTICESHIPS IN THIS SUBJECT FIELD
East London (Constr Des Mgt); Liverpool John Moores (Constr Mgt; Bld Serv Eng Proj Mgt); UWE Bristol (Constr Proj Mgt).

EXAMPLES OF COLLEGES OFFERING COURSES IN THIS SUBJECT FIELD
Accrington and Rossendale (Coll); Banbury and Bicester (Coll); Barnfield (Coll); Barnsley (Coll); Basingstoke (CT); Bath (Coll); Bedford (Coll); Birmingham Met (Coll); Blackpool and Fylde (Coll); Bournemouth and Poole (Coll); Bradford (Coll); Bury (Coll); Canterbury (Coll); Carshalton (Coll); Chelmsford (Coll); Chesterfield (Coll); Croydon (Univ Centre); Darlington (Coll); Doncaster (Coll); Dudley (Coll); Durham New (Coll); Ealing, Hammersmith and West London (Coll); East Berkshire (Coll); East Kent (Coll); East Riding (Coll); East Surrey (Coll); Eastleigh (Coll); Exeter (Coll); Furness (Coll); Gateshead (Coll); Gloucestershire (Coll); Gower Swansea (Coll); Grimsby (Inst Group); Hartlepool (CFE); Hull (Coll); Leicester (Coll); LeSoCo; Lincoln (Coll); London UCK (Coll); MidKent (Coll); Nescot; North West London (Coll); Norwich City (Coll); Plymouth City (Coll); Redcar and Cleveland (Coll); Richmond-upon-Thames (Coll); St Helens (Coll); South Cheshire (Coll); South City Birmingham (Coll); South Essex (Coll); South Leicestershire (Coll); Southampton City (Coll); Stamford New (Coll); Stephenson (Coll); Stockport (Coll); Sussex Coast Hastings (Coll); Tameside (Coll); Trafford (Coll); Wakefield (Coll); Warrington and Vale Royal (Coll); West Cheshire (Coll); West Kent (Coll); West Suffolk (Coll); Westminster City (Coll); Wigan and Leigh (Coll); Wirral Met (Coll); York (Coll).

OTHER HIGHER EDUCATION COURSES IN THIS FIELD
Nottingham (Coll).

CHOOSING YOUR COURSE (SEE ALSO CH.1)
Universities and colleges teaching quality See www.qaa.ac.uk; https://unistats.ac.uk.

Top research universities and colleges (REF 2014) See **Architecture**.

Examples of sandwich degree courses Aston; Brighton; Brunel; Coventry; Greenwich; Kingston; Leeds Beckett; Liverpool John Moores; London South Bank; Loughborough; Nottingham Trent; Portsmouth; Sheffield Hallam; Ulster; UWE Bristol; Wolverhampton.

ADMISSIONS INFORMATION
Number of applicants per place (approx) Edinburgh Napier 7; Heriot-Watt 5; Kingston 4.

Advice to applicants and planning the UCAS personal statement Details of work experience with any levels of responsibility should be included. Make contact with any building organisation to arrange a meeting with staff to discuss careers in building. Give evidence of your ability to work in a team and give details of any personal achievements in technological areas and work experience. Building also covers civil engineering, surveying, quantity surveying etc and these areas should also be explored. See also **Appendix 3**.

Selection interviews Yes Birmingham City, Loughborough, Plymouth; **Some** Greenwich; **No** Derby, Kingston, Liverpool John Moores, Northumbria, Oxford Brookes, Reading, Westminster, Wolverhampton.

Interview advice and questions Work experience in the building and civil engineering industries is important and you could be expected to describe any building project you have visited and any problems experienced in its construction. A knowledge of the range of activities to be found on a building site will be expected, for example the work of quantity and land surveyors and of the various building trades. See also **Chapter 5**.

Reasons for rejection (non-academic) Inability to communicate. Lack of motivation. Indecisiveness about reasons for choosing the course. **Loughborough** Applicant more suited to a hands-on course rather than an academic one.

AFTER-RESULTS ADVICE
Offers to applicants repeating A-levels Same Birmingham City, Brighton, Coventry, Heriot-Watt, Huddersfield, Kingston, Liverpool John Moores, London (UCL), Loughborough, Northumbria, Trinity Saint David.

GRADUATE DESTINATIONS AND EMPLOYMENT (2015/16 HESA)
Graduates surveyed 2,600 **Employed** 1,925 **In voluntary employment** 20 **In further study** 390 **Assumed unemployed** 85

Career note There is a wide range of opportunities within the building and construction industry for building technologists and managers. This subject area also overlaps into surveying, quantity surveying, civil engineering, architecture and planning and graduates from all these subjects commonly work together as members of construction teams.

OTHER DEGREE SUBJECTS FOR CONSIDERATION
Architectural Technology; Architecture; Civil Engineering; Property Planning and Development; Quantity Surveying; Surveying.

BUSINESS and MANAGEMENT COURSES

(see also Business and Management Courses (International and European), Business and Management Courses (Specialised), Economics, Hospitality and Event Management, Human Resource Management, Leisure and Recreation Management/Studies, Marketing, Retail Management, Tourism and Travel)

Business degrees attract more applicants than any other degree subject, and students should try to assess the balance between theoretical studies and hands-on approaches offered by courses. Most universities offer a range of courses such as at Durham University, where in the first year of the Business and Management course, accounting, marketing and business management are covered. Transfers between business courses is a common feature at most institutions. As for the course content, financial studies form part of all courses with additional modules which may include marketing, business law and human resources. In the following table, there is also a section focusing on European and International Business courses for those with a language ability, and a further section on more specialised courses which cover advertising, airports, engineering, music, transport, travel and sport. Since this is a vocational subject, some work experience in the field is generally required prior to application.

Useful websites www.faststream.gov.uk; www.icsa.org.uk; www.adassoc.org.uk; www.cipr.co.uk; www.ismprofessional.com; www.export.org.uk; www.ipsos.com/ipsos-mori/en-uk; www.capitaresourcing.co.uk; www.tax.org.uk; www.gov.uk/government/organisations/hm-revenue-customs; www.camfoundation.com; www.shell-livewire.org; www.iconsulting.org.uk; www.managers.org.uk; www.cipd.co.uk; www.instam.org

NB The points totals shown to the left of the institutions are for ease of reference only. It must not be assumed that Tariff points are always used by institutions or that they can be substituted for an offer in grades. The level of an offer is not necessarily indicative of the quality of a course.

Check **Chapter 3** for new university admission details and **Chapter 6** on how to read the subject tables.

COURSE OFFERS INFORMATION

Subject requirements/preferences GCSE Mathematics and English often at grade A or B (7 or 5/6) required. **AL** Mathematics required for some courses. In some cases grades A, B or C may be required.

Your target offers and examples of degree courses

152 pts   Durham – A*AA incl maths (Econ Mgt) (IB 38 pts)
Exeter – A*AA–AAB incl maths (Maths Mgt) (IB 38–34 pts HL 6 maths)
London (King's) – A*AA incl hum/soc sci (Bus Mgt) (IB 35 pts HL 766)
Manchester – A*AA (Comp Sci Bus Mgt) (IB 38 pts HL 766 incl maths)
Warwick – A*AA incl maths+phys (Phys Bus St) (IB 38 pts HL 6 maths+phys)

144 pts   Arden – (Bus Fin)
Bath – AAA/A*AB (Mgt courses) (IB 36 pts HL 666/765)
Bristol – AAA–A*AB incl maths (Acc Mgt) (IB 36–32 pts HL 6 maths)
City – AAA 144 pts (Mgt) (IB 36 pts)
Exeter – AAA–AAB (Bus Mgt; Bus Acc) (IB 36–34 pts)
Leeds – AAA (Bus Econ; Econ Mgt; Mgt Mark) (IB 35 pts HL 17 pts)
London (QM) – AAA (Bus Mgt) (IB 36 pts HL 666)
London (UCL) – AAA incl maths (Mgt Sci) (IB 38 pts HL 6 maths)
London LSE – AAA incl maths (Bus Maths Stats) (IB 38 pts HL 766 incl 7 maths); (Mgt)
      (IB 38 pts HL 766)
Loughborough – AAA incl maths (Maths Mgt) (IB 37 pts HL 6 maths)
Newcastle – AAA–AAB/A*AB–A*BB incl maths (Maths Mgt) (IB 37–35 pts HL 6 maths)
Reading – AAA–AAB (Entre Mgt; Bus Mgt) (IB 35–34 pts); AAA (Int Bus Mgt)
      (IB 35 pts)
St Andrews – AAA (Mgt Span; Mgt courses; Mgt Sci) (IB 38 pts)
Surrey – AAA–AAB (Bus Mgt) (IB 36–35 pts); AAA (Bus Econ) (IB 34 pts)
Sussex – AAA–AAB (Law Bus Mgt) (IB 34 pts)
Warwick – AAA (Mgt) (IB 38 pts)

136 pts   Aston – AAB–ABB (Acc Mgt) (IB 32 pts HL 665–655); (Bus Mgt) (IB 32 pts HL 665)
Birmingham – AAB (Bus Mgt courses) (IB 32 pts HL 665)
Cardiff – AAB–ABB (Bus St Jap) (IB 35–32 pts); AAB (Bus Mgt) (IB 35–32 pts)
Durham – AAB (Bus Mgt) (IB 36 pts)
Edinburgh – AAB (Bus Acc) (IB 43 pts HL 776); (Bus courses) (IB 43 pts)
Glasgow – AAB–BBB (Bus Mgt Comb Hons) (IB 36–34 pts)
Lancaster – AAB (Bus St courses; Mgt Org Bhv; Mgt courses; Mgt Org Bhv (Yr Ind); Acc Mgt
      St) (IB 35 pts HL 16 pts)
Leeds – AAB (Mgt) (IB 35 pts HL 17 pts)
London (RH) – AAB–ABB (Econ Mgt) (IB 32 pts HL 655)
Loughborough – AAB (Mgt Sci) (IB 35 pts HL 665)
Manchester – AAB (Bus St; Bus St Pol) (IB 32 pts HL 665); (Mgt courses; Bus St Econ; Bus St
      Sociol) (IB 35 pts HL 665)
Newcastle – AAB (Bus Mgt) (IB 35 pts)
Nottingham – AAB (Mgt) (IB 34 pts HL 18 pts)
Sheffield – AAB/ABB+aEPQ (Bus Mgt Comb Hons) (IB 34 pts)
Southampton – AAB/ABB+aEPQ (Bus Mgt; Econ Mgt Sci) (IB 34 pts HL 17 pts); AAB–BBB
      incl mus +gr 8 (Mus Mgt Sci) (IB 34–30 pts HL 6 mus)
Sussex – AAB–ABB (Mark Mgt; Comp Bus Mgt; Bus Mgt St; Econ Mgt St; Fin Bus)
      (IB 32 pts)
Warwick – AAB (Law Bus St) (IB 36 pts)

128 pts   Aston – ABB (Psy Bus) (IB 32 pts)
Bournemouth – 128–136 pts (Bus St) (IB 32–33 pts HL 55)
BPP – ABB (2 yr course) BBB (3 yr course) 128–120 pts (Bus Mgt)
Coventry – ABB–BBB (Bus Mgt) (IB 30 pts)
East Anglia – ABB (Bus Econ; Mark Mgt) (IB 32 pts)

Check **Chapter 3** for new university admission details and **Chapter 6** on how to read the subject tables.

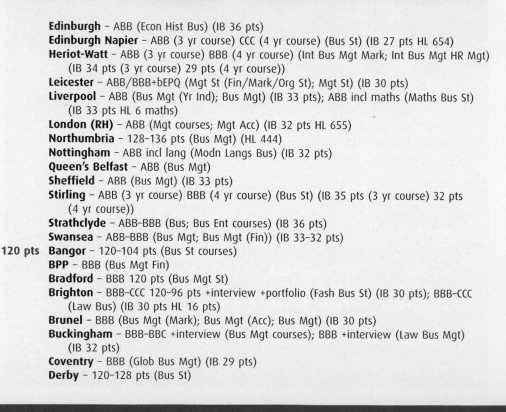

Edinburgh – ABB (Econ Hist Bus) (IB 36 pts)

Edinburgh Napier – ABB (3 yr course) CCC (4 yr course) (Bus St) (IB 27 pts HL 654)

Heriot-Watt – ABB (3 yr course) BBB (4 yr course) (Int Bus Mgt Mark; Int Bus Mgt HR Mgt) (IB 34 pts (3 yr course) 29 pts (4 yr course))

Leicester – ABB/BBB+bEPQ (Mgt St (Fin/Mark/Org St); Mgt St) (IB 30 pts)

Liverpool – ABB (Bus Mgt (Yr Ind); Bus Mgt) (IB 33 pts); ABB incl maths (Maths Bus St) (IB 33 pts HL 6 maths)

London (RH) – ABB (Mgt courses; Mgt Acc) (IB 32 pts HL 655)

Northumbria – 128–136 pts (Bus Mgt) (HL 444)

Nottingham – ABB incl lang (Modn Langs Bus) (IB 32 pts)

Queen's Belfast – ABB (Bus Mgt)

Sheffield – ABB (Bus Mgt) (IB 33 pts)

Stirling – ABB (3 yr course) BBB (4 yr course) (Bus St) (IB 35 pts (3 yr course) 32 pts (4 yr course))

Strathclyde – ABB–BBB (Bus; Bus Ent courses) (IB 36 pts)

Swansea – ABB–BBB (Bus Mgt; Bus Mgt (Fin)) (IB 33–32 pts)

120 pts **Bangor** – 120–104 pts (Bus St courses)

BPP – BBB (Bus Mgt Fin)

Bradford – BBB 120 pts (Bus Mgt St)

Brighton – BBB–CCC 120–96 pts +interview +portfolio (Fash Bus St) (IB 30 pts); BBB–CCC (Law Bus) (IB 30 pts HL 16 pts)

Brunel – BBB (Bus Mgt (Mark); Bus Mgt (Acc); Bus Mgt) (IB 30 pts)

Buckingham – BBB–BBC +interview (Bus Mgt courses); BBB +interview (Law Bus Mgt) (IB 32 pts)

Coventry – BBB (Glob Bus Mgt) (IB 29 pts)

Derby – 120–128 pts (Bus St)

Dundee – BBB (Bus Mgt) (IB 30 pts HL 555)
Edinburgh Napier – BBB (3 yr course) BCC (4 yr course) (Bus Mgt) (IB 28 pts HL 654)
Essex – BBB (Bus Mgt) (IB 30 pts)
Gloucestershire – BBB 120 pts (Bus Mgt)
Huddersfield – BBB 120 pts (Bus Law); (Bus Mgt Fin; Bus Mgt) (IB 31 pts)
Loughborough – BBB/ABC (Trans Bus Mgt) (IB 32 pts HL 555)
Northumbria – 120–128 pts (Bus Mark Mgt; Bus Econ; Bus Log Sply Chn Mgt; Bus Tour Mgt)
  (HL 444)
Oxford Brookes – BBB 120 pts (Bus Mgt) (IB 31 pts)
Plymouth – 120 pts (Law Bus) (IB 30 pts HL 4)
Queen Margaret – BBB (3 yr course) BCC (4 yr course) (Bus Mgt) (IB 28 pts)
Sheffield Hallam – 120 pts (Bus Econ)
Staffordshire – BBB 120 pts (Bus Mgt)
Ulster – BBB–AAB (Bus St) (IB 26–28 pts HL 13–14 pts)
UWE Bristol – 120 pts (Bus courses; Bus Mgt Ldrshp; Bus Mgt courses)
West Scotland – BBB (3 yr course) CCC (4 yr course) (Bus) (IB 28 pts (3 yr course) 24 pts
  (4 yr course))

112 pts **Aberystwyth** – BBC (Bus Mgt) (IB 25 pts)
Bedfordshire – 112 pts (Bus St courses; Bus Mgt)
Birmingham City – BBC 112 pts (Bus courses); BBC 112 pts +portfolio (Fash Bus Prom)
  (HL 14 pts)
Bournemouth – 112–120 pts (Acc Bus) (IB 30–31 pts HL 55)
Brighton – BBC–CCC incl maths (Maths Bus) (IB 28 pts HL 5 maths)
Cardiff Met – 112 pts (Bus Mgt St HR Mgt; Bus Mgt St courses; Bus Mgt St Law; Bus Mgt
  St Fin)
Central Lancashire – 112 pts (Bus St courses) (IB 28 pts); 112–128 pts (Bus Mgt Chin)
Chichester – BBC–CCC (Bus St) (IB 28 pts)
Cumbria – 112 pts (Bus Mgt)
De Montfort – 112 pts (Bus Mgt courses) (IB 26 pts); (Bus courses) (IB 28 pts)
East London – 112 pts (Bus Mgt) (IB 25 pts HL 15 pts)
Edge Hill – BBC 112 pts (Bus Mgt)
Glasgow Caledonian – BBC (Bus Mgt) (IB 25 pts)
Glyndŵr – 112 pts (Bus)
Greenwich – 112 pts (Bus Prchsng Sply Chn Mgt; Bus Mgt; Bus Entre Innov; PR Comms)
Hull – 112 pts (Bus courses; Bus Mgt Fin Mgt) (IB 30 pts)
Keele – BBC (Bus Mgt Comb Hons) (IB 30 pts)
Kingston – 112 pts (Bus Mgt) (IB 25 pts HL 554 incl 4 Engl lang)
Leeds Beckett – 112 pts (Bus Mgt)
Leeds Trinity – 112 pts (Bus Mark; Bus Mgt; Acc Bus)
Liverpool John Moores – BBC 112 pts (Bus St; Bus Mgt; Bus Mark; Bus Fin) (IB 26 pts)
London (Birk) – 112 pts (Mgt)
London Regent's – BBC (Glob Mgt courses) (IB 26 pts)
Middlesex – 112 pts (Bus Mgt (Mark)); (Bus Mgt) (IB 28 pts)
Nottingham Trent – BBC 112 pts (Bus Mgt Comb Hons; Law Bus; Bus)
Oxford Brookes – BBC 112 pts (Bus Mgt) (IB 30 pts)
Portsmouth – 112 pts (Law Bus; Bus Mgt) (IB 30 pts HL 17 pts)
Robert Gordon – BBC (Mgt) (IB 29 pts)
Sheffield Hallam – 112 pts (Bus courses; Bus St; Bus HR Mgt)
Southampton Solent – 112 pts (Bus Mgt)
Suffolk – BBC (Bus Mgt; Bus Mgt Law; Bus Mgt App Psy)
Sunderland – 112 pts (Bus Fin Mgt; Bus Mgt; Bus HR Mgt; Bus Mark Mgt)
Univ Law – BBC (Bus Mgt; Bus Mgt Fin; Bus Mgt Mark; Bus Mgt HR Mgt)
West London – 112 pts (Bus St; Bus St Fin); BBC 112 pts (Bus St Mark; Bus St HR Mgt)
Westminster – BBC (Bus Mgt courses; Bus Mgt (Mark)) (IB 28 pts)

Check **Chapter 3** for new university admission details and **Chapter 6** on how to read the subject tables.

166 | Business and Management Courses

Wolverhampton – BBC–CCC (Bus Mgt)
Worcester – 112 pts (Bus courses; Bus Dig Comms; Fin)

104 pts **Bangor** – 104–96 pts (Bus St Ital)
Bath Spa – BCC–CCC (Bus Mgt (Acc); Bus Mgt courses)
Bolton – 104 pts (Bus Mgt)
Brighton – BCC–CCC 104–96 pts (Bus Mgt courses; Bus Mgt Fin) (IB 28 pts HL 16 pts)
Chester – BCC–BBC (Bus Mgt) (IB 26 pts)
Greenwich – 104 pts (Bus Admin)
Kingston – 104–112 pts incl biol/chem (Pharmacol Bus)
Lincoln – BCC (Bus Mgt; Bus St; Bus Mark) (IB 28 pts)
Liverpool Hope – BCC–ABB 104–128 pts (Bus Mgt)
London South Bank – BCC (Bus Mgt Comb Hons)
Manchester Met – BCC–BBC 104–112 pts (Bus Mgt) (IB 26 pts); BCC–BBC 104–112 pts
(Bus Ent HR Mgt; PR Mark) (IB 26 pts)
Northampton – BCC (Bus Comp (Sys); Bus St; Bus Entre)
St Mary's – 104 pts (Bus Law (Comb Hons)); (Bus Mgt) (IB 28 pts)
Salford – BCC–BBC 104–112 pts (Bus Mgt) (IB 26 pts)
South Wales – BCC (Bus Mgt) (IB 29 pts HL 16 pts)
SRUC – BCC (Rur Bus Mgt)
Winchester – 104–120 pts (Bus Mgt courses) (IB 26 pts)

96 pts **Abertay** – CCC (Mark Bus; Bus Mgt) (IB 28 pts)
Anglia Ruskin – 96–112 pts (Bus Mgt) (IB 24 pts); 96–120 pts (Bus Econ) (IB 24 pts)
Derby – 96–112 pts (Bus Mgt)
Hertfordshire – 96–112 pts (Bus St; Mgt)
Leeds Beckett – 96 pts (Bus St); (Int Tour Mgt) (IB 24 pts)
London Met – CCC 96 pts (Bus Econ)
Newman – 96 pts (Bus Mgt)
Plymouth – 96 pts (Bus) (IB 26 pts HL 4)
Roehampton – 96 pts (Bus Mgt)
Royal Agricultural Univ – CCC (Int Bus Mgt) (IB 26 pts)
York St John – 96–112 pts (Bus Mgt HR Mgt; Bus Mgt); 96–112 pts incl Ger (Bus Mgt Ger);
96–116 pts (Bus IT)

88 pts **Canterbury Christ Church** – 88–112 pts (Bus St; Bus Mgt; Mgt)
Harper Adams – 88–104 pts +interview (Bus Mgt Mark)
Teesside – 88–104 pts (Law Bus Mgt)
Trinity Saint David – 88 pts +interview (Bus Mgt; Bus Fin)

80 pts **Bucks New** – 80–96 pts (Bus Mgt)
Teesside – 80–96 pts (Bus Mgt)

64 pts **UHI** – CC (Bus Mgt)
Worcester – 64 pts (Bus St)

32 pts **GSM London** – 32 pts (Bus Mgt)

Open University – contact 0300 303 0073 **or** www.open.ac.uk/contact/new (Bus St)

Alternative offers
See **Chapter 6** and **Appendix 1** for grades/UCAS Tariff points information for other examinations.

EXAMPLES OF DEGREE APPRENTICESHIPS IN THIS SUBJECT FIELD
Anglia Ruskin (Chart Mgt); Aston (Ldrshp Bus Mgt); Chester (Bus Mgt); Chichester (Chart Mgt);
Coventry (Mgt Ldrshp); De Montfort (Bus Mgt); Hertfordshire (Chart Mgt); London South Bank (Chart
Mgr); Manchester Met (Mgt); Northumbria (Bus Ldrshp Mgt); Nottingham Trent (Mgt Ldrshp);
Plymouth (Prof Mgt Chart Mgr); Portsmouth (Bus Ldrshp Mgt; Sls Ldrshp); Sheffield Hallam (Prof Prac
Mgt); Southampton Solent (Bus Mgt); Teesside (Mgt Prac); UWE Bristol (Ldrshp Mgt Prac); West
London (Mgt); Worcester (Chart Mgr).

EXAMPLES OF COLLEGES OFFERING COURSES IN THIS SUBJECT FIELD
Most colleges. See **Chapter 9**, Section 3.

CHOOSING YOUR COURSE (SEE ALSO CH.1)
Universities and colleges teaching quality See www.qaa.ac.uk; https://unistats.ac.uk.

Top research universities and colleges (REF 2014) (Business and Management Studies) Imperial London; London LSE; Cambridge; Oxford; Cardiff; Bath; City; London (King's); Leeds; London Business School; Reading; Sheffield; Warwick; East Anglia; Lancaster.

Examples of sandwich degree courses Aston; Bath; Bedfordshire; Birmingham City; Bournemouth; Bradford; Brighton; Brunel; Buckingham; Central Lancashire; Chester; Coventry; De Montfort; Derby; Glasgow Caledonian; Gloucestershire; Greenwich; Harper Adams; Hertfordshire; Huddersfield; Hull; Kingston; Liverpool John Moores; Loughborough; Manchester Met; Newcastle; Nottingham Trent; Oxford Brookes; Portsmouth; Royal Agricultural Univ; Sheffield Hallam; Staffordshire; Surrey; Teesside; Trinity Saint David; Ulster; UWE Bristol; Westminster; Wolverhampton.

ADMISSIONS INFORMATION
Number of applicants per place (approx) Abertay (Bus St) 3; Anglia Ruskin 5; Aston (Bus Mgt) 12; Bangor 3; Bath 7; Birmingham 8; Blackpool and Fylde (Coll) 2; Bolton 3; Bradford 12; Bristol 10; Buckingham 5; Cardiff 8; Central Lancashire 15; City (Bus St) 9, (Mgt) 7; Colchester (Inst) 2; De Montfort (Bus Mgt) 5; Durham 10; Edge Hill 4; Heriot-Watt 5; Hertfordshire 10; Huddersfield 4; Hull (Bus St) 5, (Mgt) 5; Kent 9; Kingston 50; Lancaster 6; Leeds 27, (Mgt St) 16; Leeds Trinity 6; Liverpool 7; London (King's) 25, (Mgt Sci) 12; London (RH) 9; London LSE 11; London Met 10; London Regent's 25; London South Bank 4; Manchester 7; Manchester Met (Bus St) 26; Middlesex 12; Newcastle 9; Oxford Brookes 7; Plymouth 21; Robert Gordon 5; Salford (Bus St) 9, (Mgt Sci) 2; Stirling 13; Strathclyde 12; Sunderland 20; Trinity Saint David 7; Warwick 22; West Scotland 5; Westminster 12; Winchester 5; Wolverhampton 7; York St John 3.

Admissions tutors' advice Buckingham Try to demonstrate that you have a genuine interest in business and explain why it fascinates you. Why have you decided to choose this particular course and how do you think it will add value to you in your pursuit of your career goals? **Leeds** Applicants taking the BTEC Extended Diploma may be required to take an additional Maths A level paper.

Advice to applicants and planning the UCAS personal statement There are many different kinds of businesses and any work experience is almost essential for these courses. This should be described in detail: for example, size of firm, turnover, managerial problems, sales and marketing aspects, customers' attitudes. Any special interests in business management should also be included, for example, personnel work, purchasing, marketing. Give details of travel or work experience abroad and, for international courses, language expertise and examples of leadership and organising skills. Reference can be made to any particular business topics you have studied in the *Financial Times*, *The Economist* and the business sections in the weekend press. Applicants need to be sociable and ambitious team players. Say why you are interested in the course, identify your academic strengths, your personal strengths and interests. Check information on the websites of the Chartered Institute of Public Relations, the Chartered Institute of Marketing and the Chartered Institute of Personnel and Development. See **Appendix 3**; see also **Accountancy/Accounting**.

Misconceptions about this course Aberystwyth Students are unaware that the course addresses practical aspects of business.

Selection interviews Yes Buckingham, Trinity Saint David; **Some** Bath, Blackpool and Fylde (Coll), Cardiff Met, Liverpool John Moores, Southampton, Warwick; **No** Aberystwyth, Anglia Ruskin, Birmingham, Birmingham City, Bradford, Brighton, City, Coventry, De Montfort, Derby, Dundee, East Anglia, Edge Hill, Essex, Glasgow Caledonian, Greenwich, Harper Adams, Hull, Kent, Leeds, London Met, Manchester Met, Middlesex, Northumbria, Nottingham, Nottingham Trent, Plymouth, Portsmouth, Robert Gordon, Roehampton, Salford, Sheffield Hallam, Staffordshire, Stirling, Strathclyde, Sunderland, Swansea, Teesside, West London, West Scotland, Winchester, Wolverhampton.

Check **Chapter 3** for new university admission details and **Chapter 6** on how to read the subject tables.

Interview advice and questions Any work experience you describe on the UCAS application will probably be the focus of questions which could include topics covering marketing, selling, store organisation and management and customer problems. Personal qualities are naturally important in a career in business, so be ready for such questions as: What qualities do you have which are suitable and important for this course? Describe your strengths and weaknesses. Why should we give you a place on this course? Is advertising fair? What qualities does a person in business require to be successful? What makes a good manager? What is a cash-flow system? What problems can it cause? How could supermarkets improve customer relations? See also **Chapter 5**. **Buckingham** Why Business? How do you see yourself in five years' time? Have you had any work experience? If so, discuss. **Wolverhampton** Mature students with no qualifications will be asked about their work experience.

Reasons for rejection (non-academic) Hadn't read the prospectus. Lack of communication skills. Limited commercial interest. Weak on numeracy and problem-solving. Lack of interview preparation (no questions). Lack of outside interests. Inability to cope with a year abroad. The candidate brought his parent who answered all the questions. See also **Marketing**. **Aberystwyth** Would have trouble fitting into the unique environment of Aberystwyth. Casual approach to learning. **Buckingham** Applicants are requested to attend an Open Day/Evening or a Tutorial Taster Day. The University believes it is very important for applicants to visit its campus. Candidates who do not respond to these invitations may be rejected, irrespective of academic achievement, as the University looks for committed, well-motivated students.

AFTER-RESULTS ADVICE

Offers to applicants repeating A-levels Higher Bradford, Greenwich, Hertfordshire, Kingston, Lancaster, Liverpool, Manchester Met, St Andrews, Sheffield, Strathclyde, Teesside, UWE Bristol; **Same** Abertay, Aberystwyth, Anglia Ruskin, Aston, Bath, Bath Spa, Birmingham City, Bolton, Brighton, Brunel, Buckingham, Cardiff, Cardiff Met, Chester, De Montfort, Derby, Durham, East Anglia, East London, Gloucestershire, Harper Adams, Huddersfield, Hull, Leeds, Lincoln, Liverpool Hope, Liverpool John Moores, Loughborough, Newman, Northumbria, Oxford Brookes, Robert Gordon, Roehampton, Royal Agricultural Univ, Salford, Sheffield Hallam, Staffordshire, Stirling, Suffolk, Sunderland, Trinity Saint David, Ulster, West London, West Scotland, Winchester, Wolverhampton, Worcester, York St John; **No** Glasgow.

GRADUATE DESTINATIONS AND EMPLOYMENT (2015/16 HESA)

Business Studies graduates surveyed 11,135 **Employed** 6,675 **In voluntary employment** 250 **In further study** 2,005 **Assumed unemployed** 675

Management Sciences graduates surveyed 5,515 **Employed** 3,575 **In voluntary employment** 105 **In further study** 835 **Assumed unemployed** 290

Career note The majority of graduates enter trainee management roles in business-related and administrative careers, many specialising in some of the areas listed in **Other degree subjects for consideration** below. The main graduate destinations are in finance, property development, wholesale, retail and manufacturing.

OTHER DEGREE SUBJECTS FOR CONSIDERATION

Accountancy; Banking; Business Information Technology; E-Business; Economics; Estate Management; Finance; Hospitality Management; Housing Management; Human Resource Management; Insurance; Leisure Management; Logistics; Marketing; Public Administration; Retail Management; Sports Management; Surveying.

BUSINESS and MANAGEMENT COURSES (INTERNATIONAL and EUROPEAN)

(including **Business Management with a European Language**; see also **Business and Management Courses, Business and Management Courses (Specialised), Hospitality and Event Management, Human Resource Management, Leisure and Recreation Management/ Studies, Marketing, Retail Management, Tourism and Travel**)

Useful websites See **Business and Management Courses**.

NB The points totals shown to the left of the institutions are for ease of reference only. It must not be assumed that Tariff points are always used by institutions or that they can be substituted for an offer in grades. The level of an offer is not necessarily indicative of the quality of a course.

COURSE OFFERS INFORMATION

Subject requirements/preferences GCSE Mathematics and English often at grade A or B (7 or 5/6) required. **AL** A language will be stipulated for most courses in this subject area. In some cases grades A, B or C may be required.

Your target offers and examples of degree courses

144 pts **Bath** – AAA–AAB+aEPQ incl Span (Int Mgt Span) (IB 36 pts HL 666); AAA/A*AB (Int Mgt) (IB 36 pts HL 765/666)

Exeter – AAA–AAB (Bus Mgt (Int St)) (IB 36–34 pts)

Leeds – AAA (Int Bus) (IB 35 pts HL 17 pts)

London (UCL) – AAA incl maths (Econ Bus E Euro St) (IB 38 pts HL 6 maths)

Reading – AAA–AAB (Int Mgt Bus Admin Fr/Ger/Ital) (IB 35 pts); AAA (Int Bus Mgt) (IB 35 pts)

Surrey – AAA–AAB (Int Bus Mgt) (IB 34 pts)

Warwick – AAA incl lang (Int Bus courses) (IB 38 pts HL 5 lang); AAA (Int Mgt) (IB 38 pts)

136 pts **Bath** – AAB/ABB+aEPQ incl Ger (Int Mgt Ger) (IB 35 pts HL 6 Ger); AAB–ABB+aEPQ incl Fr (Int Mgt Fr) (IB 36 pts HL 6 Fr)

Birmingham – AAB (Int Bus Lang; Int Bus) (IB 32 pts HL 665)

Cardiff – AAB incl lang (Bus Mgt Euro Lang) (IB 35–32 pts HL 665); AAB (Bus Mgt (Int Mgt)) (IB 35 pts)

Edinburgh – AAB incl lang (Int Bus Fr/Ger/Span) (IB 43 pts HL 776); AAB (Int Bus) (IB 43 pts HL 776)

Lancaster – AAB (Int Mgt; Int Mgt (Yr Abrd); Int Mgt (Yr Ind)) (IB 35 pts HL 16 pts)

Leeds – AAB (Int Bus Russ) (IB 35 pts HL 16 pts)

London (King's) – AAB incl Fr (Fr Mgt (Yr Abrd)) (IB 35 pts HL 665 incl 6 Fr)

London (SOAS) – AAB–ABB (Int Mgt courses) (IB 35 pts HL 665)

Loughborough – AAB (Int Bus) (IB 35 pts HL 665)

Manchester – AAB (Int Mgt; Int Mgt Am Bus St) (IB 33 pts HL 665)

Newcastle – AAB (Int Bus Mgt) (IB 35 pts)

Nottingham – AAB (Mgt Chin St) (IB 34 pts HL 18 pts)

Sheffield – AAB (Int Bus Mgt (St Abrd)) (IB 33 pts)

Southampton – AAB/ABB+aEPQ incl Fr/Ger/Span +interview (Bus Mgt Fr/Ger/Span) (IB 34 pts HL 6 Fr/Ger/Span)

Surrey – AAB incl Fr/Ger/Span (Bus Mgt Fr/Ger/Span) (IB 34 pts)

Sussex – AAB–ABB (Int Bus) (IB 32 pts)

128 pts **Aston** – ABB–BBB incl lang (Int Bus Fr/Ger/Span) (IB 32 pts HL 655–555 incl 5 lang)

Bournemouth – 128–136 pts (Int Bus St) (IB 32–33 pts HL 55)

Bradford – ABB 128 pts (Int Bus Mgt)

Coventry – ABB–BBB (Int Bus Mgt) (IB 31-30 pts)
Kent – ABB (Int Bus) (IB 34 pts)
Liverpool – ABB incl lang (Modn Lang St Bus) (IB 33 pts); ABB (Int Bus) (IB 33 pts)
London (QM) – ABB incl hum/soc sci (Russ Bus Mgt) (IB 32 pts HL 655)
London (RH) – ABB (Modn Lang Mgt; Mgt Int Bus) (IB 32 pts HL 655)
Northumbria – 128–136 pts (Int Bus Mgt) (HL 444)
Queen's Belfast – ABB (Int Bus Fr/Ger/Mand Chin)
Roehampton – 128 pts (Int Bus)
Sheffield – ABB–BBB+bEPQ (Kor St Jap) (IB 33 pts)

120 pts **Brunel** – BBB (Int Bus) (IB 30 pts)
Dundee – BBB–BCC (Int Bus Mark; Int Bus) (IB 30 pts HL 555); (Int Bus Ger; Int Bus Fin) (IB 30 pts)
Essex – BBB (Int Bus Entre) (IB 30 pts)
Gloucestershire – BBB 120 pts (Int Bus Mgt)
Greenwich – 120 pts (Int Bus)
Heriot-Watt – BBB incl lang (Int Bus Mgt Fr/Ger/Span/Chin) (IB 30 pts HL 5 lang); BBB (Int Bus Mgt (Econ/Op Mgt)) (IB 29 pts)
Huddersfield – BBB 120 pts (Int Bus) (IB 31 pts)
Nottingham Trent – BBB 120 pts (Int Bus Comb Hons)
Oxford Brookes – BBB 120 pts (Int Bus Mgt) (IB 31 pts)
Stirling – BBB (Int Mgt St Euro Langs Soty; Int Mgt St Intercult St) (IB 32 pts)
UWE Bristol – 120 pts (Int Bus)

112 pts **Bedfordshire** – 112 pts (Bus St (Int))
Brighton – BBC–CCC (Int Bus Mgt) (IB 28 pts HL 16 pts)
Cardiff Met – 112 pts (Int Bus Mgt) (IB 25 pts HL 12 pts)
Central Lancashire – 112 pts (Int Bus) (IB 28 pts)
Coventry – BBC (Int Fash Bus) (IB 30 pts)
De Montfort – 112 pts (Int Bus) (IB 28 pts)
Hull – 112 pts (Int Bus) (IB 30 pts)
Keele – BBC (Int Bus Comb Hons) (IB 30 pts)
Kingston – BBC 112 pts (Int Bus) (IB 25 pts HL 554 incl 4 Engl lang)
Liverpool John Moores – BBC 112 pts (Bus Int Bus Mgt) (IB 26 pts)
London Regent's – BBC (Glob Mgt courses) (IB 26 pts)
Middlesex – 112 pts (Bus Mgt (Mand/Span); Int Bus)
Portsmouth – 112 pts (Int Bus) (IB 30 pts HL 17 pts)
Robert Gordon – BBC (Int Bus Mgt) (IB 29 pts)
Sheffield Hallam – 112–96 pts (Int Bus); 112 pts incl Fr/Ger/Span (Langs Int Bus (Fr/Ger/Span))
Southampton Solent – 112 pts (Int Bus Mgt)
Staffordshire – BBC 112 pts (Int Bus Mgt)
Westminster – BBC (Int Bus (Arbc/Chin/Fr/Span); Int Bus) (IB 28 pts)
Wolverhampton – BBC–CCC (Int Bus Mgt)

104 pts **Chester** – BCC–BBC (Int Bus Mgt) (IB 26 pts)
Glasgow Caledonian – BCC (Int Bus) (IB 25 pts)
Lincoln – BCC (Int Bus Mgt) (IB 28 pts)
Manchester Met – BCC–BBC 104–112 pts (Int Bus Mgt) (IB 26 pts); 104–112 pts incl lang (Int Bus/Fr/Span) (IB 26 pts)
Salford – BCC–BBC 104–112 pts (Int Bus) (IB 26 pts)

96 pts **Anglia Ruskin** – 96–112 pts (Int Bus Mgt) (IB 24 pts)
Derby – 96–112 pts (Int Spa Mgt)
Edinburgh Napier – CCC incl lang (Int Bus Mgt Lang) (IB 27 pts HL 5 lang)
Euro Bus Sch London – CCC +interview (Int Bus; Int Bus (Mand Chin))
Hertfordshire – 96–112 pts (Int Mgt)
Leeds Beckett – 96 pts (Int Bus)
London Met – CCC 96 pts (Int Bus Mgt)

UCAS points Tariff: A* = 56 pts; A = 48 pts; B = 40 pts; C = 32 pts; D = 24 pts; E = 16 pts

A BUSINESS QUALIFICATION TO MATCH YOUR GLOBAL AMBITIONS

Study our BA (Hons) Business Management programmes in a unique environment, make new connections and network with people from around the world.

Study in Birmingham, Leeds, London and Manchester or online.

We bring the business world into the classroom. You'll get to meet potential future employers, participate in business games, and maximise your employability prospects.

The University of **Law**

BUSINESS SCHOOL

CMI HE Partner

For more information
law.ac.uk/business

TEF Gold

Teaching Excellence Framework
Awarded to The University of Law

London Regent's – CCC (Int Bus)
Middlesex – 96 pts (Int Tour Mgt (Span))
Plymouth – 96 pts incl Fr (Int Bus Fr) (IB 26 pts HL 4 Fr); 96 pts (Int Bus Span) (IB 26 pts HL 4 Span); (Int Bus) (IB 26 pts HL 4)
York St John – 96–112 pts (Int Bus Mgt)

Alternative offers
See **Chapter 6** and **Appendix 1** for grades/UCAS Tariff points information for other examinations.

EXAMPLES OF COLLEGES OFFERING COURSES IN THIS SUBJECT FIELD
Most colleges. Blackburn (Coll); Bristol City (Coll); Cornwall (Coll); Doncaster (Coll); Durham New (Coll); Ealing, Hammersmith and West London (Coll); HOW (Coll); Newcastle (Coll); Nottingham (Coll); Riverside (Coll); South Essex (Coll).

CHOOSING YOUR COURSE (SEE ALSO CH.1)
Universities and colleges teaching quality See www.qaa.ac.uk; https://unistats.ac.uk.

Top research universities and colleges (REF 2014) See **Business and Management Courses**.

Examples of sandwich degree courses Anglia Ruskin; Aston; Bath; Bournemouth; Bradford; Brighton; Brunel; De Montfort; Greenwich; Hertfordshire; Leeds Beckett; Loughborough; Manchester Met; Middlesex; Northumbria; Nottingham Trent; Oxford Brookes; Plymouth; Portsmouth; Sheffield Hallam; Staffordshire; Sussex.

ADMISSIONS INFORMATION
Number of applicants per place (approx) Anglia Ruskin 5; Aston (Int Bus) 6; Bath 26; Birmingham 28; Blackpool and Fylde (Coll) 2; Bradford 12; Cardiff 8; Central Lancashire 15; Colchester (Inst) 2; Derby 4; Heriot-Watt 6; Hertfordshire 10; Huddersfield 2; Kingston 50; Leeds 27; London (King's) 25;

Check **Chapter 3** for new university admission details and **Chapter 6** on how to read the subject tables.

London (RH) 9; London Met 10; London Regent's 25; Manchester Met (Int Bus) 8; Middlesex 12; Newcastle 8; Oxford Brookes 7; Plymouth 39; Robert Gordon 5; Sheffield Hallam (Int Bus) 6; Warwick 22; Westminster 12; Wolverhampton 7; York St John 3.

Advice to applicants and planning the UCAS personal statement See **Business and Management Courses**.

Misconceptions about this course Aston (Int Bus Fr) Not two separate disciplines – the two subjects are integrated involving the study of language in a business and management context.

Selection interviews Yes Euro Bus Sch London; **Some** Bath, Cardiff Met, Warwick; **No** Anglia Ruskin, Birmingham, Bradford, Brighton, Coventry, De Montfort, Derby, Glasgow Caledonian, Greenwich, Hull, Leeds, London Met, Manchester Met, Middlesex, Northumbria, Nottingham Trent, Plymouth, Robert Gordon, Roehampton, Salford, Sheffield Hallam, Staffordshire, Stirling, Wolverhampton.

Interview advice and questions See **Business and Management Courses**.

Reasons for rejection (non-academic) See **Business and Management Courses**.

AFTER-RESULTS ADVICE
Offers to applicants repeating A-levels Higher Bradford, Greenwich, Hertfordshire, Kingston, Liverpool, Manchester Met, Sheffield; **Same** Anglia Ruskin, Aston, Bath, Brighton, Cardiff, Cardiff Met, Chester, De Montfort, Derby, Gloucestershire, Huddersfield, Hull, Leeds, Lincoln, Loughborough, Northumbria, Oxford Brookes, Robert Gordon, Roehampton, Salford, Sheffield Hallam, Staffordshire, Stirling, Wolverhampton, York St John.

GRADUATE DESTINATIONS AND EMPLOYMENT (2015/16 HESA)
See **Business and Management Courses**.

Career note See **Business and Management Courses**.

OTHER DEGREE SUBJECTS FOR CONSIDERATION
Accountancy; Banking; Business Information Technology; E-Business; Economics; Estate Management; Finance; Hospitality Management; Housing Management; Human Resource Management; Insurance; Leisure Management; Logistics; Marketing; Public Administration; Retail Management; Sports Management; Surveying.

BUSINESS and MANAGEMENT COURSES (SPECIALISED)

(including **Advertising, Agri-Business Management, Business, Marketing and Consumer Behaviour, Food Science with Business, Public Relations** and **Publishing**; see also **Business and Management Courses, Business and Management Courses (International and European), Hospitality and Event Management, Human Resource Management, Leisure and Recreation Management/Studies, Marketing, Retail Management, Tourism and Travel**)

Useful websites See **Business and Management Courses**.

NB The points totals shown to the left of the institutions are for ease of reference only. It must not be assumed that Tariff points are always used by institutions or that they can be substituted for an offer in grades. The level of an offer is not necessarily indicative of the quality of a course.

COURSE OFFERS INFORMATION
Subject requirements/preferences GCSE Mathematics and English often at grade A or B (7 or 5/6) required. **AL** Mathematics required for some courses. In some cases grades A, B or C may be required. (Publ) English required for some courses.

UCAS points Tariff: A* = 56 pts; A = 48 pts; B = 40 pts; C = 32 pts; D = 24 pts; E = 16 pts

Your target offers and examples of degree courses

152 pts **Southampton** – A*AA/A*AB+aEPQ incl maths+phys (Aero Astnaut (Eng Mgt) (MEng)) (IB 38 pts HL 6 maths+phys)

144 pts **Edinburgh** – AAA incl sci/maths (Ecol Env Sci Mgt) (IB 37 pts HL 555)

London (UCL) – AAA–AAB incl chem+sci/maths +interview (Chem Mgt St) (IB 38–36 pts HL 5 chem+sci/maths)

Warwick – AAA incl maths+phys (Eng Bus Mgt) (IB 38 pts HL 6 maths+phys)

136 pts **Cardiff** – AAB (Bus Mgt (Log Ops)) (IB 35–32 pts)

Lancaster – AAB (Int Bus Mgt (Am); Adv Mark) (IB 35 pts HL 16 pts)

London (SOAS) – AAB–ABB (SE As St Int Mgt) (IB 35 pts HL 665)

Loughborough – AAB incl geog (Geog Spo Mgt) (IB 35 pts HL 665 incl 5 geog)

Newcastle – AAB–ABB (Agribus Mgt) (IB 35 pts)

Reading – AAB–ABB incl sci/maths (Fd Sci Bus) (IB 34–32 pts HL 5 sci/maths)

Ulster – AAB–AAA (Comm Adv Mark) (IB 28–29 pts HL 14 pts)

128 pts **Bournemouth** – 128–136 pts (Bus St Fin) (IB 32–33 pts HL 55)

Coventry – ABB–BBB (Disas Mgt Emer Plan) (IB 30 pts); (Int Disas Mgt; Bus Mark) (IB 31–30 pts)

Heriot-Watt – ABB (3 yr course) BBB (4 yr course) (Bus Fin) (IB 34 pts (3 yr course) 29 pts (4 yr course))

Leeds – ABB (Env Bus) (IB 34 pts HL 16 pts)

Loughborough – ABB/AAC (Air Trans Mgt) (IB 34 pts HL 655); ABB (Inf Mgt Bus) (IB 34 pts)

120 pts **Aberdeen** – BBB (Bus Mgt Inf Sys) (IB 32 pts HL 555)

Buckingham – BBB–BBC (Bus Mgt App Comp) (IB 32–31 pts)

East Anglia – BBB (Intercult Comm Bus Mgt) (IB 31 pts)

Edge Hill – BBB 120 pts (Mark PR)

Essex – BBB (Lat Am St Bus Mgt) (IB 30 pts)

Huddersfield – BBB 120 pts (Air Trans Log Mgt)

London (Royal Central Sch SpDr) – 120–64 pts +interview +portfolio (Thea Prac (Stg Mgt); Thea Prac (Tech Prod Mgt))

Middlesex – 120 pts (Mus Bus Arts Mgt); (Adv PR Brnd) (IB 28 pts)

Nottingham Trent – BBB 120 pts (Fash Mgt)

Queen Margaret – BBB (3 yr course) BCC (4 yr course) (PR Mark Evnts; PR Media) (IB 28 pts)

Ulster – BBB incl sci/maths/tech (Eng Mgt) (IB 26 pts HL 13 pts incl 5 maths+sci)

112 pts **Arts London (CFash)** – 112 pts (Fash Mgt) (IB 25 pts)

Bournemouth – 112–120 pts (PR) (IB 30–31 pts HL 55)

Cardiff Met – 112 pts (Fd Ind Mgt)

Central Lancashire – 112 pts +interview +portfolio (Adv) (IB 28 pts)

Coventry – BBC (Int Fash Bus) (IB 30 pts)

De Montfort – 112 pts (Adv Mark Comms) (IB 26 pts)

East London – 112 pts (Adv) (IB 24 pts HL 15 pts); (HR Mgt) (IB 25 pts HL 15 pts)

Glyndŵr – 112 pts (Bus Mark Consum Bhv)

Hertfordshire – 112 pts (Mus Ind Mgt) (HL 44)

Leeds Beckett – 112 pts (Spo Bus Mgt) (IB 25 pts)

Liverpool John Moores – BBC 112 pts (Mgt Trans Log; Marit Bus Mgt) (IB 26 pts)

London (Birk) – 112 pts (Env Mgt)

Nottingham Trent – BBC 112 pts (Quant Surv Constr Commer Mgt)

Oxford Brookes – BBC–BCC 112–104 pts (Quant Surv Commer Mgt) (IB 31–30 pts)

Plymouth – 112 pts (Marit Bus Log; Marit Bus Marit Law) (IB 28 pts HL 4); (Pub) (IB 28 pts)

Portsmouth – 112 pts (Bus Sys Mgt) (IB 30 pts HL 17 pts)

Robert Gordon – BBC (Fash Mgt) (IB 29 pts)

Sheffield Hallam – 112 pts (Bus Fin Mgt); 112–96 pts (PR)

Southampton Solent – 112 pts (Bus IT; Advntr Out Mgt)

Sunderland – 112 pts (Tour Mgt)
West London – 112 pts (Culn Arts Mgt; Airln Airpt Mgt; Adv PR)
104 pts **Central Lancashire** – 104 pts (Pub)
Glasgow Caledonian – BCC (Risk Mgt) (IB 25 pts)
Harper Adams – 104–120 pts +interview (Agric Frm Bus Mgt)
Manchester Met – BCC–BBC 104–112 pts (Adv Brnd Mgt; Spo Mgt) (IB 26 pts)
Northampton – BCC (Bus Entre)
Royal Agricultural Univ – BCC (Rur Lnd Mgt) (IB 26 pts)
West Scotland – BCC incl maths/sci/tech (Eng Mgt) (IB 28 pts)
96 pts **Arts London (CFash)** – 96 pts +interview +portfolio (Fash PR Comm)
Birmingham (UC) – 96 pts (Bus Ent; Culn Arts Mgt)
Derby – 96–112 pts (Int Spa Mgt; Int Tour Mgt); 96–120 pts (Bus Mgt Comb Hons)
Liverpool (LIPA) – CCC 96 pts (Mgt Mus Enter Thea Evnts)
Nottingham Trent – CCC 96 pts (Constr Mgt)
Plymouth – 96 pts (Cru Mgt) (IB 26 pts HL 4)
Royal Agricultural Univ – CCC (Int Bus Mgt (Fd Agribus)) (IB 26 pts)
Sheffield Hallam – 96–80 pts (IT Bus St)
Southampton Solent – 96 pts (Fash Mgt Mark)
UCEM – 96 pts (Rl Est Mgt)
88 pts **Trinity Saint David** – 88 pts +interview (Int Trav Tour Mgt)
80 pts **Arts London** – 80 pts (PR)
Bedfordshire – 80 pts (PR; Adv Mark Comms)
Bucks New – 80–96 pts (Airln Airpt Mgt)
Colchester (Inst) – 80 pts (Constr Mgt (Site Mgt))
Sparsholt (Coll) – CCE incl sci (Aqua Fish Mgt) (IB 24 pts HL 4 sci)
Trinity Saint David – 80 pts +interview (Spo Mgt; Tour Mgt)
64 pts **Trinity Saint David** – 64 pts +interview (Mtrspo Mgt)
UHI – CC (Glf Mgt)
24 pts **UHI** – D (Mus Bus)

Alternative offers
See **Chapter 6** and **Appendix 1** for grades/UCAS Tariff points information for other examinations.

EXAMPLES OF COLLEGES OFFERING COURSES IN THIS SUBJECT FIELD
Most colleges. See **Chapter 9**, Section 3.

CHOOSING YOUR COURSE (SEE ALSO CH.1)
Universities and colleges teaching quality See www.qaa.ac.uk; https://unistats.ac.uk.

Top research universities and colleges (REF 2014) See **Business and Management Courses**.

Examples of sandwich degree courses Birmingham (UC); Bournemouth; Central Lancashire; Coventry; De Montfort; Harper Adams; Hertfordshire; Huddersfield; Lancaster; Leeds Beckett; Liverpool John Moores; Loughborough; Manchester Met; Newcastle; Nottingham Trent; Oxford Brookes; Portsmouth; Reading; Sheffield Hallam; Southampton Solent; Trinity Saint David; Ulster.

ADMISSIONS INFORMATION
Number of applicants per place (approx) Birmingham (UC) 5; Blackpool and Fylde (Coll) 2; Cardiff 8; Central Lancashire 15; Colchester (Inst) 2; Edge Hill 4; Heriot-Watt 5; Hertfordshire 10; Huddersfield 4; Leeds 27; London (UCL) 8; London South Bank 4; Middlesex 12; Newcastle 8; Oxford Brookes 7; Plymouth 57; Robert Gordon 5; Trinity Saint David 7; Warwick 22; West Scotland 5.

Advice to applicants and planning the UCAS personal statement See **Business and Management Courses**.

Misconceptions about this course Bournemouth Advertising is not mainly a creative course but also includes strategy, planning, finance and the management of the advertising process.

Selection interviews Yes Trinity Saint David; **Some** Blackpool and Fylde (Coll), Cardiff Met, Coventry, Plymouth, Warwick; **No** De Montfort, Derby, East Anglia, Edge Hill, Glasgow Caledonian, Greenwich, Harper Adams, Leeds, Liverpool John Moores, Manchester Met, Middlesex, Nottingham Trent, Robert Gordon, Sheffield Hallam, Stirling, Sunderland, West London.

Interview advice and questions For Consumer Studies/Science, questions will stem from your special interests in this subject and in the past have included: What interests you in consumer behaviour? What are the advantages and disadvantages of measuring consumer behaviour? What is ergonomics? What do you understand by the term sustainable consumption? What world or national news has annoyed, pleased or upset you? What relevance do textiles and dress have to home economics? How would you react in a room full of fools?

Reasons for rejection (non-academic) Buckingham Applicants are requested to attend an Open Day/Evening or a Tutorial Taster Day. The University believes it is very important for applicants to visit its campus. Candidates who do not respond to these invitations may be rejected, irrespective of academic achievement, as the University looks for committed, well-motivated students.

AFTER-RESULTS ADVICE
Offers to applicants repeating A-levels Higher Hertfordshire, Lancaster, Manchester Met; **Same** Cardiff, Cardiff Met, De Montfort, Derby, East Anglia, Huddersfield, Leeds, Liverpool John Moores, Loughborough, Oxford Brookes, Robert Gordon, Royal Agricultural Univ, Sheffield Hallam, Ulster, West London, Worcester.

GRADUATE DESTINATIONS AND EMPLOYMENT (2015/16 HESA)
See **Business and Management Courses**.

Career note See **Business and Management Courses**.

OTHER DEGREE SUBJECTS FOR CONSIDERATION
Accountancy; Banking; Business Information Technology; E-Business; Economics; Estate Management; Finance; Hospitality Management; Housing Management; Human Resource Management; Insurance; Leisure Management; Logistics; Marketing; Public Administration; Retail Management; Sports Management; Surveying.

CELTIC, IRISH, SCOTTISH and WELSH STUDIES
(including Celtic and Linguistics and Gaelic Studies)

Evidence of Celtic civilisation and language exists in Ireland, Scotland, Wales, Cornwall, the Isle of Man and across the English Channel in Brittany. Welsh however is the only Celtic language classified as endangered and is spoken by 19% of the population, mainly in the border counties although there is a substantial number in North Wales, particularly in Gwynedd where it is reported that 70% of the population are Welsh speakers. Gaelic (Scottish Gaelic) is a Celtic language native to Scotland, although in addition to English, 'Scots' is a dialect which is spoken in the Lowlands and the Northern Isles. The content of courses in each of these languages, such as the Celtic option at Aberystwyth (the largest department of Welsh in the UK), will cover the history, literature and the language and its place in the modern world. Cambridge also offers a degree in Anglo Saxon, Norse and Celtic, unique in the UK for those fascinated by medieval history, literature, languages and archaeology. It is offered by all colleges and there are no specific subject requirements.

Useful websites http://gov.wales; www.bbc.com/wales; www.daltai.com; www.eisteddfod.org.uk; www.digitalmedievalist.com

NB The points totals shown to the left of the institutions are for ease of reference only. It must not be assumed that Tariff points are always used by institutions or that they can be substituted for an offer in grades. The level of an offer is not necessarily indicative of the quality of a course.

COURSE OFFERS INFORMATION

Subject requirements/preferences GCSE A foreign language or Welsh may be required. **AL** Welsh may be required for some courses.

Your target offers and examples of degree courses

152 pts **Cambridge** – A*AA +interview +ASNCAA (A-Sxn Nrs Celt) (IB 40–42 pts HL 776)

144 pts **Edinburgh** – AAA incl Engl (Engl Scot Lit) (IB 39 pts HL 666)

St Andrews – AAA (Scot Hist courses) (IB 36 pts HL 6 hist)

136 pts **Edinburgh** – ABB (P Educ Gael) (IB 36 pts)

Glasgow – AAB incl arts/lang/hum (Gael) (IB 36 pts HL 665 incl Engl+hum/lang); AAB incl arts/hum/lang (Celt Civ) (IB 36 pts HL 665 incl Eng+hum/lang); (Celt St courses; Scot Lit) (IB 36 pts HL 665 incl Engl+hum/lang)

St Andrews – AAB (Phil Scot Hist) (IB 35 pts)

128 pts **Edinburgh** – ABB incl Engl (Celt Scot Lit; Celt Engl Lit; Scot Lit) (IB 34 pts HL 655); ABB (Celt Arch; Celt Ling; Celt; Celt Scot Hist; Scot Ethnol; Scot St) (IB 34 pts HL 655)

Liverpool – ABB–BBB (Ir St Comb Hons) (IB 30 pts)

Queen's Belfast – ABB incl Ir (Ir)

Stirling – ABB (3 yr course) BBB (4 yr course) incl hist (Scot Hist) (IB 35 pts (3 yr course) 32 pts (4 yr course))

120 pts **Aberdeen** – BBB (Celt A-Sxn St Comb Hons; Gael St; Engl Scot Lit; Celt A-Sxn St) (IB 32 pts HL 555)

Aberystwyth – BBB (Hist Welsh Hist) (IB 28 pts)

Cardiff – BBB–BBC incl Welsh (Welsh) (HL 665–655)

Swansea – BBB 120 pts (Welsh courses) (IB 32 pts)

112 pts **Aberystwyth** – BBC (Ir Comb Hons) (IB 28 pts)

Bangor – 112–120 pts (Welsh Hist Comb Hons); 112 pts incl Welsh (Prof Welsh (Cym Prof))

104 pts **Aberystwyth** – BCC (Celt St; Welsh courses) (IB 28 pts)

Cardiff Met – 104 pts +interview (Educ St Welsh)

72 pts **UHI** – BC (Scot Hist; Scot Hist Arch); BC +interview (Gael Media St; Gael Dev); BC +interview +audition (Gael Trad Mus)

Alternative offers

See **Chapter 6** and **Appendix 1** for grades/UCAS Tariff points information for other examinations.

CHOOSING YOUR COURSE (SEE ALSO CH.1)

Universities and colleges teaching quality See www.qaa.ac.uk; https://unistats.ac.uk.

ADMISSIONS INFORMATION

Number of applicants per place (approx) Bangor (Welsh) 5; Cambridge 3; Cardiff 2; Swansea 7.

Advice to applicants and planning the UCAS personal statement Interests in this field largely develop through literature, museum visits or archaeology which should be fully described in the UCAS application.

Selection interviews Yes Cambridge; **No** Aberystwyth.

Interview advice and questions Past questions have included: Why do you want to study this subject? What specific areas of Celtic culture interest you? What do you expect to gain by studying unusual subjects? See **Chapter 5**.

AFTER-RESULTS ADVICE

Offers to applicants repeating A-levels Same Aberystwyth, Bangor, Cardiff, Swansea; **No** Glasgow.

GRADUATE DESTINATIONS AND EMPLOYMENT (2015/16 HESA)

Celtic Studies graduates surveyed 160 **Employed** 60 **In voluntary employment** 0 **In further study** 55 **Assumed unemployed** 5

Career note See **Combined Courses** and **Languages**.

OTHER DEGREE SUBJECTS FOR CONSIDERATION
Anthropology; Archaeology; English; History; Linguistics.

CHEMISTRY
(see also Biochemistry, Engineering (Chemical), Pharmacy and Pharmaceutical Sciences)

There is a shortage of applicants for this subject despite the fact that it's the basis of many careers in the manufacturing industries, such areas as pharmaceuticals, medicine, veterinary science and health, agriculture, petroleum, cosmetics, plastics, the food industry, colour chemistry and aspects of the environment such as pollution and recycling. Most courses will offer a range of compulsory modules (possibly up to 75% of a course) and a series of optional modules. For example, at the University of York, compulsory modules will include organic, inorganic and physical chemistry. Optional modules on offer cover air quality and human health, analytical and forensic science, atmospheric chemistry and climate, biological chemistry, environmental chemistry, green chemistry, industrial management, materials chemistry and medical chemistry. These options at all universities enable students to begin to focus on special studies and lay a foundation for possible future careers.

Useful websites www.rsc.org; www.chem.ox.ac.uk/vrchemistry

NB The points totals shown to the left of the institutions are for ease of reference only. It must not be assumed that Tariff points are always used by institutions or that they can be substituted for an offer in grades. The level of an offer is not necessarily indicative of the quality of a course.

COURSE OFFERS INFORMATION
Subject requirements/preferences GCSE English, mathematics/science subjects usually required. A/B (7/5 or 6) grades often stipulated by popular universities. **AL** Two science subjects including chemistry usually required.

Your target offers and examples of degree courses
160 pts Cambridge – A*A*A incl sci/maths +interview +NSAA (Nat Sci (Chem)) (IB 40 42 pts HL 776)

Oxford – A*A*A incl chem+maths +interview +TSA (Chem) (IB 40 pts HL 7 chem+6/7 sci/maths)

152 pts Durham – A*AA incl chem+maths (Chem) (IB 38 pts HL 666)

Imperial London – A*AA–A*A*A* incl chem+maths +interview (Chem Medcnl Chem) (IB 38–39 pts HL 7 chem 6 maths); (Chem Fr/Ger/Span Sci; Chem Mol Phys (MSci)) (IB 40–42 pts HL 7 chem 6 maths); (Chem (Yr Ind/Rsch)) (IB 40–42 pts HL 7 chem 6 maths); A*AA–AAA incl chem+maths +interview (Chem courses) (IB 39–38 pts HL 7 chem 7/6 maths)

Nottingham – A*AA–AAA incl maths+chem/phys (Cheml Eng Env Eng (Yr Ind)) (IB 36 pts)

York – A*AA–AAB incl chem+sci/maths +interview (Chem; Chem Atmos Env) (IB 36–35 pts HL 6 chem+sci/maths); A*AA–AAA incl chem+sci/maths +interview (Chem Biol Medcnl Chem) (IB 36–35 pts HL 6 chem+sci/maths)

144 pts Bath – AAA/AAB+aEPQ incl chem+sci/maths (Chem courses) (IB 36 pts HL 666)

Edinburgh – AAA incl chem+maths (Chem; Medcnl Biol Chem) (IB 37 pts HL 666); AAA incl chem+maths+phys (Cheml Phys) (IB 37 pts HL 666)

London (UCL) – AAA–AAB incl maths+chem +interview (Chem Maths) (IB 38–36 pts HL 6 maths 5 chem); AAA incl chem+maths+phys +interview (Cheml Phys) (IB 38 pts HL 5 chem+maths+phys); AAA–AAB incl chem+sci/maths +interview (Chem; Chem Mgt St; Chem Euro Lang; Medcnl Chem) (IB 38–36 pts HL 5 chem+sci/maths)

Southampton – AAA incl chem+sci/maths (Chem Medcnl Sci (MChem)) (IB 36 pts HL 6 chem+sci/maths); AAA–AAB incl chem+maths (Chem Maths (MChem)) (IB 36 pts HL 6 chem+maths)

Strathclyde – AAA incl sci/maths (Chem (MChem)) (IB 30 pts); (Foren Analyt Chem (MChem)) (IB 34 pts)

Swansea – AAA–AAB incl chem+sci/maths (Chemistry (MChem)) (IB 36–34 pts HL 6 chem)

136 pts **Birmingham** – AAB–ABB incl chem (Chem; Chem Modn Lang; Chem Pharmacol) (IB 32 pts HL 655)

Bristol – AAB–AAC incl chem+maths (Chem) (IB 34–32 pts HL 6 chem+maths)

Cardiff – AAB–BBB incl chem +interview (Chem) (IB 34–30 pts HL 5 chem+sci/maths)

Dundee – AAB incl biol+chem (Biol Chem Drug Dscvry) (IB 30 pts HL 555)

Glasgow – AAB incl chem (Chem) (IB 36 pts HL 665 incl 6 sci)

London (King's) – AAB incl chem+sci/maths (Chem Biomed; Chem) (IB 35 pts HL 665)

Manchester – AAB incl chem+sci/maths +interview (Chem; Chem Medcnl Chem) (IB 32 pts HL 665)

Newcastle – AAB incl chem (Chem (MChem)) (IB 35 pts HL 6 chem)

Nottingham – AAB incl chem+sci (Bioch Biol Chem) (IB 34 pts HL 5/6 chem+sci); AAB incl maths+phys+chem (Chem Mol Phys) (IB 34 pts HL 6 maths 6/5 phys+chem); AAB–ABB incl chem (Medcnl Biol Chem) (IB 34–32 pts Hl 6 chem); (Chem) (IB 34–32 pts HL 6 chem)

Queen's Belfast – AAB incl chem+sci+Fr/Span (Chem Fr/Span/Yr Abrd (MSci))

Reading – AAB–ABB incl chem+sci +interview (Chem (MChem) courses) (IB 34–32 pts HL 6 chem 5 sci)

St Andrews – AAB incl chem (Chem) (IB 35 pts HL 6 chem)

Sheffield – AAB incl chem+sci/maths (Chem) (IB 34 pts HL 6 chem+sci/maths)

Southampton – AAB–ABB incl chem (Chem) (IB 34 pts)

Sussex – AAB–ABB incl chem (Chem) (IB 32 pts HL 5 chem)

Warwick – AAB incl chem+maths (Chem; Chem Medcnl Chem) (IB 36 pts HL 6 chem 5 maths/sci)

128 pts **Aston** – ABB–BBB incl chem (Chem; App Chem) (IB 32 pts)

Bangor – 128–104 pts incl chem (Chem)

East Anglia – ABB (Chem Educ) (IB 32 pts HL 5 chem)

Heriot-Watt – ABB incl chem+maths (3 yr course) BBB incl chem (4 yr course) (Chem courses; Chem Bioch (MChem); Chem Mat Nanosci) (IB 35 pts (3 yr course) 30 pts (4 yr course) HL 6 chem+maths (3 yr course) 5 chem (4 yr course))

Lancaster – ABB incl chem+sci (Chem) (IB 32 pts HL 16 pts incl 6 chem+sci)

Leeds – ABB incl chem (Chem courses) (IB 32 pts HL 6 chem); ABB (Medcnl Chem) (IB 34 pts HL 6 chem)

Leicester – ABB–BBB incl chem (Chem; Chem Foren Sci) (IB 30 pts HL 5 chem); ABB–BBB/BBB–BBC+bEPQ incl chem (Pharml Chem) (IB 30 pts HL 5 chem)

Liverpool – ABB/BBB+aEPQ incl chem+sci (Medcnl Chem; Chem (Yr Ind); Chem) (IB 33 pts HL 6 chem 5 sci)

London (QM) – ABB incl chem (Chem) (IB 34 pts HL 6/5 chem)

Loughborough – ABB incl chem (Chem (MChem); Medcnl Pharml Chem; Chem) (IB 34 pts HL 655 incl 5 chem)

Newcastle – ABB incl chem (Chem Medcnl Chem; Chem (Yr Ind); Chem) (IB 34 pts HL 6 chem)

Nottingham Trent – ABB incl chem 128 pts (Chem (MChem))

Reading – ABB–BBB incl chem +interview (Chem) (IB 32–30 pts HL 5 chem)

Strathclyde – ABB incl sci/maths (Chem Teach (MChem)) (IB 34 pts)

Surrey – ABB–BBB incl chem+sci (Chem) (IB 32–34 pts); (Medcnl Chem) (IB 34–32 pts)

120 pts **Aberdeen** – BBB incl chem+sci/maths (Chem) (IB 32 pts HL 5 chem+sci/maths)

East Anglia – BBB incl chem (Chem) (IB 31 pts HL 5 chem)

Keele – ABC/BBB incl chem (Chem) (IB 32 pts HL 6 chem)

Kent – BBB incl chem (Chem) (IB 34 pts HL 5 chem)

Northumbria – 120–128 pts incl chem (Chem) (HL 444)
Nottingham Trent – BBB incl chem 120 pts (Pharml Medcnl Chem); BBB incl chem (Chem)
Queen's Belfast – BBB incl chem+sci (Chem; Medcnl Chem)
Reading – BBB–CCC (Chem Fdn)

112 pts **Bradford** – BBC incl chem 112 pts (Chem)
Central Lancashire – 112 pts incl chem (Chem) (IB 28 pts HL 5 chem)
Chester – BBC–BBB incl chem (Chem) (IB 28 pts HL 5 chem)
Coventry – BBC incl chem/biol (Analyt Chem Foren Sci) (IB 30 pts)
Glyndŵr – 112 pts incl sci (Chem Grn Nanotech)
Greenwich – 112 pts incl chem +interview (Chem)
Huddersfield – BBC incl chem 112 pts (Chem)
Hull – 112 pts incl chem (Chem) (IB 28 pts)
Manchester Met – BBC–BBB incl chem 112–120 pts (Pharml Chem (MChem) (Yr Ind)) (IB 26 pts HL 5 chem)
Sheffield Hallam – 112–96 pts incl chem (Chem)
Teesside – BBC incl chem (Chem)

104 pts **Brighton** BCC CCC incl chem (Chem) (IB 27 pts); BCC–CCC incl chem 104–96 pts (Pharml Cheml Sci) (IB 27 pts)
Kingston – 104 pts incl chem+sci (Chem)
Lincoln – BCC incl chem (Chem) (IB 28 pts HL 5 chem)
Liverpool John Moores – BCC 104 pts incl chem (Chem) (IB 26 pts)
London Met – BCC incl chem (Chem)
Manchester Met – BCC–BBC incl chem 104–112 pts (Chem) (IB 26 pts HL 5 chem); BCC–BBC incl chem+biol 104–112 pts (Medcnl Biol Chem) (IB 26 pts HL 5 chem+biol)
Plymouth – 104 pts incl chem+sci (Chem) (IB 28 pts HL 5/4 chem+sci)
South Wales – BCC–CDD incl chem+biol 104–80 pts (Foren Sci) (HL 655–445 incl 5 chem+biol); BCC–CDD incl chem+sci 104–80 pts (Chem) (HL 655–445 incl 5 chem+sci)

88 pts **Wolverhampton** – CCD incl chem (Chem) (IB 26 pts)
64 pt **West Scotland** – CC incl chem (Chem) (IB 26 pts)

Open University – contact 0300 303 0073 **or** www.open.ac.uk/contact/new (Nat Sci)

Alternative offers
See **Chapter 6** and **Appendix 1** for grades/UCAS Tariff points information for other examinations.

EXAMPLES OF DEGREE APPRENTICESHIPS IN THIS SUBJECT FIELD
Manchester Met (Cheml Sci).

EXAMPLES OF COLLEGES OFFERING COURSES IN THIS SUBJECT FIELD
Birmingham Met (Coll); Cornwall (Coll); Harrow (Coll); Leeds City (Coll); Liverpool City (Coll); Warrington and Vale Royal (Coll); Wirral Met (Coll).

CHOOSING YOUR COURSE (SEE ALSO CH.1)
Universities and colleges teaching quality See www.qaa.ac.uk; https://unistats.ac.uk.

Top research universities and colleges (REF 2014) Liverpool; Bath; East Anglia; Sheffield; Warwick; Cambridge; Cardiff; Bristol; Durham; Imperial London; Oxford; Leeds; Nottingham; Edinburgh; St Andrews.

Examples of sandwich degree courses Aston; Bangor; Bath; Cardiff; Dundee; East Anglia; Huddersfield; Kent; Kingston; Liverpool; Loughborough; Manchester; Manchester Met; Northumbria; Nottingham Trent; Queen's Belfast; St Andrews; Sheffield Hallam; Surrey; Teesside; West Scotland; York.

ADMISSIONS INFORMATION
Number of applicants per place (approx) Bangor 3; Bath 9; Birmingham 8; Bradford 10; Bristol 6; Cardiff 4; Durham 6; Edinburgh 14; Heriot-Watt 7; Hull 5; Imperial London 3; Kingston 4; Lancaster 6;

Leeds 3; Leicester 6; Liverpool 5; London (QM) 3; London (UCL) 7; Newcastle 4; Nottingham (Chem Mol Phys) 3, (Chem) 7; Oxford 4; Southampton 7; York 5.

Advice to applicants and planning the UCAS personal statement Extend your knowledge beyond your exam studies by reading scientific journals and keeping abreast of scientific developments in the news. Discuss any visits to chemical firms and laboratories, for example, pharmaceutical, food science, rubber and plastic, paper, photographic, environmental health. See also **Appendix 3**. **Bristol** Deferred entry accepted.

Misconceptions about this course Many students do not fully appreciate the strengths of a Chemistry degree for any career despite the fact that graduates regularly go into a diverse range of careers. **Durham** Students fail to realise that they require mathematics and that physics is useful. **Plymouth** Our course is accredited by the Royal Society of Chemistry, something that is highly important to employers.

Selection interviews Yes Cambridge, Imperial London, Manchester, Oxford (84% (success rate 25%)), Teesside, York; **Some** Bath, Sheffield, Southampton, Warwick; **No** Aston, Bangor, Birmingham, Bristol, Cardiff, Coventry, Dundee, East Anglia, Greenwich, Huddersfield, Hull, Keele, Kingston, Leicester, Liverpool John Moores, London (QM), London (UCL), Loughborough, Newcastle, Northumbria, Nottingham, Nottingham Trent, Plymouth, Reading, Surrey, Wolverhampton.

Interview advice and questions Be prepared for questions on your chemistry syllabus and aspects that you enjoy the most. In the past a variety of questions have been asked, for example: Why is carbon a special element? Discuss the nature of forces between atoms with varying intermolecular distances. Describe recent practicals. What is acid rain? What other types of pollution are caused by the human race? What is an enzyme? What are the general properties of benzene? Why might sciences be less popular among girls at school? What can a mass spectrometer be used for? What would you do if a river turned bright blue and you were asked how to test a sample? What would be the difference between metal and non-metal pollution? What is 'turning you on' in chemistry at the moment? See also **Chapter 5**. **Bath** Non-selective and informal interview. Why Chemistry? Discuss the practical work you are doing. **Oxford** No written work required. Evidence required of motivation, further potential, and a capacity to analyse and use information to form opinions and a willingness to discuss them. **York** Discuss your favourite areas of chemistry, some of your extra-curricular activities, your preferred learning styles – for example, small tutorials of four or fewer, or lectures.

Reasons for rejection (non-academic) Didn't attend interview. Rude and uncooperative. Arrived under influence of drink. Poor attitude and poor commitment to chemistry. Incomplete, inappropriate, illiterate personal statements. **Southampton** Applicants called for interview are not normally rejected.

AFTER-RESULTS ADVICE
Offers to applicants repeating A-levels Higher Leeds, St Andrews, Warwick; **Possibly higher** Edinburgh, Newcastle; **Same** Aston, Bangor, Bath, Bristol, Cardiff, Coventry, Dundee, Durham, East Anglia, Greenwich, Heriot-Watt, Huddersfield, Hull, Keele, Kingston, Liverpool John Moores, London (UCL), London Met, Loughborough, Northumbria, Nottingham, Plymouth, Sheffield; **No** Cambridge.

GRADUATE DESTINATIONS AND EMPLOYMENT (2015/16 HESA)
Graduates surveyed 3,195 **Employed** 1,390 **In voluntary employment** 60 **In further study** 1,190 **Assumed unemployed** 220

Career note A large number of Chemistry graduates choose to go on to further study as well as into scientific careers in research, analysis or development. Significant numbers also follow careers in a wide range of areas in management, teaching and retail work.

OTHER DEGREE SUBJECTS FOR CONSIDERATION
Agriculture; Biochemistry; Biological Sciences; Biomedical Science; Chemical Engineering;

UCAS points Tariff: A* = 56 pts; A = 48 pts; B = 40 pts; C = 32 pts; D = 24 pts; E = 16 pts

Environmental Science; Forensic Science; Genetics; Materials Science; Medicine; Microbiology; Oceanography; Pharmacology; Pharmacy.

CHINESE

(including **Korean**; see also **Asia-Pacific Studies, Languages**)

Oriental languages are not necessarily difficult languages but they differ considerably in their writing systems which present their own problems for the new student. Even so, Chinese is not a language to be chosen for its novelty and students should have a strong interest in China and its people. In all courses, students should prepare for intensive language learning, the focus being on the written and spoken word supported by studies covering the history, politics and culture of China, and at the University of Leeds, additional studies of the Asia Pacific region. At Oxford (Oriental Studies), it is possible to take an additional language from Japanese, Korean or Tibetan. The course in Chinese Studies at Durham also allows students to take modules in Japanese. It is customary in all universities to spend either the second or third year at a university in China. Several universities offer joint courses with Chinese universities.

Useful websites www.ciol.org.uk; www.bbc.co.uk/languages; www.china.org.cn; www. languageadvantage.com; www.languagematters.co.uk; www.thoughtco.com/asian-history-4133325

NB The points totals shown to the left of the institutions are for ease of reference only. It must not be assumed that Tariff points are always used by institutions or that they can be substituted for an offer in grades. The level of an offer is not necessarily indicative of the quality of a course.

COURSE OFFERS INFORMATION

Subject requirements/preferences GCSE A language is required. **AL** A modern language is usually required.

Your target offers and examples of degree courses
152 pts Cambridge – A*AA +interview (AMESAA (As Mid E St) (IB 40–42 pts HL 776)
  Nottingham – A*AA-AAA/A*ABB (Econ Chin St) (IB 38–36 pts)
144 pts Newcastle – AAA-ABB (Ling Chin/Jap) (IB 36–34 pts)
  Oxford – AAA +interview +OLAT (Orntl St) (IB 39 pts HL 666)
136 pts Birmingham – AAB incl lang (Modn Langs (Chin)) (IB 32 pts HL 665)
  Durham – AAB (Chin St (Yr Abrd)) (IB 36 pts)
  Edinburgh – AAB (Chin) (IB 36 pts HL 665)
  London (SOAS) – AAB-ABB (Chin St; Kor; Chin (Modn Class)) (IB 35 pts HL 665)
  Nottingham – AAB (Mgt Chin St) (IB 34 pts HL 18 pts)
128 pts Leeds – ABB (Chin (Modn); Chin courses; Chin Pol) (IB 34 pts HL 16 pts)
  Manchester – ABB (Chin St) (IB 33 pts HL 655); ABB incl Chin/Jap (Chin Jap) (IB 33 pts HL 655); ABB incl lang (Chin courses) (IB 33 pts HL 655-555); (Russ Chin) (IB 33 pts HL 655)
  Newcastle – ABB-BBB (Chin St) (IB 32 pts)
  Nottingham – ABB incl Span (Span Contemp Chin St) (IB 32 pts); ABB incl hist (Hist Contemp Chin St) (IB 32 pts HL 6 hist)
  Sheffield – ABB-BBB (Chin St courses) (IB 33 pts)
  Warwick – ABB incl lang (Chin Comb Hons) (IB 34 pts HL 5 lang)
120 pts De Montfort – 120 pts (Educ St Mand) (IB 28 pts)
  Essex – BBB (Mgt Mand) (IB 30 pts)
  London (Gold) – BBB (Int Rel Chin) (HL 655)
112 pts Bangor – 112-128 pts (Law Contemp Chin St)
  Central Lancashire – 112-128 pts (Bus Mgt Chin)

Check **Chapter 3** for new university admission details and **Chapter 6** on how to read the subject tables.

       Hertfordshire – 112 pts (Mand Comb Hons) (HL 44)
       Hull – 112 pts (Chin St) (IB 28 pts)
       Middlesex – 112 pts (Bus Mgt (Mand/Span))
104 pts **Chester** – BCC–BBC (Chin St Comb Hons) (26 pts)
       Manchester Met – 104–112 pts (Ling Mand Chin/Fr/Ger/Ital/Span) (IB 26 pts)
       Nottingham Trent – 104 pts (Mand Chin Comb Hons)
       Westminster – BCC incl lang (Chin Engl Lang) (IB 28 pts)

       Trinity Saint David – interview (Chin St courses)

Alternative offers
See **Chapter 6** and **Appendix 1** for grades/UCAS Tariff points information for other examinations.

CHOOSING YOUR COURSE (SEE ALSO CH.1)
Universities and colleges teaching quality See www.qaa.ac.uk; https://unistats.ac.uk.

Examples of sandwich degree courses Westminster.

ADMISSIONS INFORMATION
Number of applicants per place (approx) Durham 5; Leeds 5; London (SOAS) 8; Westminster 18.

Advice to applicants and planning the UCAS personal statement It will be necessary to demonstrate a knowledge of China, its culture, political and economic background. Visits to the Far East should be mentioned, with reference to any features which have influenced your choice of degree course. See also **Appendix 3** under Languages.

Selection interviews Yes Cambridge, Oxford; **Some** London (SOAS); **No** Leeds.

Interview advice and questions You will be expected to convince the admissions tutor why you want to study the language. Your knowledge of Chinese culture, politics and society in general, and of Far Eastern problems, could also be tested. See also **Chapter 5**.

Reasons for rejection (non-academic) Oxford Applicant's language background seemed a little weak and his written work not as strong as that of other applicants. At interview he showed himself to be a dedicated hard-working young man but lacking in the imagination, flexibility and the intellectual liveliness needed to succeed on the course.

AFTER-RESULTS ADVICE
Offers to applicants repeating A-levels Higher Leeds; **No** Cambridge.

GRADUATE DESTINATIONS AND EMPLOYMENT (2015/16 HESA)
Graduates surveyed 140 **Employed** 50 **In voluntary employment** 5 **In further study** 40 **Assumed unemployed** 20

Career note China is a country with a high economic growth rate and there are good opportunities for graduates, an increasing number being recruited by firms based in East Asia. Other opportunities exist in diplomacy, aid work and tourism throughout China, Taiwan and Mongolia as well as most non-scientific career areas in the UK. See also **Languages**.

OTHER DEGREE SUBJECTS FOR CONSIDERATION
Traditional Chinese Medicine; other Oriental languages.

CLASSICAL STUDIES/CLASSICAL CIVILISATION

(see also **Archaeology, Classics, Greek, History (Ancient), Latin**)

Classical Studies and Classical Civilisation courses tend to focus on the life of Ancient Greece and Rome, although some degrees, such as Egyptology at the University of Liverpool, cover other aspects of ancient history. At the University of Leeds, Classical Civilisation is described as a study of the Greek and Roman world ranging from the earliest Greek literature to the fall of the Roman Empire, incorporating a study of history, literature, language, art, philosophy and archaeology, whilst at Newcastle, the Classical Studies course includes the same options adding architecture and medicine. As in most university courses, students will select their subject optional topics on a modular basis alongside compulsory options. At many universities, a knowledge of Greek and Latin is not necessary since degree courses may offer these languages at beginner or advanced level, but check subject requirements before applying.

Useful websites www.britishmuseum.org; see also **History** and **History (Ancient)**.

NB The points totals shown to the left of the institutions are for ease of reference only. It must not be assumed that Tariff points are always used by institutions or that they can be substituted for an offer in grades. The level of an offer is not necessarily indicative of the quality of a course.

COURSE OFFERS INFORMATION

Subject requirements/preferences GCSE English and a foreign language often required. **AL** A modern language is required for joint language courses. Relevant subjects include classical civilisation, English literature, archaeology, Latin, Greek.

Your target offers and examples of degree courses
144 pts **Bristol** – AAA–ABB incl Engl (Engl Class St) (IB 36–32 pts HL 6 Engl)
Durham – AAA (Class Civ) (IB 37 pts)
Exeter – AAA–AAB (Class St Engl courses) (IB 36–34 pts); AAA–ABB (Class St) (IB 36–32 pts); AAA–ABB incl lang (Class St Modn Langs) (IB 36–32 pts HL 5 lang)
St Andrews – AAA (Art Hist Class St) (IB 36 pts); (Class St courses) (IB 38 pts)
136 pts **Bristol** – AAB–BBB (Class St) (IB 34–31 pts HL 17–15 pts)
Edinburgh – AAB (Class St; Class Mid E St; Class Arch Gk) (IB 36 pts HL 665)
Exeter – AAB–ABB (Class St Theol/Phil (Emp Expnc)) (IB 34–32 pts)
Leeds – AAB–ABB (Class Civ) (IB 35–34 pts HL 16 pts); AAB (Class Lit courses) (IB 35 pts HL 16 pts)
London (King's) – AAB (Class St; Class St Modn Gk St) (IB 35 pts HL 665); AAB incl Engl (Class St Engl) (IB 35 pts HL 665)
London (RH) – AAB–BBB (Class St) (IB 32 pts HL 555)
London (UCL) – AAB–ABB (Class Arch Class Civ) (IB 36–34 pts HL 17–16 pts)
Newcastle – AAB–ABB (Class St) (IB 35–32 pts HL 555)
Nottingham – AAB–ABB (Class Civ) (IB 34–32 pts)
128 pts **Birmingham** – ABB (Class Lit Civ) (IB 32 pts HL 655)
Edinburgh – ABB (Anc Medit Civ) (IB 36 pts HL 665)
Liverpool – ABB/BBB+aEPQ (Class St; Egypt) (IB 33 pts)
Manchester – ABB (Class St) (IB 33 pts HL 655)
Reading – ABB–BBB (Class St; Class Mediev St) (IB 32–30 pts)
Warwick – ABB (Class Civ) (IB 34 pts)
120 pts **Kent** – BBB (Class Arch St; Class St) (IB 34 pts)
Roehampton – 120 pts inc hist/art hist/class civ/Engl (Class Civ)
Sheffield – BBB/BBC+bEPQ (Class Hist Arch) (IB 32 pts)
Swansea – BBB 120 pts (Class Civ) (IB 32 pts)

Trinity Saint David – interview (Class St; Anc Civ)

Alternative offers
See **Chapter 6** and **Appendix 1** for grades/UCAS Tariff points information for other examinations.

CHOOSING YOUR COURSE (SEE ALSO CH.1)
Universities and colleges teaching quality See www.qaa.ac.uk; https://unistats.ac.uk.

Top research universities and colleges (REF 2014) See **Classics**.

ADMISSIONS INFORMATION
Number of applicants per place (approx) Birmingham 3; Bristol 6; Durham 10; Exeter 3; Leeds 7; London (RH) 5; London (UCL) 5; Manchester 6; Nottingham 4; Reading 10; Swansea 5; Trinity Saint David 2; Warwick 23.

Advice to applicants and planning the UCAS personal statement Discuss any A-level work and what has attracted you to this subject. Describe visits to classical sites or museums and what impressed you.

Misconceptions about this course Birmingham (Class Lit Civ) A study of classics at school is not necessary. While many people catch the classics bug by doing Classical Civilisation at A-level, others come to classics through reading the myths or seeing the plays and being fascinated by them. For others the interdisciplinary nature of the subject attracts them – literature, drama, history, politics and philosophy. **Exeter** (Class St) This is not a language degree. There is no requirement for either A-level Latin or Greek.

Selection interviews Yes Trinity Saint David; **Some** Bristol, Warwick; **No** Birmingham, Kent, London (RH), Newcastle, Nottingham.

Interview advice and questions In the past, questions have included: What special interests do you have in Classical Studies/Classics? Have you visited Greece, Rome or any other classical sites or museums and what were your impressions? These are the types of questions to expect, along with those to explore your knowledge of the culture, theatre and architecture of the period. See also **Chapter 5**.

Reasons for rejection (non-academic) Birmingham Lukewarm interest in the subject. Lack of clear idea why they wanted to do this degree.

AFTER-RESULTS ADVICE
Offers to applicants repeating A-levels Higher St Andrews, Warwick; **Same** Birmingham, Bristol, Durham, Exeter, Leeds, London (RH), Nottingham.

GRADUATE DESTINATIONS AND EMPLOYMENT (2015/16 HESA)
Classical Studies graduates surveyed 855 **Employed** 315 **In voluntary employment** 45 **In further study** 300 **Assumed unemployed** 70

Career note As with other non-vocational subjects, graduates enter a wide range of careers. In a small number of cases this may be subject-related with work in museums and art galleries. However, much will depend on how the student's interests develop during the undergraduate years and career planning should start early.

OTHER DEGREE SUBJECTS FOR CONSIDERATION
Archaeology; Ancient History; Classics; Greek; History; History of Art; Latin; Philosophy.

CLASSICS

(see also **Classical Studies/Classical Civilisation, Greek, Latin**)

These courses tend to focus on the study of Greek and Latin literature and language alongside topics such as the history, art, archaeology, drama and philosophy of Ancient Greece and Rome. Course entry requirements vary. At Oxford, with the largest Classics department in the UK, two courses which do not require a previous knowledge of Latin or Greek are offered.

Useful websites www.users.globalnet.co.uk/~loxias; www.classics.ox.ac.uk; www.cambridgescp.com; www.bbc.co.uk/history/ancient/greeks; www.bbc.co.uk/history/ancient/romans

NB The points totals shown to the left of the institutions are for ease of reference only. It must not be assumed that Tariff points are always used by institutions or that they can be substituted for an offer in grades. The level of an offer is not necessarily indicative of the quality of a course.

COURSE OFFERS INFORMATION
Subject requirements/preferences GCSE English and a foreign language usually required. Grades A*/A/B (8–9/7/5–6) may be stipulated. **AL** Check courses for Latin/Greek requirements.

Your target offers and examples of degree courses
152 pts **Cambridge** – A*AA +interview +CAA (Class) (IB 40–42 pts HL 776)
144 pts **Bristol** – AAA–ABB (Class) (IB 36–32 pts HL 18–12 pts)
Durham – AAA (Class) (IB 37 pts)
Exeter – AAA–ABB (Class (Emp Expnc)) (IB 36–32 pts); AAA–ABB incl Lat/Gk (Class) (IB 36–32 pts HL 5 Lat/Gk)
Oxford – AAA +interview +CAT +MLAT (Class Modn Langs) (IB 39 pts HL 666); AAA +interview +CAT +ELAT (Class Engl) (IB 39 pts HL 666); AAA +interview +CAT (Class; Class Orntl St) (IB 39 pts HL 666)
St Andrews – AAA (Class) (IB 36 pts)
136 pts **Edinburgh** – AAB (Class; Class Engl Lang; Class Ling) (IB 36 pts HL 665)
Leeds – AAB (Class Lit courses) (IB 35 pts HL 16 pts)
London (King's) – AAB (Class (Gk Lat)) (IB 35 pts HL 665)
London (UCL) – AAB incl Gk/Lat (Class) (IB 36 pts HL 6 Gk/Lat)
Newcastle – AAB–ABB (Class) (IB 35–32 pts HL 555)
Nottingham – AAB–ABB (Class) (IB 34–32 pts)
Warwick – AAB incl Lat/Anc Gk (Class) (IB 36 pts HL 6 Lat/Anc Gk)
128 pts **Birmingham** – ABB (Class Lit Civ) (IB 32 pts HL 655)
Liverpool – ABB/BBB+aEPQ (Class) (IB 33 pts)
London (RH) – ABB–BBB (Class) (IB 32 pts HL 555)
Manchester – ABB (Class) (IB 33 pts HL 655)
120 pts **Swansea** – BBB 120 pts (Class) (IB 32 pts)
112 pts **London (Birk)** – 112 pts incl Gk/Lat (Class)

Trinity Saint David – interview (Class)

Alternative offers
See **Chapter 6** and **Appendix 1** for grades/UCAS Tariff points information for other examinations.

CHOOSING YOUR COURSE (SEE ALSO CH.1)
Universities and colleges teaching quality See www.qaa.ac.uk; https://unistats.ac.uk.

Top research universities and colleges (REF 2014) St Andrews; Cambridge; Durham; Reading; Birmingham; Oxford; Nottingham; Warwick.

ADMISSIONS INFORMATION

Number of applicants per place (approx) Bristol 9; Cambridge 2; Durham 7; Leeds 4; London (King's) 6; London (RH) 5; London (UCL) 5; Manchester 6; Newcastle 6; Nottingham 4; Oxford 3; Swansea 6; Trinity Saint David 5.

Advice to applicants and planning the UCAS personal statement Describe any visits made to classical sites or museums, or literature which you have read and enjoyed. Discuss any significant aspects which impressed you. Classics is an interdisciplinary subject and universities are looking for people who are versatile, imaginative and independently minded, so all types of extra-curricular activities (drama, music, philosophy, creative arts, politics, other languages and cultures) will be relevant. See also **Classical Studies/Classical Civilisation**.

Misconceptions about this course While Classics can appear irrelevant and elitist, universities aim to assist students to leave with a range of transferable skills that are of importance to employers.

Selection interviews Yes Cambridge, Oxford (Class) 37%; (Class Eng) 26%; (Class Modn Langs) 25%; (Class Orntl St) 56%; **Some** Bristol, Warwick; **No** Leeds, London (RH), London (UCL), Newcastle, Nottingham, Swansea.

Interview advice and questions What do you think it means to study Classics? Do you think Classics is still a vital and central cultural discipline? What made you apply to study Classics at this university? There are often detailed questions on the texts which the students have read, to find out how reflective they are in their reading. See also **Classical Studies/Classical Civilisation** and **Chapter 5**. **Cambridge** What would happen if the Classics department burned down? Do you think feminism is dead? Emma has become a different person since she took up yoga. Therefore she is not responsible for anything she did before she took up yoga. Discuss. **Oxford** Candidates studying Latin or Greek at A-level are required to demonstrate competence in translation as part of the Classics Admissions Test. Use of dictionaries not permitted. Classics and English applicants take both the Classics Admissions Test and the English Literature Admissions Test.

Reasons for rejection (non-academic) Did not demonstrate a clear sense of why they wanted to study Classics rather than anything else.

AFTER-RESULTS ADVICE

Offers to applicants repeating A-levels Higher Leeds, St Andrews; **Same** Cambridge, Durham, Newcastle, Nottingham, Swansea.

GRADUATE DESTINATIONS AND EMPLOYMENT (2015/16 HESA)

See **Classical Studies/Classical Civilisation**.

Career note See **Classical Studies/Classical Civilisation**.

OTHER DEGREE SUBJECTS FOR CONSIDERATION

See **Classical Studies/Classical Civilisation**.

COMBINED AND LIBERAL ARTS COURSES

(see also **Art and Design (General), Social Sciences/Studies**)

Many different subjects are offered in Combined and Liberal Arts courses which are now becoming increasingly popular. These courses are particularly useful for those applicants who have difficulty in deciding on one specialist subject to follow, allowing students to mix and match according to their interests and often enabling them to embark on new subjects.

Useful websites www.artscouncil.org.uk; www.scottisharts.org.uk; www.artsprofessional.co.uk

NB The points totals shown to the left of the institutions are for ease of reference only. It must not be assumed that Tariff points are always used by institutions or that they can be substituted for an offer in grades. The level of an offer is not necessarily indicative of the quality of a course.

COURSE OFFERS INFORMATION

Subject requirements/preferences The offers listed below are average offers. Specific offers will vary depending on the relative popularity of each subject. Check with the admissions tutor of your selected institution. **GCSE** English, mathematics or science and a foreign language may be required by some universities. **AL** Some joint courses may require a specified subject.

Your target offers and examples of degree courses

160 pts **Cambridge** – A*A*A incl sci/maths +interview +NSAA (Nat Sci) (IB 40–42 pts HL 776)
152 pts **Bath** – A*AA/AAA+aEPQ incl maths+sci (Nat Sci) (IB 36 pts HL 766 incl maths+sci)
         Birmingham – A*AA–AAA +admissions essay (Librl Arts Sci) (IB 36–35 pts)
         Bristol – A*AA–AAB incl arts/hum/lang (Librl Arts) (IB 38–34 pts HL 6 arts/hum/lang)
         Durham – A*AA (Comb Hons Soc Sci) (IB 38 pts)
         Exeter – A*AA–AAB (Librl Arts (Emp Expnc); Librl Arts; Flex Comb Hons) (IB 38–34 pts)
         London (UCL) – A*AA–AAA (Arts Sci) (IB 39–38 pts)
144 pts **Imperial London** – AAA–A*AA incl chem+sci/maths (Bioch courses) (IB 39 pts HL 6
              chem+sci/maths)
         Leeds – AAA (Librl Arts) (IB 35 pts HL 17 pts)
         London (King's) – AAA (Librl Arts) (IB 35 pts HL 666)
         London (QM) – AAA incl maths (Econ Comb Hons) (IB 36 pts HL 666)
         Newcastle – AAA–AAB incl Engl (Engl Lit Comb Hons) (IB 36–35 pts HL 6 Engl)
         Nottingham – AAA (Librl Arts) (IB 36–32 pts HL 6 Engl)
         Sheffield – AAA–ABB (Comb Hons) (IB 36–34 pts); AAA–AAB incl chem+sci (Bioch Comb
              Hons) (IB 36–34 pts HL 6 chem+sci)
         Warwick – AAA (Librl Arts) (IB 38 pts)
136 pts **London (SOAS)** – AAB–ABB (Glob Librl Arts) (IB 35 pts HL 665)
         Newcastle – AAB (Comb Hons) (IB 34 pts)
128 pts **Cardiff** – ABB–BBB (Welsh Comb Hons) (HL 665–655); (Anc Hist Comb Hons)
              (IB 32–30 pts)
         East Anglia – ABB (Int Rel Comb Hons) (IB 32 pts)
         Keele – ABB (Librl Arts) (IB 34 pts)
         Kent – ABB (Librl Arts) (IB 34 pts)
         Leeds – ABB (Film St Comb Hons) (IB 34 pts HL 16 pts)
         Liverpool – ABB (Film St Comb Hons) (IB 33 pts)
         London (RH) – ABB (Librl Arts) (IB 32 pts)
         NCH London – ABB–AAA +interview (Comb Arts) (IB 34–36 pts)
         Newcastle – ABB (Film Prac) (IB 32 pts)
120 pts **Aberystwyth** – BBB–AAB (Librl Arts) (IB 30–34 pts)
         Derby – 120–128 pts (Librl Arts)
         Dundee – BBB (Librl Arts) (IB 30 pts HL 555)
         Essex – BBB (Librl Arts) (IB 30 pts)
         Heriot-Watt – BBB incl maths+sci (Comb St) (IB 29 pts)
         Hull – 120 pts (Am St)
         Kent – BBB (Cult St courses) (IB 34 pts)
112 pts **Hull** – 112 pts incl lang (Comb Three Lang) (IB 28 pts)
         Kingston – 112 pts (Cy Scrty Comp Foren Bus Comb Hons)
104 pts **Bath Spa** – BCC–CCC (Sociol Comb Hons) (IB 26 pts); (Psy Comb Hons) (IB 27 pts)
         Brighton – BCC–CCC 104–96 pts (Hum) (IB 27 pts)
         Nottingham Trent – 104 pts (Euro St Comb Hons)
         Winchester – 104–120 pts (Librl Arts; Librl Arts Engl Lit; Librl Arts Sociol) (IB 26 pts)
 96 pts **Leeds (CMus)** – 96 pts +audition +gr 5 (Mus (Comb))
         Richmond (Am Int Univ) – CCC 96 pts (Librl Arts) (IB 24 pts)

Check **Chapter 3** for new university admission details and **Chapter 6** on how to read the subject tables.

Winchester – 96–112 pts (Librl Arts Hist; Librl Arts Dr) (IB 25 pts)

Open University – contact 0300 303 0073 **or** www.open.ac.uk/contact/new (Hum Engl/Fr/Ger/Span)

Alternative offers
See **Chapter 6** and **Appendix 1** for grades/UCAS Tariff points information for other examinations.

CHOOSING YOUR COURSE (SEE ALSO CH.1)

Universities and colleges teaching quality See www.qaa.ac.uk; https://unistats.ac.uk.

Top research universities and colleges (REF 2014) See individual subject tables.

ADMISSIONS INFORMATION

Number of applicants per place (approx) Birmingham 9; Heriot-Watt 5; Newcastle 4.

Advice to applicants and planning the UCAS personal statement Refer to tables for those subjects you've chosen.

Selection interviews Some Bristol; **No** Liverpool.

Interview advice and questions Questions will focus on your chosen subjects. See under individual subject tables. See also **Chapter 5**.

Reasons for rejection (non-academic) Lack of clarity of personal goals.

AFTER-RESULTS ADVICE

Offers to applicants repeating A-levels Higher St Andrews; **Possibly higher** Newcastle; **Same** Bath Spa, Birmingham, Durham, Liverpool, Manchester Met.

GRADUATE DESTINATIONS AND EMPLOYMENT (2015/16 HESA)

Career note Graduates enter a wide range of careers covering business and administration, retail work, education, transport, finance, community and social services. Work experience during undergraduate years will help students to focus their interests.

OTHER DEGREE SUBJECTS FOR CONSIDERATION

See **Social Sciences/Studies**.

COMMUNICATION STUDIES/COMMUNICATION

(including **Communication and Media, Marketing Communication Management** and **Public Relations**; see also **Art and Design (General), Computer Courses, Engineering (Communications), Film, Radio, Video and TV Studies, Journalism, Media Studies, Speech Pathology/Sciences/Therapy**)

Communication Studies courses are often linked with Media Studies and as such attract large numbers of applicants; however the course content of your chosen course should be checked since there are several variations. Some courses are purely academic.

Useful websites www.camfoundation.com; www.aejmc.org

NB The points totals shown to the left of the institutions are for ease of reference only. It must not be assumed that Tariff points are always used by institutions or that they can be substituted for an offer in grades. The level of an offer is not necessarily indicative of the quality of a course.

COURSE OFFERS INFORMATION

Subject requirements/preferences GCSE English and mathematics grade A–C (7–4) may be required. **AL** No specific subjects required.

Your target offers and examples of degree courses

144 pts **London (King's)** – AAA (Librl Arts) (IB 35 pts HL 666)

136 pts **Leeds** – AAB (Comms Media) (IB 35 pts)
        Loughborough – AAB (Comm Media St) (IB 35 pts HL 665)
        Newcastle – AAB (Media Comm Cult St) (IB 34 pts)
        Ulster – AAB-AAA (Comm Adv Mark) (IB 28-29 pts HL 14 pts)

128 pts **Leeds** – ABB incl art/des (Graph Comm Des) (IB 34 pts HL 16 pts incl 5/6 art/vis art/des)
        Liverpool – ABB/BBB+aEPQ (Comm Media) (IB 33 pts)
        Northumbria – 128-136 pts +interview +portfolio (Fash Comm)
        Nottingham – ABB (Span Int Media Comms St) (IB 32 pts)
        Sussex – ABB (Media Comms) (IB 32 pts)

120 pts **Buckingham** – BBB-BBC +interview (Mark Media Comms) (IB 32-31 pts)
        Coventry – BBB +portfolio (Media Comms) (IB 31 pts)
        East Anglia – BBB (Intercult Comm Bus Mgt) (IB 31 pts)
        Liverpool Hope – BBB-BBC 120-112 pts (Media Comm)
        London (Gold) – BBB (Media Comms) (IB 33 pts)
        Sunderland – 120 pts (Media Cult Comm)
        UWE Bristol – 120 pts (Mark Comm Mgt) (IB 26 pts)

112 pts **Aberystwyth** – BBC-BBB (Media Comm St) (IB 28-30 pts)
        Birmingham City – BBC 112 pts +interview +portfolio (Media Comm) (HL 14 pts)
        Bournemouth – 112-120 pts (Comm Media) (IB 30-31 pts HL 55)
        Brunel – BBC (Comm Media St) (IB 29 pts)
        Greenwich – 112 pts +interview +portfolio (Media Comms)
        Keele – BBC (Media Comms Crea Prac) (IB 30 pts)
        Middlesex – 112 pts (Jrnl Comm)
        Oxford Brookes – BBC 112 pts (Engl Lang Comm; Comm Media Cult) (IB 30 pts)
        St Mary's – 112 pts (Comm Media Mark)
        Sheffield Hallam – 112 pts (Mark Comms Adv); 112-96 pts (PR Media)
        Ulster – BBC-BBB (Comm Mgt PR) (IB 25-26 pts HL 12 pts)
        Wolverhampton – BBC (Media)

104 pts **Bath Spa** – BCC-CCC (Media Comms) (IB 26 pts)
        De Montfort – 104 pts (Media Comm) (IB 24 pts)
        Glasgow Caledonian – BCC (Media Comm) (IB 25 pts)
        Leeds Beckett – 104 pts (Media Comm Cult) (IB 24 pts)
        Manchester Met – 104-112 pts (Dig Media Comms) (IB 26 pts)
        Nottingham Trent – 104 pts (Comm Soty (Comb Hons))
        Robert Gordon – BCC (PR) (IB 27 pts)

96 pts **Buckingham** – CCC +interview (Comm Media Jrnl; Comm (EFL) Media St) (IB 29 pts)

88 pts **Canterbury Christ Church** – 88-112 pts (Media Comms)

80 pts **Bedfordshire** – 80 pts (Media Comms)
        Bucks New – 80-96 pts (Adv Mgt Dig Comms)

Alternative offers

See **Chapter 6** and **Appendix 1** for grades/UCAS Tariff points information for other examinations.

CHOOSING YOUR COURSE (SEE ALSO CH.1)

Universities and colleges teaching quality See www.qaa.ac.uk; https://unistats.ac.uk.

Top research universities and colleges (REF 2014) (Communication, Cultural and Media Studies, Literary and Information Management) London LSE; Leicester (Musm St); Wolverhampton; Cardiff; London (Gold); Loughborough (Comm Media St); Westminster; De Montfort; Nottingham; London (RH); East Anglia; Leeds; Leicester (Media Comm); Newcastle.

Examples of sandwich degree courses Bournemouth; Brunel; Liverpool; Loughborough; Ulster; Westminster.

Check **Chapter 3** for new university admission details and **Chapter 6** on how to read the subject tables.

ADMISSIONS INFORMATION

Number of applicants per place (approx) Liverpool 6.

Advice to applicants and planning the UCAS personal statement Applicants should be able to give details of any work experience/work shadowing/discussions they have had in the media including, for example, in newspaper offices, advertising agencies, local radio stations or film companies (see also **Media Studies**). **London (Gold)** Interest in a study in depth of media theory plus some experience in media practice. **Manchester Met** Motivation more important than grades.

Selection interviews Yes Buckingham; **No** Glasgow Caledonian, Sheffield Hallam, Ulster.

Interview advice and questions Courses differ in this subject and, depending on your choice, the questions will focus on the type of course, either biased towards the media, or towards human communication by way of language, psychology, sociology or linguistics. See also separate subject tables and **Chapter 5**.

Reasons for rejection (non-academic) Unlikely to work well in groups. Poor writing. Misguided application, for example more practical work wanted. Poor motivation. Inability to give reasons for choosing the course. More practice needed in academic writing skills. Wrong course choice, wanted more practical work.

AFTER-RESULTS ADVICE

Offers to applicants repeating A-levels Same Brunel, Coventry, Loughborough, Nottingham Trent, Robert Gordon, Sheffield Hallam.

GRADUATE DESTINATIONS AND EMPLOYMENT (2015/16 HESA)

See **Business and Management Courses (Specialised)**, **Marketing** and **Media Studies**.

Career note Graduates have developed a range of transferable skills in their courses which open up opportunities in several areas. There are obvious links with openings in the media, public relations and advertising.

OTHER DEGREE SUBJECTS FOR CONSIDERATION

Advertising; Art and Design; Cultural Studies; Digital Communications; English; Film, Radio, Video and TV Studies; Information Studies; Journalism; Languages; Linguistics; Marketing; Media Studies; Psychology; Public Relations; Speech Sciences.

COMMUNITY STUDIES/DEVELOPMENT

(see also Health Sciences/Studies, Nursing and Midwifery, Social and Public Policy and Administration, Social Work)

These courses cover aspects of community social issues, for example housing, food, health, the elderly, welfare rights and counselling and features of community development such as education, arts, sport and leisure. Many courses are vocational in nature and often linked with youth work. Courses are in Education, Housing, Social Sciences and Public Policy. Work experience always forms part of these courses and should also take place before you apply. Most courses will lead to professional qualifications.

Useful websites http://volunteeringmatters.org.uk; http://infed.org/mobi/developing-community

NB The points totals shown to the left of the institutions are for ease of reference only. It must not be assumed that Tariff points are always used by institutions or that they can be substituted for an offer in grades. The level of an offer is not necessarily indicative of the quality of a course.

COURSE OFFERS INFORMATION

Subject requirements/preferences GCSE English and mathematics grade A–C (7–4) may be required at some institutions. **AL** No specific subjects required. **Other** Minimum age 19 plus youth work experience for some courses. Health and Disclosure and Barring Service (DBS) checks required for some courses.

Your target offers and examples of degree courses

128 pts **Edinburgh** – ABB (Commun Educ) (IB 34 pts HL 655)
        Sussex – ABB–BBB (Chld Yth (Theor Prac)) (IB 32 pts)
120 pts **Glasgow** – BBB +interview (Commun Dev) (IB 30 pts)
112 pts **Glyndŵr** – 112 pts +interview (Yth Commun Wk)
        Huddersfield – BBC 112 pts (Yth Commun Wk)
        Hull – 112 pts +interview (Yth Wk Commun Dev) (IB 28 pts)
        London (Birk) – 112 pts (Commun Dev Pblc Plcy)
        London Met – BBC 112 pts (Commun Dev Ldrshp)
        Sunderland – 112 pts (Pblc Hlth)
        Worcester – 112 pts (Dance Commun Prac)
104 pts **De Montfort** – 104 pts +interview (Yth Commun Dev) (IB 28 pts)
        West Scotland – BCC (Commun Edu) (IB 24 pts)
        Winchester – 104–120 pts (Chld Yth Commun St) (IB 26 pts)
96 pts **Cumbria** – 96–120 pts (Yth Commun Wk)
        Derby – 96–112 pts (Yth Wk Commun Dev)
        Dundee – CCC/AB (Commun Lrng Dev) (IB 29 pts HL 554)
        Leeds Beckett – 96 pts +interview (Yth Wk Commun Dev) (IB 24 pts)
        Newman – 96–88 pts (Yth Commun Wk)
        Sunderland – 96 pts +interview (Commun Yth Wk St)
88 pts **St Mark and St John** – CCD +interview (Yth Commun Wk)
80 pts **Bedfordshire** – 80 pts +interview (Yth Commun Wk)
        Cardiff Met – 80 pts +interview (Yth Commun Wk courses)
        Trinity Saint David – 80–96 pts (Yth Commun Wk)
        Ulster – CDD (Commun Yth Wk) (IB 24 pts HL 12 pts)
64 pts **London (Gold)** – CC (App Soc Sci Commun Dev Yth Wk)

Alternative offers
See **Chapter 6** and **Appendix 1** for grades/UCAS Tariff points information for other examinations.

EXAMPLES OF COLLEGES OFFERING COURSES IN THIS SUBJECT FIELD

Blackburn (Coll); Bradford (Coll); Cornwall (Coll); East Kent (Coll); Grimsby (Inst Group); North Notts (Coll); Oldham (Univ Campus); Truro and Penwith (Coll); Weston (Coll); York (Coll).

CHOOSING YOUR COURSE (SEE ALSO CH.1)

Universities and colleges teaching quality See www.qaa.ac.uk; https://unistats.ac.uk.

ADMISSIONS INFORMATION

Number of applicants per place (approx) Manchester Met 8; St Mark and St John 7.

Advice to applicants and planning the UCAS personal statement You should describe work you have done with people (elderly or young), particularly in a caring capacity, such as social work, or with the elderly or young children in schools, nursing, hospital work, youth work, community or charity work. You should also describe any problems arising and how staff dealt with them. See **Appendix 3**. **St Mark and St John** Strong multicultural policy.

Selection interviews Yes Bedfordshire, De Montfort, Manchester Met, St Mark and St John.

Interview advice and questions This subject has a vocational emphasis and work experience, or even full-time work in the field, will be expected. Community work varies considerably, so, depending on your experiences, you could be asked about the extent of your work and how you would solve the problems which occur. See also **Chapter 5**.

Reasons for rejection (non-academic) Insufficient experience. Lack of understanding of community and youth work. Uncertain career aspirations. Incompatibility with values, methods and aims of the course. No work experience.

AFTER-RESULTS ADVICE
Offers to applicants repeating A-levels Same St Mark and St John.

GRADUATE DESTINATIONS AND EMPLOYMENT (2015/16 HESA)
See **Social Work**.

Career note Social and welfare areas of employment provide openings for those wanting to specialise in their chosen field of social work. Other opportunities will also exist in educational administration, leisure and outdoor activities.

OTHER DEGREE SUBJECTS FOR CONSIDERATION
Communication Studies; Education; Health and Social Care; Nursing; Politics; Psychology; Social Policy and Administration; Social Work; Sociology; Youth Studies.

COMPUTER COURSES

(including **Artificial Intelligence, Business Information Systems, Computer Networks, Computer Science, Computing, Games Technology, Information Systems** and **Web Design and Development**; see also **Communication Studies/Communication, Information Management and Librarianship, Media Studies**)

Most universities and also colleges of further education offer Computer courses. The specialisms are many and varied, which can cause a problem when deciding which course to follow. For example, at Brunel University London, the Computer Science course has four specialisms with a choice from Artificial Intelligence, Digital Media and Games, Network Computing or Software Engineering, all with sandwich placements. At Plymouth University, there are over 17 computer courses including Computer and Information Security, Computer Science, and Computing and Games Development, whilst at Liverpool John Moores, Northumbria and other institutions, Cyber Security and Computer Forensics courses are on offer. At all universities, there are considerable opportunities for financial support and future employment by choosing sandwich courses. Courses vary in content and in the specialisations offered, which may include software engineering, programming languages, artificial intelligence, data processing and graphics.

Useful websites www.bcs.org; www.techuk.org; www.iap.org.uk; www.thetechpartnership.com

NB The points totals shown to the left of the institutions are for ease of reference only. It must not be assumed that Tariff points are always used by institutions or that they can be substituted for an offer in grades. The level of an offer is not necessarily indicative of the quality of a course.

COURSE OFFERS INFORMATION
Subject requirements/preferences GCSE Mathematics usually required. A*/A/B (8–9/7/5–6) grades may be stipulated for some subjects. **AL** Mathematics, a science subject or computer science required for some courses.

Your target offers and examples of degree courses
160 pts   **Bristol** – A*A*A–AAB incl maths+fmaths (Maths Comp Sci) (IB 40–36 pts HL
          6 maths)
          Cambridge – A*A*A incl maths +interview +CSAT (Comp Sci) (IB 40–42 pts HL 776)

Imperial London – A*AA–A*A*A* incl maths +interview (Comp (Artif Intel) (MEng)) (IB 39–41 pts HL 7 maths); (Comp (Soft Eng) (MEng)) (IB 41–43 pts HL 7 maths); A*A*A incl maths+fmaths +interview (Maths Comp Sci) (IB 41–43 pts HL 7 maths)

152 pts Birmingham – A*AA incl maths/comp (Comp Sci/Soft Eng (MEng)) (IB 32 pts HL 766 incl 6 maths/comp)

Bristol – A*AA–AAB incl maths/fmaths (Comp Sci) (IB 43–41 pts HL 6 maths)

Imperial London – A*AA incl maths +interview (Comp) (IB 41–39 pts HL 7 maths)

London (UCL) – A*AA incl maths +interview (Comp Sci) (IB 39 pts HL 6 maths); (Mathem Comput (MEng)) (IB 39 pts HL 7 maths)

Oxford – A*AA incl maths/fmaths/comp +interview +MAT (Comp Sci) (IB 39 pts HL 766)

Southampton – A*AA incl maths+phys/fmaths/tech (Electron Eng Comp Sys (MEng)); A*AA incl maths (Comp Sci Cy Scrty (MEng); Comp Sci; Comp Sci Artif Intel (MEng))

144 pts Bath – AAA–A*AB incl maths +interview (Comp Sci) (IB 36 pts HL 6 maths)

Birmingham – AAA incl maths/comp (Comp Sci) (IB 32 pts HL 666 incl 6 maths/comp)

Durham – AAA incl maths (Comp Sci) (IB 37 pts)

Edinburgh – AAA incl maths (Comp Sci courses; Artif Intel; Inform (MInf)) (IB 37 pts HL 6 maths)

Exeter – AAA–ABB incl maths (Comp Sci) (IB 36–32 pts HL 5 maths)

Leeds – AAA incl maths/comp (Comp Sci; Comp Sci Artif Intel) (IB 35 pts HL 18 pts incl 5 maths/comp)

Nottingham AAA AAB incl comp (Comp Sci) (IB 34–32 pts)

Queen's Belfast – AAA–A*AB incl maths (Maths Comp Sci (MSci))

Reading – AAA–AAB (Mgt IT) (IB 35 pts)

St Andrews – AAA incl maths+phys (Comp Sci Phys) (IB 38 pts HL 6 maths); AAA incl maths (Comp Sci Psy) (IB 38 pts HL 6 maths); (Comp Sci courses) (IB 38 pts)

Warwick – AAA incl maths (Comp Sci; Comp Mgt Sci) (IB 38 pts HL 6 maths)

136 pts Aston – AAB–ABB (Bus Comp IT) (IB 32 pts HL 665–655)

Cardiff – AAB–ABB (Comp Sci Vis Comp; Comp Sci Hi Perf Comp; Comp Sci Scrty Foren) (IB 34–30 pts HL 5)

Glasgow – AAB–BBB incl maths (Comp Sci courses) (IB 36–34 pts HL 665 incl sci)

Kent – AAB +interview (Comp Sci courses) (IB 34 pts)

Lancaster – AAB (Comp Sci courses) (IB 35 pts HL 16 pts)

Liverpool Hope – ABB–BBC 136–104 pts (Comp Sci)

London (King's) – AAB incl maths/phys/comp/electron (Comp Sci Robot; Comp Sci Mgt; Comp Sci Intel Sys) (IB 35 pts HL 665 incl 5 maths/phys/comp)

London (RH) – AAB–ABB incl maths/phys/chem/comp (Comp Sci) (IB 32 pts HL 655)

Loughborough – AAB (IT Mgt Bus) (IB 34 pts HL 655)

Manchester – AAB (IT Mgt Bus; IT Mgt Bus (Yr Ind)) (IB 35 pts HL 665)

Newcastle – AAB–ABB/AAC (Comp Sci courses) (IB 35–34 pts)

Queen's Belfast – AAB/ABB (Bus IT); AAB–AAA incl chem/phys/maths/tech/comp (Comp Sci (MEng))

Reading – AAB–ABB (Comp Sci courses) (IB 34–32 pts)

Sheffield – AAB/ABB+bEPQ incl maths (Comp Sci) (IB 34 pts HL 6 maths)

Sussex – AAB–ABB (Comp Dig Media; Comp Sci; Comp Sci Artif Intel; Gms Multim Env) (IB 32 pts)

Swansea – AAB–BBB incl sci/maths/comp/electron (Comp Sci)

York – AAB–ABB incl maths (Comp Sci) (IB 35–34 pts HL 6 maths)

128 pts Aberdeen – ABB (3 yr course) BBB (4 yr course) incl maths+sci (Comp Sci) (IB 32 pts HL 5 maths+sci)

Aston – ABB–BBB (Comp Sci) (IB 32 pts)

Bradford – ABB 128 pts (Comp Sci Gms; Comp Sci)

Cardiff – ABB–AAB (Comp Sci) (IB 33 pts)

City – ABB 128 pts (Comp Sci; Comp Sci Gms Tech) (IB 32 pts)

Coventry – ABB–BBB incl maths/phys/chem/tech/comp (Comp Sci) (IB 29 pts)

Check **Chapter 3** for new university admission details and **Chapter 6** on how to read the subject tables.

East Anglia – ABB incl maths/comp/phys/electron/econ (Comp Sci) (IB 32 pts HL 55); ABB (Comp Sci Educ) (IB 32 pts HL 5 maths); ABB incl maths/comp/econ/bus (Bus Inf Sys) (IB 32 pts HL 55)

Edge Hill – ABB–BBC 128–112 pts (Comp courses)

Heriot-Watt – ABB incl comp (3 yr course) BBB (4 yr course) (Inf Sys courses) (IB 30 pts (3 yr course) 28 pts (4 yr course) HL 6 comp (3 yr course)); ABB incl maths+comp (3 yr course) BBB incl maths (4 yr course) (Comp Sci) (IB 30 pts (3 yr course) 28 pts (4 yr course) HL 6 maths+comp (3 yr course) 5 maths (4 yr course))

Leicester – ABB/BBB+bEPQ (Comp Sci) (IB 30 pts)

Liverpool – ABB (Comp Sci (Yr Ind)) (IB 33 pts HL 5 maths/phys/comp sci); (Comp Sci) (IB 33 pts HL 5 maths)

London (QM) – ABB (Comp Sci courses) (IB 32 pts HL 655)

London (RH) – ABB (Mgt Dig Innov) (IB 32 pts HL 655)

Loughborough – ABB incl maths (Comp Sci; Comp Sci Artif Intel) (IB 34 pts HL 655 incl 5 maths)

Stirling – ABB (3 yr course) BBB (4 yr course) incl comp+bus (Bus Comp) (IB 35 pts (3 yr course) 32 pts (4 yr course)); ABB (3 yr course) BBB (4 yr course) incl comp (Comp Sci) (IB 35 pts (3 yr course) 32 pts (4 yr course))

Strathclyde – ABB (Comp Sci) (IB 34 pts HL 5 maths)

Surrey – ABB incl maths/phys/comp (Comp IT) (IB 32 pts); ABB incl maths (Comp Sci) (IB 32 pts)

120 pts **Bangor** – 120–96 pts (Comp Sci Bus; Comp Sci)

Bournemouth – 120–128 pts +interview +portfolio (Comp Animat Arts Des) (IB 31–32 pts HL 655)

Brunel – BBB (Comp Sci; Comp Sci (Dig Media Gms); Comp Sci (Net Comp); Comp Sci (Artif Intel); Bus Comp) (IB 30 pts)

Buckingham – BBB +interview (Comp courses) (IB 32 pts)

Dundee – BBB incl maths+sci (Comp Sci) (IB 30 pts HL 555)

Edinburgh Napier – BBB (3 yr course) CCC (4 yr course) (Web Des Dev) (IB 27 pts HL 654); BBB incl comp (3 yr course) CCC (4 yr course) (Comp) (IB 26 pts HL 555)

Greenwich – 120 pts (Comp Sys Net; Comp Scrty Foren)

Huddersfield – BBB 120 pts (Comp; ICT; Comp Sci Gms Prog; Comp Sci)

Keele – ABC/ABB (Comp Sci) (IB 32 pts)

Liverpool Hope – BBB–BBC 120–112 pts (IT)

London (Gold) – BBB (Crea Comp; Comp Sci) (IB 33 pts HL 655)

London South Bank – BBB (Comp Sci)

Northumbria – 120–128 pts (Comp Sci; Comp Sci Gms Dev; IT Mgt Bus) (HL 444)

Norwich Arts – BBB incl art/des/media (Gms Art Des) (IB 32 pts)

Nottingham Trent – BBB incl IT/maths/sci 120 pts (Comp Sci courses)

Plymouth – 120 pts (Comp Sci) (IB 30 pts)

Queen's Belfast – BBB–ABB incl chem/phys/math/tech/comp (Comp Sci)

Sheffield Hallam – 120–104 pts (Comp Sci)

Ulster – BBB–BCC (Bus Inf Sys) (IB 26–24 pts HL 12–13 pts); BBB (Comp Sci; Comp Sci (Soft Sys Dev)) (IB 26 pts HL 13 pts); BBB incl sci/maths/tech/eng (Comp Gms Dev) (IB 26 pts HL 13 pts)

UWE Bristol – 120 pts (Comp Sci; Comp courses); 120 pts incl maths/chem/phys/tech/comp/eng (Gms Tech)

116 pts **Plymouth** – 116 pts (Comp Inf Scrty) (IB 30 pts); 116–120 pts (Comp Gms Dev) (IB 30 pts)

112 pts **Abertay** – BBC (Comp Gms Tech) (IB 30 pts); BBC incl art/des/comp +interview +portfolio (Comp Arts) (IB 30 pts)

Aberystwyth – BBC (Intnet Comp Sys Admin; Bus IT; Comp Sci Artif Intel; Comp Sci) (IB 28 pts)

Anglia Ruskin – 112 pts (Comp Sci) (IB 24 pts)

Birmingham City – BBC incl sci/tech/maths/comp 112 pts (Comp Net Scrty; Comp Sci; Comp Gms Tech; Comp Foren); (Bus Inf Sys) (HL 14 pts)

UCAS points Tariff: A* = 56 pts; A = 48 pts; B = 40 pts; C = 32 pts; D = 24 pts; E = 16 pts

Brighton – BBC–CCC 112–96 pts (Comp Sci (Gms); Comp Sci; Bus Comp Cy Sec; Comp Sci Artif Intel; Dig Gms Dev) (IB 28 pts); (Bus Comp) (IB 28 pts)

Central Lancashire – 112 pts (Comp Gms Dev; Comp) (IB 28 pts)

Chester – BBC–BCC 112 pts (App Comp) (IB 26 pts); 112 pts (Comp Sci) (IB 26 pts)

Chichester – BBC–CCC (Bus St IT Mgt) (IB 28 pts)

De Montfort – 112 pts (Comp Sci) (IB 26 pts)

Derby – 112 pts (Comp Gms Modl Animat)

East London – 112 pts (Comp Gms Des (Stry Dev); Comp Gm Dev) (IB 25 pts HL 15 pts)

Gloucestershire – BBC 112 pts (Bus Comp; Dig Media Web Tech; Comp)

Glyndŵr – 112 pts (Comp Net Scrty)

Greenwich – 112 pts (Maths Comp)

Hull – 112 pts (Comp Sci; Comp Sci Gms Dev) (IB 28 pts)

Kingston – 112 pts (Inf Sys; Comp Sci)

Lincoln – BBC (Comp Sci; Gms Comp) (IB 29 pts)

Liverpool John Moores – BBC 112 pts (Comp Foren; Comp St; Comp Gms Dev) (IB 26 pts)

Middlesex – 112 pts (Gms Des)

Nottingham Trent – BBC incl IT/sci/maths 112 pts (Comp Sys (Foren Scrty/Net)); BBC incl IT/sci 112 pts (Inf Sys)

Oxford Brookes – BBC (Comp Sci; IT Mgt Bus) (IB 30 pts)

Salford – 112–120 pts incl maths/comp (Comp Sci) (IB 31 pts)

Southampton Solent – 112 pts (Bus IT; Net Scrty Mgt; Web Des Dev)

Staffordshire – 112 pts (Comp Sci); BBC–CCC 112 pts (Bus IT)

Suffolk – BBC 112 pts (Soft Dev; Comp Gms Tech)

Sunderland – 112 pts (Cyberscrty Dig Foren; Comp; ICT; Comp Sci; Net Comp)

Teesside – BBC incl maths/comp/IT (Comp Dig Foren)

West London – 112 pts (Comp Sci); 112–120 pts (Cy Scrty; Mbl Comp; IT Mgt Bus)

Westminster – BBC/A*A* (Bus Inf Sys) (IB 26 pts); BBC/AA (Comp Sci) (IB 26 pts)

104 pts **Anglia Ruskin** – 104 pts (Comp Gmg Tech) (IB 24 pts)

Bolton – 104 pts (Comp Net Scrty)

Bournemouth – 104–120 pts (Bus IT; Comp) (IB 28–31 pts HL 55)

Central Lancashire – 104 pts (Web Des Dev) (IB 26 pts)

Chichester – BCC incl maths (Data Sci) (IB 28 pts HL 4 maths)

De Montfort – 104 pts (Comp; Bus Inf Sys) (IB 24 pts)

Falmouth – 104–120 pts (Comp Games)

London South Bank – BCC (Bus IT)

Manchester Met – BCC–BBC incl maths/tech/sci 104–112 pts (Comp Net Tech) (IB 26 pts); BCC–BBC 104–112 pts (Comp Foren Scrty; Comp Gms Tech; Comp; Gms Des Dev; Web Tech; Comp Sci) (IB 26 pts)

Middlesex – 104 pts (Bus Inf Sys; Comp Comm Net)

Northampton – BCC (Bus Comp (Sys); Comp Gms Dev)

Portsmouth – 104–120 pts (Bus Inf Sys; Comp Sci; Comp) (IB 26 pts)

Robert Gordon – BCC (Comp Sci; Cy Scrty) (IB 27 pts)

Salford – BCC–BBC 104–112 pts (Bus IT) (IB 30 pts)

South Wales – BCC–CDD 104–80 pts (Comp Sci; ICT) (HL 655–445)

Teesside – 104–120 pts (Comp Sci); 104–120 pts incl tech/sci/maths (Comp Gms Prog); 104–120 pts +portfolio (Comp Chrctr Animat)

Trinity Saint David – 104 pts (Bus IT; Comp Gms Des; Comp Net; Comp Inf Sys; Web Dev)

Westminster – BCC/A*A (Comp Net Scrty) (IB 26 pts)

Winchester – 104–120 pts (Crea Prod) (IB 26 pts)

96 pts **Bath Spa** – CCC–CCD (Crea Comp) (IB 26 pts)

Canterbury Christ Church – 96–120 pts (Comp Sci)

Cardiff Met – 96 pts (Bus Inf Sys; Comp Sci)

Derby – 96–112 pts (Comp Foren Invstg; Comp Gms Prog; Maths Comp Sci; Comp Net Scrty; Comp Sci; IT)

   East London – 96 pts (Comp Bus) (IB 24 pts HL 15 pts); 96 pts incl maths (Comp Sci)
        (IB 25 pts HL 15 pts incl maths)
   Glasgow Caledonian – CCC incl comp/maths (IT Mgt Bus) (IB 24 pts); CCC (Comp Gms
        courses) (IB 24 pts)
   Hertfordshire – 96–112 pts (Bus Inf Sys)
   Leeds Beckett – 96 pts (Comp Foren Scrty; Comp; Comp Foren) (IB 24 pts); (Bus IT)
        (IB 25 pts)
   London Met – CCC 96 pts (Comp Gms Prog)
   London South Bank – CCC/AA 96 pts (Comp courses)
   Teesside – 96–112 pts (Web Prod; Comp; IT); 96–112 pts +interview +portfolio (Comp Gms
        Art; Comp Gms Animat); 96–112 pts +interview (Comp Gms Des)
   Winchester – 96–112 pts (Comp Aid Des) (IB 25 pts)
   Worcester – 96 pts (Comp; Comp Gms Des Dev; Bus IT)
   York St John – 96–116 pts (Bus IT)
88 pts **Canterbury Christ Church** – 88–112 pts (Comp; Bus Inf Sys)
   West Scotland – CCD incl maths/phys/comp sci (Comp Net) (IB 24 pts); CCD (Comp Gms
        Dev; Comp Sci; Web Mbl Dev) (IB 24 pts); CCD incl maths (Comp Gms Tech) (IB 24 pts)
   Wolverhampton – AB/CCD (Comp Sci (Gms Dev))
80 pts **Bangor** – 80 pts (Comp Inf Sys)
   Bedfordshire – 80 pts (Inf Data Sys)
   Bucks New – 80–96 pts (Comp courses)
   Colchester (Inst) – 80 pts (IT Sys Apps)
   London Met – BB–CCE 80 pts (Comp courses)
   Wolverhampton – BB/CDD (Comp Sci; Comp IT)
72 pts **Wolverhampton** – BC/CDE (Cyberscrty)
64 pts **Greenwich** – 64 pts (Bus IT)
24 pts **UHI** – D (Comp)

   Open University – contact 0300 303 0073 **or** www.open.ac.uk/contact/new (Comp IT;
        Comp Comb Hons)

Alternative offers
See **Chapter 6** and **Appendix 1** for grades/UCAS Tariff points information for other examinations.

EXAMPLES OF DEGREE APPRENTICESHIPS IN THIS SUBJECT FIELD
Aston (Dig Tech Sol); Birmingham (Comp Sci Dig Tech Prtshp); Birmingham City (Broad Comms Eng); BPP (Dig Tech Sol); Chichester (Dig Tech Sol (Soft Eng)); East London (Dig Tech Sol); Edinburgh Napier (Dig Tech Sol); Essex (Dig Tech Sol); Exeter (Dig Tech Sol); Greenwich (IT); Glasgow Caledonian (Dig Tech Sol); Hertfordshire (Dig Tech Sol); Leeds (Comp Sci (Dig Tech Sol)); Liverpool John Moores (Dig Tech Sol); London (QM) (Dig Tech Sol); Manchester Met (Dig Tech Sol (IT Conslt/Soft Eng/Data Analyst/Cy Scrty Analyst)); Open University (Dig Tech Sol); Plymouth (Dig Tech Sol); Queen's Belfast (Soft Eng Dig Tech); Roehampton (Dig Tech Sol); Staffordshire (Dig Tech Sol); Sunderland (Dig Tech Sol); UWE Bristol (App Comp); West London (Dig Tech Sol); Winchester (Dig Tech Sol; Dig Tech Sol (Bus Mgt)).

EXAMPLES OF COLLEGES OFFERING COURSES IN THIS SUBJECT FIELD
Most colleges, check with your local college.

CHOOSING YOUR COURSE (SEE ALSO CH.1)
Universities and colleges teaching quality See www.qaa.ac.uk; https://unistats.ac.uk.

Top research universities and colleges (REF 2014) (Computer Science and Informatics) Liverpool; Warwick; London (UCL); Imperial London; Manchester; Sheffield; Lancaster; London (QM); York; Cambridge; London (King's); Nottingham; Bristol; Newcastle; Oxford.

Examples of sandwich degree courses Aston; Bath; Birmingham City; Bournemouth; Bradford; Brighton; Brunel; Cardiff; City; Coventry; De Montfort; Derby; East Anglia; Edinburgh Napier;

Gloucestershire; Greenwich; Huddersfield; Kent; Kingston; Leeds Beckett; Lincoln; Liverpool; Liverpool John Moores; London (QM); London (RH); London South Bank; Loughborough; Manchester Met; Middlesex; Newcastle; Northumbria; Nottingham Trent; Oxford Brookes; Portsmouth; Queen's Belfast; Reading; Salford; Sheffield Hallam; South Wales; Southampton Solent; Stirling; Sunderland; Surrey; Teesside; Ulster; UWE Bristol; Westminster; Wolverhampton; York.

ADMISSIONS INFORMATION

Number of applicants per place (approx) Abertay 5; Aston (Bus Comp IT) 12; Bangor 5; Bath 10; Birmingham 9; Bradford 13; Bristol 8; Buckingham 5; Cambridge 3; Cardiff 5; City 8; Derby 5; Dundee 5; Durham 9; Edinburgh 4; Exeter 10; Heriot-Watt 9; Hull (Comp Sci) 5; Imperial London 6; Kingston 10; Lancaster 5; Leeds 10; Leicester 10; Lincoln 5; Liverpool 5; Liverpool John Moores 3; London (King's) 20; London (QM) 6; London (RH) 8; London (UCL) 12; Manchester Met 10, (Bus IT) 8; Newcastle 6; Nottingham 8; Nottingham Trent 4; Oxford Brookes 6; Plymouth 24; Robert Gordon 3; Sheffield Hallam 5; Southampton 9; Stirling 10; Strathclyde 16; Swansea 5; Teesside 4; Warwick 11; York 6.

Admissions tutors' advice Bournemouth It can be difficult for applicants to know when applying for courses what specialism they wish to follow. Our course offers a common first year with specialisms following in Years 2 and 3.

Advice to applicants and planning the UCAS personal statement Your computer and programming interests in and outside school or college should be described. It is also useful to give details of any visits, work experience and work shadowing relating to industrial or commercial organisations and their computer systems. (See **Appendix 3**.) Give details of your interests in, and knowledge of, computer hardware, software and multimedia packages. Contact the Chartered Institute for IT for information. **Bristol** Deferred entry accepted.

Misconceptions about this course That anyone who plays computer games or uses a word processor can do a degree in Computer Studies. Some think Computing degrees are just about programming; in reality, programming is only one, albeit essential, part of computing. **London (QM)** There are many misconceptions – among students, teachers and careers advisers – about what computer science entails. The main one is to confuse it with what schools call information and communication technology, which is about the use of computer applications. Computer science is all about software – ie programming – and will generally only cover a limited study of hardware. **Plymouth** Paid placements are part of some Computing courses and can lead to employment.

Selection interviews Yes Buckingham, Cambridge, Imperial London, Kent, Manchester, Northbrook Met (Coll), Oxford (Comp Sci) 9%, St Andrews, Winchester; **Some** Bath, Birmingham City, Bournemouth, Cardiff, Loughborough, Warwick; **No** Anglia Ruskin, Bradford, Brighton, Coventry, Dundee, East Anglia, Edinburgh, Falmouth, Hull, Kingston, Liverpool Hope, Liverpool John Moores, London (Gold), London (QM), London (UCL), London Met, London South Bank, Manchester Met, Newcastle, Northampton, Nottingham, Nottingham Trent, Plymouth, Portsmouth, Salford, Sheffield Hallam, Southampton, Sunderland, Surrey, UWE Bristol, West London, West Scotland.

Interview advice and questions While A-level computer studies is not usually required, you will be questioned on your use of computers and aspects of the subject which interest you. How do you organise your homework/social life? What are your strengths and weaknesses? Do you have any idea of the type of career you would like? See also **Chapter 5**. **York** Applicants are given the opportunity to attend an interview. It is not part of the selection process, but offers may be lowered if candidates perform well.

Reasons for rejection (non-academic) Little practical interest in computers/electronics. Inability to work as part of a small team. Mismatch between referee's description and performance at interview. Unsatisfactory English. Can't communicate. Inability to convince interviewer of the candidate's worth. Incoherent, unmotivated, arrogant and without any evidence of good reason. **London (QM)** Misunderstanding of what computer science involves as an academic subject – especially in personal statements where some suggest that they are interested in a course with business and administrative

Check **Chapter 3** for new university admission details and **Chapter 6** on how to read the subject tables.

skills. Lack of sufficient mathematics. Computer science is a mathematical subject and we cannot accept applicants who are unable to demonstrate good mathematical skills. **Southampton** Lack of motivation, incoherence and/or carelessness.

AFTER-RESULTS ADVICE

Offers to applicants repeating A-levels Higher Brighton, De Montfort, Greenwich, Kingston, St Andrews, Sussex, Warwick; **Possibly higher** Bath, Edinburgh, Lancaster, Leeds, Newcastle, Sheffield, Teesside; **Same** Abertay, Anglia Ruskin, Aston, Brunel, Buckingham, Cambridge, Cardiff, Cardiff Met, City, Derby, Dundee, Durham, East Anglia, East London, Exeter, Huddersfield, Hull, Lincoln, Liverpool, Liverpool Hope, Liverpool John Moores, London (RH), London (UCL), London South Bank, Loughborough, Manchester Met, Northumbria, Nottingham Trent, Oxford Brookes, Robert Gordon, Salford, Sheffield Hallam, Sunderland, West London, Wolverhampton, Worcester, York.

GRADUATE DESTINATIONS AND EMPLOYMENT (2015/16 HESA)

Computer Science graduates surveyed 7,540 **Employed** 4,525 **In voluntary employment** 195 **In further study** 1,265 **Assumed unemployed** 735

Information Systems graduates surveyed 1,890 **Employed** 1,150 **In voluntary employment** 30 **In further study** 260 **Assumed unemployed** 185

Artificial Intelligence graduates surveyed 75 **Employed** 50 **In voluntary employment** 0 **In further study** 15 **Assumed unemployed** 0

Career note A high proportion of graduates go to work in the IT sector with some degrees leading towards particular fields (usually indicated by the course title). Significant areas include software design and engineering, web and internet-based fields, programming, systems analysis and administration.

OTHER DEGREE SUBJECTS FOR CONSIDERATION

Business Studies; Communications Engineering; Computer Engineering; Electrical and Electronic Engineering; Geographical Information Systems; Information Studies; Mathematics; Physics; Software Engineering.

DANCE/DANCE STUDIES

(see also **Drama**)

Dance courses abound, most offering a balance of theoretical and practical studies across a range of dance styles. The Royal Academy of Dance for example offers ballet, adult ballet, boys' ballet, creative and contemporary dance, West End jazz, street dance, and song and dance. Other institutions offer Dance combined with other subjects equally. Some universities offer Performance Arts with many courses covering the study of choreography, acting and directing, and acting and dance. Whilst entry to Dance courses usually requires A-level grades, competitive entry to the most popular courses, such as the Contemporary Dance course at Trinity Laban, is by a demanding audition.

Useful websites https://cdmt.org.uk; www.onedanceuk.org; www.rad.org.uk; www.royalballetschool.org.uk

NB The points totals shown to the left of the institutions are for ease of reference only. It must not be assumed that Tariff points are always used by institutions or that they can be substituted for an offer in grades. The level of an offer is not necessarily indicative of the quality of a course.

COURSE OFFERS INFORMATION

Subject requirements/preferences GCSE English usually required. **AL** No specific subjects required. **Other** Disclosure and Barring Service (DBS) checks required for some courses: check websites. Practical dance experience essential.

Your target offers and examples of degree courses

136 pts **Liverpool Hope** – ABB–BBC 136–104 pts +audition (Dance)

128 pts **East London** – 128 pts +interview +audition (Dance (Urb Prac)) (IB 27 pts HL 15 pts)
Edge Hill – ABB 128 pts +audition workshop (Dance; Dance Dr)
Surrey – ABB (Dance) (IB 32 pts)

120 pts **Coventry** – BBB incl dance/perf arts +portfolio (Dance) (IB 31 pts HL 5 dance)
Leeds Beckett – 120 pts +portfolio (Dance) (IB 26 pts)
Roehampton – 120 pts (Dance; BFA Dance)
West London – BBB 120–128 pts +audition (Musl Thea)

112 pts **Bedfordshire** – 112 pts +interview +audition (Dance Prof Prac)
Cardiff Met – 112 pts +interview +audition (Dance Physl Educ)
Cumbria – 112–128 pts +interview +audition (Dance Musl Thea)
De Montfort – 112 pts +interview +workshop (Dance) (IB 26 pts)
Kingston – BBC incl dance/perf arts/Engl lit 112–128 pts +interview +workshop (Dance)
Liverpool John Moores – BBC +audition (Dance Prac) (IB 27 pts)
Middlesex – 112 pts +interview +audition (Dance St; Dance Perf)
RAc Dance – BBC 112 pts +RAD Intermediate (Dance Educ); BBC +RAD Intermediate
+interview +audition (Ballet Educ)
Wolverhampton – BBC +audition (Dance Dr; Dance)
Worcester – 112 pts (PE Dance; Dance Commun Prac)

104 pts **Central Lancashire** – 104 pts (Dance Perf Teach) (IB 28 pts)
Chester – BCC–BBC +audition (Dance) (IB 26 pts)
Chichester – 104–120 pts +interview +audition (Dance)
Falmouth – 104–120 pts +interview +audition (Dance Choreo)
Lincoln – BCC +interview +audition (Dance) (IB 28 pts)
Plymouth – 104 pts +interview +audition (Dance) (IB 26 pts)
Salford – BCC–BBB 104–120 pts +interview +audition (Dance) (IB 30 pts HL 65)

96 pts **Bath Spa** – CCC incl dance/perf arts +audition (Dance) (IB 26 pts)
Birmingham City – CCC 96 pts incl dr +interview (App Perf (Commun Educ))
Cumbria – 96–112 pts +interview +audition (Dance)
Derby – 96–128 pts (Dance Mov St Comb Hons)
Winchester – 96–112 pts (Dance Perf (Yng Ppl)) (IB 25 pts); 96–112 pts +interview
+audition (Choreo Dance) (IB 25 pts)

88 pts **Canterbury Christ Church** – 88–112 pts +interview (Dance Educ); 88–112 pts +interview
+audition (Dance)
London Met – CCD 88 pts (Spo Dance Thera)

80 pts **Bucks New** – 80–96 pts +interview +audition (Dance Perf)

64 pts **Greenwich** – 64 pts +audition (Prof Dance Musl Thea)
Liverpool (LIPA) – 64 pts +audition (Dance)

Northern (Sch Contemp Dance) – interview +audition (Dance (Contemp))
RConsvS – interview +audition (Modn Ballet)
Trinity Laban Consv – audition (Contemp Dance)

Alternative offers
See **Chapter 6** and **Appendix 1** for grades/UCAS Tariff points information for other examinations.

EXAMPLES OF COLLEGES OFFERING COURSES IN THIS SUBJECT FIELD
Barking and Dagenham (Coll); Bournemouth and Poole (Coll); Brooksby Melton (Coll); City and
Islington (Coll); Coventry (Coll); Doncaster (Coll); Ealing, Hammersmith and West London (Coll); East
Durham (Coll); Gateshead (Coll); Grimsby (Inst Group); Havering (Coll); Hull (Coll); Kingston (Coll);
Leeds City (Coll); Leicester (Coll); LeSoCo; Liverpool City (Coll); Manchester (Coll); Northbrook Met
(Coll); Nottingham (Coll); Petroc; South Essex (Coll); South Gloucestershire and Stroud (Coll);
Southampton City (Coll); Stratford-upon-Avon (Coll); Sunderland (Coll); Sussex Downs (Coll); Wakefield
(Coll); West Thames (Coll).

Check **Chapter 3** for new university admission details and **Chapter 6** on how to read the subject tables.

CHOOSING YOUR COURSE (SEE ALSO CH.1)

Universities and colleges teaching quality See www.qaa.ac.uk; https://unistats.ac.uk.

Top research universities and colleges (REF 2014) (Music, Drama, Dance and Performing Arts) Open University; Roehampton (Dance); London (QM); Warwick; London (SOAS); Durham; London (RH) (Mus); Southampton; Oxford; Birmingham (Mus); City; London (King's) (Film); Manchester (Dr); London (RH) (Dr Thea); Huddersfield; Manchester (Mus); Cardiff.

Examples of sandwich degree courses Coventry; Surrey.

ADMISSIONS INFORMATION

Number of applicants per place (approx) De Montfort (Dance) 13; Derby 4; Liverpool (LIPA) 24; Liverpool John Moores 3; Middlesex 12; Northern (Sch Contemp Dance) 6; Roehampton 8; Trinity Laban Consv 5.

Advice to applicants and planning the UCAS personal statement Full details should be given of examinations taken and practical experience in contemporary dance or ballet. Refer to your visits to the theatre and your impressions. You should list the dance projects in which you have worked, productions in which you have performed and the roles. State any formal dance training you have had and the grades achieved. Applicants need to have dedication, versatility, inventiveness and individuality, practical experience of dance, theoretical ability and language competency. **Bath Spa** Dance experience outside education should be mentioned.

Misconceptions about this course That Performing Arts is only an acting course: it also includes music.

Selection interviews Yes Bedfordshire, Bucks New, Cardiff Met, Chester, Chichester, Kingston, Northern (Sch Contemp Dance), Plymouth, Winchester, Worcester; **Some** Cumbria, RAc Dance; **No** Falmouth.

Interview advice and questions Nearly all institutions will require auditions or interviews or attendance at a workshop. The following scheme required by **Liverpool (LIPA)** may act as a guide:

1 Write a short essay (500 words) on your own views and experience of dance. You should take into account the following.
   (i)   Your history and how you have developed physically and intellectually in your run-up to applying to LIPA.
   (ii) Your main influences and what inspires you.
   (iii) What you want to gain from training as a dancer.
   (iv) Your ideas on health and nutrition as a dancer, taking into account gender and physicality.
2 All candidates must prepare **two** practical audition pieces.
   (i)   Whatever you like, in whatever style you wish, as long as the piece does not exceed two minutes (please note: panel will stop anyone exceeding this time limit). There will be no pianist at this part of the session, so if you're using music please bring it with you. This devised piece should be created by you and this means that you should feel comfortable with it and that it expresses something personal about you. You should wear your regular practice clothes for your presentation.
   (ii) You are asked to sing a musical theatre solo as part of the audition and will be accompanied by a pianist. An accompanist is provided, but you must provide the sheet music for your song, fully written out for piano accompaniment and in the key you wish to sing (the accompanist will **not** transpose at sight). **Important** Do NOT choreograph your song. You should expect to sit on a high stool or stand when singing for the audition.
3 Additionally, all candidates will participate in a class given on the day of audition.
   (i)   Please ensure that you are dressed appropriately for class with clothing you are comfortable in but allows your movement to be seen. In preparing the practical elements of the audition, please remember that audition panels are not looking for a polished performance. The panel will be looking for candidates' ability to make a genuine emotional and physical connection with the material that they are presenting which shows clear intent and focus.

UCAS points Tariff: A* = 56 pts; A = 48 pts; B = 40 pts; C = 32 pts; D = 24 pts; E = 16 pts

Remember that it is in your best interest to prepare thoroughly. Nerves inevitably play a part in any audition and can undermine even the best-prepared candidate. Your best defence is to feel confident in your preparation. See also **Chapter 5**.

Salford Audition and interview. **Wolverhampton** Audition.

Reasons for rejection (non-academic) Applicants more suitable for an acting or dance school course than a degree course. No experience of dance on the UCAS application. Limited dance skills.

AFTER-RESULTS ADVICE
Offers to applicants repeating A-levels Same Chester, Chichester, De Montfort, Liverpool John Moores, Salford, Trinity Laban Consv, Winchester, Wolverhampton.

GRADUATE DESTINATIONS AND EMPLOYMENT (2015/16 HESA)
Graduates surveyed 880 **Employed** 325 **In voluntary employment** 15 **In further study** 250 **Assumed unemployed** 40

Career note Teaching is the most popular career destination for the majority of graduates. Other opportunities exist as dance animators working in education or in the community to encourage activity and participation in dance. There is a limited number of openings for dance or movement therapists who work with the emotionally disturbed, the elderly or physically disadvantaged.

OTHER DEGREE SUBJECTS FOR CONSIDERATION
Arts Management; Drama; Education (Primary); Music; Performance Studies; Physical Education; Sport and Exercise Science.

DENTISTRY
(including Dental Hygiene and Dental Therapy and Oral Health Science)

Dentistry involves the treatment and prevention of a wide range of mouth diseases from tooth decay and gum disease to mouth cancer. Courses in Dentistry/Dental Surgery cover the basic medical sciences, human disease, clinical studies and clinical dentistry. The amount of patient contact will vary between institutions but will be considerable in all dental schools. Intercalated courses in other science subjects are offered on most courses. Courses in Oral Health Science and Dental Therapy and Hygiene lead to professional qualifications as therapists and hygienists providing advice and non-surgical treatment for children and adults to prevent tooth decay. Dental Technology courses similarly lead to a professional qualification to prepare crowns, bridges, partial and complete sets of dentures, and other orthodontic devices to replace and correct teeth.

Useful websites http://badn.org.uk; www.bsdht.org.uk; http://dla.org.uk

NB The points totals shown to the left of the institutions are for ease of reference only. It must not be assumed that Tariff points are always used by institutions or that they can be substituted for an offer in grades. The level of an offer is not necessarily indicative of the quality of a course.

COURSE OFFERS INFORMATION
Subject requirements/preferences GCSE English, mathematics and science subjects required in most cases for Dentistry courses. A*/A/B (8–9/7/5–6) grades stipulated in certain subjects by many dental schools. **AL** Chemistry plus biology or another science subject usually required for Dentistry: see offers lines below. (Dntl Tech, Oral Hlth Sci) Science subject required or preferred. Many dental schools use admissions tests (eg UKCAT: see **Chapter 5**). Evidence of non-infectivity or hepatitis B immunisation required and all new dental students screened for hepatitis C. Disclosure and Barring Service (DBS) check at enhanced level is also required.

London (King's) GCSE English and maths grade B (6) if not offered at a higher level.

Manchester GCSE Six subjects at grade A (7).

Your target offers and examples of degree courses

152 pts **London (King's)** – A*AA incl biol+chem +UKCAT (Dnstry) (IB 35 pts HL 6 biol+chem)

144 pts **Birmingham** – AAA incl chem+biol +UKCAT+interview (Dntl Srgy)

Bristol – AAA–AAC incl chem+biol/phys +UKCAT+interview (Dnstry) (IB 36–32 pts HL 18–16 incl 6 chem+sci)

Cardiff – AAA incl chem+biol +UKCAT (Dntl Srgy) (IB 36 pts HL 6 chem+biol)

Dundee – AAA incl chem+sci +UKCAT (Dnstry) (IB 37 pts)

Glasgow – AAA incl biol+chem +UKCAT (Dnstry) (IB 36 pts)

Leeds – AAA incl biol+chem +BMAT +interview (Dntl Srgy) (IB 35 pts HL 666 incl biol+chem)

Liverpool – AAA incl chem+biol +UKCAT (Dntl Srgy) (IB 36 pts HL 6 chem+biol)

London (QM) – AAA incl chem/biol+sci/maths +UKCAT (Dnstry) (IB 38 pts HL 666 incl chem/biol+sci/maths)

Manchester – AAA incl chem+biol +UKCAT (Dnstry) (IB 37 pts)

Newcastle – AAA incl chem+biol +UKCAT (Dntl Srgy) (IB 37 pts HL 6 chem+biol)

Queen's Belfast – AAA incl biol+chem/AAA incl chem+maths/phys+AS b biol +UKCAT+interview (Dnstry)

Sheffield – AAA incl chem+biol +UKCAT (Dntl Srgy) (IB 36 pts HL 6 chem+biol)

128 pts **Birmingham** – ABB incl biol (Dntl Hyg Thera)

London (QM) – ABB incl maths/phys/chem (Dntl Mat) (IB 32 pts HL 655)

Newcastle – ABB incl biol (Oral Dntl Hlth Sci) (IB 34 pts HL 5 biol)

120 pts **Cardiff** – BBB incl biol (Dntl Thera Hyg)

Dundee – BBB incl biol (Oral Hlth Sci) (IB 30 pts HL 555)

Edinburgh – BBB incl biol (Oral Hlth Sci) (IB 32 pts)

Portsmouth – 120 pts (Dntl Hyg); 120 pts incl sci (Dntl Hyg Dntl Thera) (IB 30 pts HL 17 pts incl 6 sci)

104 pts **Glasgow Caledonian** – BCC incl biol (Oral Hlth Sci) (IB 24 pts HL 6 biol)

Teesside – 104–112 pts incl biol +interview (Dntl Hyg Dntl Thera)

UHI – BCC incl sci (Oral Hlth Sci)

 96 pts **Cardiff Met** – 96 pts (Dntl Tech)

Portsmouth – 96 pts (Advnc Dntl Nurs)

Alternative offers

See **Chapter 6** and **Appendix 1** for grades/UCAS Tariff points information for other examinations.

EXAMPLES OF COLLEGES OFFERING COURSES IN THIS SUBJECT FIELD

Birmingham Met (Coll); Bury (Coll); Neath Port Talbot (Coll); Plumpton (Coll).

CHOOSING YOUR COURSE (SEE ALSO CH.1)

Universities and colleges teaching quality See www.qaa.ac.uk; https://unistats.ac.uk.

Top research universities and colleges (REF 2014) (Allied Health Professions, Dentistry, Nursing and Pharmacy) Birmingham; Sheffield (Biomed Sci); Bangor; Swansea (Allied Hlth); Aston; Coventry; Southampton; Cardiff; Surrey; Glasgow; Nottingham (Pharm); Bradford; East Anglia (Allied Hlth); London (QM); Sheffield (Dnstry); Queen's Belfast (Pharm); Bath; London (King's) (Pharm); Leeds.

Examples of sandwich degree courses London (QM).

ADMISSIONS INFORMATION

Number of applicants per place (approx) Birmingham 7, (Dntl Hyg Thera) 8; Bristol 13; Cardiff 4; Cardiff Met 1; Dundee 8, (Pre-Dntl) 5; Edinburgh (Oral Hlth Sci) 10 places every 2nd yr; Glasgow 7; Leeds 11; Liverpool 7; London (King's) 128 (offers to 1 in 9); London (QM) 4; Manchester 12, (Pre-Dntl) 21, (Oral Hlth Sci) 26; Newcastle 10; Queen's Belfast 5; Sheffield 12.

Advice to applicants and planning the UCAS personal statement UCAS applications listing four choices only should be submitted by 15 October. Applicants may add one alternative (non-Dentistry) course. On your UCAS application, show evidence of your manual dexterity, work experience and awareness of problems experienced by dentists. Details should be provided of discussions with dentists and work shadowing in dental surgeries. Employment (paid or voluntary) in any field, preferably dealing with people in an environment widely removed from your home or school, could be described. Discuss any specialised fields of dentistry in which you might be interested. See also **Appendix 3**. **Bristol** Applications are not segregated by type of educational institution. Candidates are assessed on general presentation. Work experience is expected, if possible in different fields of dentistry. Re-sit candidates are considered, but only one re-sit is allowed in each subject unless there are mitigating circumstances. **Cardiff** Applicants must be able to demonstrate: (a) evidence of, and potential for, high academic achievement, (b) an understanding of the demands of dental training and practice, (c) a caring and committed attitude towards people, (d) a willingness to accept responsibility, (e) an ability to communicate effectively, (f) evidence of broad social, cultural or sporting interests. **London (King's)** School activities desirable, for example, general reading, debating, theological interests. Community activities very desirable. General activities desirable, for example, sport, first aid, handiwork (which can be used to demonstrate manual dexterity). Work shadowing and paid or voluntary work very desirable (check website). **Manchester** Re-sit offers A*AA. Applicants are required to have observed a general dental practitioner at work before applying; a minimum of two weeks' work experience is expected.

Misconceptions about this course Cardiff Met (Dntl Tech) Some think that the course allows them to practise as a dentist. Some think the degree is entirely practical.

Selection interviews Most dental schools will interview candidates. **Yes** Aberdeen, Birmingham, Bristol, Cardiff, Dundee, Edinburgh, Glasgow, Leeds, Liverpool, London (King's), London (QM), Manchester, Newcastle, Portsmouth, Queen's Belfast, Sheffield; **No** Cardiff Met.

Interview advice and questions Dental work experience or work shadowing is essential (check with university websites) and, as a result, questions will be asked on your reactions to the work and your understanding of the different types of treatment that a dentist can offer. In the past, questions at interview have included: What is conservative dentistry? What does integrity mean? Do you think the first year syllabus is a good one? What qualities are required by a dentist? What are prosthetics, periodontics, orthodontics? What causes tooth decay? Questions asked on the disadvantages of being a dentist, the future of dentistry and how you could show that you are manually dexterous. Other questions on personal attributes and spare time activities. What are the careers within the profession open to dentists? Questions on the future of dentistry (preventative and cosmetic dentistry), the problems facing dentists, the skills needed and the advantages and disadvantages of fluoride in water. How do you relax? How do you cope with stress? See also **Chapter 5**. **Bristol** All candidates called for interview must attend in order to be considered for a place. The University uses the Multiple Mini Interview system and interviewees are asked to fill in a form detailing their work experience. Candidates are assessed on general presentation, response to questions, knowledge of dentistry, evidence of teamwork and leadership, general interests and manual dexterity. **Leeds** The interview assesses personality, verbal and communication skills and knowledge of dentistry. **London (King's)** Approximately 180 offers are made each year. All applicants receiving offers will have been interviewed. The interviews will normally take the MMI format.

Reasons for rejection (non-academic) Lack of evidence of a firm commitment to dentistry. Lack of breadth of interests. Lack of motivation for a health care profession. Unprofessional attitude. Poor manual dexterity. Poor communication skills. Poor English. Lack of evidence of ability to work in groups. Not for the faint-hearted! More interested in running a business and making money than in caring for people. **Cardiff Met** (Dntl Tech) Target numbers need to be precise so the course fills at a late stage.

Mature students The following universities/dental schools offer shortened (usually four-year) courses in Dentistry/Dental Surgery for graduates with at least 2.1 degrees in specified subjects. GCE A-level subjects and grades are also specified. Check with universities: Liverpool, London (King's), (QM).

Check **Chapter 3** for new university admission details and **Chapter 6** on how to read the subject tables.

AFTER-RESULTS ADVICE
Offers to applicants repeating A-levels Higher Leeds (very few), Manchester (AAA for applicants who firmly accepted offer of a place); **Same** Cardiff Met (Dntl Tech), Queen's Belfast; **No** Cardiff.

GRADUATE DESTINATIONS AND EMPLOYMENT (2015/16 HESA)
Clinical Dentistry graduates surveyed 910 **Employed** 835 **In voluntary employment** 0 **In further study** 20 **Assumed unemployed** 5

Career note The great majority of Dental Technology graduates gain employment in this career with job opportunities excellent in both the UK and Europe. There are openings in the NHS, commercial dental laboratories and the armed services.

OTHER DEGREE SUBJECTS FOR CONSIDERATION
Anatomy; Biochemistry; Biological Sciences; Biomedical Materials Science; Chemistry; Medical Sciences; Medicine; Nursing; Optometry; Pharmacy; Physiology; Physiotherapy; Radiography; Speech Therapy/Sciences; Veterinary Medicine/Science.

DEVELOPMENT STUDIES
(see also International Relations, Politics, Town and Country Planning)

Development Studies courses are multi-disciplinary and cover a range of subjects including economics, geography, sociology, social anthropology, politics, natural resources, with special reference to countries overseas. Courses obviously overlap with International Relations degrees which should also be checked. The main focus of Development Studies is to identify and recognise problems arising overseas and how countries may be assisted in terms of poverty and health, as well as exploring wider issues concerning social and political perspectives. The unique degree course in this category is Charity Development at the University of Chichester with either Single Honours or Joint Honours. The course covers fund-raising practices, through events and campaigns, marketing and planning.

Useful websites www.devstud.org.uk; www.gov.uk/government/organisations/department-for-international-development; www.ids.ac.uk; see also **Politics**.

NB The points totals shown to the left of the institutions are for ease of reference only. It must not be assumed that Tariff points are always used by institutions or that they can be substituted for an offer in grades. The level of an offer is not necessarily indicative of the quality of a course.

COURSE OFFERS INFORMATION
Subject requirements/preferences GCSE Mathematics, English and a foreign language may be required. **AL** Science or social science subjects may be required or preferred for some courses.

Your target offers and examples of degree courses
144 pts **London (SOAS)** – AAA–AAB (Dev St) (IB 37 pts HL 666)
    Warwick – AAA (Glob Sust Dev Bus St) (IB 38 pts)
136 pts **Bath** – AAB/ABB+aEPQ (Int Dev Econ) (IB 36 pts HL 665)
    London (King's) – AAB (Int Dev) (IB 35 pts HL 665)
    Manchester – AAB (Dev St) (IB 35 pts HL 665)
    Sussex – AAB–ABB (Econ Int Dev) (IB 32 pts); AAB (Int Rel Dev; Int Dev) (IB 34 pts)
128 pts **East Anglia** – ABB (Int Dev Pol; Int Dev; Int Dev Anth) (IB 32 pts)
    Leeds – ABB (Int Dev courses) (IB 34 pts HL 655)
    Sussex – ABB–BBB (Sociol Int Dev) (IB 30 pts)
120 pts **Birmingham** – BBB (Af St Dev) (IB 32 pts HL 555)
112 pts **Bradford** – BBC 112 pts (Glob Pol Dev)
    Chichester – BBC–CCC 112 pts +interview (Charity Dev) (IB 28 pts)

East London – 112 pts (Int Dev NGO Mgt) (IB 25 pts HL 15 pts)
London (Birk) – 112 pts (Dev Glob)
Westminster – BBC (Int Rel Dev) (IB 28 pts)
104 pts **Bath Spa** – BCC–CCC (Glob Dev Sust) (IB 26 pts)
Leeds Beckett – 104 pts (Int Rel Glob Dev) (IB 24 pts)
Northampton – BCC (Int Dev courses)
96 pts **Portsmouth** – 96–120 pts (Int Dev St) (IB 30 pts HL 17 pts)
72 pts **UHI** – BC +interview (Gael Dev)
64 pts **UHI** – CC (Sust Dev)

Alternative offers
See **Chapter 6** and **Appendix 1** for grades/UCAS Tariff points information for other examinations.

CHOOSING YOUR COURSE (SEE ALSO CH.1)
Universities and colleges teaching quality See www.qaa.ac.uk; https://unistats.ac.uk.

Top research universities and colleges (REF 2014) (Anthropology and Development Studies)
London LSE (Int Dev); Manchester (Anth); Oxford (Int Dev); Manchester (Dev St); London (Gold);
Durham; East Anglia; Cambridge; Edinburgh.

ADMISSIONS INFORMATION
Number of applicants per place (approx) Bradford 6; East Anglia 5; Leeds 8.

Admissions tutors' advice Discuss aspects of development studies which interest you, for example
in relation to geography, economics, politics. Interests in Third World countries should be mentioned.
Knowledge of current events.

Advice to applicants and planning the UCAS personal statement Some students think that
Development Studies has something to do with property, with plants or with childhood. It is none of
these and is about international processes of change, development, progress and crisis.

Interview advice and questions Since this is a multi-disciplinary subject, questions will vary
considerably. Initially they will stem from your interests and the information given on your UCAS
application and your reasons for choosing the course. In the past, questions at interview have
included: Define a Third World country. What help does the United Nations provide in the Third World?
Could it do too much? What problems does the United Nations face in its work throughout the world?
Why Development Studies? What will you do in your gap year, and what do you want to achieve?
See also **Chapter 5**.

AFTER-RESULTS ADVICE
Offers to applicants repeating A-levels Same East Anglia.

GRADUATE DESTINATIONS AND EMPLOYMENT (2015/16 HESA)
Career note The range of specialisms offered on these courses will encourage graduates to make
contact with and seek opportunities in a wide range of organisations, not necessarily limited to non-
governmental organisations and government agencies.

OTHER DEGREE SUBJECTS FOR CONSIDERATION
Economics; Environmental Science/Studies; Geography; Government; International Relations; Politics;
Sociology; Sustainable Development.

DIETETICS

(see also **Food Science/Studies and Technology, Health Sciences/Studies, Nutrition**)

Courses are often linked with nutrition and train students for a career as a dietitian. In addition to the scientific aspects of dietetics covering biochemistry, human physiology, food and clinical medicine, students are also introduced to health promotion, psychology, counselling and management skills. (See **Appendix 3**.)

Useful websites https://nutrition.org; www.bda.uk.com; www.dietetics.co.uk; www.skillsforhealth. org.uk

NB The points totals shown to the left of the institutions are for ease of reference only. It must not be assumed that Tariff points are always used by institutions or that they can be substituted for an offer in grades. The level of an offer is not necessarily indicative of the quality of a course.

COURSE OFFERS INFORMATION

Subject requirements/preferences GCSE English, mathematics and science usually required. **AL** Biology and/or chemistry may be required. **Other** Health and Disclosure and Barring Service (DBS) checks required and possible immunisation against hepatitis B for practice placements.

Your target offers and examples of degree courses

136 pts **London (King's)** – AAB incl chem+biol +interview (Nutr Diet) (IB 35 pts HL 665)
Nottingham – AAB–ABB incl sci +interview (Nutr Diet (MNutr)) (IB 34–32 pts)

128 pts **Coventry** – ABB incl biol +interview (Diet Hum Nutr) (IB 32 pts HL 7 biol)
Leeds – ABB incl sci (Fd Sci Nutr) (IB 34 pts HL 16 pts); ABB incl sci/maths (Fd Sci) (IB 34 pts HL 16 pts)
Plymouth – 128 pts incl biol+chem (Diet) (IB 31 pts HL 5 biol+chem)
Surrey – ABB incl biol+sci +interview (Nutr Diet) (IB 32 pts)

120 pts **Cardiff Met** – 120 pts incl biol+chem +interview (Hum Nutr Diet)
Hertfordshire – 120 pts incl biol+chem +interview (Diet) (HL 5 biol+chem)
Leeds Beckett – BBB incl chem+sci +interview (Diet) (IB 26 pts HL 6 chem)
London Met – BBB incl biol+chem 120 pts +interview (Diet Nutr)
Ulster – BBB incl sci/maths +HPAT (Diet)

112 pts **Chester** – BBC–BBB incl biol+sci +interview (Nutr Diet) (IB 28 pts HL 5 biol+chem)

104 pts **Bath Spa** – BCC–CCC incl biol+sci (Hum Nutr) (IB 27 pts)
Glasgow Caledonian – BCC incl chem (Hum Nutr Diet) (IB 28 pts)
Robert Gordon – BCC incl biol+chem +interview (Nutr Diet) (IB 27 pts HL 5 biol+chem)

88 pts **Queen Margaret** – AB incl chem+biol (Diet) (IB 28 pts)

Alternative offers
See **Chapter 6** and **Appendix 1** for grades/UCAS Tariff points information for other examinations.

CHOOSING YOUR COURSE (SEE ALSO CH.1)

Universities and colleges teaching quality See www.qaa.ac.uk; https://unistats.ac.uk.

Top research universities and colleges (REF 2014) See **Health Sciences/Studies**.

Examples of sandwich degree courses Glasgow Caledonian; Surrey; Ulster.

ADMISSIONS INFORMATION

Number of applicants per place (approx) Nottingham 8.

Advice to applicants and planning the UCAS personal statement Discuss the work with a hospital dietitian and describe fully work experience gained in hospital dietetics departments or with the schools meals services, and the problems of working in these fields. Admissions tutors expect applicants to have at least visited a dietetics department, and to be outgoing with good oral and written communication skills. Contact the British Dietetic Association (see **Appendix 3**).

Selection interviews Yes Chester, Coventry, Leeds Beckett; **Some** Cardiff Met; **No** Ulster.

Interview advice and questions Your knowledge of a career in dietetics will be fully explored and questions will be asked on your work experience and how you reacted to it. See also **Chapter 5**.

GRADUATE DESTINATIONS AND EMPLOYMENT (2015/16 HESA)
See **Nutrition**.

Career note Dietitians are professionally trained to advise on diets and aspects of nutrition and many degree courses combine both subjects. They may work in the NHS as hospital dietitians collaborating with medical staff on the balance of foods for patients, or in local health authorities working with GPs, or in health centres or clinics dealing with infant welfare and antenatal problems. In addition, dietitians advise consumer groups in the food industry and government and may be involved in research. Courses can lead to professional registration: check with admissions tutors.

OTHER DEGREE SUBJECTS FOR CONSIDERATION
Biological Sciences; Biochemistry; Biology; Consumer Studies; Food Science; Health Studies; Hospitality Management; Human Nutrition; Nursing; Nutrition.

DRAMA
(including **Performing Arts/Studies, Theatre Arts, Theatre Design** and **Theatre Studies**; see also **Art and Design (General), Dance/Dance Studies**)

Drama courses are popular, with twice as many women as men applying each year. Lack of confidence in securing appropriate work at the end of the course, however, tends to encourage many applicants to bid for joint courses, although these are usually far more competitive since there are fewer places available. Most schools of acting and drama provide a strong vocational bias while university drama departments offer a broader field of studies combining theory and practice. For example, at London (Goldsmiths) the Drama and Theatre Arts degree offers a balance between acting and production.

Useful websites www.equity.org.uk; www.abtt.org.uk; www.thestage.co.uk; www.uktw.co.uk; www.stagecoach.co.uk; www.rada.ac.uk; www.artscouncil.org.uk

NB The points totals shown to the left of the institutions are for ease of reference only. It must not be assumed that Tariff points are always used by institutions or that they can be substituted for an offer in grades. The level of an offer is not necessarily indicative of the quality of a course.

COURSE OFFERS INFORMATION
Subject requirements/preferences GCSE English usually required. **AL** English, drama, theatre studies may be required or preferred. (Thea Arts) English, theatre studies or drama may be required for some courses. **Other** Disclosure and Barring Service (DBS) clearance required for some courses: check websites.

Your target offers and examples of degree courses
152 pts **Cambridge** – A*AA +interview +EAA (Educ Engl Dr Arts) (IB 40–42 pts HL 776)
144 pts **Bristol** – AAA–ABB incl Engl (Thea Engl) (IB 36–32 pts HL 6 Engl)
      Exeter – AAA–AAB incl Engl lit (Engl Drama courses) (IB 36–34 pts)
      Lancaster – AAA–AAB incl Engl (Thea Engl Lit) (IB 36–35 pts HL 16 pts incl 6 Engl)
      Leeds – AAA–ABB +interview (Thea Perf) (IB 34 pts)
136 pts **Birmingham** – AAB–ABB +workshop (Dr Thea Arts) (IB 32 pts HL 665–655)
      Bristol – AAB–BBB incl lang (Thea Modn Lang) (IB 34–31 pts HL 5 lang); AAB–BBB (Thea Perf St) (IB 34–31 pts HL 17–15 pts)

East Anglia – AAB incl dr/thea st/Engl lit +interview +audition (Dr; Script Perf) (IB 33 pts HL 5 dr/thea st/Engl)

Exeter – AAB–BBB +interview +workshop (Dr) (IB 34–30 pts)

Glasgow – AAB incl arts/lang/hum (Thea St) (IB 36 pts HL 665 incl Engl+lang/hum)

Lancaster – AAB–ABB (Thea) (IB 35–32 pts HL 16 pts)

Liverpool Hope – ABB–BBC 136–104 pts +audition (Dr Thea St)

London (RH) – AAB–ABB (Dr Phil; Dr Mus) (IB 32 pts); AAB–ABB incl Engl (Engl Dr) (IB 32 pts); AAB incl Engl lit/dr thea st +portfolio (Dr Crea Writ) (IB 32 pts HL 6 Engl)

Loughborough – AAB–ABB +interview +audition (Dr) (IB 34 pts HL 655 incl 5 Engl/thea arts); AAB–ABB incl Engl +interview +audition (Engl Dr) (IB 35–34 pts HL 655 incl 6/5 Engl)

Manchester – AAB incl essay sub +interview (Dr) (IB 32 pts HL 666); AAB (Dr Engl Lit) (IB 35 pts HL 665)

Sheffield – AAB/ABB+bEPQ incl Engl/dr (Engl Thea) (IB 34 pts HL 6 Engl/dr)

Surrey (GSA) – AAB +interview +audition (Actg; Musl Thea) (IB 34 pts HL 665)

Sussex – AAB–ABB (Dr Film St) (IB 32 pts); AAB–ABB +workshop (Dr (Thea Perf)) (IB 32 pts)

Warwick – AAB incl Engl +interview (Engl Thea St) (IB 36 pts HL 6 Engl); AAB +interview (Thea Perf St) (IB 36 pts)

York – AAB (Thea (Writ Dir Perf)) (IB 35 pts)

128 pts Kent – ABB (Dr Thea) (IB 34 pts)

London (QM) – ABB incl art/hum/soc sci (Dr) (IB 32 pts HL 6 art/hum/soc sci); ABB incl art/hum/soc sci+lang (Fr/Ger/Russ Dr) (IB 32 pts HL 6/5 art/hum/soc sci)

London (RH) – ABB–BBB incl lang (Modn Lang Dr) (IB 32 pts); ABB–BBB (Dr Thea St) (IB 32 pts)

Manchester – ABB (Dr Scrn St) (IB 33 pts HL 655)

Reading – ABB–BBB +interview (Thea) (IB 32–30 pts); ABB–BBB (Engl Lit Film Thea) (IB 32–30 pts)

Surrey – ABB incl art/hum/soc sci (Thea Perf) (IB 32 pts)

120 pts Anglia Ruskin – 120 pts incl dr/thea st (Dr) (IB 24 pts); 120 pts (Dr Engl Lit) (IB 24 pts)

Bangor – 120–112 pts incl Engl (Engl Lit Thea Perf)

Brunel – BBB incl Engl +audition workshop (Thea Engl) (IB 30 pts HL 5 Engl); BBB +audition workshop (Thea Crea Writ) (IB 30 pts HL 5 Engl); (Thea) (IB 30 pts)

Edge Hill – BBB 120 pts +audition workshop (Dr)

Essex – BBB +workshop (Dr; Dr Lit) (IB 30 pts)

Huddersfield – BBB 120 pts +audition workshop (Dr Engl Lang/Lit); (Dr) (IB 31 pts)

Leeds Beckett – 120 pts +interview (Perf Arts) (IB 26 pts)

London (Birk) – 120 pts (Thea Dr St)

London (Gold) – BBB (Dr Thea Arts) (IB 33 pts)

London (Royal Central Sch SpDr) – BBB +interview (Dr App Thea Educ); 120–64 pts +interview +portfolio (Thea Prac (Thea Snd); Thea Prac (Perf Arts); Thea Prac (Pptry Des Perf); Thea Prac (Stg Mgt); Thea Prac (Tech Prod Mgt))

Northumbria – 120 pts +interview +audition (Dr (Actg Perf)) (HL 444); 120–128 pts +interview +audition (Dr (App Thea)) (IB 30 pts HL 444)

Queen's Belfast – BBB +interview +workshop (Dr courses)

Queen Margaret – BBB (Dr Perf) (IB 30 pts)

West London – BBB 120–128 pts +audition (Musl Thea); 120–128 pts +audition (Actg)

112 pts Aberystwyth – BBC–BBB (Dr Thea St; Scngrph Thea Des) (IB 28–30 pts)

Birmingham City – BBC 112 pts +portfolio (Des Perf) (HL 14 pts); BBC incl Engl 112 pts (Engl Dr) (HL 14 pts)

Bishop Grosseteste – 112 pts (App Dr courses)

Bournemouth Arts – BBC–BBB 112–120 pts +interview +audition (Actg) (IB 30–32 pts)

Chester – BBC 112 pts (Musl Thea) (IB 26 pts)

Coventry – BBC incl dr/thea/perf arts +portfolio (Thea Prof Prac) (IB 29 pts)

Cumbria – 112–128 pts +interview +audition (Perf Arts)

De Montfort – 112 pts +interview +workshop (Dr St; Perf Arts) (IB 26 pts)

East London – 112 pts +interview +audition (Dr App Thea Perf) (IB 25 pts HL 15 pts)

Glyndŵr – 112 pts +interview +audition (Thea TV Perf)
Greenwich – 112 pts (Dr)
Hull – 112 pts +interview (Dr Engl) (IB 28 pts)
London South Bank – BBC +audition (Dr Perf)
Manchester Met – 112 pts +audition (Actg) (IB 26 pts)
Middlesex – 112 pts +interview (Thea Arts)
Northampton – BBC +audition (Actg)
Oxford Brookes – BBC incl Engl 112 pts (Dr) (IB 29 pts)
Plymouth – 112 pts +interview +audition workshop (Thea Perf) (IB 28 pts)
Roehampton – 112 pts incl art/hum/soc sci (Dr Thea Perf St)
Rose Bruford (Coll) – 112 pts +interview +audition (Am Thea Arts; Euro Thea Arts)
St Mary's – 112 pts +interview +audition (Actg) (IB 28 pts)
Southampton Solent – 112 pts +audition (Actg Perf)
Sunderland – 112 pts +interview +audition (Perf Arts)
UWE Bristol – 112 pts +interview +workshop (Dr)
West London – BBC 112–128 pts (Voice Perf)
Wolverhampton – BBC +audition (Dr; Dance Dr)
Worcester – 112 pts +workshop (Dr Perf)

104 pts **Bath Spa** – BCC incl dr/thea st/Engl +interview +audition (Dr) (IB 27 pts)
Cardiff Met – 104 pts (Engl Dr)
Central Lancashire – 104 pts (Mus Thea); 104 pts +interview +audition (Thea; Actg)
     (IB 28 pts)
Chester – BCC–BBC (Dr Thea St courses) (IB 26 pts HL 5 thea)
Chichester – 104–120 pts +audition (Actg Film; Thea) (IB 28 pts); 104–120 pts (Scrn Actg
     Crea Tech) (IB 28 pts)
Falmouth – 104–120 pts +interview +audition (Actg)
Kingston – 104–112 pts incl dr/perf arts/Engl lit +interview +workshop (Dr)
Lincoln – BCC +interview (Dr) (IB 28 pts)
Liverpool John Moores – BCC 104 pts +interview +audition (Dr) (IB 24 pts)
Northampton – BCC (Dr courses)
Portsmouth – 104–120 pts +interview +workshop (Dr Perf) (IB 26 pts)
Salford – 104–120 pts incl Engl/perf/dr (Engl Dr) (IB 30–31 pts)
Sheffield Hallam – 104–88 pts incl film/TV/thea/perf (Perf Stg Scrn)
South Wales – BCC–CDD +audition workshop (Thea Dr; Perf Media) (HL 655–445)
Westminster – BCC (Thea St Engl Lit/Crea Writ) (IB 28 pts)

96 pts **Birmingham City** – 96 pts incl dr +interview (Stg Mgt)
Colchester (Inst) – 96 pts +audition (Actg Crea Perf; Musl Thea)
Cumbria – 96–112 pts +interview (Musl Thea)
Derby – 96–128 pts (Thea St Comb Hons)
Liverpool (LIPA) – CCC 96 pts (Mgt Mus Enter Thea Evnts)
London Met – CCC/BC 96 pts +interview +workshop (Thea Perf Prac)
Newman – 96 pts (Dr courses)
Rose Bruford (Coll) – 96 pts +audition (Actg; Actr Mushp); 96 pts +interview +portfolio
     (Stg Mgt; Cstm Prod)
St Mark and St John – CCC +audition (Actg)
Trinity Saint David – 96 pts +interview +workshop (Perf Arts (Contemp Perf))
Winchester – 96–112 pts +interview/workshop (Perf Arts) (IB 25 pts); 96–112 pts
     +interview +workshop (Dr) (IB 25 pts); 96–112 pts +interview (Cmdy (Perf Prod); Thea
     Chld Yng Ppl) (IB 25 pts)

88 pts **Canterbury Christ Church** – 88–112 pts (Perf Arts)
York St John – 88–104 pts (Dr Thea)

80 pts **Bedfordshire** – 80 pts +interview +audition (Thea Prof Prac)
Bucks New – 80–96 pts +interview +audition (Perf Arts (Film TV Stg))
Colchester (Inst) – 80 pts +interview +portfolio (Tech Thea)
Essex – CDD 80 pts +audition (Actg; Actg Contemp Thea)

72 pts   **Liverpool (LIPA)** – 72–80 pts +interview +audition (App Thea Commun Dr)
64 pts   **Birmingham City** – 64 pts +audition (Actg)
            Liverpool (LIPA) – CC 64 pts +interview +portfolio (Thea Perf Des; Thea Perf Tech);
               CC 64 pts +audition (Actg)
            London (Royal Central Sch SpDr) – CC +audition (Actg; Actg (Musl Thea); Actg
               (Coll Dvsd Thea))
            London Regent's – CC +interview +audition (Actg Wrld Thea)
48 pts   **Bolton** – 48 pts (Thea Fdn)
32 pts   **Arts Educ Sch** – EE +audition (Musl Thea)
            Arts London – 32 pts +audition +interview (Actg) (IB 28 pts)
            Guildhall (Sch Mus Dr) – 32 pts +audition (Actg) (IB 24 pts); 32 pts +interview
               (Stg Mgt Tech Thea) (IB 24 pts)
            RConsvS – EE +interview (Prod Arts Des) (IB 24 pts); EE +audition (Contemp Perf Prac; Actg)
               (IB 24 pts)
16 pts   **Arts London** – E +interview +portfolio (Perf Des Prac); (Thea Des) (IB 28 pts)

            Bristol Old Vic (Thea Sch) – audition (Prof Actg); interview (Prof Stg Mgt)
            LAMDA – interview +audition (Prof Actg)
            London (RADA) – audition (Actg)
            London Mountview (Ac Thea Arts) – audition (Perf (Musl Thea); Perf (Actg))
            Royal Welsh (CMusDr) – audition (Actg); interview (Stg Mgt Tech Thea)
            Trinity Saint David – audition (Actg)

Alternative offers
See **Chapter 6** and **Appendix 1** for grades/UCAS Tariff points information for other examinations.

EXAMPLES OF COLLEGES OFFERING COURSES IN THIS SUBJECT FIELD
Blackpool and Fylde (Coll); Bradford (Coll); Brooksby Melton (Coll); Buckinghamshire (Coll Group); Bury (Coll); Calderdale (Coll); Chichester (Coll); Coventry (Coll); Craven (Coll); Croydon (Univ Centre); Doncaster (Coll); Ealing, Hammersmith and West London (Coll); East Durham (Coll); Exeter (Coll); Gateshead (Coll); Gloucestershire (Coll); Grimsby (Inst Group); Guildford (Coll); Havering (Coll); Hopwood Hall (Coll); Hull (Coll); Kingston (Coll); Leicester (Coll); Liverpool City (Coll); Manchester (Coll); Middlesbrough (Coll); NCC Redbridge; Nescot; Newcastle (Coll); North Notts (Coll); North Shropshire (Coll); Northbrook Met (Coll); Nottingham (Coll); Oldham (Univ Campus); Peterborough (Coll); Plymouth City (Coll); Richmond-upon-Thames (Coll); Rotherham (CAT); St Helens (Coll); Sheffield (Coll); South Devon (Coll); South Gloucestershire and Stroud (Coll); Southampton City (Coll); Stamford New (Coll); Stratford-upon-Avon (Coll); Sunderland (Coll); Tresham (CFHE); Wakefield (Coll); Warrington and Vale Royal (Coll); West Herts (Coll); West Thames (Coll); Westminster City (Coll); Weymouth (Coll); Wigan and Leigh (Coll).

CHOOSING YOUR COURSE (SEE ALSO CH.1)
Universities and colleges teaching quality See www.qaa.ac.uk; https://unistats.ac.uk.

Top research universities and colleges (REF 2014) (Music, Drama, Dance and Performing Arts)
Open University; Roehampton (Dance); London (QM); Warwick; London (SOAS); Durham; London (RH) (Mus); Southampton; Oxford; Birmingham (Mus); City; London (King's) (Film); Manchester (Dr); London (RH) (Dr Thea); Huddersfield; Manchester (Mus); Cardiff.

ADMISSIONS INFORMATION
Number of applicants per place (approx) Arts London (Actg) 32, (Dir) 10; Bath Spa 10; Birmingham 15; Bristol 19; Cumbria 4; De Montfort (Perf Arts) 5; East Anglia 6; Edge Hill 8; Essex 15; Exeter 20; Huddersfield 5; Hull 5; Hull (Coll) 2; Kent 6; Leeds 10; Liverpool (LIPA) (Actg) 48; Liverpool John Moores 10; London (Gold) 28; London (RH) 7; London (Royal Central Sch SpDr) (Thea Prac) 5; London Met 20; London Mountview (Ac Thea Arts) (Musl Thea) 8; Manchester (Dr) 6, (Dr Engl Lit) 7; Manchester (Coll) 10; Manchester Met 48; Middlesex 26; Northampton 3; Reading 17; Roehampton 6; Royal Welsh (CMusDr) (Actg) 50, (Stg Mgt) 10; Warwick 18; Winchester 5; Worcester 4; York 4; York St John 9.

Admissions tutors' advice Emphasis is placed on academic and practical abilities.

Advice to applicants and planning the UCAS personal statement List the plays in which you have performed and specify the characters played. Indicate any experience in other areas of theatre, especially directing or writing. Add any information on projects you have initiated or developed or worked on in theatre craft, such as set design, costume design, lighting design, prop-making, scene painting. List any community arts projects such as work with youth clubs, hospital radio, amateur dramatics, music/drama workshops and voluntary work within the arts. Show your strengths in dance and theatre, and your commitment to drama in all its aspects. See **Chapter 5** and also **Appendix 3**. **Bristol** Deferred entry accepted. **London (Royal Central Sch SpDr)** (Dr App Thea Educ) We look for an interest in theatre and performance in different social and cultural settings, for example, community, schools, prisons. We also look for an enquiring mind, practical drama skills, flexibility and focus. **Manchester** Due to the detailed nature of entry requirements for Drama courses, the University is unable to include full details in the prospectus. For complete and up-to-date information on the entry requirements for these courses, please visit the website at www.manchester.ac.uk/study/undergraduate/courses. **Warwick** Applications for deferred entry considered, but candidates should bear in mind the competition for places. **York** (Thea (Writ Dir Perf)) Strong analytical ability plus experience in a related field, eg stage management/design, drama, writing are important factors.

Misconceptions about this course That a Theatre Studies course is a training for the stage: it is not. **Arts London** Provides a long-established classical conservatoire-type training for actors, and not Theatre Studies or Performance Arts courses, contrary to the views of some students. It is no longer a private school and home and EU students pay the standard degree fee. **De Montfort** (Perf Arts) Students are unaware that the course involves music. **York St John** This is not a course for intending actors.

Selection interviews Most institutions, usually with auditions which are likely to involve solo and group tests. **Yes** Anglia Ruskin, Arts London, Bath Spa, Bedfordshire, Birmingham City, Bolton (Thea), Cambridge, Central Lancashire, Chester, Chichester, Cumbria, East Anglia, East London, Edge Hill, Exeter, Greenwich, Huddersfield, Hull, Kingston, Liverpool John Moores, Loughborough, Manchester, Middlesex, Northumbria, Plymouth, Portsmouth, Queen Margaret, Sussex, UWE Bristol, Warwick, Winchester; **Some** Bristol, London (Gold), London (Royal Central Sch SpDr), Royal Welsh (CMusDr), Wolverhampton, York; **No** Bishop Grosseteste, Bucks New, Falmouth, London (QM), Reading, St Mary's.

Interview advice and questions See also **Chapter 5**. **Arts London** (Actg) Two three-minute speeches or scenes, one of which must be from the classical repertoire. (Dir) Interview and practical workshop which may involve directing actors. **Bristol** Assesses each case on its merits, paying attention to candidate's educational and cultural opportunities. Particularly interested in applicants who have already shown some evidence of commitment in their approach to drama in practical work, theatre-going, film viewing or reading. **Brunel** All applicants to whom an offer may be made will be auditioned, involving a practical workshop, voice, movement improvisation and a short prepared speech. Offers unlikely to be made to those with less than a grade B in drama or theatre studies. **De Montfort** (Perf Arts) What do you hope to gain on a three-year course in Performing Arts? Interviews involve practical workshops in drama and theatre. **East Anglia** Looks for candidates with a sound balance of academic and practical skills. Applicants will be expected to analyse performance and to understand what is entailed in the production of a drama. **Kent** No Single Honours candidate accepted without interview/group audition. Equal emphasis placed on academic and practical abilities. Questions asked to probe the applicant's creative and analytical grasp of theatre. **Loughborough** Candidates judged as individuals. Applicants with unconventional subject combinations and mature students considered. Final selection based on interview and audition. Applicants ought to show experience of practical drama, preferably beyond school plays. **Royal Welsh (CMusDr)** (Actg) Audition; (Stg Mgt) interview; (Thea Des) interview and portfolio presentation. All applicants are charged an audition/interview fee. **Warwick** Interview is important to assess academic potential and particularly commitment to, and suitability for, teaching; offers therefore variable.

Reasons for rejection (non-academic) Poor ambition. Wrong expectations of the course. Several students clearly want drama school acting training rather than a degree course. Not enough background reading. **Arts London** Insufficient clarity about career aims. **De Montfort** (Perf Arts) Candidate more suitable for a drama or dance school than for a degree course. No genuine engagement with the subject. Evidence of poor attendance at school.

AFTER-RESULTS ADVICE
Offers to applicants repeating A-levels Higher Bristol, Warwick; **Possibly higher** London (RH); **Same** Brunel, Chichester, De Montfort (Perf Arts), East Anglia, Huddersfield, Hull, Leeds (further audition required), Liverpool Hope, Liverpool John Moores, Loughborough, Manchester (Coll), Newman, Roehampton, Royal Welsh (CMusDr), St Mary's, Sunderland, Surrey (GSA), Winchester, York St John; **No** Glasgow.

GRADUATE DESTINATIONS AND EMPLOYMENT (2015/16 HESA)
Graduates surveyed 4,430 **Employed** 2,050 **In voluntary employment** 120 **In further study** 805 **Assumed unemployed** 260

Career note Some graduates develop careers in performance, writing, directing and producing as well as wider roles within the theatre. Others go on to careers such as teaching, media management and retail where their creativity and communication skills are valued.

OTHER DEGREE SUBJECTS FOR CONSIDERATION
Art and Design (Costume Design, Stage Design); Arts Management; Dance; Education (Primary); English; Performance Studies.

ECONOMICS

(including **Philosophy, Politics and Economics**; see also **Business and Management Courses, Mathematics, Statistics**)

Economics is about how society makes good use of the limited resources available. Degree courses cover all aspects of finance, taxation and monetary union between countries, aiming to equip the student to analyse economic problems in a systematic way and thus acquire an understanding of how economic systems work. Economics involves mathematics and statistics, and applicants without economics at AS or A-level should be prepared for this, although for BA courses, such as at the University of Leicester, mathematics is not required at A-level. All courses are quite flexible with specialisms coming later in the course, leading to a range of career choices. Many joint courses are often offered with combinations such as Politics, Management and Finance. The course at Cambridge in Land Economy focuses on the legal and economic aspects relative to the natural environment, covering business regulations and the financial aspects of real estate and development. The course is accredited by the Royal Institution of Chartered Surveyors and has a very high success rate of graduate employment. (See also the **Surveying and Real Estate Management** table.)

Useful websites http://iea.org.uk; www.res.org.uk; www.economist.com; http://neweconomics.org; see also **Finance**.

NB The points totals shown to the left of the institutions are for ease of reference only. It must not be assumed that Tariff points are always used by institutions or that they can be substituted for an offer in grades. The level of an offer is not necessarily indicative of the quality of a course.

COURSE OFFERS INFORMATION
Subject requirements/preferences GCSE English, mathematics and occasionally a foreign language required. A*/A/B (8–9/7/5–6) may be stipulated by some universities. **AL** Mathematics, economics or business studies may be required or preferred. Business studies may be preferred if economics is not offered. Applicants should note that many courses will accept students without economics (check prospectuses and websites).

Your target offers and examples of degree courses

160 pts **Cambridge** – A*A*A incl maths +interview +ECAA (Econ) (IB 40–42 pts HL 776)

152 pts **Bath** – A*AA–AAA+aEPQ incl maths (Econ Pol) (IB 36 pts HL 6 maths); A*AA incl maths (Econ) (IB 36 pts HL 6 maths)

Bristol – A*AA–AAB incl maths (Econ courses) (IB 38–34 pts HL 6 maths)

Cambridge – A*AA +interview +TSA (Lnd Econ) (IB 40–42 pts HL 776)

Durham – A*AA incl maths (Econ Mgt; Econ Pol; PPE; Econ) (IB 38 pts)

Edinburgh – AAA* (Econ courses; Econ Stats) (IB 43 pts); A*AA (Econ Fin) (IB 43 pts HL 776)

Exeter – A*AA–AAB incl maths (Maths Econ) (IB 38–34 pts HL 6 maths); A*AA–AAB (Bus Econ (Euro St); Econ; Econ Pol (Euro St); Bus Econ; Econ Ecomet) (IB 38–34 pts)

London (King's) – A*AA (PPE) (IB 35 pts HL 766)

London (UCL) – A*AA incl geog+maths (Econ Geog) (IB 39 pts HL 7 maths 6 geog); A*AA incl maths (Econ) (IB 39 pts HL 7 maths); A*AA–AAA incl maths (Econ Stats; Stats Econ Fin; PPE) (IB 39–38 pts HL 7 maths)

London LSE – A*AA incl maths (Ecomet Mathem Econ; Maths Econ) (IB 38 pts HL 766 incl 7 maths); (Econ) (IB 38 pts); A*AA incl A* maths (PPE) (IB 38 pts)

Nottingham – A*AA–AAA/A*ABB (Econ Chin St) (IB 38–36 pts); A*AA–AAA (Econ Fr; Econ Ger; Econ Phil) (IB 38–36 pts); A*AA–AAA incl maths (Econ courses) (IB 38–36 pts); A*AA (Econ Hisp St) (IB 36 pts); (PPE) (IB 38 pts)

Oxford – A*AA +interview +TSA (Econ Mgt) (IB 39 pts)

Warwick – A*AA (PPE) (IB 38 pts HL 5 maths); A*AA incl maths (Econ; Econ Ind Org) (IB 38 pts HL 6 maths); A*AA (Econ Pol Int St) (IB 38 pts)

York – A*AA–AAA incl maths (PPE) (IB 37 pts)

144 pts **Birmingham** – AAA (Econ; Econ Lang) (IB 32 pts HL 666); AAA incl maths (Mathem Econ Stats) (IB 32 pts HL 666)

Bristol – AAA–ABB (Phil Econ) (IB 36–32 pts); AAA–ABB incl maths (Econ Acc) (IB 36–32 pts HL 18–16 incl 6 maths)

Exeter – AAA–AAB (PPE) (IB 36–34 pts)

Leeds – AAA (Econ; PPE) (IB 35 pts HL 17 maths); (Bus Econ; Econ Fin; Econ Mgt) (IB 35 pts HL 17 pts)

Liverpool – AAA incl maths (Econ) (IB 36 pts HL 6 maths)

London (QM) – AAA incl maths (Econ Comb Hons; Econ; Econ Fin Mgt) (IB 36 pts HL 666)

London (SOAS) – AAA–AAB (Econ Comb Hons) (IB 37 pts)

London (UCL) – AAA incl maths (Econ Bus E Euro St) (IB 38 pts HL 6 maths)

London LSE – AAA (Gov Econ) (IB 38 pts HL 766)

Manchester – AAA (PPE) (IB 36 pts HL 666)

Newcastle – AAA–ABB (Pol Econ) (IB 34–32 pts)

Oxford – AAA +interview +TSA (PPE) (IB 39 pts); AAA +interview +HAT (Hist Econ) (IB 38 pts HL 666)

Queen's Belfast – AAA (PPE)

St Andrews – AAA (Econ courses) (IB 38 pts)

Southampton – AAA–AAB+aEPQ incl maths (Maths OR Stats Econ) (IB 36 pts HL 6 maths); AAA–AAB incl maths/fmaths (Econ Act Sci) (IB 34 pts HL 6 maths)

Surrey – AAA (Econ Fin; Econ; Bus Econ) (IB 34 pts)

Sussex – AAA–AAB (PPE) (IB 34 pts)

York – AAA incl hist/class civ+maths (Hist Econ) (IB 36 pts HL 6 hist); AAA incl maths (Econ Maths) (IB 36 pts HL 6 maths)

136 pts **Aston** – AAB–ABB (Econ Mgt) (IB 32 pts)

Cardiff – AAB incl Fr/Ger/Span (Bus Econ Euro Lang (Fr/Ger/Span)) (IB 35 pts); AAB (Bus Econ; Econ) (IB 35 pts)

City – AAB 136 pts (Econ Acc; Econ) (IB 33 pts); AAB incl maths 136 pts (Fin Econ) (IB 33 pts HL 5 maths)

East Anglia – AAB (Econ) (IB 32 pts)

Glasgow – AAB–BBB incl Engl (Econ Comb Hons) (IB 38–36 pts)

Check **Chapter 3** for new university admission details and **Chapter 6** on how to read the subject tables.

Lancaster – AAB incl maths (Econ (St Abrd)) (IB 35 pts HL 6 maths); AAB (Econ; Econ Comb Hons; Econ (Yr Ind); PPE; Fin Econ) (IB 35 pts HL 16 pts); (Acc Econ) (IB 35 pts HL16 pts)

London (RH) – AAB–ABB (Econ Mgt; Econ Pol Int Rel) (IB 32 pts HL 655); AAB–ABB incl maths (Econ Maths) (IB 32 pts HL 6 maths); (PPE) (IB 32 pts); AAB–BBB incl maths (Econ) (IB 32 pts HL 655); AAB–BBB (Fin Bus Econ) (IB 32 pts HL 655)

London LSE – AAB incl maths (Env Plcy Econ; Soc Plcy Econ) (IB 37 pts HL 666); (Econ Econ Hist) (IB 37 pts)

Loughborough – AAB incl geog (Geog Econ) (IB 35 pts HL 665 incl 5 geog); AAB (Econ; Bus Econ Fin; Econ Acc; Econ Pol) (IB 35 pts HL 665)

Manchester – AAB (Bus St Econ; Econ Pol; Econ Sociol; Econ) (IB 35 pts HL 665)

Newcastle – AAB (Econ Fin; Econ; Econ Bus Mgt) (IB 35 pts)

Nottingham – AAB (Ind Econ; Ind Econ Ins) (IB 34 pts HL 18 pts)

Reading – AAB–ABB (Econ; Bus Econ) (IB 34–32 pts)

Sheffield – AAB–ABB (Econ Comb Hons) (IB 34 pts)

Southampton – AAB incl maths (Econ Fin) (IB 34 pts HL 5 maths); AAB/ABBb incl maths/ phys/stats (PPE) (IB 34–32 pts HL 5 maths); AAB/ABB+aEPQ (Econ Mgt Sci) (IB 34 pts HL 17 pts); AAB–ABB (Econ Phil) (IB 34–32 pts); AAB–ABB+aEPQ incl maths/phys (Acc Econ) (IB 34 pts HL 17 pts); AAB–ABB+aEPQ incl maths (Econ) (IB 34 pts HL 5 maths)

Sussex – AAB–ABB (Econ; Econ Int Dev; Econ Int Rel; Econ Mgt St; Econ Pol) (IB 32 pts)

York – AAB incl maths (Econ Fin; Econ Ecomet Fin; Econ) (IB 35 pts HL 666)

128 pts Birmingham – ABB (Pol Econ) (IB 32 pts HL 655)

East Anglia – ABB (PPE; Econ Acc; Bus Econ; Bus Fin Econ) (IB 32 pts)

Heriot-Watt – ABB (2 yr course) BBB (3 yr course) (Econ) (IB 34 pts (2 yr course) IB 29 pts (3 yr course))

Kent – ABB incl maths (Euro Econ; Econ) (IB 34 pts)

Leicester – ABB (Econ Courses) (IB 30 pts)

Liverpool – ABB (Bus Econ) (IB 33 pts)

NCH London – ABB–AAA incl maths (Econ courses) (IB 34–36 pts)

Queen's Belfast – ABB (Econ courses)

Reading – ABB–BBB (Fd Mark Bus Econ) (IB 32–30 pts)

Southampton – ABB–BBB incl maths/phys (Pol Econ) (IB 32 pts HL 4 maths)

Stirling – ABB (3 yr course) BBB (4 yr course) (Econ; PPE) (IB 35 pts (3 yr course) 32 pts (4 yr course))

Strathclyde – ABB (3 yr course) BBB (4 yr course) incl maths (Maths Stats Econ) (IB 34 pts (3 yr course) 32 pts (4 yr course) HL 6 maths); ABB–BBB (PPE) (IB 32–30 pts); (Econ; Econ Psy) (IB 36 pts)

Swansea – ABB–BBB (Econ courses) (IB 33–32 pts)

120 pts Aberdeen – BBB (Econ) (IB 32 pts)

Aberystwyth – BBB (Econ; Bus Econ) (IB 28 pts)

Bangor – 120–104 pts (Econ Comb Hons; Bus Econ; Acc Econ)

Bradford – BBB 120 pts (Econ; Fin Econ)

Brunel – BBB (Econ Bus Fin; Econ) (IB 30 pts)

Buckingham – BBB (PPE) (IB 32 pts); BBB +interview (Law Econ) (IB 32 pts)

Coventry – BBB (Econ courses; Bus Econ; Int Econ Tr) (IB 30 pts)

Dundee – BBB–BCC incl sci/maths (Econ St) (IB 30 pts); BBB–BCC (Bus Econ Mark; Bus Econ Mark Hist) (IB 30 pts HL 555)

Essex – BBB (Econ Pol; PPE; Econ; Fin Econ; Int Econ; Mgt Econ; Econ Modn Lang) (IB 30 pts)

Greenwich – 120 pts (Econ Bank; Econ)

Huddersfield – BBB 120 pts (Econ; Econ courses)

London (Birk) – 120 pts (Econ Soc Pol)

London (Gold) – BBB (PPE) (IB 33 pts)

Nottingham Trent – BBB 120 pts (Econ; Econ Bus; Econ Int Fin Bank)

Sheffield Hallam – 120 pts (Bus Econ)

UWE Bristol – 120 pts (Econ)

Westminster – BBB (Bus Econ) (IB 28 pts)

118 pts **NCH London** – ABB–AAA (PPE) (IB 34–36 pts)
112 pts **Birmingham City** – BBC 112 pts (Fin Econ)
      Bournemouth – 112–120 pts (Fin Econ; Econ) (IB 30–31 pts HL 55)
      Cardiff Met – 112 pts (Econ; Int Econ Fin)
      Central Lancashire – 112 pts (Econ) (IB 28 pts)
      Chester – BBC–BCC 112 pts (Econ (Comb Hons)) (IB 26 pts)
      De Montfort – 112 pts (Econ Fin) (IB 28 pts)
      East London – 112 pts (Econ) (IB 25 pts HL 15 pts)
      Hull – 112 pts (PPE) (IB 28 pts); (Econ; Bus Econ) (IB 30 pts)
      Keele – BBC (Econ Comb Hons; Bus Mgt Econ) (IB 30 pts)
      Kingston – 112 pts (Fin Econ; Econ; Bus Econ)
      Leeds Beckett – 112 pts (Econ Fin) (IB 25 pts); (Bus Econ) (IB 26 pts)
      Oxford Brookes – BBC 112 pts (Acc Econ) (IB 30 pts)
      Portsmouth – 112 pts (Econ) (IB 30 pts HL 17 pts)
      Worcester – 112 pts (Bus Econ Fin)
104 pts **Manchester Met** – BCC-BBC 104–112 pts (Econ Comb Hons) (IB 26 pts);
        BCC-BBC 104–112 pts +interview (Econ) (IB 26 pts)
      Northampton – BCC (Econ courses)
      Plymouth – 104 pts (Econ courses) (IB 28–26 pts)
      Salford – 104–120 pts (Bus Econ) (IB 30 pts)
      Winchester – 104–120 pts (PPE; Econ; Econ Fin) (IB 26 pts)
96 pts **Anglia Ruskin** – 96–120 pts (Bus Econ) (IB 24 pts)
      Hertfordshire – 96–112 pts (Econ; Bus Econ; Acc Econ)
      London Met – CCC/BC (Econ); CCC 96 pts (Bus Econ)
72 pts **UHI** – BC (PPE)

      Open University – contact 0300 303 0073 **or** www.open.ac.uk/contact/new (Econ Mathem
        Sci, PPE, Comb Soc Sci (Econ/Geog/Psy/Sociol))

Alternative offers
See **Chapter 6** and **Appendix 1** for grades/UCAS Tariff points information for other examinations.

EXAMPLES OF COLLEGES OFFERING COURSES IN THIS SUBJECT FIELD
GSM London; Plymouth City (Coll).

CHOOSING YOUR COURSE (SEE ALSO CH.1)
Universities and colleges teaching quality See www.qaa.ac.uk; https://unistats.ac.uk.

Top research universities and colleges (REF 2014) (Economics and Econometrics) London (UCL); Cambridge; Warwick; Essex; London LSE; Nottingham; Oxford; Bristol; East Anglia; Edinburgh.

Examples of sandwich degree courses Aston; Bath; Birmingham City; Bournemouth; Brunel; Coventry; De Montfort; Essex; Greenwich; Hertfordshire; Leeds Beckett; Liverpool; London (QM); Loughborough; Manchester Met; Newcastle; Nottingham Trent; Portsmouth; Queen's Belfast; Salford; Sheffield Hallam; Surrey; UWE Bristol; Westminster.

ADMISSIONS INFORMATION
Number of applicants per place (approx) Anglia Ruskin 10; Aston 8; Bangor 5; Bath 8; Birmingham 3; Birmingham City 16; Bradford 5; Bristol 8; Buckingham 7; Cambridge 6; Cardiff 8; Central Lancashire 5; City 8, (Econ Acc) 6; Dundee 5; Durham 7; East Anglia 4; Essex 6; Exeter 12; Greenwich 8; Heriot-Watt 6; Hull 5; Kingston 9; Lancaster 5; Leeds 16; Leicester 8; Liverpool 7; London (RH) 6; London (UCL) 11; London LSE (Econ) 13, (Ecomet Mathem Econ) 13; Manchester 8; Manchester Met 5; Newcastle 7; Northampton 8; Nottingham (Econ Chin) 8; Nottingham Trent 2; Oxford 13; Plymouth 52; Queen's Belfast 10; Salford 6; Sheffield 6; Southampton 6; Stirling 8; Swansea 7; Warwick 16; York 4.

Advice to applicants and planning the UCAS personal statement Visits, work experience and work shadowing in banks, insurance companies, accountants' offices, etc should be described. Keep up-to-date with economic issues by reading *The Economist* and the *Financial Times* and find other sources of information. Describe any particular aspects of economics which interest you – and why. Make it clear on the statement that you know what economics is and why you want to study it. Give evidence of your interest in economics and your reasons for choosing the course and provide information about your sport/extracurricular activities and positions of responsibility.

Misconceptions about this course Bradford That the Economics course is very mathematical and that students will not get a good job, eg management. **London (UCL)** Some think the Economics course is a Business course.

Selection interviews Yes Buckingham, Cambridge, Oxford (Econ Mgt) 25% (success rate 8%); **Some** Southampton; **No** Aberystwyth, Anglia Ruskin, Bangor, Birmingham, Bristol, Coventry, Dundee, East Anglia, East London, Edinburgh, Essex, Keele, Kent, Leeds, London (RH), London (UCL), London LSE, London Met, Loughborough, Manchester Met, Nottingham, Nottingham Trent, Reading, Surrey, Swansea, UWE Bristol.

Interview advice and questions If you have studied economics at A-level or in other examinations, expect to be questioned on aspects of the subject. This is a subject which is constantly in the news, so keep abreast of developments and be prepared to be asked questions such as: What is happening to sterling at present? What is happening to the dollar? How relevant is economics today? What are your views on the government's economic policy? Do you think that the family is declining as an institution? Discuss Keynesian economics. Is the power of the Prime Minister increasing? What is a recession? How would you get the world out of recession? What causes a recession? See also **Chapter 5**. **Cambridge** What is the point of using NHS money to keep old people alive? **Oxford** (Econ Mgt) 'I was asked questions on a newspaper article I had been given to read 45 minutes beforehand, followed by a few maths problems and an economics question.' Explain why teachers might be changing jobs to become plumbers. What is the difference between the buying and selling of slaves and the buying and selling of football players? Should a Wal-Mart store be opened in the middle of Oxford?

Reasons for rejection (non-academic) Lack of knowledge about the course offered and the subject matter; lack of care in preparing personal statement; poor written English; the revelation on the statement that they want a course different from that for which they have applied! **Aberystwyth** Would have trouble fitting into the unique environment at Aberystwyth.

AFTER-RESULTS ADVICE
Offers to applicants repeating A-levels Higher Birmingham City, City, Leeds, Newcastle, Queen's Belfast, St Andrews, Warwick, York; **Possibly higher** Bradford, Durham, Lancaster; **Same** Aberystwyth, Anglia Ruskin, Bangor, Bath, Brunel, Buckingham, Cambridge, Cardiff, Coventry, Dundee, East Anglia, East London, Essex, Heriot-Watt, Hull, Kingston, Liverpool, London (RH), London Met, Loughborough, Nottingham, Nottingham Trent, Salford, Sheffield, Swansea.

GRADUATE DESTINATIONS AND EMPLOYMENT (2015/16 HESA)
Graduates surveyed 4,705 **Employed** 2,735 **In voluntary employment** 145 **In further study** 990 **Assumed unemployed** 315

Career note Most graduates work within areas of business and finance, and in a range of jobs including management and administration posts across both public and private sectors.

OTHER DEGREE SUBJECTS FOR CONSIDERATION
Accountancy; Actuarial Studies; Administration; Banking; Business Studies; Development Studies; Estate Management; Financial Services; Government; Politics; Management Sciences/Studies; Property Development; Quantity Surveying; Social Sciences; Sociology; Statistics.

EDUCATION STUDIES

(see also **Physical Education, Social Sciences/Studies, Teacher Training**)

There are four types of degree courses in Education. Firstly, there are those universities providing an academic study of the subject at Single Honours level, covering the study of childhood and aspects of education such as psychology, sociology, philosophy and history (check with your chosen institution). Secondly, there are institutions offering degrees in Education with a professional practice qualification to teach, as in the degree course in Early Years Education at Edge Hill University. Thirdly, as in all degree subjects, there are many Joint Honours and combined degrees in which Education is taken with another academic subject, in which the two subjects may be taken equally or on a Major/Minor basis. Finally, there are specific degree courses in teacher training and professional practice leading directly to the classroom (see the **Teacher Training** table).

Useful websites www.gtcs.org.uk; www.ucas.com/ucas/teacher-training; www.gov.uk/government/organisations/department-for-education; http://set.et-foundation.co.uk; www.et-foundation.co.uk

NB The points totals shown to the left of the institutions are for ease of reference only. It must not be assumed that Tariff points are always used by institutions or that they can be substituted for an offer in grades. The level of an offer is not necessarily indicative of the quality of a course.

COURSE OFFERS INFORMATION

Subject requirements/preferences GCSE English and mathematics usually required. **AL** No subjects specified.

Your target offers and examples of degree courses

152 pts Cambridge – A*AA +interview +EAA (Educ Plcy Int Dev; Educ Engl Dr Arts; Educ Psy Lrng) (IB 40–42 pts HL 776)

144 pts Loughborough – AAA incl maths (Maths Maths Educ) (IB 37 pts HL 666 incl 6 maths)

136 pts Durham – AAB (Educ St (Engl St/Geog/Hist/Phil/Psy/Sociol/Theol Relgn)) (IB 36 pts)
   Glasgow – AAB incl tech/sci/maths +interview (Technol Educ) (IB 36–32 pts HL 5 Engl+sci/maths)
   Liverpool Hope – ABB–BBC 136 pts (Educ)

128 pts Bath – ABB/BBB+aEPQ (Educ Psy) (IB 35 pts HL 655)
   Birmingham – ABB (Educ) (IB 32 pts HL 655)
   Edinburgh – ABB (Commun Educ) (IB 34 pts HL 655)
   Gloucestershire – ABB 128 pts (Physl Educ)
   Newcastle – ABB–BBB (Educ) (IB 32–30 pts HL 555)
   Sheffield – ABB (Educ Cult Chld) (IB 33 pts)
   Southampton – ABB/BBB+aEPQ (Educ) (IB 32 pts HL 16 pts)
   York – ABB (Sociol Educ) (IB 34 pts)

120 pts Aberystwyth – BBB–BBC (Educ Comb Hons) (IB 30–28 pts)
   Cardiff – BBB (Educ Sociol) (HL 17–16 pts); (Educ; Educ Welsh) (IB 32 pts)
   De Montfort – 120 pts (Educ St Mand; Educ St; Educ St Psy) (IB 28 pts)
   East Anglia – BBB (Educ) (IB 31 pts)
   Edge Hill – BBB 120 pts +interview (Ely Yrs Educ)
   Essex – BBB (Chld St) (IB 30 pts)
   Kent – BBB (Autsm St) (IB 34 pts)
   Liverpool Hope – BBB–BBC 120–112 pts (SEN) (IB 26 pts)
   Liverpool John Moores – BBB 120 pts +interview (P Educ) (IB 26 pts)
   Northumbria – 120–128 pts +interview (P Educ) (HL 444)
   Reading – BBB–BBC (Educ St) (IB 30–28 pts)
   Stirling – BBB (Prof Educ P Educ courses) (IB 32 pts)
   Sunderland – 120 pts (Educ St)
   York – BBB (Engl Educ; Educ) (IB 31 pts)

112 pts **Brighton** – BBC–CCC (Educ) (IB 28 pts)
Canterbury Christ Church – 112 pts (Ely Chld St; Educ St)
Central Lancashire – 112 pts (Educ courses) (IB 28 pts)
Dundee – BBC +interview (Educ) (IB 30 pts)
East London – 112 pts (Educ St; Spec Educ) (IB 25 pts HL 15 pts); 112 pts incl soc sci/hum (Ely Chld St) (IB 25 pts HL 15 pts)
Glyndŵr – 112 pts (Educ (ALN/SEN))
Huddersfield – BBC 112 pts (Relgn Educ)
Keele – BBC (Educ) (IB 30 pts)
London (Gold) – BBC (Educ Cult Soty) (IB 31 pts HL 655)
London Met – BBC 112 pts (Educ St)
Manchester Met – BBC +interview (P Educ) (IB 25 pts)
Oxford Brookes – BBC (Educ St) (IB 30 pts)
Plymouth – 112 pts (Ely Chld St) (IB 28 pts HL 5)
Roehampton – 112 pts (Educ St)
Suffolk – BBC 112 pts (Ely Chld St)
West London – 112 pts (Ely Yrs Educ)
104 pts **Bath Spa** – BCC–CCC (Educ St) (IB 26 pts)
Cardiff Met – 104 pts (Educ Psy SEN)
Chester – BCC–BBC (Educ St courses) (IB 26 pts); BCC 104 pts (P Educ St) (IB 26 pts)
Chichester – 104–120 pts (Educ) (IB 28 pts)
Hertfordshire – 104 pts (Educ St; Ely Chld Educ) (HL 44)
Hull – 104 pts (Educ St courses) (IB 28 pts)
Leeds Beckett – 104 pts (Chld St) (IB 24 pts)
Leeds Trinity – 104 pts (Educ St; Educ Relig St)
Liverpool John Moores – BCC 104 pts (Educ St Ely Yrs; Educ St Incln) (IB 26 pts)
Manchester Met – BCC–BBC 104–112 pts (Educ St) (IB 25 pts)
Nottingham Trent – 104 pts (Psy Spec Inclsv Educ); BCC 104 pts (Chld St; Educ St)
St Mark and St John – BCC (Ely Chld Educ)
St Mary's – 104 pts (Educ Soc Sci)
Sheffield Hallam – 104–88 pts (Educ St; Educ Psy Cnslg)
South Wales – BCC–CDD (Ely Yrs Educ Prac) (HL 655–445)
96 pts **Aberystwyth** – CCC (Chld St) (IB 28 pts)
Bangor – 96 pts (Chld Yth St)
Bedfordshire – 96 pts (Ely Chld Educ; Educ St)
Birmingham (UC) – 96 pts (Chld St)
Bishop Grosseteste – 96–112 pts (Educ St courses)
Brunel – CCC (Educ) (IB 27 pts)
Chichester – 96–120 pts +interview (Out Advntr Educ)
Derby – 96–112 pts (Ely Chld St; Maths Educ); 96–128 pts (Educ St)
Newman – 96–88 pts (St P Educ; Educ St courses; Ely Chld Educ Cr; Phil Relgn Educ)
Oldham (Univ Campus) – 96 pts (Ely Yrs)
Plymouth – 96 pts (Educ St) (IB 24 pts HL 4)
Portsmouth – 96–120 pts (Chld Yth St) (IB 26 pts); (Ely Chld St) (IB 28 pts)
Staffordshire – CCC 96 pts (Ely Chld St)
York St John – 96–112 pts (Educ St)
88 pts **St Mark and St John** – CCD (Out Advntr Educ); CCD–BCC 88 pts (Educ St); CCD 88 pts (SEN Disab St)
Trinity Saint David – 88–104 pts +interview (Ely Yrs Educ Cr); 88 pts (P Educ St; Educ St)
Worcester – 88 pts (Educ St courses)
80 pts **Bradford (Coll)** – 80 pts (Educ St)
Cardiff Met – 80 pts +interview (Yth Commun Wk courses)
72 pts **Teesside** – 72–88 pts (Ely Chld St; Chld Yth St)
64 pts **Colchester (Inst)** – 64 pts +interview (Ely Yrs)
South Essex (Coll) – 64 pts (Ely Yrs Educ)

UCAS points Tariff: A* = 56 pts; A = 48 pts; B = 40 pts; C = 32 pts; D = 24 pts; E = 16 pts

Alternative offers
See **Chapter 6** and **Appendix 1** for grades/UCAS Tariff points information for other examinations.

EXAMPLES OF COLLEGES OFFERING COURSES IN THIS SUBJECT FIELD

Most colleges, check with your local college. Barnet and Southgate (Coll); Barnfield (Coll); Barnsley (Coll); Blackburn (Coll); Blackpool and Fylde (Coll); Bournville (Coll); Bridgwater and Taunton (Coll); Bristol City (Coll); Buckinghamshire (Coll Group); Calderdale (Coll); Chesterfield (Coll); Cornwall (Coll); Craven (Coll); Derby (Coll); Duchy (Coll); East Riding (Coll); Exeter (Coll); Farnborough (CT); Grimsby (Inst Group); Grŵp Llandrillo Menai; Guildford (Coll); Harrogate (Coll); Havering (Coll); Hopwood Hall (Coll); Hull (Coll); Kensington and Chelsea (Coll); Kirklees (Coll); Lakes (Coll); Lincoln (Coll); Liverpool City (Coll); Macclesfield (Coll); Nescot; Newcastle (Coll); Newham (CFE); Norland (Coll); North Lindsey (Coll); Norwich City (Coll); Nottingham (Coll); Peter Symonds (Coll); Peterborough (Coll); Petroc; RAc Dance; Sheffield (Coll); South Cheshire (Coll); South City Birmingham (Coll); South Devon (Coll); Stockport (Coll); Sunderland (Coll); Truro and Penwith (Coll); Wakefield (Coll); Warrington and Vale Royal (Coll); Warwickshire (Coll); West Anglia (Coll); Westminster City (Coll); Wirral Met (Coll); Yeovil (Coll).

CHOOSING YOUR COURSE (SEE ALSO CH.1)

Universities and colleges teaching quality See www.qaa.ac.uk; https://unistats.ac.uk.

Top research universities and colleges (REF 2014) (Education) Sheffield; Oxford; London (King's); Queen's Belfast; Loughborough; Exeter; Nottingham; Cardiff; Durham; York; Stirling; Bristol.

ADMISSIONS INFORMATION

Number of applicants per place (approx) Anglia Ruskin 1; Bangor 5; Bath 5; Bath Spa 5; Birmingham 8; Bishop Grosseteste 12; Cambridge 2; Cardiff (Educ) 8; Cardiff Met 3; Central Lancashire 5; Derby 4; Dundee 13; Durham 3; Edge Hill 17; Gloucestershire 20; Hull 5; Hull (Coll) 4; Liverpool John Moores 3; London (Gold) 5; Manchester Met 23; Nottingham Trent 11; Oxford Brookes 6; Plymouth 14; Roehampton 3; St Mark and St John 5; St Mary's 19; Sheffield Hallam 7; Southampton 8; Trinity Saint David 10; Worcester 21; York 3.

Advice to applicants and planning the UCAS personal statement Liverpool John Moores (P Educ) Deciding to pursue a career in teaching should be based on a real commitment and passion and this should be demonstrated through your personal statement. You should have at least two weeks' recent work experience in a school or related setting before applying. In addition, we would like to see some evidence of work in the community (not as part of your course). This may be helping in sports clubs, Brownies, youth clubs or volunteering. This experience may be linked to a hobby or interest you have. Personal statements should have a clear structure with use of paragraphs and good use of grammar.

Misconceptions about this course That Childhood Studies is a childcare, child health or teaching course: it is not. That Educational Studies leads to a teaching qualification – it does not. **Bath Spa** (Educ St) Applicants should note that this is not a teacher training course – it leads on to PGCE teacher training (this applies to other Education Studies courses).

Selection interviews Yes Bangor, Brunel, Cambridge, Chichester, Glasgow, Stockport (Coll); **Some** Cardiff, Worcester; **No** Anglia Ruskin, Bishop Grosseteste, Chester, Derby, East Anglia, Glyndŵr, Manchester Met, Newman, Nottingham Trent, Oxford Brookes, Plymouth, Reading, Roehampton, St Mark and St John, Sheffield Hallam, Stirling, York St John.

Interview advice and questions Cambridge The stage is a platform for opinions or just entertainment? **Derby** Applicants are asked about an aspect of education. **Worcester** Interviewees are asked to write a statement concerning their impressions of the interview.

Reasons for rejection (non-academic) Unable to meet the requirements of written standard English. Ungrammatical personal statements.

Check **Chapter 3** for new university admission details and **Chapter 6** on how to read the subject tables.

AFTER-RESULTS ADVICE

Offers to applicants repeating A-levels Same Anglia Ruskin, Bangor, Bishop Grosseteste, Brighton, Brunel, Cambridge, Canterbury Christ Church, Cardiff, Chester, Chichester, De Montfort, Derby, Dundee, Durham, East Anglia, Liverpool Hope, Liverpool John Moores, London (Gold), Manchester Met, Newman, Northumbria, Nottingham Trent, Oxford Brookes, Roehampton, St Mark and St John, St Mary's, Sunderland, Worcester, York, York St John.

GRADUATE DESTINATIONS AND EMPLOYMENT (2015/16 HESA)

Academic Studies in Education graduates surveyed 9,760 **Employed** 3,760 **In voluntary employment** 145 **In further study** 3,560 **Assumed unemployed** 280

Career note Education Studies degrees prepare graduates for careers in educational administration although many will move into more general areas of business or into aspects of work with Social Services. Prospects are generally good. Courses in Childhood Studies could lead to work in health or childcare-related posts, in social work or administration.

OTHER DEGREE SUBJECTS FOR CONSIDERATION

Psychology; Social Policy; Social Sciences; Social Work.

ENGINEERING (ACOUSTICS and SOUND)

(including **Audio Engineering** and **Sound Technology**; see also **Engineering (Electrical and Electronic), Film, Radio, Video and TV Studies, Media Studies, Music**)

These courses, such as the one at the University of Southampton, focus on sound and vibration engineering, which covers many aspects of society, such as the motor industry, airlines, the environment, underwater communication, ultrasound, as used in medicine, and all communication systems. Courses also involve sound measurement, hearing, environmental health, and legal aspects of sound and vibration. Acoustics and sound are also extensively involved in the music industry, perhaps the most prestigious course being the Music and Sound Recording (Tonmeister) degree at the University of Surrey, which comprises music theory and practice, sound, acoustics, electronics and computer systems. The department has good links with and a high reputation in the music industry.

Engineering Council statement See **Engineering/Engineering Sciences**.

Useful websites www.ioa.org.uk; www.engc.org.uk

NB The points totals shown to the left of the institutions are for ease of reference only. It must not be assumed that Tariff points are always used by institutions or that they can be substituted for an offer in grades. The level of an offer is not necessarily indicative of the quality of a course.

COURSE OFFERS INFORMATION

Subject requirements/preferences AL Mathematics and physics usually required; music is also required for some courses. See also **Engineering/Engineering Sciences**. Offers shown below refer to BEng or BSc courses unless otherwise stated; BSc only appears as an abbreviation if the course is offered at the same institution as a BEng with different requirements.

Your target offers and examples of degree courses
144 pts Glasgow – AAA incl maths+phys (Electron Mus (MEng)) (IB 38–36 pts)
      Surrey – AAA incl maths+mus+phys (Mus Snd Rec (Tonmeister)) (IB 34 pts)
      York – AAA incl maths+phys/chem/electron (Mus Tech Sys (MEng)) (IB 32–36 pts HL 5/6
         maths+phys); AAA incl maths+phys/chem/electron +interview (Electron Eng Mus Tech
         Sys (MEng)) (IB 36–32 pts HL 6/5 maths+phys)
136 pts Glasgow – AAB–BBB incl maths+phys (Electron Mus) (IB 36–34 pts)
      Southampton – AAB incl maths+phys+mus +interview (Acoust Mus) (IB 34 pts HL 6 maths
         5 phys+mus); AAB incl maths+mus+phys (Acoust Eng) (IB 34 pts HL 6 maths)

UCAS points Tariff: A* = 56 pts; A = 48 pts; B = 40 pts; C = 32 pts; D = 24 pts; E = 16 pts

128 pts **York** – ABB incl maths+phys/chem/electron (Mus Tech Sys) (IB 32–36 pts HL 5/6 maths+phys); ABB incl maths+phys/chem/electron +interview (Electron Eng Mus Tech Sys) (IB 36–32 pts HL 6/5 maths+phys)

120 pts **Birmingham City** – BBB incl sci/tech/maths/comp 120 pts (Snd Eng Prod) (HL 15 pts)
Huddersfield – BBB 120 pts (Mus Tech Aud Sys)
London (Royal Central Sch SpDr) – 120–64 pts +interview +portfolio (Thea Prac (Thea Snd))

112 pts **Glyndŵr** – 112 pts (Snd Tech)
Lincoln – BBC (Aud Prod) (IB 29 pts)
Liverpool (LIPA) – BBC 112 pts +interview (Snd Tech)
Liverpool John Moores – BBC 112 pts (Aud Mus Prod)
Portsmouth – 112 pts (Mus Snd Tech) (IB 26 pts)
Salford – 112–120 pts incl maths/sci (Aud Acoust Eng) (IB 35 pts HL 5 maths/sci)
Southampton Solent – 112 pts (Pop Mus Prod; Aud Acoust Eng)
West London – 112–120 pts (App Snd Eng)

104 pts **Bolton** – 104 pts incl maths/sci/tech/mus +interview (Snd Eng Des)
Bournemouth – 104–120 pts incl sci/maths/mus/tech (Mus Snd Prod Tech) (IB 28–31 pts)
De Montfort – 104 pts (Aud Rec Tech) (IB 24 pts)
Hertfordshire – 104 pts incl mus tech/sci/tech (Snd Des Tech; Aud Rec Prod) (HL 44)
South Wales – BCC–CDD (Snd Eng) (HL 655–445)

96 pts **London Met** – CCC 96 pts (Mus Bus Lv Enter)
Rose Bruford (Coll) – 96 pts +interview +portfolio (Perf Snd (Lv Des Eng))

64 pts **Arts London** – 64 pts +interview +portfolio (Snd Arts Des)
Ravensbourne – CC +interview (Broad Aud Tech; Broad Comp; Broad Sys Tech; Outsd Broad Tech) (IB 28 pts)

24 pts **UHI** – D (Aud Eng)

Alternative offers
See **Chapter 6** and **Appendix 1** for grades/UCAS Tariff points information for other examinations.

EXAMPLES OF COLLEGES OFFERING COURSES IN THIS SUBJECT FIELD
Barnsley (Coll), Buckinghamshire (Coll Group); Calderdale (Coll); Leicester (Coll); Newcastle (Coll); Northbrook Met (Coll); Plymouth City (Coll); St Helens (Coll); Truro and Penwith (Coll).

CHOOSING YOUR COURSE (SEE ALSO CH.1)
Universities and colleges teaching quality See www.qaa.ac.uk; https://unistats.ac.uk.

Examples of sandwich degree courses Birmingham City; Huddersfield; Portsmouth; Surrey; York.

ADMISSIONS INFORMATION
Number of applicants per place (approx) Salford 4; Southampton 4.

Advice to applicants and planning the UCAS personal statement See **Engineering/Engineering Sciences**. See also **Appendix 3**.

Selection interviews No Salford, Southampton.

Interview advice and questions What interests you about acoustics engineering? What career do you have in mind on graduating? See also **Chapter 5**.

Reasons for rejection (non-academic) See **Engineering/Engineering Sciences**.

AFTER-RESULTS ADVICE
Offers to applicants repeating A-levels Same Salford.

GRADUATE DESTINATIONS AND EMPLOYMENT (2015/16 HESA)
See **Engineering/Engineering Sciences**.

Career note Specialist topics on these courses will enable graduates to make decisions as to their future career destinations.

OTHER DEGREE SUBJECTS FOR CONSIDERATION

Audiology; Broadcast Engineering; Communications Engineering; Computer Engineering; Computer Science; Media Technology; Music; Radio and TV; Technology; Telecommunications Engineering and Electronic Engineering.

ENGINEERING (AERONAUTICAL and AEROSPACE)

(see also Engineering (Electrical and Electronic))

Courses cover the manufacture of military and civil aircraft, theories of mechanics, thermodynamics, electronics, computing and engine design. Avionics courses include flight and energy control systems, airborne computing, navigation, optical and TV displays, airborne communications, and radar systems for navigation and power. Aeronautical Engineering involves the design, construction and powering of aircraft, and similarly Aerospace Engineering covers aerodynamics, flight design and control propulsion, and communications. Pilot training, with an additional fee, is also included in some courses as at the universities of Brunel, Leeds, Kingston, Hertfordshire and Liverpool. Some courses also include spaceflight studies and the Electronic Engineering course at Bath can be combined with Space Science and Technology. (See also under **Business and Management Courses (Specialised)** and **Transport Management and Planning** for details of Aviation Management degrees.)

Engineering Council statement See **Engineering/Engineering Sciences**.

Useful websites www.aerosociety.com; www.engc.org.uk; www.theiet.org

NB The points totals shown to the left of the institutions are for ease of reference only. It must not be assumed that Tariff points are always used by institutions or that they can be substituted for an offer in grades. The level of an offer is not necessarily indicative of the quality of a course.

COURSE OFFERS INFORMATION

Subject requirements/preferences See **Engineering/Engineering Sciences**. Offers shown below refer to BEng or BSc courses unless otherwise stated; BSc only appears as an abbreviation if the course is offered at the same institution as a BEng with different requirements.

Your target offers and examples of degree courses

160 pts **Cambridge** – A*A*A incl maths+phys +interview +ENGAA (Eng (Aerosp Aeroth Eng)) (IB 40–42 pts HL 776)

Imperial London – A*A*A incl phys+maths +interview (Aero Eng (Yr Abrd)) (IB 40 pts HL 7 maths 6 phys); A*A*A incl maths+phys +interview (Aero Eng (MEng)) (IB 40 pts HL 7 maths 6 phys)

152 pts **Bath** – A*AA/AAA+aEPQ incl maths+phys (Aerosp Eng) (IB 36 pts HL 6 maths)

Bristol – A*AA–AAB incl maths+phys (Aerosp Eng; Aerosp Eng (St Abrd) (MEng)) (IB 38–34 pts HL 6 maths+phys)

Leeds – A*AA incl maths+phys +interview (Aero Aerosp Eng) (IB 36 pts HL 18 pts incl 6 maths+phys)

Southampton – A*AA incl maths+phys (Aero Astnaut (MEng)) (IB 38 pts HL 6 math+phys); A*AA/A*AB+aEPQ incl maths+phys (Aero Astnaut (Aerodyn) (MEng); Aero Astnaut (Airvhcl Sys Des) (MEng); Aero Astnaut (Spcrft Eng) (MEng); Aero Astnaut (Mat Struct) (MEng); Aero Astnaut; Aero Astnaut (Eng Mgt) (MEng)) (IB 38 pts HL 6 maths+phys); A*AA/A*AB+aEPQ incl maths/phys (Mech Eng (Aerosp) (MEng)) (IB 38 pts HL 6 maths+phys)

Strathclyde – A*AA–AAB incl maths+phys (4 yr course) AAB–BBB incl maths+phys (5 yr course) (Aero-Mech Eng (MEng)) (IB 36 pts HL 6 maths+phys); A*AA–AAB incl maths+phys (4 yr course) ABB–BBB (5 yr course) (Mech Eng Aero (MEng)) (IB 36 pts HL 6 maths+phys)

144 pts **Brunel** – AAA incl maths+phys (Aerosp Eng (MEng); Avn Eng (MEng); Avn Eng Plt St (MEng)) (IB 34 pts HL 6 maths+phys)

City – AAA incl maths/sci 144 pts (Aero Eng (MEng)) (IB 34 pts HL 6 maths+phys)

Glasgow – AAA incl maths+phys (Mech Eng Aero (MEng)) (IB 38 pts HL 666 incl maths+phys); (Aerosp Sys (MEng)) (IB 38–36 pts HL 666 incl maths+phys)

Leeds – AAA incl maths/phys +interview (Avn Tech Mgt; Avn Tech Plt St) (IB 35 pts HL 18 pts incl 5 maths/phys)

Liverpool – AAA/AAB+aEPQ incl maths+sci (Aerosp Eng (MEng); Aerosp Eng Plt St (MEng)) (IB 35 pts HL 5 maths+phys)

London (QM) – AAA incl maths+phys/chem (Aerosp Eng (MEng)) (IB 36 pts HL 665 incl maths+phys/chem)

Manchester – AAA incl maths+phys (Aerosp Eng (MEng); Aerosp Eng Mgt (MEng)) (IB 37 pts HL 665 maths+phys)

Nottingham – AAA–AAB incl maths (Aerosp Eng) (IB 36–34 pts)

Sheffield – AAA/AAB+aEPQ incl maths+phys (Aerosp Eng (PPI) (MEng), Aerosp Eng (MEng)) (IB 36 pts HL 6 maths+phys)

Strathclyde – AAA–ABB (3 yr course) ABB–BBB (4 yr course) (Aero-Mech Eng) (IB 32 pts HL 5 maths+phys)

Surrey – AAA incl maths+phys (Aerosp Eng (MEng)) (IB 34 pts)

Swansea – AAA–AAB incl maths (Aerosp Eng (MEng)) (IB 34 pts)

136 pts **Bath** – AAB/ABB+aEPQ incl maths/sci/tech (Electron Eng Spc Sci Tech) (IB 35 pts HL 6 maths/phys+sci/tech)

Brunel – AAB incl maths+phys (Avn Eng; Aerosp Eng) (IB 33 pts HL 6 maths 5 phys); (Avn Eng Plt St) (IB 33 pts HL 6 maths+phys)

Glasgow – AAB–BBB incl maths+phys (Aero Eng; Aerosp Sys) (IB 36–34 pts HL 665 incl maths+phys)

London (QM) – AAB incl maths+phys (Aerosp Eng) (IB 34 pts HL 665)

Loughborough – AAB incl maths+phys +interview (Aero Eng) (IB 35 pts HL 665 incl 6 maths+phys)

Manchester – AAB incl maths+phys (Aerosp Eng) (IB 35 pts HL 665 maths+phys)

Queen's Belfast – AAB incl maths+sci/fmaths (Aerosp Eng (MEng)); AAB incl maths+sci/des tech (Prod Des Eng (MEng))

Sheffield – AAB/ABB+aEPQ incl maths+phys (Aerosp Eng (PPI)) (IB 34 pts HL 6 maths+sci); AAB/ABB+bEPQ incl maths+phys (Aerosp Eng; Aerosp Eng (Yr Ind)) (IB 34 pts HL 6 maths+phys)

Surrey – AAB incl maths+phys (Aerosp Eng) (IB 34 pts)

Swansea – AAB–BBB incl maths (Aerosp Eng) (IB 32 pts)

128 pts **City** – ABB incl maths+sci 128 pts (Aero Eng) (IB 32 pts HL 6 maths+phys)

Coventry – ABB–BBB incl maths+phys/des tech (Aerosp Sys Eng) (IB 31 pts); ABB–BBB (Avn Mgt) (IB 31 pts)

Hertfordshire – 128 pts incl maths+phys/tech/eng (Aerosp Eng (MEng); Aerosp Sys Eng Plt St (MEng); Aerosp Sys Eng (MEng)) (HL 555 incl maths+phys)

Kingston – 128 pts incl maths+sci (Aerosp Eng (MEng)); 128–152 pts incl maths+sci (Aerosp Eng Astnaut Spc Tech (MEng))

Leicester – ABB–BBB+bEPQ incl maths+sci (Aerosp Eng) (IB 30 pts HL 5 maths+phys)

Liverpool – ABB/BBB+aEPQ incl maths+sci (Aerosp Eng) (IB 33 pts HL 5 maths+phys)

Loughborough – ABB/AAC (Air Trans Mgt) (IB 34 pts HL 655)

UWE Bristol – 128 pts incl maths+sci/tech/eng (Aerosp Eng (MEng)) (HL 6 maths)

120 pts **Brighton** – BBB–BCC incl maths+sci (Aero Eng (MEng)) (IB 30 pts)

Queen's Belfast – BBB incl maths+sci/fmaths/tech des (Aerosp Eng)

UWE Bristol – 120 pts incl maths+sci/tech/eng (Aerosp Eng) (HL 5 maths)

112 pts **Brighton** – BBC–CCC incl maths+sci 112–96 pts (Aero Eng) (IB 28 pts HL 5 maths+phys)

Glyndŵr – 112 pts incl maths/phys (Aero Mech Eng)

Check **Chapter 3** for new university admission details and **Chapter 6** on how to read the subject tables.

Kingston – 112–144 pts incl maths+sci (Aerosp Eng Astnaut Spc Tech)

Sheffield Hallam – 112–96 pts incl maths+sci/eng/tech (Aerosp Eng)

104 pts **Hertfordshire** – 104 pts incl maths+phys/tech/eng (Aerosp Eng; Aerosp Sys Eng Plt St; Aerosp Sys Eng) (HL 4 maths+phys)

South Wales – BCC–CDD incl num sub (Aircft Mntnce Eng) (HL 655–455); BCC–CDD incl maths+sci (Aero Eng) (HL 655–445)

96 pts **Hertfordshire** – 96 pts (Aerosp Tech Mgt; Aerosp Tech Plt St) (HL 44)

Kingston – 96 pts incl maths+sci (Aerosp Eng)

Teesside – 96–112 pts incl maths+phys (Aerosp Eng)

32 pts **UHI** – C incl maths/phys (Aircft Eng)

Alternative offers

See **Chapter 6** and **Appendix 1** for grades/UCAS Tariff points information for other examinations.

EXAMPLES OF DEGREE APPRENTICESHIPS IN THIS SUBJECT FIELD

UWE Bristol (Aerosp Eng).

EXAMPLES OF COLLEGES OFFERING COURSES IN THIS SUBJECT FIELD

Blackpool and Fylde (Coll); Bristol City (Coll); Exeter (Coll); Farnborough (CT); Macclesfield (Coll); Newcastle (Coll); Solihull (Coll); Yeovil (Coll).

CHOOSING YOUR COURSE (SEE ALSO CH.1)

Universities and colleges teaching quality See www.qaa.ac.uk; https://unistats.ac.uk.

Top research universities and colleges (REF 2014) (Aeronautical, Mechanical, Chemical and Manufacturing Engineering) Cambridge; London (UCL); Manchester (Chem Eng); Bath; Imperial London; Sheffield (Mech Eng Advnc Manuf); Sheffield (Chem Biol Eng); Queen's Belfast; Birmingham (Chem Eng).

Examples of sandwich degree courses Bath; Brighton; Brunel; City; Coventry; Hertfordshire; Kingston; Leeds; London (QM); Loughborough; Queen's Belfast; Sheffield Hallam; South Wales; Surrey; Teesside; UWE Bristol.

ADMISSIONS INFORMATION

Number of applicants per place (approx) Bath 10; Bristol 7; City 11; Farnborough (CT) 7; Hertfordshire 17; Kingston 9; London (QM) 8; Queen's Belfast 6; Southampton 10.

Advice to applicants and planning the UCAS personal statement Interest in engineering and aerospace. Work experience in engineering. Flying experience. Personal attainments. Relevant hobbies. Membership of Air Training Corps. See also **Engineering/Engineering Sciences**. **Bristol** Deferred entry accepted. **Imperial London** Deferred entry acceptable.

Misconceptions about this course That Aeronautical Engineering is not a highly analytical subject: it is.

Selection interviews Yes Cambridge, Farnborough (CT), Imperial London; **Some** Loughborough; **No** Bristol, Hertfordshire, Kingston, London (QM), Southampton.

Interview advice and questions Why Aeronautical Engineering? Questions about different types of aircraft and flight principles of helicopters. Range of interests in engineering. See also **Chapter 5**.

Reasons for rejection (non-academic) See **Engineering/Engineering Sciences**.

AFTER-RESULTS ADVICE

Offers to applicants repeating A-levels Higher Bristol, Queen's Belfast; **Possibly higher** Hertfordshire; **Same** Bath, City, Farnborough (CT), Kingston, Liverpool, Loughborough, Southampton; **No** Cambridge.

GRADUATE DESTINATIONS AND EMPLOYMENT (2015/16 HESA)

Aerospace Engineering graduates surveyed 1030 **Employed** 545 **In voluntary employment** 10 **In further study** 300 **Assumed unemployed** 100

Career note Specialist areas of study on these courses will open up possible career directions. See also **Engineering/Engineering Sciences**.

OTHER DEGREE SUBJECTS FOR CONSIDERATION

Astronomy; Astrophysics; Computer Science; Electronics and Systems Engineering; Materials Science; Mathematics; Naval Architecture; Physics.

ENGINEERING (CHEMICAL)

(including **Fire Engineering**, **Nuclear Engineering** and **Petrol Engineering**; see also **Chemistry**)

Chemical engineers explore solutions to problems across the whole spectrum of industries involving oil and gas, petroleum, pharmaceuticals, cosmetics, food and drink, biotechnology, bioengineering and biomedical engineering, their role being concerned with the chemical properties of materials and also the safety aspects of projects. Petroleum engineers work in oil and gas projects which can include exploration, excavation and refining, and courses include the study of geology. Another branch is Fire Risk Engineering which invariably overlaps to some extent with Civil Engineering, as in the Fire and Leadership Studies course at the University of Central Lancashire. Finally, Nuclear Engineering focuses on the uses of nuclear energy, such as the provision of non-fossil fuels, and also covers power generation and the decommissioning of nuclear waste.

Engineering Council statement See **Engineering/Engineering Sciences**.

Useful websites www.icheme.org; www.engc.org.uk; www.whynotchemeng.com; www.bceca.org.uk; http://semta.org.uk

NB The points totals shown to the left of the institutions are for ease of reference only. It must not be assumed that Tariff points are always used by institutions or that they can be substituted for an offer in grades. The level of an offer is not necessarily indicative of the quality of a course.

COURSE OFFERS INFORMATION

Subject requirements/preferences AL Mathematics and chemistry usually required. See also **Engineering/Engineering Sciences**. Offers shown below refer to BEng or BSc courses unless otherwise stated; BSc only appears as an abbreviation if the course is offered at the same institution as a BEng with different requirements.

Your target offers and examples of degree courses

208 pts Imperial London – A*A*AA–A*A*A incl maths+chem +interview (Cheml Nucl Eng (MEng)) (IB 42–41 pts HL 7 maths+chem 6 sci/econ); A*A*AA–A*A*A* incl maths+chem+sci +interview (Cheml Eng (MEng)) (IB 41–42 pts HL 7 maths+chem 6 sci/econ)

160 pts Cambridge – A*A*A incl maths+phys +interview +ENGAA/NSAA (Cheml Eng) (IB 40–42 pts HL 776)

Oxford – A*A*A incl maths+phys +interview +PAT (Cheml Eng (MEng)) (IB 40 pts HL 776 incl 7 maths+phys)

152 pts Bath – A*AA/AAA+aEPQ incl maths+chem (Cheml Eng; Bioch Eng (MEng); Cheml Eng (MEng)) (IB 36 pts HL 766)

Birmingham – A*AA incl chem+maths (Cheml Eng; Cheml Eng (MEng) (Yr Abrd); Cheml Eng (MEng)) (IB 32 pts HL 766 incl 6 chem+maths)

Leeds – A*AA incl maths+phys/chem +interview (Chem Nucl Eng; Cheml Eng courses) (IB 36 pts HL 18 pts incl 6 maths+phys/chem)

London (UCL) – A*AA–AAA incl maths+chem (Eng (Cheml)) (IB 39–38 pts HL 5 maths+chem); A*AA–AAA incl maths+sci (Eng (Bioch) (MEng); Eng (Bioch)) (IB 39–38 pts HL 5 maths+sci)

Loughborough – A*AA incl maths+chem/phys +interview (Cheml Eng (MEng)) (IB 38 pts HL 766)

Nottingham – A*AA–AAA incl maths+chem/phys (Cheml Eng; Cheml Eng Env Eng; Cheml Eng (MEng)) (IB 36 pts)

144 pts **Aston** – AAA–AAB incl chem+maths (Cheml Eng (MEng)) (IB 34 pts HL 6 maths+chem)

Birmingham – AAA incl maths+phys (Nucl Eng (MEng)) (IB 32 pts HL 666)

Edinburgh – AAA incl maths+phys/eng/des tech (Struct Fire Sfty Eng) (IB 37 pts HL 555); AAA incl maths+chem (Cheml Eng) (IB 37 pts HL 666)

Lancaster – AAA incl maths+chem (Cheml Eng (MEng)) (IB 36 pts HL 16 pts incl 6 maths+chem)

Leeds – AAA incl maths+phys/chem +interview (Petrol Eng) (IB 35 pts HL 18 pts incl 5 maths+phys/chem)

Manchester – AAA incl maths/phys/chem +interview (Cheml Eng) (IB 37 pts HL 666 incl maths+phys/chem); AAA incl maths+sci +interview (Petrol Eng) (IB 36 pts HL 666)

Sheffield – AAA–AAB incl maths+sci (Cheml Eng Biotech (MEng)) (IB 36 pts HL 6 maths+sci); AAA incl maths+sci (Cheml Eng; Cheml Eng (MEng) Comb Hons) (IB 36 pts HL 6 maths+sci)

Strathclyde – AAA–ABB incl maths+chem+phys (3 yr course) BBB–ABB incl maths+chem+phys (4 yr course) (Cheml Eng) (IB 32 pts HL 6 maths+chem+phys)

Surrey – AAA incl maths+chem (Cheml Eng (MEng)) (IB 34 pts)

136 pts **Heriot-Watt** – AAB (4 yr course) BBC (5 yr course) incl maths+chem (Cheml Eng Ener Eng (MEng); Cheml Eng Oil Gas Tech (MEng)) (IB 29 pts); AAB (3 yr course) BBC (4 yr course) incl maths+chem (Cheml Eng) (IB 29 pts)

Lancaster – ABB incl maths+sci (Nucl Eng) (IB 32 pts HL 16 pts incl 6 maths+sci)

Newcastle – AAB incl maths+chem (Cheml Eng) (IB 37 pts HL 6 maths+chem)

Surrey – AAB incl maths+chem (Cheml Eng) (IB 34 pts)

128 pts **Aston** – ABB–BBB incl chem+maths (Cheml Eng) (IB 32 pts)

Lancaster – ABB incl maths+chem (Cheml Eng) (IB 32 pts HL 16 pts incl 6 maths+chem)

Liverpool – ABB/BBB+aEPQ incl phys+maths (Phys Nucl Sci) (IB 33 pts HL 6 phys+maths)

Swansea – ABB–BBB incl maths+chem (Cheml Eng) (IB 32 pts)

120 pts **Aberdeen** – BBB incl maths+phys/des tech/eng (Cheml Eng; Petrol Eng)

Bradford – BBB incl maths+chem 120 pts (Cheml Eng)

Queen's Belfast – BBB incl maths+sci/tech/geog (Cheml Eng)

112 pts **Central Lancashire** – 112 pts incl maths/sci (Fire Eng (MEng)) (IB 28 pts HL 5 sci)

Huddersfield – BBC incl chem 112 pts (Chem Cheml Eng)

Hull – 112 pts incl maths+chem (Cheml Eng) (IB 28 pts HL 5 maths+chem)

Portsmouth – 112–128 pts incl maths (Petrol Eng) (IB 27 pts HL 6 maths)

Teesside – 112 pts incl maths+chem (Cheml Eng MEng)

104 pts **Nottingham Trent** – 104 pts incl phys+maths (Phys Nucl Tech)

96 pts **Central Lancashire** – 96 pts incl maths/sci (Fire Eng) (IB 26 pts HL 5 sci)

Glasgow Caledonian – CCC incl maths+phys (Fire Risk Eng) (IB 25 pts)

Teesside – 96–112 pts incl maths+sci (Cheml Eng)

88 pts **West Scotland** – CCD incl maths+sci (Cheml Eng) (IB 24 pts)

Alternative offers

See **Chapter 6** and **Appendix 1** for grades/UCAS Tariff points information for other examinations.

EXAMPLES OF COLLEGES OFFERING COURSES IN THIS SUBJECT FIELD
Lakes (Coll).

CHOOSING YOUR COURSE (SEE ALSO CH.1)

Universities and colleges teaching quality See www.qaa.ac.uk; https://unistats.ac.uk.

Top research universities and colleges (REF 2014) See **Engineering (Aeronautical and Aerospace)**.

Examples of sandwich degree courses Aston; Bath; Bradford; Huddersfield; Hull; London (QM); Loughborough; Manchester; Queen's Belfast; Surrey; Teesside.

ADMISSIONS INFORMATION

Number of applicants per place (approx) Aston 4; Bath 10; Birmingham 6; Heriot-Watt 6; Huddersfield 7; Imperial London 4, (MEng) 4; Leeds 9; London (UCL) 7; Newcastle 4; Nottingham 19; Sheffield 7; Strathclyde 6; Swansea 3.

Selection interviews Yes Cambridge, Imperial London, Loughborough, Manchester, Oxford; **Some** Bath, Teesside; **No** Birmingham, Leeds, London (UCL), Newcastle, Nottingham, Surrey.

Interview advice and questions Past questions have included the following: How would you justify the processing of radioactive waste to people living in the neighbourhood? What is public health engineering? What is biochemical engineering? What could be the sources of fuel and energy in the year 2020? Discuss some industrial applications of chemistry. Regular incidents occur in which chemical spillage and other problems affect the environment – be prepared to discuss these social issues. See also **Chapter 5**. **Imperial London** Interviews can be conducted in South East Asia if necessary.

Reasons for rejection (non-academic) See **Engineering/Engineering Sciences**.

AFTER-RESULTS ADVICE

Offers to applicants repeating A-levels Higher Swansea; **Possibly higher** Bath, Leeds, Queen's Belfast; **Same** Aston, Birmingham, Cambridge, Loughborough, Newcastle, Nottingham, Sheffield, Teesside.

GRADUATE DESTINATIONS AND EMPLOYMENT (2015/16 HESA)

Chemical, Process and Energy Engineering graduates surveyed 1,250 **Employed** 680 **In voluntary employment** 30 **In further study** 310 **Assumed unemployed** 110

Career note Chemical engineering is involved in many aspects of industry and scientific development. In addition to the oil and chemical-based industries, graduates enter a wide range of careers including the design and construction of chemical process plants, food production, pollution control, environmental protection, energy conservation, waste recovery and recycling, medical science, health and safety, and alternative energy sources.

OTHER DEGREE SUBJECTS FOR CONSIDERATION

Biochemistry; Biotechnology; Chemistry; Cosmetic Science; Environmental Science; Food Science and Technology; Materials Science; Mathematics; Nuclear Engineering; Physics.

ENGINEERING (CIVIL)

(including **Architectural Engineering, Civil and Coastal Engineering, Civil and Environmental Engineering, Civil and Transportation Engineering** and **Marine Technology with Offshore Engineering**; see also **Building and Construction, Environmental Sciences**)

Civil engineers translate the work of architectural designs into reality, dealing with large scale projects such as high rise buildings, bridges, dock and harbour projects, roads, railways, dams, water supplies and reservoirs. In all major projects, civil engineers and architects work in close liaison as demonstrated at the University of Bath which has the only interdisciplinary Architecture and Civil Engineering department in the UK in which students following either degree work together. The University of Leeds also offers a common first Engineering year for all students, who can switch courses with a choice from Architectural Engineering or Civil Engineering with specialisms in either Environmental Engineering, Project Management or Structural Engineering, which focuses on the materials used in construction.

Engineering Council statement See **Engineering/Engineering Sciences**.

Useful websites www.ice.org.uk; www.engc.org.uk; www.wisecampaign.org.uk; www.istructe.org

NB The points totals shown to the left of the institutions are for ease of reference only. It must not be assumed that Tariff points are always used by institutions or that they can be substituted for an offer in grades. The level of an offer is not necessarily indicative of the quality of a course.

COURSE OFFERS INFORMATION

Subject requirements/preferences See **Engineering/Engineering Sciences**. Offers shown below refer to BEng or BSc courses unless otherwise stated; BSc only appears as an abbreviation if the course is offered at the same institution as a BEng with different requirements.

Your target offers and examples of degree courses

160 pts **Cambridge** – A*A*A incl maths+phys +interview +ENGAA (Eng (Civ Struct Env Eng)) (IB 40–42 pts HL 776)

Imperial London – A*A*A incl maths+phys (Civ Eng (MEng)) (IB 39 pts HL 7 maths 6 phys)

Oxford – A*A*A incl maths+phys +interview +PAT (Civ Eng (MEng)) (IB 40 pts HL 776 incl 7 maths+phys)

152 pts **Bath** – A*AA/AAA+aEPQ incl maths (Civ Archit Eng (MEng); Civ Eng) (IB 36 pts HL 766)

Bristol – A*AA–AAB incl maths+sci (Civ Eng (MEng); Civ Eng) (IB 38–34 pts HL 6 maths+sci)

Leeds – A*AA incl maths (Civ Env Eng) (IB 36 pts HL 6 maths+phys/chem)

London (UCL) – A*AA–AAA (Eng (Civ)) (IB 39–38 pts HL 19–18 pts)

Southampton – A*AA/A*AB+aEPQ incl maths+sci/geog (Civ Eng Archit (MEng)) (IB 36 pts HL 6 maths+sci); (Civ Eng (MEng); Civ Eng) (IB 38 pts HL 6 maths+sci)

144 pts **Birmingham** – AAA incl maths (Civ Eng (MEng)) (IB 32 pts HL 666)

Brunel – AAA incl maths+sci/geog/env/des tech (Civ Eng (MEng)) (IB 34 pts HL 6 maths+sci/geog/env/des tech)

Cardiff – AAA–ABB incl maths (Civ Eng; Civ Env Eng; Archit Eng) (IB 36–32 pts HL 5 maths+sci)

City – AAA incl maths+sci 144 pts (Civ Eng (MEng)) (IB 35 pts HL 6 maths+phys)

Edinburgh – AAA incl maths+phys/eng/des tech (Struct Eng Archit; Civ Eng) (IB 37 pts HL 555)

Exeter – AAA–AAB (Civ Eng (MEng) (Yr Ind); Civ Env Eng (MEng) (Yr Ind)) (IB 36–32 pts); AAA–ABB incl maths+sci +interview (Civ Eng (MEng)) (IB 36–32 pts HL 5 maths+sci)

Glasgow – AAA incl maths+phys (Civ Eng (MEng)) (IB 38 pts)

Newcastle – AAA incl maths+phys/chem/fmaths (Mar Tech Off Eng (MEng)) (IB 37 pts HL 6 maths+phys/chem); AAA incl maths (Civ Eng (MEng); Civ Struct Eng (MEng); Civ Eng (MEng) (Yr Ind)) (IB 37 pts HL 6 maths)

Nottingham – AAA incl maths+sci/tech/geog/fmaths (Civ Eng (MEng); Civ Eng) (IB 36 pts HL 6 maths+sci)

Sheffield – AAA/AAB+aEPQ incl maths (Civ Struct Eng (MEng); Civ Eng; Civ Eng Modn Lang (MEng)) (IB 36 pts HL 6 maths)

Warwick – AAA incl maths+phys (Civ Eng) (IB 38 pts HL 6 maths+phys)

136 pts **Birmingham** – AAB incl maths (Civ Eng) (IB 32 pts HL 665)

Coventry – AAB–ABB incl maths (Civ Eng (MEng)) (IB 30 pts)

Exeter – AAB–BBB incl maths+sci (Renew Ener Eng (MEng) (Yr Ind); Renew Ener Eng) (IB 34–30 pts HL 5 maths+sci); AAB–ABB incl maths+sci (Renew Ener Eng (MEng)) (IB 34–30 pts HL 5 maths+sci); (Civ Eng) (IB 36–32 pts HL 5 maths+sci)

Glasgow – AAB–BBB incl maths+phys (Civ Eng; Civ Eng Archit) (IB 36–34 pts HL 665)

Liverpool – AAB incl maths+phys (Civ Struct Eng (MEng)) (IB 35 pts HL 5 maths); AAB incl maths (Civ Eng (MEng); Archit Eng (MEng)) (IB 35 pts HL 5 maths)

Manchester – AAB incl maths+phys (Civ Eng) (IB 35 pts HL 6 maths+phys)

Newcastle – AAB incl maths (Civ Struct Eng; Civ Eng; Civ Eng (Yr Ind); Civ Surv Eng) (IB 35 pts HL 5 maths)

Queen's Belfast – AAB incl maths+sci/tech/geog (Civ Eng (MEng); Env Civ Eng (MEng); Struct Eng Archit (MEng))

Surrey – AAB incl sci/maths/tech (Civ Eng (MEng)) (IB 34 pts)

128 pts **Aberdeen** – ABB incl maths+phys/des tech/eng (Civ Eng (MEng); Civ Struct Eng (MEng); Civ Env Eng (MEng)) (IB 34 pts HL 6 maths+phys)

City – ABB incl maths+sci 128 pts (Civ Eng) (IB 33 pts HL 6 maths+phys)

Heriot-Watt – ABB (3 yr course) ABC/BBB (4 yr course) incl maths (Civ Eng; Civ Eng Int St) (IB 35 pts (3 yr course) 31 pts (4 yr course) HL 6 maths (3 yr course) 5 maths (4 yr course))

Hertfordshire – 128 pts incl maths (Civ Eng (MEng))

Liverpool – ABB incl maths (Civ Eng) (IB 33 pts HL 5 maths)

Liverpool John Moores – ABB 128 pts (Civ Eng (MEng)) (IB 27 pts)

Loughborough – ABB incl maths (Civ Eng) (IB 34 pts HL 655)

Surrey – ABB incl maths+sci/tech/fmaths (Civ Eng) (IB 32 pts)

Swansea – ABB–BBB incl maths (Civ Eng) (IB 32 pts)

120 pts **Brighton** – BBB–BCC incl maths 120–104 pts (Civ Eng) (IB 30 pts HL 5 maths)

Brunel – BBB incl maths+sci/geog/env/des tech (Civ Eng) (IB 30 pts HL 5 maths+sci/geog/env/des tech); (Civ Eng Sust) (IB 31 pts HL 5 maths+sci/geog/env/des tech)

Coventry – BBB–BCC incl maths (Civ Eng) (IB 30 pts)

Dundee – BBB incl maths+sci/eng (Civ Eng) (IB 30 pts HL 555)

Greenwich – 120 pts incl maths/sci (Civ Eng)

Northumbria – 120–128 pts incl maths+sci (Mech Archit Eng) (HL 444)

Nottingham Trent – BBB 120 pts (Civ Eng)

Queen's Belfast – BBB incl maths+sci/tech/geog (Civ Eng)

Strathclyde – BBB incl maths+phys/eng (Civ Eng) (IB 32 pts HL 5 maths+phys/eng)

Ulster – BBB incl sci/tech (Civ Eng) (IB 26 pts HL 13 pts)

112 pts **Bradford** – BBC incl maths 112 pts (Civ Struct Eng)

Edinburgh Napier – BBC incl maths (Civ Eng (MEng)) (IB 29 pts HL 655 incl 5 maths)

Kingston – 112 pts incl maths (Civ Infra Eng) (IB 26 pts HL 6 maths)

Leeds Beckett – 112 pts inc maths+sci (Civ Eng) (IB 25 pts)

Liverpool John Moores – BBC 112 pts (Civ Eng) (IB 26 pts); BBC incl maths/sci 112 pts (Bld Serv Eng) (IB 25 pts HL 5 maths)

London South Bank – BBC (Civ Eng)

Plymouth – 108–120 pts incl maths+sci/tech (Civ Eng; Civ Cstl Eng) (IB 28 pts HL 5 maths)

Portsmouth – 112–120 pts incl maths (Civ Eng) (IB 26 pts)

UWE Bristol – 112 pts incl maths (Civ Env Eng) (HL 5 maths)

West London – 112–120 pts incl maths/phys (Civ Env Eng)

104 pts **Bolton** – 104 pts incl maths (Civ Eng)

Coventry – BCC–CCC incl maths (Civ Eng (BSc)) (IB 30 pts)

Edinburgh Napier – BCC incl maths (Civ Trans Eng) (IB 29 pts HL 655)

Glasgow Caledonian – BCC incl maths+phys (Env Civ Eng) (IB 24 pts)

Hertfordshire – 104 pts incl maths (Civ Eng)

Nottingham Trent – BCC 104 pts (Civ Eng (BSc))

Salford – 104–112 pts incl maths+phys/des tech (Civ Eng) (IB 30 pts)

South Wales – BCC–CDD incl maths/sci/geog (Civ Eng) (HL 655–455)

Ulster – BCC incl sci/tech/geog (Civ Eng (Geoinform)) (IB 24 pts HL 12 pts)

96 pts **Abertay** – CCC incl maths (Civ Env Eng) (IB 28 pts)

Anglia Ruskin – 96 pts (Civ Eng (BSc)) (IB 24 pts)

Derby – 96–112 pts incl maths/sci (Civ Eng)

East London – 96 pts incl maths (Civ Eng) (IB 27 pts HL 15 pts incl maths+phys)

Edinburgh Napier – CCC incl maths (Civ Eng) (IB 27 pts HL 5 maths)

Teesside – 96–112 pts incl maths (Civ Eng)

Trinity Saint David – 96 pts +interview (Civ Eng Env Mgt)

Wolverhampton – AA/CCC incl maths (Civ Eng)

88 pts **West Scotland** – CCD incl maths+sci (Civ Eng) (IB 24 pts)

Check **Chapter 3** for new university admission details and **Chapter 6** on how to read the subject tables.

Alternative offers
See **Chapter 6** and **Appendix 1** for grades/UCAS Tariff points information for other examinations.

EXAMPLES OF DEGREE APPRENTICESHIPS IN THIS SUBJECT FIELD
East London (Civ Eng Site Mgt); Liverpool John Moores (Civ Eng).

EXAMPLES OF COLLEGES OFFERING COURSES IN THIS SUBJECT FIELD
Birmingham Met (Coll); Blackburn (Coll); Bolton (Coll); Bradford (Coll); Chelmsford (Coll); Chesterfield (Coll); Exeter (Coll); Guildford (Coll); Lakes (Coll); Leeds Building (Coll); Lincoln (Coll); London UCK (Coll); MidKent (Coll); Moulton (Coll); Norwich City (Coll); Plymouth City (Coll); Sheffield (Coll); South Devon (Coll); Wakefield (Coll); Wigan and Leigh (Coll).

CHOOSING YOUR COURSE (SEE ALSO CH.1)
Universities and colleges teaching quality See www.qaa.ac.uk; https://unistats.ac.uk.

Top research universities and colleges (REF 2014) (Civil and Construction Engineering) Cardiff; Imperial London; Sheffield; Manchester; Dundee.

Examples of sandwich degree courses Bath; Bradford; Brighton; Cardiff; City; Coventry; East London; Kingston; Liverpool John Moores; London South Bank; Loughborough; Nottingham Trent; Portsmouth; Queen's Belfast; Salford; Surrey; Teesside; Ulster; UWE Bristol; West Scotland; Wolverhampton.

ADMISSIONS INFORMATION
Number of applicants per place (approx) Abertay 3; Bath 7; Birmingham 11; Bradford 5; Bristol 8; Cardiff 5; City 6; Dundee 9; Edinburgh Napier 5; Greenwich 11; Heriot-Watt 7; Imperial London 4; Kingston 8; Leeds 10; Liverpool John Moores 16; London (UCL) 5; London South Bank 5; Newcastle 4, (Off Eng) 4; Nottingham 9; Nottingham Trent 11; Plymouth 3; Queen's Belfast 6; Salford 5; Sheffield 4; South Wales 6; Southampton 10; Strathclyde 4; Swansea 3; Teesside 6; West Scotland 4; Wolverhampton 3.

Advice to applicants and planning the UCAS personal statement See **Engineering/Engineering Sciences**. Also read the magazine *The New Civil Engineer* and discuss articles which interest you on your application. See also **Appendix 3**. **Bristol** Deferred entry accepted.

Selection interviews Yes Cambridge, Imperial London, Oxford; **Some** Bath, Cardiff, Southampton, Warwick; **No** Anglia Ruskin, Birmingham, Brighton, Bristol, Coventry, Dundee, Edinburgh Napier, Greenwich, Heriot-Watt, Kingston, Leeds, London (UCL), Loughborough, Newcastle, Nottingham, Nottingham Trent, Salford, Surrey.

Interview advice and questions Past questions have included: Why have you chosen Civil Engineering? Have you contacted the Institution of Civil Engineers/Institution of Structural Engineers? How would you define the difference between the work of a civil engineer and the work of an architect? What would happen to a concrete beam if a load were applied? Where would it break and how could it be strengthened? The favourite question: Why do you want to be a civil engineer? What would you do if you were asked to build a concrete boat? Do you know any civil engineers? What problems were faced in building the Channel Tunnel? See also **Chapter 5**. **Cambridge** Why did they make mill chimneys so tall?

Reasons for rejection (non-academic) Lack of vitality. Lack of interest in buildings, the built environment or in civil engineering. Poor communication skills. See also **Engineering/Engineering Sciences**.

AFTER-RESULTS ADVICE
Offers to applicants repeating A-levels Higher East London, Kingston, Queen's Belfast, Teesside, Warwick; **Possibly higher** Southampton; **Same** Abertay, Bath, Birmingham, Bradford, Brighton, Bristol, Cardiff, City, Coventry, Dundee, Greenwich, Heriot-Watt, Leeds, Liverpool John Moores, London (UCL), London South Bank, Loughborough, Newcastle, Nottingham, Nottingham Trent, Salford, Sheffield, Wolverhampton; **No** Cambridge.

UCAS points Tariff: A* = 56 pts; A = 48 pts; B = 40 pts; C = 32 pts; D = 24 pts; E = 16 pts

GRADUATE DESTINATIONS AND EMPLOYMENT (2015/16 HESA)

Graduates surveyed 2,485 **Employed** 1,660 **In voluntary employment** 15 **In further study** 465
Assumed unemployed 125

Career note The many aspects of this subject will provide career directions for graduates with many openings with local authorities and commercial organisations.

OTHER DEGREE SUBJECTS FOR CONSIDERATION

Architecture; Building; Surveying; Town and Country Planning.

ENGINEERING (COMMUNICATIONS)

(including **Business Information Systems**; see also **Communication
Studies/Communication, Engineering (Electrical and Electronic)**)

Communications engineering impacts on many aspects of the engineering and business world. Courses overlap considerably with Electronic, Computer, Digital, Media and Internet Engineering and provide graduates with expertise in such fields as telecommunications, mobile communications and microwave engineering, optoelectronics, radio engineering and internet technology. Sandwich courses and sponsorships are offered by several universities.

Engineering Council statement See **Engineering/Engineering Sciences**.

Useful websites See **Computer Courses** and **Engineering (Electrical and Electronic)**.

NB The points totals shown to the left of the institutions are for ease of reference only. It must not be assumed that Tariff points are always used by institutions or that they can be substituted for an offer in grades. The level of an offer is not necessarily indicative of the quality of a course.

COURSE OFFERS INFORMATION

Subject requirements/preferences See **Engineering/Engineering Sciences**. Offers shown below refer to BEng or BSc courses unless otherwise stated; BSc only appears as an abbreviation if the course is offered at the same institution as a BEng with different requirements.

Your target offers and examples of degree courses

152 pts Southampton – A*AA incl maths+phys (Electron Eng Wrlss Comms (MEng))

144 pts Bath – AAA/AAB+aEPQ incl maths+sci/tech (Comp Sys Eng (MEng)) (IB 36 pts HL 6 maths/phys+sci/tech); (Electron Sys Eng (MEng)) (IB 36 pts HL 6 maths+sci/tech)

Newcastle – AAA incl maths+phys/chem/electron (Electron Comms (MEng) (Yr Abrd/Ind)) (IB 37 pts HL 6 maths+phys/chem)

Sheffield – AAA/AAB+aEPQ incl maths+phys/chem/electron (Electron Comms Eng (MEng)) (IB 36 pts HL 6 maths+phys/chem/electron)

York – AAA incl maths+phys/chem/electron +interview (Electron Comm Eng (MEng)) (IB 36–32 pts HL 6/5 maths+phys)

136 pts Aston – AAB–ABB (Bus Comp IT) (IB 32 pts HL 665–655); ABB–BBB incl maths+sci/tech (Comms Eng) (IB 32 pts)

Bath – AAB–ABB+aEPQ incl maths/phys+sci/tech (Comp Sys Eng) (IB 36 pts HL 6 maths/phys+sci/tech)

Newcastle – AAB incl maths+phys/chem/electron (Electron Comms) (IB 35 pts HL 5 maths+phys/chem)

Sheffield – AAB/ABB+bEPQ incl maths+phys/chem/electron (Electron Comms Eng) (IB 34 pts HL 6 maths+phys/chem/electron)

128 pts Brunel – ABB incl maths+sci/tech (Electron Comms Eng (MEng)) (IB 31 pts HL 6 maths+sci/tech)

Heriot-Watt – ABB incl comp (3 yr course) BBB (4 yr course) (Inf Sys courses) (IB 30 pts (3 yr course) 28 pts (4 yr course) HL 6 comp (3 yr course))

       Kent – ABB incl maths+sci/tech (Electron Comms Eng (MEng)) (IB 34 pts)
       London (QM) – ABB incl maths+sci (Electron Eng Telecomm) (IB 32 pts HL 6/5 maths+sci)
       York – ABB–AAB incl maths +interview (Electron Comm Eng) (IB 32–36 pts HL 5/6
         maths+phys)

120 pts **Aberdeen** – BBB (Bus Mgt Inf Sys) (IB 32 pts HL 555)
       Brunel – BBB (Bus Comp) (IB 30 pts)
       Buckingham – BBB–BBC (Bus Mgt App Comp) (IB 32–31 pts)
       Essex – BBB incl maths (Comms Eng) (IB 30 pts HL 5 maths)
       Huddersfield – BBB incl maths+sci/tech 120 pts (Electron Comm Eng)
       Kent – BBB maths+sci/tech (Electron Comms Eng) (IB 34 pts)
       Liverpool Hope – BBB–BBC 120–112 pts (IT)
       London South Bank – BBB incl maths (Telecomm Eng)

112 pts **Birmingham City** – BBC incl sci/tech/maths/comp 112 pts (Bus Inf Sys) (HL 14 pts)
       Brighton – BBC–CCC 112–96 pts (Bus Comp) (IB 28 pts)
       Kingston – 112 pts (Comp Sci (Net Comms))
       Nottingham Trent – BBC incl IT/sci 112 pts (ICT; Inf Sys)
       Southampton Solent – 112 pts (Bus IT)
       Westminster – BBC/A*A* (Bus Inf Sys) (IB 26 pts)

104 pts **Bournemouth** – 104–120 pts (Bus IT) (IB 28–31 pts HL 55)
       Hertfordshire – 104 pts incl maths+phys/tech/eng (Electron Comm Eng) (HL 4 maths+phys)
       Middlesex – 104 pts (Bus Inf Sys)
       Northampton – BCC (Comp (Comp Net Eng))
       South Wales – BCC–CDD 104–80 pts (ICT) (HL 655–445)
       Wolverhampton – A*A/BCC incl maths+sci/tech (Electron Telecomm Eng (MEng))

96 pts **Cardiff Met** – 96 pts (Bus Inf Sys)
88 pts **London Met** – CCD 88 pts (Electron Comms Eng)
80 pts **Bangor** – 80 pts (Comp Inf Sys)
       Bedfordshire – 80 pts (Inf Data Sys; Telecomm Net Eng)

Alternative offers
See **Chapter 6** and **Appendix 1** for grades/UCAS Tariff points information for other examinations.

EXAMPLES OF COLLEGES OFFERING COURSES IN THIS SUBJECT FIELD
Birmingham Met (Coll).

CHOOSING YOUR COURSE (SEE ALSO CH.1)
Universities and colleges teaching quality See www.qaa.ac.uk; https://unistats.ac.uk.

Examples of sandwich degree courses Aston; Brunel; Kent; Kingston; Wolverhampton; York.

ADMISSIONS INFORMATION
Number of applicants per place (approx) Bradford 9; London Met 5; London South Bank 3; York 8.

Advice to applicants and planning the UCAS personal statement See **Engineering (Electrical and Electronic)** and **Appendix 3**.

Selection interviews No Hertfordshire, Kent, London Met.

Interview advice and questions See **Engineering (Electrical and Electronic)**.

Reasons for rejection (non-academic) See **Engineering (Electrical and Electronic)**.

GRADUATE DESTINATIONS AND EMPLOYMENT (2015/16 HESA)
See **Engineering (Electrical and Electronic)** and **Engineering/Engineering Sciences**.

Career note Many commercial organisations offer opportunities in the specialist areas described at the top of this table. Work placements and sandwich courses have, in the past, resulted in over 60% of graduates gaining employment with their firms.

OTHER DEGREE SUBJECTS FOR CONSIDERATION
Computer Science; Engineering (Computer, Control, Electrical, Electronic, Systems); Physics.

ENGINEERING (COMPUTER, CONTROL, SOFTWARE and SYSTEMS)

The design and application of modern computer systems is fundamental to a wide range of disciplines which also include electronic, software and computer-aided engineering. Most courses give priority to reinforcing the essential transferable skills consisting of management techniques, leadership skills, literacy, presentation skills, business skills and time management. At many universities, Computer Engineering is offered as part of a range of Electronics degree programmes where the first and even the second year courses are common to all students, who then choose to specialise later. A year in industry is a common feature of many of these courses.

Engineering Council statement See **Engineering/Engineering Sciences**.

Useful websites See **Computer Courses** and **Engineering/Engineering Sciences**.

NB The points totals shown to the left of the institutions are for ease of reference only. It must not be assumed that Tariff points are always used by institutions or that they can be substituted for an offer in grades. The level of an offer is not necessarily indicative of the quality of a course.

COURSE OFFERS INFORMATION
Subject requirements/preferences See **Engineering/Engineering Sciences**. Offers shown below refer to BEng or BSc courses unless otherwise stated; BSc only appears as an abbreviation if the course is offered at the same institution as a BEng with different requirements.

Your target offers and examples of degree courses
160 pts **Cambridge** – A*A*A incl maths+sci +interview +ENGAA (Eng (Inf Comp Eng)) (IB 40–42 pts HL 776)
Imperial London – A*AA–A*A*A* incl maths +interview (Comp (Soft Eng) (MEng)) (IB 41–43 pts HL 7 maths)
Oxford A*A*A incl maths+phys +interview +PAT (Inf Eng) (IB 40 pts HL 776 incl 7 maths+phys)
152 pts **Birmingham** – A*AA incl maths/comp (Comp Sci/Soft Eng (MEng)) (IB 32 pts HL 766 incl 6 maths/comp)
Imperial London – A*AA–A*A*A* incl maths+phys +interview (Electron Inf Eng; Electron Inf Eng (MEng) (St Abrd)) (IB 38–39 pts HL 6 maths+phys)
Manchester – A*AA incl maths +interview (Comp Sys Eng) (IB 38 pts HL 766)
Southampton – A*AA incl maths (Soft Eng)
144 pts **Bath** – AAA/AAB+aEPQ incl maths+sci/tech (Comp Sys Eng (MEng)) (IB 36 pts HL 6 maths/phys+sci/tech); (Elec Electron Eng (MEng)) (IB 36 pts HL 666)
Edinburgh – AAA incl maths (Electron Comp Sci (MEng)) (IB 37 pts HL 6 maths)
Loughborough – AAA incl maths+sci/tech/fmaths (Electron Comp Sys Eng (MEng); Sys Eng (MEng)) (IB 37 pts HL 666 incl 6 maths+sci)
Warwick – AAA incl maths (Comp Sys Eng) (IB 38 pts HL 6 maths)
136 pts **Aberystwyth** – AAB (Soft Eng (MEng)) (IB 32 pts)
Bath – AAB/ABB+aEPQ incl maths/phys+sci/tech (Electron Sys Eng) (IB 36 pts HL 6 maths/phys+sci/tech); AAB–ABB+aEPQ incl maths/phys+sci/tech (Comp Sys Eng) (IB 36 pts HL 6 maths/phys+sci/tech)
Cardiff – AAB–ABB (App Soft Eng) (33 pts)
Dyson – AAB incl A maths+sci/tech (Eng Tech)
Glasgow – AAB–BBB incl maths (Electron Soft Eng) (IB 36–34 pts HL 665 incl sci)

London (RH) – AAB–ABB incl phys/chem/comp sci/maths (Comp Sci (Soft Eng)) (IB 32 pts HL 655)

Newcastle – AAB incl maths+phys/chem/electron (Electron Comp Eng) (IB 35 pts HL 5 maths+phys/chem)

Queen's Belfast – AAB/AAA incl chem/phys/tech des/IT (Soft Eng (MEng))

Sheffield – AAB/ABB+bEPQ incl maths+sci (Sys Contr Eng; Sys Contr Eng (Eng Mgt); Mecha Robot Eng; Comp Sys Eng) (IB 34 pts HL 6 maths+sci)

Strathclyde – AAB incl maths+phys +interview (Comp Electron Sys (MEng)) (IB 36 pts HL 6 maths+phys)

York – AAB–ABB incl maths (Comp Sci Embd Sys Eng) (IB 35–34 pts HL 6 maths)

128 pts **Aberdeen** – ABB incl maths+phys/des tech/eng (Eng Electron Soft Eng (MEng)) (IB 34 pts HL 6 maths+phys)

Bradford – ABB 128 pts (Soft Eng)

Brunel – ABB incl sci/eng/maths (Comp Sys Eng (MEng)) (IB 33 pts HL 6 sci/eng/maths); ABB incl maths+sci/eng (Electron Comp Eng (MEng)) (IB 31 pts HL 6 maths+sci/eng)

East Anglia – ABB incl maths/comp/electron/econ/phys (Comp Sys Eng; Comp Sys Eng (Yr Ind)) (IB 32 pts HL 55 incl maths/comp/electron/econ/phys)

Greenwich – 128 pts (Soft Eng)

Heriot-Watt – ABB incl maths+phys (3 yr course) BBB incl maths+phys/tech/eng (4 yr course) (Comp Electron) (IB 29 pts)

Liverpool – ABB/BBB+aEPQ incl maths+sci/tech (Avion Sys; Comp Sci Electron Eng) (IB 33 pts HL 5 maths+phys/electron); (Avion Sys (MEng); Comp Sci Electron Eng (MEng)) (IB 33 pts HL 5 maths+sci); ABB incl maths/phys/comp (Comp Sci Soft Eng) (IB 33 pts HL 5 maths/phys/sci)

Loughborough – ABB incl maths+sci/tech/fmaths (Sys Eng; Electron Comp Sys Eng) (IB 34 pts HL 655 incl maths+sci)

Stirling – ABB incl comp (Soft Eng) (IB 35 pts)

Strathclyde – ABB incl maths+phys +interview (Comp Electron Sys) (IB 32 pts HL 5 maths+phys); ABB (Soft Eng) (IB 34 pts HL 5 maths)

UWE Bristol – 128 pts (Comp Embd Sys) (IB 27 pts)

120 pts **Brunel** – BBB (Comp Sci (Soft Eng); Gms Des) (IB 30 pts); BBB incl sci/eng/maths (Comp Sys Eng) (IB 30 pts HL 5 sci/eng/maths)

Edinburgh Napier – BBB (3 yr course) CCC (4 yr course) (Comp Sys Net) (IB 27 pts HL 654)

Essex – BBB (Comp Net; Comp Electron; Comp Sys Eng) (IB 30 pts)

Greenwich – 120 pts incl sci/maths (Comp Eng)

Huddersfield – BBB incl maths+sci/tech 120 pts (Comp Sys Eng)

Kent – BBB incl maths+sci/tech (Comp Sys Eng) (IB 34 pts)

Leicester – BBB (Soft Eng courses) (IB 30 pts)

London South Bank – BBB (Comp Sys Net)

Northumbria – 120–128 pts (Comp Net Cy Scrty) (HL 444)

Nottingham Trent – BBB incl IT/maths/sci 120 pts (Soft Eng)

Ulster – BBB incl sci/maths/tech (Comp Eng) (IB 26 pts HL 13 pts incl 4 maths+sci)

116 pts **Plymouth** – 116–120 pts (Comp Sys Net) (IB 30 pts)

112 pts **Aberystwyth** – BBC incl math+phys/comp sci (Spc Sci Robot) (IB 28 pts HL 5 maths+5 phys/comp sci); BBC (Soft Eng) (IB 28 pts)

Central Lancashire – 112 pts incl maths/phys/STEM (Comp Aid Eng); 112 pts incl maths+phys/STEM (Comp Aid Eng (MEng)) (HL 6 maths+phys)

Coventry – BBC–BCC incl maths+sci/tech/fmaths/eng (Comp Hard Soft Eng) (IB 29 pts)

De Montfort – 112 pts (Soft Eng) (IB 26 pts)

Hull – 112 pts (Comp Sci (Soft Eng)) (IB 28 pts)

Liverpool John Moores – BBC 112 pts (Soft Eng) (IB 26 pts)

Nottingham Trent – BBC incl IT/maths/sci 112 pts (Comp Sys Eng)

Sheffield Hallam – 112–96 pts incl sci (Comp Sys Eng); 112–96 pts (Soft Eng)

Southampton Solent – 112 pts (Net Scrty Mgt)

Staffordshire – BBC 112 pts (Soft Eng; Comp Gms Prog)
Sunderland – 112 pts (Gms Soft Dev)
Teesside – 112–128 pts incl maths+phys (Instr Contr Eng (MEng))
104 pts **Bangor** – 104–96 pts incl maths+phys (Comp Sys Eng; Comp Sys Eng (MEng))
Bournemouth – 104–120 pts (Soft Eng) (IB 28–31 pts HL 55)
Hertfordshire – 104 pts (Comp Sci (Soft Eng)) (HL 44)
Manchester Met – BCC–BBC 104–112 pts (Soft Eng) (IB 26 pts)
Middlesex – 104 pts (Comp Comm Net)
Northampton – BCC (Comp (Comp Sys Eng))
Trinity Saint David – 104 pts +interview (Soft Eng); 104 pts (Comp Sys Electron)
Westminster – BCC/A*A incl tech (Comp Sys Eng) (IB 26 pts HL 5 tech)
96 pts **Cardiff Met** – 96 pts (Soft Eng)
Southampton Solent – 96 pts (Comp Sys Net)
Teesside – 96–112 pts incl maths+sci/tech/eng (Instr Contr Eng)
88 pts **Glasgow Caledonian** – CCD incl maths+phys (Comp Aid Mech Eng) (IB 24 pts)
London Met – CCD 88 pts (Comp Sys Eng)
Wolverhampton – AB/CCD +interview (Comp Sci (Soft Eng))
80 pts **Bedfordshire** – 80 pts (Comp Sys Eng; Comp Sci Soft Eng)
Bucks New – 80–96 pts (Soft Eng)

Alternative offers
See **Chapter 6** and **Appendix 1** for grades/UCAS Tariff points information for other examinations.

EXAMPLES OF DEGREE APPRENTICESHIPS IN THIS SUBJECT FIELD
Aston (Dig Tech Sol); Chichester (Dig Tech Sol (Soft Eng)); Edinburgh Napier (Dig Tech Sol); Essex (Dig Tech Sol); Glasgow Caledonian (Dig Tech Sol); Liverpool John Moores (Contr Autom Eng; Dig Tech Sol); Queen's Belfast (Soft Eng Dig Tech); Winchester (Dig Tech Sol); UWE Bristol (Embd Electron Sys Des Dev; Dig Tech Sol).

EXAMPLES OF COLLEGES OFFERING COURSES IN THIS SUBJECT FIELD
Accrington and Rossendale (Coll); Barking and Dagenham (Coll); Barnfield (Coll); Birmingham Met (Coll); Blackburn (Coll); Blackpool and Fylde (Coll); Bristol City (Coll); Cornwall (Coll); Doncaster (Coll); Farnborough (CT); Gateshead (Coll); Highbury Portsmouth (Coll); Manchester (Coll); Newcastle (Coll); North Lindsey (Coll); Nottingham (Coll); Tyne Coast (Coll).

CHOOSING YOUR COURSE (SEE ALSO CH.1)
Universities and colleges teaching quality See www.qaa.ac.uk; https://unistats.ac.uk.

Top research universities and colleges (REF 2014) See **Computer Courses**.

Examples of sandwich degree courses Aberystwyth; Bath; Bradford; Brunel; Chester; Greenwich; Huddersfield; Kent; London (QM); London (RH); London South Bank; Loughborough; Manchester; Manchester Met; Northumbria; Nottingham Trent; Sheffield Hallam; Stirling; Westminster; York.

ADMISSIONS INFORMATION
Number of applicants per place (approx) Bath 8; Birmingham 9; Cardiff 6; Central Lancashire 12; East Anglia 5; Edinburgh 3; Huddersfield 3; Imperial London 5; Liverpool John Moores 2; London South Bank 3; Sheffield 4; Sheffield Hallam 8; Southampton 4; Staffordshire 5; Stirling 10; Strathclyde 7; Teesside 3; Trinity Saint David 4; Westminster 5; York 3.

Advice to applicants and planning the UCAS personal statement See **Computer Courses**, **Engineering (Electrical and Electronic)** and **Appendix 3**.

Selection interviews Yes Cambridge, Manchester, Trinity Saint David; **Some** Bath, Cardiff; **No** Bradford, East Anglia, Hertfordshire, Huddersfield, Kent, Liverpool John Moores, Loughborough, Nottingham Trent, Sheffield Hallam, Westminster.

Interview advice and questions See **Computer Courses**, **Engineering (Electrical and Electronic)** and **Chapter 5**.

Reasons for rejection (non-academic) Lack of understanding that the course involves engineering. See also **Computer Courses** and **Engineering (Electrical and Electronic)**.

AFTER-RESULTS ADVICE
Offers to applicants repeating A-levels Higher Strathclyde, Warwick, York; **Possibly higher** City, Sheffield; **Same** Bath, Birmingham, Coventry, East Anglia, Huddersfield, Liverpool John Moores, London South Bank, Loughborough, Teesside; **No** Cambridge.

GRADUATE DESTINATIONS AND EMPLOYMENT (2015/16 HESA)
Software Engineering graduates surveyed 645 **Employed** 410 **In voluntary employment** 10 **In further study** 75 **Assumed unemployed** 65

Career note Career opportunities extend right across the whole field of electronics, telecommunications, control and systems engineering.

OTHER DEGREE SUBJECTS FOR CONSIDERATION
Computer Science; Computing; Engineering (Aeronautical, Aerospace, Communications, Electrical and Electronic); Mathematics; Media (Systems/Engineering/Technology); Physics.

ENGINEERING (ELECTRICAL and ELECTRONIC)
(see also Engineering (Acoustics and Sound), Engineering (Aeronautical and Aerospace), Engineering (Communications))

Electrical and Electronic Engineering courses provide a sound foundation for those looking for a career in electricity generation and transmission, communications or control systems, including robotics. All courses cater for students wanting a general or more specialist engineering education and options should be considered when choosing degree courses. These could include optoelectronics and optical communication systems, microwave systems, radio frequency engineering and circuit technology. Many courses have common first years, allowing transfer in Year 2. Electronic Engineering courses also overlap closely with Information Technology and Information Systems Engineering, which involves electronic and digital information. This includes the internet and mobile phones. Most institutions have good industrial contacts and applicants should look closely at sandwich courses.

Engineering Council statement See **Engineering/Engineering Sciences**.

Useful websites www.theiet.org; www.engc.org.uk

NB The points totals shown to the left of the institutions are for ease of reference only. It must not be assumed that Tariff points are always used by institutions or that they can be substituted for an offer in grades. The level of an offer is not necessarily indicative of the quality of a course.

COURSE OFFERS INFORMATION
Subject requirements/preferences See **Engineering/Engineering Sciences**. Offers shown below refer to BEng or BSc courses unless otherwise stated; BSc only appears as an abbreviation if the course is offered at the same institution as a BEng with different requirements.

Your target offers and examples of degree courses
160 pts **Cambridge** – A*A*A incl maths+phys +interview +ENGAA (Eng (Elec Inf Sci/Elec Electron Eng)) (IB 40–42 pts HL 776)

  Oxford – A*A*A incl maths+phys +interview + PAT (Elec Eng) (IB 40 pts HL 776 incl 7 maths+phys)

152 pts **Imperial London** – A*AA–A*A*A incl maths+phys +interview (Elec Electron Eng (MEng); Elec Electron Eng Mgt (MEng); Electron Inf Eng; Electron Inf Eng (MEng) (St Abrd)) (IB 38–39 pts HL 6 maths+phys)

Manchester – A*AA incl maths +interview (Comp Sys Eng) (IB 38 pts HL 766)

Southampton – A*AA incl maths+phys (Electron Eng Wrlss Comms (MEng)); A*AA incl maths+phys/fmaths/tech (Electron Eng Comp Sys (MEng); Electron Eng Artif Intel (MEng); Electron Eng Nanotech (MEng); Electron Eng Mbl Scr Sys (MEng))

144 pts **Aston** – AAA–AAB incl maths+physl sci/tech (Elec Electron Eng (MEng)) (IB 34 pts HL 6 maths+phys)

Bath – AAA/AAB+aEPQ incl maths+sci/tech (Electron Sys Eng (MEng)) (IB 36 pts HL 6 maths+sci/tech); (Elec Electron Eng (MEng); Elec Pwr Eng (MEng)) (IB 36 pts HL 666)

Bristol – AAA–ABB incl maths (Elec Electron Eng (MEng)) (IB 36–32 pts HL 6 maths)

Cardiff – AAA–AAB incl maths (Elec Electron Eng) (IB 36–32 pts HL 5 maths)

City – AAA incl maths+sci 144 pts (Elec Electron Eng (MEng)) (IB 35 pts HL 6 maths+phys)

Edinburgh – AAA incl maths+phys/eng/des tech (Elec Mech Eng) (IB 37 pts HL 666); AAA incl maths (Electron Elec Eng; Electron Comp Sci) (IB 37 pts HL 666)

Exeter – AAA–AAB (Electron Eng (Yr Ind)) (IB 36–32 pts); AAA–ABB incl maths+sci (Electron Eng Comp Sci) (IB 36–32 pts HL 5 maths+sci)

Glasgow – AAA incl maths+phys (Electron Elec Eng (MEng)) (IB 38–36 pts HL 666 incl maths/phys); (Electron Mus (MEng)) (IB 38–36 pts)

Lancaster – AAA incl maths+physl sci (Electron Elec Eng (MEng)) (IB 36 pts HL 16 pts incl 6 maths+physl sci)

Leeds – AAA incl maths +interview (Electron Elec Eng) (IB 35 pts HL 18 pts incl 5 maths); (Electron Eng) (IB 35 pts HL 18 pts incl 5 maths)

London (UCL) – AAA incl maths+phys/fmaths (Eng (Electron Elec)) (IB 38 pts HL 6 maths)

Loughborough – AAA incl maths+sci/tech/fmaths (Electron Comp Sys Eng (MEng)) (IB 37 pts HL 666 incl 6 maths+sci); AAA incl maths+sci/tech/fmath (Electron Elec Eng (MEng)) (IB 37 pts HL 666 incl 6 maths+sci)

Newcastle – AAA incl maths+phys/chem/electron (Electron Comms (MEng) (Yr Abrd/Ind)) (IB 37 pts HL 6 maths+phys/chem)

Nottingham – AAA–ABB incl maths+sci/electron (Elec Electron Eng; Electron Comp Eng; Electron Eng) (IB 36–32 pts HL 5 maths+sci); (Elec Eng) (IB 36–32 pts)

Sheffield – AAA/AAB+aEPQ incl maths+phys/chem/electron (Electron Comms Eng (MEng); Electron Elec Eng Modn Lang (MEng)) (IB 36 pts HL 6 maths+phys/chem/electron); AAA/AAB+aEPQ incl maths+sci/electron (Dig Electron (MEng); Microelec (MEng); Elec Eng (MEng)) (IB 36 pts HL 6 maths+sci/electron); AAA–AAB+aEPQ incl maths+sci/electron (Electron Eng (MEng)) (IB 36 pts HL 6 maths+sci/electron)

Southampton – AAA incl maths+phys/fmaths/tech (Electron Eng)

Surrey – AAA–AAB incl maths+phys/electron/comp/fmaths (Electron Eng (MEng); Electron Eng Comp Sys (MEng)) (IB 34 pts)

Warwick – AAA incl maths+phys (Electron Eng) (IB 38 pts HL 6 maths/phys)

York – AAA incl maths+phys/chem/electron +interview (Electron Eng (MEng); Electron Eng Nanotech (MEng); Electron Comm Eng (MEng)) (IB 36–32 pts HL 6/5 maths+phys)

136 pts **Bath** – AAB/ABB+aEPQ incl maths/sci/tech (Electron Eng Spc Sci Tech) (IB 35 pts HL 6 maths/phys+sci/tech); AAB/ABB+aEPQ incl maths/phys+sci/tech (Electron Sys Eng; Elec Electron Eng) (IB 36 pts HL 6 maths/phys+sci/tech); AAB–ABB+aEPQ incl maths+sci/tech (Elec Pwr Eng) (IB 36 pts HL 6 maths+sci/tech)

Birmingham – AAB incl maths (Electron Elec Eng) (IB 30 pts HL 5 maths)

Brunel – AAB–ABB incl maths+sci/eng (Electron Elec Eng (MEng)) (IB 31 pts HL 6 maths+sci/eng)

Dyson – AAB incl A maths+sci/tech (Eng Tech)

Glasgow – AAB–BBB incl maths+phys (Electron Elec Eng) (IB 36–34 pts HL 665 incl maths+phys); (Electron Mus) (IB 36–34 pts)

Manchester – AAB incl maths+phys/electron +interview (Elec Electron Eng) (IB 34 pts HL 6 maths+phys)

The University Of Sheffield.

Enjoy world-class teaching and learning
Study Electronic & Electrical Engineering

At the University of Sheffield we offer a variety
of BEng and MEng degree programmes covering
the wide spectrum of Electronic and Electrical
Engineering disciplines:

- Electronic Engineering
- Electrical Engineering
- Electrical & Electronic Engineering
- Electronic & Communications Engineering
- Digital Electronics
- Microelectronics
- Electronic & Electrical Engineering with a Modern
  Language
- Foundation Year

Contact us

W: sheffield.ac.uk/eee   E: eee-rec@sheffield.ac.uk   T: 0114 222 5382

All our courses are accredited by
The Institution of Engineering and Technology

The Institution of
Engineering and Technology

Electronic Engineer or Electrical Engineer?

Electronic Engineers are concerned with the design, manufacture and management of the circuits and systems that contribute to almost all areas of our technological lives. Think of laptops, mobile phones and communication satellites.

Electrical Engineers design systems that generate and move power between distances of just a few millimetres up to miles. They need to know how to use the laws governing electromagnetics to convert energy into motion and back. Their products include machines such as rotary electric motors and power transformers.

We will teach you all the theories and tools necessary to prepare you for an exciting career in a profession that touches all areas of human civilisation.

You could be found designing computer chips, lasers, next-generation mobile communication systems, electric vehicles and their navigation systems; writing new and innovative software; building, installing and controlling robots on a production line; performing quality assurance for a bank; advising on the power requirements for a new building or the infrastructure for a wind or solar farm.

EEE graduates are the resource of the future required by forward-facing companies.

As an Electronic and Electrical Engineering graduate from The University of Sheffield you are a highly sought after individual with outstanding career prospects in all aspects of industry and commerce.

Flexibility and Choice

You can tailor your degree to suit your interests. Our flexible course structure means you can transfer from one EEE specialisation to another. For most of our degrees, the first two years offer a common core, giving you a broad educational base in the subject. You can then make an informed decision on your future specialism.

Taught by Experts

You will learn from internationally acclaimed academics in a creative and supportive environment. We work with industry to develop our courses so you acquire the knowledge and skills employers are looking for.

Our courses are very practical and you will get to grips with the sort of challenges that professionals face, exploring your ideas using the latest test facilities.

You will have workshops in our £81m Diamond building, which contains 17 state-of-the-art labs to teach the next generation of engineers in real-world environments.

The world-leading research we are doing feeds directly into your learning, so you understand the very latest innovations in the field of electrical science.

We are home to a number of research centres, including the Rolls-Royce University Technology Centre for Advanced Electrical Machines and Drives, the Sheffield-Siemens Wind Power Research Centre and the EPSRC National Epitaxy Facility.

Year in Industry & Placement Opportunities

Put theory into practice and gain industrial experience as part of your degree course. A Year in Industry will enhance your employment prospects and you will earn while you learn.

Alternatively you can choose to study abroad in one of our partner universities.

For fees information, visit the website below. Scholarships and bursaries are available.

What next?

Book online for a University Open Day: sheffield.ac.uk/undergraduate/opendays
For course content, view the online prospectus at sheffield.ac.uk/undergraduate

UNIVERSITY
of York

Department of Electronic Engineering

☏ 01904 322365   ✉ elec-ug-admissions@york.ac.uk   💻 www.york.ac.uk/electronic-engineering/undergraduate/

The Department of Electronic Engineering at the University of York has been consistently ranked amongst the best electronics departments in the country for its teaching quality and world-leading research in electromagnetic compatibility, biologically-inspired computing, music technology, wireless communications and nanotechnology. Programmes include:

- **Electronic Engineering:** provides a very wide range of knowledge and techniques in modern electronics.
- **Electronic and Communication Engineering:** gives students a strong electronics background with an emphasis on application to communication technologies.
- **Electronic and Computer Engineering:** a Computer Systems Engineering programme combining the use of electronics and computer hardware/software.
- **Music Technology Systems:** focuses on the internal design and function of contemporary music technology systems within an electronic engineering programme.
- **Music Technology Systems with a Foundation Year:** an entry route for students wishing to pursue our Music Technology Systems courses but don't have appropriate qualifications. The foundation year includes music technology work alongside maths, physics, and electronics.
- **Electronic Engineering with Nanotechnology:** gives students a strong electronics background with an emphasis on its application to nanotechnologies.
- **Electronic Engineering with Business Management:** comprises 35 percent business management, 65 percent electronics. It meets the needs of those with ambitions to progress to a management position.
- **Foundation Year:** an entry route for those who do not have relevant qualifications, particularly mature students.

The Department has a wide range of facilities used to support the teaching and research activities. Most of these facilities are also available in collaboration with industry, allowing direct input to project work.

Facilities include: interactive BioWall; Nanotechnology Clean Room; Computing Labs; Electromagnetic Test Facilities; FPGA and ARM-based Development Systems; Audio Recording Studios; Teaching Laboratories for practical work, project work and iPad/iPhone workstations. Also, the Department's Technical Support provide design and construction facilities, including PCB design and manufacture, digital manufacturing technology 3D printing and a surface-mount assembly line.

Studying Nanotechnology and Electronic Engineering

Stories about nanotechnology are commonplace, from current uses in CPU design to very speculative ideas. But what does it mean to study the engineering of nanotechnology?

At the University of York, students study nanotechnology in all 3 or 4 years of an electronic engineering degree. The applications vary widely, but to carry out such engineering it is necessary to acquire the complex fundamental knowledge. This ranges from core electronic engineering through to aspects of physics and chemistry.

The practical skills also required are considerable – at York students are taken into the clean room fabrication facilities from their First Year on. They carry out full fabrication exercises to become familiar with the many stages required to build electronic devices starting with pristine silicon wafers and finishing with devices that can be measured in a normal electronics laboratory or imaged in one of the electron microscopes.

But on top of the fundamentals, there is often surprise due to the range of applications the students may study in their course. Some applications are to core aspects of electronics – improving the performance of processors and memory. The fabrication and use of nano–wires can be studied to improve the speed of such devices. Imaging of nano–devices is challenging, so novel electron sources within electron microscopes can be investigated – perhaps using beams of electrons from carbon nano–tubes to probe the magnetic structure of devices.

Using small (10 nanometre) nano–particles within nano–fluids can give interesting effects. The physical properties of such materials can be controlled by magnetic or electric fields. Students have investigated these fluids in shock absorbers for cars – behaving fluidly or stiffly by applying voltage, giving shock absorbers with smoothly varying properties depending on the driver or the road.

Many potential medical applications exist to extend the major impact electronics has on diagnostics and treatment. Integrated electronic sensors can detect proteins, enzymes and small molecule biomarkers. With nanoelectronic devices, such as single–electron transistors, not only large samples but the properties of individual molecules can be investigated.

The diversity of nanotechnology applications is growing rapidly – what is required to sustain this are good engineering graduates with the knowledge and practical skills to push these forward!

☏ *01904 322365* ✉ *elec-ug-admissions@york.ac.uk* 🖥 *www.york.ac.uk/electronic-engineering/*

Check **Chapter 3** for new university admission details and **Chapter 6** on how to read the subject tables.

Newcastle – AAB incl maths+phys/chem/electron (Electron Comms; Electron Comp Eng; Elec Electron Eng) (IB 35 pts HL 5 maths+phys/chem)

Queen's Belfast – AAB incl maths+sci/tech/fmath (Elec Electron Eng (MEng))

Sheffield – AAB/ABB+bEPQ incl maths+sci/electron (Elec Eng; Electron Eng) (IB 34 pts HL 6 maths+sci/electron); AAB/ABB+bEPQ incl maths+phys/chem/electron (Electron Comms Eng) (IB 34 pts HL 6 maths+phys/chem/electron)

Southampton – AAB incl maths+phys (Elec Eng) (IB 34 pts)

Strathclyde – AAB incl maths+phys +interview (Electron Dig Sys (MEng)) (IB 36 pts HL 6 maths+phys)

Surrey – AAB–ABB incl maths+phys/electron/comp/fmaths (Electron Eng Comp Sys; Electron Eng) (IB 34 pts)

Swansea – AAB–BBB incl maths (Electron Elec Eng) (IB 32 pts)

128 pts **Aberdeen** – ABB incl maths+phys/des tech/eng (Elec Electron Eng (MEng)) (IB 34 pts HL 6 maths+phys)

Aston – ABB–BBB incl maths+physl sci/tech (Electron Eng Comp Sci) (IB 32 pts); ABB–BBB incl maths+phys (Electromech Eng) (IB 32 pts)

Brunel – ABB incl maths+sci/eng (Electron Comp Eng (MEng)) (IB 31 pts HL 6 maths+sci/eng)

City – ABB incl maths+sci 128 pts (Elec Electron Eng) (IB 33 pts HL 6 maths+phys)

Coventry – ABB–BBB incl maths+sci/des tech/electron/eng (Elec Electron Eng) (IB 31 pts)

Heriot-Watt – ABB (3 yr course) BBB (4 yr course) incl maths+phys/tech (Elec Electron Eng) (IB 29 pts); ABB incl maths+phys (3 yr course) BBB incl maths+phys/tech/eng (4 yr course) (Comp Electron) (IB 29 pts)

Kent – ABB incl maths+sci/tech (Electron Comms Eng (MEng)) (IB 34 pts)

Lancaster – ABB incl maths+physl sci (Electron Elec Eng) (IB 32 pts HL 16 pts incl 6 maths+physl sci)

Leicester – ABB/BBB+bEPQ incl maths+physl sci (Electron Elec Eng) (IB 30 pts HL 5 maths+phys)

Liverpool – ABB incl maths+sci/tech (Elec Electron Eng; Elec Eng Electron (Yr Ind)) (IB 33 pts HL 5 maths+phys/electron); (Elec Eng Electron (MEng)) (IB 33 pts HL 5 maths+sci)

London (QM) – ABB incl maths+sci (Elec Electron Eng; Electron Eng Telecomm) (IB 32 pts HL 6/5 maths+sci)

Loughborough – ABB incl maths+sci/tech/fmaths (Electron Comp Sys Eng) (IB 34 pts HL 655 incl maths+sci)

Plymouth – 128 pts incl maths+sci/tech (Elec Electron Eng (MEng)) (IB 32 pts HL 5 maths+sci/tech)

Strathclyde – ABB incl maths+phys+comp +interview (Electron Elec Eng) (IB 32 pts HL 5 maths+phys)

Sussex – ABB–BBB incl maths (Elec Electron Eng) (IB 30 pts HL 5 maths)

York – ABB–AAB incl maths +interview (Electron Eng; Electron Comm Eng; Electron Eng Nanotech) (IB 32–36 pts HL 5/6 maths+phys)

120 pts **Bangor** – 120–136 pts incl maths+phys/elec/electron eng (Electron Eng (MEng))

Dundee – BBB incl maths+phys (Electron Eng; Electron Eng Phys) (IB 30 pts HL 555)

Essex – BBB (Comp Electron) (IB 30 pts); BBB incl maths (Electron Eng) (IB 30 pts HL 5 maths)

Greenwich – 120 pts incl maths/physl sci (Elec Electron Eng)

Huddersfield – BBB incl maths+sci/tech 120 pts (Electron Comm Eng; Electron Eng)

Kent – BBB maths+sci/tech (Electron Comms Eng) (IB 34 pts)

London South Bank – BBB (Elec Electron Eng)

Northumbria – 120–128 pts incl maths+sci/tech/comp sci (Elec Electron Eng) (HL 444)

Plymouth – 120 pts incl maths+sci/tech (Elec Electron Eng) (IB 30 pts HL 4 sci/tech)

Queen's Belfast – BBB incl maths+sci/tech/fmaths (Elec Electron Eng)

Ulster – BBB incl sci/maths/tech/eng (Electron Eng) (IB 26 pts HL 13 pts incl 5 sci+maths)

UWE Bristol – 120 pts incl maths+sci/tech/eng (Electron Eng) (HL 5 maths+sci/tech)

112 pts **Bedfordshire** – 112 pts (Electron Eng)

Birmingham City – BBC incl maths 112 pts (Electron Eng) (IB 24 pts HL 5 maths)

Brighton – BBC–CCC incl maths+physl sci 112–96 pts (Elec Electron Eng) (IB 28 pts HL 5 maths+phys)

Central Lancashire – 112 pts incl maths/phys/STEM (Electron Eng)

De Montfort – 112 pts incl maths/phys (Elec Electron Eng) (IB 26 pts)

Glyndŵr – 112 pts incl maths/phys (Elec Electron Eng)

Hull – 112 pts incl maths (Electron Eng (MEng); Electron Eng) (IB 28 pts HL 5 maths+sci)

Liverpool John Moores – BBC incl maths+sci/tech/eng/fmaths 112 pts (Elec Electron Eng) (IB 26 pts HL 5 maths+phys)

Robert Gordon – BBC incl maths+phys/eng/des tech (Electron Elec Eng (MEng)) (IB 29 pts HL 6/5 maths+phys)

Sheffield Hallam – 112–96 pts incl maths+sci (Elec Electron Eng)

Southampton Solent – 112 pts (Electron Eng)

Staffordshire – BBC/CCC incl maths/phys/eng 112 pts (Elec Electron Eng)

Sunderland – 112 pts incl maths/phys (Electron Elec Eng)

104 pts **Bangor** – 104–96 pts incl maths+phys (Comp Sys Eng); 104–96 pts incl maths+phys/elec/electron eng (Electron Eng)

Chester – BCC–BBB incl maths+phys/chem (Electron Elec Eng) (IB 28 pts HL 5 maths+physl sci)

Hertfordshire – 104 pts incl maths+phys/tech/eng (Electron Comm Eng; Elec Electron Eng) (HL 4 maths+phys)

Manchester Met – BCC–BBC incl maths/fmaths+sci/eng/tech 104–112 pts (Elec Electron Eng) (IB 26 pts HL 5 maths+sci)

Robert Gordon – BCC incl maths+phys/eng/des tech (Electron Elec Eng) (IB 28 pts HL 5 maths+phys)

South Wales – BCC–CDD incl maths+sci/geog 104–80 pts (Elec Electron Eng) (HL 655–445 incl 5 maths+sci/geog); BCC–CDD incl maths/sci/tech 104–80 pts (Ltg Des Tech) (HL 655–445 incl 5 maths/sci/geog)

Wolverhampton – A*A/BCC incl maths+sci/tech (Electron Telecomm Eng (MEng))

96 pts **Chichester** – 96–112 pts incl maths+sci (Electron Elect Eng) (IB 28 pts incl maths+sci)

Derby – 96–112 pts incl sci/maths (Elec Electron Eng)

Edinburgh Napier – CCC incl maths+sci/tech (Electron Elec Eng) (IB 27 pts HL 5 maths+sci/tech)

Teesside – 96–112 pts incl maths+sci/tech/eng (Elec Electron Eng)

88 pts **Glasgow Caledonian** – CCD incl maths+phys (Elec Pwr Eng) (IB 24 pts)

London Met – CCD 88 pts (Electron Comms Eng)

Portsmouth – 88–112 pts incl maths (Electron Eng) (IB 26 pts)

Alternative offers
See **Chapter 6** and **Appendix 1** for grades/UCAS Tariff points information for other examinations.

EXAMPLES OF DEGREE APPRENTICESHIPS IN THIS SUBJECT FIELD
Essex (Electron Eng); London South Bank (Elec Electron Eng; Electron Eng Pwr Electron); UWE Bristol (Electron Comp Eng); Teesside (Elec Electron Eng).

EXAMPLES OF COLLEGES OFFERING COURSES IN THIS SUBJECT FIELD
Banbury and Bicester (Coll); Barking and Dagenham (Coll); Basingstoke (CT); Bedford (Coll); Birmingham Met (Coll); Blackburn (Coll); Blackpool and Fylde (Coll); Bournemouth and Poole (Coll); Bradford (Coll); Canterbury (Coll); Carshalton (Coll); Chesterfield (Coll); Darlington (Coll); Doncaster (Coll); Dudley (Coll); Ealing, Hammersmith and West London (Coll); East Surrey (Coll); Exeter (Coll); Farnborough (CT); Furness (Coll); Gateshead (Coll); Gloucestershire (Coll); Gower Swansea (Coll); Grimsby (Inst Group); Hartlepool (CFE); Havering (Coll); Highbury Portsmouth (Coll); Hopwood Hall (Coll); Hull (Coll); Leeds City (Coll); Lincoln (Coll); Liverpool City (Coll); London City (Coll); London UCK (Coll); Loughborough (Coll); MidKent (Coll); Milton Keynes (Coll); Newcastle (Coll); North Lindsey (Coll); North Notts (Coll); North Warwickshire and Hinckley (Coll); Northbrook Met (Coll); Norwich City

(Coll); Pembrokeshire (Coll); Plymouth City (Coll); St Helens (Coll); Solihull (Coll); Southport (Coll); Stephenson (Coll); Stockport (Coll); Stoke-on-Trent (Coll); Sunderland (Coll); Sussex Coast Hastings (Coll); Tameside (Coll); Tyne Coast (Coll); Uxbridge (Coll); Wakefield (Coll); Warrington and Vale Royal (Coll); Wigan and Leigh (Coll); York (Coll).

OTHER HIGHER EDUCATION COURSES IN THIS FIELD
Nottingham (Coll).

CHOOSING YOUR COURSE (SEE ALSO CH.1)
Universities and colleges teaching quality See www.qaa.ac.uk; https://unistats.ac.uk.

Top research universities and colleges (REF 2014) (Electrical and Electronic Engineering, Metallurgy and Materials) Leeds; London (QM) (Electron Elec Comp Eng); Oxford; Cambridge; Imperial London (Metal Mat); London (UCL); Sheffield (Electron Elec Comp Eng); Southampton.

Examples of sandwich degree courses Aston; Bath; Birmingham City; Brighton; Brunel; Cardiff; Central Lancashire; City; Coventry; Glasgow Caledonian; Greenwich; Hertfordshire; Huddersfield; Kent; Leicester; Liverpool; Liverpool John Moores; London (QM); London (RH); London South Bank; Loughborough; Manchester Met; Northumbria; Portsmouth; Queen's Belfast; Sheffield Hallam; South Wales; Staffordshire; Sunderland; Surrey; Teesside; Ulster; UWE Bristol; Westminster; Wolverhampton; York.

ADMISSIONS INFORMATION
Number of applicants per place (approx) Aston 6; Bangor 7; Bath 8; Birmingham 10; Birmingham City 11; Bradford (Elec Electron Eng) 8; Bristol 10; Cardiff 7; Central Lancashire 4; City 3; Derby 5; Dundee 9; Edinburgh Napier 7; Greenwich 10; Heriot-Watt 7; Hertfordshire 7; Huddersfield 3; Hull 5; Lancaster 7; Leeds 15; Leicester 8; Liverpool John Moores 2; London (UCL) 7; London South Bank 5; Manchester Met 5; Newcastle 3; Nottingham 14; Plymouth 22; Robert Gordon 3; Sheffield 6; Sheffield Hallam 2; South Wales 2; Southampton 8; Staffordshire 7; Strathclyde 7; Sunderland 6; Swansea 3; Teesside 4; Warwick 8; Westminster 5; York 5.

Advice to applicants and planning the UCAS personal statement Applicants should show enthusiasm for the subject, for example, through career ambitions, hobbies, work experience, attendance at appropriate events, competitions, etc, and evidence of good ability in mathematics and a scientific mind. Applicants should also show that they can think creatively and have the motivation to succeed on a demanding course. See also **Engineering/Engineering Sciences** and **Appendix 3**. **Bristol** Deferred entry accepted.

Selection interviews Yes Cambridge, Imperial London, Manchester, Oxford, Strathclyde; **Some** Bath, Cardiff, Leicester; **No** Aston, Bangor, Birmingham, Brighton, Bristol, Brunel, Central Lancashire, Derby, Dundee, Essex, Heriot-Watt, Hertfordshire, Huddersfield, Hull, Kent, Liverpool, Liverpool John Moores, London (UCL), Loughborough, Newcastle, Nottingham, Plymouth, Portsmouth, Southampton, Staffordshire, Sunderland, Surrey, UWE Bristol, Westminster.

Interview advice and questions Past questions have included: How does a combustion engine work? How does a trumpet work? What type of position do you hope to reach in five to 10 years' time? Could you sack an employee? What was your last physics practical? What did you learn from it? What are the methods of transmitting information from a moving object to a stationary observer? Wire bending exercise – you are provided with an accurate diagram of a shape that could be produced by bending a length of wire in a particular way. You are supplied with a pair of pliers and the exact length of wire required and you are given 10 minutes to reproduce as accurately as possible the shape drawn. A three-minute talk has to be given on one of six subjects (topics given several weeks before the interview), such as 'The best is the enemy of the good'. Is there a lesson here for British industry? 'I was asked to take my physics file and discuss some of my conclusions in certain experiments.' Explain power transmission through the National Grid. How would you explain power transmission to a friend who hasn't done physics? See also **Chapter 5**. **York** Technical questions asked.

Reasons for rejection (non-academic) Poor English. Inability to communicate. Frightened of technology or mathematics. Poor motivation and work ethic. Better suited to a less specialised engineering/science course. See also **Engineering/Engineering Sciences**.

AFTER-RESULTS ADVICE
Offers to applicants repeating A-levels Higher Brighton, Central Lancashire, Greenwich, Huddersfield, Newcastle, Queen's Belfast, Strathclyde, Warwick; **Possibly higher** Aston, City, Hertfordshire, London Met, Sheffield; **Same** Bangor, Bath, Birmingham, Cardiff, Coventry, Derby, Dundee, Hull, Leeds, Liverpool, Liverpool John Moores, London South Bank, Loughborough, Northumbria, Nottingham, Robert Gordon, Southampton, Staffordshire, Wolverhampton, York; **No** Cambridge, Glasgow.

GRADUATE DESTINATIONS AND EMPLOYMENT (2015/16 HESA)
Graduates surveyed 2,955 **Employed** 1,825 **In voluntary employment** 55 **In further study** 585 **Assumed unemployed** 200

Career note Electrical and electronic engineering is divided into two main fields – heavy current (electrical machinery, distribution systems, generating stations) and light current (computers, control engineering, telecommunications). Opportunities exist with many commercial organisations.

OTHER DEGREE SUBJECTS FOR CONSIDERATION
Computer Science; Engineering (Aeronautical, Communications, Computer, Control); Mathematics; Physics.

ENGINEERING (MANUFACTURING AND PRODUCTION)
(see also **Engineering/Engineering Sciences**)

Manufacturing engineering is sometimes referred to as production engineering. It is a branch of the subject concerned with management aspects of engineering such as industrial organisation, purchasing, and the planning and control of operations. Manufacturing Engineering courses are therefore geared to providing the student with a broad-based portfolio of knowledge in both the technical and business areas. Mechanical, product and design engineers develop systems and production processes relating to the overall progress and management of a product from its design to its final completion, including the materials used, the efficiency of the production line and development costs. For those students from an artistic background who wish to combine their design skills with the technical aspects of engineering, the BA Industrial Design and Technology course at Brunel University London is ideal. This course is taught by a cross-disciplinary team including mechanical and electrical engineers, practical designers and psychologists, and students are expected to discuss solutions to design problems. As in all Engineering courses, those offering industrial placements through sandwich courses provide many financial benefits (see **Chapter 1**).

Engineering Council statement See **Engineering/Engineering Sciences**.

Useful websites www.engc.org.uk; www.imeche.org; www.theiet.org; http://semta.org.uk

NB The points totals shown to the left of the institutions are for ease of reference only. It must not be assumed that Tariff points are always used by institutions or that they can be substituted for an offer in grades. The level of an offer is not necessarily indicative of the quality of a course.

COURSE OFFERS INFORMATION
Subject requirements/preferences See **Engineering/Engineering Sciences**. Offers shown below refer to BEng or BSc courses unless otherwise stated; BSc only appears as an abbreviation if the course is offered at the same institution as a BEng with different requirements.

Your target offers and examples of degree courses

160 pts **Cambridge** – A*A*A +interview +ENGAA (Eng (Manuf Eng)) (IB 40–42 pts HL 776)

152 pts **Bath** – A*AA/AAA+aEPQ incl maths+phys (Mech Eng Manuf Mgt (MEng)) (IB 36 pts HL 6 maths+phys)

Nottingham – A*AA–AAA incl maths (Manuf Eng (MEng)) (IB 38–36 pts)

144 pts **Glasgow** – AAA incl maths+phys (Prod Des Eng (MEng)) (IB 38–36 pts HL 666 incl maths+phys)

Newcastle – AAA incl maths+chem/phys/fmaths (Mech Des Manuf Eng (MEng)) (IB 37 pts HL 6 maths+phys/chem)

Warwick – AAA incl maths+phys (Manuf Mech Eng) (IB 38 pts HL 6 maths+phys)

136 pts **Liverpool** – AAB/ABB+aEPQ incl maths+sci/des tech (Ind Des (MEng)) (IB 35 pts HL 5 maths+phys)

Strathclyde – AAB incl maths+phys (4 yr course) BBB (5 yr course) (Prod Des Eng (MEng)) (IB 26 pts HL 5 maths+phys)

128 pts **Aston** – ABB–BBB incl sci/tech (Prod Des Mgt) (IB 32 pts)

Brunel – ABB incl art/des/tech+maths/phys +interview +portfolio (Ind Des Tech) (IB 31 pts HL 5 art/des/tech+maths/phys)

Liverpool – ABB/BBB+aEPQ incl maths+sci/des tech (Ind Des) (IB 33 pts HL 5 maths+phys)

Loughborough – ABB incl maths+phys/des/eng (Manuf Eng) (IB 34 pts HL 655)

Strathclyde – ABB (Prod Des Eng) (IB 34 HL 5 maths+phys)

112 pts **Liverpool John Moores** – BBC 112 pts incl des tech/maths/eng/chem/phys (Prod Des Eng) (IB 26 pts)

Southampton Solent – 112 pts (Eng Des Manuf)

Trinity Saint David – 112 pts incl maths/phys (Mech Manuf Eng)

104 pts **South Wales** – BCC–CDD incl maths+sci 104–80 pts (Mech Eng) (HL 655–445 incl 5 maths+sci/geog)

96 pts **Chichester** – 96–112 pts incl maths+sci (Prod Des Innov; Prod Des Innov (MEng)) (IB 28 pts incl maths+sci)

Derby – 96–112 pts (Manuf Prod Eng)

Harper Adams – CCC–BBB 96–120 pts +interview (Prod Sppt Eng)

80 pts **Portsmouth** – 80–96 pts incl maths (Mech Manuf Eng) (IB 26 pts)

Alternative offers
See **Chapter 6** and **Appendix 1** for grades/UCAS Tariff points information for other examinations.

EXAMPLES OF DEGREE APPRENTICESHIPS IN THIS SUBJECT FIELD
Liverpool John Moores (Manuf Sys Eng).

EXAMPLES OF COLLEGES OFFERING COURSES IN THIS SUBJECT FIELD
Basingstoke (CT); Birmingham Met (Coll); Blackpool and Fylde (Coll); Bristol City (Coll); Central Bedfordshire (Coll); City and Islington (Coll); Darlington (Coll); Doncaster (Coll); Dudley (Coll); Exeter (Coll); Farnborough (CT); Hartlepool (CFE); Leeds City (Coll); Newcastle (Coll); North Warwickshire and Hinckley (Coll); Petroc; Solihull (Coll); Sunderland (Coll); Tyne Coast (Coll); Warwickshire (Coll); Weymouth (Coll); Wigan and Leigh (Coll).

OTHER HIGHER EDUCATION COURSES IN THIS FIELD
Nottingham (Coll).

CHOOSING YOUR COURSE (SEE ALSO CH.1)
Universities and colleges teaching quality See www.qaa.ac.uk; https://unistats.ac.uk.

Top research universities and colleges (REF 2014) See **Engineering (Aeronautical and Aerospace)**.

Examples of sandwich degree courses Aston; Bath; Brunel; Loughborough.

ADMISSIONS INFORMATION

Number of applicants per place (approx) Aston 6; Bath 10; Nottingham 6; Strathclyde 8; Warwick 8.

Advice to applicants and planning the UCAS personal statement Work experience or work shadowing in industry should be mentioned. See **Engineering/Engineering Sciences** and **Appendix 3**.

Selection interviews Yes Cambridge, Loughborough; **No** Nottingham, Strathclyde.

Interview advice and questions Past questions include: What is the function of an engineer? Describe something interesting you have recently done in your A-levels. What do you know about careers in manufacturing engineering? Discuss the role of women engineers in industry. Why is a disc brake better than a drum brake? Would you be prepared to make people redundant to improve the efficiency of a production line? See also **Chapter 5**.

Reasons for rejection (non-academic) Mature students failing to attend interview are rejected. One applicant produced a forged reference and was immediately rejected. See also **Engineering/ Engineering Sciences**.

AFTER-RESULTS ADVICE

Offers to applicants repeating A-levels Higher Strathclyde; **Same** Cambridge, Loughborough, Nottingham.

GRADUATE DESTINATIONS AND EMPLOYMENT (2015/16 HESA)

Production and Manufacturing Engineering graduates surveyed 620 **Employed** 435 **In voluntary employment** 10 **In further study** 85 **Assumed unemployed** 30

Career note Graduates with experience in both technical and business skills have the flexibility to enter careers in technology or business management.

OTHER DEGREE SUBJECTS FOR CONSIDERATION

Business Studies; Computer Science; Engineering (Electrical, Mechanical); Physics; Technology.

ENGINEERING (MECHANICAL)

(including **Automotive Engineering**, **Mechatronics** and **Motorsport Engineering**)

Mechanical engineering is one of the most wide-ranging engineering disciplines. All courses involve the design, installation and maintenance of equipment used in industry. Whilst Automotive Engineering deals with all forms of transport, specialisms are also offered in Motorsport Engineering at several universities, in Transport Product Design at Aston University and in Mining Engineering at the University of Exeter. Several universities include a range of Engineering courses with a common first year allowing students to specialise from Year 2. Agricultural Engineering involves all aspects of off-road vehicle design and maintenance of other machinery used in agriculture.

Engineering Council statement: See **Engineering/Engineering Sciences**.

Useful websites www.imeche.org; www.engc.org.uk; http://iagre.org

NB The points totals shown to the left of the institutions are for ease of reference only. It must not be assumed that Tariff points are always used by institutions or that they can be substituted for an offer in grades. The level of an offer is not necessarily indicative of the quality of a course.

COURSE OFFERS INFORMATION

Subject requirements/preferences See **Engineering/Engineering Sciences**. Offers shown below refer to BEng or BSc courses unless otherwise stated; BSc only appears as an abbreviation if the course is offered at the same institution as a BEng with different requirements.

Your target offers and examples of degree courses

160 pts **Cambridge** – A*A*A incl maths+sci +interview +ENGAA (Eng (Mech Eng) (MEng)) (IB 40–42 pts HL 776)

Imperial London – A*A*A incl maths+phys+sci/tech/econ +interview (Mech Eng (MEng)) (IB 40 pts HL 666)

Oxford – A*A*A incl maths+phys +interview +PAT (Mech Eng) (IB 40 pts HL 776)

152 pts **Bath** – A*AA–AAA+aEPQ incl maths+phys (Mech Auto Eng (MEng); Mech Eng (MEng)) (IB 36 pts HL 766)

Bristol – A*AA–AAB incl maths+phys (Mech Eng) (IB 38–36 pts HL 6 maths+phys)

Leeds – A*AA incl maths+phys +interview (Mech Eng; Auto Eng) (IB 36 pts HL 18 pts incl 6 maths+phys)

London (UCL) – A*AA–AAA incl maths+phys (Eng (Mech) (MEng)) (IB 39–38 pts HL 6 maths+phys); A*AA–AAA incl maths (Eng (Mech Bus Fin) (MEng)) (IB 39–38 pts HL 6 maths)

Loughborough – A*AA incl maths+phys +interview (Mech Eng (MEng); Auto Eng (MEng)) (IB 38 pts HL 776 incl maths+phys)

Nottingham – A*AA–AAA incl maths (Mech Eng (MEng)) (IB 38–36 pts)

Southampton – A*AA incl maths+phys (Mech Eng (Eng Mgt) (MEng)) (IB 38 pts HL 6 maths+phys); A*AA–A*AB+aEPQ incl maths+phys (Mech Eng (Advnc Mat) (MEng); Mech Eng (Mecha) (MEng); Mech Eng (Nvl Eng) (MEng); Mech Eng (Sust Ener Sys) (MEng); Mech Eng; Mech Eng (Biomed Eng) (MEng); Mech Eng (Auto) (MEng)) (IB 38 pts HL 6 maths+phys); A*AA/A*AB+aEPQ incl maths/phys (Mech Eng (Aerosp) (MEng)) (IB 38 pts HL 6 maths+phys)

144 pts **Aston** – AAA–AAB incl maths+phys (Mech Eng (MEng)) (IB 34 pts HL 6 maths+phys)

Bath – AAA–AAB+aEPQ incl maths+phys (Integ Mech Elec Eng) (IB 36 pts HL 666)

Birmingham – AAA incl maths (Mech Eng (MEng)) (IB 32 pts HL 666)

Brunel – AAA incl maths+phys (Mech Eng (MEng)) (IB 34 pts HL 6 maths+phys)

Cardiff – AAA–ABB incl maths (Mech Eng) (IB 36–32 pts HL 5 maths+sci)

City – AAA incl maths+sci 144 pts (Mech Eng (MEng)) (IB 35 pts HL 6 maths+sci)

Edinburgh – AAA incl maths+phys/eng/des tech (Mech Eng; Elec Mech Eng) (IB 37 pts HL 666)

Exeter – AAA–AAB (Mech Eng (MEng) (Yr Ind)) (IB 36–32 pts); AAA–ABB incl sci+maths (Mech Eng (MEng); Mech Eng) (IB 36–32 pts HL 5 sci+maths)

Lancaster – AAA incl maths+physl sci (Mech Eng (MEng)) (IB 36 pts HL 16 pts)

Leeds – AAA incl maths +interview (Mecha Robot) (IB 35 pts HL 18 pts incl 5 maths)

Liverpool – AAA incl maths+sci (Mech Eng (MEng)) (IB 35 pts HL 5 maths+phys)

London (QM) – AAA incl maths+phys/chem (Mech Eng (MEng)) (IB 36 pts HL 6/5 maths+phys/chem)

London (UCL) – AAA–AAB incl maths (Eng (Mech Bus Fin)) (IB 38–36 pts HL 5 maths+phys)

Manchester – AAA incl maths+phys (Mech Eng (MEng)) (IB 37 pts HL 6 maths+phys)

Newcastle – AAA incl maths+chem/phys/fmaths (Mech Low Carbon Trans Eng (MEng)) (IB 37 pts HL 6 maths+chem/phys)

Sheffield – AAA incl maths+phys/chem (Mech Eng; Mech Eng (MEng); Mech Eng Fr/Ger/Ital (MEng)) (IB 36 pts HL 6 maths+phys/chem)

Strathclyde – AAA (3 yr course) ABB (4 yr course) (Mech Eng) (IB 32 pts HL 5 maths+phys)

Surrey – AAA incl maths+phys (Auto Eng (MEng)) (IB 34 pts); AAA–AAB incl maths+phys (Mech Eng) (IB 36–35 pts)

Warwick – AAA incl maths+phys (Auto Eng; Manuf Mech Eng; Mech Eng) (IB 38 pts HL 6 maths+phys)

136 pts **Birmingham** – AAB incl maths (Mech Eng; Mech Eng (Auto)) (IB 32 pts HL 665)

Coventry – AAB–BBB incl maths+sci/tech/eng (Mtrspo Eng) (IB 31 pts)

Dyson – AAB incl A maths+sci/tech (Eng Tech)

Exeter – AAB–BBB incl phys/chem+sci (Min Eng) (IB 34–30 pts HL 5 phys/chem/maths+sci)

Glasgow – AAB–BBB incl maths+phys (Mech Eng; Mech Des Eng; Mech Eng Aero) (IB 36–34 pts HL 665)

Glasgow (SA) – AAB incl maths+phys (Prod Des Eng) (IB 36–34 pts HL 5 maths+phys)

Huddersfield – AAB incl maths+sci/tech 136 pts (Mech Eng (MEng); Auto Mtrspo Eng (MEng))

Lancaster – AAB incl maths+physl sci (Mech Eng) (IB 35 pts HL16 pts incl 6 maths+physl sci)

Leicester – AAB incl maths+physl sci (Mech Eng (MEng)) (IB 32 pts HL 6/5 maths+phys)

London (QM) – AAB incl math+phys/chem (Mech Eng) (IB 34 pts HL 665)

Loughborough – AAB incl maths+phys (Mech Eng) (IB 35 pts HL 655)

Manchester – AAB incl maths+phys (Mech Eng Mgt; Mech Eng) (IB 35 pts HL 6 maths+phys); AAB incl maths+phys/electron/fmaths +interview (Mecha Eng) (IB 34 pts HL 6 maths+phys)

Newcastle – AAB–ABB incl maths+phys/chem/fmaths (Mech Eng) (IB 35–34 pts HL 5 maths+phys/chem)

Nottingham – AAB incl maths (Mech Eng) (IB 34 pts)

Queen's Belfast – AAB incl maths+sci/fmaths (Mech Eng (MEng))

Surrey – AAB incl maths+phys (Auto Eng) (IB 34 pts)

Swansea – AAB–BBB incl maths (Mech Eng) (IB 32 pts)

Ulster – AAB incl maths+sci/tech/eng (Mech Eng (MEng)) (IB 28 pts HL 14 pts incl 6 maths 5 sci)

128 pts **Aberdeen** – ABB incl maths+phys/des tech/eng (Mech Eng Bus Mgt (MEng)) (IB 34 pts HL 6 maths+phys)

Aston – ABB–BBB incl maths+phys (Mech Eng) (IB 32 pts); ABB–BBB incl sci/tech (Trans Prod Des) (IB 32 pts)

City – ABB 128 pts (Mech Eng) (IB 33 pts HL 6 maths+phys)

Coventry – ABB–BBB incl maths+sci/tech/eng (Mech Eng) (IB 31 pts)

Heriot-Watt – ABB (3 yr course) BBB (4 yr course) incl maths+phys/tech/eng (Mech Eng Ener Eng; Mech Eng) (IB 30 pts)

Leicester – ABB incl maths+physl sci (Mech Eng) (IB 30 pts HL 5 maths+phys)

Liverpool – ABB incl maths+sci/tech (Mecha Robot Sys (MEng)) (IB 33 pts HL 5 maths+sci); ABB incl maths+sci (Mech Eng) (IB 33 pts HL 5 maths+phys)

Liverpool John Moores – ABB incl maths+sci/tech/eng 128 pts (Mech Mar Eng (MEng)) (IB 27 pts HL 6 maths+phys); ABB 128 pts (Mech Eng (MEng)) (IB 27 pts HL 6 maths+phys)

Loughborough – ABB incl maths+phys +interview (Auto Eng) (IB 34 pts HL 655 incl 6 maths+phys)

Oxford Brookes – ABB incl maths+phys 128 pts (Mech Eng (MEng)) (IB 33 pts HL 5 maths+phys)

Sheffield Hallam – 128–112 pts incl maths+sci (Mech Eng (MEng))

Sussex – ABB–BBB incl maths (Auto Eng; Mech Eng) (IB 30 pts HL 5 maths)

120 pts **Aberdeen** – BBB incl maths+phys/des tech/eng (Eng (Mech); Eng (Mech Oil Gas St)) (IB 32 pts HL 5 maths+phys)

Brighton – BBB–BCC incl maths+physl sci 120–104 pts (Auto Eng (MEng)) (IB 30 pts HL 5 maths+phys)

Brunel – BBB incl maths+phys (Mech Eng) (IB 30 pts HL 5 maths 5 phys)

Dundee – BBB incl maths+sci/eng (Mech Eng) (IB 30 pts HL 555)

Greenwich – 120 pts incl maths/physl sci (Mech Eng)

Huddersfield – BBB incl maths+sci/tech 120 pts (Mech Eng; Auto Mtrspo Eng)

London South Bank – BBB incl maths+physl sci (Mech Eng)

Northumbria – 120–128 pts incl maths+sci/tech (Mech Eng; Mech Auto Eng) (HL 444)

Oxford Brookes – BBB incl maths+phys 120 pts (Auto Eng; Mech Eng; Mtrspo Eng) (IB 30 pts HL 5 maths+phys)

Portsmouth – 120–144 pts incl maths (Mech Eng (MEng)) (IB 27 pts HL 6 maths)

Queen's Belfast – BBB incl maths+sci/tech/fmaths (Mech Eng)

Robert Gordon – BBB incl maths+phys/eng/des tech (Mech Eng (MEng); Mech Elec Eng (MEng)) (IB 30 pts HL 6/5 maths+phys)

Salford – 120–128 pts incl maths+chem/phys/des tech (Mech Eng (MEng)) (IB 32 pts HL 6 maths+phys)

Ulster – BBB incl maths+sci/tech/eng (Mech Eng) (IB 26 pts HL 13 pts incl 5 maths+sci)

UWE Bristol – 120 pts incl maths+sci/des/tech/eng (Mech Eng; Auto Eng) (HL 5 maths)

112 pts **Birmingham City** – BBC incl maths 112 pts (Mech Eng; Auto Eng) (IB 30 pts HL 5 maths)

Bradford – BBC incl maths 112 pts (Mech Eng)

Brighton – BBC–CCC incl maths+physl sci 112–96 pts (Auto Eng; Mech Eng) (IB 28 pts HL 5 maths+phys)

Central Lancashire – 112 pts incl maths+phys/STEM (Mtrspo Eng)

De Montfort – 112 pts incl maths/phys (Mech Eng; Mecha) (IB 26 pts)

Derby – 112 pts incl maths+phys/des tech +interview (Mtrspo Eng)

Glyndŵr – 112 pts incl maths/phys (Aero Mech Eng)

Hull – 112 pts (Mech Eng (MEng); Mech Eng) (IB 28 pts HL 5 maths); 112 pts incl maths (Mech Med Eng (MEng); Mech Med Eng) (IB 28 pts HL 5 maths)

Kingston – 112 pts incl maths+sci (Mech Eng; Auto Eng)

Liverpool John Moores – BBC incl maths+phys/eng/tech 112 pts (Mech Mar Eng) (IB 26 pts HL 5 maths+phys); BBC incl maths+sci/tech/eng 112 pts (Mech Eng) (IB 26 pts HL 5 maths+phys)

Oxford Brookes – BBC 112 pts (Mech Eng (BSc)) (IB 30 pts)

Plymouth – 112–120 pts incl maths+sci/tech (Mech Eng; Mech Eng Cmpstes) (IB 30 pts HL 5 maths 4 sci/tech)

Robert Gordon – BBC incl maths+phys/eng/des tech (Mech Off Eng; Mech Eng; Mech Elec Eng) (IB 29 pts HL 6/5 maths+phys)

Sheffield Hallam – 112–96 pts incl maths+sci/eng/tech (Auto Eng); 112–96 pts incl maths+sci (Mech Eng)

Southampton Solent – 112 pts (Eng Des Manuf)

Staffordshire – BBC/CCC incl maths/phys/eng 112 pts (Mtrspo Tech; Auto Eng; Mecha; Mech Eng)

Sunderland – 112 pts incl maths/phys (Auto Eng; Mech Eng)

Trinity Saint David – 112 pts incl maths/phys (Auto Eng; Mech Eng; Mtrcycl Eng; Mtrspo Eng)

104 pts **Anglia Ruskin** – 104 pts incl maths (Mech Eng) (IB 24 pts)

Bolton – 104 pts incl maths+phys (Mech Eng)

Hertfordshire – 104 pts incl maths+phys/tech/eng (Auto Eng; Mech Eng; Auto Eng Mtrspo) (HL 4 maths+phys)

Lincoln – BCC incl maths (Mech Eng) (IB 28 pts HL 5 maths)

Manchester Met – BCC–BBC incl maths/fmaths+sci/eng/tech 104–112 pts (Mech Eng) (IB 26 pts HL 5 maths+sci)

Portsmouth – 104–120 pts incl maths (Mech Eng) (IB 26 pts HL 5 maths)

South Wales – BCC–CDD incl maths+sci 104–80 pts (Mech Eng) (HL 655–445 incl 5 maths+sci/geog)

96 pts **Bolton** – 96 pts incl maths (Auto Perf Eng (Mtrspo); Mtrspo Tech)

Chichester – 96–112 pts incl maths+sci (Mech Eng Mat) (IB 28 pts incl maths+sci)

Derby – 96 pts incl maths+phys/des tech +interview (Mtrspo Mtrcycl Manuf Eng); 96–112 pts incl maths+phys/des tech (Mech Eng)

Edinburgh Napier – CCC incl maths+sci/tech (Mech Eng) (IB 27 pts HL 654)

Teesside – 96–112 pts incl maths/phys (Mech Eng)

88 pts **Glasgow Caledonian** – CCD incl maths+phys (Comp Aid Mech Eng; Mech Sys Eng) (IB 24 pts)

West Scotland – CCD incl maths+sci (Mech Eng) (IB 24 pts)

80 pts **Portsmouth** – 80–96 pts incl maths (Mech Manuf Eng) (IB 26 pts)

Wolverhampton – BB/CDD incl maths+sci/tech (Auto Eng; Mech Eng)

Alternative offers

See **Chapter 6** and **Appendix 1** for grades/UCAS Tariff points information for other examinations.

UCAS points Tariff: A* = 56 pts; A = 48 pts; B = 40 pts; C = 32 pts; D = 24 pts; E = 16 pts

EXAMPLES OF DEGREE APPRENTICESHIPS IN THIS SUBJECT FIELD
London South Bank (Mech Eng).

EXAMPLES OF COLLEGES OFFERING COURSES IN THIS SUBJECT FIELD
Banbury and Bicester (Coll); Barking and Dagenham (Coll); Barnet and Southgate (Coll); Basingstoke (CT); Bath (Coll); Bedford (Coll); Blackburn (Coll); Blackpool and Fylde (Coll); Bradford (Coll); Bridgwater and Taunton (Coll); Canterbury (Coll); Chesterfield (Coll); Cornwall (Coll); Darlington (Coll); Doncaster (Coll); Dudley (Coll); East Surrey (Coll); Exeter (Coll); Farnborough (CT); Furness (Coll); Gateshead (Coll); Gloucestershire (Coll); Gower Swansea (Coll); Grimsby (Inst Group); Hartlepool (CFE); Highbury Portsmouth (Coll); Lincoln (Coll); Loughborough (Coll); MidKent (Coll); Newcastle (Coll); North Lindsey (Coll); North Warwickshire and Hinckley (Coll); Northbrook Met (Coll); Norwich City (Coll); Pembrokeshire (Coll); Petroc; Plymouth City (Coll); South Devon (Coll); South Gloucestershire and Stroud (Coll); Southampton City (Coll); Southport (Coll); Stephenson (Coll); Sussex Coast Hastings (Coll); Tameside (Coll); Tyne Coast (Coll); Uxbridge (Coll); Wakefield (Coll); Wigan and Leigh (Coll); Wiltshire (Coll); Wirral Met (Coll); Yeovil (Coll).

CHOOSING YOUR COURSE (SEE ALSO CH.1)
Universities and colleges teaching quality See www.qaa.ac.uk; https://unistats.ac.uk.

Top research universities and colleges (REF 2014) See **Engineering (Aeronautical and Aerospace)**.

Examples of sandwich degree courses Aston; Bath; Birmingham City; Bradford; Brighton; Cardiff; Central Lancashire; City; Coventry; De Montfort; Glasgow Caledonian; Harper Adams; Hertfordshire; Huddersfield; Kingston; Leicester; Liverpool John Moores; London South Bank; Loughborough; Manchester Met; Northumbria; Oxford Brookes; Portsmouth; Queen's Belfast; Salford; Sheffield Hallam; South Wales; Staffordshire; Sunderland; Surrey; Teesside; Ulster; UWE Bristol; West Scotland; Wolverhampton.

ADMISSIONS INFORMATION
Number of applicants per place (approx) Aston 8; Bath 10; Birmingham 9; Bradford 4; Bristol 9; Cardiff 8; City 11; Dundee 9; Heriot-Watt 10; Hertfordshire 10; Huddersfield 1; Hull 5; Kingston 8; Lancaster 8; Leeds 15; Leicester 8; Liverpool John Moores 2; London (QM) 6; London (UCL) 10; London South Bank 4; Manchester Met 6, (Mech Eng) 6; Newcastle 4; Nottingham 7; Plymouth 12; Sheffield 7; South Wales 6; Southampton 9; Staffordshire 6; Strathclyde 6; Teesside 7; Warwick 8.

Advice to applicants and planning the UCAS personal statement Work experience. Hands-on skills. An interest in solving mathematical problems related to physical concepts. Enjoyment in designing mechanical devices or components. Interest in engines, structures, dynamics or fluid flow and efficient use of materials or energy. Apply to the Year in Industry Scheme (www.etrust.org.uk) for placement. Scholarships are available to supplement the scheme. See **Engineering/Engineering Sciences** and **Appendix 3**.

Selection interviews Yes Cambridge, Harper Adams, Imperial London, Loughborough, Oxford; **Some** Blackpool and Fylde (Coll), Cardiff, Leicester; **No** Aston, Birmingham, Bolton, Bradford, Brighton, Bristol, Dundee, Hertfordshire, Huddersfield, Kingston, Leeds, Liverpool, Liverpool John Moores, London (QM), Manchester Met, Newcastle, Nottingham, Sheffield, Sheffield Hallam, Staffordshire, Strathclyde, Sunderland, Surrey.

Interview advice and questions Past questions include: What mechanical objects have you examined and/or tried to repair? How do you see yourself in five years' time? What do you imagine you would be doing (production, management or design engineering)? What engineering interests do you have? What qualities are required to become a successful mechanical engineer? Do you like sixth-form work? Describe the working of parts on an engineering drawing. How does a fridge work? What is design in the context of mechanical engineering? What has been your greatest achievement to date? What are your career plans? See also **Engineering/Engineering Sciences** and **Chapter 5**.

Check **Chapter 3** for new university admission details and **Chapter 6** on how to read the subject tables.

Reasons for rejection (non-academic) See **Engineering/Engineering Sciences**.

AFTER-RESULTS ADVICE

Offers to applicants repeating A-levels Higher Brighton, Kingston, Newcastle, Queen's Belfast, Swansea, Warwick; **Possibly higher** City, Huddersfield; **Same** Aston, Bath, Bradford, Bristol, Coventry, Derby, Dundee, Edinburgh Napier, Harper Adams, Heriot-Watt, Leeds (usually), Lincoln, Liverpool, Liverpool John Moores, London South Bank, Loughborough, Manchester Met, Northumbria, Nottingham, Oxford Brookes, Sheffield, Sheffield Hallam, Southampton, Staffordshire, Sunderland, Teesside, Wolverhampton; **No** Cambridge.

GRADUATE DESTINATIONS AND EMPLOYMENT (2015/16 HESA)

Graduates surveyed 4,340 **Employed** 2,770 **In voluntary employment** 65 **In further study** 800 **Assumed unemployed** 305

Career note Mechanical Engineering graduates have a wide choice of career options. Apart from design and development of plant and machinery, they are also likely to be involved in production processes and working at various levels of management. Mechanical engineers share interests such as structures and stress analysis with civil and aeronautical engineers, and electronics and computing with electrical and software engineers.

OTHER DEGREE SUBJECTS FOR CONSIDERATION

Engineering (Aeronautical/Aerospace, Building, Computer (Control, Software and Systems), Electrical/Electronic, Manufacturing, Marine); Materials Science; Mathematics; Physics; Product Design; Technologies.

ENGINEERING (MEDICAL)

(including **Biomedical Engineering, Mechanical and Medical Engineering** and **Medical Physics**; see also **Biotechnology**)

Biomedical engineering lies at the interface between engineering, mathematics, physics, chemistry, biology and clinical practice. This makes it a branch of engineering that has the most direct effect on human health. It is a rapidly expanding interdisciplinary field that applies engineering principles and technology to medical and biological problems. Biomedical engineers work in fields as diverse as neurotechnology, fluid mechanics of the blood and respiratory systems, bone and joint biomechanics, biosensors, medical imaging, synthetic biology and biomaterials. These can lead to the creation of novel devices such as joint replacements and heart valves, new surgical instruments, rehabilitation protocols and even prosthetic limbs.

Useful websites www.assclinsci.org; www.ipem.ac.uk; www.healthcareers.nhs.uk

NB The points totals shown to the left of the institutions are for ease of reference only. It must not be assumed that Tariff points are always used by institutions or that they can be substituted for an offer in grades. The level of an offer is not necessarily indicative of the quality of a course.

COURSE OFFERS INFORMATION

Subject requirements/preferences GCSE/AL Subjects taken from mathematics, physics, chemistry and biology. Offers shown below refer to BEng or BSc courses unless otherwise stated; BSc only appears as an abbreviation if the course is offered at the same institution as a BEng with different requirements.

Your target offers and examples of degree courses
152 pts Imperial London – A*AA–A*A*A incl maths+phys+fmaths/chem/biol (Biomed Eng (MEng))
(IB 38–40 pts HL 666 incl maths+phys)
Leeds – A*AA incl maths+phys/sci +interview (Med Eng (MEng); Med Eng) (IB 36 pts
HL 18 pts incl 6 maths+phys)

144 pts **Cardiff** – AAA–ABB incl maths (Med Eng) (IB 36–32 pts HL 5 maths+sci)
Glasgow – AAA incl maths+phys (Biomed Eng (MEng)) (IB 38–36 pts HL 666)
London (QM) – AAA incl maths+phys/chem (Biomed Eng (MEng)) (IB 36 pts HL 665 incl maths+phys/chem)
London (UCL) – AAA–AAB incl maths+phys (Med Phys (MSci)) (IB 38–36 pts HL 5 maths+phys)
Manchester – AAA–ABB incl sci/maths +interview (Biomed Sci) (IB 37–32 pts HL 5/6 sci)
Sheffield – AAA incl maths+sci (Bioeng (MEng)) (IB 36 pts HL 6 maths+sci)
Surrey – AAA incl maths+phys (Biomed Eng (MEng)) (IB 34 pts)
Swansea – AAA–AAB incl maths (Med Eng (MEng)) (IB 34–33 pts)

136 pts **Dundee** – AAB–ABB (Biomed Eng) (IB 30 pts)
Glasgow – AAB–BBB incl maths+phys (Biomed Eng) (IB 36–34 pts HL 665)
London (King's) – AAB incl maths+phys (Biomed Eng) (IB 35 pts HL 665)
London (QM) – AAB incl maths+phys/chem (Biomed Eng) (IB 34 pts HL 665)
Queen's Belfast – AAB incl maths+phys (Phys Med Apps (MSci))
Reading – AAB–ABB incl maths+sci (Biomed Eng (MEng)) (IB 34–32 pts HL 5 maths+sci)
Sheffield – AAB incl maths+sci (Bioeng) (IB 34 pts HL 6 sci)
Surrey – AAB incl maths+sci/tech (Biomed Eng) (IB 34 pts)
Swansea – AAB–BBB incl maths (Med Eng) (IB 34 pts)

128 pts **City** – ABB incl maths+sci 128 pts (Biomed Eng) (IB 33 pts HL 6 maths+sci)
Hertfordshire – 128 pts incl maths+sci/tech/eng (Biomed Eng (MEng)) (HL 5 maths+sci)
Reading – ABB–BBB incl maths+sci (Biomed Eng) (IB 32–30 pts HL 5 maths+sci)

120 pts **Queen's Belfast** – BBB incl maths+phys (Phys Med Apps)

112 pts **Bradford** – BBC incl maths 112 pts (Biomed Eng)
Hull – 112 pts incl maths (Mech Med Eng; Mech Med Eng (MEng)) (IB 28 pts HL 5 maths)

104 pts **Hertfordshire** – 104 pts incl maths+sci/eng/tech (Biomed Eng) (HL 5 maths+sci)

96 pts **Chichester** – CCC–BBC 96–112 pts (Biomed Mat Eng)

Alternative offers
See **Chapter 6** and **Appendix 1** for grades/UCAS Tariff points information for other examinations.

CHOOSING YOUR COURSE (SEE ALSO CH.1)
Universities and colleges teaching quality See www.qaa.ac.uk; https://unistats.ac.uk.

Examples of sandwich degree courses Cardiff; City; Hull; Leeds; London (QM); Surrey.

ADMISSIONS INFORMATION
Number of applicants per place (approx) Cardiff 4; London (UCL) 8; Swansea 5.

Advice to applicants and planning the UCAS personal statement Cardiff An appreciation of the typical careers available within medical engineering and an interest in engineering and anatomy would be preferable. **London (UCL)** Evidence of interest in medical physics/physics, eg visits to hospitals or internships.

Selection interviews Yes Imperial London, Kent; **No** Glasgow, Leeds, Swansea.

AFTER-RESULTS ADVICE
Offers to applicants repeating A-levels Same Cardiff, London (UCL), Swansea.

GRADUATE DESTINATIONS AND EMPLOYMENT (2015/16 HESA)
See **Biotechnology**.

Career note High rate of graduate employment. *Money* magazine ranks Biomedical Engineering number 1 for job growth prospects for the next 10 years.

OTHER DEGREE SUBJECTS FOR CONSIDERATION
Biological Sciences; Prosthetics; Orthotics.

ENGINEERING/ENGINEERING SCIENCES

(including **Engineering Design, General Engineering, Integrated Engineering** and **Product Design;** see also **Engineering (Manufacturing and Production), Transport Management and Planning)**

Mathematics and physics provide the basis of all Engineering courses, although several universities and colleges now provide one-year Foundation courses for applicants without science A-levels. Many of the Engineering courses listed below enable students to delay the decision of their final engineering specialism. Engineering courses at most universities offer a range of specialisms in which, after a common first or second year, the choice of specialism is made. The flexibility of these courses is considerable, for example, it is sometimes possible to transfer from the BEng degree to the MEng degree at the end of the first or second year. At some universities, eg Durham, the first two years of the course cover a broad engineering education for all students enabling them to decide on their specialism in Year 3 from Civil, Electronic or Mechanical Engineering. A similar scheme operates at Lancaster University, whilst at Bath, the Mechanical Engineering department offers a choice of five courses at the end of Year 2. Many institutions offer sandwich courses and firms also offer valuable sponsorships.

Engineering Council UK (ECUK) Statement

Recent developments in the engineering profession and the regulations that govern registration as a professional engineer (UK-SPEC) mean that MEng and bachelor's degrees are the typical academic routes to becoming registered.

Chartered Engineers (CEng) develop solutions to engineering problems, using new or existing technologies, through innovation, creativity and change. They might develop and apply new technologies, promote advanced designs and design methods, introduce new and more efficient production techniques, marketing and construction concepts, and pioneer new engineering services and management methods.

Incorporated Engineers (IEng) act as exponents of today's technology through creativity and innovation. They maintain and manage applications of current and developing technology, and may be involved in engineering design, development, manufacture, construction and operation. Both Chartered and Incorporated Engineers are variously engaged in technical and commercial leadership and possess effective interpersonal skills.

You should confirm with universities whether their courses are accredited for CEng or IEng by relevant professional engineering institutions. To become a Chartered or Incorporated Engineer, you will have to demonstrate competence and commitment appropriate to the registration category. On top of your academic knowledge, you will also need to demonstrate your professional development and experience. Most of this will come after you graduate but placements in industry during your degree course are also available. Both Chartered and Incorporated Engineers usually progress to become team leaders or to take other key management roles. For full information check www.engc.org.uk/ukspec.

Useful websites www.scicentral.com; www.engc.org.uk; https://epsrc.ukri.org; www.etrust.org.uk

NB The points totals shown to the left of the institutions are for ease of reference only. It must not be assumed that Tariff points are always used by institutions or that they can be substituted for an offer in grades. The level of an offer is not necessarily indicative of the quality of a course.

COURSE OFFERS INFORMATION

Subject requirements/preferences GCSE English, mathematics and a science subject required. **AL** Mathematics and/or physics, engineering or another science usually required. Design technology may be acceptable or in some cases required. Offers shown below refer to BEng or BSc courses unless otherwise stated; BSc only appears as an abbreviation if the course is offered at the same institution as a BEng with different requirements.

UCAS points Tariff: A* = 56 pts; A = 48 pts; B = 40 pts; C = 32 pts; D = 24 pts; E = 16 pts

Cambridge (Peterhouse, Trinity) STEP may be used as part of conditional offer.

Oxford AL Mathematics and mechanics modules are recommended; further mathematics is helpful.

Your target offers and examples of degree courses

160 pts **Cambridge** – A*A*A incl maths+phys +interview +ENGAA (Eng) (IB 40–42 pts HL 776)

Oxford – A*A*A incl maths+phys +interview +PAT (Eng Sci) (IB 40 pts HL 776 incl 7 maths+phys)

152 pts **Bath** – A*AA–AAA+aEPQ incl maths+phys (Mech Eng (MEng)) (IB 36 pts HL 766)

Bristol – A*AA–AAB incl maths+phys/fmaths +interview (Eng Des (Yr Ind) (MEng)) (IB 38–34 pts HL 6 maths+phys)

Nottingham – A*AA–AAA incl maths+chem/phys (Cheml Eng Env Eng (Yr Ind)) (IB 36 pts)

144 pts **Bristol** – AAA–ABB incl maths (Eng Maths) (IB 36–32 pts HL 6 maths)

City – AAA incl maths+sci (Eng (MEng)) (IB 35 pts HL 6 maths+phys)

Durham – AAA incl maths+phys (Gen Eng) (IB 37 pts)

Edinburgh – AAA incl maths+phys/eng/des tech (Eng) (IB 37 pts HL 666)

Exeter – AAA–AAB (Eng Entre; Eng Mgt (MEng) (Yr Ind); Eng Comp Sci (MEng) (Yr Ind)) (IB 36–32 pts); AAA–ABB incl sci+maths (Eng; Eng Mgt; Eng Mgt (MEng); Eng (MEng)) (IB 36–32 pts HL 5 sci+maths)

Lancaster – AAA incl maths+physl sci (Eng (St Abrd) (MEng)) (IB 36 pts HL 16 pts incl 6 maths+physl sci)

Liverpool – AAA incl maths+sci (Eng (MEng)) (IB 35 pts HL 5 maths+phys)

London (QM) – AAA incl maths/phys+sci/des tech/art des (Des Innov Crea Eng (MEng)) (IB 36 pts HL 665)

Nottingham – A*AA–AAA incl maths+chem/phys (Env Eng) (IB 36 pts)

Warwick – AAA incl maths+phys (Eng Bus Mgt; Eng) (IB 38 pts HL 6 maths+phys)

136 pts **Cardiff** – AAB incl maths (Integ Eng courses) (IB 36–32 pts HL 5 sci+maths)

Dyson – AAB incl A maths+sci/tech (Eng Tech)

Newcastle – AAB–ABB incl maths+phys/chem/fmaths (Mar Tech Off Eng) (IB 35–34 pts HL 5 maths+phys/chem)

128 pts **Aston** – ABB–BBB incl maths+phys (Des Eng) (IB 32 pts)

Brunel – ABB incl art/des/tech+maths/phys +interview +portfolio (Prod Des Eng) (IB 31 pts HL 5 art/des/tech+maths/phys)

City – ABB incl maths+sci (Eng) (IB 33 pts HL 6 maths+phys)

Coventry – ABB incl maths+sci (Env Eng (Civ) (MEng)) (IB 31–30 pts)

Lancaster – ABB incl maths+physl sci (Eng) (IB 32 pts HL 16 pts incl 6 maths+physl sci)

Leicester – ABB incl maths+physl sci (Gen Eng) (IB 30 pts HL 5 maths+phys)

Liverpool – ABB incl maths+sci (Aero Eng Plt St; Eng) (IB 33 pts HL 5 maths+phys)

Loughborough – ABB incl maths/phys/des/eng +interview (Prod Des Eng) (IB 34 pts HL 655); ABB incl maths/phys +interview (Eng Mgt) (IB 34 pts HL 655); ABB incl maths/phys+des tech/art des +interview (Prod Des Tech) (IB 34 pts HL 655 incl maths/phys+des tech/art des)

Portsmouth – 128–144 pts incl maths (Innov Eng) (IB 28 pts HL 6 maths)

Strathclyde – ABB (3 yr course) BBB (4 yr course) (Prod Eng Mgt) (IB 34 pts HL 5 maths+phys); ABB (Prod Des Eng) (IB 34 HL 5 maths+phys)

UWE Bristol – 128 pts incl maths (Archit Env Eng) (HL 5 maths)

120 pts **Aberdeen** – BBB incl maths+phys/des tech/eng (Eng) (IB 32 pts HL 5 maths+phys)

Cardiff Met – 120 pts +interview +portfolio (Prod Des)

Coventry – BBB–BBC incl maths+sci (Env Eng (Civ)) (IB 31–30 pts)

Greenwich – 120 pts incl maths/physl sci (Eng Bus Mgt)

London South Bank – BBB incl maths (Eng Prod Des)

Queen's Belfast – BBB incl maths+sci/des tech (Prod Des Eng)

Ulster – BBB incl sci/maths/tech (Eng Mgt) (IB 26 pts HL 13 pts incl 5 maths+sci)

112 pts **Central Lancashire** – 112 pts incl maths+phys/STEM (Robot Eng) (IB 28 pts)

Heriot-Watt – BBC incl maths+phys/tech (Eng) (IB 31 pts)

Portsmouth – 112–128 pts incl maths (Innov Eng (MEng)) (IB 26 pts HL 5 maths)

Staffordshire – BBC 112 pts +interview +portfolio (Prod Des)

UWE Bristol – 112 pts +portfolio (Prod Des Tech)

104 pts Bournemouth – 104–120 pts +interview +portfolio (Des Eng) (IB 28–31 pts HL 55)

Manchester Met – BCC–BBC incl maths/tech/sci 104–112 pts (Prod Des Tech) (IB 26 pts)

96 pts Derby – 96–112 pts incl art des/des tech +interview +portfolio (Prod Des)

East London – 96 pts incl art des +interview +portfolio (Prod Des) (IB 25 pts HL 15 pts)

Hertfordshire – 96 pts incl art/des tech/eng +interview +portfolio (Prod Ind Des) (HL 44)

Portsmouth – 96–120 pts (Prod Des Innov) (IB 26 pts)

64 pts Northampton – DDE (Eng)

UHI – CC incl maths (Ener Eng)

Open University – contact 0300 303 0073 **or** www.open.ac.uk/contact/new (Eng)

Alternative offers

See **Chapter 6** and **Appendix 1** for grades/UCAS Tariff points information for other examinations.

EXAMPLES OF COLLEGES OFFERING COURSES IN THIS SUBJECT FIELD

See under separate Engineering tables. Blackburn (Coll); Blackpool and Fylde (Coll); Bristol City (Coll); Bury (Coll); City and Islington (Coll); Cornwall (Coll); Coventry (Coll); East Berkshire (Coll); East Kent (Coll); East Surrey (Coll); Gŵp Llandrillo Menai; Harlow (Coll); Highbury Portsmouth (Coll); Lancaster and Morecambe (Coll); Loughborough (Coll); Manchester (Coll); Middlesbrough (Coll); Newcastle (Coll); North Kent (Coll); Northumberland (Coll); Redcar and Cleveland (Coll); Richmond-upon-Thames (Coll); St Helens (Coll); Selby (Coll); South Devon (Coll); South Essex (Coll); Stockport (Coll); Trafford (Coll); Tyne Coast (Coll); Warwickshire (Coll); West Nottinghamshire (Coll); West Suffolk (Coll); Westminster City (Coll).

CHOOSING YOUR COURSE (SEE ALSO CH.1)

Universities and colleges teaching quality See www.qaa.ac.uk; https://unistats.ac.uk.

Top research universities and colleges (REF 2014) (General Engineering) London (King's); Cardiff; Oxford; Sheffield; Cambridge; Imperial London; Liverpool; London (UCL); Glasgow.

Examples of sandwich degree courses Aston; Brunel; Cardiff; Central Lancashire; East London; Leicester; London (QM); London South Bank; Loughborough; Manchester Met; Nottingham; Portsmouth; Ulster.

ADMISSIONS INFORMATION

Number of applicants per place (approx) Aston 8; Bristol (Eng Des) 3, (Eng Maths) 5; Cambridge 7; Cardiff 5; Durham 7; Edinburgh 12; Exeter 6; Heriot-Watt 4; Lancaster 9; Leicester 8; Liverpool 7; Manchester Met 2; Northampton 3; Oxford Brookes 5; Strathclyde 5; Warwick 10.

Admissions tutors' advice Leeds Applicants taking the BTEC Extended Diploma may be required to take an additional Maths A-level paper.

Advice to applicants and planning the UCAS personal statement Details of careers in the various engineering specialisms should be obtained from the relevant engineering institutions (see **Appendix 3**). This will enable you to describe your interests in various aspects of engineering. Contact engineers to discuss their work with them. Try to visit an engineering firm relevant to your choice of specialism.

Selection interviews Yes Bournemouth, Cambridge, Loughborough, Oxford (47% (success rate 15%)); **Some** Cardiff, Leicester; **No** Bristol, London (QM), Manchester Met, Strathclyde.

Interview advice and questions Since mathematics and physics are important subjects, it is probable that you will be questioned on the applications of these subjects too, for example, the transmission of electricity, nuclear power, aeronautics, mechanics, etc. Past questions have included: Explain the theory of an arch; what is its function? What is the connection between distance and velocity and acceleration and velocity? How does a car ignition work? See also separate **Engineering** tables and **Chapter 5**.

Reasons for rejection (non-academic) Made no contribution whatsoever to the project discussions during the UCAS interview. Forged reference! Poor work ethic. Lack of motivation towards the subject area. Better suited to an alternative Engineering course. Failure to attend interview. Poor interview preparation.

AFTER-RESULTS ADVICE
Offers to applicants repeating A-levels Higher Loughborough, Warwick; **Possibly higher** Edinburgh, Lancaster, Manchester Met; **Same** Brunel, Cambridge, Cardiff, Derby, Durham, Exeter, Heriot-Watt, Liverpool.

GRADUATE DESTINATIONS AND EMPLOYMENT (2015/16 HESA)
Graduates surveyed 1,480 **Employed** 955 **In voluntary employment** 15 **In further study** 305 **Assumed unemployed** 60

Career note A high proportion of Engineering graduates go into industry as engineers, technicians, IT specialists or managers, irrespective of their engineering speciality. However, the transferable skills gained during their courses are also valued by employers in other sectors.

OTHER DEGREE SUBJECTS FOR CONSIDERATION
Computer Science; Materials Science; Mathematics; Physics; Technology; all branches of Engineering (see also following **Engineering** tables).

ENGLISH

(including Creative Writing; see also Journalism, Languages, Linguistics, Literature)

English courses continue to be extremely popular and competitive and include English Literature, English and English Language. Bear in mind that the content of courses can vary considerably. English Literature courses are popular because they are often an extension of A-level or equivalent studies and will offer a wide range of modules. At the University of Sheffield, the course covers the study of literature, poetry, fiction and drama from Old English to the 21st century along with modules such as American Literature, Gothic Literature and Renaissance literature. However, English Language courses break the mould and offer a broader interpretation of English with studies in the use of language, grammar, the meaning of words, language in the workplace, in broadcasting and other aspects of society, Pidgin and Creole English, methods of communication and linguistics. Admissions tutors will expect students to have read widely outside their A-level syllabus.

Useful websites www.bl.uk; www.lrb.co.uk; www.3ammagazine.com/3am; www.bibliomania.com

NB The points totals shown to the left of the institutions are for ease of reference only. It must not be assumed that Tariff points are always used by institutions or that they can be substituted for an offer in grades. The level of an offer is not necessarily indicative of the quality of a course.

COURSE OFFERS INFORMATION
Subject requirements/preferences GCSE English language and English literature required and a foreign language may be preferred. Grades may be stipulated. **AL** English with specific grades usually stipulated. Modern languages required for joint courses with languages.

Your target offers and examples of degree courses
152 pts **Cambridge** – A*AA +interview +ASNCAA (A-Sxn Nrs Celt) (IB 40–42 pts HL 776); A*AA incl Engl +interview +ELAT (Engl) (IB 40–42 pts HL 776); A*AA +interview +EAA (Educ Engl Dr Arts) (IB 40–42 pts HL 776)
     Durham – A*AA incl Engl (Engl Lit) (IB 38 pts)
     Edinburgh – A*AA (Engl Lit) (IB 43 pts HL 776)
     Manchester – A*AA–ABB incl Engl (Engl Lit courses) (IB 37–35 pts HL 6 Engl)

144 pts **Birmingham** – AAA incl Engl (Engl Crea Writ) (IB 32 pts HL 666)

Bristol – AAA–ABB incl Engl (Thea Engl; Engl; Engl Class St) (IB 36–32 pts HL 6 Engl)

East Anglia – AAA incl Engl (Engl Lit Crea Writ) (IB 34 pts HL 6 Engl)

Edinburgh – AAA incl Engl (Engl Scot Lit) (IB 39 pts HL 666)

Exeter – AAA–AAB incl AL Engl Lit Gr A (Engl Film (Emp Expnc)) (IB 36–34 pts); AAA–AAB (Engl (Emp Exp)) (IB 36–34 pts); AAA–AAB incl Engl lit (Engl; Engl (St Abrd)) (IB 36–34 pts HL 6 Engl); (Engl Drama courses) (IB 36–34 pts)

Lancaster – AAA–AAB incl Engl (Engl Lit) (IB 36–35 pts HL 16 pts incl 6 lit)

Leeds – AAA–AAB incl Engl (Engl Lang Lit) (IB 35 pts HL 17–16 pts incl 6 Engl)

London (UCL) – AAA incl Engl +interview (Engl) (IB 38 pts HL 6 Engl)

Newcastle – AAA–AAB incl Engl (Engl Lang Lit) (IB 36–35 pts HL 6 Engl)

Nottingham – AAA–AAB incl Engl (Engl; Engl Lang Lit; Engl Crea Writ) (IB 36–34 pts HL 6 Engl)

Oxford – AAA +interview +ELAT +MLAT (Engl Modn Langs) (IB 38 pts HL 666); AAA +interview +ELAT (Engl Lang Lit) (IB 38 pts HL 666)

St Andrews – AAA incl Engl (Engl courses) (IB 38 pts)

Strathclyde – AAA (3 yr course) ABB (4 yr course) (Engl courses) (IB 36 pts)

Warwick – AAA incl Engl (Engl Lit) (IB 38 pts HL 6 Engl); AAA incl Engl +portfolio (Engl Lit Crea Writ) (IB 38 pts HL 6 Engl)

York – AAA/A*AB incl Engl (Engl) (IB 36 pts HL 6 Engl); AAA incl Engl+hist (Engl Hist) (IB 36 pts HL 6 Engl+hist)

136 pts **Birmingham** – AAB incl Engl (Engl; Engl Lang) (IB 32 pts HL 665)

East Anglia – AAB incl dr/thea st/Engl lit +interview +audition (Script Perf) (IB 33 pts HL 5 dr/thea st/Engl); AAB (Am Engl Lit) (IB 33 pts HL 5 Engl); AAB incl Engl (Engl Lit) (IB 33 pts HL 5 Engl)

Edinburgh – AAB (Class Engl Lang; Engl Lang) (IB 36 pts HL 665)

Glasgow – AAB–BBB incl arts/hum/lang (Engl Lit; Engl Lang) (IB 36–34 pts HL 665 incl 6 Engl/hum/lang)

Lancaster – AAB incl Engl/lang (Engl Lang Crea Writ) (IB 35 pts HL 16 pts); (Engl Lang) (IB 36–35 pts HL 16 pts); AAB (Engl Lang Lit) (IB 35 pts)

Liverpool – AAB–ABB incl Engl (Engl) (IB 35–33 pts HL 6 Engl)

London (King's) – AAB incl Engl (Compar Lit) (IB 35 pts HL 6 incl Engl lit); (Class St Engl) (IB 35 pts HL 665); AAB incl Engl/lang/psy (Engl Lang Ling) (IB 35 pts HL 665 incl Engl/lang/psy)

London (RH) – AAB incl Engl lit/dr thea st +portfolio (Dr Crea Writ) (IB 32 pts HL 6 Engl); AAB–ABB incl Engl (Engl) (IB 32 pts HL 6 Engl); (Engl Dr) (IB 32 pts)

Loughborough – AAB–ABB incl Engl (Engl; Engl Spo Sci) (IB 35–34 pts HL 655 incl 6/5 Engl)

Newcastle – AAB–ABB (Engl Lang) (IB 35–34 pts)

Sheffield – AAB–ABB+bEPQ incl Engl (Engl Lang Lit; Engl Lit) (IB 34 pts HL 6 Engl); (Engl Comb Hons) (IB 34–33 pts HL 6 Engl)

Southampton – AAB–ABB incl Engl (Film Engl) (IB 32 pts HL 6 Engl); (Phil Engl) (IB 34–32 pts HL 6 Engl); AAB–ABB+aEPQ incl Engl+mus +gr 8 (Engl Mus) (IB 34 pts HL 6 Engl+mus); AAB incl Engl (Engl) (IB 34 pts HL 6 Engl); AAB–ABB+aEPQ incl Engl+hist (Engl Hist) (IB 34 pts HL 6 Engl+hist); AAB/ABB+aEPQ incl Engl+Fr/Ger/Span (Engl Fr/Ger/Span) (IB 34 pts HL 6 Engl+Fr/Ger/Span)

Sussex – AAB–ABB incl Engl (Engl Lang Lit; Engl Comb Hons; Engl) (IB 32 pts HL 6 Engl)

Warwick – AAB incl Engl lit+Fr (Engl Fr) (IB 36 pts HL 6 Engl lit 5 Fr)

York – AAB incl Engl (Engl Ling; Engl Hist Art; Engl Pol; Engl Phil) (IB 35 pts HL 6 Engl)

128 pts **Aston** – ABB–BBB incl Engl (Engl Lang) (IB 32 pts); ABB–BBB (Pol Engl Lang; Int Rel Engl Lang) (IB 32 pts)

Bangor – 128–96 pts incl Engl (Engl Lit courses); 128–112 pts incl Engl (Engl Lit Engl Lang)

Cardiff – ABB–BBB (Engl Lang) (HL 665–655); ABB incl Engl lit (Engl Lit) (HL 665)

East Anglia – ABB incl Engl (Film St Engl Lit) (IB 32 pts HL 5 Engl); (Engl Lit Comb Hons) (IB 33 pts HL 5 Engl)

Huddersfield – ABB incl Engl 128 pts (Engl Lang Lit; Engl Lang courses)

Kent – ABB incl Engl (Engl Am Postcol Lit) (IB 34 pts)

Leicester – ABB incl Engl (Engl courses) (IB 30 pts HL 6 Engl)

London (QM) – ABB incl Engl lit/Engl lang lit (Engl Lit Ling; Engl) (IB 32 pts HL 6 Engl); ABB (Engl Lang Ling) (IB 32 pts HL 655)

NCH London – ABB–AAA +interview (Engl courses) (IB 34–36 pts)

Nottingham – ABB incl Engl (Engl Hisp St) (IB 32 pts HL 5 Engl)

Queen's Belfast – ABB–BBB incl Engl (Engl courses)

Reading – ABB–BBB incl Engl (Engl Lang courses; Engl Lang Lit) (IB 32–30 pts HL 5 Engl)

Roehampton – 128 pts (Engl Lit)

Sheffield – ABB incl Engl/lang (Engl Lang Sociol) (IB 33 pts HL 6 Engl/lang); ABB–BBB+bEPQ (Engl Lang Ling) (IB 33 pts)

Stirling – ABB (3 yr course) BBB (4 yr course) incl Engl (Engl St) (IB 35 pts (3 yr course) 32 pts (4 yr course))

Surrey – ABB incl Engl (Engl Lit; Engl Lit Crea Writ) (IB 32 pts); ABB incl Engl+Fr/Ger/Span (Engl Lit Fr/Ger/Span) (IB 32 pts)

120 pts **Aberdeen** BBB (Engl Scot Lit) (IB 32 pts HL 555); (Engl) (IB 32 pts)

Aberystwyth – BBB–ABB incl Engl (Engl Lit) (IB 30 pts HL 6 Engl lit)

Anglia Ruskin – 120 pts (Engl Lang Engl Lang Teach) (IB 24 pts); 120 pts incl Engl (Writ Engl Lit; Engl Lit) (IB 24 pts)

Bangor – 120–104 pts (Engl Lang courses; Mus Crea Writ; Prof Writ Gms Des); 120–112 pts incl Engl (Engl Lit Thea Perf)

Brunel – BBB incl Engl +audition workshop (Thea Engl) (IB 30 pts HL 5 Engl); BBB incl Engl (Engl; Engl Crea Writ) (IB 30 pts HL 5 Engl); BBB +audition workshop (Thea Crea Writ) (IB 30 pts HL 5 Engl)

Buckingham – BBB (Engl Lit) (IB 32 pts)

City – BBB incl Engl (Engl) (IB 32 pts)

Derby – 120–128 pts incl Engl (Engl)

Dundee – BBB incl Engl lit (Engl Film St; Engl) (IB 30 pts HL 555)

East London – 120 pts (Engl Lit) (IB 26 pts HL 15 pts)

Edge Hill – BBB 120 pts (Engl; Crea Writ; Engl Lang; Engl Lit; Engl Film St; Engl Lit Hist)

Essex – BBB (Engl Lit; Crea Writ; Engl Lang courses; Engl Lang Lit) (IB 30 pts)

Huddersfield – BBB 120 pts +audition workshop (Dr Engl Lang/Lit); BBB incl Engl 120 pts (Engl Lit)

Hull – 120 pts (Engl) (IB 28 pts)

Keele – BBB/ABC incl Engl/dr (Engl Lit; Engl Lit Comb Hons) (IB 32 pts HL 6 Engl)

Kent – BBB incl Engl (Engl Lang Ling Engl Am Lit) (IB 34 pts); BBB (Engl Lang Ling) (IB 34 pts)

Liverpool Hope – BBB–BBC incl Engl 120–112 pts (Engl Lang; Engl Lit)

Liverpool John Moores – BBB incl Engl 120 pts (Engl) (IB 26 pts)

London (Birk) – 120 pts (Engl)

London (Gold) – BBB incl Engl (Engl Compar Lit; Engl; Engl Crea Writ) (IB 33 pts)

Northumbria – 120–128 pts (Engl Lit) (HL 444); 120–128 pts incl Engl (Engl Lang Lit; Engl Lit Crea Writ) (HL 444)

Plymouth – 120 pts incl Engl+Span (Engl Span) (IB 28 pts HL 6 Engl); 120 pts incl Engl (Engl Fr) (IB 28 pts HL 6 Engl)

Reading – BBB–BBC incl Engl +interview (P Educ Engl Spec) (IB 30–28 pts)

Sheffield Hallam – 120–104 pts incl Engl (Engl; Engl Lang); 120–104 pts (Engl Lit); 120–104 pts incl Engl/crea writ (Crea Writ)

Sunderland – 120 pts (Engl; Engl Crea Writ; Engl Lang Ling)

Swansea – BBB incl Engl (Engl Lit Lang; Pol Engl Lit) (IB 32 pts); BBB (Engl courses) (IB 32–33 pts)

York – BBB (Engl Educ) (IB 31 pts)

112 pts **Birmingham City** – 112 pts incl Engl (Engl) (IB 26 pts HL 14 pts incl 5/4 Engl); BBC incl Engl 112 pts (Engl Crea Writ) (HL 14 pts incl 5/4 Engl); (Engl Lang Lit) (IB 26 pts HL 14 pts incl 5/4 Engl)

Check **Chapter 3** for new university admission details and **Chapter 6** on how to read the subject tables.

Bournemouth – 112–120 pts incl Engl (Engl) (IB 30–31 pts HL 55)
Bournemouth Arts – BBC–BBB 112–120 pts (Crea Writ) (IB 30–32 pts)
Coventry – BBC (Engl; Engl Jrnl) (IB 31 pts)
De Montfort – 112 pts incl Engl (Engl) (IB 26 pts); 112–104 pts (Engl Lang Comb Hons; Crea Writ Comb Hons) (IB 26–24 pts)
East London – 112 pts incl Engl (Crea Prof Writ) (IB 25 pts HL 15 pts)
Edinburgh Napier – BBC incl Engl (Engl) (IB 29 pts HL 5 Engl)
Gloucestershire – BBC 112 pts (Engl Lang Crea Writ; Crea Writ; Engl Lit Crea Writ)
Glyndŵr – 112 pts (Engl; Engl Crea Writ)
Greenwich – 112 pts (Engl Lang Lit; Crea Writ)
Hertfordshire – 112 pts (Engl Lit; Engl Lang Comm) (HL 44)
Hull – 112 pts +interview (Dr Engl) (IB 28 pts)
Kingston – 112 pts (Engl Lit)
Leeds Beckett – 112 pts (Engl Lit) (IB 25 pts)
Liverpool John Moores – BBC 112 pts (Crea Writ Film St) (IB 26 pts)
London Met – BBC 112 pts (Crea Writ Engl Lit; Engl Lit)
Middlesex – 112 pts (Engl)
Nottingham Trent – 112 pts (Engl)
Oxford Brookes – BBC 112 pts (Engl Lang Comm) (IB 30 pts)
Roehampton – 112 pts (Crea Writ; Engl Lang Ling)
St Mary's – 112 pts (Engl; Crea Prof Writ)
Sheffield Hallam – 112–96 pts incl Engl lit/hist (Engl Hist)
Southampton Solent – 112 pts +interview (Engl; Engl Film)
Staffordshire – BBC 112 pts (Engl)
Suffolk – BBC 112 pts (Engl App Psy); BBC (Engl Hist)
Sunderland – 112 pts (Engl Lang Lit)
UWE Bristol – 112 pts (Engl Lit Writ; Engl Lit)
West London – BBC 112 pts (Engl Media Comms)
Winchester – 112–128 pts (Crea Writ) (IB 27 pts)
Wolverhampton – BBC (Engl courses; Crea Prof Writ courses)

104 pts **Bath Spa** – BCC incl Engl (Crea Writ) (IB 27 pts)
Brighton – BCC–CCC incl Engl 104–96 pts (Engl Lit) (IB 27 pts)
Cardiff Met – 104 pts +interview (Educ St Engl); 104 pts (Engl Media; Engl Dr; Engl Crea Writ)
Central Lancashire – 104 pts (Engl Lang Lit; Engl Lit; Engl Lang Crea Writ)
Chester – BCC–BBC incl Engl/crea writ (Crea Writ courses) (IB 26 pts HL 5 Engl); (Engl Lang Lit courses; Engl Lit; Engl Lang) (IB 28 pts HL 5 Engl)
Edinburgh Napier – BCC incl Engl (Engl Film) (IB 29 pts HL 655)
Falmouth – 104–120 pts +interview (Engl; Engl Crea Writ)
Leeds Trinity – 104 pts (Engl Film; Engl Media)
Liverpool John Moores – BCC 104 pts (Crea Writ) (IB 24 pts); BCC incl Engl 104 pts (Hist Engl) (IB 24 pts)
London South Bank – BCC (Engl Crea Writ)
Manchester Met – 104–112 pts (Engl Am Lit; Engl Crea Writ; Engl) (IB 26 pts)
Northampton – BCC (Engl courses); BCC incl Engl (Crea Writ courses)
Portsmouth – 104–112 pts (Crea Writ) (IB 29 pts)
South Wales – BCC–CDD incl Engl 104–80 pts (Engl; Engl Crea Writ) (HL 655–445)
Westminster – BCC incl Engl (Engl Lang courses) (IB 28 pts); BCC incl lang (Chin Engl Lang) (IB 28 pts)
Worcester – 104 pts (Engl Lang courses; Engl Lit courses)

96 pts **Bishop Grosseteste** – 96–112 pts (Engl courses)
Bolton – 96 pts (Crea Writ; Engl)
Chichester – 96–120 pts incl Engl/dr/crea writ (Engl Lit; Crea Writ Engl) (IB 28 pts HL 4 Engl)
Cumbria – 96–120 pts (Engl Lit; Crea Writ)

Derby – 96–112 pts (Writ Pub); 96–128 pts incl Engl (Crea Prof Writ Comb Hons); 96–112 pts incl Engl (Crea Prof Writ)

Newman – 96–88 pts incl Engl (Engl)

Portsmouth – 96–120 pts incl Engl (Engl Lang Ling) (IB 30 pts HL 17 pts incl 5 Engl)

St Mark and St John – CCC 96 pts (Engl)

Teesside – 96–112 pts incl Engl (Engl St; Engl St Crea Writ)

Winchester – 96–112 pts (Engl Am Lit) (IB 25 pts); 96–120 pts incl Engl (Engl courses) (IB 25–26 pts)

York St John – 96–112 pts (Engl Lang Ling; Engl Lit; Crea Writ)

88 pts **Canterbury Christ Church** – 88–112 pts (Engl Lang Comm); 88–112 pts incl Engl (Engl Lit)

80 pts **Arts London** – 80 pts (Mag Jrnl Pub)

Bedfordshire – 80 pts (Engl courses; Crea Writ)

Norwich City (Coll) – (Engl Soc Sci)

72 pts **UHI** – BC incl Engl (Lit)

48 pts **Anglia Ruskin** – DD (Hist Engl)

Bolton – 48 pts (Crea Writ Fdn; Engl Fdn)

Trinity Saint David – interview (Engl)

Alternative offers
See **Chapter 6** and **Appendix 1** for grades/UCAS Tariff points information for other examinations.

EXAMPLES OF COLLEGES OFFERING COURSES IN THIS SUBJECT FIELD
Accrington and Rossendale (Coll); Birmingham Met (Coll); Blackburn (Coll); Blackpool and Fylde (Coll); Bournemouth and Poole (Coll); Bradford (Coll); Craven (Coll); Doncaster (Coll); Farnborough (CT); Grimsby (Inst Group); Newham (CFE); South Devon (Coll); Truro and Penwith (Coll); West Suffolk (Coll); Yeovil (Coll).

CHOOSING YOUR COURSE (SEE ALSO CH.1)
Universities and colleges teaching quality See www.qaa.ac.uk; https://unistats.ac.uk.

Top research universities and colleges (REF 2014) (English Language and Literature) Warwick; Aberdeen; Durham; Newcastle; London (QM); York; Birmingham; Cardiff; St Andrews; Liverpool; London (UCL); Oxford Brookes.

Examples of sandwich degree courses Aston; Brighton; Coventry; Hertfordshire; Huddersfield; Loughborough; Southampton Solent; Surrey.

ADMISSIONS INFORMATION
Number of applicants per place (approx) Bangor (Engl Lit) 4, (Ling Engl Lang) 5; Bath Spa 8; Birmingham 7; Birmingham City 9; Blackpool and Fylde (Coll) 2; Bristol 7; Buckingham 5; Cambridge 4; Cardiff (Engl Lit) 6; Central Lancashire 10; Cumbria 24; De Montfort 7; Derby 6; Dundee 11; Durham 8; East Anglia (Engl Lit Crea Writ) 2; Edge Hill 4; Exeter 13; Gloucestershire 35; Hertfordshire 6; Huddersfield 4; Hull 5; Kingston 6; Lancaster 4; Leeds 10; Leeds Trinity 6; Leicester 5; Liverpool 8; London (Gold) 9; London (QM) 9; London (RH) 7; London (UCL) 10; London South Bank 5; Manchester 10; Manchester Met 7; Middlesex 8; Newman 3; Northampton 3; Nottingham 6; Nottingham Trent 21; Oxford 5; Oxford Brookes 6; Reading 11; Roehampton 6; Sheffield 6; Sheffield Hallam 4; South Wales 8; Southampton 8; Stirling 9; Sunderland 10; Teesside 5; Trinity Saint David 4; Warwick 15; Winchester 5; York 8; York St John 3.

Admissions tutors' advice Buckingham In a situation where everyone is trying to show off, it's amazing how powerful sincerity is. What poems, novels, or drama have really excited you? English Literature is a great subject, but why do you really want to read it?

Advice to applicants and planning the UCAS personal statement Applicants should read outside their subject. Details of any writing you have done (for example poetry, short stories) should be provided. Theatre visits and play readings are also important. Keep up-to-date by reading literary and theatre reviews in the national newspapers (keep a scrapbook of reviews for reference). Evidence is needed of a good writing style. Favourite authors, spare-time reading. Ability to write lucidly, accurately and succinctly. Evidence of literary enthusiasm. General interest in communications – verbal, visual, media. **Bristol** Deferred entry accepted in some cases. Late applications may not be accepted. **Manchester** Due to the detailed nature of entry requirements for English Literature courses, we are unable to include full details in the prospectus. For complete and up-to-date information on our entry requirements for these courses, please visit our website at www.manchester.ac.uk/study/undergraduate/courses.

Misconceptions about this course Birmingham City The study of English language means descriptive linguistics – the course won't necessarily enable students to speak or write better English. **Buckingham** Native speakers of English often do not realise that the EFL degree courses are restricted to non-native speakers of English.

Selection interviews Yes Anglia Ruskin, Cambridge, Cardiff Met, East Anglia, Leeds, London (UCL), Oxford (Engl Lang Lit) 22%, (Engl Modn Langs) 19%, Trinity Saint David; **Some** Blackburn (Coll), Blackpool and Fylde (Coll), Bristol, Kingston, London (Gold), Loughborough, Southampton, Truro and Penwith (Coll), Warwick; **No** Bangor, Birmingham, Birmingham City, Bishop Grosseteste, Canterbury Christ Church, Chester, Chichester, Cumbria, De Montfort, Derby, Dundee, Essex, Falmouth, Gloucestershire, Huddersfield, Hull, Leeds Trinity, London (King's), London (QM), London (RH), London Met, Middlesex, Newcastle, Nottingham, Portsmouth, Reading, Roehampton, Wolverhampton.

Interview advice and questions Questions will almost certainly be asked on set A-level texts and any essays which have been submitted prior to the interview. You will also be expected to have read outside your A-level subjects and to answer questions about your favourite authors, poets, dramatists, etc. Questions in the past have included: Do you think that class discussion plays an important part in your English course? What is the value of studying a text in depth rather than just reading it for pleasure? What is the difference between satire and comedy? Are books written by women different from those written by men? Why would you go to see a production of *Hamlet*? What are your views on the choice of novels for this year's Booker Prize? What books are bad for you? If you could make up a word, what would it be? Short verbal tests and a précis may be set. See also **Chapter 5**. **Buckingham** It is useful to know if there is any particular reason why students want a particular programme; for example, for the TEFL degree is a member of the family a teacher? **Cambridge** We look for interviewees who respond positively to ideas, can think on their feet, engage intelligently with critical issues and sustain an argument. If they don't evince any of these, we reject them. **Leeds** Interview questions based on information supplied in the personal statement, academic ability and current reading interests. **London (King's)** Interview questions are based on the information in the personal statement. **London (UCL)** The interview will focus on an ability to discuss literature in terms of language, plot, characters and genre. Following the interview applicants will be asked to write a critical commentary on an example of unseen prose or verse. **Oxford** Is there a difference between innocence and naivety? If you could make up a word, what would it be? Why? Do you think *Hamlet* is a bit long? No? Well I do. Is the Bible a fictional work? Was Shakespeare a rebel? **Warwick** We may ask students to sight-read or to analyse a text. **York** Only mature candidates and applicants with special circumstances and/or qualifications will usually be interviewed. Examples of recent essays are required at interview.

Reasons for rejection (non-academic) Some are well-informed about English literature – others are not. Inability to respond to questions about their current studies. Lack of enthusiasm for the challenge of studying familiar subjects from a different perspective. Must be able to benefit from the course. Little interest in how people communicate with each other. They don't know a single thing about our course. **Bristol** Not enough places to make offers to all those whose qualifications deserve one. **Buckingham** Applicants are requested to attend an Open Day/Evening or a Tutorial Taster Day. The University believes it is very important for applicants to visit its campus. Candidates who do not respond to these invitations may be rejected, irrespective of academic achievement, as the University looks for committed, well-motivated students. **Cambridge** See **Interview advice and questions**. **Leeds** Unsuitable predictions. **Oxford** (1) The essay she submitted was poorly written, careless and reductive and, in general, lacking in attention to the subject. She should be encouraged to write less and think more about what she is saying. She seems to put down the first thing that comes into her head. (2) We had the feeling that he rather tended to dismiss texts which did not satisfy the requirements of his personal canon and that he therefore might not be happy pursuing a course requiring the study of texts from all periods. (3) In her essay on Brontë, she took a phrase from Arnold which was metaphorical (to do with hunger) and applied it literally, writing at length about the diet of the characters. **Reading** None. If they have reached the interview we have already eliminated all other factors. **Sheffield Hallam** Apparent lack of eagerness to tackle all three strands of the course (literature, language and creative writing). **Southampton** Insufficient or patchy academic achievement. Applicants coming from non-standard academic backgrounds are assessed in terms of their individual situations.

AFTER-RESULTS ADVICE

Offers to applicants repeating A-levels Higher Sheffield Hallam, Southampton (varies), Warwick; **Possibly higher** Lancaster, Newcastle, Stirling; **Same** Bangor, Birmingham City, Blackpool and Fylde (Coll), Bristol, Cambridge, Cardiff, Cardiff Met, Chester, Chichester, Cumbria, De Montfort, Derby, Dundee, Durham, East Anglia, Edge Hill, Hull, Leeds, Leeds Trinity, Liverpool, Liverpool Hope, London (Gold), London (RH), Loughborough, Manchester Met, Newman, Nottingham, Nottingham Trent, Oxford Brookes, Reading, Roehampton, St Mary's, Sheffield, Suffolk, Trinity Saint David, Winchester, Wolverhampton, York, York St John.

GRADUATE DESTINATIONS AND EMPLOYMENT (2015/16 HESA)

English Studies graduates surveyed 8,560 **Employed** 3,735 **In voluntary employment** 395 **In further study** 2,555 **Assumed unemployed** 475

Career note English graduates work in the media, publishing, management, public and social services, business, administration and IT, retail sales, the cultural industries and the teaching profession. Those who have undertaken courses in Creative Writing could aim for careers in advertising, public relations or journalism.

OTHER DEGREE SUBJECTS FOR CONSIDERATION

Communication Studies; Drama; Language courses; Linguistics; Literature; Media Studies.

ENVIRONMENTAL SCIENCES

(including **Climate Change, Ecology, Environmental Hazards, Environmental Health, Environmental Management** and **Meteorology and Climate Science**; see also **Biological Sciences, Biology, Engineering (Civil), Geography, Geology/Geological Sciences, Health Sciences/Studies, Marine/Maritime Studies, Town and Country Planning**)

Environmental Sciences courses need to be researched carefully since the content offered by different institutions can vary considerably. The emphasis may be biological or geographical and courses can cover marine, legal, social and political issues. Some courses focus on ecological issues, either environmental or industrial, whilst others focus on environmental hazards and health, so expect some overlap in many courses. There are some vocational courses in this category with professional status which allow graduates to progress into certain professions. For example, they may choose to become an environmental health officer whose role is concerned with all aspects of public health, covering food safety, housing, health and safety, and environmental protection.

Useful websites www.cieh.org; www.ends.co.uk; www.enn.com; http://iagre.org.uk; www.gov.uk/ government/organisations/department-for-environment-food-rural-affairs; http://socenv.org.uk; www. the-ies.org; www.noc.ac.uk; www.britishecologicalsociety.org; www.rmets.org

NB The points totals shown to the left of the institutions are for ease of reference only. It must not be assumed that Tariff points are always used by institutions or that they can be substituted for an offer in grades. The level of an offer is not necessarily indicative of the quality of a course.

COURSE OFFERS INFORMATION

Subject requirements/preferences GCSE English, mathematics and a science (often chemistry or biology) usually required. **AL** One or two science subjects are usually stipulated; mathematics may be required. (Meteor) Mathematics, physics and another science may be required sometimes with specified grades, eg mathematics and physics grade B.

Your target offers and examples of degree courses

152 pts **Leeds** – A*AA incl sci/maths/geog/econ/sociol/hist/law/Engl (Sust Env Mgt (Int)) (IB 35 pts HL 19 pts); A*AA incl maths+phys/chem (Meteor Clim Sci (Int)) (IB 35 pts HL 19 pts)

York – A*AA–AAB incl chem+sci/maths +interview (Chem Atmos Env) (IB 36–35 pts HL 6 chem+sci/maths)

144 pts **Edinburgh** – AAA incl sci/maths (Ecol Env Sci Mgt) (IB 37 pts HL 555); AAA incl maths+phys (Geophys Meteor) (IB 37 pts HL 555); (Phys Meteor) (IB 37 pts HL 666); AAA incl sci/maths/geog (Ecol Env Sci) (IB 37 pts HL 555)

Imperial London – AAA incl biol+sci/maths (Ecol Env Biol) (IB 38 pts HL 6 biol+sci/maths)

Leeds – AAA–AAB incl biol (Ecol Cons Biol) (IB 35–34 pts HL 18–16 pts incl 6 biol+sci)

London (UCL) – AAA–ABB (Env Geosci) (IB 38–34 pts HL 18–16 pts)

Sheffield – AAA incl biol+sci (Ecol Cons Biol (MBiolSci)) (IB 36 pts HL 6 biol+sci)

York – AAA–AAB incl biol+chem/maths (Ecol) (IB 36–35 pts HL 6 biol+chem/maths)

136 pts **East Anglia** – AAB (Env Sci (MSci)) (IB 33 pts HL 6 sci)

Exeter – AAB–ABB incl sci/maths/geog/tech/psy/PE (Env Sci) (IB 34–32 pts HL 5 sci/maths/geog/tech/psy/PE); AAB–ABB incl sci/maths (Cons Biol Ecol) (IB 34–32 pts HL 5 sci/maths); AAB–BBB incl sci/maths/geog/tech/psy/PE (Renew Ener) (IB 34–30 pts HL 5 sci/maths/geog/tech/psy/PE)

London LSE – AAB incl maths (Env Plcy Econ) (IB 37 pts HL 666)

Reading – AAB–ABB incl maths (Maths Meteor) (IB 34–32 pts HL 6 maths); AAB–ABB incl biol+sci (Ecol Wldlf Cons) (IB 34–32 pts HL 5 biol+sci)

St Andrews – AAB incl biol+sci/maths (Env Earth Sci) (IB 36 pts)

Sheffield – AAB/ABB+aEPQ incl biol+sci (Ecol Cons Biol) (IB 34 pts HL 6 biol+sci)

Sussex – AAB–ABB incl sci/env st (Ecol Cons Env) (IB 32 pts HL 5 sci)

128 pts **Bangor** – 128–112 pts incl sci (Mar Env St)

Birmingham – ABB (Pal Palaeoenv) (IB 32 pts); ABB incl sci/maths/geog/psy/comp (Env Sci) (IB 32 pts HL 655)

Coventry – ABB–BBB (Geog Nat Haz) (IB 29 pts)

East Anglia – ABB incl sci (Env Sci) (IB 32 pts HL 5 sci); ABB (Env Sci Educ) (IB 32 pts); ABB incl maths (Meteor Ocean) (IB 32 pts HL 5 maths); ABB incl geog (Clim Chng) (IB 32 pts HL 5 geog)

Kent – ABB (Env Soc Sci; Env Soc Sci (Yr Ind)) (IB 34 pts)

Lancaster – ABB incl sci (Env Sci; Ecol Cons) (IB 32 pts HL 16 pts incl 6 sci)

Leeds – ABB incl maths/sci/geog (Env Sci) (IB 34 pts HL 16 pts); ABB incl sci/maths/geog/econ/sociol/hist/law/pol/Engl (Sust Env Mgt) (IB 34 pts HL 16 pts); ABB incl maths+phys/chem (Meteor Clim Sci) (IB 34 pts HL 16 pts)

Leicester – ABB–BBB+bEPQ incl sci/maths/geog (App Env Geol) (IB 30 pts)

Liverpool – ABB incl sci/maths/geog (Env Sci) (IB 33 pts HL 4 sci/maths/geog)

London (QM) – ABB–BBB incl geog (Env Sci) (IB 32–30 pts HL 6/5 geog)

London (RH) – ABB–BBB incl biol (Ecol Cons) (IB 32 pts HL 655)

Manchester – ABB (Env Mgt) (IB 32 pts HL 655); ABB incl sci +interview (Env Sci; Env Res Geol) (IB 33 pts HL 5 sci)

Newcastle – ABB incl sci/maths/geog/psy (Env Sci) (IB 34 pts HL 5 sci/maths/geog/psy); ABB incl maths/sci/geog/psy (Env Sci (Yr Ind)) (IB 34 pts HL 5 maths/sci/geo/psy)

Nottingham – ABB–BBB incl sci/maths (Env Sci) (IB 32–30 pts); ABB–BBB incl sci/maths/geog (Env Biol) (IB 32–30 pts)

Plymouth – 128–144 pts incl biol+sci/maths/geog/psy (Mar Biol Cstl Ecol) (IB 30 pts HL 5 biol+sci)

Reading – ABB–BBB (Env Mgt) (IB 32–30 pts); ABB–BBB incl maths+phys (Meteor Clim) (IB 32–30 pts HL 5 maths+phys); ABB–BBB incl sci/maths/geog (Env Sci) (IB 32–30 pts HL 5 sci/maths/geog)

Sheffield – ABB (Lnd Archit) (IB 33 pts); ABB incl biol/geog+chem/phys/maths (Env Sci) (IB 33 pts HL 6 geog)

Southampton – ABB incl sci/maths/geog/psy (Env Mgt Bus; Env Sci) (IB 32 pts HL 5 sci)

Stirling – ABB (3 yr course) BBB (4 yr course) incl sci/maths/geog (Env Sci) (IB 35 pts (3 yr course) 32 pts (4 yr course)); ABB (3 yr course) BBB (4 yr course) incl biol+geog/geol/env sci (Ecol; Cons Biol Mgt) (IB 35 pts (3 yr course) 32 pts (4 yr course))

York – ABB incl sci/maths/geog/psy (Env Sci) (IB 34 pts)

120 pts **Aberdeen** – BBB incl maths/sci (Env Sci; Ecol) (IB 32 pts HL 5 maths/sci)

Bangor – 120 pts (App Trstl Mar Ecol)

Dundee – BBB incl maths+sci/eng (Renew) (IB 30 pts HL 555); BBB incl sci (Env Sci) (IB 30 pts HL 555); BBB (Env Sust) (IB 30 pts HL 555)

Edge Hill – BBB incl geog/geol/env sci 120 pts (Env Sci)

Glasgow – BBB (Env Sci Sust) (IB 30 pts)

Gloucestershire – BBB 120 pts (Ecol Env Sci)

Keele – ABC/BBB (Env Sust) (IB 32 pts); ABC/BBB incl sci/geog/env st (Env Sci) (IB 32 pts HL 6 sci/geog)

Liverpool – BBB (Env Plan) (IB 31 pts)

Liverpool Hope – BBB–BBC 120–112 pts (Env Sci) (IB 24 pts)

Northumbria – 120 128 pts (Env Sci; Env Geog) (HL 444)

Reading – BBB–CCC (Ecol Wldf Cons Fdn)

Stirling – BBB incl sci/maths/geog (Env Sci Out Educ) (IB 32 pts)

Ulster – ABC incl sci/maths/geog/hm econ/hlth soc cr (Env Hlth) (IB 26 pts HL 13 pts)

112 pts **Aberystwyth** – BBC–BBB incl biol (Ecol) (IB 30 pts HL 5 biol)

Bangor – 112 pts incl sci/maths/geog/econ (Env Sci; Env Cons)

Brighton – BBC–CCC incl sci 112–96 pts (Env Sci) (IB 28 pts)

Brunel – BBC incl sci/env/maths (Env Sci) (IB 30 pts HL 5 sci/env/maths)

Greenwich – 112 pts incl sci/geog (Env Sci)

London (Birk) – 112 pts (Env Mgt)

Nottingham Trent – BBC 112 pts (Ecol Cons); BBC incl sci 112 pts (Env Sci)

Oxford Brookes – BBC 112 pts (Env Sci) (IB 30 pts)

Plymouth – 112 pts (Archit Tech Env) (IB 28 pts)

Sheffield Hallam – 112–96 pts (Env Sci)

Teesside – BBC incl sci/geog (Env Sci)

UWE Bristol – 112 pts incl sci/maths/geog (Env Sci; Wldf Ecol Cons Sci) (HL 5 sci/maths/geog)

Worcester – 112 pts (Ecol courses)

104 pts **Bath Spa** – BCC–CCC incl sci/geog (Env Sci) (IB 26 pts)

Bournemouth – 104–120 pts incl sci/maths/geog (Env Sci) (IB 28–31 pts HL 55)

Brighton – BCC–CCC incl biol 104–96 pts (Ecol) (IB 28 pts)

Cardiff Met – 104 pts (Env Hlth)

Central Lancashire – 104–112 pts (Env Mgt) (IB 28 pts)

Chester – BCC–BBC incl biol/chem/sci (Wldf Cons Ecol) (IB 26 pts HL 5 biol/chem); BCC–BBC incl geog/soc sci/app sci (Nat Haz Mgt courses) (IB 26 pts HL 5 geog)

Glasgow Caledonian – BBC (Env Mgt)

Leeds Beckett – 104 pts (Env Hlth) (IB 24 pts)

Manchester Met – BCC–BBC incl geog/sci/maths 104–112 pts (Env Sci (St Abrd)) (IB 26 pts HL 5 geog/sci/maths); (Physl Geog) (IB 26 pts HL 5 geog/sci)

Northampton – BCC (Env Sci)

Plymouth – 104–112 pts incl sci/maths/geog/psy/des tech (Env Sci) (IB 28 pts HL 5 sci); 104–112 pts (Env Mgt Sust) (IB 28 pts HL 5 sci)

Portsmouth – 104–120 pts incl sci/maths/geog (Mar Env Sci) (IB 26 pts HL 5 sci/maths/geog)

Check **Chapter 3** for new university admission details and **Chapter 6** on how to read the subject tables.

Ulster – BCC–CCD incl sci/maths/tech/hm econ/PE (Env Sci) (IB 24 pts HL 12 pts)
Worcester – 104–112 pts incl sci/geog/geol (Env Sci)
96 pts **Derby** – 96–128 pts incl sci/maths/geog (Env Haz Comb Hons)
Hertfordshire – 96 pts (Env Mgt courses; Hum Geog Env St) (HL 44)
Kingston – 96–112 pts incl chem+sci/maths/geog/psy (Env Sci)
Trinity Saint David – 96 pts (Env Cons)
Writtle (UC) – 96 pts (Glob Ecosys Mgt)
88 pts **Canterbury Christ Church** – 88–112 pts incl sci (Ecol; Env Sci)
80 pts **Sparsholt (Coll)** – CCE incl sci (Aqua Fish Mgt) (IB 24 pts HL 4 sci)
West Scotland – CCD incl sci (Env Hlth) (IB 27 pts)
Wolverhampton – BB/CCE incl sci (Env Hlth)
64 pts **UHI** – CC incl sci (Env Sci); CC (Arch Env St)

Open University – contact 0300 303 0073 **or** www.open.ac.uk/contact/new (Env St)

Alternative offers
See **Chapter 6** and **Appendix 1** for grades/UCAS Tariff points information for other examinations.

EXAMPLES OF COLLEGES OFFERING COURSES IN THIS SUBJECT FIELD
Askham Bryan (Coll); Bedford (Coll); Birmingham Met (Coll); Bishop Burton (Coll); Cornwall (Coll); Duchy (Coll); Durham New (Coll); Easton Otley (Coll); Hadlow (Coll); Hartpury (Coll); Kingston Maurward (Coll); Leeds City (Coll); Moulton (Coll); Myerscough (Coll); Petroc; Plymouth City (Coll); Sparsholt (Coll); Truro and Penwith (Coll); Weston (Coll); York (Coll).

CHOOSING YOUR COURSE (SEE ALSO CH.1)
Universities and colleges teaching quality See www.qaa.ac.uk; https://unistats.ac.uk.

Top research universities and colleges (REF 2014) (Earth Systems and Environmental Sciences) Bristol; Cambridge; Oxford; London (RH); Birmingham; Southampton; London (Birk); London (UCL); Leicester; Manchester; Leeds.

Examples of sandwich degree courses Brighton; Coventry; Glasgow Caledonian; Greenwich; Hertfordshire; Keele; Kingston; Leeds; Manchester Met; Nottingham Trent; Reading; Teesside; Ulster; UWE Bristol.

ADMISSIONS INFORMATION
Number of applicants per place (approx) Bangor 4; Bath Spa 2; Birmingham 5; Cardiff Met 4; Dundee 13; East Anglia 5; Edinburgh 1; Gloucestershire 11; Greenwich 2; Hertfordshire 5; Hull 5; Kingston 3; Lancaster 5; London LSE 8; Manchester Met (Env Sci) 5; Northampton 4; Nottingham 7; Nottingham Trent 3; Oxford Brookes 7; Plymouth 13; Sheffield Hallam 8; Southampton 4; Stirling 7; Trinity Saint David 3; Ulster 16; Wolverhampton 2; Worcester 7; York 4.

Advice to applicants and planning the UCAS personal statement 'We want doers, not just thinkers' is one comment from an admissions tutor. Describe any field courses which you have attended; make an effort to visit one of the National Parks. Discuss these visits and identify any particular aspects which impressed you. Outline travel interests. Give details of work as a conservation volunteer and other outside-school activities. Strong communication skills, people-oriented work experience. Watch your spelling and grammar! What sparked your interest in environmental science? Discuss your field trips. (Env Hlth courses) A basic knowledge of environmental health as opposed to environmental sciences. Work experience in an environmental health department is looked upon very favourably. See also **Appendix 3**. **Lancaster** (Env Sci) One A-level subject required from biology, human biology, chemistry, computing, environmental science, information technology, mathematics, physics, psychology or geography.

Misconceptions about this course Bangor Students should note that only simple mathematical skills are required for this course. **Southampton** This is not just a course for environmentalists, for example links with BP, IBM etc. **Wolverhampton** This is a course in environmental science, not environmental studies: there is a difference.

Selection interviews Yes Trinity Saint David; **Some** Cardiff Met, Plymouth; **No** Bangor, Birmingham, Coventry, Derby, Dundee, East Anglia, Gloucestershire, Greenwich, Hertfordshire, Kingston, Manchester Met, Newcastle, Nottingham, Nottingham Trent, Oxford Brookes, Reading, Sheffield Hallam, Southampton, UWE Bristol.

Interview advice and questions Environmental issues are constantly in the news, so keep abreast of developments. You could be asked to discuss particular environmental problems in the area in which you live and to justify your stance on any environmental issues on which you have strong opinions. See also **Chapter 5**.

Reasons for rejection (non-academic) Inability to be aware of the needs of others.

AFTER-RESULTS ADVICE
Offers to applicants repeating A-levels Higher Greenwich, Lancaster, Nottingham Trent; **Possibly higher** Aberystwyth; **Same** Bangor, Birmingham, Brighton, Cardiff Met, Derby, Dundee, East Anglia, Leeds, Manchester Met, Northumbria, Nottingham, Plymouth, Southampton, Wolverhampton.

GRADUATE DESTINATIONS AND EMPLOYMENT (2015/16 HESA)
See **Biological Sciences**.

Career note Some graduates find work with government departments, local authorities, statutory and voluntary bodies in areas like land management and pollution control. Others go into a range of non-scientific careers.

OTHER DEGREE SUBJECTS FOR CONSIDERATION
Biological Sciences; Biology; Chemistry; Earth Sciences; Environmental Engineering; Geography; Geology; Meteorology; Ocean Sciences/Oceanography; Town and Country Planning.

EUROPEAN STUDIES
(see also French, German, International Relations, Languages, Russian and East European Studies)

European Studies courses provide the opportunity to study one or two main languages along with a broad study of economic, political, legal, social and cultural issues within the broad context of the European community. Other similar specific courses such as European History or European Politics allow the student to focus on an individual subject area.

Useful websites http://europa.eu; www.erasmusplus.org.uk; see also **Languages**.

NB The points totals shown to the left of the institutions are for ease of reference only. It must not be assumed that Tariff points are always used by institutions or that they can be substituted for an offer in grades. The level of an offer is not necessarily indicative of the quality of a course.

COURSE OFFERS INFORMATION
Subject requirements/preferences GCSE English and a foreign language for all courses and possibly mathematics. Grades may be stipulated. **AL** A modern language usually required.

Your target offers and examples of degree courses
152 pts **London (UCL)** – A*AA (Euro Soc Pol St) (IB 39 pts HL 19 pts)
144 pts **London (King's)** – AAA (Euro St (Fr) (Yr Abrd)) (IB 35 pts HL 666)
        London (UCL) – AAA–AAB (Pol Sociol E Euro St) (IB 38–36 pts HL 18–17 pts)
        Newcastle – AAA–ABB (Gov EU St) (IB 34–32 pts)
136 pts **Glasgow** – AAB Engl/lang/hum/soc sci (Cnt E Euro St) (IB 38 pts HL 666–665 incl Engl+lang/hum)
        London (King's) – AAB (Euro St (Fr/Ger/Span) (Yr Abrd)) (IB 35 pts HL 665)
        London (UCL) – AAB incl lang (Lang Cult) (IB 36 pts HL 17 pts)

Southampton – AAB/ABB+aEPQ incl lang +interview (Langs Contemp Euro St) (IB 34 pts HL 6 lang)

128 pts **Bath** – ABB–ABC+aEPQ incl lang (Modn Langs Euro St) (IB 35 pts HL 6 lang)

Kent – ABB incl maths (Euro Econ) (IB 34 pts)

Leeds – ABB (Euro St Fr/Ger/Ital/Port/Span) (IB 34 pts HL 16 pts)

Leicester – ABB/BBB+bEPQ incl Fr/Ital/Span (Euro St) (IB 30 pts HL 6 Fr/Ital/Span)

London (RH) – ABB–BBB (Euro Int St Fr/Ger/Ital/Span) (IB 32 pts HL 555)

Nottingham – ABB (Modn Euro St) (IB 32 pts)

120 pts **Dundee** – BBB (Euro St) (IB 30 ps HL 555)

Essex – BBB (Euro St; Euro St Fr/Ger/Ital/Span) (IB 30 pts)

Kent – BBB incl lang (Euro St (Comb Langs)) (IB 34 pts); BBB (Euro St (Fr/Ger/Span)) (IB 34 pts)

104 pts **Nottingham Trent** – 104 pts (Euro St Comb Hons)

Alternative offers
See **Chapter 6** and **Appendix 1** for grades/UCAS Tariff points information for other examinations.

CHOOSING YOUR COURSE (SEE ALSO CH.1)
Universities and colleges teaching quality See www.qaa.ac.uk; https://unistats.ac.uk.

Top research universities and colleges (REF 2014) See **Languages**.

ADMISSIONS INFORMATION
Number of applicants per place (approx) Bath 6; Dundee 14; Leicester 6; London (King's) 7; London (UCL) 8; Nottingham 1; Nottingham Trent 12.

Advice to applicants and planning the UCAS personal statement Try to identify an interest you have in the country relevant to your studies. Visits to that country should be described. Read the national newspapers and magazines and keep up-to-date with political and economic developments. Show your interest in the culture and civilisation of Europe as a whole, through, for example, European travel. Show your motivation for choosing the course and give details of your personal achievements and any future career plans, showing your international awareness and perspective.

Selection interviews Yes Southampton; **No** Essex.

Interview advice and questions Whilst your interest in studying a language may be the main reason for applying for this subject, the politics, economics and culture of European countries are constantly in the news. You should keep up-to-date with any such topics concerning your chosen country and be prepared for questions. A language test may occupy part of the interview. See also **Chapter 5**.

Reasons for rejection (non-academic) Poor powers of expression. Lack of ideas on any issues. Lack of enthusiasm.

AFTER-RESULTS ADVICE
Offers to applicants repeating A-levels Same Dundee.

GRADUATE DESTINATIONS AND EMPLOYMENT (2015/16 HESA)
Graduates surveyed 160 **Employed** 80 **In voluntary employment** 10 **In further study** 40 **Assumed unemployed** 10

Career note See **Languages**.

OTHER DEGREE SUBJECTS FOR CONSIDERATION
Business and Management; History; International Relations; Politics; Language courses.

FILM, RADIO, VIDEO and TV STUDIES

(see also **Art and Design (Graphic Design), Communication Studies/Communication, Engineering (Acoustics and Sound), Media Studies, Photography**)

Many course are offered in Film, Radio, Video and TV Studies. The Film, Photography and Media course at the University of Leeds combines theory with practice, covering digital film and photography with options in TV production, film editing, and documentary production. By contrast, the Exeter course presents a broad chronological and geographical coverage from the silent film to the Hollywood classics. It's therefore important to choose courses with care, particularly the theoretical and practical content of courses. At Brunel University, practical studies occupy up to 40% of the Film and Television Studies course. It is often possible to study Film, Radio, Video and TV Studies as part of a combined degree. For example, at the University of Chester, it is possible to study Radio Production with Business Management or Television Production.

Useful websites www.bfi.org.uk; www.mtv.co.uk; www.allmovie.com; www.societyinmotion.com; www.imdb.com; www.fwfr.com; www.bafta.org; www.movingimage.us; http://film.britishcouncil.org; www.filmsite.org; www.festival-cannes.com/en; www.bbc.co.uk/careers; www.rogerebert.com; www.bectu.org.uk

NB The points totals shown to the left of the institutions are for ease of reference only. It must not be assumed that Tariff points are always used by institutions or that they can be substituted for an offer in grades. The level of an offer is not necessarily indicative of the quality of a course.

COURSE OFFERS INFORMATION

Subject requirements/preferences GCSE English usually required. Courses vary, check prospectuses. **AL** English may be stipulated for some courses.

Your target offers and examples of degree courses
144 pts **Lancaster** – AAA–AAB incl Engl (Film Engl Lit) (IB 36–35 pts HL 16 pts incl 6 lit)
      St Andrews – AAA–AAB (Film St courses) (IB 38–35 pts)
136 pts **Bristol** – AAB–BBB (Film TV) (IB 34–31 pts HL 17–15 pts)
      East Anglia – AAB (Film TV St) (IB 33 pts)
      Exeter AAB–ABB (Film St; Film St (Emp Exp)) (IB 34–32 pts)
      Glasgow – AAB–BBB incl arts/hum/lang (Film TV St Comb Hons) (IB 36 pts HL 665 incl 6 Engl/hum/lang)
      Kent – AAB (Film courses) (IB 34 pts)
      Lancaster – AAB–ABB (Film St; Film Sociol) (IB 35–32 pts HL 16 pts)
      Leeds – AAB (Film Photo Media) (IB 35 pts)
      London (King's) – AAB incl Engl+lang (Compar Lit Film St) (IB 35 pts HL 665 incl Engl lit)
      Manchester – AAB (Film St courses) (IB 35 pts HL 665)
      Southampton – AAB–ABB (Film St; Film Phil) (IB 32 pts HL 16 pts); AAB–ABB incl Engl (Film Engl) (IB 32 pts HL 6 Engl); AAB–ABB incl hist (Film Hist) (IB 32 pts HL 6 hist)
      Surrey – AAB incl maths (Film Vid Prod Tech) (IB 34 pts); AAB–ABB (Film St courses) (IB 34–32 pts)
      Sussex – AAB–ABB (Dr Film St; Film St) (IB 32 pts)
      Warwick – AAB incl Engl/film st/hist (Film St) (IB 36 pts HL 5 Engl/film st/hist); AAB incl Engl (Film Lit) (IB 36 pts HL 5 Engl)
      York – AAB (Film TV Prod) (IB 35 pts)
128 pts **East Anglia** – ABB incl Engl (Film St Engl Lit) (IB 32 pts HL 5 Engl)
      Edinburgh – ABB +portfolio (Film TV) (IB 34 pts HL 655)
      Gloucestershire – ABB 128 pts (Film Prod)
      Kent – ABB (Film) (IB 34 pts)
      Leeds – ABB (Film St Comb Hons) (IB 34 pts HL 16 pts)
      Leeds Beckett – 128 pts +portfolio (Filmm) (IB 27 pts)

Check **Chapter 3** for new university admission details and **Chapter 6** on how to read the subject tables.

Liverpool – ABB (Film St Comb Hons) (IB 33 pts)
London (QM) – ABB incl hum/soc sci (Film St) (IB 32 pts)
London (RH) – ABB–BBB +interview (Film St) (IB 32 pts HL 555)
Newcastle – ABB (Film Prac; Film Media) (IB 32 pts)
Nottingham – ABB (Film TV St Am St; Film TV St) (IB 32 pts)
Reading – ABB–BBB +interview +portfolio (Art Film Thea) (IB 32–30 pts); ABB–BBB
    (Film; Engl Lit Film Thea; Film Thea) (IB 32–30 pts)
Westminster – ABB +interview +portfolio (Film) (IB 34 pts)

120 pts **Aberdeen** – BBB (Film Vis Cult) (IB 32 pts HL 555)
Anglia Ruskin – 120 pts (Film St; Film TV Prod)
Arts London – 120 pts +interview (Film TV)
Bangor – 120–104 pts (Mus Film St; Film St courses; Film St Gms Des)
Birmingham City – BBB 120 pts (Film Prod Tech; Film Tech Vis Efcts) (IB 32 pts)
Derby – 120–128 pts +interview +portfolio (Film Prod; Media Prod)
Dundee – BBB incl Engl lit (Engl Film St) (IB 30 pts HL 555)
Edge Hill – BBB 120 pts (Film St; Film TV Prod; Media Film TV; Engl Film St)
Essex – BBB (Film St Lit; Film St) (IB 30 pts)
Greenwich – 120 pts (Film St; Film TV Prod; Dig Film Prod)
Keele – BBB/ABC (Film St) (IB 32 pts)
Kent – BBB (Art Hist Film) (IB 34 pts)
Leicester – BBB–BBC+bEPQ (Film Media St) (IB 28 pts)
Northumbria – 120–128 pts (Film TV St) (HL 444)
Norwich Arts – BBB incl art/des/media +interview +portfolio (Film Mov Imag Prod) (IB 32
    pts)
Queen's Belfast – BBB (Film St courses)
Queen Margaret – BBB (Thea Film) (IB 30 pts)
Stirling – BBB (Film Media) (IB 32 pts)
Sunderland – 120 pts (Film Media; Dig Film Prod)

112 pts **Aberystwyth** – BBC–BBB (Film TV St) (IB 28–30 pts)
Bedfordshire – 112 pts (TV Prod)
Birmingham City – BBC 112 pts +interview +portfolio (Media Comm (Rad)) (HL 14 pts)
Bournemouth – 112–128 pts (TV Prod; Film Prod Cnma) (IB 30–32 pts HL 55)
Bournemouth Arts – BBC–BBB 112–120 pts +portfolio +interview (Film Prod) (IB 30–32
    pts); BBC–BBB 112–120 pts +interview +portfolio (Animat Prod) (IB 30–32 pts)
Bradford – BBC 112 pts (Film TV Prod)
Brunel – BBC (Film TV St Engl) (IB 29 pts HL 5 Engl); (Film Prod; Film Prod Thea; Film TV St)
    (IB 29 pts)
Creative Arts – 112 pts +portfolio (Film Prod)
East London – 112 pts (Film) (IB 25 pts HL 15 pts)
Hertfordshire – 112 pts (Engl Lang Comm Film) (HL 44)
Huddersfield – BBC incl dr/thea/perf arts 112 pts (Film St courses)
Hull – 112 pts (Film St) (IB 28 pts)
Kingston – 112 pts (Filmm)
Leeds Trinity – 112 pts (Film; TV Prod)
Lincoln – BBC (Film TV) (IB 29 pts)
Liverpool John Moores – BBC 112 pts (Crea Writ Film St) (IB 26 pts); BBC 112 pts
    +interview (Film St) (IB 26 pts)
London Met – BBC 112 pts (Jrnl Film TV St; Film Broad Prod; Film TV St)
Manchester Met – 112 pts +interview +portfolio (Filmm) (IB 26 pts)
Middlesex – 112 pts +interview +portfolio (Film)
Nottingham Trent – BBC 112 pts +portfolio (Des Film TV); BBC incl IT/sci 112 pts (Dig
    Media Tech)
Oxford Brookes – BBC 112 pts (Film St) (IB 30 pts)
Plymouth – 112 pts (Film TV Prod) (IB 28 pts)
Roehampton – 112 pts (Film)

St Mary's – 112 pts (Film Scrn Media)

Sheffield Hallam – 112–96 pts (Film Media Prod)

Southampton Solent – 112 pts (Film TV; Film); 112 pts +interview (Engl Film; TV Vid Prod; TV Std Prod)

Staffordshire – BBC 112 pts (Media (Film) Prod; Film TV Rad)

Suffolk – BBC 112 pts (Dig Film Prod)

Sunderland – 112 pts (Photo Vid Dig Imag)

UWE Bristol – 112 pts (Filmm)

West London – 112 pts (Film Prod)

Wolverhampton – BBC (Film TV St courses)

104 pts Bath Spa – BCC–CCC (Film Scrn St courses) (IB 27 pts)

Central Lancashire – 104 pts (TV Prod; Scrnwrit Film TV Rad; Film Prod; Film Media Pop Cult)

Chichester – 104–120 pts (Film TV St; Dig Film Tech) (IB 28 pts)

De Montfort – 104 pts (Film St Comb Hons; Aud Rec Tech) (IB 24 pts)

Edinburgh Napier – BCC incl Engl (Engl Film) (IB 29 pts HL 655)

Falmouth – 104–120 pts +interview (Film)

Hertfordshire – 104 pts (Film TV (Prod)) (HL 44)

Leeds Trinity – 104 pts (Engl Film)

London South Bank – BCC (Film St; Film Prac)

Manchester Met – 104–112 pts (Film Media St) (IB 26 pts)

Northampton – BCC 104 pts (Film Scrn St Comb Hons)

Nottingham Trent – 104 pts (Film TV Comb Hons)

Portsmouth – 104–112 pts (Film Ind courses) (IB 26 pts)

Queen Margaret – BCC (Film Media) (IB 28 pts)

Sheffield Hallam – 104–88 pts incl Engl/film/media st (Film St); 104–88 pts incl film/Engl/hist/jrnl (Film St Scrnwrit)

South Wales – BCC–CDD incl art/film/media/IT +interview +portfolio (Film) (HL 655–445)

Worcester – 104 pts (Film St Scrn Writ); 104 pts +interview +portfolio (Film Prod)

96 pts Chester – CCC–BCC (TV Prod courses; Film St courses; Rad Prod courses) (IB 26 pts)

Cumbria – 96–112 pts (Film TV)

Derby – 96–120 pts (Film TV St Comb Hons)

Plymouth (CA) – 96 pts +portfolio +interview (Film)

Teesside – 96–112 pts +interview +portfolio (Film TV Prod)

West Scotland – CCC incl Engl (Filmm Scrnwrit; Broad Prod (TV Rad)) (IB 24 pts)

Winchester – 96–112 pts (Film St Prod); (Film St) (IB 25 pts)

York St John – 96–112 pts (Film St)

88 pts Canterbury Christ Church – 88–112 pts (Film Rad TV St; Film Prod; TV Prod)

80 pts Bucks New – 80–96 pts +portfolio (Film TV Prod)

64 pts Ravensbourne – CC (Dig Film Prod) (IB 28 pts)

32 pts RConsvS – EE (Filmm) (IB 24 pts)

Alternative offers

See **Chapter 6** and **Appendix 1** for grades/UCAS Tariff points information for other examinations.

EXAMPLES OF COLLEGES OFFERING COURSES IN THIS SUBJECT FIELD

Accrington and Rossendale (Coll); Barking and Dagenham (Coll); Barnsley (Coll); Birmingham Met (Coll); Bournemouth and Poole (Coll); Bournville (Coll); Bradford (Coll); Brooksby Melton (Coll); Buckinghamshire (Coll Group); Bury (Coll); Central Film Sch; Chesterfield (Coll); Chichester (Coll); Cleveland (CAD); Cornwall (Coll); Croydon (Univ Centre); Doncaster (Coll); East Surrey (Coll); Exeter (Coll); Farnborough (CT); Gloucestershire (Coll); Grimsby (Inst Group); Harrow (Coll); Hereford (CA); Hull (Coll); Kensington and Chelsea (Coll); Manchester (Coll); Northbrook Met (Coll); Nottingham (Coll); Rotherham (CAT); South Devon (Coll); South Staffordshire (Coll); Truro and Penwith (Coll); Warwickshire (Coll); West Thames (Coll); Weston (Coll); Wiltshire (Coll).

Check **Chapter 3** for new university admission details and **Chapter 6** on how to read the subject tables.

CHOOSING YOUR COURSE (SEE ALSO CH.1)

Universities and colleges teaching quality See www.qaa.ac.uk; https://unistats.ac.uk.

Top research universities and colleges (REF 2014) See **Drama**.

Examples of sandwich degree courses Birmingham City; Bradford; Greenwich; Hertfordshire; Huddersfield; Portsmouth; Southampton Solent; Surrey; Wolverhampton.

ADMISSIONS INFORMATION

Number of applicants per place (approx) Bournemouth Arts 8; Bristol 15; Central Lancashire 5; East Anglia (Film Engl St) 4, (Film Am St) 5; Kent 6; Leicester 9; Liverpool John Moores 17; London Met 7; Sheffield Hallam 60; Southampton 6; Staffordshire 31; Stirling 11; Warwick 18; Westminster 41; York 4; York St John 6.

Advice to applicants and planning the UCAS personal statement Bournemouth Arts Any experience in film making (beyond home videos) should be described in detail. Knowledge and preferences of types of films and the work of some producers should be included on the UCAS application. Read film magazines and other appropriate literature to keep informed of developments. Show genuine interest in a range of film genres and be knowledgeable about favourite films, directors and give details of work experience or film projects undertaken. You should also be able to discuss the ways in which films relate to broader cultural phenomena, social, literary, historical. It takes many disciplines to make a film. Bournemouth Film School is home to all of them.

Misconceptions about this course That an A-level in film or media studies is required; it is not. That it's Film so it's easy! That the course is all practical work. Some applicants believe that these are Media courses. Some applicants believe that Film and TV Studies is a form of training for production work. **Bournemouth Arts** (Animat Prod) This is not a Film Studies course but a course based on traditional animation with supported computer image processing. **De Montfort** Some believe that this is a course in practical film making: it is not, it is for analysts and historians.

Selection interviews Most institutions will interview applicants in this subject. **Yes** Bournemouth Arts, Reading; **Some** Bournemouth, Bristol, Cumbria, East Anglia, Liverpool John Moores, Southampton, Staffordshire, Warwick, York; **No** Birmingham City, Canterbury Christ Church, Chichester, Essex, Falmouth, Hertfordshire, Leeds Beckett, London South Bank, Middlesex, Nottingham, Wolverhampton.

Interview advice and questions Questions will focus on your chosen field. In the case of films, be prepared to answer questions not only on your favourite films but on the work of one or two directors you admire and early Hollywood examples. See also **Chapter 5**. **Bournemouth Arts** Applicants will be required to bring a five minute show reel of their work. **Staffordshire** We assess essay-writing skills.

Reasons for rejection (non-academic) Not enough drive or ambition. No creative or original ideas. Preference for production work rather than practical work. Inability to articulate the thought process behind the work in the applicant's portfolio. Insufficient knowledge of media affairs. Lack of knowledge of film history. Wrong course choice, wanted more practical work.

AFTER-RESULTS ADVICE

Offers to applicants repeating A-levels Higher Manchester Met; **Same** Bournemouth Arts, De Montfort, East Anglia, St Mary's, Staffordshire, Stirling, Winchester, Wolverhampton, York St John; **No** Glasgow.

GRADUATE DESTINATIONS AND EMPLOYMENT (2015/16 HESA)

See **Media Studies**.

Career note Although this is a popular subject field, job opportunities in film, TV and radio are limited. Successful graduates frequently have gained work experience with companies during their undergraduate years. The transferable skills (verbal communication etc) will open up other career opportunities.

UCAS points Tariff: A* = 56 pts; A = 48 pts; B = 40 pts; C = 32 pts; D = 24 pts; E = 16 pts

OTHER DEGREE SUBJECTS FOR CONSIDERATION
Animation; Communication Studies; Creative Writing; Media Studies; Photography.

FINANCE

(including **Finance and Investment Banking, Financial Services** and
Property, Finance and Investment; see also **Accountancy/Accounting**)

Courses involving finance are wide ranging and can involve accountancy, actuarial work, banking, economics, financial services, insurance, international finance, marketing, quantity surveying, real estate management, and risk management. Some courses are theoretical, others, such as accountancy and real estate management, are vocational, providing accreditation to professional bodies. A large number of courses are offered with commercial and industrial placements over six months or a year (which includes paid employment) and many students have found that their connection with a firm has led to offers of full-time employment upon graduation.

Useful websites www.cii.co.uk; www.financialadvice.co.uk; www.fnlondon.com; www.worldbank.org; www.libf.ac.uk; www.ft.com

NB The points totals shown to the left of the institutions are for ease of reference only. It must not be assumed that Tariff points are always used by institutions or that they can be substituted for an offer in grades. The level of an offer is not necessarily indicative of the quality of a course.

COURSE OFFERS INFORMATION

Subject requirements/preferences GCSE Most institutions will require English and mathematics grade C (4) minimum. **AL** Mathematics may be required or preferred.

Your target offers and examples of degree courses
160 pts **Imperial London** – A*A*A–A*A*A* incl maths+fmaths +MAT/STEP (Maths Stats Fin)
      (IB 39–41 pts HL 7 maths 6 phys/chem/econ)
152 pts **Edinburgh** – A*AA (Econ Fin) (IB 43 pts HL 776)
      Exeter – A*AA–AAB (Econ Fin; Econ Fin (Int St)) (IB 38–34 pts)
      London (UCL) – A*AA–AAA incl maths (Eng (Mech Bus Fin) (MEng)) (IB 39–38 pts HL 6
        maths); (Stats Econ Fin) (IB 39–38 pts HL 7 maths)
      Manchester – A*AA–AAA incl maths +interview (Maths Fin; Maths Fin Maths) (IB 34 pts
        HL 6 maths)
      Nottingham – A*AA–AAA/A*AB incl maths (Fin Maths) (IB 36 pts HL 6 maths)
144 pts **Bath** – AAA–AAB+bEPQ incl maths (Acc Fin) (IB 36 pts HL 666)
      Birmingham – AAA incl maths (Mny Bank Fin) (IB 32 pts HL 666)
      Bristol – AAA–ABB incl maths (Acc Fin) (IB 36–32 pts HL 6 maths)
      City – AAA (Bank Int Fin; Inv Fin Risk Mgt) (IB 36 pts)
      Exeter – AAA–AAB (Acc Fin) (IB 36–34 pts)
      Glasgow – AAA/A*AB incl maths (Acc Fin) (IB 38 pts HL 666 incl maths); (Fin Stats)
        (IB 38 pts HL 666)
      Lancaster – AAA–AAB incl maths/fmaths (Fin Maths) (IB 36 pts HL 16 pts incl 6 maths)
      Leeds – AAA/A*AB–AAB/A*BB incl maths (Maths Fin) (IB 35 pts HL 17 pts incl 6 maths);
        AAA (Acc Fin) (IB 35 pts HL 17 pts incl 5 maths); (Econ Fin) (IB 35 pts HL 17 pts);
        (Int Bus Fin) (IB 17 pts incl 35 pts)
      London (UCL) – AAA–AAB incl maths (Eng (Mech Bus Fin)) (IB 38–36 pts HL 5 maths+phys)
      London LSE – AAA (Acc Fin) (IB 38 pts HL 666)
      Newcastle – AAA–A*AB incl maths (Maths Fin) (IB 37–35 pts HL 6 maths)
      Reading – AAA–AAB (Fin Inv Bank) (IB 35 pts); (Acc Fin) (IB 35–34 pts)
      St Andrews – AAA (Fin Econ) (IB 38 pts)
      Southampton – AAA–AAB+aEPQ incl maths (Maths Fin) (IB 36 pts HL 6 maths)

Check **Chapter 3** for new university admission details and **Chapter 6** on how to read the subject tables.

Surrey – AAA–AAB incl maths (Fin Maths) (IB 34 pts HL 6 maths); AAA (Econ Fin) (IB 34 pts)

Warwick – AAA incl maths/fmaths (Acc Fin) (IB 38 pts HL 5 maths)

136 pts **Aston** – AAB–ABB (Fin) (IB 32 pts HL 665–655)

Birmingham – AAB (Acc Fin) (IB 32 pts HL 665)

Cardiff – AAB incl lang (Bank Fin Euro Lang) (IB 35 pts); AAB (Bank Fin; Acc Fin) (IB 35–32 pts HL 665–655)

City – AAB incl maths 136 pts (Fin Econ) (IB 33 pts HL 5 maths)

Durham – AAB (Acc Fin) (IB 36 pts)

Edinburgh – AAB (Acc Fin) (IB 43 pts HL 776)

Lancaster – AAB incl maths (Acc Fin Maths) (IB 35 pts HL 16 pts incl 6 maths); AAB (Fin; Fin Econ; Acc Fin) (IB 35 pts HL 16 pts)

LIBF – AAB–ABB (Fin Inv Risk) (IB 32–30 pts)

Liverpool – AAB incl maths (Maths Fin) (IB 35 pts HL 6 maths); AAB (Acc Fin; Acc Fin (Yr Ind)) (IB 35 pts)

London (QM) – AAB incl maths (Maths Fin Acc) (IB 34 pts HL 6/5 maths)

London (RH) – AAB–BBB (Fin Bus Econ) (IB 32 pts HL 655)

Loughborough – AAB (Bank Fin Mgt; Bus Econ Fin; Acc Fin Mgt) (IB 35 pts HL 665)

Manchester – AAB (Fin; Acc Fin) (IB 35 pts HL 665)

Newcastle – AAB (Bus Acc Fin; Acc Fin; Econ Fin) (IB 35 pts)

Nottingham – AAB (Fin Acc Mgt; Ind Econ Ins) (IB 34 pts HL 18 pts)

Sheffield – AAB incl maths (Fin Maths) (IB 34 pts HL 6 maths)

Southampton – AAB incl maths (Econ Fin) (IB 34 pts HL 5 maths); AAB/ABB+aEPQ (Acc Fin; Acc Fin (Yr Ind)) (IB 34 pts HL 17 pts)

Strathclyde – AAB (4 yr course) BBB (5 yr course) (Mech Eng Fin Mgt (MEng)) (IB 36 pts HL 6 maths+phys)

Surrey – AAB (Acc Fin) (IB 34 pts)

Sussex – AAB–ABB (Fin Bus; Acc Fin) (IB 32 pts)

York – AAB incl maths (Econ Fin; Econ Ecomet Fin) (IB 35 pts HL 666); AAB (Acc Bus Fin Mgt) (IB 35 pts)

128 pts **Abertay** – ABB (3 yr course) CCC (4 yr course) (Acc Fin) (IB 28 pts)

Bournemouth – 128–136 pts (Bus St Fin) (IB 32–33 pts HL 55)

Bradford – ABB 128 pts (Acc Fin)

East Anglia – ABB (Bus Fin Econ) (IB 32 pts)

Heriot-Watt – ABB (3 yr course) BBB (4 yr course) (Bus Fin; Acc Fin) (IB 34 pts (3 yr course) 29 pts (4 yr course))

Kent – ABB (Acc Fin (Yr Ind); Acc Fin) (IB 34 pts HL 4 maths); (Fin Econ) (IB 34 pts)

Leicester – ABB/BBB+bEPQ (Bank Fin) (IB 30 pts); ABB–BBB+bEPQ (Acc Fin) (IB 30 pts)

LIBF – ABB–BBC (Bank Fin) (IB 32–28 pts)

Liverpool – ABB (Law Acc Fin) (IB 33 pts)

London (RH) – ABB (Acc Fin) (IB 32 pts HL 655 incl maths)

Northumbria – 128–136 pts (Fin Inv Mgt) (HL 444)

Queen's Belfast – ABB–AAA (Fin (Yr Ind))

Sheffield – ABB (Acc Fin Mgt) (IB 33 pts)

Stirling – ABB incl acc+econ (3 yr course) BBB (4 yr course) (Fin) (IB 35 pts (3 yr course) 32 pts (4 yr course))

Strathclyde – ABB (Fin courses) (IB 36 pts); ABB incl maths (Acc Fin) (IB 38 pts HL 6 maths)

Swansea – ABB–BBB (Acc Fin (Yr Ind); Acc Fin; Bus Mgt (Fin)) (IB 33–32 pts)

120 pts **Aberdeen** – BBB (Fin courses) (IB 32 pts HL 555)

Aberystwyth – BBB (Bus Fin; Acc Fin) (IB 28 pts)

Bangor – 120 pts (Acc Fin); 120–104 pts (Bank Fin)

Brighton – BBB–CCC 120–96 pts (Fin Inv) (IB 30 pts HL 16 pts)

Brunel – BBB (Econ Bus Fin) (IB 30 pts); BBB incl maths (Fin Acc) (IB 30 pts HL 5 maths)

Buckingham – BBB +interview (Law Bus Mgt) (IB 32 pts); BBB–BCC +interview (Acc Fin) (IB 32–30 pts)
Dundee – BBB–BCC (Fin; Int Fin) (IB 30 pts HL 555); (Int Bus Fin) (IB 30 pts)
Essex – BBB (Fin; Fin Econ; Acc Fin; Bank Fin) (IB 30 pts)
Greenwich – 120 pts (Acc Fin; Fin Inv Bank)
Huddersfield – BBB 120 pts (Bus Fin Serv; Acc Fin)
Kingston – 120 pts (Acc Fin) (IB 27 pts HL 664 incl 4 Engl lang)
Liverpool Hope – BBB–BBC 120–112 pts (Acc Fin)
London South Bank – BBB 120 pts (Acc Fin)
Middlesex – 120 pts (Acc Fin)
Nottingham Trent – BBB (Prop Fin Inv); BBB 120 pts (Acc Fin; Econ Int Fin Bank)
Oxford Brookes – BBB 120 pts (Acc Fin) (IB 31 pts)
Plymouth – 120 pts (Acc Fin) (IB 28 pts HL 4); 120–128 pts incl maths (Maths Fin) (IB 30 pts HL 5 maths)
Sheffield Hallam – 120 pts (Acc Fin)
Staffordshire – BBB 120 pts (Acc Fin)
UWE Bristol – 120 pts (Acc Fin; Bank Fin)
112 pts **Birmingham City** – BBC 112 pts (Fin Econ); (Acc Fin; Bus Fin) (HL 14 pts)
Bournemouth – 112–120 pts (Fin Econ; Acc Fin) (IB 30–31 pts HL 55)
Brighton – BBC–CCC 112–96 pts (Acc Fin) (IB 28 pts HL 16 pts); BBC–CCC incl maths 112–96 pts (Maths Fin) (IB 28 pts HL 6 maths)
Cardiff Met – 112 pts (Bus Mgt St Fin; Int Econ Fin)
Central Lancashire – 112 pts (Acc Fin Mgt)
Chester – BBC–BCC 112 pts (Bus Fin) (IB 26 pts)
Chichester – BBC–CCC (HR Mgt Fin; Acc Fin) (IB 28 pts)
De Montfort – 112 pts (Econ Fin) (IB 28 pts)

Check **Chapter 3** for new university admission details and **Chapter 6** on how to read the subject tables.

East London – 112 pts (Acc Fin) (IB 26 pts HL 15 pts)
Gloucestershire – BBC 112 pts (Acc Fin Mgt St)
Greenwich – 112 pts (Bus Fin; Fin Maths)
Hertfordshire – 112 pts incl maths (Fin Maths) (HL 4 maths)
Hull – 112 pts (Fin Mgt; Bus Mgt Fin Mgt) (IB 30 pts)
Keele – BBC (Fin Comb Hons; Acc Fin) (IB 30 pts)
Leeds Beckett – 112 pts (Acc Fin) (IB 25 pts)
Lincoln – BBC (Acc Fin) (IB 29 pts)
Liverpool John Moores – BBC 112 pts (Acc Fin) (IB 28 pts)
London Regent's – BBC (Glob Mgt courses) (IB 26 pts)
Middlesex – 112 pts (Bank Fin)
Oxford Brookes – BBC (Econ Fin Int Bus) (IB 30 pts)
Plymouth – 112 pts (Fin Mgt) (IB 28 pts)
Portsmouth – 112 pts (Fin Mgt Bus; Acc Fin; Econ Fin Bank) (IB 30 pts HL 17 pts)
Robert Gordon – BBC (Acc Fin) (IB 29 pts)
Sheffield Hallam – 112 pts (Bus Fin Mgt)
Southampton Solent – 112 pts (Acc Fin)
Sunderland – 112 pts (Bus Fin Mgt; Acc Fin)
West London – 112 pts (Bus St Fin); 112–120 pts (Acc Fin) (IB 26 pts)
Westminster – BBC (Fin) (IB 28 pts)
Winchester – 112–120 pts (Acc Fin) (IB 26 pts)
Wolverhampton – BBC–CCC (Acc Fin)
Worcester – 112 pts (Fin)

104 pts **Coventry** – 104 pts (Fin Serv)
Glasgow Caledonian – BCC (Fin Inv Risk) (IB 25 pts)
Lincoln – BCC (Bus Fin) (IB 28 pts)
Manchester Met – BCC–BBC 104–112 pts (Acc Fin; Bank Fin) (IB 26 pts)
Northampton – BCC (Bank Fin Plan)
Plymouth – 104 pts (Fin Econ) (IB 26 pts HL 4)
Portsmouth – 104–120 pts incl maths (Maths Fin Mgt) (IB 26 pts)
Winchester – 104–120 pts (Econ Fin) (IB 26 pts); 104–120 pts incl maths (Maths Fin)
(IB 26 pts)

96 pts **Anglia Ruskin** – 96–112 pts (Bus Mgt Fin; Bank Fin) (IB 24 pts)
Edinburgh Napier – CCC (Fin Serv) (IB 27 pts HL 654)
Hertfordshire – 96–112 pts (Fin) (IB 28 pts)
London Met – CCC 96 pts (Bank Fin)
York St John – 96–112 pts (Bus Mgt Fin; Acc Fin)

88 pts **Trinity Saint David** – 88 pts +interview (Bus Fin)

80 pts **Bucks New** – 80–96 pts (Acc Fin; Bus Fin)
South Wales – BCC–CDD 104–80 pts (Acc Fin) (HL 655–445)
Teesside – 80–96 pts (Acc Fin)

Alternative offers
See **Chapter 6** and **Appendix 1** for grades/UCAS Tariff points information for other examinations.

EXAMPLES OF COLLEGES OFFERING COURSES IN THIS SUBJECT FIELD
Barnet and Southgate (Coll); Blackburn (Coll); Bradford (Coll); Croydon (Univ Centre); Manchester (Coll); Newcastle (Coll); Norwich City (Coll); Pearson (Coll); Peterborough (Coll); Plymouth City (Coll).

CHOOSING YOUR COURSE (SEE ALSO CH.1)
Universities and colleges teaching quality See www.qaa.ac.uk; https://unistats.ac.uk.

Examples of sandwich degree courses Aston; Bath; Birmingham City; Bournemouth; Bradford; Brighton; Brunel; Chichester; City; Coventry; De Montfort; Durham; Greenwich; Hertfordshire; Huddersfield; Kent; Kingston; Lancaster; Leeds Beckett; Liverpool John Moores; London Met;

UCAS points Tariff: A* = 56 pts; A = 48 pts; B = 40 pts; C = 32 pts; D = 24 pts; E = 16 pts

Loughborough; Manchester Met; Middlesex; Nottingham Trent; Oxford Brookes; Portsmouth; Queen's Belfast; Sheffield Hallam; Surrey; Sussex; Teesside; Trinity Saint David; UWE Bristol; West London; Westminster; Wolverhampton; York.

ADMISSIONS INFORMATION

Number of applicants per place (approx) Bangor 5; Birmingham 3; Birmingham City 13; Buckingham 4; Cardiff 10; Central Lancashire 6; City 9; Dundee 8; Durham 5; Manchester 11; Middlesex 3; Northampton 3; Sheffield Hallam 4.

Advice to applicants and planning the UCAS personal statement Visits to banks or insurance companies should be described, giving details of any work experience or work shadowing done in various departments. Discuss any particular aspects of finance etc which interest you. See also **Appendix 3**.

Misconceptions about this course Many applicants believe that when they graduate they can only enter careers in banking and finance. In fact, business and industry provide wide-ranging opportunities.

Selection interviews Yes Buckingham; **No** City, Dundee, Huddersfield, Staffordshire, Stirling.

Interview advice and questions Banking involves both high street and merchant banks, so a knowledge of banking activities in general will be expected. In the past mergers have been discussed and also the role of the Bank of England in the economy. The work of the accountant may be discussed. See also **Chapter 5**.

Reasons for rejection (non-academic) Lack of interest. Poor English. Lacking in motivation and determination to complete the course.

AFTER-RESULTS ADVICE

Offers to applicants repeating A-levels Same Bangor, Birmingham, Birmingham City, Bradford, Cardiff, City, Dundee, Edinburgh Napier, London Met, Loughborough, Northumbria, Stirling; **No** Glasgow.

GRADUATE DESTINATIONS AND EMPLOYMENT (2015/16 HESA)

Graduates surveyed 2,075 **Employed** 1,240 **In voluntary employment** 45 **In further study** 380 **Assumed unemployed** 150

Career note Most graduates enter financial careers. Further study is required to qualify as an accountant and to obtain other professional qualifications, eg Institute of Banking.

OTHER DEGREE SUBJECTS FOR CONSIDERATION

Accountancy; Actuarial Studies; Business Studies; Economics.

FOOD SCIENCE/STUDIES and TECHNOLOGY

(see also **Agricultural Sciences/Agriculture, Biochemistry, Dietetics, Hospitality and Event Management, Nutrition**)

Food Science courses are purely scientific and technical in their approach with the study of food composition and storage in order to monitor food quality, safety and preparation. Scientific elements cover biochemistry, chemistry and microbiology, focussing on human nutrition and, in some courses, dietetics, food processing and management. However, these courses are not to be confused with Culinary Arts subjects which lead to careers in food preparation. There are also several business courses specialising in food, such as Food Product Management and Marketing options. The unique course in this category, however, is the Viticulture and Oenology course offered at Plumpton College in partnership with the University of Brighton, which involves the study of grape growing and wine-making.

Check **Chapter 3** for new university admission details and **Chapter 6** on how to read the subject tables.

Useful websites www.sofht.co.uk; www.ifst.org; www.gov.uk/government/organisations/ department-for-environment-food-rural-affairs; http://iagre.org

NB The points totals shown to the left of the institutions are for ease of reference only. It must not be assumed that Tariff points are always used by institutions or that they can be substituted for an offer in grades. The level of an offer is not necessarily indicative of the quality of a course.

COURSE OFFERS INFORMATION

Subject requirements/preferences GCSE English, mathematics and a science. **AL** One or two mathematics/science subjects; chemistry may be required.

Your target offers and examples of degree courses

136 pts **Newcastle** – AAB–ABB (Fd Bus Mgt Mark) (IB 35–32 pts); AAB–ABB incl sci (Nutr Fd Mark) (IB 34–32 pts HL 6 biol); AAB–ABB incl biol+sci (Fd Hum Nutr) (IB 34–32 pts HL 6 biol)
Nottingham – AAB–ABB incl sci/maths (Fd Sci; Fd Sci Nutr) (IB 34–32 pts)
Reading – AAB–ABB incl sci/maths (Nutr Fd Sci; Fd Tech Bioproc; Fd Sci Bus; Fd Sci) (IB 34–32 pts HL 5 sci/maths)

128 pts **Leeds** – ABB incl sci/maths (Fd Sci) (IB 34 pts HL 16 pts)
Reading – ABB–BBB (Fd Mark Bus Econ) (IB 32–30 pts)
Surrey – ABB incl sci/maths (Fd Sci Microbiol; Nutr Fd Sci) (IB 32 pts)

120 pts **Northumbria** – 120–128 pts incl sci/fd tech/hm econ (Fd Sci Nutr) (HL 444)
Queen's Belfast – BBB–ABB incl sci (Fd Qual Sfty Nutr)

112 pts **Cardiff Met** – 112 pts (Fd Ind Mgt); 112 pts incl sci/fd tech (Fd Sci Tech)
Coventry – BBC incl biol/chem/fd tech (Fd Nutr) (IB 30 pts HL 5 biol/chem); (Fd Sfty Insp Cntrl) (IB 30 pts HL 5 biol/chem)
Glasgow Caledonian – BBC incl chem (Fd Biosci) (IB 28 pts)
Sheffield Hallam – 112 pts (Fd Nutr; Fd Mark Mgt)
Teesside – BBC incl sci/fd tech/nutr (Fd Nutr)

104 pts **Bath Spa** – BCC–CCC (Fd Nutr) (IB 26 pts)
CAFRE – 104 pts incl sci/hm econ (Food Tech; Fd Des Nutr)
Liverpool John Moores – BCC 104 pts (Fd Dev Nutr) (IB 24 pts)
Royal Agricultural Univ – BCC 104 pts (Fd Prod Sply Mgt) (IB 26 pts)
Ulster – BCC–BBB (Consum Mgt Fd Innov) (IB 24–26 pts HL 12–13 pts)

96 pts **Abertay** – CCC (Fd Consum Sci; Fd Nutr Hlth) (IB 28 pts)
Birmingham (UC) – 96 pts (Culn Arts Mgt; Fd Dev Innov)
Royal Agricultural Univ – CCC (Int Bus Mgt (Fd Agribus)) (IB 26 pts)
Ulster – CCC incl sci/maths/env tech/hm econ (Fd Nutr) (IB 24 pts HL 12 pts incl 5 sci/ maths/hm econ)

88 pts **Harper Adams** – 88–104 pts (Agri-Fd Mark Bus; Fd Prod Mark)
London South Bank – CCD incl chem (Fd Nutr)

Alternative offers
See **Chapter 6** and **Appendix 1** for grades/UCAS Tariff points information for other examinations.

EXAMPLES OF DEGREE APPRENTICESHIPS IN THIS SUBJECT FIELD
Nottingham Trent (Food Sci Tech).

EXAMPLES OF COLLEGES OFFERING COURSES IN THIS SUBJECT FIELD
Bridgwater and Taunton (Coll); CAFRE; Cornwall (Coll); Duchy (Coll); Grimsby (Inst Group); Plumpton (Coll); Westminster Kingsway (Coll).

CHOOSING YOUR COURSE (SEE ALSO CH.1)
Universities and colleges teaching quality See www.qaa.ac.uk; https://unistats.ac.uk.

Top research universities and colleges (REF 2014) See **Agricultural Sciences/Agriculture**.

Examples of sandwich degree courses Birmingham (UC); Cardiff Met; Coventry; Huddersfield; London South Bank; Northumbria; Queen's Belfast; Reading; Sheffield Hallam.

UCAS points Tariff: A* = 56 pts; A = 48 pts; B = 40 pts; C = 32 pts; D = 24 pts; E = 16 pts

ADMISSIONS INFORMATION

Number of applicants per place (approx) Bath Spa 4; Birmingham (UC) 2; Cardiff Met 1; Leeds 5; Liverpool John Moores 2; London South Bank 3; Nottingham 8; Queen's Belfast 10; Sheffield Hallam 4.

Advice to applicants and planning the UCAS personal statement Visits, work experience or work shadowing in any food manufacturing firm, or visits to laboratories, should be described on your UCAS application. Keep up-to-date with developments by reading journals relating to the industry.

Misconceptions about this course Some applicants confuse food technology with catering or hospitality management. Applicants underestimate the job prospects. **Leeds** Food Science is not food technology, catering or cooking. It aims to understand why food materials behave in the way they do, in order to improve the nutritive value, safety and quality of the food we eat.

Selection interviews Yes Harper Adams; **No** Leeds, Liverpool John Moores, Nottingham, Reading, Surrey.

Interview advice and questions Food science and technology is a specialised field and admissions tutors will want to know your reasons for choosing the subject. You will be questioned on any experience you have had in the food industry. More general questions may cover the reasons for the trends in the popularity of certain types of food, the value of junk food and whether scientific interference with food is justifiable. See also **Chapter 5**. **Leeds** Questions asked to ensure that the student understands, and can cope with, the science content of the course.

Reasons for rejection (non-academic) Too immature. Unlikely to integrate well. Lack of vocational commitment.

AFTER-RESULTS ADVICE

Offers to applicants repeating A-levels Higher Heriot-Watt, Leeds; **Same** Abertay, Liverpool John Moores, Nottingham, Queen's Belfast, Sheffield Hallam.

GRADUATE DESTINATIONS AND EMPLOYMENT (2015/16 HESA)

Food and Beverage Studies graduates surveyed 515 **Employed** 310 **In voluntary employment** 5 **In further study** 140 **Assumed unemployed** 15

Career note Employment levels for food science/studies and technology graduates are high mainly in manufacturing and retailing and increasingly with large companies.

OTHER DEGREE SUBJECTS FOR CONSIDERATION

Biochemistry; Biological Sciences; Biology; Biotechnology; Chemistry; Consumer Studies; Crop Science; Dietetics; Health Studies; Hospitality Management; Nutrition; Plant Science.

FRENCH

(see also **European Studies, Languages**)

Applicants should select courses according to the emphasis which they prefer. Courses could focus on literature or language (or both), or on the written and spoken word, as in the case of interpreting and translating courses, or on the broader study of French culture, political and social aspects found on European Studies courses.

Useful websites http://europa.eu; www.bbc.co.uk/languages; www.languageadvantage.com; www. languagematters.co.uk; www.ciol.org.uk; www.lemonde.fr; www.institut-francais.org.uk; www. academie-francaise.fr; www.institut-de-france.fr; www.sfs.ac.uk; https://academic.oup.com/fs

NB The points totals shown to the left of the institutions are for ease of reference only. It must not be assumed that Tariff points are always used by institutions or that they can be substituted for an offer in grades. The level of an offer is not necessarily indicative of the quality of a course.

COURSE OFFERS INFORMATION

Subject requirements/preferences GCSE French, mathematics (for business courses), grade levels may be stipulated. **AL** French is usually required at a specific grade and in some cases a second language may be stipulated.

Your target offers and examples of degree courses

152 pts **Imperial London** – A*AA–A*A*A* incl chem+maths +interview (Chem Fr/Ger/Span Sci) (IB 40–42 pts HL 7 chem 6 maths)

Nottingham – A*AA–AAA (Econ Fr) (IB 38–36 pts)

144 pts **Durham** – AAA incl lang (Modn Langs Cult (Yr Abrd)) (IB 37 pts)

London (King's) – AAA (Euro St (Fr) (Yr Abrd)) (IB 35 pts HL 666)

Newcastle – AAA–ABB incl Fr (Ling Fr) (IB 36–34 pts HL 5 Fr)

Oxford – AAA incl Fr +interview +MLAT (Fr) (IB 38 pts HL 666)

Southampton – AAA–AAB+aEPQ incl maths+Fr/Ger/Span (Maths Fr/Ger/Span) (IB 36 pts HL 6 maths)

Strathclyde – AAA–BBB (Fr courses) (IB 36 pts)

136 pts **Bath** – AAB–ABB+aEPQ incl Fr (Int Mgt Fr) (IB 36 pts HL 6 Fr)

Birmingham – AAB incl Fr (Fr St Comb Hons) (IB 32 pts HL 665)

Edinburgh – AAB incl lang (Fr) (IB 40 pts HL 766); (Int Bus Fr/Ger/Span) (IB 43 pts HL 776)

Exeter – AAB–ABB incl Fr (Fr Arbc) (IB 34–32 pts HL 5 Fr); AAB–ABB incl Fr+Lat (Fr Lat) (IB 34–32 pts HL 5 Fr+Lat)

Glasgow – AAB–BBB incl arts/lang/hum (Fr) (IB 36–34 pts HL 665 incl Engl+lang/hum)

Lancaster – AAB–ABB (Fr St) (IB 35–32 pts HL 16 pts)

Leeds – AAB incl Fr+maths (Fr Maths) (IB 35 pts HL 16 pts incl 6 Fr+maths)

London (King's) – AAB incl Fr (Fr Mgt (Yr Abrd); Fr Ger (Yr Abrd); Fr Span (Yr Abrd)) (IB 35 pts HL 665 incl 6 Fr); (Fr; Fr Phil (Yr Abrd)) (IB 35 pts HL 665 incl Fr); AAB (Euro St (Fr/ Ger/Span) (Yr Abrd)) (IB 35 pts HL 665); AAB incl Fr+hist (Fr Hist (Yr Abrd)) (IB 35 pts HL 665 incl Fr+hist)

London (RH) – AAB–BBB (Modn Lang Lat) (IB 32 pts HL 555)

London (UCL) – AAB incl Fr (Fr As Af Lang; Fr) (IB 36 pts HL 6 Fr)

Northumbria – AAB incl Fr (Int Bus Mgt Fr) (IB 34 pts HL 18 pts incl 5 Fr)

St Andrews – AAB (Fr courses) (IB 36 pts HL 6 Fr)

Southampton – AAB/ABB+aEPQ incl Fr +interview (Fr) (IB 34 pts HL 6 Fr); AAB incl sci/ maths/geog +interview (Ocean Fr (MSci)); AAB–ABB incl Fr/Ger/Span (Film Fr/Ger/ Span) (IB 32 pts HL 6 Fr/Ger/Span); AAB/ABB+aEPQ incl Engl+Fr/Ger/Span (Engl Fr/ Ger/Span) (IB 34 pts HL 6 Engl+Fr/Ger/Span)

Surrey – AAB–ABB incl Fr (Fr courses) (IB 34–32 pts)

Warwick – AAB incl Fr (Fr Ger St; Fr Comb Hons) (IB 36 pts HL 5 Fr)

York – AAB–ABB incl Fr (Fr Ling (Yr Abrd); Fr Ger Lang (Yr Abrd)) (IB 34 pts); (Fr Ital Lang (Yr Abrd); Fr Sp Lang (Yr Abrd)) (IB 35–34 pts)

128 pts **Aston** – ABB–BBB incl lang (Int Bus Fr/Ger/Span) (IB 32 pts HL 655–555 incl 5 lang); ABB–BBB incl Fr (Fr courses) (IB 33–32 pts HL 6 Fr)

Bath – ABB–ABC+aEPQ incl lang (Modn Langs Euro St) (IB 35 pts HL 6 lang)

Bristol – AAB–BBC incl Fr (Fr courses) (IB 32–29 pts HL 5 Fr)

Cardiff – ABB–BBC incl lang (Fr courses) (IB 32–30 pts HL 665–655)

Dundee – ABB incl lang (Law Langs) (IB 32 pts HL 655)

Leeds – ABB incl Fr (Fr) (IB 34 pts HL 16 pts incl 6 Fr)

Leicester – ABB/BBB+bEPQ (Fr Comb Hons) (IB 30 pts)

Liverpool – ABB incl Fr (Fr; Fr Comb Hons) (IB 33 pts HL 6 Fr)

London (Inst Paris) – ABB incl Fr +interview (Fr St) (IB 34 pts HL 6 Fr)

London (QM) – ABB incl art/hum/soc sci+lang (Fr/Ger/Russ Dr) (IB 32 pts HL 6/5 art/ hum/soc sci)

London (RH) – ABB–BBB incl lang (Modn Lang Dr) (IB 32 pts); ABB–BBB (Euro Int St Fr/ Ger/Ital/Span; Modn Lang Mus; Modn Lang) (IB 32 pts HL 555); ABB (Modn Lang Mgt) (IB 32 pts HL 655)

      Manchester – ABB (Fr courses) (IB 33 pts HL 655)

      Nottingham – ABB (Fr Comb Hons) (IB 32 pts HL 5 Fr); ABB incl Fr (Fr St) (IB 32 pts HL 5 Fr)

      Queen's Belfast – ABB incl Fr (Fr Comb Hons); ABB (Fr)

      Reading – ABB–BBB (Fr courses) (IB 30–32 pts)

      Sheffield – ABB–BBB incl Fr (Fr Comb Hons) (IB 33–32 pts HL 6 Fr); ABB/BBB+bEPQ incl Fr (Fr St) (IB 33 pts HL 6 Fr)

      Stirling – ABB (3 yr course) BBB (4 yr course) incl Fr (Fr) (IB 35 pts (3 yr course) 32 pts (4 yr course))

      Sussex – ABB–BBB incl Fr (Fr Ital/Span (Yr Abrd)) (IB 30 pts HL 5 Fr)

      Warwick – ABB incl Fr (Fr St) (IB 34 pts HL 5 Fr)

120 pts **Aberdeen** – BBB (Fr St; Anth Fr/Ger) (IB 32 pts HL 555)

      Aberystwyth – BBB–ABB (Fr Comb Hons) (IB 30 pts)

      Buckingham – BBB–BBC (Mark Fr) (IB 32–31 pts); BBB +interview (Law Fr) (IB 32 pts)

      Essex – BBB (Fr St Modn Langs) (IB 30 pts)

      Heriot-Watt – BBB incl lang (App Langs Transl (Fr/Span)/(Ger/Span)) (IB 30 pts HL 5 lang)

      Kent – BBB incl Fr (Fr) (IB 34 pts)

      London (QM) – BBB incl Fr (Fr courses) (IB 30 pts HL 5 Fr)

      Plymouth – 120 pts incl Engl (Engl Fr) (IB 28 pts HL 6 Engl)

      Swansea – BBB incl lang 120 pts (Fr)

112 pts **Central Lancashire** – 112 pts (Mod Lang Int Bus); 112 pts incl lang (Modn Langs (Fr/Ger/Span/Jap))

      Chester – 112 pts incl art des+Fr +interview +portfolio (Fn Art Fr) (IB 26 pts HL 5 vis arts+Fr)

      Coventry – BBC (Fr Int Rel) (IB 29 pts)

      Hertfordshire – 112 pts (Fr Comb Hons; Engl Lit Fr) (HL 44)

      Hull – 112 pts incl lang (Hist Modn Lang; Fr St; Fr Comb Hons) (IB 28 pts)

104 pts **Chester** – BCC–BBC incl Fr (Fr) (IB 26 pts HL 5 Fr)

      London (Birk) – 104 pts incl lang (Modn Langs (Fr/Ger/Ital/Jap/Port/Span)); 104 pts (Fr Mgt); 104 pts incl Fr (Fr St)

      Manchester Met – 104–112 pts (Ling Mand Chin/Fr/Ger/Ital/Span) (IB 26 pts); 104–112 pts incl Fr (Fr St) (IB 26 pts)

      Nottingham Trent – 104 pts incl Fr (Fr Comb Hons)

      Westminster – BCC (Fr courses) (IB 28 pts)

 96 pts **Bangor** – 96–104 pts incl lang (Fr courses)

      Portsmouth – 96–120 pts (Modn Lang)

 88 pts **Canterbury Christ Church** – 88–112 pts incl Fr (Fr)

Alternative offers

See **Chapter 6** and **Appendix 1** for grades/UCAS Tariff points information for other examinations.

EXAMPLES OF COLLEGES OFFERING COURSES IN THIS SUBJECT FIELD

Richmond-upon-Thames (Coll).

CHOOSING YOUR COURSE (SEE ALSO CH.1)

Universities and colleges teaching quality See www.qaa.ac.uk; https://unistats.ac.uk.

Top research universities and colleges (REF 2014) See **Languages**.

Examples of sandwich degree courses Bangor.

ADMISSIONS INFORMATION

Number of applicants per place (approx) Aston 6; Bangor 5; Bath (Modn Langs Euro St) 6; Birmingham 5; Bristol 4; Cardiff 6; Central Lancashire 5; Durham 5; Exeter 8; Hull 5; Kent 6; Lancaster 7; Leicester (Fr Ital) 6; Liverpool 6; London (Inst Paris) 9; London (King's) 9; London (RH) 7; London (UCL) 5; Manchester Met 13; Newcastle (Modn Langs) 7; Nottingham 8; Warwick 7; York 8.

Advice to applicants and planning the UCAS personal statement Visits to France (including exchange visits) should be described, with reference to any particular cultural or geographical features of the region visited. Providing information about your contacts with French friends and experience in speaking the language are also important. Express your willingness to work/live/travel abroad and show your interests in French life and culture. Read French newspapers and magazines and keep up-to-date with news stories etc. See also **Appendix 3**. **Bristol** Deferred entry accepted in some cases. Late applications may not be accepted.

Misconceptions about this course Leeds See **Languages**. **Swansea** Some applicants are not aware of the range of subjects which can be combined with French in our flexible modular system. They sometimes do not know that linguistics and area studies options are also available as well as literature options in French.

Selection interviews Yes Leeds, London (Inst Paris), Oxford; **Some** London (UCL), Warwick; **No** Bangor, Birmingham, Canterbury Christ Church, Essex, Heriot-Watt, Hull, Liverpool, Nottingham, Portsmouth, Reading, Surrey.

Interview advice and questions Questions will almost certainly be asked on your A-level texts, in addition to your reading outside the syllabus – books, magazines, newspapers etc. Part of the interview may be conducted in French and written tests may be involved. See also **Chapter 5**. **Leeds** See **Languages**.

Reasons for rejection (non-academic) Unstable personality. Known alcoholism. Poor motivation. Candidate unenthusiastic, unmotivated, ill-informed about the nature of the course (had not read the prospectus). Not keen to spend a year abroad.

AFTER-RESULTS ADVICE
Offers to applicants repeating A-levels Higher Aberystwyth, Leeds, Warwick; **Possibly higher** Aston; **Same** Chester, Durham, Lancaster, Liverpool, Newcastle, Nottingham, Sheffield, Sussex; **No** Glasgow.

GRADUATE DESTINATIONS AND EMPLOYMENT (2015/16 HESA)
Graduates surveyed 1,115 **Employed** 570 **In voluntary employment** 55 **In further study** 280 **Assumed unemployed** 65

Career note See **Languages**.

OTHER DEGREE SUBJECTS FOR CONSIDERATION
European Studies; International Business Studies; Literature; other language.

GENETICS
(see also Biological Sciences, Microbiology)

Genetics is at the cutting edge of modern biology, as demonstrated by the recent developments in genomics and biotechnology leading to considerable advances in the treatment of disease and genetic engineering. Studies can cover such fields as genetic counselling, population genetics, pharmaceuticals, pre-natal diagnoses, cancer biology, evolution, forensic genetics, plant biology and food quality. Possibly an ideal option for keen science students looking for a degree allied to medicine.

Useful websites www.genetics.org; www.nature.com/genetics; www.genetics.org.uk; see also **Biological Sciences**.

NB The points totals shown to the left of the institutions are for ease of reference only. It must not be assumed that Tariff points are always used by institutions or that they can be substituted for an offer in grades. The level of an offer is not necessarily indicative of the quality of a course.

COURSE OFFERS INFORMATION

Subject requirements/preferences GCSE English, mathematics and science subjects. **AL** Chemistry and/or biology are usually required or preferred.

Your target offers and examples of degree courses

160 pts **Cambridge** – A*A*A incl sci/maths +interview +NSAA (Nat Sci (Genet)) (IB 40–42 pts HL 776)

144 pts **Leeds** – AAA–AAB incl biol (Genet) (IB 35–34 pts HL 18–16 pts incl 6 biol+sci)

Manchester – AAA–ABB incl sci/maths +interview (Genet Modn Lang; Genet; Genet (Yr Ind)) (IB 37–32 pts HL 6/5 sci)

Newcastle – AAA–AAB incl biol/chem+maths/sci (Biomed Genet) (IB 35–34 pts HL 5 biol/chem+maths/sci)

Sheffield – AAA–AAB incl sci (Genet; Genet Mol Cell Biol; Med Genet; Genet Microbiol) (IB 36–34 pts HL 6 chem+sci)

York – AAA–AAB incl biol+chem/maths (Genet (Yr Abrd); Genet) (IB 36–35 pts HL 6 biol+chem/maths)

136 pts **Birmingham** – AAB incl biol+sci (Biol Sci (Genet)) (IB 32 pts HL 665); AAB incl chem+sci (Bioch (Genet)) (IB 32 pts HL 665)

Cardiff – AAB–ABB incl biol+sci (Bio Sci (Genet)) (IB 34 pts HL 6 biol+chem)

Dundee – AAB incl biol+chem (Mol Genet) (IB 34 pts (3 yr course) 30 pts (4 yr course) HL 665 (3 yr course) 555 (4 yr course))

Glasgow – AAB–BBB incl biol/chem (Genet) (IB 36–34 pts HL 665 incl 6 biol/chem)

Lancaster – AAB incl chem+sci (Bioch Genet) (IB 35 pts HL 16 pts incl 6 chem+sci)

Leicester – AAB–ABB incl sci/maths (Med Genet) (IB 32–30 pts HL 6 sci)

London (King's) – AAB incl chem+biol (Mol Genet; Pharmacol Mol Genet) (IB 35 pts HL 665)

Nottingham – AAB incl biol+sci/geog/psy (Genet) (IB 34 pts HL 5/6 biol+sci); AAB incl chem+sci (Bioch Genet) (IB 34 pts HL 5/6 chem+sci)

Swansea – AAB–BBB incl biol+chem 136–120 pts (Med Genet; Bioch Genet) (IB 33–32 pts); AAB–BBB incl biol 136–120 pts (Genet) (IB 33–32 pts)

128 pts **East Anglia** – ABB incl biol (Mol Biol Genet) (IB 32 pts HL 55 incl biol)

Liverpool – ABB/BBB+aEPQ incl biol+sci (Genet) (IB 33 pts HL 6 biol 5 sci)

London (QM) – ABB incl biol (Genet) (IB 34 pts HL 6/5 biol)

120 pts **Aberdeen** – BBB incl maths/sci (Genet; Genet (Immun)) (IB 32 pts HL 5 maths/sci)

Brunel – BBB incl sci (Biomed Sci (Genet)) (IB 30 pts HL 5 sci)

112 pts **Aberystwyth** – BBC–BBB incl biol (Genet) (IB 30 pts HL 5 biol)

Huddersfield – BBC incl sci 112 pts (Med Genet)

104 pts **Essex** – BCC incl biol (Genet) (IB 28 pts HL 5 biol)

Hertfordshire – 104 pts incl biol/chem+sci/maths/geog/psy (Mol Biol) (HL 44 incl biol/chem+sci)

80 pts **Wolverhampton** – BB/CDD incl sci (Genet Mol Biol)

Alternative offers
See **Chapter 6** and **Appendix 1** for grades/UCAS Tariff points information for other examinations.

CHOOSING YOUR COURSE (SEE ALSO CH.1)

Universities and colleges teaching quality See www.qaa.ac.uk; https://unistats.ac.uk.

Top research universities and colleges (REF 2014) See **Biological Sciences**.

Examples of sandwich degree courses See also **Biological Sciences**. Brunel; Essex; Huddersfield; Leeds; Manchester; York.

ADMISSIONS INFORMATION

Number of applicants per place (approx) Bath 8; Dundee 8; Leeds 7; Leicester (Biol Sci) 10; Nottingham 8; Swansea 7; Wolverhampton 4; York 9.

Advice to applicants and planning the UCAS personal statement See **Biological Sciences**.

Misconceptions about this course York Some fail to realise that chemistry (beyond **GCSE**) is essential to an understanding of genetics.

Selection interviews Yes Cambridge, Manchester; **No** Dundee, Liverpool, Swansea, Wolverhampton.

Interview advice and questions Likely questions will focus on your A-level science subjects, particularly biology, why you wish to study genetics, and on careers in genetics. See also **Chapter 5**.

AFTER-RESULTS ADVICE
Offers to applicants repeating A-levels Higher Aberystwyth, Leeds, Swansea; **Same** Dundee, Nottingham, Wolverhampton, York; **No** Cambridge.

GRADUATE DESTINATIONS AND EMPLOYMENT (2015/16 HESA)
Graduates surveyed 300 **Employed** 105 **In voluntary employment** 5 **In further study** 150 **Assumed unemployed** 15

Career note See **Biological Sciences**.

OTHER DEGREE SUBJECTS FOR CONSIDERATION
Biochemistry; Biological Sciences; Biology; Biotechnology; Human Sciences; Immunology; Life Sciences; Medical Biochemistry; Medical Biology; Medicine; Microbiology; Molecular Biology; Natural Sciences; Physiology; Plant Sciences.

GEOGRAPHY

(see also **Environmental Sciences**)

The content and focus of Geography courses will vary between universities, although many similarities exist between BA and BSc courses apart from entry requirements. For example, at the University of Birmingham, the course is flexible offering topics from migration and urban and social changes, to natural hazards and global environmental changes, with decisions on the paths to take between human and physical geography being delayed. At Leeds, the BA course focuses on human geography and the BSc course on physical aspects. This is a subject deserving real research between the offerings of a wide range of institutions in view of the variety of topics on offer, for example, rural, historical, political or cultural geography at Exeter, environmental geography and climate change at East Anglia, and physical oceanography as part of the BSc course at Plymouth.

Useful websites www.metoffice.gov.uk; www.rgs.org; www.ordnancesurvey.co.uk; http://geographical.co.uk; www.nationalgeographic.com; www.cartography.org.uk; www.gov.uk/government/organisations/natural-england; www.geography.org.uk; www.publicprofiler.org; www.esri.com/what-is-gis

NB The points totals shown to the left of the institutions are for ease of reference only. It must not be assumed that Tariff points are always used by institutions or that they can be substituted for an offer in grades. The level of an offer is not necessarily indicative of the quality of a course.

COURSE OFFERS INFORMATION
Subject requirements/preferences GCSE Geography usually required. Mathematics/sciences often required for BSc courses. **AL** Geography is usually required for most courses. Mathematics/science subjects required for BSc courses.

Your target offers and examples of degree courses
152 pts Bristol – A*AA–AAB (Geog) (IB 38–34 pts HL 18–17 pts)
        Cambridge – A*AA +interview +GAA (Geog) (IB 40–42 pts HL 776)
        Durham – A*AA–AAA (Geog courses) (IB 38–37 pts); A*AA (Comb Hons Soc Sci) (IB 38 pts)

London (UCL) – A*AA incl geog+maths (Econ Geog) (IB 39 pts HL 7 maths 6 geog)

Oxford – A*AA +interview +TSA (Geog) (IB 39 pts HL 766)

144 pts **Cardiff** – AAA–AAB incl geog (Geog (Hum)) (IB 36–35 pts HL 666); AAA–ABB incl geog (Geog (Hum) Plan) (HL 666)

Edinburgh – AAA incl sci+maths (Geol Physl Geog) (IB 37 pts HL 555)

Exeter   AAA AAB incl hum/soc sci (Geog) (IB 36–34 pts HL 5 hum/soc sci)

Lancaster – AAA (Hum Geog (Yr Abrd)) (IB 36 pts)

Leeds – AAA–AAB (Geog courses) (IB 35 pts HL 18–16 pts)

London (UCL) – AAA–AAB incl geog (Geog) (IB 38–36 pts HL 6 geog)

London LSE – AAA (Geog) (IB 38 pts HL 766); AAA incl maths (Geog Econ) (IB 38 pts HL 766)

St Andrews – AAA (Geog Int Rel; Geog; Geog Lang) (IB 38 pts)

136 pts **Birmingham** – AAB (Geog) (IB 32 pts HL 665)

Glasgow – AAB–BBB incl sci (Geog) (IB 36–34 pts HL 665)

Lancaster – AAB incl geog (Geog; Physl Geog) (IB 35 pts HL 16 pts incl 6 geog)

London (King's) – AAB (Geog) (IB 35 pts HL 665)

London (RH) – AAB–ABB (Geog; Hum Geog; Physl Geog) (IB 32 pts HL 655)

Loughborough – AAB incl geog (Geog Spo Mgt; Geog Spo Sci; Geog Econ) (IB 35 pts HL 665 incl 5 geog); AAB incl geog/hist (Geog) (IB 35 pts HL 665 incl geog)

Manchester – AAB (Geog) (IB 32 pts HL 665)

Newcastle – AAB–ABB incl geog (Geog) (IB 35–32 pts HL 6 geog); AAB–ABB incl sci/maths/ geog (Earth Sci) (IB 35–33 pts)

Nottingham – AAB incl geog (Geog Bus) (IB 34 pts HL 5 geog)

St Andrews – AAB (Psy Geog) (IB 35 pts)

Sheffield – AAB–ABB+aEPQ incl sci/geog (Geog) (IB 34 pts HL 6 sci/geog)

Southampton – AAB/ABB+aEPQ incl geog (Geog) (IB 34 pts HL 17 pts)

Sussex – AAB–ABB (Geog; Geog Anth) (IB 32 pts)

Swansea – AAB–BBB incl geog (Geog; Geog Geoinform) (IB 34–32 pts HL 5 geog)

York – AAB incl geog+sci/maths/env st/psy (Env Geog) (IB 35 pts)

128 pts **Bangor** – 128–112 pts incl sci/maths/geog (Mar Geog)

Birmingham – ABB (Geog Urb Reg Plan Comb Hons) (IB 32 pts HL 655)

Coventry – ABB–BBB (Geog; Geog Nat Haz) (IB 29 pts); (Disas Mgt Emer Plan) (IB 30 pts); (Int Disas Mgt) (IB 31–30 pts)

East Anglia – ABB incl geog (Clim Chng; Geog) (IB 32 pts HL 5 geog); ABB (Geog (Yr Ind)) (IB 32 pts)

Leicester – ABB–BBB+bEPQ (Geog; Hum Geog; Physl Geog) (IB 30 pts)

Liverpool – ABB (Geog) (IB 33 pts)

London (QM) – ABB–BBB incl geog (Hum Geog; Geog) (IB 32–30 pts HL 655–555 incl geog)

Newcastle – ABB (Geog Info Sci) (IB 34 pts); ABB incl geog+sci/maths/geol (Physl Geog) (IB 32 pts HL 6 geog); ABB–BBB incl geog (Geog Plan) (IB 32–30 pts)

Nottingham – ABB–BBB incl geog (Arch Geog) (IB 32–30 pts HL 5 geog)

Reading – ABB–BBB incl geog (Hum Geog; Physl Geog; Geog Econ (Reg Sci); Hum Physl Geog) (IB 32–30 pts HL 5 geog)

Southampton – ABB incl geog+sci/maths +interview (Ocean Physl Geog; Geol Physl Geog); ABB incl geog+sci/maths/env st +interview (Ocean Physl Geog) (IB 32 pts); ABB incl geog (Popn Geog) (IB 32 pts HL 16 pts)

120 pts **Aberdeen** – BBB (Geog) (IB 32 pts HL 555)

Aberystwyth – BBB–ABB (Hum Geog; Physl Geog; Geog) (IB 28 pts HL 5 geog)

Bangor – 120 pts incl geog (Geog)

Dundee – BBB (Geog) (IB 30 pts HL 555)

Edge Hill – BBB incl geog/env sci 120 pts (Physl Geog Geol; Physl Geog)

Gloucestershire – BBB 120 pts (Geog courses)

Heriot-Watt – ABC/BBB (Geog) (IB 29 pts)

Keele – ABC/BBB incl geog (Geog; Physl Geog; Hum Geog) (IB 32 pts HL 6 geog)

Liverpool Hope – BBB–BBC 120–112 pts (Geog)

Check **Chapter 3** for new university admission details and **Chapter 6** on how to read the subject tables.

Northumbria – 120–128 pts (Geog; Env Geog) (HL 444)

Queen's Belfast – BBB incl geog (Geog)

Sheffield Hallam – 120–104 pts incl geog/soc sci (Hum Geog); 120–104 pts incl geog/env sci (Geog)

116 pts **Plymouth** – 116–128 pts incl sci/maths/geog/tech (Physl Geog Geol) (IB 28–30 pts HL 4 sci)

112 pts **Brighton** – BBC–CCC incl geog 112–96 pts (Geog) (IB 28 pts)

Chester – BBC–BBB incl geog/soc sci/app sci 112 pts (Geog) (IB 26 pts HL 5 geog)

Edge Hill – BBC incl geog/env sci 112 pts (Geog; Hum Geog)

Greenwich – 112 pts incl geog/sci (Geog)

Hull – 112 pts (Physl Geog; Hum Geog; Geog) (IB 28 pts); 112 pts incl sci/maths/geol (Geol Physl Geog) (IB 28 pts HL 5 sci/maths/geol)

Leeds Beckett – 112 pts (Hum Geog; Hum Geog Plan) (IB 25 pts)

Liverpool John Moores – BBC incl sci/geog 112 pts (Geog) (IB 26 pts)

London (Birk) – 112 pts (Geog)

Nottingham Trent – BBC incl geog 112 pts (Geog; Geog (Physl))

Oxford Brookes – BBC incl geog 112 pts (Geog) (IB 30 pts)

UWE Bristol – 112 pts (Geog)

Worcester – 112 pts (Geog Spo St)

108 pts **Plymouth** – 108–112 pts incl geog (Geog) (IB 28 pts HL 5 geog)

104 pts **Bath Spa** – BCC–CCC incl geog/sociol/econ/sci (Geog) (IB 26 pts)

Bournemouth – 104–120 pts (Geog) (IB 28–31 pts HL 55)

Central Lancashire – 104–112 pts (Geog)

Manchester Met – BCC–BBC incl geog/sci/maths 104–112 pts (Physl Geog) (IB 26 pts HL 5 geog/sci); BCC–BBC incl geog 104–112 pts (Hum Geog (St Abrd)) (IB 26 pts HL 5 geog/hum); BCC–BBC incl geog/sci 104–112 pts (Geog (St Abrd)) (IB 26 pts HL 5 geog/sci)

Northampton – BCC (Geog (Physl Geog); Geog)

Portsmouth – 104–120 pts (Geog) (IB 26 pts)

South Wales – BCC–CDD incl sci/maths/geog 104–80 pts (Geog) (HL 655–445); BCC–CDD incl sci/geog/maths 104–80 pts (Geol Physl Geog) (HL 655–445)

Winchester – 104–120 pts (Geog) (IB 26 pts)

Worcester – 104–120 pts (Geog; Hum Geog)

96 pts **Derby** – 96–112 pts incl sci/soc sci (Geog)

Hertfordshire – 96 pts (Geog; Hum Geog) (HL 44)

Kingston – 96–112 pts (Hum Geog); 96–112 pts incl geog/wrld dev (Geog Comb Hons)

Staffordshire – CCC 96 pts (Geog; Geog Mntn Ldrshp)

88 pts **Canterbury Christ Church** – 88–112 pts incl geog (Geog)

Ulster – CCD–BCC incl geog (Geog) (IB 24 pts HL 12 pts)

Open University – contact 0300 303 0073 **or** www.open.ac.uk/contact/new (Geog Env Sci; Comb Soc Sci (Econ/Geog/Psy/Sociol))

Alternative offers

See **Chapter 6** and **Appendix 1** for grades/UCAS Tariff points information for other examinations.

EXAMPLES OF COLLEGES OFFERING COURSES IN THIS SUBJECT FIELD

Hopwood Hall (Coll); Truro and Penwith (Coll).

CHOOSING YOUR COURSE (SEE ALSO CH.1)

Universities and colleges teaching quality See www.qaa.ac.uk; https://unistats.ac.uk.

Top research universities and colleges (REF 2014) (Geography, Environmental Studies and Archaeology) Glasgow (Geog); London (RH); London LSE; Bristol (Geog); Cambridge (Geog); Oxford (Geog Env St); London (QM); St Andrews; Newcastle (Geog); Southampton (Geog); London (UCL) (Geog); Reading (Arch); Sheffield (Geog); Oxford (Arch).

Examples of sandwich degree courses Brighton; Cardiff; Coventry; Hertfordshire; Kingston; Loughborough; Manchester Met; Northumbria; Nottingham Trent; Sheffield Hallam; Ulster.

ADMISSIONS INFORMATION

Number of applicants per place (approx) Birmingham 5; Bristol 6; Cambridge 3; Cardiff 5; Central Lancashire 3; Derby 5; Dundee 9; Durham 4; Edge Hill 8; Edinburgh 9; Exeter 10; Gloucestershire 40; Greenwich 2; Hull 5; Kingston 7; Lancaster 13; Leeds 12; Leicester 7; Liverpool 6; Liverpool John Moores 6; London (King's) 5; London (QM) 5; London (RH) 5; London (SOAS) 5; London (UCL) 4; London LSE 8; Manchester 6; Newcastle 7; Northampton 4; Nottingham 9; Oxford Brookes 9; Sheffield 6; South Wales 5; Southampton 7; Staffordshire 10; Swansea 5; Worcester 5.

Advice to applicants and planning the UCAS personal statement Visits to, and field courses in, any specific geographical region should be fully described. Study your own locality in detail and get in touch with the area planning office to learn about any future developments. Read geographical magazines and describe any special interests you have – and why. Be aware of world issues and have travel experience. **Bristol** Deferred entry accepted.

Misconceptions about this course Birmingham Some students think that the BA and BSc Geography courses are very different; in fact they do not differ from one another. All course options are available for both degrees. **Liverpool** Some applicants assume that a BSc course restricts them to physical geography modules. This is not so since human geography modules can be taken. Some students later specialise in human geography. **Plymouth** Our course has shared BA and BSc modules in the first year, allowing students to choose between courses and degrees at a later stage.

Selection interviews Yes Cambridge, Oxford (26%), Worcester; **Some** Cardiff, Coventry, London (SOAS), Loughborough, Nottingham; **No** Birmingham, Bristol, Canterbury Christ Church, Central Lancashire, Dundee, East Anglia, Edge Hill, Greenwich, Kingston, Liverpool, London (King's), London (RH), London (UCL), Manchester, Manchester Met, Newcastle, Northumbria, Reading, Southampton, Staffordshire.

Interview advice and questions Geography is a very broad subject and applicants can expect to be questioned on their syllabus and those aspects which they find of special interest. Some questions in the past have included: What fieldwork have you done? What are your views on ecology? What changes In the landscape have you noticed on the way to the interview? Explain in simple meteorological terms today's weather. Why are earthquakes almost unknown in Britain? What do you enjoy about geography and why? Are there any articles of geographical importance in the news at present? Discuss the current economic situation in Britain and give your views. Questions on the Third World, on world ocean currents and drainage and economic factors worldwide. What do you think about those people who consider global warming nonsense? Expect to comment on local geography and on geographical photographs and diagrams. See also **Chapter 5**. **Cambridge** Are Fairtrade bananas really fair? Imagine you are hosting the BBC radio show on New Year's day, what message would you send to listeners? **Oxford** Is nature natural? **Southampton** Applicants selected on academic ability only.

Reasons for rejection (non-academic) Lack of awareness of the content of the course. Failure to attend interview. Poor general knowledge. Lack of geographical awareness. **Liverpool** Personal statement gave no reason for choosing Geography.

AFTER-RESULTS ADVICE

Offers to applicants repeating A-levels Higher Kingston, St Andrews; **Possibly higher** Edinburgh; **Same** Aberystwyth, Birmingham, Brighton, Bristol, Cardiff, Chester, Coventry, Derby, Dundee, Durham, East Anglia, Edge Hill, Hull, Lancaster, Leeds, Liverpool, Liverpool Hope, Liverpool John Moores, London (RH), London (SOAS), Loughborough, Manchester Met, Newcastle, Northumbria, Nottingham, Oxford Brookes, Southampton, Staffordshire; **No** Cambridge, Glasgow.

GRADUATE DESTINATIONS AND EMPLOYMENT (2015/16 HESA)

Human and Social Geography graduates surveyed 2,380 **Employed** 1,155 **In voluntary employment** 80 **In further study** 625 **Assumed unemployed** 135

Physical Geographical Sciences graduates surveyed 2,785 **Employed** 1,390 **In voluntary employment** 90 **In further study** 740 **Assumed unemployed** 130

Career note Geography graduates enter a wide range of occupations, many in business and administrative careers. Depending on specialisations, areas could include agriculture, forestry, hydrology, transport, market research and retail. Teaching is also a popular option.

OTHER DEGREE SUBJECTS FOR CONSIDERATION

Agriculture; Anthropology; Civil Engineering; Countryside Management; Development Studies; Environmental Engineering/Science/Studies; Forestry; Geology; Geomatic Engineering; Surveying; Town Planning; Urban Land Economics; Urban Studies.

GEOLOGY/GEOLOGICAL SCIENCES

(including Earth Sciences, Geophysics and Geoscience; see also Astronomy and Astrophysics, Environmental Sciences)

Topics in Geology courses include the physical and chemical constitution of the earth, exploration geophysics, oil and marine geology (oceanography) and seismic interpretation. Earth Sciences covers geology, environmental science, physical geography and can also include business studies and language modules. No previous knowledge of geology is required for most courses.

Useful websites www.geolsoc.org.uk; www.bgs.ac.uk; www.noc.ac.uk; www.scicentral.com; http://britgeophysics.org

NB The points totals shown to the left of the institutions are for ease of reference only. It must not be assumed that Tariff points are always used by institutions or that they can be substituted for an offer in grades. The level of an offer is not necessarily indicative of the quality of a course.

COURSE OFFERS INFORMATION

Subject requirements/preferences GCSE English, mathematics and a science required. **AL** One or two mathematics/science subjects usually required. Geography may be accepted as a science subject.

Your target offers and examples of degree courses

160 pts Cambridge – A*A*A incl sci/maths +interview +NSAA (Nat Sci (Earth Sci)) (IB 40–42 pts HL 776)

152 pts Leeds – A*AA incl maths+phys (Geophysl Sci (Int) (MGeophys)) (IB 35 pts HL 19 pts); A*AA incl sci/maths/geog (Geol Sci (Int) (MGeol)) (IB 35 pts HL 19 pts)

   Oxford – A*AA/AAAA +interview (Earth Sci (Geol)) (IB 39 pts HL 766)

144 pts Cardiff – AAA incl sci/maths/geog (Explor Res Geol (Int) (MESci); Geol (Int) (MESci)) (IB 35 pts)

   Durham – AAA incl sci (Earth Sci (MSci)) (IB 37 pts)

   Edinburgh – AAA incl maths+phys (Geophys; Geophys Meteor; Geophys Geol) (IB 37 pts HL 555); AAA incl sci+maths (Geol Physl Geog) (IB 37 pts HL 555); AAA incl sci/maths/geog (Geol) (IB 37 pts HL 555)

   Imperial London – AAA–A*AA incl sci/maths/geog +interview (Geol; Geol Geophys (MSci); Petrol Geosci (MSci)) (IB 38–39 pts HL 6 sci/maths/geog); AAA–A*AA incl maths+phys +interview (Geophys) (IB 38–39 pts HL 6 maths+phys)

   London (UCL) – AAA–ABB incl sci/maths (Earth Sci (Int) (MSci)) (IB 38–34 pts HL 5 sci/maths); AAA–ABB (Env Geosci; Geol; Earth Sci) (IB 38–34 pts HL 18–16 pts); AAA–ABB incl maths+phys (Geophys) (IB 38–34 pts HL 5 maths+phys)

136 pts Birmingham – AAB incl sci (Geol (MSci) (Yr Abrd)) (IB 32 pts HL 665)

   Bristol – AAB–ABC incl sci (Env Geosci; Geol) (IB 34–31 pts HL 17–15 pts)

   Cardiff – AAB incl sci/maths/geog (Env Geosci (Int) (MESci); Geol (MESci)) (IB 35 pts)

   Durham – AAB incl sci (Geosci; Geol) (IB 36 pts); AAB incl sci+maths (Geophys Geol) (IB 36 pts)

Exeter – AAB–ABB incl sci/geol (App Geol; Geol (Cornwall)) (IB 34–32 pts HL 5 sci)

Glasgow – AAB–BBB incl sci (Earth Sci) (IB 36–34 pts HL 665 incl 6 sci)

Leeds – AAB incl sci/maths/geog (Geol Sci) (IB 35 pts HL 17 pts)

Leicester – AAB incl sci/maths/geog (Geol (MGeol); Geol Pal (MGeol)) (IB 32 pts)

Liverpool – AAB incl maths+phys (Geol Geophys (MESci)) (IB 35 pts HL 4 maths+phys); AAB incl sci (Geol (MESci); Geol Physl Geog (MESci)) (IB 35 pts HL 4 sci)

Manchester – AAB incl sci +interview (Earth Sci (MEarthSci)) (IB 34 pts HL 665)

St Andrews – AAB incl sci/maths/geog (Geol) (IB 36 pts); AAB incl biol+sci/maths (Env Earth Sci) (IB 36 pts)

Southampton – AAB incl maths+phys +interview (Geophys (MSci))

128 pts **Bangor** – 128–112 pts incl sci/maths/geog (Geol Ocean)

Birmingham – ABB incl sci (Geol) (IB 32 pts HL 655)

Cardiff – ABB incl sci/maths/geog (Explor Res Geol (MESci)) (IB 32 pts)

Lancaster – ABB incl sci (Earth Env Sci) (IB 32 pts HL 16 pts incl 6 sci)

Leicester – ABB–BBB+bEPQ incl sci/maths/comp sci/geog (Geol) (IB 30 pts); ABB–BBB+bEPQ incl maths/phys (Geol Geophys) (IB 30 pts); ABB–BBB+bEPQ incl sci/maths/geog (App Env Geol) (IB 30 pts)

Liverpool – ABB incl sci (Geol Physl Geog) (IB 33 pts HL 4 sci); (Geol) (IB 33 pts)

London (RH) – ABB incl sci (Geosci (MSci)) (IB 32 pts HL 655); ABB incl sci/maths/geog +interview (Geol (Yr Ind); Geol) (IB 32 pts HL 655)

Manchester – ABB incl chem +interview (Geochem) (IB 33 pts HL 5 chem); ABB incl maths/phys (Geol Planet Sci) (IB 33 pts HL 5 maths/phys); ABB incl sci +interview (Geog Geol; Geol; Env Res Geol) (IB 33 pts HL 5 sci)

Southampton – ABB incl geog+sci/maths +interview (Geol Physl Geog); ABB incl maths+phys +interview (Geophysl Sci); ABB incl sci/maths/geog +interview (Geol)

Swansea – ABB–BBB incl geog (Physl Earth Sci) (IB 34–32 pts HL 5 geog)

120 pts **Aberdeen** – BBB incl maths/sci (Geol Petrol Geol) (IB 32 pts HL 5 maths/sci)

Cardiff – BBB incl sci/maths/geog (Explor Res Geol; Geol) (IB 30 pts); (Env Geosci) (IB 32–30 pts)

Edge Hill – BBB incl geog/env sci 120 pts (Physl Geog Geol)

London (Birk) – 120 pts (Geol)

116 pts **Plymouth** – 116–128 pts incl sci/maths/geog/tech (Physl Geog Geol) (IB 28–30 pts HL 4 sci); 116–128 pts (Geol Ocn Sci; App Geol) (IB 28–30 pts)

112 pts **Aberystwyth** – BBC incl sci (Env Earth Sci) (IB 28 pts HL 4 sci)

Brighton – BBC–CCC incl geog/sci (Physl Geog Geol) (IB 28 pts); BBC–CCC incl sci 112–96 pts (Geol) (IB 28 pts)

Hull – 112 pts incl sci/maths/geol (Geol Physl Geog) (IB 28 pts HL 5 sci/maths/geol)

Keele – BBC incl sci/geog/maths (Geol Comb Hons) (IB 30 pts HL 6 sci/geog)

Portsmouth – 112–136 pts incl sci/maths/geog/tech (Eng Geol Geotech) (IB 26 pts)

104 pts **Portsmouth** – 104–120 pts incl sci/maths/geog (Geol) (IB 27 pts)

South Wales – BCC CCD incl sci/maths/geog 104–96 pts (Geol) (HL 655–445)

96 pts **Derby** – 96–112 pts incl sci/maths/geog (Geol)

Open University – contact 0300 303 0073 **or** www.open.ac.uk/contact/new (Nat Sci (Earth Sci))

Alternative offers
See **Chapter 6** and **Appendix 1** for grades/UCAS Tariff points information for other examinations.

CHOOSING YOUR COURSE (SEE ALSO CH.1)

Universities and colleges teaching quality See www.qaa.ac.uk; https://unistats.ac.uk.

Top research universities and colleges (REF 2014) See **Environmental Sciences**.

Examples of sandwich degree courses Brighton; Cardiff; Leeds; London (RH); Portsmouth.

ADMISSIONS INFORMATION

Number of applicants per place (approx) Bangor 5; Birmingham 4; Bristol 6; Cardiff 5; Derby 5; Durham 3; Edinburgh 19; Exeter 5; Imperial London 5; Leeds 8; Leicester 5; Liverpool 8; London (RH) 5; London (UCL) 5; Oxford 4; Plymouth 14; Southampton 5.

Advice to applicants and planning the UCAS personal statement Visits to any outstanding geological sites and field courses you have attended should be described in detail. Apart from geological formations, you should also be aware of how geology has affected humankind in specific areas in the architecture of the region and artefacts used. Evidence of social skills could be given. See also **Appendix 3**. **Bristol** Only accepting a limited number of deferred applicants in fairness to next year's applicants. Apply early.

Misconceptions about this course London (UCL) Environmental geoscience is sometimes mistaken for environmental science; they are two different subjects.

Selection interviews Yes Cambridge, Imperial London, Oxford (86% (success rate 27%)), Southampton; **Some** Aberystwyth (mature students only); **No** Birmingham, Bristol, Derby, East Anglia, Edinburgh, Liverpool, London (RH).

Interview advice and questions Some knowledge of the subject will be expected and applicants could be questioned on specimens of rocks and their origins. Past interviews have included questions on the field courses attended, and the geophysical methods of exploration in the detection of metals. How would you determine the age of this rock (sample shown)? Can you integrate a decay curve function and would it help you to determine the age of rocks? How many planes of crystallisation could this rock have? What causes a volcano? What is your local geology? See also **Chapter 5**. **Oxford** (Earth Sci (Geol)) Candidates may be asked to comment on specimens of a geological nature, based on previous knowledge of the subject.

Reasons for rejection (non-academic) Exeter Outright rejection uncommon but some applicants advised to apply for other programmes.

AFTER-RESULTS ADVICE

Offers to applicants repeating A-levels Higher Bristol, St Andrews; **Possibly higher** Cardiff; **Same** Aberystwyth, Derby, Durham, East Anglia, Leeds, London (RH), Plymouth, Southampton; **No** Cambridge.

GRADUATE DESTINATIONS AND EMPLOYMENT (2015/16 HESA)

Graduates surveyed 1,345 **Employed** 515 **In voluntary employment** 30 **In further study** 520 **Assumed unemployed** 95

Career note Areas of employment include mining and quarrying, the oil and gas industry, prospecting and processing.

OTHER DEGREE SUBJECTS FOR CONSIDERATION

Archaeology; Civil and Mining Engineering; Environmental Science; Geography; Meteorology; Oceanography; Physics.

GERMAN

(see also European Studies, Languages)

There are fewer Single Honours German courses than formerly, although the subject is offered jointly with other subjects, particularly other languages and business and management studies, at many universities. German courses range from those which focus on language and literature (eg Edinburgh), those which emphasise fluency of language and communication (eg Hull) and those offering translation studies (eg Heriot-Watt).

Useful websites www.goethe.de; www.bbc.co.uk/languages; www.ciol.org.uk; www.
languageadvantage.com; www.languagematters.co.uk; www.faz.net; www.sueddeutsche.de; http://
europa.eu; www.gslg.org.uk; www.wigs.ac.uk

*NB The points totals shown to the left of the institutions are for ease of reference only. It must not
be assumed that Tariff points are always used by institutions or that they can be substituted for an
offer in grades. The level of an offer is not necessarily indicative of the quality of a course.*

COURSE OFFERS INFORMATION
Subject requirements/preferences GCSE English and German are required. **AL** German required
usually at a specified grade.

Your target offers and examples of degree courses

152 pts **Bristol** – A*AA/A*A*B–AAB incl Ger +LNAT (Law Ger) (IB 38–34 pts HL 6 Ger)

Cambridge – A*AA incl lang +interview +MMLAA (Modn Mediev Langs) (IB 40–42 pts HL
776)

Imperial London – A*AA–A*A*A* incl chem+maths +interview (Chem Fr/Ger/Span Sci)
(IB 40–42 pts HL 7 chem 6 maths)

Nottingham – A*AA–AAA (Econ Ger) (IB 38–36 pts)

144 pts **Birmingham** – AAA (Law Ger Law) (IB 32 pts HL 666)

Imperial London – AAA incl biol+sci/maths (Biol Sci Ger Sci) (IB 38 pts HL 6 biol+sci/
maths)

Lancaster – AAA–ABB (Ger St courses) (IB 35–32 pts HL 16 pts)

London (UCL) – AAA–ABB incl lang (Modn Langs) (IB 34–36 pts HL 6 lang)

Oxford – AAA +interview +MLAT (Ger courses) (IB 39–38 pts HL 666)

Reading – AAA–BBB/ABC (Ger courses) (IB 32–30 pts)

Southampton – AAA–AAB+aEPQ incl maths+Fr/Ger/Span (Maths Fr/Ger/Span)
(IB 36 pts HL 6 maths)

136 pts **Bath** – AAB/ABB+aEPQ incl Ger (Int Mgt Ger) (IB 35 pts HL 6 Ger); AAB–ABB+aEPQ incl Ger
(Ger courses) (IB 36 pts HL 6 Ger)

Birmingham – AAB (Ger St courses) (IB 32 pts HL 665)

Edinburgh – AAB incl lang (Int Bus Fr/Ger/Span) (IB 43 pts HL 776); AAB (Ger) (IB 37 pts
HL 666)

Exeter – AAB–ABB incl Ger (Ger) (IB 34–32 pts HL 5 Ger)

Glasgow – AAB–BBB incl arts/lang/hum (Ger Comb Hons) (IB 36–34 pts HL 6 Engl/lang/
hum)

Leeds – AAB–ABB incl Ger (Ger courses) (IB 35–34 pts HL 16 pts incl 6 Ger)

London (King's) – AAB incl Fr (Fr Ger (Yr Abrd)) (IB 35 pts HL 665 incl 6 Fr); AAB incl mus
(Ger Mus (Yr Abrd)) (IB 35 pts HL 665 incl 6 mus); AAB (Euro St (Fr/Ger/Span) (Yr
Abrd)) (IB 35 pts HL 665)

London (RH) – AAB–BBB (Modn Lang Lat) (IB 32 pts HL 555)

St Andrews – AAB (Ger courses) (IB 36 pts)

Sheffield – AAB–BBB incl lang (Ger St Comb Hons) (IB 34–32 pts HL 6 lang)

Southampton – AAB/ABB+aEPQ incl Engl+Fr/Ger/Span (Engl Fr/Ger/Span) (IB 34 pts
HL 6 Engl+Fr/Ger/Span); AAB–ABB incl Fr/Ger/Span (Film Fr/Ger/Span) (IB 32 pts
HL 6 Fr/Ger/Span)

Surrey – AAB–ABB incl Ger (Ger courses) (IB 32–34 pts)

Warwick – AAB incl Fr (Fr Ger St) (IB 36 pts HL 5 Fr); AAB incl Engl lit+lang (Engl Ger) (IB
36 pts HL 5 Engl lit+lang); AAB incl Ger (Ger Ital) (IB 36 pts HL 5 Ger/Ital); AAB incl
lang (Ger Comb Hons) (IB 36 pts HL 5 lang)

York – AAB–ABB (Ger courses) (IB 34 pts); AAB–ABB incl Fr (Fr Ger Lang (Yr Abrd))
(IB 34 pts)

128 pts **Aston** – ABB–BBB incl lang (Int Bus Fr/Ger/Span) (IB 32 pts HL 655–555 incl 5 lang);
ABB–BBB (Ger courses) (IB 32–33 pts)

Bath – ABB–ABC+aEPQ incl lang (Modn Langs Euro St) (IB 35 pts HL 6 lang)

Check **Chapter 3** for new university admission details and **Chapter 6** on how to read the subject tables.

Bristol – ABB–BBC incl Ger (Ger) (IB 32–29 pts HL 5 Ger); ABB–BBC incl lang (Ger courses) (IB 32–29 pts HL 5 lang)

Cardiff – ABB–BBC incl lang (Ger) (IB 32–30 pts HL 665–655)

Dundee – ABB incl lang (Law Langs) (IB 32 pts HL 655)

Liverpool – ABB (Ger courses) (IB 33 pts)

London (QM) – ABB incl art/hum/soc sci+lang (Fr/Ger/Russ Dr) (IB 32 pts HL 6/5 art/ hum/soc sci)

London (RH) – ABB–BBB incl lang (Modn Lang Dr) (IB 32 pts); ABB–BBB (Euro Int St Fr/ Ger/Ital/Span; Modn Lang Mus; Modn Lang) (IB 32 pts HL 555); ABB (Modn Lang Mgt) (IB 32 pts HL 655)

Manchester – ABB (Ger courses; Ger St) (IB 33 pts HL 655)

Nottingham – ABB (Ger; Ger Comb Hons) (IB 32 pts)

Warwick – ABB incl Ger (Ger St courses) (IB 34 pts HL 5 Ger)

120 pts Aberdeen – BBB (Ger St; Anth Fr/Ger) (IB 32 pts HL 555)

Aberystwyth – ABC/BBB (Ger Comb Hons) (IB 28–30 pts)

Dundee – BBB–BCC (Int Bus Ger) (IB 30 pts); BBB (Phil Ger; Ger courses) (IB 30 pts HL 555)

Heriot-Watt – BBB incl lang (App Langs Transl (Fr/Span)/(Ger/Span)) (IB 30 pts HL 5 lang)

Kent – BBB incl lang (Ger) (IB 34 pts HL 4 lang); BBB (Ger courses) (IB 34 pts)

London (QM) – BBB incl hum/soc sci (Ger Ling; Ger Compar Lit) (IB 30 pts HL 5 hum/soc sci); BBB–ABB incl hum/soc sci/lang (Ger courses) (IB 30–32 pts HL 6/5 hum/soc sci/ lang)

Sheffield – BBB/BBC+bEPQ incl lang (Ger St) (IB 32 pts HL 6 lang)

Swansea – BBB incl lang (Ger courses) (IB 32 pts)

112 pts Central Lancashire – 112 pts (Mod Lang Int Bus); 112 pts incl lang (Modn Langs (Fr/Ger/ Span/Jap))

Hertfordshire – 112 pts (Ger Comb Hons) (IB 28 pts HL 44)

Hull – 112 pts incl lang (Hist Modn Lang; Ger Comb Hons; Ger St) (IB 28 pts)

104 pts Chester – BCC–BBC incl Ger (Ger courses) (IB 26 pts HL 5 Ger)

London (Birk) – 104 pts (Ger); 104 pts incl lang (Modn Langs (Fr/Ger/Ital/Jap/Port/Span))

Manchester Met – 104–112 pts (Ling Mand Chin/Fr/Ger/Ital/Span) (IB 26 pts)

Nottingham Trent – 104 pts incl Ger (Ger Comb Hons)

96 pts Bangor – 96–104 pts (Ger courses)

Portsmouth – 96–120 pts (Modn Lang)

York St John – 96–112 pts incl Ger (Bus Mgt Ger)

Alternative offers

See **Chapter 6** and **Appendix 1** for grades/UCAS Tariff points information for other examinations.

CHOOSING YOUR COURSE (SEE ALSO CH.1)

Universities and colleges teaching quality See www.qaa.ac.uk; https://unistats.ac.uk.

Top research universities and colleges (REF 2014) See **Languages**.

Examples of sandwich degree courses Bangor.

ADMISSIONS INFORMATION

Number of applicants per place (approx) Aston 4; Bath 6 (Mod Langs Eur St); Birmingham 6; Bristol 4; Cardiff 6; Central Lancashire 2; Exeter 4; Heriot-Watt 10; Hull 5; Kent 5; Lancaster 7; Leeds (Comb Hons) 8; London (King's) 5; London (QM) 6; London (RH) 7; London (UCL) 5; Nottingham 5; Swansea 4; Warwick 8; York 6.

Advice to applicants and planning the UCAS personal statement Describe visits to Germany or a German-speaking country and the particular cultural and geographical features of the region. Contacts with friends in Germany and language experience should also be mentioned, and if you are bilingual, say so. Read German newspapers and magazines and keep up-to-date with national news.

indigo.

From trotman t

NEW from the trusted leaders in careers guidance publishing, **Indigo** is a complete, integrated solution for careers leaders with modules for choosing uni courses, managing work experience, exploring over 600 careers, planning and delivering careers lessons for Y7-13, events management and much more.

Simple to use and with personalised teacher and student dashboards, Indigo saves schools valuable time and helps you to:

✓ deliver inspiring **careers education**

✓ meet new **policy requirements**

✓ **monitor and report** student progress

✓ demonstrate impact to **Ofsted**

✓ achieve the **Gatsby Benchmarks**

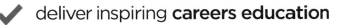

Contact us on
indigo@trotman.co.uk
to arrange a demo

trotman.co.uk/indigo

Misconceptions about this course Leeds See **Languages**. **Swansea** Some students are afraid of the year abroad, which is actually one of the most enjoyable parts of the course.

Selection interviews Yes Cambridge, Leeds, Oxford, Southampton; **Some** Cardiff, London (UCL); **No** Bangor, Birmingham, Heriot-Watt, Hull, Liverpool, Nottingham, Portsmouth, Sheffield, Surrey, Swansea.

Interview advice and questions Questions asked on A-level syllabus. Part of the interview may be in German. What foreign newspapers and/or magazines do you read? Questions on German current affairs, particularly politics and reunification problems, books read outside the course, etc. See also **Chapter 5**. **Leeds** See **Languages**.

Reasons for rejection (non-academic) Unstable personality. Poor motivation. Insufficient commitment. Unrealistic expectations. Not interested in spending a year abroad.

AFTER-RESULTS ADVICE
Offers to applicants repeating A-levels Higher Birmingham, Leeds, Warwick; **Same** Aston, Cardiff, Chester, Nottingham, Swansea, York; **No** Cambridge, Glasgow.

GRADUATE DESTINATIONS AND EMPLOYMENT (2015/16 HESA)
Graduates surveyed 395 **Employed** 180 **In voluntary employment** 15 **In further study** 120 **Assumed unemployed** 25

Career note See **Languages**.

OTHER DEGREE SUBJECTS FOR CONSIDERATION
East European Studies; European Studies; International Business Studies.

GREEK
(see also Classical Studies/Classical Civilisation, Classics, Languages, Latin)

Courses are offered in Ancient and Modern Greek, covering the language and literature from ancient times to the present day. Some Classics and Classical Studies courses (see separate tables) also provide the opportunity to study Greek from scratch.

Useful websites www.greek-language.com; www.greek-gods.org; www.fhw.gr; www.culture.gr; www.greeklanguage.gr

NB The points totals shown to the left of the institutions are for ease of reference only. It must not be assumed that Tariff points are always used by institutions or that they can be substituted for an offer in grades. The level of an offer is not necessarily indicative of the quality of a course.

COURSE OFFERS INFORMATION
Subject requirements/preferences GCSE English and a foreign language required. Greek required by some universities. **AL** Latin, Greek or a foreign language may be specified by some universities.

Your target offers and examples of degree courses
152 pts **Cambridge** – A*AA +interview (Modn Mediev Langs (Class Gk)) (IB 40–42 pts HL 776); A*AA +interview +CAA (Class) (IB 40–42 pts HL 776)
144 pts **Oxford** – AAA +interview +MLAT (Modn Langs (Modn Gk)) (IB 38 pts HL 666)
    St Andrews – AAA–AAB (Gk courses) (IB 38–36 pts)
136 pts **Edinburgh** – AAB (Anc Hist Gk) (IB 36 pts HL 665); (Gk St) (IB 38 pts HL 666)
    Glasgow – AAB–BBB incl arts/lang/hum (Gk) (IB 36–34 pts HL 665 incl Engl+lang/hum)
    London (King's) – AAB (Class St Modn Gk St) (IB 35 pts HL 665)
    London (UCL) – AAB incl Gk (Gk Lat) (IB 36 pts HL 6 Gk); AAB incl Lat (Lat Gk) (IB 36 pts HL 6 Lat)
128 pts **London (RH)** – ABB–BBB (Gk) (IB 32 pts HL 555)

Alternative offers
See **Chapter 6** and **Appendix 1** for grades/UCAS Tariff points information for other examinations.

CHOOSING YOUR COURSE (SEE ALSO CH.1)

Universities and colleges teaching quality See www.qaa.ac.uk; https://unistats.ac.uk.

Top research universities and colleges (REF 2014) See **Classics**.

ADMISSIONS INFORMATION

Number of applicants per place (approx) London (King's) 3; London (UCL) 5.

Advice to applicants and planning the UCAS personal statement See **Classical Studies/Classical Civilisation**.

Selection interviews Yes Cambridge; **No** London (RH).

Interview advice and questions Questions asked on A-level syllabus. Why do you want to study Greek? What aspects of this course interest you? (Questions will develop from answers.) See also **Chapter 5**.

Reasons for rejection (non-academic) Poor language ability.

AFTER-RESULTS ADVICE

Offers to applicants repeating A-levels Higher St Andrews; **Same** Leeds; **No** Cambridge.

GRADUATE DESTINATIONS AND EMPLOYMENT (2015/16 HESA)

Classical Greek Studies graduates surveyed 10 **Employed** 0 **In voluntary employment** 0 **In further study** 0 **Assumed unemployed** 0

Career note See **Languages**.

OTHER DEGREE SUBJECTS FOR CONSIDERATION

Ancient History; Classical Studies; Classics; European Studies; Philosophy.

HEALTH SCIENCES/STUDIES

(including **Deaf Studies, Nutrition and Public Health, Orthoptics, Osteopathy, Paramedic Science, Prosthetics and Orthotics** and **Public Health**; see also **Community Studies/Development, Dietetics, Environmental Sciences, Nursing and Midwifery, Nutrition, Pharmacology, Pharmacy and Pharmaceutical Sciences, Physiotherapy, Radiography, Social Sciences/Studies, Speech Pathology/Sciences/Therapy**)

Health Sciences/Studies is a broad subject field which includes courses covering both practical applications concerning health and well-being (some of which border on nursing) and also the administrative activities involved in the promotion of health in the community. Also included are some specialised courses which include chiropractic, involving the healing process by way of manipulation, mainly in the spinal region, and osteopathy in which joints and tissues are manipulated to correct abnormalities. See **Physiotherapy**. Audiology is concerned with the treatment and diagnosis of hearing and balance disorders while prosthetics involves the provision and fitting of artificial limbs and orthotics is concerned with making and fitting braces, splints and special footwear to ease pain and to assist movement.

Useful websites www.rsph.org.uk; www.bmj.com; www.aor.org.uk; www.baap.org.uk; https://chiropractic-uk.co.uk; www.osteopathy.org.uk; www.who.int; www.csp.org.uk; www.baaudiology.org; www.thebsa.org.uk; www.healthcareers.nhs.uk; www.gcc-uk.org; www.uco.ac.uk; www.osteopathy.org.uk; www.collegeofparamedics.co.uk

UCL FACULTY OF POPULATION HEALTH SCIENCES

BSc Population Health

The Lifecourse Degree

For further information:

www.ucl.ac.uk/bsc-population-health

Email: bscpopulationhealth@ucl.ac.uk

Twitter: @bscpophealth

Q-Step — A step-change in quantitative social science skills. Funded by the Nuffield Foundation, ESRC and HEFCE

UCL Q-STEP

UCL FACULTY OF POPULATION HEALTH SCIENCES

BSc Population Health | The Lifecourse Degree

WHAT IS POPULATION HEALTH?

Population health studies the factors that shape our health – the social and physical environment, the way we live, health care systems and our genes.

This BSc programme will ground you in the different social science disciplines used to study population health and prepare you for research and professional practice in the health sector and beyond.

For further information:

www.ucl.ac.uk/bsc-population-health

Email: bscpopulationhealth@ucl.ac.uk

Twitter: @bscpophealth

WHAT WILL I LEARN?

- World leading researchers will teach you the social, economic and demographic distribution of health and disease, and train you to analyse data to address health inequalities.

- You will develop quantitative data analysis skills, which are in high demand by employers, especially in the health sector and beyond.

- Complementing this you will also learn the theory, history and policy of population health creating a unique multidisciplinary educational experience.

Q-Step — A step-change in quantitative social science skills. Funded by the Nuffield Foundation, ESRC and HEFCE

UCL Q-STEP

Check **Chapter 3** for new university admission details and **Chapter 6** on how to read the subject tables.

NB The points totals shown to the left of the institutions are for ease of reference only. It must not be assumed that Tariff points are always used by institutions or that they can be substituted for an offer in grades. The level of an offer is not necessarily indicative of the quality of a course.

COURSE OFFERS INFORMATION

Subject requirements/preferences GCSE English, mathematics and a science important or essential for some courses. **AL** Mathematics, chemistry or biology may be required for some courses. **Other** Health checks and Disclosure and Barring Service (DBS) clearance required for many courses. (Paramed Sci) Full clean manual UK driving licence with at least a provisional C1 category required by some universities.

Your target offers and examples of degree courses

136 pts Durham – AAB (Hlth Hum Sci) (IB 36 pts)
Exeter – AAB–ABB incl biol+sci (Med Sci) (IB 34–32 pts HL 6 biol/sci)
London (UCL) – AAB–ABB (Popn Hlth) (IB 36–34 pts HL 17–16 pts)

128 pts Aston – ABB incl sci (Hlthcr Sci (Audiol)) (IB 32 pts)
Leeds – ABB incl sci/maths +interview (Hlthcr Sci (Audiol)) (IB 34 pts HL 555)
Manchester – ABB incl sci/maths/psy +interview (Hlthcr Sci (Audiol)) (IB 34–33 pts HL 655)
Plymouth – ABB incl sci 128 pts (Paramed Practnr) (IB 30 pts HL 5 sci)
Sheffield – ABB–BBB (Hlth Hum Sci) (IB 33–32 pts)
Southampton – ABB incl sci (Hlthcr Sci (Cardiov Respir Slp Sci)) (IB 32 pts HL 16 pts)
South Wales – ABB incl biol+sci (MChiro) (IB 32 pts)
Strathclyde – ABB–BBB incl maths+sci +interview (Pros Orthot) (IB 34 pts HL 6 maths)
UWE Bristol – 128 pts incl sci/soc sci (Paramed Sci) (+interview HL 6 sci/soc sci)

120 pts Bradford – BBB incl biol+chem 120 pts (Clin Sci)
Brighton – BBB incl sci/soc sci +interview (Paramed Prac) (IB 30 pts)
Brunel – BBB incl sci (Biomed Sci (Hum Hlth)) (IB 30 pts HL 5 sci)
Cardiff Met – 120 pts incl biol +interview (Hlthcr Sci)
Dundee – BBB incl biol (Oral Hlth Sci) (IB 30 pts HL 555)
East Anglia – BBB incl biol/chem/PE +interview (Paramed Sci) (IB 31 pts HL 5 sci)
European Sch Ost – BBB incl sci/maths/PE/psy +interview (MOst) (IB 31 pts HL 5 sci)
Glasgow – BBB–CCC (Hlth Soc Plcy) (IB 28–30 pts)
Glasgow Caledonian – BBB incl sci (Orth) (IB 28 pts HL 6 sci+maths)
Kent – BBB (Hlth Soc Cr) (IB 34 pts)
Liverpool – BBB incl biol (Orth) (IB 30 pts HL 6 biol)
Liverpool Hope – BBB–BBC 120–112 pts (Hlth Wlbng)
London (St George's) – BBB incl biol +interview (Hlthcr Sci (Physiol Sci))
Manchester Met – BBB 120 pts incl biol +interview (Hlthcr Sci (Lf Sci/Physiol Sci))
   (IB 26 pts HL 5 biol)
Salford – 120 pts incl maths/phys/eng (Pros Orthot) (IB 28 pts)
Sheffield – BBB incl sci/maths (Orth) (IB 32 pts HL 6 sci/maths)
Surrey – BBB incl sci +interview (Paramed Sci) (IB 32 pts HL 555)
Swansea – BBB +interview (Ost); BBB incl sci/maths (Hlthcr Sci (Audiol))
UWE Bristol – 120 pts incl sci +interview (Hlthcr Sci (Physiol Sci)) (HL 5 sci); 120 pts incl
   biol/chem+sci +interview (Hlthcr Sci (Lf Sci)) (HL 6 biol/chem 5 sci)

112 pts Bangor – 112–96 pts (Hlth Soc Cr)
Brit Coll Ost Med – 112 pts incl biol +interview (MOst)
East London – 112 pts (Publc Hlth Hlth Prom) (IB 25 pts HL 15 pts)
Edge Hill – BBC 112 pts (Hlth Soc Wlbng)
Greenwich – 112 pts (Pblc Hlth)
Hertfordshire – 112–128 pts incl sci (Paramed Sci) (IB 30 pts HL 54)
Liverpool John Moores – BBC 112 pts (Pblc Hlth); (Hlth Soc Cr Indiv Fmly Commun)
   (IB 26 pts)
London Met – BBC 112 pts (Hlth Soc Cr; Hlth Soc Plcy)
Middlesex – 112 pts +interview (Hlthcr Sci (Audiol))

UCAS points Tariff: A* = 56 pts; A = 48 pts; B = 40 pts; C = 32 pts; D = 24 pts; E = 16 pts

Nottingham Trent – BBC incl sci/PE 112 pts (Exer Nutr Hlth)
Portsmouth – 112 pts incl sci/PE +interview (Paramed Sci) (IB 26 pts HL 5 sci/PE)
Salford – 112 pts incl sci/spo/sociol/psy (Exer Nutr Hlth) (IB 31 pts)
Sheffield Hallam – 112 pts (Nutr Pblc Hlth)
Southampton Solent – 112 pts (Hlth Nutr Exer Sci)
Sunderland – 112 pts (Hlthcr Sci (Physiol/Lf Sci); Pblc Hlth)
Swansea – BBC (Hlth Soc Cr)
Ulster – BBC incl sci/maths (Hlth Physiol/Hlthcr Sci); BBC (Hlth Soc Cr Plcy)
    (IB 25 pts HL 12 pts)
Westminster – BBC incl sci/maths/psy/geog (Herb Med) (IB 26 pts HL 4 sci)
Wolverhampton – BBC–CCC (Df St courses)
104 pts **AECC (UC)** – BCC (MChiro) (IB 28 pts)
Chester – BCC–BBC (Hlth Soc Cr) (IB 26 pts)
Kingston – 104–144 pts incl sci/psy/PE (Nutr (Exer Hlth))
Lincoln – BCC +interview (Hlth Soc Cr) (IB 28 pts)
London (St George's) – BCC (Paramed Sci) (HL 544)
Northampton – BCC (Hlth St Comb Hons)
Nottingham Trent – BCC 104 pts (Hlth Soc Cr)
St Mary's – 104 pts incl sci (Hlth Exer Sci)
Sunderland – 104 pts (Hlth Soc Cr)
UHI – BCC incl sci (Oral Hlth Sci)
96 pts **Bangor** – 96–112 pts (Hlth Wlbng)
BPP – CCC incl sci (MChiro)
Cardiff Met – 96 pts (Hlth Soc Cr)
Derby – 96–112 pts +interview (Hlth Soc Cr)
Nescot – 96 pts incl sci (Ost Med)
Oldham (Univ Campus) – 96 pts (Commun St Hlth)
Trinity Saint David – 96 pts +interview (Hlth Nutr Lfstl)
West London – 96 pts (Hlth Prom Pblc Hlth)
Worcester – 96 pts +interview (Paramed Sci) (IB 24 pts)
88 pts **Canterbury Christ Church** – 88–112 pts (Hlth St)
Winchester – 88–104 pts (Hlth Commun Soc Cr St) (IB 24 pts)
80 pts **Anglia Ruskin** – 80 pts (Pblc Hlth)
West Scotland – CCD incl sci (Env Hlth) (IB 27 pts)
Wolverhampton – CDD (Soc Cr Hlth St; Hlth St)
64 pts **UHI** – CC (Hlth St)

Open University – contact 0300 303 0073 **or** www.open.ac.uk/contact/new
    (Hlth Soc Cr)

Alternative offers
See **Chapter 6** and **Appendix 1** for grades/UCAS Tariff points information for other examinations.

EXAMPLES OF COLLEGES OFFERING COURSES IN THIS SUBJECT FIELD
See also **Social and Public Policy and Administration**. Most colleges, check with your local college.
Accrington and Rossendale (Coll); Bedford (Coll); Blackburn (Coll); Blackpool and Fylde (Coll); Bradford (Coll); Bridgwater and Taunton (Coll); Bristol City (Coll); Buckinghamshire (Coll Group); Chesterfield (Coll); City of Oxford (Coll); Cornwall (Coll); Doncaster (Coll); Duchy (Coll); Durham New (Coll); Exeter (Coll); Grimsby (Inst Group); Gŵp Llandrillo Menai; Hugh Baird (Coll); Hull (Coll); Leeds City (Coll); Lincoln (Coll); London South East (Coll); Manchester (Coll); Myerscough (Coll); Newcastle (Coll); Norwich City (Coll); Petroc; St Helens (Coll); Sir Gâr (Coll); Sparsholt (Coll); Stockport (Coll); Tresham (CFHE); Truro and Penwith (Coll); Wakefield (Coll); Warwickshire (Coll); West Cheshire (Coll); Westminster City (Coll); Weston (Coll); Wigan and Leigh (Coll); York (Coll).

CHOOSING YOUR COURSE (SEE ALSO CH.1)
Universities and colleges teaching quality See www.qaa.ac.uk; https://unistats.ac.uk.

Top research universities and colleges (REF 2014) (Public Health, Health Services and Primary Care) Cambridge; Liverpool; Oxford; Imperial London; Keele; London (UCL); Southampton; Bristol; London (King's); London (QM).

(Allied Health Professions, Dentistry, Nursing and Pharmacy) Birmingham; Sheffield (Biomed Sci); Bangor; Swansea (Allied Hlth); Aston; Coventry; Southampton; Cardiff; Surrey; Glasgow; Nottingham (Pharm); Bradford; East Anglia (Allied Hlth); London (QM); Sheffield (Dnstry); Queen's Belfast (Pharm); Bath; London (King's) (Pharm); Leeds.

ADMISSIONS INFORMATION
Number of applicants per place (approx) Bangor 5; Brit Coll Ost Med 5; Central Lancashire 6; European Sch Ost 3; Liverpool John Moores 10; London Met 7; Manchester 18; Manchester Met 10; Northampton 3; Salford 8; Southampton 4; Swansea 1.

Admissions tutors' advice You should describe any work with people you have done, particularly in a caring capacity, for example, working with the elderly, nursing, hospital work. Show why you wish to study this subject. You should give evidence of your ability to communicate and to work in a group. Evidence needed of applicants' understanding of the NHS and health care systems. Osteopathy applicants should provide clear evidence of why they want to work as an osteopath: work shadowing in an osteopath's practice is important and should be described. Give details of any work using your hands.

London (St George's) Work experience required.

Misconceptions about this course There is a mistaken belief that Health Science courses include nursing. **Bangor** (Hlth Soc Cr) This is an administration course, not a nursing course. **Bournemouth** Students should ultimately only apply to one type of health professional degree, eg all adult nursing courses, or all child health nursing courses – not a mixture. This is because admissions are looking for students who are dedicated to a specific health career that they can demonstrate insight into. **Bournemouth** Many think that being passionate about babies is what midwifery is all about, but really it is about the care of the adult (ie mothers through pregnancy), not the child. **Brit Coll Ost Med** Some students think that we offer an orthodox course in medicine. **European Sch Ost** Some applicants think we teach in French: we do not although we do have a franchise with a French school based in St Etienne and a high percentage of international students. All lectures are in English. Applicants should note that cranial osteopathy – one of our specialisms – is only one aspect of the programme.

Selection interviews Yes Anglia Ruskin, Bolton, Brighton, Dundee, European Sch Ost, London (St George's), Portsmouth, Worcester; **Some** Cardiff Met, Nottingham Trent; **No** Canterbury Christ Church, Derby, Lincoln, Liverpool John Moores, Southampton, Swansea, West Scotland.

Interview advice and questions Courses vary considerably and you are likely to be questioned on your reasons for choosing the course at that university or college. If you have studied biology, then questions on the A-level syllabus are possible and you could also be asked to discuss any work experience you have had. (Ost) What personal qualities would you need to be a good osteopath? What have you done that you feel demonstrates a sense of responsibility? What would you do if you were not able to secure a place on an Osteopathy course this year? See also **Chapter 5**.

Reasons for rejection (non-academic) Some students are mistakenly looking for a professional qualification in, for example, occupational therapy or nursing.

AFTER-RESULTS ADVICE
Offers to applicants repeating A-levels Same Bangor, Brighton, Chester, Derby, European Sch Ost, Lincoln, Liverpool John Moores, Salford, Swansea.

GRADUATE DESTINATIONS AND EMPLOYMENT (2015/16 HESA)
See also **Biotechnology**, **Dentistry**, **Medicine**, **Nursing and Midwifery**, **Nutrition** and **Optometry**.

Complementary Medicines, Therapies and Well-being graduates surveyed 560 **Employed** 145 **In voluntary employment** 0 **In further study** 220 **Assumed unemployed** 10

Aural and Oral Sciences graduates surveyed 630 **Employed** 495 **In voluntary employment** 0 **In further study** 35 **Assumed unemployed** 10

Career note Graduates enter a very broad variety of careers depending on their specialism. Opportunities exist in the public sector, for example, management and administrative positions with health and local authorities and in health promotion.

OTHER DEGREE SUBJECTS FOR CONSIDERATION

Audiology; Biological Sciences; Biology; Community Studies; Consumer Studies; Dentistry; Dietetics; Medicine; Environmental Health; Nursing; Nutrition; Occupational Therapy; Optometry; Physiotherapy; Psychology; Podiatry; Radiography; Speech Therapy; Sport Science.

HISTORY

(including **Heritage Studies** and **Medieval Studies**; see also **History (Ancient)**, **History (Economic and Social)**, **History of Art**)

Degrees in History cover a very broad field with many courses focusing on British and European history. However, specialised History degrees are available which cover other regions of the world and all courses will offer a wide range of modules.

Useful websites www.english-heritage.org.uk; www.historytoday.com; www.archives.com; www. historynet.com; www.archives.org.uk; http://royalhistsoc.orq; www.nationalarchives.gov.uk; www. history.ac.uk

NB The points totals shown to the left of the institutions are for ease of reference only. It must not be assumed that Tariff points are always used by Institutions or that they can be substituted for an offer in grades. The level of an offer is not necessarily indicative of the quality of a course.

COURSE OFFERS INFORMATION

Subject requirements/preferences GCSE English and a foreign language may be required or preferred. **AL** History usually required at a specified grade. (Mediev St) History or English Literature required for some courses.

Your target offers and examples of degree courses

152 pts **Cambridge** – A*AA +interview +HAA (Hist) (IB 40–42 pts HL 776)
Durham – A*AA incl hist (Hist) (IB 38 pts HL 666)
Exeter – A*AA–AAB (Hist; Hist (Emp Expnc)) (IB 38–34 pts)
London (UCL) – A*AA–AAA incl hist+Euro lang (Hist Euro Lang) (IB 39–38 pts HL 6 hist+Euro lang); A*AA–AAA incl hist (Hist; Hist (Yr Abrd)) (IB 39–38 pts HL 6 hist)

144 pts **Birmingham** – AAA–AAB incl hist (Hist) (IB 32 pts HL 666–665); AAA–ABB incl hist (Hist Comb Hons) (IB 32 pts HL 666–655)
Bristol – AAA–ABB incl hist (Hist) (IB 36–32 pts HL 6 hist)
Cardiff – AAB–ABB incl hist (Hist) (HL 665)
Edinburgh – AAA (Hist; Hist Pol) (IB 40 pts HL 766)
Exeter – AAA–AAB (Hist Int Rel courses) (IB 36–34 pts)
Lancaster – AAA–AAB (Hist Pol; Hist Int Rel; Mediev Ren St; Hist Phil) (IB 36–35 pts HL 16 pts); (Hist) (IB 36–35 pts)
Leeds – AAA incl hist (Hist) (IB 35 pts HL 17 pts incl 6 hist)
Liverpool – AAA–AAB (Hist) (IB 36–35 pts)
London (King's) – AAA incl hist (Hist; War St Hist) (IB 35 pts HL 666 incl hist)
London LSE – AAA (Gov Hist; Int Rel Hist; Hist) (IB 38 pts HL 766)

Check **Chapter 3** for new university admission details and **Chapter 6** on how to read the subject tables.

Manchester – AAA incl hist (Hist) (IB 37 pts HL 6 hist); AAA–ABB incl hist (Hist courses) (IB 37–33 pts HL 7/6 hist)

Newcastle – AAA–AAB incl hist (Hist) (IB 37–35 pts HL 6 hist)

Nottingham – AAA–AAB incl Engl+hist (Engl Hist) (IB 36–34 pts); AAA–AAB incl hist (Hist) (IB 36 pts HL 6 hist)

Oxford – AAA +interview +HAT (Hist Econ; Hist Pol; Hist; History (Anc Modn)) (IB 38 pts HL 666); AAA +interview +HAT +MLAT (Hist Modn Langs) (IB 38 pts HL 666); AAA +interview (Class Arch Anc Hist) (IB 39 pts HL 666)

St Andrews – AAA (Mediev Hist courses; Scot Hist courses; Mediev Hist Arch) (IB 36 pts HL 6 hist); (Modn Hist courses) (IB 38 pts HL 6 hist)

Strathclyde – AAA (3 yr course) ABB (4 yr course) (Hist) (IB 36 pts)

Warwick – AAA incl hist (Hist (Ren/Modn Modn)) (IB 38 pts HL 6 hist)

York – AAA/A*AB incl hist (Hist) (IB 36 pts HL 6 hist); AAA incl Fr+hist/class civ (Hist Fr) (IB 36 pts HL 6 Fr+hist); AAA incl Engl+hist (Engl Hist) (IB 36 pts HL 6 Engl+hist)

136 pts Birmingham – AAB incl hist (Hist Russ St) (IB 32 pts HL 665)

East Anglia – AAB incl hist (Hist; Modn Hist; Hist Pol) (IB 33 pts HL 5 hist)

Edinburgh – AAB (Archit Hist Herit) (IB 36 pts HL 665)

Glasgow – AAB–BBB incl arts/lang (Scot Hist; Hist) (IB 36–34 pts)

Leeds – AAB–ABB (Hist Phil Sci courses) (IB 35–34 pts HL 16 pts)

London (King's) – AAB incl Fr+hist (Fr Hist (Yr Abrd)) (IB 35 pts HL 665 incl Fr+hist)

London (RH) – AAB–ABB (Hist) (IB 32 pts HL 655)

London (SOAS) – AAB–ABB (Hist) (IB 35 pts HL 665)

London (UCL) – AAB–ABB incl hist (Russ Hist) (IB 36–34 pts HL 5 hist); AAB–ABB (Hist Phil Sci) (IB 36–34 pts HL 17–16 pts)

Manchester – AAB incl hist/pol/gov (Pol Modn Hist) (IB 35 pts HL 6 hist/pol/gov)

Nottingham – AAB incl hist (Hist Hist Art; Anc Hist Hist) (IB 34 pts HL 6 hist)

Reading – AAB–ABB incl hist/anc hist (Hist) (IB 32–34 pts HL 5 hist)

Sheffield – AAB–ABB incl hist/class civ (Hist Comb Hons) (IB 34–33 pts HL 6 hist); AAB–ABB+bEPQ incl hist/class civ (Hist Pol; Hist) (IB 34 pts HL 6 hist)

Southampton – AAB–ABB incl hist (Film Hist) (IB 32 pts HL 6 hist); (Hist; Modn Hist Pol) (IB 34 pts HL 6 hist); (Phil Hist) (IB 34–32 pts HL 6 hist); AAB–ABB+aEPQ incl Engl+hist (Engl Hist) (IB 34 pts HL 6 Engl+hist); AAB–ABB incl hist +interview (Arch Hist) (IB 34–32 pts HL 6 hist)

Sussex – AAB–ABB (Hist) (IB 32 pts); AAB–BBB (Hist Comb Hons) (IB 32–30 pts)

128 pts Cardiff – ABB incl hist (Modn Hist Pol) (IB 35 pts HL 6 hist)

Chichester – ABB–CCC (Hist; Modn Hist) (IB 28 pts)

East Anglia – ABB incl Engl+hist (Lit Hist) (IB 32 pts HL 5 Engl+hist); ABB incl hist (Am Hist; Hist Hist Art; Phil Hist) (IB 32 pts HL 5 hist)

Edinburgh – ABB (Celt Scot Hist) (IB 34 pts HL 655)

Kent – ABB incl hist/class (Hist courses; Mltry Hist) (IB 34 pts); ABB incl hist (Am St (Hist)) (IB 34 pts)

Leeds – ABB incl biol (Biol Hist Phil Sci) (IB 34 pts HL 6 biol)

Leicester – ABB–BBB+bEPQ (Hist; Hist Am St; Contemp Hist) (IB 30 pts HL 6); (Anc Hist Hist) (IB 30 pts)

Liverpool – ABB (Hist Comb Hons) (IB 33 pts)

London (QM) – ABB incl hist (Hist Pol; Hist; Mediev Hist; Hist Compar Lit) (IB 32 pts HL 655 incl hist)

London (UCL) – ABB (Scand St Hist) (IB 34 pts HL 16 pts); ABB incl hist (Hist (Cnt E Euro) Jew St) (IB 34 pts HL 5 hist)

Loughborough – ABB (Hist; Hist Pol; Hist Int Rel) (IB 34 pts HL 655)

NCH London – ABB–AAA +interview (Hist courses) (IB 34–38 pts)

Nottingham – ABB (Am Can Lit Hist Cult) (IB 32 pts); ABB incl hist (Am St Hist; Hist E Euro Cult St) (IB 32 pts HL 5 hist); (Hisp St Hist) (IB 32 pts HL 5); (Hist Contemp Chin St) (IB 32 pts HL 6 hist)

Queen's Belfast – ABB–BBB (Hist courses); ABB incl Fr (Fr Comb Hons)

COMBINING RESEARCH EXCELLENCE WITH INSPIRATIONAL TEACHING

The School of History at the University of Kent is recognised as one of the leading history departments in the country. Ranked eighth for Research Intensity in the most recent Research Excellence Framework, students are taught by world-class academics, actively working at the forefront of their fields.

The School prides itself on its flexible programmes, offering students the opportunity to tailor their degree to their own interests. Undergraduate students have access to over 80 modules covering British, Irish, European, American, Pacific and African history, as well as a wide range of courses on military history. An unparalleled range of joint honours degrees are also on offer, for those wishing to pursue a cross-disciplinary programme.

For the past five years, the School of History has consistently scored over 90% for student satisfaction in the National Student Survey – reflecting its inspiring teaching, lively and engaging student body and fantastic student support. A student-led History Society maintains a vibrant undergraduate community, organising extra-curricular lectures, field trips to places such as Rome and Vienna, and a host of social events.

The School is situated on Canterbury's leafy campus, where students have access to the University library, which holds over one million items, as well as the British Cartoon Archive. The medieval city provides a dramatic backdrop to the study of history, and students have privileged access to the Canterbury Cathedral Library and archives. High-speed trains link Canterbury to London and the continent, placing many of the most influential and historic sites in Europe a stone's throw away.

The School of History also has strong and established links with institutions across Europe as well as in Canada, the United States and South Africa allowing for a truly global outlook and opportunities to study abroad.

The strength of the School's degrees means that graduates are highly sought after; in 2016 96% of students who responded to a national survey were in employment or further study shortly after graduation (DLHE).

A superb student experience

"Every part of the School of History made my time at Kent exciting and enjoyable. The School offers a wide range of modules to choose from, and staff are always there to help you with any questions you might have.

Kent is a brilliant place to go for a History degree. It is one of the most exciting and innovative Universities in the UK and is at the forefront of research. The amount of extracurricular activities available to you is brilliant. Having a degree from the University of Kent is brilliant for my future career prospects, and in many job interviews employers have commented on Kent being a great University to have been to.

Since graduating I have completed a work placement with Channel 5 in their PR department, and have recently begun an internship with Sony Music."

Jessie Martin
History graduate

Fantastic prospects

"I was attracted to Kent by the modules available, the fact that it was a campus university, and the impressive student satisfaction rating. Kent is second in the country for History too, so I felt I'd be in safe hands.

My course was great; the teaching was one of its finest features. I always felt my seminars were valuable to my learning, and really built my confidence in each topic.

My studies have definitely helped my career prospects. The day after results day I was offered a full time job as a Trainee Oral Historian, working for an organisation which provides cultural, educational and historical activities. The work involves setting up exhibitions, interviewing people, conducting research, and archiving material. I am proud to be able to directly put my degree to use."

Emily Richards
History graduate

Further details

For more information please contact:
history@kent.ac.uk
01227 823710
www.kent.ac.uk/history

Roehampton – 128 pts incl hum (Hist)

Sheffield – ABB–BBB+bEPQ (Jap St Comb Hons) (IB 33 pts)

Stirling – ABB (3 yr course) BBB (4 yr course) incl hist (Scot Hist; Hist) (IB 35 pts (3 yr course) 32 pts (4 yr course))

120 pts **Aberdeen** – BBB (Hist) (IB 32 pts HL 555)

Aberystwyth – BBB (Hist; Hist Welsh Hist; Mediev Ely Modn Hist; Modn Contemp Hist) (IB 28 pts)

Anglia Ruskin – 120 pts (Hist) (IB 24 pts)

Brunel – BBB (Hist; Mltry Int Hist) (IB 30 pts)

Buckingham – BBB +interview (Engl Lit Hist) (IB 32 pts)

City – BBB (Hist) (IB 32 pts)

De Montfort – 120 pts incl hist (Hist) (IB 28 pts)

Dundee – BBB–BCC (Bus Econ Mark Hist) (IB 30 pts HL 555); BBB (Hist; Scot Hist St) (IB 30 pts HL 555)

Edge Hill – BBB 120 pts (Hist; Engl Lit Hist; Hist Pol)

Essex – BBB (Hist; Modn Hist) (IB 30 pts)

Huddersfield – BBB incl hist 120 pts (Hist); BBB 120–112 pts (Hist Comb Hons)

Hull – 120 pts (Hist; Hist Arch) (IB 28 pts)

Keele – BBB/ABC (Hist) (IB 32 pts)

Leicester – BBB–BBC+bEPQ (Int Rel Hist) (IB 28 pts)

Liverpool Hope – BBB–BBC 120–112 pts (Hist) (IB 26 pts)

London (Birk) – 120–128 pts (Pol Phil Hist)

London (Gold) – BBB (Hist Pol; Hist) (IB 33 pts HL 655)

Northumbria – 120–128 pts incl hist (Hist) (HL 444 incl hist); 120–128 pts incl hist/pol (Hist Pol) (HL 444 incl hist/pol)

Oxford Brookes – BBB–BBC 120–112 pts (Hist) (IB 30 pts)

Sunderland – 120 pts (Hist courses)

Swansea – BBB 120 pts (Hist) (IB 32 pts)

UWE Bristol – 120 pts (Hist)

112 pts **Bangor** – 112–120 pts (Hist; Mediev Ely Modn Hist; Modn Contemp Hist; Welsh Hist Comb Hons; Herit Arch Hist)

Chester – BBC–BBB incl hist/class civ/pol/sociol 112 pts (Hist) (IB 28 pts HL 5 hist)

Coventry – 112 pts incl hist (Hist courses) (IB 26 pts); BBC (Hist Pol) (IB 29 pts)

East London – 112 pts (Hist) (IB 25 pts HL 15 pts)

Gloucestershire – BBC 112 pts (Hist)

Glyndŵr – 112 pts (Hist)

Greenwich – 112 pts (Hist)

Hertfordshire – 112 pts (Hist) (HL 44)

Hull – 112 pts incl lang (Hist Modn Lang) (IB 28 pts)

Kingston – 112–128 pts (Hist)

Leeds Beckett – 112 pts (Hist) (IB 25 pts)

Lincoln – BBC (Hist) (IB 29 pts)

Liverpool John Moores – BBC 112 pts (Hist) (IB 26 pts)

London (Birk) – 112 pts (Hist)

Manchester Met – BBC 112 pts (Mediev Ely Modn Hist; Modn Hist; Hist) (IB 26 pts)

Nottingham Trent – 112 pts (Hist)

Plymouth – 112 pts (Hist courses) (IB 28 pts); 112 pts incl hist (Hist Pol) (IB 28 pts)

St Mary's – 112 pts (Hist)

Sheffield Hallam – 112–96 pts incl hist/class civ/relig st/sociol (Hist); 112–96 pts incl Engl lit/hist (Engl Hist)

Staffordshire – BBC 112 pts (Modn Hist)

Suffolk – BBC 112 pts (Hist Law; Hist Eth)

Wolverhampton – BBC–CCC (Pol Hist; Hist)

104 pts **Bath Spa** – BCC–CCC (Hist) (IB 26 pts)

Brighton – BCC–CCC 104–96 pts +interview (Hist Lit Cult) (IB 27 pts)

Central Lancashire – 104 pts (Hist)
Leeds Trinity – 104 pts (Hist)
Manchester Met – 104–112 pts (Hist Comb Hons) (IB 26 pts)
Newman – 104–96 pts (Hist)
Northampton – BCC (Hist courses)
Nottingham Trent – 104 pts (Hist Pol)
South Wales – BCC–CDD 104–80 pts (Hist) (HL 655–445)
Westminster – BCC incl Engl/hum (Engl Lit Hist) (IB 28 pts HL 5 Engl)
Winchester – 104–120 pts incl hist/arch/econ/pol (Hist; Hist Mediev Wrld) (IB 26 pts HL 5)
Worcester – 104 pts (Hist courses)

96 pts Bishop Grosseteste – 96–112 pts (Hist courses; Arch Hist)
Derby – 96–112 pts incl class st/hist/pol (Hist)
Portsmouth – 96–120 pts incl hist (Hist) (IB 30 pts HL 17 pts incl 5 hist)
Teesside – 96–112 pts incl hist (Hist)
York St John – 96–112 pts (Hist)

88 pts Canterbury Christ Church – 88–112 pts (Hist)
72 pts UHI – BC (Scot Hist Arch; Hist Pol; Scot Hist)
48 pts Anglia Ruskin – DD (Hist Engl)

Trinity Saint David – interview (Hist courses; Mediev St Comb Hons; Herit St courses)

Alternative offers
See **Chapter 6** and **Appendix 1** for grades/UCAS Tariff points information for other examinations.

EXAMPLES OF COLLEGES OFFERING COURSES IN THIS SUBJECT FIELD
North Lindsey (Coll); Peterborough (Coll); Petroc; South Devon (Coll); Stockton Riverside (Coll); Truro and Penwith (Coll).

CHOOSING YOUR COURSE (SEE ALSO CH.1)
Universities and colleges teaching quality See www.qaa.ac.uk; https://unistats.ac.uk.

Top research universities and colleges (REF 2014) York; Birmingham; Southampton; London (King's); Sheffield; London (Birk); Hertfordshire; Leeds; Leicester; Queen's Belfast; Sussex; Warwick; Edinburgh; Cardiff.

ADMISSIONS INFORMATION
Number of applicants per place (approx) Anglia Ruskin 4; Bangor 4; Bath Spa 6; Birmingham 8; Bristol 7; Buckingham 10; Cambridge 3; Cardiff 7; Central Lancashire 5; De Montfort 10; Dundee 8; Durham 7; East Anglia 3; Edge Hill 8; Exeter 9; Gloucestershire 26; Huddersfield 3; Hull 5; Kent 5; Kingston 6; Lancaster 4; Leeds 12; Leeds Trinity 6; Leicester 5; Liverpool 4; London (Gold) 6; London (King's) 10; London (QM) 5; London (RH) 6; London (UCL) 5; London LSE 11; Manchester 6; Manchester Met 8; Newcastle 5; Newman 2; Northampton 4; Nottingham 5; Oxford Brookes 9; Roehampton 4; St Mary's 5; Sheffield Hallam 21; Southampton 8; Staffordshire 8; Stirling 10; Teesside 4; Trinity Saint David 6; Warwick 17; York 5; York St John 3.

Advice to applicants and planning the UCAS personal statement Show your passion for the past! Visits to places of interest should be mentioned, together with any particular features which impressed you. Read historical books and magazines outside your A-level syllabus. Mention these and describe any special areas of study which interest you. (Check that these areas are covered in the courses for which you are applying!) **Bristol** Only accepting a limited number of deferred applicants in fairness to next year's applicants. Apply early. **Manchester** Due to the detailed nature of entry requirements for History courses, we are unable to include full details in the prospectus. For complete and up-to-date information on our entry requirements for these courses, please visit our website at www.manchester.ac.uk/study/undergraduate/courses.

Misconceptions about this course Students sometimes underestimate the amount of reading required. **Lincoln** Some students expect the subject to be assessed only by exams and essays. It is not – we use a wide range of assessment methods. **Stirling** Some applicants think that we only teach British history. We also cover European, American, African and environmental history.

Selection interviews Yes Brighton, Buckingham, Cambridge, Oxford (Hist) 23%, (Hist Econ) 11%, (Hist Modn Lang) 21%, (Hist Pol) 13%, Trinity Saint David; **Some** Bristol, Cardiff, Leeds Trinity, London (QM), Southampton, Warwick, Wolverhampton; **No** Anglia Ruskin, Bangor, Birmingham, Bishop Grosseteste, Canterbury Christ Church, Chichester, De Montfort, Dundee, East Anglia, Edge Hill, Essex, Hertfordshire, Huddersfield, Hull, Kent, Liverpool, London (King's), London (RH), London (UCL), London LSE, Nottingham, Oxford Brookes, Portsmouth, Reading, Roehampton, Sheffield Hallam, Staffordshire, Winchester.

Interview advice and questions Questions are almost certain to be asked on those aspects of the history A-level syllabus which interest you. Examples of questions in previous years have included: Why did imperialism happen? If a Martian arrived on Earth what aspect of life would you show him/her to sum up today's society? Has the role of class been exaggerated by Marxist historians? What is the difference between power and authority and between patriotism and nationalism? Did Elizabeth I have a foreign policy? What is the relevance of history in modern society? Who are your favourite monarchs? How could you justify your study of history to the taxpayer? What are the origins of your Christian name? See also **Chapter 5**. **Cambridge** How would you compare Henry VIII to Stalin? In the 1920s did the invention of the Henry Ford car lead to a national sub-culture or was it just an aspect of one? Is there such a thing as 'race'? Should historians be allowed to read sci-fi novels? **Oxford** Questions on submitted work and the capacity to think independently. What are the origins of your name? Why are you sitting in this chair?

Reasons for rejection (non-academic) Personal statements which read like job applications, focusing extensively on personal skills and saying nothing about the applicant's passion for history. Poor use of personal statement combined with predicted grades. Little commitment and enthusiasm. No clear reason for choice of course. Little understanding of history. Absence or narrowness of intellectual pursuits. Deception or concealment on the UCAS application. Knowledge of 19th century history (chosen subject) did not have any depth. Unwillingness to learn. Narrow approach to subject. Failure to submit requested information. **Birmingham** Commitment insufficient to sustain interest over three years. **London (King's)** Inability to think analytically and comparatively. **London (UCL)** The vast majority of applications are of a very high standard, many applicants being predicted AAA grades. We view each application as a complete picture, taking into account personal statement, reference and performance at any interview as well as actual and predicted academic performance. There is no single rule by which applicants are selected and therefore no single reason why they are rejected.

AFTER-RESULTS ADVICE
Offers to applicants repeating A-levels Higher Exeter, Huddersfield, Leeds, Liverpool, St Andrews, Trinity Saint David, Warwick; **Possibly higher** Aberystwyth, Birmingham, Cambridge; **Same** Anglia Ruskin, Bangor, Bristol, Buckingham, Cardiff, Chester, Chichester, De Montfort, Dundee, Durham, East Anglia, Edge Hill, Hull, Lancaster, Lincoln, Liverpool Hope, Liverpool John Moores, London (QM), London (RH), London (SOAS), Newcastle, Newman, Nottingham Trent, Oxford Brookes, Roehampton, St Mary's, Staffordshire, Stirling, Suffolk, Winchester, Wolverhampton, York, York St John; **No** Glasgow.

GRADUATE DESTINATIONS AND EMPLOYMENT (2015/16 HESA)
Graduates surveyed 8,520 **Employed** 3,490 **In voluntary employment** 365 **In further study** 2,650 **Assumed unemployed** 520

Career note Graduates enter a broad spectrum of careers. Whilst a small number seek positions with museums and galleries, most will enter careers in management, public and social services and retail as well as the teaching profession.

OTHER DEGREE SUBJECTS FOR CONSIDERATION
Ancient History; Anthropology; Archaeology; Economic and Social History; Government; History of Art; International Relations; Medieval History; Politics.

UCAS points Tariff: A* = 56 pts; A = 48 pts; B = 40 pts; C = 32 pts; D = 24 pts; E = 16 pts

HISTORY (ANCIENT)

(see also **Arabic and Ancient Near and Middle Eastern Studies, Archaeology, Classical Studies/Classical Civilisation, History**)

Ancient History covers the Greek and Roman world, the social, religious, political and economic changes taking place in the Byzantine period and the medieval era which followed.

Useful websites http://royalhistsoc.org; www.guardians.net; www.ancientworlds.net; www.bbc.co. uk/history/ancient

NB The points totals shown to the left of the institutions are for ease of reference only. It must not be assumed that Tariff points are always used by institutions or that they can be substituted for an offer in grades. The level of an offer is not necessarily indicative of the quality of a course.

COURSE OFFERS INFORMATION

Subject requirements/preferences GCSE A foreign language or classical language may be required. **AL** History or Classical Civilisation may be preferred subjects.

Your target offers and examples of degree courses

152 pts **Cambridge** – A*AA +interview +HSPSAA (Hum Soc Pol Sci (Assyr Egypt)) (IB 40–42 pts HL 776)

144 pts **Durham** – AAA (Anc Hist Arch; Anc Hist) (IB 37 pts)
Exeter – AAA–ABB (Anc Hist) (IB 36–32 pts)
London (UCL) – AAA incl hist/class civ (Anc Hist) (IB 38 pts HL 6 hist)
Oxford – AAA +interview +HAT (History (Anc Modn)) (IB 38 pts HL 666)
St Andrews – AAA (Anc Hist Comb Hons) (IB 36 pts HL 666)

136 pts **Bristol** – AAB–BBB (Anc Hist) (IB 34–31 pts HL 17–16 pts)
Edinburgh – AAB (Anc Hist Lat; Anc Hist; Anc Hist Gk; Anc Hist Class Arch) (IB 36 pts HL 665)
London (King's) – AAB (Anc Hist) (IB 35 pts HL 665)
London (RH) – AAB–ABB (Anc Hist Phil) (IB 32 pts HL 655)
London (UCL) – AAB (Anc Wrld) (IB 36 pts HL 17 pts)
Nottingham – AAB incl hist (Anc Hist Hist) (IB 34 pts HL 6 hist)

128 pts **Birmingham** – ABB (Arch Anc Hist; Anc Mediev Hist; Anc Hist) (IB 32 pts HL 655)
Cardiff – ABB–BBB (Anc Hist Comb Hons) (IB 32–30 pts)
Edinburgh – ABB (Anc Medit Civ) (IB 36 pts HL 665)
Leicester – ABB–BBB+bEPQ (Anc Hist Arch; Anc Hist Hist) (IB 30 pts)
Liverpool – ABB (Anc Hist; Arch Anc Civ) (IB 33 pts)
London (RH) – ABB–BBB (Anc Hist) (IB 32 pts HL 555)
Manchester – ABB (Anc Hist) (IB 33 pts HL 655)
Nottingham – ABB (Anc Hist Arch) (IB 32 pts)
Swansea – ABB–BBB 128–120 pts (Anc Hist Hist) (IB 32–30 pts)
Warwick – ABB (Anc Hist Class Arch) (IB 34 pts)

120 pts **Kent** – BBB (Anc Hist) (IB 34 pts)
Swansea – BBB (Egypt Anc Hist) (IB 32 pts); BBB 120 pts (Anc Mediev Hist) (IB 32 pts)
Trinity Saint David – interview (Anc Mediev Hist; Anc Hist)

Alternative offers
See **Chapter 6** and **Appendix 1** for grades/UCAS Tariff points information for other examinations.

CHOOSING YOUR COURSE (SEE ALSO CH.1)

Universities and colleges teaching quality See www.qaa.ac.uk; https://unistats.ac.uk.

Top research universities and colleges (REF 2014) See **Classics**.

Check **Chapter 3** for new university admission details and **Chapter 6** on how to read the subject tables.

ADMISSIONS INFORMATION

Number of applicants per place (approx) Birmingham 7; Bristol 6; Cardiff 4; Durham 6; Leicester 5; London (RH) 5; London (UCL) 5; Manchester 7; Nottingham 4; Oxford 4.

Advice to applicants and planning the UCAS personal statement Any information about experience of excavation or museum work should be given. Visits to Greece and Italy to study archaeological sites should be described. Show how your interest in, for example, Ancient Egypt developed through, for example, reading, television and the internet. Be aware of the work of the career archaeologist, for example, sites and measurement officers, field officers and field researchers (often specialists in pottery, glass, metalwork). See also **History**.

Misconceptions about this course Liverpool (Egypt) Some students would have been better advised looking at V400 Archaeology or VV16 Ancient History and Archaeology, both of which offer major pathways in the study of Ancient Egypt.

Selection interviews Yes Oxford (23%); **Some** Bristol, Cardiff; **No** Birmingham, London (RH).

Interview advice and questions See **History**.

AFTER-RESULTS ADVICE

Offers to applicants repeating A-levels Same Birmingham, Cardiff, Durham, Newcastle.

GRADUATE DESTINATIONS AND EMPLOYMENT (2015/16 HESA)

See **History**.

Career note See **History**.

OTHER DEGREE SUBJECTS FOR CONSIDERATION

Anthropology; Archaeology; Classical Studies; Classics; Greek; History of Art; Latin.

HISTORY (ECONOMIC and SOCIAL)

(see also History)

Economic and Social History is a study of societies and economies and explores the changes that have taken place in the past and the causes and consequences of those changes. The study can cover Britain, Europe and other major powers.

Useful websites http://royalhistsoc.org; www.ehs.org.uk; see also **Economics** and **History**.

NB The points totals shown to the left of the institutions are for ease of reference only. It must not be assumed that Tariff points are always used by institutions or that they can be substituted for an offer in grades. The level of an offer is not necessarily indicative of the quality of a course.

COURSE OFFERS INFORMATION

Subject requirements/preferences GCSE Mathematics usually required and a language may be preferred. **AL** History preferred.

Your target offers and examples of degree courses
144 pts **Edinburgh** – AAA–AAB (Soc Hist courses) (IB 40–39 pts HL 766–666)
　　　　　York – AAA incl hist/class civ+maths (Hist Econ) (IB 36 pts HL 6 hist)
136 pts **Edinburgh** – AAB (Soc Plcy Soc Econ Hist) (IB 39 pts HL 666)
　　　　　Glasgow – AAB–BBB incl Engl/hum (Econ Soc Hist) (IB 36–34 pts HL 665)
　　　　　London LSE – AAB incl maths (Econ Econ Hist) (IB 37 pts)
128 pts **Manchester** – ABB incl hist/sociol (Hist Sociol) (IB 33 pts HL 655)

Alternative offers
See **Chapter 6** and **Appendix 1** for grades/UCAS Tariff points information for other examinations.

CHOOSING YOUR COURSE (SEE ALSO CH.1)
Universities and colleges teaching quality See www.qaa.ac.uk; https://unistats.ac.uk.

ADMISSIONS INFORMATION
Number of applicants per place (approx) London LSE (Econ Hist) 7, (Econ Hist Econ) 12; York 8.

Advice to applicants and planning the UCAS personal statement See **History**.

Interview advice and questions See **History**.

AFTER-RESULTS ADVICE
Offers to applicants repeating A-levels Higher York.

GRADUATE DESTINATIONS AND EMPLOYMENT (2015/16 HESA)
See **History**.

Career note See **History**.

OTHER DEGREE SUBJECTS FOR CONSIDERATION
Economics; Government; History; Politics; Social Policy and Administration; Sociology.

HISTORY OF ART
(see also History)

History of Art (and Design) courses differ slightly between universities although most will focus on the history and appreciation of European art and architecture from the 14th to 20th centuries. Some courses also cover the Egyptian, Greek and Roman periods and at London (SOAS), Asian, African and European Art. The history of all aspects of design and film can also be studied in some courses. There has been an increase in the popularity of these courses in recent years.

Useful websites www.artchive.com; www.artcyclopedia.com; http://theartguide.com; www.galleries. co.uk; www.fine-art.com; www.nationalgallery.org.uk; www.britisharts.co.uk; www.tate.org.uk

NB The points totals shown to the left of the institutions are for ease of reference only. It must not be assumed that Tariff points are always used by institutions or that they can be substituted for an offer in grades. The level of an offer is not necessarily indicative of the quality of a course.

COURSE OFFERS INFORMATION
Subject requirements/preferences GCSE English required and a foreign language usually preferred. **AL** History is preferred for some courses.

Your target offers and examples of degree courses
152 pts **Cambridge** – A*AA +interview +HAAA (Hist Art) (IB 40–42 pts HL 776)
144 pts **Exeter** – AAA–AAB (Art Hist Vis Cult; Art Hist courses) (IB 36–32 pts)
         London (Court) – AAA–AAB +interview (Hist Art) (IB 35 pts)
         London (UCL) – AAA–ABB (Hist Art) (IB 38–34 pts HL 17–16 pts)
         Oxford – AAA +interview (Hist Art) (IB 38 pts HL 666)
         St Andrews – AAA (Art Hist Mid E St) (IB 36 pts HL 6 hist); (Art Hist Class St) (IB 36 pts)
136 pts **Bristol** – AAB–BBB incl lang (Hist Art Modn Lang) (IB 34–31 pts HL 5 lang); AAB–BBB (Hist Art) (IB 34–31 pts HL 17–15 pts)
         East Anglia – AAB (Arch Anth Art Hist (St Abrd); Hist Art) (IB 33 pts)
         Edinburgh – AAB incl mus (Hist Art Hist Mus) (IB 38 pts HL 666); AAB (Hist Art) (IB 38 pts HL 666)
         Glasgow – AAB incl arts/hum/lang (Hist Art) (IB 36 pts HL 665 incl 6 Engl/hum/lang)
         Leeds – AAB (Hist Art) (IB 35–34 pts)

Nottingham – AAB incl hist (Hist Hist Art) (IB 34 pts HL 6 hist); AAB incl Engl (Hist Art Engl) (IB 34 pts HL 6 Engl)

St Andrews – AAB (Art Hist Psy; Art Hist; Art Hist Lang) (IB 35 pts)

Sussex – AAB–ABB (Art Hist) (IB 32 pts)

York – AAB–ABB (Hist Art) (IB 35–34 pts); AAB incl hist/class civ (Hist Hist Art) (IB 35 pts HL 6 hist); AAB incl Engl (Engl Hist Art) (IB 35 pts HL 6 Engl)

128 pts **Birmingham** – ABB incl lang (Modn Langs Hist Art) (IB 32 pts HL 655); ABB (Hist Art) (IB 32 pts HL 655)

East Anglia – ABB incl hist (Hist Hist Art) (IB 32 pts HL 5 hist)

London (SOAS) – ABB (Hist Art (As Af Euro)) (IB 35 pts HL 555); ABB–BBB (Hist Art; Hist Art Arch courses) (IB 33 pts HL 555)

Manchester – ABB (Hist Art) (IB 33 pts HL 655)

Nottingham – ABB (Hist Art) (IB 34 pts); ABB–BBB (Arch Hist Art) (IB 32–30 pts)

Warwick – ABB (Hist Art) (IB 34 pts)

120 pts **Aberdeen** – BBB (Hist Art) (IB 32 pts HL 555)

Buckingham – BBB +interview (Hist Art Herit Mgt) (IB 32 pts)

Essex – BBB (Art Hist; Lit Art Hist) (IB 30 pts)

Kent – BBB (Art Hist Film) (IB 34 pts); BBB +interview (Art Hist) (IB 34 pts)

Leicester – BBB (Hist Art) (IB 28 pts)

112 pts **Aberystwyth** – BBC incl art +portfolio (Fn Art Art Hist) (IB 30 pts); BBC (Art Hist) (IB 30 pts)

Liverpool John Moores – BBC 112 pts (Hist Art Musm St) (IB 26 pts)

London (Birk) – 112 pts (Hist Art)

Manchester Met – 112–120 pts (Art Hist) (IB 26 pts)

104 pts **Brighton** – BCC–CCC +interview (Fash Drs Hist) (IB 27 pts); BCC–CCC 104–96 pts (Hist Art Des) (IB 27 pts)

Plymouth – 104 pts (Art Hist) (IB 26 pts); 104 pts +interview +portfolio (Fn Art Art Hist) (IB 26 pts)

Alternative offers
See **Chapter 6** and **Appendix 1** for grades/UCAS Tariff points information for other examinations.

EXAMPLES OF COLLEGES OFFERING COURSES IN THIS SUBJECT FIELD
South Gloucestershire and Stroud (Coll).

CHOOSING YOUR COURSE (SEE ALSO CH.1)
Universities and colleges teaching quality See www.qaa.ac.uk; https://unistats.ac.uk.

Top research universities and colleges (REF 2014) See **Art and Design (General)**.

ADMISSIONS INFORMATION
Number of applicants per place (approx) Birmingham 14; Bristol 4; Cambridge 4; East Anglia 5; Essex 5; Leeds 29; Leicester 9; London (Court) 320; London (SOAS) 4; London (UCL) 6; Manchester 3; Manchester Met 10; Nottingham 2; York 4.

Advice to applicants and planning the UCAS personal statement Applicants for History of Art courses should have made extensive visits to art galleries, particularly in London, and should be familiar with the main European schools of painting. Evidence of lively interest required. Discuss your preferences and say why you prefer certain types of work or particular artists. You should also describe any visits to museums and any special interests in furniture, pottery or other artefacts. **Bristol** Deferred entry may be considered. **London (Court)** Everyone is surrounded by visual materials, from buildings and works of art to films, photography, fashion, advertisements and computer games. Ideally, your personal statement includes an explanation of why some visual materials you have seen really interest you. Admissions tutors look for an expression and explanation of enthusiasm for the topic of art history and for the study of the visual material as evidence of historical circumstances and human activity. You might include an account of how your understanding of visual materials has been affected by an article or book you have read (not necessarily art history). A-levels in History, History of Art, English, and modern European languages are the most relevant; however, other subjects are considered. Art offered as an A-level should include a history of art paper.

Misconceptions about this course London (Court) The BA History of Art programme does not have fine art/practice based components. **York** Students do not need a background in art or art history. It is not a course with a studio element in it.

Selection interviews Yes Buckingham, Cambridge, Manchester, Oxford (10%), Warwick; **Some** Bristol; **No** Birmingham, Brighton, East Anglia, Essex, Kent, London (UCL), Manchester Met, Nottingham.

Interview advice and questions Some universities set slide tests on painting and sculpture. Those applicants who have not taken History of Art at A-level will be questioned on their reasons for choosing the subject, their visits to art galleries and museums and their reactions to the art work which has impressed them. See **Chapter 5**. **Kent** Do they visit art galleries? Have they studied art history previously? What do they expect to get out of the degree? Sometimes they are given images to compare and discuss. **London (Court)** If selected for interview, candidates are asked to attend an interview day, first completing a 30 minute test comparing two images, then an informal interview with two members of academic staff. This exercise is a chance for our academic members of staff to assess candidates' visual comprehension. Candidates are not expected to exercise specific history of art knowledge at this stage.

Reasons for rejection (non-academic) Poorly presented practical work. Students who do not express any interest or enthusiasm in contemporary visual arts are rejected.

AFTER-RESULTS ADVICE
Offers to applicants repeating A-levels Possibly higher St Andrews; **Same** Aberystwyth, East Anglia, Leeds, Warwick, York; **No** Cambridge.

GRADUATE DESTINATIONS AND EMPLOYMENT (2015/16 HESA)
Career note Work in galleries, museums and collections will be the objective of many graduates, who should try to establish contacts by way of work placements and experience during their undergraduate years. The personal skills acquired during their studies, however, open up many opportunities in other careers.

OTHER DEGREE SUBJECTS FOR CONSIDERATION
Art; Archaeology; Architecture; Classical Studies; Photography.

HORTICULTURE

(including **Garden Design**; see also **Agricultural Sciences/Agriculture, Landscape Architecture, Plant Sciences**)

Horticulture is a broad subject area covering amenity or landscape horticulture, production horticulture and retail horticulture.

Useful websites http://iagre.org; www.rhs.org.uk; www.horticulture.org.uk; www.sgd.org.uk

NB The points totals shown to the left of the institutions are for ease of reference only. It must not be assumed that Tariff points are always used by institutions or that they can be substituted for an offer in grades. The level of an offer is not necessarily indicative of the quality of a course.

COURSE OFFERS INFORMATION
Subject requirements/preferences GCSE Mathematics sometimes required. **AL** A science subject may be required or preferred for some courses.

Your target offers and examples of degree courses
104 pts **SRUC** – BCC incl sci (Hort Plntsmn; Hort)
96 pts **Hadlow (Coll)** – 96 pts (Gdn Des; Hort (Commer))
Writtle (UC) – 96 pts (Hort) (IB 24 pts)
80 pts **Duchy (Coll)** – 80 pts (Hort (Gdn Lnd Des))

Alternative offers
See **Chapter 6** and **Appendix 1** for grades/UCAS Tariff points information for other examinations.

EXAMPLES OF COLLEGES OFFERING COURSES IN THIS SUBJECT FIELD

Askham Bryan (Coll); Bicton (Coll); Bishop Burton (Coll); Bridgend (Coll); Bridgwater and Taunton (Coll); Brooksby Melton (Coll); CAFRE; Capel Manor (Coll); Craven (Coll); Myerscough (Coll); Warwickshire (Coll).

CHOOSING YOUR COURSE (SEE ALSO CH.1)

Universities and colleges teaching quality See www.qaa.ac.uk; https://unistats.ac.uk.

ADMISSIONS INFORMATION

Number of applicants per place (approx) SRUC 1; Writtle (UC) 3.

Advice to applicants and planning the UCAS personal statement Practical experience is important and visits to botanical gardens (the Royal Botanic Gardens, Kew or Edinburgh and the Royal Horticultural Society gardens at Wisley) could be described. Contact your local authority offices for details of work in parks and gardens departments. See also **Appendix 3**.

Selection interviews Some SRUC; **No** Greenwich.

Interview advice and questions Past questions have included: How did you become interested in horticulture? How do you think this course will benefit you? Could you work in all weathers? What career are you aiming for? Are you interested in gardening? Describe your garden. What plants do you grow? How do you prune rose trees and fruit trees? Are there any EU policies at present affecting the horticulture industry? Topics relating to the importance of science and horticulture. See also **Chapter 5**.

AFTER-RESULTS ADVICE

Offers to applicants repeating A-levels Same SRUC.

GRADUATE DESTINATIONS AND EMPLOYMENT (2015/16 HESA)

See **Agricultural Sciences/Agriculture**.

Career note Graduates seeking employment in horticulture will look towards commercial organisations for the majority of openings. These will include positions as growers and managers with fewer vacancies for scientists involved in research and development and advisory services.

OTHER DEGREE SUBJECTS FOR CONSIDERATION

Agriculture; Biology; Crop Science; Ecology; Forestry; Landscape Architecture; Plant Sciences.

HOSPITALITY and EVENT MANAGEMENT

(see also **Business and Management Courses, Business and Management Courses (International and European), Business and Management Courses (Specialised), Food Science/Studies and Technology, Leisure and Recreation Management/Studies, Tourism and Travel**)

Courses cover the full range of skills required for those working in the industry. Specific studies include hotel management, food and beverage supplies, equipment design, public relations and marketing. Depending on the course, other topics may include events management, tourism and the international trade.

Useful websites www.thebapa.org.uk; www.cordonbleu.edu; www.instituteofhospitality.org; www.people1st.co.uk; www.abpco.org

NB The points totals shown to the left of the institutions are for ease of reference only. It must not be assumed that Tariff points are always used by institutions or that they can be substituted for an offer in grades. The level of an offer is not necessarily indicative of the quality of a course.

COURSE OFFERS INFORMATION
Subject requirements/preferences GCSE English and mathematics usually required together with a foreign language for International Management courses. **AL** No specified subjects.

Your target offers and examples of degree courses
144 pts **Strathclyde** – AAA–ABB incl maths (Acc Hspty Tour Mgt) (IB 38 pts HL 6 maths)
128 pts **Strathclyde** – ABB (Hspty Tour Mgt) (IB 36 pts)
Surrey – ABB (Int Hspty Mgt; Int Hspty Tour Mgt) (IB 32 pts)
120 pts **Coventry** – BBB (Int Hspty Tour Mgt) (IB 29 pts)
112 pts **Bournemouth** – 112–120 pts (Evnts Mgt) (IB 30–31 pts HL 55)
Bournemouth Arts – BBC–BBB 112–120 pts +interview (Crea Evnts Mgt) (IB 30–32 pts)
Central Lancashire – 112 pts (Int Hspty Mgt; Evnt Mgt) (IB 28 pts)
Chester – BBC–BCC 112 pts (Evnts Mgt) (IB 26 pts)
Chichester – BBC–CCC (Evnt Mgt) (IB 28 pts)
Coventry – BBC (Evnt Mgt) (IB 29 pts)
De Montfort – 112 pts (Arts Fstvl Mgt) (IB 26 pts)
East London – 112 pts (Hspty Mgt) (IB 25 pts HL 15 pts)
Euro Bus Sch London – BBC (Int Evnts Mgt)
Gloucestershire – BBC 112 pts (Evnts Mgt)
Greenwich – 112 pts (Evnt Mgt)
Huddersfield – BBC 112 pts (Evnts Mgt; Hspty Bus Mgt)
Liverpool John Moores – BBC 112 pts (Evnts Mgt) (IB 26 pts)
London Regent's – BBC (Int Evnts Mgt)
Oxford Brookes – BBC 112 pts (Int Hspty Mgt) (IB 30 pts)
Plymouth – 112 pts (Evnts Mgt) (IB 28 pts HL 4)
Robert Gordon – BBC (Evnts Mgt) (IB 29 pts)
Sheffield Hallam – 112 pts (Int Htl Rsrt Mgt)
Southampton Solent – 112 pts (Evnts Mgt)
Sunderland – 112 pts (Int Tour Hspty Mgt)
Ulster – BBC–BBB (Int Hspty Mgt) (IB 25–26 pts HL 12–13 pts)
West London – BBC 112 pts (Hspty Mgt; Evnt Mgt)
Wolverhampton – BBC–CCC (Int Hspty Mgt; Evnt Vnu Mgt)
104 pts **Birmingham (UC)** – 104 pts (Evnts Mgt)
Brighton – BCC–CCC 104–96 pts (Int Evnt Mgt; Int Hspty Mgt) (IB 27 pts)
CAFRE – 104 pts incl bus/sci/hm econ (Fd Bus Mgt)
Edinburgh Napier – BCC (Int Fstvl Evnt Mgt) (IB 28 pts)
Glasgow Caledonian – BCC (Int Evnts Mgt) (IB 25 pts)
Lincoln – BCC (Evnts Mgt) (IB 28 pts)
Northampton – BCC (Evnts Mgt; Evnts Mgt Comb Hons)
Queen Margaret – BCC 104 pts (Evnts Mgt) (IB 28 pts)
Salford – BCC 104–112 pts (Int Evnts Mgt) (IB 26 pts)
South Wales – BCC–CCD 104–88 pts (Evnt Mgt) (HL 655–445)
96 pts **Birmingham (UC)** – 96 pts (Culn Arts Mgt; Hspty courses; Spec Hair Media Mkup)
Cardiff Met – 96–112 pts (Evnts Mgt; Int Hspty Tour Mgt)
Derby – 96–112 pts (Int Hspty Mgt; Evnts Mgt)
Edinburgh Napier – CCC (Int Hspty Mark Mgt) (IB 27 pts)
Essex – CCC 96 pts (Htl Mgt)
Hertfordshire – 96–112 pts (Evnt Mgt)
Leeds Beckett – 96 pts (Spo Evnt Mgt; Evnts Mgt) (IB 24 pts)

London Met – CCC/BC 96 pts (Evnts Mgt)
Manchester Met – CCC–BBC 96–112 pts (Hspty Bus Mgt) (IB 26 pts); CCC–BBC 96–112 pts (Evnts Mgt) (IB 26 pts)
Plymouth – 96 pts (Int Hspty Mgt; Hspty Mgt) (IB 24 pts HL 4); (Cru Mgt) (IB 26 pts HL 4)
Robert Gordon – CCC (Int Hspty Mgt) (IB 26 pts)
Staffordshire – 96 pts (Evnts Mgt)
West Scotland – CCC (Evnts Mgt) (IB 24 pts)
Winchester – 96–112 pts (Evnt Mgt) (IB 25 pts)
88 pts **Canterbury Christ Church** – 88–112 pts (Evnts Mgt)
Portsmouth – 88 pts (Hspty Mgt; Hspty Mgt Tour) (IB 28 pts HL 15 pts)
Trinity Saint David – 88 pts +interview (Evnts Mgt)
80 pts **Bedfordshire** – 80 pts (Evnt Mgt)
Bucks New – 80–96 pts (Evnts Fstvl Mgt; Mus Lv Evnts Mgt)
64 pts **UHI** – CC (Hosp Mgt)

Alternative offers
See **Chapter 6** and **Appendix 1** for grades/UCAS Tariff points information for other examinations.

EXAMPLES OF COLLEGES OFFERING COURSES IN THIS SUBJECT FIELD
Accrington and Rossendale (Coll); Barnsley (Coll); Bedford (Coll); Birmingham Met (Coll); Bishop Burton (Coll); Blackburn (Coll); Blackpool and Fylde (Coll); Bournemouth and Poole (Coll); Bournville (Coll); Bradford (Coll); Brighton Met (Coll); Bury (Coll); Cornwall (Coll); Craven (Coll); Darlington (Coll); Derby (Coll); Doncaster (Coll); Durham New (Coll); Ealing, Hammersmith and West London (Coll); East Riding (Coll); Furness (Coll); Grimsby (Inst Group); Grŵp Llandrillo Menai; Guildford (Coll); Hartlepool (CFE); Highbury Portsmouth (Coll); Hull (Coll); Leicester (Coll); Liverpool City (Coll); London City (Coll); London UCK (Coll); Loughborough (Coll); LSST; Macclesfield (Coll); Manchester (Coll); MidKent (Coll); NCC Redbridge; Neath Port Talbot (Coll); Nescot; Newcastle (Coll); North Notts (Coll); Northumberland (Coll); Norwich City (Coll); Petroc; Plymouth City (Coll); Reaseheath (Coll); Richmond-upon-Thames (Coll); Sheffield (Coll); South Cheshire (Coll); South Devon (Coll); South Essex (Coll); Stratford-upon-Avon (Coll); Walsall (Coll); Warwickshire (Coll); West Cheshire (Coll); West Herts (Coll); West Suffolk (Coll); Westminster Kingsway (Coll); Weymouth (Coll); Wirral Met (Coll).

CHOOSING YOUR COURSE (SEE ALSO CH.1)
Universities and colleges teaching quality See www.qaa.ac.uk; https://unistats.ac.uk.

Examples of sandwich degree courses Birmingham (UC); Bournemouth; Brighton; Cardiff Met; Central Lancashire; Derby; Gloucestershire; Huddersfield; Leeds Beckett; Manchester Met; Oxford Brookes; Portsmouth; Salford; Sheffield Hallam; Staffordshire; Sunderland; Surrey; Ulster; Wolverhampton.

ADMISSIONS INFORMATION
Number of applicants per place (approx) Cardiff Met 12; Central Lancashire 8; Edinburgh Napier 10; London Met 10; Manchester Met (Hspty Mgt) 12; Oxford Brookes 5; Robert Gordon 3; Strathclyde 8.

Advice to applicants and planning the UCAS personal statement Experience in dealing with members of the public is an important element in this work which, coupled with work experience in cafés, restaurants or hotels, should be described fully. All applicants are strongly recommended to obtain practical experience in catering or hotel work. Admissions tutors are likely to look for experience in industry and for people who are ambitious, sociable and team players. See also **Appendix 3**.

Misconceptions about this course Cardiff Met The course is not about cooking! We are looking to create managers, not chefs.

Selection interviews No Bucks New, Cardiff Met, Manchester Met, Portsmouth, Robert Gordon, Salford, Surrey.

Interview advice and questions Past questions have included: What books do you read? What do you know about hotel work and management? What work experience have you had? What kind of job do you have in mind when you have qualified? How did you become interested in this course? Do you eat in restaurants? What types of restaurants? Discuss examples of good and bad restaurant organisation. What qualities do you have which make you suitable for management? See also **Chapter 5**.

Reasons for rejection (non-academic) Lack of suitable work experience or practical training. Inability to communicate. Lack of awareness of workload, for example shift working, weekend work. **Cardiff Met** Students looking specifically for licensed trade courses or a cookery course.

AFTER-RESULTS ADVICE
Offers to applicants repeating A-levels Same Brighton, Cardiff Met, Huddersfield, Manchester Met, Oxford Brookes, Salford, Strathclyde, Suffolk, Ulster, West London, Wolverhampton.

GRADUATE DESTINATIONS AND EMPLOYMENT (2015/16 HESA)
Including Leisure, Tourism and Transport graduates surveyed 4,420 **Employed** 2,650 **In voluntary employment** 70 **In further study** 740 **Assumed unemployed** 210

Career note These business-focused hospitality programmes open up a wide range of employment and career opportunities in both hospitality and other business sectors. The demand for employees has been high in recent years. Events management is currently a growth area with graduates working in sports and the arts, tourist attractions, hospitality, business and industry.

OTHER DEGREE SUBJECTS FOR CONSIDERATION
Business; Consumer Studies; Dietetics; Food Science; Health Studies; Leisure and Recreation Management; Management; Tourism and Travel.

HOUSING
(see also Building and Construction, Surveying and Real Estate Management, Town and Country Planning)

These courses prepare students for careers in housing management although topics covered will also be relevant to other careers in business and administration. Modules will be taken in housing, law, finance, planning policy, public administration and construction.

Useful websites www.gov.uk/government/topics/housing; www.rtpi.org.uk; www.freeindex.co.uk/categories/property/construction/Property_Development

NB The points totals shown to the left of the institutions are for ease of reference only. It must not be assumed that Tariff points are always used by institutions or that they can be substituted for an offer in grades. The level of an offer is not necessarily indicative of the quality of a course.

COURSE OFFERS INFORMATION
Subject requirements/preferences GCSE English and mathematics required. **AL** No specified subjects.

Your target offers and examples of degree courses
112 pts Central Lancashire – 112 pts (Commun Soc Care Plcy Prac) (IB 28 pts)
104 pts London South Bank – BCC (Hous St)
 88 pts Cardiff Met – 88 pts +interview (Hous St)

Alternative offers
See **Chapter 6** and **Appendix 1** for grades/UCAS Tariff points information for other examinations.

EXAMPLES OF COLLEGES OFFERING COURSES IN THIS SUBJECT FIELD
Blackburn (Coll); St Helens (Coll).

CHOOSING YOUR COURSE (SEE ALSO CH.1)
Universities and colleges teaching quality See www.qaa.ac.uk; https://unistats.ac.uk.

ADMISSIONS INFORMATION

Number of applicants per place (approx) Cardiff Met 1.

Advice to applicants and planning the UCAS personal statement An interest in people, housing problems, social affairs and the built environment is important for this course. Contacts with local housing managers (through local authority offices or housing associations) are important. Describe any such contacts and your knowledge of the housing types and needs in your area. The planning department in your local council office will be able to provide information on the various types of developments taking place in your locality and how housing needs have changed during the past 50 years. See also **Appendix 3**.

Misconceptions about this course Applicants do not appreciate that the course is very close to social work/community work and is most suitable for those wishing to work with people.

Selection interviews Yes Cardiff Met.

Interview advice and questions Since the subject is not studied at school, questions are likely to be asked on reasons for choosing this degree. Other past questions include: What is a housing association? Why were housing associations formed? In which parts of the country would you expect private housing to be expensive and, by comparison, cheap? What is the cause of this? Have estates of multi-storey flats fulfilled their original purpose? If not, why not? What causes a slum? What is an almshouse? See also **Chapter 5**.

Reasons for rejection (non-academic) Lack of awareness of current social policy issues.

AFTER-RESULTS ADVICE

Offers to applicants repeating A-levels Same Cardiff Met, London South Bank.

GRADUATE DESTINATIONS AND EMPLOYMENT (2015/16 HESA)

See **Building and Construction**.

Career note Graduates aiming for openings in housing will be employed mainly as managers with local authorities; others will be employed by non-profit-making housing associations and trusts and also by property companies owning blocks of flats.

OTHER DEGREE SUBJECTS FOR CONSIDERATION

Architecture; Building; Business Studies; Community Studies; Environmental Planning; Estate Management; Property Development; Social Policy and Administration; Social Studies; Surveying; Town Planning; Urban Regeneration.

HUMAN RESOURCE MANAGEMENT

(see also Business and Management Courses, Business and Management Courses (International and European), Business and Management Courses (Specialised))

This is one of the many branches of the world of business and has developed from the role of the personnel manager. HR managers may be involved with the induction and training of staff, disciplinary and grievance procedures, redundancies and equal opportunities issues. In large organisations, some HR staff may specialise in one or more of these areas. Work experience dealing with the public should be stressed in the UCAS personal statement.

Useful websites www.hrmguide.co.uk; www.cipd.co.uk

NB The points totals shown to the left of the institutions are for ease of reference only. It must not be assumed that Tariff points are always used by institutions or that they can be substituted for an offer in grades. The level of an offer is not necessarily indicative of the quality of a course.

GRADUATE CAREER READY

The University of **Law**

BUSINESS SCHOOL

Develop the knowledge and skills employers are looking for. Choose our BA (Hons) Business Management (Human Resource Management) to start your career in HRM.

Study in Birmingham, Leeds, London and Manchester or online.

We bring the business world into the classroom. You'll get to meet potential future employers, participate in business games, and maximise your employability prospects.

CMI
HE Partner

For more Information
law.ac.uk/business

TEF Gold Teaching Excellence Framework
Awarded to The University of Law

COURSE OFFERS INFORMATION

Subject requirements/preferences GCSE English and mathematics at C (4) or above. **AL** No subjects specified.

Your target offers and examples of degree courses

136 pts **Aston** – AAB–ABB (HR Mgt) (IB 32 pts HL 665–655)
Cardiff – AAB (Bus Mgt (HR)) (IB 35–32 pts HL 665–655)
Lancaster – AAB (Mgt HR) (IB 35 pts HL 16 pts)
Leeds – AAB (HR Mgt) (IB 35 pts HL 17 pts)
Manchester – AAB (Mgt HR) (IB 35 pts HL 665)

128 pts **Bournemouth** – 128–136 pts (Bus St HR Mgt) (IB 32 pts HL 55)
Coventry – ABB–BBB (Bus HR Mgt) (IB 31–30 pts)
Heriot-Watt – ABB (3 yr course) BBB (4 yr course) (Int Bus Mgt HR Mgt) (IB 34 pts (3 yr course) 29 pts (4 yr course))
London (RH) – ABB (Mgt HR) (IB 32 pts HL 655)
Stirling – ABB (3 yr course) BBB (4 yr course) (HR Mgt) (IB 35 pts (3 yr course) 32 pts (4 yr course))
Swansea – ABB–BBB (Bus Mgt (HR Mgt)) (IB 33–32 pts)

120 pts **Bradford** – BBB 120 pts (HR Mgt)
Edinburgh Napier – BBB (3 yr course) BCC (4 yr course) (Bus St HR Mgt) (IB 28 pts HL 654)
Huddersfield – BBB 120 pts (Bus HR Mgt)
Northumbria – 120–128 pts (HR Mgt) (HL 444)
Ulster – BBB (HR Mgt) (IB 26 pts HL 13 pts)

112 pts **Birmingham City** – BBC 112 pts (HR Mgt)
Cardiff Met – 112 pts (Bus Mgt St HR Mgt)

Check **Chapter 3** for new university admission details and **Chapter 6** on how to read the subject tables.

Chichester – BBC–CCC (Evnt Mgt HR Mgt; HR Mgt Fin) (IB 28 pts)
De Montfort – 112 pts (HR Mgt) (IB 26 pts)
East London – 112 pts (HR Mgt) (IB 25 pts HL 15 pts)
Greenwich – 112 pts (HR Mgt)
Keele – BBC (HR Mgt Comb Hons) (IB 30 pts)
Leeds Beckett – 112 pts (HR Mgt Bus) (IB 25 pts)
Nottingham Trent – BBC 112 pts (Bus Mgt HR)
Portsmouth – 112 pts (HR Mgt Psy) (IB 30 pts HL 17 pts)
Robert Gordon – BBC (Mgt HR Mgt) (IB 29 pts)
Sheffield Hallam – 112 pts (Bus HR Mgt)
Sunderland – 112 pts (Bus HR Mgt)
West London – BBC 112 pts (Bus St HR Mgt; Hum Res Mgt)
Westminster – BBC (Bus Mgt HR Mgt) (IB 28 pts)
Wolverhampton – BBC–CCC (HR Mgt)

104 pts **Bath Spa** – BCC–CCC (Bus Mgt (HR Mgt)) (IB 26 pts)
Brighton – BCC–CCC 104–96 pts (Bus HR Mgt) (IB 28 pts HL 16 pts)
Liverpool John Moores – BCC 104 pts (HR Mgt) (IB 24 pts)
Northampton – BCC (HR Mgt courses)
South Wales – BCC–CDD 104–80 pts (HR Mgt) (HL 655–445)

96 pts **Anglia Ruskin** – 96–112 pts (Bus HR Mgt) (IB 24 pts)
Derby – 96–128 pts (HR Mgt Comb Hons)
Hertfordshire – 96–112 pts (HR Mgt; Bus HR)
Middlesex – 96 pts (HR Mgt; Bus Mgt (HR))
York St John – 96–112 pts (Bus Mgt HR Mgt)

88 pts **Canterbury Christ Church** – 88–112 pts (HR Mgt)
Trinity Saint David – 88 pts +interview (HR Mgt)

80 pts **Bedfordshire** – 80 pts (HR Mgt)
Bucks New – 80–96 pts (Bus HR Mgt)

32 pts **GSM London** – 32 pts (HR Mgt)

Alternative offers
See **Chapter 6** and **Appendix 1** for grades/UCAS Tariff points information for other examinations.

EXAMPLES OF COLLEGES OFFERING COURSES IN THIS SUBJECT FIELD

Barking and Dagenham (Coll); Basingstoke (CT); Bath (Coll); Birmingham Met (Coll); Bournemouth and Poole (Coll); Croydon (Univ Centre); GSM London; London City (Coll); Manchester (Coll); Newcastle (Coll); North Lindsey (Coll); Plymouth City (Coll); St Helens (Coll); South Gloucestershire and Stroud (Coll).

CHOOSING YOUR COURSE (SEE ALSO CH.1)

Universities and colleges teaching quality See www.qaa.ac.uk; https://unistats.ac.uk.

Examples of sandwich degree courses Aston; Bath Spa; Bedfordshire; Birmingham City; Bournemouth; Bradford; Brighton; Chichester; Coventry; De Montfort; Hertfordshire; Huddersfield; Leeds; Leeds Beckett; Liverpool John Moores; Manchester Met; Northampton; Northumbria; Portsmouth; Sheffield Hallam; Ulster; Westminster; Wolverhampton; Worcester.

ADMISSIONS INFORMATION

Number of applicants per place (approx) Anglia Ruskin 10; Aston 10.

Advice to applicants and planning the UCAS personal statement See **Business and Management Courses**.

Selection interviews No Anglia Ruskin, De Montfort.

Interview advice and questions See **Business and Management Courses**.

Reasons for rejection (non-academic) See **Business and Management Courses**.

AFTER-RESULTS ADVICE
Offers to applicants repeating A-levels **Higher** Anglia Ruskin.

GRADUATE DESTINATIONS AND EMPLOYMENT (2015/16 HESA)
Graduates surveyed 665 **Employed** 425 **In voluntary employment** 25 **In further study** 100
Assumed unemployed 30

Career note See under **Business and Management Courses**.

OTHER DEGREE SUBJECTS FOR CONSIDERATION
Business Studies; Information Systems; Management Studies/Sciences; Marketing; Psychology; Retail
Management; Sociology; Sports Management.

HUMAN SCIENCES/HUMAN BIOSCIENCES
(see also Medicine, Neuroscience)

Human Sciences is a multi-disciplinary study relating to biological and social sciences and focuses on
social and cultural behaviour. Topics range from genetics and evolution to health, disease, social
behaviour and industrial societies. A typical course may include anatomy, physiology, bio-mechanics,
anthropology and psychology.

Useful websites www.bbsrc.ac.uk; www.becominghuman.org; see also **Biology** and **Geography**.

*NB The points totals shown to the left of the institutions are for ease of reference only. It must not
be assumed that Tariff points are always used by institutions or that they can be substituted for an
offer in grades. The level of an offer is not necessarily indicative of the quality of a course.*

COURSE OFFERS INFORMATION
Subject requirements/preferences GCSE Science essential and mathematics usually required. **AL**
Chemistry/biology usually required or preferred for some courses.

Your target offers and examples of degree courses
144 pts   **Exeter** – AAA–ABB (Hum Sci (Cornwall)) (IB 36–32 pts)
        London (UCL) – AAA incl sci (Hum Sci) (IB 38 pts HL 6 sci)
        Oxford – AAA +interview +TSA (Hum Sci) (IB 38 pts HL 666)
        Sussex – AAA–AAB (Psy Cog Sci; Psy Neuro) (IB 34 pts)
        Swansea – AAB–ABB incl biol+STEM (App Med Sci)
136 pts   **Durham** – AAB (Hlth Hum Sci) (IB 36 pts)
128 pts   **Cardiff** – ABB (Hum Soc Sci) (IB 34–33 pts HL 17 pts)
        Sheffield – ABB–BBB (Hlth Hum Sci) (IB 33–32 pts)
120 pts   **Aberdeen** – BBB incl sci/maths (Hum Emb Dev Biol) (IB 32 pts HL 5 sci/maths)
        Plymouth – 120 pts incl biol+maths/sci (Hum Biosci) (IB 28 pts HL 5 biol/chem)
112 pts   **Coventry** – BBC incl biol (Hum Biosci) (IB 30 pts HL 5 biol)
104 pts   **Manchester Met** – BCC–BBC incl biol/app sci 104–112 pts (Hum Biol) (IB 26 pts HL 5 biol);
        BCC–BBC incl geog 104–112 pts (Hum Geog (St Abrd)) (IB 26 pts HL 5 geog/hum)
  88 pts   **West Scotland** – CCD incl chem (Foren Sci) (IB 27 pts incl chem); CCD incl biol+sci (Biomed
        Sci; App Biomed Sci) (IB 24 pts)

Alternative offers
See **Chapter 6** and **Appendix 1** for grades/UCAS Tariff points information for other examinations.

EXAMPLES OF COLLEGES OFFERING COURSES IN THIS SUBJECT FIELD
Blackpool and Fylde (Coll).

CHOOSING YOUR COURSE (SEE ALSO CH.1)
Universities and colleges teaching quality See www.qaa.ac.uk; https://unistats.ac.uk.

ADMISSIONS INFORMATION
Number of applicants per place (approx) London (UCL) 4; Oxford 8.

Advice to applicants and planning the UCAS personal statement See **Biology** and **Anthropology**.

Selection interviews Yes Oxford (11%); **No** London (UCL).

Interview advice and questions Past questions have included: What do you expect to get out of a degree in Human Sciences? Why are you interested in this subject? What problems do you think you will be able to tackle after completing the course? Why did you drop PE as an A-level given that it's relevant to Human Sciences? How do you explain altruism, given that we are surely programmed by our genes to be selfish? How far is human behaviour determined by genes? What do you think are the key differences between animals and human beings? See also **Chapter 5**. **Oxford** Are there too many people in the world?

GRADUATE DESTINATIONS AND EMPLOYMENT (2015/16 HESA)
See **Biology**.

Career note As a result of the multi-disciplinary nature of these courses, graduates could focus on openings linked to their special interests or look in general at the scientific and health sectors. Health administration, social services work and laboratory-based careers are some of the more common career destinations of graduates.

OTHER DEGREE SUBJECTS FOR CONSIDERATION
Anthropology; Biology; Community Studies; Environmental Sciences; Life Sciences; Psychology; Sociology.

INFORMATION MANAGEMENT and LIBRARIANSHIP

(including **Informatics**; see also **Computer Courses, Media Studies**)

Information Management and Library Studies covers the very wide field of information. Topics covered include retrieval, indexing, computer and media technology, classification and cataloguing.

Useful websites www.emeraldinsight.com/journal/ajim; www.cilip.org.uk; www.bl.uk

NB The points totals shown to the left of the institutions are for ease of reference only. It must not be assumed that Tariff points are always used by institutions or that they can be substituted for an offer in grades. The level of an offer is not necessarily indicative of the quality of a course.

COURSE OFFERS INFORMATION
Subject requirements/preferences GCSE English, mathematics and occasionally a foreign language. **AL** No specified subjects.

Your target offers and examples of degree courses
144 pts **Edinburgh** – AAA incl maths (Inform (MInf)) (IB 37 pts HL 6 maths)
 London (UCL) – AAA (Inf Mgt Bus) (IB 38 pts HL 18 pts)
 Reading – AAA–AAB (Mgt IT) (IB 35 pts)
136 pts **Lancaster** – AAB (Mgt IT) (IB 35 pts HL 16 pts)
 Loughborough – AAB (IT Mgt Bus) (IB 34 pts HL 655)
 Manchester – AAB (IT Mgt Bus; IT Mgt Bus (Yr Ind)) (IB 35 pts HL 665)
128 pts **Kent** – ABB (Comp) (IB 34 pts)
 Loughborough – ABB (Inf Mgt Bus) (IB 34 pts)

120 pts **Huddersfield** – BBB 120 pts (ICT)
Northumbria – 120–128 pts (IT Mgt Bus) (HL 444)
UWE Bristol – 120 pts (IT Mgt Bus)
112 pts **Chichester** – BBC–CCC (Bus St IT Mgt) (IB 28 pts)
Edge Hill – BBC 112 pts (IT Mgt Bus)
Oxford Brookes – BBC (IT Mgt Bus) (IB 30 pts)
Southampton Solent – 112 pts (Bus IT)
104 pts **Bournemouth** – 104–120 pts (IT Mgt) (IB 28–30 pts HL 55)

Alternative offers
See **Chapter 6** and **Appendix 1** for grades/UCAS Tariff points information for other examinations.

EXAMPLES OF COLLEGES OFFERING COURSES IN THIS SUBJECT FIELD
Most colleges offer ICT courses. Birmingham Met (Coll); Grŵp Llandrillo Menai; Totton (Coll).

CHOOSING YOUR COURSE (SEE ALSO CH.1)
Universities and colleges teaching quality See www.qaa.ac.uk; https://unistats.ac.uk.

Top research universities and colleges (REF 2014) (Communication, Cultural and Media Studies, Library and Information Management) London LSE; Leicester (Musm St); Wolverhampton; Cardiff; London (Gold); Loughborough (Comm Media St); Westminster; De Montfort; Nottingham; London (RH); East Anglia; Leeds; Leicester (Media Comm); Newcastle.

Examples of sandwich degree courses Bournemouth; Huddersfield; Kent; Lancaster; Loughborough; Manchester; Reading; UWE Bristol.

ADMISSIONS INFORMATION
Number of applicants per place (approx) London (UCL) 8; Southampton 5.

Advice to applicants and planning the UCAS personal statement Work experience or work shadowing in local libraries is important but remember that reference libraries provide a different field of work. Visit university libraries and major reference libraries and discuss the work with librarians. Describe your experiences in the personal statement. See also **Appendix 3**.

Misconceptions about this course Read the prospectus carefully. The course details can be confusing. Some courses have a bias towards the organisation and retrieval of information, others towards information systems technology.

Selection interviews Yes London (UCL); **Some** Loughborough; **No** Southampton.

Interview advice and questions Past questions include: What is it about librarianship that interests you? Why do you think you are suited to be a librarian? What does the job entail? What is the role of the library in school? What is the role of the public library? What new developments are taking place in libraries? Which books do you read? How often do you use a library? What is the Dewey number for the history section in the library? (Applicant studying A-level history.) See also **Chapter 5**.

AFTER-RESULTS ADVICE
Offers to applicants repeating A-levels Higher Loughborough.

GRADUATE DESTINATIONS AND EMPLOYMENT (2015/16 HESA)
Career note Graduates in this subject area and in communications enter a wide range of public and private sector jobs where the need to process information as well as to make it easily accessible and user-friendly is very high. Areas of work could include web content, design and internet management and library management.

OTHER DEGREE SUBJECTS FOR CONSIDERATION
Business Information Systems; Communication Studies; Computer Science; Geographic Information Systems; Media Studies.

INTERNATIONAL RELATIONS

(including **International Development, Peace Studies and International Relations** and **War Studies**; see also **Development Studies, European Studies, Politics**)

A strong interest in international affairs is a prerequisite for these courses which often allow students to focus on a specific area such as African, Asian or West European politics.

Useful websites www.sipri.org; www.un.org; www.un.int; rightweb.irc-online.org; see also **Politics**.

NB The points totals shown to the left of the institutions are for ease of reference only. It must not be assumed that Tariff points are always used by institutions or that they can be substituted for an offer in grades. The level of an offer is not necessarily indicative of the quality of a course.

COURSE OFFERS INFORMATION

Subject requirements/preferences GCSE English; a foreign language usually required. **AL** No specified subjects. (War St) History may be required.

Your target offers and examples of degree courses

152 pts **Cambridge** – A*AA +interview +HSPSAA (Hum Soc Pol Sci (Pol Int Rel)) (IB 40–42 pts HL 776)
Edinburgh – A*AA (Int Rel) (IB 43 pts); A*AA incl Engl (Law Int Rel) (IB 43 pts HL 776)
Warwick – A*AA (Econ Pol Int St) (IB 38 pts)

144 pts **Bath** – AAA–AAB+aEPQ (Pol Int Rel) (IB 36 pts HL 666)
Bristol – AAA–ABB (Pol Int Rel) (IB 36–32 pts HL 18–16 pts)
Durham – AAA incl soc sci/hum (Int Rel) (37 pts)
Exeter – AAA–AAB (Hist Int Rel (St Abrd); Hist Int Rel) (IB 36–34 pts); AAA–ABB incl lang (Int Rel Modn Langs) (IB 36–32 pts HL 5 lang)
Lancaster – AAA–AAB (Hist Int Rel) (IB 36–35 pts HL 16 pts)
London (King's) – AAA incl hist (War St Hist) (IB 35 pts HL 666 incl hist); AAA (War St Phil; War St) (IB 35 pts HL 666)
London LSE – AAA (Int Rel Hist; Int Rel) (IB 38 pts HL 766)
Nottingham – AAA (Int Rel Glob Is MSci) (IB 36 pts)
St Andrews – AAA (Geog Int Rel; Int Rel courses) (IB 38 pts)
Sussex – AAA–AAB (Law Int Rel) (IB 34 pts)

136 pts **Cardiff** – AAB incl lang (Int Rel Pol (Lang)) (IB 34 pts HL 665)
Exeter – AAB–BBB (Pol Int Rel (Cornwall)) (IB 34–30 pts)
Lancaster – AAB–ABB (Pce St Int Rel; Pol Int Rel) (IB 35–32 pts HL 16 pts)
Leeds – AAB (Int Rel) (IB 35 pts HL 655)
London (RH) – AAB–ABB (Pol Int Rel; Econ Pol Int Rel) (IB 32 pts HL 655)
Manchester – AAB (Pol Int Rel) (IB 35 pts HL 665)
Reading – AAB–ABB (Int Dev) (IB 34–32 pts); AAB–BBB (Int Rel courses) (IB 32–30 pts)
Sheffield – AAB–ABB+bEPQ (Int Rel Pol) (IB 34 pts); AAB–ABB+bEPQ incl hist/class civ (Hist Pol) (IB 34 pts HL 6 hist)
Sussex – AAB–ABB (Econ Int Rel) (IB 32 pts); AAB (Int Rel; Int Rel Dev) (IB 34 pts)
York – AAB (Pol Int Rel) (IB 35 pts)

128 pts **Aston** – ABB (Pol Int Rel) (IB 32 pts); ABB–BBB (Bus Int Rel; Int Rel Engl Lang) (IB 32 pts)
Birmingham – ABB (Int Rel; Int Rel Comb Hons; Pol Sci Int Rel) (IB 32 pts HL 655)
East Anglia – ABB (Int Rel; Int Rel Comb Hons) (IB 32 pts)
Heriot-Watt – ABB (3 yr course) ABC/BBB (4 yr course) incl maths (Civ Eng Int St) (IB 35 pts (3 yr course) 31 pts (4 yr course) HL 6 maths (3 yr course) 5 maths (4 yr course))
Leeds – ABB (Int Rel Thai St) (IB 34 pts HL 16 pts)
London (QM) – ABB (Int Rel) (IB 32 pts HL 655)
Loughborough – ABB (Int Rel; Hist Int Rel) (IB 34 pts HL 655)
Queen's Belfast – ABB (Int Pol Cnflct St)

UCAS points Tariff: A* = 56 pts; A = 48 pts; B = 40 pts; C = 32 pts; D = 24 pts; E = 16 pts

       Reading – ABB–BBB (Pol Int Rel; War Pce Int Rel) (IB 32–30 pts)
       Southampton – ABB–BBB+aEPQ (Pol Int Rel; Int Rel) (IB 32 pts HL 16 pts)
       Stirling – ABB (3 yr course) BBB (4 yr course) incl pol/modn st (Pol (Int Pol)) (IB 35 pts
          (3 yr course) 32 pts (4 yr course))
       Surrey – ABB (Law Int St) (IB 32 pts)
120 pts **Aberdeen** – BBB (Int Rel courses) (IB 32 pts HL 555)
       Aberystwyth – BBB (Int Pol; Int Pol Strat St) (IB 28 pts)
       Bradford – BBB 120 pts (App Pce Cnflct St; Int Rel)
       Brunel – BBB (Int Pol; Mltry Int Hist) (IB 30 pts)
       Dundee – BBB (Int Rel Pol) (IB 30 pts HL 555)
       Essex – BBB (Pol Hum Rts; Int Rel; Sociol Hum Rts) (IB 30 pts)
       Keele – BBB/ABC (Int Rel) (IB 32 pts)
       Kent – BBB (War Cnflct) (IB 34 pts)
       Leicester – BBB–BBC+bEPQ (Int Rel Hist; Int Rel) (IB 28 pts)
       Liverpool Hope – BBB–BBC 120 pts (Int Rel) (IB 26 pts)
       London (Birk) – 120–128 pts (Glob Pol Int Rel)
       London (Gold) – BBB (Int Rel) (IB 33 pts)
       Nottingham Trent – BBB 120 pts (Int Law)
       Swansea – BBB 120 pts (Int Rel; Int Rel Am St; War Soty) (IB 32 pts)
112 pts **Bradford** – BBC 112 pts (Glob Pol Dev)
       Coventry – BBC (Fr Int Rel; Int Rel) (IB 29 pts)
       De Montfort – 112 pts (Int Rel) (IB 26 pts)
       Greenwich – 112 pts (Pol Int Rel; Langs Int Rel)
       Hull – BBC 112 pts (Pol Int Rel) (IB 28 pts)
       London Met – CCC/BC 112 pts (Int Rel Pce Cnflct St); BBC 112 pts (Law (Int Rel)); BBC/BC
          112 pts (Int Rel)
       Middlesex – 112 pts (Int Pol)
       Oxford Brookes – BBC 112 pts (Int Rel) (IB 31 pts)
       Portsmouth – 112 pts (Law Int Rel) (IB 30 pts HL 17 pts)
       Westminster – BBC (Int Rel) (IB 28 pts)
       Wolverhampton – BBC–CCC (War St; War St Phil)
104 pts **Brighton** – BCC–CCC 104–96 pts +interview (Hum War Cnflct Modnty) (IB 27 pts)
       Buckingham – BCC (Int St) (IB 30 pts)
       Chester – BCC–BBC (Int Dev St courses) (IB 26 pts)
       De Montfort – 104 pts (Int Rel Pol) (IB 24 pts)
       Leeds Beckett – 104 pts (Int Rel Glob Dev; Int Rel Pce St) (IB 24 pts)
       Lincoln – BCC 104 pts (Int Rel) (IB 28 pts)
       Manchester Met – 104–112 pts (Int Pol Langs (Fr/Ger/Ital/Span); Int Pol Phil) (IB 26 pts)
       Nottingham Trent – 104 pts (Glob St Comb Hons; Int Rel Comb Hons); BCC 104 pts
          (Pol Int Rel)
       Plymouth – 104 pts (Int Bus Econ) (IB 24 pts HL 4); (Int Rel Law; Int Rel; Pol Int Rel)
          (IB 26 pts HL 4)
96 pts **Canterbury Christ Church** – 96–112 pts (Int Rel)
       Derby – 96–128 pts (Int Rel Dipl Comb Hons); 96–128 pts geog/sci/soc sci (Glob Dev Comb
          Hons)
       Portsmouth – 96–120 pts (Int Rel) (IB 30 pts HL 17 pts)

       Open University – contact 0300 303 0073 **or** www.open.ac.uk/contact/new (Int St)

Alternative offers
See **Chapter 6** and **Appendix 1** for grades/UCAS Tariff points information for other examinations.

CHOOSING YOUR COURSE (SEE ALSO CH.1)
Universities and colleges teaching quality See www.qaa.ac.uk; https://unistats.ac.uk.

Top research universities and colleges (REF 2014) See **Politics**.

Examples of sandwich degree courses Aston; Bath; Brunel; Coventry; Nottingham Trent; Oxford Brookes; Portsmouth; Westminster.

ADMISSIONS INFORMATION

Number of applicants per place (approx) Bath 7; Birmingham 10; De Montfort 6; Derby 3; Exeter 8; Leeds 13; London (King's) 6; London (RH) 8; London LSE 14; Nottingham 5; Reading 5; Southampton (Int Rel) 6.

Advice to applicants and planning the UCAS personal statement Describe any special interests you have in the affairs of any particular country. Contact embassies for information on cultural, economic and political developments. Follow international events through newspapers and magazines. Give details of any voluntary work you have done. **London (King's)** Substantial experience required in some area of direct relevance to War Studies.

Misconceptions about this course Some students think that this degree will give direct entry into the Diplomatic Service. **Bradford** The teaching and research in Peace Studies aims to be applied to real-life problems such as the control of Weapons of Mass Destruction, sexual violence in conflict and the influence of environmental threats.

Selection interviews Some Nottingham Trent, Wolverhampton; **No** Birmingham, De Montfort, East Anglia, London (King's), London Met, Nottingham.

Interview advice and questions Applicants are likely to be questioned on current international events and crises between countries. See also **Chapter 5**. **Nottingham Trent** Be prepared to be challenged on your existing views!

AFTER-RESULTS ADVICE

Offers to applicants repeating A-levels Same Chester, De Montfort, Lincoln, Wolverhampton.

GRADUATE DESTINATIONS AND EMPLOYMENT (2015/16 HESA)

See **Politics**.

Career note See **Politics**.

OTHER DEGREE SUBJECTS FOR CONSIDERATION

Development Studies; Economics; European Studies; Government; Politics.

ITALIAN

(see also Languages)

The language and literature of Italy will feature strongly on most Italian courses. The majority of applicants have no knowledge of Italian. They will need to give convincing reasons for their interest and to show that they have the ability to assimilate language quickly. See also **Appendix 3** under **Languages**.

Useful websites http://europa.eu; www.governo.it; www.bbc.co.uk/languages; www.languageadvantage.com; http://italianstudies.org.uk; www.languagematters.co.uk; see also **Languages**.

NB The points totals shown to the left of the institutions are for ease of reference only. It must not be assumed that Tariff points are always used by institutions or that they can be substituted for an offer in grades. The level of an offer is not necessarily indicative of the quality of a course.

COURSE OFFERS INFORMATION

Subject requirements/preferences GCSE English and a foreign language required. **AL** Italian may be required for some courses.

Your target offers and examples of degree courses

152 pts **Cambridge** – A*AA incl lang +interview +MMLAA (Modn Mediev Langs) (IB 40–42 pts HL 776)

144 pts **Durham** – AAA incl lang (Modn Langs Cult (Yr Abrd)) (IB 37 pts)

Edinburgh – AAA (Ital Ling; Ital) (IB 39 pts HL 666)

Oxford – AAA +interview +MLAT (Ital courses) (IB 38 pts HL 666)

136 pts **Exeter** – AAB–ABB incl Ital/Arbc (Ital Arbc) (IB 34–32 pts HL 5 Ital/Arbc)

Glasgow – AAB–BBB incl arts/hum/lang (Ital Comb Hons) (IB 36–34 pts HL 665 incl 6 Engl/hum/lang)

Leeds – AAB–ABB (Ital Comb Hons) (IB 35–34 pts HL 16 pts)

London (UCL) – AAB (Ital) (IB 36 pts HL 17 pts)

St Andrews – AAB (Ital courses) (IB 36 pts)

Swansea – AAB–BBB (Ital courses) (IB 33–32 pts)

Warwick – AAB incl Fr (Fr Ger St) (IB 36 pts HL 5 Fr); AAB incl Engl lit+lang (Engl Ital Lit) (IB 36 pts HL 5 Engl lit+lang); AAB incl Ger (Ger Ital) (IB 36 pts HL 5 Ger/Ital); AAB incl lang (Ital Comb Hons) (IB 36 pts HL 5 lang)

York – AAB–ABB incl Fr (Fr Ital Lang (Yr Abrd)) (IB 35–34 pts)

128 pts **Bangor** – 128–112 pts (Law Ital (Euro Expnc))

Bath – ABB–ABC+aEPQ incl lang (Modn Langs Euro St) (IB 35 pts HL 6 lang)

Bristol – ABB–BBC incl lang (Ital) (IB 32–29 pts HL 5 lang)

Cardiff – ABB–BBC incl lang (Ital) (IB 32–30 pts)

Leeds – ABB (Ital) (IB 34 pts)

Leicester – ABB–BBB+aEPQ (Ital Comb Hons) (IB 30 pts)

London (RH) – ABB–BBB incl lang (Modn Lang Dr) (IB 32 pts); ABB–BBB (Euro Int St Fr/Ger/Ital/Span; Modn Lang; Modn Lang Mus) (IB 32 pts HL 555); ABB (Modn Lang Mgt) (IB 32 pts HL 655)

Manchester – ABB +interview (Ital courses; Ital St) (IB 33 pts HL 655)

Sussex – ABB–BBB incl Ital/Span (Ital Span (Yr Abrd)) (IB 30 pts HL 5 Ital/Span)

Warwick – ABB incl lang (Ital courses) (IB 34 pts HL 5 lang)

120 pts **Kent** – BBB (Ital courses) (IB 34 pts)

Reading – BBB/ABC (Ital) (IB 30 pts)

112 pts **Hull** – 112 pts incl lang (Ital Comb Hons; Hist Modn Lang) (IB 28 pts)

104 pts **Bangor** – 104–96 pts (Bus St Ital; Hist Ital; Acc Ital)

Manchester Met – 104–112 pts (Ling Mand Chin/Fr/Ger/Ital/Span) (IB 26 pts)

Nottingham Trent – 104 pts (Ital Comb Hons)

96 pts **Portsmouth** – 96–120 pts (Modn Lang)

Alternative offers
See **Chapter 6** and **Appendix 1** for grades/UCAS Tariff points information for other examinations

CHOOSING YOUR COURSE (SEE ALSO CH.1)

Universities and colleges teaching quality See www.qaa.ac.uk; https://unistats.ac.uk.

Top research universities and colleges (REF 2014) See **Languages**.

ADMISSIONS INFORMATION

Number of applicants per place (approx) Birmingham 5; Bristol 4; Cardiff 3; Durham 5; Hull 5; Leeds 3; London (RH) 7; London (UCL) 5.

Advice to applicants and planning the UCAS personal statement Describe any visits to Italy and experience of speaking the language. Interests in Italian art, literature, culture, society and architecture could also be mentioned. Read Italian newspapers and magazines and give details if you have a bilingual background. Give evidence of your interest and your reasons for choosing the course. See also **Appendix 3** under **Languages**.

Misconceptions about this course Leeds See **Languages**.

Selection interviews Yes Cambridge, Oxford; **No** Birmingham, Reading.

Interview advice and questions Past questions include: Why do you want to learn Italian? What foreign newspapers or magazines do you read (particularly if the applicant has taken A-level Italian)? Have you visited Italy? What do you know of the Italian people, culture, art? See also **Chapter 5**. **Leeds** See **Languages**.

AFTER-RESULTS ADVICE
Offers to applicants repeating A-levels Higher Birmingham, Warwick; **Same** Cardiff, Hull, Leeds; **No** Glasgow.

GRADUATE DESTINATIONS AND EMPLOYMENT (2015/16 HESA)
Graduates surveyed 195 **Employed** 90 **In voluntary employment** 20 **In further study** 55 **Assumed unemployed** 10

Career note See **Languages**.

OTHER DEGREE SUBJECTS FOR CONSIDERATION
European Studies; International Business Studies; other languages.

JAPANESE
(see also **Asia-Pacific Studies, Languages**)

A strong interest in Japan and its culture is expected of applicants. A number of four-year joint courses are now offered, all of which include a period of study in Japan. Potential employers are showing an interest in Japanese. Students report that 'it is not a soft option'. They are expected to be firmly committed to a Japanese degree (for example, by listing only Japanese on the UCAS application), to have an interest in using their degree in employment and to be prepared for a lot of hard work. See **Appendix 3** under **Languages**.

Useful websites www.ciol.org.uk; www.bbc.co.uk/languages; www.languageadvantage.com; www.languagematters.co.uk; www.japanese-online.com; www.gojapango.com; www.thejapanesepage.com; www.japanesestudies.org.uk

NB The points totals shown to the left of the institutions are for ease of reference only. It must not be assumed that Tariff points are always used by institutions or that they can be substituted for an offer in grades. The level of an offer is not necessarily indicative of the quality of a course.

COURSE OFFERS INFORMATION
Subject requirements/preferences GCSE A foreign language usually required. **AL** Modern language required for some courses.

Your target offers and examples of degree courses
152 pts Cambridge – A*AA +interview +AMESAA (As Mid E St) (IB 40–42 pts HL 776)
144 pts Leeds – AAA–ABB (Jap courses) (IB 35–34 pts HL 16 pts)
      Oxford – AAA +interview +OLAT (Orntl St) (IB 39 pts HL 666); AAA +interview +CAT (Class Orntl St) (IB 39 pts HL 666)
136 pts Birmingham – AAB incl lang (Modn Langs) (IB 32 pts HL 665)
      Cardiff – AAB–ABB (Bus St Jap) (IB 35–32 pts)
      Edinburgh – AAB (Jap Ling; Jap) (IB 36 pts HL 665)
128 pts Manchester – ABB +interview (Jap St) (IB 33 pts HL 655); ABB incl Russ/Jap +interview (Russ Jap) (IB 33 pts HL 655); ABB incl Chin/Jap (Chin Jap) (IB 33 pts HL 655)
      Newcastle – ABB–BBB (Jap St) (IB 32 pts)
      Sheffield – ABB–BBB+bEPQ (Jap St; Kor St Jap; Jap St Comb Hons) (IB 33 pts)

112 pts Central Lancashire – 112 pts (Mod Lang Int Bus); 112 pts incl lang (Modn Langs (Fr/Ger/Span/Jap))

104 pts London (Birk) – 104 pts incl lang (Modn Langs (Fr/Ger/Ital/Jap/Port/Span))

Alternative offers
See **Chapter 6** and **Appendix 1** for grades/UCAS Tariff points information for other examinations.

CHOOSING YOUR COURSE (SEE ALSO CH.1)
Universities and colleges teaching quality See www.qaa.ac.uk; https://unistats.ac.uk.

ADMISSIONS INFORMATION
Number of applicants per place (approx) Cardiff 8; Sheffield 6.

Advice to applicants and planning the UCAS personal statement Discuss your interest in Japan and your reasons for wishing to study the language. Know Japan, its culture and background history. Discuss any visits you have made or contacts with Japanese nationals. See also **Appendix 3** under **Languages**. **Leeds** See **Languages**.

Selection interviews Yes Cambridge, Oxford; **No** Leeds.

Interview advice and questions Japanese is an extremely demanding subject and applicants are most likely to be questioned on their reasons for choosing this degree. They will be expected also to have some knowledge of Japanese culture, history and current affairs. See also **Chapter 5**.

Reasons for rejection (non-academic) Insufficient evidence of genuine motivation.

AFTER-RESULTS ADVICE
Offers to applicants repeating A-levels No Cambridge.

GRADUATE DESTINATIONS AND EMPLOYMENT (2015/16 HESA)
Graduates surveyed 120 **Employed** 50 **In voluntary employment** 0 **In further study** 30 **Assumed unemployed** 15

Career note See **Languages**.

OTHER DEGREE SUBJECTS FOR CONSIDERATION
Asia-Pacific Studies; International Business Studies; Oriental Languages; South East Asia Studies.

JOURNALISM
(see also Communication Studies/Communication, English, Media Studies)

A passion for writing, good spelling, grammar and punctuation and the ability to work under pressure are some of the qualities which all journalists require. The opportunities within journalism range from covering day-to-day news stories in the local and national press to periodicals and magazines covering specialist subjects. Journalism is also the foundation for work in local radio.

Useful websites www.journalism.co.uk; www.bjtc.org.uk; www.nctj.com; www.nuj.org.uk

The points totals shown to the left of the institutions are for ease of reference only. It must not be assumed that Tariff points are always used by institutions or that they can be substituted for an offer in grades. The level of an offer is not necessarily indicative of the quality of a course.

COURSE OFFERS INFORMATION
Subject requirements/preferences GCSE English and maths often required. **AL** No specific subjects required.

Your target offers and examples of degree courses

136 pts **City** – AAB 136 pts +interview (Jrnl) (IB 33 pts)

Leeds – AAB (Jrnl) (IB 35 pts)

Newcastle – AAB (Jrnl Media Cult) (IB 34 pts)

128 pts **Cardiff** – ABB incl Engl (Jrnl Media Engl Lit) (HL 6 Engl); ABB (Jrnl Media Sociol) (HL 17 pts)

Kent – ABB +interview (Jrnl) (IB 34 pts)

Sheffield – ABB (Jrnl St) (IB 33 pts)

Strathclyde – ABB (Jrnl Crea Writ courses) (IB 36 pts)

Sussex – ABB +Skype interview (Jrnl) (IB 32 pts)

120 pts **Bangor** – 120–104 pts (Jrnl Media St)

Gloucestershire – BBB 120 pts +interview (Jrnl)

London (Gold) – BBB (Jrnl) (IB 33 pts)

Northumbria – 120–128 pts incl Engl (Jrnl Engl Lit) (HL 444)

Stirling – BBB (Jrnl St) (IB 32 pts)

Trinity Saint David – 120 pts +interview (Photojrnl Doc Photo)

UWE Bristol – 120 pts (Jrnl; Jrnl PR)

Westminster – BBB (Jrnl) (IB 28 pts)

112 pts **Birmingham City** – BBC 112 pts +interview +portfolio (Jrnl) (HL 14 pts)

Bournemouth – 112–128 pts (Multim Jrnl) (IB 30–32 pts HL 55)

Brighton – BBC–CCC 112–96 pts (Multim Broad Jrnl; Spo Jrnl) (IB 28 pts)

Brunel – BBC incl Engl/hist/soc sci +interview (Jrnl Cult) (IB 29 pts HL 5 Engl/hist/soc sci)

Buckingham – BBC–BCC (Jrnl Comm St) (IB 31–30 pts)

Chester – BBC–BCC 112 pts (Spo Jrnl) (IB 26 pts)

Coventry – BBC (Jrnl) (IB 29 pts); (Engl Jrnl) (IB 31 pts)

Creative Arts – 112 pts +portfolio (Fash Jrnl; Jrnl Media Prod); 112 pts +interview (Mus Jrnl)

East London – 112 pts (Jrnl; Spo Jrnl) (IB 25 pts HL 15 pts)

Edinburgh Napier – BBC (3 yr course) BCC (4 yr course) (Jrnl) (IB 28 pts HL 5 Engl)

Gloucestershire – BBC 112 pts +interview +portfolio (Photojrnl Doc Photo)

Glyndŵr – 112 pts (Broad Jrnl Media Comms)

Hertfordshire – 112 pts (Jrnl Comb Hons) (HL 44)

Huddersfield – BBC 112 pts (Spo Jrnl; Jrnl)

Leeds Beckett – 112 pts (Jrnl) (IB 25 pts)

Leeds Trinity – 112 pts (Jrnl; Spo Jrnl; Broad Jrnl)

Lincoln – BBC +interview (Jrnl) (IB 29 pts)

Liverpool John Moores – BBC 112 pts (Spo Jrnl) (IB 27 pts); BBC 112 pts +interview (Jrnl) (IB 26 pts)

London Met – BBC 112 pts (Jrnl Film TV St; Fash Mark Jrnl); BBC 112 pts +interview (Jrnl)

Middlesex – 112 pts (Crea Writ Jrnl; Jrnl Comm)

Nottingham Trent – BBC 112 pts (Jrnl; Broad Jrnl)

Portsmouth – 112 pts +interview (Broad Jrnl) (IB 26 pts)

Robert Gordon – BBC incl Engl (Jrnl) (IB 29 pts HL 5 Engl)

Roehampton – 112 pts incl hum (Jrnl)

Sheffield Hallam – 112–96 pts (Jrnl)

Southampton Solent – 112 pts +interview (Jrnl; Spo Jrnl)

Staffordshire – BBC 112 pts +interview (Jrnl)

Sunderland – 112–120 pts (Fash Jrnl; Spo Jrnl; Jrnl)

UWE Bristol – 112 pts (Engl Lit Writ)

West London – BBC 112 pts (Broad Dig Jrnl)

104 pts **Central Lancashire** – 104 pts +interview (Spo Jrnl; Jrnl)

Chester – BCC–BBC (Jrnl) (IB 26 pts)

De Montfort – 104 pts +interview (Jrnl) (IB 24 pts)

Falmouth – 104–120 pts +interview (Jrnl; Spo Jrnl)

Glasgow Caledonian – BCC +interview (Multim Jrnl) (IB 25 pts)

Leeds Trinity – 104 pts (Jrnl Pol)

London South Bank – BCC (Jrnl)

Northampton – BCC incl Engl/hum (Multim Jrnl)
South Wales – BCC–CDD +interview (Jrnl) (HL 655–445)
Winchester – 104–120 pts +interview (Jrnl) (IB 26 pts HL 5); 104–120 pts (Media Comm Jrnl) (IB 26 pts)
Worcester – 104 pts (Jrnl)
96 pts **Derby** – 96–112 pts (Spec Spo Jrnl; Mag Jrnl); 96–112 pts +interview (Jrnl)
Leeds Beckett – 96 pts (PR Jrnl) (IB 25 pts)
Portsmouth – 96–120 pts +interview (Jrnl) (IB 26 pts HL 17 pts)
St Mark and St John – CCC (Spo Jrnl; Jrnl)
Teesside – 96–112 pts +interview (Jrnl); 96–112 pts +interview +portfolio (Broad Media Prod)
West Scotland – CCC incl Engl (Jrnl) (IB 24 pts)
Wolverhampton – CCC +interview (Multim Jrnl)
88 pts **Canterbury Christ Church** – 88–112 pts (Multim Jrnl)
80 pts **Arts London** – 80 pts (Jrnl)
Bedfordshire – 80 pts (Jrnl)
72 pts **Anglia Ruskin** – 72–96 pts +portfolio (Jrnl (Multim))

Alternative offers
See **Chapter 6** and **Appendix 1** for grades/UCAS Tariff points information for other examinations.

EXAMPLES OF COLLEGES OFFERING COURSES IN THIS SUBJECT FIELD
Cornwall (Coll); Darlington (Coll); Exeter (Coll); Harlow (Coll); Peterborough (Coll); South Essex (Coll).

CHOOSING YOUR COURSE (SEE ALSO CH.1)
Universities and colleges teaching quality See www.qaa.ac.uk; https://unistats.ac.uk.

Examples of sandwich degree courses City; Coventry; Hertfordshire; Huddersfield; Leeds; Portsmouth; Southampton Solent.

ADMISSIONS INFORMATION
Number of applicants per place (approx) Strathclyde (Jrnl) 20.

Admissions tutors' advice Buckingham As far as journalism and media are concerned you can't be just a wannabe any more. Keeping a blog (on any theme) is great; so is producing video for YouTube. Writing for school magazine or newspaper is also well regarded. Active knowledge of current affairs and a wide frame of reference is to be commended. Having an interest in people is absolutely key.

Advice to applicants and planning the UCAS personal statement Buckingham Do not begin your personal statement with 'I've always been fascinated by media...' This is now a cliché and suggests slack-jawed drooling on a sofa rather than engaging actively.

Include the URLs of your blogs, YouTube channels, Tableau projects, Instagram albums or anything that will show me that you engage with media as a producer rather than a consumer. Make me really want to watch, see or read it. I will have a look at your content for sure. It will give you a firm base for discussion when I call you for interview.

Tell me whether your content lived up to your expectations. Trying, failing and learning a lesson are signs of character.

Tell me about what you've done outside the classroom – that will reveal to me what kind of person you are and create an opportunity for meaningful conversation at interview.

Tell me the kind of news media you love: whose byline thrills you, whose journalism takes you there, who you love to read in order to disagree with.

Show me a wide range of reference – sometimes as journalists we have to become instant experts.

City In your personal statement you should demonstrate a clear passion and enthusiasm for Journalism. This can be shown in a variety of ways, particularly demonstrated by the extra-curricular activities you do. Try and have an online presence through writing or blogging about a topic that interests you, or writing for your school's student paper or magazine. Immerse yourself in different types of media by reading newspapers, listening to news reports on TV and radio, and understanding how news is portrayed through different forms of social media. Try and get some relevant work experience with a radio station, TV company or local news provider, or make your own work experience by running your own website or blog. We are also interested in hearing about your influences, such as journalists and foreign correspondents who inspire you; let us know why their work interests you. It is also important to view and read news critically, as this will be something you will do whilst studying at university.

From a Journalism applicant we are looking for the following qualities:

1 be curious and interested in news;

2 be determined – don't take no for an answer;

3 good communication skills;

4 be keen to find out more;

5 enjoy writing and develop a style.

Also, do not be afraid to aim high with your university choices; you might be surprised where you receive offers from. Some universities, such as City, will invite you to a Selection Day as part of the application process, so you will have another opportunity to show why you are suitable for the degree, and have a chance to see the University and find out more details about the course.

Hertfordshire Many of the tutors who teach Journalism have also been journalists and they will expect students to listen to/watch the news or read articles. So when you write your personal statement, do make sure you refer to news stories or documentaries you have read. A vague statement such as 'I enjoy reading news tweets' tells the reader nothing. A much better example would be: 'Since my grandmother became ill I have been following stories about the NHS with great interest, particularly ones about bed-blocking. A news item on my local radio station about a woman who had been waiting to leave hospital for a month was really interesting because...'

If your passion is fashion journalism, then, again, give examples of articles you have read and why they have interested you or what you like about particular fashion magazines or fashion bloggers. Be specific and make sure you watch/read/listen to the news regularly as well.

Tutors won't expect professional experience but if you have a blog, make videos about things that interest you, or if you have written for the school or community website or magazine, then tell them about it. If you have researched a particular project, write about that research. This is because writing and research are important journalistic skills. Similarly, if you've watched a TV programme being made or spent a day shadowing a local journalist, mention this. Journalism tutors hope to teach the journalists of the future and showing that you have already taken the time to learn about some aspects of journalism shows the sort of enthusiasm they like to see.

Robert Gordon In regard to their personal statements we would be looking for applicants to display their passion for Journalism and the media in general – what sparked their interest in the field? What understanding do they have of the role of a journalist? Why would they like to work in this industry?

Any work or shadowing experience they may have is certainly a plus, though this is not mandatory.

Winchester We are typically looking for applicants to demonstrate a keen interest in becoming a journalist in their personal statement, ideally by talking about any relevant work experience that they may have had or whether they write on a daily basis, for example in a blog. We see a lot of applicants who have their own blogs which provide a very helpful starting point for discussions at interview.

Selection interviews Yes Brunel, Canterbury Christ Church, Edinburgh Napier, Kent, Leeds Trinity, Worcester; most institutions will interview candidates, some requiring auditions and/or a portfolio. **Some** Sussex, Winchester; **No** Bedfordshire, Falmouth, London South Bank, Northumbria.

Interview advice and questions Buckingham I will ask you to tell me a funny story because:

1 it shows me you can tell a story – what we do every day of our journalistic lives;

2 it shows me you keep a narrative thread;

3 it breaks the ice;

4 I like a chuckle/laughter can be a potent journalistic weapon.

I will ask you about all the practical efforts you describe in your personal statement. I will ask you in detail about the content of the A-levels/BTECs you are taking. I will ask you what makes you angry in life. Good journalists always carry a little fire in their bellies.

Hertfordshire Questions you might meet at interview include the following.

1 Tell me about some news stories or documentaries you've read/listened to/watched in the past week. Which have interested you and why?

2 What do you think a journalist does?

3 What skills do you think you will learn?

4 Here is an article. How do you think the writer might have found out these facts?

Winchester During interviews we are looking for students to be fully aware of current events and understand the power of the media for social change. Some applicants may talk about who or what (for example, a particular news story) inspired them to consider journalism as a profession and this is also helpful.

During the course of the interview applicants are also expected to perform a short piece in front of a camera, in addition to the more formal question and answer section.

Finally, interviews are as much about the applicants selecting the right university as the University selecting the right applicants, so there are always opportunities to ask the programme team questions about the course and life at the University.

Reasons for rejection (non-academic) Buckingham Applicants are requested to attend an Open Day/Evening or Tutorial Taster Days. The University believes it is very important for applicants to visit its campus. Candidates who do not respond to these invitations may be rejected, irrespective of academic achievement, as the University looks for committed, well-motivated students.

GRADUATE DESTINATIONS AND EMPLOYMENT (2015/16 HESA)
Graduates surveyed 1,860 **Employed** 1,105 **In voluntary employment** 100 **In further study** 180 **Assumed unemployed** 115

Career note Some graduates go on to work directly in journalism for local, regional and national newspapers, magazines, broadcasting corporations and creative digital media agencies as journalists, press editors and publishing copy-editors. Many enter others areas, including PR, advertising, marketing, management, charity work, education, law and politics.

OTHER DEGREE SUBJECTS FOR CONSIDERATION
Communication Studies; English; Media Studies

LANDSCAPE ARCHITECTURE

(including **Garden Design**; see also **Agricultural Sciences/Agriculture, Architecture, Horticulture**)

Landscape architects shape the world you live in. They are responsible for urban design, the integration of ecology and the quality of the built environment. Courses in Landscape Architecture include project-based design, landscape theory, management, planning and design, ecology, construction, plant design and design practice. After completing the first three years leading to a BSc (Hons) or BA (Hons), students aiming for full professional status take a further one year in practice and one year to achieve their Master of Landscape Architecture (MLA).

Useful websites www.landscapeinstitute.org; www.bealandscapearchitect.com; www.bali.org.uk

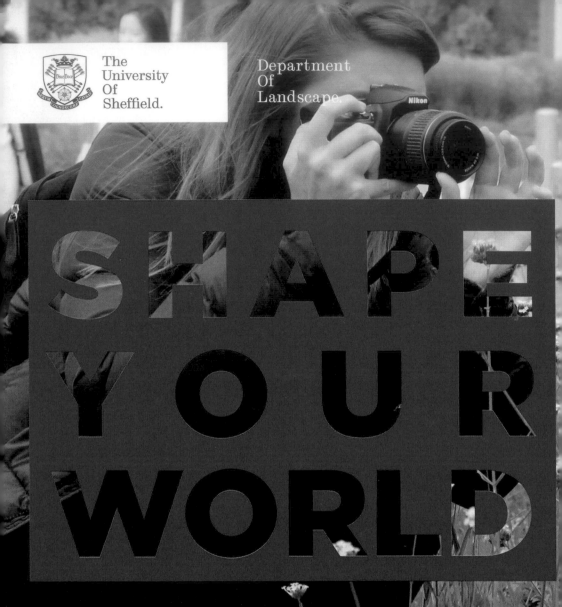

The University Of Sheffield.

Department Of Landscape.

SHAPE YOUR WORLD

Study at the UK's largest and only independent department of Landscape Architecture.

www.sheffield.ac.uk/landscape

*DLHE 2015-16

SHEFFIEL
LANDSCAP
ARCHITECTUR

STUDYING LANDSCAPE ARCHITECTURE AT SHEFFIELD

The Department of Landscape at the University of Sheffield is the largest and only independent department of Landscape Architecture in the UK. We offer internationally renowned research and taught courses that span arts, design, social sciences, geography, planning, ecology and management.

Come to the Department of Landscape and you will be joining one of the world's leading departments for landscape education and research. Our staff are involved in some of the most exciting contemporary landscape design projects. They are committed to developing the next generation of Landscape Architects to create lasting, functional and inspirational places.

100% of students secured graduate jobs in Landscape Architecture in 2016*

BA Hons Landscape Architecture
UCAS code: K3K4

This course aims to educate Landscape Architects who, as well as being skilled designers, have a sound understanding of landscape issues at the large scale. If you enjoy subjects such as geography, politics, economics or history you will appreciate the scope and challenge of this course. By learning about urban design theory, planning and practice, you will acquire a better understanding of the context in which design takes place and the wider implications of your design proposals. On completing this course, you will be uniquely placed to understand the wider societal picture, into which fits inspiring design.

BSc Hons Landscape Architecture
UCAS code: KC39

This course aims to educate Landscape Architects to have an in-depth understanding of ecology and habitat creation. If you are interested in the natural world or enjoy biology or environmental sciences, you will enjoy the focus of this course. You will learn about ecological processes and how they work within designed landscape to give you an understanding of the impact that design proposals have on habitat. In a world of increasing environmental pressure, this course will give you the specialist training to protect and restore existing habitats as well as create new places where nature thrives.

SHAPE YOUR WORLD.

The Department of Landscape at the University of Sheffield is the top rated Landscape Architecture department in the UK[1].

1. Research Excellence Framework, 2014

Why study Landscape Architecture?

"I was initially looking into Architecture, but discovered Landscape Architecture at a careers meeting in year 12 and as soon as I visited the department I knew this is where I wanted to go. I was so impressed with the facilities and the staff were all really friendly.

The course is so varied and dynamic beyond anything I really expected, you learn about everything across the whole Landscape Architecture discipline.

The best thing about the course at Sheffield is how it has really encouraged my graphic skills. I had no idea how to use Photoshop or Indesign before I started the course and now I would consider my graphic skills as one of my main strengths."

Daniel Bilsborough, BA Landscape Architecture

Landscape Architecture involves the design, planning and management of places that benefit people and nature. Landscape Architects create spaces between buildings that are inspirational and functional. If you have a flair for creativity and a passion for improving the environment and people's lives, Landscape Architecture could be for you.

Join the Department of Landscape and you will be joining one of the world's leading departments for landscape education and research. Our staff are involved in some of the most exciting contemporary landscape design projects and are committed to developing the next generation of Landscape Architects.

Sheffield is the ideal place to study Landscape Architecture, whether large-scale urban renewal, complex planning issues or natural habitat. More than a third of our city is within the boundary of the breathtaking Peak District National Park.

Our students are highly sought after within the Landscape profession. We aim to develop graduates with outstanding skills, who are able to take the lead in multidisciplinary projects. Study with us and you will develop design skills as well as the ability to understand the cultural, social and ecological drivers that underpin successful landscapes.

Our courses also equip students with excellent transferable skills. Through working in teams, undertaking live projects for community groups and developing your personal portfolio, you will acquire professional standards in communication, graphic design, report writing and presentation.

Our graduates are in demand. Alumni work in the private sector, where many have set up their own companies. Others work in the public or Third sectors, helping to improve local communities.

Whatever path you choose, a degree in Landscape Architecture from Sheffield will set you up to make a real, positive difference to the world around you.

100% of students secured graduate jobs in Landscape Architecture in 2016*

Contact Us

Email: landscape@sheffield.ac.uk

Telephone: +44 (0)114 222 0600

Website: www.sheffield.ac.uk/landscape

Twitter: @LandscapeSheff

SHEFFIELD
LANDSCAPE
ARCHITECTURE

NB The points totals shown to the left of the institutions are for ease of reference only. It must not be assumed that Tariff points are always used by institutions or that they can be substituted for an offer in grades. The level of an offer is not necessarily indicative of the quality of a course.

COURSE OFFERS INFORMATION

Subject requirements/preferences GCSE English, geography, art and design, mathematics and at least one science usually required. **AL** Preferred subjects for some courses include biology, geography and environmental science. A portfolio may also be required.

Your target offers and examples of degree courses
144 pts **Sheffield** – AAA +portfolio (Archit Lnd) (IB 36 pts)
128 pts **Edinburgh** – ABB (Lnd Archit) (IB 34 pts HL 655)
          Greenwich – 128 pts +interview +portfolio (Lnd Archit)
          Sheffield – ABB (Lnd Archit) (IB 33 pts)
120 pts **Leeds Beckett** – 120 pts +interview +portfolio (Lnd Archit Des) (IB 26 pts)
112 pts **Birmingham City** – BBC 112 pts (Land Archit) (HL 16–14 pts)
          Gloucestershire – BBC 112 pts (Lnd Archit)
 96 pts **Hadlow (Coll)** – 96 pts (Gdn Des)
          Writtle (UC) – 96 pts +interview +portfolio (Lnd Gdn Des; Lnd Archit) (IB 24 pts)
 80 pts **Duchy (Coll)** – 80 pts (Hort (Gdn Lnd Des))

Alternative offers
See **Chapter 6** and **Appendix 1** for grades/UCAS Tariff points information for other examinations.

EXAMPLES OF COLLEGES OFFERING COURSES IN THIS SUBJECT FIELD
Craven (Coll); Duchy (Coll).

CHOOSING YOUR COURSE (SEE ALSO CH.1)
Universities and colleges teaching quality See www.qaa.ac.uk; https://unistats.ac.uk.

ADMISSIONS INFORMATION
Number of applicants per place (approx) Edinburgh 19; Gloucestershire 9; Greenwich 3; Writtle (UC) 5.

Advice to applicants and planning the UCAS personal statement Knowledge of the work of landscape architects is important. Arrange a visit to a landscape architect's office and try to organise some work experience. Read up on historical landscape design and visit country house estates with examples of outstanding designs. Describe these visits in detail and your preferences. Membership of the National Trust could be useful. See also **Appendix 3**.

Selection interviews Yes Greenwich, Writtle (UC); **No** Birmingham City, Gloucestershire, Sheffield.

Interview advice and questions Applicants will be expected to have had some work experience and are likely to be questioned on their knowledge of landscape architectural work and the subject. Historical examples of good landscaping could also be asked for. See also **Chapter 5**.

Reasons for rejection (non-academic) Lack of historical knowledge and awareness of current developments. Poor portfolio.

AFTER-RESULTS ADVICE
Offers to applicants repeating A-levels Same Birmingham City, Edinburgh, Greenwich.

GRADUATE DESTINATIONS AND EMPLOYMENT (2015/16 HESA)
Landscape Design graduates surveyed 155 **Employed** 100 **In voluntary employment** 5 **In further study** 25 **Assumed unemployed** 0

Career note Opportunities at present in landscape architecture are good. Openings exist in local government or private practice and may cover planning, housing, and conservation.

OTHER DEGREE SUBJECTS FOR CONSIDERATION

Architecture; Art and Design; Environmental Planning; Forestry; Horticulture.

LANGUAGES

(including **British Sign Language, European Studies, Modern Languages** and **Translation Studies;**
see separate language tables; see also **African Studies, Asia-Pacific Studies, Chinese, English,
European Studies, French, German, Greek, Italian, Japanese, Latin, Linguistics, Russian and East
European Studies, Scandinavian Studies, Spanish**)

Modern language courses usually offer three main options: a single subject degree commonly based
on literature and language, a European Studies course, or two-language subjects which can often
include languages different from those available at school (such as Scandinavian Studies, Russian and
the languages of Eastern Europe, the Middle and Far East).

Useful websites www.ciol.org.uk; www.iti.org.uk; http://europa.eu; www.bbc.co.uk/languages;
www.languageadvantage.com; www.omniglot.com; www.languagematters.co.uk

*NB The points totals shown to the left of the institutions are for ease of reference only. It must not
be assumed that Tariff points are always used by institutions or that they can be substituted for an
offer in grades. The level of an offer is not necessarily indicative of the quality of a course.*

COURSE OFFERS INFORMATION

Subject requirements/preferences GCSE English and a modern language required. In some cases
grades A (7) and/or B (5 or 6) may be stipulated. **AL** A modern foreign language required usually
with a specified grade.

Your target offers and examples of degree courses

152 pts Cambridge – A*AA incl lang +interview +MMLAA (Modn Mediev Langs) (IB 40–42 pts HL
776); A*AA +interview +AMESAA (As Mid E St) (IB 40–42 pts HL 776)

Imperial London – A*AA–A*A*A* incl chem+maths +interview (Chem Fr/Ger/Span Sci) (IB
40–42 pts HL 7 chem 6 maths)

London (UCL) – A*AA–AAA incl hist+Euro lang (Hist Euro Lang) (IB 39–38 pts HL 6 hist+Euro
lang)

Nottingham – A*AA–AAA incl maths+phys (Phys Euro Lang) (IB 36 pts HL 6 maths+phys)

St Andrews – A*AA incl maths (Maths Langs) (IB 36 pts HL 6 maths)

144 pts Birmingham – AAA (Econ Lang) (IB 32 pts HL 666)

Durham – AAA incl lang+hist (Modn Euro Langs Hist (Yr Abrd)) (IB 37 pts); AAA incl lang
(Modn Langs Cult (Yr Abrd)) (IB 37 pts)

Exeter – AAA–ABB incl lang (Int Rel Modn Langs) (IB 36–32 pts HL 5 lang)

London (UCL) – AAA–ABB incl lang (Modn Langs) (IB 34–36 pts HL 6 lang)

Manchester – AAA–ABB incl sci/maths +interview (Anat Sci Modn Lang) (IB 37–32 pts HL 5
chem+sci); (Microbiol Modn Lang; Plnt Sci Modn Lang) (IB 37–32 pts HL 5 sci); (Biol
Modn Lang) (IB 37–32 pts HL 5/6 sci+chem); (Genet Modn Lang) (IB 37–32 pts HL 6/5
sci)

Newcastle – AAA–ABB incl Fr (Ling Fr) (IB 36–34 pts HL 5 Fr)

Oxford – AAA +interview +MLAT (Modn Langs Ling) (IB 38 pts HL 666); (Phil Modn Langs)
(IB 39 pts HL 666); AAA +interview +CAT +MLAT (Class Modn Langs) (IB 39 pts HL 666);
AAA +interview +HAT +MLAT (Hist Modn Langs) (IB 38 pts HL 666); AAA +interview
+ELAT +MLAT (Engl Modn Langs) (IB 38 pts HL 666); AAA +interview +OLAT (Orntl St) (IB
39 pts HL 666)

St Andrews – AAA (Heb courses) (IB 36 pts HL 666)

Sheffield – AAA/AAB+aEPQ incl maths (Civ Eng Modn Lang (MEng)) (IB 36 pts HL 6 maths);
AAA/AAB+aEPQ incl maths+phys/chem/electron (Electron Elec Eng Modn Lang (MEng))
(IB 36 pts HL 6 maths+phys/chem/electron)

136 pts **Bath** – AAB–ABB+aEPQ (Lang Pol) (IB 36 pts HL 6 lang)

Birmingham – AAB incl lang (Modn Langs) (IB 32 pts HL 665)

Bristol – AAB–ABC incl langs (Modn Langs) (IB 34–31 pts HL 6/5 langs); AAB–BBB incl lang (Phil Modn Lang; Hist Art Modn Lang; Pol Modn Lang) (IB 34–31 pts HL 5 lang)

Edinburgh – AAB incl Span/Port (Span Port) (IB 39 pts HL 666)

Exeter – AAB–ABB (Modn Lang Arab) (IB 34–32 pts); AAB–ABB incl Fr+Lat (Fr Lat) (IB 34–32 pts HL 5 Fr+Lat)

Lancaster – AAB–ABB incl lang (Modn Langs) (IB 35–32 pts HL 16 pts)

London (RH) – AAB–BBB (Modn Lang Lat) (IB 32 pts HL 555)

London (SOAS) – AAB–ABB (Kor; Swli Comb Hons; Turk) (IB 35 pts HL 665)

London (UCL) – AAB incl lang (Lang Cult) (IB 36 pts HL 17 pts)

St Andrews – AAB (Art Hist Lang) (IB 35 pts)

Southampton – AAB/ABB+aEPQ incl Fr/Ger/Span +interview (Bus Mgt Fr/Ger/Span) (IB 34 pts HL 6 Fr/Ger/Span); AAB/ABB+aEPQ incl lang +interview (Langs Contemp Euro St) (IB 34 pts HL 6 lang)

128 pts **Aston** – ABB–BBB incl Fr/Ger/Span (Transl St (Fr/Ger/Span)) (IB 33–32 pts HL 6 Fr/Ger/Span)

Bath – ABB–ABC+aEPQ incl lang (Modn Langs Euro St) (IB 35 pts HL 6 lang)

Bristol – ABB–BBC incl lang (Span Modn Lang) (IB 32–29 pts HL 5 lang); ABB–BBC incl mus+lang (Mus Modn Lang) (IB 32–29 pts HL 5 mus+lang); ABB–BBC incl Russ/Port (Russ Port) (IB 32–29 pts HL 5 Russ/Port)

East Anglia – ABB (Modn Langs; Transl Media Modn Lang) (IB 32 pts); ABB incl Fr/Span/Jap (Transl Interp Modn Langs (Yr Abrd)) (IB 32 pts HL 6 Fr/Span/Jap)

Leeds – ABB (Port Russ) (IB 34 pts HL 16 pts)

Liverpool – ABB incl maths+Fr/Ger/Span (Mathem Sci Euro Lang) (IB 33 pts HL 6 maths+Fr/Ger/Span); ABB (Lat Am Hisp St Comb Hons) (IB 33 pts); ABB incl lang (Modn Euro Langs) (IB 33 pts HL 6 lang); (Modn Lang St Bus) (IB 33 pts)

London (RH) – ABB–BBB (Modn Lang) (IB 32 pts HL 555)

London (SOAS) – ABB (Burm (Myan) courses; Indsn Comb Hons; Thai Comb Hons) (IB 33 pts HL 555)

Manchester – ABB incl lang (Span Port) (IB 33 pts HL 655)

Newcastle – ABB–BBB incl Fr/Ger/Span (Modn Langs; Modn Langs Ling) (IB 32 pts HL 6 Fr/Ger/Span); ABB incl Fr/Ger/Span (Mod Langs Transl Interp) (IB 32 pts HL 6 Fr/Ger/Span)

Nottingham – ABB incl lang (Modn Langs Bus; Modn Lang St) (IB 32 pts); ABB (Modn Euro St) (IB 32 pts)

Sheffield – ABB–BBB+bEPQ incl lang (Modn Langs) (IB 33 pts HL 6 lang)

120 pts **Aberdeen** – BBB (Lang Ling) (IB 32 pts)

Dundee – BBB (Euro St) (IB 30 pts HL 555)

Essex – BBB (Modn Langs; Lang St; Euro St Fr/Ger/Ital/Span; Span St Modn Langs) (IB 30 pts)

Greenwich – 120 pts (Adv Dig Mark Comm Lang)

Heriot-Watt – BBB incl lang (App Langs Transl (Fr/Span)/(Ger/Span)) (IB 30 pts HL 5 lang); (Langs (Interp Transl) (Fr/Ger)/(Ger/Span)) (IB 30 pts); BBB (Brit Sign Lang (Interp Transl App Lang St)) (IB 30 pts)

Stirling – BBB (Modn Langs; Int Mgt St Euro Langs Soty) (IB 32 pts)

Swansea – BBB incl lang (Modn Lang Transl Inter) (IB 32–30 pts)

112 pts **Aberystwyth** – BBC (Euro Langs) (IB 28 pts)

Central Lancashire – 112 pts (Mod Lang Int Bus; Modn Langs)

Greenwich – 112 pts (Langs Int Rel)

Hull – 112 pts incl lang (Comb Three Lang; Hist Modn Lang) (IB 28 pts)

Roehampton – 112 pts (Lang Glob Comm)

Wolverhampton – BBC–CCC (Interp (Brit Sign Lang/Engl))

104 pts **Chester** – BCC–BBC incl Span/Fr/Ger (Modn Langs) (IB 26 pts HL 5 Span/Fr/Ger)

London (Birk) – 104 pts (Ling Lang)

Nottingham Trent – 104 pts incl Fr (Fr Comb Hons)

Westminster – BCC (Transl St (Span); Transl St (Fr)) (IB 28 pts HL 4 lang)

UCAS points Tariff: A* = 56 pts; A = 48 pts; B = 40 pts; C = 32 pts; D = 24 pts; E = 16 pts

96 pts   **Edinburgh Napier** – CCC incl lang (Int Bus Mgt Lang) (IB 27 pts HL 5 lang)
London Met – CCC/BC 96 pts (Transl)
Plymouth – 96 pts incl Fr (Int Bus Fr) (IB 26 pts HL 4 Fr)
Portsmouth – 96–120 pts (Modn Lang)
York St John – 96–112 pts (Langs)

Open University – contact 0300 303 0073 **or** www.open.ac.uk/contact/new (Lang St)

Alternative offers
See **Chapter 6** and **Appendix 1** for grades/UCAS Tariff points information for other examinations.

CHOOSING YOUR COURSE (SEE ALSO CH.1)
Universities and colleges teaching quality See www.qaa.ac.uk; https://unistats.ac.uk.

Top research universities and colleges (REF 2014) (Modern Languages and Linguistics) London (QM) (Ling); Queen Margaret; Edinburgh (Ling); Kent; York; Queen's Belfast; Southampton; Cardiff; Essex; Warwick; Glasgow (Celt St); Cambridge; Manchester; London (RH).

Examples of sandwich degree courses Bangor.

ADMISSIONS INFORMATION
Number of applicants per place (approx) Aston 4; Bangor 6; Bath 6 (Mod Langs Eur St); Birmingham 5; Bristol 15; Cambridge 2; Durham 5; East Anglia 5; Heriot-Watt 6; Lancaster 7; Leeds 8; Leicester 6; Liverpool 6; London (SOAS) (Thai) 2, (Burm) 1; London (UCL) 5; Newcastle 7; Swansea 4; Wolverhampton 10.

Advice to applicants and planning the UCAS personal statement Discuss any literature studied outside your course work. Students applying for courses in which they have no previous knowledge (for example, Italian, Portuguese, Modern Greek, Czech, Russian) would be expected to have done a considerable amount of language work on their own in their chosen language before starting the course. See also **Appendix 3**.

Misconceptions about this course Leeds Some applicants think that studying languages means studying masses of literature – wrong. At Leeds, generally speaking, it's up to you; you study as much or as little literature as you choose. Residence abroad does not inevitably mean a university course (except where you are taking a language from scratch). Paid employment is usually another option.

Selection interviews Yes Cambridge, Oxford (Modn Lang) 34%, (Modn Lang Ling) 33%, Southampton; **No** Aston, Dundee, East Anglia, Heriot-Watt, Leeds, Liverpool, London (RH), Swansea.

Interview advice and questions See also **Chapter 5**. **Cambridge** Think of a painting of a tree. Is the tree real? **Leeds** Give an example of something outside your studies that you have achieved over the past year.

Reasons for rejection (non-academic) Lack of commitment to spend a year abroad. Poor references. Poor standard of English. No reasons for why the course has been selected. Poor communication skills. Incomplete applications, for example missing qualifications and reference.

AFTER-RESULTS ADVICE
Offers to applicants repeating A-levels Possibly higher Aston; **Same** Birmingham, Bristol, Durham, East Anglia, Leeds, Liverpool, Newcastle, Nottingham Trent, Stirling, Wolverhampton; **No** Cambridge.

GRADUATE DESTINATIONS AND EMPLOYMENT (2015/16 HESA)
See separate language tables.

Career note The only career-related fields for language students are teaching, which attracts some graduates, and the demanding work of interpreting and translating, to which only a small number aspire. The majority will be attracted to work in management and administration, financial services and a host of other occupations which may include the social services, law and property development.

OTHER DEGREE SUBJECTS FOR CONSIDERATION

Communication Studies; Linguistics; Modern Languages Education/Teaching.

LATIN

(see also Classical Studies/Classical Civilisation, Classics, Greek, Languages)

Latin courses provide a study of the language, art, religion and history of the Roman world. This table should be read in conjunction with the **Classical Studies/Classical Civilisation** and **Classics** tables.

Useful websites www.thelatinlibrary.com; www.arlt.co.uk; www.cambridgescp.com

NB The points totals shown to the left of the institutions are for ease of reference only. It must not be assumed that Tariff points are always used by institutions or that they can be substituted for an offer in grades. The level of an offer is not necessarily indicative of the quality of a course.

COURSE OFFERS INFORMATION

Subject requirements/preferences GCSE English, a foreign language and Latin may be stipulated. **AL** Check courses for Latin requirement.

Your target offers and examples of degree courses

152 pts **Cambridge** – A*AA +interview +test (Modn Mediev Langs (Class Lat)) (IB 40–42 pts HL 776); A*AA +interview +CAA (Class) (IB 40–42 pts HL 776)

144 pts **St Andrews** – AAA (Lat Mediev Hist; Lat courses) (IB 36 pts)

136 pts **Edinburgh** – AAB (Anc Hist Lat; Lat St) (IB 36 pts HL 665)

Exeter – AAB–ABB incl Fr+Lat (Fr Lat) (IB 34–32 pts HL 5 Fr+Lat)

Glasgow – AAB incl arts/hum/lang (Lat Comb Hons) (IB 36 pts HL 665 incl 6 Engl/hum/lang)

London (RH) – AAB–BBB (Modn Lang Lat) (IB 32 pts HL 555)

London (UCL) – AAB incl Gk (Gk Lat) (IB 36 pts HL 6 Gk); AAB incl Lat (Lat Gk) (IB 36 pts HL 6 Lat)

Nottingham – AAB–ABB (Lat) (IB 34–32 pts)

Warwick – AAB inc Engl lit+Lat (Engl Lat Lit) (IB 36 pts HL 6 Engl lit+Lat)

128 pts **London (RH)** – ABB–BBB (Lat) (IB 32 pts HL 555)

120 pts **Swansea** – BBB 120 pts (Lat Comb Hons) (IB 32 pts)

Trinity Saint David – interview (Lat courses)

Alternative offers

See **Chapter 6** and **Appendix 1** for grades/UCAS Tariff points information for other examinations.

CHOOSING YOUR COURSE (SEE ALSO CH.1)

Universities and colleges teaching quality See www.qaa.ac.uk; http://unistats.ac.uk.

Top research universities and colleges (REF 2014) See **Classics**.

ADMISSIONS INFORMATION

Number of applicants per place (approx) London (UCL) 5; Nottingham 4; Trinity Saint David 6.

Advice to applicants and planning the UCAS personal statement See **Classical Studies/Classical Civilisation** and **Classics**.

Selection interviews Yes Cambridge, London (UCL), Trinity Saint David; **No** London (RH), Nottingham.

Interview advice and questions See **Classical Studies/Classical Civilisation** and **Classics**.

UCAS points Tariff: A* = 56 pts; A = 48 pts; B = 40 pts; C = 32 pts; D = 24 pts; E = 16 pts

AFTER-RESULTS ADVICE
Offers to applicants repeating A-levels Higher St Andrews, Warwick.

GRADUATE DESTINATIONS AND EMPLOYMENT (2015/16 HESA)
Graduates surveyed 15 **Employed** 5 **In voluntary employment** 0 **In further study** 5 **Assumed unemployed** 0

Career note Graduates enter a broad range of careers within management, the media, commerce and tourism as well as social and public services. Some graduates choose to work abroad and teaching is a popular option.

OTHER DEGREE SUBJECTS FOR CONSIDERATION
Ancient History; Archaeology; Classical Studies; Classics.

LATIN AMERICAN STUDIES

(including **Hispanic Studies**; see also **American Studies, Spanish**)

Latin American courses provide a study of Spanish and of Latin American republics, covering both historical and present-day conditions and problems. Normally a year is spent in Latin America.

Useful websites www.ciol.org.uk; www.bbc.co.uk/languages; www.languageadvantage.com; www.languagematters.co.uk; www.wola.org; http://thelaa.org; see also **Languages** and **Spanish**.

NB The points totals shown to the left of the institutions are for ease of reference only. It must not be assumed that Tariff points are always used by institutions or that they can be substituted for an offer in grades. The level of an offer is not necessarily indicative of the quality of a course.

COURSE OFFERS INFORMATION
Subject requirements/preferences GCSE English and a foreign language required by most universities. **AL** Spanish may be required for some courses.

Your target offers and examples of degree courses
152 pts Nottingham – A*AA (Econ Hisp St) (IB 36 pts)
136 pts Birmingham – AAB incl hist (Hisp St Hist) (IB 32 pts HL 665)
  London (UCL) – AAB incl Span (Span Lat Am St) (IB 36 pts HL 6 Span)
  Sheffield – AAB–BBB incl lang (Hisp St Comb Hons) (IB 34–32 pts HL 6 lang)
  Southampton – AAB incl Span/Port +interview (Pol Span/Port Lat Am St) (IB 34 pts HL 6 Span/Port); AAB incl Span +interview (Span (Lat Am St)) (IB 34 pts HL 6 Span)
  Warwick – AAB incl lang (Hisp St courses) (IB 36 pts HL 5 lang)
128 pts Bristol – ABB–BBC incl Span (Hisp St) (IB 32–29 pts HL 5 Span)
  Liverpool – ABB (Lat Am Hisp St Comb Hons) (IB 33 pts)
  Manchester – ABB incl Span +interview (Span Port Lat Am St) (IB 33 pts HL 655)
  Newcastle – ABB–BBB incl Span (Span Port Lat Am St) (IB 32 pts HL 6 Span)
  Nottingham – ABB (Am St Lat Am St) (IB 32 pts); ABB incl hist (Hisp St Hist) (IB 32 pts HL 5)
  Sheffield – ABB incl lang (Hisp St) (IB 33 pts HL 6 lang)
  Stirling – ABB (3 yr course) BBB (4 yr course) (Span Lat Am St) (IB 35 pts (3 yr course) 32 pts (4 yr course))
120 pts Aberdeen – BBB (Hisp St (Lat Am/Spn)) (IB 32 pts HL 555)
  Essex – BBB (Lat Am St courses) (IB 30 pts)
  Kent – BBB (Hisp St courses) (IB 34 pts)
  London (QM) – BBB–ABB incl lang/hum/soc sci (Hisp St courses; Hisp St) (IB 30–32 pts HL 6/5 lang/hum/soc sci)
112 pts Chester – 112 pts incl Span (Span Port Lat Am St) (IB 26 pts HL 5 Span)
  Hull – 112 pts incl lang (Span Lat Am St) (IB 28 pts)

Check **Chapter 3** for new university admission details and **Chapter 6** on how to read the subject tables.

342 | Law

Alternative offers
See **Chapter 6** and **Appendix 1** for grades/UCAS Tariff points information for other examinations.

CHOOSING YOUR COURSE (SEE ALSO CH.1)
Universities and colleges teaching quality See www.qaa.ac.uk; https://unistats.ac.uk.

ADMISSIONS INFORMATION
Number of applicants per place (approx) Essex 3; Nottingham 4; Southampton 8.

Advice to applicants and planning the UCAS personal statement Visits and contacts with Spain and Latin American countries should be described. An awareness of the economic, historical and political scene of these countries is also important. Information may be obtained from respective embassies.

Selection interviews Yes Southampton; **No** Portsmouth.

Interview advice and questions Past questions include: Why are you interested in studying Latin American Studies? What countries related to the degree course have you visited? What career are you planning when you finish your degree? Applicants taking Spanish are likely to be asked questions on their syllabus and should also be familiar with some Spanish newspapers and magazines. See also **Chapter 5**.

AFTER-RESULTS ADVICE
Offers to applicants repeating A-levels Same Essex.

GRADUATE DESTINATIONS AND EMPLOYMENT (2015/16 HESA)
See **American Studies**.

Career note See **Languages**.

OTHER DEGREE SUBJECTS FOR CONSIDERATION
American Studies; Portuguese; Spanish.

LAW

(including **Criminology**; see also **Social Sciences/Studies**)

Law courses are usually divided into two parts. Part I occupies the first year and introduces the student to criminal and constitutional law and the legal process. Thereafter, many different specialised topics can be studied in the second and third years. Consult the subsection **Interview advice and questions** in order to gain a flavour of the types of questions raised in studying this subject. The course content is very similar for most courses. Applicants are advised to check with universities for their current policies concerning their use of the National Admissions Test for Law (LNAT). See **Subject requirements/preferences** below and also **Chapter 5**.

Useful websites www.barcouncil.org.uk; www.cilex.org.uk; www.lawcareers.net; www.lawsociety.org. uk; www.cps.gov.uk; www.gov.uk/government/organisations/hm-courts-and-tribunals-service; www. lawscot.org.uk; www.lawsoc-ni.org; www.rollonfriday.com; www.lnat.ac.uk

NB The points totals shown to the left of the institutions are for ease of reference only. It must not be assumed that Tariff points are always used by institutions or that they can be substituted for an offer in grades. The level of an offer is not necessarily indicative of the quality of a course.

COURSE OFFERS INFORMATION
Subject requirements/preferences GCSE Many universities will expect high grades. **AL** Arts, humanities, social sciences and sciences plus languages for courses combined with a foreign

The
University of
Law

WE SHARE YOUR AMBITION

Want to change the world,
be big in business or serve
your community? A degree
from The University of Law
gives you the skills to help
you achieve your ambitions.

FIND OUT MORE
law.ac.uk/undergraduate

TEF Gold — Teaching Excellence Framework

91% | EMPLOYMENT*
(Work or Further Education)

WE SHARE YOUR AMBITION

EXPERIENCE AND EXPERTISE

The University of Law is the UK's longest-established specialist provider of legal education. In fact, we've trained more lawyers than anyone else. We can trace our origins to 1876 with the formation of leading tutorial firm Gibson & Weldon. With a rich heritage and a reputation for innovation and contemporary teaching practices, we continuously focus on developing the best legal minds.

With campuses based in 7 of the UK's most vibrant and interesting cities, The University of Law offers a diverse choice of locations to study in. Whether it's the bustling metropolitans of London and Manchester or the heritage-rich Guildford and Chester that appeal, all of our centres provide the same first-class, professional learning environment. Our well-equipped IT suites, award-winning comprehensive law libraries and quiet study and social areas cater to all your study needs.

INNOVATIVE TEACHING

We specialise in teaching, not research, and focus our energy on developing innovative and highly effective teaching methods, all endorsed by employers. With over 250 qualified and experienced solicitors, barristers and judges as your tutors, we can provide you with the practical skills that can make all the difference when starting your career.

The refined syllabus of courses we offer has been purposely developed to complement your career needs. From the undergraduate LLB all the way through to the barrister-level BPTC, our courses are specifically designed by some of the country's top law academics – the majority of whom have previously practised law – so you can be confident in the knowledge that you're learning real-world legal skills from real lawyers.

TEF Gold Teaching Excellence Framework

91% **EMPLOYMENT*** (Work or Further Education)

FOLLOW US:

f 🐦 in ▶️ YouTube 📷

\# liveprospectus.com

*91% of our full-time LLB students who graduated in 2016, are in work/further education six months after completing the course.

The University of **Law**

ENHANCED EMPLOYABILITY

What really sets us apart from other universities is the guiding principle that the students we teach should only ever learn in a realistic, professional and contemporary context. We focus on practice-based training and give our students access to our market leading law careers service and legal vacancy database. Through our pro bono programme, you'll have the opportunity to get an authentic experience of life in a firm before graduating.

STIMULATING ENVIRONMENT

From business games to mock trials and negotiation competitions, you can enhance your learning and boost your CV without it feeling like work. Of course, you'll need time to switch off from studying too and our centres have a range of activities such as debating societies, sports teams, fundraising events, balls, parties, and social activities to make sure you have a full and well-rounded student experience.

FIND OUT MORE
law.ac.uk/undergraduate

language. **All universities** Applicants offering art and music A-levels should check whether these subjects are acceptable.

Your target offers and examples of degree courses

152 pts **Bristol** – A*AA/A*A*B–AAB incl Fr +LNAT (Law Fr) (IB 38–34 pts HL 6 incl Fr); A*AA/A*A*B–AAB +LNAT (Law) (IB 38–34 pts); A*AA/A*A*B–AAB incl Ger +LNAT (Law Ger) (IB 38–34 pts HL 6 Ger)

Cambridge – A*AA +interview +CLT (Law) (IB 40–42 pts HL 776); A*AA +interview +TSA (Lnd Econ) (IB 40–42 pts HL 776)

Durham – A*AA +LNAT (Law) (IB 38 pts)

Edinburgh – A*AA (Law courses; Law Acc) (IB 43 pts HL 776)

London (King's) – A*AA incl Fr/Ger +LNAT (Engl Law Fr Law/Ger Law) (IB 35 pts HL 766 incl 6 Fr/Ger); A*AA +LNAT (Pol Phil Law; Law) (IB 35 pts HL 766)

London (QM) – A*AA (Law) (IB 37 pts HL 18 pts)

London (SOAS) – A*AA–AAB (Law) (IB 37 pts HL 666)

London (UCL) – A*AA incl Fr/Ger/Span +LNAT (Law Fr Law/Ger Law/Hisp Law) (IB 39 pts HL 6 Fr/Ger/Span); A*AA +LNAT (Law) (IB 39 pts HL 19 pts)

London LSE – A*AA (Law) (IB 38 pts HL 776)

144 pts **Birmingham** – AAA +LNAT (Law Bus St) (IB 32 pts HL 666); AAA (Law; Law Ger Law) (IB 32 pts HL 666)

East Anglia – AAA (Law Am Law; Law Euro Leg Sys; Law) (IB 34 pts)

Exeter – AAA–AAB (Law; Law (Euro St)) (IB 36–34 pts)

Glasgow – AAA incl Engl +LNAT (Law Comb Hons) (IB 38–34 pts)

Kent – AAA–ABB (Law; Law Comb Hons) (IB 34 pts); AAA (Int Legal St (Yr Abrd)) (IB 34 pts); AAA–AAB incl Fr (Engl Fr Law) (IB 34 pts)

Leeds – AAA (Law) (IB 35 pts HL 665)

London (QM) – AAA (Law Pol) (IB 37 pts HL 18 pts)

Manchester – AAA (Law; Law Crimin (Yr Abrd); Law Pol) (IB 37 pts HL 666)

Newcastle – AAA (Law) (IB 34 pts HL 666)

Nottingham – AAA incl Fr/Ger/Span +LNAT (Law Fr Fr Law/Ger Ger Law/Span Span Law) (IB 36 pts); AAA +LNAT (Law) (IB 36 pts)

Oxford – AAA +interview +LNAT (Law; Law Law St Euro) (IB 38 pts HL 666)

Queen's Belfast – AAA (Law)

Reading – AAA–AAB (Law) (IB 35–34 pts)

Sheffield – AAA/AAB+aEPQ (Law; Law (Euro Int)) (IB 36 pts)

Southampton – AAA–AAB+aEPQ (Euro Leg St; Int Leg St) (IB 36 pts HL 18 pts); AAA (Law) (IB 36 pts HL 18 pts)

Sussex – AAA–AAB (Law; Law Am St; Law Bus Mgt; Law Int Rel; Law Pol; Law Lang (Yr Abrd)) (IB 34 pts)

Warwick – AAA (Law; Law (St Abrd)) (IB 38 pts); AAA incl Fr/Ger (Law Fr Law/Ger Law) (IB 38 pts HL 6 Fr/Ger)

York – AAA/A*AB/A*A*C +interview (Law) (IB 36 pts)

136 pts **Aston** – AAB–ABB (Law Mgt) (IB 32 pts HL 665); AAB–ABB (Law) (IB 35–34 pts HL 665)

Bangor – 136 pts (Law Crea Media Writ)

Cardiff – AAB (Law; Law Crimin) (IB 35 pts HL 666)

Durham – AAB (Crimin) (IB 36 pts)

Huddersfield – AAB 136 pts (Law (Exmp))

Lancaster – AAB (Law Crimin; Law (St Abrd)) (IB 35 pts HL 16 pts); (Law) (IB 36 pts HL 16 pts)

Leicester – AAB incl Fr (Engl Fr Law (Mait)) (IB 33 pts HL 6 Fr); AAB (Law) (IB 33 pts); AAB incl lang (Law Modn Lang (Fr/Span/Ital)) (IB 33 pts)

London (RH) – AAB (Law) (IB 32 pts HL 665)

London LSE – AAB (Anth Law) (IB 37 pts HL 666)

Sheffield – AAB/ABB+bEPQ (Law Crimin) (IB 34 pts)

Strathclyde – AAB (Scots Engl Law (Clin)) (IB 38 pts HL 5 Engl)

Check **Chapter 3** for new university admission details and **Chapter 6** on how to read the subject tables.

Swansea – AAB–BBB (Law Am St; Bus Law; Law Span)

Warwick – AAB (Law Bus St; Law Sociol) (IB 36 pts)

128 pts **Aberdeen** – ABB (Law) (IB 34 pts)

Bangor – 128–120 pts (Law courses); 128–112 pts (Law Media St; Law Crimin)

BPP – ABB 128 pts (Law)

Brunel – ABB (Law) (IB 31 pts)

City – ABB 128 pts (Law) (IB 29 pts)

Coventry – ABB (Law) (IB 31 pts)

Dundee – ABB incl lang (Law Langs) (IB 32 pts HL 655); ABB (Law (Scot Engl); Scot Law)
  (IB 32 pts HL 655)

Essex – ABB incl Fr (Engl Fr Law (Mait)) (IB 32 pts HL 6 Fr)

Keele – ABB (Law courses) (IB 34 pts)

Leicester – ABB–BBB+bEPQ (Crimin) (IB 30 pts)

Liverpool – ABB (Law; Law Acc Fin) (IB 33 pts)

London South Bank – ABB (Law)

Middlesex – 128 pts +interview (Law)

NCH London – ABB–AAA +interview (Law) (IB 34–36 pts)

Northumbria – 128–136 pts (Law) (HL 444)

Portsmouth – 128 pts (Law) (IB 30 pts HL 17 pts)

Stirling – ABB (Law) (IB 36 pts)

Surrey – ABB (Law; Law Int St; Law Crimin) (IB 32 pts)

120 pts **Aberystwyth** – BBB (Law; Crim Law; Euro Law) (IB 30 pts)

Bournemouth – 120 pts (Law) (IB 31 pts HL 555)

Bradford – BBB 120 pts (Bus St Law; Law)

Brighton – BBB–CCC (Law Bus) (IB 30 pts HL 16 pts)

Buckingham – BBB +interview (Law Fr) (IB 32 pts); (Law Bus Mgt; Law Econ; Law Bus Mgt;
  Law; Law Pol) (IB 32 pts)

De Montfort – 120 pts (Law) (IB 28 pts)

Derby – 120–128 pts (Law; Law Crimin)

Edge Hill – BBB 120 pts (Law; Law Crimin; Crimin)

Essex – BBB (Phil Law; Law Hum Rts; Law) (IB 30 pts)

Gloucestershire – BBB 120 pts (Law)

Greenwich – 120 pts (Crimin; Law)

Huddersfield – BBB 120 pts (Bus Law; Law)

Hull – 120 pts (Law; Law Pol) (IB 28 pts)

Keele – ABC–BBB incl sci (Biol Law) (IB 32 pts HL 6 sci/maths)

Kingston – 120 pts (Law)

Liverpool Hope – BBB–BBC 120–112 pts (Law Comb Hons)

Liverpool John Moores – BBB 120 pts (Law; Law Crim Just) (IB 26 pts)

London (Birk) – 120 pts (Law; Crimin Crim Just)

Nottingham Trent – BBB 120 pts (Law)

Plymouth – 120 pts (Law; Law Bus) (IB 30 pts HL 4)

Portsmouth – 120 pts (Law Crimin) (IB 30 pts HL 17 pts)

Sheffield Hallam – 120–104 pts (Law; Law Crimin)

Ulster – BBB (Law; Law Ir; Law Mark) (IB 26 pts HL 13 pts)

Univ Law – BBB–ABB (Law; Law Bus) (IB 29–31 pts)

UWE Bristol – 120 pts (Crimin Law; Law)

Westminster – BBB (Euro Leg St; Law) (IB 28 pts); BBB incl Fr (Law Fr Law) (IB 28 pts)

Worcester – BBB 120 pts (Law; Law Crimin; Law Foren Psy)

112 pts **Anglia Ruskin** – 112 pts (Law)

Birmingham City – BBC 112 pts (Sociol Crimin; Law; Law Am Leg St; Law Crimin) (HL 14 pts)

Bournemouth – 112–120 pts (Acc Law; Law Tax; Bus Law; Enter Law) (IB 30–31 pts HL 55)

Cardiff Met – 112 pts (Bus Mgt St Law)

Central Lancashire – 112 pts (Law Crimin; Law)

Chester – BCC–BBC 112 pts (Law Crimin) (IB 26 pts); BBC–BBB (Law) (IB 28 pts)

Cumbria – 112–128 pts (Law)
De Montfort – 112 pts (Law Hum Rts Soc Just) (IB 26 pts)
East London – 112 pts (Law) (IB 26 pts HL 15 pts)
Glyndŵr – 112 pts (Crimin Crim Just)
Kingston – 112–120 pts (Crimin courses)
Leeds Beckett – 112 pts (Law) (IB 25 pts)
Lincoln – BBC (Law) (IB 29 pts)
London Met – BBC 112 pts (Bus Law; Law (Int Rel); Law)
Manchester Met – BBC–BBB 112–120 pts (Law) (IB 26 pts)
Middlesex – 112 pts (Crimin courses)
Northampton – BBC–BCC (Law courses)
Nottingham Trent – BBC 112 pts (Law Bus; Law Crimin; Law Psy)
Oxford Brookes – BBC–BBB 112–120 pts (Law) (IB 30–32 pts)
Plymouth – 112 pts (Marit Bus Marit Law) (IB 28 pts HL 4)
Portsmouth – 112 pts (Law Int Rel; Law Bus) (IB 30 pts HL 17 pts)
Robert Gordon – BBC (Law) (IB 29 pts)
Roehampton – 112 pts (Crimin)
St Mary's – 112 pts (Law)
Southampton Solent – 112 pts (Law; Crimin)
Staffordshire – 112–120 pts (Crimin)
Sunderland – 112 pts (Law)
West London – BBC 112–120 pts (Crimin); 112–128 pts (Law)
Wolverhampton – BBC (Law; Law Phil)

104 pts **Abertay** – BCC (Law) (IB 29 pts)
Chester – BCC–BBC (Law Comb Hons) (IB 26–28 pts)
De Montfort – 104 pts (Crimin; Bus Mgt Law) (IB 24 pts)
Edinburgh Napier – BCC (Law) (IB 29 pts HL 655); BCC incl Engl (Crimin) (IB 29 pts HL 655)
Lincoln – BCC (Crimin) (IB 28 pts)
Plymouth – 104 pts (Int Rel Law) (IB 26 pts HL 4)
St Mary's – 104 pts (Bus Law (Comb Hons))
South Wales – BCC–CDD 104–80 pts (Law Crimin Crim Just; Law) (HL 655–445)
Winchester – 104–120 pts (Law) (IB 26 pts)

96 pts **Bucks New** – 96–112 pts (Law; Bus Law)
Canterbury Christ Church – 96–120 pts (Law)
Cumbria – 96–112 pts (Crimin Law)
Derby – 96–128 pts (Law Comb Hons)
Hertfordshire – 96–112 pts (Law; Law (Gov Pol)) (HL 44)
West Scotland – CCC (Law Bus) (IB 24 pts HL 44)
Winchester – 96–112 pts (Law Comb Hons) (IB 25 pts)

88 pts **Teesside** – 88–104 pts (Law Bus Mgt; Law)
80 pts **Bedfordshire** – 80 pts (Law; Crimin)
Bucks New – 80–96 pts (Crimin)
Teesside – 80–96 pts (Crimin courses)

Open University – contact 0300 303 0073 **or** www.open.ac.uk/contact/new (Law)

Alternative offers
See **Chapter 6** and **Appendix 1** for grades/UCAS Tariff points information for other examinations.

EXAMPLES OF DEGREE APPRENTICESHIPS IN THIS SUBJECT FIELD
City (Leg Prac); Manchester Met (Leg Prac).

EXAMPLES OF COLLEGES OFFERING COURSES IN THIS SUBJECT FIELD
Barnsley (Coll); Birmingham Met (Coll); Blackburn (Coll); Blackpool and Fylde (Coll); Bury (Coll); Croydon (Univ Centre); Nottingham (Coll); Pearson (Coll); Petroc; St Helens (Coll); South Devon (Coll); South Thames (Coll); Truro and Penwith (Coll).

Check **Chapter 3** for new university admission details and **Chapter 6** on how to read the subject tables.

CHOOSING YOUR COURSE (SEE ALSO CH.1)

Universities and colleges teaching quality See www.qaa.ac.uk; https://unistats.ac.uk.

Top research universities and colleges (REF 2014) Durham; London (King's); York; Sheffield; Cambridge; Leeds; London LSE; Ulster; London (QM); Warwick; Bristol; Exeter.

Examples of sandwich degree courses Aston; Bournemouth; Bradford; Brighton; Brunel; Coventry; De Montfort; Essex; Greenwich; Hertfordshire; Huddersfield; Leeds; London (RH); Nottingham Trent; Portsmouth; Surrey; UWE Bristol; Westminster.

ADMISSIONS INFORMATION

Number of applicants per place (approx) Abertay 4; Anglia Ruskin 10; Aston 10; Bangor 5; Birmingham 6; Birmingham City 20; Bradford 2; Bristol 5; Buckingham 10; Cambridge 5; Cardiff 12; Central Lancashire 36; City 6; De Montfort 6; Derby 7; Dundee 6; Durham 7; East Anglia 7; East London 13; Edinburgh 9; Edinburgh Napier 11; Essex 26; Exeter 15; Glasgow 8; Huddersfield 6; Hull 5; Kent 6; Kingston 25; Lancaster 4; Leeds 15; Leicester 6; Liverpool 12; Liverpool John Moores 10; London (King's) 14; London (QM) 17; London (RH) 6; London (SOAS) 8; London (UCL) 14; London LSE 15; London Met 13; London South Bank 4; Manchester 7; Manchester Met 21; Middlesex 25; Newcastle 7; Northampton 4; Nottingham 7; Nottingham Trent 15; Oxford Brookes 7; Plymouth 21; Robert Gordon 4; Sheffield 6; Sheffield Hallam 6; Southampton 7; Staffordshire 16; Stirling 11; Strathclyde 10; Sussex 10; Teesside 3; Warwick 20; Westminster 29; Wolverhampton 12; York 8.

Admissions tutors' advice Buckingham A personal statement should demonstrate (at least a potential for) some of the key skills for the study of law: a passion or desire to study the subject, interest in other people and the world around us, powers of synthesis and analysis. Above all a statement should be articulate and succinct and show the applicant has an aptitude for effective communication.

Advice to applicants and planning the UCAS personal statement Visit the law courts and take notes on cases heard. Follow leading legal arguments in the press. Read the law sections in *The Independent*, *The Times* and the *Guardian*. Discuss the career with lawyers and, if possible, obtain work shadowing in lawyers' offices. Describe these visits and experiences and indicate any special areas of law which interest you. (Read *Learning the Law* by Glanville Williams.) Commitment is essential to the study of law as an academic discipline, not necessarily with a view to taking it up as a career.

When writing to admissions tutors, especially by email, take care to present yourself well: text language is not acceptable. You should use communication as an opportunity to demonstrate your skill in the use of English. Spelling mistakes, punctuation errors and bad grammar suggest that you will struggle to develop the expected writing ability (see **Misconceptions about this course**) and may lead to your application being rejected. When writing to an admissions tutor, do not demand an answer immediately or by return or urgently. If your query is reasonable, the tutor will respond without such urging. Adding these demands is bad manners and suggests that you are doing everything at the last minute and increases your chances of a rejection.

The criteria for admission are: motivation and capacity for sustained and intense work; the ability to analyse and solve problems using logical and critical approaches; the ability to draw fine distinctions, to separate the relevant from the irrelevant; the capacity for accurate and critical observation, for sustained and cogent argument; creativity and flexibility of thought and lateral thinking; competence in English; the ability to express ideas clearly and effectively; a willingness to listen and to be able to give considered responses. See also **Appendix 3**. **Deferred entry** Check with your university choices since deferred entry will not necessarily be accepted. **Bristol** Deferred entry is limited. Second time applicants rarely considered. **Manchester** Deferred entry is accepted. **Warwick** Deferred entry is usually acceptable.

Misconceptions about this course Aberystwyth Some applicants believe that all Law graduates enter the legal profession – this is incorrect. **Birmingham** Students tend to believe that success in Law centres on the ability to learn information. Whilst some information does necessarily have to be learnt, the most important skills involve (a) developing an ability to select the most relevant pieces of information and (b) developing the ability to write tightly argued, persuasively reasoned essays on the basis of such information. **Bristol** Many applicants think that most of our applicants have been privately educated: the reverse is true. **Derby** Many applicants do not realise the amount of work involved to get a good degree classification.

Selection interviews Approximately four well-qualified candidates apply for every place on undergraduate Law courses in the UK and the National Admissions Test for Law (LNAT) is used by a number of universities (see Your target offers and examples of degree courses and **Chapter 5**). **Yes** Anglia Ruskin, Buckingham, Cambridge, Oxford (Law) 15%, (Law Law St Euro) 11%, York; **Some** Cardiff, Liverpool John Moores, London (King's), London (UCL), Southampton Solent, Warwick; **No** Aberystwyth, Bangor, Birmingham, Bristol, Canterbury Christ Church, Central Lancashire, Coventry, Derby, Dundee, East Anglia, East London, Essex, Huddersfield, Kent, Liverpool, Northumbria, Nottingham, Nottingham Trent, Oxford Brookes, Reading, Sheffield Hallam, Southampton, Staffordshire, Sunderland, Surrey, Teesside, UWE Bristol, West London.

Interview advice and questions Law is a highly competitive subject and applicants will be expected to have a basic awareness of aspects of law and to have gained some work experience, on which they are likely to be questioned. It is almost certain that a legal question will be asked at interview and applicants will be tested on their responses. Questions in the past have included: What interests you in the study of law? What would you do to overcome the problem of prison overcrowding if you were (a) a judge, (b) a prosecutor, (c) the Prime Minister? What legal cases have you read about recently? What is jurisprudence? What are the causes of violence in society? A friend bought a bun which, unknown to him, contained a stone. He gave it to you to eat and you broke a tooth. Could you sue anyone? Have you visited any law courts? What cases did you see? A person arrives in England unable to speak the language. He lights a cigarette in a restaurant where smoking is not allowed. Can he be charged and convicted? What should be done in the case of an elderly person who steals a bar of soap? What, in your opinion, would be the two basic laws in Utopia? Describe, without using your hands, how you would do the butterfly stroke. What would happen if there were no law? Should we legalise euthanasia? If you could change any law, what would it be? How would you implement the changes? If a person tries to kill someone using black magic, are they guilty of attempted murder? If a jury uses a ouija board to reach a decision, is it wrong? If so, why? Jane attends a university interview. As she enters the building she sees a diamond brooch on the floor. She hands it to the interviewer who hands it to the police. The brooch is never claimed. Who is entitled to it? Jane? The interviewer? The police? The University authorities? The Crown? Mr Grabbit who owns the building? Where does honesty fit into law? For joint courses: What academic skills are needed to succeed? Why have you applied for a joint degree? See also **Chapter 5**. **Cambridge** Logic questions. If I returned to the waiting room and my jacket had been taken and I then took another one, got home and actually discovered it was mine, had I committed a crime? If the interviewer pulled out a gun and aimed it at me, but missed as he had a bad arm, had he committed a crime? If the interviewer pulled out a gun and aimed it at me, thinking it was loaded but, in fact, it was full of blanks and fired it at me with the intention to kill, had he committed a crime? Which of the three preceding situations are similar and which is the odd one out? If a law is immoral, is it still a law and must people abide by it? For example, when Hitler legalised the systematic killing of Jews, was it still law? **Oxford** Should the use of mobile phones be banned on public transport? Is wearing school uniform a breach of human rights? If you could go back in time to any period of time, when would it be and why? Would you trade your scarf for my bike, even if you have no idea what state it's in or if I even have one? Is someone guilty of an offence if they did not set out to commit a crime but ended up doing so? Does a girl who joins the Scouts have a political agenda?

Reasons for rejection (non-academic) 'Dreams' about being a lawyer! Poorly informed about the subject. Badly drafted application. Underestimated workload. Poor communication skills. **Buckingham** Applicants are requested to attend an Open Day/Evening or a Tutorial Taster Day. The University believes it is very important for applicants to visit its campus. Candidates who do not respond to these invitations may be rejected, irrespective of academic achievement, as the University looks for committed, well-motivated students. **Manchester Met** Some were rejected because they were obviously more suited to Psychology.

Check **Chapter 3** for new university admission details and **Chapter 6** on how to read the subject tables.

AFTER-RESULTS ADVICE
Offers to applicants repeating A-levels Higher Aberystwyth, Leeds, London Met, Manchester Met, Newcastle, Queen's Belfast, Sheffield, Sheffield Hallam, Strathclyde, Warwick; **Possibly higher** Liverpool; **Same** Anglia Ruskin, Bangor, Birmingham, Bradford, Brighton, Bristol, Brunel, Cardiff, Coventry, De Montfort, Derby, Dundee, Durham, East Anglia, Essex, Huddersfield, Hull, Kingston, Lincoln, Liverpool Hope, Liverpool John Moores, Northumbria, Nottingham, Nottingham Trent, Oxford Brookes, Staffordshire, Stirling, Sunderland, Wolverhampton; **No** Cambridge, Glasgow.

GRADUATE DESTINATIONS AND EMPLOYMENT (2015/16 HESA)
Graduates surveyed 10,415 **Employed** 4,135 **In voluntary employment** 300 **In further study** 4,175 **Assumed unemployed** 500

Career note Training places for the bar and solicitors' examinations remain extremely competitive. There are, however, alternative legal careers such as legal journalism, patent law, legal publishing and teaching. The course also proves a good starting point for careers in industry, commerce and the public service, whilst the study of consumer protection can lead to qualification as a Trading Standards officer.

OTHER DEGREE SUBJECTS FOR CONSIDERATION
Criminology; Economics; Government; History; International Relations; Politics; Social Policy and Administration; Sociology.

LEISURE and RECREATION MANAGEMENT/STUDIES

(see also **Business and Management Courses, Business and Management Courses (International and European), Business and Management Courses (Specialised), Hospitality and Event Management, Sports Sciences/Studies, Tourism and Travel**)

The courses cover various aspects of leisure and recreation and in particular, a wide range of outdoor activities. Specialist options include Recreation Management, Tourism and Countryside Management, all of which are offered as individual degree courses in their own right. Look out for other 'outdoor' activities in sport such as the two-year Foundation course in Surf Science and Technology offered at Cornwall College in partnership with Plymouth University. There is also an obvious link with Sports Studies, Physical Education and Tourism and Travel courses. See also **Appendix 3**.

Useful websites www.cimspa.co.uk; www.leisuremanagement.co.uk; www.thebapa.org.uk; www.leisureopportunities.co.uk; www.recmanagement.com; www.uksport.gov.uk

NB The points totals shown to the left of the institutions are for ease of reference only. It must not be assumed that Tariff points are always used by institutions or that they can be substituted for an offer in grades. The level of an offer is not necessarily indicative of the quality of a course.

COURSE OFFERS INFORMATION
Subject requirements/preferences GCSE Normally English and mathematics grades A–C (7–4). **AL** No specified subjects. **Other** Disclosure and Barring Service (DBS) clearance and health checks required for some courses.

Your target offers and examples of degree courses
128 pts **Manchester** – ABB (Mgt Ldrshp Leis) (IB 32 pts HL 655)
120 pts **Stirling** – BBB incl sci/maths/geog (Env Sci Out Educ) (IB 32 pts)
112 pts **Central Lancashire** – 112–128 pts (Out Advntr Ldrshp)
　　　　Leeds Beckett – 112 pts (Enter Mgt) (IB 25 pts)
　　　　Southampton Solent – 112 pts (Advntr Out Mgt)
104 pts **Cumbria** – 104–120 pts (Out Ldrshp; Out Advntr Env)
　　　　Gloucestershire – BCC 104 pts (Spo Mgt)

Stranmillis (UC) – BCC (Hlth Physl Actvt Spo)
Ulster – BCC–BBB (Leis Evnts Mgt) (IB 24–26 pts HL 12–13 pts)
96 pts **Derby** – 96–112 pts (Out Ldrshp Mgt)
Worcester – 96 pts (Out Advntr Ldrshp Mgt)
88 pts **Canterbury Christ Church** – 88–112 pts (Tour St)
Trinity Saint David – 88 pts +interview (Leis Mgt)
80 pts **Bucks New** – 80–96 pts (Spo Bus Mgt)
64 pts **UHI** – CC (Advntr Tour Mgt)

Alternative offers
See **Chapter 6** and **Appendix 1** for grades/UCAS Tariff points information for other examinations.

EXAMPLES OF COLLEGES OFFERING COURSES IN THIS SUBJECT FIELD
See also **Tourism and Travel**. Bedford (Coll); Blackburn (Coll); Bradford (Coll); Brighton Met (Coll); Cornwall (Coll); Durham New (Coll); Exeter (Coll); Grimsby (Inst Group); Leicester (Coll); Loughborough (Coll); Manchester (Coll); MidKent (Coll); Myerscough (Coll); Newcastle (Coll); Norwich City (Coll); South Devon (Coll); SRUC; Totton (Coll); Wakefield (Coll); West Herts (Coll); Wirral Met (Coll).

CHOOSING YOUR COURSE (SEE ALSO CH.1)
Universities and colleges teaching quality See www.qaa.ac.uk; https://unistats.ac.uk.

Top research universities and colleges (REF 2014) See **Sports Sciences/Studies**.

Examples of sandwich degree courses Bournemouth; Trinity Saint David; Ulster.

ADMISSIONS INFORMATION
Number of applicants per place (approx) Gloucestershire 7.

Advice to applicants and planning the UCAS personal statement Work experience, visits to leisure centres and national parks and any interests you have in particular aspects of leisure should be described, for example, art galleries, museums, countryside management, sport. An involvement in sports and leisure as a participant or employee is an advantage. See also **Appendix 3**.

Misconceptions about this course The level of business studies in Leisure Management courses is higher than many students expect.

Interview advice and questions In addition to sporting or other related interests, applicants will be expected to have had some work experience and can expect to be asked to discuss their interests. What do you hope to gain by going to university? See also **Chapter 5**.

Reasons for rejection (non-academic) Poor communication or presentation skills. Relatively poor sporting background or knowledge.

GRADUATE DESTINATIONS AND EMPLOYMENT (2015/16 HESA)
See **Hospitality and Event Management**.

Career note Career opportunities exist in public and private sectors within leisure facilities, health clubs, the arts, leisure promotion, marketing and events management. Some graduates work in sports development and outdoor activities.

OTHER DEGREE SUBJECTS FOR CONSIDERATION
Business Studies; Events Management; Hospitality Management; Sports Studies; Tourism.

LINGUISTICS
(see also **English, Languages**)

Hi/Hello/Good day/Good morning – Linguistics is the study of language, the way we speak to our friends, or at an interview, the expressions we use, how we express ideas or emotions. The way in which children speak, the types of language used in advertising, or in sports reporting. Courses will include morphology (the formation of words), phonetics (the study of sounds), and semantics (the study of meanings). OK?/Understand?/Cheers!

Useful websites www.ciol.org.uk; www.cal.org; https://academic.oup.com/applij; www.linguisticsociety.org; www.sil.org; www.baal.org.uk

NB The points totals shown to the left of the institutions are for ease of reference only. It must not be assumed that Tariff points are always used by institutions or that they can be substituted for an offer in grades. The level of an offer is not necessarily indicative of the quality of a course.

COURSE OFFERS INFORMATION
Subject requirements/preferences GCSE English required and a foreign language preferred. **AL** English may be required or preferred for some courses.

Your target offers and examples of degree courses
152 pts Cambridge – A*AA +interview +LAA (Ling) (IB 40–42 pts HL 776)
144 pts Edinburgh – AAA (Ital Ling) (IB 39 pts HL 666)
    Lancaster – AAB incl Engl/lang/maths/comp/psy (Ling) (IB 35 pts HL 16 pts)
    Newcastle – AAA–ABB (Ling; Ling Chin/Jap) (IB 36–34 pts); AAA–ABB incl Fr (Ling Fr)
        (IB 36–34 pts HL 5 Fr)
136 pts Edinburgh – AAB (Ling; Jap Ling; Class Ling; Ling Engl Lang) (IB 36 pts HL 665)
    Lancaster – AAB incl Engl/lang (Ling Psy) (IB 35 pts HL 16 pts); AAB incl Engl/lang/maths/
        comp/psy (Ling (St Abrd); Ling Phil) (IB 35 pts HL 16 pts)
    Leeds – AAB–ABB (Ling Comb Hons; Ling Phon) (IB 35–34 pts HL 16 pts)
    London (SOAS) – AAB–ABB (Ling) (IB 35 pts HL 665)
    Southampton – AAB/ABB+aEPQ incl lang +interview (Lang Soty) (IB 34 pts HL 6 lang)
    York – AAB–ABB (Ling) (IB 34 pts); AAB (Phil Ling) (IB 35 pts); AAB–ABB incl Fr (Fr Ling
        (Yr Abrd)) (IB 34 pts)
128 pts Edinburgh – ABB (Phil Ling) (IB 37 pts HL 666)
    London (QM) – ABB incl Engl lit/Engl lang lit (Engl Lit Ling) (IB 32 pts HL 6 Engl); ABB
        (Engl Lang Ling) (IB 32 pts HL 655)
    Manchester – ABB (Ling courses) (IB 33 pts)
    Newcastle – ABB–BBB incl Fr/Ger/Span (Modn Langs Ling) (IB 32 pts HL 6 Fr/Ger/Span)
    Queen's Belfast – ABB incl Engl (Engl Ling)
    Sheffield – ABB incl Engl (Ling Comb Hons) (IB 33 pts); ABB–BBB+bEPQ (Engl Lang Ling)
        (IB 33 pts)
120 pts Aberdeen – BBB (Lang Ling) (IB 32 pts)
    Anglia Ruskin – 120 pts (Engl Lang Ling)
    Bangor – 120–104 pts (Ling Engl Lang; Ling; Ling Engl Lit)
    Essex – BBB (Ling) (IB 30 pts)
    Kent – BBB incl Engl (Engl Lang Ling Engl Am Lit) (IB 34 pts); BBB (Engl Lang Ling)
        (IB 34 pts)
    London (QM) – BBB incl hum/soc sci (Ger Ling) (IB 30 pts HL 5 hum/soc sci)
    UWE Bristol – 120 pts (Engl Lang Ling)
112 pts Roehampton – 112 pts (Engl Lang Ling)
    Wolverhampton – BBC–CCC (Ling courses)
104 pts Brighton – BCC–CCC incl Engl 104–96 pts (Engl Lang Ling) (IB 27 pts)
    Central Lancashire – 104 pts (Engl Lang Ling)

UCAS points Tariff: A* = 56 pts; A = 48 pts; B = 40 pts; C = 32 pts; D = 24 pts; E = 16 pts

London (Birk) – 104 pts (Ling Lang)
Manchester Met – 104–112 pts (Ling Mand Chin/Fr/Ger/Ital/Span) (IB 26 pts)
Nottingham Trent – 104 pts (Ling Comb Hons)
Ulster – BCC–BBC (Lang Ling) (IB 24–25 pts HL 12 pts)
Westminster – BCC (Engl Lang Ling) (IB 28 pts HL 5 Engl); (Arbc Ling) (IB 28 pts)
Winchester – 104–120 pts (Engl Ling) (IB 26 HL 5); (Engl Ling Foren Ling) (IB 26 pts HL 5)
80 pts **Bedfordshire** – 80 pts (Engl Lang Ling)

Alternative offers
See **Chapter 6** and **Appendix 1** for grades/UCAS Tariff points information for other examinations.

CHOOSING YOUR COURSE (SEE ALSO CH.1)

Universities and colleges teaching quality See www.qaa.ac.uk; https://unistats.ac.uk.

Top research universities and colleges (REF 2014) (Modern Languages and Linguistics) London (QM) (Ling); Queen Margaret; Edinburgh (Ling); Kent; York; Queen's Belfast; Southampton; Cardiff; Essex; Warwick; Glasgow (Celt St); Cambridge; Manchester; London (RH).

Examples of sandwich degree courses Leeds; Nottingham Trent; Westminster.

ADMISSIONS INFORMATION

Number of applicants per place (approx) Bangor 5; Cambridge 3; Essex 1; Lancaster 6; Leeds 12; York 11.

Advice to applicants and planning the UCAS personal statement Give details of your interests in language and how it works, and about your knowledge of languages and their similarities and differences.

Selection interviews Yes Cambridge; **No** Brighton, Essex, Newcastle, Sheffield.

Interview advice and questions Past questions include: Why do you want to study linguistics? What does the subject involve? What do you intend to do at the end of your degree course? What answer do you give to your parents or friends when they ask why you want to study the subject? How and why does language vary according to sex, age, social background and regional origins? See also **Chapter 5**.

Reasons for rejection (non-academic) Lack of knowledge of linguistics. Hesitation about the period to be spent abroad.

AFTER-RESULTS ADVICE

Offers to applicants repeating A-levels Same Brighton, Essex, Leeds, Newcastle, York.

GRADUATE DESTINATIONS AND EMPLOYMENT (2015/16 HESA)

Graduates surveyed 620 **Employed** 275 **In voluntary employment** 30 **In further study** 180 **Assumed unemployed** 30

Career note Students enter a wide range of careers, with information management and editorial work in publishing offering some interesting and useful outlets.

OTHER DEGREE SUBJECTS FOR CONSIDERATION

Cognitive Science; Communication Studies; Education Studies; English; Psychology; Speech Sciences.

LITERATURE

(see also **English**)

This is a very broad subject introducing many aspects of the study of literature and aesthetics. Courses will vary in content. Degree courses in English and foreign languages will also include a study of literature.

Useful websites www.lrb.co.uk; www.3ammagazine.com/3am; www.bibliomania.com; www.bl.uk; www.acla.org

NB The points totals shown to the left of the institutions are for ease of reference only. It must not be assumed that Tariff points are always used by institutions or that they can be substituted for an offer in grades. The level of an offer is not necessarily indicative of the quality of a course.

COURSE OFFERS INFORMATION

Subject requirements/preferences GCSE English and a foreign language usually required. **AL** English may be required or preferred for some courses.

Your target offers and examples of degree courses

152 pts **Durham** – A*AA incl Engl+hist (Engl Lit Hist) (IB 38 pts); A*AA incl Engl (Engl Lit; Engl Lit Phil) (IB 38 pts)

Edinburgh – A*AA (Engl Lit) (IB 43 pts HL 776)

Manchester – A*AA–ABB incl Engl (Engl Lit courses) (IB 37–35 pts HL 6 Engl)

144 pts **Lancaster** – AAA–AAB incl Engl (Thea Engl Lit) (IB 36–35 pts HL 16 pts incl 6 Engl); (Film Engl Lit; Engl Lit) (IB 36–35 pts HL 16 pts incl 6 lit)

Leeds – AAA–AAB incl Engl (Engl Lang Lit) (IB 35 pts HL 17–16 pts incl 6 Engl)

Newcastle – AAA–AAB incl Engl (Engl Lit; Engl Lang Lit; Engl Lit Comb Hons) (IB 36–35 pts HL 6 Engl)

Nottingham – AAA–AAB incl Engl (Engl Lang Lit) (IB 36–34 pts HL 6 Engl)

Oxford – AAA +interview +ELAT (Engl Lang Lit) (IB 38 pts HL 666)

Warwick – AAA incl Engl (Engl Lit) (IB 38 pts HL 6 Engl); AAA incl Engl +portfolio (Engl Lit Crea Writ) (IB 38 pts HL 6 Engl)

136 pts **East Anglia** – AAB (Am Engl Lit) (IB 33 pts HL 5 Engl); (Am Lit Crea Writ) (IB 33 pts); AAB incl Engl (Engl Lit) (IB 33 pts HL 5 Engl)

Glasgow – AAB–BBB incl arts/hum/lang (Engl Lit) (IB 36–34 pts HL 665 incl 6 Engl/hum/ lang); AAB incl arts/hum/lang (Compar Lit Comb Hons) (IB 36 pts HL 665 incl 6 Engl/ hum/lang); (Scot Lit) (IB 36 pts HL 665 incl Engl+hum/lang)

Lancaster – AAB (Engl Lang Lit) (IB 35 pts)

Leeds – AAB (Class Lit courses) (IB 35 pts HL 16 pts)

London (King's) – AAB incl Engl (Compar Lit) (IB 35 pts HL 6 incl Engl lit); AAB incl Engl+lang (Compar Lit Film St) (IB 35 pts HL 665 incl Engl lit)

Sheffield – AAB–ABB+bEPQ incl Engl (Engl Lang Lit; Engl Lit) (IB 34 pts HL 6 Engl)

Sussex – AAB–ABB incl Engl (Engl Lang Lit) (IB 32 pts HL 6 Engl)

Warwick – AAB incl Engl (Film Lit) (IB 36 pts HL 5 Engl); AAB incl Engl lit+lang (Engl Ital Lit; Engl Ger) (IB 36 pts HL 5 Engl lit+lang)

128 pts **Bangor** – 128–112 pts incl Engl (Engl Lit Engl Lang)

Cardiff – ABB incl Engl (Jrnl Media Engl Lit) (HL 6 Engl); ABB incl Engl lit (Engl Lit) (HL 665)

East Anglia – ABB incl Engl (Engl Lit Comb Hons) (IB 33 pts HL 5 Engl); ABB incl Engl+hist (Lit Hist) (IB 32 pts HL 5 Engl+hist); ABB (Cult Lit Pol) (IB 32 pts HL 5 Engl)

Edinburgh – ABB incl Engl (Celt Scot Lit; Scot Lit) (IB 34 pts HL 655)

Kent – ABB incl Engl (Contemp Lit; Engl Am Postcol Lit) (IB 34 pts)

London (QM) – ABB incl Engl lit/Engl lang lit (Engl Lit Ling) (IB 32 pts HL 6 Engl); ABB incl hist (Hist Compar Lit) (IB 32 pts HL 655 incl hist)

London (RH) – ABB–BBB (Compar Lit Cult) (IB 32 pts HL 555)

Nottingham – ABB (Am Can Lit Hist Cult) (IB 32 pts)
Reading – ABB–BBB incl Engl (Engl Lang Lit) (IB 32–30 pts HL 5 Engl); ABB–BBB (Engl Lit Film Thea) (IB 32–30 pts)
Roehampton – 128 pts (Engl Lit)
Surrey – ABB incl Engl (Engl Lit; Engl Lit Crea Writ) (IB 32 pts)

120 pts **Aberdeen** – BBB (Engl Scot Lit) (IB 32 pts HL 555)
Aberystwyth – BBB–ABB incl Engl (Engl Lit Crea Writ; Engl Lit) (IB 30 pts HL 6 Engl lit)
Anglia Ruskin – 120 pts (Phil Engl Lit; Dr Engl Lit) (IB 24 pts); 120 pts incl Engl (Writ Engl Lit) (IB 24 pts)
Bangor – 120–104 pts (Ling Engl Lit)
Buckingham – BBB (Engl Lit) (IB 32 pts); BBB +interview (Engl Lit Hist) (IB 32 pts)
East London – 120 pts (Engl Lit) (IB 26 pts HL 15 pts)
Edge Hill – BBB 120 pts (Engl Lit)
Essex – BBB (Lit Art Hist; Film St Lit; Engl Lit; Engl Lang Lit) (IB 30 pts); BBB +workshop (Dr Lit) (IB 30 pts)
Huddersfield – BBB incl Engl 120 pts (Engl Lit; Engl Lit Crea Writ)
Hull – 120 pts (Engl Am Lit Cult) (IB 28 pts)
Kent – BBB incl Engl (Engl Lang Ling Engl Am Lit) (IB 34 pts); BBB (Compar Lit; Wrld Lit) (IB 34 pts)
Liverpool Hope – BBB–BBC incl Engl 120–112 pts (Engl Lit)
London (Gold) – BBB incl Engl (Engl Am Lit; Engl Compar Lit) (IB 33 pts)
London (QM) – BBB incl hum/soc sci (Ger Compar Lit) (IB 30 pts HL 5 hum/soc sci)
Northumbria – 120–128 pts (Engl Lit) (HL 444); 120–128 pts incl Engl (Jrnl Engl Lit; Engl Lang Lit; Engl Lit Crea Writ) (HL 444); 120–128 pts incl Engl/hist (Engl Lit Hist) (HL 444)
Sheffield Hallam – 120–104 pts (Engl Lit)
Swansea – BBB incl Engl (Engl Lit Lang) (IB 32 pts)
York – BBB (Engl Educ) (IB 31 pts)

112 pts **Birmingham City** – BBC incl Engl 112 pts (Engl Lit courses) (HL 14 pts)
Gloucestershire – BBC 112 pts (Engl Lit Crea Writ)
Greenwich – 112 pts (Engl Lit)
Hertfordshire – 112 pts (Engl Lit Fr; Engl Lit) (HL 44)
Kingston – 112 pts (Engl Lit)
Leeds Beckett – 112 pts (Engl Lit) (IB 25 pts)
London Met – BBC 112 pts (Engl Lit)
Sunderland – 112 pts (Engl Lang Lit)

104 pts **Bath Spa** – BCC incl Engl (Engl Lit) (IB 27 pts)
Brighton – BCC–CCC 104–96 pts +interview (Hist Lit Cult) (IB 27 pts); BCC–CCC incl Engl 104–96 pts (Engl Lit; Media Engl Lit) (IB 27 pts)
Central Lancashire – 104 pts (Engl Lit)
Manchester Met – 104–112 pts (Engl Am Lit) (IB 26 pts)
Westminster – BCC incl Engl/hum (Engl Lit Hist) (IB 28 pts HL 5 Engl)
Worcester – 104 pts (Engl Lit courses)

96 pts **Bishop Grosseteste** – 96–112 pts (Engl courses)
Portsmouth – 96–120 pts incl Engl (Engl Lit) (IB 26 pts)
Winchester – 96–112 pts (Engl Am Lit) (IB 25 pts)
York St John – 96–112 pts (Engl Lit; Crea Writ)

72 pts **UHI** – BC incl Engl (Lit)

Alternative offers
See **Chapter 6** and **Appendix 1** for grades/UCAS Tariff points information for other examinations.

CHOOSING YOUR COURSE (SEE ALSO CH.1)
Universities and colleges teaching quality See www.qaa.ac.uk; https://unistats.ac.uk.

Top research universities and colleges (REF 2014) See **English**.

Check **Chapter 3** for new university admission details and **Chapter 6** on how to read the subject tables.

ADMISSIONS INFORMATION

Number of applicants per place (approx) Bangor 4; East Anglia 5; Essex 4.

Advice to applicants and planning the UCAS personal statement See **English**. **Kent** An interest in literatures other than English.

Interview advice and questions See **English**. See also **Chapter 5**. **Kent** Which book would you take on a desert island, and why? What is the point of doing a Literature degree in the 21st century?

GRADUATE DESTINATIONS AND EMPLOYMENT (2015/16 HESA)

See **English**.

Career note Students enter a wide range of careers, with information management and editorial work in publishing offering some interesting and useful outlets. See also **English**, **Linguistics** and **Celtic, Irish, Scottish and Welsh Studies**.

MARINE/MARITIME STUDIES

(including **Marine Biology, Marine Geography** and **Oceanography**; see also **Environmental Sciences, Naval Architecture**)

A wide range of courses come under this category. These include Marine Business; Marine Law (world shipping, transport of goods, shipbroking, salvage rights, piracy); Marine Technology (marine engineering/nautical design); Marine Technology Offshore Engineering (marine structures, oil rigs, offshore engineering); Navigation Marine Science (merchant navy, yachts, superyachts); Naval Architecture with High Performance Crafts (design, construction, operation, large and small vessels, hydrofoils, hovercrafts); Shipping Port Management (international shipping, shipbroking, ship agency work) and Yacht and Powercraft Design (powerboats, yachts, superyachts). Other scientific courses cover marine applications with biology, chemistry, freshwater biology and geography.

Useful websites www.ukchamberofshipping.com; https://uksa.org; www.rya.org.uk; www.royalnavy. mod.uk; www.sstg.org; www.noc.ac.uk; www.nautinst.org; www.mcsuk.org; www.nmm-stena.com; www.imo.org; www.gov.uk/government/organisations/maritime-and-coastguard-agency; www.gov.uk/government/organisations/centre-for-environment-fisheries-and-aquaculture-science; www.mba.ac.uk

NB The points totals shown to the left of the institutions are for ease of reference only. It must not be assumed that Tariff points are always used by institutions or that they can be substituted for an offer in grades. The level of an offer is not necessarily indicative of the quality of a course.

COURSE OFFERS INFORMATION

Subject requirements/preferences GCSE Mathematics and science are required for several courses.
AL Science or mathematics will be required or preferred for some courses.

Your target offers and examples of degree courses

152 pts **Strathclyde** – A*AA incl maths+phys (Nvl Archit Ocn Eng (MEng)) (IB 36 pts HL 6 maths+phys)

144 pts **Newcastle** – AAA incl maths+phys/chem/fmaths (Mar Tech Off Eng (MEng)) (IB 37 pts HL 6 maths+phys/chem)

136 pts **Cardiff** – AAB incl sci/geog/maths (Mar Geog (Int) (MESci)) (IB 34 pts)

East Anglia – AAB incl maths (Meteor Ocean (MSci); Meteor Ocean (Yr Abrd)) (IB 33 pts HL 6 maths)

Glasgow – AAB incl biol/chem (Mar Frshwtr Biol) (IB 36 pts)

Newcastle – AAB–ABB incl biol+sci/maths (Mar Biol Ocean) (IB 35–34 pts HL 6 biol); AAB–ABB incl biol+sci (Mar Biol) (IB 35–34 pts HL 6 biol); AAB–ABB incl maths+phys/chem/fmaths (Mar Tech Mar Eng; Mar Tech Sml Crft Tech) (IB 35–34 pts HL 5 maths+phys/chem)

St Andrews – AAB incl biol+sci/maths (Mar Biol) (IB 36 pts)
Southampton – AAB incl sci/maths/geog +interview (Ocean Fr (MSci)); (Mar Biol (MSci)) (IB 34 pts)

128 pts **Bangor** – 128–112 pts incl sci/maths/geog (Ocn Sci; Geol Ocean; Mar Geog); 128–112 pts incl biol (App Mar Biol); 128–112 pts incl sci (Mar Env St)
Cardiff – ABB incl sci/geog/maths (Mar Geog (MESci)) (IB 32 pts)
East Anglia – ABB incl maths (Meteor Ocean) (IB 32 pts HL 5 maths)
Heriot-Watt – ABB (3 yr course) BBB (4 yr course) (Mar Biol) (IB 32 pts (3 yr course) 27 pts (4 yr course) HL 6 biol (3 yr course) 5 biol (4 yr course))
Liverpool – ABB incl sci (Ocn Sci) (IB 33 pts); ABB incl biol+sci/maths/geog (Mar Biol Ocean) (IB 33 pts HL 5 biol)
Plymouth – 128–144 pts incl biol+sci/maths/geog/psy (Mar Biol Cstl Ecol; Mar Biol Ocean) (IB 30 pts HL 5 biol+sci)
Southampton – ABB incl biol+sci/maths/geog +interview (Mar Biol Ocean) (IB 32 pts); ABB incl geog+sci/maths +interview (Ocean Physl Geog); ABB incl geog+sci/maths/env st +interview (Ocean Physl Geog) (IB 32 pts); ABB incl sci/maths/geog +interview (Ocean) (IB 32 pts)
Stirling – ABB (3 yr course) BBB (4 yr course) incl sci/maths (Mar Biol) (IB 35 pts (3 yr course) 32 pts (4 yr course))

120 pts **Aberdeen** – BBB incl maths/sci (Mar Biol) (IB 32 pts HL 5 maths/sci)
Bangor – 120 pts (App Trstl Mar Ecol); 120 pts incl biol (Physl Geog Ocean)
Cardiff – BBB incl sci/geog/maths (Mar Geog) (IB 30 pts)
Plymouth – 120 pts incl sci/maths/geog (Ocn Sci (MSci)) (IB 28 pts HL 5 sci/maths/geog)
Queen's Belfast – BBB–ABB incl biol/app sci (Mar Biol)
Strathclyde – BBB incl maths+phys (Nvl Archit Mar Eng; Nvl Archit Ocn Eng) (IB 32 pts HL 5 maths+phys)

112 pts **Aberystwyth** – BBC–BBB incl biol (Mar Frshwtr Biol) (IB 30 pts HL 5 biol)
Anglia Ruskin – 112 pts incl biol (Mar Biol Biodiv Cons) (IB 24 pts)
Hull – 112 pts incl biol/app sci (Mar Biol) (IB 28 pts HL 5 biol)
Liverpool John Moores – BBC incl maths+phys/eng/tech 112 pts (Mech Mar Eng) (IB 26 pts HL 5 maths+phys); BBC 112 pts (Marit Bus Mgt) (IB 26 pts)
Plymouth – 112 pts (Marit Bus Log; Marit Bus Marit Law) (IB 28 pts HL 4); 112–128 pts incl sci/maths/geog/psy/des tech (Ocn Explor Surv) (IB 26–28 pts HL 5 sci); 112–120 pts incl maths+sci/tech (Mar Tech) (IB 30 pts HL 5 maths 4 sci/tech)
Portsmouth – 112 pts incl biol (Mar Biol) (IB 30 pts HL 17 pts incl 6 biol)
Southampton Solent – 112 pts (Ycht Des Prod; Ship Pt Mgt)

104 pts **Edinburgh Napier** – BCC incl sci (Mar Frshwtr Biol) (IB 28 pts HL 5 sci)
Essex – BCC (Mar Biol) (IB 28 pts HL 5 biol)
Falmouth – 104–120 pts +portfolio +interview (Mar Nat Hist Photo)
Portsmouth – 104–120 pts incl sci/maths/geog (Mar Env Sci) (IB 26 pts HL 5 sci/maths/geog)
UHI – BCC incl sci (Mar Sci)

80 pts **Plymouth** – 80–112 pts incl sci (Navig Marit Sci) (IB 26 pts HL 5 sci)

Alternative offers
See **Chapter 6** and **Appendix 1** for grades/UCAS Tariff points information for other examinations.

EXAMPLES OF COLLEGES OFFERING COURSES IN THIS SUBJECT FIELD
Blackpool and Fylde (Coll); Cornwall (Coll); Plymouth City (Coll); South Devon (Coll); Southampton City (Coll); Sparsholt (Coll).

CHOOSING YOUR COURSE (SEE ALSO CH.1)
Universities and colleges teaching quality See www.qaa.ac.uk; https://unistats.ac.uk.

Examples of sandwich degree courses Anglia Ruskin; Bangor; Cardiff; Essex; Liverpool John Moores; Portsmouth; Southampton Solent.

ADMISSIONS INFORMATION

Number of applicants per place (approx) Bangor 4; Glasgow 2; Liverpool John Moores (Marit St) 3; Southampton 6.

Advice to applicants and planning the UCAS personal statement This is a specialised field and, in many cases, applicants will have experience of marine activities. Describe these experiences, for example, sailing, snorkelling, fishing. See also **Appendix 3**.

Selection interviews No Southampton, UHI.

Interview advice and questions Most applicants will have been stimulated by their studies in science or will have strong interests or connections with marine activities. They are likely to be questioned on their reasons for choosing the course. See also **Chapter 5**.

AFTER-RESULTS ADVICE

Offers to applicants repeating A-levels Same Bangor, Liverpool John Moores, Plymouth, UHI.

GRADUATE DESTINATIONS AND EMPLOYMENT (2015/16 HESA)

Maritime Technology graduates surveyed 215 **Employed** 140 **In voluntary employment** 0 **In further study** 40 **Assumed unemployed** 15

Career note This subject area covers a wide range of vocational courses, each offering graduates an equally wide choice of career openings in either purely scientific or very practical areas.

OTHER DEGREE SUBJECTS FOR CONSIDERATION

Biology; Civil Engineering; Environmental Studies/Sciences; Geography; Marine Engineering; Marine Transport; Naval Architecture; Oceanography.

MARKETING

(including **Public Relations**; see also **Business and Management Courses, Business and Management Courses (International and European), Business and Management Courses (Specialised), Retail Management**)

Marketing courses are very popular and applications should include evidence of work experience or work shadowing. Whilst marketing is also a subject included in all Business Studies courses, specialist marketing courses are also available focussing on Advertising (also included in Marketing and Graphic Design courses), Agriculture, Consumer Behaviour, Design, Fashion, Food, Leisure, Retail and Sport.

Useful websites www.adassoc.org.uk; www.cim.co.uk; www.camfoundation.com; www.ipa.co.uk; www.ipsos.com/ipsos-mori/en-uk; www.marketingtoday.com

NB The points totals shown to the left of the institutions are for ease of reference only. It must not be assumed that Tariff points are always used by institutions or that they can be substituted for an offer in grades. The level of an offer is not necessarily indicative of the quality of a course.

COURSE OFFERS INFORMATION

Subject requirements/preferences GCSE English and mathematics. **AL** No specified subjects required.

Your target offers and examples of degree courses
144 pts **Exeter** – AAA–AAB (Mgt Mark) (IB 36–34 pts)
Leeds – AAA (Mgt Mark) (IB 35 pts HL 17 pts)
136 pts **Aston** – AAB–ABB (Mark) (IB 32 pts)
Cardiff – AAB (Bus Mgt (Mark)) (IB 35–32 pts)

UCAS points Tariff: A* = 56 pts; A = 48 pts; B = 40 pts; C = 32 pts; D = 24 pts; E = 16 pts

Durham – AAB (Mark Mgt) (IB 36 pts)
Lancaster – AAB (Adv Mark; Mark; Mark Mgt; Mark Des; Mark (St Abrd); Mark Mgt (St Abrd)) (IB 35 pts HL 16 pts)
Loughborough – AAB (Rtl Mark Mgt) (IB 35 pts HL 665)
Manchester – AAB +interview (Fash Mark) (IB 35 pts HL 665); AAB (Mgt (Mark)) (IB 35 pts HL 665)
Newcastle – AAB (Mark; Mark Mgt) (IB 35 pts)
Reading – AAB–ABB (Consum Bhv Mark) (IB 34–32 pts)
Southampton – AAB/ABB+aEPQ (Mark (Yr Ind)) (IB 34 pts HL 17 pts)
Sussex – AAB–ABB (Mark Mgt) (IB 32 pts)
Ulster – AAB–AAA (Comm Adv Mark) (IB 28–29 pts HL 14 pts)
128 pts **Coventry** – ABB (Mark) (IB 31 pts); ABB–BBB (Adv Mark) (IB 31–30 pts)
Heriot-Watt – ABB (3 yr course) BBB (4 yr course) (Int Bus Mgt Mark) (IB 34 pts (3 yr course) 29 pts (4 yr course))
Kent – ABB (Mark) (IB 34 pts)
Liverpool – ABB (Mark) (IB 33 pts)
London (RH) – ABB (Mgt Mark) (IB 32 pts HL 655)
Northumbria – 128–136 pts +interview +portfolio (Fash Des Mark) (HL 444); 128–136 pts (Mark Mgt) (HL 444)
Reading – ABB–BBB (Fd Mark Bus Econ) (IB 32–30 pts)
Stirling – ABB (3 yr course) BBB (4 yr course) (Mark; Rtl Mark) (IB 35 pts (3 yr course) 32 pts (4 yr course))
Strathclyde – ABB (Mark courses) (IB 36 pts)
Swansea – ABB–BBB (Bus Mgt (Mark); Mark) (IB 33–32 pts)
120 pts **Bournemouth Arts** – BBB 120 pts (Fash Brnd Comm) (IB 30 pts)
Bradford – BBB 120 pts (Mark)

Check **Chapter 3** for new university admission details and **Chapter 6** on how to read the subject tables.

Buckingham – BBB–BBC (Mark Span; Mark Fr) (IB 32–31 pts); BBB–BBC +interview (Mark Media Comms) (IB 32–31 pts)

Dundee – BBB–BCC (Bus Econ Mark Hist; Int Bus Mark; Bus Econ Mark) (IB 30 pts HL 555)

Edge Hill – BBB 120 pts (Mark; Adv)

Edinburgh Napier – BBB (3 yr course) CCC (4 yr course) (Mark Mgt; Mark Dig Media) (IB 27 pts HL 654)

Essex – BBB (Mark; Mgt Mark) (IB 30 pts)

Greenwich – 120 pts (Adv Dig Mark Comm Lang; Adv Dig Mark Comms)

Huddersfield – BBB 120 pts (Adv Mark Comm; Mark; Mark PR); BBB 120 pts +interview +portfolio (Fash Brnd Mark)

Liverpool Hope – BBB–BBC 120–112 pts (Mark) (IB 26 pts)

Middlesex – 120 pts (Adv PR Brnd) (IB 28 pts)

Northumbria – 120–128 pts (Bus Mark Mgt) (HL 444)

Nottingham Trent – BBB 120 pts (Mark; Fash Mark Brnd; Fash Comm Prom)

Oxford Brookes – BBB 120 pts (Bus Mark Mgt) (IB 31 pts)

Queen Margaret – BBB (3 yr course) BCC (4 yr course) (PR Mark Evnts) (IB 28 pts)

Southampton (Winchester SA) – BBB (Fash Mark) (IB 30 pts HL 16 pts)

Trinity Saint David – 120 pts +interview +portfolio (Adv Brnd Des) (IB 32 pts)

Ulster – BBB (HR Mgt; Law Mark) (IB 26 pts HL 13 pts); BBB–ABB (Mark) (IB 26–27 pts HL 13 pts)

UWE Bristol – 120 pts (Mark Comm Mgt) (IB 26 pts)

Westminster – BBB (PR Adv) (IB 28 pts HL 5 Engl)

112 pts   **Aberystwyth** – BBC (Mark) (IB 28 pts)

Birmingham City – BBC 112 pts (Mark; Mark Adv PR)

Bournemouth – 112–120 pts (Adv) (IB 30–31 pts HL 55); 112–128 pts (Mark) (IB 30–32 pts HL 55)

Cardiff Met – 112 pts (Mark Mgt)

Central Lancashire – 112 pts (Mark Mgt)

Chester – BBC–BCC 112 pts (Mark Mgt) (IB 26 pts)

Chichester – BBC–CCC (Mark) (IB 28 pts)

Coventry – BBC (Spo Mark) (IB 29 pts)

Creative Arts – 112 pts (Adv); 112 pts +interview (Fash Mgt Mark); 112 pts +portfolio (Fash Prom Imag)

De Montfort – 112 pts (Int Mark Bus) (IB 24 pts); (Mark; Adv Mark Comms) (IB 26 pts)

East London – 112 pts (Mark) (IB 25 pts); 112 pts +interview +portfolio (Fash Mark) (IB 24 pts HL 15 pts)

Gloucestershire – BBC 112 pts (Adv)

Greenwich – 112 pts (Mark Mgt)

Hull – 112 pts (Mark) (IB 30 pts)

Keele – BBC (Mark Comb Hons) (IB 30 pts)

Leeds Arts – BBC incl art/des 112 pts +portfolio (Crea Adv)

Leeds Beckett – 112 pts (Mark; Mark Adv Mgt) (IB 25 pts)

Liverpool John Moores – BBC 112 pts (Mark) (IB 26 pts); (Bus PR) (IB 28 pts)

London Met – BBC 112 pts (Fash Mark Jrnl)

Middlesex – 112 pts (Mark)

Plymouth – 112 pts (Mark) (IB 28 pts HL 4)

Portsmouth – 112 pts (Mark; Mark Psy) (IB 30 pts HL 17 pts)

Robert Gordon – BBC (Mgt Mark) (IB 29 pts)

Roehampton – 112 pts (Mark)

St Mary's – 112 pts (Comm Media Mark)

Sheffield Hallam – 112 pts (Mark; Mark Comms Adv; Bus Mark)

Southampton Solent – 112 pts (Mark; Adv; PR Comm; Mark Adv Mgt)

Staffordshire – BBC 112 pts +interview (Mark Mgt)

Sunderland – 112 pts (Bus Mark Mgt); 112 pts +portfolio (Adv Des; Fash Prod Prom)

West London – BBC 112 pts (Bus St Mark; Fash Brnd Mark)

 Westminster – BBC (Mark Mgt; Bus Mgt (Mark); Mark Comms) (IB 28 pts)
 Wolverhampton – BBC–CCC (Mark Mgt)
 Worcester – 112 pts (Mark Adv PR)
104 pts **Bath Spa** – BCC–CCC (Bus Mgt (Mark)) (IB 28 pts)
 Brighton – BCC–CCC 104–96 pts (Mark Mgt) (IB 28 pts HL 16 pts)
 Chester – BCC–CCC 104 pts (Mark Adv Mgt) (IB 26 pts)
 Falmouth – 104–120 pts +interview (Crea Adv)
 Glasgow Caledonian – BCC (Int Mark) (IB 25 pts)
 Lincoln – BCC (Adv Mark; Mark Mgt; Bus Mark) (IB 28 pts)
 London South Bank – BCC (Bus Mgt Mark; Mark)
 Manchester Met – BCC–BBC 104–112 pts (Dig Media Mark; Spo Mark Mgt; PR Mark; Int Fash
  Prom; Mark Mgt; Rtl Mgt Mark) (IB 26 pts)
 Northampton – BCC (Psy Mark Comb Hons; Fash Mark; Evnts Mgt Comb Hons; Adv Comb
  Hons); BCC 104 pts (Mark Comb Hons)
 South Wales – BCC–CCD (Fash Mark Rtl Des) (HL 655–445); BCC–CDD incl art des +interview
  +portfolio (Adv Des) (HL 655–445); BCC–CDD 104–80 pts (Mark) (HL 655–445); BCC–CCD
  incl art des +interview +portfolio (Fash Prom) (HL 655–445)
 Winchester – 104–120 pts (Media Comm Adv) (IB 26 pts)
96 pts **Abertay** – CCC (Mark Bus) (IB 28 pts)
 Anglia Ruskin – 96–112 pts (Mark) (IB 24 pts)
 Bedfordshire – 96 pts (Mark)
 Birmingham (UC) – 96 pts (Mark Mgt)
 Derby – 96–112 pts (Mark courses; Mark (PR Adv))
 Hertfordshire – 96–112 pts (Mark; Mark Adv)
 London Met – CCC/BC 96 pts (Fash Mark Bus Mgt); CCC 96 pts (Adv Mark Comms PR)
 Plymouth (CA) – 96–120 pts +interview +portfolio (Crea Adv Brnd)
 York St John – 96–112 pts (Mark Mgt; Tour Mgt Mark)
88 pts **Canterbury Christ Church** – 88–112 pts (Mark; Adv)
 Harper Adams – 88–104 pts +interview (Bus Mgt Mark); 88–104 pts (Agri-Fd Mark Bus)
 Trinity Saint David – 88 pts +interview (Bus Mgt (Mark))
80 pts **Bedfordshire** – 80 pts (PR; Adv Mark Comms)
 Bucks New – 80–96 pts (Mark)
 Teesside – 80–96 pts (Mark)
64 pts **Ravensbourne** – CC +interview +portfolio (Fash Prom) (IB 28 pts)

Alternative offers
See **Chapter 6** and **Appendix 1** for grades/UCAS Tariff points information for other examinations.

EXAMPLES OF COLLEGES OFFERING COURSES IN THIS SUBJECT FIELD
Arts London (CFash); Bath (Coll); Birmingham Met (Coll); Blackpool and Fylde (Coll); Bradford (Coll);
Croydon (Univ Centre); Doncaster (Coll); ESE; Grimsby (Inst Group); Kensington Bus (Coll); Leeds
City (Coll); Loughborough (Coll); LSST; Manchester (Coll); Newcastle (Coll); Nottingham (Coll);
Pearson (Coll); Petroc; Plymouth City (Coll); South City Birmingham (Coll); South Essex (Coll);
Yeovil (Coll).

CHOOSING YOUR COURSE (SEE ALSO CH.1)
Universities and colleges teaching quality See www.qaa.ac.uk; https://unistats.ac.uk.

Examples of sandwich degree courses Aston; Bath Spa; Bedfordshire; Birmingham City;
Bournemouth; Bradford; Cardiff Met; Central Lancashire; Chester; Chichester; Coventry; De Montfort;
Derby; Durham; Greenwich; Harper Adams; Hertfordshire; Huddersfield; Lancaster; Leeds Beckett;
Liverpool John Moores; London (RH); London South Bank; Loughborough; Manchester Met; Newcastle;
Northumbria; Nottingham Trent; Oxford Brookes; Portsmouth; Sheffield Hallam; Southampton Solent;
Staffordshire; Sussex; Teesside; Trinity Saint David; Ulster; UWE Bristol; Westminster; Wolverhampton;
Worcester.

ADMISSIONS INFORMATION

Number of applicants per place (approx) Abertay 3; Anglia Ruskin 5; Aston 9; Birmingham City 4; Central Lancashire 13; De Montfort 3; Derby 4; Harper Adams 3; Huddersfield 4; Lancaster 5; Lincoln 3; London Met 10; Manchester 7; Northampton 4; Nottingham Trent 2; Plymouth 7; Staffordshire 6; Stirling 13; Teesside 3.

Advice to applicants and planning the UCAS personal statement See **Business and Management Courses** and **Appendix 3**.

Misconceptions about this course Bournemouth This course is not restricted to advertising but covers a much wider field.

Selection interviews Yes Buckingham; **No** Aberystwyth, Anglia Ruskin, Aston, De Montfort, Essex, Harper Adams, Manchester Met, Middlesex, Staffordshire.

Interview advice and questions Past questions include: What is marketing? Why do you want to take a Marketing degree? Is sales pressure justified? How would you feel if you had to market a product which you considered to be inferior? See also **Chapter 5**. **Buckingham** What job do you see yourself doing in five years' time?

Reasons for rejection (non-academic) Little thought of reasons for deciding on a Marketing degree. Weak on numeracy and problem solving. Limited commercial awareness. Poor interpersonal skills. Lack of leadership potential. No interest in widening their horizons, either geographically or intellectually. 'We look at appearance, motivation and the applicant's ability to ask questions.' Not hungry enough. Limited understanding of the career. No clear reasons for wishing to do the course.

AFTER-RESULTS ADVICE

Offers to applicants repeating A-levels Same Abertay, Aberystwyth, Anglia Ruskin, Aston, Buckingham, De Montfort, Lincoln, Manchester Met, Queen Margaret, Staffordshire.

GRADUATE DESTINATIONS AND EMPLOYMENT (2015/16 HESA)

Graduates surveyed 3,190 **Employed** 2,205 **In voluntary employment** 100 **In further study** 300 **Assumed unemployed** 170

Career note See **Business and Management Courses**.

OTHER DEGREE SUBJECTS FOR CONSIDERATION

Advertising; Art and Design; Business courses; Communications; Graphic Design; Psychology; Public Relations.

MATERIALS SCIENCE/METALLURGY

Materials Science is a broad subject which covers physics, chemistry and engineering at one and the same time! From its origins in metallurgy, materials science has now moved into the processing, structure and properties of materials – ceramics, polymers, composites and electrical materials. Materials science and metallurgy are perhaps the most misunderstood of all careers and applications for degree courses are low with very reasonable offers. Valuable bursaries and scholarships are offered by the Institute of Materials, Minerals and Mining (check with Institute – see **Appendix 3**). Polymer science is a branch of materials science and is often studied in conjunction with chemistry. It covers such topics as polymer properties and processing relating to industrial applications with, for example, plastics, paints, adhesives. Other courses under this heading include Fashion and Leather Technology. See also **Appendix 3**.

Useful websites www.eef.org.uk/uksteel; www.iom3.org; www.epsrc.ac.uk; www.imm.org; www.icme.org.uk

NB The points totals shown to the left of the institutions are for ease of reference only. It must not be assumed that Tariff points are always used by institutions or that they can be substituted for an offer in grades. The level of an offer is not necessarily indicative of the quality of a course.

COURSE OFFERS INFORMATION

Subject requirements/preferences GCSE (Eng/Sci courses) Science/mathematics subjects. **AL** Mathematics, physics and/or chemistry required for most courses. (Poly Sci) Mathematics and/or physics usually required; design technology encouraged.

Your target offers and examples of degree courses

160 pts Cambridge – A*A*A incl sci/maths +interview +NSAA (Nat Sci (Mat Sci)) (IB 40–42 pts HL 776)

152 pts Imperial London – A*AA–A*A*A incl maths+phys+chem +interview (Mat Mgt; Mat Nucl Eng; Mat Sci Eng; Biomat Tiss Eng (MEng)) (IB 38–40 pts HL 6 maths+phys+chem)

Oxford – A*AA incl maths+phys +interview +PAT (Mat Sci) (IB 40 pts HL 766 incl 7 maths+phys/chem)

Southampton – A*AA–A*AB+aEPQ incl maths+phys (Mech Eng (Advnc Mat) (MEng)) (IB 38 pts HL 6 maths+phys)

144 pts Birmingham – AAA incl maths+phys/chem/des tech (Mat Sci Eng (MEng)) (IB 32 pts HL 666)

Exeter – AAA–ABB (Mat Eng (Yr Ind)) (IB 36–32 pts); AAA–ABB incl maths+sci (Mat Eng; Mat Eng (MEng)) (IB 36–32 pts HL 5 maths+sci)

London (QM) – AAA incl maths/phys/chem (Mat Sci Eng (MEng) (Yr Ind)) (IB 36 pts HL 665); (Dntl Mat (MEng)) (IB 36 pts HL 666)

Loughborough – AAA incl maths/phys/chem +interview (Mat Sci Eng (MEng)) (IB 37 pts HL 666); AAA incl maths/phys/chem (Auto Mat (MEng)) (IB 37 pts HL 666)

Sheffield – AAA–AAB+bEPQ incl sci/maths (Biomat Sci Eng (MEng)) (IB 36 pts HL 6 sci/maths); AAA incl maths/phys/chem (Mat Sci Eng (MEng); Metal (MEng)) (IB 36 pts HL 6 maths/phys/chem)

Southampton – AAB–AAB+aEPQ (Ship Sci (Advncd Mat) (MEng)) (IB 36 pts HL 6 maths+phys)

Swansea – AAA–AAB (Mat Sci Eng (MEng)) (IB 34–33 pts)

136 pts Birmingham – AAB incl maths+phys/chem/des tech (Metal) (IB 32 pts HL 665); AAB incl maths+phys (Nucl Sci Mat) (IB 32 pts HL 665)

Exeter – AAB–BBB incl phys/chem+sci (Min Eng) (IB 34–30 pts HL 5 phys/chem/maths+sci)

Manchester – AAB incl maths/phys/chem +interview (Mat Sci Eng) (IB 35 pts HL 665)

St Andrews – AAB incl chem (Mat Chem) (IB 35 pts)

Sheffield – AAB incl maths/phys/chem (Mat Sci Eng) (IB 34 pts HL 6 maths/phys/chem); AAB incl sci/maths (Biomat Sci Eng) (IB 34 pts HL 6 sci/maths)

Swansea – AAB–BBB (Mat Sci Eng) (IB 34 pts)

128 pts Heriot-Watt – ABB incl chem+maths (3 yr course) BBB incl chem (4 yr course) (Chem Mat Nanosci) (IB 35 pts (3 yr course) 30 pts (4 yr course) HL 6 chem+maths (3 yr course) 5 chem (4 yr course))

London (QM) – ABB incl sci/maths/des tech (Mat Des) (IB 32 pts HL 655); ABB incl maths/phys/chem (Mat Sci Eng; Dntl Mat) (IB 32 pts HL 655)

Loughborough – ABB incl maths/phys/chem +interview (Mat Sci Eng; Auto Mat) (IB 34 pts HL 655); ABB incl maths+sci +interview (Biomat Eng) (IB 34 pts HL 655)

120 pts Strathclyde – BBB incl maths+physics (Mech Eng Mat Eng (MEng)) (IB 36 pts HL 6 maths+phys)

112 pts Sheffield Hallam – 112–96 pts (Mat Eng)

96 pts Chichester – CCC–BBC 96–112 pts (Biomed Mat Eng)

88 pts Northampton – CCD incl physl sci (Lea Tech (Lea Sci/Mark/Bus))

Check **Chapter 3** for new university admission details and **Chapter 6** on how to read the subject tables.

Alternative offers
See **Chapter 6** and **Appendix 1** for grades/UCAS Tariff points information for other examinations.

EXAMPLES OF COLLEGES OFFERING COURSES IN THIS SUBJECT FIELD
Hereford (CA).

CHOOSING YOUR COURSE (SEE ALSO CH.1)
Universities and colleges teaching quality See www.qaa.ac.uk; https://unistats.ac.uk.

Top research universities and colleges (REF 2014) See **Engineering (Electrical and Electronic)**.

Examples of sandwich degree courses Exeter; London (QM); Loughborough; St Andrews; Sheffield Hallam.

ADMISSIONS INFORMATION
Number of applicants per place (approx) Birmingham 8; Imperial London 3; Southampton 8; Swansea 4.

Advice to applicants and planning the UCAS personal statement Read scientific and engineering journals and describe any special interests you have. Try to visit chemical or technological installations (rubber, plastics, glass, etc) and describe your visits. See also **Appendix 3**.

Misconceptions about this course Students are generally unaware of what this subject involves or the opportunities within the industry.

Selection interviews Yes Imperial London, Oxford (22%); **No** Birmingham.

Interview advice and questions Questions are likely to be based on AS/A-level science subjects. Recent examples include: Why did you choose Materials Science? How would you make each part of this table lamp (on the interviewer's desk)? Identify this piece of material. How was it manufactured? How has it been treated? (Questions related to metal and polymer samples.) What would you consider the major growth area in materials science? See also **Chapter 5**. **Oxford** Tutors look for an ability to apply logical reasoning to problems in physical science and an enthusiasm for thinking about new concepts in science and engineering.

AFTER-RESULTS ADVICE
Offers to applicants repeating A-levels Higher Swansea; **Same** Birmingham; **No** Cambridge.

GRADUATE DESTINATIONS AND EMPLOYMENT (2015/16 HESA)
Metallurgy graduates surveyed 15 **Employed** 0 **In voluntary employment** 0 **In further study** 5 **Assumed unemployed** 0

Polymers and Textiles graduates surveyed 110 **Employed** 85 **In voluntary employment** 5 **In further study** 5 **Assumed unemployed** 10

Materials Science graduates surveyed 35 **Employed** 15 **In voluntary employment** 0 **In further study** 10 **Assumed unemployed** 0

Career note Materials scientists are involved in a wide range of specialisms in which openings are likely in a range of industries. These include manufacturing processes in which the work is closely linked with that of mechanical, chemical, production and design engineers.

OTHER DEGREE SUBJECTS FOR CONSIDERATION
Aerospace Engineering; Biotechnology; Chemistry; Dentistry; Engineering Sciences; Mathematics; Mechanical Engineering; Medical Engineering; Plastics Technology; Physics; Product Design and Materials; Prosthetics and Orthotics; Sports Technology.

MATHEMATICS

(including Mathematical Sciences; see also Economics, Statistics)

Mathematics at degree level is an extension of A-level mathematics, covering pure and applied mathematics, statistics, computing, mathematical analysis and mathematical applications. Mathematics is of increasing importance and is used in the simplest of design procedures and not only in applications in the physical sciences and engineering. It also plays a key role in management, economics, medicine and the social and behavioural sciences.

Useful websites www.ima.org.uk; www.theorsociety.com; www.m-a.org.uk; www.mathscareers.org. uk; www.imo-official.org; http://bmos.ukmt.org.uk; http://maths.org; www.ukmt.org.uk

NB The points totals shown to the left of the institutions are for ease of reference only. It must not be assumed that Tariff points are always used by institutions or that they can be substituted for an offer in grades. The level of an offer is not necessarily indicative of the quality of a course.

COURSE OFFERS INFORMATION

Subject requirements/preferences GCSE English often required and mathematics is obviously essential at a high grade for leading universities. **AL** Mathematics, in several cases with a specified grade, required for all courses. **Other** Mathematics AEA or STEP papers may be required by some universities (eg Imperial, Warwick). See also **Chapter 4**. NB The level of an offer may depend on whether an applicant is taking AS/A-level further maths; check websites.

Your target offers and examples of degree courses

168 pts Warwick – A*A*A*–A*AA incl maths (Maths Comb Hons; MORSE) (IB 38 pts HL 7 maths); A*A*A* incl maths+fmaths (Maths (MMath); Maths) (IB 39 pts HL 766–666)

160 pts Bristol – A*A*A-AAA incl maths+fmaths/sci/econ/comp (Maths Stats) (IB 40–36 pts HL 6 maths+sci/econ/comp); A*A*A-AAA incl maths+fmaths/sci/econ/comp sci (Maths) (IB 40–36 pts HL 6 maths+sci/econ/comp sci); A*A*A-AAB incl maths+fmaths (Maths Comp Sci) (IB 40–36 pts HL 6 maths)

Cambridge – A*A*A incl maths +interview +STEP (Maths; Maths Phys) (IB 40–42 pts HL 776)

Durham – A*A*A incl maths+fmaths (Maths) (IB 38 pts)

Imperial London – A*A*A incl maths+fmaths +interview (Maths Comp Sci) (IB 41–43 pts HL 7 maths); A*A*A A*A*A* incl maths+fmaths +interview (Maths Mathem Comput) (IB 39–41 pts HL 7 maths 6 phys/chem/econ); A*A*A-A*A*A* incl maths+fmaths +MAT/ STEP (Maths Stats; Maths; PMaths; Maths Optim Stats; Maths Stats Fin) (IB 39–41 pts HL 7 maths 6 phys/chem/econ)

London (UCL) – A*A*A-A*AA incl maths+fmaths (Maths) (IB 40–39 pts HL 7 maths)

Manchester – A*A*A-A*AA incl phys+maths +interview (Maths Phys) (IB 37 pts HL 776–766)

Oxford – A*A*A incl maths +interview +MAT (Maths Stats) (IB 39 pts HL 766 incl 7 maths); (Maths; Maths Phil) (IB 39 pts HL 766)

152 pts Bath – A*AA-AAA+aEPQ incl maths+phys (Maths Phys) (IB 36 pts HL 766); A*AA incl maths (Mathem Sci) (IB 36 pts HL 765–666 incl 7/6 maths)

Bristol – A*AA-AAB incl maths (Maths Phil) (IB 38–34 pts HL 6 maths)

Edinburgh – A*AA incl maths+phys (Mathem Phys) (IB 37 pts HL 666); A*AA incl maths (Maths Stats) (IB 37 pts HL 6 maths); A*AA-AAB (Maths; Maths Mgt; Maths (MA); Maths Mus) (IB 37 pts HL 666); A*AA-AAB incl maths (App Maths) (IB 37 pts HL 666)

Exeter – A*AA-AAB incl maths (Maths; Maths Acc; Maths Fin; Maths Econ; Maths Mgt) (IB 38–34 pts HL 6 maths); A*AA-AAB incl maths+phys +interview (Maths Phys) (IB 38–34 pts HL 6 maths/phys)

London (UCL) – A*AA incl maths +interview (Mathem Comput (MEng)) (IB 39 pts HL 7 maths)

London LSE – A*AA incl maths (Ecomet Mathem Econ; Maths Econ) (IB 38 pts HL 766 incl 7 maths)

Manchester – A*AA–AAA incl maths +interview (Maths Fin; Maths Fin Maths) (IB 34 pts HL 6 maths); A*AA–AAA incl maths (Maths; Act Sci Maths; Maths Phil) (IB 34 pts HL 6 maths); A*AA incl maths +interview (Comp Sci Maths) (IB 38 pts HL 766)

Nottingham – A*AA–AAA incl maths+phys (Mathem Phys) (IB 36 pts HL 6 maths+phys); A*AA–AAA/A*AB incl maths (Maths; Fin Maths) (IB 36 pts HL 6 maths)

St Andrews – A*AA (Anc Hist Maths) (IB 36 pts); A*AA incl maths (Maths Langs; Arbc Maths) (IB 36 pts HL 6 maths); (Maths Span; App Maths; PMaths (MMath)) (IB 36 pts)

Southampton – A*AA–AAB incl maths (Maths; Maths (MMath)) (IB 37 pts HL 6 maths)

Surrey – A*AA–AAA incl maths (Maths (MMath)) (IB 36 pts HL 6 maths)

Warwick – A*AA incl maths/fmaths (Dscrt Maths) (IB 38 pts HL 666)

144 pts **Birmingham** – AAA incl maths (Maths; Maths Bus Mgt) (IB 32 pts HL 666)

Bristol – AAA–ABB incl maths (Eng Maths) (IB 36–32 pts HL 6 maths)

Cardiff – AAA–A*BB incl maths (Maths; Maths OR Stats) (IB 36–34 pts HL 6 maths)

Glasgow – AAA/A*AB incl maths (Acc Maths) (IB 38 pts HL 666 incl maths)

Lancaster – AAA (Maths OR Stats Econ (MORSE)) (IB 36 pts HL 16 pts); AAA incl maths/fmaths (Maths Stats) (IB 36 pts HL 6 maths); AAA–AAB incl maths/fmaths (Fin Maths) (IB 36 pts HL 16 pts incl 6 maths); (Maths) (IB 36 pts HL 6 maths)

Leeds – AAA/A*AB–AAB/A*BB incl maths (Maths Fin) (IB 35 pts HL 17 pts incl 6 maths); (Maths Stats; Maths) (IB 35 pts HL 6 maths); AAA–A*AB incl maths/AAB–A*BB incl maths+fmaths (Act Maths) (IB 35 pts HL 17 pts incl 6 maths)

London (King's) – AAA incl maths+fmaths (Maths) (IB 35 pts HL 666); (Maths Phil) (IB 35 pts HL 666)

London (QM) – AAA incl maths (Maths Stats Fin Econ; Maths MSci) (IB 36 pts HL 6 maths)

London (UCL) – AAA–AAB incl maths+chem +interview (Chem Maths) (IB 38–36 pts HL 6 maths 5 chem)

Loughborough – AAA incl maths (Maths Mgt) (IB 37 pts HL 6 maths); (Maths Maths Educ) (IB 37 pts HL 666 incl 6 maths); (Maths) (IB 37 pts HL 666)

Newcastle – AAA/A*AB–AAB/A*BB incl maths (Maths (MMath)) (IB 37 pts HL 6 maths); (Maths; Maths Stats) (IB 37–35 pts HL 6 maths); AAA–AAB/A*AB–A*BB incl maths (Maths Mgt) (IB 37–35 pts HL 6 maths); AAA–A*AB incl maths (Maths Fin) (IB 37–35 pts HL 6 maths)

Nottingham – AAA–AAB incl comp (Comp Sci) (IB 34–32 pts)

Queen's Belfast – AAA/A*AB incl maths (Maths Comp Sci (MSci); Maths (MSci); Maths Stats OR (MSci); App Maths Phys (MSci))

St Andrews – AAA (Maths) (IB 36 pts)

Sheffield – AAA/AAB+aEPQ incl maths (Maths (MMath)) (IB 36 pts HL 6 maths)

Southampton – AAA/AAB+aEPQ incl maths (Maths Act Sci) (IB 36 pts HL 6 maths); AAA incl maths+phys (Phys Maths (MPhys)) (IB 36 pts HL 6 maths+phys); (Maths Phys (MMath)) (IB 37 pts HL 6 maths+phys); AAA–AAB incl maths+mus (Maths Mus) (IB 36 pts HL 6 maths); AAA–AAB+aEPQ incl maths+Fr/Ger/Span (Maths Fr/Ger/Span) (IB 36 pts HL 6 maths); AAA–AAB+aEPQ incl maths (Maths Stats; Maths OR Stats Econ; Maths Fin; Maths Comp Sci) (IB 36 pts HL 6 maths)

Strathclyde – AAA–ABB (Maths courses) (IB 36–32 pts)

Surrey – AAA–AAB incl maths (Fin Maths) (IB 34 pts HL 6 maths); (Maths courses) (IB 36–35 pts); AAA incl maths (Maths Stats) (IB 34 pts)

Sussex – AAA incl maths+fmaths (Maths (MMath)) (IB 35 pts HL 6 maths)

Swansea – AAA incl maths (Maths (MMath)) (IB 36 pts HL 6 maths)

York – AAA–AAB incl maths (Maths; Maths Stats) (IB 36 pts HL 6 maths); AAA incl maths (Econ Maths; Maths Fin) (IB 36 pts HL 6 maths)

136 pts **City** – AAB incl maths/fmaths 136 pts (Maths Fin; Maths) (IB 34 pts HL 6 maths)

East Anglia – AAB–ABB incl maths (Maths (MMath); Maths) (IB 33 pts HL 6 maths)

Glasgow – AAB incl maths (Maths) (IB 36 pts HL 665 incl 6 sci)

Heriot-Watt – AAB (3 yr course) ABB (4 yr course) incl maths (Maths Comb Hons; Maths) (IB 30 pts (3 yr course) 28 pts (4 yr course) HL 6 maths (3 yr course) 5 maths (4 yr course))

Kent – AAB incl maths (Fin Maths; Maths) (IB 34 pts)

Lancaster – AAB incl maths (Acc Fin Maths) (IB 35 pts HL 16 pts incl 6 maths); AAB–ABB incl maths/fmaths (Maths Phil) (IB 35 pts HL 6 maths); AAB incl phys+maths (Theor Phys Maths) (IB 35 pts HL 16 pts)

Leicester – AAB/ABB+bEPQ incl maths (Maths) (IB 32 pts HL 6 maths)

Liverpool – AAB incl maths (Maths Fin) (IB 35 pts HL 6 maths); AAB/ABB+aEPQ incl maths+phys (Mathem Phys (MMath)) (IB 35 pts HL 6 maths+phys)

London (QM) – AAB incl maths (Maths Fin Acc; Maths) (IB 34 pts HL 6/5 maths); (Maths Stats) (IB 34 pts HL 6/5 maths)

London (RH) AAB ABB incl maths (Econ Maths; Maths) (IB 32 pts HL 6 maths); (Maths Stats) (IB 32 pts HL 6 maths)

Reading – AAB–ABB incl maths (Maths; Maths Stats; Maths Meteor; Comput Maths) (IB 34–32 pts HL 6 maths)

Sheffield – AAB incl maths (Fin Maths) (IB 34 pts HL 6 maths); AAB/ABB+bEPQ incl maths (Maths; Comp Sci Maths; Maths Comb Hons) (IB 34 pts HL 6 maths)

Southampton – AAB–ABB+aEPQ incl maths (Phil Maths) (IB 34–32 pts HL 6 maths)

Sussex – AAB–ABB incl maths (Maths Econ; Maths courses) (IB 32 pts HL 5 maths)

Swansea – AAB–BBB incl maths (Maths) (IB 34–32 pts HL 6 maths)

York – AAB incl maths+phys +interview (Maths Phys) (IB 36 pts HL 6 maths+phys)

128 pts **Aston** – ABB–AAB incl maths (Maths; Maths Comb Hons) (IB 32 pts HL 6 maths)

Brunel – ABB incl maths/fmaths (Fin Maths (MMath)) (IB 31 pts HL 6 maths)

Coventry – ABB–BBB incl maths (Maths courses) (IB 31 pts HL 5 maths)

Heriot-Watt – ABB incl maths (Maths Span) (IB 28 pts HL 5 maths)

Liverpool – ABB/BBB+aEPQ incl maths (Maths; Maths Econ) (IB 33 pts HL 6 maths); (Maths Stats) (IB 33 pts HL 6 maths); ABB incl maths (Maths Bus St) (IB 33 pts HL 6 maths); ABB incl maths+Fr/Ger/Span (Mathem Sci Euro Lang) (IB 33 pts HL 6 maths+Fr/Ger/Span)

Loughborough – ABB incl maths+phys (Phys Maths) (IB 34 pts HL 6 maths/phys 5 maths/phys)

Portsmouth – 128–144 pts incl maths (Maths (MMath)) (IB 27 pts)

Queen's Belfast – ABB incl maths+Fr/Ger (Maths Ext St Euro); ABB incl maths (App Maths Phys; Maths Comp Sci; Maths; Maths Stats OR)

Stirling – ABB (3 yr course) BBB (4 yr course) incl maths (App Maths) (IB 35 pts (3 yr course) 32 pts (4 yr course))

Strathclyde – ABB (3 yr course) BBB (4 yr course) incl maths (Maths Stats Econ) (IB 34 pts (3 yr course) 32 pts (4 yr course) HL 6 maths)

120 pts **Aberdeen** – BBB incl maths (Maths; App Maths) (IB 32 pts HL 5 maths)

Aberystwyth – ABC/BBB incl maths (App Maths Stats) (IB 28–30 pts HL 5/4 maths); (Maths; App Maths PMaths) (IB 30–28 pts HL 5/4 maths)

Brunel – BBB incl maths/fmaths (Maths Stats Mgt; Maths Comp Sci; Maths) (IB 30 pts HL 5 maths)

Central Lancashire – 120 pts incl maths (Maths)

Coventry – BBB–BBC incl maths (Maths Stats) (IB 31 pts HL 4 maths)

Dundee – BBB incl maths+sci (Mathem Biol) (IB 30 pts HL 555); BBB incl maths (Maths) (IB 30 pts HL 555)

Essex – BBB (Maths) (IB 30 pts)

Keele – ABC incl maths (Maths) (IB 32 pts HL 6 maths)

Liverpool Hope – BBB–BBC 120–112 pts (Maths)

Northumbria – 120–128 pts incl maths (Maths) (HL 444)

Nottingham Trent – 120 pts incl maths (Maths)

Oxford Brookes – ABC incl maths (Maths courses; Mathem Sci) (IB 30 pts HL 5 maths)

Plymouth – 120–128 pts incl maths (Maths Fin) (IB 30 pts HL 5 maths)

Check **Chapter 3** for new university admission details and **Chapter 6** on how to read the subject tables.

South Wales – BBB incl maths +interview (Maths) (IB 29 pts HL 5 maths)
UWE Bristol – 120 pts incl maths (Maths)
West London – 120 pts incl maths (Maths Stats)

112 pts **Brighton** – BBC–CCC incl maths (Maths Bus) (IB 28 pts HL 5 maths); BBC–CCC incl maths
112–96 pts (Maths Fin; Maths) (IB 28 pts HL 6 maths)
Canterbury Christ Church – 112 pts incl maths (Maths S Educ QTS)
Chester – BBC–BCC 112 pts (Maths) (IB 26 pts HL 5 maths)
Coventry – BBC incl maths (Maths Data Analyt) (IB 29 pts HL 4 maths)
De Montfort – 112 pts incl maths (Maths) (IB 26 pts HL 6 maths)
Greenwich – 112 pts (Maths Comp; Fin Maths); 112 pts incl maths (Maths)
Hertfordshire – 112 pts incl maths (Fin Maths) (HL 4 maths); (Maths) (HL 554)
Kingston – 112 pts incl maths (Maths)
Liverpool John Moores – BBC incl maths 112 pts (App Maths Eng; Maths Data Sci; Maths
Fin; Maths) (IB 26 pts)
London (Birk) – BBC incl maths 112 pts (Maths Stats)
Sheffield Hallam – 112–96 pts incl maths (Maths)
Wolverhampton – BBC incl maths (Maths)
Worcester – 112 pts incl maths (Maths)

104 pts **Bolton** – 104 pts incl maths (Maths)
Manchester Met – BCC–BBC incl maths 104–112 pts (Maths) (IB 26 pts HL 5 maths)
Nottingham Trent – 104 pts incl maths+PE/sci (Spo Sci Maths)
Portsmouth – 104–120 pts incl maths (Maths; Maths Stats; Maths Fin Mgt) (IB 26 pts)
Winchester – 104–120 pts incl maths (Maths; Maths Fin) (IB 26 pts)

96 pts **Bishop Grosseteste** – 96–112 pts (Spo Maths)
Derby – 96–112 pts (Maths Comp Sci; Maths Educ); 96–112 pts incl maths (Maths)

80 pts **Bedfordshire** – 80 pts (Comp Maths)
London Met – CCE incl maths 80 pts (Maths)

72 pts **London Met** – CDE/BC 72 pts (Mathem Sci)

Open University – contact 0300 303 0073 **or** www.open.ac.uk/contact/new (Maths)

Alternative offers
See **Chapter 6** and **Appendix 1** for grades/UCAS Tariff points information for other examinations.

EXAMPLES OF COLLEGES OFFERING COURSES IN THIS SUBJECT FIELD
Accrington and Rossendale (Coll); Bournemouth and Poole (Coll); Bradford (Coll); Bury (Coll).

CHOOSING YOUR COURSE (SEE ALSO CH.1)
Universities and colleges teaching quality See www.qaa.ac.uk; https://unistats.ac.uk.

Top research universities and colleges (REF 2014) (Mathematical Sciences) Oxford; Dundee;
Cambridge; Warwick; Imperial London; Lancaster; London (RH); St Andrews; Manchester; Cardiff;
Sheffield; Glasgow; Bath; Newcastle; Nottingham.

Examples of sandwich degree courses Aston; Bath; Brighton; Brunel; Cardiff; Coventry; East Anglia;
Greenwich; Hertfordshire; Kent; Kingston; Lancaster; Liverpool John Moores; London (QM);
Loughborough; Northumbria; Nottingham Trent; Portsmouth; Reading; Surrey; UWE Bristol;
Wolverhampton; York.

ADMISSIONS INFORMATION
Number of applicants per place (approx) Aston 8; Bath 7; Birmingham 6; Bristol 8; Cambridge 5;
Cardiff 5; Central Lancashire 7; City 5; Derby 5; Dundee 8; Durham 6; East Anglia 5; Edinburgh 13;
Exeter 6; Greenwich 2; Heriot-Watt 6; Hertfordshire 9; Lancaster 6; Leeds (Maths) 5, (Maths Fin) 4;
Leicester 6; Liverpool 6; London (King's) 8; London (QM) 5; London (RH) 7; London (UCL) 8; London
LSE 8; London Met 3; Manchester Met 3; Newcastle 5; Nottingham Trent 7; Oxford Brookes 6;
Plymouth 10; Sheffield 6; Sheffield Hallam 3; Southampton 10; Stirling 6; Strathclyde 6; Warwick 6;
York 6.

UCAS points Tariff: A* = 56 pts; A = 48 pts; B = 40 pts; C = 32 pts; D = 24 pts; E = 16 pts

Admissions tutors' advice Leeds Applicants taking the BTEC Extended Diploma may be required to take an additional Maths A-level paper.

Advice to applicants and planning the UCAS personal statement Any interests you have in careers requiring mathematical ability could be mentioned, for example, engineering, computers (hardware and software) and business applications. Show determination, love of mathematics and an appreciation of the rigour of the course. Give details of your skills, work experience, positions of responsibility. A variety of non-academic interests to complement the applicant's academic abilities preferred. For non-UK students, fluency in oral and written English required. **Manchester** Unit grades may form part of an offer. **Warwick** Offers for courses in Statistics (eg MORSE) include achievement requirements in STEP and other requirements. Check University website for latest information. See also **Appendix 3**.

Misconceptions about this course London (QM) Some believe that a study of mechanics is compulsory – it is not. **York** Further maths is not required.

Selection interviews Yes Cambridge, Manchester, Oxford (Maths) 15%; (Maths Phil) 14%; (Maths Stats) 7%; **Some** Bath, Cardiff, London (UCL), Warwick, York; **No** Aberystwyth, Birmingham, Bishop Grosseteste, Brighton, Bristol, Central Lancashire, City, Coventry, Dundee, East Anglia, Essex, Greenwich, Heriot-Watt, Imperial London, Kent, Kingston, Leeds, Liverpool, Liverpool John Moores, London (King's), London (RH), London LSE, London Met, Loughborough, Manchester Met, Newcastle, Nottingham, Reading, Sheffield, Southampton, UWE Bristol.

Interview advice and questions Questions are likely to be asked arising from the information you have given in your UCAS application and about your interests in the subject. Questions in recent years have included: How many ways are there of incorrectly setting up the back row of a chess board? A ladder on a rough floor leans against a smooth wall. Describe the forces acting on the ladder and give the maximum possible angle of inclination possible. There are three particles connected by a string; the middle one is made to move – describe the subsequent motion of the particles. What mathematics books have you read outside your syllabus? Why does a ball bounce? Discuss the work of any renowned mathematician. Balance a pencil on your index fingers and then try to move both towards the centre of the pencil. Explain what is happening in terms of forces and friction. See also **Chapter 5**. **Cambridge** If you could spend half an hour with any mathematician past or present, who would it be? **Oxford** What makes you think I'm having thoughts? What was the most beautiful proof in A-level mathematics? I am an oil baron in the desert and I need to deliver oil to four different towns which happen to lie in a straight line. In order to deliver the correct amount to each town I must visit each town in turn, returning to my warehouse in between each visit. Where would I position my warehouse in order to drive the shortest possible distance? Roads are no problem since I have a friend who will build me as many roads as I like for free. **Southampton** Personal statements generate discussion points. Our interviews are informal chats and so technical probing is kept low key.

Reasons for rejection (non-academic) Usually academic reasons only. Lack of motivation. Uneasiness about how much mathematics will be remembered after a gap year. **Birmingham** A poorly written and poorly organised personal statement.

AFTER-RESULTS ADVICE
Offers to applicants repeating A-levels Higher Brighton, London Met, Strathclyde, Swansea, Warwick; **Possibly higher** Cambridge (Hom), Durham, Lancaster, Leeds, Newcastle, Sheffield; **Same** Aberystwyth, Aston, Bath, Birmingham, Bristol, Brunel, Chester, Coventry, East Anglia, Essex, Liverpool, Liverpool Hope, London (RH), Loughborough (usually), Manchester Met, Nottingham, Nottingham Trent, Sheffield Hallam, Southampton, Stirling, Wolverhampton, York; **No** Cambridge, Glasgow.

GRADUATE DESTINATIONS AND EMPLOYMENT (2015/16 HESA)
Graduates surveyed 5,160 **Employed** 2,520 **In voluntary employment** 125 **In further study** 1,485 **Assumed unemployed** 390

Career note Graduates enter a range of careers. Whilst business, finance and retail areas are popular options, mathematicians also have important roles in the manufacturing industries. Mathematics offers the pleasure of problem-solving, the satisfaction of a rigorous argument and the most widely employable non-vocational degree subject. A student's view: 'Maths trains you to work in the abstract, to think creatively and to come up with concrete conclusions.' These transferable skills are much sought-after by employers. Employment prospects are excellent, with high salaries.

OTHER DEGREE SUBJECTS FOR CONSIDERATION

Accountancy; Actuarial Studies; Astronomy; Astrophysics; Computer Science; Economics; Engineering Sciences; Operational Research; Physics; Statistics.

MEDIA STUDIES

(including **Broadcast Media Technologies**; see also **Art and Design (General), Communication Studies/Communication, Computer Courses, Engineering (Acoustics and Sound), Film, Radio, Video and TV Studies, Information Management and Librarianship, Journalism, Photography**)

Intending Media applicants need to check course details carefully since this subject area can involve graphic design, illustration and other art courses as well as the media in the fields of TV, radio and journalism.

Useful websites www.bbc.co.uk/careers; www.newsmediauk.org; www.ppa.co.uk; www. thomsonreuters.com/en/careers.html; www.nctj.com; www.ipa.co.uk; www.camfoundation.com; www.mediastudies.com

NB The points totals shown to the left of the institutions are for ease of reference only. It must not be assumed that Tariff points are always used by institutions or that they can be substituted for an offer in grades. The level of an offer is not necessarily indicative of the quality of a course.

COURSE OFFERS INFORMATION

Subject requirements/preferences GCSE English and mathematics often required. **AL** No specified subjects required.

Your target offers and examples of degree courses
136 pts **Lancaster** – AAB–ABB (Media Cult St) (IB 35–32 pts HL 16 pts)
　　　　Leeds – AAB (Comms Media) (IB 35 pts)
　　　　Loughborough – AAB (Comm Media St) (IB 35 pts HL 665)
　　　　Newcastle – AAB (Media Comm Cult St; Jrnl Media Cult) (IB 34 pts)
　　　　York – AAB (Interact Media) (IB 36 pts)
128 pts **Cardiff** – ABB (Jrnl Media Sociol) (HL 17 pts)
　　　　East Anglia – ABB incl arts/hum (Media St) (IB 32 pts); ABB (Media Int Dev; Transl Media Modn Lang) (IB 32 pts)
　　　　Kent – ABB (Media St) (IB 34 pts HL 16 pts)
　　　　Leicester – ABB/BBB+bEPQ (Media Soty) (IB 30 pts); AAB–BBB+bEPQ (Media Comm) (IB 30 pts)
　　　　Liverpool – ABB/BBB+aEPQ (Comm Media) (IB 33 pts)
　　　　Nottingham – ABB (Int Media Comm St; Span Int Media Comms St) (IB 32 pts)
　　　　Surrey – ABB (Media Cult Soty) (IB 32 pts)
　　　　Sussex – ABB (Media Cult St) (IB 32 pts)
120 pts **Anglia Ruskin** – 120 pts (Media St courses) (IB 24 pts)
　　　　Bangor – 120–104 pts (Media St Gms Des; Jrnl Media St; Media St courses)
　　　　Brunel – BBB incl art+tech (Vis Efcts Mtn Graph) (IB 30 pts HL 5 art+tech)
　　　　Coventry – BBB incl media/film st (Media Prod) (IB 31 pts); BBB +portfolio (Media Comms) (IB 31 pts)
　　　　Derby – 120–128 pts +interview +portfolio (Media Prod)

Edge Hill – BBB 120 pts (Media Mus Snd)
Leicester – BBB–BBC+bEPQ (Film Media St) (IB 28 pts)
Lincoln – BBB (Media Prod) (IB 30 pts)
Liverpool Hope – BBB–BBC 120–112 pts (Media Comm)
London (Gold) – BBB (Media Comms) (IB 33 pts)
Northumbria – 120–128 pts (Media Jrnl) (HL 444)
Oxford Brookes – BBB 120 pts (Pub Media) (IB 31 pts)
Queen Margaret – BBB (3 yr course) BCC (4 yr course) (PR Media) (IB 28 pts)
Sunderland – 120 pts (Media Cult Comm)
Swansea – BBB 120 pts (Media courses) (IB 32 pts)
112 pts **Aberystwyth** – BBC–BBB (Media Comm St) (IB 28–30 pts)
Arts London (CFash) – 112 pts +interview +portfolio (Fash Jrnl)
Birmingham City – BBC 112 pts +interview +portfolio (Jrnl) (HL 14 pts); (Media Comm (Mus Ind)) (HL 16–14 pts)
Bournemouth – 112–120 pts (Comm Media) (IB 30–31 pts HL 55); 112–128 pts (Film Prod Cnma; Media Prod) (IB 30–32 pts HL 55)
Brighton – BBC–CCC 112–96 pts (Media Env Comm; Media St) (IB 28 pts)
Brunel – BBC (Sociol (Media); Comm Media St) (IB 29 pts)
Buckingham – BBC–BCC (Jrnl Comm St) (IB 31–30 pts)
East London – 112 pts (Media Comm) (IB 25 pts HL 15 pts)
Glyndŵr – 112 pts (Broad Jrnl Media Comms)
Greenwich – 112 pts +interview +portfolio (Media Comms)
Hull – 112 pts (Media St) (IB 28 pts)
Keele – BBC (Media Comms Crea Prac) (IB 30 pts)
Kingston – 112 pts (Media Comm)
Leeds Trinity – 112 pts (Media)
London Met – BBC 112 pts (Media Comms)
Middlesex – 112 pts (Jrnl Comm)
Nottingham Trent – 112 pts (Media)
Oxford Brookes – BBC 112 pts (Comm Media Cult) (IB 30 pts)
Plymouth – 112 pts (Media Arts; Pub) (IB 28 pts)
Portsmouth – 112 pts (Dig Media) (IB 26 pts)
St Mary's – 112 pts (Comm Media Mark)
Sheffield Hallam – 112–96 pts (PR Media; Media)
UWE Bristol – 112 pts (Media Cult Prac; Media Jrnl)
West London – BBC 112 pts (Engl Media Comms; Soc Media Mark; Media Comms)
Wolverhampton – BBC (Media Engl; Media)
104 pts **Bath Spa** – BCC–CCC (Media Comms) (IB 26 pts)
Brighton – BCC–CCC incl Engl 104–96 pts (Media Engl Lit) (IB 27 pts)
Cardiff Met – 104 pts (Engl Media)
Central Lancashire – 104 pts (Film Media Pop Cult; Pub; Media Prod)
Chichester – 104–120 pts (Media Comms; Spo Media) (IB 28 pts)
De Montfort – 104 pts +interview (Jrnl) (IB 24 pts); 104 pts (Media Comm) (IB 24 pts)
Falmouth – 104–120 pts +interview (Jrnl)
Glasgow Caledonian – BCC (Media Comm) (IB 25 pts)
Huddersfield – 104 pts (Media Pop Cult) (IB 30 pts)
Leeds Beckett – 104 pts (Media Comm Cult) (IB 24 pts)
Leeds Trinity – 104 pts (Engl Media)
Liverpool John Moores – BCC 104 pts (Int Jrnl; Media Cult Comm) (IB 24 pts)
Manchester Met – 104–112 pts (Film Media St; Dig Media Comms) (IB 26 pts); BCC–BBC 104–112 pts (Dig Media Mark) (IB 26 pts)
Northampton – BCC (Media Prod Mov Imag)
Nottingham Trent – 104 pts (Media Comb Hons)
Portsmouth – 104–120 pts (Media St) (IB 25–30 pts)
Robert Gordon – BCC (Media) (IB 28 pts)

Check **Chapter 3** for new university admission details and **Chapter 6** on how to read the subject tables.

Sheffield Hallam – 104–96 pts (Dig Media Prod)

South Wales – BCC–CDD incl art/film/media +interview +portfolio (Media Prod) (HL 655–445); BCC–CDD +audition workshop (Perf Media) (HL 655–445)

Winchester – 104–120 pts (Media Comm Jrnl; Media Comm courses; Media Comm Adv) (IB 26 pts)

Worcester – 104 pts (Media Cult)

96 pts **Bolton** – 96 pts +interview +portfolio (Media Writ Prod)

Buckingham – CCC +interview (Comm (EFL) Media St; Comm Media Jrnl) (IB 29 pts)

Chester – CCC–BCC (Media) (IB 26 pts)

Cumbria – 96–112 pts +interview +portfolio (Wldlf Media)

Derby – 96–128 pts (Media St Comb Hons)

Edinburgh Napier – CCC incl des/mus/media (Dig Media Interact Des Glob) (IB 27 pts HL 654)

Hull (Coll) – 96 pts +interview +portfolio (Filmm Crea Media Prod; Jrnl Dig Media)

Leeds Beckett – 96 pts (Broad Media Tech; Crea Media Tech) (IB 24 pts)

Plymouth (CA) – 96–120 pts +portfolio (Fash Media Mark)

Roehampton – 96 pts (Media Cult Idnty)

Teesside – 96–112 pts +interview +portfolio (Broad Media Prod)

Winchester – 96–112 pts (Dig Media Des courses) (IB 25 pts)

York St John – 96–112 pts (Media courses)

88 pts **Canterbury Christ Church** – 88–112 pts (Media Comms)

80 pts **Arts London** – 80 pts (Contemp Media Cult; Mag Jrnl Pub)

Bedfordshire – 80 pts (Media Comms; Media Prod courses)

72 pts **UHI** – BC +interview (Gael Media St)

64 pts **Ravensbourne** – CC (Edit Pst Prod) (IB 28 pts)

Alternative offers

See **Chapter 6** and **Appendix 1** for grades/UCAS Tariff points information for other examinations.

EXAMPLES OF COLLEGES OFFERING COURSES IN THIS SUBJECT FIELD

Most colleges, check with your local college. Accrington and Rossendale (Coll); Blackpool and Fylde (Coll); Bridgwater and Taunton (Coll); Brooksby Melton (Coll); Central Film Sch; East Riding (Coll); Farnborough (CT); Gloucestershire (Coll); Grimsby (Inst Group); HOW (Coll); Hugh Baird (Coll); Kingston (Coll); Leeds City (Coll); Macclesfield (Coll); Newcastle (Coll); Northbrook Met (Coll); Peterborough (Coll); South Essex (Coll); Stratford-upon-Avon (Coll); Truro and Penwith (Coll); Westminster Kingsway (Coll); Weston (Coll); Yeovil (Coll).

CHOOSING YOUR COURSE (SEE ALSO CH.1)

Universities and colleges teaching quality See www.qaa.ac.uk; https://unistats.ac.uk.

Top research universities and colleges (REF 2014) See **Communication Studies/Communication**.

Examples of sandwich degree courses Bedfordshire; Bournemouth; Brighton; Brunel; Coventry; De Montfort; Huddersfield; Leeds; Leeds Beckett; Liverpool John Moores; Manchester Met; Nottingham Trent; Portsmouth; Sheffield Hallam; Stirling; Surrey.

ADMISSIONS INFORMATION

Number of applicants per place (approx) Bath Spa 4; Bradford 13; Cardiff 11; Cardiff Met 3; Central Lancashire 33; Cumbria 4; De Montfort 11; East London 27; Falmouth 4; Greenwich 12; Lincoln 4; London (Gold) 13; Northampton 4; Nottingham Trent 5; Oxford Brookes (Pub) 5; Sheffield Hallam 56; South Essex (Coll) 10; Teesside 33; Winchester 5.

Advice to applicants and planning the UCAS personal statement Work experience or work shadowing is important. Contact local newspaper offices to meet journalists and to discuss their work. Contact local radio stations and advertising agencies, read newspapers (all types) and be able to describe the different approaches of newspapers. Watch TV coverage of news stories and the way in which the interviewer deals with politicians or members of the public. Give your opinions on the various forms of media. School magazine and/or any published work should be mentioned. A balance of academic and practical skills preferred. Creativity, problem-solving, cultural awareness, communication skills and commitment required. (International students: Fluency in written and spoken English required.) See also **Communication Studies/Communication** and **Appendix 3**.

Misconceptions about this course Birmingham City That Media courses are soft options: they are not! **Cardiff Met** Some applicants believe that the course will automatically lead to a job in the media: it won't. This depends on the student developing other employment skills and experience. **Cumbria** This is not a Media Studies course: it is a highly practical media production course. **Lincoln** (Media Prod) BTEC applicants may think that this is a technology-based course.

Selection interviews Yes Anglia Ruskin, Bolton, Cardiff Met, East Anglia; **Some** Bournemouth, Edge Hill, Liverpool John Moores, Southampton Solent, Westminster, Winchester, Wolverhampton; **No** Birmingham City, Cardiff, Huddersfield, London (Gold), Nottingham, Nottingham Trent, Portsmouth, Sheffield Hallam, South Essex (Coll), Sunderland, West London.

Interview advice and questions Past questions include: Which newspapers do you read? Discuss the main differences between the national daily newspapers. Which radio programmes do you listen to each day? Which television programmes do you watch? Should the BBC broadcast advertisements? What do you think are the reasons for the popularity of *EastEnders*? Film or video work, if required, should be edited to a running time of 15 minutes unless otherwise stated. See also **Chapter 5**. **Cardiff Met** What is your favourite area in respect of popular culture? Are you considering taking up the work placement module? If so where would you plan to go? **Cumbria** Role of journalism in society. What is today's main news story? Who is Rupert Murdoch?

Reasons for rejection (non-academic) No clear commitment (to Broadcast Journalism) plus no evidence of experience (now proving to be essential). Mistaken expectations of the nature of the course. Can't write and doesn't work well in groups. Too specific and narrow areas of media interest, for example, video or scriptwriting. Lack of knowledge of current affairs. **Cardiff Met** Lack of experience in the field. Application arrived too late.

AFTER-RESULTS ADVICE
Offers to applicants repeating A-levels Same Birmingham City, Cardiff, Cardiff Met, Chester, De Montfort, Huddersfield, Lincoln, Loughborough, Manchester Met, Nottingham Trent, St Mary's, South Essex (Coll), Sunderland, Winchester, Wolverhampton.

GRADUATE DESTINATIONS AND EMPLOYMENT (2015/16 HESA)
Graduates surveyed 4,345 **Employed** 2,130 **In voluntary employment** 210 **In further study** 645 **Assumed unemployed** 375

Career note See **Film, Radio, Video and TV Studies**.

OTHER DEGREE SUBJECTS FOR CONSIDERATION
Advertising; Communication; English; Film, Radio, Video and TV Studies; Journalism; Photography; Public Relations.

MEDICINE

(including Medical Sciences; see also Biological Sciences, Human Sciences/Human Biosciences)

Medicine is a highly popular choice of degree subject and career. All courses listed below include the same areas of study and all lead to a qualification and career in medicine. Medical schools aim to produce doctors who are clinically competent, who are able to see patients as people and have a holistic and ethical approach (including the ability to understand and manage each patient's case in a family and social context as well as in hospital), who treat patients and colleagues with respect, dignity and sensitivity, are skilled at teamwork and are prepared for continual learning. In several ways, these aims reflect the qualities selectors seek when interviewing applicants. In all cases, close attention will be paid to the confidential report on the UCAS application to judge the applicant's personality, communication skills, academic potential and commitment to a medical career. Methods of teaching may vary slightly, depending on the medical school. To achieve these aims, some medical schools adopt the system of self-directed learning (SDL) in which objectives are set to assess students' progress, and problem-based learning (PBL) which helps students to develop critical thinking and clinical problem-solving skills.

Whilst there is a core curriculum of knowledge, the first three years integrate scientific and clinical experience, and there are fewer formal lectures than before, with more group and individual work. For outstanding students without science A-levels, some pre-medical courses are available. Most medical schools also offer an extra year of study, usually in the middle of the medical degree, to enable students to research a scientific subject leading to an 'intercalated' BSc degree. Additionally, elective periods abroad in the final year can sometimes be taken.

Medical students' and doctors' advice to applicants

'I did not fully appreciate how diverse medicine is as a career. Everyone has their own particular reasons for wishing to pursue it, but these will change as you progress through your career. There are many different pathways you can take which makes it all the more exciting ... and daunting! Choose your university carefully; in most medical degrees, you will only be based at university for the first two years, and thereafter you will be in hospitals around the area so choose a city or an area you want to work and live in.'

'Medicine is a career which can open many doors – as a family or hospital doctor, working in Africa treating children with infectious diseases, in a war zone, in a laboratory, in sport, in journalism, and in law, going on to study law, to specialise in medical law, I have friends who have done all of these things.'

'Get to know what the real working lives of doctors are. The attributes needed to see sick and needy people. The fact that the NHS is a public and not a private organisation and what this means in the changing world of medical knowledge. Some of this is very difficult to learn in sixth form but periods of work experience will help. In addition to talking to medical students and family friends who are doctors, browse through medical journals and medical websites. Every doctor has had their own individual experiences, good and bad, but the majority would still apply to medicine again if they were 17!'

Useful websites www.scicentral.com; www.ipem.ac.uk; www.bmj.com; www.admissionstesting.org; www.gmc-uk.org; www.healthcareers.nhs.uk; www.bma.org.uk; www.rcgp.org.uk; www.rcpath.org

NB The points totals shown to the left of the institutions are for ease of reference only. It must not be assumed that Tariff points are always used by institutions or that they can be substituted for an offer in grades. The level of an offer is not necessarily indicative of the quality of a course.

COURSE OFFERS INFORMATION

Subject requirements/preferences GCSE In all cases, a good spread of science and non-science subjects will be expected at high grades.

Aberdeen Grade C (4) in English and mathematics. Biology and physics or dual award science recommended.
Anglia Ruskin Check the university's website.
Aston Grade B (6) or above in English language, mathematics, chemistry, biology or double science (or overseas equivalent).
Birmingham Minimum of grade B (6) in **GCSE** English language, English literature, mathematics, biology and chemistry. Dual science award acceptable as an alternative to biology and chemistry.
Brighton and Sussex (MS) Mathematics and English at grade B or grade 6, or above.
Bristol Five A (7) grades including mathematics, English and two sciences.
Buckingham Grade C (4) in English and mathematics.
Cambridge Mathematics and dual science award (or biology and physics).

Medicine
Consult the Specialist

MPW is one of the UK's best known groups of independent sixth-form colleges. We offer a range of specialist services to those who have chosen a career in Medicine.

M|P|W

Mander Portman Woodward

London	020 7835 1355
Birmingham	0121 454 9637
Cambridge	01223 350158

Specialist two-year and one-year A level courses

Detailed UCAS advice

Seminars on application procedures and interview preparation

Interview training

Getting into Medical School by MPW is published by Trotman Publishing

Check **Chapter 3** for new university admission details and **Chapter 6** on how to read the subject tables.

Canterbury Christ Church Check the university's website.

Cardiff B in nine subjects (minimum). English or Welsh at grade B (6), mathematics at grade B (6), grades AA in dual science or AAB in three sciences.

Central Lancashire GCSE or equivalent to include English and mathematics at grade B (6) or higher with a broad study of sciences.

Dundee Grade B/6 (minimum) in biology, mathematics and English.

East Anglia Six subjects at grade A or grade 7 or above including mathematics, English and two science subjects.

Edge Hill Check the university's website.

Edinburgh English, mathematics, biology, chemistry or dual science award at grade B/6 or higher.

Exeter Minimum grade C (4) in English and mathematics. Higher grades may be specified for individual programmes of study. International students should view requirements on the website.

Glasgow Grade B or grade 6 or above in English.

Hull York (MS) Eight subjects at grades A*–C including English language and mathematics at grade B or higher, or grade 6 or above in the reformed **GCSE**s.

Imperial For advice on the requirements please contact the School of Medicine.

Keele Chemistry, physics, biology, English and mathematics at grade B (6) minimum. A broad spread of subjects is expected with a minimum of five at grade A.

Kent Check the university's website.

Lancaster Applicants must provide evidence of excellent attainment in **GCSE**s. See the university's website for further details.

Leeds Six subjects at grade B minimum including English language, mathematics, chemistry and biology or dual science award.

Leicester Grade B (6) (minimum) in English language, mathematics and two sciences (including chemistry) or dual science award.

Lincoln For the University of Nottingham Lincoln Medical School, check the university's website.

Liverpool Nine **GCSE** subjects at grades A–C, including dual science (or biology, chemistry and physics), English language and mathematics at grade B (6) minimum.

London (King's) Grade B/6 (minimum) in English and mathematics.

London (QM) Six subjects at A–B (7–6) minimum grades including English, mathematics and science subjects.

London (St George's) Typically eight subjects at grade A (7) are required including English language, mathematics and science subjects. Contact the admissions team for a more detailed breakdown of grade requirements.

London (UCL) English and mathematics at grade B or 6 minimum plus grade C or 5 in a foreign language.

Manchester Seven subjects with five at grades A/A* or 7/6. Biology and physics required at grade C (or AS) minimum, with English and mathematics at grade B minimum.

Newcastle Grade A or 7 in biology/chemistry (or dual science award) if not offered as AS or A-level.

Nottingham Minimum of six **GCSE**s at grade A (7) including chemistry, physics and biology or dual science award. Grade B (5) in English and mathematics. For the University of Nottingham Lincoln Medical School, check the university's website.

Oxford Mathematics, biology and physics or dual science award if not taken at A-level.

Plymouth Seven subjects at grades A*–C (9–4) including English language, mathematics and either **GCSE** double award science or two from single award chemistry, biology or physics.

Sheffield At least eight subjects at grades A*–C (9–4), including six A (7) grades. You must achieve **GCSE** passes at grade C (4) or above in mathematics, English and the sciences (which may be dual awards).

Queen's Belfast GCSE mathematics and physics (or dual science award) at grade C (4) (or CC).

St Andrews Minimum of five A grades (7).

Southampton A minimum of seven subjects at grade B (6) including English, mathematics and dual science award or equivalent. (Widening Access course BM6) Five at grade C (4) including English, mathematics and dual science award or equivalent. (Students join the five-year programme on completion of Year Zero.)

Sunderland Check the university's website.

Swansea Mathematics and English/Welsh at grade C (4) or above.
Warwick GCSE results not considered; this is a graduate entry course.

AL See **Your target offers and examples of degree courses** below. Mathematics and further mathematics will not both be counted towards three AL subjects by some universities. Applicants should note that A-levels in general studies and critical thinking may not be accepted for entry.

Medicine Foundation courses Some of these courses, such as the one at Manchester, are designed for students who have demonstrated high academic potential but who have taken non-science subjects or a combination including no more than one of biology, chemistry and physics. Others, such as the course at **Bristol** are designed to widen access.

Other requirements: See **Health requirements** below; DBS clearance is also required.

NB Home and EU-funded students applying for entry to Medicine are required by many universities to sit either the UKCAT or BMAT tests before applying. See **Your target offers and examples of degree courses** below and **Chapter 5** for further information.

Your target offers and examples of degree courses

164 pts **Queen's Belfast** – AAAa/AAAB/AAA+aEPQ incl chem+sci/maths (Check offer) +interview +UKCAT (Med 5 yrs)

160 pts **Cambridge** – A*A*A incl chem+sci/maths +interview +BMAT (Med 6 yrs) (IB 40–42 pts HL 776)
Lancaster – AAAb/AAA–A*AA incl biol+chem (Check offer) +interview +BMAT (Med Srgy 5 yrs) (IB 36 pts HL 6 biol+chem)

152 pts **Birmingham** – A*AA incl chem+biol +interview +UKCAT (Med Srgy 5 yrs) (IB 32 pts HL 766)
Exeter – A*AA–AAA incl biol+chem +interview +UKCAT (Med) (IB 38–36 pts HL 6 biol+chem)
Imperial London – A*AA incl biol+chem +interview +BMAT (Med 6 yrs) (IB 38 pts HL 6 biol+chem)
Keele – A*AA incl chem/biol+sci/maths +interview +UKCAT (Med 5 yrs) (IB 35 pts HL 666 incl chem/biol+sci/maths)
London (King's) – A*AA incl chem+biol +interview +UKCAT (Med 6 yrs) (IB 35 pts HL 766 incl chem/biol)
London (UCL) – A*AA incl chem+biol +interview +BMAT (Med 6 yrs) (IB 39 pts HL 7 biol/chem 6 biol/chem)
Oxford – A*AA incl chem+sci/maths +interview +BMAT (Med 6 yrs) (IB 39 pts HL 766)
Plymouth – A*AA–AAB incl chem+biol +UKCAT (Med Srgy 5 yrs) (IB 36–38 pts HL 6 biol+chem)

144 pts **Aberdeen** – AAA incl chem+sci/maths +interview +UKCAT (Med 5 yrs) (IB 36 pts HL 6 chem+sci/maths)
Brighton and Sussex (MS) – AAA incl biol+chem +interview +BMAT (Med 5 yrs) (IB 36 pts HL 6 biol+chem)
Bristol – AAA–AAC incl chem+sci +interview +UKCAT (Med 5 yrs) (IB 36–32 pts HL 6 chem+sci)
Cardiff – AAA incl chem+biol +interview +UKCAT (Med 5 yrs) (IB 36 pts HL 666 incl chem/biol+sci/maths)
Dundee – AAA incl chem+sci/maths +interview +UKCAT (Med 5 yrs) (IB 37 pts HL 666)
East Anglia – AAA incl biol+phys/chem +interview +UKCAT (Med 5 yrs) (IB 36 pts HL 666 incl biol+phys/chem)
Edinburgh – AAA incl chem+maths/sci +UKCAT (Med 6 yrs) (IB 37 pts HL 667)
Glasgow – AAA incl chem+sci/maths +interview +UKCAT (Med 5 yrs) (IB 38 pts HL 6 chem 6 biol)
Hull York (MS) – AAA incl chem+biol +interview +UKCAT (Med 5 yrs) (IB 36 pts HL 665 incl chem+biol)
Leeds – AAA incl chem +interview +UKCAT (Med Srgy 5 yrs) (IB 35 pts HL 666 incl chem)
Leicester – AAA incl chem +interview +UKCAT (Med 5 yrs) (IB 36 pts HL 6 chem+biol)
Liverpool – AAA incl chem+biol +interview +UKCAT (Med Srgy 5 yrs) (IB 36 pts HL 666 incl biol+chem)
London (QM) – AAA incl chem/biol+sci/maths +interview +UKCAT (Med 5 yrs) (IB 38 pts HL 6 chem/biol+sci/maths)

London (St George's) – AAA incl chem+biol +interview +UKCAT (Med 5 yrs) (IB 36 pts HL 18 pts incl 6 chem+biol)

Manchester – AAA +interview +UKCAT (Med 6 yrs) (IB 37 pts HL 666); AAA incl chem+sci/maths +interview +UKCAT (Med 5 yrs) (IB 37 pts HL 766 incl chem)

Newcastle – AAA incl chem/biol +interview +UKCAT (Med Srgy 5 yrs) (IB 38 pts HL 6 chem/biol)

Nottingham – AAA incl chem+biol +interview +UKCAT (Med 5 yrs) (IB 36 pts HL 666 incl chem+biol)

St Andrews – AAA incl chem+sci/maths +interview +UKCAT (Med 6 yrs) (IB 38 pts HL 666)

Sheffield – AAA incl chem+sci/maths/psy +interview +UKCAT (Med 5 yrs) (IB 36 pts HL 6 chem+sci/maths/psy)

Southampton – AAA incl chem+biol +interview +UKCAT (Med 5 yrs) (IB 36 pts)

136 pts Aston – AAB incl chem+biol +interview +UKCAT (Med 5 yrs) (IB 35 pts HL 665)

Buckingham – AAB incl chem+maths/biol (Med) (IB 34 pts HL 6 chem+biol)

Central Lancashire – AAB incl chem+sci +interview (Med 5 yrs) (IB 36 pts HL 5 chem 5 sci)

Exeter – AAB–ABB incl biol+sci (Med Sci) (IB 34–32 pts HL 6 biol/sci)

120 pts South Wales – BBB incl biol (Med Sci) (IB 32 pts HL 18 pts incl 6 biol+sci)

Widening Access and Foundation Courses (Check websites)
LWP – Local Widening Participation
Bradford (Leeds) – BCC/104 pts (Course B991) LWP
Bristol – BBC incl chem+sci/maths +UKCAT (A108) (IB 29 pts) LWP
Cardiff – AAA +UKCAT (Course A104)
Dundee – AAA +UKCAT (Course A104) (IB 37 pts)
Dundee – AAB incl chem+sci +UKCAT (Course A104) LWP
East Anglia – BBB +UKCAT (Course A104) (IB 32 pts) LWP
Keele – A*AA +UKCAT (Course A104) (IB 35 pts)
London (King's) – ABB incl biol+chem +UKCAT (Course A101) LWP
Manchester – AAA incl arts/hum (Course A104) (IB 35 pts)
Nottingham – BBC incl biol+chem +UKCAT (Course A108) (IB 28 pts) LWP
Southampton – BBB incl biol+chem +UKCAT (Course A102) LWP
St Andrews – 85%/3.2 GPA incl chem +UKCAT (Int students only)

Graduate entry for Medicine – A-levels and degrees stipulated
(In most cases a degree in science would be required (Check with university))
Birmingham – BBB or higher +2.1
Cambridge – AAA +2.1
London (QM) – 2.1 +UKCAT
London (St George's) – 2.1 any degree +GAMSAT
Oxford – 2.1 +BMAT
Swansea – 2.1+GAMSAT
Warwick – 2.1+UKCAT

Alternative offers
See **Chapter 6** and **Appendix 1** for grades/UCAS Tariff points information for other examinations.

CHOOSING YOUR COURSE (SEE ALSO CH.1)
Universities and colleges teaching quality See www.qaa.ac.uk; https://unistats.ac.uk.

Top research universities and colleges (REF 2014) (Clinical Medicine) London (King's); Oxford; London (QM); Cardiff; Edinburgh; Cambridge; Imperial London; Sheffield; Leeds; Manchester.

ADMISSIONS INFORMATION
Number of applicants per place (approx) Brighton and Sussex (MS) 10; Bristol 15; Cambridge 6; Cardiff 9; Dundee 10; East Anglia 9; Edinburgh 8; Glasgow 8; Hull York (MS) 9; Imperial London 8; Lancaster 11; Leicester 11; Liverpool 8; London (King's) 12; London (QM) 4; London (UCL) 7; Manchester 5; Newcastle 10; Nottingham 8; Oxford 10; Sheffield 9.

Numbers of applicants (**a** UK **b** EU (non-UK) **c** non-EU **d** mature) Birmingham **a**5 **b**25, (Grad entry) 12; Leeds **a**17; Queen's Belfast **a**4 **c**(a small number of places are allocated); Cambridge **c**22.

Admissions tutors' advice Policies adopted by all medical schools are very similar, although some medical schools use the Multiple Mini-Interview (MMI) format in which candidates rotate around different question stations, each one devoted to one question. Each interview lasts seven minutes. However, a brief outline of the information provided by admissions tutors is given below. Further information should be obtained direct from institutions. Applicants wishing to contact medical schools should do so by telephone and not by email.

Aberdeen Applicants must take the UKCAT in the year of application. A cut-off score is not used. Overseas applicants may be interviewed abroad or in Aberdeen. The University uses the MMI format and interviews last up to an hour. Total intake for 2017 was 181 including 19 international students. Most offers are made by end of March. Points equivalent results not accepted. Re-sits only accepted in exceptional circumstances. These must be submitted in good time to be considered. Feedback for unsuccessful applicants upon request. International students English language entry requirement (or equivalent): IELTS 7.0 and 7.0 in speaking.

Anglia Ruskin For entry requirements to this new School of Medicine, see the university's website.

Aston Deferred entry and gap years are accepted, however interviews, UKCAT and academic qualifications must be obtained in the year of the application. General studies and critical thinking not accepted.

Birmingham UKCAT required. Non-academic interests and extra-curricular activities noted in addition to academic factors. General studies and critical thinking not accepted. MMI format used. Approximately 1,200 called for interview. Approximately 10% take a year off which does not jeopardise the chances of an offer, but candidates must be available for interview. Re-sit candidates who failed by a small margin are only considered in exceptional circumstances. Transfers of undergraduates from other medical schools not considered. International applicants must show a good standard of written and spoken English. Second time applicants considered if not previously rejected at interview.

Brighton and Sussex (MS) BMAT used to assess each applicant. All applicants required to have grade B (grade 6) in maths and English **GCSE**. Candidates are interviewed if they have passed the first two stages of assessment (academic and personal statement if international; academic and BMAT score if a Home/EU applicant). Work experience necessary, but this does not need to be any given length or in particular health sector. Interviews for Medicine are Multi Mini Interviews (MMI) and are currently held in January, February and March. Resit applicants are welcome to apply but only if they have dropped in one grade and one subject (eg AAB). Applicants with lower grades but resitting can apply to us once they have re-sat their subjects and obtained AAA. All Year 1 medical school students are guaranteed accommodation as long as they apply by the deadline (some students who live in the local area may not be able to apply for accommodation due to more applicants requiring housing than rooms available). Teaching is 'systems integrated' so students are exposed to the clinical environment from Year 1. Cadaver dissection is also part of the course from Year 1, so students get a real understanding of human anatomy, enhancing their learning experience. As the medical school is small, so are class sizes, meaning that students have a strong relationship with academic and support staff.

Bristol No places are offered without an interview. MMI interview format (see above). Second time applicants rarely considered. The top applicants are called for an interview lasting an hour; the remainder grouped into two categories: 'hold' and 'unsuccessful' – some from the first two categories will be interviewed. Full details of the interview process are offered on the Bristol website. Widening participation panel considers appropriate candidates. Criteria for selection: UKCAT, realistic and academic interest in medicine, commitment to helping others, wide range of interests, contribution to school/college activities, personal achievements. Interview criteria: reasons for wanting to study Medicine, awareness of current developments, communication skills, self-confidence, enthusiasm and determination to study, ability to cope with stress, awareness of the content of the course and career. General studies and critical thinking not acceptable. Subject content overlap (eg biology/PE/sports science) not allowed. Deferred entry welcomed (except for A101 (Graduate Entry)), but applicants must be available for interview. Points equivalent results not accepted. International students English language requirement (or equivalent): IELTS 7.5. Some candidates are still applying without the right subjects or grade predictions. Their medicine curriculum is being reviewed. Visit www.bristol.ac.uk/study/undergraduate for up-to-date course and entry information.

Cambridge Most applicants for Medicine at Cambridge have at least three science/mathematics A-levels and some colleges require this or ask for particular A-level subject(s). BMAT used to assess each applicant. The standard undergraduate course is offered at all colleges except Hughes Hall. Normally two interviews lasting 20 minutes each. Films of interviews can be found on www.undergraduate.study.cam.ac.uk/applying/interviews. Approximately 80% of applicants are interviewed. Applicants are not usually required to submit examples of written work. Gap year acceptable but for positive reasons. Clinical studies from Year 4 at the Cambridge Clinical School (Addenbrooke's Hospital).

Canterbury Christ Church For entry requirements for the new forthcoming medical school, check the university's website.

Cardiff Admission is determined by a combination of academic performance, non-academic skills, knowledge and completion of the UKCAT test. Applications can be made in the Welsh language. Approximately 1,500 of the 3,500 applicants are called for interview. Cardiff uses the MMI format for interviews. Applications are assessed and scored as follows: 1. Medical motivation and awareness of career. 2. Caring ethos. 3. Sense of responsibility. 4. Evidence of a balanced approach to life. 5. Evidence of self-directed learning. 6. Referee's report.

Central Lancashire Interview format is MMI with 10 activity stations. All applicants invited to interview must provide a satisfactory enhanced DBS check or international equivalent and proof of ID. All applicants successful at interview will need to undergo occupational health screening as part of the enrolment process.

Dundee No minimum UKCAT cut-off score used, although candidates receiving offers in recent years have typically achieved around 2,720 pts. A fully integrated hospital and Medical School. Preference given to candidates who achieve the right grades at the first sitting. A system of 10 seven-minute mini-interviews has been introduced which gives students separate opportunities to sell themselves. Deferred entry acceptable. Clinical attachments in Year 4. World-wide experience in final year electives.

East Anglia Criteria include academic requirements and UKCAT. MMI format (see above) are used for the interviews, candidates visit each station for one question with five minutes at each station. English entry requirement IELTS 7.5. Clinical experience from Year 1.

Edge Hill For entry requirements to the university's new access to medicine course, see the university's website.

Edinburgh All examination grades must be achieved at the first sitting; only in extenuating circumstances will re-sits be considered. All UKCAT scores considered. The situation judgement section of the UKCAT test is also considered. Equal weighting given to academic and non-academic criteria. Non-academic criteria score based on personal qualities and skills, evidence of career exploration prior to application, breadth and level of non-academic achievements and interests. Work experience and work shadowing, particularly in a hospital, viewed positively but the admissions panel recognises that not all applicants have equal opportunities to gain such experience. School-leaving applicants are not normally interviewed so references are important. Shortlisted graduate and mature applicants will be interviewed; 190 UK/EU fee rate places available, around one in eleven receive an offer. International applicants not normally called for interview. Some clinical experience from Year 1. The six-year programme includes an intercalated research Honours year in Year 3.

Exeter Selection procedures include the assessment of UKCAT or GAMSAT. Mini interviews are used.

Glasgow The initial screening process considers the applicant's academic achievement, personal statement and reference. The UKCAT is the final part of the screening process and is used for allocation of interview. The range of UKCAT scores considered changes each year as the performance of each admissions cohort varies. Approximately 750 applicants are interviewed. The interview session will last around 30 minutes and candidates are made aware of what to expect on the day in the invite to interview. Normally applicants will be interviewed by two panels, with two interviewers on each panel. Candidates will be given the option to select one of two scenarios immediately prior to their interview and will be expected to discuss the issues around the scenario with their panel. Obtaining work experience in a medical setting is not necessary to study or obtain entry to Medicine at Glasgow, but it is expected that candidates will have a realistic understanding of what a career in medicine entails and be aware of current issues facing the medical profession. Given the competitive nature of entry to medicine, unsuccessful applicants are welcome to reapply to Glasgow in future admissions cycles, providing they meet minimum academic entry requirements within seven years of entry. All potential applicants should be encouraged to visit the Medical School prior to applying.

Hull York (MS) Students apply to HYMS, not to either the University of Hull or York. Students allocated places at Hull or York by ballot for Years 1 and 2. Transfers from other medical schools not accepted. Disabilities listed on UCAS application do not affect the assessment of the application. UKCAT required; approximately 670 called for interview, 440 offered places. MMI system involving a group interview of 20 minutes and two semi-structured individual interviews of 10 minutes, plus a 'scenario station' used. During the interview process, applicants will be scored on their motivation for a medical career, critical thinking skills, awareness and understanding of healthcare issues, communication skills, empathy, tolerance and resilience. A-level re-sits not usually accepted. Clinical placements from Year 1. Non-EU applicants English language (or equivalent requirement) IELTS 7.5 with at least 7 in each component.

Imperial London Approximately 750 candidates interviewed. Fifteen-minute interviews with panel of four or five selectors. Not aimed at being an intimidating experience – an evaluation of motivation, capacity to deal with stress, evidence of commitment to the values of the NHS constitution, evidence of working as a leader and team member, ability to multitask, likely contribution to university life, communication skills and maturity. BMAT test cut-off scores calculated each year depending on applications. Admissions tutor's comment: 'We look for resourceful men and women with wide interests and accomplishments, a practical concern for others and for those who will make a contribution to the life of the school and hospital.' Results within two weeks. Re-sits are only considered for candidates with extenuating circumstances. Approximately 480 offers made. Clinical contact in Year 1.

Keele Please check our website for details of our application process www.keele.ac.uk/medicine/mbchb5years/entryrouteshowtoapply/.

Kent For entry requirements for the new forthcoming medical school, check the university's website.

Lancaster The University delivers the curriculum at the academic base at Lancaster University and clinical placements in Years 2–5 at acute hospitals and primary care settings in Lancashire and Cumbria. BMAT required. Interviews in the MMI format with 12–14 different stations.

Leeds BMAT required. No cut-off point when assessing the results. 219 home students plus 18 non-EU students. Admissions tutor's comment: 'We use the MMI format for interviews [see above]. Consider your motivation carefully – we do!' Good verbal, non-verbal and presentational skills required. Candidates should: (i) be able to report on some direct experience of what a career in medicine is about; (ii) show evidence of social activities on a regular basis (eg part-time employment, organised community experiences); (iii) show evidence of positions of responsibility and interests outside medical and school activities. Disabled students should indicate their disability status on the UCAS form. Candidates must be available for interview; approximately 500 applicants interviewed. Points-equivalent results not accepted. International students' English language requirement (or equivalent): IELTS 7.5 including 7.5 in spoken English. Re-applications accepted from students who have achieved the right grades. Resits only considered in exceptional circumstances and with good supporting evidence; offer AAA. Transfers from other medical schools not encouraged. Ward based attachments begin in Year 1 and 2; clinical practice from Year 3. Applicants should hold the required A-level grades or a high class science or medically related degree.

Leicester New purpose-built Medical School opened in 2016. UKCAT required. Interview is MMI format – 8 stations assessing verbal and written communication, listening skills, compassion and respect, emotional intelligence, problem solving skills, motivation and ethical judgement. Deferred entry considered. Resits rarely considered and only on prior agreement from the admissions tutors. Transfers from other medical schools not considered. Patient contact in first semester, full body dissection. Integrated course.

Lincoln For entry requirements for the new University of Nottingham Lincoln Medical School, check the university's website.

Liverpool UKCAT is required for all non-graduate applicants applying to the A100 programme. Graduate applicants to the A100 programme must offer GAMSAT. 255 Home/EU places are available on the A100 Liverpool medical programme. Evidence of healthcare insight and awareness, caring contribution to the community, excellent communication and values that embody and underpin good healthcare practice is necessary. Interview is via MMI. Applicants wishing to take a gap year may be considered, but applicants must be available for interview. The Liverpool A100 medical programme usually has 23 places available for international students. Under-qualified international students may be able to apply to Liverpool International College prior to placing an application for the Liverpool A100 medical programme. The selection process at Liverpool is a three stage process which is competitive at each stage. Applications are placed via UCAS. For international students, certain minimum language requirements for the course may exist (IELTS of no less than 7.0 in each component).

London (King's) UKCAT required. Personal statement a significant factor in selection. Emphasis placed on appreciation of academic, physical and emotional demands of the course, commitment, evidence of working in a caring environment, communication skills and interaction with the general public. Approximately 400 out of 6,000 applications are successful. The University interviews around 1,300 applicants every year using the MMI format and makes offers to approximately a third of them. Clinical contact in Year 1.

London (St George's) Applicants must be taking A-level Chemistry and Biology or Human Biology. You will be required to complete your A-levels within two years of study and the standard offer is AAA. Applicants must have an average grade of A (7) across their top eight **GCSE**s including English language, maths and dual award or the three single sciences. Applicants are also required to take the UKCAT test in the year of application. Applicants who meet our A-level and **GCSE** requirements and achieve our required overall and section scores in UKCAT will be offered an interview. All offers are made post-interview. Applicants are expected to have relevant work experience which is assessed at interview. The value of work experience lies with reflection. What have you gained? How has the experience affected your journey to study Medicine? What skills do you need to work on as a result of carrying out this experience? The English language requirement for international students is IELTS 7.0 with 7.0 in writing and no section less than 6.5. Deferred entry welcome. Medicine (six years, including Foundation year) is for mature non-graduate students only. Medicine (four years, Graduate stream) is for graduates with a 2.1 Hons degree in any discipline. Graduates are not eligible for the five-year Medicine programme.

London (UCL) All candidates are required to take the BMAT. Two or three selectors interview applicants, each interview lasting 15–20 minutes; approximately 30% of applicants interviewed. Qualities sought include motivation, awareness of scientific and medical issues, ability to express and defend opinions, maturity and individual strengths. Deferred entry for good reason is acceptable. Minimum age of entry 18 years. Transfers from other medical schools considered. International students may take the University Preparation Certificate for Science and Engineering (UPCSE) which is the minimum entry requirement for entry to Medicine. 24 places for non-EU applicants. Patient contact starts in Year 1.

Manchester 372 places for around 2,000 applicants. UKCAT scores important. Threshold not disclosed. Seven interviews based on the MMI format (see above). Mitigating circumstances regarding the health or disposition of the candidate should appear in the referee's report. Any applicant who feels unwell before the interview should inform the admissions team and the interview will be re-scheduled; pleas of infirmity cannot be accepted after the interview! Candidates should be aware of the advantages and disadvantages of enquiry-based learning and opinions may be asked. Ethical questions may be raised. Decisions will be made by the end of March. Resit offers only made to applicants with extenuating circumstances; having AAB at first attempt A-level. Clinical attachments from Year 3. Application details on www.bmh.manchester.ac.uk/study/undergraduate.

Newcastle 367 places. The University runs multiple mini interviews. It does not stipulate its UKCAT threshold until after the recruitment cycle has ended, and it only accepts resits in extenuating circumstances. Decisions on resits are made on an individual basis by the Sub-Dean of Admissions. The University accepts deferred entry. Clinical placements start in Year 3. Check the website for the latest up-to-date information before applying.

Nottingham Up to date information on the Medicine programmes at the University of Nottingham and the application process is provided on the University's website, including for the new University of Lincoln Medical School.

Oxford Critical thinking and general studies are not acceptable. BMAT required. Approximately 30% of applicants called for interview on the basis of academic performance, test score and information on the application form. Ratio of interviewees to places approximately 2.5 to 1. No student admitted without an interview. All colleges use a common set of selection criteria. 11% success rate. Candidate's comment (Lincoln College): 'Two interviewers and two interviews. Questions covered my hobbies and social life, and scientific topics to test my logical train of thought. A great university, but it's not the be-all and end-all if you don't get in.' Clinical experience commences in Year 4.

Plymouth The typical offers published are not necessarily the threshold for selection for interview, which takes approximately 20 minutes. UKCAT must be taken; thresholds vary (approx 2,550–2,600 pts).

Queen's Belfast Majority of applicants are school-leavers. When considering applicants' **GCSE** performance, the best nine subjects will be scored on the basis of 4 points for an A* and 3 points for an A. Points will also be given or deducted on each UKCAT paper. Offers for re-sitting applicants will be restricted. These applicants will have been expected to have missed their offer by one grade. A proportion of candidates will be called for interview. Interviews based on the MMI format. A small number of places are allocated to non-EU applicants. Number of places restricted for re-sit applicants who have narrowly missed an offer at Queen's. Clinical experience from Year 1.

St Andrews Medicine students take a full three-year programme leading to BSc (Hons), followed by clinical medicine at one of its partner medical schools. UKCAT required. MMI format (see above) with six or more mini interviews or stations. Special attention given to international students and those who achieve qualifications at more than one sitting. As far as possible, the interview panel will reflect the gender and ethnic distribution of candidates for interview.

Sheffield Applications processed between October and end of March. Candidates may send additional information concerning extenuating circumstances or health problems via the University's Disrupted Studies form, which can be found at: www.sheffield.ac.uk/undergraduate/apply/applying/disrupted. UKCAT required; threshold available at: www.sheffield.ac.uk/medicine/prospective_ug/applying/entryrequire. MMI format used. A-level resits are not accepted. Gap year acceptable; medicine-related work very helpful. Clinical experience from Year 1. For more information, please see: www.sheffield.ac.uk/medicine/prospective_ug/applying.

Southampton 202 places available for five-year course. Please refer to the website for further information: www.southampton.ac.uk/medicine.

Sunderland For entry requirements to this new School of Medicine, see the university's website.

Swansea Graduate entry only.

Warwick Selection includes interview and group activities. UKCAT, work experience and a reference required. You should have, or be predicted to gain, a minimum of a 2.1 degree or overseas equivalent in any subject. Candidates with a 2.2 degree should hold a master's or doctoral qualification to be considered for entry.

Advice to applicants and planning the UCAS personal statement (See also **Admissions tutors' advice**) Nearly all universities now require either the UKCAT or BMAT entry tests to be taken before applying for Medicine. Check websites (www.ukcat.ac.uk; www.admissiontesting.org/for-test-takers/bmat) for details of test dates and test centres and with universities for their requirements. It is essential that you check for the latest information before applying and that you give yourself plenty of time to make arrangements for sitting these tests (see also **Chapter 5**).

Admissions tutors look for certain personal qualities (see **Admissions tutors' advice**) and these will emerge in your personal statement, at the interview and on your school or college reference. There should be evidence of scientific interest, commitment, enthusiasm, determination, stability, self-motivation, ability to organise your own work, interest in the welfare of others, communication skills, modesty (arrogance and over-confidence could lead to rejection!), breadth of interest, leadership skills, stamina, and good physical and mental health.

Some kind of first-hand experience in a medical setting is almost obligatory for those applying for Medicine (see also under **Admissions tutors' advice**). Depending on your personal contacts in the medical profession, this could include observing operations (for example, orthopaedic surgery), working in hospitals and discussing the career with your GP. Remember that your friends and relatives may have medical conditions that they would be willing to discuss with you – and all this will contribute to your knowledge and show that you are informed and interested. Read medical and scientific magazines and keep up-to-date with important current issues – AIDS, Ebola, assisted dying, abortion. Community work, clubs, societies, school and social activities should be mentioned. Show that you have an understanding of the role of health professionals in society and the social factors that influence health and disease. And finally, a comment from one admissions tutor: 'Don't rush around doing things just for your CV. If you are a boring student, be an incredibly well-read boring student! You can play netball, rugby, hockey, make beautiful music and paint with your feet, but if you fail to get the grades you'll be rejected.' **Bristol** Deferred places are limited. Late applications may not be accepted.

Misconceptions about this course Liverpool Some applicants think that three science subjects at A-level are required to study Medicine – wrong! **London (St George's)** That you should be white, middle class and male: 60% of medical students are now female and 53% of our students are not white.

Selection interviews Yes Aberdeen, Birmingham, Bristol, Cambridge, Dundee, East Anglia, Exeter, Glasgow, Hull York (MS), Keele, Lancaster, London (King's), London (St George's), Manchester, Newcastle, Nottingham, Oxford (11%), Plymouth, Queen's Belfast, St Andrews, Sussex; **Some** Edinburgh.

Interview advice and questions Questions will vary between applicants, depending on their UCAS statements and their A-level subjects. Questions are likely to relate to A-level specific subjects, general medicine topics and unconnected topics (see also **Admissions tutors' advice**). The following questions will provide a guide to the range of topics covered in past interviews. Outline the structure of DNA. What is meant by homeostasis? Is a virus a living organism? What has been the most important advance in biology in the last 50 years? What interests you about (i) science, (ii) biology, (iii) chemistry? Why did you choose the particular A-level subjects you are doing? Why do you want to study Medicine/become a doctor? Do you expect people to be grateful? Why do you want to study here? Why should we take you? What do you do to relax? What do you do when you have three or four things to do, and they are all equally urgent? How do you balance work and all the outside activities you do? Do you agree with the concept of 'foundation trusts'? What do you think about polyclinics? Do you think NHS doctors and staff should be able to take private patients? If you were in charge of finances for a large health authority, what would be your priorities for funding? If you had to decide between saving the life of a young child and that of an old person, what would you do? Would you treat lung cancer patients who refuse to give up smoking? What do you understand by 'gene therapy'? Can you give any examples? In your opinion, what is the most serious cause for concern for the health of the UK? What do you want to do with your medical degree? What do you think the human genome project can offer medicine? Should we pay for donor organs? Where do you see yourself in 15 years' time? What was the last non-technical book you read? What is your favourite piece of classical music? List your top five novels. What is your favourite play? What politician do you admire the most? Who made the most valuable contribution to the 20th century? Why do you think research is important? Why is teamwork important? What do you think about the NHS's problems? Do you think that sport is important? What did you gain from doing work experience in a nursing home? What were the standards like? How does the medical profession deal with social issues? What societies will you join at university? How could you compare your hobby of rowing to medicine? Do you agree that it is difficult to balance the demands of being a doctor with those of starting a family? In doing a medical course, what would you find the most emotionally challenging aspect? How would you cope with emotional strain? Who should have priority for receiving drugs in a flu epidemic/pandemic? How would you deal with the death of a patient? What are stem cells? Why are they controversial? How is cloning done? What constitutes a human being? Describe an egg. How can you measure intelligence? How do we combat genetic diseases? How are genes actually implanted? What do you want to talk about? If you were a cardiothoracic surgeon, would you perform a heart by-pass operation on a smoker? What are the negative aspects of becoming a doctor? At some interviews, essays may be set, eg (i) 'A scientific education is a good basis for a medical degree: discuss'; (ii) 'Only drugs that are safe and effective should be prescribed to patients: discuss'. Should someone sell their kidney? How would you describe a human to a person from Mars? Should obese people have treatment on the NHS? Occasionally applicants at interview may be given scenarios to discuss (see **Glasgow** under **Admissions tutors' advice**). See also **Chapter 5**. **Oxford** Tell me about drowning. What do you think of assisted suicide? Would you give a 60-year-old woman IVF treatment? When are people dead?

Reasons for rejection (non-academic) Insufficient vocation demonstrated. No steps taken to gain practical experience relevant to medicine. Doubts as to the ability to cope with the stress of a medical career. Not enough awareness about the career. Lack of knowledge about the course. Applicant appears dull and lacking in enthusiasm and motivation. Lacking a caring, committed attitude towards people. No evidence of broad social, cultural or sporting interests or of teamwork. Poor or lack of communication skills. Arrogance. Over-confident at interview. Unrealistic expectations about being a doctor. **Buckingham** Applicants are requested to attend an Open Day/Evening or a Tutorial Taster Day. The University believes it is very important for applicants to visit its campus. Candidates who do not respond to these invitations may be rejected, irrespective of academic achievement, as the University looks for committed, well-motivated students.

Age at entry Applicants must be 17 years old on 30 September of the year of entry. However, some medical schools stipulate 17 years and six months, and a small number stipulate 18 years. Those considering entry at 17 would probably be advised to take a gap year.

Health requirements Medical schools require all students to have their immunity status for hepatitis B, tuberculosis and rubella checked on entry. Offers are usually made subject to satisfactory health screening for hepatitis B. In line with advice from the General Medical Council, students will not be admitted to courses who are found to be e-antigen positive when screened within the first week of the course. Candidates accepting offers should assure themselves of their immunity status.

Mature students Medical schools usually accept a small number of mature students each year. However, several, if not the majority, reject applicants over 30 years of age. Some medical schools accept non-graduates although A-level passes at high grades are usually stipulated. The majority of applicants accepted are likely to be graduates with a first or 2.1 degree. **Birmingham** Applications from mature candidates are welcomed, but the length of training which has be to taken will be considered when assessing applications. **Leeds** There is no upper age limit for the course. Applicants should hold the required A-level grades or a high class science degree. **Southampton** Applicants with nursing qualifications should hold two grade A A-levels including chemistry and biology.

Advice to graduate applicants Graduate applicants are considered by all medical schools. At some medical schools the Graduate Australian Medical Schools Admission Test (GAMSAT) and the Medical Schools Admissions Test (MSAT) are now being used to assess the aptitude of prospective applicants. Applicants at some institutions are selected on the basis of three criteria: (i) an Honours degree at 2.2 or above; (ii) the GAMSAT score; (iii) performance at interview. All applicants must be EU students. **London (St George's)** Some students think that science graduates are the only ones to do well in GAMSAT: 40% of those on the course do not have a science degree or A-levels; however, work experience is essential.

AFTER-RESULTS ADVICE
Offers to applicants repeating A-levels Same Brighton and Sussex (MS).

GRADUATE DESTINATIONS AND EMPLOYMENT (2015/16 HESA)
Clinical Medicine graduates surveyed 4,680 **Employed** 4,520 **In voluntary employment** 10 **In further study** 90 **Assumed unemployed** 10

Career note Applicants should also bear in mind that while most doctors do work in the NHS, either in hospital services or in general practice, many graduates choose to work in other fields such as public health, pharmacology, the environment, occupational medicine with industrial organisations, the armed services and opportunities abroad.

OTHER DEGREE SUBJECTS FOR CONSIDERATION

Biomedical/Medical Materials Science; Biology; Biotechnology; Clinical Sciences; Dentistry; Dietetics; Genetics; Health Sciences; Immunology; Medical Biochemistry; Medical Engineering; Medical Microbiology; Medical Physics; Medical Product Design; Medical Sciences; Medicinal Chemistry; Midwifery; Nursing; Nutrition; Occupational Therapy; Optometry; Osteopathy; Pharmacology; Pharmacy; Physiology; Physiotherapy; Psychology; Radiography; Speech Sciences; Sports Medicine; Veterinary Medicine; Virology – and Law! (The work of doctors and lawyers is similar: both are required to identify the relevant information – clinical symptoms or legal issues!)

MICROBIOLOGY

(see also Biological Sciences, Biology, Biotechnology, Genetics)

Microbiology is a branch of biological science specialising in the study of micro-organisms: bacteria, viruses and fungi. The subject covers the relationship between these organisms and disease and industrial applications such as food and drug production, waste-water treatment and future biochemical uses.

Useful websites www.microbiologysociety.org; www.nature.com/subjects/microbiology; www.asm. org; www.microbiologynetwork.com; see also **Biochemistry**, **Biological Sciences** and **Biology**.

NB The points totals shown to the left of the institutions are for ease of reference only. It must not be assumed that Tariff points are always used by institutions or that they can be substituted for an offer in grades. The level of an offer is not necessarily indicative of the quality of a course.

COURSE OFFERS INFORMATION

Subject requirements/preferences GCSE English and mathematics and science subjects. **AL** One or two mathematics/science subjects including chemistry and/or biology required or preferred; grades sometimes specified.

Your target offers and examples of degree courses

144 pts **Edinburgh** – AAA incl biol+chem (Biol Sci (Dev Regn Stem Cells); Biol Sci (Mol Biol))
(IB 37 pts HL 666)

Imperial London – AAA incl biol+sci/maths (Microbiol) (IB 38 pts HL 6 biol+chem/maths)

Leeds – AAA–ABB incl chem/biol+sci (Microbiol) (IB 35–33 pts HL 18–17 pts incl 6 chem/biol+sci); (Med Microbiol) (IB 37–32 pts HL 18–17 pts incl 6 chem/biol+sci)

Manchester – AAA–ABB incl sci/maths +interview (Microbiol (Yr Ind); Microbiol Modn Lang) (IB 37–32 pts HL 5 sci)

Sheffield – AAA–AAB incl sci (Genet Microbiol; Genet Mol Cell Biol) (IB 36–34 pts HL 6 chem+sci); (Mol Biol; Microbiol; Med Microbiol) (IB 36–34 pts HL 6 sci)

York – AAA–AAB incl biol+chem/maths (Biotech Microbiol) (IB 36–35 pts HL 6 biol+chem/maths)

136 pts **Bristol** – AAB–BBB incl chem+sci/maths (Med Microbiol) (IB 34–31 pts HL 6/5 chem+sci); (Cell Mol Med) (IB 34–31 pts HL 6–5 chem+sci/maths)

Dundee – AAB incl biol+chem (Microbiol) (IB 34 pts (3 yr course) 30 pts (4 yr course) HL 665 (3 yr course) 555 (4 yr course))

Glasgow – AAB incl biol/chem (Microbiol; Mol Cell Biol (Plnt Sci)) (IB 36 pts HL 665 incl 6 sci); (Mol Cell Biol (Biotech)) (IB 36–34 pts)

Leicester – AAB–ABB+bEPQ incl sci/maths (Med Microbiol) (IB 32–30 pts)

Nottingham – AAB–ABB incl sci/maths/geog (Microbiol) (IB 34–32 pts)

128 pts **Aston** – ABB–BBB incl biol (Biol Sci (Cell Mol Biol); Microbiol Immun) (IB 32 pts HL 6 biol)

UCAS points Tariff: A* = 56 pts; A = 48 pts; B = 40 pts; C = 32 pts; D = 24 pts; E = 16 pts

Liverpool – ABB incl biol+sci (Microbiol) (IB 33 pts HL 6 biol)
Reading – ABB–BBB incl biol+sci (Microbiol) (IB 32–30 pts)
Stirling – ABB (3 yr course) BBB (4 yr course) incl sci/maths (Cell Biol) (IB 35 pts (3 yr course) 32 pts (4 yr course))
Strathclyde – ABB (3 yr course) BBB (4 yr course) incl biol/chem+sci (Immun Microbiol) (IB 32 pts HL 5 biol/chem+sci)
Surrey – ABB incl sci/maths (Fd Sci Microbiol) (IB 32 pts); ABB incl biol+sci/maths/geog (Microbiol; Microbiol (Med)) (IB 32 pts)

120 pts **Aberdeen** – BBB incl maths/sci (Microbiol) (IB 32 pts HL 5 maths/sci)
Heriot-Watt – BBB incl sci/maths (Biol Sci (Microbiol)) (IB 27 pts HL 5 biol)
Nottingham Trent – BBB incl biol 120 pts (Microbiol)
Queen's Belfast – BBB–ABB incl sci (Microbiol)
Strathclyde – BBB incl chem+biol (Microbiol (MSci)) (IB 34 pts HL 5 sci)

112 pts **Aberystwyth** – BBC–BBB incl biol (Microbiol) (IB 30 pts HL 5 biol)
Chester – BBC–BCC 112 pts (Microbiol) (IB 26 pts HL 5 biol/chem)
Glasgow Caledonian – BBC incl chem (Microbiol) (IB 28 pts)
Huddersfield – BBC incl sci 112 pts (Biol (Mol Cell))
Leeds Beckett – 112 pts incl biol+sci (Biomed Sci (Microbiol/Mol Biol)) (IB 25 pts HL 6 biol)

104 pts **Edinburgh Napier** – BCC incl sci (App Microbiol) (IB 28 pts HL 5 sci)
Glasgow Caledonian – BCC incl chem (Cell Mol Biol) (IB 24 pts)
Hertfordshire – 104 pts incl biol/chem+sci/maths/geog/psy (Mol Biol) (HL 44 incl biol/chem+sci)
Manchester Met – BCC–BBC incl biol 104–112 pts (Microbiol Mol Biol (St Abrd)) (IB 26 pts HL 5 biol)

80 pts **Wolverhampton** – BB/CDD incl sci (Microbiol)

Alternative offers
See **Chapter 6** and **Appendix 1** for grades/UCAS Tariff points information for other examinations.

EXAMPLES OF COLLEGES OFFERING COURSES IN THIS SUBJECT FIELD
St Helens (Coll).

CHOOSING YOUR COURSE (SEE ALSO CH.1)
Universities and colleges teaching quality See www.qaa.ac.uk; https://unistats.ac.uk.

Top research universities and colleges (REF 2014) See **Biological Sciences**.

Examples of sandwich degree courses See also **Biochemistry** and **Biological Sciences**. Aston; Leeds; Manchester; Manchester Met; Nottingham Trent; Queen's Belfast; Surrey; York.

ADMISSIONS INFORMATION
Number of applicants per place (approx) Bradford 6; Bristol 8; Cambridge 4; Dundee 8; Leeds 7; Liverpool (Lf Sci) 7; Nottingham 7; Strathclyde 10; Wolverhampton 4.

Advice to applicants and planning the UCAS personal statement Relevant experience, particularly for mature students. See **Biological Sciences** and also **Appendix 3**.

Selection interviews Yes Leeds, Manchester, Wolverhampton; **Some** Aberystwyth (mature students only); **No** Bristol, Dundee, Nottingham, Surrey.

Interview advice and questions Examples of past questions include: How much does the country spend on research and on the armed forces? Discuss reproduction in bacteria. What do you particularly like about your study of biology? What would you like to do after your degree? Do you have any strong views on vivisection? Discuss the differences between the courses you have applied for. What important advances have been made in the biological field recently? How would you describe microbiology? Do you know anything about the diseases caused by micro-organisms? What symptoms would be caused by which particular organisms? See also **Chapter 5**.

AFTER-RESULTS ADVICE
Offers to applicants repeating A-levels Higher Bristol, Strathclyde; **Same** Aberystwyth, Leeds, Liverpool, Nottingham, Wolverhampton.

GRADUATE DESTINATIONS AND EMPLOYMENT (2015/16 HESA)
Graduates surveyed 390 **Employed** 155 **In voluntary employment** 5 **In further study** 155 **Assumed unemployed** 15

Career note See **Biology**.

OTHER DEGREE SUBJECTS FOR CONSIDERATION
Animal Sciences; Biochemistry; Biological Sciences; Biology; Biotechnology; Genetics; Medical Sciences; Medicine; Molecular Biology; Pharmacology; Physiology.

MUSIC
(including **Music Technology**; see also **Engineering (Acoustics and Sound)**)

Theory and practice are combined to a greater or lesser extent in most university Music courses, and about 50% or more of graduates will go on to non-music careers. However, courses are also offered by conservatoires and schools of music where the majority of applicants are aiming to become professional musicians. For these courses, the ability to perform on an instrument is more important than academic ability and offers are therefore likely to be lower. When choosing music courses, the applicant should also be aware of the specialisms offered, such as classical, jazz, new music, popular music and film music (Leeds College of Music) in addition to courses in music production and music business. Music Journalism is also an option on some courses. See also **Appendix 2**. Some applications are made through UCAS Conservatoires (formerly CUKAS): see **Chapter 4** for details.

Useful websites www.ism.org; www.roh.org.uk; www.nyo.org.uk; www.ucas.com/ucas/conservatoires; www.artscouncil.org.uk; www.soundandmusic.org; http://gb.abrsm.org/en/home

NB The points totals shown to the left of the institutions are for ease of reference only. It must not be assumed that Tariff points are always used by institutions or that they can be substituted for an offer in grades. The level of an offer is not necessarily indicative of the quality of a course.

COURSE OFFERS INFORMATION
Subject requirements/preferences GCSE A foreign language and mathematics may be required. A good range of As and Bs for popular universities. **AL** Music plus an instrumental grade usually required.

Your target offers and examples of degree courses
160 pts Imperial London – A*A*A incl maths+phys +interview +audition +gr 8 (Phys Mus Perf) (IB 40 pts HL 766)
152 pts Cambridge – A*AA incl mus +interview (Mus) (IB 40–42 pts HL 776)
        Edinburgh – A*AA–AAB (Maths Mus) (IB 37 pts HL 666)
144 pts Edinburgh – AAA incl maths+phys (Phys Mus) (IB 37 pts HL 666)
        Oxford – AAA incl mus +interview (Mus) (IB 38 pts HL 666)
        Southampton – AAA–AAB incl maths+mus (Maths Mus) (IB 36 pts HL 6 maths)
        Surrey – AAA incl maths+mus+phys (Mus Snd Rec (Tonmeister)) (IB 34 pts)
136 pts Birmingham – AAB (Mus) (IB 32 pts HL 665)
        Cardiff – AAB–BBB incl mus +gr 8 (Mus courses) (IB 32 pts HL 6 music)
        Durham – AAB incl mus (Mus) (IB 36 pts)
        Edinburgh – AAB incl mus (Hist Art Hist Mus) (IB 38 pts HL 666)
        Glasgow – AAB incl arts/hum/lang +gr 5 (Mus) (IB 36 pts HL 6 Engl/hum/lang)
        Leeds – AAB +interview +audition +gr 8 (Mus (Perf)) (IB 35 pts HL 6 mus); AAB (Mus) (IB 35 pts HL 6 mus); AAB–ABB incl mus (Mus Comb Hons) (IB 35–34 pts HL 6 music)

London (King's) – AAB incl mus (Ger Mus (Yr Abrd)) (IB 35 pts HL 665 incl 6 mus); AAB (Mus) (IB 35 pts HL 665)

London (RH) – AAB incl maths+phys (Phys Mus) (IB 32 pts HL 665); AAB–ABB (Mus Pol St) (IB 32 pts HL 6 mus); (Mus Phil) (IB 32 pts HL 655); (Dr Mus) (IB 32 pts)

Manchester – AAB incl mus +gr 8 (Mus) (IB 35 pts HL 6 mus); AAB incl mus +interview +gr 8 (Mus Dr) (IB 35 pts HL 665)

Newcastle – AAB–BBB (Folk Trad Mus) (IB 34–32 pts)

Nottingham – AAB–ABB incl mus/mus tech (Mus) (IB 32 pts HL 5 mus); AAB–ABB incl mus (Mus Phil) (IB 32 pts HL 5 mus)

Southampton – AAB–ABB incl mus +gr 8 (Phil Mus) (IB 34–32 pts HL 6 mus); AAB–ABB+aEPQ incl Engl+mus +gr 8 (Engl Mus) (IB 34 pts HL 6 Engl+mus); AAB incl maths+phys+mus +interview (Acoust Mus) (IB 34 pts HL 6 maths 5 phys+mus); AAB–BBB incl mus +gr 8 (Mus Mgt Sci; Mus) (IB 34–30 pts HL 6 mus)

York – AAB–ABB (Mus) (IB 35–34 pts HL 6 mus)

128 pts **Bangor** – 128–120 pts incl mus (Mus)

Bristol – ABB–BBC incl mus (Mus) (IB 32–29 pts HL 6/5 mus)

City – ABB incl mus 128 pts +gr 7 (Mus) (IB 32 pts HL 6 mus)

Edinburgh – ABB (Mus) (IB 39 pts HL 666)

Glasgow – ABB incl mus +gr 8 +audition +interview (BMus) (IB 34 pts)

Liverpool – ABB/BBB+aEPQ (Mus Pop Mus) (IB 33 pts)

London (Gold) – BBB +interview (Mus) (IB 33 pts HL 655); (Pop Mus) (IB 33 pts)

London (RH) – ABB–BBB (Modn Lang Mus) (IB 32 pts HL 555)

Newcastle – ABB–BBB incl mus (Mus) (IB 32 pts)

Sheffield – ABB/BBB+bEPQ (Mus; Mus Comb Hons) (IB 33 pts)

Surrey – ABB incl mus/mus tech (Crea Mus Tech) (IB 32 pts); ABB incl mus +interview (Mus) (IB 32 pts)

Sussex – ABB–BBB (Mus Tech; Mus) (IB 30 pts HL 5 mus)

120 pts **Aberdeen** – BBB (Mus St courses) (IB 32 pts HL 555)

Anglia Ruskin – 120 pts incl mus/mus tech +interview/audition (Mus)

Bangor – 120–104 pts (Mus Crea Writ; Mus Film St)

Coventry – BBB incl maths/phys/tech/mus +portfolio (Mus Tech) (IB 31 pts)

Derby – 120–128 pts +interview (Pop Mus Mus Tech); 120–128 pts incl sci/maths/mus/tech +interview (Mus Tech Prod)

Edge Hill – BBB 120 pts (Media Mus Snd)

Gloucestershire – BBB 120 pts (Mus Bus)

Huddersfield – BBB 120 pts (Mus Tech Aud Sys); BBB incl mus/mus tech 120 pts (BMus)

Hull – 120 pts incl mus/mus tech (Mus) (IB 28 pts)

Leeds Beckett – 120 pts +interview (Perf Arts) (IB 26 pts)

Liverpool Hope – BBB–BBC incl mus 120–112 pts +interview +audition (Mus)

London (SOAS) – BBB (Mus Comb Hons) (IB 31 pts HL 554)

Middlesex – 120 pts (Mus Bus Arts Mgt)

Queen's Belfast – BBB incl mus (Mus)

Reading – BBB–BBC incl mus +interview (P Ed Mus Spec) (IB 30–28 pts HL 5 mus)

Trinity Saint David – 120 pts +interview +portfolio (Mus Tech) (IB 32 pts)

West London – BBB 120–128 pts +audition (Musl Thea)

112 pts **Brighton** – BBC–CCC 112–96 pts +interview +portfolio (Dig Mus Snd Arts) (IB 28 pts)

Chester – BBC 112 pts (Musl Thea) (IB 26 pts); 112 pts +audition (Pop Mus Perf) (IB 26 pts)

Coventry – BBC +interview +audition (Mus) (IB 29 pts)

Creative Arts – 112 pts +interview (Mus Jrnl)

East London – 112 pts incl mus (Mus Perf Prod) (IB 25 pts HL 15 pts)

Gloucestershire – BBC 112 pts +interview +portfolio (Pop Mus)

Glyndŵr – 112 pts (Mus Tech)

Huddersfield – BBC 112 pts (Mus Jrnl)

Kent – BBC (Mus Bus Prod; Mus Tech Aud Prod; Mus Perf Prod) (IB 34 pts)

Kingston – 112–128 pts incl mus/mus tech +interview (Mus Tech; Pop Mus)

Check **Chapter 3** for new university admission details and **Chapter 6** on how to read the subject tables.

Leeds Beckett – 112 pts (Mus Prod; Mus Tech) (IB 25 pts)

Liverpool (LIPA) – BBC 112 pts +interview (Snd Tech)

Middlesex – 112 pts (Pop Mus); 112 pts +audition (Mus)

Plymouth – 112 pts +interview (P (Mus)) (IB 28 pts)

Portsmouth – 112 pts (Mus Snd Tech) (IB 26 pts)

Southampton Solent – 112 pts (Mus Prom; Pop Mus Prod)

Staffordshire – BBC 112 pts (Mus Tech)

Sunderland – 112 pts (Jazz Pop Commer Mus)

UWE Bristol – 112 pts incl mus+sci/mus tech +audition (Crea Mus Tech)

West London – BBC 112–128 pts incl mus (Mus Cmpsn Rec); BBC 112–128 pts +gr 8 (Mus Tech Pop Mus Perf); BBC 112–128 pts (Voice Perf; Mus Perf Tech)

West Scotland – BBC (3 yr course) CCC (4 yr course) (Commer Mus) (IB 28 pts (3 yr course) 24 pts (4 yr course))

Wolverhampton – BBC +audition (Mus; Mus Pop Mus); BBC +interview (Mus Tech)

104 pts **Anglia Ruskin** – 104 pts (Aud Mus Tech) (IB 24 pts)

Bath Spa – BCC incl mus/mus tech +interview +portfolio (Commer Mus) (IB 27 pts)

Brunel – BCC incl mus +audition (Mus) (IB 28 pts)

Central Lancashire – 104 pts (Mus; Mus Prod; Mus Thea)

Chichester – 104–120 pts +audition (Musl Thea (Trpl Threat)) (IB 28 pts)

De Montfort – 104 pts incl mus/mus tech (Crea Mus Tech) (IB 24 pts HL 5 mus/mus tech); (Mus Tech Perf) (IB 28 pts HL 5 mus/mus tech); 104 pts (Mus Tech) (IB 24 pts)

Edinburgh Napier – BCC incl mus+Engl (Mus) (IB 27 pts HL 5 mus/Engl); (Mus (Pop)) (IB 27 pts HL 5 mus+Engl)

Falmouth – 104–120 pts +interview +audition (Crea Mus Tech; Pop Mus); 104–120 pts (Mus)

Hertfordshire – 104 pts incl mus/mus tech (Mus Cmpsn Tech) (HL 44)

Keele – BCC (Mus Tech) (IB 28 pts); BCC +gr 7 (Mus) (IB 28 pts)

Northampton – BCC +interview (Pop Mus courses)

Oxford Brookes – BCC 104 pts +audition (Mus) (IB 29 pts)

Plymouth – 104 pts incl mus (Mus) (IB 26 pts HL 4 mus)

RConsvS – BCC incl mus +audition (Mus (BEd))

South Wales – BCC–CDD +interview (Pop Commer Mus) (HL 655–445)

Winchester – 104–120 pts (Mus Snd Prod)

96 pts **Chichester** – 96–112 pts +audition (Choral Dir; Mus) (IB 26 pts)

Derby – 96–128 pts (Pop Mus Prod Comb Hons)

Leeds (CMus) – 96 pts +audition +gr 5 (Mus (Comb)); 96 pts +portfolio +gr 5 (Mus (Prod)); 96 pts +audition +gr 8/6 (Mus (Class Mus); Mus (Jazz); Mus (Pop Mus))

Liverpool (LIPA) – CCC incl mus/mus tech 96 pts +audition (Mus); CCC 96 pts (Mgt Mus Enter Thea Evnts)

Middlesex – 96 pts +audition (Jazz)

Rose Bruford (Coll) – 96 pts +audition (Actr Mushp)

88 pts **Canterbury Christ Church** – 88–112 pts (Mus (Commer Mus)); 88–112 pts incl mus (Mus)

Teesside – 88–112 pts +interview (Mus Tech)

West Scotland – CCD incl mus+maths (Mus Tech) (IB 24 pts)

York St John – 88–104 pts (Mus courses)

80 pts **Bedfordshire** – 80 pts +interview (Mus Tech)

Birmingham City – 80 pts +interview +portfolio (Mus Bus)

Bucks New – 80–96 pts (Aud Mus Prod; Mus Perf Mgt)

72 pts **UHI** – BC +interview +audition (Gael Trad Mus)

64 pts **London (Royal Central Sch SpDr)** – CC +audition (Actg (Musl Thea))

Ravensbourne – CC (Mus Snd Prod) (IB 28 pts)

32 pts **Guildhall (Sch Mus Dr)** – EE (Perf Crea Ent) (IB 24 pts); EE +audition (Mus) (IB 24 pts)

London (RAcMus) – EE incl mus +audition (BMus)

RCMus – EE +audition (BMus) (IB 24 pts)

RConsvS – EE +audition (BMus courses; Musl Thea) (IB 24 pts)

RNCM – EE +audition (BMus)

UCAS points Tariff: A* = 56 pts; A = 48 pts; B = 40 pts; C = 32 pts; D = 24 pts; E = 16 pts

Royal Welsh (CMusDr) – EE incl mus +interview/audition (BMus)
Trinity Laban Consv – EE incl mus +audition +gr 8 check with admissions tutor (Mus)
24 pts UHI – D +interview +audition (Pop Mus)

Alternative offers
See **Chapter 6** and **Appendix 1** for grades/UCAS Tariff points information for other examinations.

EXAMPLES OF COLLEGES OFFERING COURSES IN THIS SUBJECT FIELD

Most colleges, check with your local college. Accrington and Rossendale (Coll); Barnfield (Coll); Barnsley (Coll); Bath (Coll); Bedford (Coll); Birmingham Met (Coll); Blackpool and Fylde (Coll); Bournemouth and Poole (Coll); Bradford (Coll); Brighton Met (Coll); Buckinghamshire (Coll Group); Calderdale (Coll); Canterbury (Coll); Carshalton (Coll); City and Islington (Coll); Colchester (Inst); Cornwall (Coll); Coventry (Coll); Doncaster (Coll); Dudley (Coll); Ealing, Hammersmith and West London (Coll); East Surrey (Coll); Exeter (Coll); Fareham (Coll); Gateshead (Coll); Gloucestershire (Coll); Grimsby (Inst Group); Havant and South Downs (Coll); Havering (Coll); Hertford (Reg Coll); HOW (Coll); Hull (Coll); Kingston (Coll); Leicester (Coll); Liverpool City (Coll); Manchester (Coll); MidKent (Coll); Neath Port Talbot (Coll); Nescot; Newcastle (Coll); Northbrook Met (Coll); Oaklands (Coll); Petroc; Rotherham (CAT); Sheffield (Coll); South Essex (Coll); South Gloucestershire and Stroud (Coll); Telford New (Coll); Tresham (CFHE); Truro and Penwith (Coll); Westminster City (Coll); Wigan and Leigh (Coll).

CHOOSING YOUR COURSE (SEE ALSO CH.1)

Universities and colleges teaching quality See www.qaa.ac.uk; https://unistats.ac.uk.

Top research universities and colleges (REF 2014) (Music, Drama, Dance and Performing Arts) Open University; Roehampton (Dance); London (QM); Warwick; London (SOAS); Durham; London (RH) (Mus); Southampton; Oxford; Birmingham (Mus); City; London (King's) (Film); Manchester (Dr); London (RH) (Dr Thea); Huddersfield; Manchester (Mus); Cardiff.

Examples of sandwich degree courses Birmingham City; Bournemouth; Coventry; Hertfordshire; Huddersfield; Leeds; Leeds Beckett; Oxford Brookes; Portsmouth; Staffordshire; Surrey; UWE Bristol.

ADMISSIONS INFORMATION

Number of applicants per place (approx) Anglia Ruskin 5; Bangor 4; Bath Spa 8; Birmingham 8; Bristol 8; Cambridge 2; Cardiff 6; City 7; Colchester (Inst) 4; Cumbria 7; Durham 6; Edinburgh 6; Edinburgh Napier 8; Glasgow 4; Huddersfield 2; Hull 5; Kingston 18; Leeds 18; Liverpool 6; Liverpool (LIPA) 12; London (Gold) 7; London (King's) 10; London (RAcMus) 7; London (RH) 6; London (SOAS) 4; Manchester 6; Middlesex 23; Newcastle 3; Northampton 3; Nottingham 5; Oxford Brookes 7; Queen's Belfast 6; RCMus 10; RConsvS 6; RNCM 8; Rose Bruford (Coll) 15; Southampton 6; Trinity Laban Consv 4; Ulster 8; York 8; York St John 2.

Advice to applicants and planning the UCAS personal statement In addition to your ability and expertise with your chosen musical instrument(s), it is also important to know your composers and to take a critical interest in various kinds of music. Reference should be made to these, visits to concerts listed and any special interests indicated in types of musical activity, for example, opera, ballet. Work with orchestras, choirs and other musical groups should also be included and full details given of any competitions entered and awards obtained. See **Chapter 4** for details of applications for Music courses at conservatoires. **Guildhall (Sch Mus Dr)** International applicants sending extra documentation from overseas must make sure that for Customs purposes they indicate that they will pay any import tax charged. **London (Gold)** We encourage students to bring examples of their written and creative work. **London (SOAS)** Candidates are judged on individual merits. Applicants are expected to have substantial practical experience of musical performance, but not necessarily Western music. **Royal Welsh (CMusDr)** Evidence of performance-related experience, eg youth orchestras, solo work, prizes, scholarships etc. Our course is a conservatoire course as opposed to a more academic university course. We offer a very high standard of performance tuition balanced with academic theory modules.

Misconceptions about this course Cardiff Some mistakenly think that the BMus scheme is either performance-based or something inferior to the principal music-based degree.

Check **Chapter 3** for new university admission details and **Chapter 6** on how to read the subject tables.

Selection interviews Most institutions, plus audition to include a performance of a prepared piece (or pieces) on main instrument. **Yes** Aberdeen, Anglia Ruskin, Bath Spa, Birmingham City, Bucks New, Cambridge, Cardiff, Chichester, Edinburgh Napier, Glasgow, Guildhall (Sch Mus Dr), Leeds, Liverpool (LIPA), London (Gold), Manchester, Oxford (36%), York; **Some** Bristol, Canterbury Christ Church, Coventry, Surrey, West London; **No** Birmingham, Chester, Edinburgh, Falmouth, Hertfordshire, Huddersfield, Leeds Beckett, Staffordshire.

Interview advice and questions See also **Chapter 4** under Applications for Music Courses at Conservatoires. **Bangor** Offer depends on proven ability in historical or compositional fields plus acceptable performance standard. Options include music therapy, recording techniques and jazz. **Bath Spa** Candidates are required to submit three examples of their work prior to audition and then perform an original piece at audition. Discussion of previous performing, composing and academic experience. **Bristol** (Mus Fr/Ger/Ital) No in-depth interviews; candidates invited to Open Days. **Cambridge** (St Catharine's) At interview, candidates have to undergo some simple keyboard or aural tests (including harmonisation of an unseen melody and memorisation of a rhythm). They will also have to comment on some unseen musical extracts from a stylistic and analytical point of view and a passage of musicological literature. Candidates are usually asked to submit some examples of work before the interview, which can be from the fields of harmony and counterpoint, history and analysis; they are also encouraged to send any other material such as compositions, programme notes or an independent essay on a subject of interest to the candidate. (Taking the STEP examination is not a requirement for admission.) Above all this, though, the main prerequisite for reading Music at St Catharine's is an academic interest in the subject itself. **Colchester (Inst)** Great stress laid on candidate's ability to communicate love of the subject. **Durham** Grade 7 or 8 in first instrument and keyboard skills advisable. **Edinburgh Napier** Most candidates are called for interview, although very well-qualified candidates may be offered a place without interview. All are asked to submit samples of their work. Associated Board or Trinity Guildhall Grade 5 theory required. **Hull (Coll)** Good instrumental grades can improve chances of an offer and of confirmation in August. Students are not normally required to attend an audition/interview. Decisions will be made according to the information supplied on the UCAS application. Successful applicants will be invited to attend a departmental Open Day. We welcome applications from mature students and those with unconventional qualifications: in such cases an interview may be required. **Leeds** Intending students should follow an academic rather than practical-oriented A-level course. Interviews and auditions last approximately 20 minutes. Grade 8 Associated Board on an instrument is a normal expectation. **Liverpool (LIPA)** In addition to performing in orchestras etc, give details of any compositions you have completed (the number and styles). Instrumentalists (including vocalists) should describe any performance/gig experience together with any musical instrument grades achieved. (Mus) Candidates should prepare two pieces of contrasting music to play on their chosen instrument. They are likely to be asked to send three music tracks and a biography prior to audition. (Snd Tech) Applicants will be expected to analyse a sound recording of their choice, highlighting the technical and production values that they think are the most important. Examples of recorded work they have undertaken should also be available at interview, eg on CD. **London (Gold)** The interview will include a discussion of music and the personal interests of the applicant. **London (RAcMus)** All candidates are called for audition; places are usually offered later, subject to the minimum **GCSE** requirements being achieved. (BMus) Applicants sit a 50-minute written paper, and may also be tested on keyboard and aural performance. **RCMus** All UK and Eire candidates are required to attend an audition in person, but recordings are acceptable from overseas applicants. It must be stressed, however, that personal audition is preferable and those students offered places on the basis of a recorded audition may be required to take a confirmatory audition on arrival. Candidates are required to perform on the principal study instrument, and may also be required to undertake sight-reading, aural tests and paperwork. There is also an interview. Potential scholars sometimes proceed to a second audition, usually on the same day. The academic requirement for the BMus (RCM) course is two A-levels at pass grades. Acceptance is ultimately based on the quality of performance at audition, performing experience and perceived potential as a performer. As a guide, applicants should be of at least Grade 8 distinction standard. **RNCM** All applicants are called for audition. Successful applicants proceed to an academic interview which will include aural tests and questions on music theory and history. Student comment: 'A 45-minute interview with a panel of three. Focus was on portfolio of compositions sent in advance. Prior to interview was asked to harmonise a short passage and study an orchestral excerpt followed up at interview. Aural test waived.' **Royal Welsh (CMusDr)** All UK and Eire applicants are called to audition and/or interview in person; overseas candidates may audition by sending a recording. Candidates may be required to demonstrate their sight-reading ability or complete a short aural test. Composers are required to send recent examples of their work to discuss at interview. **Trinity Laban Consv** Applicants for the BMus degree must attend an audition and show that they have attained a certain level of competence in their principal and second studies, musical subjects and in musical theory. Grade 8 practical and theory can count as one A-level, but not if the second A-level is in music. Overseas applicants may submit a tape recording of their audition; video recordings are preferred. They must also show evidence of good aural perception in musical techniques and musical analysis. **Wolverhampton** The audition will involve playing/singing a piece of own-choice music (up to five minutes – no longer). Accompanists may be brought along or the department may be able to provide one if requested in advance. Candidates will be requested to produce a short piece of written work. It would be helpful to see any music certificates if available, together with examples of recent work in music (an essay, harmony, composition etc).

Reasons for rejection (non-academic) Usually academic (auditions, practical, aural/written test). Dull, unenthusiastic students, ignorant about their subject, showing lack of motivation and imagination. **Cambridge** Her harmony was marred by elementary technical errors and her compositions lacked formal and stylistic focus. **London (King's)** Apparent lack of interest, performance not good enough, lack of music history knowledge. Foreign students: language skills inadequate. **Royal Welsh (CMusDr)** Performing/technical ability not of the required standard.

AFTER-RESULTS ADVICE
Offers to applicants repeating A-levels Higher Leeds; **Same** Anglia Ruskin, Bath Spa, Bristol, Cardiff, City, Colchester (Inst), De Montfort, Durham, Guildhall (Sch Mus Dr), Huddersfield, Hull, Kingston, Leeds (CMus), London (RAcMus), London (RH), Nottingham, Rose Bruford (Coll), Royal Welsh (CMusDr), Staffordshire, York, York St John.

GRADUATE DESTINATIONS AND EMPLOYMENT (2015/16 HESA)
Graduates surveyed 4,055 **Employed** 1,465 **In voluntary employment** 110 **In further study** 1190 **Assumed unemployed** 215

Career note Some graduates go into performance-based careers, many enter the teaching profession and others go into a wide range of careers requiring graduate skills.

OTHER DEGREE SUBJECTS FOR CONSIDERATION
Acoustics; Drama; Musical Theatre; Performance Arts.

NATURAL SCIENCES
(see also **Biological Sciences**)

These are flexible courses allowing the student to gain a broad view of the origins and potential of sciences in general and then to focus in Years 2 and 3 on a specialist area of scientific study.

Useful websites www.scicentral.com; www.nature.com; see also **Biology**, **Chemistry** and **Physics**.

NB The points totals shown to the left of the institutions are for ease of reference only. It must not be assumed that Tariff points are always used by institutions or that they can be substituted for an offer in grades. The level of an offer is not necessarily indicative of the quality of a course.

COURSE OFFERS INFORMATION
Subject requirements/preferences GCSE Strong results, particularly in the sciences. **AL** Science subjects required.

Your target offers and examples of degree courses

160 pts **Cambridge** – A*A*A incl sci/maths +interview +NSAA (Nat Sci (Astro)) (IB 40–42 pts HL 776); (Nat Sci (Physiol Dev Neuro); Nat Sci (Bioch); Nat Sci (Biol Biomed Sci); Nat Sci (Chem); Nat Sci (Genet); Nat Sci (Earth Sci); Nat Sci (Mat Sci); Nat Sci (Hist Phil Sci); Nat Sci (Zool); Nat Sci (Neuro); Nat Sci) (IB 40–42 pts HL 776)

152 pts **Bath** – A*AA incl maths/sci (Nat Sci (St Abrd)) (IB 36 pts HL 776 maths+sci); A*AA/AAA+aEPQ incl maths+sci (Nat Sci) (IB 36 pts HL 766 incl maths+sci)

Birmingham – A*AA–AAA +admissions essay (Librl Arts Sci (Nat Sci)) (IB 36–35 pts)

Durham – A*AA incl sci (Nat Sci) (IB 38 pts)

East Anglia – A*AA incl sci (Nat Sci (MNatSci)) (IB 35 pts HL 6 sci/maths); (Nat Sci (Yr Ind/St Abrd)) (IB 35 pts HL 6 sci)

Exeter – A*AA–AAB incl maths+sci (Nat Sci) (IB 38–34 pts HL 5 maths+sci)

Lancaster – A*AA–AAA incl sci (Nat Sci) (IB 38–36 pts HL 6 sci)

Leeds – A*AA (Nat Sci) (IB 36 pts)

London (UCL) – A*AA–AAA incl sci/maths/geol (Nat Sci) (IB 39–38 pts HL 5 sci/maths)

Nottingham – A*AA incl sci/maths (Nat Sci) (IB 38 pts HL 6/7 sci/maths)

144 pts **East Anglia** – AAA incl sci +interview (Nat Sci) (IB 34 pts HL 6 sci)

136 pts **Loughborough** – AAB incl sci (Nat Sci) (IB 37 pts HL 666)

Open University – contact 0300 303 0073 **or** www.open.ac.uk/contact/new (Nat Sci)

Alternative offers
See **Chapter 6** and **Appendix 1** for grades/UCAS Tariff points information for other examinations.

CHOOSING YOUR COURSE (SEE ALSO CH.1)

Universities and colleges teaching quality See www.qaa.ac.uk; https://unistats.ac.uk.

Top research universities and colleges (REF 2014) See separate science tables.

Examples of sandwich degree courses Bath; East Anglia; Leeds.

ADMISSIONS INFORMATION

Number of applicants per place (approx) Bath 8; Birmingham 10; Cambridge 4; Durham 6; Lancaster 4; London (UCL) 4; Nottingham 7.

Advice to applicants and planning the UCAS personal statement See **Biology**, **Chemistry**, **Physics** and **Appendix 3**.

Selection interviews Yes Cambridge, East Anglia; **Some** Bath; **No** Birmingham.

Interview advice and questions See also **Chapter 5**. **Cambridge** Questions depend on subject choices and studies at A-level and past questions have included the following: Discuss the setting up of a chemical engineering plant and the probabilities of failure of various components. Questions on the basic principles of physical chemistry, protein structure and functions and physiology. Questions on biological specimens. Comment on the theory of evolution and the story of the Creation in Genesis. What are your weaknesses? Questions on electro-micrographs. What do you talk about with your friends? How would you benefit from a university education? What scientific magazines do you read? Questions on atoms, types of bonding and structures. What are the problems of being tall? What are the differences between metals and non-metals? Why does graphite conduct? Questions on quantum physics and wave mechanics. How could you contribute to life here? What do you see yourself doing in five years' time? If it is common public belief that today's problems, for example industrial pollution, are caused by scientists, why do you wish to become one? Questions on the gyroscopic motion of cycle wheels, the forces on a cycle in motion and the design of mountain bikes. What do you consider will be the most startling scientific development in the future? What do you estimate is the mass of air in this room? If a carrot can grow from one carrot cell, why not a human?

AFTER-RESULTS ADVICE

Offers to applicants repeating A-levels No Cambridge.

GRADUATE DESTINATIONS AND EMPLOYMENT (2015/16 HESA)
See **Biology**, **Chemistry**, **Mathematics** and **Physics**.

Career note These courses offer a range of science and in some cases non-scientific subjects, providing students with the flexibility to develop particular interests as they progress through the course.

OTHER DEGREE SUBJECTS FOR CONSIDERATION
Anatomy; Anthropology; Archaeology; Astrophysics; Biochemistry; Biological Sciences; Biology; Chemistry; Earth Sciences; Ecology; Genetics; Geography; Geology; History and Philosophy of Science; Neuroscience; Pharmacology; Physics; Plant Sciences; Psychology; Zoology.

NAVAL ARCHITECTURE
(including **Mechanical and Marine Engineering** and **Ship Science**; see also **Marine/Maritime** Studies)

Professional naval architects or marine engineers are responsible for the design, construction and repair of cruise liners, yachts, submarines, container ships and oil tankers. Ship Science focuses on, for example, vehicles and structures that use the oceans for transport, recreation and energy generation. Courses cover marine structures, transport and operations, design, propulsion and mathematics. Ship design has many similarities to the design of aircraft.

Useful websites www.rina.org.uk; www.naval-architecture.co.uk

NB The points totals shown to the left of the institutions are for ease of reference only. It must not be assumed that Tariff points are always used by institutions or that they can be substituted for an offer in grades. The level of an offer is not necessarily indicative of the quality of a course.

COURSE OFFERS INFORMATION
Subject requirements/preferences GCSE Grades A–C (7–4) in mathematics and physics are normally required. **AL** Mathematics and physics usually required.

Your target offers and examples of degree courses

152 pts **Strathclyde** – A*AA incl maths+phys (Nvl Archit Mar Eng (MEng); Nvl Archit Ocn Eng (MEng)) (IB 36 pts HL 6 maths+phys)

144 pts **Newcastle** – AAA incl maths+phys/chem/fmaths (Mar Tech Sml Crft Tech (MEng); Mar Tech Off Eng (MEng)) (IB 37 pts HL 6 maths+phys/chem); (Mar Tech Mar Eng (MEng)) (IB 37 pts HL 6 phys/chem)

Southampton – AAA–AAB+aEPQ incl maths+phys (Ship Sci (Eng Mgt) (MEng); Ship Sci (Nvl Archit) (MEng); Ship Sci (Nvl Eng) (MEng); Ship Sci (Ycht Sml Crft) (MEng); Ship Sci) (IB 36 pts HL 6 maths+phys); AAB–AAB+aEPQ (Ship Sci (Advncd Mat) (MEng)) (IB 36 pts HL 6 maths+phys)

136 pts **Newcastle** – AAB–ABB incl maths+phys/chem/fmaths (Mar Tech Sml Crft Tech; Mar Tech Mar Eng) (IB 35–34 pts HL 5 maths+phys/chem)

128 pts **Liverpool John Moores** – ABB incl maths+sci/tech/eng 128 pts (Mech Mar Eng (MEng)) (IB 27 pts HL 6 maths+phys)

120 pts **Plymouth** – 120 pts incl sci/maths/geog (Ocn Sci (MSci)) (IB 28 pts HL 5 sci/maths/geog)

Strathclyde – BBB incl maths+phys (Nvl Archit Mar Eng; Nvl Archit Ocn Eng) (IB 32 pts HL 5 maths+phys)

112 pts **Liverpool John Moores** – 112 pts (Naut Sci); BBC incl maths+phys/eng/tech 112 pts (Mech Mar Eng) (IB 26 pts HL 5 maths+phys)

Plymouth – 112–120 pts incl maths+sci/tech (Mar Tech) (IB 30 pts HL 5 maths 4 sci/tech)

Southampton Solent – 112 pts (Ycht Des Prod)

Alternative offers
See **Chapter 6** and **Appendix 1** for grades/UCAS Tariff points information for other examinations.

EXAMPLES OF COLLEGES OFFERING COURSES IN THIS SUBJECT FIELD
Cornwall (Coll); Plymouth City (Coll).

CHOOSING YOUR COURSE (SEE ALSO CH.1)
Universities and colleges teaching quality See www.qaa.ac.uk; https://unistats.ac.uk.

ADMISSIONS INFORMATION
Number of applicants per place (approx) Southampton 4.

Advice to applicants and planning the UCAS personal statement Special interests in this subject area should be described fully. Visits to shipyards and awareness of ship design from the *Mary Rose* in Portsmouth to modern speedboats should be fully explained and the problems noted. See also **Engineering/Engineering Sciences**, **Marine/Maritime Studies** and **Appendix 3**.

Selection interviews No Newcastle, Southampton.

Interview advice and questions Because of the highly vocational nature of this subject, applicants will naturally be expected to discuss any work experience and to justify their reasons for choosing the course. See also **Chapter 5**.

AFTER-RESULTS ADVICE
Offers to applicants repeating A-levels Higher Newcastle.

GRADUATE DESTINATIONS AND EMPLOYMENT (2015/16 HESA)
Graduates surveyed 50 **Employed** 35 **In voluntary employment** 0 **In further study** 0 **Assumed unemployed** 0

Career note A small proportion of naval architects work in the shipbuilding and repair industry, others are involved in the construction of oil rigs or may work for ship-owning companies. There are also a number of firms of marine consultants employing naval architects as managers or consultants.

OTHER DEGREE SUBJECTS FOR CONSIDERATION
Aeronautical Engineering; Civil Engineering; Electrical/Electronic Engineering; Geography; Marine Biology; Marine Engineering; Marine/Maritime Studies; Marine Technology; Mechanical Engineering; Oceanography; Physics; Shipping Operations; Transport Management.

NEUROSCIENCE

(including **Anatomical Science**; see also **Biological Sciences, Human Sciences/Human Biosciences, Physiology, Psychology**)

Courses in Neuroscience include the study of biochemistry, cell and molecular biology, genetics and physiology and focus on the structure and functions of the brain. It also overlaps into neurobiology, neuroanatomy, neurophysiology, pharmacology and psychology which in turn can involve the study of behavioural problems and mental processes, both conscious and unconscious. It is a field of research contributing to the treatment of such medical conditions as Parkinson's disease, Alzheimer's, schizophrenia, epilepsy and autism. Studies will cover anatomical structures such as skeletal, muscular, cardiovascular and nervous systems and components such as muscle cells.

Useful websites www.innerbody.com; www.instantanatomy.net

NB The points totals shown to the left of the institutions are for ease of reference only. It must not be assumed that Tariff points are always used by institutions or that they can be substituted for an offer in grades. The level of an offer is not necessarily indicative of the quality of a course.

COURSE OFFERS INFORMATION

Subject requirements/preferences GCSE Mathematics usually required. **AL** One or two mathematics/science subjects usually required; biology and chemistry preferred.

Your target offers and examples of degree courses

160 pts **Cambridge** – A*A*A incl sci/maths +interview +NSAA (Nat Sci (Neuro)) (IB 40–42 pts HL 776)

144 pts **Birmingham** – AAA incl biol (Hum Neuro) (IB 32 pts HL 666 incl biol)

Bristol – AAA/A*AB–ABB incl sci/maths +interview (Neuro) (IB 36–32 pts HL 66–65 sci/maths)

Leeds – AAA–AAB incl biol/chem+sci (Neuro) (IB 35–34 pts HL 6 biol/chem+sci)

London (RH) – AAA–AAB (Psy Clin Cog Neuro) (IB 32 pts HL 665)

London (UCL) – AAA incl chem+sci/maths (Neuro) (IB 38 pts HL 5 chem+sci/maths)

Manchester – AAA–ABB incl sci/maths (Anat Sci; Neuro; Anat Sci (Yr Ind)) (IB 37–32 pts HL 5/6 biol+chem); AAA–ABB incl sci/maths (Cog Neuro Psy) (IB 37–32 pts HL 5/6 biol+chem)

Reading – AAA–AAB incl sci (Psy Neuro) (IB 35–34 pts)

Sussex – AAA–AAB (Psy Cog Sci; Psy Neuro) (IB 34 pts)

136 pts **Bangor** – 136–112 pts incl sci (Psy Neuropsy)

Cardiff – AAB–ABB incl biol+sci (Biomed Sci; Neuro; Biomed Sci (Anat)) (IB 34 pts HL 6 biol+chem)

Glasgow – AAB–BBB incl biol/chem (Neuro; Anat) (IB 36–34 pts HL 665 biol/chem+sci)

Leicester – AAB–ABB/BBB+bEPQ (Psy Cog Neuro) (IB 32–30 pts)

Liverpool – AAB incl biol (Anat Hum Biol) (IB 34 pts HL 6 biol)

London (King's) – AAB incl chem+biol (Neuro; Anat Dev Hum Biol) (IB 35 pts HL 665 chem+biol)

Nottingham – AAB incl biol/chem+sci/maths (Neuro) (IB 34 pts)

St Andrews – AAB incl sci/maths (Neuro) (IB 35 pts)

Sussex – AAB–ABB incl sci/psy (Neuro Cog Sci; Med Neuro) (IB 32 pts HL 5 sci/psy)

128 pts **Edinburgh** – ABB (Neuro) (IB 36 pts HL 6 biol+chem)

Keele – ABB incl sci/maths/stats (Neuro) (IB 34 pts HL 6 chem)

120 pts **Aberdeen** – BBB incl maths+sci (Neuro Psy) (IB 32 pts HL 5 maths+sci)

Dundee – BBB–BCC incl biol (Anat Sci) (IB 30 pts HL 555 biol)

Essex – BBB (Psy Cog Neuro) (IB 30 pts)

London (Gold) – BBB (Psy Cog Neuro) (IB 33 pts)

112 pts **Central Lancashire** – 112–128 pts (Neuropsy)

Middlesex – BBC incl biol/chem 112 pts (Med Physiol (Neuro))

Alternative offers

See **Chapter 6** and **Appendix 1** for grades/UCAS Tariff points information for other examinations.

CHOOSING YOUR COURSE (SEE ALSO CH.1)

Universities and colleges teaching quality See www.qaa.ac.uk; https://unistats.ac.uk.

Top research universities and colleges (REF 2014) See **Biological Sciences**.

Examples of sandwich degree courses Bristol; Cardiff; Leeds; Manchester.

ADMISSIONS INFORMATION

Number of applicants per place (approx) Bristol 10; Cardiff 9; London (UCL) 7.

Advice to applicants and planning the UCAS personal statement Give reasons for your interest in this subject (usually stemming from school work in biology). Discuss any articles in medical and other scientific journals which have attracted your attention and any new developments in medicine related to neuroscience.

Selection interviews Yes Bristol, Liverpool; **Some** Cardiff.

Check **Chapter 3** for new university admission details and **Chapter 6** on how to read the subject tables.

Interview advice and questions Questions are likely on your particular interests in biology and anatomy, why you wish to study the subject and your future career intentions. See also **Chapter 5**.

AFTER-RESULTS ADVICE
Offers to applicants repeating A-levels Higher Bristol; **Same** Cardiff.

GRADUATE DESTINATIONS AND EMPLOYMENT (2015/16 HESA)
Including Pathology and Physiology graduates surveyed 2,880 **Employed** 1,750 **In voluntary employment** 30 **In further study** 675 **Assumed unemployed** 105

Career note The subject leads to a range of careers in various laboratories, in government establishments, the NHS, pharmaceutical and food industries. It can also lead to postgraduate studies in physiotherapy, nursing, osteopathy and, in exceptional cases, in medicine, dentistry and veterinary science.

OTHER DEGREE SUBJECTS FOR CONSIDERATION
Biological Sciences; Biology; Genetics; Microbiology; Osteopathy; Physiology; Physiotherapy.

NURSING and MIDWIFERY

(see also **Biological Sciences, Community Studies/Development, Health Sciences/Studies**)

Nursing and Midwifery courses are designed to equip students with the scientific and caring skills demanded by medical science in the 21st century. Courses follow a similar pattern with an introductory programme of study covering clinical skills, nursing practice and the behavioural and social sciences. Thereafter, specialisation starts in adult, child or mental health nursing, or with patients with learning disabilities. Throughout the three-year course, students gain extensive clinical experience in hospital wards, clinics, accident and emergency and high-dependency settings. UCAS handles applications for Nursing degree courses. Nursing is an all-graduate profession.

Useful websites www.scicentral.com; www.healthcareers.nhs.uk; www.nursingtimes.net; www.nmc.org.uk; www.rcn.org.uk; www.rcm.org.uk; see also **Health Sciences/Studies** and **Medicine**.

NB The points totals shown to the left of the institutions are for ease of reference only. It must not be assumed that Tariff points are always used by institutions or that they can be substituted for an offer in grades. The level of an offer is not necessarily indicative of the quality of a course.

COURSE OFFERS INFORMATION
Subject requirements/preferences GCSE English and a science subject. Mathematics required at several universities. **AL** Science subjects required for some courses. **Other** All applicants holding firm offers will require an occupational health check and Disclosure and Barring Service (DBS) clearance and are required to provide documentary evidence that they have not been infected with hepatitis B.

Your target offers and examples of degree courses
144 pts **Southampton** – AAA/AAB+aEPQ incl sci +interview (Midwif) (IB 36 pts)
136 pts **Edinburgh** – AAB–ABB +interview (Nurs St) (IB 36–34 pts HL 665)
        Manchester – AAB–ABB +interview (Midwif) (IB 32 pts HL 665 biol/chem)
        UWE Bristol – 136 pts incl sci/soc sci (Midwif)
128 pts **Birmingham City** – ABB 128 pts +interview (Midwif) (IB 32 pts)
        Bournemouth – 128–136 pts incl biol +interview (Midwif) (IB 32–33 pts HL 55)
        Bradford – ABB 128 pts +interview (Midwif St)
        Cardiff – ABB +MMI (Midwif) (IB 28 pts)
        City – ABB 128 pts (Midwif) (IB 33 pts)
        East Anglia – ABB incl sci/PE/maths +interview (Midwif) (IB 32 pts)
        Edge Hill – ABB 128 pts +interview (Midwif)
        Glasgow – ABB incl sci/maths +interview (Nurs) (IB 36 pts HL 6 chem/biol)

Huddersfield – ABB incl biol 128 pts (Midwif St)
Keele – ABB incl biol/hlth soc cr/psy/sociol +interview (Midwif) (IB 27 pts)
Kingston – ABB incl sci 128 pts +interview (Midwif)
Leeds – ABB incl biol +interview (Midwif) (IB 34 pts HL 5 biol)
Liverpool John Moores – 128 pts +interview (Midwif) (IB 27 pts)
London (King's) – ABB +interview (Midwif Reg) (IB 34 pts HL 655)
Sheffield Hallam – 128 pts incl nat/soc sci +interview (Midwif)
Surrey – ABB +MMI (Midwif) (IB 34 pts)
York – ABB (Midwif) (IB 34 pts)

120 pts **Anglia Ruskin** – 120 pts +interview (Midwif) (IB 26 pts)
Bangor – 120 pts +interview (Nurs A/C/LD/MH; Midwif)
Birmingham – BBB incl biol/psy/sociol +interview (Nurs A/MH/C) (IB 32 pts HL 555)
Birmingham City – BBB 120 pts interview (Nurs A/C/LD/MH) (IB 30 pts)
Bradford – BBB 120 pts +interview (Nurs A/C/MH)
Brighton – BBB incl sci/soc sci +interview (Midwif; Nurs A/C/MH) (IB 30 pts)
Canterbury Christ Church – BBB +interview (Midwif)
Cardiff – BBB +MMI (Nurs A/C/MH) (IB 28 pts)
Chester – BBB–BBC incl biol/app sci 120 pts (Midwif) (IB 28 pts HL 5 biol)
Coventry – BBB incl sci/soc sci (Midwif) (IB 30 pts)
De Montfort – 120 pts +interview (Midwif) (IB 30 pts HL sci/psy)
Derby – 120–128 pts +interview (Nurs A/MH)
East Anglia – BBB +interview (Nurs A/LD/MH) (IB 31 pts)
Greenwich – 120 pts +interview +test (Midwif)
Hertfordshire – 120 pts incl biol sci/bhv sci/soc sci (Midwif) (HL 5 biol sci/bhv sci)
Huddersfield – BBB incl biol/psy/maths/soc sci 120 pts +interview (Nurs A/C/MH)
Leeds Beckett – 120 pts +interview (Nurs A/MH) (IB 26 pts)
Liverpool – BBB incl biol +interview (Nurs) (IB 30 pts HL 555)
Liverpool John Moores – BBB 120 pts +interview (Nurs C)
London (King's) – BBB incl sci +interview (Nurs A/C/MH) (IB 32 pts HL 555)
London South Bank – BBB 120 pts +interview (Midwif)
Northumbria – 120–128 pts +interview (Nurs St A/C/LD/MH) (HL 444); 120–128 pts incl sci/hlth (Midwif) (HL 444 sci/hlth)
Nottingham – BBB incl sci/PE/psy/sociol (Nurs A/C/MH) (IB 30 pts HL 555 sci)
Oxford Brookes – BBB incl biol 120 pts +interview (Midwif) (IB 32 pts HL 4 biol)
Southampton – BBB incl sci/soc sci +interview (Nurs A/C/MH) (IB 30 pts)
South Wales – BBB +interview (Midwif; Nurs A/C/LD/MH) (IB 32 pts)
Staffordshire – BBB incl sci/hlth +interview (Midwif Prac)
Swansea – BBB +interview (Nurs A/C/MH; Midwif)
UWE Bristol – 120 pts incl sci/soc sci +interview (Nurs A/C/LD/MH)
West London – 120 pts +interview (Midwif)
Worcester – 120 pts +interview (Nurs (A/C/MH)); BBB incl sci/PE/sociol/hlth 120 pts +interview (Midwif)
York – BBB (Nurs A/C/LD/MH) (IB 31 pts)

112 pts **Anglia Ruskin** – 112 pts +interview (Nurs A/C/MH)
Bedfordshire – 112 pts +interview (Nurs A/C/MH; Midwif)
Bucks New – 112–128 pts +interview (Nurs A/C/MH)
Canterbury Christ Church – BBC +interview (Nurs A/C/MH)
Central Lancashire – 112 pts (Nurs (A/MH)); 112–128 pts incl biol (Midwif)
Chester – BBC–BCC (Nurs A/C/LD/MH) (IB 26 pts)
City – BBC 112 pts +interview +test (Nurs A/C/MH) (IB 32 pts)
Cumbria – 112–120 pts incl biol +interview (Midwif)
De Montfort – 112 pts +interview (Nurs A/C/MH/LD)
Edge Hill – BBC 112 pts +interview (Nurs A/C/LD/MH)
Greenwich – 112 pts +interview +test (Nurs A/C/LD/MH)
Hertfordshire – 112–120 pts +interview (Nurs (A/LD))

Check **Chapter 3** for new university admission details and **Chapter 6** on how to read the subject tables.

Hull – 112 pts +interview (Nurs A/MH/LD) (IB 24 pts)
Keele – BBC +interview (Nurs A/C/LD/MH) (IB 25 pts)
Kingston – BBC incl sci/hlth 112 pts +interview (Nurs A/C/LD/MH) (IB 26 pts)
Leeds – BBC incl sci/maths/soc sci +interview (Nurs A/C/MH) (IB 30 pts HL 555)
Lincoln – BBC +interview (Nurs A/MH) (IB 29 pts)
Liverpool John Moores – BBC 112 pts +interview (Nurs (MH/A)) (IB 26 pts)
London South Bank – BBC +interview (Nurs A/C/MH)
Manchester – BBC incl sci/psy/hlth/app sci +interview (Nurs A) (IB 30 pts HL 555)
Middlesex – 112 pts +interview (Nurs A/C/MH); 112 pts + interview (Midwif)
Northampton – BBC incl sci/psy/sociol (Midwif)
Oxford Brookes – BBC incl sci 112 pts +interview (Nurs A/MH) (IB 30 pts)
Queen's Belfast – BBC–BCC incl sci/maths (Midwif Sci)
Salford – 112–128 pts (Midwif) (IB 31 pts)
Sheffield Hallam – 112 pts +interview (Nurs A/MH)
Staffordshire – BBC +interview (Nurs Prac A/C/MH)
Teesside – 112–128 pts incl sci +interview (Midwif)
Ulster – BBC (Nurs A/MH) (IB 25 pts)
West London – 112–120 pts +interview (Nurs A/C/LD/MH)
Wolverhampton – BBC–BCC +interview (Nurs A/C/MH); BBC incl sci +interview (Midwif)

104 pts **Abertay** – BCC (Nurs MH) (IB 29 pts)
Bournemouth – 104–120 pts +interview (Nurs A/C/MH) (IB 28–31 pts HL 55); 104–120 pts (Chld Yng Ppl Nurs) (IB 28–31 pts HL 55)
Coventry – BCC (Nurs A/LD/MH) (IB 27 pts)
Cumbria – 104–112 pts incl sci/soc sci +interview (Nurs A/C/LD/MH)
Edinburgh Napier – BCC incl biol +interview (Midwif)
Manchester Met – BCC–BBC 104–112 pts +interview (Nurs A) (IB 29 pts)

Northampton – BCC (Nurs A/C/MH/LD)
Queen's Belfast – BCC–BBC incl sci +interview (Nurs A/C/LD/MH)
Queen Margaret – BCC incl biol +interview (Nurs) (IB 30 pts)
Robert Gordon – BCC incl Engl+sci +interview (Midwif; Nurs A/C/MH) (IB 27 pts)
96 pts **Stirling** – CCC +interview (Nurs A/MH) (IB 28 pts)
Suffolk – CCC 96 pts +interview (Nurs A)
Teesside – 96–112 pts +interview (Nurs St A/C/LD/MH)
West Scotland – CCC incl sci (Midwif)
72 pts **Glasgow Caledonian** – BC +interview (Nurs St (A/C/MH)) (IB 24 pts)
West Scotland – BC (Nurs A/MH) (IB 24 pts)
64 pts **Dundee** – CC +interview (Nurs A/C/MH) (IB 24 pts)
Edinburgh Napier – CC incl sci+Engl +interview (Nurs A/C/LD/MH)

Open University – contact 0300 303 0073 **or** www.open.ac.uk/contact/new (Nurs Prac)

Abbreviations used in this table A – Adult; C – Child; LD – Learning Disability; MH – Mental Health.

Alternative offers
See **Chapter 6** and **Appendix 1** for grades/UCAS Tariff points information for other examinations.

EXAMPLES OF COLLEGES OFFERING COURSES IN THIS SUBJECT FIELD
Central Campus, Sandwell (Coll); East Kent (Coll); MidKent (Coll); Norwich City (Coll); Oaklands (Coll).

CHOOSING YOUR COURSE (SEE ALSO CH.1)
Universities and colleges teaching quality See www.qaa.ac.uk; https://unistats.ac.uk.

Top research universities and colleges (REF 2014) (Allied Health Professions, Dentistry, Nursing and Pharmacy) Birmingham; Sheffield (Biomed Sci); Bangor; Swansea (Allied Hlth); Aston; Coventry; Southampton; Cardiff; Surrey; Glasgow; Nottingham (Pharm); Bradford; East Anglia (Allied Hlth); London (QM); Sheffield (Dnstry); Queen's Belfast (Pharm); Bath; London (King's) (Pharm); Leeds.

ADMISSIONS INFORMATION
Number of applicants per place (approx) Abertay 5; Anglia Ruskin 10; Bangor 4; Birmingham 8; Birmingham City 15; Cardiff 7; Central Lancashire (Midwif) 14; City (Nurs MH) 14, (Nurs C) 11, (Midwif) 9, (Nurs Adult) 12; Cumbria 8; De Montfort 10; Huddersfield (Midwif St) 8; Hull 10; Leeds (Midwif) 12; Liverpool John Moores (Nurs) 5; London (King's) 4; London South Bank 16; Middlesex 10; Northampton 17; Nottingham 9; Oxford Brookes 7; Salford 10; Sheffield Hallam 8; Southampton (Nurs) 15, (Midwif) 25; Staffordshire (Midwif Prac) 10; Stirling 5; Swansea 10; York (Midwif) 2.

Numbers of applicants (**a** UK **b** EU (non-UK) **c** non-EU **d** mature) Cardiff **c**6.

Advice to applicants and planning the UCAS personal statement Experience of care work – for example in hospitals, old people's homes, children's homes – is important. Describe what you have done and what you have learned. Read nursing journals in order to be aware of new developments in the treatment of illnesses. Note, in particular, the various needs of patients and the problems they experience. Try to compare different nursing approaches with, for example, children, people with learning disabilities, old people and terminally ill people. If you underperformed at **GCSE**, give reasons. If you have had work experience or a part-time job, describe how your skills have developed, for example responsibility, communication, team building, organisational skills. How do you spend your spare time? Explain how your interests help with stress and pressure. See also **Appendix 3**. Contact NHS Student Bursaries for information about financial support; tel 0300 330 1345. **Liverpool John Moores** (Nurs C) The candidate needs to have clear evidence of experience in caring for children/young people aged 0–17. This can be paid employment, voluntary work or work experience within a health or social care setting within the last three years. Their experience needs to include working with a variety of age ranges (not just one), such as babies through to young people, as well as those children and young people who have a range of physical and intellectual abilities. **West Scotland** Research the role of a nurse and the essential qualities needed.

Misconceptions about this course That Nursing programmes are not demanding. Midwives and nurses don't do shift work and are not involved in travelling! **Bournemouth** Many think that being passionate about babies is what midwifery is all about, but really it is about the care of the adult (ie mothers through pregnancy), not the child. **Bradford** Mental Health nurses are not just trained to keep patients sedated with drugs. The work involves supporting a patient's recovery and enabling them to have involvement and control in their recovery. **City** Midwives are only involved at the birth stage and not at the antenatal and postnatal stages, or in education and support.

Selection interviews Most institutions **Yes** Abertay, Anglia Ruskin, Bangor, Bedfordshire, Birmingham, Birmingham City, Bolton, Bournemouth, Brighton, Cardiff, Chester, City, Cumbria, Dundee, East Anglia, Edge Hill, Edinburgh, Edinburgh Napier, Greenwich, Hertfordshire, Huddersfield, Hull, Leeds Beckett, Lincoln, Liverpool John Moores, London (King's), London South Bank, Manchester, Middlesex, Nottingham, Oxford Brookes, Plymouth, Queen Margaret, Queen's Belfast, Robert Gordon, Salford, Sheffield Hallam, Southampton, Stirling, Suffolk, Surrey, Swansea, UWE Bristol, West London, West Scotland, Wolverhampton, Worcester; **Some** Bucks New, Coventry, Keele; **No** Central Lancashire.

Interview advice and questions Past questions have included: Why do you want to be a nurse? What experience have you had in nursing? What do you think of the nurses' pay situation? Should nurses go on strike? What are your views on abortion? What branch of nursing most interests you? How would you communicate with someone who can't speak English? What is the nurse's role in the community? How should a nurse react in an emergency? How would you cope with telling a patient's relative that the patient was dying? Admissions tutors look for communication skills, team interaction and the applicant's understanding of health/society-related subjects. See also **Chapter 5**. **London South Bank** What do you understand by equal opportunities? **Swansea** What is your perception of the role of the nurse? What qualities do you have that would be good for nursing?

Reasons for rejection (non-academic) Insufficient awareness of the roles and responsibilities of a midwife or nurse. Lack of motivation. Poor communication skills. Lack of awareness of nursing developments through the media. (Detailed knowledge of the NHS or nursing practice not usually required.) Failed medical. Unsatisfactory health record. Not fulfilling the hepatitis B requirements or police check requirements. Poor preparation for the interview. Too shy. Only wants nursing as a means to something else, for example commission in the armed forces. Too many choices on the UCAS application, for example Midwifery, Physiotherapy, Occupational Therapy. No care experience. Some applicants have difficulty with maths – multiplication and division – used in calculating dosage for medicines. **De Montfort** No insight as to nursing as a career or the various branches of nursing. **Swansea** Poor communication skills. **Ulster** Reasons relating to health and/or police checks.

AFTER-RESULTS ADVICE
Offers to applicants repeating A-levels Higher Cardiff; **Same** De Montfort, Huddersfield, Hull, Liverpool John Moores, London South Bank, Queen Margaret, Salford, Staffordshire, Stirling, Suffolk, Swansea, Wolverhampton; **No** Birmingham City.

GRADUATE DESTINATIONS AND EMPLOYMENT (2015/16 HESA)
Nursing graduates surveyed 19,140 **Employed** 15,800 **In voluntary employment** 20 **In further study** 1,015 **Assumed unemployed** 195

Career note The majority of Nursing graduates aim to enter the nursing profession.

OTHER DEGREE SUBJECTS FOR CONSIDERATION
Audiology; Biological Sciences; Biology; Community Studies; Dietetics; Education; Health Studies; Medicine; Nutrition; Occupational Therapy; Optometry; Pharmacology; Pharmacy; Physiotherapy; Podiatry; Psychology; Radiography; Social Policy and Administration; Social Work; Sociology; Speech Therapy; Veterinary Nursing.

Check **Chapter 3** for new university admission details and **Chapter 6** on how to read the subject tables.

NUTRITION
(see also Dietetics, Food Science/Studies and Technology, Health Sciences/Studies)

Nutrition attracts a great deal of attention in society and whilst controversy, claim and counter-claim seem to focus daily on the merits and otherwise of food, it is, nevertheless, a scientific study in itself. Courses involve topics relating to diet, health, nutrition and food policy and are designed to prepare students to enter careers as specialists in nutrition and dietetics.

Useful websites www.nutrition.org.uk; www.nutritionsociety.org; see also under **Dietetics**.

NB The points totals shown to the left of the institutions are for ease of reference only. It must not be assumed that Tariff points are always used by institutions or that they can be substituted for an offer in grades. The level of an offer is not necessarily indicative of the quality of a course.

COURSE OFFERS INFORMATION
Subject requirements/preferences GCSE Mathematics and science usually required. **AL** Science subjects required for most courses, biology and/or chemistry preferred.

Your target offers and examples of degree courses

136 pts Leeds – AAB incl sci/maths (Nutr) (IB 35 pts)
  London (King's) – AAB incl chem+biol +interview (Nutr Diet) (IB 35 pts HL 665)
  Newcastle – AAB–ABB incl sci (Nutr Fd Mark) (IB 34–32 pts HL 6 biol); AAB–ABB incl biol+sci (Fd Hum Nutr) (IB 34–32 pts HL 6 biol)
  Nottingham – AAB–ABB incl sci/maths (Fd Sci Nutr) (IB 34–32 pts); AAB–ABB incl sci +interview (Nutr Diet (MNutr)) (IB 34–32 pts)
  Reading – AAB–ABB incl sci/maths (Fd Sci; Nutr Fd Sci) (IB 34–32 pts HL 5 sci/maths); (Nutr Fd Consum Sci) (IB 32–34 pts HL 5 sci)

128 pts Leeds – ABB incl sci (Fd Sci Nutr) (IB 34 pts HL 16 pts)
  London (King's) – ABB incl chem+biol (Nutr) (IB 34 pts)
  Nottingham – ABB–BBB incl sci (Nutr) (IB 32–30 pts)
  Surrey – ABB incl biol+sci (Nutr) (IB 32 pts HL 6 biol 5 sci); ABB incl sci/maths (Nutr Fd Sci) (IB 32 pts); ABB incl biol+sci +interview (Nutr Diet) (IB 32 pts)

120 pts Cardiff Met – 120 pts incl biol+chem +interview (Hum Nutr Diet)
  Leeds Beckett – BBB incl chem+sci +interview (Diet) (IB 26 pts HL 6 chem)
  Liverpool Hope – BBB–BBC 120–112 pts (Nutr)
  London Met – BBB incl biol+chem 120 pts +interview (Diet Nutr)
  Northumbria – 120–128 pts incl sci/fd tech/hm econ (Fd Sci Nutr) (HL 444)
  Plymouth – 120 pts incl biol+sci (Nutr Exer Hlth) (IB 28 pts HL 5 biol+sci)
  Queen's Belfast – BBB–ABB incl sci (Fd Qual Sfty Nutr)

112 pts Cardiff Met – 112 pts (Spo Biomed Nutr)
  Central Lancashire – 112–128 pts (Nutr Exer Sci)
  Chester – BBC–BBB incl biol+sci +interview (Nutr Diet) (IB 28 pts HL 5 biol+chem); BBC–BCC incl biol/chem/env sci 112 pts (Hum Nutr) (IB 26 pts HL 5 biol/chem); BBC–BCC 112 pts (Nutr Exer Sci) (IB 26 pts)
  Coventry – BBC incl biol/chem/fd tech (Fd Nutr; Nutr Hlth) (IB 30 pts HL 5 biol/chem)
  Edge Hill – BBC 112 pts (Nutr Hlth)
  Greenwich – 112 pts (Hum Nutr)
  Hull – 112 pts (Spo Exer Nutr) (IB 28 pts)
  Leeds Beckett – 112 pts incl biol/chem (Nutr) (IB 25 pts HL 6 biol)
  Leeds Trinity – 112 pts (Spo Exer Sci (Spo Nutr))
  Nottingham Trent – BBC incl sci/PE 112 pts (Exer Nutr Hlth)
  Oxford Brookes – BBC 112 pts (Nutr) (IB 30 pts)
  Roehampton – 112 pts (Nutr Hlth)
  Sheffield Hallam – 112 pts (Nutr Pblc Hlth; Nutr Diet Lfstl; Fd Nutr)

Teesside – BBC incl sci/fd tech/nutr (Fd Nutr)
Westminster – BBC incl sci (Hum Nutr) (IB 26 pts HL 5 sci)
104 pts **Bath Spa** – BCC–CCC incl biol+sci (Hum Nutr) (IB 27 pts); BCC–CCC (Fd Nutr) (IB 26 pts)
Bournemouth – 104–112 pts (Nutr) (IB 28–30 pts HL 55)
CAFRE – 104 pts incl sci/hm econ (Fd Des Nutr)
Glasgow Caledonian – BCC incl chem (Hum Nutr Diet) (IB 28 pts)
Kingston – 104–144 pts incl sci/psy/PE (Nutr (Exer Hlth)); 104–112 pts (Nutr (Hum Nutr))
Liverpool John Moores – BCC 104 pts (Fd Dev Nutr) (IB 24 pts)
Robert Gordon – BCC incl biol+chem +interview (Nutr Diet) (IB 27 pts HL 5 biol+chem)
St Mary's – 104 pts (Nutr)
Ulster – BCC incl sci/maths/tech (Hum Nutr) (IB 24 pts)
96 pts **Abertay** – CCC (Fd Nutr Hlth) (IB 28 pts)
Bedfordshire – 96 pts (Hlth Nutr Exer)
Hertfordshire – 96 pts incl chem+biol (Nutr) (HL 44)
London Met – CCC 96 pts incl biol (Hum Nutr)
Manchester Met CCC BBC 96 112 pts (Nutr Sci) (IB 26 pts)
Robert Gordon – CCC incl chem+sci (Nutr) (IB 26 pts)
Trinity Saint David – 96 pts +interview (Hlth Nutr Lfstl)
Ulster – CCC incl sci/maths/env tech/hm econ (Fd Nutr) (IB 24 pts HL 12 pts incl 5 sci/ maths/hm econ)
Worcester – 96–104 pts incl biol+sci/maths (Hum Nutr)
80 pts **London South Bank** – CDD (Hum Nutr)
Queen Margaret – BB incl chem/biol 80 pts (Nutr) (IB 26 pts)

Alternative offers
See **Chapter 6** and **Appendix 1** for grades/UCAS Tariff points information for other examinations.

EXAMPLES OF COLLEGES OFFERING COURSES IN THIS SUBJECT FIELD
Bradford (Coll); Truro and Penwith (Coll).

CHOOSING YOUR COURSE (SEE ALSO CH.1)
Universities and colleges teaching quality See www.qaa.ac.uk; https://unistats.ac.uk.

Top research universities and colleges (REF 2014) See **Agricultural Sciences/Agriculture**.

Examples of sandwich degree courses Bedfordshire; Coventry; Glasgow Caledonian; Harper Adams; Huddersfield; Kingston; Leeds; Leeds Beckett; Liverpool John Moores; Manchester Met; Newcastle; Northumbria; Queen's Belfast; Reading; Sheffield Hallam; Surrey; Teesside; Ulster.

ADMISSIONS INFORMATION
Number of applicants per place (approx) Cardiff Met 5; Liverpool John Moores 10; London (King's) 6; London Met 9; London South Bank 5; Newcastle 5; Nottingham 9; Robert Gordon 4.

Advice to applicants and planning the UCAS personal statement Information on relevant experience, reasons for wanting to do the degree and careers sought would be useful. See also **Dietetics** and **Appendix 3**.

Misconceptions about this course Some applicants do not realise that this is a science course.

Selection interviews Some Chester, London Met, Surrey; **No** Liverpool John Moores, Nottingham, Robert Gordon, Roehampton.

Interview advice and questions Past questions have focused on scientific A-level subjects studied and aspects of subjects enjoyed by the applicants. Questions then arise from answers. Extensive knowledge expected of nutrition as a career and candidates should have talked to people involved in this type of work, for example dietitians. They will also be expected to discuss wider problems such as food supplies in developing countries and nutritional problems resulting from famine. See also **Chapter 5**.

AFTER-RESULTS ADVICE

Offers to applicants repeating A-levels Same Liverpool John Moores, Manchester Met, Nottingham, Roehampton, St Mary's.

GRADUATE DESTINATIONS AND EMPLOYMENT (2015/16 HESA)

Graduates surveyed 785 **Employed** 445 **In voluntary employment** 15 **In further study** 150 **Assumed unemployed** 40

Career note Nutritionists work in retail, health promotion and sport; others specialise in dietetics.

OTHER DEGREE SUBJECTS FOR CONSIDERATION

Biological Sciences; Biology; Consumer Studies; Dietetics; Food Sciences; Health Studies/Sciences.

OCCUPATIONAL THERAPY

Everyday life involves washing, dressing, eating, walking, driving, shopping and going to work, all aspects which we take for granted – until we have an injury or illness. If this happened to you then during the recovery period, you would realise the importance of the occupational therapist's role. They assist people of all ages, not only those being treated with physical injuries/illness but others with mental health issues, the work being to identify the special problems they face and the practical solutions that are required to help them recover and maintain their daily living and working skills. The focus of the OT is on meaningful and functional activity. This may be achieved by advising on physical modifications to the home environment and potentially introducing new equipment and devices to make various activities easier along with task analysis. In the case of mental health OTs, they assist clients to re-establish routines and skills to allow them to return to living fulfilling lives. To achieve these results, occupational therapists often work with physiotherapists, psychologists, speech therapists and social workers amongst others. Most courses therefore involve anatomy, physiology, psychology, sociology, mental health and ethics. OTs can work in a very wide range of settings, acute care, long term care, social services and mental health plus many more. There are opportunities to specialise in burns, hand therapy, oncology and surgery, forensic psychology and prison rehabilitation to name but a few. Selectors look for maturity, initiative, tact, sound judgement, team work and organising ability.

Useful websites www.rcot.co.uk

NB The points totals shown to the left of the institutions are for ease of reference only. It must not be assumed that Tariff points are always used by institutions or that they can be substituted for an offer in grades. The level of an offer is not necessarily indicative of the quality of a course.

COURSE OFFERS INFORMATION

Subject requirements/preferences GCSE English, mathematics and science grade A–C (7–4). **AL** A social science or science subjects required or preferred for most courses. **Other** All applicants need to pass an occupational health check and obtain Disclosure and Barring Service (DBS) clearance.

Your target offers and examples of degree courses

136 pts **Plymouth** – 136 pts incl sci (Occ Thera) (IB 33 pts)
     Southampton – AAB–ABB+aEPQ incl sci/soc sci (Occ Thera) (IB 32 pts)
     UWE Bristol – 136 pts incl sci/soc sci (Occ Thera)
128 pts **Bournemouth** – 128–136 pts (Occ Thera) (IB 32–33 pts HL 55)
     Bradford – ABB 128 pts (Occ Thera)
     Cardiff – ABB (Occ Thera) (IB 35 pts)
120 pts **Brunel** – BBB +interview (Occ Thera) (IB 30 pts)
     Coventry – BBB–CCC (Occ Thera)
     East Anglia – BBB (Occ Thera) (IB 31 pts HL 655)
     Huddersfield – BBB incl biol/psy 120 pts (Occ Thera)

Liverpool – BBB incl soc sci/biol/PE (Occ Thera) (IB 30 pts)
London (St George's) – BBB (Occ Thera) (IB 32 pts HL 15 pts)
London South Bank – BBB (Occ Thera)
Northumbria – 120 pts incl sci/hlth (Occ Thera) (HL 444)
Oxford Brookes – BBB 120 pts (Occ Thera) (IB 30 pts)
Ulster – BBB +HPAT (Occ Thera)
Worcester – BBB 120 pts incl biol/soc sci (Occ Thera)
York St John – 120 pts +interview (Occ Thera)

112 pts **Canterbury Christ Church** – BBC (Occ Thera)
Cumbria – 112–120 pts (Occ Thera)
Derby – 112 pts (Occ Thera)
Glyndŵr – 112 pts (Occ Thera)
Northampton – BBC (Occ Thera)
Teesside – 112–128 pts incl sci (Occ Thera)

104 pts **Glasgow Caledonian** – BCC (Occ Thera) (IB 24 pts)
Robert Gordon – BCC incl Engl+biol (Occ Thera) (IB 27 pts)

32 pts **Brighton** – interview p/t, individual offers may vary, NHS bursaries are available for all courses (Occ Thera)

Alternative offers
See **Chapter 6** and **Appendix 1** for grades/UCAS Tariff points information for other examinations.

CHOOSING YOUR COURSE (SEE ALSO CH.1)

Universities and colleges teaching quality See www.qaa.ac.uk; https://unistats.ac.uk.

Top research universities and colleges (REF 2014) See **Health Sciences/Studies**.

ADMISSIONS INFORMATION

Number of applicants per place (approx) Cardiff 10; Cumbria 20; Derby 5; East Anglia 6; Northampton 4; Oxford Brookes 11; Robert Gordon 6; Southampton 7; Ulster 13; York St John 5.

Admissions tutors' advice London (St George's) Work experience required.

Advice to applicants and planning the UCAS personal statement Contact your local hospital and discuss this career with the occupational therapists. Try to obtain work shadowing experience and make notes of your observations. Describe any such visits in full (see also **Reasons for rejection (non-academic)**). Applicants are expected to have visited two occupational therapy departments, one in a physical or social services setting, one in the mental health field. Good interpersonal skills. Breadth and nature of health-related work experience is important. Also skills, interests (for example, sports, design). Applicants should have a high standard of communication skills and experience of working with people with disabilities. See also **Appendix 3**. **York St John** Contact with the profession essential; very competitive course.

Selection interviews Most institutions. **Yes** Bournemouth, Brighton, Brunel, Canterbury Christ Church, Coventry, Cumbria, East Anglia, Huddersfield, Oxford Brookes, Queen Margaret, Robert Gordon, Worcester; **No** Glyndŵr, Ulster, York St John.

Interview advice and questions Since this is a vocational course, work experience is nearly always essential and applicants are likely to be questioned on the types of work involved and the career. Some universities may use admissions tests: check websites and see **Chapter 5**.

Reasons for rejection (non-academic) Poor communication skills. Lack of knowledge of occupational therapy. Little evidence of working with people. Uncertain about their future career. Lack of maturity. Indecision regarding the profession.

AFTER-RESULTS ADVICE

Offers to applicants repeating A-levels Same Derby, York St John.

GRADUATE DESTINATIONS AND EMPLOYMENT (2015/16 HESA)
Career note Occupational therapists (who work mostly in hospital departments) are involved in the rehabilitation of those who have required medical treatment and work with the young, aged and, for example, people with learning difficulties.

OTHER DEGREE SUBJECTS FOR CONSIDERATION
Audiology; Community Studies; Dietetics; Education; Health Studies/Sciences; Nursing; Nutrition; Physiotherapy; Podiatry; Psychology; Radiography; Social Policy and Administration; Social Work; Sociology; Speech Sciences.

OPTOMETRY (OPHTHALMIC OPTICS)
(including Ophthalmic Dispensing and Orthoptics)

Optometry courses (which are becoming increasingly popular) lead to qualification as an optometrist (previously known as an ophthalmic optician). They provide training in detecting defects and diseases in the eye and in prescribing treatment with, for example, spectacles, contact lenses and other appliances to correct or improve vision. Orthoptics includes the study of general anatomy, physiology and normal child development and leads to a career as an orthoptist. This involves the investigation, diagnosis and treatment of defects of binocular vision and other eye conditions. The main components of degree courses include the study of the eye, the use of diagnostic and measuring equipment and the treatment of eye abnormalities. See also **Appendix 3**.

Useful websites www.optical.org; www.abdo.org.uk; www.college-optometrists.org

NB The points totals shown to the left of the institutions are for ease of reference only. It must not be assumed that Tariff points are always used by institutions or that they can be substituted for an offer in grades. The level of an offer is not necessarily indicative of the quality of a course.

COURSE OFFERS INFORMATION
Subject requirements/preferences GCSE Good grades in English and science subjects usually required. **AL** Science subjects required for all Optometry courses. Mathematics usually acceptable.

Your target offers and examples of degree courses
144 pts **Aston** – AAA–AAB incl sci (Optom) (IB 32 pts HL 6 biol+chem/phys 5 maths)
        Cardiff – AAA–AAB incl sci/maths (Optom) (IB 34 pts incl sci/maths)
        Plymouth – AAA–AAB incl maths/sci 144–136 pts (Optom) (IB 36–34 pts HL 6 maths/sci)
136 pts **Anglia Ruskin** – AAB incl sci/maths (Optom) (IB 33 pts HL 6 sci/maths)
        Bradford – AAB 136 pts (Optom)
        City – AAB 136 pts (Optom) (IB 34 pts)
        Glasgow Caledonian – AAB incl sci/maths (Optom) (IB 30 pts HL 4 sci+maths)
        Hertfordshire – 136 pts incl sci/maths (MOptom)
        Manchester – AAB incl sci/maths (Optom) (IB 35 pts)
        Ulster – AAB incl sci/maths (Optom) (IB 28 pts)
120 pts **Liverpool** – BBB incl biol (Orth) (IB 30 pts HL 6 biol)
        Sheffield – BBB incl sci/maths (Orth) (IB 32 pts HL 6 sci/maths)
104 pts **Anglia Ruskin** – 104 pts incl sci (Oph Disp) (IB 24 pts)
 64 pts **Bradford (Coll)** – 64 pts incl sci/maths (Oph Disp)

Alternative offers
See **Chapter 6** and **Appendix 1** for grades/UCAS Tariff points information for other examinations.

EXAMPLES OF COLLEGES OFFERING COURSES IN THIS SUBJECT FIELD
Bradford (Coll); City and Islington (Coll).

CHOOSING YOUR COURSE (SEE ALSO CH.1)

Universities and colleges teaching quality See www.qaa.ac.uk; https://unistats.ac.uk.

ADMISSIONS INFORMATION

Number of applicants per place (approx) Anglia Ruskin 12; Aston 7; Bradford 6; Cardiff 13; City 8.

Advice to applicants and planning the UCAS personal statement For Optometry courses, contact with optometrists is essential, either work shadowing or gaining some work experience. Make notes of your experiences and the work done and report fully on the UCAS application on why the career interests you. See also **Appendix 3**.

Selection interviews Yes Aston, Manchester, Sheffield; **Some** Cardiff; **No** Anglia Ruskin, Bradford, City, Glasgow Caledonian.

Interview advice and questions Optometry is a competitive subject requiring applicants to have had some work experience on which they will be questioned. See also **Chapter 5**.

AFTER-RESULTS ADVICE

Offers to applicants repeating A-levels Higher City; **Possibly higher** Aston; **Same** Anglia Ruskin, Cardiff.

GRADUATE DESTINATIONS AND EMPLOYMENT (2015/16 HESA)

Graduates surveyed 745 **Employed** 630 **In voluntary employment** 10 **In further study** 80 **Assumed unemployed** 5

Career note The great majority of graduates enter private practice either in small businesses or in larger organisations (which have been on the increase in recent years). A small number work in eye hospitals. Orthoptists tend to work in public health and education dealing with children and the elderly.

OTHER DEGREE SUBJECTS FOR CONSIDERATION

Health Studies; Nursing; Occupational Therapy; Physics; Physiotherapy; Radiography; Speech Studies.

PHARMACOLOGY

(including **Physiology and Pharmacology**; see also **Biological Sciences, Health Sciences/Studies**)

Pharmacology is the study of drugs and medicines and courses focus on physiology, biochemistry, toxicology, immunology, microbiology and chemotherapy. Pharmacologists are not qualified to work as pharmacists. Toxicology involves the study of the adverse effects of chemicals on living systems. See also **Appendix 3** under Pharmacology.

Useful websites www.thebts.org; www.bps.ac.uk

NB The points totals shown to the left of the institutions are for ease of reference only. It must not be assumed that Tariff points are always used by institutions or that they can be substituted for an offer in grades. The level of an offer is not necessarily indicative of the quality of a course.

COURSE OFFERS INFORMATION

Subject requirements/preferences GCSE English, science and mathematics. **AL** Chemistry and/or biology required for most courses.

Your target offers and examples of degree courses

160 pts Cambridge – A*A*A incl sci/maths +interview +NSAA (Nat Sci (Pharmacol)) (IB 40–42 pts HL 776)

144 pts Leeds – AAA–ABB incl biol/chem+sci (Pharmacol) (IB 35–34 pts HL 6 chem/biol+sci)

London (UCL) – AAA–AAB incl chem+sci/maths (Pharmacol) (IB 38–36 pts HL 5 chem+sci/maths)

Manchester – AAA–ABB incl sci/maths (Pharmacol; Pharmacol (Yr Ind)) (IB 37–32 pts HL 5/6 sci); (Pharmacol Physiol (Yr Ind)) (IB 37–32 pts)

Newcastle – AAA–AAB incl biol (Pharmacol) (IB 35–34 pts HL 5 chem+biol)

136 pts **Bath** – AAB–ABB+aEPQ incl chem+sci/maths (Pharmacol) (IB 36 pts)

Birmingham – AAB–ABB incl chem (Chem Pharmacol) (IB 32 pts HL 655)

Bristol – AAB–ABC incl chem+sci/maths (Pharmacol (Yr Ind)) (IB 34–31 pts HL 6/5 chem+sci/maths)

Edinburgh – AAB incl biol+chem (Pharmacol) (IB 36 pts HL 6 biol+chem)

Glasgow – AAB–BBB incl biol/chem (Pharmacol) (IB 36–34 pts)

Liverpool – AAB incl chem+sci (Pharmacol) (IB 34 pts HL 6 chem)

London (King's) – AAB incl chem+biol (Pharmacol Mol Genet) (IB 35 pts HL 665); (Pharmacol) (IB 35 pts)

Southampton – AAB incl chem+sci/maths (Pharmacol) (IB 34 pts HL 6 chem+sci/maths)

128 pts **Dundee** – ABB incl biol+chem (Pharmacol) (IB 30 pts)

Leicester – ABB–BBB+bEPQ incl sci/maths (Biol Sci (Physiol Pharmacol)) (IB 30 pts)

Strathclyde – ABB–BBB incl chem+biol (Pharmacol (MSci)) (IB 34 pts HL 6 chem+biol)

120 pts **Aberdeen** – BBB incl maths/sci (Pharmacol) (IB 32 pts HL 5 maths/sci)

Medway Sch Pharm – BBB 120 pts (Pharmacol Physiol) (IB 26–30 pts HL 12–14 pts)

Nottingham Trent – BBB incl biol 120 pts (Pharmacol)

112 pts **Central Lancashire** – 112 pts incl chem/biol/env sci (Physiol Pharmacol)

Chester – BBC–BCC incl biol/chem/sci 112 pts (Pharm) (IB 26 pts HL 5 chem)

Coventry – BBC incl biol (Med Pharmacol Sci) (IB 30 pts)

East London – 112 pts incl biol+chem (Pharmacol) (IB 25 pts HL 15 pts incl biol+chem)

Glasgow Caledonian – BBC incl chem (Pharmacol) (IB 28 pts)

Leeds Beckett – 112 pts incl biol+sci (Biomed Sci (Physiol/Pharmacol)) (IB 25 pts HL 6 biol)

Portsmouth – BBC incl biol/chem+sci/maths (Pharmacol) (IB 30 pts HL 665 incl biol+chem/maths)

Westminster – BBC incl sci (Pharmacol Physiol) (IB 26 pts HL 5 sci); BBC incl sci/maths/ psy/geog (Herb Med) (IB 26 pts HL 4 sci)

104 pts **Hertfordshire** – 104 pts incl sci/maths/geog (Pharmacol) (HL 44)

Kingston – 104–112 pts (Pharmacol) (IB 26–28 pts); 104–112 pts incl biol/chem (Pharmacol Bus)

96 pts **Worcester** – 96–104 pts incl sci (Pharmacol)

88 pts **London Met** – CCD incl biol+chem 88 pts (Pharmacol)

80 pts **Queen Margaret** – BB incl chem/biol 80 pts (App Pharmacol) (IB 26 pts)

Wolverhampton – BB/CDD incl chem/biol (Pharmacol)

Alternative offers

See **Chapter 6** and **Appendix 1** for grades/UCAS Tariff points information for other examinations.

CHOOSING YOUR COURSE (SEE ALSO CH.1)

Universities and colleges teaching quality See www.qaa.ac.uk; https://unistats.ac.uk.

Examples of sandwich degree courses Bath; Bristol; East London; Kingston; Leeds; Manchester; Medway Sch Pharm; Nottingham Trent; Southampton.

ADMISSIONS INFORMATION

Number of applicants per place (approx) Bath 7; Birmingham 6; Bristol 7; Dundee 8; East London 4; Hertfordshire 10; Leeds 7; Liverpool 7; London (King's) 6; London (UCL) 8; Southampton 8; Strathclyde 10; Wolverhampton 4.

Advice to applicants and planning the UCAS personal statement Contact with the pharmaceutical industry is important in order to be aware of the range of work undertaken. Read pharmaceutical journals (although note that Pharmacology and Pharmacy courses lead to different careers). See also **Pharmacy and Pharmaceutical Sciences**. **Bath** Interests outside A-level studies. Important to produce evidence that there is more to the student than A-level ability. **Bristol** Be aware that a Pharmacology degree is mainly biological rather than chemical although both subjects are important.

Misconceptions about this course Mistaken belief that pharmacology and pharmaceutical sciences are the same as pharmacy and that a Pharmacology degree will lead to work as a pharmacist.

Selection interviews Yes Cambridge, Manchester; **Some** Bath; **No** Birmingham, Dundee, Newcastle, Portsmouth.

Interview advice and questions Past questions include: Why do you want to do Pharmacology? Why not Pharmacy? Why not Chemistry? How are pharmacologists employed in industry? What are the issues raised by anti-vivisectionists on animal experimentation? Questions relating to the A-level syllabus in chemistry and biology. See also **Chapter 5**.

Reasons for rejection (non-academic) Confusion between pharmacology, pharmacy and pharmaceutical sciences. One university rejected two applicants because they had no motivation or understanding of the course (one had A-levels at AAB!). Insurance against rejection for Medicine. Lack of knowledge about pharmacology as a subject.

AFTER-RESULTS ADVICE
Offers to applicants repeating A-levels Higher Bristol, Leeds; **Same** Bath, Dundee; **No** Glasgow.

GRADUATE DESTINATIONS AND EMPLOYMENT (2015/16 HESA)
Pharmacology, Toxicology and Pharmacy graduates surveyed 2,950 **Employed** 2,175 **In voluntary employment** 75 **In further study** 560 **Assumed unemployed** 60

Career note The majority of pharmacologists work with the large pharmaceutical companies involved in research and development. A small number are employed by the NHS in medical research and clinical trials. Some will eventually diversify and become involved in marketing, sales and advertising.

OTHER DEGREE SUBJECTS FOR CONSIDERATION
Biochemistry; Biological Sciences; Biology; Biotechnology; Chemistry; Life Sciences; Medical Biochemistry; Medicinal Chemistry; Microbiology; Natural Sciences; Pharmaceutical Sciences; Pharmacy; Physiology; Toxicology.

PHARMACY and PHARMACEUTICAL SCIENCES
(including **Herbal Medicine**; see also **Biochemistry, Chemistry, Health Sciences/Studies**)

Pharmacy is the science of medicines, involving research into chemical structures and natural products of possible medicinal value, the development of dosage and the safety testing of products. This table also includes information on courses in Pharmaceutical Science (which should not be confused with Pharmacy) which is a multi-disciplinary subject covering chemistry, biochemistry, pharmacology and medical issues. Pharmaceutical scientists apply their knowledge of science and the biology of disease to the design and delivery of therapeutic agents. Note: All Pharmacy courses leading to MPharm are four years. Only Pharmacy degree courses accredited by the Royal Phamaceutical Society of Great Britain lead to a qualification as a pharmacist. Check prospectuses and websites.

Useful websites www.rpharms.com; www.chemistanddruggist.co.uk

NB The points totals shown to the left of the institutions are for ease of reference only. It must not be assumed that Tariff points are always used by institutions or that they can be substituted for an offer in grades. The level of an offer is not necessarily indicative of the quality of a course.

COURSE OFFERS INFORMATION
Subject requirements/preferences GCSE English, mathematics and science subjects. **AL** Chemistry and one or two other sciences required for most courses.

Your target offers and examples of degree courses

144 pts London (UCL) – AAA–AAB incl chem+sci/maths +interview (MPharm) (IB 38–36 pts
     HL 18–17 pts)

136 pts Aston – AAB–ABB incl chem+sci/maths +interview (MPharm) (IB 32 pts HL 6 chem+biol/
     phys)
     Bath – AAB–ABB+aEPQ incl chem+sci/maths +interview (MPharm) (IB 36 pts HL 665)
     Birmingham – AAB incl chem+sci/maths (MPharm) (IB 32 pts HL 665)
     Cardiff – AAB–ABB incl chem+sci/maths (MPharm) (IB 34 pts HL 6 chem+sci/maths)
     East Anglia – AAB incl chem+sci/maths +interview (MPharm) (IB 33 pts HL 6 chem+sci/
     maths)
     Huddersfield – AAB–ABB incl chem+sci/maths (MPharm) (IB 32 pts HL 6 chem 6/5
     maths+biol)
     Keele – AAB–ABB incl biol/chem (MPharm) (IB 36–34 pts HL 6 biol/chem)
     London (King's) – AAB incl chem+sci/maths (MPharm) (IB 35 pts HL 665)
     Newcastle – AAB incl chem+sci/maths (MPharm) (IB 36 pts HL 5 chem+sci/maths)
     Nottingham – AAB incl chem+sci/maths (MPharm) (IB 34 pts HL 665)
     Queen's Belfast – AAB incl chem+sci/maths (MPharm)
     Reading – AAB–ABB incl chem+sci (MPharm) (IB 34–32 pts HL 6/5 chem+sci)
     Strathclyde – AAB incl chem+biol (MPharm) (IB 36 pts HL 7 chem 6 biol)
     Ulster – AAB incl chem+sci/maths (MPharm) (IB 28 pts HL 14 pts incl 6 chem 7 sci)

128 pts Bradford – ABB incl chem/biol+sci 128 pts +interview (MPharm)
     Brighton – ABB–BBB incl chem 128–120 pts +interview (MPharm) (IB 32 pts HL 5
     chem+biol)
     Central Lancashire – ABB incl chem+sci/maths +interview (MPharm)
     De Montfort – 128 pts incl chem+sci/maths/psy +interview (MPharm) (IB 30 pts HL 6
     chem+sci/maths/psy)
     Kingston – 128 pts incl chem+sci/maths (MPharm)
     Leicester – ABB–BBB/BBB–BBC+bEPQ incl chem (Pharml Chem) (IB 30 pts HL 5 chem)
     London (QM) – ABB incl chem (Pharml Chem) (IB 34 pts HL 6/5 chem)
     Loughborough – ABB incl chem (Medcnl Pharml Chem) (IB 34 pts HL 655 incl 5 chem)
     Manchester – ABB–AAA incl chem+maths/biol +interview (MPharm) (IB 35 pts HL 6 chem
     6/5 maths/biol)
     Medway Sch Pharm – ABB incl chem+sci/maths 128 pts (MPharm) (IB 32 pts HL 15 pts
     incl 5 chem+sci)
     Portsmouth – 128 pts incl chem+sci +interview (MPharm) (IB 30 pts HL 17 pts incl 5
     chem+sci/maths)
     Robert Gordon – ABB incl chem+maths/sci (MPharm) (IB 32 pts HL 6 chem 5 sci/maths)
     Sunderland – 128–120 pts incl chem+sci (MPharm)

120 pts Hertfordshire – 120 pts incl chem+sci/maths (MPharm) (+interview HL 5 chem+sci/maths)
     Liverpool John Moores – BBB 120 pts incl chem +interview (MPharm) (IB 27 pts)
     Nottingham Trent – BBB incl chem 120 pts (Pharml Medcnl Chem)
     Reading – BBB–CCC (MPharm Fdn)
     Wolverhampton – BBB incl chem+sci/maths (MPharm)

112 pts East London – 112 pts incl biol/chem (Pharml Sci) (IB 25 pts HL 15 pts incl biol+chem)
     Greenwich – 112 pts incl chem +interview (Pharml Sci)
     Hertfordshire – 112 pts incl chem+sci/maths/geog (Pharml Sci) (HL 4 chem+sci/maths/
     geog)
     Huddersfield – BBC incl chem 112 pts (Pharml Chem)
     Manchester Met – BBC–BBB incl chem 112–120 pts (Pharml Chem (MChem) (Yr Ind))
     (IB 26 pts HL 5 chem)
     Westminster – BBC incl sci/maths/psy/geog (Herb Med) (IB 26 pts HL 4 sci)

104 pts Brighton – BCC–CCC incl chem 104–96 pts (Pharml Cheml Sci) (IB 27 pts)
     De Montfort – 104 pts incl chem+sci (Pharml Cos Sci) (IB 24 pts HL 6 chem+sci)
     Kingston – 104 pts incl chem+sci (Pharml Sci)
     South Wales – BCC–CDD incl chem+sci (Pharml Sci) (HL 655–445)

96 pts **London Met** – CCC incl biol+chem 96 pts (Pharml Sci)
80 pts **Wolverhampton** – BB/CDD incl chem (Pharml Sci)

Alternative offers
See **Chapter 6** and **Appendix 1** for grades/UCAS Tariff points information for other examinations.

EXAMPLES OF COLLEGES OFFERING COURSES IN THIS SUBJECT FIELD
Birmingham Met (Coll).

CHOOSING YOUR COURSE (SEE ALSO CH.1)
Universities and colleges teaching quality See www.qaa.ac.uk; https://unistats.ac.uk.

Top research universities and colleges (REF 2014) (Allied Health Professions, Dentistry, Nursing and Pharmacy) Birmingham; Sheffield (Biomed Sci); Bangor; Swansea (Allied Hlth); Aston; Coventry; Southampton; Cardiff; Surrey; Glasgow; Nottingham (Pharm); Bradford; East Anglia (Allied Hlth); London (QM); Sheffield (Dnstry); Queen's Belfast (Pharm); Bath; London (King's) (Pharm); Leeds.

Examples of sandwich degree courses Bradford; De Montfort; Greenwich; Hertfordshire.

ADMISSIONS INFORMATION
Number of applicants per place (approx) Aston 10; Bath 7; Bradford 10; Cardiff 8; De Montfort 14; Liverpool John Moores (Pharm) 7; London (King's) 15, (Sch Pharm) 6; Manchester 9; Nottingham 10; Robert Gordon 11; Strathclyde 10; Sunderland 20.

Advice to applicants and planning the UCAS personal statement Work experience and work shadowing with a retail and/or hospital pharmacist is important, and essential for Pharmacy applicants. Read pharmaceutical journals, extend your knowledge of well-known drugs and antibiotics. Read up on the history of drugs. Attend Open Days or careers conferences. See also **Appendix 3**. **Manchester** Students giving preference for Pharmacy are likely to be more successful than those who choose Pharmacy as an alternative to Medicine or Dentistry.

Misconceptions about this course That a degree in Pharmaceutical Science is a qualification leading to a career as a pharmacist. It is not: it is a course which concerns the application of chemical and biomedical science to the design, synthesis and analysis of pharmaceuticals for medicinal purposes. See also **Pharmacology**.

Selection interviews Yes Aston, Bath, Bradford, Cardiff, East Anglia, Huddersfield, Liverpool John Moores, London (UCL), Manchester, Nottingham, Sussex; **Some** Brighton; **No** De Montfort, Keele, Portsmouth, Reading, Robert Gordon, Strathclyde, Wolverhampton.

Interview advice and questions As work experience is essential for Pharmacy applicants, questions are likely to focus on this and what they have discovered. Other relevant questions could include: Why do you want to study Pharmacy? What types of work do pharmacists do? What interests you about the Pharmacy course? What branch of pharmacy do you want to enter? Name a drug – what do you know about it (formula, use, etc)? Name a drug from a natural source and its use. Can you think of another way of extracting a drug? Why do fungi destroy bacteria? What is an antibiotic? Can you name one and say how it was discovered? What is insulin? What is its source and function? What is diabetes? What type of insulin is used in its treatment? What is a hormone? What drugs are available over the counter without prescription? What is the formula of aspirin? What is genetic engineering? See also **Chapter 5**. **Bath** Informal and relaxed; very few rejected at this stage. **Cardiff** Interviews cover both academic and vocational aspects; candidates must reach a satisfactory level in both areas. **Liverpool John Moores** Aptitude test and interview. No specific preparation required. **Manchester** Candidates failing to attend interviews will have their applications withdrawn. The majority of applicants who are called for interview are made offers.

Reasons for rejection (non-academic) Poor communication skills. Poor knowledge of pharmacy and the work of a pharmacist.

AFTER-RESULTS ADVICE
Offers to applicants repeating A-levels Higher Bradford, Cardiff, De Montfort, London (UCL), Queen's Belfast, Strathclyde; **Possibly higher** Aston; **Same** Bath, Brighton, East Anglia, Liverpool John Moores, Nottingham, Robert Gordon, Sunderland, Wolverhampton.

GRADUATE DESTINATIONS AND EMPLOYMENT (2015/16 HESA)
See **Pharmacology**.

Career note The majority of Pharmacy graduates proceed to work in the commercial and retail fields, although opportunities also exist with pharmaceutical companies and in hospital pharmacies. There are also opportunities in agricultural and veterinary pharmacy.

OTHER DEGREE SUBJECTS FOR CONSIDERATION
Biochemistry; Biological Sciences; Biology; Biotechnology; Chemistry; Drug Development; Life Sciences; Medicinal Chemistry; Microbiology; Natural Sciences; Pharmacology; Physiology.

PHILOSOPHY

(including **Philosophy, Politics and Economics**; see also **Psychology**)

Philosophy is one of the oldest and most fundamental disciplines, which examines the nature of the universe and humanity's place in it. Philosophy seeks to discover the essence of the mind, language and physical reality and discusses the methods used to investigate these topics.

Useful websites www.iep.utm.edu; www.philosophypages.com; http://royalinstitutephilosophy.org; see also **Religious Studies**.

NB The points totals shown to the left of the institutions are for ease of reference only. It must not be assumed that Tariff points are always used by institutions or that they can be substituted for an offer in grades. The level of an offer is not necessarily indicative of the quality of a course.

COURSE OFFERS INFORMATION
Subject requirements/preferences GCSE English and mathematics. A foreign language may be required. **AL** No specific subjects except for joint courses.

Your target offers and examples of degree courses

160 pts **Cambridge** – A*A*A incl sci/maths +interview +NSAA (Nat Sci (Hist Phil Sci)) (IB 40–42 pts HL 776)
Oxford – A*A*A incl maths +interview +MAT (Maths Phil) (IB 39 pts HL 766)

152 pts **Bristol** – A*AA–AAB incl maths+phys (Phys Phil) (IB 38–34 pts HL 6 maths 6 phys); A*AA–AAB incl maths (Maths Phil) (IB 38–34 pts HL 6 maths)
Cambridge – A*AA +interview +PAA (Phil) (IB 40–42 pts HL 776)
Durham – A*AA incl maths (PPE) (IB 38 pts); A*AA incl Engl (Engl Lit Phil) (IB 38 pts)
London (King's) – A*AA +LNAT (Pol Phil Law) (IB 35 pts HL 766); A*AA (PPE) (IB 35 pts HL 766)
London (UCL) – A*AA–AAA incl maths (PPE) (IB 39–38 pts HL 7 maths)
London LSE – A*AA incl A* maths (PPE) (IB 38 pts)
Manchester – A*AA–AAA incl maths (Maths Phil) (IB 34 pts HL 6 maths)
Nottingham – A*AA (PPE) (IB 38 pts)
Oxford – A*AA +interview +TSA (Psy Phil Ling) (IB 39 pts)
Warwick – A*AA (PPE) (IB 38 pts HL 5 maths)
York – A*AA–AAA incl maths (PPE) (IB 37 pts)

144 pts **Bristol** – AAA–ABB (Phil) (HL 665); (Phil Theol; Phil Econ) (IB 36–32 pts)
Durham – AAA incl soc sci/hum (Phil Pol) (IB 37 pts); AAA (Phil; Phil Psy) (IB 37 pts)
Exeter – AAA–AAB (Phil Pol; Phil; PPE) (IB 36–34 pts)
Leeds – AAA (PPE) (IB 35 pts HL 17 maths)

UCAS points Tariff: A* = 56 pts; A = 48 pts; B = 40 pts; C = 32 pts; D = 24 pts; E = 16 pts

London (King's) – AAA (War St Phil) (IB 35 pts HL 666); (Phil courses) (IB 35 pts); AAA incl maths+fmaths (Maths Phil) (IB 35 pts HL 666)

London (UCL) – AAA (Phil) (IB 38 pts)

London LSE – AAA (Pol Phil) (IB 38 pts HL 766); (Phil Lgc Sci Meth) (IB 38 pts); AAA incl maths (Phil Econ) (IB 38 pts)

Manchester – AAA (PPE) (IB 36 pts HL 666)

NCH London – AAA–ABB +interview (Phil courses) (IB 36–34 pts)

Oxford – AAA +interview +TSA (PPE) (IB 39 pts); AAA +interview +MLAT (Phil Modn Langs) (IB 39 pts HL 666); AAA +interview +test (Phil Theol) (IB 39 pts)

Queen's Belfast – AAA (PPE)

Sussex – AAA–AAB (PPE) (IB 34 pts)

Warwick – AAA–AAB (Phil Comb Hons) (IB 38–36 pts)

York – AAA (Phil Pol) (IB 36 pts)

136 pts **Birmingham** – AAB (Phil) (IB 32 pts HL 665)

Bristol – AAB–BBB incl lang (Phil Modn Lang) (IB 34–31 pts HL 5 lang); AAB–BBB (Sociol Phil) (IB 34–31 pts)

Edinburgh – AAB (Phil) (IB 36 pts)

Glasgow – AAB–BBB incl arts/lang (Phil) (IB 36–34 pts)

Lancaster – AAB–ABB (Phil; Phil Relig St; Eth Phil Relgn) (IB 35–32 pts); AAB incl Engl/lang/maths/comp/psy (Ling Phil) (IB 35 pts HL 16 pts); AAB–ABB incl maths/fmaths (Maths Phil) (IB 35 pts HL 6 maths); AAB (PPE) (IB 35 pts HL 16 pts)

Leeds – AAB–ABB (Hist Phil Sci courses) (IB 35–34 pts HL 16 pts); AAB (Phil; Phil Comb Hons) (IB 35 pts)

London (King's) – AAB (Relgn Phil Eth) (IB 35 pts); AAB incl Fr (Fr Phil (Yr Abrd)) (IB 35 pts HL 665 incl Fr)

London (RH) – AAB–ABB incl maths (PPE) (IB 32 pts); AAB–ABB (Mus Phil) (IB 32 pts HL 655); (Pol Phil) (IB 32 pts)

London (UCL) – AAB–ABB (Hist Phil Sci) (IB 36 34 pts HL 17–16 pts)

Newcastle – AAB (Phil Comb Hons) (IB 35 pts)

Nottingham – AAB/A*BB (Phil; Phil Theol; Class Civ Phil; Psy Phil) (IB 34 pts); AAB/A*BB incl Engl (Engl Phil) (IB 34 pts); AAB (Relgn Phil Eth) (IB 34 pts)

St Andrews – AAB (Phil courses; Phil Scot Hist) (IB 35 pts)

Sheffield – AAB–ABB+bEPQ (Phil; Pol Phil) (IB 34 pts)

Southampton – AAB–ABB incl mus +gr 8 (Phil Mus) (IB 34–32 pts HL 6 mus); AAB–ABB incl hist (Phil Hist) (IB 34–32 pts HL 6 hist); AAB/ABBb incl maths/phys/stats (PPE) (IB 34–32 pts HL 5 maths); AAB–ABB (Film Phil) (IB 32 pts HL 16 pts); (Econ Phil; Phil Sociol; Phil Pol; Phil) (IB 34–32 pts); AAB–ABB incl Engl (Phil Engl) (IB 34–32 pts HL 6 Engl); AAB–ABB+aEPQ incl maths (Phil Maths) (IB 34–32 pts HL 6 maths)

Sussex – AAB–ABB (Phil) (IB 32 pts)

Warwick – AAB (Phil) (IB 36 pts)

York – AAB incl maths+phys +interview (Phys Phil); AAB (Phil; Phil Ling) (IB 35 pts); AAB incl Engl (Engl Phil) (IB 35 pts HL 6 Engl)

128 pts **Cardiff** – ABB (Phil) (IB 34 pts)

East Anglia – ABB (Phil Pol; PPE; Phil) (IB 32 pts); ABB incl hist (Phil Hist) (IB 32 pts HL 5 hist)

Edinburgh – ABB (Phil Ling) (IB 37 pts HL 666)

Kent – ABB (Phil Joint courses) (IB 34 pts)

Leeds – ABB incl biol (Biol Hist Phil Sci) (IB 34 pts HL 6 biol)

Liverpool – ABB (Phil Comb Hons) (IB 33 pts HL 665); (Phil) (IB 33 pts)

London (RH) – ABB (Phil) (IB 32 pts)

Manchester – ABB (Theol St Phil Eth; Phil) (IB 33 pts)

Reading – ABB–BBB (Art Phil; Phil courses) (IB 32–30 pts)

Sheffield – ABB (Phil Comb Hons) (IB 34 pts)

Stirling – ABB (3 yr course) BBB (4 yr course) (PPE) (IB 35 pts (3 yr course) 32 pts (4 yr course)); ABB (Phil) (IB 35 pts)

Check **Chapter 3** for new university admission details and **Chapter 6** on how to read the subject tables.

Strathclyde – ABB–BBB (PPE) (IB 32–30 pts)

Warwick – ABB (Class Civ Phil) (IB 34 pts)

120 pts Aberdeen – BBB (Phil Comb Hons) (IB 32 pts); BBB incl maths+phys (Nat Phil)
  (IB 32 pts HL 5 maths+phys)

Anglia Ruskin – 120 pts (Phil; Phil Engl Lit) (IB 24 pts)

Buckingham – BBB (PPE) (IB 32 pts)

Dundee – BBB–BCC (Phil; Euro Phil) (IB 30 pts)

Essex – BBB (Phil; Phil Hist; PPE; Phil Law) (IB 30 pts)

Keele – BBB/ABC (Phil) (IB 32 pts)

Liverpool Hope – BBB–BBC 120–112 pts (Phil Eth; Phil Eth Relgn)

London (Birk) – 120 pts (Phil); 120–128 pts (Pol Phil Hist)

London (Gold) – BBB (PPE) (IB 33 pts)

Queen's Belfast – BBB (Phil courses)

Roehampton – 120 pts (Phil)

UWE Bristol – 120 pts (Phil)

118 pts NCH London – ABB–AAA (PPE) (IB 34–36 pts)

112 pts Bangor – 112–96 pts (Phil Relgn)

Gloucestershire – BBC 112 pts (Relgn Phil Eth)

Hertfordshire – 112 pts (Phil) (HL 44)

Hull – 112 pts (Phil Pol; Phil; PPE) (IB 28 pts)

Manchester Met – BBC–BBB (Phil Psy) (IB 26 pts)

Oxford Brookes – BBC 112 pts (Phil) (IB 30 pts)

Wolverhampton – BBC–CCC (Pol Phil; War St Phil); BBC (Law Phil; Phil Sociol; Relig
  St Phil)

104 pts Bath Spa – BCC–CCC (Relgn Phil Eth) (IB 26 pts)

Brighton – BCC–CCC 104–96 pts (Phil Pol Eth) (IB 27 pts)

Central Lancashire – 104 pts (Pol Phil Soty; Phil)

Chichester – 104–120 pts (Phil Eth) (IB 28 pts)

Leeds Trinity – 104 pts (Phil Eth Relgn)

Manchester Met – 104–112 pts (Phil; Int Pol Phil) (IB 26 pts)

Nottingham Trent – 104 pts (Phil Comb Hons)

Winchester – 104–120 pts (PPE) (IB 26 pts)

 96 pts Bishop Grosseteste – 96–112 pts (Theol Eth Soty)

Newman – 96–88 pts (Phil Relgn Educ)

York St John – 96–112 pts (Relgn Phil Eth)

 88 pts Canterbury Christ Church – 88–112 pts (Relgn Phil Eth)

 72 pts UHI – BC (PPE)

Open University – contact 0300 303 0073 **or** www.open.ac.uk/contact/new
  (PPE; Phil Psy)

Trinity Saint David – interview (Phil; Phil Comb Hons)

Alternative offers

See **Chapter 6** and **Appendix 1** for grades/UCAS Tariff points information for other examinations.

CHOOSING YOUR COURSE (SEE ALSO CH.1)

Universities and colleges teaching quality See www.qaa.ac.uk; https://unistats.ac.uk.

Top research universities and colleges (REF 2014) Warwick; Essex; Sheffield; Edinburgh;
Birmingham; London LSE; St Andrews; Bristol; Oxford; Cambridge (Hist Phil Sci); London (King's).

ADMISSIONS INFORMATION

Number of applicants per place (approx) Bangor 4; Birmingham 4; Bristol 19; Cambridge 4; Cardiff
8; Dundee 10; Durham 5; East Anglia 6; Hull 5; Lancaster 6; Leeds 10; Liverpool 5; London (King's) 6;
London (UCL) 6; London LSE 13; Manchester 6; Nottingham 5; Oxford (PPE) 7; Oxford Brookes 7;
Sheffield 8; Southampton 6; Stirling 10; Trinity Saint David 4; Warwick 9; York 6.

UCAS points Tariff: A* = 56 pts; A = 48 pts; B = 40 pts; C = 32 pts; D = 24 pts; E = 16 pts

Advice to applicants and planning the UCAS personal statement Read Bertrand Russell's *Problems of Philosophy*. Refer to any particular aspects of philosophy which interest you (check that these are offered on the courses for which you are applying). Selectors will expect applicants to have read around the subject. Explain what you know about the nature of studying philosophy. Say what you have read in philosophy and give an example of a philosophical issue that interests you. Universities do not expect applicants to have a wide knowledge of the subject, but evidence that you know what the subject is about is important. **Bristol** Deferred entry considered.

Misconceptions about this course Applicants are sometimes surprised to find what wide-ranging Philosophy courses are offered.

Selection interviews Yes Cambridge, Oxford (Phil Mod Lang) 27%, (PPE) 14%, (Phil Theol) 22%, Trinity Saint David; **Some** Bristol, Cardiff, Southampton, Warwick; **No** Birmingham, Dundee, East Anglia, Essex, Hull, Leeds, Liverpool, London (UCL), London LSE, Newcastle, Nottingham, Reading.

Interview advice and questions Philosophy is a very wide subject and initially applicants will be asked for their reasons for their choice and their special interests in the subject. Questions in recent years have included: Is there a difference between being tactless and being insensitive? Can you be tactless and thin-skinned? Define the difference between knowledge and belief. Was the vertical distortion of El Greco's paintings a product of a vision defect? What is the point of studying philosophy? What books on philosophy have you read? Discuss the work of a renowned philosopher. What is a philosophical novel? Who has the right to decide your future – yourself or another? What do you want to do with your life? What is a philosophical question? John is your husband, and if John is your husband then necessarily you must be his wife. If you are necessarily his wife then it is not possible that you could not be his wife, so it was impossible for you not to have married him – you were destined for each other. Discuss. What is the difference between a man's entitlements, his deserts and his attributes? What are morals? A good understanding of philosophy is needed for entry to degree courses, and applicants are expected to demonstrate this if they are called to interview. As one admissions tutor stated, 'If you find Bertrand Russell's *Problems of Philosophy* unreadable – don't apply!' See also **Chapter 5**. **Cambridge** If you were to form a government of philosophers, what selection process would you use? Is it moral to hook up a psychopath (whose only pleasure is killing) to a really stimulating machine so that he can believe he is in the real world and kill as much as he likes? **Oxford** If you entered a teletransporter and your body was destroyed and instantly recreated on Mars in exactly the same way with all your memories intact etc, would you be the same person? Tutors are not so much concerned with what you know as how you think about it. Evidence required concerning social and political topics and the ability to discuss them critically. (PPE) Is being hungry the same thing as wanting to eat? Why is there not a global government? What do you think of teleport machines? Should there be an intelligence test to decide who should vote? **York** Do human beings have free will? Do we perceive the world as it really is?

Reasons for rejection (non-academic) Evidence of severe psychological disturbance, criminal activity, drug problems (evidence from referees' reports). Lack of knowledge of philosophy. **Oxford** He was not able to explore his thoughts deeply enough or with sufficient centrality. **York** No evidence of having read any philosophical literature.

AFTER-RESULTS ADVICE
Offers to applicants repeating A-levels Higher Bristol (Phil Econ), Leeds, Warwick; **Same** Birmingham, Bristol, Cardiff, Dundee, Durham, East Anglia, Essex, Hull, Liverpool Hope, Newcastle, Nottingham (in some cases), Nottingham Trent, St Mary's, Southampton, Stirling, Wolverhampton, York; **No** Cambridge, Glasgow.

GRADUATE DESTINATIONS AND EMPLOYMENT (2015/16 HESA)
Graduates surveyed 1,705 **Employed** 725 **In voluntary employment** 60 **In further study** 520 **Assumed unemployed** 105

Career note Graduates have a wide range of transferable skills that can lead to employment in many areas, eg management, public administration, publishing, banking and social services.

OTHER DEGREE SUBJECTS FOR CONSIDERATION

Divinity; History and Philosophy of Science; History of Art; Human Sciences; Psychology; Religious Studies; Science; Theology.

PHOTOGRAPHY

(see also **Art and Design (Fine Art), Art and Design (General), Film, Radio, Video and TV Studies, Media Studies**)

Photography courses offer a range of specialised studies involving commercial, industrial and still photography, portraiture and film, digital and video work. Increasingly this subject is featuring in Media courses. See also **Appendix 3**.

Useful websites www.the-aop.org; www.rps.org; www.bjp-online.com; www.bipp.com

NB The points totals shown to the left of the institutions are for ease of reference only. It must not be assumed that Tariff points are always used by institutions or that they can be substituted for an offer in grades. The level of an offer is not necessarily indicative of the quality of a course.

COURSE OFFERS INFORMATION

Subject requirements/preferences GCSE Art and/or a portfolio usually required. **AL** One or two subjects may be required, including an art/design or creative subject. Most institutions will make offers on the basis of a portfolio of work.

Your target offers and examples of degree courses

136 pts **Leeds** – AAB (Film Photo Media) (IB 35 pts)

128 pts **Brighton** – ABB–BBB 128–120 pts +interview +portfolio (Photo) (IB 30 pts)
Edinburgh – ABB +portfolio (Photo) (IB 34 pts)
Glasgow (SA) – ABB +interview +portfolio (Fn Art Photo)

120 pts **Bournemouth Arts** – BBB 120 pts +portfolio +interview (Photo; Commer Photo) (IB 30 pts)
Coventry – BBB incl art/media/photo (Photo) (IB 31 pts)
Derby – 120–128 pts +portfolio +interview (Photo; Commer Photo)
Huddersfield – BBB 120 pts (Photo)
Norwich Arts – BBB incl art/des (Photo) (IB 32 pts)
Trinity Saint David – 120 pts +interview (Photojrnl Doc Photo); 120 pts (Photo Arts) (IB 32 pts)

112 pts **Anglia Ruskin** – 112 pts (Photo) (IB 24 pts)
Birmingham City – BBC 112 pts +interview +portfolio (Photo) (HL 14 pts)
Central Lancashire – 112 pts +interview +portfolio (Fash Prom)
Chester – BBC–BCC incl art/des/photo 112 pts +interview (Photo) (IB 26 pts HL 5 vis arts)
Creative Arts – 112 pts (Photo)
De Montfort – 112 pts incl art des (Photo Vid) (IB 26 pts)
Gloucestershire – BBC 112 pts +interview +portfolio (Photojrnl Doc Photo); 112 pts +interview +portfolio (Photo)
Leeds Arts – BBC 112 pts +portfolio (Photo)
Lincoln – BBC incl art/des/media (Photo) (IB 29 pts HL 5 art/des/media)
Manchester Met – 112 pts +interview +portfolio (Photo) (IB 26 pts)
Middlesex – 112 pts +interview +portfolio (Photo)
Nottingham Trent – BBC 112 pts (Photo)
Plymouth – 112 pts (Photo; Doc Photo) (IB 28 pts)
Roehampton – 112 pts (Photo)
Sheffield Hallam – 112–96 pts (Photo)

Southampton Solent – 112 pts (Photo)
Staffordshire – BBC 112 pts (Photo)
Sunderland – 112 pts (Photo Vid Dig Imag)
UWE Bristol – 112 pts (Photo)
West London – BBC 112 pts incl art des (Photo)
Wolverhampton – BBC 112 pts +portfolio (Photo)

104 pts **Bath Spa** – BCC +portfolio +interview (Photo) (IB 27 pts)
Central Lancashire – 104 pts (Photo)
Falmouth – 104–120 pts +portfolio +interview (Photo; Press Edit Photo; Mar Nat Hist Photo); 104–120 pts +interview +portfolio (Fash Photo)
Kingston – 104 pts (Photo)
Northampton – BCC incl art/des/photo 104 pts (Photo)
Portsmouth – 104–112 pts (Photo) (IB 26 pts)
South Wales – BCC–CDD 104–80 pts +interview +portfolio (Photo) (HL 655–445); BCC–CDD incl art des 104–80 pts +interview +portfolio (Doc Photo) (HL 655–445)

96 pts **Bolton** – 96 pts (Photo)
Bournemouth – 96–104 pts (Photo) (IB 26–29 pts HL 55)
Cleveland (CAD) – 96 pts (Commer Photo)
Cumbria – 96–112 pts (Photo)
East London – 96 pts (Photo) (IB 24 pts)
Hertfordshire – 96 pts incl art +portfolio +interview (Photo) (HL 44)
Plymouth (CA) – 96 pts +portfolio (Photo)
Ulster – BCC BBB incl art des (Photo Vido) (IB 24 pts)
Westminster – CCC–BB incl photo (Photo) (IB 28 pts)

88 pts **Canterbury Christ Church** – 88–112 pts (Photo)
80 pts **Arts London** – 80 pts (Photo)
Bedfordshire – 80 pts +portfolio (Photo Vid Art)
Hereford (CA) – 80 pts +portfolio +interview (Photo)

64 pts **Arts London (CFash)** – CC 64 pts +interview +portfolio (Fash Photo)
Colchester (Inst) – 64 pts +portfolio (Photo)
Ravensbourne – CC (Dig Photo) (IB 28 pts)
Stockport (Coll) – 64 pts +portfolio (Contemp Photo)

Alternative offers
See **Chapter 6** and **Appendix 1** for grades/UCAS Tariff points information for other examinations.

EXAMPLES OF COLLEGES OFFERING COURSES IN THIS SUBJECT FIELD

Barking and Dagenham (Coll); Bedford (Coll); Birmingham Met (Coll); Blackburn (Coll); Blackpool and Fylde (Coll); Bournemouth and Poole (Coll); Bradford (Coll); Brighton Met (Coll); Bristol City (Coll); Buckinghamshire (Coll Group); Canterbury (Coll); Central Bedfordshire (Coll); Central Campus, Sandwell (Coll); City and Islington (Coll); Coventry (Coll); Doncaster (Coll); East Coast (Coll); East Surrey (Coll); Exeter (Coll); Farnborough (CT); Gloucestershire (Coll); Grimsby (Inst Group); Grŵp Llandrillo Menai; Havering (Coll); Hugh Baird (Coll); Hull (Coll); Kensington and Chelsea (Coll); Kirklees (Coll); Leeds City (Coll); Leicester (Coll); LeSoCo; Lincoln (Coll); Manchester (Coll); Milton Keynes (Coll); Myerscough (Coll); Nescot; Newcastle (Coll); North Shropshire (Coll); North Warwickshire and Hinckley (Coll); Northbrook Met (Coll); Northumberland (Coll); Nottingham (Coll); Rotherham (CAT); St Helens (Coll); Sheffield (Coll); Sir Gâr (Coll); Solihull (Coll); South Devon (Coll); South Essex (Coll); South Gloucestershire and Stroud (Coll); South Staffordshire (Coll); Southampton City (Coll); Southport (Coll); Stamford New (Coll); Stockport (Coll); Sussex Coast Hastings (Coll); Tresham (CFHE); Truro and Penwith (Coll); Wakefield (Coll); Walsall (Coll); West Kent (Coll); Westminster City (Coll); Weston (Coll); Weymouth (Coll); Wiltshire (Coll); Wirral Met (Coll); Yeovil (Coll).

CHOOSING YOUR COURSE (SEE ALSO CH.1)

Universities and colleges teaching quality See www.qaa.ac.uk; https://unistats.ac.uk.

Examples of sandwich degree courses Coventry; Hertfordshire; Leeds; Portsmouth; Wolverhampton.

ADMISSIONS INFORMATION

Number of applicants per place (approx) Arts London 10; Birmingham City 6; Blackpool and Fylde (Coll) 3; Bournemouth Arts 3; Cleveland (CAD) 2; Derby 4; Falmouth 3; Nottingham Trent 4; Plymouth 6; Plymouth (CA) 7; Staffordshire 3; Stockport (Coll) 6; Trinity Saint David 12.

Advice to applicants and planning the UCAS personal statement Discuss your interest in photography and your knowledge of various aspects of the subject, for example, digital, video, landscape, medical, wildlife and portrait photography. Read photographic journals to keep up-to-date on developments, particularly in photographic technology. You will also need first-hand experience of photography and to be competent in basic skills. See also **Appendix 3**. **Derby** (Non-UK students) Fluency in written and spoken English important. Portfolio of work essential.

Misconceptions about this course Some believe that courses are all practical work with no theory. **Cumbria** They didn't realise the facilities were so good!

Selection interviews Most institutions will interview applicants and expect to see a portfolio of work. **Yes** Brighton, Chester, Cumbria, Huddersfield, Plymouth, Southampton Solent; **No** Falmouth, West London.

Interview advice and questions Questions relate to the applicant's portfolio of work which, for these courses, is of prime importance. Who are your favourite photographers? What is the most recent exhibition you have attended? Have any leading photographers influenced your work? Questions regarding contemporary photography. Written work sometimes required. See **Chapter 5**.

Reasons for rejection (non-academic) Lack of passion for the subject. Lack of exploration and creativity in practical work. Poorly presented portfolio.

AFTER-RESULTS ADVICE

Offers to applicants repeating A-levels Same Birmingham City, Blackpool and Fylde (Coll), Chester, Cumbria, Manchester Met, Nottingham Trent, Staffordshire.

GRADUATE DESTINATIONS AND EMPLOYMENT (2015/16 HESA)

Cinematics and Photography graduates surveyed 3,890 **Employed** 1,950 **In voluntary employment** 165 **In further study** 385 **Assumed unemployed** 305

Career note Opportunities for photographers exist in a range of specialisms, including advertising and editorial work, fashion, medical, industrial, scientific and technical photography. Some graduates also go into photojournalism and other aspects of the media.

OTHER DEGREE SUBJECTS FOR CONSIDERATION

Art and Design; Digital Animation; Film, Radio, Video and TV Studies; Media Studies; Moving Image; Radiography.

PHYSICAL EDUCATION

(see also Education Studies, Sports Sciences/Studies, Teacher Training)

Physical Education courses are very popular and unfortunately restricted in number. Ability in gymnastics or an involvement in sport are obviously important factors.

Useful websites www.afpe.org.uk; www.uksport.gov.uk; see also **Education Studies** and **Teacher Training**.

NB The points totals shown to the left of the institutions are for ease of reference only. It must not be assumed that Tariff points are always used by institutions or that they can be substituted for an offer in grades. The level of an offer is not necessarily indicative of the quality of a course.

COURSE OFFERS INFORMATION

Subject requirements/preferences GCSE English, mathematics and a science. **AL** PE, sports studies and science are preferred subjects and for some courses one of these may be required. Disclosure and Barring Service (DBS) check before starting the course. Declaration of Health usually required.

Your target offers and examples of degree courses

144 pts **Birmingham** – AAA–ABB incl maths/sci (Spo PE Coach Sci) (IB 32 pts HL 666–665)

128 pts **Bangor** – 128–112 pts (Spo Hlth PE)

East Anglia – ABB (PE) (IB 32 pts)

Edge Hill – ABB 128 pts (PE Sch Spo)

Edinburgh – ABB (PE) (IB 34 pts)

Sheffield Hallam – 128–112 pts (PE Sch Spo)

120 pts **Cardiff Met** – 120 pts (Spo PE)

Liverpool Hope – BBB–BBC 120–112 pts (Spo PE)

112 pts **Brighton** – BBC–CCC 112–96 pts (PE) (IB 28 pts)

Brunel – BBC (Spo Hlth Exer Sci (Spo Dev); PE Yth Spo) (IB 29 pts)

Canterbury Christ Church – 112 pts (PE Spo Exer Sci)

Chichester – BBC–CCC incl PE (PE Spo Coach)

East London – 112 pts incl PE/spo/sci (Spo PE Dev) (IB 25 pts)

Leeds Beckett – 112 pts incl sci (PE Out Educ) (IB 25 pts); 112 pts incl sci/PE (PE courses)
    (IB 25 pts)

Leeds Trinity – 112 pts (PE; S PE courses)

Liverpool John Moores – 112 pts (Spo Dev)

Newman 112 pts (Spo Educ)

Oxford Brookes – BBC 112 pts (Spo Coach PE) (IB 30 pts)

Plymouth – 112 pts (P PE BEd (QTS))

Staffordshire – BBC 112 pts (PE Yth Spo Coach)

Winchester – 112–120 pts (P Educ PE QTS)

Wolverhampton – BBC (PE)

Worcester – 112 pts (PE Spo St; PE Dance)

104 pts **Anglia Ruskin** – 104 pts (Spo Coach PE) (IB 24 pts)

Bedfordshire – 104 pts +interview (PE S)

Greenwich – 104 pts incl sci (Spo Sci Coach); 104 pts (PE Spo)

96 pts **Cumbria** – 96–112 pts (Spo Coach PE)

London Met – BC/CCC incl biol/PE/spo sci 96 pts (Spo Psy Coach PE)

St Mark and St John – CCC incl PE/sci 96 pts (PE); CCC 96 pts (Spo Coach PE)

Trinity Saint David – 96 pts (PE)

Wolverhampton – CCC (Exer Hlth)

York St John – 96–112 pts (PE Spo Coach)

80 pts **Bedfordshire** – 80 pts (Spo Sci; Spo St)

Alternative offers

See **Chapter 6** and **Appendix 1** for grades/UCAS Tariff points information for other examinations.

EXAMPLES OF COLLEGES OFFERING COURSES IN THIS SUBJECT FIELD

City and Islington (Coll); Doncaster (Coll); Hartpury (Coll); Peterborough (Coll).

CHOOSING YOUR COURSE (SEE ALSO CH.1)

Universities and colleges teaching quality See www.qaa.ac.uk; https://unistats.ac.uk.

Top research universities and colleges (REF 2014) See **Sports Sciences/Studies**.

ADMISSIONS INFORMATION

Number of applicants per place (approx) Bangor 4; Birmingham 5; Edge Hill 40; Leeds Trinity 6; Liverpool John Moores 4; Newman 5; St Mark and St John 18; Sheffield Hallam 60; Worcester 31.

Advice to applicants and planning the UCAS personal statement Ability in gymnastics, athletics and all sports and games is important. Full details of these activities should be given on the UCAS application – for example, teams, dates and awards achieved, assisting in extra-curricular activities. Involvement with local sports clubs, health clubs, summer camps, gap year. Relevant experience in coaching, teaching, community and youth work. **Liverpool John Moores** Commitment to working with children and a good sports background.

Selection interviews Most institutions. In most cases, applicants will take part in physical education practical tests and games/gymnastics, depending on the course. The results of these tests could affect the level of offers. See also **Chapter 5**. **Yes** Worcester.

Interview advice and questions The applicant's interests in physical education will be discussed, with specific questions on, for example, sportsmanship, refereeing, umpiring and coaching. Questions in the past have also included: What qualities should a good netball goal defence possess? How could you encourage a group of children into believing that sport is fun? Do you think that physical education should be compulsory in schools? Why do you think you would make a good teacher? What is the name of the Education Minister?

Reasons for rejection (non-academic) Poor communication and presentational skills. Relatively poor sporting background or knowledge. Lack of knowledge about the teaching of physical education and the commitment required. Lack of ability in practicalities, for example, gymnastics, dance when relevant. Poor self-presentation. Poor writing skills.

AFTER-RESULTS ADVICE
Offers to applicants repeating A-levels Same Liverpool John Moores, Newman.

GRADUATE DESTINATIONS AND EMPLOYMENT (2015/16 HESA)
See **Sports Sciences/Studies**.

Career note The majority of graduates go into teaching although, depending on any special interests, they may also go on into the sport and leisure industry.

OTHER DEGREE SUBJECTS FOR CONSIDERATION
Coach Education; Exercise and Fitness; Exercise Physiology; Human Biology; Leisure and Recreation; Physiotherapy; Sport and Exercise Science; Sport Health and Exercise; Sport Studies/Sciences; Sports Coaching; Sports Development; Sports Engineering; Sports Psychology; Sports Therapy.

PHYSICS
(see also Astronomy and Astrophysics)

Physics is an increasingly popular subject and a wide variety of courses are available which enables students to follow their own interests and specialisations. Some course options are nanotechnology, medical physics, cosmology, environmental physics and biophysics.

Useful websites www.myphysicscourse.org; www.iop.org; www.physics.org; www.scicentral.com; www.ipem.ac.uk; www.epsrc.ac.uk; https://jobs.newscientist.com; www.nature.com/subjects/physics

NB The points totals shown to the left of the institutions are for ease of reference only. It must not be assumed that Tariff points are always used by institutions or that they can be substituted for an offer in grades. The level of an offer is not necessarily indicative of the quality of a course.

COURSE OFFERS INFORMATION
Subject requirements/preferences GCSE English, mathematics and science. **AL** Physics and mathematics are required for most courses.

LOVE
PHYSICS?

Pass on the passion. *Teach.*

iop.org/teach

IOP Institute of Physics

Department of Physics
Faculty of Science

- Our lectures, laboratories and small group teaching are designed to increase your future employability

- Student-led research projects in Nano and Nuclear Physics, Plasma and Astrophysics

- Industrial placements and study abroad options available

- Our courses are offered as an integrated masters or bachelors degree and accredited by the Institute of Physics

Find out more:
For further information on studying at York:
york.ac.uk/physics
+44 (0)1904 322241
physics-admissions@york.ac.uk

STUDY PHYSICS
at the University of York

At the University of York we know that our graduates have broad ranging aspirations. With destinations spanning academic research, education, industrial and financial sectors, the need for a well rounded university education is clear. That is why we ensure that our courses combine an education in cutting edge physics with the practical and professional skills required to succeed in your chosen career.

Our recently redesigned undergraduate programmes offer you a thorough grounding in core physics topics, leading to all of our degrees being accredited by the Institute of Physics. This is combined with advanced modules in topics closely aligned with our research (95% of which was rated internationally excellent in the latest REF exercise). Whether your interest lies in fusion energy, nuclear and plasma astrophysics, smart materials research, biophysics or quantum information theory, we have modules and final year research projects to suit you.

All of this is supported by practical experience in our laboratory facilities. This includes our recently renovated undergraduate teaching laboratories, our dedicated Astrocampus and computational laboratories, as well as our cutting-edge research laboratories. In addition, professional skills are integrated in to our curriculum via tutorials and training. We also host the White Rose Industrial Physics

Academy (WRIPA), a collaboration between the Universities of York and Sheffield. By working with our technical industry partners we improve the industry-relevant skills of physics graduates by facilitating industry led projects and internships

You will be taught by world leading academics at the cutting edge of their field who possess an enthusiasm for teaching. This fosters excellent student-staff rapport and ensures a friendly, inclusive and supportive atmosphere. You have access to our distinctive 'research-informed' teaching via regular supervision meetings, small group classes and an 'open door' policy for approaching academic staff. We are holders of the Juno Champion Award and have achieved a Silver Athena SWAN accreditation for our active support of women in science.

We offer integrated Year Abroad or Year in Industry programmes alongside the majority of our Physics programs. Studying or working abroad during your degree is a life-enhancing experience that can boost your self-confidence, independence and ambition. It also broadens your cultural and social perspectives, develops language skills and significantly increases your employability in the global jobs market. By working in industry you can learn how to apply your enthusiasm for physics, and to develop the skills and experience desired by leading employers.

All of this means that you will have excellent career prospects, with 91% of graduates in a professional job or graduate level study 6 months after graduation according to the latest DLHE survey. We pride ourselves on being a friendly and supportive department, helping students to unlock their academic potential and develop skills that are increasingly sought after by employers.

Campus West. University of York

UNIVERSITY of York

Find out more:
For further information on studying at York:
york.ac.uk/physics
+44 (0)1904 322241
physics-admissions@york.ac.uk

Your target offers and examples of degree courses

160 pts **Cambridge** – A*A*A incl sci/maths +interview +NSAA (Nat Sci (Phys/Physl Sci/Astro)) (IB 40–42 pts HL 776)

Durham – A*A*A incl phys+maths (Phys; Theor Phys (MPhys)) (IB 38 pts HL 776); A*A*A incl maths+phys (Phys Astron (MPhys)) (IB 38 pts HL 776 incl maths+phys)

Imperial London – A*A*A incl maths+phys +interview +audition +gr 8 (Phys Mus Perf) (IB 40 pts HL 766); A*A*A incl maths+phys +interview (Phys; Phys (Yr Abrd) (MSci)) (IB 40 pts HL 766)

Manchester – A*A*A–A*AA incl phys+maths +interview (Phys) (IB 37 pts HL 776–766); A*A*A–A*AA incl maths+phys (Phys Astro) (IB 37 pts HL 776–766 incl maths+phys)

152 pts **Bath** – A*AA–AAA+aEPQ incl maths+phys (Phys; Maths Phys) (IB 36 pts HL 766)

Birmingham – A*AA incl maths+phys (Phys) (IB 32 pts HL 766)

Bristol – A*AA–AAB incl maths+phys (Phys; Phys Phil) (IB 38–34 pts HL 6 maths 6 phys); (Phys Astro) (IB 38–34 pts HL 6 maths+phys)

Durham – A*AA incl sci (Nat Sci) (IB 38 pts)

Edinburgh – A*AA incl maths+phys (Mathem Phys) (IB 37 pts HL 666)

Exeter – A*AA–AAB incl maths+phys +interview (Phys; Phys Astro (MPhys); Maths Phys) (IB 38–34 pts HL 6 maths/phys)

Nottingham – A*AA–AAA incl maths+phys (Phys Euro Lang; Phys Med Phys; Phys Theor Phys; Phys; Mathem Phys) (IB 36 pts HL 6 maths+phys); (Phys Theor Astro; Phys Astron) (IB 36 pts HL 666 incl maths+phys)

Oxford – A*AA incl phys+maths +interview +PAT (Phys) (IB 39 pts HL 766)

Warwick – A*AA incl maths+phys (Phys Bus St) (IB 38 pts HL 6 maths+phys); A*AA incl maths/fmaths+phys (Phys) (IB 38 pts HL 6 maths+phys)

144 pts **Cardiff** – AAA–AAB incl maths+phys (Phys Astron (MPhys)) (IB 36–34 pts HL 6 maths+phys); AAA–AAB incl phys+maths (Phys MPhys) (IB 36–34 pts HL 6 phys+maths)

East Anglia – AAA incl sci +interview (Nat Sci) (IB 34 pts HL 6 sci)

Edinburgh – AAA incl maths+phys (Geophys; Geophys Meteor) (IB 37 pts HL 555); (Phys Meteor; Theor Phys; Phys Mus; Phys; Comput Phys) (IB 37 pts HL 666)

Lancaster – AAA incl maths+phys (Phys (MPhys)) (IB 36 pts HL 16 pts); (Phys Astro Cosmo (MPhys)) (IB 36 pts HL 16 pts incl maths/phys); (Phys Ptcl Phys Cosmo (MPhys)) (IB 36 pts HL 16 pts incl maths+phys)

London (RH) – AAA–ABB incl maths+phys +interview (Phys; Theor Phys; Phys Ptcl Phys) (IB 32 pts HL 6 maths 5 phys)

London (UCL) – AAA–AAB incl maths+phys (Med Phys (MSci); Phys Med Phys) (IB 38–36 pts HL 5 maths+phys); AAA incl maths+phys (Phys) (IB 38 pts HL 6 maths+phys); AAA incl chem+maths+phys +interview (Cheml Phys) (IB 38 pts HL 5 chem+maths+phys)

St Andrews – AAA incl maths+phys (Comp Sci Phys) (IB 38 pts HL 6 maths); (Phys) (IB 38 pts)

Sheffield – AAA–AAB incl maths+phys (Phys (MPhys)) (IB 36 pts HL 6 maths+phys)

Southampton – AAA incl maths+phys (Phys Nanotech (MPhys); Phys Photon (MPhys); Phys Spc Sci (MPhys)) (IB 34 pts HL 6 maths+phys); (Phys Maths (MPhys)) (IB 36 pts HL 6 maths+phys); (Maths Phys (MMath)) (IB 37 pts HL 6 maths+phys)

Surrey – AAA incl maths+mus+phys (Mus Snd Rec (Tonmeister)) (IB 34 pts)

Swansea – AAA–AAB incl maths+phys (Phys (MPhys)) (IB 36–34 pts HL 6 maths+phys)

York – AAA incl maths+phys +interview (Phys (MPhys)) (IB 36 pts HL 6 maths+phys)

136 pts **Cardiff** – AAB–ABB incl phys+maths (Phys) (IB 34–30 pts HL 6 maths+phys); (Phys Med Phys; Theor Comput Phys) (IB 34–30 pts HL 6 phys+maths); AAB–ABB incl maths+phys (Phys Astron) (IB 34–30 pts HL 6 maths+phys)

East Anglia – AAB incl maths+phys (Phys (MPhys)) (IB 33 pts HL 6 maths+phys)

Glasgow – AAB incl maths+phys (Phys) (IB 36 pts HL 665); AAB–BBB incl maths+phys (Phys Astro) (IB 36 pts HL 665 incl 6 maths+phys)

Heriot-Watt – AAB (3 yr course) BBB (4 yr course) incl maths+phys (Phys courses) (IB 30–28 pts)

Lancaster – AAB incl maths+phys (Phys Astro Cosmo; Phys Ptcl Phys Cosmo) (IB 35 pts HL 16 pts); AAB incl phys+maths (Phys; Theor Phys Maths) (IB 35 pts HL 16 pts)

Leeds – AAB incl maths+phys (Phys Astro) (IB 35 pts HL 16 pts incl 5 maths+phys); AAB incl phys+maths (Theor Phys; Phys) (IB 35 pts HL 5 phys+maths)

Leicester – AAB incl maths+phys (Phys Spc Sci) (IB 32 pts HL 5 maths+phys); (Phys Astro) (IB 32 pts); AAB incl phys+maths (Phys) (IB 32 pts HL 5 phys+maths)

Liverpool – AAB/ABB+aEPQ incl maths+phys (Mathem Phys (MMath)) (IB 35 pts HL 6 maths+phys); (Theor Phys (MPhys)) (IB 35 pts HL 6 phys+maths); AAB/ABB+aEPQ incl phys+maths (Phys (MPhys)) (IB 35 pts HL 6 phys+maths)

Liverpool John Moores – AAB incl maths+phys 136 pts (Astro (MPhys))

London (King's) – AAB incl maths+phys (Phys Phil; Phys; Phys Theor Phys) (IB 35 pts HL 6 maths+phys)

London (QM) – AAB incl maths+phys 136 pts (Phys (MSci)) (IB 34 pts HL 6 maths+phys); AAB incl maths+phys (Astro (MSci); Theor Phys (MSci)) (IB 34 pts HL 6 maths+phys)

London (RH) – AAB incl maths+phys (Phys Mus) (IB 32 pts HL 665)

Newcastle – AAB–A*BB incl maths+phys (Theor Phys) (IB 37–35 pts HL 6 maths+phys); AAB/A*BB incl maths+phys (Phys (MPhys)) (IB 37 pts HL 6 maths+phys)

Nottingham – AAB incl maths+phys+chem (Chem Mol Phys) (IB 34 pts HL 6 maths 6/5 phys+chem)

Queen's Belfast – AAB incl maths+phys (Phys Med Apps (MSci); Phys Astro (MSci); Phys (MSci))

Sheffield – AAB incl maths+phys (Phys Astro) (IB 35 pts HL 6 maths+phys); AAB/ABB+bEPQ incl maths+phys (Phys Comb Hons; Theor Phys) (IB 34 pts HL 6 maths+phys); (Phys) (IB 35 pts HL 6 maths+phys)

Southampton – AAB incl maths+phys (Phys) (IB 34 pts HL 6 maths 5 phys)

Sussex – AAB–ABB incl maths+phys (Phys; Theor Phys; Phys Astro) (IB 32 pts HL 5 maths+phys)

Swansea – AAB–BBB incl maths+phys (Phys; Phys Ptcl Phys Cosmo; Theor Phys) (IB 34–32 pts HL 6 maths 6/5 phys)

York – AAB incl maths+phys +interview (Phys Phil); (Theor Phys; Phys; Maths Phys; Phys Astro) (IB 36 pts HL 6 maths+phys)

128 pts **East Anglia** – ABB (Phys Educ) (IB 32 pts HL 5 maths+phys); ABB incl maths+phys (Phys) (IB 32 pts HL 5 maths+phys)

Hertfordshire – 128 pts incl maths+phys (Phys) (HL 555)

Liverpool – ABB/BBB+aEPQ incl maths+phys (Geophys (Geol/Phys)) (IB 33 pts HL 4 maths+phys); ABB/BBB+aEPQ incl phys+maths (Phys Med Apps; Phys; Phys Nucl Sci) (IB 33 pts HL 6 phys+maths)

Liverpool John Moores – ABB incl maths+phys 128 pts (Phys Astron)

London (QM) – ABB incl maths+phys (Phys Ptcl Phys) (IB 32 pts HL 6 maths+phys); (Theor Phys) (IB 32 pts HL 6 phys+maths); (Astro) (IB 32 pts HL 6/5 maths+phys 6/5 phys+maths)

Loughborough – ABB incl maths+phys (Phys; Phys Maths) (IB 34 pts HL 6 maths/phys 5 maths/phys); (Eng Phys) (IB 34 pts HL 6/5 maths+phys)

Queen's Belfast – ABB incl maths+phys (Phys); ABB incl maths (Theor Phys)

Reading – ABB–AAC incl maths+phys (Env Phys) (IB 30–32 pts HL 65 maths+phys/56 maths+phys)

Strathclyde – ABB incl phys+maths (Phys) (IB 32 pts HL 5 phys+maths)

Surrey – ABB incl maths+phys (Phys Nucl Astro; Phys Qntm Tech; Phys; Phys Astron) (IB 32 pts)

120 pts **Aberdeen** – BBB incl maths+phys (Phys; Nat Phil) (IB 32 pts HL 5 maths+phys)

Central Lancashire – 120 pts incl phys+maths (Phys)

Dundee – BBB incl maths/phys (App Phys) (IB 30 pts HL 555); BBB incl maths+phys/eng (Phys) (IB 30 pts HL 555)

East Anglia – BBB incl chem+maths (Cheml Phys) (IB 31 pts HL 6 chem+maths)

Kent – BBB (Phys Astro (Yr Ind)) (IB 34 pts HL 15 pts); BBB incl maths+phys (Phys) (IB 34 pts)

Queen's Belfast – BBB incl maths+phys (Phys Med Apps; Phys Astro)

Check **Chapter 3** for new university admission details and **Chapter 6** on how to read the subject tables.

432 | Physics

112 pts **Aberystwyth** – BBC incl math+phys/comp sci (Spc Sci Robot) (IB 28 pts HL 5 maths+5 phys/comp sci); BBC incl maths+phys (Phys courses) (IB 28 pts HL 5 maths+phys)

Hull – 112 pts incl maths+phys (Phys) (IB 28 HL 5 maths+phys); (Phys Astro) (IB 28 pts HL 5 maths+phys)

Keele – BBC incl phys/maths (Phys Comb Hons) (IB 30 pts HL 5 phys/5 maths+4 phys)

Nottingham Trent – 112 pts incl maths+phys (Phys Astro)

Portsmouth – 112–128 pts incl maths+phys (Phys (MPhys)) (IB 29 pts HL 17 pts incl 5 maths+phys)

104 pts **Nottingham Trent** – 104 pts incl phys+maths (Phys Nucl Tech); 104 pts (Phys); 104 pts incl maths+phys (Phys Math)

St Mary's – 104 pts incl phys +interview (App Phys)

Salford – 104–112 pts incl maths+phys (Phys; Phys Acoust) (IB 30 pts HL 5 maths+phys)

88 pts **West Scotland** – CCD incl maths+phys (Phys) (IB 24 pts)

Open University – contact 0300 303 0073 **or** www.open.ac.uk/contact/new (Nat Sci (Phys))

Alternative offers
See **Chapter 6** and **Appendix 1** for grades/UCAS Tariff points information for other examinations.

CHOOSING YOUR COURSE (SEE ALSO CH.1)
Universities and colleges teaching quality See www.qaa.ac.uk; https://unistats.ac.uk.

Top research universities and colleges (REF 2014) Cardiff; Durham; Nottingham; Edinburgh; St Andrews; Strathclyde; Southampton; Warwick; Imperial London; Manchester; Oxford; Bath; Cambridge; Leeds.

Examples of sandwich degree courses Bath; Bristol; Cardiff; East Anglia; Hertfordshire; Kent; Loughborough; Nottingham Trent; Portsmouth; Surrey; Sussex; West Scotland.

ADMISSIONS INFORMATION
Number of applicants per place (approx) Bath 7; Birmingham 6; Bristol 7; Cardiff 4, (Phys Astron) 6; Dundee 10; Durham 6; Edinburgh 10; Exeter 5; Heriot-Watt 5; Hull 5; Imperial London 3; Lancaster 4; Leeds 7; Leicester 5; Liverpool 10; London (King's) 7; London (QM) 6; London (RH) 5; London (UCL) 7; Manchester 4; Nottingham 4; Salford 5; Southampton 6; Strathclyde 5; Swansea 3; Warwick 8; York 5.

Advice to applicants and planning the UCAS personal statement Admissions tutors look for potential, enthusiasm and interest in the subject so interests relating to maths and physics must be mentioned. An awareness of the range of careers in which physics is involved should also be mentioned on the UCAS application together with a demonstration of any particular interests, such as details on a physics or maths book you have read recently (not science fiction!). Make sure to mention if you have attended any courses, summer schools or day conferences on physics and engineering. See also **Appendix 3**. **Bristol** Deferred entry accepted.

Selection interviews Yes Cambridge, Exeter, Imperial London, Manchester, Oxford (Phys) 17%, York; **Some** Bath, Heriot-Watt, Lancaster, St Andrews, Surrey, Warwick; **No** Aberystwyth, Birmingham, Bristol, Cardiff, Dundee, East Anglia, Hull, Liverpool, London (QM), London (RH), Loughborough, Nottingham, Salford, Sheffield, Strathclyde, Swansea.

Interview advice and questions Questions will almost certainly focus on those aspects of the physics A-level course that the student enjoys. See also **Chapter 5**. **Bristol** Why Physics? Questions on mechanics, physics and pure maths. Given paper and calculator and questions asked orally; best to take your own calculator. Tutors seek enthusiastic and highly motivated students and the physicist's ability to apply basic principles to unfamiliar situations.

AFTER-RESULTS ADVICE
Offers to applicants repeating A-levels Higher Bristol, St Andrews, Warwick; **Possibly higher** Aberystwyth, Leeds, Loughborough, York; **Same** Birmingham, Cardiff, Dundee, Durham, East Anglia, Exeter, Hull, Lancaster, Leicester, Liverpool, Salford, Swansea; **No** Cambridge, Glasgow.

GRADUATE DESTINATIONS AND EMPLOYMENT (2015/16 HESA)
Graduates surveyed 2,705 **Employed** 1,080 **In voluntary employment** 65 **In further study** 1,060 **Assumed unemployed** 220

Career note Many graduates go into scientific and technical work in the manufacturing industries. However, in recent years, financial work, management and marketing have also attracted many seeking alternative careers.

OTHER DEGREE SUBJECTS FOR CONSIDERATION
Astronomy; Astrophysics; Computer Science; Earth Sciences; Engineering subjects; Geophysics; Materials Science and Metallurgy; Mathematics; Meteorology; Natural Sciences; Oceanography; Optometry; Radiography.

PHYSIOLOGY
(see also Animal Sciences, Neuroscience, Psychology)

Physiology is the study of body function. Courses in this wide-ranging subject will cover the central nervous system, special senses and neuro-muscular mechanisms, and body-regulating systems such as exercise, stress and temperature regulation. The Bristol course is available for intercalation in which it is possible to follow a one-year stand-alone degree in any of the following subjects: Functional and Clinical Anatomy, Genomic Medicine, Global Health, Health Sciences Research, Medical Humanities, or Transfusion and Transplanting Science.

Useful websites www.physoc.org; www.physiology.org; www.bases.org.uk/Physiology; see also **Biological Sciences**.

NB The points totals shown to the left of the institutions are for ease of reference only. It must not be assumed that Tariff points are always used by institutions or that they can be substituted for an offer in grades. The level of an offer is not necessarily indicative of the quality of a course.

COURSE OFFERS INFORMATION
Subject requirements/preferences GCSE Science and mathematics at grade A (7). **AL** Two science subjects are usually required; chemistry and biology are the preferred subjects.

Your target offers and examples of degree courses
160 pts Cambridge – A*A*A incl sci/maths +interview +NSAA (Nat Sci (Physiol Dev Neuro)) (IB 40–42 pts HL 776)

144 pts Leeds – AAA–AAB (Hum Physiol) (IB 35–34 pts); AAA–ABB incl sci (Spo Sci Physiol) (IB 35–33 pts HL 6 sci)
Manchester – AAA–ABB incl maths/sci (Physiol (Yr Ind)) (IB 37–32 pts); AAA–ABB incl sci/maths (Pharmacol Physiol (Yr Ind); Physiol) (IB 37–32 pts)
Newcastle – AAA–AAB incl biol (Physiol Sci) (IB 35–34 pts HL 5 biol+chem)

136 pts Bristol – AAB–ABC incl sci/maths (Physiol Sci) (IB 34–31 pts HL 6/5 sci/maths)
Cardiff – AAB incl biol+sci (Biomed Sci (Physiol)) (IB 34 pts HL 6 biol+chem)
Dundee – AAB incl biol+chem (Physiol Sci) (IB 30 pts)
Edinburgh – AAB (Physiol) (IB 36 pts)
Glasgow – AAB–BBB incl biol/chem (Physiol) (IB 36–34 pts)
Leicester – AAB–BBB+bEPQ incl sci/maths (Med Physiol) (IB 32/30 pts)
London (King's) – AAB incl chem+biol (Med Physiol) (IB 35 pts)

128 pts Aberdeen – ABB incl maths/sci (Physiol (Yr Ind)) (IB 34 pts HL 6 maths/sci)
Leeds – ABB incl sci (Hlthcr Sci (Crdc Physiol)) (IB 34 pts HL 5 sci)

120 pts Aberdeen – BBB incl maths/sci (Physiol) (IB 32 pts HL 5 maths+sci)
London (St George's) – BBB incl biol +interview (Hlthcr Sci (Physiol Sci))
Medway Sch Pharm – BBB 120 pts (Pharmacol Physiol) (IB 26–30 pts HL 12–14 pts)

Plymouth – 120 pts incl biol+sci (Hlthcr Sci (Physiol Sci))

UWE Bristol – 120 pts incl sci +interview (Hlthcr Sci (Physiol Sci)) (HL 5 sci); 120 pts incl biol/chem+sci +interview (Hlthcr Sci (Lf Sci)) (HL 6 biol/chem 5 sci)

112 pts **Central Lancashire** – 112 pts incl chem/biol/env sci (Physiol Pharmacol)

East London – 112 pts incl biol/chem (Med Physiol) (IB 25 pts HL 15 pts incl biol+chem)

Sunderland – 112 pts incl biol/chem (Physiol Sci)

UCO – BBC incl biol+sci (MOst)

Ulster – BBC incl sci/maths (Hlth Physiol/Hlthcr Sci)

Westminster – BBC incl sci (Pharmacol Physiol) (IB 26 pts HL 5 sci)

104 pts **Manchester Met** – BCC–BBC incl biol 104–112 pts (Physiol (Physl Actvt Hlth)) (IB 26 pts HL 5 biol)

Alternative offers

See **Chapter 6** and **Appendix 1** for grades/UCAS Tariff points information for other examinations.

CHOOSING YOUR COURSE (SEE ALSO CH.1)

Universities and colleges teaching quality See www.qaa.ac.uk; https://unistats.ac.uk.

Top research universities and colleges (REF 2014) See **Biological Sciences**.

Examples of sandwich degree courses Cardiff; Leeds; Manchester Met; Medway Sch Pharm.

ADMISSIONS INFORMATION

Number of applicants per place (approx) Bristol 6; Cardiff 8; Dundee 8; Leeds 4; Leicester 5; London (King's) 5.

Advice to applicants and planning the UCAS personal statement See **Neuroscience** and **Biological Sciences**.

Selection interviews Yes Cambridge, Manchester; **No** Bristol, Cardiff, Dundee, Leeds, Leicester, Newcastle.

Interview advice and questions Past questions include: What made you decide to do a Physiology degree? What experimental work have you done connected with physiology? What future career do you have in mind? What is physiology? Why not choose Medicine instead? What practicals do you do at school? See also **Chapter 5**.

AFTER-RESULTS ADVICE

Offers to applicants repeating A-levels Higher Bristol, Leeds, Leicester; **Same** Cardiff, Dundee; **No** Cambridge, Glasgow.

GRADUATE DESTINATIONS AND EMPLOYMENT (2015/16 HESA)

See **Neuroscience**.

Career note See **Biology**.

OTHER DEGREE SUBJECTS FOR CONSIDERATION

Anatomy; Biochemistry; Biological Sciences; Biotechnology; Dentistry; Genetics; Health Studies; Medicine; Microbiology; Neuroscience; Nursing; Optometry; Pharmacology; Radiography; Sports Science.

PHYSIOTHERAPY

(including **Chiropractic, Sports Therapy** and **Veterinary Physiotherapy**; see also **Health Sciences/Studies**)

Physiotherapists work as part of a multi-disciplinary team with other health professionals and are involved in the treatment and rehabilitation of patients of all ages and with a wide variety of medical problems. Degree courses include periods of clinical practice. On successful completion of the three-year course, graduates are eligible for State Registration and Membership of the Chartered Society of Physiotherapy. Courses are very competitive. A-levels in biology or human biology and PE are usually specified with high grades. Check websites. Tuition fees are paid by the NHS Bursary Scheme in England (and similar support is available in the rest of the UK, but arrangements differ so it is important to consult the relevant authority). Bursaries are available based on individual circumstances. All courses expect applicants to have gained some work experience which can include caring and voluntary work.

Useful websites www.csp.org.uk; www.thephysiotherapysite.co.uk; www.healthcareers.nhs.uk; www.physio-pedia.com; www.hpc-uk.org

NB The points totals shown to the left of the institutions are for ease of reference only. It must not be assumed that Tariff points are always used by institutions or that they can be substituted for an offer in grades. The level of an offer is not necessarily indicative of the quality of a course.

COURSE OFFERS INFORMATION
Subject requirements/preferences GCSE English, mathematics and science subjects. Many universities stipulate A/B (7/5-6) grades in specific subjects. **AL** One or two science subjects are required. **Other** Occupational health check and Disclosure and Barring Service (DBS) clearance.

Your target offers and examples of degree courses
144 pts **Southampton** – AAA incl sci +interview (Physio) (IB 36 pts HL 18 pts)
136 pts **Birmingham** – AAB incl biol/PE (Physio) (IB 32 pts HL 665)
Bournemouth – 136-144 pts incl biol/PE (Physio) (IB 33-34 pts HL 55)
Bradford – AAB incl biol/spo 136 pts +interview (Physio)
Cardiff – AAB incl biol (Physio) (IB 34 pts HL 665 incl 6 biol)
East Anglia – AAB incl biol/PE +interview (Physio) (IB 33 pts HL 666)
Glasgow Caledonian – AAB incl sci (Physio) (IB 32 pts HL 6 biol+sci)
Hertfordshire – AAB incl lf sci 136-152 pts +interview (Physio) (IB 33 pts HL 655)
Liverpool – AAB incl biol/PE (Physio) (IB 32 pts HL 655 incl 6 biol)
London (King's) – AAB incl sci/maths/soc sci (Physio) (IB 35 pts HL 666)
Nottingham – AAB incl biol/PE +interview (Physio) (IB 34 pts HL 6 biol)
Oxford Brookes – AAB incl biol 136 pts +interview (Physio) (IB 34 pts HL 6 biol)
Plymouth – AAB incl biol/app sci 136 pts (Physio) (IB 33 pts HL 6 biol)
Queen Margaret – AAB incl sci/maths (Physio) (IB 32 pts)
UWE Bristol – 136 pts incl biol +interview (Physio) (HL 6 biol)
128 pts **Brighton** – ABB incl biol/PE +interview (Physio) (IB 32 pts)
Canterbury Christ Church – ABB (Physio)
Central Lancashire – ABB incl biol/psy/PE (Physio)
Coventry – ABB inc biol +interview (Physio) (IB 34 pts HL 666)
Harper Adams – ABB incl biol+sci +interview (Vet Physio) (IB 29 pts HL 6 biol)
Huddersfield – ABB incl biol/PE 128 pts +interview (Physio)
Keele – ABB/A*BC/AAC incl biol/PE (Physio) (IB 34 pts HL 6 biol)
Kingston – ABB +interview Delivered with London (St George's) (Physio) (IB 34 pts HL 16 pts)
Leeds Beckett – 128 pts incl sci +interview (Physio) (IB 27 pts HL 6 sci)
London (St George's) – ABB +interview (Physio) (IB 34 pts HL 16 pts)
Manchester Met – ABB incl biol/spo +interview (Physio) (IB 29 pts)
Northumbria – 128-136 pts incl sci/hlth (Physio) (HL 5 sci/hlth)
Robert Gordon – ABB incl sci/maths +interview (Physio) (IB 32 pts HL 5 sci/maths)
Sheffield Hallam – 128 pts incl biol/PE +interview (Physio)
South Wales – ABB incl biol+sci (MChiro) (IB 32 pts)
York St John – ABB incl biol/PE +interview (Physio)
120 pts **Chichester** – 120-136 pts incl biol/PE (Spo Thera)
Cumbria – 120-128 pts incl biol/PE +interview (Physio)
East London – BBB incl biol/chem 120 pts (Physio) (IB 28 pts HL 15 pts incl biol+chem)

        Teesside – 120–144 pts incl sci/soc sci +interview (Physio)
        Ulster – BBB incl sci/maths +HPAT (Physio)
        Worcester – 120–136 pts incl biol/PE +interview (Physio)

104 pts **AECC (UC)** – BCC (MChiro) (IB 28 pts)
 96 pts **BPP** – CCC incl sci (MChiro)
        Winchester – 96–112 pts incl sci (Physio) (IB 25 pts)

Alternative offers
See **Chapter 6** and **Appendix 1** for grades/UCAS Tariff points information for other examinations.

EXAMPLES OF COLLEGES OFFERING COURSES IN THIS SUBJECT FIELD
Warwickshire (Coll).

CHOOSING YOUR COURSE (SEE ALSO CH.1)
Universities and colleges teaching quality See www.qaa.ac.uk; https://unistats.ac.uk.

Top research universities and colleges (REF 2014) See **Health Sciences/Studies**.

ADMISSIONS INFORMATION
Number of applicants per place (approx) Birmingham 9; Bradford 22; Cardiff 17; East Anglia 16; East London 10; Hertfordshire 13; Huddersfield 12; Kingston 9; Liverpool 20; London (King's) 16; Oxford Brookes 14; Robert Gordon 13; Sheffield Hallam 12; Southampton 36; Teesside 33; Ulster 12.

Admissions tutors' advice London (St George's) Work experience required.

Advice to applicants and planning the UCAS personal statement Visits to, and work experience in, hospital physiotherapy departments are important, although many universities publicly state that this is not necessary. However, with the level of competition for this subject I would regard this as doubtful (see Reasons for rejection). Applicants must demonstrate a clear understanding of the nature of the profession. Give details of voluntary work activities. Take notes of the work done and the different aspects of physiotherapy. Explain your experience fully on the UCAS application. Outside interests and teamwork are considered important. Good communication skills are required. Observation placement within a physiotherapy department. See also **Appendix 3**. **Manchester Met** We need to know why you want to be a physiotherapist. We also look for work shadowing a physiotherapist or work experience in another caring role. Evidence is also required of good communication skills, ability to care for people and of teamwork and leadership.

Misconceptions about this course Some applicants think that Physiotherapy has a sports bias.

Selection interviews Most institutions. **Yes** Birmingham, Bournemouth, Bradford, Brighton, Brunel, Cardiff, Coventry, Cumbria, East Anglia, East London, Huddersfield, Kingston, London (St George's), Nottingham, Oxford Brookes, Plymouth, Robert Gordon, Sheffield Hallam, Worcester, York St John; **Some** Keele; **No** Northumbria, Southampton, Ulster.

Interview advice and questions Physiotherapy is one of the most popular courses at present and work experience is very important, if not essential. A sound knowledge of the career, types of treatment used in physiotherapy and some understanding of the possible problems experienced by patients will be expected. Past interview questions include: How does physiotherapy fit into the overall health care system? If one patient was a heavy smoker and the other not, would you treat them the same? What was the most emotionally challenging thing you have ever done? Give an example of teamwork in which you have been involved. Why should we make you an offer? What is chiropractic? What is osteopathy? See also **Chapter 5**.

Reasons for rejection (non-academic) Lack of knowledge of the profession. Failure to convince the interviewers of a reasoned basis for following the profession. Failure to have visited a hospital physiotherapy unit. Lack of awareness of the demands of the course. **Birmingham** Poor communication skills. Lack of career insight. **Cardiff** Lack of knowledge of physiotherapy; experience of sports injuries only.

AFTER-RESULTS ADVICE
Offers to applicants repeating A-levels Higher East Anglia, East London, Kingston, Teesside; **Same** Coventry, Queen Margaret, Southampton.

GRADUATE DESTINATIONS AND EMPLOYMENT (2015/16 HESA)
See **Health Sciences/Studies**.

Career note The professional qualifications gained on graduation enable physiotherapists to seek posts in the NHS where the majority are employed. A small number work in the community health service, particularly in rural areas, whilst others work in residential homes. In addition to private practice, there are also some opportunities in professional sports clubs.

OTHER DEGREE SUBJECTS FOR CONSIDERATION
Anatomy; Audiology; Biological Sciences; Health Studies; Leisure and Recreation; Nursing; Occupational Therapy; Osteopathy; Physical Education; Psychology; Sport Science/Studies.

PLANT SCIENCES

(including **Arboriculture and Urban Forestry**; see also **Biological Sciences, Biology, Horticulture**)

Plant Sciences cover such areas as plant biochemistry, plant genetics, plant conservation and plant geography. Botany encompasses all aspects of plant science and also other subject areas including agriculture, forestry and horticulture. Botany is basic to these subjects and others including pharmacology and water management. As with other biological sciences, some universities introduce Plant Sciences by way of a common first year with other subjects. Plant sciences has applications in the agricultural, biotechnological, horticultural and food industries.

Useful websites www.kew.org; www.anbg.gov.au; https://bsbi.org; www.theplantlist.org; www.botany.org

NB The points totals shown to the left of the institutions are for ease of reference only. It must not be assumed that Tariff points are always used by institutions or that they can be substituted for an offer in grades. The level of an offer is not necessarily indicative of the quality of a course.

COURSE OFFERS INFORMATION
Subject requirements/preferences GCSE Mathematics if not offered at A-level. **AL** One or two science subjects are usually required.

Your target offers and examples of degree courses
160 pts **Cambridge** – A*A*A incl sci/maths +interview +NSAA (Nat Sci (Plnt Sci)) (IB 40–42 pts HL 776)
144 pts **Manchester** – AAA–ABB incl sci/maths (Plnt Sci; Plnt Sci (Yr Ind)) (IB 37–33 pts); AAA–ABB incl sci/maths +interview (Plnt Sci Modn Lang) (IB 37–32 pts HL 5 sci)
        Sheffield – AAA–AAB+bEPQ incl biol+sci (Plnt Sci (MBiolSci)) (IB 36 pts HL 6 biol+sci)
136 pts **Glasgow** – AAB incl biol/chem (Mol Cell Biol (Plnt Sci)) (IB 36 pts HL 665 incl 6 sci)
        Newcastle – AAB–ABB incl biol (App Plnt Sci) (IB 35–32 pts)
        Nottingham – AAB–ABB incl biol+sci (Plnt Sci) (IB 34–32 pts)
        Sheffield – AAB–ABB+bEPQ incl biol+sci (Plnt Sci) (IB 34 pts HL 6 biol+sci)
120 pts **Aberdeen** – BBB incl maths+sci (Plnt Soil Sci) (IB 32 pts HL 5 maths+sci)
        Edge Hill – BBB 120 pts (Plnt Sci)
112 pts **Aberystwyth** – BBC–BBB incl biol (Plnt Biol) (IB 30 pts HL 5 biol)
104 pts **Myerscough (Coll)** – 104 pts (Arbor Urb Frsty) (IB 24 pts)
 96 pts **Worcester** – 96–104 pts incl biol+sci/maths (Plnt Sci)
 88 pts **Canterbury Christ Church** – 88–112 pts (Plnt Sci)

Alternative offers
See **Chapter 6** and **Appendix 1** for grades/UCAS Tariff points information for other examinations.

CHOOSING YOUR COURSE (SEE ALSO CH.1)

Universities and colleges teaching quality See www.qaa.ac.uk; https://unistats.ac.uk.

Top research universities and colleges (REF 2014) See **Biological Sciences**.

Examples of sandwich degree courses Manchester.

ADMISSIONS INFORMATION

Number of applicants per place (approx) Edinburgh 6; Glasgow 4; Nottingham 6; Sheffield 8.

Advice to applicants and planning the UCAS personal statement Visit botanical gardens. See also **Biological Sciences** and **Appendix 4**.

Selection interviews Yes Cambridge; **No** Nottingham.

Interview advice and questions You are likely to be questioned on your biology studies, your reasons for wishing to study Plant Sciences and your ideas about a possible future career. In the past, questions have been asked about Darwin's theory of evolution, photosynthesis and DNA and the value of gardening programmes on TV! See also **Chapter 5**.

AFTER-RESULTS ADVICE

Offers to applicants repeating A-levels Same Birmingham, Nottingham, Sheffield; **No** Cambridge.

GRADUATE DESTINATIONS AND EMPLOYMENT (2015/16 HESA)

Botany graduates surveyed 70 **Employed** 20 **In voluntary employment** 0 **In further study** 25 **Assumed unemployed** 5

Career note See **Biology** and **Horticulture**.

OTHER DEGREE SUBJECTS FOR CONSIDERATION

Agriculture; Biochemistry; Biological Sciences; Biology; Crop Science (Agronomy); Ecology; Food Science; Forestry; Herbal Medicine; Horticulture; Landscape Architecture; Traditional Chinese Medicine.

PODIATRY (CHIROPODY)

A podiatrist's primary aim is to improve the mobility, independence and quality of life for their patients. They are autonomous healthcare professionals who deliver preventative, palliative, biomechanical, pharmacological and surgical interventions for lower limb problems. They work alone or are part of a multidisciplinary team. Courses lead to the eligibility for registration with the Health and Care Professions Council and some work shadowing prior to application is preferred by admissions tutors.

Useful websites www.careersinpodiatry.com; www.healthcareers.nhs.uk; www.podiatrynetwork.com; www.podiatrytoday.com; www.healthcommunities.com/health-topics/foot-health.shtml; www.scpod.org

NB The points totals shown to the left of the institutions are for ease of reference only. It must not be assumed that Tariff points are always used by institutions or that they can be substituted for an offer in grades. The level of an offer is not necessarily indicative of the quality of a course.

COURSE OFFERS INFORMATION

Subject requirements/preferences GCSE Mathematics and science subjects. **AL** Biology usually required or preferred. **Other** Hepatitis B, tuberculosis and tetanus immunisation; Disclosure and Barring Service (DBS) clearance (a pre-existing record could prevent a student from participating in the placement component of the course and prevent the student from gaining state registration).

Your target offers and examples of degree courses
120 pts East London – 120 pts incl sci/maths/PE (Pod) (IB 28 pts HL 15 pts incl biol+chem)
       Huddersfield – BBB incl biol/spo sci/PE 120 pts +interview (Pod)

Plymouth – BBB incl biol 120 pts (Pod) (IB 28 pts HL 5 biol)
Southampton – BBB incl sci/soc sci +interview (Pod) (IB 30 pts HL 16 pts)
Ulster – BBB incl sci/maths +HPAT (Pod)
112 pts **Birmingham Met (Coll)** – 112 pts incl sci (Pod)
Brighton – BBC (Pod) (IB 28 pts)
Cardiff Met – 112 pts incl biol +interview (Pod)
Northampton – BBC (Pod)
96 pts **Glasgow Caledonian** – CCC incl sci (Pod) (IB 24 pts)
Queen Margaret – CCC (Pod) (IB 28 pts)
64 pts **Durham New (Coll)** – 64 pts (Pod)

Alternative offers
See **Chapter 6** and **Appendix 1** for grades/UCAS Tariff points information for other examinations.

EXAMPLES OF COLLEGES OFFERING COURSES IN THIS SUBJECT FIELD
Birmingham Met (Coll); Durham New (Coll).

CHOOSING YOUR COURSE (SEE ALSO CH.1)
Universities and colleges teaching quality See www.qaa.ac.uk; https://unistats.ac.uk.

ADMISSIONS INFORMATION
Number of applicants per place (approx) Birmingham Met (Coll) 4; Cardiff Met 8; Huddersfield 3; Northampton 2; Southampton 4.

Advice to applicants and planning the UCAS personal statement Visit a podiatrist's clinic to gain work experience/work shadowing experience. Applicants need the ability to communicate with all age ranges, to work independently, to be resourceful and to possess a focused approach to academic work. Admissions tutors look for evidence of an understanding of podiatry, some work experience, good people skills, and effective communication. Mature applicants must include an academic reference (not an employer reference). See also **Appendix 3**.

Misconceptions about this course Cardiff Met Prospective students are often not aware of the demanding requirements of the course: 1,000 practical clinical hours augmented by a rigorous academic programme. Applicants are often unaware that whilst the elderly are a significant sub-population of patients with a variety of foot problems, increasingly the role of the podiatrist is the diagnosis and management of biomechanical/developmental disorders as well as the management of the diabetic or rheumatoid patient and those who require surgical intervention for nail problems. **Huddersfield** Many people think that podiatry is limited in its scope of practice to treating toe nails, corns and calluses: FALSE. As professionals, we do treat such pathologies but the scope of practice is much wider. It now includes surgery, biomechanics, sports injuries, treating children and high-risk patients. Because offers are low it is considered an easier course than, for example, Physiotherapy: FALSE. The course is academically demanding in addition to the compulsory clinical requirement.

Selection interviews Most institutions. **Yes** Cardiff Met, Huddersfield, Plymouth; **No** Southampton, Ulster.

Interview advice and questions Past questions include: Have you visited a podiatrist's surgery? What do your friends think about your choice of career? Do you think that being a podiatrist could cause you any physical problems? With which groups of people do podiatrists come into contact? What are your perceptions of the scope of practice of podiatry? What transferable skills do you think you will need? See also **Chapter 5**. **Cardiff Met** What made you consider podiatry as a career? Have you researched your career choice and where did you find the information? What have you discovered and has this altered your original perception of podiatry? What personal characteristics do you think you possess which might be useful for this work? **Southampton** Applicants should show an interest in medical topics. Communication skills are important, as is an insight into the implications of a career in podiatry.

Reasons for rejection (non-academic) Unconvincing attitude; poor communication and interpersonal skills; lack of motivation; medical condition or physical disabilities which are incompatible with professional practice; no knowledge of chosen profession; lack of work experience.

AFTER-RESULTS ADVICE
Offers to applicants repeating A-levels Same Cardiff Met, Huddersfield.

GRADUATE DESTINATIONS AND EMPLOYMENT (2015/16 HESA)
Career note Many state-registered podiatrists are employed by the NHS whilst others work in private practice or commercially run clinics.

OTHER DEGREE SUBJECTS FOR CONSIDERATION
Audiology; Biological Sciences; Health Studies; Nursing; Occupational Therapy; Osteopathy; Physiotherapy.

POLITICS

(including **European Politics, Government** and **Philosophy, Politics and Economics;** see also **Development Studies, International Relations, Social Sciences/Studies**)

Politics is often described as the study of 'who gets what, where, when and how'. Courses have become increasingly popular in recent years and usually cover the politics and government of the major powers. Because of the variety of degree courses on offer, it is possible to study the politics of almost any country in the world.

Useful websites http://europa.eu; www.gov.uk/government/organisations/foreign-commonwealth-office; www.psa.ac.uk; www.parliament.uk; www.whitehouse.gov; www.amnesty.org; www.gov.uk; www.un.org; www.un.int

NB The points totals shown to the left of the institutions are for ease of reference only. It must not be assumed that Tariff points are always used by institutions or that they can be substituted for an offer in grades. The level of an offer is not necessarily indicative of the quality of a course.

COURSE OFFERS INFORMATION
Subject requirements/preferences GCSE English, mathematics and a foreign language may be required. **AL** No subjects specified; history useful but an arts or social science subject also an advantage.

Your target offers and examples of degree courses
152 pts **Bath** – A*AA–AAA+aEPQ incl maths (Econ Pol) (IB 36 pts HL 6 maths)
 Cambridge – A*AA +interview +HSPSAA (Hum Soc Pol Sci; Hum Soc Pol Sci (Pol Int Rel)) (IB 40–42 pts HL 776)
 Durham – A*AA incl maths (Econ Pol; PPE) (IB 38 pts)
 Exeter – A*AA–AAB (Econ Pol (Euro St)) (IB 38–34 pts)
 London (King's) – A*AA +LNAT (Pol Phil Law) (IB 35 pts HL 766); A*AA (PPE) (IB 35 pts HL 766)
 London (UCL) – A*AA–AAA incl maths (PPE) (IB 39–38 pts HL 7 maths)
 London LSE – A*AA incl A* maths (PPE) (IB 38 pts)
 Nottingham – A*AA (PPE) (IB 38 pts)
 Warwick – A*AA (Econ Pol Int St) (IB 38 pts); A*AA (PPE) (IB 38 pts HL 5 maths)
 York – A*AA–AAA incl maths (PPE) (IB 37 pts)
144 pts **Bath** – AAA–AAB+aEPQ (Pol Int Rel) (IB 36 pts HL 666)
 Bristol – AAA–ABB (Pol Int Rel) (IB 36–32 pts HL 18–16 pts)
 Durham – AAA incl soc sci/hum (Phil Pol; Pol) (IB 37 pts)
 Edinburgh – AAA–ABB (Pol) (IB 40–34 pts); AAA (Hist Pol) (IB 40 pts HL 766)
 Exeter – AAA–AAB (PPE; Pol) (IB 36–34 pts)
 Lancaster – AAA–AAB (Hist Pol) (IB 36–35 pts HL 16 pts); (Pol (St Abrd)) (IB 36–35 pts)
 Leeds – AAA (PPE) (IB 35 pts HL 17 maths)
 London (King's) – AAA (War St) (IB 35 pts HL 666)
 London (QM) – AAA (Law Pol) (IB 37 pts HL 18 pts)
 London (SOAS) – AAA (Pol) (IB 37 pts)

London (UCL) – AAA–AAB (Pol Sociol E Euro St) (IB 38–36 pts HL 18–17 pts)

London LSE – AAA (Gov Hist; Pol Phil; Gov; Gov Econ; Int Rel) (IB 38 pts HL 766)

Manchester – AAA (PPE) (IB 36 pts HL 666)

NCH London – AAA–ABB (Pol Int Rel) (IB 36–34 pts)

Newcastle – AAA–ABB (Pol Econ; Gov EU St; Pol) (IB 34–32 pts)

Nottingham – AAA–ABB (Pol courses) (IB 36–32 pts)

Oxford – AAA +interview +TSA (PPE) (IB 39 pts); AAA +interview +HAT (Hist Pol) (IB 38 pts HL 666)

Queen's Belfast – AAA (PPE; Law Pol)

Reading – AAA–AAB (PPE) (IB 35–34 pts)

Strathclyde – AAA–BBB (Pol courses) (IB 36 pts incl maths)

Sussex – AAA–AAB (PPE; Law Pol) (IB 34 pts)

Warwick – AAA (Pol courses) (IB 38 pts)

York – AAA (Phil Pol) (IB 36 pts)

136 pts **Bath** – AAB–ABB+aEPQ (Lang Pol) (IB 36 pts HL 6 lang)

Bristol – AAB–BBB incl lang (Pol Modn Lang) (IB 34–31 pts HL 5 lang); AAB–BBB (Soc Plcy Pol) (IB 34–31 pts HL 17–15 pts); (Pol Sociol) (IB 34–31 pts)

Cardiff – AAB incl lang (Int Rel Pol (Lang)) (IB 34 pts HL 665); ABB (Pol) (IB 34 pts)

East Anglia – AAB incl hist (Hist Pol) (IB 33 pts HL 5 hist)

Edinburgh – AAB (Persn Pol) (IB 37 pts HL 666)

Exeter – AAB–BBB (Pol Int Rel (Cornwall)) (IB 34–30 pts)

Glasgow – AAB–BBB incl Engl (Pol) (IB 38–36 pts)

Lancaster – AAB–ABB (Pol Int Rel) (IB 35–32 pts HL 16 pts); (Pol Sociol; Pol Relig St; Pol) (IB 35–32 pts); AAB (PPE) (IB 35 pts HL 16 pts)

Leeds – AAB (Pol) (IB 35 pts)

London (King's) – AAB (Euro Pol) (IB 35 pts)

London (RH) – AAB–ABB incl maths (PPE) (IB 32 pts); AAB–ABB (Mus Pol St) (IB 32 pts HL 6 mus); (Pol; Econ Pol Int Rel; Pol Int Rel) (IB 32 pts HL 655); (Pol Phil) (IB 32 pts)

London LSE – AAB (Soc Plcy Gov) (IB 37 pts HL 666)

Loughborough – AAB (Econ Pol) (IB 35 pts HL 665)

Sheffield – AAB–ABB+bEPQ (Int Rel Pol; Pol Phil; Pol) (IB 34 pts); AAB–ABB+bEPQ incl hist/class civ (Hist Pol) (IB 34 pts HL 6 hist)

Southampton – AAB incl Span/Port +interview (Pol Span/Port Lat Am St) (IB 34 pts HL 6 Span/Port); AAB/ABBb incl maths/phys/stats (PPE) (IB 34–32 pts HL 5 maths); AAB–ABB incl hist (Modn Hist Pol) (IB 34 pts HL 6 hist); AAB–ABB (Phil Pol) (IB 34–32 pts); AAB–ABB+aEPQ incl Fr/Ger (Pol Fr/Ger) (IB 34 pts HL 6 Fr/Ger)

Sussex – AAB–ABB (Pol courses; Econ Pol) (IB 32 pts)

Warwick – AAB (Pol Sociol) (IB 36 pts)

York – AAB (Pol; Soc Pol Sci; Pol Int Rel) (IB 35 pts); AAB incl Engl (Engl Pol) (IB 35 pts HL 6 Engl)

128 pts **Aston** – ABB (Pol Soc Plcy; Pol Sociol; Pol Int Rel) (IB 32 pts); ABB–BBB (Pol Engl Lang) (IB 32 pts)

Birmingham – ABB (Pol Sci; Pol Econ; Pol Sci Int Rel; Pol Sci Soc Plcy (Yr Abrd)) (IB 32 pts HL 655)

Cardiff – ABB (Int Rel Pol) (IB 34 pts)

Chichester – ABB–CCC (Pol Contemp Hist) (IB 28 pts); ABB–CCC incl pol/hist (Pol)

City – ABB–BBB 128–120 pts (Int Pol) (IB 32 pts)

East Anglia – ABB (Pol; PPE) (IB 32 pts)

Kent – ABB (Econ Pol) (IB 34 pts)

Leeds – ABB (Chin Pol) (IB 34 pts HL 16 pts); (Int Dev courses) (IB 34 pts HL 655); (Pol Port/Russ/Span) (IB 34 pts)

Liverpool – ABB (Int Pol Plcy; Pol) (IB 33 pts)

London (QM) – ABB (Pol) (IB 32 pts HL 655); ABB incl hist (Hist Pol) (IB 32 pts HL 655 incl hist)

Loughborough – ABB (Hist Pol; Pol courses) (IB 34 pts HL 655)

Manchester – ABB (Pol Soc Anth) (IB 33 pts HL 655); (Pol Sociol) (IB 33 pts)

Check **Chapter 3** for new university admission details and **Chapter 6** on how to read the subject tables.

Newcastle – ABB–BBB (Pol Sociol) (IB 32–30 pts)
Queen's Belfast – ABB incl Fr (Fr Comb Hons)
Reading – ABB–BBB (Pol Int Rel; War Pce Int Rel) (IB 32–30 pts)
Sheffield – ABB–BBB+bEPQ (Pol Sociol) (IB 33 pts)
Southampton – ABB–BBB incl maths/phys (Pol Econ) (IB 32 pts HL 4 maths); ABB–
    BBB+aEPQ (Pol Int Rel) (IB 32 pts HL 16 pts); ABB–BBB (Pol) (IB 32 pts)
Stirling – ABB (3 yr course) BBB (4 yr course) (PPE) (IB 35 pts (3 yr course) 32 pts
    (4 yr course)); ABB (3 yr course) BBB (4 yr course) incl pol/modn st (Pol (Int Pol))
    (IB 35 pts (3 yr course) 32 pts (4 yr course))
Strathclyde – ABB–BBB (PPE) (IB 32–30 pts)
Surrey – ABB incl soc sci/hum (Int Pol; Pol) (IB 32 pts)
120 pts **Aberdeen** – BBB (Pol courses) (IB 32 pts)
Aberystwyth – BBB (Int Pol; Pol; Pol courses) (IB 28 pts)
Brunel – BBB (Int Pol; Pol) (IB 30 pts)
Buckingham – BBB (PPE) (IB 32 pts)
Dundee – BBB–BCC incl sci (Geopol) (IB 30 pts); BBB–BCC (Pol) (IB 30 pts)
Edge Hill – BBB 120 pts (Hist Pol)
Essex – BBB (Pol; Econ Pol; PPE; Pol Hum Rts) (IB 30 pts)
Hull – 120 pts (Law Pol) (IB 28 pts)
Keele – BBB/ABC (Pol) (IB 32 pts)
Kent – BBB (Pol) (IB 34 pts); (Pol Int Rel (Yr Abrd)) (IB 35 pts)
Leicester – BBB–BBC+bEPQ (Pol Econ; Pol) (IB 28 pts)
Liverpool Hope – BBB–BBC 120–112 pts (Pol; Pol Int Rel) (IB 26 pts)
London (Birk) – 120–128 pts (Pol Phil Hist)
London (Gold) – BBB (PPE; Pol; Int Rel) (IB 33 pts)
Northumbria – 120–128 pts incl hist/pol (Hist Pol) (HL 444 incl hist/pol)
Queen's Belfast – BBB–ABB (Pol Comb Hons)
Stirling – BBB (Pol) (IB 32 pts)
Swansea – BBB (Pol; Pol Soc Plcy) (IB 32 pts); BBB 120 pts (War Soty) (IB 32 pts);
    BBB incl Engl (Pol Engl Lit) (IB 32 pts)
118 pts **NCH London** – ABB–AAA (PPE) (IB 34–36 pts)
112 pts **Bradford** – BBC 112 pts (Pol Scrty St)
Brighton – BBC–CCC 112–96 pts (Pol) (IB 28 pts)
Chester – BBC–BCC 112 pts (Pol) (IB 26 pts)
Coventry – BBC (Pol; Hist Pol) (IB 29 pts)
De Montfort – 112 pts (Pol Comb Hons) (IB 28 pts)
Greenwich – 112 pts (Pol Int Rel)
Huddersfield – BBC 112 pts (Int Pol; Pol)
Hull – 112 pts (PPE; Phil Pol) (IB 28 pts)
Kingston – 112 pts (Glob Pol Int Rel)
London Met – BBC 112 pts (Pol); CCC/BC 112 pts (Int Rel Pce Cnflct St)
Middlesex – 112 pts (Int Pol)
Nottingham Trent – BBC 112 pts (Pol)
Oxford Brookes – BBC 112 pts (Pol; Econ Pol Int Rel; Int Rel Pol) (IB 30 pts)
Plymouth – 112 pts incl hist (Hist Pol) (IB 28 pts)
Westminster – BBC (Pol Int Rel; Pol) (IB 28 pts)
Wolverhampton – BBC–CCC (Pol Phil; Pol Hist; Sociol Pol)
104 pts **Brighton** – BCC–CCC 104–96 pts (Phil Pol Eth) (IB 27 pts)
Central Lancashire – 104 pts (Pol courses; Pol Phil Soty)
De Montfort – 104 pts (Int Rel Pol) (IB 24 pts)
Leeds Beckett – 104 pts (Pol) (IB 24 pts)
Leeds Trinity – 104 pts (Pol Int Rel)
Lincoln – BCC 104 pts (Int Rel Pol); (Pol) (IB 28 pts)
London South Bank – BCC (Pol)

Manchester Met – 104–112 pts (Int Pol Phil; Pol; Int Pol) (IB 26 pts)
Northampton – BCC (Int Rel Pol)
Nottingham Trent – 104 pts (Hist Pol); BCC 104 pts (Pol Int Rel)
Plymouth – 104 pts (Pol Int Rel) (IB 26 pts HL 4)
Sheffield Hallam – 104–88 pts (Pol)
Sunderland – 104 pts (Pol Comb Hons)
Ulster – BCC–BBC (Sociol Pol; Pol)
West London – 104–120 pts (Pol Int Rel)
Winchester – 104–120 pts (PPE) (IB 26 pts)
Worcester – 104 pts (Pol)

96 pts **Canterbury Christ Church** – 96–120 pts (Pol)
Portsmouth – 96–120 pts (Pol) (IB 26 pts)
West Scotland – CCC incl Engl (Soty Pol Plcy) (IB 24 pts)

72 pts **UHI** – BC (Hist Pol; PPE; Sociol Pol); BC incl Engl/hist/pol (Scot Hist Pol)

Open University – contact 0300 303 0073 **or** www.open.ac.uk/contact/new (PPE)

Alternative offers
See **Chapter 6** and **Appendix 1** for grades/UCAS Tariff points information for other examinations.

EXAMPLES OF COLLEGES OFFERING COURSES IN THIS SUBJECT FIELD
Blackburn (Coll); Newham (CFE).

CHOOSING YOUR COURSE (SEE ALSO CH.1)
Universities and colleges teaching quality See www.qaa.ac.uk; https://unistats.ac.uk.

Top research universities and colleges (REF 2014) (Politics and International Studies) London LSE; London (UCL); Sheffield; Essex; Exeter; Oxford; Cardiff; Warwick; York.

Examples of sandwich degree courses Aston; Bath; Brunel; Coventry; De Montfort; Essex; Leeds; Loughborough; Middlesex; Oxford Brookes; Surrey.

ADMISSIONS INFORMATION
Number of applicants per place (approx) Aston 4; Bath 7; Birmingham 5; Bradford 10; Bristol 14; Cambridge 5; Cardiff 14; De Montfort 6; Dundee 13; Durham (Pol) 11, (PPE) 8; East Anglia 4; Exeter 8; Hull (Pol) 5, (PPE) 5; Kent 9; Lancaster 14; Leeds 18; Leicester 6; Liverpool 8; London (QM) 10; London (RH) 8; London (SOAS) 5; London LSE (Gov) 7, (Gov Econ) 8, (Gov Hist) 6; London Met 5; Newcastle 5; Northampton 4; Nottingham 5; Nottingham Trent 3; Oxford (PPE) 7; Oxford Brookes 7; Southampton 6; Stirling 10; Swansea 3; Warwick 10; York 6, (PPE) 9.

Advice to applicants and planning the UCAS personal statement Study the workings of government in the UK, Europe and other areas of the world, such as the Middle East, the Far East, America and Russia. Describe visits to the Houses of Commons and Lords and the debates taking place. Attend council meetings – county, town, district, village halls. Describe these visits and agendas. Read current affairs avidly. Be aware of political developments in the major countries and regions of the world including the Middle East, South America, the UK, Europe, USA, China, Korea and Russia. Keep abreast of developments in theatres of war, for example, Afghanistan. Explain your interests in detail. **Aberystwyth** We look for degree candidates with a strong interest in political and social issues and who want to inquire into the way in which the world is organised politically, socially and economically. **Bristol** Deferred entry accepted. **De Montfort** Demonstration of active interest in current affairs and some understanding of how politics affects our daily lives.

Misconceptions about this course Aberystwyth Many students believe that they need to study politics at A-level for Politics courses – this is not the case. **De Montfort** Some applicants believe that a Politics course only covers the mechanics of government and parliament.

Selection interviews Yes Cambridge, Kent, Oxford; **Some** Bath, Bristol, London (SOAS), Nottingham, Warwick; **No** Aberystwyth, Birmingham, De Montfort, Dundee, East Anglia, Essex, Huddersfield, Hull,

Leeds, Leicester, Liverpool, London (Gold), London LSE, London Met, Loughborough, Portsmouth, Reading, Sheffield, Surrey, Swansea, Ulster.

Interview advice and questions Questions may stem from A-level studies but applicants will also be expected to be up-to-date in their knowledge and opinions of current events. Questions in recent years have included: What constitutes a 'great power'? What is happening at present in the Labour Party? Define capitalism. What is a political decision? How do opinion polls detract from democracy? Is the European Union a good idea? Why? What are the views of the present government on the European Union? What is a 'spin doctor'? Are politicians hypocrites? See also **Chapter 5**.

AFTER-RESULTS ADVICE
Offers to applicants repeating A-levels Higher Leeds, Newcastle, Warwick, York; **Possibly higher** Lancaster, Swansea; **Same** Aberystwyth, Birmingham, Bristol, De Montfort, Dundee, Durham, East Anglia, Essex, Hull, Lincoln, Liverpool Hope, London (SOAS), London Met, London South Bank, Loughborough, Nottingham, Nottingham Trent, Oxford Brookes, Stirling, Sussex, Wolverhampton; **No** Cambridge, Glasgow.

GRADUATE DESTINATIONS AND EMPLOYMENT (2015/16 HESA)
Graduates surveyed 4,400 **Employed** 2,075 **In voluntary employment** 220 **In further study** 1,245 **Assumed unemployed** 295

Career note The transferable skills gained in this degree open up a wide range of career opportunities. Graduates seek positions in management, public services and administration and in some cases in political activities.

OTHER DEGREE SUBJECTS FOR CONSIDERATION
Development Studies; Economics; Government; History; International Relations; Public Policy and Administration; Social Policy and Administration; Sociology.

PSYCHOLOGY
(including **Autism Studies, Cognitive Science, Counselling Psychology** and **Forensic Psychology**; see also **Animal Sciences, Biological Sciences, Neuroscience, Philosophy, Physiology, Social Sciences/Studies**)

Psychology is a very popular subject, with the number of applications rising by 40,000 in the last 10 years. The study attracts three times more women than men. It covers studies in development, behaviour, perception, memory, language, learning and personality as well as social relationships and abnormal psychology. Psychology is a science and you will be involved in experimentation and statistical analysis. The degree is usually offered as a BSc or a BA course and there are many similarities between them; the differences are in the elective subjects which can be taken in the second and third years. Contrary to popular belief, psychology is not a study to enable you to psycho-analyse your friends – psychology is not the same as psychiatry!

To qualify as a chartered psychologist (for which a postgraduate qualification is required), it is necessary to obtain a first degree (or equivalent) qualification which gives eligibility for both Graduate Membership (GM) and the Graduate Basis for Chartered Membership (GBC) of the British Psychological Society (BPS). A full list of courses accredited by the British Psychological Society is available on the Society's website www.bps.org.uk. Specialisms in the subject include Educational, Clinical, Occupational and Forensic Psychology (see **Appendix 3**).

Behavioural Science covers the study of animal and human behaviour and offers an overlap between Zoology, Sociology, Psychology and Biological Sciences. Psychology, however, also crosses over into Education, Management Sciences, Human Resource Management, Counselling, Public Relations, Advertising, Artificial Intelligence, Marketing, Retail and Social Studies.

Useful websites www.psychology.org; www.bps.org.uk; www.socialpsychology.org; www.psychcentral.com

NB The points totals shown to the left of the institutions are for ease of reference only. It must not be assumed that Tariff points are always used by institutions or that they can be substituted for an offer in grades. The level of an offer is not necessarily indicative of the quality of a course.

COURSE OFFERS INFORMATION

Subject requirements/preferences GCSE English, mathematics and a science. **AL** A science subject is usually required. Psychology may be accepted as a science subject.

Your target offers and examples of degree courses

160 pts Cambridge – A*A*A incl sci/maths +interview +NSAA (Nat Sci (Psy)) (IB 40–42 pts HL 776)

152 pts Bath – A*AA–AAA+aEPQ (Psy) (IB 36 pts)

Bristol – A*AA–AAB incl sci/psy/geog (Psy) (IB 38–34 pts)

Cambridge – A*AA +interview +PBSAA (Psy Bhv Sci) (IB 40–42 pts HL 776)

London (UCL) – A*AA–AAA incl sci/maths/psy (Psy) (IB 39–38 pts HL 6 sci/maths/psy)

Oxford – A*AA +interview +TSA (Psy (Expmtl)) (IB 39 pts); A*AA +interview +TSA (Psy Phil Ling) (IB 39 pts)

144 pts Birmingham – AAA (Psy) (IB 32 pts HL 666)

Cardiff – AAA (Psy) (IB 36 pts)

Durham – AAA (Psy; Phil Psy) (IB 37 pts)

Exeter – AAA–AAB (Psy (Yr Abrd)) (IB 36–34 pts); AAA–AAB incl sci (App Psy (Clin) (MSci); Psy Spo Exer Sci; Psy) (IB 36–34 pts HL 5 sci)

Leeds – AAA (Psy) (IB 35 pts)

Liverpool – AAA/AAB+aEPQ (Psy (MPsycholSci)) (IB 36 pts)

London (RH) – AAA–AAB (Psy; Psy Clin Cog Neuro) (IB 32 pts HL 665)

Manchester – AAA–ABB incl sci/maths (Cog Neuro Psy) (IB 37–32 pts HL 5/6 biol+chem)

Newcastle – AAA–ABB incl biol (Psy Biol) (IB 35 pts HL 6 biol); AAA–ABB incl sci (Psy) (IB 35 pts)

Nottingham – AAA–AAB (Psy Cog Neuro) (IB 36–34 pts); AAA–AAB incl sci (Psy) (IB 36–34 pts)

Reading – AAA–AAB (Psy) (IB 35–34 pts); AAA–AAB +interview +portfolio (Art Psy) (IB 35 pts); AAA–AAB incl sci (Psy Neuro) (IB 35–34 pts)

St Andrews – AAA (Econ Psy) (IB 38 pts); AAA incl maths (Comp Sci Psy) (IB 38 pts HL 6 maths)

Southampton – AAA–AAB incl sci/maths (Psy) (IB 34 pts)

Sussex – AAA–AAB (Psy; Psy Cog Sci; Psy Neuro) (IB 34 pts)

York – AAA incl sci/maths (Psy) (IB 36 pts)

136 pts Bangor – 136–112 pts incl sci (Psy Neuropsy); 136–128 pts (Spo Exer Psy); 136–112 pts (Psy; Psy Clin Hlth Psy)

City – AAB 136 pts (Psy) (IB 33 pts)

Edinburgh – AAB incl sci/maths (Cog Sci (Hum)) (IB 36 pts HL 665); (Psy) (IB 38 pts HL 666)

Glasgow – AAB–BBB incl sci (Psy) (IB 38–36 pts)

Kent – AAB incl Fr/Ger (Psy St Euro) (IB 34 pts); AAB (Psy Clin Psy; Soc Psy; Psy) (IB 34 pts)

Lancaster – AAB incl Engl/lang (Ling Psy) (IB 35 pts HL 16 pts); AAB (Psy) (IB 35 pts)

Leicester – AAB–ABB/ABB+bEPQ (Psy) (IB 32–30 pts); AAB–ABB/BBB+bEPQ (Psy Cog Neuro) (IB 32–30 pts)

Lincoln – AAB incl sci (Psy Clin Psy) (IB 32 pts HL 5 sci)

London (QM) – AAB incl sci/maths (Psy) (IB 35 pts HL 6/5 sci/maths)

Loughborough – AAB (Psy; Soc Psy; Spo Exer Psy) (IB 35 pts)

Manchester – AAB (Psy) (IB 35 pts)

Newcastle – AAB–ABB (Nutr Psy) (IB 35 pts HL 6 biol)

Nottingham – AAB/A*BB (Psy Phil) (IB 34 pts)

St Andrews – AAB (Art Hist Psy; Psy Geog; Psy) (IB 35 pts)

Sheffield – AAB (Psy) (IB 34 pts)

Check **Chapter 3** for new university admission details and **Chapter 6** on how to read the subject tables.

Join now as a Subscriber

The British Psychological Society is the representative body for psychology and psychologists in the UK. We are responsible for the development, promotion and application of psychology for the public good.

As a Subscriber you can:

- Receive full online access to *The Psychologist*, our monthly magazine;
- Keep up-to-date with the latest developments affecting psychology;
- Contribute to our discussion groups;
- Attend our events to find out more about a career in psychology;
- Benefit from high street discounts.

Find out more and to join online

www.bps.org.uk/join

Once you're studying an accredited undergraduate degree, membership will broaden your appreciation and understanding of psychology, and open up a network of like-minded students, academics and professionals, not to mention future opportunities.

For more information on Student membership visit **www.bps.org.uk/student**

The British
Psychological Society

PRIFYSGOL
BANGOR
UNIVERSITY

The British
Psychological Society
Accredited

EXPLORE THE MIND AT BANGOR

Why Psychology at Bangor?

We're one of very few UK Psychology departments able to boast a consistent track record of being highly ranked for 'Student Satisfaction', 'Research Excellence' and 'Employability'. That means we're confident our students are happy, study with world leading academics and are well placed to get a job when they graduate. Not a bad combination!

Student satisfaction and student life

We offer our students an exceptional lifestyle, a few highlights of which are:

- Bangor is top 10 for 'Student Satisfaction' - National Student Survey 2017
- Top 15 for Research Quality – CUG 2018
- Bangor is a friendly, safe city whose nightlife is dominated by the influx of over 11,000 students. About 1 in 3 of the town's inhabitants are students!
- WhatUni? Awards- Best Clubs & Societies (2017), which are free to join & best Accommodation (2016)
- Bangor is "one of the cheapest places in Britain" to be a student (*The Independent's A-Z of Universities*)
- 4th best place in the world to visit – Lonely Planet 2017

Teaching excellence

We offer unique learning opportunities that currently include 'gamified lectures' and human brain practical. We focus on caring for and supporting our students with specialist International, Employability and Disability Tutors who can help you reach your maximum potential. Our independent external examiner has said we're "*producing some of the best quality psychology graduates in the UK.*"

Bangor boosts your job prospects

To help you go further with your Bangor degree, you can develop additional skills, gain qualifications and complete work experience that's relevant both to your degree and to your future career.

- Top 15 for Graduate Prospects – Complete University Guide 2018
- 95% working or in further study within six months of graduating (*Psychology with Clunical & Health Psychology, UniStats*).

BSc/MSci
Psychology
Psychology with Clinical and Health Psychology

BSc
Psychology with Neuropsychology
Psychology with Business

"Bangor was recommended to me by my psychology teacher for having excellent ratings for psychology students and once I had taken a look online at the uni and the city itself was hard to resist the appeal of Bangor! However, being told I will be able to hold a human brain in my 1st year is the final factor that swung it for me!"

SAMANTHA POWELL BSc Psychology, Wiltshire

t: 01248 388453 e: psychology@bangor.ac.uk
www.bangor.ac.uk/psychology 🐦 PsychBangor

TEF Gold Teaching Excellence Framework

There are lots of reasons why we think you should explore the mind with us. Here are just a few:

- Bangor is top 10 for 'Student Satisfaction' – NSS 2017
- Unique learning opportunities that currently include 'gamified lectures' and human brain practical
- Top 15 for Graduate Employment – Complete University Guide 2018
- Top 20 for Research – CUG 2018
- 1st for student clubs & societies (& free to join!) – WHATUNI? 2017
- Affordable living costs in a beautiful, safe location with good transport links
- 4th best place in the world to visit – Lonely Planet 2017

THINK PSYCHOLOGY THINK BANGOR

TEF Gold Teaching Excellence Framework

School of Psychology, Bangor University, Gwynedd LL57 2AS
t. +44(0)1248 388453 e. psychology@bangor.ac.uk
www.bangor.ac.uk/psychology 🐦 PsychBangor

SEICOLEG BANGOR PSYCHOLOGY

PRIFYSGOL BANGOR UNIVERSITY

Southampton – AAB (Educ Psy) (IB 34 pts)
Surrey – AAB (Psy) (IB 34 pts)
Sussex – AAB–ABB incl sci/psy (Neuro Cog Sci) (IB 32 pts HL 5 sci/psy)
Swansea – AAB–ABB (Psy) (IB 34–33 pts)
Warwick   AAB (Psy) (IB 36 pts)

128 pts **Aston** – ABB (Psy) (IB 32 pts)
De Montfort – 128 pts (Psy; Psy Crimin) (IB 30 pts)
East Anglia – ABB (Psy) (IB 32 pts)
Lincoln – ABB incl sci (Psy) (IB 32 pts HL 5 sci)
Liverpool – ABB (Psy) (IB 33 pts)
Liverpool John Moores – ABB 128 pts (Foren Psy Crim Just) (IB 30 pts)
Northumbria – 128–136 pts (Psy) (HL 444)
Queen's Belfast – ABB (Psy)
Strathclyde – ABB–BBB (Psy; Econ Psy) (IB 36 pts)
UWE Bristol – 128 pts (Psy courses) (HL 6)
York – ABB   (Sociol Soc Psy) (IB 34 pts)

120 pts **Aberdeen** – BBB (Psy) (IB 32 pts); BBB incl maths+sci (Neuro Psy) (IB 32 pts HL 5 maths+sci)
Aston – BBB (Psy Sociol) (IB 31 pts)
Brunel – BBB (Psy; Psy (Spo Hlth Exer)) (IB 30 pts)
Buckingham – BBB (Psy; Psy Span) (IB 32 pts)
Coventry – BBB (Psy) (IB 30 pts); (Spo Exer Psy) (IB 31 pts)
De Montfort – 120 pts (Educ St Psy) (IB 28 pts)
Derby – 120–128 pts (Psy)
Dundee – BBB–BCC (Psy) (IB 30 pts)
Edge Hill – BBB 120 pts (Psy)
Essex – BBB (Psy; Psy Cog Neuro) (IB 30 pts)

Check **Chapter 3** for new university admission details and **Chapter 6** on how to read the subject tables.

Greenwich – 120 pts (Psy; Crimin Crim Psy)
Heriot-Watt – BBB (Psy courses) (IB 27 pts)
Huddersfield – BBB 120 pts (Psy; Psy Crimin; Psy Cnslg)
Keele – ABC/BBB (Psy) (IB 32 pts)
Kent – BBB (Autsm St) (IB 34 pts)
Kingston – 120 pts (Foren Psy)
Liverpool Hope – BBB–BBC 120–112 pts (Psy; Psy Comb Hons)
London (Birk) – 120 pts (Psy)
London (Gold) – BBB (Psy Cog Neuro) (IB 33 pts); BBB (Psy) (IB 33 pts)
London South Bank – BBB (Psy (Clin Psy); Psy; Psy (Chld Dev))
Middlesex – 120 pts (Psy Comb courses)
Northumbria – 120–128 pts (Gdnc Cnslg) (HL 444)
Nottingham Trent – BBB 120 pts (Psy)
Oxford Brookes – BBB 120 pts (Psy) (IB 32 pts)
Plymouth – BBB 120 pts (Psy; Psy Sociol) (IB 28 pts)
Portsmouth – 120 pts incl sci (Psy; Foren Psy) (IB 30 pts HL 17 pts incl 6 sci)
Roehampton – 120 pts (Psy Cnslg; Psy)
St Mary's – 120 pts (Psy)
Sheffield Hallam – 120–104 pts (Psy)
Staffordshire – BBB 120 pts (Psy Crimin; Psy; Foren Psy)
Stirling – BBB (Psy) (IB 32 pts)
UWE Bristol – 120 pts (Crimin Psy)
Westminster – BBB (Psy) (IB 32 pts); BBB incl sci/maths (Psy Cnslg) (IB 32 pts)
Worcester – BBB 120 pts (Law Foren Psy)
York St John – 120 pts (Psy)

112 pts   **Aberystwyth** – BBC (Psy Crimin; Psy) (IB 30 pts)
Bedfordshire – 112 pts (Psy; Psy Crim Bhv)
Birmingham City – 112 pts (Psy) (HL 14 pts)
Bolton – 112 pts (Psy; Psy Psytrpy Cnslg)
Bournemouth – 112–120 pts (Psy) (IB 30–31 pts HL 55)
BPP – BBC 112 pts (Psy)
Bradford – BBC 112 pts (Psy)
Brighton – BBC–CCC 112–96 pts (App Psy Sociol; App Psy Crimin) (IB 28 pts)
Cardiff Met – 112 pts (Psy)
Central Lancashire – 112–128 pts (Foren Psy; Hlth Psy; Psy; Neuropsy)
Chester – BBC–BCC 112 pts (Cnslg Sk Psy) (IB 26 pts)
East London – 112 pts (Psy; Foren Psy) (IB 25 pts)
Glyndŵr – 112 pts (Psy)
Hertfordshire – 112 pts incl sci (Psy) (HL 44)
Hull – 112 pts (Psy; Psy Crimin) (IB 28 pts)
Kingston – 112 pts (Psy courses)
Leeds Beckett – 112 pts incl sci/maths (Psy courses) (IB 25 pts HL 6 sci)
Leeds Trinity – 112 pts (Psy; Foren Psy; Cnslg Psy)
Liverpool John Moores – BBC 112 pts (Crimin Psy) (IB 26 pts); 112 pts (App Spo Psy)
    (IB 25 pts); (Psy) (IB 26 pts)
Manchester Met – BBC–BBB (Psy; Psy Sociol) (IB 26 pts)
Northampton – BBC (Psy courses)
Nottingham Trent – BBC 112 pts (Law Psy)
Portsmouth – 112 pts (Mark Psy) (IB 30 pts HL 17 pts)
Queen Margaret – BBC 112 pts (Psy) (IB 30 pts)
Salford – 112 pts (Psy) (IB 31 pts)
Sheffield Hallam – 112–96 pts (Crimin Psy)
Southampton Solent – 112 pts (Psy)
Suffolk – BBC 112 pts (Psy Sociol)
Sunderland – 112 pts (Psy; Psy Cnslg)

Trinity Saint David – 112 pts (Psy)
Ulster – BBC–BBB (Psy courses) (IB 25–26 pts)
West London – BBC 112–120 pts (Psy; Psy Crimin/Cnslg Theor)
Worcester – 112 pts (Psy)

104 pts **Abertay** – BCC incl sci (Psy Foren Biol) (IB 29 pts); BCC (Psy; Psy Cnslg) (IB 29 pts)
Anglia Ruskin – 104 pts (Psy; Psy Crimin) (IB 24 pts)
Bath Spa – BCC–CCC (Psy Comb Hons) (IB 27 pts); BCC (Psy) (IB 27 pts)
Bournemouth – 104–120 pts (Spo Psy Coach Sci) (IB 28–31 pts)
Chester – BCC–BBC (Psy courses) (IB 26 pts)
Chichester – 104–120 pts incl psy/sci/soc sci (Psy) (IB 28 pts HL 4 sci)
Coventry – BCC +interview (Cnslg Coach Ment) (IB 27 pts)
Cumbria – 104–120 pts (App Psy)
Edinburgh Napier – BCC incl Engl (Psy; Psy Sociol) (IB 28 pts HL 5 Engl)
Leeds Beckett – 104 pts (Crimin Psy) (IB 24 pts)
London Met – BCC 104 pts (Psy)
Newman – 104–96 pts (Psy)
Northampton – BCC (Psy Mark Comb Hons)
Nottingham Trent – 104 pts (Psy Spec Inclsv Educ); BCC 104 pts (Ely Yrs Psy)
Sheffield Hallam – 104–88 pts (Educ Psy Cnslg)
South Wales – BCC–CDD (Psy; Psy Dev Diso; Psy Cnslg) (HL 655–445)

96 pts **Bishop Grosseteste** – 96–112 pts (Psy Comb Hons)
Bucks New – 96–112 pts (Psy; Psy Crimin)
Canterbury Christ Church – 96–112 pts (Psy)
Derby – 96–112 pts (Crea Expr Thera (Dance/Dr/Mus/Art))
Portsmouth – 96–120 pts (Sociol Psy) (IB 26 pts)
West Scotland – CCC (Psy) (IB 24 pts)

88 pts **Queen Margaret** – CCD (Psy Sociol) (IB 26 pts)
Teesside – 88–104 pts (Psy; Foren Psy; Psy Cnslg; Psy Crimin)
Trinity Saint David – 88 pts (Cnslg St Psy)
Wolverhampton – CCD (Psy (Cnslg Psy)); CCD 88 pts (Psy)

80 pts **Bedfordshire** – 80 pts (App Psy; Hlth Psy)
72 pts **UHI** – BC (Psy)

Open University – contact 0300 303 0073 **or** www.open.ac.uk/contact/new (Comb Soc Sci (Econ/Geog/Psy/Sociol); Psy)

Alternative offers
See **Chapter 6** and **Appendix 1** for grades/UCAS Tariff points information for other examinations.

EXAMPLES OF COLLEGES OFFERING COURSES IN THIS SUBJECT FIELD
Barking and Dagenham (Coll); Bedford (Coll); Birmingham Met (Coll); Blackburn (Coll); Bradford (Coll); Bury (Coll); Canterbury (Coll); Chesterfield (Coll); Colchester (Inst); Cornwall (Coll); Croydon (Univ Centre); Doncaster (Coll); Durham New (Coll); East Coast (Coll); Eastleigh (Coll); Farnborough (CT); Grimsby (Inst Group); Guildford (Coll); Haringey, Enfield and North East London (Coll); Harrogate (Coll); Havering (Coll); Lambeth (Coll); Metanoia (Inst); Milton Keynes (Coll); Nescot; Newham (CFE); North Lindsey (Coll); North Notts (Coll); Norwich City (Coll); Oldham (Coll); Oldham (Univ Campus); Peter Symonds (Coll); Peterborough (Coll); Petroc; Riverside (Coll); South Devon (Coll); South Gloucestershire and Stroud (Coll); Southport (Coll); Sussex Downs (Coll); Totton (Coll); Truro and Penwith (Coll); Tyne Coast (Coll); Warwickshire (Coll); West Anglia (Coll); West Thames (Coll); Wirral Met (Coll).

CHOOSING YOUR COURSE (SEE ALSO CH.1)
Universities and colleges teaching quality See www.qaa.ac.uk; https://unistats.ac.uk.

Top research universities and colleges (REF 2014) (Psychology, Psychiatry and Neuroscience) Oxford; York; Cambridge; London (RH); Imperial London; Cardiff; Sussex; Warwick; Essex; London (Birk); Birmingham; Dundee; Bangor.

Examples of sandwich degree courses Aston; Bath; Bedfordshire; Bournemouth; Brunel; Cardiff; Coventry; Hertfordshire; Kent; Leeds; Loughborough; Middlesex; Newcastle; Nottingham Trent; Portsmouth; Reading; Surrey; Ulster; UWE Bristol; Westminster.

ADMISSIONS INFORMATION

Number of applicants per place (approx) Abertay 4; Aston 6; Bangor 4; Bath 9; Bath Spa 10; Birmingham 6; Bolton 5; Bradford 2; Bristol 8; Buckingham 7; Cambridge 7; Cardiff 5; Cardiff Met 5; Central Lancashire 13; City 7; De Montfort 10; Derby 5; Dundee 8; Durham 8; Edinburgh Napier 13; Exeter 14; Greenwich 8; Heriot-Watt 5; Hertfordshire 22; Huddersfield 3; Hull 5; Kent 7; Lancaster 6; Leeds 12; Leeds Trinity 6; Leicester 6; Liverpool 6; Liverpool John Moores 8; London (RH) 7; London (UCL) 10; London South Bank 7; Manchester 7; Manchester Met 14; Middlesex 10; Newcastle 9; Newman 3; Northampton 4; Nottingham 11; Nottingham Trent 3; Oxford Brookes 11; Plymouth 17; Roehampton 5; Salford 4; Sheffield 6; Sheffield Hallam 10; Southampton 10; Staffordshire 6; Stirling 8; Sussex 5; Swansea 7; Teesside 10; Ulster 4; Warwick 13; Westminster 6; Worcester 9; York 9; York St John 3.

Advice to applicants and planning the UCAS personal statement Psychology is heavily over-subscribed so prepare well in advance by choosing suitable A-level subjects. Contact the Education and Social Services departments in your local authority office to arrange meetings with psychologists to gain a knowledge of the work. Make notes during those meetings and of any work experience gained and describe these fully on the UCAS application. Reference to introductory reading in psychology is important (many students have a distorted image of it). Demonstrate your interest in psychology through, for example, voluntary or other work experience. See also **Appendix 3**. **Bristol** General scientific interests are important. Only consider this course if you have some aptitude and liking for scientific study (either in biological or physical sciences). Deferred entry accepted. **Leeds** One A-level subject must be taken from psychology, geography, maths, chemistry, physics, biology, geology, economics, statistics, environmental science or computing.

Misconceptions about this course Some believe a Psychology course will train them as therapists or counsellors – it will not. **Bath** They think that they are going to learn about themselves. **Birmingham** Some applicants underestimate the scientific nature of the course. **Exeter** Students should be aware that it is a rigorous scientific discipline. **Lincoln** Applicants should be aware that this is a science-based course. Academic psychology is an empirical science requiring research methodologies and statistical analysis. **Reading** Not all applicants are aware that it is a science-based course and are surprised at the high science and statistics content. **Sussex** Applicants should note that the BSc course is not harder than the BA course. Many students mistakenly believe that Psychology consists of counselling and that there is no maths. Psychology is a science. **York** Some students think psychology means Freud, which it hasn't done for 50 years or more. They do not realise that psychology is a science in the same vein as biology, chemistry or physics. Only 20% of Psychology graduates become professional psychologists. This involves taking a postgraduate degree in a specialist area of psychology.

Selection interviews Yes Anglia Ruskin, Buckingham, Cambridge, Oxford (Psy (Expmtl)) 19%; (Psy Phil Ling) 16%; **Some** Cardiff, East Anglia, Exeter, Leeds Trinity, Liverpool John Moores, Nottingham Trent, Reading; **No** Aston, Bangor, Birmingham, Bishop Grosseteste, Bolton, Bristol, Chichester, Derby, Dundee, Essex, Glyndŵr, Huddersfield, Keele, Leeds, Leicester, London (QM), London (UCL), London Met, Manchester, Middlesex, Newcastle, Northampton, Nottingham, Oxford Brookes, Plymouth, Roehampton, Salford, Southampton, Sunderland, Surrey, Swansea.

Interview advice and questions Although some applicants will have studied the subject at A-level and will have a broad understanding of its coverage, it is still essential to have gained some work experience or to have discussed the career with a professional psychologist. Questions will focus on this and in previous years they have included: What have you read about psychology? What do you expect to gain by studying psychology? What are your parents' and teachers' views on your choice of subject? Are you interested in any particular branch of the subject? Is psychology an art or a science? Do you think you are well suited to this course? Why? Do you think it is possible that if we learn enough about the functioning of the brain we can create a computer that is functionally the same? What is counselling? Is it necessary? Know the differences between the various branches of psychology and discuss any specific interests, for example, in clinical, occupational, educational, criminal psychology and cognitive, neuro-, social or physiological psychology. What influences young children's food choices? What stereotypes do we have of people with mental illness? See also **Chapter 5**. **Oxford** Ability to evaluate evidence and to have the capacity for logical and creative thinking.

Reasons for rejection (non-academic) Lack of background reading and lack of awareness of psychology; poor communication skills; misunderstanding of what is involved in a degree course. Poor personal statement. Poor grades, especially in **GCSE** mathematics. **Exeter** Competition for places – we can only select those with exceptional grades. **Warwick** (BSc) Lack of science background.

AFTER-RESULTS ADVICE
Offers to applicants repeating A-levels Higher Birmingham, City, Loughborough, Newcastle, Southampton, Swansea, Warwick, York; **Possibly higher** Aston, Northampton; **Same** Bangor, Bolton, Brunel, Cardiff, Cardiff Met, Chester, Derby, Dundee, Durham, East Anglia, Huddersfield, Hull, Lincoln, Liverpool Hope, Liverpool John Moores, London (RH), London South Bank, Manchester Met, Newman, Nottingham, Nottingham Trent, Oxford Brookes, Roehampton, Salford, Sheffield Hallam, Staffordshire, Stirling, Suffolk, Sunderland, West London, Wolverhampton, York St John; **No** Cambridge.

GRADUATE DESTINATIONS AND EMPLOYMENT (2015/16 HESA)
Graduates surveyed 11,860 **Employed** 4,985 **In voluntary employment** 445 **In further study** 3,505 **Assumed unemployed** 590

Career note Clinical, educational and occupational psychology are the three main specialist careers for graduate psychologists, all involving further study. Ergonomics, human/computer interaction, marketing, public relations, human resource management, advertising, the social services, the prison and rehabilitation services also provide alternative career routes.

OTHER DEGREE SUBJECTS FOR CONSIDERATION
Anthropology; Behavioural Science; Cognitive Sciences; Education; Health Studies; Neuroscience; Sociology.

RADIOGRAPHY
(including **Medical Imaging** and **Radiotherapy**; see also **Health Sciences/Studies**)

Many institutions offer both Diagnostic and Therapeutic Radiography but applicants should check this, and course entry requirements, before applying. Information on courses is also available from the Society of Radiographers (see **Appendix 3**). Diagnostic Radiography is the demonstration on film (or other imaging materials) of the position and structure of the body's organs using radiation or other imaging media. Therapeutic Radiography is the planning and administration of treatment for patients suffering from malignant and non-malignant disease using different forms of radiation. Courses lead to state registration.

Useful websites www.sor.org; https://radiographycareers.co.uk; www.healthcareers.nhs.uk

NB The points totals shown to the left of the institutions are for ease of reference only. It must not be assumed that Tariff points are always used by institutions or that they can be substituted for an offer in grades. The level of an offer is not necessarily indicative of the quality of a course.

COURSE OFFERS INFORMATION

Subject requirements/preferences GCSE Five subjects including English, mathematics and a science subject (usually at one sitting). **AL** One or two sciences required; mathematics may be acceptable. (Radiothera) One science subject required for some courses. Psychology may not be considered a science subject at some institutions. **Other** Applicants required to have an occupational health check and a Disclosure and Barring Service (DBS) clearance. Visit to, or work experience in, a hospital imaging department often required/expected.

Your target offers and examples of degree courses

136 pts **Exeter** – AAB–BBB incl sci (Med Imag (Diag Radiog)) (IB 34–30 pts HL 4 sci)

128 pts **Leeds** – ABB incl sci (Diag Radiog) (IB 34 pts HL 5 sci)

Sheffield Hallam – 128 pts incl sci/maths (Diag Radiog)

120 pts **Bangor** – 120 pts incl biol/phys (Diag Radiog)

Birmingham City – BBB incl sci 120 pts (Radiothera; Diag Radiog) (IB 30 pts)

Cardiff – BBB (Diag Radiog Imag; Radiothera Onc) (IB 32 pts)

City – BBB 120 pts (Radiog (Radiothera Onc); Radiog (Diag Imag)) (IB 33 pts)

Cumbria – 120–128 pts incl sci (Diag Radiog)

Derby – 120–128 pts incl sci (Diag Radiog)

Hertfordshire – 120–136 pts incl sci/maths (Radiothera Onc) (HL 4 sci/maths); 120–136 pts incl sci (Diag Radiog Imag) (HL 4 sci/maths)

Liverpool – BBB incl biol sci (Diag Radiog) (IB 30 pts HL 6 maths+biol/phys); BBB incl sci/ maths/PE (Radiothera) (IB 30 pts HL 5 maths+biol/phys)

London (St George's) – BBB incl sci 120 pts (Diag Radiog; Ther Radiog) (HL 554)

London South Bank – BBB (Diag Radiog; Thera Radiog)

Sheffield Hallam – 120 pts incl sci (Radiothera Onc)

UWE Bristol – 120 pts incl sci (Diag Imag) (HL 5 sci)

112 pts **Portsmouth** – 112 pts incl sci +interview (Diag Radiog Med Imag; Radiog Onc) (IB 30 pts HL 17 pts incl 5 sci/maths)

104 pts **Glasgow Caledonian** – BCC incl sci (Radiothera Onc; Diag Imag) (IB 24 pts)

Robert Gordon – BCC incl sci/maths (Diag Radiog) (IB 27 pts)

96 pts **Queen Margaret** – CCC incl sci 96 pts (Ther Radiog) (IB 28 pts)

Alternative offers

See **Chapter 6** and **Appendix 1** for grades/UCAS Tariff points information for other examinations.

EXAMPLES OF COLLEGES OFFERING COURSES IN THIS SUBJECT FIELD

Birmingham Met (Coll).

CHOOSING YOUR COURSE (SEE ALSO CH.1)

Universities and colleges teaching quality See www.qaa.ac.uk; https://unistats.ac.uk.

Top research universities and colleges (REF 2014) See **Health Sciences/Studies**.

ADMISSIONS INFORMATION

Number of applicants per place (approx) Bangor 6; Birmingham City (Radiothera) 8; Cardiff 3; Derby 9; Hertfordshire (Diag Radiog Imag) 8; Leeds 10; London (St George's) 7; London South Bank 9; Robert Gordon 5; Sheffield Hallam 8, (Radiothera Onc) 3.

Admissions tutors' advice London (St George's) Work experience required.

Advice to applicants and planning the UCAS personal statement Contacts with radiographers and visits to the radiography departments of hospitals should be discussed in full on the UCAS application. See also **Appendix 3**. **Birmingham City** Evidence needed of a visit to at least one imaging department or oncology (radiotherapy) department before completing the UCAS application. Evidence of good research into the career. **Liverpool** Choice between therapeutic and diagnostic pathways should be made before applying.

Misconceptions about this course There is often confusion between radiotherapy and diagnostic imaging and between diagnostic and therapeutic radiography.

Selection interviews Yes Bangor, Birmingham City, Cardiff, City, Cumbria, Derby, Exeter, Hertfordshire, London (St George's), London South Bank, Portsmouth, Queen Margaret, Sheffield Hallam.

Interview advice and questions All applicants should have discussed this career with a radiographer and visited a hospital radiography department. Questions follow from these contacts. Where does radiography fit into the overall healthcare system? See also **Chapter 5**.

Reasons for rejection (non-academic) Lack of interest in people. Poor communication skills. Occasionally students may be unsuitable for the clinical environment, for example, they express a fear of blood and needles; poor grasp of radiography as a career. Unable to meet criteria for employment in the NHS, for example, health factors, criminal convictions, severe disabilities.

AFTER-RESULTS ADVICE
Offers to applicants repeating A-levels Higher London (St George's); **Same** Derby.

GRADUATE DESTINATIONS AND EMPLOYMENT (2015/16 HESA)
See **Health Sciences/Studies**.

Career note Most radiographers work in the NHS in hospital radiography departments undertaking diagnostic or therapeutic treatment. Others work in private healthcare.

OTHER DEGREE SUBJECTS FOR CONSIDERATION
Audiology; Forensic Engineering; Health Studies; Medical Physics; Nursing; Occupational Therapy; Physics; Podiatry; Speech Sciences.

RELIGIOUS STUDIES

(including **Biblical Studies, Divinity, Hebrew, Islamic Studies** and **Theology**; see also
Arabic and Ancient Near and Middle Eastern Studies)

The subject content of these courses varies and students should check prospectuses carefully. They are not intended as training courses for ministry; an adherence to a particular religious denomination is not a necessary qualification for entry. Courses offer the study of the major religions – Christianity, Judaism, Islam, Buddhism and Hinduism. The comprehensive Lancaster course offers optional modules covering theological, sociological, anthropological, psychological and philosophical perspectives.

Useful websites www.theguardian.com/world/religion; www.jewfaq.org; www.virtualreligion.net; https://academic.oup.com/jis; www.sikhs.org; www.buddhanet.net; www.religionfacts.com/hinduism; www.islaminfocentre.org.uk; www.christianity.com

NB The points totals shown to the left of the institutions are for ease of reference only. It must not be assumed that Tariff points are always used by institutions or that they can be substituted for an offer in grades. The level of an offer is not necessarily indicative of the quality of a course.

COURSE OFFERS INFORMATION
Subject requirements/preferences GCSE English and mathematics. For teacher training, English, mathematics and science. **AL** Religious studies or theology may be required or preferred for some courses.

Your target offers and examples of degree courses
152 pts **Cambridge** – A*AA +interview +TAA (Theol Relig St) (IB 40–42 pts HL 776)
144 pts **Durham** – AAA (Phil Theol) (IB 37 pts)
        Oxford – AAA +interview (Relig Orntl St) (IB 38 pts HL 666); (Theol Relgn) (IB 38 pts); AAA
         +interview +test (Phil Theol) (IB 39 pts)

Check **Chapter 3** for new university admission details and **Chapter 6** on how to read the subject tables.

St Andrews – AAA incl Engl (Bib St Engl) (IB 36 pts); AAA (Heb courses) (IB 36 pts HL 666); (Bib St; Theol St; Theol) (IB 36 pts)

136 pts Birmingham – AAB (Pol Relgn Phil) (IB 32 pts HL 665)
Bristol – AAB–BBB (Relgn Theol) (IB 34–31 pts HL 17–15 pts)
Durham – AAB (Theol courses) (IB 36 pts)
Edinburgh – AAB (Islam St) (IB 37 pts HL 666)
Exeter – AAB–BBB (Theol Relgn) (IB 34–30 pts)
Glasgow – AAB–BBB incl arts/lang (Theol Relig St) (IB 36–34 pts)
Lancaster – AAB–ABB (Phil Relig St; Relig St; Pol Relig St; Relig St Sociol) (IB 35–32 pts)
London (King's) – AAB (Relgn Pol Soty; Theol Relgn Cult; Relgn Phil Eth) (IB 35 pts)
Nottingham – AAB (Relgn Phil Eth) (IB 34 pts)

128 pts Birmingham – ABB (Theol Relgn) (IB 32 pts HL 655)
Cardiff – ABB–BBC (Relig Theol) (IB 28–36 pts); ABB–BBB (Relig St Ital) (HL 665–655)
Edinburgh – ABB (Relig St; Div Class) (IB 34 pts HL 655)
Leeds – ABB (Russ Civ Theol Relig St; Islam St; Theol Relig St) (IB 34 pts)
London (SOAS) – ABB–BBB (St Relgns) (IB 33 pts)
London (UCL) – ABB incl hist (Hist (Cnt E Euro) Jew St) (IB 34 pts HL 5 hist)
Manchester – ABB (Relgns Theol) (IB 33 pts)
Nottingham – ABB (Relgn Cult Eth) (IB 32 pts)
Sheffield – ABB–BBB+bEPQ (Phil Relgn) (IB 33 pts)

120 pts Aberdeen – BBB (Theol; Div; Theol Relig St) (IB 32 pts)
Cardiff – BBB–BBC incl Span (Relig St Span) (HL 655); BBB–BBC (Relig St Ger) (HL 665–655)
Essex – BBB (Phil Relgn Eth) (IB 30 pts)
Kent – BBB (Relig St) (IB 34 pts)
Liverpool Hope – BBB–BBC 120–112 pts (Phil Eth Relgn; Theol Relig St)
Queen's Belfast – BBB (Theol)
Stirling – BBB (Relgn) (IB 32 pts)

112 pts Bangor – 112–96 pts (Phil Relgn)
Chester – BBC–BCC 112 pts (Relig St; Theol Relig St; Theol) (IB 26 pts)
Gloucestershire – BBC 112 pts (Relgn Phil Eth)
Huddersfield – BBC 112 pts (Relgn Educ)
Hull – 112 pts (Phil Relgn) (IB 28 pts)
Roehampton – 112 pts (Theol Relig St)
St Mary's – 112 pts (Theol Relig St)
Wolverhampton – BBC (Relig St courses; Relig St Phil; Relig St Sociol)

104 pts Bath Spa – BCC–CCC (Relgn Phil Eth; St Relgn Comb) (IB 26 pts)
Central Lancashire – 104 pts (Relgn Cult Soty)
Chichester – BCC–BBB (Theol) (IB 28 pts)
Leeds Trinity – 104 pts (Theol Relig St; Phil Eth Relgn)
Winchester – 104–120 pts +interview (Theol Relgn Eth) (IB 26 pts)

96 pts Bishop Grosseteste – 96–112 pts (Theol Eth Soty)
Islamic (Coll) – CCC (Islam St; Hawza St)
Newman – 96 pts (Theol); 96–88 pts (Phil Relgn Educ)
York St John – 96–112 pts (Relgn Phil Eth; Theol Relig St)

88 pts Canterbury Christ Church – 88–112 pts (Theol)
64 pts UHI – CC (Theol St)

Trinity Saint David – interview (Theol Comb Hons; Relig St Theol; Relig St Islam St)

Alternative offers
See **Chapter 6** and **Appendix 1** for grades/UCAS Tariff points information for other examinations.

CHOOSING YOUR COURSE (SEE ALSO CH.1)
Universities and colleges teaching quality See www.qaa.ac.uk; https://unistats.ac.uk.

UCAS points Tariff: A* = 56 pts; A = 48 pts; B = 40 pts; C = 32 pts; D = 24 pts; E = 16 pts

Top research universities and colleges (REF 2014) (Theology and Religious Studies) Durham; Exeter; Leeds; Cambridge; Birmingham; London (UCL); London (SOAS); Edinburgh.

ADMISSIONS INFORMATION

Number of applicants per place (approx) Bangor 4; Birmingham 4; Bristol 9; Cambridge 2; Durham 4; Edinburgh 3; Exeter 7; Glasgow 4; Hull 5; Kent 4; Lancaster 6; Leeds 4; Leeds Trinity 6; London (King's) 6; Manchester 4; Newman 2; Nottingham 4; Sheffield 8; Trinity Saint David 7; Winchester 5; York St John 2.

Advice to applicants and planning the UCAS personal statement An awareness of the differences between the main religions is important as is any special research you have done to help you decide on your preferred courses. Interests in the religious art and architecture of various periods and styles should be noted. Applicants should have an open-minded approach to studying a diverse range of religious traditions. **Bristol** Deferred entry accepted.

Misconceptions about this course Some students think that you must be religious to study Theology – in fact, people of all faiths and none study the subject. A study of religions is not Christian theology. **Leeds** Some applicants are not aware of the breadth of the subject. We offer modules covering New Testament, Christian theology, Islamic studies, Hinduism, Buddhism, Sikhism, Christian ethics and sociology of religion. **Newman** That the Theology course only concentrates on the Christian/Catholic religions – all major religions are covered.

Selection interviews Yes Cambridge, Manchester, Oxford (Theol Relgn) 29%, Trinity Saint David, Winchester; **Some** Bristol, Cardiff, London (SOAS); **No** Birmingham, Bishop Grosseteste, Chester, Chichester, Edinburgh, Hull, Leeds, Leeds Trinity, Nottingham, Sheffield.

Interview advice and questions Past questions have included: Why do you want to study Theology/ Biblical Studies/Religious Studies? What do you hope to do after obtaining your degree? Questions relating to the A-level syllabus. Questions on current theological topics. Do you have any strong religious convictions? Do you think that your religious beliefs will be changed at the end of the course? Why did you choose Religious Studies rather than Biblical Studies? How would you explain the miracles to a 10-year old? (BEd course.) Do you agree with the National Lottery? How do you think you can apply theology to your career? See also **Chapter 5**. **Cambridge** There is a Christian priest who regularly visits India and converted to a Hindu priest. When he is in England he still practises as a Christian priest. What problems might this pose? Do you believe we should eradicate Christmas on the basis that it offends other religious groups? **Oxford** The ability to defend one's opinions and willingness to engage in a lively dialogue are both important.

Reasons for rejection (non-academic) Students not attending Open Days may be rejected. Too religiously conservative. Failure to interact. Lack of motivation to study a subject which goes beyond A-level. **Cardiff** Insufficiently open to an academic study of religion.

AFTER-RESULTS ADVICE

Offers to applicants repeating A-levels Higher Manchester, St Andrews; **Possibly higher** Cambridge (Hom); **Same** Bangor, Birmingham, Cardiff, Chester, Durham, Hull, Lancaster, Leeds, Liverpool Hope, London (SOAS), Nottingham, St Mary's, Sheffield, Stirling, Trinity Saint David, Winchester, Wolverhampton, York St John; **No** Cambridge, Glasgow.

GRADUATE DESTINATIONS AND EMPLOYMENT (2015/16 HESA)

Theology and Religious Studies graduates surveyed 1,270 **Employed** 460 **In voluntary employment** 95 **In further study** 460 **Assumed unemployed** 55

Career note Although a small number of graduates may regard these courses as a preparation for entry to religious orders, the great majority enter other careers, with teaching particularly popular.

OTHER DEGREE SUBJECTS FOR CONSIDERATION

Community Studies; Education; History; Philosophy; Psychology; Social Policy and Administration; Social Work.

RETAIL MANAGEMENT

(see also **Business and Management Courses, Business and Management Courses (International and European), Business and Management Courses (Specialised), Marketing**)

This subject attracts a large number of applicants each year and it is necessary to have work experience before applying. The work itself varies depending on the type of retail outlet. After completing their courses graduates in a large department store will be involved in different aspects of the business, for example supervising shop assistants, warehouse and packing staff. They could also receive special training in the sales of particular goods, for example food and drink, clothing, furniture. Subsequently there may be opportunities to become buyers. In more specialised shops, for example shoes, fashion and food, graduates are likely to work only with these products, with opportunities to reach senior management.

Useful websites https://brc.org.uk; www.retail-week.com; www.theretailbulletin.com; www.retailchoice.com; www.nrf.com

NB The points totals shown to the left of the institutions are for ease of reference only. It must not be assumed that Tariff points are always used by institutions or that they can be substituted for an offer in grades. The level of an offer is not necessarily indicative of the quality of a course.

COURSE OFFERS INFORMATION

Subject requirements/preferences GCSE English and mathematics at grade C or above (4 or above). **AL** No subjects specified.

Your target offers and examples of degree courses
136 pts **Loughborough** – AAB (Rtl Mark Mgt) (IB 35 pts HL 665)
128 pts **Stirling** – ABB (3 yr course) BBB (4 yr course) (Rtl Mark) (IB 35 pts (3 yr course) 32 pts (4 yr course))
Surrey – ABB (Bus Rtl Mgt) (IB 32 pts)
120 pts **Heriot-Watt** – BBB (Fash Mark Rtl) (IB 29 pts)
Huddersfield – BBB 120 pts (Int Fash Buy Mgt)
Nottingham Trent – BBB 120 pts (Fash Mgt)
112 pts **Arts London** – 112 pts (Fash Mgt) (IB 25 pts)
Birmingham City – BBC 112 pts +portfolio (Fash Bus Prom) (HL 14 pts)
Cardiff Met – 112 pts (Mark Mgt)
De Montfort – 112 pts (Fash Buy courses) (IB 26 pts)
104 pts **Bournemouth** – 104–120 pts (Rtl Mgt) (IB 28–31 pts HL 55)
Manchester Met – BCC–BBC 104–112 pts (Rtl Mgt Mark) (IB 26 pts)
96 pts **Leeds Beckett** – 96 pts (Rtl Mark Mgt) (IB 24 pts)
Roehampton – 96 pts (Rtl Mark Mgt)
88 pts **Canterbury Christ Church** – 88–112 pts (Bus Mgt (Rtl))

Alternative offers
See **Chapter 6** and **Appendix 1** for grades/UCAS Tariff points information for other examinations.

EXAMPLES OF COLLEGES OFFERING COURSES IN THIS SUBJECT FIELD

Blackburn (Coll); Blackpool and Fylde (Coll); Durham New (Coll); Grŵp Llandrillo Menai; Hugh Baird (Coll); Hull (Coll); Leeds City (Coll); Newcastle (Coll).

CHOOSING YOUR COURSE (SEE ALSO CH.1)

Universities and colleges teaching quality See www.qaa.ac.uk; https://unistats.ac.uk.

Examples of sandwich degree courses Arts London; Birmingham City; Bournemouth; Brighton; Central Lancashire; Huddersfield; Leeds Beckett; Manchester Met; Surrey.

UCAS points Tariff: A* = 56 pts; A = 48 pts; B = 40 pts; C = 32 pts; D = 24 pts; E = 16 pts

ADMISSIONS INFORMATION

Number of applicants per place (approx) See also **Business and Management Courses**. Manchester Met 10.

Advice to applicants and planning the UCAS personal statement See also **Business and Management Courses**. **Manchester Met** (Rtl Mgt Mark) Evidence of working with people or voluntary work experience (department unable to assist with sponsorships).

Misconceptions about this course See **Business and Management Courses**.

Interview advice and questions See **Business and Management Courses**.

Reasons for rejection (non-academic) See **Business and Management Courses**.

GRADUATE DESTINATIONS AND EMPLOYMENT (2015/16 HESA)

See **Business and Management Courses**.
Career note Majority of graduates work in business involved in marketing and retail work. Employment options include brand design, product management, advertising, PR, sales and account management.

OTHER DEGREE SUBJECTS FOR CONSIDERATION

Business Studies; Consumer Sciences/Studies; E-Commerce; Human Resource Management; Psychology; Supply Chain Management.

RUSSIAN and EAST EUROPEAN STUDIES

(including **History and East European Cultural Studies**, **Russian and Arabic** and **Russian and History**; see also **European Studies, Languages**)

East European Studies cover a wide range of the less popular language courses and should be considered by anyone with a love of and gift for languages. Many natural linguists often devote themselves to one of the popular European languages studied up to A-level, when their language skills could be extended to the more unusual languages, thereby increasing their future career opportunities.

Useful websites www.ciol.org.uk; www.bbc.co.uk/languages; www.languageadvantage.com; www.languagematters.co.uk

NB The points totals shown to the left of the institutions are for ease of reference only. It must not be assumed that Tariff points are always used by institutions or that they can be substituted for an offer in grades. The level of an offer is not necessarily indicative of the quality of a course.

COURSE OFFERS INFORMATION

Subject requirements/preferences GCSE A foreign language. **AL** One or two modern languages may be stipulated.

Your target offers and examples of degree courses

152 pts **Cambridge** – A*AA incl lang +interview +MMLAA (Modn Mediev Langs) (IB 40–42 pts HL 776)

Durham – A*AA (Comb Hons Soc Sci (Russ)) (IB 38 pts)

144 pts **Oxford** – AAA +interview +MLAT (Modn Langs (Russ+2nd Lang)) (IB 38 pts); AAA +interview +MLAT +OLAT (Euro Mid E Langs (Cz/Russ)) (IB 38 pts)

136 pts **Birmingham** – AAB incl lang (Modn Langs) (IB 32 pts HL 665); AAB incl hist (Hist Russ St) (IB 32 pts HL 665)

Exeter – AAB–ABB incl Russ/Arbc (Russ Arbc) (IB 34–32 pts HL 5 Russ/Arbc)

Glasgow – AAB–BBB incl arts/lang (Russ) (IB 36–34 pts); AAB Engl/lang/hum/soc sci (Cnt E Euro St) (IB 38 pts HL 666–665 incl Engl+lang/hum)

Leeds – AAB (Int Bus Russ) (IB 35 pts HL 16 pts)

London (UCL) – AAB–ABB incl hist (Russ Hist) (IB 36–34 pts HL 5 hist); AAB–ABB (Bulg/Czech/Finn/Hung/Polh/Romn/Slovak E Euro St; Russ St) (IB 36–34 pts)

St Andrews – AAB (Russ courses) (IB 36 pts)

Sheffield – AAB–BBB incl lang (Russ St Comb Hons) (IB 34–32 pts HL 6 lang)

128 pts **Bristol** – ABB–BBC incl Russ/Port (Russ Port) (IB 32–29 pts HL 5 Russ/Port); ABB–BBC incl lang (Russ) (IB 32–29 pts HL 5 lang)

Edinburgh – ABB (Russ St) (IB 34 pts HL 655)

Leeds – ABB (Russ Sociol; Russ Civ Theol Relig St; Russ) (IB 34 pts)

London (QM) – ABB incl hum/soc sci (Russ Bus Mgt) (IB 32 pts HL 655); ABB incl art/hum/soc sci+lang (Fr/Ger/Russ Dr) (IB 32 pts HL 6/5 art/hum/soc sci)

Manchester – ABB incl lang (Russ Chin) (IB 33 pts HL 655); ABB incl Russ/Jap +interview (Russ Jap) (IB 33 pts HL 655)

Nottingham – ABB (Russ St) (IB 32 pts); ABB incl hist (Hist E Euro Cult St) (IB 32 pts HL 5 hist)

Sheffield – ABB–BBB incl lang (Russ St) (IB 33 pts HL 6 lang); ABB–BBB+bEPQ (Jap St Comb Hons) (IB 33 pts)

120 pts **London (QM)** – BBB incl hum/soc soci (Russ) (IB 30 pts HL 5 hum/soc sci)

Alternative offers
See **Chapter 6** and **Appendix 1** for grades/UCAS Tariff points information for other examinations.

CHOOSING YOUR COURSE (SEE ALSO CH.1)
Universities and colleges teaching quality See www.qaa.ac.uk; https://unistats.ac.uk.

ADMISSIONS INFORMATION
Number of applicants per place (approx) Bath 6 (Mod Langs Eur St); Birmingham 3; Bristol 4; Durham 5; Leeds 3; London (UCL) 3; Nottingham 3.

Advice to applicants and planning the UCAS personal statement Visits to Eastern Europe should be mentioned, supported by your special reasons for wishing to study the language. A knowledge of the cultural, economic and political scene could be important. Fluent English important for non-UK students. Evidence of wide reading, travel and residence abroad. See also **Appendix 3** under Languages.

Selection interviews Yes Cambridge, Oxford (Euro Mid E Langs) 41%; **No** London (UCL), Nottingham.

Interview advice and questions Since many applicants will not have taken Russian at A-level, questions often focus on their reasons for choosing a Russian degree, and their knowledge of, and interest in, Russia. Those taking A-level Russian are likely to be questioned on the course and on any reading done outside A-level work. East European Studies applicants will need to show some knowledge of their chosen country/countries and any specific reasons why they wish to follow the course. See also **Chapter 5**. **Leeds** See **Languages**.

Reasons for rejection (non-academic) Lack of perceived commitment for a demanding *ab initio* subject.

AFTER-RESULTS ADVICE
Offers to applicants repeating A-levels Higher Bristol, Leeds, St Andrews; **Same** Durham; **No** Cambridge, Glasgow.

GRADUATE DESTINATIONS AND EMPLOYMENT (2015/16 HESA)
Graduates surveyed 110 **Employed** 45 **In voluntary employment** 5 **In further study** 25 **Assumed unemployed** 10

Career note See **Languages**.

OTHER DEGREE SUBJECTS FOR CONSIDERATION
Economics; European Studies; International Relations; Linguistics; Politics; other languages.

SCANDINAVIAN STUDIES

(see also Languages)

Scandinavian Studies provides students who enjoy languages with the opportunity to extend their language expertise to learn a modern Scandinavian language – Danish, Norwegian or Swedish – from beginner's level to Honours level in four years, including a year in Scandinavia. The three languages are very similar to each other and a knowledge of one makes it possible to access easily the literature and cultures of the other two. Viking Studies includes Old Norse, runology and archaeology.

Useful websites www.ciol.org.uk; www.bbc.co.uk/languages; www.languageadvantage.com; www.languagematters.co.uk; www.scandinaviahouse.org; https://scandinavianstudy.org

NB The points totals shown to the left of the institutions are for ease of reference only. It must not be assumed that Tariff points are always used by institutions or that they can be substituted for an offer in grades. The level of an offer is not necessarily indicative of the quality of a course.

COURSE OFFERS INFORMATION

Subject requirements/preferences GCSE Foreign language preferred for all courses. **AL** A modern language may be required.

Your target offers and examples of degree courses
152 pts Cambridge – A*AA +interview +ASNCAA (A-Sxn Nrs Celt) (IB 40–42 pts HL 776)
136 pts Edinburgh – AAB (Scand St; Scand St (Dan); Scand St (Nor); Scand St (Swed))
         (IB 36 pts HL 665)
128 pts Edinburgh – ABB (Celt) (IB 34 pts HL 655)
         London (UCL) – ABB (Vkg Old Nrs St; Ice; Scand St) (IB 34 pts)

Alternative offers
See **Chapter 6** and **Appendix 1** for grades/UCAS Tariff points information for other examinations.

CHOOSING YOUR COURSE (SEE ALSO CH.1)

Universities and colleges teaching quality See www.qaa.ac.uk; https://unistats.ac.uk.

ADMISSIONS INFORMATION

Number of applicants per place (approx) London (UCL) 5.

Advice to applicants and planning the UCAS personal statement Visits to Scandinavian countries could be the source of an interest in studying these languages. You should also be aware of cultural, political, geographical and economic aspects of Scandinavian countries. Knowledge of these should be shown in your statement.

Selection interviews Yes Cambridge.

Interview advice and questions Applicants in the past have been questioned on why they have chosen this subject area, on their visits to Scandinavia and on their knowledge of the country/ countries and their people. Future career plans are likely to be discussed. See also **Chapter 5**.

Reasons for rejection (non-academic) One applicant didn't know the difference between a noun and a verb.

AFTER-RESULTS ADVICE

Offers to applicants repeating A-levels No Cambridge.

GRADUATE DESTINATIONS AND EMPLOYMENT (2015/16 HESA)

See **Languages**.

Career note See **Languages**.

OTHER DEGREE SUBJECTS FOR CONSIDERATION
Archaeology; European History/Studies; History; other modern languages, including, for example, Russian and East European languages.

SOCIAL and PUBLIC POLICY and ADMINISTRATION

(see also **Community Studies/Development, Social Work, Sociology**)

Social Policy is a multi-disciplinary degree that combines elements from sociology, political science, social and economic history, economics, cultural studies and philosophy. It is a study of the needs of society and how best to provide such services as education, housing, health and welfare services.

Useful websites www.local.gov.uk

NB The points totals shown to the left of the institutions are for ease of reference only. It must not be assumed that Tariff points are always used by institutions or that they can be substituted for an offer in grades. The level of an offer is not necessarily indicative of the quality of a course.

COURSE OFFERS INFORMATION

Subject requirements/preferences GCSE English and mathematics normally required. **AL** No subjects specified.

Your target offers and examples of degree courses

152 pts **Cambridge** – A*AA +interview +HSPSAA (Hum Soc Pol Sci) (IB 40–42 pts HL 776)
  Durham – A*AA (Comb Hons Soc Sci) (IB 38 pts)

136 pts **Bath** – AAB–ABB+bEPQ (Soc Plcy) (IB 35 pts HL 665)
  Bristol – AAB–BBB (Soc Plcy Pol) (IB 34–31 pts HL 17–15 pts)
  Edinburgh – AAB (Soc Plcy courses) (IB 39 pts HL 666)
  Glasgow – AAB–BBB (Soc Pblc Plcy) (IB 38–34 pts)
  London LSE – AAB incl maths (Soc Plcy Econ) (IB 37 pts HL 666); AAB (Soc Plcy Gov; Soc Plcy Sociol; Soc Plcy) (IB 37 pts HL 666)

128 pts **Aston** – ABB (Pol Soc Plcy) (IB 32 pts); ABB–BBB (Bus Mgt Pblc Plcy) (IB 33 pts)
  Birmingham – ABB (Pol Sci Soc Plcy (Yr Abrd)) (IB 32 pts HL 655)
  Bristol – ABB–BBC (Soc Plcy; Soc Plcy Sociol) (IB 32–29 pts HL 16–14 pts)
  Cardiff – ABB (Crimin Soc Plcy) (HL 17 pts)
  Leeds – ABB (Soc Pol Sociol; Soc Plcy courses) (IB 34 pts HL 655)
  Loughborough – ABB (Crimin Soc Plcy) (IB 34 pts HL 655)
  Nottingham – ABB +interview (Soc Wk) (IB 32 pts); ABB (Sociol Soc Plcy) (IB 32 pts)
  Southampton – ABB–BBB+aEPQ (Sociol Soc Plcy) (IB 32 pts HL 16 pts)
  Stirling – ABB (3 yr course) BBB (4 yr course) (Sociol Soc Plcy) (IB 35 pts (3 yr course) 32 pts (4 yr course))

120 pts **Aston** – BBB (Sociol Soc Pol) (IB 32 pts)
  Birmingham – BBB (Soc Plcy) (IB 32 pts HL 555)
  Cardiff – BBB (Sociol Soc Plcy) (HL 17–16 pts)
  Kent – BBB (Soc Plcy) (IB 34 pts)
  Liverpool – BBB (Sociol Soc Plcy) (IB 30 pts)
  Liverpool Hope – BBB–BBC 120–112 pts (Soc Plcy courses)
  London (Gold) – BBB (Econ Pol Pblc Plcy) (IB 33 pts)
  Queen's Belfast – BBB (Soc Plcy courses)
  Sheffield – BBB (Sociol Soc Plcy) (IB 32 pts)
  Swansea – BBB (Crimin Soc Plcy); (Soc Plcy) (IB 32–33 pts)
  York – BBB (Soc Plcy (Chld Yng Ppl/Crm Crim Just); Soc Plcy) (IB 31 pts)

112 pts **Bangor** – 112–96 pts (Soc Plcy Comb Hons; Sociol Soc Pol)

UCAS points Tariff: A* = 56 pts; A = 48 pts; B = 40 pts; C = 32 pts; D = 24 pts; E = 16 pts

      Central Lancashire – 112 pts (Soc Plcy Sociol)
      London Met – BBC 112 pts (Hlth Soc Plcy); BBC/BC 112 pts (Sociol Soc Plcy)
      Wolverhampton – BBC–CCC (Soc Plcy courses)
104 pts **Bath Spa** – BCC–CCC (Educ St) (IB 26 pts)
      Lincoln – BCC (Crimin Soc Plcy) (IB 28 pts)
      Manchester Met – 104–112 pts (Pblc Serv) (IB 26 pts)
      Ulster – BCC (Soc Plcy) (IB 24 pts HL 12 pts)
  96 pts **Lincoln** – CCC (Soc Plcy) (IB 27 pts)
      West Scotland – CCC incl Engl (Soty Pol Plcy) (IB 24 pts)
  88 pts **Canterbury Christ Church** – 88–112 pts (Sociol Soc Plcy)
  80 pts **Anglia Ruskin** – 80 pts (Soc Plcy) (IB 24 pts)
      Trinity Saint David – 80 pts +interview (Pblc Serv)

Alternative offers
See **Chapter 6** and **Appendix 1** for grades/UCAS Tariff points information for other examinations.

EXAMPLES OF COLLEGES OFFERING COURSES IN THIS SUBJECT FIELD
Barnfield (Coll); Blackburn (Coll); Canterbury (Coll); Central Bedfordshire (Coll); Chesterfield (Coll); Craven (Coll); Dearne Valley (Coll); Derby (Coll); Dudley (Coll); Durham New (Coll); East Surrey (Coll); Exeter (Coll); Grŵp Llandrillo Menai; Hull (Coll); Macclesfield (Coll); Manchester (Coll); Milton Keynes (Coll); Norwich City (Coll); Plymouth City (Coll); St Helens (Coll); South Gloucestershire and Stroud (Coll); Walsall (Coll); Weston (Coll).

CHOOSING YOUR COURSE (SEE ALSO CH.1)
Universities and colleges teaching quality See www.qaa.ac.uk; https://unistats.ac.uk.

Top research universities and colleges (REF 2014) See **Social Work**.

Examples of sandwich degree courses Aston; Bath; Leeds.

ADMISSIONS INFORMATION
Number of applicants per place (approx) Aston 8; Bangor 6; Bath 6; Birmingham 5; Bristol 3; Cardiff 4; Central Lancashire 6; Leeds 10; London LSE (Soc Plcy) 10, (Soc Plcy Sociol) 13, (Soc Plcy Econ) 18, (Soc Plcy Gov) 9; Manchester Met 4; Nottingham 5; Southampton 6; Swansea 6; York 3.

Advice to applicants and planning the UCAS personal statement Careers in public and social administration are covered by this subject; consequently a good knowledge of these occupations and contacts with the social services should be discussed fully on your UCAS application. Gain work experience if possible. (See **Appendix 3** for contact details of some relevant organisations.) **Bangor** Ability to communicate and work in a group. **Bristol** Deferred entry accepted.

Misconceptions about this course York Some applicants imagine that the course is vocational and leads directly to social work – it does not. Graduates in this field are well placed for a wide range of careers.

Selection interviews Some Bath, Cardiff, Southampton; **No** Anglia Ruskin, Bangor, Birmingham, Kent, Leeds, London LSE, Loughborough, Nottingham, Swansea.

Interview advice and questions Past questions have included: What relevance has history to social administration? What do you understand by 'public policy'? What advantage do you think studying social science gives when working in policy fields? How could the image of public management of services be improved? Applicants should be fully aware of the content and the differences between all the courses on offer, why they want to study Social Policy and their career objectives. See also **Chapter 5**.

Reasons for rejection (non-academic) Some universities require attendance when they invite applicants to Open Days (check). Lack of awareness of current social issues. See also **Social Work**. **Bath** Applicant really wanted Business Studies: evidence that teacher, careers adviser or parents are pushing the applicant into the subject or higher education.

AFTER-RESULTS ADVICE
Offers to applicants repeating A-levels Higher Leeds; **Same** Anglia Ruskin, Bangor, Bath, Birmingham, Cardiff, Loughborough, Southampton, York; **No** Glasgow.

GRADUATE DESTINATIONS AND EMPLOYMENT (2015/16 HESA)
Social Policy graduates surveyed 1,450 **Employed** 675 **In voluntary employment** 40 **In further study** 330 **Assumed unemployed** 85

Career note See **Social Sciences/Studies**.

OTHER DEGREE SUBJECTS FOR CONSIDERATION
Behavioural Science; Community Studies; Criminology; Economic and Social History; Economics; Education; Government; Health Studies; Human Resource Management; Law; Politics; Psychology; Social Work; Sociology; Women's Studies.

SOCIAL SCIENCES/STUDIES

(including **Combined Social Sciences, Criminal Justice, Criminology, Human Rights** and **Police Studies**; see also **Combined and Liberal Arts Courses, Education Studies, Health Sciences/Studies, Law, Politics, Psychology, Teacher Training**)

Most Social Sciences/Studies courses take a broad view of aspects of society, for example, economics, politics, history, social psychology and urban studies. Applied Social Studies usually focuses on practical and theoretical preparation for a career in social work. These courses are particularly popular with mature students and some universities and colleges offer shortened degree courses for those with relevant work experience.

Useful websites https://volunteeringmatters.org.uk

NB The points totals shown to the left of the institutions are for ease of reference only. It must not be assumed that Tariff points are always used by institutions or that they can be substituted for an offer in grades. The level of an offer is not necessarily indicative of the quality of a course.

COURSE OFFERS INFORMATION
Subject requirements/preferences GCSE Usually English and mathematics; a science may be required. **AL** No subjects specified. **Other** A Disclosure and Barring Service (DBS) check and relevant work experience required for some courses.

Your target offers and examples of degree courses
152 pts Durham – A*AA (Comb Hons Soc Sci) (IB 38 pts)
144 pts Exeter – AAA–ABB (Crimin) (IB 36–32 pts)
        Manchester – AAA–ABB incl sci/maths +interview (Biol Sci Soty) (IB 37–32 pts HL 5/6 sci); AAA (Law Crimin (Yr Abrd)) (IB 37 pts HL 666)
136 pts Cardiff – AAB (Crimin) (HL 18 pts)
        Durham – AAB (Crimin) (IB 36 pts)
        Lancaster – AAB (Law Crimin) (IB 35 pts HL 16 pts); (Crimin Psy) (IB 35 pts)
        London (UCL) – AAB–ABB (Popn Hlth; Sci Soty) (IB 36–34 pts HL 17–16 pts)
        York – AAB (Soc Pol Sci; Crimin) (IB 35 pts)
128 pts Bath – ABB–BBB+bEPQ (Soc Sci) (IB 34 pts)
        Bristol – ABB–BBC (Chld St) (IB 32–29 pts HL 16–14 pts)
        Cardiff – ABB (Crimin Soc Plcy; Crimin Sociol) (HL 17 pts)
        City – ABB 128 pts (Crimin Sociol) (IB 32 pts)
        Lancaster – ABB (Crimin) (IB 32 pts HL 16 pts)
        Leeds – ABB (Chld St) (IB 34 pts HL 655); (Soc Plcy Crm) (IB 35 pts HL 655)
        Leicester – ABB–BBB+bEPQ (Crimin) (IB 30 pts)
        Liverpool John Moores – ABB 128 pts (Foren Psy Crim Just) (IB 30 pts)

UCAS points Tariff: A* = 56 pts; A = 48 pts; B = 40 pts; C = 32 pts; D = 24 pts; E = 16 pts

London (RH) – ABB–BBB (Crimin Sociol) (IB 32 pts HL 555)
Loughborough – ABB (Crimin Soc Plcy) (IB 34 pts HL 655)
Manchester – ABB (Soc Anth Crimin; Crimin) (IB 33 pts HL 655)
Queen's Belfast – ABB (Crimin)
Stirling – ABB (3 yr course) BBB (4 yr course) (Crimin Sociol) (IB 35 pts (3 yr course) 32 pts (4 yr course))
Surrey – ABB (Law Crimin; Crimin Sociol) (IB 32 pts)

120 pts **Aberystwyth** – BBB (Hum Rts) (IB 30 pts)
Anglia Ruskin – 120 pts (Crimin courses) (IB 24 pts)
Cardiff – BBB (Soc Sci) (HL 17–16 pts)
Central Lancashire – 120 pts (Plcg Crim Invstg)
Coventry – BBB (Soc Sci) (IB 27 pts)
Derby – 120–128 pts (Plcg); 120–128 pts incl biol/chem (Foren Sci Crimin)
Edge Hill – BBB 120 pts (Crimin)
Edinburgh Napier – BBB (3 yr course) BCC (4 yr course) (Soc Sci) (IB 28 pts HL 654)
Essex – BBB (Crimin Am St; Sociol Crimin; Law Hum Rts; Crimin) (IB 30 pts)
Gloucestershire – BBB 120 pts (Crimin)
Greenwich – 120 pts (Crimin; Crimin Crim Psy)
Huddersfield – BBB 120 pts (Psy Crimin)
Kent – BBB (Crimin; Crimin Comb Hons) (IB 34 pts)
Liverpool – BBB (Crimin) (IB 30 pts)
Liverpool Hope – BBB–BBC 120–112 pts (Crimin)
Liverpool John Moores – BBB 120 pts (Law Crim Just) (IB 26 pts)
London (Birk) – 120 pts (Crimin Crim Just)
Northumbria – 120–128 pts (Crimin; Crimin Foren Sci; Integ Hlth Soc Cr) (HL 444)
Staffordshire – BBB 120 pts (Psy Crimin)
Stranmillis (UC) – BBB (Ely Chld St)
Ulster – BBB–ABB (Crimin Crim Just) (IB 26–27 pts HL 13 pts)
UWE Bristol – 120 pts (Crimin Psy; Crimin)
York – BBB (App Soc Sci) (IB 31 pts)

112 pts **Aberystwyth** – BBC (Crimin) (IB 28 pts)
Bangor – 112–96 pts (Crimin Crim Just)
Birmingham City – BBC 112 pts (Crimin courses; Crimin Plcg Invstg) (HL 14 pts)
Bolton – 112 pts (Crm Crim Just)
Brighton – BBC–CCC 112–96 pts (Soc Sci; Crimin Sociol; App Psy Crimin) (IB 28 pts)
Central Lancashire – 112 pts (Crimin courses)
Chester – BBC–BCC 112 pts (Crimin) (IB 26 pts); BCC–BBC 112 pts (Law Crimin) (IB 26 pts)
Coventry – BBC (Sociol Crimin) (IB 29 pts)
De Montfort – 112 pts (Law Hum Rts Soc Just) (IB 26 pts)
East London – 112 pts (Crimin Crim Just) (IB 25 pts HL 15 pts)
Glyndŵr – 112 pts (Crimin Crim Just)
Greenwich – 112 pts incl maths/sci (Foren Sci Crimin)
Huddersfield – BBC 112 pts (Crimin)
Hull – 112 pts (Psy Crimin; Crimin) (IB 28 pts)
Keele – BBC (Crimin; Crimin Comb Hons) (IB 30 pts)
Kent – BBC (Crim Just Crimin; Soc Sci) (IB 34 pts)
Kingston – 112 pts (Hum Rts); 112–120 pts (Crimin courses)
Liverpool John Moores – BBC 112 pts (Crim Just; Crimin Psy; Crimin) (IB 26 pts)
London Met – BBC 112 pts (Crimin courses)
Manchester Met – 112 pts incl soc sci/hum (Crimin) (IB 26 pts); 112–120 pts (Crimin Comb Hons) (IB 26 pts)
Middlesex – 112 pts (Crimin courses; Crimin (Plcg); Crimin (Yth Just))
Nottingham Trent – BBC 112 pts (Crimin; Law Crimin)
Roehampton – 112 pts (Crimin)
Sheffield Hallam – 112–96 pts (Crimin Psy; Crimin; Crimin Sociol)

Check **Chapter 3** for new university admission details and **Chapter 6** on how to read the subject tables.

Southampton Solent – 112 pts (Crimin; Crim Invstg Psy)
Staffordshire – BBC 112 pts (Plcg Crim Invstg)
Teesside – BBC (Crm Scn Sci)
West London – BBC 112–120 pts (Crimin; Psy Crimin/Cnslg Theor)
Westminster – BBC (Crimin) (IB 28 pts)
Wolverhampton – BBC–CCC (Plcg Intel; Crimin Crim Just)
Worcester – 112 pts (Crimin Pol)

104 pts **Abertay** – BCC (Crimin) (IB 29 pts)
Brighton – BCC–CCC 104–96 pts +interview (Hum War Cnflct Modnty) (IB 27 pts)
Coventry – BCC (Crimin) (IB 27 pts)
De Montfort – 104 pts (Crimin) (IB 24 pts)
Edinburgh Napier – BCC incl Engl (Plcg Crimin) (IB 28 pts HL 654); (Crimin) (IB 29 pts HL 655)
Leeds Beckett – 104 pts (Crimin Psy; Crimin) (IB 24 pts)
Leeds Trinity – 104 pts (Crimin Sociol)
Lincoln – BCC (Crimin Soc Plcy; Crimin) (IB 28 pts)
Liverpool John Moores – 104 pts (Crimin Sociol) (IB 24 pts)
London (Birk) – 104 pts (Soc Sci)
London South Bank – BCC (Crimin)
Northampton – BCC (Crimin)
Nottingham Trent – 104 pts (Comm Soty (Comb Hons))
Plymouth – 104 pts (Crimin Crim Just St) (IB 26 pts HL 4)
Robert Gordon – BCC (App Soc Sci) (IB 28 pts)
St Mary's – 104 pts (Educ Soc Sci)
Sheffield Hallam – 104–88 pts (App Soc Sci)
South Wales – BCC–CDD (Plcg Sci; Crimin Crim Just) (HL 655–445)
Sunderland – 104 pts (Crimin)
Winchester – 104–120 pts (Crimin) (IB 26 pts)

96 pts **Bishop Grosseteste** – 96–112 pts (Ely Chld St courses)
Bucks New – 96–112 pts (Plcg St courses)
Canterbury Christ Church – 96–120 pts (App Crimin; Plcg)
Cumbria – 96–112 pts (Crimin Plcg Invstg; Crimin Soc Sci; Crimin Law)
Derby – 96–112 pts (Crimin)
Portsmouth – 96–128 pts (Crimin Crim Just) (IB 30 pts HL 17 pts); (Crimin Cybercrim)
(IB 30 pts)
West Scotland – CCC incl Engl (Crim Just) (IB 24 pts)

88 pts **Teesside** – 88–104 pts (Psy Crimin)

80 pts **Bedfordshire** – 80 pts (Crimin; Soc St)
Bucks New – 80–96 pts (Crimin)
Teesside – 80–96 pts (Crim Invstg; Crimin courses)
Wolverhampton – BB/CDD incl biol/chem +interview (Foren Sci Crimin)

72 pts **Farnborough (CT)** – 72 pts (Psy Crimin)
UHI – BC (Soc Sci)

64 pts **London (Gold)** – CC (App Soc Sci Commun Dev Yth Wk)

Open University – contact 0300 303 0073 **or** www.open.ac.uk/contact/new
(Crimin Psy; Comb Soc Sci (Econ/Geog/Psy/Sociol))

Alternative offers
See **Chapter 6** and **Appendix 1** for grades/UCAS Tariff points information for other examinations.

EXAMPLES OF DEGREE APPRENTICESHIPS IN THIS SUBJECT FIELD
Liverpool John Moores (Plcg).

EXAMPLES OF COLLEGES OFFERING COURSES IN THIS SUBJECT FIELD
See also **Social and Public Policy and Administration**. Accrington and Rossendale (Coll); Blackburn
(Coll); Blackpool and Fylde (Coll); Bolton (Coll); Cornwall (Coll); Coventry (Coll); Derby (Coll); Doncaster

(Coll); Ealing, Hammersmith and West London (Coll); Exeter (Coll); Gloucestershire (Coll); Grŵp Llandrillo Menai; Lincoln (Coll); Middlesbrough (Coll); MidKent (Coll); North Lindsey (Coll); Norwich City (Coll); Peterborough (Coll); Richmond-upon-Thames (Coll); Sir Gâr (Coll); South Essex (Coll); Stamford New (Coll); Truro and Penwith (Coll); Warwickshire (Coll); West Anglia (Coll); Wirral Met (Coll); York (Coll).

CHOOSING YOUR COURSE (SEE ALSO CH.1)
Universities and colleges teaching quality See www.qaa.ac.uk; https://unistats.ac.uk.

Top research universities and colleges (REF 2014) See individual social science subjects.

Examples of sandwich degree courses Bath; Coventry; Middlesex; Portsmouth; Surrey; Teesside.

ADMISSIONS INFORMATION
Number of applicants per place (approx) Abertay 4; Bangor 5; Bath 6; Bradford 15; Bristol (Chld St) 6; Cardiff 5; Cornwall (Coll) 2; Cumbria 4; De Montfort 1; Durham 6; East London 10; Edge Hill 5; Hull 5; Kingston 5; Leicester (Crimin) 5; Liverpool 10; London South Bank 3; Manchester Met 10; Middlesex 26; Northampton 5; Nottingham Trent 2; Roehampton 6; Sheffield Hallam 7; Staffordshire 2; Sunderland 11; West Scotland 5; Westminster 14; Winchester 5; York 5.

Advice to applicants and planning the UCAS personal statement The Social Sciences/Studies subject area covers several topics. Focus on these (or some of these) and state your main areas of interest, outlining your work experience, personal goals and motivation to follow the course. Show your interest in current affairs and especially in social issues and government policies.

Misconceptions about this course Cornwall (Coll) That students transfer to Plymouth at the end of Year 1: this is a three-year course in Cornwall.

Selection interviews Yes Anglia Ruskin; **Some** Bath, Cornwall (Coll), Kingston, Robert Gordon; **No** Bangor, Birmingham City, Coventry, Cumbria, Edge Hill, Essex, Glasgow Caledonian, Hull, Nottingham Trent, Roehampton, Staffordshire, Sunderland, West London, West Scotland, Westminster, Winchester.

Interview advice and questions Past questions have included: Define democracy. What is the role of the Church in nationalistic aspirations? Does today's government listen to its people? Questions on current affairs. How would you change the running of your school? What are the faults of the Labour Party/Conservative Party? Do you agree with the National Lottery? Is money from the National Lottery well spent? Give examples of how the social services have failed. What is your understanding of the social origins of problems? See also **Chapter 5**.

Reasons for rejection (non-academic) Stated preference for other institutions. Incompetence in answering questions.

AFTER-RESULTS ADVICE
Offers to applicants repeating A-levels Same Abertay, Anglia Ruskin, Bangor, Bradford, Chester, Cornwall (Coll), Coventry, Cumbria, Durham, Essex, Gloucestershire, Leeds, Liverpool, London Met, London South Bank, Manchester Met, Nottingham Trent, Roehampton, Sheffield Hallam, Staffordshire, Stirling, Winchester, Wolverhampton; **No** Glasgow.

GRADUATE DESTINATIONS AND EMPLOYMENT (2015/16 HESA)
See **Law**, **Politics** and **Psychology**

Career note Graduates find careers in all aspects of social provision, for example health services, welfare agencies such as housing departments, the probation service, police forces, the prison service, personnel work and residential care and other careers not necessarily linked with their degree subjects.

OTHER DEGREE SUBJECTS FOR CONSIDERATION
Business Studies; Community Studies; Economics; Education; Geography; Government; Health Studies; Law; Politics; Psychology; Public Administration; Social Policy; Social Work; Sociology; Urban Studies.

SOCIAL WORK

(see also **Community Studies/Development, Social and Public Policy and Administration**)

Social Work courses (which lead to careers in social work) have similarities to those in Applied Social Studies, Social Policy and Administration, Community Studies and Health Studies. If you are offered a place on a Social Work course which leads to registration as a social worker, you must undergo the Disclosure and Barring Service (DBS) check. You will also have to provide health information and certification. Check for full details of training and careers in social work with the Health and Care Council (see **Appendix 3**). Students from England may be eligible for student bursaries from the NHS Business Services Authority.

Useful websites www.ageuk.org.uk; www.samaritans.org; https://socialcare.wales; www.sssc. uk.com; www.niscc.info; www.basw.co.uk

NB The points totals shown to the left of the institutions are for ease of reference only. It must not be assumed that Tariff points are always used by institutions or that they can be substituted for an offer in grades. The level of an offer is not necessarily indicative of the quality of a course.

COURSE OFFERS INFORMATION

Subject requirements/preferences GCSE English and mathematics usually required. **AL** No subjects specified. **Other** Disclosure and Barring Service (DBS) check and an occupational health check required. Check also with universities for applicant minimum age requirements.

Your target offers and examples of degree courses

128 pts **Bath** – ABB–BBB/BBC+aEPQ (Soc Wk App Soc St) (IB 34 pts)

Birmingham – ABB (Soc Wk) (IB 32 pts HL 655)

Brighton – ABB–BBC 128–112 pts +interview (Soc Wk) (IB 32 pts)

Edinburgh – ABB (Soc Wk) (IB 36 pts)

Lancaster – ABB (Soc Wk) (IB 32 pts)

Leeds – ABB (Soc Wk) (IB 34 pts)

Nottingham – ABB +interview (Soc Wk) (IB 32 pts)

Queen's Belfast – ABB (Soc Wk)

Strathclyde – ABB–BBB (Soc Wk)

Sussex – ABB–BBB (Soc Wk) (IB 30 pts); (Chld Yth (Theor Prac)) (IB 32 pts)

120 pts **Bournemouth** – 120–128 pts +interview (Soc Wk) (IB 31–32 pts)

Bradford – BBB 120 pts +interview (Soc Wk)

Coventry – BBB (Soc Wk) (IB 30 pts)

East Anglia – BBB (Soc Wk) (IB 31 pts)

East London – 120 pts (Soc Wk) (IB 33 pts)

Edge Hill – BBB 120 pts (Soc Wk)

Greenwich – 120 pts (Soc Wk)

Huddersfield – BBB 120 pts (Soc Wk)

Hull – 120 pts (Soc Wk) (IB 28 pts)

Keele – BBB–BBC (Soc Wk) (IB 32–30 pts)

Kent – BBB (Soc Wk) (IB 34 pts)

Leeds Beckett – 120 pts (Soc Wk) (IB 26 pts)

Liverpool Hope – BBB–BBC 120–112 pts (Soc Wk) (IB 26 pts)

London (Gold) – BBB (Soc Wk) (IB 33 pts)

London South Bank – BBB (Soc Wk)

Middlesex – 120 pts (Soc Wk)

Northumbria – 120–128 pts (Soc Wk) (HL 444)

Nottingham Trent – BBB 120 pts (Soc Wk)

Plymouth – 120 pts (Soc Wk) (IB 24 pts)

Sheffield Hallam – 120 pts (Soc Wk)

Stirling – BBB (Soc Wk) (IB 32 pts)
Sunderland – 120 pts (Soc Wk)
UWE Bristol – 120 pts (Soc Wk)
York – BBB +interview (Soc Wk) (IB 31 pts)

112 pts **Anglia Ruskin** – 112 pts +interview (Soc Wk)
Bedfordshire – 112 pts (Soc Wk)
Birmingham City – 112 pts (Soc Wk) (IB 28 pts)
Canterbury Christ Church – BBC (Soc Wk)
Central Lancashire – 112 pts (Soc Wk)
Chester – 112 pts +interview (Soc Wk) (IB 26 pts)
Glyndŵr – 112 pts (Soc Wk)
Hertfordshire – 112–128 pts (Soc Wk) (HL 44)
Kingston – 112 pts (Soc Wk)
Liverpool John Moores – BBC 112 pts (Hlth Soc Cr Indiv Fmly Commun) (IB 26 pts)
London Met – BBC 112 pts (Soc Wk)
Manchester Met – BBC–BBB 112–120 pts +interview (Soc Wk) (IB 29 pts)
Oxford Brookes – BBC 112 pts (Soc Wk) (IB 30 pts)
Portsmouth – 112 pts +interview (Soc Wk) (IB 26 pts)
Southampton Solent – 112 pts (Soc Wk)
South Wales – BBC (Soc Wk) (IB 29 pts)
Staffordshire – BBC 112 pts (Soc Wk)
Teesside – 112–128 pts +interview (Soc Wk)
West London – BBC 112 120 pts (Soc Wk)
Worcester – 112 pts +interview (Soc Wk)

104 pts **Cumbria** – 104–120 pts (Soc Wk)
Gloucestershire – BCC 104 pts +interview (Soc Wk)
Northampton – BCC (Soc Cr Hlth St); 104–120 pts (Soc Wk)
Nottingham Trent – BCC 104 pts (Yth St)
South Wales – BCC–CDD +interview (Yth Commun Wk) (HL 655–445)
Swansea – BCC (Soc Wk) (IB 33–34 pts)
Wolverhampton – BCC +interview (Soc Wk)

96 pts **Birmingham (UC)** – 96 pts (Hlth Soc Cr)
Bucks New – 96–112 pts (Soc Wk)
Cardiff Met – 96 pts (Soc Wk; Hlth Soc Cr)
Chichester – 96–120 pts (Soc Wk) (IB 28 pts)
Cumbria – 96–112 pts (Wkg Chld Fmly)
Derby – 96–112 pts (App Soc Wk; Yth Wk Commun Dev)
Glasgow Caledonian – CCC (Soc Wk) (IB 24 pts)
HOW (Coll) – 96 pts (Soc Wk)
Newman – 96 pts (Wk Chld Yng Ppl Fmly)
Robert Gordon – CCC (Soc Wk) (IB 26 pts)
West Scotland – CCC (Soc Wk) (IB 24 pts)
Winchester – 96–112 pts (Soc Wk) (IB 25 pts)

88 pts **Dundee** – AB–CCC (Soc Wk) (IB 29 pts)
St Mark and St John – CCD +interview (Yth Commun Wk)
Winchester – 88–104 pts (Hlth Commun Soc Cr St) (IB 24 pts)

80 pts **Bedfordshire** – 80 pts (Hlth Soc Cr)

64 pts **Colchester (Inst)** – 64 pts +interview (Hlth Soc Cr)
London (Gold) – CC (App Soc Sci Commun Dev Yth Wk)

Open University – contact 0300 303 0073 **or** www.open.ac.uk/contact/new (Soc Wk)

Alternative offers
See **Chapter 6** and **Appendix 1** for grades/UCAS Tariff points information for other examinations.

EXAMPLES OF COLLEGES OFFERING COURSES IN THIS SUBJECT FIELD

See also **Social and Public Policy and Administration**. Barnfield (Coll); Birmingham Met (Coll); Blackburn (Coll); Bradford (Coll); Cornwall (Coll); Durham New (Coll); East Coast (Coll); Exeter (Coll); Furness (Coll); Gateshead (Coll); Grimsby (Inst Group); Gŵp Llandrillo Menai; Harrogate (Coll); Hartlepool (CFE); HOW (Coll); Hull (Coll); Leeds City (Coll); Liverpool City (Coll); MidKent (Coll); Newcastle (Coll); North Lindsey (Coll); Norwich City (Coll); Nottingham (Coll); Sir Gâr (Coll); South Cheshire (Coll); South City Birmingham (Coll); South Gloucestershire and Stroud (Coll); South Thames (Coll); Southport (Coll); Stockport (Coll); Truro and Penwith (Coll); Warrington and Vale Royal (Coll); Warwickshire (Coll); Wiltshire (Coll); Wirral Met (Coll).

CHOOSING YOUR COURSE (SEE ALSO CH.1)

Universities and colleges teaching quality See www.qaa.ac.uk; https://unistats.ac.uk.

Top research universities and colleges (REF 2014) (Social Work and Social Policy) London LSE; Oxford; East Anglia; Kent; Teesside; York; Leicester; London (UCL); Southampton; Glasgow; Edinburgh; Bath; Bristol.

ADMISSIONS INFORMATION

Number of applicants per place (approx) Bath 6; Birmingham 13; Bradford 10; Dundee 4; London Met 27; Northampton 7; Nottingham Trent 6; Sheffield Hallam 4; Staffordshire 3.

Advice to applicants and planning the UCAS personal statement The statement should show motivation for social work, relevant work experience, awareness of the demands of social work and give relevant personal information, for example disabilities. Awareness of the origins of personal and family difficulties, commitment to anti-discriminatory practice. Most applicants will have significant experience of a statutory care agency or voluntary/private organisation providing a social work or social care service. See also **Social and Public Policy and Administration** and **Appendix 4**.

Selection interviews Yes Anglia Ruskin, Bath, Bedfordshire, Birmingham, Birmingham City, Bolton, Bournemouth, Bradford, Brighton, Canterbury Christ Church, Cardiff Met, Central Lancashire, Chichester, Coventry, Cumbria, East Anglia, Edge Hill, Glyndŵr, Greenwich, Hertfordshire, Huddersfield, Hull, Keele, Kent, Leeds Beckett, Liverpool Hope, London Met, Middlesex, Newman, Northumbria, Nottingham, Nottingham Trent, Plymouth, Portsmouth, Queen's Belfast, Robert Gordon, Sheffield Hallam, South Wales, Suffolk, Sussex, UWE Bristol, West London, Wolverhampton, Worcester, York; **Some** Winchester; **No** Chester, Dundee, Edinburgh, Gloucestershire, Lancaster, Liverpool John Moores, Staffordshire, Sunderland, Swansea, West Scotland.

Interview advice and questions What qualities are needed to be a social worker? What use do you think you will be to society as a social worker? Why should money be spent on prison offenders? Your younger brother is playing truant and mixing with bad company. Your parents don't know. What would you do? See also **Social and Public Policy and Administration** and **Chapter 5**.

Reasons for rejection (non-academic) Criminal convictions.

AFTER-RESULTS ADVICE

Offers to applicants repeating A-levels Same Lincoln, Liverpool Hope, Staffordshire, Suffolk, Wolverhampton.

GRADUATE DESTINATIONS AND EMPLOYMENT (2015/16 HESA)

Graduates surveyed 7,195 **Employed** 4,040 **In voluntary employment** 80 **In further study** 1,425 **Assumed unemployed** 300

Career note See **Social Sciences/Studies**.

OTHER DEGREE SUBJECTS FOR CONSIDERATION

Community Studies; Conductive Education; Criminology; Economics; Education; Health Studies; Law; Psychology; Public Sector Management and Administration; Social Policy; Sociology; Youth Studies.

SOCIOLOGY

(see also **Anthropology, Social and Public Policy and Administration**)

Sociology is the study of social organisation, social structures, systems, institutions and practices. Courses are likely to include the meaning and structure of, for example, race, ethnicity and gender, industrial behaviour, crime and deviance, health and illness. **NB** Sociology is not a training course for social workers, although some graduates take additional qualifications to qualify in social work.

Useful websites www.britsoc.co.uk; www.asanet.org; www.sociology.org.uk; www.sociology.org

NB The points totals shown to the left of the institutions are for ease of reference only. It must not be assumed that Tariff points are always used by institutions or that they can be substituted for an offer in grades. The level of an offer is not necessarily indicative of the quality of a course.

COURSE OFFERS INFORMATION

Subject requirements/preferences GCSE English and mathematics usually required. **AL** No subjects specified.

Your target offers and examples of degree courses

152 pts **Cambridge** – A*AA +interview +HSPSAA (Hum Soc Pol Sci (Pol Sociol)) (IB 40–42 pts HL 776)

144 pts **Exeter** – AAA–ABB (Sociol Comb Hons) (IB 34–32 pts)

136 pts **Bath** – AAB–ABB+aEPQ (Sociol) (IB 35 pts)
Bristol – AAB–BBB (Sociol; Sociol Phil; Pol Sociol) (IB 34–31 pts)
Durham – AAB (Anth Sociol; Sociol) (IB 36 pts)
Edinburgh – AAB (Sociol; Soc Plcy Soc Econ Hist) (IB 39 pts HL 666)
Exeter – AAB–ABB (Sociol) (IB 34–32 pts)
Glasgow – AAB–BBB incl arts/lang (Sociol) (IB 36–34 pts)
Lancaster – AAB–ABB (Film Sociol) (IB 35–32 pts HL 16 pts); (Sociol; Pol Sociol; Relig St Sociol) (IB 35–32 pts)
London LSE – AAB (Soc Plcy Sociol; Sociol) (IB 37 pts HL 666)
Manchester – AAB (Econ Sociol; Bus St Sociol) (IB 35 pts HL 665)
Southampton – AAB–ABB (Phil Sociol) (IB 34–32 pts)
Warwick – AAB (Law Sociol) (IB 36 pts)

128 pts **Aston** – ABB (Pol Sociol) (IB 32 pts); ABB–BBB (Sociol courses) (IB 33–32 pts)
Bath – ABB–BBB+bEPQ (Soc Sci) (IB 34 pts)
Birmingham – ABB (Educ Sociol) (IB 32 pts HL 655)
Bristol – ABB–BBC (Soc Plcy Sociol) (IB 32–29 pts HL 16–14 pts)
Cardiff – ABB (Sociol Hist; Jrnl Media Sociol; Sociol) (HL 17 pts)
City – ABB–BBB 128–120 pts (Sociol Psy) (IB 32 pts); ABB–BBB (Sociol) (IB 32 pts)
Essex – BBB (Sociol) (IB 30 pts)
Lancaster – ABB (Crimin Sociol) (IB 32 pts)
Leeds – ABB (Sociol; Soc Pol Sociol) (IB 34 pts HL 655); (Russ Sociol) (IB 34 pts)
Leicester – BBB–BBC+bEPQ (Sociol) (IB 28 pts)
Loughborough – ABB (Sociol) (IB 34 pts)
Manchester – ABB (Sociol; Pol Sociol) (IB 33 pts)
Newcastle – ABB–BBB (Sociol) (IB 32–30 pts)
Nottingham – ABB (Sociol; Sociol Soc Plcy) (IB 32 pts)
Sheffield – ABB–BBB+bEPQ (Pol Sociol) (IB 33 pts); ABB incl Engl/lang (Engl Lang Sociol) (IB 33 pts HL 6 Engl/lang)
Southampton – ABB–BBB (Sociol) (IB 32 pts); ABB–BBB+aEPQ (Sociol Soc Plcy) (IB 32 pts HL 16 pts)
Stirling – ABB (3 yr course) BBB (4 yr course) (Sociol Soc Plcy) (IB 35 pts (3 yr course) 32 pts (4 yr course))
Surrey – ABB (Sociol) (IB 32 pts)

Sussex – ABB–BBB (Sociol) (IB 30 pts)

Warwick – ABB (Sociol) (IB 34 pts)

York – ABB (Sociol; Sociol Soc Psy; Sociol Educ) (IB 34 pts)

120 pts **Aberdeen** – BBB (Sociol) (IB 32 pts)

Anglia Ruskin – 120 pts (Sociol) (IB 24 pts)

Aston – BBB (Psy Sociol) (IB 31 pts)

Brunel – BBB (Anth Sociol) (IB 30 pts)

Cardiff – BBB (Educ Sociol) (HL 17–16 pts)

Essex – BBB (Sociol Crimin; Sociol Hum Rts) (IB 30 pts)

Kent – BBB (Sociol; Sociol (Yr Abrd)) (IB 34 pts)

Liverpool – BBB (Sociol) (IB 30 pts)

London (Gold) – BBB (Sociol) (IB 33 pts)

Northumbria – 120–128 pts (Sociol) (HL 444)

Plymouth – BBB 120 pts (Psy Sociol) (IB 28 pts)

Queen's Belfast – BBB–ABB (Sociol courses)

Sheffield – BBB (Sociol Soc Plcy) (IB 32 pts)

112 pts **Bangor** – 112–96 pts (Sociol Soc Pol; Sociol; Sociol Comb Hons)

Birmingham City – BBC 112 pts (Sociol; Sociol Crimin) (HL 14 pts)

Brighton – BBC–CCC 112–96 pts (Sociol courses; Crimin Sociol; App Psy Sociol) (IB 28 pts)

Brunel – BBC (Sociol (Media); Sociol) (IB 29 pts)

Chester – BBC–BCC 112 pts (Sociol) (IB 26 pts)

Coventry – BBC (Sociol; Sociol Crimin) (IB 29 pts)

East London – 112 pts (Sociol) (IB 25 pts)

Edge Hill – BBC 112 pts (Sociol)

Gloucestershire – BBC 112 pts (Sociol)

Greenwich – 112 pts (Sociol)

Huddersfield – BBC 112 pts (Sociol)

Hull – 112 pts (Sociol) (IB 28 pts)

Keele – BBC (Sociol; Sociol Comb Hons) (IB 30 pts)

Kingston – 112 pts (Sociol)

London Met – BBC 112 pts (Sociol)

Manchester Met – BBC–BBB (Psy Sociol) (IB 26 pts); 112 pts incl soc sci/hum (Sociol) (IB 26 pts)

Nottingham Trent – BBC 112 pts (Sociol)

Oxford Brookes – BBC 112 pts (Sociol) (IB 30 pts)

Roehampton – 112 pts (Sociol)

Sheffield Hallam – 112–96 pts (Sociol)

Staffordshire – BBC 112 pts (Sociol)

Suffolk – BBC (Sociol Law; App Sociol Relig St)

UWE Bristol – 112 pts (Sociol)

Westminster – BBC (Sociol) (IB 28 pts)

Wolverhampton – BBC–CCC (Sociol Pol; Sociol); BBC (Relig St Sociol; Phil Sociol)

104 pts **Abertay** – BCC (Sociol) (IB 29 pts)

Bath Spa – BCC–CCC (Sociol; Sociol Comb Hons) (IB 26 pts)

Bournemouth – 104–120 pts (Sociol) (IB 30 pts HL 55)

Central Lancashire – 104 pts (Sociol)

Edinburgh Napier – BCC incl Engl (Psy Sociol) (IB 28 pts HL 5 Engl)

Leeds Beckett – 104 pts (Sociol) (IB 24 pts)

Liverpool John Moores – 104 pts (Sociol; Crimin Sociol) (IB 24 pts)

London South Bank – BCC (Sociol)

Northampton – BCC (Sociol)

Plymouth – 104–120 pts (Sociol) (IB 26 pts)

Salford – 104–112 pts (Sociol) (IB 30–31 pts)

South Wales – BCC–CCD (Sociol Crimin Crim Just) (HL 655–445)

Sunderland – 104 pts (Sociol)

Ulster – BCC–BBC (Sociol Pol); (Sociol) (IB 24–25 pts)
Winchester – 104–120 pts (Sociol) (IB 26 pts)
Worcester – 104 pts (Sociol)
96 pts **Bedfordshire** – 96 pts (Crimin Sociol)
Bishop Grosseteste – 96–112 pts (Sociol)
Bradford – CCC 96 pts (Sociol)
Derby – 96–112 pts (Sociol); 96–128 pts (Sociol Comb Hons)
Middlesex – 96 pts (Sociol)
Portsmouth – 96–120 pts (Sociol; Sociol Psy) (IB 26 pts)
88 pts **Canterbury Christ Church** – 88–112 pts (Sociol Soc Plcy; Sociol)
Queen Margaret – CCD (Psy Sociol) (IB 26 pts)
72 pts **Teesside** – 72–88 pts +interview (Sociol)

Alternative offers
See **Chapter 6** and **Appendix 1** for grades/UCAS Tariff points information for other examinations.

EXAMPLES OF COLLEGES OFFERING COURSES IN THIS SUBJECT FIELD
Blackburn (Coll); Bury (Coll); Cornwall (Coll); Farnborough (CT); Lincoln (Coll); Milton Keynes (Coll); Newham (CFE); Norwich City (Coll); Peterborough (Coll); Petroc; Richmond-upon-Thames (Coll); South Devon (Coll); Totton (Coll); West Anglia (Coll).

CHOOSING YOUR COURSE (SEE ALSO CH.1)
Universities and colleges teaching quality See www.qaa.ac.uk; https://unistats.ac.uk.

Top research universities and colleges (REF 2014) York; Cardiff; Manchester; Lancaster; Edinburgh; Oxford; London LSE; Essex; Exeter.

Examples of sandwich degree courses Aston; Bath; Brunel; Coventry; Middlesex; Surrey.

ADMISSIONS INFORMATION
Number of applicants per place (approx) Aston 8; Bangor 6; Bath 6; Birmingham 8; Birmingham City 12; Bristol 6; Cardiff 5; City 6; Durham 4; East London 8; Exeter 5; Gloucestershire 8; Greenwich 5; Hull 5; Kent 5; Kingston 9; Lancaster 6; Leeds 14; Leicester 4; Liverpool 10; Liverpool John Moores 10; London (Gold) 5; London LSE 8; London Met 3; Manchester 8; Northampton 3; Nottingham 5; Oxford Brookes 8; Plymouth 5; Roehampton 5; Sheffield Hallam 7; Southampton 4; Staffordshire 10; Sunderland 5; Warwick 20; Worcester 5; York 5.

Advice to applicants and planning the UCAS personal statement Show your ability to communicate and work as part of a group and your curiosity about issues such as social conflict and social change between social groups. Discuss your interests in sociology on the personal statement. Demonstrate an intellectual curiosity about sociology and social problems. See also **Social Sciences/ Studies**. **Bristol** Deferred entry accepted.

Misconceptions about this course Some applicants believe that all sociologists want to become social workers. **Birmingham** Students with an interest in crime and deviance may be disappointed that we do not offer modules in this area. **London Met** That it is the stamping ground of student activists and has no relevance to the real world.

Selection interviews Yes Anglia Ruskin, Cambridge; **Some** Bath, Cardiff, Liverpool John Moores, London (Gold), Southampton, Warwick; **No** Aston, Birmingham, Birmingham City, Bristol, City, Derby, East London, Essex, Hull, Kent, Leeds, Leicester, Liverpool, Loughborough, Newcastle, Nottingham, Nottingham Trent, Portsmouth, St Mary's, Salford, Sheffield Hallam, Staffordshire, Surrey.

Interview advice and questions Past questions have included: Why do you want to study Sociology? What books have you read on the subject? How do you see the role of women changing in the next 20 years? See also **Chapter 5**.

Reasons for rejection (non-academic) Evidence of difficulty with written work. Non-attendance at Open Days (find out from your universities if your attendance will affect their offers). 'In the middle of an interview for Sociology, a student asked us if we could interview him for Sports Studies instead!' See also **Social and Public Policy and Administration**. **Durham** No evidence of awareness of what the course involves. **London Met** References which indicated that the individual would not be able to work effectively within a diverse student group; concern that the applicant had not put any serious thought into the choice of subject for study.

AFTER-RESULTS ADVICE
Offers to applicants repeating A-levels Higher East London, Newcastle, Nottingham Trent, Warwick, York; **Possibly higher** Leeds, Liverpool; **Same** Aston, Bangor, Bath, Birmingham, Birmingham City, Bristol, Brunel, Cardiff, Coventry, Derby, Durham, Essex, Gloucestershire, Hull, Kingston, Lancaster, Liverpool John Moores, London Met, Loughborough, Northumbria, Roehampton, St Mary's, Salford, Sheffield Hallam, Southampton, Staffordshire; **No** Cambridge, Glasgow.

GRADUATE DESTINATIONS AND EMPLOYMENT (2015/16 HESA)
Graduates surveyed 6,095 **Employed** 2,860 **In voluntary employment** 195 **In further study** 1,515 **Assumed unemployed** 360

Career note See **Social Sciences/Studies**.

OTHER DEGREE SUBJECTS FOR CONSIDERATION
Anthropology; Economic and Social History; Economics; Education; Geography; Government; Health Studies; History; Law; Politics; Psychology; Social Policy; Social Work.

SPANISH

(including Hispanic Studies and Portuguese; see also Languages, Latin American Studies)

Spanish can be studied by focusing on the language and literature of Spain. Broader courses in Hispanic Studies (see also **Latin American Studies**) are available which also include Portuguese and Latin American studies. See also **Appendix 3** under Languages.

Useful websites www.donquijote.co.uk; http://europa.eu; www.ciol.org.uk; www.bbc.co.uk/languages; www.languageadvantage.com; www.languagematters.co.uk; https://studyspanish.com; www.spanishlanguageguide.com; see also **Latin American Studies**.

NB The points totals shown to the left of the institutions are for ease of reference only. It must not be assumed that Tariff points are always used by institutions or that they can be substituted for an offer in grades. The level of an offer is not necessarily indicative of the quality of a course.

COURSE OFFERS INFORMATION
Subject requirements/preferences GCSE English, mathematics or science and a foreign language. **AL** Spanish required for most courses.

Your target offers and examples of degree courses
152 pts **Cambridge** – A*AA incl lang +interview +MMLAA (Modn Mediev Langs) (IB 40–42 pts HL 776)

Imperial London – A*AA–A*A*A incl sci/maths (Span Sci courses) (IB 40–42 pts HL 766 incl 7/6 sci+maths); A*AA–A*A*A* incl chem+maths +interview (Chem Fr/Ger/Span Sci) (IB 40–42 pts HL 7 chem 6 maths)

St Andrews – A*AA incl maths (Maths Span) (IB 36 pts)
144 pts **Bath** – AAA–AAB+aEPQ incl Span (Int Mgt Span) (IB 36 pts HL 666)

London (UCL) – AAA–ABB incl lang (Modn Langs) (IB 34–36 pts HL 6 lang)

Oxford – AAA incl Span +interview +MLAT (Span courses) (IB 38 pts); AAA +interview +MLAT (Port courses) (IB 38 pts)

St Andrews – AAA (Mgt Span) (IB 38 pts)

UCAS points Tariff: A* = 56 pts; A = 48 pts; B = 40 pts; C = 32 pts; D = 24 pts; E = 16 pts

Southampton – AAA–AAB+aEPQ incl maths+Fr/Ger/Span (Maths Fr/Ger/Span) (IB 36 pts HL 6 maths)

Strathclyde – AAA–BBB (Span courses) (IB 36 pts)

Surrey – AAA–AAB incl Span (Span courses) (IB 34–32 pts)

136 pts Birmingham – AAB incl hist (Hisp St Hist) (IB 32 pts HL 665)

Edinburgh – AAB incl lang (Int Bus Fr/Ger/Span) (IB 43 pts HL 776)

Exeter – AAB–ABB incl Span/Arbc (Span Arbc) (IB 34–32 pts HL 5 Span/Arbc)

Glasgow – AAB–BBB incl arts/hum/lang (Span) (IB 36–34 pts HL 665 incl Eng+hum/lang)

Lancaster – AAB–ABB (Span St) (IB 35–32 pts); AAB incl geog (Span St Geog) (IB 35 pts HL 6 geog)

London (King's) – AAB (Euro St (Fr/Ger/Span) (Yr Abrd)) (IB 35 pts HL 665); AAB incl Fr (Fr Span (Yr Abrd)) (IB 35 pts HL 665 incl 6 Fr)

London (RH) – AAB–BBB (Modn Lang Lat) (IB 32 pts HL 555)

London (UCL) – AAB incl Span (Span Lat Am St) (IB 36 pts HL 6 Span)

St Andrews – AAB (Span courses) (IB 36 pts)

Southampton – AAB incl Span/Port +interview (Pol Span/Port Lat Am St) (IB 34 pts HL 6 Span/Port); AAB–ABB incl Fr/Ger/Span (Film Fr/Ger/Span) (IB 32 pts HL 6 Fr/Ger/Span); AAB–ABB incl Span (Span courses) (IB 34 pts HL 6 Span); AAB incl Span +interview (Span (Lat Am St)) (IB 34 pts HL 6 Span); AAB/ABB+aEPQ incl Engl+Fr/Ger/Span (Engl Fr/Ger/Span) (IB 34 pts HL 6 Engl+Fr/Ger/Span)

Swansea – AAB–BBB (Law Span)

Warwick – AAB incl lang (Hisp St courses) (IB 36 pts HL 5 lang)

York – AAB–ABB (Span courses) (IB 35–34 pts); AAB–ABB incl Fr (Fr Sp Lang (Yr Abrd)) (IB 35–34 pts)

128 pts Aston – ABB–BBB incl lang (Int Bus Fr/Ger/Span) (IB 32 pts HL 655–555 incl 5 lang); ABB–BBB incl Span (Span courses) (IB 33–32 pts HL 6 Span)

Bath – ABB–ABC+aEPQ incl lang (Modn Langs Euro St) (IB 35 pts HL 6 lang)

Birmingham – ABB incl lang (Modn Langs Hist Art) (IB 32 pts HL 655)

Bristol – ABB–BBC incl Span (Span) (IB 32–29 pts HL 5 Span); (Hisp St) (IB 32–29 pts HL 5 Span)

Cardiff – ABB–BBC incl Span (Span) (IB 32–30 pts HL 665–655)

Dundee – ABB incl lang (Law Langs) (IB 32 pts HL 655)

Edinburgh – AAB incl lang (Span courses) (IB 39 pts HL 666 incl lang)

Heriot-Watt – ABB incl maths (Maths Span) (IB 28 pts HL 5 maths)

Leeds – ABB incl Span (Span; Span Port Lat Am St) (IB 34 pts HL 6 Span)

Liverpool – ABB incl Span (Hisp St) (IB 33 pts HL 6 Span)

London (RH) – ABB–BBB incl lang (Modn Lang Dr) (IB 32 pts); ABB–BBB (Modn Lang Mus; Euro Int St Fr/Ger/Ital/Span; Modn Lang) (IB 32 pts HL 555)

Manchester – ABB incl lang (Span courses; Span Port) (IB 33 pts HL 655); ABB incl Span +interview (Span Port Lat Am St) (IB 33 pts HL 655)

Northumbria – 128–136 pts (Int Bus Mgt Span) (HL 444)

Nottingham – ABB incl Engl (Engl Hisp St) (IB 32 pts HL 5 Engl); ABB (Span Int Media Comms St) (IB 32 pts); ABB incl Span (Hisp St) (IB 32 pts)

Queen's Belfast – ABB incl Span (Span; Span Port St)

Reading – ABB–BBB (Span) (IB 32–30 pts HL 5 Span)

Sheffield – ABB–BBB+bEPQ (Jap St Comb Hons) (IB 33 pts); ABB incl lang (Hisp St) (IB 33 pts HL 6 lang)

Stirling – ABB (3 yr course) BBB (4 yr course) (Span Lat Am St) (IB 35 pts (3 yr course) 32 pts (4 yr course))

Sussex – ABB–BBB incl Ital/Span (Ital Span (Yr Abrd)) (IB 30 pts HL 5 Ital/Span)

120 pts Dundee – BBB–BCC (Span courses) (IB 30 pts)

Essex – BBB (Span St Modn Langs; Lat Am St courses) (IB 30 pts)

Heriot-Watt – BBB incl lang (App Langs Transl (Fr/Span)/(Ger/Span)) (IB 30 pts HL 5 lang); (Span App Lang St) (IB 30 pts)

London (QM) – BBB–ABB incl lang/hum/soc sci (Hisp St courses; Hisp St) (IB 30–32 pts HL 6/5 lang/hum/soc sci)

Plymouth – 120 pts incl Engl+Span (Engl Span) (IB 28 pts HL 6 Engl)

Swansea – BBB incl lang (Span)

112 pts **Aberystwyth** – BBC–ABB (Span Comb Hons) (IB 28–30 pts)

Central Lancashire – 112 pts (Mod Lang Int Bus); 112 pts incl lang (Modn Langs (Fr/Ger/Span/Jap))

Chester – BBC–BCC incl Span 112 pts (Span courses) (IB 26 pts HL 5 Span)

Hull – 112 pts incl lang (Hist Modn Lang; Span) (IB 28 pts)

Middlesex – 112 pts (Bus Mgt (Mand/Span))

104 pts **London (Birk)** – 104 pts (Span Port Lat Am St); 104 pts incl lang (Modn Langs (Fr/Ger/Ital/Jap/Port/Span))

Manchester Met – 104–112 pts (Ling Mand Chin/Fr/Ger/Ital/Span) (IB 26 pts); 104–112 pts incl Span (Span St) (IB 26 pts)

Nottingham Trent – 104 pts (Span Comb Hons)

Sunderland – 104 pts (Span Comb Hons)

Westminster – BCC (Transl St (Span)) (IB 28 pts HL 4 lang)

96 pts **Bangor** – 96–104 pts incl Span (Span courses)

Plymouth – 96 pts (Int Bus Span) (IB 26 pts HL 4 Span)

Portsmouth – 96–120 pts (Modn Lang)

Alternative offers
See **Chapter 6** and **Appendix 1** for grades/UCAS Tariff points information for other examinations.

EXAMPLES OF COLLEGES OFFERING COURSES IN THIS SUBJECT FIELD
Euro Bus Sch London; Richmond-upon-Thames (Coll).

CHOOSING YOUR COURSE (SEE ALSO CH.1)
Universities and colleges teaching quality See www.qaa.ac.uk; https://unistats.ac.uk.

Top research universities and colleges (REF 2014) See **Languages**.

Examples of sandwich degree courses Bangor.

ADMISSIONS INFORMATION
Number of applicants per place (approx) Birmingham 9; Bristol 4; Cardiff 3; Exeter 5; Hull 5; Leeds 10; Liverpool 6; London (King's) 6; London (QM) 5; London (UCL) 5; Middlesex 2; Nottingham 5; Southampton 8.

Advice to applicants and planning the UCAS personal statement Visits to Spanish-speaking countries should be discussed. Study the geography, culture, literature and politics of Spain (or Portugal) and discuss your interests in full. Further information could be obtained from embassies in London. See also **Appendix 3** under **Languages**.

Selection interviews Yes Cambridge, Leeds, Oxford, Southampton; **Some** Cardiff, London (UCL); **No** Hull, London (QM), Nottingham, Swansea.

Interview advice and questions Candidates offering A-level Spanish are likely to be questioned on their A-level work, their reasons for wanting to take the subject and on their knowledge of Spain and its people. Interest in Spain is important for all applicants. Student comment: 'Mostly questions about the literature I had read and I was given a poem and asked questions on it.' Questions were asked in the target language. 'There were two interviewers for the Spanish interview; they did their best to trip me up and to make me think under pressure by asking aggressive questions.' See **Chapter 5**.

AFTER-RESULTS ADVICE
Offers to applicants repeating A-levels Higher Leeds; **Same** Cardiff, Chester, Hull, Liverpool, Nottingham, Roehampton, Swansea; **No** Cambridge, Glasgow.

GRADUATE DESTINATIONS AND EMPLOYMENT (2015/16 HESA)

Spanish Studies graduates surveyed 820 **Employed** 390 **In voluntary employment** 25 **In further study** 210 **Assumed unemployed** 45

Career note See **Languages**.

OTHER DEGREE SUBJECTS FOR CONSIDERATION

International Business Studies; Latin American Studies; Linguistics; see other language tables.

SPEECH PATHOLOGY/SCIENCES/THERAPY

(including **Healthcare Science**; see also **Communication Studies/Communication, Health Sciences/Studies**)

Speech Pathology/Sciences/Therapy is the study of speech defects caused by accident, disease or psychological trauma. These can include failure to develop communication at the usual age, voice disorders, physical and learning disabilities and stammering. Courses lead to qualification as a speech therapist. This is one of many medical courses. See also **Medicine** and **Appendix 3**.

Useful websites www.rcslt.org; www.speechteach.co.uk; www.asha.org

NB The points totals shown to the left of the institutions are for ease of reference only. It must not be assumed that Tariff points are always used by institutions or that they can be substituted for an offer in grades. The level of an offer is not necessarily indicative of the quality of a course.

COURSE OFFERS INFORMATION

Subject requirements/preferences GCSE English language, a modern foreign language and biology/dual award science at grade B or above (5/6 or above). **AL** At least one science subject; biology may be stipulated, psychology and English language may be preferred. **Other** Disclosure and Barring Service (DBS) and occupational health checks essential for Speech Sciences/Speech Therapy applicants.

Your target offers and examples of degree courses
144 pts **Reading** – AAA–AAB (Sp Lang Thera (MSci)) (IB 35–34 pts)
136 pts **East Anglia** – AAB (Sp Lang Thera) (IB 33 pts HL 666)
         Manchester – AAB (Sp Lang Thera) (IB 35 pts)
         Queen Margaret – AAB incl sci/maths (Sp Lang Thera) (IB 32 pts)
         Strathclyde – AAB–ABB incl Engl+maths+sci (Sp Lang Path) (IB 32 pts HL 6 Engl+maths+sci)
128 pts **Cardiff Met** – ABB (Sp Lang Thera)
         City – ABB 128 pts (Sp Lang Thera) (IB 33 pts)
         Leeds Beckett – 128 pts incl sci/psy/sociol/lang (Sp Lang Thera) (IB 27 pts)
         Sheffield – ABB–BBB+bEPQ (Sp Lang Sci) (IB 33 pts)
120 pts **Birmingham City** – BBB incl sci 120 pts (Sp Lang Thera) (IB 30 pts)
         Essex – BBB (Sp Lang Thera) (IB 30 pts)
         St Mark and St John – BBB (Sp Lang Thera) (IB 28–30 pts)
112 pts **Middlesex** – 112 pts +interview (Hlthcr Sci (Audiol))
         St Mark and St John – 112 pts (Sp Lang Sci)

Alternative offers
See **Chapter 6** and **Appendix 1** for grades/UCAS Tariff points information for other examinations.

CHOOSING YOUR COURSE (SEE ALSO CH.1)

Universities and colleges teaching quality See www.qaa.ac.uk; https://unistats.ac.uk.

ADMISSIONS INFORMATION

Number of applicants per place (approx) Birmingham City 28; Cardiff Met 10; City 6; Manchester 13; Manchester Met 21; Newcastle 5.

Advice to applicants and planning the UCAS personal statement Contact with speech therapists and visits to their clinics are an essential part of the preparation for this career. Discuss your contacts in full, giving details of any work experience or work shadowing you have done and your interest in helping people to communicate, showing evidence of good 'people skills'. See also **Appendix 3** and **Chapter 5**. **Manchester** Selectors look for some practical experience with individuals who have communication or swallowing difficulties. (International students) Good English required because of placement periods.

Misconceptions about this course Some students fail to differentiate between speech therapy, occupational therapy and physiotherapy. They do not realise that to study speech and language therapy there are academic demands, including the study of linguistics, psychology, medical sciences and clinical dynamics, so the course is intensive. **Cardiff Met** Some are under the impression that good grades are not necessary, that it is an easy option and one has to speak with a standard pronunciation.

Selection interviews Yes Birmingham City, Cardiff Met, East Anglia, Leeds Beckett, Manchester Met, Reading, St Mark and St John; **No** Sheffield.

Interview advice and questions Have you visited a speech and language therapy clinic? What did you see there? What made you want to become a speech therapist? What type of speech problems are there? What type of person would make a good speech therapist? Interviews often include an ear test (test of listening ability). See also **Chapter 5**. **Cardiff Met** Interviewees must demonstrate an insight into communication problems and explain how one speech sound is produced.

Reasons for rejection (non-academic) Insufficient knowledge of speech and language therapy. Lack of maturity. Poor communication skills. Written language problems.

AFTER-RESULTS ADVICE
Offers to applicants repeating A-levels Higher Birmingham City, Cardiff Met; **Possibly higher** Manchester Met; **Same** City, Newcastle.

GRADUATE DESTINATIONS AND EMPLOYMENT (2015/16 HESA)
Career note Speech therapists work mainly in NHS clinics, some work in hospitals and others in special schools or units for the mentally or physically handicapped. The demand for speech therapists is high.

OTHER DEGREE SUBJECTS FOR CONSIDERATION
Audiology; Communication Studies; Deaf Studies; Education; Health Studies; Linguistics; Psychology.

SPORTS SCIENCES/STUDIES
(see also Leisure and Recreation Management/Studies, Physical Education)

In addition to the theory and practice of many different sporting activities, Sports Sciences/Studies courses also cover the psychological aspects of sports and sports business administration. The geography, economics and sociology of recreation may also be included. The University Centres of Cricketing Excellence, part of a scheme introduced by the England and Wales Cricket Board, are funded by Marylebone Cricket Club and collectively known as MCC Universities.

Useful websites www.uksport.gov.uk; www.laureus.com; www.wsff.org.uk; www.sta.co.uk; www.olympic.org; https://sportscotland.org.uk; www.thebapa.org.uk; www.planet-science.com; www.olympic.org/london-2012; www.bases.org.uk; www.eis2win.co.uk

NB The points totals shown to the left of the institutions are for ease of reference only. It must not be assumed that Tariff points are always used by institutions or that they can be substituted for an offer in grades. The level of an offer is not necessarily indicative of the quality of a course.

COURSE OFFERS INFORMATION
Subject requirements/preferences GCSE English, mathematics and, often, a science subject. **AL**

Science required for Sport Science courses. PE required for some Sport Studies courses. **Other** Disclosure and Barring Service (DBS) disclosure required for many courses. Evidence of commitment to sport.

Your target offers and examples of degree courses

144 pts **Bath** – ∧∧∧–∧∧B+aEPQ incl maths/sci (Spo Exer Sci) (IB 36 pts HL 666)
Birmingham – AAA-ABB incl sci/maths (Spo Exer Sci) (IB 32 pts HL 666-665)
Exeter – AAA-ABB incl sci (Exer Spo Sci) (IB 36-32 pts HL 5 sci)
Leeds – AAA-ABB incl sci (Spo Exer Sci; Spo Sci Physiol) (IB 35-33 pts HL 6 sci)
Loughborough – AAA (Spo Exer Sci) (IB 37 pts HL 666)
Newcastle – AAA-AAB incl sci/maths (Spo Exer Sci) (IB 35-34 pts HL 5 sci)

136 pts **Bangor** – 136-128 pts (Spo Exer Psy)
Bath – AAB/A*AC/A*BB (Hlth Exer Sci) (IB 36 pts HL 665); (Spo Soc Sci) (IB 36 pts)
Birmingham – AAB-ABB (App Glf Mgt St) (IB 32 pts HL 665-655)
Durham – AAB (Spo Exer Physl Actvt) (IB 36 pts)
Loughborough – AAB-ABB incl Engl (Engl Spo Sci) (IB 35-34 pts HL 655 incl 6/5 Engl); AAB incl geog (Geog Spo Sci) (IB 35 pts HL 665 incl 5 geog)
Strathclyde – AAB-BBB (Spo Physl Actvt) (IB 36 pts)
Ulster – AAB incl hum/soc sci/spo (Spo St); AAB incl sci/maths/spo (Spo Exer Sci)

128 pts **Bangor** – 128-112 pts (Spo Sci; Spo Hlth PE; Spo Sci (Out Actvts); Spo Hlth Exer Sci)
Bournemouth – 128-136 pts incl biol/PE (Spo Thera) (IB 32-33 pts HL 55)
Brighton – ABB-BBC 128-112 pts (Spo Exer Sci) (IB 32 pts)
Edge Hill – ABB 128 pts (Spo Thera; Spo Exer Sci)
Edinburgh – ABB (App Spo Sci; Spo Recr Mgt) (IB 37 pts HL 666)
Gloucestershire – ABB (Spo Dev Coach); ABB 128 pts (Spo Thera; Physl Educ)
Kent – ABB incl sci/maths (Spo Thera; Spo Exer Sci) (IB 34 pts)
Loughborough – ABB (Spo Mgt) (IB 34 pts)
Northumbria – 128-136 pts (Spo Mgt; App Spo Exer Sci) (HL 444)
Nottingham Trent – ABB incl sci/PE 128 pts (Spo Exer Sci)
Portsmouth – 128 pts incl sci (Spo Exer Sci) (IB 27 pts HL 5 sci)
Sheffield Hallam – 128-112 pts incl PE/soc sci/sci (Spo Exer Sci); 128-112 pts incl PE/spo sci/sci (Spo Coach; Physl Actvt Spo Hlth)
Swansea – ABB-BBB (Spo Exer Sci) (IB 32 pts)
UWE Bristol – 128 pts incl biol/PE (Spo Rehab) (HL 5 biol/PE)

120 pts **Aberdeen** – BBB incl maths/sci (Spo Exer Sci) (IB 32 pts HL 5 maths/sci)
Brunel – BBB (Psy (Spo Hlth Exer)) (IB 30 pts)
Cardiff Met – 120 pts (Spo Exer Sci; Spo PE; Spo Condit Rehab Msg)
Chester – 120 pts (Spo Exer Sci) (IB 28 pts)
Coventry – BBB (Spo Exer Psy) (IB 31 pts)
Derby – 120-128 pts (Spo Thera Rehab); 120-128 pts incl biol/PE (Spo Exer Sci)
Edge Hill – BBB 120 pts (Spo Dev Mgt)
Gloucestershire – BBB 120 pts (Spo Exer Sci)
Huddersfield – BBB 120 pts (Spo Sci)
Kent – BBB (Spo Exer Mgt) (IB 34 pts); BBB incl sci/maths (Spo Exer Hlth) (IB 34 pts)
Lincoln – BBB incl sci/spo (Spo Exer Sci) (IB 30 pts)
Liverpool Hope – BBB-BBC 120-112 pts (Spo Psy; Spo Exer Sci) (IB 26 pts)
Liverpool John Moores – BBB 120 pts (Spo Exer Sci) (IB 26 pts)
Nottingham Trent – BBB incl sci/PE 120 pts (Spo Sci Mgt)
Robert Gordon – BBB incl Engl+sci (App Spo Exer Sci) (IB 28 pts HL 5 sci)
Stirling – BBB (Spo St; Spo Exer Sci) (IB 32 pts)

112 pts **Aberystwyth** – BBC (Spo Exer Sci) (IB 28 pts)
Birmingham City – 112 pts (Spo Exer Sci)
Bolton – 112 pts incl spo/PE/sci (Spo Rehab; Spo Exer Sci)
Brighton – BBC-CCC 112-96 pts (Spo Jrnl; Spo Coach) (IB 28 pts)
Brunel – BBC (Spo Hlth Exer Sci (Spo Dev); Spo Hlth Exer Sci; Spo Hlth Exer Sci (Hum Perf); Spo Hlth Exer Sci (Coach)) (IB 29 pts)

ARE YOU ONE OF LIFE'S EXPLORERS?

EXPLORE **BANGOR** FOR SPORT SCIENCE

At Bangor, you'd be studying at one of the best research-led Sport Science Schools in the UK. Established in 1978 we're also one of the oldest and we've attracted world-leading academic staff who have ongoing links at the highest levels of sport, elite performance and health. Our research, **rated 7th** in the UK, and our professional links contribute to an exciting range of up-to-date degree programmes. This leads to high student engagement and means we are regularly in the **Top Ten in the UK.** Ranked 8th in the UK for Student Satisfaction in the Sport Science subject area (NSS 2017).

Opportunity of a Lifetime – Study Abroad as part of your degree and gain valuable 'real life' experience to enhance your CV. Our students have been to universities in West **Florida, Maine and Iowa, USA and Melbourne, Australia.**

With the **Bangor Employability Award**, you have the opportunity to gain additional qualifications and complete work experience relevant to your future career aspirations. This means you not only graduate with an excellent degree but with a CV full of transferable skills that will help you to excel in today's competitive job market.

Sport and Outdoor Activities at Bangor. You will be studying in one of the best university locations in the UK. Our award-winning clubs and societies offer **free membership** so there are no expensive subscriptions to pay.

Explore more at
bangor.ac.uk/sport
🐦 @sportsscibangor

PRIFYSGOL
BANGOR
UNIVERSITY

GO BEYOND

Cardiff Met – 112 pts (Spo Coach)

Central Lancashire – 112–128 pts incl biol/PE/spo sci (Spo Thera); 112–128 pts (Out Advntr Ldrshp; Spo Exer Sci)

Chester – BBC–BCC 112 pts (Spo Jrnl) (IB 26 pts); BBC–BCC (Spo Dev Coach) (IB 26 pts)

Coventry – BBC (Spo Mgt; Spo Mark) (IB 29 pts); BBC incl biol/PE (Spo Thera) (IB 28 pts)

East London – 112 pts incl PE/spo/sci (Spo Exer Sci) (IB 25 pts); 112 pts (Spo Jrnl) (IB 25 pts HL 15 pts)

Glyndŵr – 112 pts (Spo Coach Part Perf Dev; Spo Exer Sci)

Hertfordshire – 112 pts incl sci (Spo Exer Sci) (HL 44)

Huddersfield – BBC 112 pts (Spo Jrnl)

Hull – 112 pts (Spo Coach Perf; Spo Exer Nutr; Spo Rehab) (IB 28 pts)

Leeds Beckett – 112 pts incl sci/PE (Physl Actvt Hlth) (IB 25 pts)

Leeds Trinity – 112 pts (Spo Exer Sci; Exer Hlth Nutr; Exer Hlth Fit; Spo Psy; Spo Jrnl; Spo Exer Sci (Spo Nutr))

Liverpool John Moores – BBC 112 pts (Sci Ftbl; Spo Coach) (IB 26 pts); (Spo Jrnl) (IB 27 pts)

Middlesex – 112 pts (Spo Exer Rehab; Spo Exer Sci)

Newman – 112 pts (Spo Educ; Spo Exer St)

Nottingham Trent – BBC incl sci/PE 112 pts (Coach Spo Sci)

Oxford Brookes – BBC 112 pts (Spo Exer Sci) (IB 30 pts)

Portsmouth – 112 pts (Spo Mgt Dev) (IB 26 pts)

Roehampton – 112 pts incl sci/PE (Spo Exer Sci)

St Mary's – 112 pts (Spo Sci; Spo Coach Sci); 112 pts incl biol/PE+spo/sci (Spo Rehab); 112 pts incl sci (Strg Condit Sci)

Sheffield Hallam – 112–96 pts (Spo Bus Mgt; Spo Dev Coach)

Southampton Solent – 112 pts (App Spo Sci)

Staffordshire – BBC 112 pts (Spo Coach; Spo Exer Sci)

Sunderland – 112 pts (Spo Exer Sci; Spo Coach; Spo Comb Hons)

Ulster – BBC incl sci/maths/spo (Spo Physl Actvt Hlth) (IB 25 pts HL 12 pts)

Worcester – 112 pts (Spo St; Spo Bus Mgt; Geog Spo St); 112 pts incl PE/hum biol (Spo Thera)

104 pts **Abertay** – BCC incl sci/PE/maths (Spo Exer) (IB 29 pts)

Anglia Ruskin – 104 pts (Spo Exer Sci) (IB 24 pts)

Birmingham (UC) – 104 pts (Spo Thera)

Bournemouth – 104–112 pts (Spo Dev Coach Sci) (IB 28–31 pts HL 55); 104–120 pts (Spo Mgt; Spo Psy Coach Sci) (IB 28–31 pts)

Brighton – BCC–CCC 104–96 pts (Spo St) (IB 27 pts)

Central Lancashire – 104 pts +interview (Spo Jrnl)

Chichester – 104–120 pts incl sci (Spo courses) (IB 28 pts HL 5 sci); 104–120 pts (Spo Tour) (IB 28 pts)

Cumbria – 104–120 pts (Spo Exer Sci)

Edinburgh Napier – BCC incl sci/psy (Spo Exer Sci courses) (IB 28 pts HL 5 sci)

Essex – BCC (Spo Exer Sci) (IB 28 pts)

Greenwich – 104 pts incl sci (Spo Sci Coach); 104 pts (Spo Sci)

Kingston – 104–128 pts (Spo Sci; Spo Sci (Coach))

Manchester Met – BCC–BBC 104–112 pts incl biol (Spo Sci Hum Biol; Spo Sci Physiol) (IB 26 pts HL 5 biol); BCC–BBC 104–112 pts (Spo Mgt; Spo Mark Mgt) (IB 26 pts)

Northampton – BCC (Spo St courses)

Nottingham Trent – 104 pts incl maths+PE/sci (Spo Sci Maths)

South Wales – BCC–CDD (Spo Coach Dev; Spo Psy) (HL 655–445); BCC–CCD incl sci/PE (Spo Exer Sci) (HL 655–445); BCC–CDD incl sci/maths/PE (Rgby Coach Perf) (HL 655–445); BCC–CDD incl sci/maths (Ftbl Coach Perf) (HL 655–445)

West Scotland – BCC incl sci 104 pts (Spo Exer Sci) (IB 27 pts)

96 pts **Cumbria** – 96–112 pts (Spo Rehab)

Derby – 96–112 pts (Spo Coach Dev); 96–128 pts incl biol/PE (Spo Exer St Comb Hons)

Hertfordshire – 96 pts (Spo St) (HL 44)

UCAS points Tariff: A* = 56 pts; A = 48 pts; B = 40 pts; C = 32 pts; D = 24 pts; E = 16 pts

St Mark and St John – 96 pts (Spo Dev); CCC (Spo Coach; Spo Thera)
Winchester – 96–112 pts (Spo Bus Mark; Spo Coach) (IB 25 pts)
Wolverhampton – CCC incl sci (Spo Exer Sci); CCC (Spo Coach Prac)
Writtle (UC) – 96 pts (Spo Exer Perf)
York St John – 96–112 pts (PE Spo Coach; Spo Exer Thera)

88 pts Canterbury Christ Church – 88–112 pts (Spo Exer Sci courses)
London South Bank – CCD (Spo Exer Sci)
Teesside – 88–104 pts incl spo/sci/PE (Spo Thera Rehab); 88–104 pts (Spo Exer
    (App Spo Sci); Spo Exer (Coach Sci))

80 pts Bedfordshire – 80 pts (Ftbl St; Spo Sci)
London Met – BB incl biol/PE/spo sci (Spo Exer Sci)
Trinity Saint David – 80 pts +interview (Spo Mgt)

Alternative offers
See **Chapter 6** and **Appendix 1** for grades/UCAS Tariff points information for other examinations.

EXAMPLES OF COLLEGES OFFERING COURSES IN THIS SUBJECT FIELD

Most colleges, check with your local college. Accrington and Rossendale (Coll); Askham Bryan (Coll); Bishop Burton (Coll); Blackpool and Fylde (Coll); Bradford (Coll); Colchester (Inst); Easton Otley (Coll); Hartpury (Coll); Lakes (Coll); Leeds City (Coll); Manchester (Coll); Myerscough (Coll); NCC Hackney; Newcastle (Coll); North Kent (Coll); North Lindsey (Coll); Peterborough (Coll); Plumpton (Coll); Reaseheath (Coll); Sir Gâr (Coll); South Devon (Coll); South Essex (Coll); Stamford New (Coll); Tameside (Coll); Warwickshire (Coll); Westminster City (Coll); Weston (Coll); York (Coll).

CHOOSING YOUR COURSE (SEE ALSO CH.1)

Universities and colleges teaching quality See www.qaa.ac.uk; https://unistats.ac.uk.

Top research universities and colleges (REF 2014) (Sports and Exercise Science, Leisure and Tourism) Bristol; Liverpool John Moores; Leeds; Bath; Birmingham; Exeter; London (King's); Bangor; Cardiff Met.

Examples of sandwich degree courses Bath; Bedfordshire; Bournemouth; Brighton; Brunel; Central Lancashire; Coventry; Essex; Hertfordshire; Kingston; Leeds; Loughborough; Manchester Met; Nottingham Trent; Portsmouth; Southampton Solent; Trinity Saint David; Ulster.

ADMISSIONS INFORMATION

Number of applicants per place (approx) Bangor 4; Bath 10; Birmingham 7; Cardiff Met 10; Cumbria 14, (Spo St) 6; Durham 6; Edinburgh 6; Exeter 23; Gloucestershire 8; Kingston 13; Leeds 25; Leeds Trinity 6; Liverpool John Moores 4; Manchester Met 16; Northampton 4; Nottingham Trent 8; Oxford Brookes 6; Roehampton 5; St Mary's 4; Sheffield Hallam 7; South Essex (Coll) 1; Staffordshire 12; Stirling 8; Strathclyde 28; Sunderland 2; Swansea 6; Teesside 15; Winchester 5; Wolverhampton 4; Worcester 10; York St John 4.

Advice to applicants and planning the UCAS personal statement See also **Physical Education** and **Appendix 3**. **Cardiff Met** A strong personal statement required which clearly identifies current performance profile and indicates a balanced lifestyle.

Misconceptions about this course Birmingham (App Glf Mgt St) Applicants do not appreciate the academic depth required across key areas (it is, in a sense, a multiple Honours course covering business management, sports science, coaching theory and materials science). **Swansea** (Spo Sci) Applicants underestimate the quantity of maths on the course. Many applicants are uncertain about the differences between Sports Studies and Sports Science.

Selection interviews Yes Bolton, Chichester, Robert Gordon, Stirling, Worcester; **Some** Bath, Leeds Trinity; **No** Anglia Ruskin, Birmingham, Cardiff Met, Cumbria, Derby, Edinburgh, Essex, Leeds, Liverpool John Moores, Nottingham Trent, Roehampton, St Mary's, Sheffield Hallam, Staffordshire, West Scotland, Wolverhampton.

Interview advice and questions Applicants' interests in sport and their sporting activities are likely to be discussed at length. Past questions include: How do you strike a balance between sport and academic work? How many, and which, sports do you coach? For how long? Have you devised your own coaching programme? What age range do you coach? Do you coach unsupervised? See also **Chapter 5**. **Loughborough** A high level of sporting achievement is expected.

Reasons for rejection (non-academic) Not genuinely interested in outdoor activities. Poor sporting background or knowledge. Personal appearance. Inability to apply their science to their specialist sport. Illiteracy. Using the course as a second option to Physiotherapy. Arrogance. Expectation that they will be playing sport all day. When the course is explained to them, some applicants realise that a more arts-based course would be more appropriate. **Ulster** Reasons relating to health and/or police checks.

AFTER-RESULTS ADVICE
Offers to applicants repeating A-levels Higher Swansea; **Same** Cardiff Met, Chichester, Derby, Lincoln, Liverpool John Moores, Loughborough, Roehampton, St Mary's, Sheffield Hallam, Staffordshire, Stirling, Sunderland, Winchester, Wolverhampton, York St John.

GRADUATE DESTINATIONS AND EMPLOYMENT (2015/16 HESA)
Graduates surveyed 8,895 **Employed** 3,895 **In voluntary employment** 230 **In further study** 2,690 **Assumed unemployed** 310

Career note Career options include sport development, coaching, teaching, outdoor centres, sports equipment development, sales, recreation management and professional sport.

OTHER DEGREE SUBJECTS FOR CONSIDERATION
Anatomy; Biology; Human Movement Studies; Leisure and Recreation Management; Nutrition; Physical Education; Physiology; Physiotherapy; Sports Equipment Product Design.

STATISTICS
(see also Economics, Mathematics)

Statistics has mathematical underpinnings but is primarily concerned with the collection, interpretation and analysis of data. Statistics are used to analyse and solve problems in a wide range of areas, particularly in the scientific, business, government and public services.

Useful websites www.rss.org.uk; www.gov.uk/government/statistics/announcements; www.ons.gov.uk

NB The points totals shown to the left of the institutions are for ease of reference only. It must not be assumed that Tariff points are always used by institutions or that they can be substituted for an offer in grades. The level of an offer is not necessarily indicative of the quality of a course.

COURSE OFFERS INFORMATION
Subject requirements/preferences GCSE English and mathematics. **AL** Mathematics required for all courses.

Your target offers and examples of degree courses
168 pts **Warwick** – A*A*A*–A*AA incl maths (MORSE) (IB 38 pts HL 7 maths)
160 pts **Bristol** – A*A*A–AAA incl maths+fmaths/sci/econ/comp (Maths Stats) (IB 40–36 pts HL 6 maths+sci/econ/comp)
         Imperial London – A*A*A–A*A*A* incl maths+fmaths +MAT/STEP (Maths Stats; Maths Optim Stats; Maths Stats Fin) (IB 39–41 pts HL 7 maths 6 phys/chem/econ)
         Oxford – A*A*A incl maths +interview +MAT (Maths Stats) (IB 39 pts HL 766 incl 7 maths)
152 pts **Bath** – A*AA incl maths (Stats) (IB 36 pts HL 6 maths)
         Edinburgh – A*AA incl maths (Maths Stats) (IB 37 pts HL 6 maths)

London (UCL) – A*AA–AAA/A*AB incl maths (Stats Mgt Bus; Stats) (IB 39–38 pts HL 7 maths); A*AA–AAA incl maths (Stats Sci (Int); Stats Econ Fin) (IB 39–38 pts HL 7 maths)

London LSE – A*AA incl maths (Fin Maths Stats) (IB 38 pts HL 766 incl 7 maths)

Manchester – A*AA–AAA incl maths (Maths Stats) (IB 34 pts HL 6 maths)

St Andrews – A*AA incl maths (Stats) (IB 36 pts)

144 pts **Birmingham** – AAA incl maths (Mathem Econ Stats) (IB 32 pts HL 666)

Cardiff – AAA–A*BB incl maths (Maths OR Stats) (IB 36–34 pts HL 6 maths)

Glasgow – AAA/A*AB incl maths (Fin Stats) (IB 38 pts HL 666)

Lancaster – AAA incl maths/fmaths (Maths Stats; Stats) (IB 36 pts HL 6 maths); AAA–AAB incl maths/fmaths (Stats (St Abrd) MSci) (IB 36 pts HL 6 maths)

Leeds – AAA/A*AB–AAB/A*BB incl maths (Maths Stats) (IB 35 pts HL 6 maths)

London LSE – AAA incl maths (Bus Maths Stats) (IB 38 pts HL 766 incl 7 maths)

Newcastle – AAA/A*AB–AAB/A*BB incl maths (Maths Stats) (IB 37–35 pts HL 6 maths)

Queen's Belfast – AAA/A*AB incl maths (Maths Stats OR (MSci))

Southampton – AAA–AAB+aEPQ incl maths (Maths OR Stats Econ; Maths Stats) (IB 36 pts HL 6 maths)

Surrey – AAA incl maths (Maths Stats) (IB 34 pts)

York – AAA–AAB incl maths (Maths Stats) (IB 36 pts HL 6 maths)

136 pts **Glasgow** – AAB–BBB incl maths (Stats) (IB 36–34 pts)

Heriot-Watt – AAB incl maths (Stats Modl) (IB 28 pts HL 6 maths)

London (QM) – AAB incl maths (Maths Stats) (IB 34 pts HL 6/5 maths)

London (RH) – AAB–ABB incl maths (Maths Stats) (IB 32 pts HL 6 maths)

Newcastle – AAB/A*BB incl maths (Stats) (IB 37 35 pts HL 6 maths)

Reading – AAB–ABB incl maths (Maths Stats; Comput Maths) (IB 34–32 pts HL 6 maths); AAB–ABB (Consum Bhv Mark) (IB 34–32 pts)

128 pts **Queen's Belfast** – ABB incl maths (Maths Stats OR)

Strathclyde – ABB (3 yr course) BBB (4 yr course) incl maths (Maths Stats Econ) (IB 34 pts (3 yr course) 32 pts (4 yr course) HL 6 maths)

120 pts **Aberystwyth** – ABC/BBB incl maths (App Maths PMaths) (IB 30–28 pts HL 5/4 maths)

Brunel – BBB incl maths/fmaths (Maths Stats Mgt) (IB 30 pts HL 5 maths)

Coventry – BBB–BBC incl maths (Maths Stats) (IB 31 pts HL 4 maths)

Plymouth – 120–128 pts incl maths (Maths Stats) (IB 30 pts HL 5 maths)

UWE Bristol – 120 pts inc maths (Maths Stats) (HL 6 maths)

West London – 120 pts incl maths (Maths Stats)

112 pts **Greenwich** – 112 pts (Stats OR)

London (Birk) – BBC incl maths 112 pts (Maths Stats)

104 pts **Chichester** – 104–120 pts incl C Maths (Maths Stats) (IB 28 pts)

Portsmouth – 104–120 pts incl maths (Maths Stats) (IB 26 pts)

Alternative offers

See **Chapter 6** and **Appendix 1** for grades/UCAS Tariff points information for other examinations.

CHOOSING YOUR COURSE (SEE ALSO CH.1)

Universities and colleges teaching quality See www.qaa.ac.uk; https://unistats.ac.uk.

Top research universities and colleges (REF 2014) See **Mathematics**.

Examples of sandwich degree courses Bath; Brunel; Cardiff; Coventry; Greenwich; Kent; Kingston; Portsmouth; Reading; Surrey; UWE Bristol.

ADMISSIONS INFORMATION

Number of applicants per place (approx) Bath 7; Heriot-Watt 6; Lancaster 6; London (UCL) 9; London LSE 8; Southampton 10; York 5.

Advice to applicants and planning the UCAS personal statement Love mathematics, don't expect an easy life. See also **Mathematics** and **Appendix 3**.

Selection interviews Some Bath, Greenwich, London (UCL); **No** Birmingham, East Anglia, Newcastle, Reading.

Interview advice and questions Questions could be asked on your A-level syllabus (particularly in mathematics). Applicants' knowledge of statistics and their interest in the subject are likely to be tested, together with their awareness of the application of statistics in commerce and industry. See also **Chapter 5**.

AFTER-RESULTS ADVICE
Offers to applicants repeating A-levels Higher Leeds, Newcastle; **Same** Birmingham.

GRADUATE DESTINATIONS AND EMPLOYMENT (2015/16 HESA)
Graduates surveyed 345 **Employed** 180 **In voluntary employment** 0 **In further study** 90 **Assumed unemployed** 20

Career note See **Mathematics**.

OTHER DEGREE SUBJECTS FOR CONSIDERATION
Accountancy; Actuarial Sciences; Business Information Technology; Business Studies; Computer Science; Economics; Financial Services; Mathematical Studies; Mathematics.

SURVEYING and REAL ESTATE MANAGEMENT

(including **Building Surveying**, **Property Development**, **Quantity Surveying** and **Rural Property Management. For Property, Finance** and **Investment see under Finance;** see also **Agricultural Sciences/Agriculture, Building and Construction, Housing, Town and Country Planning**)

Surveying covers a very diverse range of careers and courses and following a Royal Institution of Chartered Surveyors (RICS) accredited course is the accepted way to become a Chartered Surveyor. There are three main specialisms – the Built Environment (Building Surveying, Project Management and Quantity Surveying); Land Surveying (Rural, Planning, Environmental, Minerals and Waste Management); and Property Surveying (Commercial and Residential Property and Valuation, Facilities Management, Art and Antiques). Student membership of the RICS is possible. Not all the courses listed below receive RICS accreditation; check with the university or college prior to applying.

Useful websites www.rics.org/ru/join/student; www.cstt.org.uk

NB The points totals shown to the left of the institutions are for ease of reference only. It must not be assumed that Tariff points are always used by institutions or that they can be substituted for an offer in grades. The level of an offer is not necessarily indicative of the quality of a course.

COURSE OFFERS INFORMATION
Subject requirements/preferences GCSE English and mathematics grade A–C (7–4). **AL** No subjects specified; mathematics useful.

Your target offers and examples of degree courses
152 pts **Cambridge** – A*AA +interview +TSA (Lnd Econ) (IB 40–42 pts HL 776)
144 pts **Reading** – AAA–AAB (Rl Est) (IB 35 pts)
136 pts **Edinburgh Napier** – AAB (3 yr course) CCC (4 yr course) (Bld Surv) (IB 26 pts HL 555)
　　　　　London (UCL) – AAB (Plan Rl Est Mgt) (IB 36 pts HL 17 pts)
　　　　　Ulster – AAB (Quant Surv Commer Mgt) (IB 28 pts)
128 pts **London South Bank** – ABB (Rl Est)
　　　　　Manchester – ABB (Plan Rl Est) (IB 32 pts HL 655)
　　　　　Newcastle – ABB (Surv Map Sci) (IB 34 pts)
　　　　　Oxford Brookes – ABB–BBB (Rl Est Mgt) (IB 33–32 pts)
　　　　　Reading – ABB–BBB (Quant Surv; Bld Surv) (IB 32–30 pts)

120 pts **Aberdeen** – BBB (Rl Est Mgt)

Coventry – BBB (Quant Surv Commer Mgt) (IB 30 pts); BBB–BBC (Bld Surv) (IB 29 pts)

Huddersfield – BBB 120 pts (Surv (Bld Surv))

Leeds Beckett – 120 pts (Bld Surv) (IB 25 pts)

Loughborough – 120 pts (Commer Mgt Quant Surv) (IB 32 pts)

Northumbria – 120–128 pts (Bld Surv); (Quant Surv) (HL 444); (Rl Est) (IB 30 pts HL 444)

Nottingham Trent – 120 pts (Rl Est); BBB 120 pts (Bld Surv)

Plymouth – 120 pts (Bld Surv Env) (IB 28 pts)

Ulster – BBB (Bld Surv) (IB 26 pts HL 13 pts)

112 pts **Anglia Ruskin** – 112 pts (Bld Surv) (IB 25 pts)

Birmingham City – BBC 112 pts (Bld Surv) (HL 14 pts); (Quant Surv; Rl Est) (IB 30 pts)

Brighton – BBC–CCC 112–96 pts (Bld Surv) (IB 28 pts)

Central Lancashire – 112 pts incl maths (Quant Surv) (IB 28 pts HL 5 maths)

Glasgow Caledonian – BBC (Bld Surv) (IB 24 pts)

Kingston – BBC 112 pts (Rl Est Mgt) (IB 25 pts incl 4 maths HL 554 incl 4 Engl lang); 112–120 pts (Bld Surv)

Leeds Beckett – 112 pts (Quant Surv) (IB 25 pts)

Liverpool John Moores – BBC 112 pts (Bld Surv; Rl Est; Quant Surv) (IB 26 pts)

London South Bank – BBC (Quant Surv)

Nottingham Trent – BBC 112 pts (Quant Surv Constr Commer Mgt)

Oxford Brookes – BBC–BCC 112–104 pts (Quant Surv Commer Mgt) (IB 31–30 pts); BBC (Plan Prop Dev) (IB 31 pts)

Portsmouth – 112–120 pts (Prop Dev) (IB 26 pts)

Sheffield Hallam – 112 pts (Quant Surv); 112–96 pts (Bld Surv)

Ulster – BBC (Rl Est) (IB 25 pts HL 12 pts)

UWE Bristol – 112 pts (Bld Surv); (Rl Est; Quant Surv Commer Mgt) (IB 25 pts)

Westminster – BBC (Rl Est; Bld Surv) (IB 28 pts); (Quant Surv Commer Mgt) (IB 29 pts)

108 pts **Anglia Ruskin** – 108 pts (Quant Surv) (IB 25 pts)

Portsmouth – 108–120 pts (Quant Surv) (IB 26 pts)

104 pts **Glasgow Caledonian** – BCC (Prop Mgt Val) (IB 24 pts)

Greenwich – 104 pts (Quant Surv)

Harper Adams – 104 pts (Rl Est)

Royal Agricultural Univ – 104 pts (Rl Est)

Salford – 104 pts (Prop Rl Est)

South Wales – BCC (Quant Surv Commer Mgt; Proj Mgt (Surv)) (IB 29 pts)

96 pts **Derby** – 96–112 pts (Constr Mgt Prop Dev)

East London – 96 pts (Surv Map Sci) (IB 24 pts)

Edinburgh Napier – CCC (Rl Est Surv) (IB 27 pts HL 5 maths); (Quant Surv) (IB 27 pts)

London South Bank – CCC (Commer Mgt (Quant Surv); Prop Mgt (Bld Surv))

Nottingham Trent – 96 pts (Quant Surv)

Robert Gordon – CCC (Surv) (IB 28 pts)

UCEM – 96 pts (Bld Serv; Quant Surv; Rl Est Mgt)

Wolverhampton – 96 pts (Quant Surv)

88 pts **Derby** – 88–120 pts (Prop Dev Comb Hons)

Harper Adams – 88 pts +interview (Rur Prop Mgt)

80 pts **Wolverhampton** – BB/CCE (Bld Surv)

72 pts **Trinity Saint David** – 72 pts (Quant Surv Commer Mgt)

Alternative offers

See **Chapter 6** and **Appendix 1** for grades/UCAS Tariff points information for other examinations.

EXAMPLES OF DEGREE APPRENTICESHIPS IN THIS SUBJECT FIELD

Liverpool John Moores (Rl Est; Quant Surv; Bld Surv; Facil Mgt); Salford (Quant Surv); Sheffield Hallam (Quant Surv); UCEM (Build Surv; Quant Surv; Rl Est Mgt); UWE Bristol (Quant Surv Commer Mgt; Rl Est).

Check **Chapter 3** for new university admission details and **Chapter 6** on how to read the subject tables.

EXAMPLES OF COLLEGES OFFERING COURSES IN THIS SUBJECT FIELD
Blackburn (Coll); South Cheshire (Coll); UCEM.

CHOOSING YOUR COURSE (SEE ALSO CH.1)
Universities and colleges teaching quality See www.qaa.ac.uk; https://unistats.ac.uk. Check on RICS accreditation.

Examples of sandwich degree courses Anglia Ruskin; Birmingham City; Central Lancashire; Coventry; Glasgow Caledonian; Kingston; Leeds Beckett; Liverpool John Moores; London South Bank; Loughborough; Northumbria; Nottingham Trent; Oxford Brookes; Sheffield Hallam; Ulster; UWE Bristol; Wolverhampton.

ADMISSIONS INFORMATION
Number of applicants per place (approx) Anglia Ruskin 2; Birmingham City 4; Cambridge 4; Edinburgh Napier 7; Greenwich 8; Harper Adams 3; London South Bank 2; Nottingham Trent (Quant Surv) 10; Oxford Brookes 4; Robert Gordon 5; Royal Agricultural Univ 3; Sheffield Hallam (Quant Surv) 7; Westminster 10; Wolverhampton 6.

Admissions tutors' advice Nottingham Trent Candidates should demonstrate that they have researched the employment opportunities in the property and construction sectors.

Advice to applicants and planning the UCAS personal statement Surveyors work with architects and builders as well as in their own consultancies dealing with commercial and residential property. Work experience with various firms is strongly recommended depending on the type of surveying speciality preferred. Read surveying magazines. **Cambridge** Statements should be customised to the overall interests of students, not to the Land Economy Tripos specifically. **Oxford Brookes** Apply early. Applicants should be reflective. We are looking for at least 50%–60% of the personal statement to cover issues surrounding why they want to do the course, what motivates them about the subject, how they have developed their interest, how their A-levels have helped them and what they have gained from any work experience. Extracurricular activities are useful but should not dominate the statement.

Misconceptions about this course Students underestimate the need for numerical competence.

Selection interviews Yes Birmingham City, Cambridge, Loughborough; **No** Anglia Ruskin, Glasgow Caledonian, Harper Adams, Kingston, Liverpool John Moores, Nottingham Trent, Oxford Brookes, Robert Gordon, Royal Agricultural Univ, Salford, Ulster.

Interview advice and questions What types of work are undertaken by surveyors? How do you qualify? What did you learn on your work experience? See also **Chapter 5**. **Cambridge** (Lnd Econ) Questions on subsidies and the euro and economics. Who owns London? How important is the modern day church in town planning? How important are natural resources to a country? Is it more important to focus on poverty at home or abroad? Is the environment a bigger crisis than poverty? Do you think that getting involved with poverty abroad is interfering with others 'freedoms'? (The questions were based on information given in the personal statement.) Students sit the TSA at interview.

Reasons for rejection (non-academic) Inability to communicate. Lack of motivation. Indecisiveness about reasons for choosing the course. **Loughborough** Applicants more suited to a practical type of course rather than an academic one. **Nottingham Trent** Incoherent and badly written application.

AFTER-RESULTS ADVICE
Offers to applicants repeating A-levels Higher Bolton, Nottingham Trent; **Same** Coventry, Edinburgh Napier, Liverpool John Moores, Oxford Brookes, Robert Gordon, Salford.

GRADUATE DESTINATIONS AND EMPLOYMENT (2015/16 HESA)
Career note See **Building and Construction**.

OTHER DEGREE SUBJECTS FOR CONSIDERATION
Architecture; Building and Construction; Civil Engineering; Estate Management; Town Planning; Urban Studies.

TEACHER TRAINING

(see also **Education Studies, Physical Education, Social Sciences/Studies**)

Abbreviations used in this table: ITE - Initial Teacher Education; ITT - Initial Teacher Training; P - Primary Teaching; QTS - Qualified Teacher Status; S - Secondary Teaching; STQ - Scottish Teaching Qualification.

Teacher training courses are offered in subject areas such as Art and Design (P); Biology (P S); Chemistry (S); Childhood (P); Computer Education (P); Creative and Performing Arts (P); Dance (P); Design and Technology (P S); Drama (P); English (P S); Environmental Science (P S); Environmental Studies (P); French (S); General Primary; Geography (P S); History (P S); Maths (P S); Music (P S); Physical Education/Movement Studies (P S); Religious Studies (P); Science (P S); Sociology (S); Textile Design (S); Welsh (S). For further information on teaching as a career see websites below and **Appendix 3** for contact details. Over 50 taster courses are offered each year to those considering teaching as a career. Early Childhood Studies has been introduced in recent years by a number of universities. The courses focus on child development, from birth to eight years of age, and the provision of education for children and their families. It is a multi-disciplinary subject and can cover social problems and legal and psychological issues. Note that many institutions listed below also offer one-year Postgraduate Certificate in Education (PGCE) courses which qualify graduates to teach other subjects.

Useful websites www.gtcs.org.uk; www.ucas.com/ucas/teacher-training; http://teachertrainingcymru.org; www.gov.uk/government/organisations/department-for-education

NB The points totals shown to the left of the institutions are for ease of reference only. It must not be assumed that Tariff points are always used by institutions or that they can be substituted for an offer in grades. The level of an offer is not necessarily indicative of the quality of a course.

COURSE OFFERS INFORMATION

Subject requirements/preferences See **Education Studies**.

Your target offers and examples of degree courses

152 pts **Cambridge** - A*AA +interview +EAA (Educ Psy Lrng; Educ Engl Dr Arts; Educ Plcy Int Dev) (IB 40-42 pts HL 776)

136 pts **Durham** - AAB (Educ St (Engl St/Geog/Hist/Phil/Psy/Sociol/Theol Relgn)) (IB 36 pts)
Edinburgh - ABB (P Educ Gael) (IB 36 pts)
Glasgow - AAB-BBB incl Engl (Educ P QTS; Relig Phil Educ) (IB 36-32 pts)
Stranmillis (UC) - AAB (P Educ QTS)

128 pts **Durham** - ABB (P Educ) (IB 34 pts)
Strathclyde - ABB incl sci/maths (Chem Teach (MChem)) (IB 34 pts); ABB-BBB (P Educ) (IB 36 pts)

120 pts **Brighton** - BBB (P Educ) (IB 30 pts)
Edge Hill - BBB 120 pts (P Educ QTS)
Gloucestershire - BBB 120 pts +interview (P Educ BEd QTS)
Leeds Beckett - 120 pts (P Educ (QTS)) (IB 26 pts)
Liverpool Hope - BBB-BBC 120-112 pts (Disab St Educ); (P Educ QTS) (IB 26 pts)
Nottingham Trent - BBB 120 pts (P Educ QTS)
Reading - BBB-BBC incl mus +interview (P Ed Mus Spec) (IB 30-28 pts HL 5 mus); BBB-BBC incl Engl +interview (P Educ Engl Spec) (IB 30-28 pts); BBB-BBC (P Educ Art Spec) (IB 30-28 pts)
Sheffield Hallam - 120-104 pts (P Educ QTS)
Stirling - BBB (Educ P; Educ S; Prof Educ P Educ courses) (IB 32 pts)
Sunderland - 120 pts (P Educ)
West Scotland - BBB incl Engl (Educ) (IB 32 pts)

Worcester – 120 pts (P ITE)
York St John – 120 pts +interview (P Educ)
112 pts **Bedfordshire** – 112 pts (P Educ BEd QTS)
Birmingham City – BBC 112 pts (P Educ QTS) (IB 28 pts)
Bishop Grosseteste – 112 pts (P Educ QTS)
Canterbury Christ Church – 112 pts (P Educ); 112 pts incl maths (Maths S Educ QTS)
Edge Hill – BBC 112 pts (S Educ QTS courses)
Gloucestershire – BBC 112 pts (Educ)
Greenwich – 112 pts (Educ P BA QTS)
Hertfordshire – 112 pts (Educ P BEd QTS) (HL 44)
Huddersfield – BBC 112 pts (Ely Yrs)
Hull – 112 pts (P Teach) (IB 28 pts)
Kingston – 112 pts (P Teach QTS)
Leeds Trinity – BBC (P Educ courses (QTS))
Manchester Met – BBC incl maths +interview (S Maths Educ QTS) (IB 25 pts)
Middlesex – 112 pts +interview (P Educ QTS)
Oxford Brookes – BBC 112 pts (P Teach Educ) (IB 30 pts)
Plymouth – 112 pts (P PE BEd (QTS)); 112 pts +interview (P (Mus)) (IB 28 pts)
RAc Dance – BBC +RAD Intermediate +interview +audition (Ballet Educ)
Roehampton – 112 pts (P Educ QTS)
St Mark and St John – 112 pts (PE (S Educ QTS); P Educ QTS)
South Wales – BBC (P St QTS) (IB 29 pts)
UWE Bristol – 112 pts (P Educ ITE)
Winchester – 112–120 pts +interview (P Educ QTS); 112–120 pts (P Educ Geog QTS;
    P Educ PE QTS)
Wolverhampton – BBC +interview (P Educ)
104 pts **Bath Spa** – BCC–CCC (P Educ (BA + PGCE))
Cardiff Met – 104 pts (S Educ (Mus/Welsh) QTS)
Chester – BCC 104 pts (P Educ St) (IB 26 pts)
Chichester – BCC–CCC (Maths Teach KS 2+3) (IB 28 pts); 104–120 pts (P Teach Ely Yrs QTS)
    (IB 30 pts)
Cumbria – 104–128 pts (P Educ QTS)
Gloucestershire – BCC 104 pts (Ely Chld St)
Leeds Beckett – 104 pts (Chld St) (IB 24 pts)
Northampton – BCC (Educ St courses)
Nottingham Trent – BCC 104 pts (Ely Yrs Spec Inclsv Educ; Educ St Spec Inclsv Educ)
RConsvS – BCC incl mus +audition (Mus (BEd))
St Mary's – 104 pts (P Educ QTS)
Winchester – 104–120 pts (Educ St (Ely Chld); Educ St courses) (IB 26 pts)
96 pts **Bangor** – 96 pts (P Educ QTS); 96–80 pts (Des Tech S Educ QTS)
Bedfordshire – 96 pts (Ely Chld Educ; Educ St)
Birmingham City – 96 pts (Cond Educ)
Middlesex – 96 pts (Educ St)
Northampton – CCC (Ely Chld St; Chld Yth)
Portsmouth – 96–120 pts (Ely Chld St) (IB 28 pts)
Staffordshire – CCC 96 pts (Ely Chld St)
88 pts **Trinity Saint David** – 88–104 pts +interview (Ely Yrs Educ Cr)
80 pts **Anglia Ruskin** – 80 pts (P Educ St) (IB 24 pts)
72 pts **Teesside** – 72–88 pts (Ely Chld St; Chld Yth St)

Alternative offers
See **Chapter 6** and **Appendix 1** for grades/UCAS Tariff points information for other examinations.

EXAMPLES OF COLLEGES OFFERING COURSES IN THIS SUBJECT FIELD
Most colleges, check with your local college. Bedford (Coll); Bishop Burton (Coll); Bradford (Coll);

UCAS points Tariff: A* = 56 pts; A = 48 pts; B = 40 pts; C = 32 pts; D = 24 pts; E = 16 pts

Carshalton (Coll); Cornwall (Coll); Grŵp Llandrillo Menai; Kensington Bus (Coll); Leeds City (Coll); Loughborough (Coll); Myerscough (Coll); Nottingham (Coll); Sir Gâr (Coll); South Cheshire (Coll); South Devon (Coll); South Essex (Coll); Wakefield (Coll); Warwickshire (Coll); Wigan and Leigh (Coll); Wiltshire (Coll); Yeovil (Coll).

CHOOSING YOUR COURSE (SEE ALSO CH.1)

Universities and colleges teaching quality See www.qaa.ac.uk; https://unistats.ac.uk.

Top research universities and colleges (REF 2014) See **Education Studies**.

ADMISSIONS INFORMATION

Number of applicants per place (approx) Bangor 4; Bishop Grosseteste 12; Cardiff Met 3; Durham 3; Edge Hill 17; Gloucestershire 20; Greenwich 3; Hull 5; Kingston 9, Middlesex 7; Northampton 7; Nottingham Trent 11; Oxford Brookes 6; Plymouth 26; Roehampton 6; St Mark and St John 5; St Mary's 19; Sheffield Hallam 7; Strathclyde 7; West Scotland 7; Winchester 5; Wolverhampton 4; Worcester 21.

Advice to applicants and planning the UCAS personal statement Too many candidates are applying without the required **GCSE** requirements in place or pending (maths, English, science). Any application for teacher training courses requires candidates to have experience of observation in schools and with children relevant to the choice of age range. Describe what you have learned from this. Any work with young people should be described in detail, indicating any problems which you may have seen which children create for the teacher. Applicants are strongly advised to have had some teaching practice prior to interview and should give evidence of time spent in a primary or secondary school and an analysis of activity undertaken with children. Give details of music qualifications, if any. Admissions tutors look for precise, succinct, well-reasoned, well-written statements (no mistakes!). See also **Chapter 5**. **Chichester** Minimum of two weeks spent observing or helping out in a state school required. **West Scotland** Review the General Teaching Council for Scotland website for the latest news. It is important to know the current teaching policy and processes, the impact of technology, changes within the classroom and Curriculum for Excellence. Visit a school and ask about 'the day in the life of a teacher'.

Selection interviews Check all institutions. It is a requirement that all candidates for teacher training are interviewed. Some related courses, such as Early Childhood Studies, do not require interviews. **Yes** Brighton, Edge Hill, Edinburgh, Glasgow, Hertfordshire, Huddersfield, Hull, Leeds Trinity, Middlesex, Oxford Brookes, Reading, Roehampton, St Mark and St John, South Wales, Sunderland, Sussex, UWE Bristol, Wolverhampton, York St John; **Some** Cumbria, Durham, Greenwich, Leeds Beckett, Winchester; **No** Birmingham City, Cardiff Met, Gloucestershire.

Interview advice and questions Questions invariably focus on why you want to teach and your experiences in the classroom. In some cases, you may be asked to write an essay on these topics. Questions in the past have included: What do you think are important issues in education at present? Discussion of coursework will take place for Art applicants.

Reasons for rejection (non-academic) Unable to meet the requirements of written standard English. Ungrammatical personal statements. Lack of research about teaching at primary or secondary levels. Lack of experience in schools. Insufficient experience of working with people; tendency to be racist.

AFTER-RESULTS ADVICE

Offers to applicants repeating A-levels Possibly higher Cumbria; **Same** Bangor, Bishop Grosseteste, Brighton, Canterbury Christ Church, Chester, Durham, Liverpool Hope, Nottingham Trent, Oxford Brookes, Roehampton, St Mark and St John, St Mary's, Stirling, Sunderland, Winchester, Wolverhampton, Worcester, York St John; **No** Kingston.

GRADUATE DESTINATIONS AND EMPLOYMENT (2015/16 HESA)

Graduates surveyed 9,420 **Employed** 7,270 **In voluntary employment** 45 **In further study** 590 **Assumed unemployed** 155

Check **Chapter 3** for new university admission details and **Chapter 6** on how to read the subject tables.

Career note See **Education Studies**.

OTHER DEGREE SUBJECTS FOR CONSIDERATION
Education Studies; Psychology; Social Policy; Social Sciences; Social Work.

TOURISM and TRAVEL

(see also **Business and Management Courses, Business and Management Courses (International and European), Business and Management Courses (Specialised), Hospitality and Event Management, Leisure and Recreation Management/Studies)**

Tourism and Travel courses are popular; some are combined with Hospitality Management which thus provides students with two possible career paths. Courses involve business studies and a detailed study of tourism and travel. Industrial placements are frequently involved and language options are often included. See also **Appendix 3**.

Useful websites www.wttc.org; http://abta.com; www.thebapa.org.uk; www.itt.co.uk; www.tmi.org.uk

NB The points totals shown to the left of the institutions are for ease of reference only. It must not be assumed that Tariff points are always used by institutions or that they can be substituted for an offer in grades. The level of an offer is not necessarily indicative of the quality of a course.

COURSE OFFERS INFORMATION
Subject requirements/preferences GCSE English and mathematics required. **AL** No subjects specified.

Your target offers and examples of degree courses
144 pts Strathclyde – AAA–ABB incl maths (Acc Hspty Tour Mgt) (IB 38 pts HL 6 maths)
136 pts Surrey – AAB (Int Tour Mgt) (IB 35 pts)
128 pts Strathclyde – ABB (Hspty Tour Mgt) (IB 36 pts)
　　　　　Surrey – ABB (Int Hspty Tour Mgt) (IB 32 pts)
120 pts Liverpool Hope – BBB–BBC 120–112 pts (Tour)
　　　　　Northumbria – 120–128 pts (Bus Tour Mgt; Tour Evnts Mgt) (HL 444)
112 pts Aberystwyth – BBC (Tour Mgt) (IB 28 pts)
　　　　　Bournemouth – 112–120 pts (Tour Mgt) (IB 30–31 pts HL 55)
　　　　　Central Lancashire – 112 pts (Int Tour Mgt)
　　　　　East London – 112 pts (Tour Mgt) (IB 25 pts HL 15 pts)
　　　　　Gloucestershire – BBC 112 pts (Htl Rsrt Tour Mgt)
　　　　　Greenwich – 112 pts (Tour Mgt)
　　　　　Middlesex – 112 pts (Int Tour Mgt)
　　　　　Southampton Solent – 112 pts (Int Tour Mgt; Int Tour Mgt)
　　　　　Suffolk – 112 pts (Tour Mgt)
　　　　　Sunderland – 112 pts (Tour Mgt; Int Tour Hspty Mgt)
　　　　　West London – BBC 112 pts (Trav Tour Mgt)
　　　　　Westminster – BBC (Tour Bus; Tour Plan Mgt) (IB 28 pts)
　　　　　Wolverhampton – BBC–CCC (Tour Mgt)
104 pts Bath Spa – BCC–CCC (Bus Mgt (Tour Mgt)) (IB 26 pts)
　　　　　Birmingham (UC) – 104 pts (Int Tour Mgt)
　　　　　Brighton – BCC–CCC 104–96 pts (Int Tour Mgt) (IB 27 pts)
　　　　　Coventry – 104 pts (Glob Tour Hspty Mgt)
　　　　　Lincoln – BCC (Int Tour Mgt) (IB 28 pts)
　　　　　London South Bank – BCC 104 pts (Tour Hspty Mgt)
　　　　　Queen Margaret – BCC (Int Hspty Tour Mgt) (IB 28 pts)
　　　　　St Mary's – 104 pts (Tour; Tour Mgt)
　　　　　Ulster – BCC–BBB (Int Trav Tour Mgt) (IB 26–28 pts)

UCAS points Tariff: A* = 56 pts; A = 48 pts; B = 40 pts; C = 32 pts; D = 24 pts; E = 16 pts

96 pts **Anglia Ruskin** – 96–112 pts (Tour Mgt) (IB 24 pts)
Birmingham (UC) – 96 pts (Int Tour Bus Mgt)
Cardiff Met – 96–112 pts (Int Hspty Tour Mgt)
Chichester – 96–112 pts (Tour Mgt) (IB 28 pts)
Derby – 96–112 pts (Int Tour Mgt)
Edinburgh Napier – CCC (Int Tour Mgt) (IB 27 pts)
Hertfordshire – 96–112 pts (Tour Mgt; Int Tour Mgt)
Leeds Beckett – 96 pts (Int Tour Mgt) (IB 24 pts)
London Met – CCC 96 pts (Tour Trav Mgt)
Manchester Met – CCC–BBC 96–112 pts (Tour Mgt) (IB 26 pts)
Plymouth – 96 pts (Cru Mgt) (IB 26 pts HL 4); (Tour Mgt; Int Tour Mgt) (IB 26 pts)
Robert Gordon – CCC (Int Tour Mgt) (IB 26 pts)
Staffordshire – 96 pts (Tour Hosp Mgt)
York St John – 96–112 pts (Tour Mgt; Tour Mgt Mark)
88 pts **Canterbury Christ Church** – 88–112 pts (Tour St; Tour Mgt)
Portsmouth – 88 pts (Hspty Mgt Tour) (IB 28 pts HL 15 pts)
Trinity Saint David – 88 pts +interview (Int Trav Tour Mgt)
80 pts **Bedfordshire** – 80 pts (Trav Tour; Int Tour Mgt)
Trinity Saint David – 80 pts +interview (Tour Mgt)
64 pts **UHI** – CC (Advntr Tour Mgt)
32 pts **GSM London** – 32 pts (Trav Tour)

Alternative offers
See **Chapter 6** and **Appendix 1** for grades/UCAS Tariff points information for other examinations.

EXAMPLES OF COLLEGES OFFERING COURSES IN THIS SUBJECT FIELD

Barnet and Southgate (Coll); Barnsley (Coll); Basingstoke (CT); Bedford (Coll); Birmingham Met (Coll); Bishop Burton (Coll); Blackburn (Coll); Blackpool and Fylde (Coll); Bournemouth and Poole (Coll); Bournville (Coll); Bradford (Coll); Brighton Met (Coll); Bury (Coll); Central Bedfordshire (Coll); Chelmsford (Coll); Cornwall (Coll); Craven (Coll); Dearne Valley (Coll); Derby (Coll); Dudley (Coll); Durham New (Coll); East Berkshire (Coll); East Surrey (Coll); Grimsby (Inst Group); Gŵp Llandrillo Menai; Guildford (Coll); Highbury Portsmouth (Coll); Hugh Baird (Coll); Hull (Coll); Kingston (Coll); Lancaster and Morecambe (Coll); Leeds City (Coll); Leicester (Coll); Liverpool City (Coll); London City (Coll); London UCK (Coll); Loughborough (Coll); Manchester (Coll); MidKent (Coll); Neath Port Talbot (Coll); Nescot; Newcastle (Coll); North Kent (Coll); North Notts (Coll); North Warwickshire and Hinckley (Coll); Northumberland (Coll); Norwich City (Coll); Nottingham (Coll); Redcar and Cleveland (Coll); South Cheshire (Coll); South Devon (Coll); Sunderland (Coll); Uxbridge (Coll); West Cheshire (Coll); West Herts (Coll); West Nottinghamshire (Coll); West Thames (Coll); Westminster City (Coll); Westminster Kingsway (Coll); Weston (Coll); Wirral Met (Coll).

CHOOSING YOUR COURSE (SEE ALSO CH.1)

Universities and colleges teaching quality See www.qaa.ac.uk; https://unistats.ac.uk.

Examples of sandwich degree courses Birmingham (UC); Bournemouth; Brighton; Chester; Chichester; Gloucestershire; Greenwich; Hertfordshire; Leeds Beckett; Lincoln; Liverpool John Moores; Manchester Met; Middlesex; Northumbria; Portsmouth; Southampton Solent; Stirling; Sunderland; Surrey; Trinity Saint David; Ulster; Wolverhampton.

ADMISSIONS INFORMATION

Number of applicants per place (approx) Birmingham (UC) 10; Derby 4; Sunderland 2.

Advice to applicants and planning the UCAS personal statement Work experience in the travel and tourism industry is important – in agencies, the airline industry or hotels. This work should be described in detail. Any experience with people in sales work, dealing with the public – problems and complaints – should also be included. Travel should be outlined, detailing places visited. Genuine interest in travel, diverse cultures and people. Good communication skills required. See also **Appendix 3**.

Misconceptions about this course Wolverhampton Some applicants are uncertain whether or not to take a Business Management course instead of Tourism Management. They should be aware that the latter will equip them with a tourism-specific knowledge of business.

Selection interviews Yes Plymouth; **No** Anglia Ruskin, Brighton, Derby, Sunderland, Surrey.

Interview advice and questions Past questions have included: What problems have you experienced when travelling? Questions on places visited. Experiences of air, rail and sea travel. What is marketing? What special qualities do you have that will be of use in the travel industry? See also **Chapter 5**.

Reasons for rejection (non-academic) Wolverhampton English language competence.

AFTER-RESULTS ADVICE
Offers to applicants repeating A-levels Same Anglia Ruskin, Birmingham (UC), Chester, Derby, Lincoln, Manchester Met, Northumbria, St Mary's, Wolverhampton.

GRADUATE DESTINATIONS AND EMPLOYMENT (2015/16 HESA)
See **Hospitality and Event Management**.

Career note See **Business and Management Courses**.

OTHER DEGREE SUBJECTS FOR CONSIDERATION
Airline and Airport Management; Business Studies; Events Management; Heritage Management; Hospitality Management; Leisure and Recreation Management; Travel Management.

TOWN and COUNTRY PLANNING

(including **Environmental Management** and **Urban Studies**; see also **Development Studies, Environmental Sciences, Housing, Surveying and Real Estate Management, Transport Management and Planning**)

Town and Country Planning courses are very similar and some lead to qualification or part of a qualification as a member of the Royal Town Planning Institute (RTPI). Further information from the RTPI (see **Appendix 3**).

Useful websites www.rtpi.org.uk

NB The points totals shown to the left of the institutions are for ease of reference only. It must not be assumed that Tariff points are always used by institutions or that they can be substituted for an offer in grades. The level of an offer is not necessarily indicative of the quality of a course.

COURSE OFFERS INFORMATION
Subject requirements/preferences GCSE English and mathematics required. **AL** Geography may be specified.

Your target offers and examples of degree courses
152 pts **Cambridge** – A*AA +interview +TSA (Lnd Econ) (IB 40–42 pts HL 776)
144 pts **Cardiff** – AAA–ABB (Urb Plan Dev) (HL 666–665); AAA–ABB incl geog (Geog (Hum) Plan) (HL 666)
        Reading – AAA–AAB (Rl Est) (IB 35 pts); (Rl Est Urb Plan Dev) (IB 35–34 pts)
136 pts **London LSE** – AAB (Env Dev) (IB 37 pts HL 666)
128 pts **Birmingham** – ABB (Geog Urb Reg Plan Comb Hons) (IB 32 pts HL 655)
        Liverpool – ABB (Twn Reg Plan) (IB 33 pts)
        London (UCL) – ABB (Urb St; Urb Plan Des Mgt) (IB 34 pts)
        Manchester – ABB (Env Mgt) (IB 32 pts HL 655)
        Newcastle – ABB–BBC (Urb Plan) (IB 28–32 pts)

Sheffield – ABB–BBB+bEPQ incl geog (Geog Plan) (IB 33 pts HL 6 geog)
120 pts **Dundee** – BBB (Twn Reg Plan) (IB 30 pts)
Heriot-Watt – ABC–BBB (Urb Plan Prop Dev) (IB 29 pts)
Liverpool – BBB (Env Plan; Urb Regn Plan) (IB 31 pts)
Nottingham Trent – BBB 120 pts (Prop Dev Plan)
Queen's Belfast – BBB (Plan Env Dev)
Sheffield – BBB–BBC+bEPQ (Urb St; Urb St Plan) (IB 32 pts)
112 pts **Leeds Beckett** – 112 pts (Hum Geog Plan) (IB 25 pts)
Oxford Brookes – BBC (Urb Des Plan Dev; Plan Prop Dev) (IB 31 pts)
Westminster – BBC (Prop Plan) (IB 28 pts)
104 pts **London South Bank** – BCC (Urb Env Plan)

Alternative offers
See **Chapter 6** and **Appendix 1** for grades/UCAS Tariff points information for other examinations.

CHOOSING YOUR COURSE (SEE ALSO CH.1)

Universities and colleges teaching quality See www.qaa.ac.uk; https://unistats.ac.uk.

Top research universities and colleges (REF 2014) See **Architecture**.

Examples of sandwich degree courses Cardiff; Nottingham Trent.

ADMISSIONS INFORMATION

Number of applicants per place (approx) Birmingham 2; Cardiff 6; Dundee 8; London (UCL) 6; London South Bank 3; Manchester 9; Newcastle 4; Oxford Brookes 4.

Advice to applicants and planning the UCAS personal statement Visit your local planning office and discuss the career with planners. Know plans and proposed developments in your area and any objections to them. Study the history of town planning worldwide and the development of new towns in the UK during the 20th century, for example Bournville, Milton Keynes, Port Sunlight, Welwyn Garden City, Cumbernauld, and the advantages and disadvantages which became apparent. See also **Appendix 3**. **Oxford Brookes** See **Surveying and Real Estate Management**.

Selection interviews Some Cardiff; **No** Dundee, Harper Adams, London (UCL), Newcastle, Oxford Brookes.

Interview advice and questions Since Town and Country Planning courses are vocational, work experience in a planning office is relevant and questions are likely to be asked on the type of work done and the problems faced by planners. Questions in recent years have included: If you were re-planning your home county for the future, what points would you consider? How are statistics used in urban planning? How do you think the problem of inner cities can be solved? Have you visited your local planning office? See also **Chapter 5**.

Reasons for rejection (non-academic) Lack of commitment to study for a professional qualification in Town Planning.

AFTER-RESULTS ADVICE

Offers to applicants repeating A-levels Higher Newcastle; **Same** Cardiff, Dundee, London South Bank, Oxford Brookes.

GRADUATE DESTINATIONS AND EMPLOYMENT (2015/16 HESA)

Planning (urban, rural and regional) graduates surveyed 470 **Employed** 295 **In voluntary employment** 5 **In further study** 90 **Assumed unemployed** 35

Career note Town Planning graduates have a choice of career options within local authority planning offices. In addition to working on individual projects on urban development, they will also be involved in advising, co-ordinating and adjudicating in disputes and appeals. Planners also work closely with economists, surveyors and sociologists and their skills open up a wide range of other careers.

OTHER DEGREE SUBJECTS FOR CONSIDERATION
Architecture; Countryside Management; Environmental Studies; Geography; Heritage Management; Housing; Land Economy; Property; Public Administration; Real Estate; Sociology; Surveying; Transport Management.

TRANSPORT MANAGEMENT and PLANNING

(including **Aviation Management, Cruise Management** and **Transport Design**;
see also **Engineering/Engineering Sciences, Town and Country Planning**)

Transport Management and Planning is a specialised branch of business studies with many applications on land, sea and air. It is not as popular as the less specialised Business Studies courses but is just as relevant and will provide the student with an excellent introduction to management and its problems.

Useful websites www.transportweb.com; www.nats.aero; www.ciltuk.org.uk

NB The points totals shown to the left of the institutions are for ease of reference only. It must not be assumed that Tariff points are always used by institutions or that they can be substituted for an offer in grades. The level of an offer is not necessarily indicative of the quality of a course.

COURSE OFFERS INFORMATION
Subject requirements/preferences GCSE English and mathematics required. **AL** No subjects specified.

Your target offers and examples of degree courses
136 pts **Cardiff** – AAB (Bus Mgt (Log Ops)) (IB 35–32 pts)
        Leeds – AAB (Geog Trans Plan) (IB 35 pts)
128 pts **Coventry** – ABB–BBB (Avn Mgt) (IB 31 pts)
        Loughborough – ABB/AAC (Air Trans Mgt) (IB 34 pts HL 655)
120 pts **Aston** – BBB (Log Trans Mgt) (IB 32 pts)
        Huddersfield – BBB 120 pts (Air Trans Log Mgt)
        Loughborough – BBB/ABC (Trans Bus Mgt) (IB 32 pts HL 555)
        Northumbria – 120–128 pts (Bus Log Sply Chn Mgt) (HL 444)
112 pts **Coventry** – BBC incl art/des (Auto Trans Des) (IB 29 pts)
        Greenwich – 112 pts (Bus Log Trans Mgt)
        Huddersfield – BBC 112 pts (Trans Log Mgt)
        Liverpool John Moores – BBC 112 pts (Mgt Trans Log) (IB 26 pts)
        Staffordshire – 112 pts +interview +portfolio (Trans Des)
        West London – BBC 112 pts (Strat Trans Mgt)
 96 pts **Bucks New** – 96–112 pts (Air Trans Commer Plt Trg)
        Plymouth – 96 pts (Cru Mgt) (IB 26 pts HL 4)
 80 pts **Bucks New** – 80–96 pts (Airln Airpt Mgt)
 64 pts **Trinity Saint David** – 64 pts (Log Sply Chn Mgt)

Alternative offers
See **Chapter 6** and **Appendix 1** for grades/UCAS Tariff points information for other examinations.

EXAMPLES OF COLLEGES OFFERING COURSES IN THIS SUBJECT FIELD
Bedford (Coll); Blackburn (Coll); Craven (Coll); Grimsby (Inst Group); MidKent (Coll); Myerscough (Coll); Newcastle (Coll); Norwich City (Coll); Wirral Met (Coll).

CHOOSING YOUR COURSE (SEE ALSO CH.1)
Universities and colleges teaching quality See www.qaa.ac.uk; https://unistats.ac.uk.

Examples of sandwich degree courses Aston; Coventry; Huddersfield; Liverpool John Moores; Loughborough.

UCAS points Tariff: A* = 56 pts; A = 48 pts; B = 40 pts; C = 32 pts; D = 24 pts; E = 16 pts

ADMISSIONS INFORMATION
Number of applicants per place (approx) Aston 5; Huddersfield 3.

Advice to applicants and planning the UCAS personal statement Air, sea, road and rail transport are the main specialist areas. Contacts with those involved and work experience or work shadowing should be described in full. See also **Appendix 3**.

Selection interviews Yes Plymouth; **No** Aston, Bucks New, Huddersfield, Loughborough.

Interview advice and questions Some knowledge of the transport industry (land, sea and air) is likely to be important at interview. Reading around the subject is also important, as are any contacts with management staff in the industries. Past questions have included: What developments are taking place to reduce the number of cars on the roads? What transport problems are there in your own locality? How did you travel to your interview? What problems did you encounter? How could they have been overcome? See also **Chapter 5**.

AFTER-RESULTS ADVICE
Offers to applicants repeating A-levels Same Aston.

GRADUATE DESTINATIONS AND EMPLOYMENT (2015/16 HESA)
Career note Many graduates will aim for openings linked with specialisms in their degree courses. These could cover air, rail, sea, bus or freight transport in which they will be involved in the management and control of operations as well as marketing and financial operations.

OTHER DEGREE SUBJECTS FOR CONSIDERATION
Air Transport Engineering; Civil Engineering; Environmental Studies; Logistics; Marine Transport; Town and Country Planning; Urban Studies.

VETERINARY SCIENCE/MEDICINE

(including **Bioveterinary Sciences** and **Veterinary Nursing**; see also **Animal Sciences**)

Veterinary Science/Medicine degrees enable students to acquire the professional skills and experience to qualify as veterinary surgeons. Courses follow the same pattern and combine rigorous scientific training with practical experience. The demand for these courses is considerable (see below) and work experience is essential prior to application. Graduate entry programmes provide a route to qualifying as a vet to graduates with good degrees in specified subjects. See also **Appendix 3**. Veterinary Nursing Honours degree courses combine both the academic learning and the nursing training required by the Royal College of Veterinary Surgeons, and can also include practice management. Foundation degrees in Veterinary Nursing are more widely available. Bioveterinary Sciences are usually three-year full-time BSc degree courses focusing on animal biology, management and disease, but do not qualify graduates to work as vets. For places in Veterinary Science/Medicine, applicants may select only four universities. Applicants to the University of Cambridge Veterinary School are required to sit the BioMedical Admissions Test (BMAT) (see **Chapter 5**).

Useful websites www.rcvs.org.uk; www.admissionstesting.org; www.bvna.org.uk; https://spvs.org.uk; www.bva.co.uk

NB The points totals shown to the left of the institutions are for ease of reference only. It must not be assumed that Tariff points are always used by institutions or that they can be substituted for an offer in grades. The level of an offer is not necessarily indicative of the quality of a course.

COURSE OFFERS INFORMATION
Subject requirements/preferences GCSE (Vet Sci/Med) Grade B (5/6) English, mathematics, physics, dual science if not at A-level. **AL** (Vet Sci/Med) See offers below. (Vet Nurs) Biology and another science may be required. **Other** Work experience essential for Veterinary Science/Medicine and

Veterinary Nursing courses and preferred for other courses: check requirements. Health checks may be required.

Bristol (Vet Sci) **GCSE** Grade A in five subjects. Grade A (7) in mathematics if neither mathematics nor physics is offered at grade A at AS/A-level.

Glasgow (Vet Med) **GCSE** Grade B (6) in English.

Liverpool (Vet Sci) Minimum of seven **GCSE**s at grades AAABBBB (A/7 and B/6) or above, including English, mathematics and physics (either as a separate subject or as dual award science) are required.

London (RVC) (Vet Med) **GCSE** Grade A (7) in five subjects.

Nottingham (Vet Med) **GCSE** Grade A (7) in five subjects.

Your target offers and examples of degree courses
160 pts **Cambridge** – A*A*A +interview +BMAT (Vet Med) (IB 40–42 pts)
152 pts **Glasgow** – A*AA incl chem+biol (Vet Med Srgy) (IB 38 pts)
144 pts **Bristol** – AAA–AAB incl chem+biol 144–136 pts (Vet Sci) (IB 36–34 pts HL 6 chem 6/5 biol)
        Edinburgh – AAA incl chem+biol+maths/phys (Vet Med) (IB 38 pts)
        Liverpool – AAA incl biol+chem (Vet Sci) (IB 36 pts HL 6 biol+chem)
        London (RVC) – AAA–AAB incl chem+biol +BMAT (Vet Med)
        Surrey – AAA incl chem+biol (Vet Med Sci) (IB 36 pts HL 6 chem+biol)
136 pts **Glasgow** – AAB incl chem+biol (Vet Biosci) (IB 36–34 pts)
        Nottingham – AAB incl chem+biol (Vet Med Srgy) (IB 34 pts); AAB (Vet Med +Prelim Yr)
             (IB 34 pts)
        Surrey – AAB incl biol+sci (Vet Biosci) (IB 35 pts)
128 pts **Harper Adams** – ABB incl biol+sci +interview (Vet Physio) (IB 29 pts HL 6 biol)
        Liverpool – ABB incl biol+sci (Biovet Sci) (IB 33 pts)
        London (RVC) – ABB–BBB incl chem/biol+sci/maths (Biovet Sci)
120 pts **Aberystwyth** – BBB–ABB incl biol (Vet Biosci) (IB 32 pts HL 5 biol)
        Lincoln – 120 pts incl biol/chem (Biovet Sci)
112 pts **Bristol** – BBC incl chem+sci/maths +interview (Gateway Vet Sci) (IB 29 pts HL 5 chem+sci/
             maths); BBC incl biol+chem (Vet Nurs Biovet Sci) (IB 29 pts HL 5 biol+chem)
        Nottingham – BBC incl biol+chem (Vet Med Gateway Yr) (IB 28 pts HL 554 incl 5 biol+chem)
104 pts **Edinburgh Napier** – BCC incl sci 4 weeks work expnc req (Vet Nurs) (IB 28 pts HL 5 sci)
        Harper Adams – 104–120 pts incl biol +interview (Biovet Sci; Biovet Sci (MSci))
 96 pts **Harper Adams** – 96–112 pts incl biol +interview (Vet Nurs courses)
        London (RVC) – BCD incl biol (Vet Nurs); CCC incl chem+biol (Vet Gateway)
        Middlesex – CCC (Vet Nurs)
        Writtle (UC) – 96 pts (Biovet Sci) (IB 24 pts)
 80 pts **Sparsholt (Coll)** – CCE incl lf sci (Vet Nurs (FdSc)) (IB 25 pts HL 5 biol)

Alternative offers
See **Chapter 6** and **Appendix 1** for grades/UCAS Tariff points information for other examinations.

EXAMPLES OF COLLEGES OFFERING COURSES IN THIS SUBJECT FIELD
Askham Bryan (Coll); (Vet Nurs) Bishop Burton (Coll); (Biovet Sci) Canterbury (Coll); Chichester (Coll); Cornwall (Coll); Derby (Coll); Duchy (Coll); (Vet Nurs) Easton Otley (Coll); Hartpury (Coll); (Vet Nurs); (Biovet Sci) Kingston Maurward (Coll); Leeds City (Coll); Myerscough (Coll); (Vet Nurs) Northumberland (Coll); (Vet Nurs) Plumpton (Coll); (Vet Nurs) Sheffield (Coll); Sir Gâr (Coll); Sparsholt (Coll); Warwickshire (Coll); (Vet Nurs FdSci) West Anglia (Coll).

CHOOSING YOUR COURSE (SEE ALSO CH.1)
Author's note Veterinary Science/Medicine is an intensely competitive subject and, as in the case of Medicine, one or two offers and three rejections are not uncommon. As a result, the Royal College of Veterinary Surgeons has raised a number of points which are relevant to applicants and advisers.

UCAS points Tariff: A* = 56 pts; A = 48 pts; B = 40 pts; C = 32 pts; D = 24 pts; E = 16 pts

1 Every candidate for a Veterinary Medicine/Science degree course should be advised to spend a suitable period with a veterinarian in practice.

2 A period spent in veterinary work may reveal a hitherto unsuspected allergy or sensitivity following contact with various animals.

3 Potential applicants should be under no illusions about the difficulty of the task they have set themselves: at least five applicants for every available place, with no likelihood of places being increased at the present time.

4 There are so many candidates who can produce the necessary level of scholastic attainment that other considerations have to be taken into account in making the choice. In most cases, the number of **GCSE** grade As (7s) will be crucial. This is current practice. Head teachers' reports and details of applicants' interests, activities and background are very relevant and are taken fully into consideration; applicants are reminded to include details of periods of time spent with veterinary surgeons.

5 Any applicant who has not received an offer but who achieves the grades required for admission ought to get in touch, as soon as the results are known, with the schools and enquire about the prospects of entry at the Clearing stage. All courses cover the same subject topics.

Universities and colleges teaching quality See www.qaa.ac.uk; https://unistats.ac.uk.

Top research universities and colleges (REF 2014) (Agriculture, Veterinary and Food Science) Warwick; Aberdeen; Glasgow; East Anglia; Bristol; Stirling; Queen's Belfast; Liverpool; Reading; Cambridge; Nottingham.

Examples of sandwich degree courses Harper Adams.

ADMISSIONS INFORMATION
Number of applicants per place (approx) Bristol (Vet Sci) 9, (Vet Nurs Biovet Sci) 12; Cambridge 4; Edinburgh 12; Glasgow 20; Liverpool 6; London (RVC) 5; Nottingham 10.

Advice to applicants and planning the UCAS personal statement Applicants for Veterinary Science must limit their choices to four universities and submit their applications by 15 October. They may add one alternative course. Work experience is almost always essential so discuss this in full, giving information about the size and type of practice and the type of work in which you were involved. As described below, there are several alternative options for work experience. These include work at a veterinary practice involving domestic animals, city and rural farms with dairy, beef cattle, sheep, pigs or poultry, kennels, catteries, laboratories, pet shops, wildlife parks, abattoirs and zoos. See also **Appendix 3**. **Bristol** Eight weeks of work experience, preferably including four weeks of veterinary experience in more than one practice and four weeks in a range of animal establishments. **Cambridge** Work experience expected. **Edinburgh** Competition for places is intense: 125 places are available for the 5-year programme and there are approximately 1,000 applicants each year. The strongest candidates are invited to an interview consisting of seven 10 minute stations that will focus on the applicants' work experience, awareness of animal welfare, career exploration, numeracy skills, data interpretation, ethical issues and a practical manual task.

Edinburgh Napier For Vet Nursing, applicants must have 4 weeks' work experience in a veterinary practice and this must be stated in their personal statement. **Glasgow** A minimum of two weeks in a veterinary practice plus experience of work on a dairy farm, working at a stables, assisting at lambing, work at a cattery or kennels and if possible a visit to an abattoir. Additional experience at a zoo or wildlife park. **Liverpool** The selection process involves three areas: academic ability to cope with the course; knowledge of vocational aspects of veterinary science acquired through work experience in veterinary practice and 10 further weeks of experience working with animals; personal attributes that demonstrate responsibility and self-motivation. **London (RVC)** (Vet Med) Hands-on experience needed: two weeks in a veterinary practice, and two weeks in another animal environment, such as a riding school, zoo or kennels. **Nottingham** Six weeks (minimum) of work experience required.

Check **Chapter 3** for new university admission details and **Chapter 6** on how to read the subject tables.

Misconceptions about this course Liverpool (Biovet Sci) Some applicants think that the course allows students to transfer to Veterinary Science: it does not.

Selection interviews (Vet Sci and Vet Nurs) All institutions **Yes** Cambridge, Edinburgh, Edinburgh Napier, Glasgow, Harper Adams, London (RVC), Nottingham, Surrey.

Interview advice and questions Past questions have included: Why do you want to be a vet? Have you visited a veterinary practice? What did you see? Do you think there should be a Vet National Health Service? What are your views on vivisection? What are your views on intensive factory farming? How can you justify thousands of pounds of taxpayers' money being spent on training you to be a vet when it could be used to train a civil engineer? When would you feel it your responsibility to tell battery hen farmers that they were being cruel to their livestock? What are your views on vegetarians? How does aspirin stop pain? Why does it only work for a certain length of time? Do you eat beef? Outline the bovine TB problem. Questions on A-level science syllabus. See also **Chapter 5**. **Glasgow** Applicants complete a questionnaire prior to interview. Questions cover experience with animals, reasons for choice of career, animal welfare, teamwork, work experience, stressful situations.

Reasons for rejection (non-academic) Failure to demonstrate motivation. Lack of basic knowledge or understanding of ethical and animal issues.

AFTER-RESULTS ADVICE
Offers to applicants repeating A-levels Higher Liverpool; **Same** London (RVC); **No** Cambridge, Edinburgh, Glasgow.

GRADUATE DESTINATIONS AND EMPLOYMENT (2015/16 HESA)
Graduates surveyed 600 **Employed** 555 **In voluntary employment** 15 **In further study** 10 **Assumed unemployed** 10

Career note Most veterinary surgeons work in private practice with the remainder involved in research in universities, government-financed research departments and in firms linked with farming, foodstuff manufacturers and pharmaceutical companies.

OTHER DEGREE SUBJECTS FOR CONSIDERATION
Agricultural Science; Agriculture; Animal Sciences; Biological Sciences; Biology; Dentistry; Equine Dental Science; Equine Management; Equine Studies; Medicine; Zoology.

ZOOLOGY

(including **Animal Biology**; see also **Agricultural Sciences/Agriculture, Animal Sciences, Biological Sciences, Biology**)

Zoology courses have a biological science foundation and could cover animal ecology, marine and fisheries biology, animal population, development and behaviour and, on some courses, wildlife management and fisheries.

Useful websites www.biaza.org.uk; www.zsl.org; www.abwak.org

NB The points totals shown to the left of the institutions are for ease of reference only. It must not be assumed that Tariff points are always used by institutions or that they can be substituted for an offer in grades. The level of an offer is not necessarily indicative of the quality of a course.

COURSE OFFERS INFORMATION
Subject requirements/preferences GCSE English and science/mathematics required or preferred. **AL** One or two sciences will be required.

Your target offers and examples of degree courses

160 pts **Cambridge** – A*A*A incl sci/maths +interview +NSAA (Nat Sci (Zool)) (IB 40–42 pts HL 776)

144 pts **Birmingham** – AAA–AAB incl biol+sci (Biol Sci (Zool)) (IB 32 pts HL 666–665)

Edinburgh – AAA–ABB (Zool) (IB 37–32 pts)

Leeds – AAA–AAB incl biol+sci (Zool) (IB 35–34 pts HL 6 biol+sci)

London (UCL) – AAA incl biol+sci/maths (Biol Sci (Zool)) (IB 38 pts)

Manchester – AAA–ABB incl sci/maths (Zool (Yr Ind)) (IB 37–33 pts); AAA–ABB 144–128 pts (Zool) (IB 37–33 pts); AAA–ABB (Zool Modn Lang) (IB 37–32 pts HL 5 sci)

Sheffield – AAA incl biol+sci (Zool (MBiol)) (IB 37 pts HL 6 biol+sci)

136 pts **Bristol** – AAB–BBB incl sci/maths (Zool) (IB 34–31 pts HI 6/5 sci/maths)

Cardiff – AAB–ABB incl biol (Zool) (IB 34 pts HL 6 biol+chem)

Exeter – AAB–ABB incl sci/maths (Zool (Cornwall)) (IB 34–32 pts HL 5 sci/maths)

Glasgow – AAB incl biol/chem (Zool) (IB 36–34 pts)

Newcastle – AAB–ABB incl biol (Zool) (IB 35 pts HL 6 biol); AAB–ABB incl biol+sci (Mar Zool) (IB 35–34 pts HL 6 biol)

Nottingham – AAB ABB incl biol i sci (Zool) (IB 34–32 pts)

St Andrews – AAB incl biol+sci/maths (Zool) (IB 36 pts)

Sheffield – AAB–ABB+bEPQ incl biol+sci (Zool) (IB 34 pts HL 6 biol+sci)

Southampton – AAB incl biol+sci/maths (Zool) (IB 34 pts HL 6 biol+sci/maths)

Sussex – AAB–ABB (Zool) (IB 32 pts HL 5 sci)

128 pts **Leicester** – ABB incl sci/maths (Biol Sci (Zool)) (IB 30 pts)

Liverpool – ABB incl biol+sci (Zool) (IB 33 pts HL 6 biol)

London (QM) – ABB incl biol (Zool) (IB 34 pts HL 6/5 biol)

London (RH) – ABB–BBB incl biol (Zool) (IB 32 pts HL 5 biol)

Reading – ABB–BBB (Zool) (IB 32–30 pts)

Roehampton – 128 pts incl biol+sci (Zool)

Stirling – ABB incl sci/maths (3 yr course) BBB incl biol+sci (4 yr course) (Anim Biol) (IB 35 pts (3 yr course) 32 pts (4 yr course))

Swansea – ABB–BBB incl biol (Zool) (IB 33–32 pts)

120 pts **Aberdeen** – BBB–ABB incl maths/sci (Zool) (IB 32–34 pts HL 5 maths/sci)

Gloucestershire – BBB 120 pts (Anim Biol)

Lincoln – 120 pts incl biol (Zool)

Queen's Belfast – BBB–ABB incl biol+sci/maths/geog (Zool)

Reading – BBB–CCC (Zool Fdn)

112 pts **Aberystwyth** – BBC–BBB incl biol (Zool); (Anim Bhv) (IB 30 pts HL 5 biol)

Bangor – 112–136 pts incl biol (Mar Biol Zool); 112–136 pts incl biol+sci (Zool; Zool Cons; Zool Mar Zool; Mar Vert Zool)

Derby – 112 pts incl biol (Zool)

Hull – 112 pts incl biol (Zool) (IB 28 pts HL 5 biol)

Liverpool John Moores – 112 pts (Zool) (IB 26 pts)

Nottingham Trent – BBC incl biol 112 pts (Zoo Biol)

Oxford Brookes – BBC 112 pts (Anim Biol Cons) (IB 30 pts)

Staffordshire – 112 pts (Anim Biol Cons)

104 pts **Chester** – BCC–BBC incl biol/chem/psy (Anim Bhv Biol/Psy) (IB 26 pts HL 5 biol)

Harper Adams – 104–120 pts (App Zool; Zool Env Mgt; Zool Entomol)

Manchester Met – BCC–BBC incl biol 104–112 pts (Anim Bhv (St Abrd); Wldlf Biol (St Abrd)) (IB 26 pts HL 5 biol)

Northampton – 104–120 pts (Wldlf Cons)

South Wales – BCC–CDD incl biol+sci 104–80 pts (Int Wldlf Biol) (HL 655–445 incl biol); BCC–CDD incl sci 104–80 pts (Nat Hist) (HL 5 geog/maths)

96 pts **Anglia Ruskin** – 96 pts (Zool) (IB 24 pts)

Cumbria – 96–112 pts +interview +portfolio (Wldlf Media)

Worcester – 96–104 pts incl biol+sci/maths/stats (Anim Biol)

88 pts **West Scotland** – CCD incl biol (App Biosci Zool) (IB 24 pts)

Check **Chapter 3** for new university admission details and **Chapter 6** on how to read the subject tables.

Alternative offers
See **Chapter 6** and **Appendix 1** for grades/UCAS Tariff points information for other examinations.

EXAMPLES OF COLLEGES OFFERING COURSES IN THIS SUBJECT FIELD
See also **Animal Sciences**. Bishop Burton (Coll); Cornwall (Coll); Craven (Coll); Dudley (Coll); Easton Otley (Coll); Guildford (Coll); South Gloucestershire and Stroud (Coll); Sparsholt (Coll).

CHOOSING YOUR COURSE (SEE ALSO CH.1)
Universities and colleges teaching quality See www.qaa.ac.uk; https://unistats.ac.uk.

Examples of sandwich degree courses Cardiff; Leeds; Liverpool John Moores; Manchester; Nottingham Trent.

ADMISSIONS INFORMATION
Number of applicants per place (approx) Bangor 5; Bristol 6; Leeds 7; Liverpool John Moores 6; London (RH) 5; Newcastle 5; Nottingham 9; Southampton 7; Swansea 6.

Advice to applicants and planning the UCAS personal statement Interests in animals should be described, together with any first-hand experience gained. Visits to zoos, farms, fish farms, etc and field courses attended should be described, together with any special points of interest you noted.

Selection interviews Yes Manchester; **Some** Southampton; **No** Derby, Hull, Liverpool, London (RH), Newcastle, Roehampton, Swansea.

Interview advice and questions Past questions have included: Why do you want to study Zoology? What career do you hope to follow on graduation? Specimens may be given to identify. Questions usually asked on A-level subjects. See also **Chapter 5**.

AFTER-RESULTS ADVICE
Offers to applicants repeating A-levels Higher Bristol, Leeds, Swansea; **Same** Aberystwyth, Bangor, Derby, Hull, Liverpool, Liverpool John Moores, London (RH), Roehampton.

GRADUATE DESTINATIONS AND EMPLOYMENT (2015/16 HESA)
Graduates surveyed 1,045 **Employed** 340 **In voluntary employment** 60 **In further study** 335 **Assumed unemployed** 80

Career note See **Biology**.

OTHER DEGREE SUBJECTS FOR CONSIDERATION
Animal Ecology; Animal Sciences; Aquaculture; Biological Sciences; Biology; Ecology; Fisheries Management; Marine Biology; Parasitology; Veterinary Science; Wildlife Management.

INFORMATION FOR INTERNATIONAL STUDENTS

The choice of a subject to study (from over 50,000 degree courses) and of a university or college (from more than 150 institutions) is a major task for students living in the UK. For overseas and EU applicants it is even greater, and the decisions that have to be made need much careful planning, preferably beginning two years before the start of the course. **NB** Beware that there are some private institutions offering bogus degrees: check www.ucas.com to ensure your university and college choices are legitimate.

APPLICATIONS AND THE POINTS-BASED IMMIGRATION SYSTEM

In addition to submitting your application through UCAS (see **Chapter 4**) a Points-based Immigration System is now in operation for overseas students. The main features of this system include:

- **Confirmation of Acceptance for Studies (CAS) number** When you accept an offer the institution will send you a CAS number which you will need to include on your visa application.
- **Maintenance** Students will need to show that they are able to pay for the first year's tuition fees, plus £1,265 per month for accommodation and living expenses if you are studying in London (which includes the University of London, institutions fully or partially in London, or in parts of Surrey, Hertfordshire and Essex), and £1,015 per month if you are studying in the rest of the UK. Additional funds and regulations apply for those bringing dependants into the UK.
- **Proof of qualifications** Your visa letter will list all the qualifications that you submitted to obtain your university place and original proof will be required of these qualifications when submitting your visa application. These documents will be checked by the Home Office. Any fraudulent documents will result in your visa application being rejected and a possible ban from entering the UK for 10 years.
- **Attendance** Once you have started your course, your attendance will be monitored. Non-attending students will be reported to the UK Border Agency.

Full details can be obtained from www.ukcisa.org.uk.

SELECTION, ADMISSION AND FINANCE

The first reason for making early contact with your preferred institution is to check their requirements for your chosen subject and their selection policies for overseas applicants. For example, for most Art and some Architecture courses you will have to present a portfolio of work or slides. For Music courses your application often will have to be accompanied by a recording you have made of your playing or singing and, in many cases, a personal audition will be necessary. Attendance at an interview in this country is compulsory for some universities and for some courses. At other institutions the interview may take place either in the UK or with a university or college representative in your own country.

The ability to speak and write good English is essential and many institutions require evidence of competence, for example scores from the International English Language Testing System (IELTS) or from the Trinity College London test (see www.ielts.org and www.trinitycollege.com/site?id=3218). For some institutions, you may have to send examples of your written work. Each institution provides information about its English language entry requirements and a summary of this is given for each university listed below. International students should note that the recommended threshold for minimum English language requirements is IELTS 6.5–7.0 and an overall score of 5.5 (including 5.5 in each of the four skills) is a requirement for the visa application. Recent research indicates that students with a lower score may have difficulty in dealing with their course.

In the next chapter you will find a directory of universities and colleges in the UK, together with their contact details. Most universities and colleges in the UK have an overseas student adviser who can advise you on these and other points you need to consider, such as passports, visas, entry certificates, evidence of financial support, medical certificates, medical insurance, and the numbers of overseas students in the university from your own country. All these details are very important and need to be considered at the same time as choosing your course and institution.

The subject tables in **Chapter 7** provide a comprehensive picture of courses on offer and of comparative entry levels. However, before making an application, other factors should be considered, such as English language entry requirements (see above), the availability of English language teaching, living costs, tuition fees and any scholarships or other awards which might be offered. Detailed information about these can be obtained from the international offices in each university or college, British higher education fairs throughout the world, the British Council offices abroad and from websites: see www.britishcouncil.org; www.education.org.

Below is a brief summary of the arrangements made by each university in the UK for international students aiming to take a full-time degree programme. The information is presented as follows:

- Institution.
- International student numbers.
- English language entry requirements for degree programmes, shown in IELTS scores. These vary between universities and courses, and can range from 5.5 to 7.5. For full details, contact the university or college.
- Arrangements for English tuition courses.
- International Foundation courses.
- Annual tuition fees (approximate) for full-time undergraduate degree courses. Tuition fees also usually include fees for examinations and graduation. These figures are approximate and are subject to change each year. EU students currently pay 'home student' fees, except for those from the Channel Islands and the Isle of Man; students from an Overseas Territory may be eligible to pay home fees at universities and other institutions of higher education, provided that they meet any residence requirements. For a list of British and other EU member states Overseas Territories, see page 516. More information for international students is available at the UK Council for International Student Affairs, www.ukcisa.org.uk. In the wake of the UK's decision to leave the EU, EU students starting their course in September 2018 will pay 'home student' fees for the duration of their course. EU students starting their courses in September 2018 also remain eligible to apply for student funding under the current terms. Fees for EU students starting courses in the UK beyond 2018 are to be negotiated as part of the exit proceedings with the EU, which will be taking place over the course of the next year. Therefore, for the time being, until it is announced otherwise, EU students will continue to pay the same fees as home students.
- Annual living costs. These are also approximate and represent the costs for a single student over the year. The living costs shown cover university accommodation (usually guaranteed for the first year only), food, books, clothing and travel in the UK, but not travel to or from the UK. (Costs are likely to rise year by year in line with the rate of inflation in the UK.) Overseas students are normally permitted to take part-time work for a period of up to 20 hours per week if they are studying at degree level in the UK.
- Scholarships and awards for non-EU students (most universities offer awards for EU students).

UNIVERSITY INFORMATION AND FEES FOR UNDERGRADUATE INTERNATIONAL STUDENTS

Applicants should check university websites before applying. **The fees published below (unless otherwise stated) are those being charged to students in 2018/19 (check websites for 2019/20 fees).**

Aberdeen Approximately 27% of students come from 120 nationalities. *English language entry requirement (or equivalent):* IELTS 6.0; Medicine 7.0. Four-week English course available in August before the start of the academic year. *Fees:* £14,600–£18,400; Clinical Medicine £39,000. *Living costs:* £1,015 per month.

Abertay International students are represented from over 60 countries around the world. *English language entry requirement (or equivalent):* IELTS 6.0 (no band less than 5.5). Pre-sessional English course available, also full-time English course September to May and free English tuition throughout degree course. *Fees:* £12,250–£14,250. *Living costs:* £820 per month.

Aberystwyth International students make up approximately 13% of the undergraduate student population. *English language entry requirement (or equivalent):* IELTS 6.0 7.5. Full-time tuition in English available. *Fees:* Arts and Social Science subjects £13,450, Science subjects £15,000. *Living costs:* £800 per month. International scholarships available.

AECC (UC) English language entry requirement (or equivalent): IELTS 6.0.

Anglia Ruskin Students from 177 countries. *English language entry requirement (or equivalent):* IELTS 6.0, with minimum of 5.5 in each element. A one-year International Foundation programme available. *Fees:* Arts and Science subjects £11,700–£12,000; Business subjects £11,900–£12,200. Scholarships available. *Living costs:* £8,750.

Arden This private university offers career-focused online distance learning courses worldwide, as well as blended learning study at their following UK study centres: Ealing, Tower Hill, Holborn, Birmingham and Manchester. *Fees:* Contact the University.

Arts London A large number of international students. *English language entry requirement (or equivalent):* IELTS 6.0 for practice-based courses, 6.5 for theory-based courses. Language Centre courses in academic English for four to 24 weeks. *Fees:* £19,350. *Living costs:* £16,120–£18,200. Scholarships and bursaries available.

Aston International students from over 130 countries, with 3,000 of the total student population from overseas. *English language entry requirement (or equivalent):* IELTS 7.5–6.0. International Foundation programme offered as a bridge to the degree courses. Pre-sessional English classes also available for four, eight, 12, 16, 20 and 30 weeks. *Fees:* Languages and Social Science courses £14,000–£14,630; Engineering and Applied Science courses £13,300–£17,200; Life and Health Sciences £14,630–£17,200; Aston Business School £14,950. *Living costs:* £820 per month. Scholarships offered, including bursaries for Engineering and Science subjects.

Bangor Around 13% of the student population are international students. *English language entry requirement (or equivalent):* IELTS 5.5–7.0. Pre-study English course available starting September, January or April depending on level of English proficiency, leads to International Foundation course. One-month or two-month courses before commencement of degree course also offered. *Fees:* Arts, Social Sciences and Education £12,750; Bangor Business School courses £13,500–£14,000; Engineering £14,800; Law £13,000; Science (including Health and Behavioural) £14,300. *Living costs:* £6,000–£8,000. International entrance scholarships available.

Bath Over 1,500 international students from around 100 countries. *English language entry requirement (or equivalent):* IELTS 6.5–7.0. *Fees:* £15,900–£19,800 *Living costs:* £9,700. Scholarships, bursaries and awards available.

Bath Spa Staff and students from over 40 countries. *English language entry requirement (or equivalent):* IELTS 6.0 (minimum of 5.5 in all bands). Pre-sessional English courses for four or five weeks and 11 or 12 weeks. *Fees:* Classroom-based courses £12,9500; laboratory/studio-based courses £13,900. *Living costs:* £7,400–£9,840.

Bedfordshire Over 3,000 EU and international students. *English language entry requirement (or equivalent):* IELTS 5.5. General English programmes are offered, including a summer school. *Fees:* £11,500. *Living costs:* £6,500–£7,500.

Birmingham Over 4,500 international students from 150 countries. *English language entry requirement (or equivalent):* IELTS 6.0–7.0, depending on programme of study. Pre-sessional English language programmes last between six and 42 weeks depending on language proficiency (IELTS 4.0–7.0). *Fees:* Non-laboratory subjects £15,720–£17,520; Laboratory subjects £20,280; Clinical courses £36,840. *Living* *costs:* £7,140–£8,316. Awards are offered by some subject departments including all Engineering subjects, Computer Science, Earth Sciences, Law, and Psychology.

Birmingham (UC) A quarter of the student population are from overseas and come from 65 countries. Specific entry requirements for each country are found on the College website. *English language entry requirement (or equivalent):* IELTS 6.0, with minimum of 5.5 in each band. Pre-sessional English programme for six or 10 weeks depending on language ability. *Fees:* £9,700. *Living costs:* £7,380.

Birmingham City Large number of international students. *English language entry requirement (or equivalent):* IELTS 6.0, with minimum of 5.5 in each band. Pre-sessional language courses of six and 10 weeks. Orientation programme for all students. *Fees:* All undergraduate courses £12,000; Conservatoire/ Acting courses £19,500. *Living costs:* £8,840. Music bursaries.

Bishop Grosseteste *Fees:* Contact the University.

Bolton International students make up approximately 7% of the student population. *English language entry requirement (or equivalent):* IELTS 6.0. English pre-sessional programmes for six, 12, 18 and 24 weeks. Subject-specific Foundation programmes also available. *Fees:* £11,250. *Living costs:* £6,826.

Bournemouth A large number of international students. *English language entry requirement (or equivalent):* IELTS 6.0, with a minimum of 5.5 in each component. Pre-sessional English programmes from two to 39 weeks. *Fees:* £13,500. *Living costs:* £7,000–£9,000 per year. Some subject awards available.

Bournemouth Arts IELTS: 6.0–6.5 overall, with a minimum of 5.5 in each band. *Fees:* £15,000. *Living costs:* £6,500–£8,500.

BPP A private university dedicated to business and the professions with several study centres spread across England. Contact the University for information. *Fees:* Contact the University.

Bradford Over 150 countries represented (15%). *English language entry requirement (or equivalent):* IELTS 6.0, with minimum of 5.5 in each element. Pre-sessional English language courses for six, 10, 20, 30 and 40 weeks. *Fees:* Lab-based courses £17,800; Classroom-based courses £14,950; Health Studies courses £14,950–£18,440. *Living costs:* £6,490–£10,915. Scholarships available.

Brighton Some 1,400 international students from over 100 countries. *English language entry requirement (or equivalent):* IELTS 6.5, with no less than 5.5 for each component. Pre-sessional English courses for four to 30 weeks. *Fees:* Classroom-based courses £12,900; Laboratory and studio-based courses £14,040. *Living costs:* £800 per month. Merit-based scholarships available.

Brighton and Sussex (MS) *English language entry requirement (or equivalent):* IELTS 7.0, with no less than 7.0 in each section. *Fees:* £30,450. *Living costs:* £8,500. Scholarships based on merit and financial need available.

Bristol Approximately 1,500 students from over 100 countries. *English language entry requirement (or equivalent):* IELTS 6.0–7.5 depending on programme of study. Pre-sessional language courses lasting six, 10 and 14 weeks and a year-long International Foundation programme. *Fees:* Arts and Social Sciences courses £16,500 (excluding Archaeology, Film, Theatre, Innovation and Liberal Arts, for which the Science course fees apply); Science and Engineering courses £20,300; Clinical courses £31,800. *Living costs:* £9,000–£14,500. Scholarships and bursaries available.

Brunel More than 2,500 international students from over 110 countries. *English language entry requirement (or equivalent):* IELTS 6.0–7.0. Pre-sessional English language courses available from four to 50 weeks. *Fees:* £14,800–£178,000. *Living costs:* £11,385. International, academic excellence and country-specific scholarships available.

Buckingham Eighty nationalities represented at this small university. *English language entry requirement (or equivalent):* IELTS 6.5, with a minimum of 6.0 in each component. Foundation English courses offered. *Fees:* Eight-term degrees £17,400; nine-term degrees £15,468 for Years 1 and 2 and £3,864 for Year 3. *Living costs:* £8,200. International higher achiever scholarship and some bursaries available.

Bucks New Around 8% of the student population are international students coming from over 50 countries. *English language entry requirement (or equivalent):* IELTS 6.0, with a minimum of of 5.5 in each element. English foundation programme available for one year. *Fees:* (2017/18) £10,500. *Living costs:* £6,000–£7,000. Academic achievement scholarships available.

Cambridge Over 800 international undergraduate students. *English language entry requirement (or equivalent):* IELTS 7.5 overall, with minimum of 7.0 in each element. Pre- and in-sessional English support is available. *Fees:* Tuition fees range between £19,197 and £50,130, depending on the course studied. College fees vary between £6,580 and £12,264 per year, depending on the college. *Living costs:* £10,310. Financial awards are offered to international students through the University of Cambridge and by some colleges. Scholarships for students from Canada and Hong Kong are also available.

Canterbury Christ Church International students from over 80 countries. *English language entry requirement (or equivalent):* IELTS 6.0, with a minimum of 5.5 in each section. Some non-standard programmes require IELTS 6.5 overall. *Fees:* £11,500. *Living costs:* £9,000. International student scholarship of £1,500 per year for up to three years of study.

Cardiff Over 4,500 international students from 100 countries. *English language entry requirement (or equivalent):* IELTS 6.5–7.0. Pre-sessional language courses from eight to 12 weeks. In-sessional support is also available. Induction course for all students. International Foundation courses for Business, Engineering and Health and Life Sciences. *Fees:* Arts-based courses £15,950; Business School courses £16,950; science-based courses £19,950; clinical courses £35,250; healthcare sciences £24,938. *Living costs:* £6,756–£7,340. Scholarships available.

Cardiff Met The University has over 1,200 international students enrolled from more than 143 countries. *English language entry requirement (or equivalent):* IELTS 6.0, with a minimum of 5.5 in each section. International Foundation course and pre-sessional English courses available. *Fees:* £12,000. *Living costs:* £6,800–£7,600. Academic and sports scholarships available.

Central Lancashire Over 2,000 international students from over 100 countries. *English language entry requirement (or equivalent):* IELTS 6.0, with a minimum of 5.5 in each element. *Fees:* Non-laboratory courses £12,450; Laboratory courses £13,450. *Living costs:* £820 per month. Scholarships and bursaries available for international students. Scholarships for students from Indonesia and Palestine are also available.

Chester Over 20,000 students in total from over 130 countries globally. *English language entry requirement (or equivalent):* IELTS 6.0, with a minimum of 5.5 in each element. International Foundation programmes available in Business, Law and Social Sciences, Engineering and Computing, Life Sciences and Creative Arts. Pre- and in-sessional English language courses also available. *Fees:* £11,950. *Living costs:* £9,135. International students are automatically considered for the University of Chester International Scholarship upon application.

Chichester International students from several countries. *English language entry requirement (or equivalent):* IELTS 6.0 or 5.5 if taking a joint degree with International English Studies. No component may be less than 5.5. Pre-sessional programme for five and 10 weeks available. International Academic and Language Support (IALS) is offered alongside any degree. *Fees:* £12,600. *Living costs:* £1,000 per month.

City A large international community with students from over 160 countries. *English language entry requirement (or equivalent):* IELTS 6.0 (6.5 for Law and Journalism). Pre-sessional English language courses are available as four-, eight- and 12-week programmes. International Foundation programme pathways in Actuarial Science, Business, Humanities and Law, Engineering and Mathematics, and Computer Science. *Fees:* £16,830–£17,000. *Living costs:* £1,140 per month. Academic scholarships available.

Coventry About 2,500 international students. *English language entry requirement (or equivalent):* IELTS 6.0–7.0. International Foundation and pre-sessional English programmes available. *Fees:* £12,600–£14,850. *Living costs:* £6,000–£7,000. Scholarships available.

Creative Arts *English language entry requirement (or equivalent):* IELTS 6.0 (no band less than 5.5). *Fees:* £13,540. *Living costs:* £5,000–£8,000. Undergraduate creative scholarships available.

Cumbria *English language entry requirement (or equivalent):* IELTS 6.0, with at least 5.5 in each component (7.0 for Nursing, Midwifery, Occupational Therapy and Social Work). International Foundation Programme and pre- and in-sessional English language courses available. *Fees:* £10,500–£15,500. *Living costs:* £5,500. International scholarships available.

De Montfort Over 1,000 international students from more than 100 countries. *English language entry requirement (or equivalent):* IELTS 6.0–7.0. Pre-sessional English language courses and one-year International Foundation Certificate available. *Fees:* £12,750–£15,500. *Living costs:* £9,000–£11,000. Some scholarships for overseas students.

Derby Students from 100 countries. *English language entry requirement (or equivalent):* IELTS 6.0, with a minimum of 5.5 in all areas. Courses offered to those needing tuition in English language. International Foundation Programme and pre-sessional English courses available. Language development sessions available throughout the course. *Fees:* £12,500; Occupational Therapy courses £13,500. *Living costs:* £208 per week. International scholarships available.

Dundee Students from approximately 83 countries. *English language entry requirement (or equivalent):* IELTS 6.0. Foundation programme pathways in Art and Design, Business, Physical Science and Engineering, Life and Biomedical Sciences, and Social Sciences available. Pre-sessional programmes of four, five and 10 weeks also available. *Fees:* £16,450–£32,000. *Living costs:* £7,000–£8,000. International scholarships available.

Durham Over 4,500 international students from 156 countries. *English language entry requirement (or equivalent):* IELTS 6.5, with no component under 6.0. Pre- and in-sessional English language programmes available. *Fees:* £18,300–£23,100. *Living costs:* £5,000–£7,000. University-administered scholarships and bursaries as well as College and Departmental Prizes available.

Dyson Check the website for details: www.dysoninstitute.com/apply/.

East Anglia Over 4,000 international students from 120 countries. *English language entry requirement (or equivalent):* IELTS 6.0 (higher for some courses). International Foundation and pre-sessional programmes available. *Fees:* Classroom-based subjects £15,300; laboratory-based subjects £19,400; Medicine £30,000. *Living costs:* £7,200. International scholarships available.

East London International students from more than 120 countries. *English language entry requirement (or equivalent):* IELTS 5.5–6.0. Pre-sessional English courses of five, 10 and 15 weeks. *Fees:* £11,880. *Living costs:* £9,000. Range of international scholarships available.

Edge Hill There is a small number of international students. *English language entry requirement (or equivalent):* IELTS 6.0, with a minimum of 5.5 in each element. International Foundation Programme available. *Fees:* £11,800. *Living costs:* £7,000–£8,000. International students will automatically be considered for a scholarship upon application.

Edinburgh Some 4,000 international students from 120 countries. *English language entry requirement (or equivalent):* IELTS 7.0–7.5. English language courses offered throughout the year. *Fees:* £18,800–£24,600; Medicine £32,100–£49,900; Veterinary Medicine £30,800. *Living costs:* £655–£1,340 per month. International maths scholarship available.

Edinburgh Napier Approximately 4,000 international students. *English language entry requirement (or equivalent):* IELTS 6.0 overall with no component below 5.5. Pre- and in-sessional language support. *Fees:* Classroom-based and journalism courses £12,350; Laboratory-based courses £14,350. *Living costs:* £890 per month. Merit-based scholarships available as well as scholarships for students from Hong Kong and India.

Essex International students from over 135 countries. *English language entry requirement (or equivalent):* IELTS 6.0. Pre-sessional English language programmes from five to 25 weeks and academic English classes provided during the year. *Fees:* Laboratory-based courses in Biological Sciences, Health and Human Sciences and Psychology £16,170; all other full-time undergraduate degrees £14,020. *Living* *costs:* £258–£300 per week. A comprehensive package of scholarships and bursaries is available. See www1.essex.ac.uk/fees-and-funding.

Exeter International students from over 140 countries. *English language entry requirement (or equivalent):* IELTS 6.5–7.5. International Foundation and Diploma programmes available as well as pre-sessional English language programmes of six and 10 weeks. *Fees:* Arts, Humanities and Social Sciences (including Business, Economics and Law) £16,900; Accounting and Finance £17,500; Biosciences, Mathematics, Geography, Psychology and Sports Sciences £19,700; Physics, Geology, Mining and Engineering £22,500; Combined Honours programmes that combine a science and a non-science subject £17,995; Medicine £33,000. *Living costs:* £9,500. A range of scholarships and awards are available. Further information is available at www.exeter.ac.uk/studying/funding/prospective.

Falmouth *English language entry requirement (or equivalent):* IELTS 6.0. Discipline-specific academic English courses available throughout the year. *Fees:* £15,000. *Living costs:* £320–£540 per week. International scholarships available.

Glasgow Over 2,000 international students. *English language entry requirement (or equivalent):* IELTS 6.5 (higher for some courses). Pre- and in-sessional English language courses available. *Fees:* Arts and Social Sciences programmes £15,500; Engineering, Science, College of Medical, Veterinary and Life Sciences programmes £20,150; Clinical courses £42,000; Veterinary Medicine and Surgery £28,500. *Living costs:* £12,100. Fee-waiver scholarships and automatic Fourth Year scholarships available (not for Dentistry, Medicine or Veterinary Science).

Glasgow Caledonian Students from more than 100 countries. *English language entry requirement (or equivalent):* IELTS 6.0, with minimum 5.5 in each element. English language programmes available. *Fees:* £11,500. *Living costs:* £1,015 per month. Merit-based scholarships as well as a guaranteed scholarship of £1,000 for full-time self-funded students.

Gloucestershire International students from more than 60 countries. *English language entry requirement (or equivalent):* IELTS 5.5. English language support and mentor scheme with other international students. *Fees:* £13,840. *Living costs:* £7,000–£9,135. International scholarships and bursaries available.

Glyndŵr The University welcomes students from Europe and worldwide. *English language entry requirement (or equivalent):* IELTS 6.0, with a minimum of 5.5 in each element. In-sessional and intensive English language courses available. *Fees:* £11,750. *Living costs:* £7,500. Scholarships available.

Greenwich 4,200 international students from over 140 countries. *English language entry requirement (or equivalent):* IELTS 6.0, with a minimum of 5.5 in each component. Pre-sessional English courses and International Foundation programmes available. *Fees:* (2017/18) £11,500. *Living costs:* £9,500–£10,500. Scholarships open to applicants from 25 countries.

Harper Adams Students from around 30 different countries. *English language entry requirement (or equivalent):* 6.0, with a minimum of 5.5 in each component. Pre-sessional English language programmes available from six weeks to six months. *Fees:* £10,400. *Living costs:* £9,250. Scholarships available.

Heriot-Watt One third of the student population are from outside of the UK. *English language entry requirement (or equivalent):* IELTS 6.0. Several English language courses are offered; these range in length depending on students' requirements. *Fees:* Laboratory-based Science and Engineering courses £17,960; Non-laboratory-based courses £14,200. *Living costs:* £8,970. Some international scholarships are available.

Hertfordshire More than 2,800 international students from over 100 countries are at present studying at the University. *English language entry requirement (or equivalent):* IELTS 6.0–7.0. English language tuition is offered in the one-year International Foundation course and in a pre-sessional intensive English course held during the summer months. *Fees:* £11,950. *Living costs:* £190–£240 per week. International scholarships available.

Huddersfield International students from over 80 countries. *English language entry requirement (or equivalent):* IELTS 6.0, with a minimum of 5.5 in each element. English language courses available and a one-year International Foundation course in English language with options in Business, Computing,

Engineering, Mathematics and Music. Students guaranteed entry to Huddersfield courses on completion. *Fees:* Computing, Engineering and Science courses £14,000; all other courses £15,000. *Living costs:* £9,135. International students are automatically considered for a scholarship of up to £2,000 per year upon application.

Hull Ten per cent of students are from outside the EU. *English language entry requirement (or equivalent):* IELTS 6.0. English summer study programmes available. *Fees:* Non-science programmes £13,500; Science programmes £16,000. *Living costs:* £6,500–£8,500. Excellent overseas scholarship provisions depending on the chosen subject and the student's country of origin.

Hull York (MS) *English language entry requirement (or equivalent):* 7.5, with a minimum of 7.0 in each component. *Fees:* £33,000.

Imperial London International students from over 125 countries. *English language entry requirement (or equivalent):* IELTS 6.5–7.0. Pre-sessional English course available for three weeks. *Fees:* Engineering £29,000; Medicine £40,000; Medical Biosciences £29,000; Chemistry £29,100; Mathematics £26,000; Physics £28,000; Life Sciences £28,650. *Living costs:* £11,184–£14,496. Scholarships available.

Keele Large number of overseas students. *English language entry requirement (or equivalent):* IELTS 6.0–7.0. English language summer school before the start of degree course. International Foundation year degree programmes (entry IELTS 5.0). *Fees:* £13,200–£17,000; Medicine £29,000. *Living costs:* £7,300–£11,200. General, course-specific and country-specific scholarships available for international students. Bursaries also available.

Kent Over 150 different nationalities represented at the University. English language requirement (or equivalent): IELTS 6.5–7.0. Pre-sessional courses and International Foundation programme available. *Fees:* £15,200–£18,400. *Living costs:* £7,000–£13,000. International scholarships worth £5,000 for each year of study available.

Kingston More than 2,000 international students. *English language entry requirement (or equivalent):* IELTS 6.0–7.0. Pre-sessional English language and subject-specific Foundation-level courses available. Free English support during degree studies. *Fees:* Classroom-based courses £12,300; Art and Design courses £13,400; Pharmacy and studio-based courses £13,800; Laboratory-based courses £13,800. *Living costs:* £6,500–£10,000. International scholarship worth £4,000 per year of study.

Lancaster Twenty-five per cent of student population from over 100 countries. *English language entry requirement (or equivalent):* IELTS 6.0–7.0. Pre-sessional and in-session English language courses cover reading, writing, listening and speaking skills. *Fees:* £15,680–£30,300. *Living costs:* £7,840.

Leeds More than 6,000 students from outside the UK. *English language entry requirement (or equivalent):* IELTS 7.0–7.5, with a minimum of 5.5–6.5 in each component. *Fees:* £17,500–£31,250. *Living costs:* £575–£760 per month. International subject-specific scholarships available.

Leeds Arts *English language entry requirement (or equivalent):* IELTS 5.5. *Fees:* £15,000.

Leeds Beckett Students from 125 countries and territories. *English language entry requirement (or equivalent):* IELTS 6.0 (IELTS 5.0 for the International Foundation programme, starting September or February). Also general English courses. *Fees:* £12,000. *Living costs:* £9,135. Scholarships available.

Leeds Trinity *English language entry requirement (or equivalent):* IELTS 6.0 overall, with a minimum of 5.5 in each component (may be higher for some courses). Pre-sessional English course available. *Fees:* £11,250. *Living costs:* £9,135. International scholarship worth £1,000 awarded based on academic and professional merit.

Leicester Over 4,000 international students from 110 countries. *English language entry requirement (or equivalent):* IELTS 6.5–7.5 (5.0 for the Foundation year). English language preparatory programmes and on-going support Foundation programme. *Fees:* Non-science degrees £15,980; science degrees £19,070; Geography £16,640; Medicine £19,705–£41,945. *Living costs:* £800 per month. International scholarships available.

LIBF The Institute offers a range of finance courses leading to professional qualifications. See the website for details: www.libf.ac.uk. *Fees:* £10,500.

Lincoln International students from over 100 countries. *English language entry requirement (or equivalent):* IELTS 6.0. Pre- and in-sessional English language courses available. *Fees:* £13,800–£15,600. *Living costs:* £800 per month. Scholarships for high-achieving international students. Engineering bursaries also available.

Liverpool Over 7,500 international students from more than 120 countries. *English language entry requirement (or equivalent):* Science and Engineering: IELTS 6.0 (minimum 5.5 in each component); Humanities and Social Sciences, Health and Life Sciences, Geography, Planning and Carmel College: IELTS 6.5 (minimum 5.5 in each component). *Fees:* £15,750–£19,700; Dentistry, Medicine and Veterinary Science £33,600. *Living costs:* £440–£1,090 per month. Scholarships available, including special awards for students from Hong Kong.

Liverpool Hope Approximately 700 international students. *English language entry requirement (or equivalent):* IELTS 6.0. Language courses available. *Fees:* £11,200–£12,000. *Living costs:* £7,380. International Excellence bursary and Music scholarship available.

Liverpool John Moores A large number of overseas students. *English language entry requirement (or equivalent):* IELTS 6.0. Pre-sessional and in-session English tuition available. *Fees:* Laboratory-based courses £14,000; Classroom-based courses £13,250. *Living costs:* £1,015 per month. International scholarships available.

London (Birk) Over 100,000 international students from more than 200 countries. *English language entry requirement (or equivalent):* IELTS 6.5. Pre-sessional English courses and free online study skills materials available. *Fees:* £13,000. *Living costs:* £12,000–£13,000. Scholarships available.

London (Court) Students from around the world. *English language entry requirement (or equivalent):* IELTS 7.0. *Fees:* £18,180. *Living costs:* £1,500 per month. Scholarships available.

London (Gold) Students from more than 140 countries. *English language entry requirement (or equivalent):* IELTS 6.5. Pre-sessional programmes available. *Fees:* £13,910–£20,590. *Living costs:* £640–£1,760 per month. Country-specific scholarships available.

London (Inst Paris) *English language entry requirement (or equivalent):* IELTS 6.5, with a minimum of 5.5 in each element. *Fees:* (2017/18) £14,500. *Living costs:* £296–£817 per month. Bursaries available.

London (King's) Thousands of international students from over 150 countries. *English language entry requirement (or equivalent):* IELTS 6.0–7.5. Pre-sessional summer courses and a one-year Foundation course available. *Fees:* Classroom-based £17,900; Laboratory-based £23,900; Pharmacy £20,600. *Living costs:* £1,000–£1,200 per month. Awards available.

London (QM) Students from over 162 countries. *English language entry requirement (or equivalent):* IELTS 6.0–7.0. International Foundation course covering English language tuition and specialist courses in Business, Management, Economics, Mathematics, Spanish, Geography and European Studies. The course guarantees progression to linked degree courses including Law. *Fees:* £16,900–£19,000; Dentistry and Medicine £34,300. *Living costs:* £1,050 per month. Subject-specific bursaries and scholarships available.

London (RH) Over 1,900 overseas students from nearly 100 countries. *English language entry requirement (or equivalent):* IELTS 6.5–7.0. Pre-sessional English course available. Ten-month Foundation course with studies in English language and introduction to specialist studies in a range of degree subjects. *Fees:* £16,500–£18,900. *Living costs:* £11,960–£12,129. Bursaries and scholarships available.

London (RVC) Many international students from countries all over the world. *English language entry requirement (or equivalent):* IELTS 6.5–7.0. *Fees:* £13,380–£33,990. *Living costs:* £13,388–£20,900. International scholarships available.

London (St George's) There are a variety of courses that international and non-EU students can apply to. Full details on entry requirements for each individual course are available on the University website. *English language entry requirement (or equivalent):* a language level of at least CEFR B2. Pre-sessional English courses available. *Fees:* Physiotherapy £15,250; Biomedical Science £17,000; Diagnostic Radiography £15,000; Medicine £32,500. *Living costs:* £1,200 per month.

London (SOAS) Students from more than 133 countries. *English language entry requirement (or equivalent):* IELTS 7.0. A one-year Foundation programme and English language courses available with an entry requirement of IELTS 6.0–6.5 depending on the length. *Fees:* £16,907. *Living costs:* Over £1,000 per month.

London (UCL) Overseas students make up 25% of the population. *English language entry requirement (or equivalent):* IELTS 6.5–7.5. *Fees:* £17,890–£33,650. *Living costs:* £15,103. Scholarships available.

London LSE International students represent 150 countries. *English language entry requirement (or equivalent):* IELTS 7.0. Academic English language courses available. *Fees:* £19,152. *Living costs:* £12,000. A limited number of international scholarships available.

London Met Students from 147 countries. *English language entry requirement (or equivalent):* IELTS 6.0. One-year International Foundation programme. Full range of English courses. *Fees:* £11,800. *Living costs:* £1,265 per month.

London Regent's Students from over 140 countries around the world. *English language entry requirement (or equivalent):* A range of English language qualifications accepted. *Fees:* £17,000. *Living costs:* £1,000–£1,200 per month. Scholarships available.

London South Bank Almost 2,000 international students from over 130 countries. *English language entry requirement (or equivalent):* IELTS 6.0. Pre-study English course and a University Foundation course for overseas students. *Fees:* From £13,125. *Living costs:* £820–£2,200 per month. Range of scholarships available.

Loughborough Some 1,000 undergraduate students from outside the UK. *English language entry requirement (or equivalent):* IELTS 6.5 with a minimum of 6.0 in all sub-tests. Special pre-sessional courses offered by the Student Support Centre. *Fees:* Classroom-based subjects and School of Business £17,500; Laboratory-based subjects £20,500. *Living costs:* £8,000. Self-funded international students are automatically considered for an international scholarship upon application.

Manchester A high proportion of international students from over 160 countries. *English language entry requirement (or equivalent):* IELTS 6.0–7.0. Foundation Year programme available as well as pre- and in-sessional English language courses. *Fees:* Non-laboratory £18,000; Laboratory £22,000; Clinical £40,000. *Living costs:* £9,255. Some scholarships and bursaries are available.

Manchester Met A large number of international students. *English language entry requirement (or equivalent):* IELTS 6.0. General, academic and pre-sessional English language courses available. *Fees:* Classroom-based courses £13,500; Laboratory-based courses £15,000; Architecture £22,000. *Living costs:* £7,380. Variety of international scholarships and awards available.

Middlesex Over 8,000 international students. *English language entry requirement (or equivalent):* IELTS 6.0. Pre-sessional English course available. *Fees:* £12,500. *Living costs:* £950–£1,500 per month. Scholarships available.

NCH London *English language entry requirement (or equivalent):* IELTS 7.0, with a minimum of 6.5 in each component. *Fees:* £19,750. *Living costs:* £1,250 per month. International scholarship of £2,000 awarded based on academic ability.

Newcastle Over 2,500 students from outside the UK. *English language entry requirement (or equivalent):* IELTS 6.5. Pre- and in-sessional English language courses as well as an International Foundation programme. *Fees:* Non-science subjects £16,200; science subjects £21,000; Dentistry £21,000 (Phase 1) £35,200 (Phase 2); Medicine £32,000. *Living costs:* £9,500–£10,500. International scholarships available.

Newman *English language entry requirement (or equivalent):* IELTS 6.0. *Fees:* (2017/18) £11,100. *Living costs:* £600–£1,015 per month. Scholarships available.

Northampton Over 1,000 international students from over 100 countries. *English language entry requirement (or equivalent):* IELTS 6.0. English language courses available. *Fees:* £12,000 for all BA/BSc courses, except Podiatry and Occupational Therapy (£13,000). *Living costs:* £8,000–£10,000. Scholarships and bursaries are available, please see our website for more details.

Northumbria Students from over 100 countries. *English language entry requirement (or equivalent):* IELTS 5.5–7.0. English language and Foundation courses available. *Fees:* £13,000–£15,000. *Living costs:* £1,015 per month. Country scholarships for students from over 15 countries; some merit-based course scholarships.

Norwich Arts Students from over 40 countries. *English language entry requirement (or equivalent):* IELTS 6.0 (with a minimum of 5.5 in all sections). English language study and pre-course training offered. *Fees:* £13,700.

Nottingham Students and staff from over 150 countries. *English language entry requirement (or equivalent):* IELTS 6.0–7.0 (7.5 for Medicine). Pre- and in-sessional English language courses available. *Fees:* £16,350–£21,060; Medicine £22,170. *Living costs:* £1,015 per month. Scholarships for siblings and science applicants.

Nottingham Trent Large number of overseas students. *English language entry requirement (or equivalent):* IELTS 6.0–7.0. English language courses (six to 30 weeks) available. *Fees:* £13,450. *Living costs:* £8,000. International scholarships available.

Open University Courses are open to students throughout the world with study online or with educational partners. Tutorial support is by telephone, fax, computer conferencing or email. *Fees:* Non-EU students' fees vary depending on type of course.

Oxford Students from 140 countries and territories. *English language entry requirement (or equivalent):* IELTS 7.0. English language courses available. *Fees:* Tuition fee £16,230–£23,885, Clinical Medicine £36,007; College fee £7,570. *Living costs:* £1,014–£1,556 per month. University and college scholarships and awards are available.

Oxford Brookes Large number of international students. *English language entry requirement (or equivalent):* IELTS 6.0–6.5. Large number of English language support courses offered. *Fees:* £13,150–£14,000. *Living costs:* £11,130. Partner scholarships available for students from North America and Norway as well as family awards.

Plymouth *English language entry requirement (or equivalent):* IELTS 6.0. Pre-sessional English courses available. *Fees:* £13,000. *Living costs:* £1,000 per month. International scholarships available.

Portsmouth Over 4,000 international students from 130 different countries. *English language entry requirement (or equivalent):* IELTS 6.0. Induction, academic skills and language courses available. *Fees:* Classroom-based courses £13,200; mixed classroom- and laboratory-based courses £14,000; laboratory-based courses £15,100. *Living costs:* £7,000–£8,000. International scholarships available.

Queen Margaret Around 25% of students are international coming from over 70 countries. *English language entry requirement (or equivalent):* IELTS 6.5. English language support available. *Fees:* Classroom-based courses £12,000; Laboratory/studio-based courses £13,000. *Living costs:* £7,380. Scholarships for students from China, Canada, USA and India as well as other international scholarships.

Queen's Belfast International students from over 80 countries. *English language entry requirement (or equivalent):* IELTS 6.5–7.5. Special English language summer schools and pre-university language courses are provided, also weekly language courses. Orientation programme held before the start of the academic year. *Fees:* Classroom-based courses £15,550; Laboratory component courses £19,500; Pre-clinical courses £19,950; Clinical courses £37,695. *Living costs:* £197 per week. International scholarships available.

Reading More than 5,000 students from over 140 countries. *English language entry requirement (or equivalent):* IELTS 6.5. International Foundation programme offering English language tuition and a choice of 15 specialist pathways. Other pre-sessional English courses offered. *Fees:* Non-laboratory courses £16,070; Laboratory courses £19,330. *Living costs:* £876–£1,116 per month. Some scholarships offered.

Robert Gordon Over 1,000 international students from more than 65 countries. *English language entry requirement (or equivalent):* IELTS 6.0. Pre-sessional English programme available as well as language classes and one-to-one support during the year. *Fees:* £12,360–£15,760. *Living costs:* £7,000–£9,000. Merit scholarships for specific subjects available.

Roehampton Students from more than 140 countries. *English language entry requirement (or equivalent):* IELTS 6.0, with a minimum of 5.5 in each component. International Foundation programme and pre-sessional English courses available. *Fees:* £13,520. *Living costs:* £7,500–£8,500. International scholarships available.

Rose Bruford (Coll) International students from over 25 different countries. Throughout the year staff hold interviews and auditions in Asia, Canada, Europe and USA. See the website for more details.

Royal Agricultural Univ International students from 45 different countries. *English language entry requirement (or equivalent):* IELTS 6.0. International Foundation Year and English language courses available. *Fees:* £10,000. *Living costs:* £8,000–£10,000. International scholarships available.

St Andrews Over 1,500 international students from more than 120 different nationalities. *English language entry requirement (or equivalent):* IELTS 7.0–8.0. International Foundation programme available as well as pre- and in-sessional English language courses. *Fees:* £21,290; Medicine £30,080. *Living costs:* £14,000–£16,000. Scholarships available.

St Mark and St John *English language entry requirement (or equivalent):* IELTS 6.0. English Preparation Programme available. *Fees:* £11,000; Speech and Language Therapy £11,750. *Living costs:* £1,000 per month.

St Mary's Qualifications from any country will be considered and measured against British equivalents. Almost 10% of the student population are international. *English language entry requirement (or equivalent):* IELTS 6.0 (minimum 5.5 in each component); Nutrition BSc 6.5 (minimum 6.0 in each component). In-sessional English language programme available. *Fees:* £11,220. *Living costs:* £7,000–£8,000.

Salford More than 3,000 international students from over 100 countries. *English language entry requirement (or equivalent):* IELTS 6.0–7.0. English study programmes and a very comprehensive International Foundation year. *Fees:* £8,225–£13,300. *Living costs:* £7,624–£9,545. Scholarships and bursaries available.

Sheffield Over 6,500 international students from 150 countries. *English language entry requirement (or equivalent):* IELTS 7.0. Preparatory English courses and an international summer school with English classes. *Fees:* £16,800–£21,450; Clinical Medicine £37,300. *Living costs:* £9,135. Faculty scholarships and international merit scholarships available.

Sheffield Hallam Over 100 countries represented by thousands of international students. *English language entry requirement (or equivalent):* IELTS 6.0–7.0. Pre-sessional and academic English language courses available. *Fees:* £12,750. *Living costs:* £800 per month. International scholarships available as well as country-specific scholarships for students from South Asia and South East Asia.

South Wales *English language entry requirement (or equivalent):* IELTS from 6.0. Pre-sessional course offered in English with course lengths of between five and 10 weeks depending on the applicant's proficiency. An International Foundation Programme is also offered. *Fees:* £13,500. *Living costs:* £4,788–£8,820. International students automatically considered for a scholarship upon application.

Southampton Over 6,500 international students from more than 135 countries. *English language entry requirement (or equivalent):* IELTS 5.5–7.0. English courses offered and also an International Foundation course covering Arts, Humanities, Social Sciences and Law. *Fees:* £16,536–£20,320; Clinical Medicine £40,230. *Living costs:* £7,200–£8,800. International Merit scholarship available.

Southampton Solent Over 14% of the student population come from overseas, representing more than 100 different nationalities. *English language entry requirement (or equivalent):* IELTS 6.0. Induction programme and language tuition available. *Fees:* £12,500. *Living costs:* £8,000.

Staffordshire Students from over 70 countries. *English language entry requirement (or equivalent):* IELTS 6.0. English tuition available. *Fees:* £11,100. *Living costs:* £7,000. International scholarships available.

Stirling Students from 120 nationalities. *English language entry requirement (or equivalent):* IELTS 6.0. English language tuition available as well as an International Foundation in Business, Finance, Economics and Marketing. *Fees:* £12,140–£14,460. *Living costs:* £5,000–£6,000. Some scholarships are available. Please see www.stir.ac.uk/scholarships.

Stranmillis (UC) *Fees:* £15,550. *Living costs:* £7,500.

Strathclyde Students from 100 countries. *English language entry requirement (or equivalent):* IELTS 6.5. Pre-entry and pre-sessional English tuition available. *Fees:* £14,050–£18,750. *Living costs:* £8,000–£12,700.

Suffolk *Fees:* Classroom-based courses £11,500; Laboratory/studio/IT-based courses £13,000.

Sunderland International students come from over 100 countries. *English language entry requirement (or equivalent):* IELTS 6.0. English language tuition available. *Fees:* £11,000. *Living costs:* £485–£1,164 per month. International students are automatically considered for a £1,500 scholarship upon application.

Surrey Students from over 120 different countries. *English language entry requirement (or equivalent):* IELTS 6.5–7.5. English language courses and summer courses offered. *Fees:* £17,500–£20,500; Veterinary Medicine £31,500. *Living costs:* £6,883.50. Scholarships and bursaries offered, including awards for students on Civil Engineering courses.

Sussex More than 3,000 international students from over 140 countries. *English language entry requirement (or equivalent):* IELTS 6.5–7.0 (7.5 for Medicine). English language and study skills courses available. International Foundation courses offered, covering English language tuition and a choice from Humanities, Law, Media Studies, Social Sciences and Cultural Studies and Science and Technology. *Fees:* £15,500–£19,200; Medicine £30,450. *Living costs:* £550–£1,120 per week. International scholarships available.

Swansea Students from over 100 countries. *English language entry requirement (or equivalent):* IELTS 6.0–6.5. Pre-sessional English language courses available and on-going support during degree courses. *Fees:* £13,350–£35,700. *Living costs:* £6,000–£9,000. Some overseas scholarships and prizes.

Teesside Students from over 100 countries. *English language entry requirement (or equivalent):* IELTS 5.5–7.0. Free English courses available throughout the year while following degree programmes. International summer school available. *Fees:* £11,825. *Living costs:* £1,015 per month. Scholarships available for self-funded students.

Trinity Saint David International students are well represented at the University. *English language entry requirement (or equivalent):* IELTS 6.5. International Foundation programme available. *Fees:* (2017/18) £10,400. *Living costs:* £6,500–£7,500. International scholarships available.

UCO Students from across the world including Australia, Brazil and Europe. English language entry requirement (or equivalent): IELTS 6.5 or above.

UHI *English language entry requirement (or equivalent):* IELTS 6.0; minimum 5.5 in all four components. *Fees:* Art, Humanities, Social Science and Business courses £11,100; Science and Technology courses £12,200. *Living costs:* £610–£850 per month.

Ulster Students from over 100 countries. *English language entry requirement (or equivalent):* IELTS 6.0. Pre- and in-sessional English language courses available. *Fees:* (2017/18) £13,240. *Living costs:* £6,000–£7,000. International scholarships available.

Univ Law More than 1,200 students from over 100 countries. *English language entry requirement (or equivalent):* IELTS 7.0. *Fees:* £13,000–£18,000. *Living costs:* £6,000–£8,000. International scholarships available.

UWE Bristol More than 1,750 international students. *English language entry requirement (or equivalent):* IELTS 6.0, with a minimum of 5.5 in each component. Pre- and in-sessional English language courses offered. *Fees:* £13,000. *Living costs:* £1,015 per month. Scholarships based on academic, sports and entrepreneurial excellence available as well as country- and programme-specific scholarships.

Warwick Over 3,500 international students. *English language entry requirement (or equivalent):* IELTS 6.0 for Science courses, 6.5 for Arts courses, 6.5 for MORSE courses, and 7.0 for Social Studies and Business courses. English language support available. *Fees:* Classroom-based courses £18,330; Laboratory-based courses, plus Theatre and Performance Studies, Economics and Business courses (with a few exceptions) £23,380; Medicine £21,390–£37,290. *Living costs:* £7,250–£12,040. More than 20 awards available for overseas students.

West London A large number of international students. *English language entry requirement (or equivalent):* IELTS 6.0. International Foundation programme and English language support available. *Fees:* £12,000. *Living costs:* £13,700. International scholarships available.

West Scotland Over 1,100 international students from around 70 countries. *English language entry requirement (or equivalent):* IELTS 6.0. English language Foundation course available. *Fees:* Classroom-based courses £10,600; laboratory-based courses £12,100. *Living costs:* £600 per month. International scholarships available.

Westminster Over 20,000 students from over 169 nations. *English language entry requirement (or equivalent):* IELTS 6.0. Pre- and in-sessional English courses available. *Fees:* £12,750. *Living costs:* £800 per month (minimum). International scholarships available.

Winchester Some 600 international students from over 60 countries. *English language entry requirement (or equivalent):* IELTS 6.0. Language courses available. *Fees:* £12,950. *Living costs:* £7,500–£8,500. International scholarships available.

Wolverhampton Over 2,500 international students from over 100 countries. *English language entry requirement (or equivalent):* IELTS 6.0. Four week English course available. International student programme. *Fees:* £11,700. *Living costs:* £7,200. Scholarships and bursaries available.

Worcester *English language entry requirement (or equivalent):* IELTS 6.0. English language support available. *Fees:* £12,100. *Living costs:* £6,000–£7,500. International scholarships of up to £3,000 available.

Writtle (UC) *Fees:* £11,400.

York 15% of students from outside the UK. *English language entry requirement (or equivalent):* IELTS 6.0–7.0 (7.5 for Medicine). Pre-sessional English language courses. *Fees:* £16,620–£20,910; Medicine £33,000. *Living costs:* £7,624–£9,665. Several scholarships for overseas students.

York St John *English language entry requirement (or equivalent):* IELTS 6.0. Pre-sessional courses and International Foundation Programme available. *Fees:* £14,000; Health Programmes £14,500. *Living costs:* £1,015 per month.

BRITISH OVERSEAS TERRITORIES STUDENTS
Students from British Overseas Territories are now treated as home students for fee purposes at universities and other institutions of higher education in England, Wales and Northern Ireland, provided they meet residency requirements. The territories to which this policy applies are:

British Overseas Territories Anguilla, Bermuda, British Antarctic Territory, British Indian Ocean Territory, British Virgin Islands, Cayman Islands, Falkland Islands, Montserrat, Pitcairn, Henderson, Ducie and Oeno Islands, South Georgia and the South Sandwich Islands, St Helena and Dependencies (Ascension Island and Tristan de Cunha), Turks and Caicos Islands.

Overseas Territories of other EU member states Aruba, Faroe Islands, French Polynesia, French Southern and Antarctic Territories, Greenland, Netherland Antilles (Bonaire, Curaçao, Saba, Sint Eustatius and Sint Maarten), the Territory of New Caledonia and Dependencies, St-Barthélemy (St Barth), St Pierre et Miquelon, Wallis and Futuna Islands.

SECTION 1: UNIVERSITIES AND UNIVERSITY COLLEGES

Listed below are universities and university colleges in the United Kingdom that offer degree and diploma courses at higher education level. Applications to these institutions are submitted through UCAS except for part-time courses, private universities and colleges, and further education courses. For current information refer to the websites shown and also to www.ucas.com for a comprehensive list of degree and diploma courses (see **Appendix 4**)

Aberdeen Tel 01224 272090; www.abdn.ac.uk

Abertay (Dundee) Tel 01382 308045; www.abertay.ac.uk

Aberystwyth Tel 01970 622021; www.aber.ac.uk

AECC (UC) (Bournemouth) Tel 01202 436200; www.aecc.ac.uk

Anglia Ruskin (Chelmsford) Tel 01245 686868; www.anglia.ac.uk

Arden (London; Brmingham; Manchester) Tel 0800 268 7737; https://arden.ac.uk/

Arts London Tel 020 7514 6000; www.arts.ac.uk

Aston (Birmingham) Tel 0121 204 4444; www.aston.ac.uk

Bangor Tel 01248 383717; www.bangor.ac.uk

Bath Tel 01225 383019; www.bath.ac.uk

Bath Spa Tel 01225 876180; www.bathspa.ac.uk

Bedfordshire (Luton) Tel 01582 743500; www.beds.ac.uk

Birmingham Tel 0121 414 3344; www.birmingham.ac.uk

Birmingham (UC) Tel 0121 604 1040; www.ucb.ac.uk

Birmingham City Tel 0121 331 5595; www.bcu.ac.uk

Bishop Grosseteste (Lincoln) Tel 01522 583658; www.bishopg.ac.uk

Bolton Tel 01204 903394; www.bolton.ac.uk

Bournemouth (Poole) Tel 01202 961916; www1.bournemouth.ac.uk

Bournemouth Arts (Poole) Tel 01202 533011; https://aub.ac.uk

BPP (Manchester) Tel 03331 224359; www.bpp.com

Bradford Tel 01274 236088; www.bradford.ac.uk

Brighton Tel 01273 644644; www.brighton.ac.uk

Brighton and Sussex (MS) Tel 01273 643528; www.bsms.ac.uk

Bristol Tel 0117 394 1649; www.bristol.ac.uk

Brunel (Uxbridge) Tel 01895 265265; www.brunel.ac.uk

Buckingham Tel 01280 820313; www.buckingham.ac.uk

Bucks New (High Wycombe) Tel 0330 123 2023; www.bucks.ac.uk

Cambridge Tel 01223 333308; www.cam.ac.uk

Canterbury Christ Church Tel 01227 782900; www.canterbury.ac.uk

Cardiff Tel 029 2087 9999; www.cardiff.ac.uk

Cardiff Met Tel 029 2041 6010; www.cardiffmet.ac.uk

Central Lancashire (Preston) Tel 01772 201201; www.uclan.ac.uk

Chester Tel 01244 511000; www1.chester.ac.uk

Chichester Tel 01243 816002; www.chi.ac.uk

City (London) Tel 020 7040 8716; www.city.ac.uk

Coventry Tel 024 7765 2222; www.coventry.ac.uk

Creative Arts (Farnham) Tel 01252 892960; www.uca.ac.uk

Cumbria Tel 0333 920 9243; www.cumbria.ac.uk

De Montfort (Leicester) Tel 0116 250 6070; www.dmu.ac.uk

Derby Tel 01332 591167; www.derby.ac.uk

Dundee Tel 01382 383838; www.dundee.ac.uk

Durham Tel 0191 334 6128; www.dur.ac.uk

Dyson (Malmesbury) Tel 0800 298 0298; www.dysoninstitute.com

East Anglia (Norwich) Tel 01603 591515; www.uea.ac.uk

East London Tel 020 8223 3333; www.uel.ac.uk

Edge Hill (Ormskirk) Tel 01695 657000; www.edgehill.ac.uk

Edinburgh Tel 0131 650 4360; www.ed.ac.uk

Edinburgh Napier Tel 0333 900 6040; www.napier.ac.uk

Essex (Colchester) Tel 01206 873666; www.essex.ac.uk

Exeter Tel 0300 555 6060; www.exeter.ac.uk

Falmouth Tel 01326 213730; www.falmouth.ac.uk

Glasgow Tel 0141 330 2000; www.gla.ac.uk

Glasgow Caledonian Tel 0141 331 8630; www.gcu.ac.uk

Gloucestershire (Cheltenham) Tel 01242 714845; www.glos.ac.uk

Glyndŵr (Wrexham) Tel 01978 293439; www.glyndwr.ac.uk

Greenwich (London) Tel 020 8331 9000; www.gre.ac.uk

Harper Adams (Newport) Tel 01952 815000; www.harper-adams.ac.uk

Heriot-Watt (Edinburgh) Tel 0131 449 5111; www.hw.ac.uk

Hertfordshire (Hatfield) Tel 01707 284800; www.herts.ac.uk

Huddersfield Tel 01484 473969; www.hud.ac.uk

Hull Tel 01482 466100; www.hull.ac.uk

Hull York (MS) Tel 01904 321690; www.hyms.ac.uk

Imperial London Tel 020 7589 5111; www.imperial.ac.uk

Keele Tel 01782 734010; www.keele.ac.uk

Kent (Canterbury) Tel 01227 827272; www.kent.ac.uk

Kingston (Kingston upon Thames) Tel 0844 855 2177; www.kingston.ac.uk

Lancaster Tel 01524 592028; www.lancaster.ac.uk

Leeds Tel 0113 343 2336; www.leeds.ac.uk

Leeds Arts Tel 0113 202 8000; www.leeds-art.ac.uk

Leeds Beckett Tel 0113 812 3113; www.leedsbeckett.ac.uk

Leeds Trinity Tel 0113 283 7123; www.leedstrinity.ac.uk

Leicester Tel 0116 252 5281; https://le.ac.uk

LIBF (London) Tel 012 2781 8609; www.libf.ac.uk

Lincoln Tel 01522 886644; www.lincoln.ac.uk

Liverpool Tel 0151 794 5927; www.liverpool.ac.uk

Liverpool Hope Tel 0151 291 3111; www.hope.ac.uk

Liverpool John Moores Tel 0151 231 5090; www.ljmu.ac.uk

London (Birk) Tel 020 7631 6000; www.bbk.ac.uk

London (Court) Tel 020 7848 2645; www.courtauld.ac.uk

London (Gold) Tel 020 7078 5300; www.gold.ac.uk

London (Inst Paris) Tel +33 (0) 1 44 11 73 83; https://ulip.london.ac.uk

London (King's) Tel 020 7836 5454; www.kcl.ac.uk

London (QM) Tel 020 7882 5511; www.qmul.ac.uk

London (RH) (Egham) Tel 01784 414944; www.royalholloway.ac.uk

London (RVC) Tel 020 7468 5147; www.rvc.ac.uk

London (St George's) Tel 020 8725 2333; www.sgul.ac.uk

London (SOAS) Tel 020 7898 4306; www.soas.ac.uk

London (UCL) Tel 020 7679 2000; www.ucl.ac.uk

London LSE Tel 020 7955 6613; www.lse.ac.uk

London Met Tel 020 7133 4200; www.londonmet.ac.uk

London Regent's Tel 020 7487 7505; www.regents.ac.uk

London South Bank Tel 0800 923 8888; www.lsbu.ac.uk

Loughborough Tel 01509 223522; www.lboro.ac.uk

Manchester Tel 0161 275 2077; www.manchester.ac.uk

Manchester Met Tel 0161 247 6969; www2.mmu.ac.uk

Medway Sch Pharm (Chatham) Tel 01634 202936; www.msp.ac.uk

Middlesex (London) Tel 020 8411 5555; www.mdx.ac.uk

NCH London Tel 020 7637 4550; www.nchlondon.ac.uk

Newcastle (Newcastle-upon-Tyne) Tel 0191 208 3333; www.ncl.ac.uk

Newman (Birmingham) Tel 0121 476 1181; www.newman.ac.uk

Northampton Tel 0300 303 2772; www.northampton.ac.uk

Northumbria (Newcastle-upon-Tyne) Tel 0191 349 5600; www.northumbria.ac.uk

Norwich Arts Tel 01603 610561; www.nua.ac.uk

Nottingham Tel 0115 951 5559; www.nottingham.ac.uk

Nottingham Trent Tel 0115 848 4200; www.ntu.ac.uk

Open University (Milton Keynes) Tel 0300 303 5303; www.open.ac.uk

Oxford Tel 01865 288000; www.ox.ac.uk

Oxford Brookes Tel 01865 483040; www.brookes.ac.uk

Plymouth Tel 01752 585858; www.plymouth.ac.uk

Portsmouth Tel 023 9284 5566; www.port.ac.uk

Queen Margaret (Edinburgh) Tel 0131 474 0000; www.qmu.ac.uk

Queen's Belfast Tel 028 9097 3838; www.qub.ac.uk

Reading Tel 0118 378 8372; www.reading.ac.uk

Richmond (Am Int Univ) (Richmond-upon-Thames) Tel 020 8332 8200; www.richmond.ac.uk

Robert Gordon (Aberdeen) Tel 01224 262728; www.rgu.ac.uk

Roehampton (London) Tel 020 8392 3232; www.roehampton.ac.uk

Rose Bruford (Coll) (Sidcup) Tel 020 8308 2600; www.bruford.ac.uk [D]

Royal Agricultural Univ (Cirencester) Tel 01285 889912; www.rau.ac.uk

St Andrews Tel 01334 462150; www.st-andrews.ac.uk

St Mark and St John (Plymouth) Tel 01752 636890; www.marjon.ac.uk

St Mary's (Twickenham) Tel 020 8240 4029; www.stmarys.ac.uk

Salford Tel 0161 295 4545; www.salford.ac.uk

Sheffield Tel 0114 222 8030; www.sheffield.ac.uk

Sheffield Hallam Tel 0114 225 5555; www.shu.ac.uk

South Wales (Pontypridd) Tel 03455 767778; www.southwales.ac.uk

Southampton Tel 023 8059 4732; www.southampton.ac.uk

Southampton Solent Tel 023 8201 5066; www.solent.ac.uk

Staffordshire (Stoke-on-Trent) Tel 01782 294400; www.staffs.ac.uk

Stirling Tel 01786 467044; www.stir.ac.uk

Stranmillis (UC) (Belfast) Tel 028 9038 4263; www.stran.ac.uk

Strathclyde (Glasgow) Tel 0141 548 3195; www.strath.ac.uk

Suffolk (Ipswich) Tel 01473 338833; www.uos.ac.uk

Sunderland Tel 0191 515 3154; www.sunderland.ac.uk

Surrey (Guildford) Tel 01483 682222; www.surrey.ac.uk

Sussex (Brighton) Tel 01273 678416; www.sussex.ac.uk

Swansea Tel 01792 295111; www.swansea.ac.uk

Teesside (Middlesbrough) Tel 01642 218121; www.tees.ac.uk

Trinity Saint David (Lampeter) Tel 01267 676767 (Camarthen) 01570 422351 (Lampeter) 07192 481000 (Swansea) 0207 5826297 (London); www.uwtsd.ac.uk

UCO (London) Tel 020 7089 5316; www.uco.ac.uk

UHI (Inverness) Tel 0845 272 3600; www.uhi.ac.uk

Ulster (Belfast) Tel 028 7012 3456; www.ulster.ac.uk

Univ Law (Guildford) Tel 0800 289 997; www.law.ac.uk

UWE Bristol Tel 0117 328 3333; www.uwe.ac.uk

Warwick (Coventry) Tel 024 7652 3723; www.warwick.ac.uk

West London Tel 0800 036 8888; www.uwl.ac.uk

West Scotland (Paisley) Tel 0800 027 1000; www.uws.ac.uk

Westminster (London) Tel 020 7915 5511; www.westminster.ac.uk

Winchester Tel 01962 827234; www.winchester.ac.uk

Wolverhampton Tel 01902 323505; www.wlv.ac.uk

Worcester Tel 01905 855111; www.worcester.ac.uk

Writtle (UC) (Chelmsford) Tel 01245 424200; www.writtle.ac.uk

York Tel 01904 324000; www.york.ac.uk

York St John Tel 01904 876598; www.yorksj.ac.uk

SECTION 2: SPECIALIST COLLEGES OF AGRICULTURE AND HORTICULTURE, ART, DANCE, DRAMA, FASHION, MUSIC, OSTEOPATHY AND SPEECH

Many colleges and institutes provide undergraduate and postgraduate courses in a wide range of subjects. While many universities and university colleges offer courses in art, design, music, drama, agriculture, horticulture and courses connected to the land-based industries, the specialist colleges listed below provide courses at many levels, often part-time, in these separate fields.

It is important that you read prospectuses and check websites carefully and go to Open Days to find out as much as you can about these colleges and about their courses which interest you. Applications for full-time courses at the institutions listed below are through UCAS.

Abbreviations used below A = Art and Design; **Ag** = Agriculture, Animals and Land-related courses; **C** = Communication; **D** = Drama, Performing and Theatre Arts; **Da** = Dance; **F** = Fashion; **H** = Horticulture and Lanscape-related courses; **M** = Music.

Academy of Live and Recorded Arts (ALRA) (London and Wigan) Tel 020 8870 6475; https://alra. co.uk [**D**]

Architectural Association School of Architecture (London) Tel 020 7887 4051; www.aaschool.ac.uk

Arts Educational Schools London Tel 020 8987 6666; https://artsed.co.uk [**A**]

Askham Bryan College Tel 01904 772277; www.askham-bryan.ac.uk [**Ag**]

Banbury and Bicester College Tel 0808 1686 626; www.banbury-bicester.ac.uk

Belfast Metropolitan College Tel 028 9026 5265; www.belfastmet.ac.uk

Berkshire College of Agriculture (Maidenhead) Tel 01628 827479; www.bca.ac.uk [**Ag**]

Bicton College (East Budleigh) Tel 01395 562400; www.bicton.ac.uk [**Ag**]

Bishop Burton College (Beverley) Tel 01964 553000; www.bishopburton.ac.uk [**Ag**]

Bristol Old Vic Theatre School Tel 0117 973 3535; www.oldvic.ac.uk [**D**]

British College of Osteopathic Medicine (London) Tel 020 7435 6464; www.bcom.ac.uk

British Institute of Technology, England (London) Tel 020 8552 3071; www.bite.ac.uk

Brooksby Melton College (Melton Mowbray) Tel 01664 855444; www.brooksbymelton.ac.uk [**Ag**]

Camberwell College of Arts, University of the Arts London Tel 020 7514 6302; www.arts.ac.uk/ camberwell [**A**]

Capel Manor College (Enfield) Tel 08456 122122; www.capel.ac.uk [**H**]

Central Saint Martins College, University of the Arts London Tel 020 7514 7023; www.arts.ac.uk/ csm [**A**]

Chelsea College of Arts, University of the Arts London Tel 020 7514 7751; www.arts.ac.uk/chelsea [**A**]

City and Guilds of London Art School Tel 020 7735 2306; www.cityandguildsartschool.ac.uk [**A**]

Cleveland College of Art and Design (Hartlepool) Tel 01429 422000; www.ccad.ac.uk [**A**]

College of Agriculture, Food & Rural Enterprise (CAFRE) (Muckamore) Tel 0800 028 4291; www. cafre.ac.uk [**Ag**]

Drama Centre London, University of the Arts London Tel 020 7514 2354; www.arts.ac.uk/csm/ drama-centre-london [**D**]

Duchy College (Callington) Tel 01579 372222; www.duchy.ac.uk [**Ag**]

East 15 Acting School (Loughton) Tel 020 8418 7731; www.east15.ac.uk [**D**]

Easton and Otley College (East Anglia) Tel 08000 224556; www.eastonotley.ac.uk [**Ag**]

European School of Osteopathy (Maidstone) Tel 01622 671558; www.eso.ac.uk

Fashion Retail Academy (London) Tel 0300 247 4000; www.fashionretailacademy.ac.uk [**F**]

Glasgow Clyde College Tel 0141 272 9000; www.glasgowclyde.ac.uk

Glasgow School of Art Tel 0141 353 4500; www.gsa.ac.uk [**A**]

Gray's School of Art, Robert Gordon University (Aberdeen) Tel 01224 262728; https://graysartschoolaberdeen.com [**A**]

Guildford School of Acting, University of Surrey Tel 01483 682222; www.gsauk.org [**D**]

Guildhall School of Music and Drama (London) Tel 020 7628 2571; www.gsmd.ac.uk [**M**]

Hadlow College Tel 01732 850551; www.hadlow.ac.uk [**Ag**]

Hartpury College Tel 01452 702345; www.hartpury.ac.uk [**Ag**]

Heatherley School of Fine Art (London) Tel 020 7351 4190; www.heatherleys.org [**A**]

Hereford College of Arts Tel 01432 273359; www.hca.ac.uk [**A**]

Kingston Maurward College (Dorset) Tel 01305 215000; www.kmc.ac.uk [**Ag**]

Leeds College of Music Tel 0113 222 3416; www.lcm.ac.uk [**M**]

Liverpool Institute for Performing Art Tel 0151 330 3000; www.lipa.ac.uk [**D**]

London Academy of Music and Dramatic Art Tel 020 8834 0500; www.lamda.org.uk [**M**]

London College of Communication, University of the Arts London Tel 020 7514 6599; www.arts.ac.uk/lcc [**C**]

London College of Fashion, University of the Arts London Tel 020 7514 7400; www.arts.ac.uk/fashion [**F**]

Metanoia Institute (London) Tel 020 8579 2505; www.metanoia.ac.uk

Mountview Academy of Theatre Arts (London) Tel 020 8881 2201; www.mountview.org.uk [**D**]

Myerscough College (Preston) Tel 01995 642222; www.myerscough.ac.uk [**Ag**]

Northern School of Contemporary Dance (Leeds) Tel 0113 219 3000; www.nscd.ac.uk [**Da**]

Plumpton College Tel 01273 890454; www.plumpton.ac.uk [**Ag**]

Plymouth College of Art Tel 01752 203434; www.plymouthart.ac.uk [**A**]

Ravensbourne (London) Tel 020 3040 3500; www.ravensbourne.ac.uk [**C**]

Reaseheath College Tel 01270 625131; www.reaseheath.ac.uk [**Ag**]

Royal Academy of Dance (London) Tel 020 7326 8000; www.rad.org.uk [**Da**]

Royal Academy of Dramatic Art (RADA) (London) Tel 020 7636 7076; www.rada.ac.uk [**D**]

Royal Academy of Music, University of London Tel 020 7873 7373; www.ram.ac.uk [**M**]

Royal Central School of Speech and Drama, University of London Tel 020 7722 8183; www.cssd.ac.uk [**D**]

Royal College of Music (London) Tel 020 7591 4300; www.rcm.ac.uk [**M**]

Royal Conservatoire of Scotland (Glasgow) Tel 0141 332 4101; www.rcs.ac.uk [**M**]

Royal Northern College of Music (Manchester) Tel 0161 907 5200; www.rncm.ac.uk [**M**]

Royal Welsh College of Music and Drama (Cardiff) Tel 029 2039 1361; www.rwcmd.ac.uk [**M**]

Ruskin School of Art, University of Oxford Tel 01865 276940; www.rsa.ox.ac.uk [**A**]

SAE Institute (London; Oxford; Liverpool; Glasgow) Tel 03330 112 315; www.sae.edu

Scotland's Rural College (Ayr) Tel 0800 269 453; www.sruc.ac.uk [**Ag**]

Slade School of Fine Art, University College London Tel 020 7679 2313; www.ucl.ac.uk/slade [**A**]

Sparsholt College Hampshire Tel 01962 776441; www.sparsholt.ac.uk [**H**]

Trinity Laban Conservatoire of Music and Dance (London) Tel 020 8305 4444; www.trinitylaban.ac.uk [**M**]

University College of Estate Management (Reading) Tel 0800 019 9697; www.ucem.ac.uk

Wimbledon College of Arts, University of the Arts London Tel 020 7514 9641; www.arts.ac.uk/wimbledon [**A**]

Winchester School of Art, University of Southampton Tel 023 8059 6900; www.southampton.ac.uk/wsa [**A**]

SECTION 3: FURTHER EDUCATION AND OTHER COLLEGES OFFERING HIGHER EDUCATION COURSES

Changes are taking place fast in this sector, with the merger of colleges and the introduction of University Centres. These are linked to further education colleges and to one or more universities, and provide Foundation and Honours degree courses (often part-time) and sometimes postgraduate qualifications.

The following institutions appear under various subject headings in the tables in **Chapter 7** and are in UCAS for some of their courses. See prospectuses and websites for application details.

Abingdon and Witney College Tel 01235 555585; www.abingdon-witney.ac.uk

Accrington and Rossendale College Tel 01254 389933; www.accross.ac.uk

Andover College Tel 01264 360000; www.andover.ac.uk

Argyll College, University of the Highlands and Islands (Dunoon) Tel 0845 230 9969; www.argyll.uhi.ac.uk

Ayrshire College (Ayr) Tel 0300 303 0303; www1.ayrshire.ac.uk

Barking and Dagenham College (Romford) Tel 020 3667 0294; www.barkingdagenhamcollege.ac.uk

Barnet and Southgate College Tel 020 8266 4000; www.barnetsouthgate.ac.uk

Barnfield College (Luton) Tel 01582 569569; www.barnfield.ac.uk

Barnsley College Tel 01226 216123; www.barnsley.ac.uk

Basingstoke College of Technology Tel 01256 354141; www.bcot.ac.uk

Bath College Tel 01225 312191; www.bathcollege.ac.uk

Bedford College Tel 01234 291000; www.bedford.ac.uk

Birmingham Metropolitan College Tel 0121 446 4545; 01384 344 344; www.bmet.ac.uk

Bishop Auckland College Tel 01388 443000; www.bacoll.ac.uk

Blackburn College Tel 01254 292929; www.blackburn.ac.uk

Blackpool and The Fylde College Tel 01253 504343; www.blackpool.ac.uk

Bolton College Tel 01204 482000; www.boltoncollege.ac.uk

Boston College Tel 01205 365701; www.boston.ac.uk

Bournemouth and Poole College (Poole) Tel 01202 205180; www.thecollege.co.uk

Bournville College (Birmingham) Tel 0800 111 6311; www.sccb.ac.uk

Bracknell and Wokingham College Tel 01344 868600; www.bracknell.ac.uk

Bradford College Tel 01274 433333; www.bradfordcollege.ac.uk

Bridgend College Tel 01656 302302; www1.bridgend.ac.uk

Bridgwater and Taunton College (Bridgwater) Tel 01278 455464; www.bridgwater.ac.uk

Brighton Metropolitan College Tel 01273 667759; www.gbmc.ac.uk/brighton

Brockenhurst College Tel 01590 625555; www.brock.ac.uk

Brooklands College (Weybridge) Tel 01932 797797; www.brooklands.ac.uk

Buckinghamshire College Group (Amersham; Aylesbury; High Wycombe) Tel 0800 614016; 01296 588595; www.buckscollegegroup.ac.uk

Burnley College Tel 01282 733373; www.burnley.ac.uk

Burton and South Derbyshire College (Burton-upon-Trent) Tel 01283 494400; www.bsdc.ac.uk

Bury College (Bury) Tel 0161 280 8280; www.burycollege.ac.uk

Buxton and Leek College (Leek) Tel 0800 074 0099; www.blc.ac.uk

Calderdale College (Halifax) Tel 01422 399399; www.calderdale.ac.uk

Cambridge Regional College Tel 01223 226315; 01480 379100; www.camre.ac.uk

Canterbury College Tel 01227 811111; www.canterburycollege.ac.uk

Carlisle College Tel 01228 822700; www.carlisle.ac.uk

Carmel College (St Helens) Tel 01744 452200; www.carmel.ac.uk

Carshalton College Tel 0208 544 4501; www.carshalton.ac.uk

CECOS London College Tel 020 7359 3316; www.cecos.co.uk

Central Bedfordshire College (Dunstable) Tel 01582 477776; www.centralbeds.ac.uk

Central Film School London Tel 0207 377 6060; www.centralfilmschool.com

Chelmsford College Tel 01245 293031; www.chelmsford.ac.uk

Cheshire College (Chester, Crewe, Ellesmere Port) Tel 01270 654654; www.scc.ac.uk

Chesterfield College Tel 01246 500500; www.chesterfield.ac.uk

Chichester College Tel 01243 786321; www.chichester.ac.uk

City and Islington College (London) Tel 020 7700 9200; www.candi.ac.uk

City College Norwich Tel 01603 773311; www.ccn.ac.uk

City College Plymouth Tel 01752 305300; www.cityplym.ac.uk

City College Southampton Tel 023 8048 4848; www.southampton-city.ac.uk

City of Bristol College Tel 0117 312 5000; www.cityofbristol.ac.uk

City of Liverpool College Tel 0151 252 3000; www.liv-coll.ac.uk

City of London College Tel 020 7247 2177; www.clc-london.ac.uk

City of Oxford College Tel 01865 550550; www.cityofoxford.ac.uk

City of Westminster College Tel 020 7258 2721; www.cwc.ac.uk

City of Wolverhampton College Tel 01902 836000; www.wolvcoll.ac.uk

Cliff College (Calver) Tel 01246 584202; www.cliffcollege.ac.uk

Colchester Institute Tel 01206 712000; www.colchester.ac.uk

Coleg Sir Gâr (Carmarthenshire) Tel 01554 748000; www.colegsirgar.ac.uk

Coleg y Cymoedd (Aberdare) Tel 01685 887500; www.cymoedd.ac.uk

College of Haringey, Enfield and North East London (Enfield) Tel 020 8442 3055; www.conel.ac.uk

College of North West London (Brent) Tel 020 8208 5050; www.cnwl.ac.uk

College of West Anglia (King's Lynn) Tel 01553 761144; www.cwa.ac.uk

Cornwall College (Redruth) Tel 01209 617698; www.cornwall.ac.uk

Coventry College Tel 024 7693 2932; www.coventrycollege.ac.uk

Craven College (Skipton) Tel 01756 791411; www.craven-college.ac.uk

Croydon College Tel 020 8760 5934; www.croydon.ac.uk

Darlington College Tel 01325 503030; www.darlington.ac.uk

Dearne Valley College (Rotherham) Tel 01709 513355; www.dearne-coll.ac.uk

Derby College Tel 0800 028 0289; www.derby-college.ac.uk

Derwentside College (Consett) Tel 01207 585900; www.derwentside.ac.uk

Doncaster College Tel 0800 358 7474; www.don.ac.uk

Dudley College Tel 01384 363000; www.dudleycol.ac.uk

Ealing, Hammersmith and West London College Tel 020 8741 1688; www.wlc.ac.uk

East Berkshire College (Langley) Tel 01753 793000; www.eastberks.ac.uk

East Coast College (Great Yarmouth; Lowestoft) Tel 0800 854 695; www.eastcoast.ac.uk

East Durham College (Peterlee) Tel 0191 518 2000; www.eastdurham.ac.uk

East Kent College (Broadstairs) Tel 01843 605049; www.eastkent.ac.uk

East Riding College (Beverley) Tel 0345 120 0044; www.eastridingcollege.ac.uk

East Surrey College (Redhill) Tel 01737 788445; www.esc.ac.uk

Eastleigh College Tel 023 8091 1299; www.eastleigh.ac.uk

Edinburgh College Tel 0131 660 1010; www.edinburghcollege.ac.uk

European Business School London Tel 020 7487 7505; www.regents.ac.uk

European School of Economics (London) Tel 020 7245 6148; www.europeanschoolofeconomics.com

Exeter College Tel 01392 400500; www.exe-coll.ac.uk

Fareham College Tel 01329 815200; www.fareham.ac.uk

Farnborough College of Technology Tel 01252 407040; www.farn-ct.ac.uk

Forth Valley College (Falkirk) Tel 0845 634 4444; www.forthvalley.ac.uk

Furness College (Barrow-in-Furness) Tel 01229 825017; www.furness.ac.uk

Gateshead College Tel 0191 490 2246; www.gateshead.ac.uk

Gloucestershire College (Gloucester) Tel 0345 155 2020; www.gloscol.ac.uk

Gower College Swansea Tel 01792 284000; www.gcs.ac.uk

Grantham College Tel 0800 0521 577; www.grantham.ac.uk

Grimsby Institute Group (Grimsby; Scarborough; Skegness; Louth) Tel 0800 315002; www.grimsbyinstitutegroup.co.uk

Grŵp Llandrillo Menai Tel 01492 546666 (Coleg Llandrillo); 01341 422827 (Coleg Meirion-Dwyfor); 01248 370125 (Coleg Menai); www.gllm.ac.uk

GSM London Tel 020 3432 5486; www.gsmlondon.ac.uk

Guildford College Tel 01483 448500; www.guildford.ac.uk

Halesowen College Tel 0121 602 7777; www.halesowen.ac.uk

Harlow College Tel 01279 868100, www.harlow-college.ac.uk

Harrogate College Tel 01423 878211; www.harrogate.ac.uk

Harrow College Tel 020 8909 6000; www.harrow.ac.uk

Hartlepool College of Further Education Tel 01429 295111; www.hartlepoolfe.ac.uk

Havant and South Downs College (Waterlooville; Havant) Tel 023 9387 9999; www.hsdc.ac.uk

Havering College Tel 01708 455011; www.havering-college.ac.uk

Heart of Worcestershire College (Redditch) Tel 08448 802500; www.howcollege.ac.uk

Herefordshire and Ludlow College (Hereford) Tel 0800 032 1986; www.hlcollege.ac.uk

Hertford Regional College (Ware) Tel 01992 411400; www.hrc.ac.uk

Highbury College Portsmouth Tel 023 9238 3131; www.highbury.ac.uk

Highland Theological College, University of the Highlands and Islands (Dingwall) Tel 01349 780000; www.htc.uhi.ac.uk

Hillcroft College (Surbiton) Tel 020 8399 2688; www.hillcroft.ac.uk

Hopwood Hall College (Rochdale) Tel 01706 345346; www.hopwood.ac.uk

Hugh Baird College (Bootle) Tel 0151 353 4654; www.hughbaird.ac.uk

Hull College Tel 01482 598744; www.hull-college.ac.uk

Isle of Wight College Tel 01983 526631; www.iwcollege.ac.uk

Kendal College Tel 01539 814700; www.kendal.ac.uk

Kensington and Chelsea College Tel 020 7573 5333; www.kcc.ac.uk

Kensington College of Business Tel 020 7404 6330; www.kensingtoncoll.ac.uk

Kidderminster College Tel 01562 820811; http://kidderminster.ac.uk

Kingston College Tel 020 8546 2151; www.kingston-college.ac.uk

Kirklees College (Huddersfield) Tel 01484 437070; www.kirkleescollege.ac.uk

Knowsley Community College (Kirkby) Tel 0151 477 5850; www.knowsleycollege.ac.uk

Lakes College, West Cumbria (Workington) Tel 01946 839300; www.lcwc.ac.uk

Lambeth College Tel 020 7501 5010; www.lambethcollege.ac.uk

Lancaster and Morecambe College Tel 01524 66215; 0800 306 306; www.lmc.ac.uk

Leeds City College Tel 0113 386 1997; www.leedscitycollege.ac.uk

Leeds College of Building Tel 0113 222 6000; www.lcb.ac.uk

Leicester College Tel 0116 224 2240; www.leicestercollege.ac.uk

Leo Baeck College (London) Tel 020 8349 5600; www.lbc.ac.uk

Lewisham Southwark College Tel 020 3757 3000; www.lscollege.ac.uk

Lews Castle College, University of the Highlands and Islands (Stornoway) Tel 01851 770000; www.lews.uhi.ac.uk

Lincoln College Tel General Enquiries 01522 876000; Course Enquiries 030 030 32435; www.lincolncollege.ac.uk

London School of Commerce Tel 020 7357 0077; www.lsclondon.co.uk

London School of Science and Technology Tel 020 8795 3863; www.lsst.ac

London South East Colleges (Bromley; Erith; Greenwich) Tel 0300 303 2554; www.lsec.ac.uk

Loughborough College Tel 01509 618375; www.loucoll.ac.uk

Macclesfield College of Further and Higher Education Tel 01625 410002; www.macclesfield.ac.uk

Middlesbrough College Tel 01642 333333; www.mbro.ac.uk

MidKent College (Gillingham) Tel 01634 402020; www.midkent.ac.uk

Milton Keynes College Tel 01908 684444; www.mkcollege.ac.uk

Mont Rose (Coll) (London) Tel 020 8556 5009; https://mrcollege.ac.uk

Moray College, University of the Highlands and Islands (Elgin) Tel 01343 576000; www.moray.uhi.ac.uk

Moulton College Tel 01604 491131; www.moulton.ac.uk

NAFC Marine Centre, University of the Highlands and Islands (Port Arthur) Tel 01595 772000; www.nafc.uhi.ac.uk

Nazarene Theological College (Manchester) Tel 0161 445 3063; www.nazarene.ac.uk

Neath Port Talbot College Tel 01639 648000; www.nptcgroup.ac.uk

Nelson and Colne College (Nelson) Tel 01282 440272; www.nelson.ac.uk

Nescot, North East Surrey College of Technology (Epsom) Tel 020 8394 3038; www.nescot.ac.uk

New City College Hackney Tel 020 7613 9123; www.hackney.ac.uk

New City College Redbridge (Romford) Tel 020 8548 7400; www.redbridge-college.ac.uk

New City College Tower Hamlets Tel 020 7510 7777; www.tower.ac.uk

New College Durham Tel 0191 375 4000; www.newcollegedurham.ac.uk

New College Stamford Tel 01780 484300; www.stamford.ac.uk

New College Swindon Tel 01793 611470; www.newcollege.ac.uk

New College Telford Tel 01952 641892; www.nct.ac.uk

Newbury College Tel 01635 845000; www.newbury-college.ac.uk

Newcastle College Tel 0191 200 4000; www.ncl-coll.ac.uk

Newcastle-under-Lyme College Tel 01782 715111; www.nulc.ac.uk

Newham College London Tel 020 8257 4446; www.newham.ac.uk

Norland College (Bath) Tel 01225 904040; www.norland.co.uk

North East Scotland College (Aberdeen) Tel 0300 330 5550; www.nescol.ac.uk

North Hertfordshire College (Stevenage) Tel 01462 424242; www.nhc.ac.uk

North Highland College, University of the Highlands and Islands Tel 01847 889000; www.northhighland.uhi.ac.uk

North Kent College (Dartford) Tel 01322 629400; Course enquiries 0800 074 1447; www.northkent.ac.uk

North Lindsey College (Scunthorpe) Tel 01724 281111; www.northlindsey.ac.uk

North Notts College (Worksop) Tel 01909 504504; www.nnc.ac.uk

North Shropshire College (Oswestry) Tel 01691 688000; www.nsc.ac.uk

North Warwickshire and Hinckley College (Nuneaton) Tel 024 7624 3000; www.nwhc.ac.uk

Northampton College Tel 0300 123 2344; www.northamptoncollege.ac.uk

Northbrook Metropolitan College (Worthing) Tel 0845 155 6060; www.northbrook.ac.uk

Northern Regional College (Ballymena) Tel 028 2563 6221; www.nrc.ac.uk

Northumberland College (Ashington). Tel 01670 841200; www.northumberland.ac.uk

Nottingham College Tel 01159 100100; www.nottinghamcollege.ac.uk

Oaklands College (St Albans) Tel 01727 737000; www.oaklands.ac.uk

Oldham College Tel 0161 785 4000; www.oldham.ac.uk

Orkney College, University of the Highlands and Islands (Kirkwall) Tel 01856 569000; www.orkney.uhi.ac.uk

Pearson College (London) Tel 020 7348 1920; www.pearsoncollegelondon.ac.uk

Pembrokeshire College (Haverfordwest) Tel 01437 753000; www.pembrokeshire.ac.uk

Perth College, University of the Highlands and Islands Tel 0845 270 1177; www.perth.uhi.ac.uk

Peter Symonds College (Winchester) Tel 01962 857500; www.psc.ac.uk

Peterborough Regional College Tel 0345 872 8722; www.peterborough.ac.uk

Petroc (Barnstaple) Tel 01271 345291; www.petroc.ac.uk

Portsmouth College Tel 023 9266 7521; www.portsmouth-college.ac.uk

Preston's College Tel 01772 225000; www.preston.ac.uk

Redcar and Cleveland College Tel 01642 473132; www.cleveland.ac.uk

Richmond-upon-Thames College (Twickenham) Tel 020 8607 8000; www.rutc.ac.uk

Riverside College (Widnes) Tel 0151 257 2800; www.riversidecollege.ac.uk

Rotherham College of Arts and Technology Tel 01709 722777; www.rotherham.ac.uk

Royal National College for the Blind (Hereford) Tel 01432 376621; www.rnc.ac.uk

Runshaw College (Chorley) Tel 01772 642040; www.runshaw.ac.uk

Ruskin College (Oxford) Tel 01865 759600; www.ruskin.ac.uk

Sabhal Mòr Ostaig, University of the Highlands and Islands (Sleat) Tel 01471 888304; www.smo.uhi.ac.uk

St Helens College Tel 0800 996699; www.sthelens.ac.uk

Sandwell College (West Bromwich) Tel 0800 622006; www.sandwell.ac.uk

School of Advanced Study, University of London Tel 020 7862 8653; www.sas.ac.uk

School of Audio Engineering Institute (Oxford) Tel 03330 112315; www.sae.edu

Scottish Association for Marine Science, University of the Highlands and Islands (Oban) Tel 01631 559000; www.sams.ac.uk

Selby College Tel 01757 211000; www.selby.ac.uk

Sheffield College Tel 0114 260 2600; www.sheffcol.ac.uk

Shetland College, University of the Highlands and Islands (Lerwick) Tel 0845 272 3600; www.shetland.uhi.ac.uk

Shrewsbury College Tel 01743 342342; www.shrewsbury.ac.uk

Solihull College Tel 0121 678 7000; www.solihull.ac.uk

South and City College Birmingham (Digbeth) Tel 0800 111 6311; www.sccb.ac.uk

South Devon College (Paignton) Tel 08000 21 31 81; www.southdevon.ac.uk

South Essex College (Basildon) Tel 0845 521 2345; www.southessex.ac.uk

South Gloucestershire and Stroud College Tel 01453 763424; www.sgscol.ac.uk

South Lanarkshire College (East Kilbride) Tel 01355 270750; www.south-lanarkshire-college.ac.uk

South Leicestershire College (South Wigston) Tel 0116 264 3535; www.slcollege.ac.uk

South Staffordshire College (Cannock) Tel 0300 456 2424; www.southstaffs.ac.uk

South Thames College (London) Tel 020 8918 7777; www.south-thames.ac.uk

Southern Regional College (Portadown) Tel 0300 123 1223; www.src.ac.uk

Southport College Tel 01704 392704; www.southport.ac.uk

Stafford College Tel 01785 223800; www.staffordcoll.ac.uk

Stephenson College (Coalville) Tel 01530 836136; www.stephensoncoll.ac.uk

Stockport College Tel 0161 296 5000; www.stockport.ac.uk

Stockton Riverside College Tel 01642 865400; www.stockton.ac.uk

Stoke-on-Trent Colleg Tel 01782 208208; www.stokecoll.ac.uk

Stratford-upon-Avon College Tel 01789 417414; www.stratford.ac.uk

Strode College (Street) Tel 01458 844400; www.strode-college.ac.uk

Strode's College (Egham) Tel 01784 437506; www.strodes.ac.uk

Sunderland College Tel 0191 511 6000; https://sunderlandcollege.ac.uk

Sussex Coast College Tel 01424 442222; www.sussexcoast.ac.uk

Sussex Downs College (Eastbourne) Tel 030 3003 9300; www.sussexdowns.ac.uk

Tameside College (Ashton-under-Lyne) Tel 0161 908 6789; www.tameside.ac.uk

Telford College Tel 01952 642200; www.tcat.ac.uk

The Islamic College (London) Tel 020 8451 9993; www.islamic-college.ac.uk

The London College UCK Tel 020 7243 4000; www.lcuck.ac.uk

The Manchester College Tel 03333 222 444; www.tmc.ac.uk

Tottenham Hotspur Foundation (London) Tel 020 8365 5138; www.tottenhamhotspur.com/foundation

Totton College Tel 02380 874874; www.totton.ac.uk

Trafford College (Stretford) Tel 0161 886 7092; www.trafford.ac.uk

Tresham College (Kettering) Tel 0345 658 8990; www.tresham.ac.uk

Truro and Penwith College Tel 01872 267061; www.truro-penwith.ac.uk

Tyne Coast College (South Shields; Wallsend) Tel 0191 427 3500; 0191 229 5000; www.tynecoast.ac.uk

University Campus Oldham Tel 0161 334 8800; www.uco.oldham.ac.uk

Uxbridge College Tel 01895 853333; www.uxbridge.ac.uk

Wakefield College Tel 01924 789111; 01924 789110; www.wakefield.ac.uk

Walsall College Tel 01922 657000; www.walsallcollege.ac.uk

Waltham Forest College Tel 020 8501 8501; www.waltham.ac.uk

Warrington and Vale Royal College (Warrington; Northwich) Tel 01925 494 400; www.warrington. ac.uk

Warwickshire College Group (Royal Leamington Spa) Tel 0300 456 0047; www.wcg.ac.uk

West Herts College (Watford) Tel 01923 812345; www.westherts.ac.uk

West Highland College, University of the Highlands and Islands (Fort William) Tel 01397 874000; www.whc.uhi.ac.uk

West Kent College (Tonbridge) Tel 0845 207 8220; www.westkent.ac.uk

West Nottinghamshire College (Mansfield) Tel 0808 100 3626; www.wnc.ac.uk

West Suffolk College (Bury St Edmunds) Tel 01284 716333; www.westsuffolkcollege.ac.uk

West Thames College (London) Tel 020 8326 2020; www.west-thames.ac.uk

Westminster Kingsway College Tel 020 7963 4181; www.westking.ac.uk

Weston College (Weston super Mare) Tel 01934 411411; www.weston.ac.uk

Weymouth College Tel 01305 761100; www.weymouth.ac.uk

Wigan and Leigh College Tel 01942 761600; www.wigan-leigh.ac.uk

Wiltshire College (Chippenham) Tel 01249 466806; www.wiltshire.ac.uk

Wirral Metropolitan College (Birkenhead) Tel 0151 551 7777; www.wmc.ac.uk

Yeovil College Tel 01935 423921; www.yeovil.ac.uk

Yeovil College University Centre Tel 01935 845454; www.ycuc.ac.uk

York College Tel 01904 770200; www.yorkcollege.ac.uk

A-LEVELS AND AS • SCOTTISH HIGHERS/ADVANCED HIGHERS • ADVANCED WELSH BACCALAUREATE – SKILLS CHALLENGE CERTIFICATE • IB INTERNATIONAL BACCALAUREATE DIPLOMA (IB CERTIFICATE IN HIGHER LEVEL; IB CERTIFICATE IN STANDARD LEVEL; IB CERTIFICATE IN EXTENDED ESSAY; IB CERTIFICATE IN THEORY OF KNOWLEDGE) • BTEC LEVEL 3 NATIONAL EXTENDED DIPLOMA • EXTENDED PROJECT • MUSIC EXAMINATIONS • ART AND DESIGN FOUNDATION STUDIES

A-levels and AS

Grade					Tariff points
GCE & AVCE Double Award	A-level with additional AS	GCE A-level and AVCE	GCE AS Double Award	GCE AS & AS VCE	
A*A*					112
A*A					104
AA					96
AB					88
BB					80
	A*A				76
BC					72
	AA				68
CC	AB				64
CD	BB	A*			56
	BC				52
DD		A			48
	CC				44
	CD				42
DE		B	AA		40
			AB		36
	DD				34
EE		C	BB		32
	DE				30
			BC		28
		D	CC		24
	EE		CD		22
			DD	A	20
		E	DE	B	16
			EE	C	12
				D	10
				E	6

Scottish Highers/Advanced Highers

Grade	Higher	Advanced Higher
A	33	56
B	27	48
C	21	40
D	15	32

Advanced Welsh Baccalaureate – Skills Challenge Certificate

Grade	Tariff points
A*	56
A	48
B	40
C	32
D	24
E	16

IB International Baccalaureate Diploma

While the IB Diploma does not attract UCAS Tariff points, the constituent qualifications of the IB Diploma do, so the total Tariff points for an IB Diploma can be calculated by adding together each of the following four components:

IB Certificate in Higher Level

Grade	Tariff points
H7	56
H6	48
H5	32
H4	24
H3	12
H2	0
H1	0

Size band: 4
Grade bands: 3–14

IB Certificate in Standard Level

Grade	Tariff points
S7	28
S6	24
S5	16
S4	12
S3	6
S2	0
S1	0

Size band: 2
Grade bands: 3–14

IB Certificate in Extended Essay

Grade	Tariff points
A	12
B	10
C	8
D	6
E	4

Size band: 1
Grade bands 4–12

IB Certificate in Theory of Knowledge

Grade	Tariff points
A	12
B	10
C	8
D	6
E	4

Size band: 1
Grade bands: 4–12

Certificates in Extended Essay and Theory of Knowledge are awarded Tariff points when the certificates have been taken individually.

BTEC Level 3 National Extended Diploma

Grade	Tariff points
D*D*D*	168
D*D*D	160
D*DD	152
DDD	144
DDM	128
DMM	112
MMM	96
MMP	80
MPP	64
PPP	48

Size band: 4+4+4 = 12
Grade bands: 4–14

Extended Project – Stand alone

Grade	Tariff points
A*	28
A	24
B	20
C	16
D	12
E	8

Music examinations

Performance			Theory			Tariff points
Grade 8	Grade 7	Grade 6	Grade 8	Grade 7	Grade 6	
D						30
M						24
P						18
	D					16
	M	D				12
	P	M	D			10
			M			9
			P	D		8
				M		7
		P		P	D	6
					M	5
					P	4

Additional points will be awarded for music examinations from the Associated Board of the Royal Schools of Music (ABRSM), University of West London, Rockschool and Trinity Guildhall/Trinity College London (music examinations at grades 6, 7, 8 (D=Distinction; M=Merit; P=Pass)).

Art and Design Foundation Studies

Grade	Tariff points
D	112
M	96
P	80

Size band: 4+4 = 8
Grade bands: 10–14

NB Full acknowledgement is made to UCAS for this information. For further details of all qualifications awarded UCAS Tariff points see www.ucas.com/advisers/guides-and-resources/information-new-ucas-tariff-advisers. Note that the Tariff is constantly updated and new qualifications are introduced each year.

Universities in the UK accept a range of international qualifications and those which normally satisfy the minimum general entrance requirements are listed below. However, the specific levels of achievement or grades required for entry to degree courses with international qualifications will vary, depending on the popularity of the university or college and the chosen degree programme. The subject tables in **Chapter 7** provide a guide to the levels of entry to courses although direct comparisons between A-level grades and international qualifications are not always possible except for the three European examinations listed at the end of this Appendix. Students not holding the required qualifications should consider taking an International Foundation course.

International students whose mother tongue is not English and/or who have not studied for their secondary education in English will be required to pass a secure English language test (SELT) such as IELTS (International English Language Testing System) or the Trinity College London tests. Entry requirements vary between universities and courses. For the IELTS, scores can range from bands 1–9, but most universities' requirements range from 5.5 to 7.5.

Algeria Baccalauréat
Argentina Completion of Year One of an Argentinian University degree (Licenciado)
Australia Completion of Senior Secondary Certificate of Education
Austria Reifeprüfungszeugnis/Maturazeugnis
Bahrain Secondary School Leaving Certificate plus A levels/bridging course
Bangladesh Bachelor of Arts, Science and Commerce
Belgium Certificat d'Enseignement Secondaire Superieur
Bermuda Diploma of Arts and Science
Bosnia-Herzegovina Secondary School Leaving Diploma
Brazil Completion of Ensino Medio and a good pass in the Vestibular plus Foundation year
Brunei Brunei GCE A-level
Bulgaria Diploma za Zavarsheno Sredno Obrazovanie (Diploma of Completed Secondary Education)
Canada Completion of Grade 12 secondary/high school certificate or equivalent
Chile Completion of Year one of a Bachelor degree
China Gaokao plus Foundation degree
Croatia Državna Matura (Secondary school leaving diploma)
Cyprus Apolytirion/Lise Bitirme Diploma with good grades
Czech Republic Vysvedceni o Maturitni Zkousce/Maturita
Denmark Studentereksamen (HF), (HHX), (HTX), STX
Egypt General Secondary School Certificate plus A-levels or two-year Diploma
Finland Ylioppilastutkinotodistus/Studentexamen (Matriculation certificate)
France French Baccalauréat
Gambia West African Senior Secondary Certificate Exam (WASSCE) Advanced Level
Georgia Successful completion of Year One of a Bachelor degree plus bridging programme
Germany Abitur
Ghana West African Senior Secondary Certificate Exam (WASSCE) plus bridging programme/A-levels
Greece Apolytirion of Geniko Lykeio (previously Apolytirion of Eniaio Lykeio)
Hong Kong A-levels/HKDSE
Hungary Érettségi Bizonyítvány/Matura
Iceland Studentsprof
India Higher Secondary School Certificate
Ireland Irish Leaving Certificate Higher Level

Israel Bagrut
Italy Diploma di Esame di Stato (formerly the Diploma di Matura) with good grades
Japan Associate Degree (Jun-Gakushi)/Vocational Degree (Senmon-shi)/Kotogakko Sotsugyo Shomeisho plus Foundation year
Kenya Kenya Certificate of Secondary Education
Lebanon Lebanese Baccalaureate plus Foundation year/A-levels
Malaysia Sijil Tinggi Persekolahan Malaysia (STPM, Malaysia Higher School Certificate)
Mauritius Cambridge Overseas Higher School Certificate or A-levels
Mexico Bachillerato plus Foundation year
Netherlands Diploma Voorbereidend Wetenschappelijk Onderwijs (VWO)
Nigeria Senior School Certificate Education (SSCE)/West African Senior School Certificate Examination plus bridging programme
Norway Certificate of Upper Secondary Education
Pakistan Higher Secondary School Certificate plus A-levels
Poland Matura
Portugal Diploma de Ensino Secundario
Russian Federation Certificate of Secondary Education plus A-levels/bridging course
Saudi Arabia General Secondary Education Certificate plus A-levels/bridging course
Serbia Secondary School Leaving Diploma
Singapore Singapore-Cambridge A-level
South Korea General High School Diploma plus access/Foundation programme
Spain Bachillerato
Sri Lanka A-levels
Sweden Slutbetyg fran Gymnasieskolan
Taiwan Senior High school Diploma plus A-levels/bridging course
Thailand Successful completion of year one of a Bachelor degree
Turkey Devlet Lise Diplomasi (State High School Diploma) with good grades
Uganda Uganda Advanced Certificate of Education (UACE)
Ukraine Successful completion of year one of a Bachelor degree
USA Good grades from the High School Graduation Diploma with SAT and/or APT/ACT

COMPARISONS BETWEEN A-LEVEL GRADES AND THE FOLLOWING EUROPEAN EXAMINATIONS

A-level grades	European Baccalaureate	French Baccalauréat	German Abitur
AAA	82–84%	14	1.2–1.3
AAB	79–81%	13.5	1.5
ABB	76–78%	13	1.8
BBB	74–75%	12.5	2.0
BBC	72–73%	12	2.2–2.3
BCC	70–71%	11.5	2.4

APPENDIX 3
PROFESSIONAL ASSOCIATIONS

Professional associations vary in size and function and many offer examinations to provide members with vocational qualifications. However, many of the larger bodies do not conduct examinations but accept evidence provided by the satisfactory completion of appropriate degree and diploma courses. When applying for courses in vocational subjects, therefore, it is important to check whether your chosen course is accredited by a professional association, since membership of such bodies is usually necessary for progression in your chosen career after graduation.

Information about careers, which you can use as background information for your UCAS application, can be obtained from the organisations below listed under the subject table headings used in **Chapter 7**. Full details of professional associations, their examinations and the degree courses accredited by them are published in *British Qualifications* (see **Appendix 4**).

Some additional organisations that can provide useful careers-related information are listed below under the subject table headings and other sources of relevant information are indicated in the subject tables of **Chapter 7** and in **Appendix 4**.

Accountancy/Accounting
Accounting Technicians Ireland www.accountingtechniciansireland.ie
Association of Accounting Technicians www.aat.org.uk
Association of Chartered Certified Accountants www.accaglobal.com
Association of International Accountants www.aiaworldwide.com
Chartered Accountants Ireland www.charteredaccountants.ie
Chartered Institute of Internal Auditors www.iia.org.uk
Chartered Institute of Management Accountants www.cimaglobal.com
Chartered Institute of Public Finance and Accountancy www.cipfa.org
Chartered Institute of Taxation www.tax.org.uk
Institute of Chartered Accountants in England and Wales www.icaew.com
Institute of Chartered Accountants of Scotland www.icas.com
Institute of Financial Accountants www.ifa.org.uk

Actuarial Science/Studies
Institute and Faculty of Actuaries www.actuaries.org.uk

Agricultural Sciences/Agriculture
Innovation for Agriculture www.innovationforagriculture.org.uk
Institute of Chartered Foresters www.charteredforesters.org
Royal Forestry Society www.rfs.org.uk
Wood Technology Society www.iom3.org/wood-technology-society

Animal Sciences
British Horse Society www.bhs.org.uk
British Society of Animal Science www.bsas.org.uk

Anthropology
Association of Social Anthropologists of the UK and Commonwealth www.theasa.org
Royal Anthropological Institute www.therai.org.uk

Archaeology
Chartered Institute for Archaeologists www.archaeologists.net
Council for British Archaeology new.archaeologyuk.org

Architecture
Chartered Institute of Architectural Technologists www.ciat.org.uk
Royal Incorporation of Architects in Scotland www.rias.org.uk
Royal Institute of British Architects www.architecture.com

Art and Design
Arts Council England www.artscouncil.org.uk
Association of Illustrators www.theaoi.com
Association of Photographers www.the-aop.org
British Association of Art Therapists www.baat.org
British Association of Paintings Conservator-Restorers www.bapcr.org.uk
British Institute of Professional Photography www.bipp.com
Chartered Society of Designers www.csd.org.uk
Crafts Council www.craftscouncil.org.uk
Creative Scotland www.creativescotland.com
Design Council www.designcouncil.org.uk
Institute of Conservation www.icon.org.uk
Institute of Professional Goldsmiths www.ipgoldsmiths.com
National Society for Education in Art and Design www.nsead.org
Royal British Society of Sculptors www.rbs.org.uk
Textile Institute www.texi.org

Astronomy/Astrophysics
Royal Astronomical Society www.ras.org.uk

Biochemistry (see also Chemistry)
Association for Clinical Biochemistry and Laboratory Medicine www.acb.org.uk
Biochemical Society www.biochemistry.org
British Society for Immunology www.immunology.org

Biological Sciences/Biology
British Society for Genetic Medicine www.bsgm.org.uk
Genetics Society www.genetics.org.uk
Institute of Biomedical Science www.ibms.org
Royal Society of Biology www.rsb.org.uk

Building and Construction
Chartered Institute of Building www.ciob.org
Chartered Institution of Building Services Engineers www.cibse.org
Construction Industry Training Board www.citb.co.uk

Business and Management Courses
Chartered Institute of Personnel and Development www.cipd.co.uk
Chartered Institute of Public Relations www.cipr.co.uk
Chartered Management Institute www.managers.org.uk
Communications Advertising and Marketing Education Foundation
    www.camfoundation.com
Department for Business, Energy and Industrial Strategy www.gov.uk/government/organisations/
    department-for-business-energy-and-industrial-strategy
ICSA: The Governance Institute www.icsa.org.uk

Institute of Administrative Management www.instam.org
Institute of Consulting www.iconsulting.org.uk
Institute of Export & International Trade www.export.org.uk
Institute of Practitioners in Advertising www.ipa.co.uk
Institute of Sales Management www.ismprofessional.com
Skills CFA www.skillscfa.org

Chemistry
National Nanotechnology Initiative www.nano.gov
Royal Society of Chemistry www.rsc.org

Computer Courses
BCS The Chartered Institute for IT www.bcs.org
Institution of Analysts and Programmers www.iap.org.uk
Learning and Performance Institute www.thelpi.org

Dance
Council for Dance Education and Training www.cdet.org.uk

Dentistry
British Association of Dental Nurses www.badn.org.uk
British Association of Dental Therapists www.badt.org.uk
British Dental Association www.bda.org
British Society of Dental Hygiene and Therapy www.bsdht.org.uk
Dental Laboratories Association www.dla.org.uk
Dental Technologists Association www.dta-uk.org
General Dental Council www.gdc-uk.org

Dietetics
British Dietetic Association www.bda.uk.com

Drama
Equity www.equity.org.uk
Society of British Theatre Designers www.theatredesign.org.uk

Economics
Royal Economic Society www.res.org.uk

Education and Teacher Training
Department for Education www.education.gov.uk
Education Workforce Council www.ewc.wales
General Teaching Council for Northern Ireland www.gtcni.org.uk
General Teaching Council for Scotland www.gtcs.org.uk

Engineering/Engineering Sciences
Energy Institute www.energyinst.org
Engineering Council UK www.engc.org.uk
Institute for Manufacturing www.ifm.eng.cam.ac.uk
Institute of Acoustics www.ioa.org.uk
Institute of Marine Engineering, Science and Technology www.imarest.org
Institution of Agricultural Engineers www.iagre.org
Institution of Civil Engineers www.ice.org.uk
Institution of Engineering Designers www.institution-engineering-designers.org.uk
Institution of Engineering and Technology www.theiet.org

Institution of Mechanical Engineers www.imeche.org
Nuclear Institute www.nuclearinst.com
Royal Aeronautical Society www.aerosociety.com

Environmental Science/Studies
Chartered Institute of Ecology and Environmental Management www.cieem.net
Chartered Institute of Environmental Health www.cieh.org
Chartered Institution of Wastes Management www.ciwm.co.uk
Chartered Institution of Water and Environmental Management www.ciwem.org
Environment Agency www.gov.uk/government/organisations/environment-agency
Institution of Environmental Sciences www.the-ies.org
Institution of Occupational Safety and Health www.iosh.co.uk
Royal Environmental Health Institute of Scotland www.rehis.com
Society for the Environment www.socenv.org.uk

Film, Radio, Video and TV Studies
British Film Institute www.bfi.org.uk
Creative Skillset (National Training Organisation for broadcast, film, video and multimedia) www.creative
    skillset.org

Finance (including Banking and Insurance)
Chartered Banker Institute www.charteredbanker.com
Chartered Institute of Loss Adjusters www.cila.co.uk
Chartered Insurance Institute www.cii.co.uk
Chartered Institute for Securities and Investment www.cisi.org
London Institute of Banking and Finance www.libf.ac.uk
Personal Finance Society www.thepfs.org

Food Science/Studies and Technology
Institute of Food Science and Technology www.ifst.org
Society of Food Hygiene and Technology www.sofht.co.uk

Forensic Science
Chartered Society of Forensic Sciences www.csofs.org

Geography
British Cartographic Society www.cartography.org.uk
Royal Geographical Society with IBG www.rgs.org
Royal Meteorological Society www.rmets.org

Geology/Geological Sciences
Geological Society www.geolsoc.org.uk

Health Sciences/Studies
British Academy of Audiology www.baaudiology.org
British and Irish Orthoptic Society www.orthoptics.org.uk
British Association of Prosthetists and Orthotists www.bapo.com
British Chiropractic Association https://chiropractic-uk.co.uk
British Occupational Hygiene Society www.bohs.org
General Osteopathic Council www.osteopathy.org.uk
Institute for Complementary and Natural Medicine www.icnm.org.uk
Institution of Occupational Safety and Health www.iosh.co.uk
Institute of Osteopathy www.osteopathy.org
Society of Homeopaths www.homeopathy-soh.org

History
Royal Historical Society www.royalhistsoc.org

Horticulture
Chartered Institute of Horticulture www.horticulture.org.uk

Hospitality and Event Management
Institute of Hospitality www.instituteofhospitality.org
People 1st www.people1st.co.uk

Housing
Chartered Institute of Housing www.cih.org

Human Resource Management
Chartered Institute of Personnel and Development www.cipd.co.uk

Information Management and Librarianship
Chartered Institute of Library and Information Professionals www.cilip.org.uk

Landscape Architecture
Landscape Institute www.landscapeinstitute.org

Languages
Chartered Institute of Linguists www.ciol.org.uk
Institute of Translation and Interpreting www.iti.org.uk

Law
Bar Council www.barcouncil.org.uk
Chartered Institute of Legal Executives www.cilex.org.uk
Faculty of Advocates www.advocates.org.uk
Law Society of England and Wales www.lawsociety.org.uk
Law Society of Northern Ireland www.lawsoc-ni.org
Law Society of Scotland www.lawscot.org.uk

Leisure and Recreation Management/Studies
Chartered Institute for the Management of Sport and Physical Activity www.cimspa.co.uk

Linguistics
British Association for Applied Linguistics www.baal.org.uk
Royal College of Speech and Language Therapists www.rcslt.org

Marine/Maritime Studies
Nautical Institute www.nautinst.org

Marketing (including Public Relations)
Chartered Institute of Marketing www.cim.co.uk
Chartered Institute of Public Relations www.cipr.co.uk
Institute of Sales Management www.ismprofessional.com

Materials Science/Metallurgy
Institute of Materials, Minerals and Mining www.iom3.org

Mathematics
Council for the Mathematical Sciences www.cms.ac.uk
Institute of Mathematics and its Applications www.ima.org.uk
London Mathematical Society www.lms.ac.uk
Mathematical Association www.m-a.org.uk

Media Studies
British Broadcasting Corporation www.bbc.co.uk/careers/home
National Council for the Training of Journalists www.nctj.com
Creative Skillset (National training organisation for broadcast, film, video and multimedia) www.creative
    skillset.org
Society for Editors and Proofreaders www.sfep.org.uk
Society of Authors www.societyofauthors.org

Medicine
British Medical Association www.bma.org.uk
General Medical Council www.gmc-uk.org
Institute for Complementary and Natural Medicine www.icnm.org.uk

Microbiology (see also Biological Sciences/Biology)
Microbiology Society www.microbiologysociety.org

Music
Incorporated Society of Musicians www.ism.org
Institute of Musical Instrument Technology www.imit.org.uk

Naval Architecture
Royal Institution of Naval Architects www.rina.org.uk

Neuroscience
InnerBody www.innerbody.com
Instant Anatomy www.instantanatomy.net

Nursing and Midwifery
Community Practitioners' and Health Visitors' Association www.unitetheunion.org/cphva
Health and Social Care in Northern Ireland http://online.hscni.net
Nursing and Midwifery Council www.nmc.org.uk
Royal College of Midwives www.rcm.org.uk
Royal College of Nursing www.rcn.org.uk

Nutrition (see Dietetics)

Occupational Therapy
British Association and College of Occupational Therapists www.cot.co.uk

Optometry
Association of British Dispensing Opticians www.abdo.org.uk
British and Irish Orthoptic Society www.orthoptics.org.uk
College of Optometrists www.college-optometrists.org
General Optical Council www.optical.org

Pharmacology
British Toxicology Society www.thebts.org

Pharmacy and Pharmaceutical Sciences
Royal Pharmaceutical Society of Great Britain www.rpharms.com

Photography
Association of Photographers www.the-aop.org
British Institute of Professional Photography www.bipp.com
Royal Photographic Society www.rps.org

Physical Education (see Education and Teacher Training and Sports Sciences/Studies)

Physics
Institute of Physics www.iop.org
Institute of Physics and Engineering in Medicine www.ipem.ac.uk

Physiotherapy
Association of Chartered Physiotherapists in Animal Therapy www.acpat.org
Chartered Society of Physiotherapy www.csp.org.uk

Plant Sciences (see Biological Sciences/Biology)

Podiatry (Chiropody)
Society of Chiropodists and Podiatrists and College of Podiatry www.scpod.org

Psychology
British Psychological Society www.bps.org.uk

Radiography
Society and College of Radiographers www.sor.org

Social Work
Health and Care Professions Council www.hcpc-uk.org
Northern Ireland Social Care Council www.niscc.info
Scottish Social Services Council www.sssc.uk.com
Social Care Wales www.socialcare.wales

Sociology
British Sociological Association www.britsoc.co.uk

Speech Pathology/Sciences/Therapy
Royal College of Speech and Language Therapists www.rcslt.org

Sports Sciences/Studies
British Association of Sport and Exercise Sciences www.bases.org.uk
Chartered Institute for the Management of Sport and Physical Activity www.cimspa.co.uk
English Institute of Sport www.eis2win.co.uk
Society of Sports Therapists www.society-of-sports-therapists.org
Sport England www.sportengland.org
Sportscotland www.sportscotland.org.uk
Sport Wales http://sport.wales
Sports Institute Northern Ireland www.sportni.net/performance/sports-institute-northern-ireland
UK Sport www.uksport.gov.uk

Statistics
Royal Statistical Society www.rss.org.uk

Surveying and Real Estate Management
Chartered Institute of Building www.ciob.org
Chartered Surveyors Training Trust www.cstt.org.uk
National Association of Estate Agents www.naea.co.uk
Royal Institution of Chartered Surveyors www.rics.org

Tourism and Travel
Institute of Travel and Tourism www.itt.co.uk

Town and Country Planning
Royal Town Planning Institute www.rtpi.org.uk

Transport Management and Planning
Chartered Institute of Logistics and Transport www.cilluk.org.uk

Veterinary Science/Medicine/Nursing
Association of Chartered Physiotherapists in Animal Therapy www.acpat.org
British Veterinary Nursing Association www.bvna.org.uk
Royal College of Veterinary Surgeons www.rcvs.org.uk
Royal Veterinary College www.rvc.ac.uk

Zoology
Royal Entomological Society www.royensoc.co.uk
Zoological Society of London www.zsl.org

APPENDIX 4
BOOKLIST AND USEFUL WEBSITES

Unless otherwise stated, the publications in this list are all available from Trotman Publishing.

STANDARD REFERENCE BOOKS
British Qualifications 2018, 48th edition, Kogan Page
British Vocational Qualifications, 12th edition, Kogan Page

OTHER BOOKS AND RESOURCES
Choosing Your Degree Course & University, 14th edition, Brian Heap
Destinations of Leavers from Higher Education 2015/16, Higher Education Statistics Agency Services (available from HESA)
Getting into course guides: Art & Design Courses, Business & Economics Courses, Dental School, Engineering Courses, Law, Medical School, Nursing & Midwifery, Oxford & Cambridge, Pharmacy and Pharmacology Courses, Physiotherapy Courses, Psychology Courses, Veterinary School
A Guide to Uni Life, Lucy Tobin
How to Complete Your UCAS Application: 2019 Entry, Beryl Dixon
How to Write a Winning UCAS Personal Statement, 3rd edition, Ian Stannard
Studying Abroad, 5th edition
Studying and Learning at University, Alan Pritchard, SAGE Study Skills Series
The Times Good University Guide 2018, John O'Leary, Times Books
Your Gap Year, 7th edition, Susan Griffith, Crimson Publishing

USEFUL WEBSITES
Education, course and applications information
www.gov.uk/browse/education
www.erasmusplus.org.uk
Higher Education Statistics Agency www.hesa.ac.uk
www.opendays.com (information on university and college Open Days)
https://unistats.ac.uk (official information from UK universities and colleges for comparing courses)
www.ucas.com
www.disabilityrightsuk.org

Careers information
www.army.mod.uk
www.aspire-igen.com/aspire-international
www.careerconnect.org.uk
www.insidecareers.co.uk
www.inspiringfutures.org.uk
www.milkround.com
www.healthcareers.nhs.uk
www.prospects.ac.uk
www.socialworkandcarejobs.com
www.tomorrowsengineers.org.uk
www.trotman.co.uk

Gap years
www.etrust.org.uk/the-year-in-industry
www.gapyear.com
www.gap-year.com

Study overseas
Association of Commonwealth Universities www.acu.ac.uk
www.allaboutcollege.com
Fulbright Commission www.fulbright.org.uk
www.globalgraduates.com

COURSE INDEX

INDEX OF ADVERTISERS